ANCIENT EUROPE
8000 B.C.–A.D. 1000

ANCIENT EUROPE
8000 B.C.–A.D. 1000
ENCYCLOPEDIA OF THE BARBARIAN WORLD

VOLUME II
BRONZE AGE TO EARLY MIDDLE AGES
(C. 3000 B.C.–A.D. 1000)

INDEX

Peter Bogucki & Pam J. Crabtree
Editors in Chief

CHARLES SCRIBNER'S SONS®

New York • Detroit • San Diego • San Francisco • Cleveland • New Haven, Conn. • Waterville, Maine • London • Munich

Ancient Europe 8000 B.C.–A.D. 1000: Encyclopedia of the Barbarian World
Peter Bogucki and Pam J. Crabtree, Editors in Chief

LIBRARY OF CONGRESS CATALOGING-IN-PUBLICATION DATA

Ancient Europe 8000 B.C.–A.D. 1000 : encyclopedia of the Barbarian world / Peter Bogucki, Pam J. Crabtree, editors.
        p. cm.
    Includes bibliographical references and index.
    ISBN 0-684-80668-1 (set : hardcover : alk. paper) — ISBN 0-684-80669-X (vol. 1) — ISBN 0-684-80670-3 (vol. 2) — ISBN 0-684-31421-5 (e-book)
    1. Antiquities, Prehistoric—Europe—Encyclopedias. 2. Prehistoric peoples—Europe—Encyclopedias. 3. History, Ancient—Encyclopedias. 4. Europe—History—To 476—Encyclopedias. 5. Europe—History—392-814—Encyclopedias. I. Bogucki, Peter I. II. Crabtree, Pam J.

D62 .A52 2004
936—dc22   2003015251

This title is also available as an e-book.
ISBN 0-684-31421-5

Contact your Gale sales representative for ordering information

Printed in the United States of America
10 9 8 7 6 5 4 3 2 1

EDITORIAL AND PRODUCTION STAFF

Project Editor
Alja Kooistra Collar

Assisting Editors
Cindy Clendenon, Shawn Corridor, Sharon Malinowski

Copy Editors
Marcia Merryman Means
Lisa Dixon, Gretchen Gordon, Jeffrey J. Hill, Jean Fortune Kaplan,
Jane Marie Todd

Proofreader
Carol Holmes

Indexer
J. Naomi Linzer

Image Researcher
Deanna Raso

Senior Art Director
Pamela Galbreath

Imaging
Lezlie Light, Leitha Etheridge-Sims, Mary Grimes, Dan Newell, Dave
Oblender, Christine O'Bryan, Kelly A. Quin, Denay Wilding

Cartographer
XNR Productions

Line Illustrator
GGS Information Services

Composition
Datapage Technologies International

Manufacturing
Wendy Blurton

Senior Editor
John Fitzpatrick

Publisher
Frank Menchaca

CONTENTS

VOLUME I

1: DISCOVERING BARBARIAN EUROPE

4: CONSEQUENCES OF AGRICULTURE, 5000–2000 B.C.

VOLUME II

5: MASTERS OF METAL, 3000–1000 B.C.

6: THE EUROPEAN IRON AGE, C. 800 B.C.–A.D. 400

7: EARLY MIDDLE AGES/MIGRATION PERIOD

MAPS

VOLUME I

VOLUME II

VOLUME II

MAPS OF ANCIENT EUROPE, 3000 B.C.–A.D. 1000

Human geography is an essential dimension of archaeology. The locations that ancient people chose for their settlements, cemeteries, and ritual activities are very important for understanding how European societies developed and declined.

Archaeological sites are found throughout Europe. The maps on the following pages show the locations of selected sites mentioned in the text and give an overview of their distribution on a large scale. Smaller and more detailed maps accompany many specific entries.

For clarity, we have divided Europe into five major regions: Northwestern Europe, which covers the British Isles and nearby portions of the Continent; Northern Europe, which includes the North European Plain and Scandinavia; Southwestern Europe, the Iberian Peninsula and the lands around the western Mediterranean; Southeastern Europe, which includes the Danube Basin and Greece; and Eastern Europe, the area east of the Bug River and the Carpathians. Areas beyond these maps, such as the Caucasus and Cyprus, are covered in smaller maps in the relevant articles.

Maps in this volume cover some of the sites mentioned in parts 5 through 7, from the Bronze Age to the Early Middle Ages.

Northwestern Europe and the British Isles, 3000 B.C.–A.D. 1000

Northern Europe, 3000 B.C.–A.D. 1000

0   100   200 mi.
0   100   200 km

N

Norwegian Sea

Vesterålen
Lofoten

Inari

Muonio River
Lainedheen River
Ouras River
Kalixälven
Torneälven
Kemi River
Luleälven
Piteälven
Oulu River
Oulujärvi
Skellefteälven
Pyhä River
Vindelälven
Umedälven
Lesti River
Angermanälven

Trondheim
(Nidaros)

Gene ■

Indalsälven

Ljungan River

Gulf of Bothnia

Hamar ■

Begna River
Glåma River
Klarälven
Ljusnan River

Lågen River

Otra River

Varikkoniemi ■

Dalälven

Åland Is.

Kaupang ■

Lake Vänern

Vendel ■
Valsgärde ■ Gamla Uppsala ■
Lake Mälaren   Sigtuna ■
Tuna ■   Hundhamra ■
Adelsö ■ ■ Helgö
Birka

Hiiumaa

Gulf of Finland

Lake Vättern

Saaremaa

Broa ■
Gotland
Paviken ■   ■ Torsburgen
Fröjel ■   ■ Uggårde Röjr

Skagerrak

Kattegat

Skedemosse ■
Ismanstorp ■
Öland
Eketorp ■

Gulf of Riga

Dvina River

Jutland
Tollund ■ ■ Borum Eshøj

Löddeköpinge ■
Åhus ■
Lund ■ Kivik ■
Uppåkra ■
Trelleborg ■

Baltic Sea

North Sea

Hodde ■
Jelling ■
Egtved ■
Ribe ■   *Fyn*
Drengsted ■
Hjortspring ■   *Als*
Hedeby ■
(Haithabu)

Roskilde ■
Zealand

Bornholm

Rügen

Neman River
Courland Lagoon

Gulf of Gdańsk

Truso ■

Frisian Islands

Feddersen ■
Wierde ■

Wolin ■

IJsselmeer

Elbe River
Ems River
Weser River

Oder R.

Biskupin ■

Narew River
Vistula River
Bug R.

Dorestad ■

Rhine River

Oder River
Warta River

Saale River

Holzhausen ■

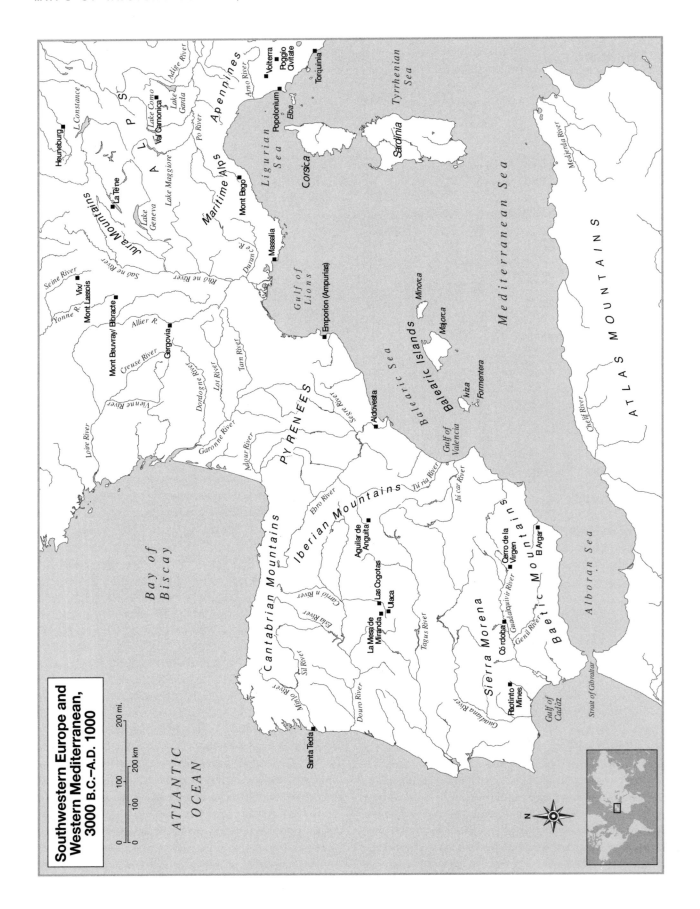

Southwestern Europe and Western Mediterranean, 3000 B.C.–A.D. 1000

Italy, Southeastern Europe,
and the Aegean,
3000 B.C.–A.D. 1000

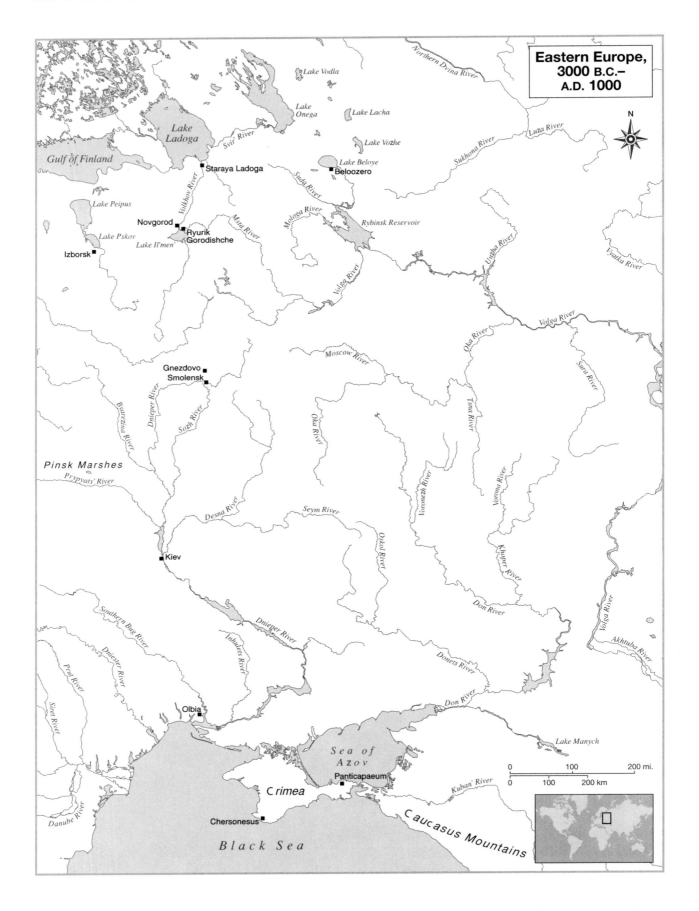

Eastern Europe,
3000 B.C.–
A.D. 1000

N

Northern Dvina River

Luza River

Lake Vodla

Lake Onega

Lake Lacha

Lake Vozhe

Sukhona River

Lake Ladoga

Svir River

Gulf of Finland

Vyatka River

Untzha River

Staraya Ladoga ■

Beloozero ■
Lake Beloye

Suda River

Rybinsk Reservoir

Lake Peipus

Volkhov River

Mologa River

Novgorod ■
Msta River

■ Ryurik
Gorodishche

Lake Pskov
Lake Il'men'

Izborsk ■

Volga River

Moscow River

Oka River

Volga River

Sura River

Gnezdovo ■
Smolensk ■

Dnieper River

Berezina River

Sozh River

Oka River

Tsna River

Voronezh River

Vorona River

Pinsk Marshes

Prypyats' River

Desna River

Seym River

Oskol River

Khoper River

Kiev ■

Don River

Volga River

Southern Bug River

Dniester River

Prut River

Siret River

Inhulets River

Dnieper River

Donets River

Don River

Akhtuba River

Olbia ■

Lake Manych

*Sea of
Azov*

Panticapaeum ■

C rimea

Kuban' River

0   100   200 mi.

0   100   200 km

Chersonesus ■

Caucasus Mountains

Danube River

Black Sea

CHRONOLOGY OF ANCIENT EUROPE, 2000 B.C.–A.D. 1000

Archaeologists need to make sense of how the archaeological record fits together in time and space. A simple tool for organizing this information is a chronological chart, which can be thought of as a timeline running vertically, with the oldest developments at the bottom and the most recent at the top. The vertical lines indicate the duration of cultures and people, whose date of first appearance is indicated by the label at the bottom of the line. The horizontal lines indicate cultures and events that spanned more than one geographic region. Historical events or milestones appear in boldface type.

During the last two millennia B.C. and the first millennium A.D., the archaeological record in Europe gets progressively more detailed. The broad developments of the earlier period discussed in volume I now take on greater specificity in time and space. For that reason, the following chronological chart is organized somewhat differently from the one in volume I: instead of large regions, it is now necessary to view the past in terms of particular countries or smaller regions and in 500-year increments. The chronological chart should be used in conjunction with the individual articles on these topics to give the reader a sense of the larger picture across Europe and through time.

DATE	IRELAND	BRITAIN	FRANCE/ BELGIUM/ SWITZERLAND	GERMANY
A.D. 1000		Norman conquest A.D. 1066		Ottonian/Holy Roman Empire
	Viking Age	Late Saxon period	Carolingian Dynastsy	Carolingian empire
		EMPORIA	Charlemagne crowned	
	early monasteries	Middle Saxon period		
A.D. 500		Early Saxon period	Merovingian Franks	Merovingian Franks
	Early Christian period			
	Late Iron Age	Roman period		
A.D. 1			Roman period	Roman Iron Age/Roman period
	Irish royal sites	Late Iron Age	OPPIDA	
	Middle Iron Age	Middle Iron Age		
500 B.C.			La Tène period	La Tène period
			Greek colonies established	
	Early Iron Age hillforts	hillforts		
		Early Iron Age	Hallstatt period	Hallstatt period
1000 B.C.				
	Late Bronze Age	Late Bronze Age		
			Late Bronze Age	Late Bronze Age
1500 B.C.			Middle Bronze Age	Middle Bronze Age
		Middle Bronze Age		
2000 B.C.	Early Bronze Age	Early Bronze Age	Early Bronze Age	Early Bronze Age

SCANDINAVIA	POLAND	RUSSIA/ UKRAINE	IBERIA	DATE
				A.D. 1000
Settlement of Iceland and Greenland	Formation of early Polish state	Viking settlements in Russia		
Viking Age	EMPORIA			
	Expansion of early Slav culture		Arab conquest	
		Expansion of early Slav culture	Suevian and Visigothic kingdoms	A.D. 500
Germanic Iron Age	Migration period			
three-aisled longhouses		Later Sarmatians		
Roman Iron Age	Wielbark culture / Roman Iron Age		Roman period	A.D. 1
		Pontic kingdom		
Tollund Man		Sarmatians	Carthaginian control	
		Scythians / Bosporan kingdom		
Early Iron Age	Pre-Roman Iron Age / Scythian raids	Greek colonies established	Greek colonies established	500 B.C.
	Iron use appears		Iron Age / Establishment of Phoenician colonies	
		Early Scythians	urnfields	
Later Bronze Age				1000 B.C.
	Lusatian culture			
			Late Bronze Age	1500 B.C.
	Middle Bronze Age			
Older Bronze Age				
		Late Bronze Age		
Late Neolithic	Early Bronze Age	Middle Bronze Age	Classic Bronze Age	2000 B.C.

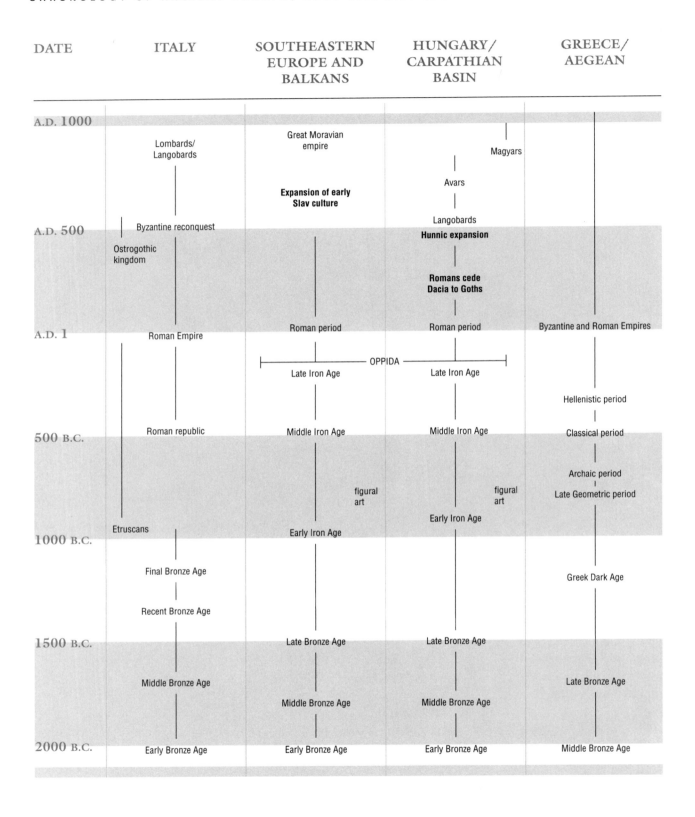

DATE	ITALY	SOUTHEASTERN EUROPE AND BALKANS	HUNGARY/ CARPATHIAN BASIN	GREECE/ AEGEAN
A.D. 1000		Great Moravian empire	Magyars	
	Lombards/ Langobards		Avars	
		Expansion of early Slav culture	Langobards	
A.D. 500	Byzantine reconquest		Hunnic expansion	
	Ostrogothic kingdom		Romans cede Dacia to Goths	
A.D. 1	Roman Empire	Roman period	Roman period	Byzantine and Roman Empires
		OPPIDA		
		Late Iron Age	Late Iron Age	
				Hellenistic period
500 B.C.	Roman republic	Middle Iron Age	Middle Iron Age	Classical period
				Archaic period
		figural art	figural art	Late Geometric period
	Etruscans	Early Iron Age	Early Iron Age	
1000 B.C.				
	Final Bronze Age			Greek Dark Age
	Recent Bronze Age			
1500 B.C.		Late Bronze Age	Late Bronze Age	
	Middle Bronze Age			Late Bronze Age
		Middle Bronze Age	Middle Bronze Age	
2000 B.C.	Early Bronze Age	Early Bronze Age	Early Bronze Age	Middle Bronze Age

MASTERS OF METAL,
3000–1000 B.C.

INTRODUCTION

During the third and second millennia B.C., societies emerged from the Atlantic to the Urals that were characterized by the use of bronze for a wide variety of weapons, tools, and ornaments and, perhaps more significantly, by pronounced and sustained differences in status, power, and wealth. The period that followed is known as the Bronze Age, a somewhat arbitrary distinction based on the widespread use of the alloy of copper and tin. It is the second of Christian Jürgensen (C. J.) Thomsen's tripartite division of prehistory into ages of Stone, Bronze, and Iron based on his observations of the Danish archaeological record.

Society did not undergo a radical transformation at the onset of the Bronze Age. Many of the social, economic, and symbolic developments that mark this period have their roots in the Late Neolithic. Similarly, many of the characteristics of the Bronze Age persist far longer than its arbitrary end in the first millennium B.C. with the development of ironworking. The Bronze Age in Europe is of tremendous importance, however, as a period of significant change that continued to shape the European past into the recognizable precursor of the societies that we eventually meet in historical records. Professor Stuart Piggott, in his 1965 book *Ancient Europe from the Beginnings of Agriculture to Classical Antiquity: A Survey,* calls it "a phase full of interest" in which the preceding "curious amalgam of traditions and techniques" was transformed into the world "we encounter at the dawn of European history."

CONTINUITY FROM LATE NEOLITHIC

In most parts of Europe, the Late Neolithic societies described in the previous section blend imperceptibly into the Early Bronze Age communities. No one living in the late third millennium B.C. would have suspected that archaeologists of the nineteenth century A.D. would assign such significance to a modest metallurgical innovation. At the beginning of the second millennium B.C., people continued to inhabit generally the same locations, live in similar types of houses, grow more or less the same crops, and go about their lives not much differently from the way they lived in previous centuries. There were, of course, some subtle yet significant differences. For example, in Scandinavia, Bronze Age burial mounds generally occur on the higher points in the landscape, while Neolithic ones are in lower locations.

The major changes of the Early Bronze Age are not a radical departure from patterns observed in the later Neolithic. Rather, they are an amplification of some trends that began during the earlier period, including the use of exotic materials like bronze, gold, amber, and jet, and the practice of elaborate ceremonial behavior, not only as part of mortuary rituals but also in other ways that remain mysterious. These changes reflected back into society during the following millennium to cause a transformation in the organization of the valuables and the ways in which the possession of these goods served as symbols of power and status. Thus, by the end of the Bronze Age, prehistoric society in much of Europe was indeed different from that of the Neolithic.

MAKING BRONZE

Bronze is an alloy of copper with a small quantity of another element, most commonly tin but sometimes arsenic. The admixture of the second metal, which can form up to 10 percent of the alloy, provides the soft copper with stiffness and strength. Bronze is also easier to cast than copper, allowing the crafting of a wide variety of novel and complex shapes not hitherto possible. The development of bronze fulfilled the promise of copper, a bright and attractive metal that was unfortunately too soft and pliable by itself to make anything more than simple tools and ornaments.

During the course of the Bronze Age, we see a progressive increase of sophistication in metallurgical techniques. Ways were found to make artifacts that were increasingly complicated and refined. Now it was possible to make axes, sickles, swords, spearheads, rings, pins, and bracelets, as well as elaborate artistic achievements such as the Trundholm "sun chariot" and even wind instruments such as the immense horns found in Denmark and Ireland. The ability to cast dozens of artifacts from a single mold makes it possible to speak of true manufacturing as opposed to the individual crafting of each piece. Some scholars have proposed that metalsmithing was a specialist occupation in certain places. Such emergent specialization would have had profound significance for the agrarian economy, still largely composed of self-sufficient households. Some metal artifacts, such as the astonishing Irish gold neck rings, seem to be clearly beyond the ability of an amateur to produce.

Copper and tin rarely, if ever, occur naturally in the same place. Thus one or the other—or both—must be brought some distance from their source areas to be alloyed. Copper sources are widely distributed in the mountainous zones of Europe, but known tin sources are only found in western Europe, in Brittany, Cornwall, and Spain. Thus, tin needed to be brought from a considerable distance to areas of east-central Europe, such as Hungary and Romania, where immense quantities of bronze artifacts had been buried deliberately in hoards. Similarly, Denmark has no natural sources of copper or tin, but it has yielded more bronze artifacts per square kilometer than most other parts of Europe.

It is in this need to acquire critical supplies of copper and tin, as well as the distribution of materials such as amber, jet, and gold, that we see the rise of long-distance trading networks during the Bronze Age. Trade was no longer something that happened sporadically or by chance. Instead, materials and goods circulated along established routes. The Mediterranean, Baltic, Black, and North Seas were crossed regularly by large boats, while smaller craft traversed shorter crossings like the English Channel.

BURIALS, RITUAL, AND MONUMENTS

Much more than both earlier and later periods, the Bronze Age is known largely from its burials. In large measure, this is due to the preferences of early archaeologists to excavate graves that contained spectacular bronze and gold trophies. Settlements of the period, in contrast, were small and unremarkable. This imbalance is slowly being corrected, as new ways are developed to extract as much information as possible from settlement remains.

Bronze burials are remarkable both for their regional and chronological diversity, although occasionally mortuary practices became uniform over broad areas. The practice of single graves under barrows or tumuli (small mounds) is widespread during the first half of the Bronze Age, although flat cemeteries are also found in parts of central Europe. Some of the Early Bronze Age barrows are remarkably rich, such as Bush Barrow near Stonehenge and Leubingen in eastern Germany. Occasional graves with multiple skeletons, such as the ones at Amesbury in southern England and Wassenaar in the Netherlands, may reflect a more violent side to Bronze Age life. Around 1200 B.C., there was a marked shift in burial practices in much of central and southern Europe, and cremation burial in urns became common. The so-called urnfields are large cemeteries, sometimes with several thousand individual burials.

Alongside the burial sites, other focal points in the landscape grew in importance. The megalithic tradition in western Europe continued the practice of building large stone monuments. Stonehenge, begun during the Late Neolithic, reached its zenith during the Bronze Age, when the largest upright sarsen stones and lintels still visible today were erected, and other features of the surrounding sacred landscape, such as the Avenue, were expanded.

At widely separated parts of Europe, in southern Scandinavia and the southern Alps, large rock outcrops were covered with images of people, animals, boats, and chariots, as well as abstract designs. Offerings were made by depositing weapons and body armor into rivers, streams, bogs, and especially springs.

STATUS, POWER, WEALTH

The variation in the burials has led to the very reasonable view that the Bronze Age was characterized by increasing differences in the access by individuals to status, power, and wealth. Admittedly, burial evidence may overemphasize such differences, but a compelling case can be made that certain burials, such as the oak-coffin tombs of Denmark, reflect the high status of their occupants. The amount of effort that went into the construction of some Bronze Age mortuary structures and the high value ascribed to the goods buried with the bodies—and thus taken out of use by the living—is consistent with the expectations for such a stratified society. These are not the earliest examples of astonishingly rich burials in European prehistory, as the Copper Age cemetery at Varna attests. The displays of wealth in some Bronze Age burials are so elaborate and the practice is so widespread, however, that it is difficult not to conclude that society was increasingly differentiated into elites and commoners.

Evidence for such social differentiation appears late in the third millennium B.C. in widely separated areas. Among these are the Wessex culture of southern England, builders of Stonehenge; the Unětice culture of central Europe, whose hoards of bronze artifacts reflect the ability to acquire tin from a considerable distance; and the El Argar culture of southern Spain, who buried many of their dead in large ceramic jars. Somewhat later, in places such as Denmark and Ireland, lavish displays of wealth provided an opportunity for the elite to demonstrate their status.

Archaeologists have pondered the question of what form these differentiated societies took. Some have advanced the hypothesis that they were organized into chiefdoms, a form of social organization known from pre-state societies around the world. In chiefdoms, positions of status and leadership are passed from one generation to the next, and this elite population controls the production of farmers, herders, and craft specialists, whose products they accumulate, display, and distribute to maintain their social preeminence. As an alternative to such a straightforwardly hierarchical social structure, other archaeologists have advanced the notion that Bronze Age society had more complicated and fluid patterns of differences in authority and status, which changed depending on the situation and the relationships among individuals and groups. Whatever position one accepts, it is clear that social organization was becoming increasingly complex throughout Europe during the Bronze Age.

The most complex societies were found in the Aegean beginning in the third millennium B.C. On the island of Crete, the Minoan civilization developed a political and economic system dominated by several major palaces in which living quarters, storerooms, sanctuaries, and ceremonial rooms surrounded a central courtyard. Clearly, these were the seats of a powerful elite. During the mid-second millennium B.C., the fortified town of Mycenae on the Greek mainland, with its immense royal burial complexes, became the focus of an Aegean civilization that was celebrated by later Greek writers such as Homer and Thucydides. Bronze Age developments in the Aegean proceeded much more quickly than in the rest of Europe, and the Minoans and Mycenaeans were true civilizations with writing and an elaborate administrative structure.

The Bronze Age continues to pose many challenges to archaeologists. In particular, the significance of age and gender differences in Bronze Age society will need to be explored to a greater degree, as will the possible meanings of the remarkable sacred landscapes created by monuments and burials. The roles of small farmsteads and fortified sites need to be better understood. The European Bronze Age is a classic example of how new archaeological finds, rather than providing definitive answers, raise more questions for archaeologists to address.

PETER BOGUCKI

THE SIGNIFICANCE OF BRONZE

Bronze is an alloy, a crystalline mixture of copper and tin. The ratio is set ideally at 9:1, though it varied in prehistory as a result of either manufacturing conditions or the deliberate choice of the metalworker. Bronze can be cast or hammered into complex shapes, including sheets, but cold hammering has an additional effect: it elongates the crystals and causes work hardening. Through work hardening, effective edges can be produced on blades, but the process can be exaggerated, leading to brittleness and cracking. Heating, or annealing, causes recrystallization and eliminates the distortion of the crystals, canceling the work hardening but enabling an artifact to be hammered into the desired shape. Moreover, the presence of tin improves the fluidity of the molten metal, making it easier to cast and permitting the use of complex mold shapes.

Because of the long history of research on the topic of European prehistory, the sequence of metallurgical development is well known. Newer work, particularly in the southern Levant, has shed fresh light on the context of metallurgy in a milieu of developing social complexity. Bronze production on a significant scale first appeared in about 2400 B.C. in the Early Bronze Age central European Únětice culture, distributed around the Erzgebirge, or "Ore mountains," on the present-day border between Germany and the Czech Republic. It is no accident that these mountains have significant tin reserves, which many archaeologists believe probably were exploited in antiquity, although this point is the subject of controversy. Farther west, tin bronze was introduced rapidly to Britain from about 2150 B.C.,

so that there was no real Copper Age. Here, the earliest good evidence for tin production is provided by tin slag from a burial at Caerloggas, near Saint Austell in Cornwall, dated to 1800 B.C. Significantly, Cornwall is a major tin source.

ARSENICAL COPPER: THE FIRST STEP

An issue that divides many modern scholars is the extent to which ancient metalworkers were aware of the processes taking place as they smelted, refined, melted, and cast: Were the metalwork and its compositions achieved by accident or by design? This controversy is an aspect of the modernist versus primitivist debate, which pits those who see the people of prehistory as very much like ourselves, practicing empirical experimentation, against those who doubt the complexity of former societies and their depth of knowledge.

This is particularly the case with respect to arsenical copper, an alloy containing between 2 percent and 6 percent arsenic, which was used in the Copper Age of Europe during the fourth and third millennium B.C. It. continued to be produced and to circulate for some time after the introduction of tin bronze. Like bronze, arsenical copper is superior in its properties to unalloyed copper. The arsenic acts as a deoxidant. It makes the copper more fluid and thus improves the quality of the casting. Experimental work has shown that cold working of the alloy leads to work hardening. Thus, while arsenical coppers in the as-cast or annealed state can have a hardness of about 70 HV (Vickers hardness), this

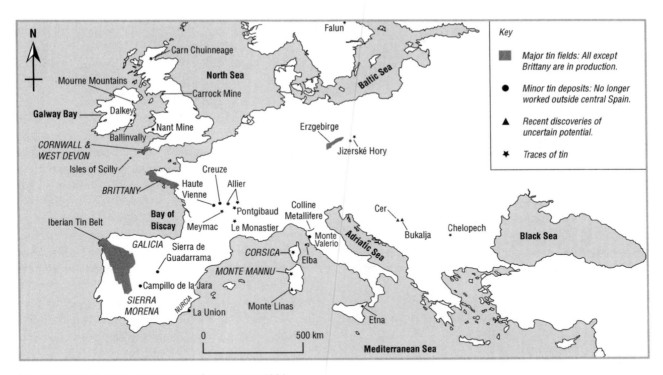

Tin deposits in Europe. ADAPTED FROM PENHALLURICK 1986.

hardness can be work hardened to 150 HV. In prehistoric practice hardness rarely exceeded 100 HV, however; this hardness compares favorably to that of copper, which also can be work hardened. It has been claimed, however, that many of the artifacts in arsenical copper were produced accidentally and that their properties were not as advantageous, as is sometimes claimed. This is argued not least because of the tendency of arsenic to segregate during casting (to form an arsenic-rich phase within the matrix of the alloy and, in particular, close to the surface of the artifact).

Some copper ores are rich in arsenic, such as the metallic gray tennantite or enargite, and it is argued that arsenical copper was first produced accidentally using such ores; the prehistoric metalworkers then would have noticed that the metal produced was mechanically superior to normal copper. Furthermore, arsenic-rich ores could have been recognized from the garlic smell they emit when heated or struck. Arsenic, however, is prone to oxidation, producing a fume of arsenious oxide; this fume is toxic and would deplete the arsenic content of the molten metal unless reducing conditions (i.e., an oxygen-poor environment) were maintained at all times. The "white arsenic smoke" and white residue pro-

duced during melting and hot working probably would have been noticed by metalworkers as correlating with certain properties of the material. This loss probably explains the greatly varying arsenic content of Copper Age arsenical copper.

Whether or not arsenical copper was produced deliberately, it has been noted that daggers were made preferentially of arsenical copper in numerous early copper-using cultural groups of the circum-Alpine area, such as Altheim, Pfyn, Cortaillod, Mondsee, and Remedello. Similar patterns have been noticed in Wales, and in the Copper Age southern Levant there was differentiation between utilitarian metalwork in copper and prestige/cultic artifacts in arsenical copper. Although arsenical copper produces harder edges than does copper, this deliberate choice of raw material may have been based on color rather than mechanical properties. As a result of segregation, arsenic-rich liquid may exude at the surface ("sweating") during the casting of an artifact in arsenical copper, resulting in a silvery coating.

THE COMING OF TIN

Cassiterite, tin oxide ore, is present in various areas of Europe in placer deposits. These are secondary

Fig. 1. Sheet-bronze armor from Marmesses, France. RÉUNION DES MUSÉES NATIONAUX/ART RESOURCE, NY. REPRODUCED BY PERMISSION.

deposits that are produced by the erosion of ore-bearing rock, and the cassiterite is then redeposited in alluvial sands and gravels. The high-density, hard, dark pebbles of "stream tin" presumably would have been known to prehistoric people searching for gold. Stannite, a sulfide of tin, sometimes occurs in ore bodies in association with chalcopyrite and pyrite, and the weathered part of such deposits would contain cassiterite.

Tin, however, is very rare. Although some placer deposits probably would been worked out and are therefore not known today, tin's distribution is very uneven in Europe. Indeed, it is perhaps no accident that its earliest regular use appeared in the Únětice culture, around the tin-rich Erzgebirge. It has been suggested that the rich "Wessex" graves of the early second millennium in south-central England owe their wealth to their control of the rich Cornish tin of the southwest peninsular. The gold Rillaton cup, from Cornwall, tends to support such a hypothesis as it documents the accumulation of

wealth presumably amassed through the tin trade. Other major sources occur in western Iberia and Brittany, although there is no hard evidence for their working in the Bronze Age. In Anatolia Early Bronze Age mining is known at Kestel and tin processing nearby at Göltepe, in the Taurus Mountains of southern Turkey.

It is thought that the complex societies of the Aegean and eastern Mediterranean obtained their tin from Turkey, Afghanistan, or the eastern desert of Egypt. The presence of tin ingots in the Ulu Burun shipwreck, which sank about 1300 B.C. near Kaş off the southern coast of Turkey, shows that metallic tin was circulating in the Late Bronze Age Mediterranean. Tin smelting is relatively inefficient (the slags at Caerloggas contain 45 percent tin oxide), but it can be added easily to copper by putting cassiterite and a flux (to facilitate the chemical reaction) on the surface of molten copper under charcoal. Bronze Age metallic tin (which is, in fact, unstable) is found rarely, which supports the hypothesis that the direct addition of tinstone (cassiterite) to molten copper was preferred. This process also guarantees a consistent alloy, whereas arsenical copper production could not be controlled so easily.

As noted, bronze presents distinct mechanical advantages over copper. The presence of tin improves the fluidity of the molten metal, making it better suited for casting, and lowers its melting point: 10 percent tin will lower the melting point of bronze by some 200 degrees. Bronze in its as-cast state has a hardness of about 100 HV, which can be improved to about 170 HV by cold working. It is probably no accident that the widespread use of stone arrowheads and daggers declines only with the change from arsenical copper to bronze in the Early Bronze Age (as, for example, in northern Italy). This is partly because bronze becomes more widely available as a result of increased production but also as metal edge tools increase in effectiveness.

LEAD ADDITIVES

During the Late Bronze Age lead was used as an additive to bronze. Lead certainly improves casting, lowering the melting point of the alloy and improving its viscosity, but the main reason for its use may have been to bulk out copper in a period of metal shortage. Breton socketed axes often have high lead contents, and in Slovenia it is noticeable that different artifact types contained varying amounts of lead, axes having 6–7 percent and sickles 3–4 percent. Deliberately added lead appears in British bronze in the Wilburton phase (1140–1020 B.C.), continuing in the succeeding Ewart Park (1020–800 B.C.) and Llyn Fawr (800 B.C. onward) phases.

COPPER PROCUREMENT

Copper is more common in Europe than is tin, and it is likely that prehistoric miners worked outcrops that are of no economic significance today. Bronze Age mines are known at Ross Island (2400–2000 B.C.) and Mount Gabriel (1700–1500 B.C.) in southwest Ireland, and workings at Alderley Edge in England date to the first half of the second millennium B.C. There are extensive contemporary underground workings at Great Orme's Head, Llandudno, on the north coast of Wales, and mining also is documented at Cwmystwyth and Nantyreira in the west of the country and at Parys Mountain on the island of Anglesey.

In Spain mining is documented at Chinflon in the south and at El Aramo and El Milagro in the north, while in southern France it is known at Cabrières and Saint-Véran–les Clausis. There is Copper Age mining in Liguria, in northwestern Italy, at Libiola and Monte Loreto, and the ores around Rudna Glava, near Bor in Serbia were exploited from a very early date (fifth millennium B.C.). There are also fifth millennium dates for the mines at Ai Bunar, and Bronze Age working is indicated at Tymnjanka in Bulgaria. There is some evidence for Copper and Bronze Age mining at Špania Dolina and Slovinky in central Slovakia. None of these mines, however, seems to be on the same scale as Bronze Age workings in Austria and Russia. The Mitterberg mines are situated in the Salzach valley, near Salzburg in Austria; here, there are Bronze Age adits up to 100 meters long, and it has been calculated that as much as 18,000 tons of copper were produced in prehistory. At Kargaly, southwest of the Urals in European Russia, it seems that mining was conducted on a massive scale, with an estimated 1.5–2 million tons of ore produced.

METALS ANALYSIS AND PROVENANCE

A large body of metals analysis exists for prehistoric Europe; the Stuttgart program of spectrographic analysis, for example, effected some 22,000 analyses. Many of the sampled artifacts date to the Copper and Early Bronze Age, as it was thought that compositional analysis would be particularly useful in shedding light on the emergence of metallurgy in Europe. Statistical analyses of these data have thrown up metal composition groups, although these are contested. There are numerous methodological problems. Prehistoric artifacts do not have homogeneous compositions, not least because of segregation of elements in cast artifacts. Unfortunately, some of the elements determined by these analyses show this characteristic, such as arsenic, whose segregation we have already discussed. Furthermore, ore bodies vary in composition through the outcrop, so that provenance is difficult to ascertain. Recycling seems to have been practiced from the Early Bronze Age (because one of the advantages that metal presents over stone tools is that broken artifacts can be repaired easily and the raw material reused), which means that metals from different sources may have been melted together. Finally, the effect of alloying on the composition of impurities in metal is not understood completely.

Sometimes compositional groups correspond with artifact types. The Early Bronze Age ingot rings (*Ösenhalsringe* or *Ösenringe*), very commonly found to the north of the eastern Alps in southern Bavaria, lower Austria, and Moravia, represent one example. They frequently are made from a metal that is conventionally referred to as "C2," or "*Ösenring* metal," and which probably is linked to Austrian copper sources. Peter Northover has used data on impurity groups and alloy types to argue convincingly about metal circulation zones in Britain and northwestern Europe. He also was able to suggest sources for the supply—for example, the earliest metal used in Britain seems to have come from Ireland, and, in the Late Bronze Age, metal from central European sources was used.

METAL AND SOCIETY

It is a commonplace of prehistory that the development of the metals industry is linked to the growth of social complexity. It is, however, worth noting that it was the Australian prehistorian Vere Gordon Childe, in his *The Dawn of European Civilization*, who saw the "qualities . . . which distinguish the Western world" as beginning in the Bronze Age. It is, however, debatable whether the metals trade caused the emergence of elites or whether, conversely, their emergence favored the development of metallurgy.

Metal is a medium for producing efficient tools and weapons that could be repaired without the loss of material, but it also is uniquely suitable as a mark of status. It was scarce, particularly in the earlier phases of its use, and this rarity was compounded by the use of tin, which was even scarcer than copper. Metalworkers with the requisite skills to perform the "magical" transformation of green copper ore into metal may have been equally scarce. Metal would have caught the light in a way that no other substance in use at the time did; bronze, in particular, could be formed, by casting or working, into complex shapes to make ornaments, tools, and weapons but also sheet metal. The latter material could be used in the production of armor—helmets, grieves, and shields—and vessels. Sheet armor, which is arguably less efficient than leather or wood, would have had a definite display function, as would bronze vessels, not least because of the expertise required for their manufacture. The Greek epic poet Homer, author of the *Iliad* and the *Odyssey,* who wrote in the first half of the first millennium B.C., gives us a picture of the heroic warriors at the siege of Troy. His Late Bronze Age Aegean warriors bear impressive bronze sheet armor, helmets, and shields, which are regularly described as "shining" or "flashing,"

The use and possession of metal therefore can be seen as a measure of wealth, and this is particularly true for an area such as Denmark, which was entirely dependent on outside sources for its copper and tin. Such attempts to ascribe value to prehistoric commodities are risky, because we can only speculate on the relative scarcities of raw materials or the cost of labor input and guess at the ritual significance or the biographies of artifacts. For example, in much epic literature weapons acquire value by virtue of their previous owner, like Achilles' spear in Homer's *Iliad.*

Because copper and tin are distributed unevenly, the desire for raw materials bound together European society in a metals trade. We are not sure which organic commodities were traded for metal, but control of resources and craft specialists seems to have acquired increasing importance. Thus, Late

Bronze Age fortified settlements of the Urnfield period appear to have acted as regional metallurgical centers, and some smaller settlements seem to have had no production of their own. The importation of Continental scrap metal into Late Bronze Age Britain is evidenced by the cargo of the Middle Bronze Age Langdon Bay ship, wrecked off Dover in the English Channel. Mining gave upland communities, naturally poor in agricultural resources, such as the Late Bronze Age Luco/Laugen groups of Trentino–Alto Adige in the Italian Alps, a commodity to tie them in to wider economic and status networks.

THE SOCIAL POSITION OF BRONZEWORKERS

A key concept in understanding the growth of social complexity is that of craft specialization, where individuals are dedicated to specific economic tasks rather than participating in domestic food production. As copper metallurgy developed, many crafts emerged, including prospecting, mining and ore dressing, smelting, and refining, casting, and finishing. It is likely that at least some of these crafts were protected, secret knowledge. Gordon Childe (in *The Bronze Age*) suggests that bronzesmiths were an itinerant caste, outside the social structures of society, who traveled from settlement to settlement to ply their trade. Increasing documentation for metalworking within settlements, as at the Italian lake villages of Ledro and Fiavé, coupled with the lack of support for this model in the ethnographic literature, has led archaeologists to argue for permanent workshops: community-based and possibly part-time production. Thus, Michael Rowlands has suggested locally based seasonal production. Metal types can have surprisingly wide distributions, and the transmission of models or ideas (rather than itinerant smiths) is documented, for example, by the early Urnfield flange-hilted swords, which show close similarities from the east Mediterranean to western Europe.

Excavations by Stephen Shennan at an Early Bronze Age mining village in the Salzach valley, Sankt Veit–Klinglberg, indicate that the metal smelters were already craft specialists, importing foodstuffs and using ores won from various outcrops. In the Late Bronze Age the massive concentrations of smelting slag found, for example, on the

Lavarone-Vezzena plateau in the Trentino Alps, in southern Italy, or on Cyprus suggest large-scale industrial production, although it is significant that both are tied in to the Mediterranean markets of the period.

METALS MAKE THE WORLD GO ROUND

It is not clear to what extent bronze and the metals trade in general were responsible for the growth of social complexity in Bronze Age Europe. Was bronze a relatively minor component in complex patterns of wealth display involving many perishable elements (such as livestock, furs, and textiles), which do not survive in the archaeological record? Is the significance of bronze that it provided the catalyst for the development of complexity, as has been claimed for the southern Levant, or was the emergence of the elites of barbarian Europe an independent phenomenon? It seems that social stratification already had begun to develop in Neolithic Europe, and copper and then bronze gave the emergent elites a useful and rare raw material whose control enabled them to consolidate their power as well as a perfect vehicle for display. The "beauty" of the Bronze Age warrior was very much bound up in his armor, his shining bronze.

See also **Origins and Growth of European Prehistory** (*vol. 1, part 1*); **Early Copper Mines at Rudna Glava and Ai Bunar** (*vol. 1, part 4*).

BIBLIOGRAPHY

Budd, Paul. "Eneolithic Arsenical Copper: Heat Treatment and the Metallographic Interpretation of Manufacturing Process." In *Archaeometry '90*. Edited by Ernst Pernicka and Günther A. Wagner, pp. 35–44. Boston: Birkhäuser, 1991. (Budd doubts that arsenical copper was as advantageous as has been claimed and whether it was produced deliberately.)

Charles, James A. "The Coming of Copper and Copper-Base Alloys and Iron: A Metallurgical Sequence." In *The Coming of the Age of Iron*. Edited by Theodore A. Wertime and James D. Muhly, pp. 151–181. New Haven, Conn.: Yale University Press, 1980. (An excellent treatment, exploring hypotheses to explain developments, with particular attention to arsenical copper.)

Chernykh, Evgenii N. *Ancient Metallurgy in the USSR: The Early Metal Age*. Translated by Sarah Wright. New Studies in Archaeology. Cambridge, U.K.: Cambridge University Press, 1992.

Childe, Vere Gordon. *The Bronze Age*. Cambridge, U.K.: Cambridge University Press, 1930. (An influential, but very dated account of the Bronze Age.)

———. *The Dawn of European Civilization*. London: Kegan Paul, 1925. (A dated account, but containing interesting ideas.)

Coghlan, Herbert H. *Notes on the Prehistoric Metallurgy of Copper and Bronze in the Old World*. 2d ed. Occasional Papers on Technology, no. 4. Oxford: Pitt Rivers Museum, 1975.

Harding, Anthony F. *European Societies in the Bronze Age*. Cambridge World Archaeology. Cambridge, U.K.: Cambridge University Press, 2000. (See, in particular, pp. 197–241.)

Northover, J. Peter. "The Exploration of the Long-Distance Movement of Bronze in Bronze and Early Iron Age Europe." *Bulletin of the Institute of Archaeology, London* 19 (1982): 45–72.

Pearce, Mark. "Metals Make the World Go Round: The Copper Supply for Frattesina." In *Metals Make the World Go Round: The Supply and Circulation of Metals in Bronze Age Europe*. Edited by Christopher F. E. Pare, pp. 108–115. Oxford: Oxbow Books, 2000.

———. "Reconstructing Prehistoric Metallurgical Knowledge: The Northern Italian Copper and Bronze Ages." *European Journal of Archaeology* 1, no. 1 (1998): 51–70.

Penhallurick, Roger D. *Tin in Antiquity: Its Mining and Trade throughout the Ancient World with Particular Reference to Cornwall*. London: Institute of Metals, 1986.

Rowlands, Michael J. *The Production and Distribution of Metalwork in the Middle Bronze Age in Southern Britain*. BAR British Series, no. 31. Oxford: British Archaeological Reports, 1976.

Shennan, Stephen. *Bronze Age Copper Producers of the Eastern Alps: Excavations at St. Veit–Klinglberg*. Universitätsforschungen zur prähistorischen Archäologie 27. Bonn, Germany: Habelt, 1995.

Tylecote, Ronald F. *The Prehistory of Metallurgy in the British Isles*. London: Institute of Metals 1986. (Despite the British focus, a useful review of technological change.)

MARK PEARCE

THE EARLY AND MIDDLE BRONZE AGES IN TEMPERATE SOUTHEASTERN EUROPE

The earlier part of the Bronze Age in temperate southeastern Europe (c. 2200–1500 B.C.) presents a confusing picture to the unwary archaeologist. Although over the years more publications have appeared in English, German, and French, many basic site reports and syntheses are only fully available in Hungarian, Romanian, Bulgarian, Serbian, or other indigenous languages. Often the names of apparently identical archaeological cultures change with bewildering abandon as one crosses modern national borders or even moves between regions of the same country. This part of the world has a history (beginning in the mid-nineteenth century) of antiquarian collecting and detailed specialist typological studies, especially of ceramics and metal objects, with far less effort expended on the more mundane aspects of prehistoric life. Only since the 1980s have studies become available that incorporate the analysis of plant and animal material from Bronze Age sites, and these are far from the rule.

To some extent, this is due to the nature of the archaeological record, that is, the sites and material that have survived from the Early and Middle Bronze Ages. With the exception of habitation mounds (tells) and burial mounds (tumuli), both of which have a limited distribution in the earlier part of the Bronze Age, most sites are shallow, close to the modern ground surface, and easily disturbed. Farming and urban development have been more destructive to these sites than to the more deeply buried sites of earlier periods. The typically more dispersed settlement pattern of the Bronze Age in most of this region results in smaller sites, more vulnerable to the vagaries of history than the more concentrated nucleated sites of the later Neolithic or Eneolithic (sometimes called Copper Age) of the fifth and fourth millennia B.C. Sometimes only cemeteries or only settlements are known from a region during the Early or Middle Bronze Age, thus preserving only a part of the remains of the once-complete cultural system and making synchronization with other regions and reconstruction of Bronze Age life difficult. Radiocarbon (carbon-14) dates, although becoming more common for this period, are not abundant. They are rarely the product of a research program that stresses good archaeological context and high-precision dating of short-lived samples. The absolute chronology of the period is therefore somewhat lacking in precision, although the broad outlines are clear.

Taking the above strictures into account, this article treats the Early and Middle Bronze Ages in temperate southeastern Europe as a single "period," although it distinguishes discrete Early and Middle Bronze Age "cultures," as they are defined by archaeologists working in the area. In this the article follows John Coles and Anthony Harding in *The Bronze Age in Europe* (1979), who point out that the distinction between Early and Middle Bronze Ages, while chronologically valid, is arbitrary in cultural terms and that both of these periods (lasting a total of 500 to 750 years to the middle of the second millennium B.C.) are much more similar to each other than to the succeeding Late Bronze and Early Iron Ages.

GEOGRAPHY AND LANDSCAPE

Southeastern Europe, as the term will be used here, includes the Hungarian Plain, the southern part of the Carpathian arc and its interior, and the drainage of the Middle and Lower Danube and its tributaries. This diverse area encompasses territory found in the modern states of Hungary, Romania, Bulgaria, and the former Yugoslavia (Slovenia, Croatia, Bosnia and Herzegovina, Macedonia, and Serbia and Montenegro). The phrase "temperate southeastern Europe" specifically excludes Greece and those parts of the southern Balkan Peninsula that have a Mediterranean climate. By contrast, temperate southeastern Europe has a Continental climatic regime: hot summers and cold winters, with rainfall distributed throughout the year. Vegetation is highly variable, from deciduous forests (with evergreens at the higher elevations) to grassy plains and swampy lowlands. In the earlier part of the Bronze Age, from about 4000 to 3500 B.P., the climate was slightly warmer, cooling off toward the period's end to a climate roughly similar to that of modern times. The malarial swamps along the slower lowland rivers and the Lower Danube were undrained, and the uncleared mountain slopes were more heavily forested. Before modern drainage projects, flooding was common on the Hungarian Plain, and the area between the Danube and the Tisza Rivers was inhospitable to settlement, marshy, and difficult to cross. This landscape must have patterned Bronze Age settlements and contact in ways that differed from what is seen today.

Four thousand years ago the rivers and their valleys served as important routes through the difficult terrain of the Dinaric Alps, the Balkans, and the Carpathian mountain ranges. Although a determined cross-country walker could traverse most of these mountains, following the river valleys was probably the preferred route, especially when carrying burdens or leading pack animals. The broad alluvial flats were also favored farming terrain, with farmsteads and larger settlements located on the terraces above. Thus contact between sites seems to have been easier and more intense in the Bronze Age along larger rivers and their tributaries than it was with equally distant sites across the mountains.

Archaeologically this is often evident in the characteristic decoration of pottery or the shapes of metal objects, which may be limited to an area bounded by a river valley or mountain range. While such a distribution has sometimes been taken to be coterminous with a prehistoric ethnic or political boundary, this conclusion is not necessarily warranted.

The mountains of temperate southeastern Europe contain resources that were in great demand in the earlier part of the Bronze Age. Their forests provided wood for fires and for construction and sometimes wild game for furs and food (as the bones from mountain sites such as Ljuljaci in central Serbia seem to indicate). The Carpathians of Romania and the mountains of eastern Serbia had metal ores—copper, lead, and silver among them—that are known to have been worked at this time and even earlier. Although the exact mechanism of the trade for these ores and their products, both finished and unfinished, is still a matter of discussion among archaeologists, the ubiquity of metal objects throughout the entire region is indicative of the importance of these resources.

The landscape of the earlier part of the Bronze Age was not only natural but also culturally constructed. The inhabitants of temperate southeastern Europe in the early second millennium were not the earliest people to occupy that territory. Farming settlements had been established some four thousand to five thousand years earlier along the river valleys and the adjacent fertile loess plains (whose soil originally was windblown dust from the glaciers). Reoccupied over the years, some of these had grown to mounds of imposing stature, looming over the flatter river valleys or the Hungarian Plain. While some of those in eastern Hungary and western Romania, such as Pecica and Tószeg, remained occupied during the Early Bronze Age, most of the large habitation mounds of the rest of southeastern Europe were abandoned by 4000 B.C., well before the Bronze Age began. Such is the case with the tell sites of northeastern and north central Bulgaria and southern Romania. The looming presence of these abandoned sites and their former inhabitants may well have played a part in Bronze Age worldview and mythology. Like the modern inhabitants, the prehistoric peoples could have used these sites as topographical reference points that tied a mythic past to their present. Even more immediate, the tumulus burials of the earlier Bronze Age bound the land to known and imagined ancestors, real or fictive progenitors of living people.

LIFE IN THE EARLIER BRONZE AGE: COMMONALITIES

The beginning of the Bronze Age in temperate southeastern Europe in the centuries around 2000 B.C. is in many senses an arbitrary point. Bronze ornaments and tools do become more common. However, neither the smelting of copper ores, the production and use of copper implements, nor the alloying of copper (with either arsenic or tin) to make a harder, more easily worked metal is the defining characteristic of this period. Copper mines (as at Rudna Glava in eastern Serbia and Ai Bunar in south central Bulgaria) and copper artifacts (such as those from Vinča on the Middle Danube) are known from the Eneolithic or Copper Age (4500–2500 B.C.), up to two millennia before the onset of the Bronze Age. Easily made useful small flint blades were still common. The beginnings of metal technology did not apparently cause a major change in the productive technology of southeastern Europe. Indeed some of the earliest Early Bronze Age metal artifacts are ornaments, such as pins, torcs, and hair rings, which may have immediately indicated the status of the wearer while making the most economical use of the metal. The bronze flat axes and riveted triangular daggers of the earliest period may also have conveyed and conferred a degree of status to the possessor. Certainly the more highly decorated examples of the metalsmith's art seem to have been prized more for show than for work.

By the earlier part of the Bronze Age, this region had been occupied for some four millennia by societies that based their subsistence on agriculture and stock raising. Several types of wheat and barley as well as legumes, fruits, and berries are found on Early Bronze Age sites. Although the mix of animals varied somewhat from site to site, possibly due to local geographic and ecological factors, bones from most of the Early and Middle Bronze Age sites that have been analyzed from this region indicate that cattle predominate, followed by sheep or goats and then pigs. Wild animals were of only minor importance for food in most cases, although deer and even aurochs were still being hunted. Transhumant pastoralism, moving the flocks to the uplands in the summer and lowlands in the winter, might have been practiced in the Balkans, but this remains unproven.

The transition from Late Neolithic and Chalcolithic societies to those of the Bronze Age was not sudden but rather a gradual accretion of small interconnected changes in economy, ideology, and social structure that produced a distinctly different picture by the beginning of the second millennium B.C. As Peter Bogucki points out in his *Origins of Human Society* (1999), one of the important ways in which Bronze Age societies differed from those found earlier in the same region relates to the development of animal traction. This builds on Andrew Sherratt's idea of a Secondary Products Revolution, which envisions a major change in the utilization of animals occurring in the fourth millennium B.C. Prior to this time, according to Sherratt, domestic animals, such as sheep, goats, and cattle, were important primarily as food. They were part of a system of food resources that worked synergistically, each part contributing to and amplifying the results of the effort as a whole. Thus domestic animals were "food on the hoof," partial insurance against bad crop years, able to live on uncleared or agriculturally marginal land and able to graze on harvested fields, which they improved by reducing the stubble and producing fertilizer. This model of mixed agriculture and animal husbandry, which was developed by archaeologists based on data from the prehistoric Near East, was also generally valid for the farming ecology of southeastern Europe. Sherratt's model of a Secondary Products Revolution retains this important food-system role for domestic animals but adds further, "secondary," uses: milk and milk products from cattle, goats, and sheep; wool from sheep; traction from cattle (and horses a bit later, in the late fourth millennium). Bogucki sees this latter use of domestic animals as crucial to the developments that led to Bronze Age society, in which social inequality and differences in wealth are generally agreed to be greater than those of the preceding periods.

In modern economic terms, using cattle for traction transformed them from food resources to productive assets. Thus ownership or access to cattle (as well as to land and the human labor force, possibly displacing the latter) became a way in which households and larger kin groups could negotiate their influence and social power. Like differences in land productivity or control of labor, it became another way in which inequality among households and kin groups might be engendered and maintained. Animal traction, first appearing in this region in contexts of the Eneolithic Baden culture (fourth millennium B.C.), made it possible to transport bulky loads (especially wood and stone) more easily as well as speeding up forest clearance and plowing. Wagon models and wooden disk wheels have been found in very Early Bronze Age (around 2000 B.C.) contexts in Hungary (Somogyvar-Vinkovci culture) and Romania (early Wietenberg); plows of this time are not attested for temperate southeastern Europe but are known from other parts of the Continent.

With animal traction decreasing the necessity of a large human labor pool for critical agricultural and subsistence tasks, households could be more widely distributed over the landscape. By 2000–1500 B.C. the settlement pattern of dispersed farmsteads of several related families who shared draft animals and participated together in time-critical agricultural tasks, such as plowing and reaping, contrasts sharply with the more nucleated settlements of the fifth and fourth millennia. With a few exceptions, such as the Early Bronze Age Hungarian Plain tell settlements and some reoccupied fifth millennium tells in south central Bulgaria, "villages" are unknown. The typical inhabitant of southeastern Europe in the earlier Bronze Age lived in a farmstead or hamlet of ten to fifty people. Demographically, in order to survive and reproduce the next generation, the breeding population must be larger than this. Thus although the people of this time lived in small communities, they were necessarily cognizant of other such communities around them. In fact one could think of this settlement pattern, in the words of Anthony Harding, as a "dispersed village." Not all households of this village were equal; some had access to resources denied to others and may have indicated this in various ways by dress, ornaments, or behavior. Many of the households must have been related by blood or marriage over several generations, providing transgenerational pathways to power and recognition, cohesive "institutional memory," and multiple role models for mundane and specialized statuses and tasks.

The structures that households occupied, whether in "dispersed villages" or tell settlements, were generally similar in plan and construction. With few exceptions, they are built of wattle and daub, characterized by weaving or tying smaller sticks to an armature of larger posts and covering the resultant wall with a thick plaster of mud, often with chaff or other plant material mixed in. Houses so constructed probably had thatched roofs with center poles supported by a line of posts. Easy to make, the construction provided insulation from the cold and was (aside from the roof) relatively fireproof. House interiors were either one room or were subdivided by wattle walls; floors were of beaten earth. Storage pits for grain and often an interior hearth completed the inventory. The usually rectangular houses vary in size, possibly reflecting the number of inhabitants and the stage of household development, but most are about 8 to 10 by 4 to 6 meters. Other notable structures of the earlier Bronze Age of this region are "semisubterranean" houses, whose remains are found as pits dug into the subsoil. These tend to be smaller than the aboveground wattle-and-daub houses and may in some cases represent cellar holes or special function structures.

Archaeologists have disagreed over the characterization of the political system of earlier Bronze Age societies. It is generally acknowledged that they cannot be called bands (the technologically simplest, most "egalitarian," smallest-scale type of society in an evolutionary hierarchy) and do not fit into the category of states (the largest, most complex, ranked or socially stratified societal type). Most agree that true states did not emerge in Europe until late in the Iron Age, at least a thousand years later. The societies of the earlier Bronze Age have been called tribes or chiefdoms. As defined by Elman Service in *Primitive Social Organization* (1962), tribes, larger than a band, are made up of a larger number of groups that are self-sufficient and provide their own protection. Leadership is personal and charismatic and usually temporary; there are no permanent political offices that contain real power. The tribal society is made up of discrete "segments," from families to lineages, which combine when necessary to oppose "segments" of equal size. A chiefdom, according to Service and others, is a centrally organized regional population that numbers in the thousands. This population is characteristically more dense than that of simple segmented tribes and usually has evidence of heritable social ranking and economic stratification along with "central places" that coordinate economic, social, and religious activity. The social and political system is hierarchical and pyramidal, with a small, powerful group of elite decision makers and a large mass of lower-status subjects. Religion and legitimate coercion act to assure social control, and craft specialization and redistribution characterize the economic system.

The question of which type of political system best describes the polity of the earlier Bronze Age in temperate southeastern Europe remains open. Its importance lies in the tantalizing nature of the fragmentary data about the social forms of this period and the illusory explanatory power of this evolutionary socioeconomic model. Thus archaeologists often emphasize the supposed ranked nature of Bronze Age society. This ranking is most evident in cemetery assemblages, where some graves are "richer" than others, as judged by the material, the number, or the workmanship of grave goods. The association of mortuary variability with status differences in such prehistoric contexts is far from simple or proven, but one cannot deny that such variability exists and seems to increase as the Bronze Age develops. Similar patterned variety is not generally found in other aspects of the archaeological record of the earlier Bronze Age, except possibly at the very end of the Middle Bronze Age. In multistructure settlements or in "dispersed villages," houses are usually of roughly similar size and construction. Importance or social ranking of a household or kin group does not seem to be able to be inferred from intrasettlement patterning or house location. Except in a very small number of cases, the domestic inventories of cooking and storage vessels, tools, and food preparation implements give little clue as to the ranking of the occupants.

LIFE IN THE EARLIER BRONZE AGE: PARTICULARS

The local groups of the earlier Bronze Age are, above all, identifiable by their ceramics and, to a lesser degree, their metal inventory. Much research since the mid-nineteenth century has been devoted to distinguishing the types and styles of these artifacts and their distributions in time and space. This is connected with an emphasis on collectible artifacts, the excavation of cemeteries (where such artifacts are more often found complete than in settlements), and a stress on local differences rather than areawide similarities. In fact, as has been pointed out above, attention to the lifeways of this period clearly indicates the areawide shared characteristics of these societies. Moreover the (often casually implicit) assumption that communities with shared ceramic or metal types correspond to ethnic groups in the modern sense has been objected to on both theoretical and ethnographic grounds. Nonetheless most archaeologists working in the area continue to speak of the spatial and temporal distributions of these favored artifact types and styles as delineating "cultures" and "cultural groups."

Encompassing an area from Budapest to the Balkans and the Carpathians, the earliest sites considered to be Bronze Age on the Hungarian Plain and its lowland extensions are occupied by people using Somogyvar, Vinkovci, Kisapostag, Nagyrev, and Hatvan ceramics. These wares are found in small settlements and tells such as Tószeg, near Szolnok (Hungary) on the Tisza River, the epynomous sites of Vinkovci (Serbia) or Nagyrev (Hungary), and cemeteries such as Kisapostag (Hungary). Vinkovci pottery is known from sites as far south as the Morava Valley of central Serbia. Although the regional typologies are complex, in general the handmade pottery is smoothed and often burnished, plain or decorated with combed or brushlike exterior surface roughening (especially Hatvan and Nagyrev) or sometimes with simple linear motifs of incised (often with white chalk filling) or applied lines. Widemouthed jugs, bowls, and cups with one or sometimes two handles are common forms as well as simple larger urn shapes. The houses in the habitation sites conform to the typical Early Bronze Age wattle-and-daub construction and form. Cremation burials are the rule in Hatvan and Nagyrev cemeteries, while the people using Kisapostag and Somogyvar pottery practiced inhumation.

The Early Bronze Age sites of the lower Maros (Romanian, Mures) River, with a ceramic tradition closely associated with Hatvan and Nagyrev, are among the most extensively studied of any sites of this time. Settlements are found on the river terraces and ridges lifted above the plain. Tell settlements, such as Periam or Pecica near Arad (Romania), have been known and investigated for more than a century. Aside from the ceramic inventory and relative chronology, these excavations have provided only a small glimpse into the lives of these people. Wattle-and-daub house remains, apparently of large rectangular houses with interior plaster hearths, and storage pits later used for refuse indicate that they shared the common mixed farming economy of the earlier Bronze Age, supplemented by hunting and fishing. A wide variety of points, punches, awls, and needles were made of bone, but little metal was found in the settlements.

Almost on the modern border between Serbia, Hungary, and Romania, the cemeteries of Mokrin (in Serbia) and Szöreg and Deszk (in Hungary) are the last resting places of these Maros villagers of four thousand years ago. These are inhumation cemeteries, sometimes containing several hundred skeleton graves (Mokrin has 312) and associated grave goods of pottery and metal. This type of burial was the most common in the earlier Bronze Age of temperate southeastern Europe and indeed throughout Europe as a whole at this time. The dead were laid in the earth in a contracted position, often with the males oriented one direction and the females the other, usually with the head turned to face the same way. Grave goods were variable, allowing archaeologists to distinguish "rich" from "poor" graves. Typically at least some ornaments (pins, necklaces, bracelets, hair rings, beads), weapons or tools (daggers, axes), or pottery were interred with most of the burials. The ornamental metal objects, such as large curved knot-headed pins and hair rings worn by women, were often made of copper; necklaces, bracelets, and implements were made of bronze. The pottery was handmade, fine burnished black ware, made into graceful biconical shapes of small jugs with flaring rims and two handles or lugs on the shoulder or wider-mouthed bowls. Incised decoration on the pottery, although present, was rare.

As noted above, the association of mortuary variability with status differences in such prehistoric contexts is far from simple or proven. The richest graves contain gold, as well as copper and bronze, while the poorest contain only pottery or no grave goods at all. Some of the women were buried with extensive grave goods, possibly reflecting their own

or their husband's status. The skeletons themselves provide information concerning health and nutrition. At Mokrin, in at least eleven cases, evidence was found for trephination, a procedure where an opening was made in the skull while the person was alive. Its purpose is unknown; relief of some mental or physical illness has been suggested. The number of children's graves indicates high childhood mortality, and pathologies caused by illnesses, such as meningitis, osteomyelitis, sinusitis, and otitis media, have been documented. With high perinatal and childhood mortality, the chances for living into the teens was predictably low. Survivors to adulthood were old at thirty-five, and few lived beyond fifty.

Deeper in the Balkans, the transition to the Bronze Age is still murky. A few burials under tumuli with ceramic grave goods reminiscent of Vinkovci or typologically earliest Vatin (Early to Middle Bronze Age from the area south of the Maros) pottery have been found in western Serbia. Novacka Cuprija in the mountains bordering the Morava River valley in central Serbia is a small farmstead or hamlet site. Pottery from a series of pits dating to about 1900 B.C. bears close resemblance to Vinkovci-style pottery across the Danube. Botanical and zooarchaeological analyses indicate that the Early Bronze Age inhabitants were practicing mixed farming and animal husbandry, growing several types of wheat, barley, lentils, and fruits. Even farther into the mountainous Balkan region, the scatter of small sites in western Bulgaria, although using a different style of pottery, seem to document a similar way of life. Only in central and southern Bulgaria did stable farming settlements with substantial houses, as at Ezero or Yunacite, persist for long enough to form sizable tells.

From about 1800 to 1500 B.C. changes in the habitation and burial sites in temperate southeastern Europe delineate the period that is traditionally called the Middle Bronze Age. These changes include a general preference for cremation burial rather than inhumation, an increase of metal objects and weapons in graves and hoards, and a stronger tendency to place at least some sites on defensible locations, often surrounded with a wall. These changes were long explained as betokening times of more unrest. More recent studies have emphasized the multiple possible reasons for these phenomena, including gradual development of chiefly or tribal societies, emulation of developing Mediterranean societies, economic and social changes that promoted an ideology of male display (involving weapons, but not necessarily large-scale or widespread warfare), changes in metallurgy and technology, or shifts in religious beliefs. The names given to Middle Bronze Age "cultures" vary from region to region, but as in earlier Bronze Age times, the main distinctions seem to be those of ceramic decoration, while the general pattern of life exhibits many commonalities. Thus the people using Incrusted Ware in central Hungary do not differ in many respects (except their preference for certain pottery shapes and designs) from their Vatya Ware neighbors to the east or their Fuzesabony or Otomani contemporaries across the Tisza River. These in turn bear recognizable similarities to the sites in Oltenia and the southern Banat (from the Maros south to the Danube in Serbia) occupied by people using (respectively) Tei and almost identical Vatin pottery. The investigation of many of the excavated settlement sites has emphasized stratigraphic and typological analysis over the analysis of the more mundane foodways and domestic activities.

Initial Hungarian-American excavations at Szazhalombatta, along the Danube south of Budapest, and more complete German-Serbian excavations at Feudvar near Mosorin illustrate a trend toward broader-based research designs that investigate the household economy and everyday life. At Feudvar excavators uncovered a Middle Bronze Age settlement surrounded by a strong wattle-and-daub palisaded wall. Rows of rectangular wattle-and-daub houses of varying sizes (up to 12 by 6 meters) separated by narrow alleys filled the occupied area. Some of these had plastered low-relief designs around the windows and doors. Most had interior plastered hearths and grain storage vessels; some had loom weights and grinding stones on the floors. The pottery is of Vatin type, finely polished carinated vessels with incised and sometimes white-filled geometric and linear patterns. This was a farming settlement, as indicated by the common finds of carbonized one-row and two-row wheat and barley, beans, and legumes, harvested with the help of bronze and flint sickles. At least some of this grain, according to the excavators, went into beer production; no trace of wine or grapes has been found. Aside from the common domestic animals, wild cat-

tle, deer, and wild pigs were hunted. Fishing with harpoon or hooks (and probably nets) was also an important source of food. Animal bone, horn, and antler, found in large numbers in the refuse pits of Feudvar, were worked into tools and ornaments, often decorated with intricate designs of concentric circles and meanders. Similar designs are found on contemporaneous Middle Bronze Age metal shaft-hole axes and swords. While some archaeologists see Mycenaean influence in such motifs, they may equally well have been developed locally.

These were by no means urban societies. Middle Bronze Age settlements like Feudvar, Zidovar, or Dupljaja in the Yugoslav Banat region or the Otomani settlement of Salacea in the Transylvania region of Romania were the largest population centers of their time, possibly numbering a hundred or more people. They usually chose locations that had not been previously inhabited or at least had been abandoned for some time. Nucleated settlements are not numerous; the majority of the population still lived in smaller dispersed hamlets or farmsteads. Goods seem to have moved freely across the landscape. Bronze tools and weapons are found in some abundance several hundred kilometers distant from the nearest ore sources. Textiles and food products may have formed an archaeological invisible part of exchange networks. Cremation burial is the rule, often in burnished biconical urns with incised designs accompanied by smaller vessels whose carinated shapes may imitate metal.

The pattern of life developed in temperate southeastern Europe in the earlier Bronze Age is distinctively European in flavor. In this microcosm one can already perceive the later landscape of hamlets and small towns, farmsteads and fields almost lost in the forested mass of the Continent. The artwork of Bronze Age peoples on metal and ceramics emphasizes a strong local identity within a wider, perhaps only indirectly and hazily perceived community. Their names, their gods, their lives gone for millennia, the people of the Early and Middle Bronze Ages of southeastern Europe left a legacy lasting to early modern times.

See also **Transition to Farming in the Balkans** (vol. 1, part 3); **The Early and Middle Bronze Ages in Central Europe** (vol. 2, part 5).

BIBLIOGRAPHY

Bailey, Douglass. *Balkan Prehistory: Exclusion, Incorporation, and Identity*. London: Routledge, 2000.

Bailey, Douglass, and Ivan Panayotov, eds. *Prehistoric Bulgaria*. Monographs in World Archaeology, no. 22. Madison, Wis.: Prehistory Press, 1995.

Bogucki, Peter. *The Origins of Human Society*. Oxford: Blackwell, 1999.

Coles, John, and Anthony Harding. *The Bronze Age in Europe*. London: Methuen, 1979. (A basic source for information about this period; dated, but still very useful.)

Gimbutas, Marija. *Bronze Age Cultures in Central and Eastern Europe*. The Hague: Mouton, 1965.

Girić, Miodrag. *Mokrin: Nekropola ranog bronzanog doba* [Mokrin: A cemetery of the Early Bronze Age]. Belgrade: Serbian Academy of Arts and Sciences, 1971. (Basic site report on a large Early Bronze Age cemetery; Serbian and English text.)

Hänsel, Bernhard, and Predrag Medović, eds. *Feudvar I: Das Plateau von Titel und die Šajkaška: Titelski Plato I Šajkaška*. Kiel, Germany: Verlag Oetker/Voges, 1998.

Harding, Anthony. *European Societies in the Bronze Age*. Cambridge, U.K.: Cambridge University Press, 2000.

———. "Bronze Age in Central and Eastern Europe." *Advances in World Archaeology* 2 (1983): 1–50.

Mohen, Jean-Pierre, and Christiane Eluère. *The Bronze Age in Europe*. New York: Harry Abrams, 1999. (Although containing only a small section of southeastern temperate Europe, this small volume has some very good artifact illustrations.)

O'Shea, John M. *Villagers of the Maros: A Portrait of a Bronze Age Society*. New York: Plenum Press, 1996.

Service, Elman. *Primitive Social Organization*. New York: Random House, 1962.

Sherratt, Andrew. "Plough and Pastoralism: Aspects of the Secondary Products Revolution." In *Pattern of the Past: Studies in Honour of David Clarke*. Edited by Ian Hodder, Glyn Isaac, and Nicholas Hammond, pp. 261–305. Cambridge, U.K.: Cambridge University Press, 1981.

Tasić, Nikola, ed. *Kulturen der Frühbronzezeit des Karpatenbeckens und Nordbalkans*. Belgrade: Prosveta, 1984. (Good collection of articles on the Bronze Age of temperate southeastern Europe by Hungarian, Yugoslav, and Romanian scholars.)

H. ARTHUR BANKOFF

THE EARLY AND MIDDLE BRONZE AGES IN CENTRAL EUROPE

FOLLOWED BY FEATURE ESSAY ON:

Spišský Štvrtok *31*

The definition and chronological framework of the Bronze Age is by no means uniform within the archaeological literature. Various areas had different paths and rhythms of change and development, and regional traditions of research influenced the labeling and periodization of the archaeological material in many ways. Thus, the Bronze Age begins in the last centuries of the fourth millennium B.C. in the Near East and the Aegean, around the middle of the third millennium B.C. in the northern Balkans and the Carpathian Basin, and around 2300 B.C. in central Europe—despite the fact that bronze itself became widespread a few centuries later. The Early Bronze Age of central Europe can be divided up into an early phase from about 2300 to 2000 B.C. and a later phase from about 2000 to 1600 B.C. The Middle Bronze Age (with its own subdivisions) spanned the time between about 1600 and 1350 B.C.

Central Europe will be taken here to consist of modern-day Germany, Switzerland, Austria, the Czech Republic, Poland, and Slovakia. The geography of this vast area varies widely. It is dominated by large alluvial plains—the Danube Valley, the North European Plain, the Carpathian Basin—and bordered by high mountains, namely the Alps in the south and the Carpathians in the east, along with lower mountainous areas in central Germany, Bohemia, and southern Poland. The large rivers of central Europe (the Danube, Rhine, Oder, and Elbe) and their tributaries provided natural corridors for communication, travel, and trade. The area has a temperate Continental climate: cold, wet winters and warm, moist summers, with precipitation evenly distributed throughout the year. The Bronze Age falls into the so-called Subboreal climatic phase (about 3000–1000 B.C.), with only a slightly lower average temperature and a drier climate than that of today. Climatic changes altered vegetation during this period. Although deciduous forests continued to dominate most of the area, their composition changed: previous forests of oak, linden, and elm gave way to beech, with lime disappearing almost entirely. Human impact had its effect on the landscape as well. Deforestation due to opening up arable land and pasture reached its peak in the Late Neolithic and Early Bronze Age during the phase of initial occupation of various environmental niches and decreased afterward. Local variation was, however, caused by different scales of wood use: copper mining in the eastern Alps and central Germany required a large amount of wood, as did the continuous rebuilding of timber houses in the Alpine lake settlements, to the extent that regeneration of local forests did not occur.

MATERIAL REMAINS

Pottery Styles. The various environmental zones of central Europe—despite the natural routes connecting neighboring regions—accommodated human groups with fairly diverse material cultures. The most frequent trace of this diversity is evident in the pottery of these communities, and its study constitutes the bulk of traditional archaeological studies. Pottery is classified into regional stylistic groups, often named after "type-sites" or some important characteristic of the style. These groupings are sometimes referred to as "archaeological cultures," a dubious, normative category often equated with prehistoric ethnic groups. Although such an interpretation has come to be strongly questioned, some knowledge of these groupings is essential because archaeological material from various regions is often referred to by these labels.

In Slovakia, for example, the first half of the Early Bronze Age in the western part of the country is characterized by Nitra pottery; in the east we find the so-called Košt'any material. Later on the Nitra develops into Únětice and Mad'arovce styles, whereas Košt'any is followed by Otomani style in the east, with similar or identical material from east Hungary (Füzesabony, Gyulavarsánd) and northwest Romania (Otomani). In Austria, the Czech Republic, Germany, and Switzerland the final phase of Bell Beaker assemblages appear at the very beginning of the Early Bronze Age, which later gives way to various local developments: Straubing and Adlerberg in Germany; Unterwölbing and Wieselburg in Austria; and Únětice (or Aunjetitz) in the Czech Republic, some parts of Germany, and southwestern Poland—the final phase of which is termed *Böheimkirchen* in Austria and *Věteřov* in the Czech Republic. The Middle Bronze Age shows a more unified picture in terms of pottery styles, with most of central Europe covered by Tumulus culture type or related material with some local variation.

Settlements. The material remains of the period come from various contexts and locations—settlements, burials, and metal hoards—and show significant differences in their geographical and temporal distribution. As for settlements, their occurrence during the Early and Middle Bronze Ages varies considerably both spatially and temporally. Large areas show no signs of settlement at all, and the extension of occupation can only be reconstructed on the basis of the distribution of graves and hoards. In many cases, where settlement remains are found, they only consist of pits dug into the subsoil. There are, however, some areas where archaeologists have good knowledge of house forms, internal settlement organization, and larger settlement patterns as well, especially from the later part of the Early Bronze Age.

The most widespread house form of the Early Bronze Age appears to have been a rectangular timber-frame construction with large posts in the corners and along the longer sides of the houses. The walls were formed by these posts, which were set roughly 1 to 2 meters apart and the gaps filled with reed or wattle and daub. Houses like these were found in the Czech Republic (e.g., at Pospoloprty, Blšany, or Březno), Austria (at Franzhausen or Böheimkirchen), or on the so-called tell settlements (multilayered settlement mounds) of Slovakia. Sizes could vary considerably even within settlements—from smaller buildings, measuring 4 by 6 meters, to larger ones, like a house at Březno that measured 32 by 6.5 meters. Some houses might have internal divisions into two or three rooms (e.g., at Nitriansky Hrádok in Slovakia) or have central posts to support a ridged roof. Other techniques of construction are known as well. Houses might have stone foundations or foundation ditches, they might have wooden plank floors, or they might have been entirely made of wood with the so-called *Blockbau* technique resulting a "log cabin."

Some of the best-preserved buildings come from lake dwellings in the Alps (southern Germany and Switzerland) preserved in the waterlogged environment. At Zurich-Mozarstrasse rectangular buildings were excavated that had sleeper beams laid directly on the floor and perforated by mortise holes through which posts were inserted and rammed into the ground. A number of various house types have been recovered in Cham-Obervil on Lake Zug and at Padnal near Savognin in Switzerland as well. In Padnal the earliest settlement layer had post-and-plank-built houses, sometimes with stone foundations, in one case with a floor of wooden planks. In later phases houses had stone foundations and wooden walls, and their floors were sometimes paved with stone.

In the Middle Bronze Age evidence for house forms becomes much scarcer. Some earlier settlements in Switzerland (e.g., Bodaman-Schachen) and Slovakia (e.g., Veselé) continued uninterrupted until the end of the initial phase of the Middle Bronze Age, with house types described above. A few other finds—for example from Tannhausen in Bavaria—also confirm the existence of post-built houses with wattle-and-daub walls. Other sites, as at Nitra in Slovakia, show new types: small semisubterranean houses about 3.5 meters wide and 5 meters long.

By looking at larger patterns, a number of different settlement types might be distinguished. Aside from the rarely detectable—small and short-lived—villages and hamlets, one special class is hilltop sites such as those found, for example, in southern Germany and Moravia, located on strategically important locations and rising above and controlling their immediate environment. Similar locations were chosen for larger settlements with impressive fortifications of ditches, ramparts, and palisades. About thirty such sites are known from Slovakia alone, the excavated ones displaying a well-organized, almost urbanistic internal layout, sometimes having narrow alleys between houses that line up in rows; comparable settlements make their appearance in southern Poland, the Czech Republic, and southern Germany.

Such sites were part of a settlement system with a hierarchy of at least two levels. They emerged in the later phase of the Early Bronze Age and indicate an increase both in local warfare and social complexity. They usually occupy easily defendable locations along important trade routes along river valleys, usually at distances of some 10 to 20 kilometers from each other, and were surrounded by smaller, undefended sites.

Burial. In many cases evidence of burial is the only record attesting the prehistoric occupation of an area during the Early and Middle Bronze Ages in central Europe. In this period, burial was usually by inhumation, either under or without a mound. The standard rite in the Early Bronze Age was flat inhumation in cemeteries of various sizes. Bodies were interred either on their sides in a crouched position with their legs bent and pulled upward, or they were placed flat on their backs. Specific details, however,

varied from region to region. In this respect, two large groups may be discerned. In the Danube Valley burial rites show a strict gender differentiation in terms of the orientation of the body: men were placed on one side, and women were placed on the other side with their heads lying in the opposite direction. In both groups, resultingly, the face was looking in the same direction. Cemeteries with this kind of burial ritual include the one at Gemeinlebarn in Austria, with grave numbers reaching into the hundreds; at Franzhausen, with well over one thousand graves; and a large number of smaller cemeteries in southern Germany (e.g., at Singen). Graves are arranged in a similar manner in eastern Slovakia, northeast Hungary, and around the area of the borders between Hungary, Romania, and Serbia, although the specific orientation of graves varies regionally. Sometimes even cemeteries near each other show differences in this respect. In the Rhine Valley and in Switzerland graves containing similar material culture do not observe such a differentiation between the sexes, nor do the many smaller cemeteries of the Únětice (or Aunjetitz) area.

In addition to the regular burial rites, exceptional modes of interment have also been observed. Cremation became more frequent around the end of the Early Bronze Age, especially in southwest Slovakia, most probably due to more intense connections with the rest of the Carpathian Basin, where this rite had been practiced since the beginning of the Bronze Age. A number of special burials have been found within the previously described inhumation cemeteries as well. In cemeteries with Únětice-type material, sometimes double or multiple burials occur, usually containing the bodies of a man and a women or an adult and a child or children, suggesting a close relationship between the buried persons. At some Bohemian sites these multiple burials contained the remains of dismembered skeletons; in other cases the head of the deceased was cut off before burial. In many cases traces of wooden coffins or other wooden constructions were found. Sometimes grave pits were walled by stone slabs or marked by stone stelae on the surface.

Grave goods are usually sex-specific in all these burials. Most graves contain personal ornaments, weapons, tools, and pottery. In the earlier part of the Early Bronze Age (c. 2300–2000 B.C.) metal items—usually made of copper—were rare. Male graves were sometimes furnished with triangular copper or bronze daggers, sometimes flat or flanged axes, and (rarely) pins or earrings or hair rings. Female graves contained mostly ornaments, like copper earrings and bracelets. Nonmetal items included flint tools and weapons (arrowheads, scrapers, etc.), bone objects (e.g., awls, pins), or beads made of various materials (such as faience, amber, bone, antler, shells). In the later part of the Early Bronze Age (c. 2000–1600 B.C.) bronze grave goods become more widespread and numerous. New types included various pins, bronze axes, neck rings, bronze pendants, and diadems.

A number of Early Bronze Age graves stand out among the others both in terms of their construction and the richness of their grave goods: these are the so-called princely burials of the Únětice area. Two famous burial mounds are located in Saxo-Thuringia in central Germany. At Leubingen, a barrow about 35 meters in diameter and 8–9 meters high was excavated in 1877. Under the earthen mound a circular ditch surrounded a stone cairn covering a rectangular wooden chamber. A skeleton of an elderly man was laid on the oak planks covering the floor. Another skeleton, probably that of a child, was laid across his hips. Grave goods consisted of a pot, a halberd, three small triangular daggers, two flanged axes, three chisels, two gold "eyelet" pins, one gold spiral bead, a massive gold bracelet, and two gold hair rings.

The other famous barrow near Helmsdorf, excavated in 1907, had a similar size. Here, a stone wall surrounded the central cairn, under which a wooden chamber was found. The floor of the chamber was paved with stone slabs in the northern half and covered with reed in the southern end. The skeleton of an adult man was laid down in a contracted position on its right side on the floor of the chamber. The grave goods—a broken clay vessel, a stone hammer, remains of a bronze dagger and a chisel, a bronze flat axe, a gold spiral bead, two gold earrings, and two gold pins—were placed on the bier as well. At various places, the construction showed traces of burning, probably the results of burial feasts or an attempt at firing the whole structure. (Excavation at a similar barrow, near Dieskau, could only confirm that it had been robbed. However, a gold "hoard" from the same site—three

bracelets and a flanged axe—was most probably part of the grave goods deposited in the barrow.)

Because they were made of wood, the burial chambers could be analyzed using dendrochronological methods, providing a date of about 1800 B.C. for the burial at Helmsdorf and about 1900 B.C. for that at Leubingen, putting both at the beginning of the later part of the Early Bronze Age.

Interment under barrows became the standard burial rite in the Middle Bronze Age throughout central Europe. Forms and structure of grave construction differed from region to region, sometimes even within one barrow cemetery. Interment was usually by inhumation; cremation, however, became more and more frequent in some areas, such as Bavaria and eastern Slovakia. Barrows might consist of a simple earthen mound above a grave pit; they might have circular ditches around them; or they might be covered by stones. In some instances stone cist graves were used as well. Grave goods in the Middle Bronze Age still usually consisted of personal ornaments, weapons, and tools. Richer male graves contained a sword, a dagger, and an axe, poorer graves have only one or two of these items. Female graves were furnished with ornaments and jewelry—mostly pins, bracelets, pendants, or belt buttons.

Often these grave goods provide an opportunity to reconstruct prehistoric clothing and the various ways ornaments and jewelry were worn, especially by women. An elaborate bronze headgear for women could be reconstructed based on the finds from three graves from the Early Bronze Age cemetery at Franzhausen in Austria. In the Middle Bronze Age, round spiked or heart-shaped pendants might be worn hanging from a necklace or sewn on the neck of a dress. Bronze pins fastened the dresses in the front at the height of the chest; decorated spiral-ended bands were worn on the ankle; and small bronze buttons were attached to belts or skirts. Bracelets and spiral-ended finger rings were common ornaments as well.

METALLURGY

A development in metallurgical techniques and raw materials used for the production of metal objects is one of the main characteristics of the Bronze Age. Although copper had already been in use since the seventh and sixth millennia B.C. in Anatolia, bronze (copper alloyed with tin) makes its appearance much later, in the third millennium B.C., giving its name to a whole prehistoric period. Bronze first appeared in the Near East; the largest concentration of finds appears in Mesopotamia, Iran, and Anatolia, in the early third millennium B.C.—paradoxically in areas without the necessary raw materials. It appears in the Carpathian Basin by the middle of the third millennium B.C. and by the end of the millennium it was the most commonly used metal from the Atlantic coast to Southeast Asia.

What caused such a fast adoption of the new material and the techniques of its production? Bronze is easier to work, especially to cast, than pure copper. It has a lower melting point and is less prone to subsequent fragmentation due to blistering during casting. Tin also hardens the metal, both after casting and hammering, resulting in more efficient tools and weapons. However, in the earliest phase of bronze metallurgy, bronze was rarely used to produce weapons and tools; rather, it was used for jewelry, ornaments, or vessels. This suggests the value placed on other qualities of the metal: possibly its texture and color, since the addition of tin gave copper a golden-brownish shine similar to that of gold, which was also greatly valued in prehistoric times. Furthermore, tin is a rare material with few sources in Europe, and it must have been procured separately from copper from great distances. This could have significantly contributed to its value and attraction as raw material for precious objects.

Procurement. Major sources of tin in Europe are found in Cornwall in Great Britain and in the Bohemian Erzgebirge (Ore Mountains), both of great importance in prehistoric times. Less significant deposits are in Bretagne, the French Massif Central, and northwestern Iberia. Copper sources are more numerous and had already been exploited from the Late Neolithic. One important development, however, was that, whereas in earlier times surface deposits of copper oxides had been used, in the Early Bronze Age sulphide copper ores began to be extracted from greater depths, triggering an intensification of mining activities. Central Europe probably was supplied from a number of different copper sources: the eastern Alpine area, the Harz Mountains in central Germany, the northern Carpathians in eastern Slovakia, and the eastern Carpathians in Transylvania. This latter area probably provided

most of the gold used in the Bronze Age of central Europe as well. Although direct traces of prehistoric exploitation are rare, a fairly well studied Bronze Age mining area is known in the Austrian Alps at Mitterberg, southwest of Salzburg. In order to extract the sulphide ores, large pits were created in the rock—with picks, stone hammers, and the help of fire (causing cracks in the rock)—and those pits sometimes later turned into shafts running up to 100 meters long. The separation of the ores took place outside the shafts, probably with the help of water, and the smelting of metal from the ore was usually carried out farther down the mountain slopes. Such intensity of extraction required tremendous organization, especially to facilitate the lighting, ventilation, and drainage of the shafts. The specialized communities carrying out the actual mining were dependent on others for food production and for the procurement of the huge amount of wood that was needed during cracking the rocks, extraction, supporting the shafts, and smelting the ores.

Production. The production of bronze artifacts by bronzesmiths could take place anywhere in local workshops. Based on finds of metallurgical equipment (molds, crucibles, small conical clay nozzles for bellows, stone hammers, and so forth) and the distribution of various types of objects, it seems certain that all areas had their own metalworking centers even when no raw materials were available locally. Based on typological differences, three major metalworking provinces may be discerned in the Early Bronze Age: a Danubian group in the north Alpine area; the Únětice province in central Germany, Bohemia, Moravia, and western Poland; and a Carpathian group in Slovakia with strong ties to more southerly centers within the Carpathian Basin. Early Bronze Age bronze objects include ring ingots, sheet bronze bosses (round, decorated bronze sheets with a half-spherical knob/boss in the middle), spectacle spiral pendants, spiral bracelets and finger rings, metal plaques, arm and leg spirals, simple and solid-hilted triangular daggers, flat and flanged axes, and racket-headed pins with folded tops.

In the later Early Bronze Age there was an even greater variety of metalwork. Daggers became longer and ogival in shape; flanged axes, shaft-hole axes, and halberds appeared, and a number of new pin forms came into use, the most important of which was the pin with perforated spherical head. An important innovation was the manufacture of bronze vessels, of which so far only one is known, found in Skeldal, Denmark, but produced in the Únětice area. The Middle Bronze Age witnessed a typological unification of the area, and the introduction of new types, like longer pins with seal-shaped heads or pins with sickle-shaped twisted shafts, wide ribbed bracelets, heart-shaped pendants, small two- or four-riveted daggers with rounded or trapezoid heels, palstaves, tweezers, and, importantly, new forms of swords.

Hoards. One of the most striking phenomena of the Bronze Age is the deposition of metalwork in hoards. The hoards vary greatly from each other in terms of number of items, number of types buried, or the locations in which they were buried, among other elements. One very important aspect of hoards, however, was the burial of ingots and fragmented objects. Ingots seem to be intermediate forms well suited for transport and easy to cast, serving mainly the purpose of enabling the movement of the raw material to a smith's workshop. However, another aspect seems to be just as significant. The so-called ring ingots of the Early Bronze Age show a remarkable uniformity in their weight (usually 180–200 grams), similar to some forms of early flanged axes and, later, rib-shaped ingots. This might suggest that they played the role of standard weights and units of exchange within a pre-monetary economic system. The copper in the ingots exhibits a uniform and unusual composition that might be a result of some unique treatment that made it appropriate for such a special use. This interpretation, however, still does not explain the burial of these ingots and axes in hoards containing hundreds of identical pieces. Was such a withdrawal from circulation the result of overproduction beyond the propensity of local consumption? Or was the practice of hoarding intended as an offering for gods, in the hope of receiving a supernatural "guarantee" for the hoarded items' value as currency in the secular sphere? Whatever their purpose, these kinds of hoards soon disappear from the archaeological record, and a similar function seems to have been transferred to bronze fragments broken to pieces of identical weight that appear in hoards from the turn of the Early to Middle Bronze Age (e.g.,

in the famous hoards of Bühl and Ackenbach) and that have a long history through the Late Bronze Age.

Gold and Silver. Although objects made of bronze abound in the material of this period, artifacts of precious metals are much scarcer. Whereas silver is extremely rare, there are a few important and well-known examples of the use of gold. The finds of "chiefly graves" with gold grave goods from Leubingen and Helmsdorf are perhaps the most famous. In other, less spectacular, graves gold hair rings are sometimes found, and occasionally hoards of gold objects are recovered as well, like that from a fortified settlement at Bernstorf in Bavaria. The most impressive products of Early Bronze Age gold metallurgy, however, are the gold beakers from Fritzdorf near Bonn and Gölenkamp near Hannover in Germany and from Eschenz in Switzerland, dated to around 1600/1500 B.C. They show some similarity to silver beakers found in Brittany and other golden beakers from France and Great Britain, thus connecting them to an Atlantic network of workshops.

AGRICULTURE

The wealthiest segment of Bronze Age society—the chiefs and their immediate retinue—had easy access to the prestigious products of the local and faraway metalworking centers, but most of the population lived under much more modest circumstances. Their most important daily concern was the production of food—the maintenance of the subsistence economy. The communities of central Europe at this time practiced mixed farming: growing crops and raising stock. The most commonly cultivated plants of the Bronze Age were those of the Neolithic as well: emmer, einkorn, and barley. Somewhat less significant were flax, peas, and lentils. Newly introduced species included spelt, millet, broad beans, and oats. There might have been an increase in barley cultivation during the Bronze Age, possibly due to its use as a raw material for making the alcoholic beverages consumed at important social occasions and rituals. Most domesticated animals—cattle, sheep, goats, pigs, and dogs—were inherited from Neolithic times as well. One major change was an increase in the exploitation of the horse—which remained fairly rare after its introduction in the Final

Neolithic—suggesting an increase in its use as a traction animal and for riding.

The Bronze Age witnessed an intensification in the agricultural practices carried down from the Neolithic, a process that began in the Final Neolithic with the introduction of a number of important innovations sometimes termed the "Secondary Products Revolution": the exploitation of animals for secondary products (milk and other dairy products, power for traction, wool for textile production) and the introduction of plowing with wooden ards (primitive light plows). These innovations made possible a greater diversification of subsistence strategies reflected by changes in land use, occupying a wider range of locations. In many areas pastoralism and transhumance seem to have gained greater importance, with possibly larger numbers of animals kept for their primary and secondary products. This tendency seems to be even more pronounced in the Middle Bronze Age, as reflected by a much more dispersed settlement pattern.

RITUAL AND RELIGION

Although the reconstruction of agricultural practices can be carried out fairly straightforwardly based on plant and animal remains, the observation and interpretation of prehistoric rituals and religious life is a much more difficult task. Without written documents archaeologists can only rely on the recognition of special contexts in which some of the material remains occur, and from this they must try to reconstruct complex systems of beliefs that influenced most spheres of life.

The multilayered settlement mounds of Slovakia and the central and eastern part of the Carpathian Basin provide an interesting case to point out for description. These tells were built up during hundreds of years through the cyclical burning of houses and their rebuilding at the same location, on top of the ruins of their predecessors. This cyclical, constantly recurring practice is best explained as a conscious action, the deliberate destruction of living place, most probably connected to the life cycles of their owners. The rebuilding of the same structures in the same places can be viewed as connected to the worship of ancestors and ancestral places. Although destruction implies discontinuity, the rebuilding reinforces continuity and legitimation through a connection with the past and the ancestors. Special

places having some significance in local mythologies were probably also singled out for settlement and continuous (re)occupation.

These settlements were the location of many special depositions, in pits or wells. At Gánovce in central Slovakia, for example, a deep well apparently containing ritual depositions was found in the middle of a settlement. The fill contained a large amount of pottery, plant and animal remains, burned ashes, human bones, birch bark cups, and one of the earliest iron objects in Europe: a sickle blade. Other settlements contain similar depositions of pottery and of bronze and gold objects in pits among houses or under the house floors. Some of these hoards contain only pottery—usually sets of intact drinking cups, which makes clear that the hoards were not simply rubbish pits. The cups seem to be the remains of feasts and rituals connected to various social occasions, like rites of passage, and suggest the consumption of alcoholic beverages on such events, after which the vessels used were buried.

Indeed, one of the most important, archaeologically visible, prehistoric ritual activities was the deposition of hoards of copper, bronze, and gold objects. Although previous generations of archaeologists tended to interpret these as personal or communal property buried in times of danger and never subsequently retrieved, an interpretation that views the hoarding as an element of ritual is becoming more and more accepted. Many of the hoards were buried in special, isolated locations in the landscape: in rivers, lakes, or fens; under large rocks; in caves; in mountain passes; on top of hills or mountains. Sometimes the contents and the mode of deposition of the hoards point at their ritual nature as well. Objects were deposited in waters or fens from where they could never be retrieved. The arrangement of the buried objects sometimes shows a great degree of care, which contradicts the interpretation that the items were hastily hidden valuables. In other cases the objects were deliberately damaged or fragmented, seemingly in order to avoid further profane use. The deposition of such votive assemblages now appears to represent a gift exchange between humans and supernatural forces through which people hoped to establish reciprocal obligations and influence the gods. At some of these sacred places the burial of hoards continued through hundreds of years; such places later became sanctuaries dedicated to gods. For example, around Melz in northern Germany a large concentration of Early Bronze Age hoards was observed. At Dresden-Dobritz four metal hoards, one pottery deposition, and a hoard of metal vessels were found within a small area, on a strip of land 200–300 meters long and 80 meters wide along the river Elbe. At Berlin-Spandau remains of a post-built structure, a sort of pier leading into the water, were recovered. A selected group of objects had been deposited here in the Early and Middle Bronze Ages, probably not at the same time, but over a long period. All the artifacts were weapons, and some of them arrived here from longer distances. Two swords came from northern Germany or Scandinavia, a solid-hilted dagger came from Denmark, and another sword came from eastern France. This and similar sites show that these sacred locations had interregional significance, similar to the famous sanctuaries of classical Greece.

A unique and highly significant find from the Bronze Age fortified settlement of Mittelberg near Nebra in central Germany shows again that such settlements were indeed ritual centers as well. Beside a hoard of bronze objects (two swords, two flanged axes, a chisel, and fragments of arm spirals) dated to around 1600 B.C., a bronze disk with gold inlays was recovered in a stone cist (fig. 1). The inlays represent the sun, the crescent moon, and the starry sky, with the Pleiades constellation of seven stars clearly recognizable. Two gold bands on the rim present the horizon while a third band between them seems to be a representation of a ship—an object that will gain significant ritual connotation in the later history of the Bronze Age—traveling across the nocturnal celestial ocean. Although a full study of this new find has not been published yet, it will most certainly enrich our understanding of prehistoric astronomy, mythology, and cosmology.

EXCHANGE NETWORKS

Trade and exchange were important factors in the social and economic development of any given area, triggering important changes and contributing to the increase of social complexity. In addition to the flow of raw materials and finished objects, exchange networks also provided a framework for the flow of information through which important inventions,

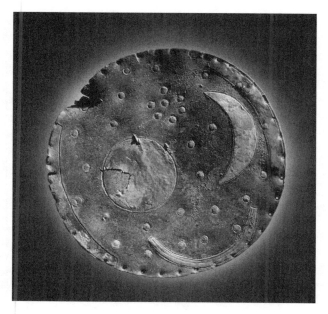

Fig. 1. The "celestial disk" of Nebra (Germany). PHOTOGRAPH BY JURAJ LIPTÁK. LANDESAMT FÜR ARCHÄOLOGIE SACHSEN-ANHALT, LANDESMUSEUM FÜR VORGESCHICHTE. REPRODUCED BY PERMISSION.

innovations and new technologies spread throughout Europe. These networks can be mapped by identifying the distribution of rare materials (e.g., amber, tin, copper, and gold) or the appearance of objects outside their densest distribution area where they were most probably manufactured.

The most important and widely exchanged raw materials of the Bronze Age were, obviously, tin and copper, used to manufacture bronze objects. Although the sole source of tin in central Europe is the Erzgebirge (Ore Mountains) in Bohemia, copper is more widely found, as described above. Amber is found on the shores of the Baltic Sea and western Jutland in Denmark. Other traded raw materials must have included gold, probably from Transylvanian sources, and salt from seashores and surface deposits, for example in the area around Halle on the Saale River in central Germany. Exchanged finished products include bronze objects, sometimes pottery, and also archaeologically invisible, or almost untraceable, items like textiles, furs, and possibly foodstuffs.

Although traffic in these commodities wove a web of connections throughout central Europe on the basis of already existing trade patterns, by the Bronze Age central Europe also had become part of a much larger exchange network that is sometimes

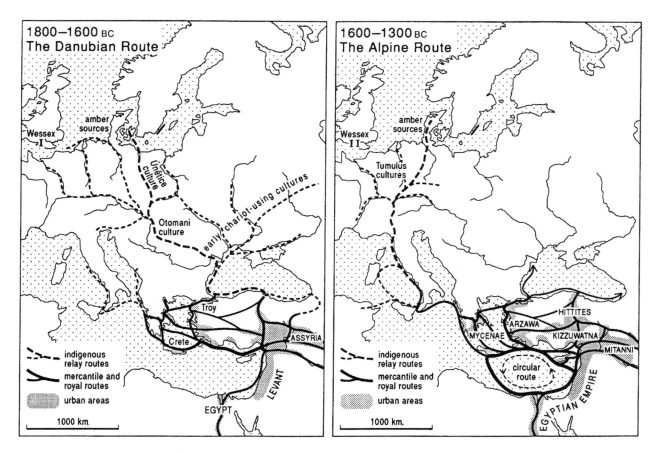

Principal trade routes of the Early (left) and Middle (right) Bronze Ages. MAPS BY ANDREW SHERRATT. REPRODUCED BY PERMISSION.

labeled a "prehistoric world-system." Although temperate Europe played only the role of a "margin" in the system of the Near Eastern "core area" and an important "periphery" in Anatolia, these links were a significant factor in the development of social and economic complexity.

It seems that emerging urban centers in Anatolia established connections with European communities around the mouth of the Danube and beyond. During the Early Bronze Age (c. 2300–1600 B.C.), the Danube became an important axis of exchange along which objects and information about new technologies were exchanged. Ring ingots and so-called Cypriot wound-wire pins reached Troy (in northwest Asia Minor), Egypt, and Byblos (modern Jubayl, Lebanon) on the Levantine coast. Transylvanian gold might have traveled to Anatolia. The systematic use of copper alloys might have been begun as a result of Anatolian contacts: indeed, a non-European source for the tin of the earliest European bronze artifacts, produced before the exploi-

tation of Bohemian tin started, cannot be excluded. A few exotic items—like a slotted dagger of Anatolian or Aegean origin found together with amber beads, wound-wire pins, and an ingot ring at Kyhna in Saxony—made their ways into the center of the Continent. These stimulated already existing local exchange cycles and triggered a demand for prestige items obtained through long-distance connections.

In the later Early Bronze Age another innovation reached the Carpathian Basin and central Europe via this route: the two-wheeled "chariot." Although constructions probably remained simple, these were still elite items and remained so for a long time, as rich wagon burials of the Late Bronze Age and Early Iron Age show. Decorated antler cheekpieces for bridle bits found in Slovakian and Moravian fortified sites also attest their connection to the local elites. These fortified sites along the tributaries of the Danube were located on the most important trade routes to the north: the source of amber. Prestigious bronze objects such as decorated shaft-hole axes and solid-hilted swords produced in the Carpathian Basin or a small bronze vessel manufactured in the Únětice area reached Denmark via this network (fig. 2, left). Central Europe also had important connections with the Atlantic area, as shown by the appearance of so-called Armorico-British-type daggers in the cemetery of Singen in southwestern Germany or two amber beads from Switzerland: one with gold casing found at Zurich-Mozartstrasse and a star-shaped one from Arbon-Bleiche, both probably manufactured in the Wessex area in Great Britain.

In the Middle Bronze Age this axis of trade shifted. The Danube became less important, routes to northern Europe realigned along a north-south axis via Germany, and the passes through the Alps from central Europe to Italy gained significance. Through this route European communities came into indirect contact with Mycenaean communities establishing connections with the Tyrrhenian coast in western Italy. Baltic amber reached Mycenae and was found in the famous Shaft Graves. Since at this time no other amber finds are known to Greece, this seems to be an instance of directional trade with only few intermediaries (fig. 2, right). At Bernstorf (Bavaria, southern Germany), in a Middle Bronze Age fortified hilltop settlement dated to about 1600–1400 B.C., a number of amber beads were found (together with the hoard of gold objects mentioned above), two of which deserve special attention. One of them had a face of a man carved on one side with a few incised signs on the other side. The other one had four incised signs on it, three of which have been identified as Linear B signs—the writing of the Late Bronze Age Mycenaean kingdoms of Greece—whereas the fourth probably represents a ship. It seems that the raw material—amber—reached the Aegean world from the Baltic area where it was written on using the local writing system. Later on it returned to central Europe and was deposited at a local fortified center.

SOCIETY AND COMMUNITY

In the early third millennium B.C. a new concern with prestige and social stratification, and the representation of these through the deposition of copper objects, is observable in the archaeological record. In the first phase of the Early Bronze Age (c. 2300–2000 B.C.), this tendency continues, although with regional differences: in Bohemia and central Germany, only a narrow range of variation in grave goods is observable, whereas in the Danube Valley an increase in the differentiation of grave goods—suggesting slightly greater social differentiation—is apparent from the beginning of the Bronze Age. This incipient social ranking seems based on an increasing intensification of the subsistence economy, since greater social stratification seems to emerge in fertile and agriculturally very productive regions not too far away from metal sources. Later on, however, with the increase of bronze production, metal artifacts do not simply reflect social status. It seems that access to, and control of, metal sources and prestige items circulating in exchange networks became necessary sources of political and economic control.

In the later phase of the Early Bronze Age (c. 2000–1600 B.C.), the different nature of economic and political power and a greater social differentiation is also reflected by the emergence of two-level settlement hierarchies in certain regions, where one or two fortified sites surrounded by a number of smaller, undefended settlements dominated and controlled smaller areas, usually along river valleys. These settlements were probably the residences of local chiefs and their immediate retinue and served as nodal points in exchange networks and as centers of economic production. Various regions, however, reacted in various ways to the intensification of bronze production. In the northern periphery, in central Germany and Poland, the chiefly burial mounds and their rich grave goods are probably witnesses of the emergence of the monopolistic position of local elites in terms of access to metal and prestige-goods exchange. Such a monopoly of the elite could not develop in areas closer to metal sources with more dense exchange networks. In those areas a much more competitive situation emerged, leading to warfare and the construction of fortifications around local centers. This was accompanied by the crystallization of a male warrior ethos, expressed in the much more elaborate and richly decorated weaponry of the elite, deposited in large numbers in graves and hoards.

The Middle Bronze Age (c. 1600–1350 B.C.) saw again a transformation of these structures. It has been argued that the changes in material cultural distributions during this period, showing a much greater uniformity throughout the whole of central

Europe, are characteristic of more expansive communities with an economy placing greater emphasis on stock raising and mobility. The warrior ideology seems to have spread to the west and was adapted to a more decentralized social and political environment, as monumental burial mounds furnished with weaponry and other symbols of wealth show. Similarities not just in material cultural in general, but also in the combination of weapons and status symbols over large areas, indicate the existence of a warrior elite without centralized leadership. These communities probably formed loose alliances strengthened by the exogamous marriage practices of their leaders. This phenomenon is easily reconstructable on the basis of the appearance of foreign female ornament sets in various areas. These connections delineate a north-south axis of connections and movement of women that coincides with the main axis of trade relations. This may be related to new strategies of transmitting properties as well. Exogamous marriage is usually a characteristic of decentralized, expansionist societies and is accompanied by the paying of bride wealth mostly consisting of movable wealth (instead of land). Thus, in this period marriage patterns were more open, enabling the formation of alliances between smaller chiefdoms and establishing long-distance exchange networks.

Similar changes are observable during the later prehistoric development of European societies as well. The processes of centralization (with an emphasis on access to land and characterized by fortified centers) and decentralization (with greater mobility and dispersed settlements) return almost cyclically, leading finally to the emergence of archaic states just before the expansion of the Roman Empire, which substantially transformed the social and economic landscape of the Continent.

See also **Milk, Wool, and Traction: Secondary Animal Products** (*vol. 1, part 4*); **Late Neolithic/Copper Age Central Europe** (*vol. 1, part 4*); **Bell Beakers from West to East** (*vol. 1, part 4*); **The Significance of Bronze** (*vol. 2, part 5*); **Spišský Štvrtok** (*vol. 2, part 5*); **Late Bronze Age Urnfields of Central Europe** (*vol. 2, part 5*).

BIBLIOGRAPHY

Coles, J. M., and A. F. Harding. *The Bronze Age in Europe: An Introduction to the Prehistory of Europe c. 2000–700 B.C.* London: Methuen, 1979.

Harding, A. F. "The Bronze Age." In *European Prehistory. A Survey.* Edited by Sarunas Milisauskas, pp. 271–334. New York: Kluwer Academic/Plenum, 2002.

———. *European Societies in the Bronze Age.* Cambridge, U.K.: Cambridge University Press, 2000.

Kadrow, Slawomir. "Social Structures and Social Evolution among Early-Bronze-Age Communities in South-Eastern Poland." *Journal of European Archaeology* 2, no. 2 (1994): 229–248.

Kristiansen, Kristian. *Europe before History.* Cambridge, U.K.: Cambridge University Press, 1998.

———. "The Emergence of the European World System in the Bronze Age: Divergence, Convergence, and Social Evolution during the First and Second Millennium B.C. in Europe." In *Europe in the First Millennium B.C.* Edited by Kristian Kristiansen and Jorgen Jensen, pp. 7–30. Sheffield Archaeological Monographs 6. Sheffield, U.K.: Collis, 1994.

Pare, Chris, ed. *Metals Make the World Go Round: The Supply and Circulation of Metals in Bronze Age Europe.* Oxford: Oxbow, 2000.

Primas, Margarita. "Bronze Age Economy and Ideology: Central Europe in Focus." *Journal of European Archaeology* 5, no. 1 (1997): 115–130.

Shennan, Stephen J. "Settlement and Social Change in Central Europe, 3500–1500 B.C." *Journal of World Prehistory* 7, no. 2 (1993): 121–161.

———. "Central Europe in the Third Millennium B.C.: An Evolutionary Trajectory for the Beginning of the European Bronze Age." *Journal of Anthropological Archaeology* 5 (1986): 115–146.

Sherratt, A. G. "The Emergence of Élites: Earlier Bronze Age Europe, 2500–1300 B.C." In *Prehistoric Europe: An Illustrated History.* Edited by Barry Cunliffe, pp. 244–276. Oxford: Oxford University Press, 1998.

———. "What Would a Bronze-Age World System Look Like? Relations between Temperate Europe and the Mediterranean in Later Prehistory." *Journal of European Archaeology* 1, no. 2 (1993): 1–57.

Sørensen, M. L. S. "Reading Dress: The Construction of Social Categories and Identities in Bronze Age Europe." *Journal of European Archaeology* 5, no. 1 (1997): 93–114.

Treherne, Paul. "The Warrior's Beauty: The Masculine Body and Self-Identity in Bronze-Age Europe." *Journal of European Archaeology* 3, no. 1 (1995): 105–144.

VAJK SZEVERÉNYI

SPIŠSKÝ ŠTVRTOK

The fortified hilltop settlement of Spišský Štvrtok is one of the most significant sites of the earlier prehistory of central Europe. It dates to the transitional period between the Early and the Middle Bronze Age with a cultural affiliation to the Otomani-Füzesabony culture, c. 1700–1500 B.C. The village of Spišský Štvrtok (located in an area called Spišská Nová Ves, which is also a town) is situated on an oblong hill adjacent to a valley in the undulated country of eastern Slovakia at Myšia Hôrka in the Carpathian Basin. The hill rises very steeply on the western side and more gradually on the east, in modern times with a growth of forest. The fortification on the summit, about 625 meters above sea level, comprises about 6,600 square meters with thirty-nine houses and a cult place in addition to a complex system of ramparts, bastions, and ditches. There are two occupation phases: the end phase of the Early Bronze Age and the first phase of the Middle Bronze Age.

The site became known to the scientific community in the 1930s due to still-visible walls and several spectacular surface finds. It was systematically excavated in 1968–1974 under the direction of Dr. J. Vladar from the Archaeological Institute of the Slovakian Academy of Science in Nitra. The site is wholly examined and is in an excellent state of preservation. Vladar has described the excavation results in several small reports while the final report still awaits.

A stone wall encircles the entire settlement except at the gate, which is located at the eastern, more accessible, side. Here the fortification is reinforced with two additional walls and with a broad stone-lined ditch, which may have been water-filled. The intervals between the walls were filled in with gravel probably derived from digging the broad ditch. The latter runs north to south, uninterrupted, along the outer side of the rampart and a wooden bridge presumably existed at the gate.

The walls are built of thin stone slabs, which were brought in from the neighborhood at a distance of 2–3 kilometers. At the base, the rampart had a total width of 7.5 meters. The height is estimated at about 4 meters. Possibly a wooden palisade was erected on the top as a further reinforcement. The entrance to the settlement is flanked by two circular bastions of nearly 6 meters across—probably watchtowers. The gate itself widens considerably toward the outside, probably to make room for a defensive unit of warriors in case the settlement was attacked.

Only a minor part of the area encircled by the fortification was built up. The settlement consisted of stone houses, the foundations of which had been preserved, and streets divided the occupied space. According to the excavator the settlement had a clear bipartite division suggesting the existence of an elite and a broader stratum occupied with crafts. Finds from the craftsmen's quarter indicated the manufacture of a whole series of different products in cloth, stone, pottery, bone, antler, gold, and bronze. Houses inhabited by the privileged part of the population were of a much better quality, were situated in the best-protected part of the stronghold, and contained various treasures. Valuables of weapons and ornaments in bronze and gold had been deposited in chests below the floors. These finer houses were organized in a U shape around a slab-plastered "town square."

Spišský Štvrtok is merely one of several contemporary sites with fortifications known from southeast Slovakia, notably Bárca, Nižná Myšľa, Streda nad Bodrogom, and Gánovce. Similar sites belonging to the Otomani-Füzesabony culture—and broadly dating to the span 1700–1500 B.C.—exist in adjoining regions of Hungary and Romania. Some settlements were fortified and situated on hilltops, such as the strongholds of Otomani and Sălacea in Romania and several of the Slovakian sites. Fortified sites may be situated also in the swampy areas between rivers. Moreover, there are so-called tell settlements with ring walls, such as Tószeg-Laposhalom at the river Tisza on the Hungarian Plain and the nearby tells of Gyulavarsánd and Socodor just across the border in Romania. Large open settlements are also known, apparently without fortifications, but situated in naturally defendable locations.

Fortified settlements also occur in related cultural groupings in nearby southwest Slovakia (Nitriansky Hradok, Maďarovce, Malé Kosihy, Veselé), Moravia (Blučina, Hradisko, Věteřov), and lower Austria (Böheimkirschen). The phenomenon apparently has a wide geographical distribution over

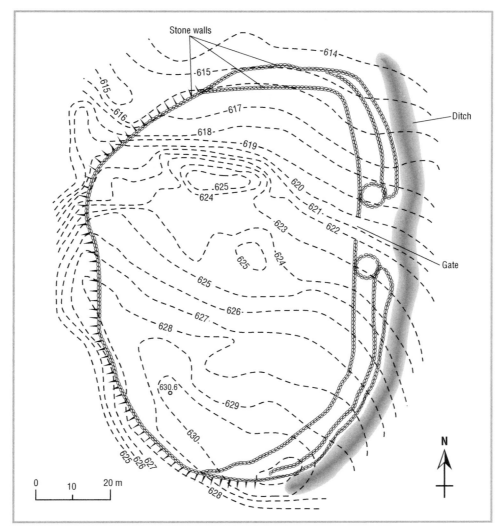

Fig. 1. Plan of the ramparts of the fortified hilltop settlement at Spišský Štvrtok in present-day Slovakia. ADAPTED FROM VLADAR 1975.

eastern central Europe and the Balkans especially in the period c. 1700–1500 B.C.

Some of the principal paraphernalia of the Bronze Age have roots in the complex cultural mosaic of the Carpathian Basin at the threshold to the Middle Bronze Age. The hillforts were mediators of inventions that passed through this region on their way to central and northern Europe from Eurasia and the Aegean. The spearhead, the sword, the four-spoked wheel, the chariot, and horse management are among these innovations. The first swords appeared in the Carpathian Basin in eastern Hungary and Romania around 1600 B.C.—only one hundred years after the appearance of the bronze spearhead in roughly the same region. Such quality

metalwork was in high demand all over central and northern Europe at this time. Exotica such as amber beads were traded in from the north and people of the Otomani-Füzesabony culture made contacts with stratified palace-based societies in early Mycenaean Greece.

Excavations suggest that all these sites should indeed be interpreted as protected centers of crafts and trade. They were probably also residences of local elites, who identified more closely with neighboring elites than with nonelite groupings in their local area. This identification involved more than peaceful communication through networks of alliance and exchange. The frequency of fortified sites, the occurrence of mass graves, the energy invested in ramparts and earthen works, the emphasis on horse culture and bronze weaponry—the entire cultural picture provided by the excavations indicates ongoing rivalries and hostilities between elite groups, probably about the control of valuables, their production, and distribution. Ritual depositions of weapons and ornament at the sites, or near them, probably also connect to the waging of wars. Hoards have been found for instance at Hajdúsámson, Apa, Bárca, Věteřov, Böheimkirschen, and Mad'arovce. The central position of these fortified sites, surrounded by satellite villages and hamlets, bears witness to increased inequality and hierarchy: in other words, to an extremely hot social climate. Finally, around 1600–1500 B.C., this volatile social climate gave rise to the emergence of the Tumulus culture, which brought new forms of social conduct, ideology, and personal appearance among the elite. The rapid spread of Tumulus material and immaterial culture across temperate Europe should probably be seen in light of this strategic background of exchange, alliance, and warfare in the Carpathian Basin and around the Middle Danubian region.

See also **The Early and Middle Bronze Ages in Central Europe** (*vol. 2, part 5*).

BIBLIOGRAPHY

Bader, T. "Bemerkungen zur Bronzezeit im Karpatenbecken, Otomani/Füzesabony-Komplex." *Jahresschrift für Mitteldeutsche Vorgeschichte* 80 (1998): 43–108.

Jockenhövel, Albrecht. "Bronzezeitliche Burgenbau in Mitteleuropa. Untersuchrungen zur Struktur frühmetalzeitlicher Gesellschaften." In *Orientalisch-Ägäische Einflüsse in der europäischen Bronzezeit*, pp 209–228. Monograph 15. Mainz, Germany: Römisch-Germanischen Zentralmuseums, 1990.

Neugebauer, J.-W.. "Die Stellung der Veterovkultur bzw. ihrer Böheimkirchner Gruppe am Übergang von der frühen zur mittleren Bronzezeit Niederösterreichs." *Archäologisches Korrespondenzblatt* 9 (1979): 35–52.

Shennan, S. E. "From Minimal to Moderate Ranking." In *Ranking, Resource, and Exchange: Aspects of the Archaeology of Early European Study.* Edited by Colin Renfrew and Stephen J. Shennan, pp. 27–32. Cambridge, U.K.: Cambridge University Press, 1982.

Sherratt, Andrew. "What Would a Bronze Age World System Look Like? Relations between Temperate Europe and the Mediterranean in Later Prehistory." *Journal of European Archaeology* 1, no. 2 (1993): 1–58.

Tihelka, Karel. "Der Veterover (Witterschauer) Typus in Mähren." In *Kommision für das Äneolithikum und die ältere Bronzezeit, Nitra 1958*, pp. 77–109. Bratislava, Slovakia: Slovakian Academy of Science, 1961.

Vladar, J. "Spišský Štvrtok. Befestigte Siedlung der Otomani-kultur." In *III. Internaler Kongress für slawische Archäologie Bratislava 7.–14. September 1975*, pp. 2–24. Nitra, Slovakia: Slovakian Academy of Science, 1975.

HELLE VANDKILDE

THE ITALIAN BRONZE AGE

Italy lies between the east and west Mediterranean, but it also represents the point of contact between the Mediterranean world and Europe north of the Alps, a point of contact especially important during the Bronze Age. The easy passes across the mountains north from the Po plain make the northern Adriatic basin a key area for understanding European prehistory, and indeed the key site of Frattesina is to be understood in this context. The themes that dominate the Italian Bronze Age are the wetland sites of the north—both lake villages and *terremare* settlements—and the pastoral economy which adapted so effectively to the mountainous peninsula. The Bronze Age saw two cycles of development: the first comes to an end at about 1200 B.C. and the second lays the foundation for Iron Age urbanism and social complexity. Connections between the Italian Bronze Age and the Aegean World will also be discussed here.

The Italian Bronze Age has traditionally been dated by reference to central European metalwork and to eastern Mediterranean imports. The growing availability of radiocarbon dates (although these are still quite rare) and, more importantly, dendro-chronological dating of Alpine wetland sites, both in Italy and farther north, has meant that a more accurate dating scheme is being worked out. The dating of the end of the Bronze Age is still quite con-troversial, with most scholars arguing for a point between 1000 and 900 B.C. The Italian Bronze Age is conventionally divided into four segments: the Early Bronze Age (2300–1700 B.C.), the Middle Bronze Age (1700–1350 B.C.), the Recent Bronze Age (1350–1150 B.C.), and the Final Bronze Age (1150–950 B.C.). Italian scholars generally describe the Recent and Final Bronze Ages as the "Late" Bronze Age, a matter of confusion for English speakers, who would normally refer to the Recent Bronze Age as the Late Bronze Age. The Italian convention will be used here, as it aids understanding of the literature.

For the purposes of discussion, Italy is divided into three regions: (1) the north, roughly the Po Valley and the Alpine valleys, but including Liguria in the west; (2) the center; and (3) the south, Sicily and the smaller islands. For much of its history, northern Italy has been culturally closer to central Europe than to the Mediterranean world.

EARLY BRONZE AGE

The Early Bronze Age begins at about 2300 B.C. and marks the start of a new cultural cycle in northern Italy, which continues with few substantial changes until the end of the Recent Bronze Age. The Early Bronze Age is characterized by the Polada culture, which has roots in the preceding Bell

Beaker phenomenon and shows strong links to central Europe. Polada settlements seem to be preferentially in wetland locations, both in the morainic hills along the Alpine margin (where Cavriana is located) and around the larger lakes, but also in the plain to the north of the Po River (where Lagazzi del Vhò and Canàr are found). The choice of wetland locations—which were common in northern Italy during the Early, Middle, and Recent Bronze Ages—is difficult to explain, but they seem to be a cultural constant. Little is known of settlement in the plain to the south of the Po, though this area was inhabited in the Copper Age and densely settled in the Middle and Recent Bronze Ages. Interestingly, evidence of metal hoards has been found in this area. Burial evidence, however, is almost completely absent in the Early Bronze Age of northern Italy, though the presence of human skulls at some sites (such as Barche di Solferino) suggests alternative methods of disposing of the dead, perhaps by exposure.

Metalworking seems to have taken place in settlements, as indicated at Ledro, Rivoli, and Monte Covolo. The hoards, which seem to have been deposited away from settlements, often consist of assemblages of a single artifact. For example, the Savignano hoard consists of ninety-six flanged axes. The Pieve Albignola hoard, from the western plain to the north of the Po, comprised thirty-seven axes, both finished and unfinished, some from the same mold. Such hoards are usually interpreted as traders' hoards. Prestige artifacts, in amber and faience, are found in settlements, but there is little evidence for overt social ranking.

In central Italy, the eastern seaboard is characterized by the Ripatransone culture, whereas to the west, the Rinaldone culture continues from the Copper Age into the early phases of the Early Bronze Age, to be followed by the Montemerano-Scoglietto-Palidoro culture. The economy seems to show a growing reliance on pastoralism, with the presence of grazing camps both on the coastal plain and the uplands. Settlements include defended sites, like Crostoletto di Lamone and Luni sul Mignone, as well as caves, valley-bottom sites, and wetland sites, such as Ortucchio in the Fucino Basin. Social differentiation is indicated by the Tomba della Vedova (Tomb of the Widow), at Ponte San Pietro, where the warrior chief is accompanied by

his sacrificed bride with a dog guarding the entrance to the grave. A dagger and halberd are used to signal burials at Montemerano II, at Teramo, and at Popoli. Cave cults continue from the preceding Copper Age, as at Cetona, a cave with a *stillicide* (continuous) water drip, where seeds were offered in pots.

In southern Italy, the Early Bronze Age Laterza culture of the early part of the period is succeeded by the Palma Campania culture. The Proto-Apennine phase sees the appearance of sites, such as Toppo Daguzzo and La Starza, that may be central places. Tufariello, near Buccino, and Coppa Nevigata have defensive, stone-built walls. Bronze artifacts are rare, except in grave assemblages, and rich tombs are infrequent—an example is the warrior burial at Parco dei Monaci, Matera, accompanied by a flanged axe and two daggers. Olive and vine cultivation, as seen in Proto-Apennine levels at Tufariello as well as at La Maculufa in Sicily, indicate agricultural intensification—the cultivation of fruit trees requires high levels of labor input.

In Sicily, Castelluccio culture sites indicate the spread of settlement in central and southeastern areas—the upland locations of many sites suggesting a pastoral economy based on the raising of sheep. The multiple-burial ritual makes the recognition of social hierarchy difficult, but stone-walled fortified sites, such as Branco Grande and Timpa Dieri, at Melilli, are known on the coast. In contrast, Manfria in western Sicily is an undefended village with oval huts.

The situation in the Lipari Islands (also known as the Aeolian Islands), which lie between Sicily and Italy, seems to indicate growing insecurity, and the low-lying sites of the early Capo Graziano phase, such as Casa Lopez and Filo Braccio on Filicudi or Contrada di Diana on the island of Lipari, give way to later defensive sites, such as La Montagnola on Filicudi or the acropolis on Lipari. The material culture of the islands shows parallels with Tarxien material on Malta.

MIDDLE BRONZE AGE
The Middle Bronze Age begins at about 1700 B.C. Its inception is traditionally fixed as marked by the appearance of Aegean pottery in peninsular Italy, but it corresponds to clear historical phenomena.

In the central Po Plain, many settlements, such as Lagazzi del Vhò, are abandoned at the beginning of the Middle Bronze Age and others, such as Castellaro del Vhò immediately to the north, are founded. The period sees large numbers of settlements established in the central area both to the north and to the south of the Po. The banked and ditched settlements of the plain are generally referred to as *terremare*. It is clear from the material culture and the choice of wetland locations that the *terremare* are closely related to the circum-Alpine lake villages (*palafitte*) to the north, even though the Swedish archaeologist Gösta Säflund argued against this relationship in 1939. In the western Po Valley, there seems to be less attraction to water, although there are wetland sites, such as Mercurago. In the east, the fortified hilltop sites, known as *castellieri*, of the Venezia-Giulia Karst show clear connections with developments farther east.

It has been argued that the wetland societies of the central Po Plain, the Alpine *palafitte,* and the *terremare* of the plain show evidence of contact with the Danubian-Carpathian region. Artifacts underlying this theory include antler horse bits and sword burials (as at Povegliano). What is certain is that the *terremare* of Emilia show a dramatic increase in settlement density, reaching levels of up to 1 site per 25 square kilometers. Nineteenth-century reports of urban planning were widely disregarded as fantasy, but evidence from modern excavations at the Santa Rosa di Poviglio *terremare* and from the Alpine lake village at Fiavè has confirmed these assertions. The complex drainage works and the pile-built dwellings indicate that this society must have been highly organized. However, little evidence exists for overt social ranking. Simple and undifferentiated cremation burial begins in the Late Middle Bronze Age *terremare,* and the sword burials that appear in the Veneto Plain to the north may be indicative of male warrior status rather than social ranking. Metal production seems to have been settlement based, as demonstrated at Castellaro del Vhò.

In central and southern peninsular Italy, the Middle Bronze Age is conventionally referred to as the Apennine Bronze Age. This period sees the establishment of a settlement pattern based on the exploitation of both lowland and upland areas. In 1959, Salvatore M. Puglisi proposed a model, based on ethnographic analogy, of transhumant pastoralists using lowland pasture in winter and upland pasture (often snow-covered in the winter) during the summer. This was criticized in 1967 by Carl Eric Östenberg, who, on the basis of his excavation results from Luni sul Mignone, argued that sedentary agricultural communities existed during this period. Most scholars now accept the integrated economic system proposed by Graeme Barker in 1981. This model maintains that some groups or communities moved into the Apennine uplands during the summer months to exploit the grazing, while others remained at their permanent cereal-dependent settlements in the lowlands. Indeed, the evidence of sheep, goats, pigs, and cattle at most lowland sites suggests a mixed form of animal husbandry. Whatever its exact form, transhumant pastoralism allowed the carrying capacity of sites to be raised by moving flocks for part of the year and thus represented a form of economic intensification. The close cultural connections of the material culture of the peninsula, albeit with local aspects, argue for the importance of this mobility in establishing social relations between groups. Metalwork seems to have had a relatively limited distribution in central Italy, and this picture of low-level trade is reflected in the lack of Aegean material in this part of Italy. Likewise, there is little evidence for social hierarchy, although two rock-cut longhouses with hearths were found at Luni sul Mignone.

Three monumental tombs at Toppo Daguzzo show the emergence of elite groups. In Tomb 3 there were two levels of inhumations—an upper level of about ten disarticulated skeletons without grave goods and a lower level that consisted of eleven burials, six males accompanied by bronze weapons, four females (three with precious beads), and a child.

The site of Thapsos is situated on an islet linked by an isthmus to the mainland just north of Syracuse in eastern Sicily. There, in the early part of the Middle Bronze Age, circular and sub-circular huts were built, their roofs supported by a central post. The second phase at the site, which extends into the Recent Bronze Age, is claimed to be semi-urban and to be of eastern inspiration. There are rectangular buildings arranged around paved courtyards and streets, and the settlement seems to have been defended by stone walls. The regular planning seems to indicate some degree of political control, and Sebastiano Tusa has drawn attention to its formal similarities with Gla in Boeotia. Like the settlement on the islet of Ognina, south of Syracuse, which dates to the same period, Thapsos was probably sited for maritime trade. This seems to be confirmed by the fact that most Middle Bronze Age settlements in eastern Sicily are close to the coast.

The Middle Bronze Age type site on the Lipari Islands is Punta Milazzese on the island of Lipari. Situated on a rocky headland, it consists of about fifty drystone huts. This site and the settlements at Portella on Salina and the acropolis at Lipari, both defensively located, met with violent destruction at the end of the period. Casting molds on Lipari and Salina indicate a local metalworking industry.

RECENT BRONZE AGE
In northern Italy, the Recent Bronze Age (c. 1350–1150 B.C.) saw substantial continuity from the preceding period. In the west, the cremation cemeteries of the Middle Bronze Age Scamozzina-Monza group are succeeded by the Canegrate group, which show strong Transalpine affinities. Their relatively dense settlement pattern, which seem to be based on dryland villages, are in some cases relatively large. One of these is Boffolora at Garlasco, which measures 5 hectares. Although dry locations were preferred for settlements, river depositions of metalwork, in the Adda in the west and in the Livenza in the east, suggest a ritual focus on water. It is interesting, however, that this practice did not seem to occur in the central area, which is characterized by wetland settlement.

While in the early part of the Middle Bronze Age the *terremare* of the central Po Plain were usually no larger than 2 hectares, in the Recent Bronze Age some *terremare* were abandoned and others became quite large. Santa Rosa di Poviglio goes from 1 hectare to 7 hectares, Fondo Paviani is 16 hectares, and Case del Lago is 22.5 hectares. This apparent settlement hierarchy is not supported by evidence from *terremare* cremation cemeteries, though the presence in some sites of inner fortified "keeps" may identify the residence of elite groups. On the other hand, they may be nothing but community refuges. The *palafitte-terremare* system collapsed dramatically at around 1200 B.C., with a rapid depopulation of the central Po Plain. Although there is no satisfying explanation for this catastrophic event, its chronological contemporaneity with the collapse of the palace societies of the eastern Mediterranean may suggest some sort of connection between the two areas. Although direct evidence of contact is rare, it is interesting that stone weights identified in the *terremare* show the use of eastern Mediterranean measures.

The Recent Bronze Age of central Italy, a period sometimes referred to as the Sub-Apennine, sees the relocation of sites to defended locations. The suspicion that this may be at the behest of emerging elites is confirmed by larger than average huts at, for example, Narce. The settlement at Luni sul Mignone expands dramatically, and a clear settlement hierarchy appears in Latium and Tuscany. The increase of settlement in the Monti della Tolfa may be linked to the presence of copper resources, while wetland and cave sites are abandoned. Metalwork depositions in rivers and lakes and also in caves, as at Cetona, indicate a ritual focus on such locations. Separate groups of tombs in cemeteries at Crostoletto di Lamone and Castelfranco Lamoncello, in the Fiora Valley, indicate the importance of group (perhaps family) identity.

In southern Italy there are a number of fortified coastal settlements at ports, such as Porto Perone, Coppa Nevigata, and Scoglio del Tonno, along the Apulian coast (see fig. 1). These sites seem to have participated in trade with the eastern Mediterranean and show evidence of craft specialization. In the interior, Sub-Apennine sites are often found in locations that provide good natural defenses. Some of these are sites, like Toppo Daguzzo or La Starza, that show continuity from previous periods, while others, such as Timmari and Botromagno, are new sites. However, the inland sites did not seem to participate in the maritime trade or the developments seen on the coast. Vivara, an island site in the Gulf of Naples, also shows important links with the Aegean.

The earliest Late Helladic pottery found at the site of Broglio di Trebisacce in the plain of Sybaris, excavated by Renato Peroni, dates to the end of the Middle Bronze Age. The Recent Bronze Age saw the production of Aegean-type storage jars (*dolia*). These jars and the introduction of olive cultivation suggest the presence of a redistributive economy or at least a centralized storage economy. The central

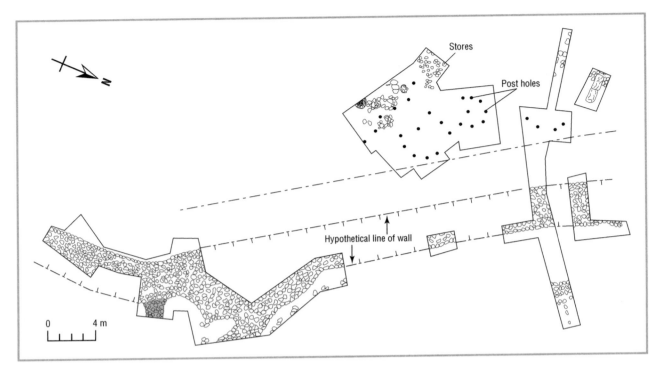

Fig. 1. Plan of the Late Bronze Age levels of the settlement at Porto Perone. ADAPTED FROM PERONI 1989.

hut at the site had Late Helladic IIIB and IIIC wares and local, wheel-made gray ware.

In 1973 Anna Maria Bietti Sestieri argued that the development of a local bronze industry in the Recent Bronze Age of southern Italy was a consequence of trade with the Aegean. Although this external stimulus may not be the full explanation, the period certainly sees an increase in bronze goods. There is also direct evidence for local production in the form of molds found at Scoglio del Tonno, Grotta Manaccora, and other sites.

In Sicily there is very little evidence for Recent Bronze Age coastal settlement, with the exception of the late phases of the Thapsos sites and some communities on the north coast. The north coast sites are characterized by the Ausonian culture, which is also known on the Lipari Islands. The tendency was for relatively few, large sites to be located inland. One example is Pantalica, situated in the upper reaches of the River Anapo. Although the stone-built "palace," or *anaktoron,* which has evidence for metalworking, may not date to this period, the site is surrounded by a large cemetery of rock-cut tombs, some individual burials, others with multiple occupancy. Upland defended settle-

ments include the stone-wall site at Monte Dessueri.

The Ausonian culture of the Lipari Islands seems to follow directly after the destruction of the Milazzese villages, particularly at the Lipari acropolis (see fig. 2). Two phases are recognized, the first corresponding to the Recent Bronze Age. Occupation during that period is marked by Aegean Late Helladic IIIB and C material.

FINAL BRONZE AGE
The Final Bronze Age (1150–950 B.C.) sees the beginning of a new cultural cycle. Much of peninsular Italy is united by the Protovillanovan culture, which is best known from urnfields of central European character.

The central Po Plain seems to be largely abandoned during this period, though a number of *terremare* in the Grandi Valli Veronesi, north of the river, continue into the early phases of the period. These include Fondo Paviani (16 hectares), Fabbrica dei Soci (6 hectares), and Castello del Tartaro (11 hectares). In these settlements, Late Helladic IIIC middle potsherds indicate contacts with the eastern Mediterranean, which have been confirmed

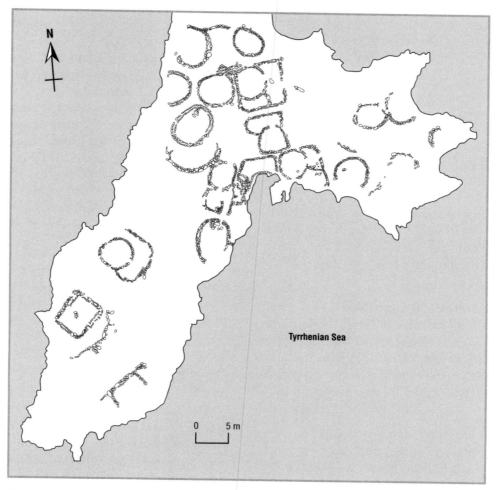

Fig. 2. Plan of the later Middle Bronze Age settlement at Milazzese, Panarea (Lipari Islands). ADAPTED FROM PERONI 1989.

by chemical analysis. Bronze, glass, bone, and antler working take place on-site.

The 20-hectare site of Frattesina, on a branch of the Po, was occupied from the twelfth to the ninth centuries B.C. and shows impressive evidence of craft production in glass, glazed pottery, bone, antler, elephant ivory, bronze, iron, and amber. The settlement seems to have played an active role in the Mediterranean trade system, importing raw materials, such as amber, ivory, and ostrich eggs, and exporting finished goods. Like the similar site of Montagnana on the Adige, it has Late Helladic IIIC late potsherds, probably of southern Italian manufacture. Montagnana appears to be the predecessor of the Iron Age site of Este, and indeed, the first millennium B.C. Protovenetic Este culture shows conti-

nuity from the Final Bronze Age of the Veneto. Cemetery evidence for groups of tombs gives very little support for the identification of ranking, though it is likely that sword burials at Frattesina mark out elite graves.

To the north, in the southern Alps, there is a massive expansion of copper production documented by smelting sites that are associated with the Luco–Laugen A culture group, which seems ancestral to the Iron Age Raeti. Both the southern Alps and Tuscany in central Italy supplied copper to Frattesina and, through that center, the east and central Mediterranean.

The western Po Plain sees a drop in settlement density, with a concentration of sites around Lake Como and Lake Maggiore. In this area, the origins of the Golasecca polities, which would continue into the Early Iron Age, are evident. Sword burials and other types of rich burials suggest a ranked society.

In central Italy, too, the emerging pattern of the Final Bronze Age has clear links with the succeeding phase of state formation. Most of the places that would become major centers of the Iron Age were occupied during the Final Bronze Age. There is a marked abandonment of lowland sites and a preference for locations with natural defenses, often on tufa outcrops. One such site is Sorgenti della Nova, which is set on a 5-hectare hilltop. Nuccia Negroni Catacchio, who excavated the site, has argued that a separate area at the top of the hill was occupied by the elite.

Most Protovillanovan cemeteries in central Italy are relatively small, with little evidence for social differentiation. An exception to this is the cemetery of Pianello di Genga, which had more than five hundred burials. It remained in use for two centuries and probably served a number of different communities.

There is a major change in metal production, with an increase in the range and quantity of metal artifacts produced. Many of these types show a distribution that suggests the exploitation of the copper ores of Tuscany. The nature of the economy at this time is very controversial, with a dispute between those who prefer to see a formal economy in place and those, more primitivist, who prefer a substantivist model. Certainly it should be noted that the period sees a major increase in hoard deposition, often associated with what seems to be ritual destruction, as in the Rimessone hoard.

In southern Italy, hoards of bronze, generally consisting of axes, become more common. There is also an increased presence of metalwork in graves, which signals an emerging warrior elite. In southern Italy and Sicily, there is evidence for early ironworking at Broglio di Trebisacce that is associated with the Final Bronze Age phase of the site. This settlement was defended by a wall and a ditch. An iron spearhead is known from the inhumation cemetery of Castellace, Oppido Mamertina, where a group of elite burials, male warriors and females, were perhaps grouped under a tumulus, an arrangement also found in Albania, to the east. Two iron knives were also found at the cemetery of Madonna del Piano, Molino della Badia, in eastern Sicily.

The emergence of a settlement hierarchy in the Plain of Sybaris, perhaps associated with competing warrior groups, is attested at Broglio di Trebisacce, where the total number of settlements diminishes. Indeed, the Castellace cemetery seems to represent the burial place of such a group. The period is certainly one of change. Some of the principal settlements of the southeast, like Porto Perone and later Scoglio del Tonno, were abandoned, while others, such as Toppo Daguzzo, were completely rebuilt.

In contrast to the earlier ritual use of caves, which Ruth Whitehouse has called "underground religion," there is a move to more open and visible forms of cult, such as the anthropomorphic statue-stelae of northern Apulia, representing both males and females, as at Castelluccio dei Sauri. Likewise, the rock-cut Sicilian tombs, as at Pantalica, which have architectural features and are visible from a distance, indicate a growing emphasis on the individual in burial rituals.

The settlement of Sabucina, overlooking the River Salso in central Sicily, consists of fifteen or so circular huts. Cannatello, on the south coast, which has both Aegean (Late Helladic IIIA and IIIB) and Cypriot pottery, is probably a trading settlement on the route passing to the south of the island. It consists of 6 huts arranged around a central open area with a diameter of about 60 meters. Five of the dwellings are circular, while the sixth is square. There is also evidence for a roughly paved road.

Luigi Bernabò Brea has argued that the Ausonian culture of the Lipari Islands is linked to groups from peninsular Italy who were eager to secure these important staging posts for trade. In the later phase, documented also in north and central Sicily, the form of huts changes from circular to much larger oval shapes. Construction is still by drystone walls but with upright posts inserted into the walls to give height to the structure.

THE AEGEAN CONNECTION

It has been argued that there were Mycenaean potters in Apulia and Lucania, and it has even be suggested that Broglio di Trebisacce might represent Mycenaean colonists, but it should be emphasized that the presence of Aegean (Late Helladic) sherds in Italy and the islands does not necessarily indicate the presence of Mycenaeans, even if this is likely. Certainly, the Italian-type winged-axe mold from the House of the Oil Merchant at Mycenae attests to very close relations between the Italian Peninsula and Bronze Age Greece. It should be noticed that in the Final Bronze Age, after the collapse of the palace societies of the eastern Mediterranean, these contacts continue. Indeed, the exceptional site of Frattesina dates from this very period.

The distribution of Aegean and Aegean-type pottery in Italy and the islands varies through time. In the sixteenth and fifteenth centuries B.C. (the Early Middle Bronze Age–Late Helladic I and II), it occurs in the Lipari Islands, on the coasts of Apulia and Calabria (facing northern Greece and Albania) and at Vivara in the Bay of Naples. In the fourteenth and thirteenth century B.C. (later Middle and Late Bronze Age–Late Helladic IIIA and B), there is an increase in the number of locations where the pottery has been found. Material is known from the Bay of Naples, Tuscany, and Latium but particularly from Southeast Italy and Southeast Sicily (where the Mycenaean influence on the Thapsos culture has been noted), Sardinia, and the Lipari Islands. Twelfth-century B.C. material (Final Bronze Age–Late Helladic IIIC) shows a differing pattern. The Ionian Sea seems to have become a key area, and the decrease in finds in the Lipari Islands and Sicily may suggest a new route to Sardinia passing south of Sicily. The presence of five finds in the Po Plain in northern Italy is the major novelty of the Final Bronze Age.

CONCLUSIONS

The Italian Bronze Age saw a cycle of development, from the Early to the Recent Bronze Age, and then, in the Final Bronze Age, the beginning of a new cycle that led to the complex urban societies of the Iron Age. Although the evidence for social differentiation is patchy, it is clear that, for example, the *terremare* and lake-village societies of central northern Italy reached high levels of complexity in the Recent Bronze Age. Indeed, the sword-bearing warriors who appeared about this time represented the visible signs of the elite groups who became increasingly important as the Bronze Age drew to a close.

See also **Bell Beakers from West to East** (*vol. 1, part 4*); **The Early and Middle Bronze Ages in Central**

Europe (*vol. 2, part 5*); **Poggiomarino** (*vol. 2, part 5*); **Late Bronze Age Urnfields of Central Europe** (*vol. 2, part 5*); **Mycenaean Greece** (*vol. 2, part 5*); **Etruscan Italy** (*vol. 2, part 6*).

BIBLIOGRAPHY

Barfield, Lawrence. *Northern Italy before Rome.* Ancient Peoples and Places 76. New York: Praeger, 1972.

Barker, Graeme. *Landscape and Society: Prehistoric Central Italy.* London and New York: Academic Press, 1981.

Bernabò Brea, Maria, Andrea Cardarelli, and Mauro Cremaschi, eds. *Le Terramare: La più antica civiltà padana.* Exhibition catalog. Milan: Electa, 1997.

Bietti Sestieri, Anna Maria. *Protostoria: Teoria e pratica.* Studi Superiori NIS 301. Rome: La Nuova Italia Scientifica, 1996.

Cocchi Genick, Daniela, ed. *L'antica età del bronzo: Atti del Congresso di Viareggio, 9–12 Gennaio 1995.* Florence, Italy: OCTAVO, Franco Cardini Editore, 1996.

Guidi, Alessandro, and Marcello Piperno, eds. *Italia preistorica.* Rome and Bari: Laterza, 1992. (Contains three useful essays: Andrea Cardarelli, "Le età dei metalli nell'Italia settentrionale," pp. 366–419; Alessandro Guidi, "Le età dei metalli nell'Italia centrale e in Sardegna," pp. 420–470; and Enrico Pellegrini, "Le età dei metalli nell'Italia meridionale e in Sicilia," pp. 471–516.)

Harari, Maurizio, and Mark Pearce. *Il protovillanoviano al di qua e al di là dell'Appennino: Atti della giornata di studio: Pavia, Collegio Ghislieri, 17 giugno 1995.* Biblioteca di "Athenaeum" 38. Como, Italy: Edizioni New Press, 2000.

Leighton, Robert. *Sicily before History: An Archaeological Survey from the Palaeolithic to the Iron Age.* Ithaca, N.Y.: Cornell University Press; London: Duckworth, 1999.

"L'età del bronzo in Italia nei secoli dal XVI al XIV a.C. Viareggio 26–30 ottobre 1989." *Rassegna di Archeologia* (1991–1992): 10. (Conference proceedings on the Middle Bronze Age in Italy published as a single volume of the journal.)

Mathers, Clay, and Simon Stoddart, eds. *Development and Decline in the Mediterranean Bronze Age.* Sheffield Archaeological Monographs, no. 8. Sheffield, U.K.: J. R. Collis, 1994. (Contains three useful essays: Lawrence Barfield, "The Bronze Age of Northern Italy: Recent Work and Social Interpretation," pp. 129–144; Graeme Barker and Simon Stoddart, "The Bronze Age of Central Italy: c. 2000–900 B.C.," pp. 145–165; and Caroline Malone, Simon Stoddart, and Ruth Whitehouse, "The Bronze Age of Southern Italy, Sicily, and Malta c. 2000–800 B.C.," pp. 167–194.)

Pearce, Mark. "New Research on the *Terremare* of Northern Italy." *Antiquity* 72 (1998): 743–746.

Fig. 1. One of the various excavated islets of Poggiomarino, Italy. SOPRINTENDENZA ARCHEOLOGICA DI POMPEI. REPRODUCED BY PERMISSION.

Peroni, Renato. *L'Italia alle soglie della storia.* Rome and Bari: Laterza, 1996. (A good chrono-typological outline of the key sites and assemblages.)

———. *Protostoria dell'Italia continentale: La penisola italiana nelle età del Bronzo e del ferro.* Popoli e Civiltà dell'Italia Antica vol. 9. Rome: Biblioteca di Storia Patria, 1989.

Ridgway, David, and Francesca R. Ridgway, eds. *Italy before the Romans: The Iron Age, Orientalizing, and Etruscan Periods.* London and New York: Academic, 1979. (Contains some important, if a little dated, papers on the Bronze-Iron transition.)

Skeates, Robin, and Ruth Whitehouse, eds. *Radiocarbon Dating and Italian Prehistory.* Archaeological Monographs of the British School at Rome vol. 8; Accordia Specialist Studies on Italy vol. 3. London: British School at Rome and Accordia Research Centre, 1994. (The date lists are regularly updated in the journal *Accordia Research Papers.*)

Tusa, Sebastiano. *La Sicilia nella preistoria.* Palermo, Italy: Sellerio, 1983.

MARK PEARCE

POGGIOMARINO

The remarkable discovery of the Bronze Age wetland site of Poggiomarino is rewriting the history of southern Italy's Bronze Age. The peculiarity of this riverine settlement consists of its location and the way in which it was constructed. In fact the village was built on a multitude of little artificially created islands linked by a navigable network of canals, hence its nickname the "Bronze Age Venice."

The fortunate discovery of this prehistoric village was made during the construction of a water-purification system for the Sarno River in October 2000. The settlement is situated near the Sarno River in a place called Longola-Poggiomarino (Naples), about 10 kilometers northeast of Pompeii. It is believed that the site covers an area of about 7 hectares, of which only 4,800 square meters are being investigated. The prehistoric settlement, believed to have been one of the major Bronze Age industrial centers in southern central Italy, was occu-

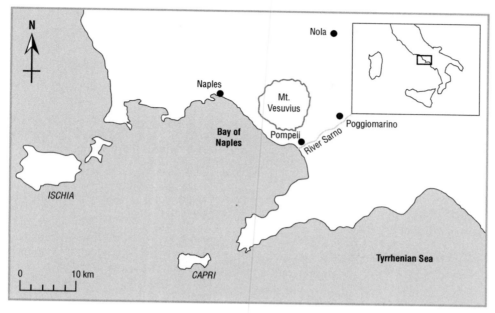

Poggiomarino, Italy, and environs.

pied continuously from around the sixteenth to the sixth century B.C., when environmental factors forced the Poggiomarino community to abandon the area. According to Renato Peroni, archaeological evidence supports the theory that the same people moved westward toward the coast and started to build the city of Pompeii.

By 2003 the Soprintendenza Archeologica di Pompei in conjunction with the Centre National de la Recherche Scientifique in Paris had excavated no more than 1,600 square meters of the village. There are seven main trenches (five measuring 20 by 40 meters and two measuring 20 by 20 meters) plus a series of small test pits. On average, the anthropogenic strata lie 2.8–7 meters below the modern terrain surface, but in some areas they can be even deeper. The settlement, a fairly large area, consists mainly of an agglomerate of small, artificially built islands set in a network of manually dug waterways. Eight circular islands had been discovered, ranging in size between 120 and 240 square meters.

Each island contained a hut and a modest landing stage for small watercraft and probably was connected to the rest of the settlement by either permanent bridges or drawbridges. The engineering was quite sophisticated. The banks along the canals were raised using a multitude of trunks of oak trees and wooden panels as bulwark, creating structures of is-

lets, which subsequently were filled in and reinforced in order to build habitations on them (fig. 1). In the majority of cases, the surfaces of these islands were paved with pebbles and slabs of volcanic rock quarried in the area. Finally, the water level was maintained at a constant level by a series of drainage trenches and sluices built around the settlement.

Poggiomarino has yielded an enormous quantity of artifacts, which range from wooden construction material to the finest metal products. The large amount of well-preserved wood (mostly oak) was found in the form of posts, flat planks, worked and semiworked beams, wooden tools, and a few dugout canoes used to navigate the canal network.

The richness of the material culture is astonishing. More than 500,000 fragments of pottery and 100,000 animal bones (mainly wild boar, deer, and bear) and antlers have been found, along with more than 600 coarse and fine artifacts made of bronze, lead, iron, glass, amber, bone, and antler. Important finds in the archaeological assemblage are unworked chunks of amber, a furnace for smelting copper, and a few mold casts for bronze objects. They suggest that Poggiomarino was an important industrial center, where large quantities of various goods were produced for trade all over southern Italy and the central Mediterranean. Another vital characteristic of the archaeological material is the presence of a significant quantity of botanical and faunal remains, which will allow archaeologists to reconstruct the climate and vegetation of the site.

Despite the large quantity of wood found on the site, absolute dates based on dendrochronology are not yet available. A research team from Cornell University led by Peter Kuniholm has begun analysis of a selection of 122 posts of long-lived oak from the islands to place them within the Mediterranean dendrochronological sequence. Chronology still relies on relative dates obtained from pottery typological analyses, which place the settlement between the sixteenth and sixth centuries B.C.

In conclusion, Poggiomarino promises to revolutionize the chronology of later southern Italian prehistory and protohistory and, as the largest Bronze Age and Iron Age wetland site found in the Mediterranean, shed light on the occupational patterns and chronology of later prehistoric wetland settlements in Europe. Surprisingly there are quite a few gaps in the southern Italian chronologies that precede the Pompeii period. The long occupation of Poggiomarino along with Nola, an Early Bronze Age settlement situated only 25 kilometers north of Poggiomarino and destroyed by the eruption of Mount Vesuvius in the eighteenth century B.C., will help fill in the gaps and clarify cultural aspects of local populations that occupied the area well before Pompeii was built. The settlement also will shed light on important aspects of local and long-distance trade and social interaction in later prehistoric Europe. In fact, having been a large and important industrial center, it might well have been connected to the long-distance trade route (in the Aegean area of the Baltic Sea) through southern Italy and the Alpine region. Finally, Poggiomarino might play an important role in solving the mystery of the disappearance of the Alpine wetland settlements at the beginning of the Iron Age. The majority of European Iron Age wetland populations decided to become more "terrestrial," and for some reason that does not seem to be fully environmen-

tal, this trend started around the Alpine lakes and subsequently spread over Europe.

See also **The Italian Bronze Age** (*vol. 2, part 5*).

BIBLIOGRAPHY

Carancini, Gian Luigi, and Renato Peroni. *L'eta' del bronzo in Italia: Per una cronologia della produzione metallurgica.* Perugia, Italy: Alieno, 1999.

Kuniholm, Peter Ian. "Aegean Dendrochronology Project December 2002 Progress Report." http://www.arts.cornell.edu / dendro / 2002news / 2002adp.html.

Manning, Sturt W., Bernd Kromer, Peter Ian Kuniholm, and Maryanne W. Newton. "Confirmation of Near-Absolute Dating of East Mediterranean Bronze-Iron Dendrochronology." *Antiquity* 77, no. 295 (2003). http:// antiquity.ac.uk / ProjGall / Manning / manning.html.

Menotti, Francesco. "Climatic Change, Flooding, and Occupational Hiatus in the Lake-Dwelling Central European Bronze Age." In *Natural Disasters and Cultural Change.* Edited by Robin Torrence and John Grattan, pp. 235–249. London: Routledge, 2002.

———. The *"Missing Period": Middle Bronze Age Lake-Dwellings in the Alps.* BAR International Series, no. 968. Oxford: Archeopress, 2001.

———. "The Abandonment of the ZH-Mozartstrasse Early Bronze Age Lake-Settlement: GIS Computer Simulations of the Lake-Level Fluctuation Hypothesis." *Oxford Journal of Archaeology* 18, no. 2 (1999): 143–155.

Peroni, Renato. *L'Italia alle soglie della storia.* Rome: Editori Laterza, 1996.

Pruneti, P. "Palafitte a Poggiomarino sul Sarno: Protostoria ai piedi del Vesuvio." *Archeologia Viva* 94 (July–August 2002): 72–76.

Schlichtherle, Helmut. *Pfahlbauten rund um die Alpen.* Stuttgart, Germany: Konrad Theiss Verlag, 1997.

Sherratt, A. G. "The Human Geography of Europe: A Prehistoric Perspective." In *An Historical Geography of Europe.* Edited by Robin A. Butlin and Robert A. Dodgshon, pp. 1–25. Oxford: Clarendon Press, 1998.

FRANCESCO MENOTTI

EL ARGAR AND RELATED BRONZE AGE CULTURES
OF THE IBERIAN PENINSULA

FOLLOWED BY FEATURE ESSAY ON:

The Bronze Age of the southeastern quadrant of the Iberian Peninsula constitutes an archaeologically well-documented example of the barbarian social formations of later prehistoric Europe. The rich body of mortuary evidence first developed in the late nineteenth century by the Belgian mining engineers Henri Siret and Louis Siret has been supplemented by a number of settlement excavations that have taken place since the 1970s. As a result, one can reconstruct the major lines of the economic and social organization of southeastern Iberia in the late third millennium and early second millennium B.C. Radiocarbon dates for the classic Bronze Age cultures of southeastern Iberia generally fall between about 2200 to 1500 B.C. There are three regional variants: the El Argar culture of eastern Andalusia and Murcia, the Bronce Valenciano of the Spanish Levant and southern Aragon, and the Mancha Bronze Age of the southern Meseta. Of these, the Argaric is the best known.

EL ARGAR

The bulk of the evidence for the El Argar complex comes from coastal lowlands of the provinces of Almería and Murcia. The Siret brothers' mining operations were based in this region, and the most important modern excavations, at Gatas and Fuente Álamo, have been carried out at sites first excavated by the Sirets. The coastal zone of southeastern Spain lies in the rain shadow of the Betic mountain systems (the Sierra Nevada, the Sierra de Segura, and so forth). In the present, this is the most arid region of Europe, with mean annual rainfall of less than 400 millimeters, so that irrigation is a prerequisite for stable agriculture. The El Argar culture area extends westward into the uplands of eastern Andalusia, windward of the mountain systems, where higher precipitation permits reliably productive dry farming. The available paleoenvironmental evidence indicates that the climate during the Bronze Age was similar to that of the present. The modern environmental contrasts within the area are caused by the mountainous geography and would have been diminished during the Bronze Age only by changes in atmospheric circulation patterns greater than can be plausibly postulated for the Holocene period.

Settlement. The Bronze Age archaeology of southeastern Iberia is an archaeology of settlements. Hundreds of Argaric villages are documented: in areas that have been surveyed systematically they are found every 2 or 3 kilometers along the watercourses. The villages typically consist of tight clus-

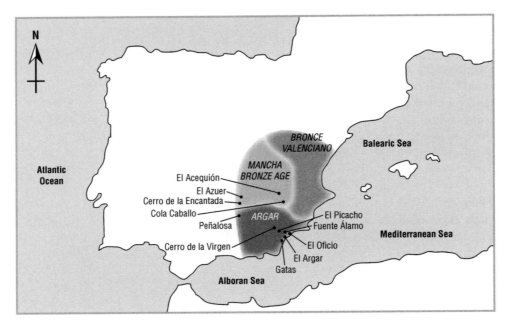

Selected sites in southeast Iberia.

ters of rectangular houses packed on the crests of steep hills and terraced on the upper slopes of the hillsides. Almost all of these sites are small (a fraction of a hectare), limited in size by their emplacements, but they are often deeply stratified, reflecting long occupations that cover much of the seven hundred–year span of the Argaric Bronze Age. A few sites, Cerro de la Virgen, for example, were occupied in the preceding Copper Age, but most were newly established in the Bronze Age. Argaric settlement strategies were apparently governed by defensive considerations of unprecedented severity.

Production. The long-term occupations characteristic of the Argaric were based on stably productive mixed farming. The staple grains were wheat and barley, supplemented by legumes, such as peas, broad beans, and lentils. Animal species included (in descending order of frequency) sheep and goats, cattle, pigs, and horses. A variety of intensifications of agricultural production had been initiated in the preceding Copper Age, and these were maintained in the Argaric. The evidence indicates the exploitation of sheep, goats, cattle, and horses for their secondary products (wool, milk, traction). There may have been some cultivation of olives. It also seems likely that there was some development of hydraulic agriculture: throughout the Argaric culture area, sites are oriented toward land that could be irrigat-

ed, and in the arid sector the cultivation of crops, such as flax and broad beans, would have required irrigation.

Argaric households engaged in a complete suite of production activities, none of them exhibiting a significant degree of craft specialization. The ceramic industry generally exhibits a low degree of artisan investment. Vessels were coil-made and generally coarsely tempered pottery that was fired at low temperatures under reducing conditions. Ceramic decoration is generally rare except for digitations (finger impressions) on the rims and appliqué buttons. The range of forms (carinated vases, bowls, baggy storage jars of various sizes) is monotonous and repetitive but not apparently standardized. The fragments of linen and woolen textiles that have been recovered are homespun, and loom weights are found in most domestic spaces. Esparto grass was used to make baskets and cords. The chipped-stone tool industry consists mainly of unmodified blades and flakes, the main distinctive tool type being backed and denticulated sickle teeth. Typologically nondescript milling stones and groundstone axes were also produced. Even metallurgy appears to be a household industry. Arsenical copper ores were smelted in small ceramic crucibles found in otherwise ordinary-seeming domestic contexts; the overall number of artifacts produced was very small (particularly in comparison to other regions of Europe at the same time), and the trace-element signatures of slags and finished artifacts varied from site to site (suggesting that the circulation and recasting of metal was minimal). Metallurgical production was devoted primarily to making arms (daggers, halberds, swords, projectile points) and ornaments (such as bracelets) to be interred with the dead. Tools such as chisels were produced in smaller quantities.

Social and Political Organization. The Argarics buried their dead under the floors of their houses in natural cavities, stone cists, or large jars. These were individual interments, but in some cases there were double (male and female) burials. Radiocarbon dates on the skeletons of a series of five of these double burials indicate that in all cases the female skeleton was a century or more older than the male, suggesting a matrilocal residence pattern. Argaric grave goods consist of the personal finery of the dead, such as ceramic drinking vessels and bronze weapons and ornaments, and they show considerable differences in wealth. These wealth differentials are more marked at sites in the arid sector of the Argaric culture area and have generally been interpreted as evidence of hereditary stratification, but analyses of the skeletal evidence provide no clear evidence that individuals with wealthier grave goods grew taller or were healthier in childhood.

Systematic, extensive excavations of Argaric villages are still few, but the results from the most completely published sites—El Picacho, Gatas, Peñalosa, and Fuente Álamo—do not suggest marked internal differentiation in residential facilities. Some houses are bigger than others to be sure, but there is no prima facie evidence for chiefly residences. It is of particular interest, for example, that no claims have been made for the association of wealthier burials with larger residences. Likewise, there is little monumentality in public architecture. Large public spaces or plazas are not evident (if only because the packing of the houses onto hilltops would have made these difficult to establish). The only buildings interpretable as public or official buildings—the freestanding rectangular structures H and O, built during phases III and IV of the Fuente Álamo occupation—are both relatively modest in size (about 50 meters squared and 80 meters squared, respectively).

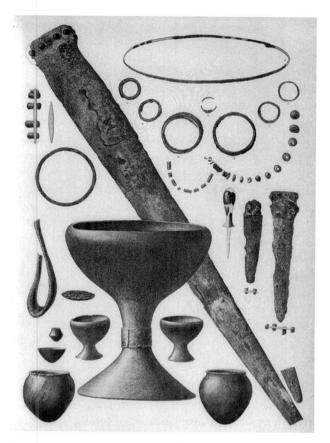

Fig. 1. Grave contents of Fuente Álamo grave 9. PHOTOGRAPH COURTESY OF HARVARD COLLEGE LIBRARY.

Argaric settlements show some differentiation in size. Robert Chapman interprets this as evidence of a two-tier settlement hierarchy, which in turn would suggest a chiefdom level of social organization. Roberto Risch suggests that at Fuente Álamo large-scale grain milling was out of proportion to the agricultural resources found in the immediate vicinity and infers from this that its residents must have received grain from lower-ranking communities elsewhere. Similar claims have been made on the basis of as yet incompletely published survey projects. The difficulty with such claims is the limited scale of differentiation involved. The range of site sizes is from villages of at most 6 or 7 hectares (not necessarily occupied simultaneously) to hamlets of a fraction of a hectare. This is not what one would expect of a society with a well-established social hierarchy.

The general consensus of students of the Argaric has been that it was a culture that showed signs of "emerging complexity" (this term serves as the title for Chapman's study). Most scholars feel that it was certainly a chiefdom and even perhaps a state. The evidence accumulated by the functionalist archaeology of the past generation to test this view suggests a more "tribal" form of social organization, however. Households were self-sufficient and undifferentiated in their production. The multiplicity of small settlements found throughout the Argaric zone suggests that small groups of households enjoyed the freedom to establish themselves in new communities. Considerable wealth differentials may have arisen in the context of the competition over the resources, including herds and irrigated plots. These differentials might have become more pronounced in the course of agricultural intensification. They appear to be larger in the arid zone (where environmental constraints would have sharpened such competition), but there is little to suggest that commoners were caged by powerful aristocrats.

Ideology. The burial of the dead under the houses of the living strongly suggests the existence of clan ideologies that legitimated household property claims in terms of ancestry. Apart from the mortuary record, Argaric archaeology is conspicuously lacking in direct evidence of systems of beliefs. There is no art; there are no figurines or other nonfunctional objects interpretable as fetishes; there are no evident cult spaces, apart from a possible altar from the site of El Oficio. This is in sharp contrast to the abundant evidence of religious practice that characterized the communal institutions of the preceding Copper Age and the civic ones of the succeeding Iron Age.

THE BRONCE VALENCIANO AND THE MANCHA BRONZE AGE

The Bronce Valenciano and the Mancha Bronze Age cultures are broadly contemporaneous to the Argaric and grade into it seamlessly along their "frontier" in northern Jaén and Murcia Provinces. They are differentiated from the Argaric (and from each other) more to facilitate didactic archaeological classification than because of differences in their principal features. The main substantive contrast, in fact, is the scarcity of burials inside the settlements.

The Bronce Valenciano is distributed in the mountainous zone and coastal areas of eastern Spain between the Rivers Ebro and Segura, an area whose climate and resources are broadly similar to the less-arid portions of the Argaric domain. The Mancha Bronze Age is found in the southeastern Meseta north of the Sierra Morena and Betic mountain systems. This region has a more arid and Continental climate than the Spanish Levant, but conditions are in no way as unfavorable to agriculture as in the coastal Argaric zone.

Settlement. Both the Bronce Valenciano and the Mancha Bronze Age are characterized by their large numbers of small settlements, usually placed on hilltops, promontories, or other defensible positions. In the Alto Palancia district (within the Bronce Valenciano area), for example, 50 open settlements (open-air settlements, as opposed to caves or rock shelters) are documented in an area of a little over 1,000 square kilometers. A survey of 10,000 square kilometers in northern Albacete Province (in the Mancha Bronze Age area) documented the existence of some 250 Bronze Age settlements. Site densities of a similar order of magnitude are found wherever archaeologists have worked systematically. The Mancha Bronze Age is distinguished by the construction of fortified settlements built on a circular plan in areas where the natural relief affords insufficient protection (El Azuer and El Acequión are the best-known examples).

Production. The lack of published, functionally oriented excavations means less is known about the organization of productive activities for the Bronce Valenciano and Mancha Bronze Age than for the Argaric, but the available evidence suggests that subsistence patterns were broadly similar. The same range of domesticates were husbanded, the pattern being one of mixed farming with intensifications, such as the use of the plow and other exploitations of animals for their secondary products. In terms of artifact technology, what mainly distinguishes the Bronce Valenciano and Mancha Bronze Age from the Argaric is the absence of some of the more distinctive Argaric productions, such as ceramic chalices and bronze swords and halberds. In the Argaric, these are only found in burials, and burials are scarce in the Bronce Valenciano and Mancha Bronze Age areas.

Social and Political Organization. The scarcity of mortuary evidence from the Bronce Valenciano and Mancha Bronze Age areas deprives archaeologists of one of the principal avenues for assessing social distinctions. Cerro de la Encantada, in the Mancha Bronze Age area, contains burials, but it is often considered an Argaric outlier because it has as many as twenty burials, which falls far short of the more than one thousand found at El Argar itself. The evidence elsewhere is too sparse to permit assessment of its central tendencies. The Mancha Bronze Age circular fortified settlements are sometimes interpreted as being occupied by elites, and some of them have yielded items that are suggestive of an elite presence (such as the 107-gram ivory button from El Acequión). But systematic testing of this hypothesis would require comparison of the contents of habitational spaces found at these large sites with their counterparts at smaller sites. Our most reliable avenue for assessing social differentiation is restricted to the settlement-pattern evidence obtained in systematic surveys. The multiplicity of small sites and the small size of the larger ones (Cola Caballo, the largest site documented in the area surveyed by Antonio Gilman, Manuel Fernández-Miranda, María Dolores Fernández-Posse, and Concepción Martín, measures 1.4 hectares) argues strongly for a segmentary social organization.

Ideology. José Sánchez Meseguer's interpretation of one of the constructional spaces at Cerro de la Encantada as a cult space, even if accepted, would be an isolated exception to the general absence of overt ideological manifestations in the Bronce Valenciano and Mancha Bronze Age cultures. The overall pattern of absence of overt "superstructural" activities is similar to what is found in the Argaric.

COMMENTARY

The rich archaeological record available for the El Argar culture permits one to sketch out its principal features. The makers of that record were largely self-sufficient households of socially segmentary mixed farmers engaged in intense competition over land and other factors of production. In the course of that competition, they developed incipient social ranking. The evidence for the Bronce Valenciano and Mancha Bronze Age cultures is less complete, but it is clearly indicative of social groups operating along similar lines. This reconstruction is very different, however, from those that can be obtained for societies that are historically documented. One can-

not tell, for example, what language (or languages) the Bronze Age people of southeastern Iberia spoke. (One might speculate that they spoke an ancestral version of the non-Indo-European Iberian spoken in the same area of the peninsula fifteen hundred years later, but the changes in the artifactual inventory from the Bronze to the Iron Age is so pervasive that tracing a direct archaeological filiation is impossible.) This, in turn, makes any ethnic interpretation of the Iberian Bronze Age a dubious proposition: the archaeological record does not document an ancient society but rather an ancient way of life that may have been shared by groups that would have considered themselves (and would have been considered by contemporary observers) to be quite different. It is important to realize, therefore, that this deep prehistoric case is in some important respects not comparable to ones documented ethnohistorically.

See also **Late Neolithic/Copper Age Iberia** (*vol. 1, part 4*); **Iberia in the Iron Age** (*vol. 2, part 6*); **Early Medieval Iberia** (*vol. 2, part 7*).

BIBLIOGRAPHY

Buikstra, Jane, et al. "Approaches to Class Inequalities in the Later Prehistory of South-East Iberia: The Gatas Project." In *The Origins of Complex Societies in Late Prehistoric Iberia.* Edited by Katina T. Lillios, pp. 153–168. Ann Arbor, Mich.: International Monographs in Prehistory, 1995.

Chapman, Robert. *Emerging Complexity: The Later Prehistory of South-East Spain, Iberia, and the West Mediterranean.* Cambridge, U.K.: Cambridge University Press, 1990.

Contreras Cortés, Francisco, and Juan Antonio Cámara Serrano. *La jerarquización social en la del Bronce del alto Guadalquivir (España): El poblado de Peñaloso (Baños de la Encina, Jaén).* BAR International Series, vol. 1025. Oxford: John and Erica Hedges, 2002.

Gilman, Antonio. "Assessing Political Development in Copper and Bronze Age Southeast Spain." In *From Leaders to Rulers.* Edited by Jonathan Haas, pp. 59–81. New York: Kluwer Academic/Plenum, 2001.

Gilman, Antonio, and John B. Thornes. *Land-Use and Prehistory in South-East Spain.* London: Allen and Unwin, 1985.

Gilman, Antonio, Manuel Fernández-Miranda, María Dolores Fernández-Posse, and Concepción Martín. "Preliminary Report on a Survey Program of the Bronze Age of Northern Albacete Province, Spain." In *Encounters and Transformations: The Archaeology of Iberia in Transition.* Edited by Miriam S. Balmuth, Antonio Gilman, and Lourdes Prados-Torreira, pp. 33–50. Monographs in Mediterranean Archaeology, vol. 7. Sheffield, U.K.: Sheffield Academic, 1997.

Harrison, R. J. "The 'Policultivo Ganadero': or, the Secondary Products Revolution in Spanish Agriculture, 5000–1000 B.C." *Proceedings of the Prehistoric Society* 51 (1985): 75–102.

Lull, Vicente. "Argaric Society: Death at Home." *Antiquity* 74 (2000): 581–590.

Martín, Concepción, Manuel Fernández-Miranda, María Dolores Fernández-Posse, and Antonio Gilman. "The Bronze Age of La Mancha." *Antiquity* 67 (1993): 23–45.

Mathers, Clay. "Goodbye to All That? Contrasting Patterns of Change in the South-East Iberian Bronze Age c. 24/2200–600 B.C." In *Development and Decline in the Mediterranean Bronze Age*. Edited by Clay Mathers and Simon Stoddart, pp. 21–71. Sheffield Archaeological Monographs, no. 8. Sheffield, U.K.: J. R. Collis Publications, 1994.

Montero Ruiz, Ignacio. "Bronze Age Metallurgy in Southeast Spain." *Antiquity* 67 (1993): 46–57.

Risch, Roberto. "Análisis paleoeconómico y medios de producción líticos: El caso de Fuente Alamo." In *Minerales y metales en la prehistoria reciente: Algunos testimonios de su explotación y laboreo en la Península Ibérica*. Edited by Germán Delibes de Castro, pp. 105–154. Studia Archaeologica, no. 88. Valladolid, Spain: Secretariado de Publicaciones e Intercambio Científico, Universidad de Valladolid, Fundación Duques de Soria, 1998.

Ruiz, Matilde, et al. "Environmental Exploitation and Social Structure in Prehistoric Southeast Spain." *Journal of Mediterranean Archaeology* 5 (1992): 3–38.

Sánchez Meseguer, José. "El altar de cuernos de La Encantada y sus paralelos orientales." *Oretum* 1 (1985): 125–174.

ANTONIO GILMAN

SARDINIA'S BRONZE AGE TOWERS

During the Bronze Age and the Early Iron Age, from 2000 to 600 B.C., the western Mediterranean island of Sardinia, now part of Italy, was home to a remarkable people, the Nuragic culture. For much of their history the Nuragic people lived in scattered farmsteads, practiced intensive small-scale farming and stock raising, and communicated without writing. In these respects they resembled many of their contemporaries in the western Mediterranean and Europe. However, the Nuragic people distinguished themselves from their mainland neighbors by channeling their creative energies into their architecture: the dramatic conical stone towers, known as *nuraghi* (singular, *nuraghe*), that give their name to the culture. To modern time these towers, some seven thousand of them, dot the island's landscape. Even after some four thousand years of wear and tear, they remain impressive and beautiful monuments. The neighboring islands of Corsica, the Balearic Islands, and Pantelleria all have monumental towers akin to the *nuraghi*. But their numbers are fewer, and they appear slightly later in history, so they are thought to be copies of the Sardinian towers. The Sardinian examples, then, justly have received the most study. Twentieth-century investigations of the towers greatly expanded understanding of the origins, construction, and development of the *nuraghi* and their social significance.

CONSTRUCTION AND DISTRIBUTION

The *nuraghi* are composed of large stone blocks constructed without benefit of mortar or any other binding agent. Construction styles vary: the blocks may be well dressed or only roughly hewn, and they may be arranged in horizontal courses of walling or stacked with progressively smaller stones used as the wall gets higher. The towers average 12 meters in external diameter and reached an estimated 15 to 20 meters in height when they were complete (most have lost the upper portions). Inside the towers typically consist of a windowless central circular chamber on the ground floor, with two or three shallow niches off it. The ceiling took the form of a corbeled vault. To the side of the entrance is a small niche, commonly called a "guard's chamber," though its function remains obscure. Often these towers had an upper story, and in the case of the largest ones two upper stories, reached by a staircase built inside the double walls. The builders used local stone: basalt and granite were preferred, but in some cases limestone was used. Although the *nuraghi*'s ground plans are quite homogeneous, there is enormous variety in their appearance. The variation in size and building techniques suggests that these towers were not built under the direction of an islandwide authority but instead were the result of local decision making.

The *nuraghi* are found all over the island though in greatest densities in the hilly central region. Their distribution is dispersed, positioned no less than half a kilometer apart. Stone tombs known as "giants' tombs," consisting of an elongated chamber of large stone slabs and fronted by a semicircular forecourt, are found near many *nuraghi* and were the sites of communal burials.

QUESTIONS OF FUNCTION

Theories abound to explain the function of the *nuraghi*. For several hundred years scholars have proposed that they were temples, tombs, farms, storehouses, and forts. But finds from excavations over the twentieth century suggest fairly conclusively that the towers were habitations. Remains of vessels for cooking, serving, and storing food; animal bones and seeds; traces of hearths; stone tools; and implements for weaving and spinning all point to domestic activities in the towers. Given their rural setting, the towers seem to have been farmsteads, each, in all likelihood, occupied by a family who grew crops or herded sheep and goats on the surrounding land. However, this does not explain their monumental size. The towers' height, their location in prominent places such as hilltops, and the fact that many towers seem positioned to be in sight of each other all suggest that they functioned as watchtowers. Their solidity points to self-defense. In the absence of any evidence of external threats, many scholars think of them as fortresses for a society prone to chronic feuding between families, interspersed with moments of cooperation. Clearly such cooperation was needed from neighbors in order to construct these towers: a single family could not have done this alone. The towers took an estimated 3,600 person-days to build. However, this theory remains somewhat tentative as there is little evidence of warfare apart from the towers themselves, and it is perplexing why neighbors would help to build structures that would then be used as defense against them.

ORIGINS AND CHRONOLOGY

Until the late twentieth century the *nuraghi* were thought to be Greek in origin: their vaulted ceilings and conical shapes resemble the *tholoi*, or "beehive" tombs, of Mycenae. However, subsequent work has laid this theory to rest. New dating has shown that the *nuraghi* are earlier than the Mycenaean structures, which date from the Late Bronze Age or fifteenth century B.C., and the construction techniques of the two types of monuments are different. It is widely accepted that the *nuraghi* emerged independently on the island rather than copied from somewhere else.

Dating the *nuraghi* themselves is difficult, and so the chronology for the emergence of the *nuraghi* is still hotly debated. There is no method for dating the construction itself, so the ages of the *nuraghi* are determined by carbon-14 dates from associated organic deposits and from the chronologies of the artifacts found in the towers. Unfortunately linking the artifacts or organic deposits to the moment of construction of the towers is problematic because of their long period of occupation. Still scholars have reached some consensus on the chronology and nature of the towers' development. The classic conical *nuraghe* is the product of a gradual architectural evolution. This evolution is evident from the remains of older structures labeled "proto-*nuraghi*" that are composed of monumental stone blocks but lack the interior vault and conical form. Most scholars favor a date for the appearance of the conical towers around 2000 B.C., though the ranges given vary from as early as 2300 B.C. to as late as 1700 B.C.

The *nuraghi* continued to be occupied for around a thousand years, and likewise Nuragic culture carried on, though with some changes to the social structure that are reflected in the architecture. After 1300 B.C. some of the simple single towers were expanded: new features included surrounding bastions, walls, and additional towers. In some cases these complexes were built from scratch, without having an older tower as a base. Though clearly belonging to the same architectural family as the simple *nuraghi*, these new multitowered *nuraghi*, numbering around two thousand, greatly exceed them in scale and grandeur. While the earlier homogeneous single towers were strong evidence that Nuragic society was egalitarian, these new complex towers suggest the emergence of a social hierarchy, with the elites residing in the grand *nuraghi*. These large complexes would have required considerable numbers of people to build them, far more than the cooperative neighboring families envisaged for the single towers' construction. Around the *nuraghi*, both the complex and the simpler ones, circular huts appear in the second half of the second millen-

Fig. 1. Nuraghe Su Nuraxi, Barumini. © GIANNI DAGLI ORTI/CORBIS. REPRODUCED BY PERMISSION.

nium B.C., suggesting a general population growth. The relationship between these modest huts and the complex *nuraghi* was perhaps akin to that between a medieval village and its castle. The clearest account of the progressive development of these towers is given at Nuraghe Su Nuraxi di Barumini, a site excavated in the 1950s. As the excavation showed, the complex began as a simple single tower and gradually expanded out to become an urban settlement (fig. 1).

In conjunction with these architectural and settlement changes, Nuragic life was changing in other respects in the late second century B.C., and the stimulus was perhaps due to greater contacts with the rest of the Mediterranean world through trade. There is evidence of increasing metallurgical activity at Nuragic sites: a variety of weapons, tools, and fig-

urines in copper and bronze as well as some iron and some lead have been found. By 1300 B.C. the Nuragic people were clearly participating in the vast Mediterranean trading network, as evidenced by the pottery from Mycenaean Greece and Cypriot copper ingots found at Nuragic sites on Sardinia. In turn, Sardinian ceramics have been found in Greece as well as on the island of Lipari off the north coast of Sicily and in two Etruscan burials in central Italy. Phoenician colonies were established along Sardinia's western and southern coasts in the eighth century B.C., further influencing the island culture.

At this time, in the Late Bronze Age and the Early Iron Age, from 1100 to 900 B.C., a new type of building appears that points to a change in ritual practices: a water cult practiced at newly constructed well temples. This period is also characterized by the introduction of ashlar masonry techniques and new pottery forms and decoration. No new *nuraghi* seem to have been built, and some were destroyed and abandoned at this time. The Nuragic period was on the wane, ending historically when the Carthaginians conquered the island in the late sixth century B.C. Since then the island's inhabitants have been under the rule of various foreign groups. However, the towers live on as extraordinary and enduring testaments to the creative vitality of this insular society.

See also **El Argar and Related Bronze Age Cultures of the Iberian Peninsula** (*vol. 2, part 5*).

BIBLIOGRAPHY

Balmuth, Miriam S. "The Nuraghi of Sardinia: An Introduction." In *Studies in Sardinian Archaeology*. Edited by Miriam S. Balmuth and R. J. Rowland, pp. 23–52. Ann Arbor: University of Michigan Press, 1984.

Lilliu, Giovanni. *La civiltà dei Sardi: Dal Paleolitico all'età dei nuraghi*. Turin, Italy: Nuova ERI, 1988.

Trump, David. *Nuraghe Noeddos and the Bonu Ighinu Valley: Excavation and Survey in Sardinia*. Oxford: Oxbow, 1990.

Tykot, Robert H., and Tamsey K. Andrews, eds. *Sardinia in the Mediterranean: A Footprint in the Sea*. Sheffield, U.K.: Sheffield Academic Press, 1992.

Webster, Gary S. *A Prehistory of Sardinia 2300–500 B.C.* Sheffield, U.K.: Sheffield Academic Press, 1996.

Whitehouse, Ruth. "Megaliths of the Central Mediterranean." In *The Megalithic Monuments of Western Europe*. Edited by Colin Renfrew, pp. 42–63. London: Thames and Hudson, 1983.

EMMA BLAKE

BRONZE AGE BRITAIN AND IRELAND

In Britain and Ireland the beginning of the Bronze Age is marked by the appearance of metalworking, new burial practices, and an increase in trade and exchange. What is significant about these developments is their social impact: they facilitated the emergence of hierarchical societies in which social difference was marked out through the ownership and display of bronze artifacts and other exotic objects.

MINING AND METALWORKING

The earliest evidence for metalworking in the British Isles can be dated to c. 2500 B.C. This technology was introduced from the Continent, possibly via contacts with the Low Countries. At first, unalloyed copper was used to create a limited range of simple tools, weapons, and ornaments. These included such items as flat axes, knives, halberds, and rings. Unalloyed copper is a relatively soft metal, however, and tools and weapons made from this material will blunt quickly. By c. 2200 B.C., metalworkers had learned to alleviate this problem by mixing tin with copper to create bronze. Bronze is a harder metal consisting of approximately 90–95 percent copper and 5–10 percent tin.

Sources of both copper and tin were known and used in the British Isles in the Bronze Age. Copper is found in southwest Ireland, Wales, and the northwest of Scotland, and major sources of tin are located in southwest England. During the Bronze Age it is likely that tin was panned from river gravels, a process that does not leave traces in the archaeological record; our evidence for the exploitation of tin during this period is scanty. Copper, however, was mined, and several Bronze Age copper mines have been identified. In southwest Ireland the copper mines at Ross Island and Mount Gabriel have produced evidence for activity spanning much of the Early Bronze Age (c. 2200–1650 B.C.).

A series of short shafts following veins of mineralized rock into the hillside have been identified at these sites. Stone mauls, wooden picks, and wooden shovels were recovered from the mines at Mount Gabriel, providing evidence for the kinds of tools that would have been used. Once the ore had been won from the rock face and brought to the surface, it was crushed and sorted, allowing the most visibly mineralized pieces to be separated from waste material. The ore was then smelted. No evidence for kilns has been identified at either Mount Gabriel or Ross Island, however, and it is likely that simple bowl furnaces (shallow scoops in the ground lined with clay) were employed for this purpose. Mining does not seem to have been carried out on an industrial scale. Calculations indicate that the mines at Mount Gabriel would have produced little more than 15–20 kilograms of copper per year. It seems likely that mining was seasonal work carried out by small groups of people, perhaps at quiet times in the agricultural cycle.

Evidence for the casting of bronze objects is provided by molds, crucibles, and bronze waste. High-status settlements, such as Runnymede in Surrey, have produced particular concentrations of metalworking debris, suggesting that elite groups might have controlled the production of bronze. Stone, ceramic, and metal molds have all been identified. The earliest molds are of one piece, although two-piece molds were introduced by c. 1700 B.C. These molds facilitated the production of more complex and varied forms of bronze objects, including socketed implements. Over time, innovations in bronzeworking facilitated the production of an array of new types of artifact. Such tools as chisels, hammers, gouges, punches, and sickles became common during the Middle Bronze Age (1650–1200 B.C.). Developments in weaponry include spearheads, which appeared at the end of the Early Bronze Age, and swords, which were introduced by c. 1200 B.C. By the Late Bronze Age (1200–700 B.C.), the presence of highly complex and finely crafted items of sheet metal, such as cauldrons, horns, and shields, may indicate the existence of full-time specialist bronzesmiths.

TRADE AND EXCHANGE
Because of the localized distribution of sources of copper and tin, most communities were reliant on trade to acquire metal. The importance of bronze to the Bronze Age economy resulted in a marked increase in the scale of trading activities during this period. Lead isotope analysis of metal objects shows that Ross Island was the main source of copper used throughout the British Isles during much of the Early Bronze Age, although in later centuries communities in southern Britain became more dependent on imported scrap metal from the Continent. Other materials that have been traced to particular sources include amber from the Baltic and jet from east Yorkshire; both materials were used widely for the production of ornaments in Britain and Ireland. Finished items also were exchanged over long distances. For example, a Middle Bronze Age axe from Bohemia was found at Horridge Common in Devon, and a hoard of bronzes from Dieskau in eastern Germany included an Irish axe of Early Bronze Age date. During the Late Bronze Age evidence for the production of salt at sites near the coast, such as Mucking North Ring in Essex, indicates that staples were exchanged alongside prestige goods. Ideas also traveled. Similarities in the pottery styles used in different areas suggest significant interregional contacts. For example, bowl food vessels from Ireland, southwest Scotland, the Isle of Man, and southwest Wales are extremely similar stylistically, although petrographic analysis argues that they were manufactured from local clays in each region.

There is good evidence for the movement of goods and people by both land and sea. Significant deforestation occurred during the Bronze Age, so that travel by land perhaps became easier than it had been during the preceding Neolithic period. Wooden trackways were constructed to facilitate passage across marshy or boggy land. Some of these were light structures, built purely for small-scale traffic on foot. Others were more substantial and would have been able to accommodate wheeled transport. It is during the Late Bronze Age that the first evidence for wheeled vehicles is found in Britain and Ireland, for example, the block wheel from Doogarymore, County Roscommon. Knowledge of horse riding also spread into these islands at this time, although this activity may have been restricted to high-status people. For example, antler cheekpieces (parts of horse bridles) tend to be found at wealthy settlement sites, such as Runnymede in Surrey.

Over longer distances waterborne transport was a vital means of communication. Dugout canoes fashioned from single oak trunks provided a suitable mode of transport in estuarine and riverine contexts. Seagoing plank-built boats also are known, for instance, from North Ferriby, North Humberside (fig. 1). Occasionally, shipwrecks give vivid insight into the cargo of such vessels. At Langdon Bay near Dover a cluster of more than three hundred bronze objects was found some 500 meters offshore, although the ship itself had not survived. Many of the items recovered were French, provid-

Fig. 1. Excavation of the Dover boat. The boat was abandoned in a creek near a river over 3,000 years ago. CANTERBURY ARCHAEOLOGICAL TRUST. REPRODUCED BY PERMISSION.

ing evidence for the importation of goods into Britain from abroad.

Although the Langdon Bay shipwreck hints at large-scale and highly organized trading ventures, commercial exchange as we know it today is unlikely to have existed during the Bronze Age. There is little evidence for the presence of a specialist merchant class, for dedicated marketplaces, or for early forms of currency. Instead, most goods would have changed hands as gifts between neighbors, kinsfolk, or chiefly elites—perhaps to forge new friendships or to cement long-standing alliances.

BURIAL PRACTICES

During the Early Bronze Age, the communal mortuary monuments of the Neolithic were replaced by traditions of individual burial with grave goods. Although single burials of Late Neolithic date are known, it was during the Early Bronze Age that this form of mortuary rite became widespread across

much of Britain and Ireland. Funerary practices at this time seem to have been greatly influenced by developments abroad. In many parts of continental western Europe, the so-called Beaker burial rite had become the dominant mortuary tradition by the middle of the third millennium B.C. This rite appears to have been introduced into the British Isles, probably via the Low Countries, around 2500 B.C.

Beaker burials are so called because the dead were accompanied by a pottery beaker, or drinking-vessel, of a distinctive S-shaped profile. Other characteristic grave goods include copper knives and daggers; archer's equipment, such as stone wrist guards and barbed-and-tanged arrowheads made of flint; stone battle-axes; antler "spatulas" (probably used to produce flint tools); and buttons of jet or shale. Usually, the dead were inhumed, their bodies laid on their sides with their legs and arms drawn up, as if asleep. The precise positioning of the body in the grave evidently was important. In northeast Scotland, for example, men were placed on their left sides, with their heads pointing to the east. Women, however, were laid on their right sides, with their heads oriented to the west. In some cases wooden mortuary houses were erected over the graves.

Beaker burials have produced some of the earliest metal items known from these islands. In the past archaeologists believed that these burials indicated the immigration or invasion of a large group of Beaker folk from abroad, who brought with them the new metalworking technology. Current theories, however, stress that although there is likely to have been small-scale movement of people during this period, knowledge of Beaker mortuary rites probably was acquired through preexisting networks of trade and exchange. For elite groups in the British Isles individual burial with exotic artifacts, such as copper knives, represented an appealing new way of expressing personal status.

Once the practice of individual burial with grave goods had been introduced, local variants of this form of mortuary rite were quick to emerge. In Ireland, for example, very few Beaker burials are known. Instead, single burials were accompanied by indigenous forms of pottery, such as food vessels. Toward the end of the Early Bronze Age, inhumation was replaced by cremation as the dominant mortuary practice. The cremated remains of the dead were collected from the pyre and placed in a ceramic vessel, such as a collared urn or cordoned urn.

Both inhumation and cremation burials were accompanied by grave goods indicative of the social status of the deceased person. The wealthiest Early Bronze Age burials included not only copper or bronze objects, such as daggers and awls, but also ornaments, decorative fittings, and small items of exotic materials, such as amber, jet, faience, and gold. These rich burials have been termed "Wessex burials," after a region of southern England in which there is a particular concentration. Rich graves are found elsewhere, too. For example, the cremation burial from Little Cressingham, Norfolk, produced two bronze daggers, an amber necklace, a rectangular gold plate with incised decoration, and four other small decorative fittings of gold, including a possible pommel mount for one of the daggers. Such wealthy burials may indicate the presence of a chiefly class whose status depended at least

in part on their ability to acquire prestige goods through exchange.

Round barrows and round cairns were the dominant form of mortuary monument during the Early Bronze Age. Although the mounds raised over Beaker burials usually were small, by the later part of the Early Bronze Age, large and elaborate barrows were being constructed. These barrows could be up to 40 meters in diameter and often were built in several phases. Some have lengthy histories of construction and appear to have been enlarged over successive generations. In many parts of Britain barrows cluster together into cemeteries. Linear arrangements of barrows in such areas as the Dorset Ridgeway hint at the importance of genealogical succession in Early Bronze Age society; the relative positioning of different barrows within a barrow cemetery may have been a means of expressing kinship relationships.

Not all burials were provided with such a marker, however. Some were left unmarked by any form of monument, whereas others were inserted into preexisting mounds. Within individual barrows or cairns archaeologists often distinguish between "primary" and "secondary" burials, that is, between the interment over which the mound originally was raised (the primary burial) and burials that were inserted into the mound at a later point (secondary burials). It has been suggested that people interred in secondary positions within a monument were not of sufficient importance to have a barrow or cairn constructed for them alone. Alternatively, such people may have wished to underscore their links with significant ancestors buried in preexisting monuments.

During the Middle Bronze Age cremation was the dominant mode of treatment of the dead. In some cases burials were grouped together into small, flat cemeteries. Elsewhere, they were inserted into earlier barrows or had their own small, simple mound raised over them. Grave goods accompanied few burials during this period. Some archaeologists see this change in funerary rites as indicating the collapse of Early Bronze Age chiefdoms. It is more likely, however, that status was simply expressed in a different way outside the mortuary arena. During the Late Bronze Age burial rites become archaeologically invisible, and we do not know how the bodies of the dead were disposed of. The discovery of unburned, disarticulated, and fragmentary human bone on settlement sites, however, may hint that exposure to the elements became the normal mode of mortuary treatment during this period.

SETTLEMENTS

Bronze Age settlements in Britain and Ireland generally were small in scale. There is no evidence for the construction of hamlets or villages. Instead, the settlement pattern is predominantly one of scattered farmsteads, each providing a home for a single nuclear or small extended family group. In most areas the dominant house form was the roundhouse, circular in shape and usually some 6–12 meters in diameter. A central ring of stout timber posts gave support to a thatched roof. The walls were constructed of wattle and daub, although in many upland areas, stone was used. The doorway usually faced east or southeast and often was protected by a porch structure (fig. 2). Hut 3 at Black Patch in Sussex provides interesting evidence for the internal spatial arrangement of activities. A hearth located toward the front of the building was the focus for a range of craft activities. At the back of the house were a number of storage pits as well as a line of loom weights, which may indicate the original location of an upright weaving loom.

Most Bronze Age settlements comprise several roundhouses set within an enclosure formed by lengths of bank, ditch, and palisade. Analysis of the distribution of finds indicates that settlements included a main residential structure along with one or more ancillary structures. The latter provided specialized working areas for a variety of tasks, as well as storage facilities and housing for animals.

The settlement at Black Patch is a good example. At this site five roundhouses were set within small yards defined by lines of fencing. The main residential structure was hut 3, which contains evidence for such activities as the serving and consumption of food, storage of grain, leatherworking, and cloth production. A large number of cooking vessels, along with quern stones and animal bone, were recovered from hut 1, suggesting that this was an area dedicated to food preparation. Both hut 3 and hut 1 had their own water sources, in the form of a small pond. Hut 4 produced evidence for a combination of the activities carried out in huts 3 and 1, but this structure did not have its own pond,

hinting that it may have been the home of a dependent relative of the household head, perhaps a younger sibling or elderly parent. Huts 2 and 5 produced few artifacts and may have been used as shelters for animals. The excavator, Peter Drewett, suggested that there may have been a gendered aspect to the use of space at this site. A razor was found in hut 3, the main residential structure, and two finger rings were recovered from hut 1, the cooking hut. Drewett argues that these finds indicate a male head of household whose wife had her own hut.

During the Late Bronze Age, there is increasing evidence for the development of settlement hierarchies. Hillforts began to be constructed during this period, hinting at the large-scale mobilization of labor for certain projects. Some of these sites appear to have had high-status inhabitants. The hillfort known as Haughey's Fort, in County Armagh, Ireland, was occupied between c. 1100 and 900 B.C. Three concentric ditches enclosed an area of about 340 by 310 meters, inside of which were located several very substantial timber structures. The site produced several small decorative articles of gold, among them, a stud, pieces of wire, and fragments of sheet gold, as well as glass beads and bracelets of bronze and lignite.

In southern England, a category of very rich midden sites can be identified during this period. At Potterne in Wiltshire, a 2-meter-thick deposit of refuse covering approximately 3.5 hectares hints at large gatherings of people at certain times of the year. Much of this midden consisted of cattle dung, barn waste, and domestic refuse, although the site also produced 186 bronze objects, along with decorative items of antler, jet, shale, amber, gold, and glass. Analysis of the animal bones and ceramics recovered attest that feasting activities were carried out on a large scale at Potterne. The accumulation of such large middens may in itself have been an indicator of social status, providing physical evidence for the keeping of large herds of animals, feasting, and craft production.

In eastern England a lower level in the settlement hierarchy may be indicated by a class of sites known as ringworks, or ringforts. These are small, defended settlements enclosed by a circular bank and ditch. They have produced copious evidence for craft-working activities, such as the production of bronze objects; salt; and cloth, although "exotic"

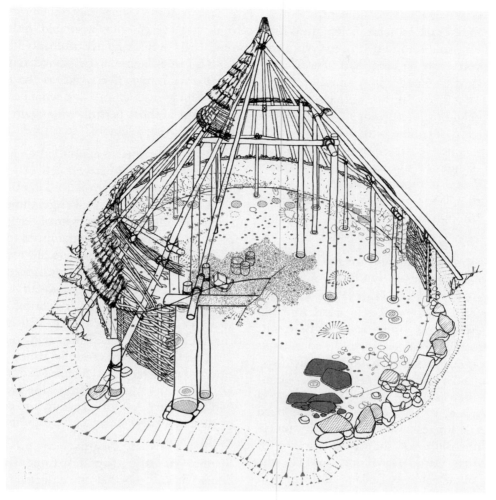

Fig. 2. Artist's reconstruction of house 2222 at Trethellan Farm, Cornwall, showing the different structural elements of the building. COPYRIGHT ROSEMARY ROBERTSON. REPRODUCED BY PERMISSION.

materials, such as amber, gold, or glass, generally are not found on these sites.

THE ECONOMY

Bronze Age farmers practiced mixed agriculture. Cattle and sheep or goats were the most important domestic animals, although pigs also were kept. At some sites horses were present, but usually in very small numbers. Over time there was an increase in the relative proportion of sheep to cattle. The recovery of large numbers of spindle whorls and loom weights from Middle and Late Bronze Age settlements suggests that sheep generally were kept for their wool rather than their meat. Wheat and barley were the main cereals grown, and peas, beans, and lentils also were cultivated. During the Middle and Late Bronze Ages, several new crops were intro-

duced, including spelt wheat, rye, and flax; the latter was a source of fiber and oil. Agricultural implements, such as digging sticks, hoes, and ards, probably were manufactured from wood and therefore rarely survive, although during the Middle and Late Bronze Ages, bronze sickles became relatively common. Ard marks are known from several sites, most famously, Gwithian in Cornwall.

Bronze Age field systems have been identified in several regions. On Dartmoor in Devon a series of field systems covering thousands of hectares of land were constructed around the fringes of the moor. These systems appear to have been carefully laid out during a single planned phase of expansion into the uplands around 1700 B.C. The boundaries themselves were built of earth and stone and enclose rectilinear fields of varying sizes. Individual boundaries can be up to several kilometers in length. Within each field system, roundhouses, droveways, cairns, and other features can be identified. The roundhouses were not distributed evenly among the various parcels of land, however, but were clustered together into "neighborhood groups," suggesting a communal pattern of landholding. The large-scale, organized, and cohesive nature of land division on Dartmoor has suggested to some researchers that a centralized political authority must have been responsible for the planning and construction of the boundaries, although the possibility of intercommunity cooperation also has been raised.

In other parts in Britain and Ireland rather different forms of land enclosure can be identified. On the East Moors of the Peak District, for example, small field systems 1–25 hectares in area have been identified. These systems comprise groups of irregular fields of broadly curvilinear form. In contrast to the situation on Dartmoor, such individual field systems were not laid out during a single phase of construction but seem to have grown and developed over time, with new plots enclosed as the need arose. Their scale suggests that they probably represent the landholdings of individual families or household groups. As on Dartmoor, however, the development of new forms of land management may indicate the intensification of agricultural production.

HOARDS
Although settlements and burials sometimes produce bronze objects, the vast majority of Bronze Age metalwork has been recovered either as single finds—unassociated with any other artifacts—or as part of a larger collection (a hoard) of metalwork buried in the ground or deposited in a river, lake, or bog. Metalwork deposited in wetland contexts would not have been easily recoverable, and such finds can be interpreted as a form of sacrifice to gods, spirits, or ancestors. Votive offerings of this type often include particularly fine metalwork. For example, in the Dowris hoard from County Offaly there were bronze buckets, cauldrons, horns, and swords along with many other items, all found in an area of reclaimed bog in the 1820s. More than two hundred items were recovered. It seems unlikely that all of these items were deposited as part of a sin-

gle event. Rather, they may be the material remains of periodic ceremonies at a location that was visited repeatedly over a long period of time. Richard Bradley has made the point that the act of throwing fine metalwork into a river, lake, or bog would have been highly ostentatious and would have enhanced the status of those persons who could afford to sacrifice such valuable items.

In comparison, items buried or hidden in dryland contexts would have been easier to recover. These finds usually are explained in utilitarian terms. Collections of worn, broken, or miscast bronzes often are interpreted as "smiths' hoards"—scrap metal accumulated for recycling into new artifacts. This type of hoard can include ingots, waste metal, and fragments of crucibles and molds. At Petters Sports Field in Surrey, seventy-eight bronze objects, among them, numerous broken items and other scrap metal, were buried in two small pits cut into the upper silts of a Late Bronze Age ditch. This material had been sorted carefully: the size and composition of the scrap metal from each of these deposits was different, suggesting that the two collections had been intended for recycling into different types of object.

Some dryland hoards have produced several identical items, perhaps cast from the same mold, along with objects that do not appear to have been used. Such hoards often have been interpreted as "merchant's hoards"—the stock of a trader who, for one reason or another, was unable to recover this material from its hiding place. Other hoards consist of a single set of tools or ornaments probably belonging to one person. For example, the Mountrivers hoard from County Cork comprised two socketed axes, a bronze penannular bracelet, a string of amber beads, and two gold dress fasteners. The owners of such "personal hoards" may have hidden them for safekeeping in times of unrest.

SOCIETY AND POLITICS
Many archaeologists have argued that the appearance of rich individual burials during the Early Bronze Age indicates an increase in social stratification. Burials accompanied by items of gold, amber, faience, and the like may signify the emergence of a chiefly class. Undoubtedly, the development of metalworking and the associated increase in trade and exchange played a significant role. Metal, an

eye-catching and adaptable material, provided novel ways of displaying personal status. Control over the distribution of prestige goods and the materials from which they were produced would have facilitated the accumulation of wealth by particular people.

Rich burials had disappeared by the end of the Early Bronze Age. This does not indicate a return to a more egalitarian political order, however. High-quality metalwork continued to be produced. During the Middle and Late Bronze Ages, it was deposited into rivers, lakes, and bogs as part of the conspicuous consumption of wealth by high-status persons. The Late Bronze Age saw the development of a distinct settlement hierarchy. High-status settlements, such as Runnymede in Surrey, furnish copious evidence for metalworking and other craft activities, as well as exotic items imported from distant parts of Britain and beyond, indicating that control over production and exchange continued to be important.

See also **Trackways and Boats** (*vol. 1, part 4*); **Stonehenge** (*vol. 2, part 5*).

BIBLIOGRAPHY

Barnatt, J. "Bronze Age Settlement on the East Moors of the Peak District of Derbyshire and South Yorkshire." *Proceedings of the Prehistoric Society* 53 (1987): 393–418.

Barrett, John C. "Mortuary Archaeology." In *Landscape, Monuments and Society: The Prehistory of Cranborne Chase.* Edited by John C. Barrett, Richard Bradley, and Martin Green, pp. 120–128. Cambridge, U.K.: Cambridge University Press, 1991.

Bradley, Richard. *The Passage of Arms: An Archaeological Analysis of Prehistoric Hoards and Votive Deposits.* Oxford: Oxbow Books, 1999.

———. *The Social Foundations of Prehistoric Britain: Themes and Variations in the Archaeology of Power.* London: Longman, 1984.

Clarke, David V., Trevor G. Cowie, and Andrew Foxon. *Symbols of Power at the Time of Stonehenge.* Edinburgh: National Museum of Antiquities of Scotland, 1985.

Cooney, Gabriel, and Eoin Grogan. *Irish Prehistory: A Social Perspective.* Dublin: Wordwell, 1994.

Darvill, Timothy. *Prehistoric Britain.* London: Batsford, 1987.

Drewett, P. "Later Bronze Age Downland Economy and Excavations at Black Patch, East Sussex." *Proceedings of the Prehistoric Society* 48 (1982): 321–400.

Fleming, Andrew. *The Dartmoor Reaves: Investigating Prehistoric Land Divisions.* London: Batsford, 1988.

Lawson, Andrew. *Potterne 1982–5: Animal Husbandry in Later Prehistoric Wiltshire.* Salisbury, U.K.: Trust for Wessex Archaeology, 2000.

Mallory, J. P. "Haughey's Fort and the Navan Complex in the Late Bronze Age." In *Ireland in the Bronze Age.* Edited by John Waddell and Elizabeth Shee-Twohig, pp. 73–86. Dublin: Stationery Office, 1995.

Muckleroy, K. "Two Bronze Age Cargoes in British Waters." *Antiquity* 54 (1980): 100–109.

Needham, S. "The Structure of Settlement and Ritual in the Late Bronze Age of South-East Britain." In *L'habitat et l'occupation du sol à l'Âge du Bronze en Europe.* Edited by C. Mordant and A. Richard, pp. 49–69. Paris: Éditions du Comité des Travaux Historiques et Scientifiques, 1993.

Needham, Stuart, and Tony Spence. *Runnymede Bridge Research Excavations.* Vol. 2, *Refuse and Disposal at Area 16 East Runnymede.* London: British Museum Press, 1996.

Northover, J. P., W. O'Brien, and S. Stos. "Lead Isotopes and Metal Circulation in Beaker/Early Bronze Age Ireland." *Journal of Irish Archaeology* 10 (2001): 25–47.

O'Brien, William. *Bronze Age Copper Mining in Britain and Ireland.* Princes Risborough, U.K.: Shire Archaeology, 1996.

Parker Pearson, Michael. *English Heritage Book of Bronze Age Britain.* London: Batsford/English Heritage, 1993.

Waddell, John. *The Prehistoric Archaeology of Ireland.* Galway, Ireland: Galway University Press, 1998.

Wright, Edward. *The Ferriby Boats: Seacraft of the Bronze Age.* London: Routledge, 1990.

JOANNA BRÜCK

STONEHENGE

Stonehenge in Wiltshire, England, is a unique Neolithic monument that combines several episodes of construction with various monument classes. The final monument, as seen in the early twenty-first century, represents an extraordinary level of sophistication in design, material, construction, and function rarely found at other prehistoric sites in Europe. Stonehenge evolved slowly over a millennium or longer and was embellished and rebuilt according to changing styles, social aspirations, and beliefs in tandem with the local political landscape of Wiltshire. The various stages, which archaeology identifies in three main phases and at least eight constructional episodes, link closely with monument building and developments seen elsewhere in Britain and Europe (fig. 1).

Stonehenge began its development in the early third millennium B.C., a period of transition between the earlier Neolithic, with its monuments of collective long barrows and communal causewayed enclosures, and the later Neolithic world of henges, avenues, ceremonial enclosures, circles, and megalithic monuments. Across Britain and western Europe, this period signaled the closure of many of the megalithic tombs and seems to indicate changes in society, from small-scale, apparently egalitarian farming groups to more hierarchical and territorially aware societies. Burial especially reflected these changes, with the abandonment of collective rites and the emergence over the third millennium B.C. of individual burials furnished with personal ornaments, weapons, and tools. Landscape also showed changes, including more open landscapes cleared of trees, growing numbers of settlements, and an apparent preoccupation with the creation of ceremonial and monumental areas incorporating numerous sites within what is described as "sacred geography," or monuments arranged intentionally to take advantage of other sites and views, creating an arena for ceremonial activities.

Toward the end of the third millennium B.C., the later Neolithic and Bell Beaker periods evidenced increasing numbers of individual burials and ritual deposits and the growing use of megalithic stones and building of henges. Early metal objects, first of copper and then of bronze and gold, appeared in burials, and these items have close parallels with material developments in western Europe and across the British Isles. The quest for metals, with a related rise in interaction between groups, is reflected in rapidly changing fashions in metalwork, ornaments, and ritual practices. Wessex and its so-called Wessex culture lay at the junction between the metal-rich west of Britain and consumers in central eastern Britain and Europe. Through political, ritual, and economic control, these communities acquired materials and fine objects for use and burial in the tombs of elites on Salisbury Plain and the chalk lands of southern Britain.

The main building phases of Stonehenge reveal the growing importance of the Stonehenge area as a focus for burial and ritual. Earlier sites either were abandoned or, as in the case of Stonehenge, were massively embellished and rebuilt; many other very large and prominent monuments were located within easy sight of Stonehenge. Geographic Information Systems studies suggest the Stonehenge was visible to all its contemporary neighbors and thus strategically located at the center of a monumental landscape. The significance of its location may stem from Stonehenge's special function as an observatory for the study of lunar and solar movements. Without doubt, the later phases of Stonehenge's construction focused on the orientation of the structures, which aligned with observations of the solstices and equinoxes, especially the rising of the midsummer and midwinter sun. Few other prehistoric sites appear to have had comparable structures, although several were observatories, such as the passage graves at Maes Howe on Orkney, Newgrange (rising midwinter sun) and Knowth in County Meath, Ireland, and many of the stone circles across Britain and Ireland.

CONSTRUCTION SEQUENCE AND CHRONOLOGY

Stonehenge was constructed over some fifteen hundred years, with long periods between building episodes. The first stage, c. 2950–2900 B.C., included a small causewayed enclosure ditch with an inner and outer surrounding bank, which had three entrances (one aligned roughly northeast, close to the present one). At this time, the construction of the fifty-six Aubrey Holes probably took place; these manmade holes filled with rubble may have supported a line of timber posts. Deposits and bones were placed at the ends of the ditch, signifying ritual activity. At the same time, the Greater and Lesser Cursus monuments, termed "cursus" after their long, linear form, suggestive of a racetrack, were constructed to the north of the Stonehenge enclosure. Some 4 kilometers north, the causewayed enclosure of Robin Hood's Ball probably was still in use. The surrounding landscape was becoming increasingly clear of tree cover, as farming communities continued to expand across the area. Survey has identified many potential settlement sites.

The second phase of building took place over the next five hundred years, until 2400 B.C., and represented a complex series of timber settings

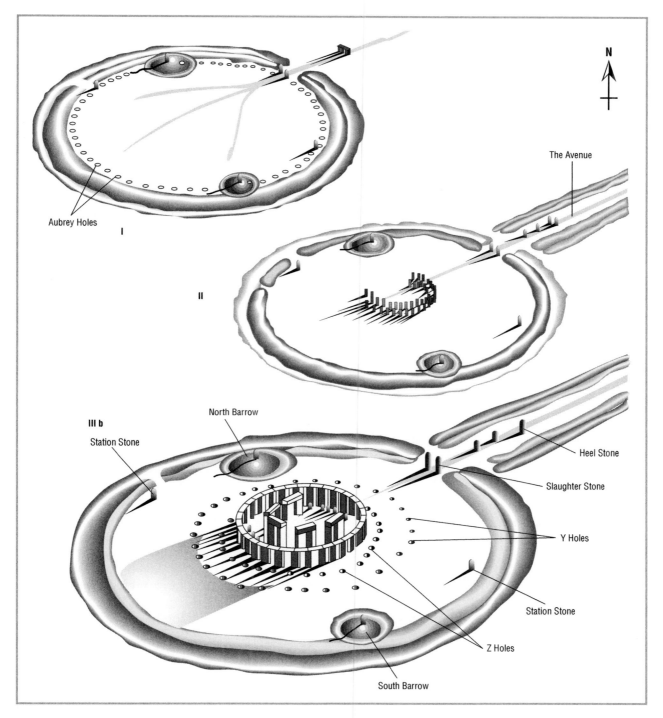

Aubrey Holes

I

II

III b

North Barrow

Station Stone

The Avenue

Heel Stone

Slaughter Stone

Y Holes

Station Stone

Z Holes

South Barrow

N

Fig. 1. Phases in the construction of Stonehenge. REDRAWN FROM HTTP://ZEBU.UOREGON.EDU/~JS/AST122/IMAGES/STONEHENGE_MAP.JPG.

within and around the ditched enclosure. Subsequent building has obscured the plan, but the northeastern entrance comprised a series of post-built corridors that allowed observation of the sun and blocked access to the circle. The interior included a central structure—perhaps a building—and a southern entrance with a post corridor and barriers. Cremations were inserted into the Aubrey Holes and ditch, along with distinctive bone pins. During this phase a palisade was erected between Stonehenge and the Cursus monuments to the north, dividing the landscape into northern and southern sections. To the east, 3 kilometers distant, the immense Durrington Walls Henge and the small Woodhenge site beside it, incorporating large circular buildings, seem to have represented the major ceremonial focus during this period.

The third and major phase of building lasted from 2550–2450 to about 1600 B.C., with several intermittent bursts of construction and modification. The earth avenue was completed, leading northeastward from what was by then a single northeastern entrance. Sight lines focused on two stones in the entrance area (the surviving Heel Stone and another now lost) that aligned on the Slaughter Stone and provided a direct alignment to the center of the circle. Four station stones were set up against the inner ditch on small mounds, forming a quadrangular arrangement around the main circle.

The first stone phase (stage 3i) was initiated with the erection of bluestones in a crude circle (at least twenty-five stones) at the center of the henge, but lack of evidence and the subsequent removal of the stones leave the form of the possibly unfinished structure unclear. It was followed (stage 3ii), c. 2300 B.C., by the erection of some 30 huge (4 meters high) sarsen stones, capped and held together by a continuous ring of lintels, in a circle enclosing a horseshoe-shaped inner setting of 10 stones 7 meters high. These were "dressed," or shaped, in situ with stone mauls (hammers).

This arrangement was further modified with the insertion of bluestone within the sarsen circle (stage 3iii), but it was dismantled and rearranged by c. 2000 B.C. (stage 3iv), and more than twenty of the original stones probably were dressed and set in an oval around the inner sarsen horseshoe. Another ring of rougher bluestones was assembled between this and the outer sarsen circle, and an altar stone of Welsh sandstone was set at the center. Between 1900 and 1800 B.C. there was further rearrangement (stage 3v) of the bluestone, and stones in the northern section were removed. A final stage (stage 3vi) saw the excavation of two rings of pits around the main sarsen circle—the so-called Y and Z Holes, which may have been intended for additional settings. Material at the bases dates to c. 1600 B.C., and several contained deliberate deposits of antler. In parallel with these final phases of rebuilding, Stonehenge became the main focus of burial for the area, with about five hundred Bronze Age round barrows, some of which contain prestigious grave goods.

RAW MATERIALS AND DEBATES

The raw materials that comprise Stonehenge were selected deliberately and transported over great distances, which suggests that the materials themselves were symbolically important. The sarsen stone that forms the main massive trilithons and circle derived from areas north and east of Salisbury Plain, some 20 to 30 kilometers distant. Sarsen is a very hard Tertiary sandstone, formed as a capping over the Wiltshire chalk and dispersed as shattered blocks over the Marlborough Downs and in the valleys. The shaping of this extremely hard material at Stonehenge represents a remarkable and very unusual exercise for British prehistory, when stones generally were selected in their natural form and utilized without further work. The bluestones have long been the focus of discussion, since they derive only from the Preseli Mountains of Southwest Wales, located 240 kilometers from Salisbury Plain. Collectively, the stones are various forms of dolerite and rhyolite, occurring in large outcrops. Many theories have been proposed, and in the 1950s Richard Atkinson demonstrated the ease by which these quite small stones could be transported by raft to the Stonehenge area. Later geological study suggested that glacial ice probably transported considerable quantities of bluestone in a southeasterly direction and deposited it in central southern Britain.

The debate continues, but the carefully selected shape and size of the bluestones at Stonehenge seem to indicate that it would have been difficult to find so many similar stones deposited by natural agencies in Wiltshire. One theory suggests that the original bluestones were taken wholesale from an existing circle and removed to Stonehenge, perhaps as tribute or a gift. Other materials also have been found at Stonehenge, including the green sandstone altar stone, which may derive from the Cosheston Beds in southern Wales. Other local sites, such as West Kennet Long Barrow, include stone selected some distance away, such as Calne (Wiltshire) limestone. The interesting and complex dispersal of exotic stone axes and flint from early in the Neolithic further supports the idea that exotic materials were highly prized and had special symbolic properties.

SURROUNDING LANDSCAPE AND SITES

The landscape surrounding Stonehenge is a dry, rolling chalk plateau, with the broad Avon Valley and its floodplain to the east. The valley areas were attractive to early settlement, but perhaps because of its bleakness and lack of water, the area immediately surrounding Stonehenge was little settled. The special ritual status afforded the location also may have deterred settlement over much of prehistory. Initially (4000–3000 B.C.), the landscape at the beginning of the Neolithic was heavily wooded, and clearances made by early farmers were the main open spaces. By the transition from the earlier to the later Neolithic, c. 2900 B.C., it seems that well over half the landscape was open, and monuments such as the Cursus were widely visible. Over the next millennium, increasing clearance reduced tree cover to belts of woodland around the edge of the Avon Valley and sparse scrub, allowing Stonehenge and the surrounding monuments to be visible one from another and to gain prominence in a largely manmade landscape.

Late Mesolithic activity has been identified in the parking area of Stonehenge, where four large postholes were located. They may have demarcated an early shrine, but a relationship to activity more than four thousand years later seems remote. The two-ditched causewayed enclosure of Robin Hood's Ball represents the earliest major site in the Stonehenge landscape in the early fourth millennium B.C., alongside some ten or more long barrows in the immediate area. Such a concentration is typical of these ceremonial foci and is repeated around other causewayed enclosures. Other sites developed over the late fourth and third millennia B.C., including an enclosure on Normanton Down, which may have been a mortuary site. Contemporary with the building of the enclosure in Stonehenge phase I is the Coneybury Henge located to the southeast. It was small and oval-shaped and contained settings of some seven hundred wooden posts arranged around the inner edge and in radiating lines around a central point. Its ditches contained grooved-ware pottery, and, significantly, among the animal bone deposits was a white-tailed sea eagle, a rare bird never found inland, so its placement would appear to be intentional and ritual.

To the west of Stonehenge lies another very small henge, only about 7 meters in diameter—the Fargo Plantation, which surrounded inhumation and cremation burials. Such concerns also were reflected at Woodhenge, located 3 kilometers northeast of Stonehenge, where the central focus is on the burial of a child with Bell Beaker grave goods, who might have been killed in a ritual sacrifice. The site formed the ditched enclosure of a large structure—probably a circular building supported on six concentric rings of posts. Immediately north lies Durrington Walls, the second largest of all the henges of Britain, with a maximum diameter of 525 meters and covering some 12 hectares within an immense ditch and bank. Only a small linear area of this site had been investigated before road building took place, but this study revealed two more large, wooden, circular buildings. A great quantity of grooved-ware pottery was found together with animal remains and fine flint, suggesting offerings had been placed in the ditch and at the base of the timber posts. The henge sites all seem to have been occupied until the end of the third millennium. The Early Bronze Age saw an increasing emphasis on burial landscapes and the construction of monuments.

Over the course of only half a millennium, the five hundred or so round barrows were constructed in groups at prominent places in the Stonehenge landscape. Dramatic locales, such as the King Barrow Ridge, were chosen for linear cemeteries of as many as twenty large, round barrows. Another example, Winterbourne Stoke, west of Stonehenge, was the site of an earlier long barrow. To the south of Stonehenge, the Normanton Down cemetery, with more than twenty-five barrows, included very rich burials, such as Bush Barrow. Excavations at many sites in the nineteenth century emptied the tombs and destroyed much of the evidence; nevertheless, much artifactual information was gathered. This information formed the basis of studies by Stuart Piggott and others that helped define the Wessex culture of the Early Bronze Age, which lasted from c. 1900 to 1550 B.C. Corpses were inhumed in burial pits accompanied by collared urns, a variety of small vessels used for offerings and incense, and personal ornaments, which sometimes were made of valuable amber, shale, copper, gold, and jet. Many of the finest objects were fashioned from exotic materials, some of which have electrostatic properties (materials that can take an electrical charge and spark, such as amber and coal shale). Bronze weapons and tools, including daggers and axes, were buried with the dead and provide a means of relative dating and sequencing. The goldwork of the Wessex tombs is especially distinctive, with linear geometric patterns incised into sheets of hammered gold. Particularly rich burials are known from Bush Barrow and Upton Lovell as well as farther afield.

As the Bronze Age developed, the focus on Stonehenge waned, and by the middle of the second millennium B.C. both the monument and its surrounding cemeteries were abandoned. Cremation cemeteries took the place of barrow cemeteries, and fields and settlements replaced earthwork monuments. These changes have not been fully explained, but it seems that the availability of metal tools and weapons through increased interaction across wide areas of Britain and Europe, together with growing populations and more productive agriculture, reduced the significance of ritual in megalithic sites and their calendar observations.

OTHER HENGES AND STANDING STONE MONUMENTS

Stonehenge is a comparatively small henge site and, with its curious inner bank and outer ditch, one of a small, rare group within the eight different henge forms that have been identified. Most henges have outer banks and inner ditches, crossed by one to four causewayed entrances. With the largest henges spanning 500 meters in diameter, Stonehenge measures only 110 meters; clearly, its size is not a significant factor. Stonehenge's ceremonial complex of sites is repeated as a distinctive "module" elsewhere in Neolithic Britain. At Avebury, Dorchester, Cranborne Chase, the Thames area, and the Fenland, similar associations of successive enclosures, barrows, monuments, and henges have been documented. In the uplands, tor (high granite outcrop) enclosures seem to represent comparable ceremonial foci, and elsewhere in Britain and Ireland, pit enclosures, palisade sites, and cursus and other structures similarly cluster around concentrations of early burials and megalithic tombs. Research shows that

the distribution of these complexes is related closely to the parent rock and draws on local traditions. Eastern Britain tended toward monuments built of ditches and pits, earth, wood, and gravel, whereas the rockier north and west invariably made use of local stone, with fewer attempts to excavate deep ditches. Common to all areas was construction of manmade landscapes of ritual significance, focused on a series of ceremonial sites.

The use of megalithic stones in monument building was adopted from the beginning of tomb building in the west and north of Britain, soon after 3900–3800 B.C. Megalithic cemeteries, such as Carrowmore and Carrowkeel in County Sligo, Ireland, employed large boulders and stones in early passage graves. The use of large stones in other types of ceremonial monuments is difficult to date, as the complex succession of Stonehenge demonstrates, but it seems likely that standing stones became common as ceremonial markers and components of structures during the first half of the third millennium B.C. For example, the stone circles at Avebury in Wiltshire, Stanton Drew in Somerset, Arbor Low in Derbyshire, the Ring of Brodgar on Orkney, Callanais on Lewis, or the Grange circle in Limerick, Ireland, seem to have been constructed in the second half of the third millennium B.C., in the Late Neolithic, with additions in the Bronze Age. Beaker burials inserted at the base of some standing stones show that these structures were erected before the end of the third millennium B.C. Many of the stone circles of the west of Britain, Ireland, Wales, and Scotland—such as Machrie Moor on Arran (an island off the west coast of Scotland)—and the recumbent stone circles of northeastern Scotland—such as Easter Aquhorthies—date from the earlier Bronze age, contemporary with the final stages of Stonehenge. Although local practices clearly continued in remote areas, the use and construction of stone-built circles, rows, alignments, and individual menhirs seem to have faded in the mid-second millennium B.C.

The range of megalithic structures across the British Isles is varied and often regional in distribution. In Scotland complexes of stone rows, often in elaborate fanlike arrangements, as at Lybster in Caithness, appear to have had observational functions. Similarly, the concentrations of stone rows in southwestern England and Wales represent alignments on major focal points, such as barrows and ceremonial sites. The equivalent structures in the lowlands and in eastern Britain are represented by earth avenues and post alignments, both of which are found at Stonehenge and many other sites that have been identified through aerial photography.

The interpretation of Stonehenge and thus, by association, many of the other stone-and-earth ceremonial complexes across Britain suggests that these monuments were focused on mortuary, death, ancestral, and funerary concerns. Barrows, deposits, stone and timber structures, and ritual activity indicate dimensions of a spiritual and symbolic worldview. Analysis has indicated that the use of stone was itself symbolic of the dead, whereas the living were represented by wood and earth.

See also **The Origins and Growth of European Prehistory** (*vol. 1, part 1*); **Ritual and Ideology** (*vol. 1, part 1*); **The Megalithic World** (*vol. 1, part 4*); **Avebury** (*vol. 1, part 4*).

BIBLIOGRAPHY

Chippindale, Christopher. *Stonehenge Complete.* London: Thames and Hudson, 1983.

Cleal, Rosamund M. J., K. E. Walker, and R. Montague. *Stonehenge in Its Landscape: Twentieth-Century Excavations.* London: English Heritage, 1995.

Cunliffe, Barry, and Colin Renfrew. *Science and Stonehenge.* Oxford: Oxford University Press, 1997.

Malone, Caroline. *Neolithic Britain and Ireland.* Stroud, U.K.: Tempus, 2001.

Piggott, Stuart. "The Early Bronze Age in Wessex." *Proceedings of the Prehistoric Society* 4 (1935): 52–106.

Richards, Julian. *The English Heritage Book of Stonehenge.* London: Batsford, 1991.

———. *The Stonehenge Environs Project.* London: Historic Buildings and Monuments Commission for England, 1990.

Souden, David. *Stonehenge: Mysteries of the Stones and Landscape.* London: Collins and Brown, 1987.

Woodward, Ann. *British Barrows: A Matter of Life and Death.* Stroud, U.K.: Tempus, 2000.

CAROLINE MALONE

FLAG FEN

The site at Flag Fen sits in a basin of low-lying land on the western margins of the Fens of eastern En-

gland, at the outskirts of the city of Peterborough. Before their drainage in the seventeenth century the Fens were England's largest area of natural wetland, comprising about a million acres, to the south and west of the Wash. The Fen margins immediately east of Peterborough have been the subject of nearly continuous archaeological research since about 1900. In 1967 the central government designated Peterborough a New Town, which resulted in additional government funding and rapid commercial development. Most of the archaeological research described here took place as a response to new building projects in the last three decades of the twentieth century.

A ditched field system in use from 2500–900 B.C. is situated on the dry land to the west of the Flag Fen basin (an area known as Fengate). A similar field system has been revealed at Northey, on the eastern side of the basin. The fields of Northey and Fengate were defined by ditches and banks, on which hedges were probably planted. The fields were grouped into larger holdings by parallel-ditched droveways (specialized farm tracks along which animals were driven), which led down to the wetland edge. It is widely accepted that the fields at Fengate and Northey were laid out for the control and management of large numbers of livestock, principally sheep and cattle. Animals grazed on the rich wetland pastures of Flag Fen during the drier months of the year and returned to flood-free grazing around the fen edge to overwinter.

The center of the Fengate Bronze Age field system was laid out in a complex pattern of droveways, yards, and paddocks. This area, centered on a major droveway, is interpreted as a communal "marketplace" for the exchange of livestock and for regular social gatherings. The droveway through these communal stockyards continued east until it encountered the edge of the regularly flooded land. Here the line of the drove was continued by five parallel rows of posts, which ran across the gradually encroaching wetland of Flag Fen to Northey, some 1,200 meters to the east.

The five rows of posts are collectively termed the "post alignment." The post alignment was primarily a causeway constructed from timbers laid on the surface of the peat within and around the posts. These horizontal timbers were pegged into position, and their surfaces were dusted with coarse sand

Fig. 1. Timbers of the Flag Fen post alignment (a ceremonial causeway), 1300–900 B.C. COURTESY OF FRANCIS PRYOR. REPRODUCED BY PERMISSION.

and fine gravel to make them less slippery. The upstanding posts, which may have projected more than 3 meters above the causeway surface, would have marked out and drawn attention to the route of the causeway, especially when water levels were very high. Dendrochronology shows the post alignment to have been in use for some 400 years, between approximately 1300 and 900 B.C. About 200 meters west of the Northey landfall, the post alignment crossed a large artificial platform also constructed of timber; both platform and post alignment were contemporary and part of the same integral construction. The nature, use, and development of the platform is as yet poorly understood, but it undoubtedly was linked closely both physically and functionally to the post alignment.

Conditions of preservation were excellent in the wetter parts of Flag Fen, and it was possible to study woodworking in some detail. The earliest timbers were generally of alder and other wet-loving species, but in later phases oak was used too. Wood chips

and other debris suggest that most of the woodworking was of large timbers, and there was little processing of coppice (trees or shrubs that periodically were cut off at ground level), except in the lower levels of the timber construction of the platform. Examination of tool marks indicates that socketed axes were used almost exclusively. There were numerous wooden artifacts and reused pieces, including part of a tripartite wheel, an axle, and a scoop.

Study of the animal bones and pottery showed two distinct assemblages at the edge of Flag Fen (at a site on which a power station subsequently was constructed) and within the wetland proper. One was dominated by domestic material that may have derived from settlement(s) on the fen edge nearby. There was also a significant ritual component at both sites, but principally at Flag Fen; ritual finds included complete ceramic vessels and the remains of several dogs. Some 275 "offerings" of metal objects clearly demonstrated the importance of ritual at

Flag Fen. The bronze and tin objects included weaponry, ornaments, and several Continental imports (mainly from France and central Europe). There was evidence that many of the items had been smashed or broken deliberately, before being placed in the water. A significant proportion of the assemblage could be dated to the Iron Age and must have been placed in the waters around the post alignment long after the structure itself had been abandoned.

The posts of the alignment were interwoven with five levels of horizontal wood, which served as reinforcement, as foundation, and, in places, as a path with associated narrow tracks. The posts, too, served many purposes: as a guide for travelers along the tracks, as a near-solid wall, and as a palisade. There also was evidence of transverse timber and wattle partitions, which may have divided the alignment into segments 5 to 6 meters in length. It is suggested that these segments had an important ritual role. The partitions were emphasized further by the placing of "offerings" or boundary deposits of valuable items, such as weaponry or unused quern stones [hand mills]. It has been suggested that the segments may have been used to structure rituals in some way—perhaps by providing different kin groups with distinctive foci for family-based ceremonies. It has also been suggested that the private or kin group rites at Flag Fen took place at times of the year when the main community stockyards at the western end of the post alignment were the scene of much larger social gatherings.

BIBLIOGRAPHY

Chippindale, C., and F. M. M. Pryor, eds. "Special Section: Current Research at Flag Fen, Peterborough." *Antiquity* 66 (1992): 439–531.

Pryor, F. M. M. *The Flag Fen Basin: Archaeology and Environment of a Fenland Landscape.* English Heritage Archaeological Report. London: English Heritage, 2001.

———. *Farmers in Prehistoric Britain.* Stroud, U.K.: Tempus Publications, 1998.

———. "Sheep, Stockyards, and Field Systems: Bronze Age Livestock Populations in the Fenlands of Eastern England." *Antiquity* 70 (1996): 313–324.

———. "Look What We've Found: A Case-Study in Public Archaeology." *Antiquity* 63 (1989): 51–61.

Pryor, F. M. M., C. A. I. French, and M. Taylor. "Flag Fen, Fengate, Peterborough. I. Discovery, Reconnaissance, and Initial Excavation." *Proceedings of the Prehistoric Society* 52 (1986): 1–24.

FRANCIS PRYOR

IRISH BRONZE AGE GOLDWORK

In Europe the earliest evidence for goldworking dates to the fifth millennium B.C. By the end of the third millennium goldworking had become well established in Ireland and Britain, together with a highly productive copper- and bronzeworking industry. While it is not known precisely how the Late Neolithic people of Ireland became familiar with the use of metal, it is clear that it was introduced as a fully developed process. Essential metalworking skills must have been introduced by people already experienced at all levels of production, from identification and recovery of ores through every stage of the manufacturing process.

During the Early Bronze Age, between 2200 and 1700 B.C., goldsmiths produced a limited range of ornaments. The principal products were sun discs, usually found in pairs, such as those from Tedavnet, County Monaghan; plain and decorated bands; and especially the crescent gold collars called *lunulae* (singular *lunula,* "little moon"). These objects were all made from sheet gold—a technique that is particularly well represented by the *lunulae,* many of which are beaten extremely thin. A *lunula* such as the one from Rossmore Park, County Monaghan exemplifies the high level of control and skill achieved by the earliest goldsmiths. During this early period decoration consisted mainly of geometric motifs, such as triangles, lozenges, and groups of lines arranged in patterns. Incision using a sharp tool and repoussé (working from behind to produce a raised pattern) were the principal techniques employed. Sheet-gold objects continued to be produced up to about 1400 B.C.

By about 1200 B.C. there was a remarkable change in the types of ornaments made in the workshops. New goldworking methods were developed, and new styles began to appear. Twisting of bars or strips of gold became the most commonly used technique, and a great variety of twists can be seen. By altering the form of the bar or strip of gold and

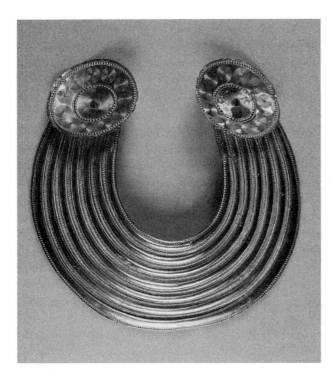

Fig. 1. Gold collar from Gleninsheen, County Clare, Ireland. NATIONAL MUSEUM OF IRELAND. REPRODUCED BY PERMISSION.

by controlling the degree of torsion, a wide range of styles could be produced. Torcs (torques) might be as small as earrings or as large as the exceptionally grand pair from Tara, County Meath, which are 37.3 centimeters and 43.0 centimeters in diameter and weigh 385 grams and 852 grams respectively. Many of these ornaments necessitated very large amounts of gold, suggesting that a new source for gold had been discovered. Between 1000 and 850 B.C. there seems to have been a lull in goldworking, as few gold objects can be dated to that time. It may be that this apparent gap is caused by changes in deposition practices, which have made it difficult to identify objects of this period.

The succeeding phase was extremely productive, however, and is noted for the great variety and quality of both goldwork and bronzework. Goldsmiths had developed to a very high degree all the skills necessary to make a range of ornaments that differed in form and technique. The same care and attention to detail were applied to objects large and small, irrespective of whether they required the expenditure of vast quantities of gold or only a few grams.

The goldwork of this period can be divided into two main types. Solid objects, cast or made from bars and ingots, such as bracelets, dress fasteners, and split-ring ornaments (incomplete circular objects for use in the ears, nose, hair, and so forth), contrast dramatically with delicate collars (fig. 1) and ear spools made of sheet gold. Gold wire also was used in numerous ways but especially to produce the ornaments called lock rings (elaborate, biconical ornaments made from wire probably used as hair ornaments). Thin gold foil, sometimes highly decorated, was used to cover objects made from other metals, such as copper, bronze, or lead. The best example of this technique is the bulla from the Bog of Allen, a heart-shaped lead core covered by a highly decorated fine gold foil. The purpose of this and other similar objects is not fully understood, but they may have been used as amulets or charms.

Decoration is an important feature of Late Bronze Age goldwork. Many different motifs were used to achieve the complicated patterns that often cover the entire surface of the object, consisting of geometric shapes, concentric circles, raised bosses (domed or conical), and rope and herringbone designs. The goldsmiths produced these motifs through combinations of repoussé and chasing, stamping with specially made punches, as well as incising the surface of the gold.

Knowledge of Bronze Age goldwork from Ireland is largely dependent on the discovery of groups of objects in hoards. At least 160 hoards of the Late Bronze Age have been recorded from Ireland. Several different types of hoards have been found, including founders' hoards consisting of scrap metal, merchants' hoards containing objects for trade, and ritual or votive hoards deliberately deposited with no intention and, in many cases, no possibility of recovery. Hoards can contain tools, weapons, and personal ornaments using bronze, gold, and amber. Where tools and weapons occur together with ornaments or jewelry, it may be that they represent the personal regalia of an individual. In Ireland there is little or no evidence from burials to show how or by whom certain ornaments were worn.

The number of spectacular discoveries from bogs suggests that the people of the Bronze Age, particularly during its later phases, regarded them as special places. In the eighteenth century a remarkable series of discoveries was made in the Bog of

Cullen in County Tipperary. Very many bronze and gold objects were found during turf cutting over a period of about seventy years. Only one gold object can be positively identified from the Bog of Cullen. It is a decorated terminal, the only surviving fragment of a once magnificent dress fastener. This is one of a series of exceptionally large objects weighing up to 1 kilogram apiece.

A large hoard of gold ornaments found in 1854 in marshy ground close to a lake at Mooghaun North, County Clare, contained more than two hundred objects, most of which were melted down. The hoard consisted mainly of bracelets but also included at least six gold collars and two neck rings. It is difficult to explain the reason for the deposition of such a huge wealth of gold. Its discovery close to a lake suggests that is was a ritual deposit.

During the Bronze Age, Irish goldsmiths did not function as an isolated group of specialist craftspeople on the western shores of Europe. While they maintained links with Britain and Europe, drawing some of their inspiration from trends that were current abroad, they always imparted a characteristically Irish style to each product. At the same time they likewise expressed their individuality and creativity by producing gold ornaments that are unparalleled elsewhere.

See also **Bronze Age Britain and Ireland** (*vol. 2, part 5*); **Jewelry** (*vol. 2, part 7*); **Early Christian Ireland** (*vol. 2, part 7*).

BIBLIOGRAPHY

Armstrong, Edmund Clarence Richard. *Catalogue of Irish Gold Ornaments in the Collection of the Royal Irish Academy.* Dublin: National Museum of Science and Art, 1933.

Cahill, Mary. "Before the Celts—Treasures in Gold and Bronze." In *Treasures of the National Museum of Ireland: Irish Antiquities.* Edited by Patrick F. Wallace and Raghnall Ò Floinn, pp. 86–124. Dublin: Gill and Macmillan, 2002.

Eogan, George. *The Accomplished Art: Gold and Gold Working in Britain and Ireland during the Bronze Age.* Oxford: Oxbow Books, 1994.

MARY CAHILL

BRONZE AGE SCANDINAVIA

The Bronze Age was first acknowledged as a separate period, and thus as an object of study in 1836, when Christian Jürgensen Thomsen published his famous Three Age System. In this system, the Bronze Age was sandwiched between the Stone Age and the Iron Age. The latter periods built on indigenous materials of stone and iron. The Bronze Age, by contrast, was founded on an artificial, and thus truly innovative, alloy of copper and tin, metals that were traded into metal-poor Scandinavia from metal-rich regions of central Europe. Thomsen's system evidenced an evolutionary logic that was virtually Darwinian, and it became the foundation of all later research, which has progressed mostly in leaps.

The investigation, during the later nineteenth and early twentieth centuries, of numerous extremely well-preserved bodies of persons buried in oak coffins below earthen mounds is of special significance. The thousands of mounds in the cultural landscape thus became linked to the Bronze Age and gave rise to the notion of "the Mound People." Likewise, a growing awareness of the past among peasants and the bourgeoisie, in conjunction with nationalistic trends and more effective agricultural and industrial production, brought increasing numbers of bronze artifacts to museums. Then, in 1885,

Oscar Montelius was able to establish subdivisions of the Bronze Age into periods I–III for the Older Bronze Age and periods IV–VI for the Late Bronze Age. Later scholars have regulated the content of this system, which nonetheless still stands, surprisingly intact. Current research endeavors to improve our understanding of Bronze Age society. These interests have been prompted by improvements in theoretical tools, in absolute chronology, and in methods of data recording and analysis. Scandinavia in the Bronze Age stands as one of the most bronze-rich areas in Europe, despite the fact that every bit had to be imported.

GEOGRAPHICAL FRAMEWORK

The core region of the classic Nordic Bronze Age is southern Scandinavia, consisting of Denmark, Schleswig, and Scania. The adjoining northern European lowland in present-day Germany, as well as southern Norway and south-central Sweden, can be considered to be closely associated. Within this region cultural coherence was mediated through particular practices in the domains of metalwork style and personal appearance, sacrificial and funerary rituals, cosmology, economy, and social conduct and organization. The Bronze Age to us nevertheless is very much the culture of a social elite.

Northern Scandinavia is culturally distinct, if not unaffected by the general Bronze Age idea. The border is fluid and changeable, however. With increasing distance northward, cairns for burial replaced mounds, bronzework becomes rare, and eastern patterns of communication toward Russia, Finland, and the eastern Baltic region become prevalent. Moreover, the focus of pictures carved on rock changes from food production to hunting and fishing, hence also reflecting differences in subsistence economy, ideology, social organization, and probably ethnicity.

CHRONOLOGICAL FRAMEWORK

Among more recent research advances, count the "revolutions" of carbon-14 dating and dendrochronology, which have been applied to Bronze Age materials with astonishingly precise results. The small group of oak-coffin graves, notably, could be dated to a brief period between 1396 and 1260 B.C. The Bronze Age proper commenced c. 1700 B.C. and concluded c. 500 B.C., but metals became socially integrated by about 2000 B.C., during the Late Neolithic period—already a bronze age in all but name. Approximate dates in calendar years are as follows: Late Neolithic I, 2350–1950 B.C.; Late Neolithic II, 1950–1700 B.C.; period I, 1700–1500 B.C.; period II, 1500–1300 B.C.; period III, 1300–1100 B.C.; period IV, 1100–900 B.C.; period V, 900–700 B.C.; and period VI, 700–500 B.C.

Metal was brought in from metal-controlling societies in central Europe. Comparative chronology therefore is the foundation for assessments of social networks and dependencies across Europe. The Late Neolithic period and the earliest Bronze Age (period IA) are contemporaneous with the Danubian and Ünětician Early Bronze Age cultures in central Europe (c. 2300–1600 B.C.). Periods IB–II correspond to the Middle Bronze Age Tumulus culture (1600–1300 B.C.). Periods III–V are parallel to the Late Bronze Age Urnfield culture (1300–700 B.C.). The final Bronze Age, period VI, corresponds to the Early Iron Age Hallstatt culture (700–500 B.C.).

THE BEGINNING

The first copper objects appeared in southern Scandinavia in the fourth millennium B.C., along with the consolidation of food production. They presumably were accompanied by experiments with metallurgy, but the knowledge was not maintained. At the end of the third millennium B.C. metallurgy was reintroduced, together with the northward dispersal of Bell Beaker material cultures; this time, production and use of metals were integrated permanently into culture and society.

The period around 2000 B.C. is an important turning point in the social history of early Europe, with, for instance, innovations in tin-bronze technology and consolidation of social hierarchies. In southern Scandinavia there was a veritable boom in metal use, which was connected to a powerful metal-producing center in the Ünětice culture across the Baltic Sea on the river plains of the Elbe-Saale area of Germany. Overt presentation of salient individuals was avoided, perhaps because social practices were rooted in principles of communality. This view finds support in the continued emphasis on sacrificial practices in sacred wetlands; at least, this is where some of most prominent finds of early metalwork have been discovered, notably, the hoards of Gallemose and Skeldal in Jutland and Pile in Scania. There are small signs of an elite group, which appears to have interacted closely with neighboring elites.

It was not until about 1600 B.C. that social structure and the material world shifted manifestly toward patterns that came to characterize the Nordic Bronze Age. Precisely at this time large earthen mounds began to be built, and identities of wealth, rank, age, and gender began to be presented overtly. One probably must understand these presentations as forming part of an aristocratic and highly competitive lifestyle among a social elite and not necessarily in terms of rigid positions of rank within this elite.

Copper as raw material prevailed for a while, but from c. 2000 B.C. objects were more consistently made of bronze, which by 1700 B.C. had become absolutely dominant. Flint and stone, accordingly, were valued less. The local production of metalwork initially was very one-sided: flat axe heads were favorites from the onset and were put to traditional social and practical uses. In about 1600 B.C., however, a much more varied repertoire of bronzework was produced, circulated, and consumed in a variety of new or altered contexts. This variance coincided with the first overt elite manifestations and with the spread of new social habits, ideas, and fashions— part of the so-called Tumulus culture.

METALS AND SOCIAL INEQUALITY

It has been claimed that in early Europe it was not money that made the world go around, but metals. It is certainly true that when the technique was first discovered and became part of the fabric of social life, European societies were altered in the process. Social hierarchy can exist easily without metals, but it is harder to find profoundly metal-using societies that maintain an egalitarian way of life. The reasons for this are not straightforward, but one can speculate on such factors as differential access to and control of key resources and of exchange networks. Copper ore, in fact, is unevenly distributed geographically, with a few major concentrations, hence providing a natural barrier against uniform circulation of raw copper and finished objects in Europe. Tin is distributed even more narrowly, with only one major source in central Europe, located in the mountains between Saxo-Thuringia and Bohemia.

Craft specialization is another important factor, because it creates divisions in society beyond those of gender and age. Producing items of copper is a difficult and prolonged process, demanding divisions of labor and specialist knowledge and thus an institutionalized system of apprenticeship. The fantastic transformation of raw copper into finished objects is difficult to comprehend and may well have been surrounded by secrecy and mythical imaginations, again a possible medium for gaining control. In a sense, metallurgy is the exercise of power over material and human resources. Social hierarchy and elitism thus walk hand in hand with metallurgical production in metal-poor as well as metal-rich regions of Europe. Most important, however, the metal objects themselves—owing to their inherent attraction and ascribed functions and meanings— actively built social identity. Metal objects soon assumed important roles in creating and maintaining individual identities relating to gender, status, and rank, hence accentuated social distinctions of various kinds.

ORGANIZATION OF METALWORK PRODUCTION

The basic technique employed by the Scandinavian metalworker was casting. Hammering the bronze rarely was used as a primary technique. This is unlike the situation in central Europe, where, for instance, vessels and shields were beaten into shape rather than cast. Cold and hot hammering nevertheless was not unknown in Scandinavia, indispensable as these techniques are to harden, for instance, the cutting edge of an axe or a sword. Remains of melting and fragments of tuyeres and crucibles of baked clay are known from some settlements, especially from the Late Bronze Age. Composite stone molds of Bronze Age date exist, but their rarity suggests that they usually were made of more perishable clay and sand. This is consistent with details on the bronze objects implying that they often were cast using the lost-wax method (*cire perdue*). In addition, so-called *Überfangsguss* or over-casting was used, for example, when the hilt of a dagger or sword needed to be attached securely to the blade or when repairing broken objects. Skills in metalworking were considerable, and the objects created in bronze were far more complex than earlier objects in copper.

Manufacturing objects of bronze is specialist work and therefore, as mentioned earlier, required divisions of labor within society. The quality of Scandinavian metalwork and remains from the production process suggest that further specialization soon came about: from c. 1600 B.C. there was a division into ordinary metalworkers producing for kin and community and specialist metalworkers retained by the social elite. A patron-supported craft production is suggested by findings in the large period II longhouse at Store Tyrrestrup (Vendsyssel, Denmark). There, unfinished axes had been deposited, together with casting residues, under the floor, close to the fireplace. The smith is a curiously anonymous person throughout the Bronze Age, and this may sustain the interpretation of a patron relationship. In fact, only one burial of a bronzesmith is known, at Galgehøj (Hesselager, Denmark).

THE DEAD AND THE LIVING

Funerary practices are embedded in society as a statement of the way things are or should be. They are performed by the living in memory of the dead and as a mixture of habitual ritual action and social strategy; quite often one aspect dominates the other. Inhumation in stone cists or oak trunks was the dominant burial custom in the Older Bronze

Age, whereas cremation in urns took over in the Late Bronze, with period III as transitional. These two major funerary customs of the Bronze Age broadly reflect the situation in Europe, first in the Tumulus Bronze Age and, from about 1300 B.C., the Urnfield culture. Both probably must be understood as the rapid spread over geographic space of particular social and religious practices among an "international" elite.

In the Older Bronze Age mounds of turf or cairns of stone were erected to cover the inhumed remains of the deceased, who was placed in the coffin wholly dressed and with various accessories, regulated by such parameters as age, gender, profession, and rank. Borum Eshøj near Århus and Hohøj at Mariager Fjord in Denmark and the Bredarör cairn at Kivik in Sweden are examples of large tumuli. The tumulus-covered burials from the Older Bronze Age can have represented only a segment of the population, no doubt chosen among the elite. The new custom of tumulus burial was first used to commemorate certain heroes of war and only later came to incorporate other social identities.

In the Late Bronze Age fewer tumuli were built, but existent ones continued in use as the family burial place, celebrating the recent dead and the ancestors. Small houses sometimes were built at the mound periphery, probably indicating that the corpse lay in state before the cremation ceremony took place. The cremated bones usually were placed in a pottery urn together with a few personal items of bronze. The conspicuous display of the previous period is mostly absent. A large number of urns typically were placed in the side of a tumulus or near it, and it is likely that more people than in previous years received a proper burial. The cremation custom contributed to making people more equal in death, but still the level of wealth varied quite a lot. It therefore is likely that the cremation custom concealed a reality of considerable social inequality. This view is supported by the existence of chieftains' burials below giant tumuli, notably Lusehøj in the central region of southwestern Fyn and the mound of Håga near present-day Uppsala in central Sweden.

PERSONAL APPEARANCE AND SOCIAL IDENTITY

Material culture, and, in fact, all sorts of cultural consumption, is predisposed to fulfil a social function: namely, that of legitimating social differences. In the Bronze Age elite identity was signified outwardly through forms of personal appearance that included particular types of dress and personal equipment. Objects of bronze and gold formed an integral part of an aristocratic outfit, which varied according to status, gender, and probably also age. The inhumations of the older Bronze Age reflect ideal social structure within the privileged group of people who received a mound burial. Skeletons, unfortunately, have been preserved only rarely, but the small group of well-preserved oak coffins provides valuable information not least on gender distinctions. In the Late Bronze Age the custom of cremation made it difficult to assess personal appearance and thus the social identities the deceased had maintained in life. Principles of dress and accessories appear to have remained the same throughout the Bronze Age, whereas the style of metalwork changed systematically from period to period, notably with spirals in period IB–II and wavy bands in period V.

The first rich mound burials appeared in period IB, c. 1600 B.C. They commemorated certain persons with a warrior identity, presumably males, as, for instance, at Buddinge (Copenhagen, Denmark) and Strandtved (Svendborg, Denmark). Notably, it was not until period II that females became visible as persons of rank. Early elite warriors carried a sword or dagger, a weapon axe, and sometimes a spearhead or a long pointed weapon for stabbing (fig. 1). Dress accessories of bronze included a dress pin and belt hook and sometimes a frontlet of gold sheet, as well as such personal items as tweezers, palstave (an axe-like implement), or chisel for work and a fishhook. Running spirals quite often adorned the weaponry of period IB, but the real breakthrough of this ornamental style did not occur until period II, when it became especially associated with female trinkets and worship of the sun.

Several hundred burials testify to personal appearances in periods II and III. The small group of oak coffins from the peninsula of Jutland in Denmark is particularly valuable as a source for Bronze Age social life, because they preserve organic materials, such as wood, wool, and antler. These burials contained such personalities as the Egtved Girl, the Skrydstrup Woman, the Mulbjerg Man, the

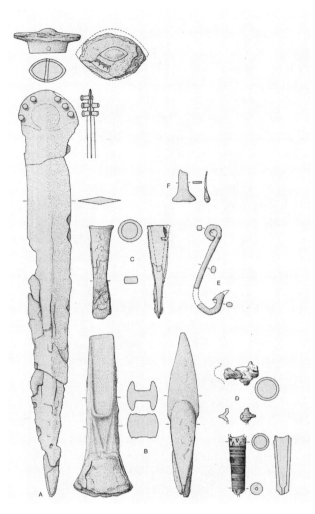

Fig. 1. Warrior's equipment of sword, axe, chisel, pointed weapon, tweezers, and fish hook from mound burial dating to the earliest Bronze Age, c. 1600 B.C., at Strandtved near Svendborg in Denmark. THE NATIONAL MUSEUM OF DENMARK. REPRODUCED BY PERMISSION.

Trindhøj and Borum Eshøj bodies, and the Guldhøj Man.

High-ranking women and men wore woolen dresses of superior quality, including shoes and headdress. Over a belted kiltlike coat the males wore a mantle and, on the head, a round-crowned hat. One or more additional objects of bronze and sometimes of gold accompanied the deceased or completed the dress, among them, arm ring, belt hook, dress pin, fibula (a clasp resembling a safety pin), double buttons, tweezers, razor, dagger, and hafted axe for work or for war. Bronze swords in a finely cut wooden sheath symbolized high male

rank in addition to adulthood and warrior status. The sword was suspended at the waist or arranged diagonally across the chest. Buckets of birch bark, wooden bowls with or without tin nail ornamentation, folding stools of wood with otter skin seats, antler spoons, and blankets of wool and oxhide add to this picture of social superiority.

The female dress seems to have varied according to position within an age cycle, with a major division at the transition to womanhood. The miniskirt of strings worn by the sixteen-year-old girl from Egtved may have shown that she was unmarried. The long skirts worn by the eighteen- to twenty-year-old young woman from Skrydstrup and the middle-aged woman from Borum Eshøj may have signaled their status as married women. Similarly, elaborate hairstyles stabilized by a hairnet or a cap might well be associated mainly with married women. A short blouse with long sleeves, by contrast, appears to have been worn by women of all ages. A spiral-decorated belt plate of bronze—later a belt box—fastened to the stomach with a belt of wool or leather also was nearly a standard dress accessory. Smaller, button-like plates (*tutuli*), fibulae, neck collars, and various rings of gold and bronze for the ears, arms, legs, neck, or hair completed the female dress. Small personal items, such as antler combs and bronze awls and strange objects perhaps carrying magical meanings, sometimes were added to the outfit, contained in a small purse or box or suspended at the belt.

SETTLEMENT AND LANDSCAPE
The sources for subsistence economy notably consist of pollen diagrams, preserved fields, plow furrows, wooden plows, bones of livestock, charred remains of domesticated plants, and tools of stone and metal. Sources for settlement organization include the remains of wooden longhouses, four-post structures, and storage pits in addition to many other fragments of human activities in the cultural landscape. It was only within the last decades of the twentieth century that Bronze Age settlements began to emerge in the archaeological record. Important fieldwork has been undertaken, notably in Thy, on Djursland; in Sønderjylland and southwestern Fyn in Denmark; and in the regions of Malmö and Ystad in Scania. Important sites are Fosie IV near Malmö and Apalle near Stockholm in Sweden.

In addition, there are Højgård in southern Jutland, Bjerre and Legård in Thy, Grøntoft and Spjald in western Jutland, and Hemmed on Djursland, all in western Denmark.

The Bronze Age falls within the Subboreal period, which was on the whole warm and dry. In the settled regions, especially near the coast, the landscape was open, with mounds prominently occupying the top of the low hills. The forested inlands, far from the coast, were only thinly settled. The economy was agrarian, based on the cultivation of cereals in small oval fields close to the settlements and on herds of livestock grazing in nearby pastures. Cow dung probably was collected as manure for the fields. Domestic animals, such as cattle, sheep, and horses, contributed immensely to keeping the land open, as did felling of trees with metal axes for the building of houses, ships, wagons, and burial coffins. The coast rarely was far removed from settlements in the Bronze Age, and fishing is known to have contributed to the basic economy.

The farm usually consisted merely of one wooden longhouse, which in the beginning of period II developed from having two aisles to having three aisles (divided by posts). Longhouses were of a variety of sizes, the largest covering 400 square meters and the smallest about 50 square meters, with a range of intermediate sizes. In analogy with royal buildings of the Late Iron Age, the largest longhouses have been designated "halls" and interpreted as residences of chiefly families, for instance, at Brødrene Gram, Spjald, and Skrydstrup in Jutland (Denmark). Some houses were so well preserved that internal divisions could be observed into a living area with hearth and a barn area with small compartments for the stalling of cattle or horses.

The basic settlement unit was the single farm, consisting of a longhouse and typically also a small, four-posted building, perhaps used for the storage of hay (figs. 2 and 3). The last decades of excavations have demonstrated a predominantly rather dispersed settlement organization, with farmsteads each occupying a micro-territory of a few square kilometers within a larger social and economic macro-territory. Sometimes the family cemetery of mounds is located on the manor; in other cases, the mounds are placed in particular community cemeteries. Macro-territories were separated from each other by bogs, lakes, streams, and rivers, which were considered liminal places inhabited by spirits and gods.

Excavations often reveal several houses in the same area, but this pattern does not necessarily indicate the existence of a village, as all these houses hardly stood at the same time. Old houses were left to decay when new houses were built. Single farms seem to be a dominant feature, and villages in the form known from the Early Iron Age, with fenced-in clusters of buildings, have so far not been ascertained in the Bronze Age. Still, however, the people occupying the single farmsteads could well have shared some of the routines of daily life and work.

In the Late Bronze Age a settlement hierarchy, with a large central farmstead surrounded by smaller farmsteads, is apparent in one well-examined and very wealthy region in southwest Fyn, with the site of Kirkebjerget as a nodal point. The giant mound of Lusehøj, with its two rich cremation burials from period V, is located nearby, among a group of larger and smaller mounds. A settlement hierarchy may well have existed in the Older Bronze Age, especially in regions with large concentrations of burial mounds. Future research will show whether the hierarchical model is generally applicable to the organization of social space in the Bronze Age.

RITUALS AND COSMOLOGY

The Bronze Age is rich in pictures, relics, and fragments of practices with a ritual character. Together they deliver certain clues to a complex world of myth, cult, and religion, which was entangled with the social world of the elite. One motive, in particular, dominated the cosmology, that is, the journey of the sun across the sky, day and night, throughout the year. This motif formed part of the pictures carved on metalwork and on rock, for instance, in Bohuslän in Sweden. The famous sun chariot from Trundholm Mose in northwest Zealand (Denmark) must be understood as a cult object. The sun disk, with its day-golden and night-dark sides, is pulled by a horse, but the sun horse is placed upon a six-wheeled wagon. The Trundholm chariot probably played a role in religious ceremonies and processions. Through depictions on rock carvings and on bronze razors the sun horse is related to other sacred signs, mainly ships.

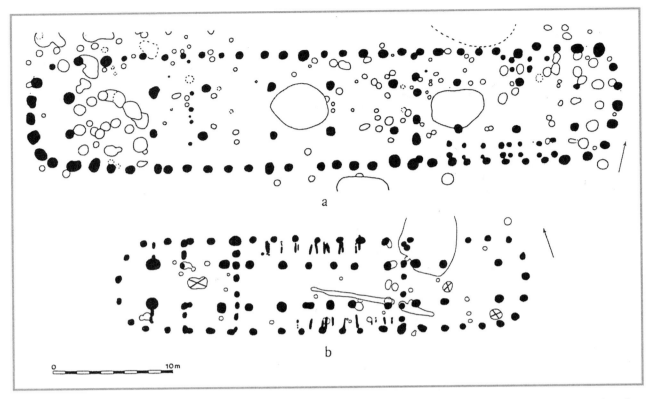

Fig. 2. Plans of three-aisled longhouses from the Danish Period II localities of Brødrene Gram in southern Jutland (upper) and Legård in northwestern Jutland (lower). The Gram house measures 50 × 10 meters with living quarters in the western part and byre in the eastern part. The Legård house is 33 meters long and seems to have accommodated two households, one at each end separated by a barn for stalling of livestock in the center. THE NATIONAL MUSEUM OF DENMARK. REPRODUCED BY PERMISSION.

Feasts with cultic activities, sport games, and processions seem to have taken place regularly, in spring and autumn and at the solstices of winter and summer. They probably also occurred on other occasions, such as when important people died or when war victories were celebrated. The end point of these activities frequently was marked by the deposition in watery places of valuables of bronze and gold as gifts to the gods. The latter often are located at the boundary between settled territories, thus hinting at the communal intention of these sacred depositions. Instead of bronze valuables, ritual killing and sacrifice of humans took place on rare occasions in sacred liminal places thought to be inhabited by spirits and gods. Other offerings of valuables were connected to the settlements; in particular, it was customary to deposit small hoards in a posthole when building a new house. Still other cult activities were carried out in specific houses—cult houses or temples—known from the sites of Sandagergård in Denmark and Kivik and Håga in Sweden.

SOCIAL NETWORKS AND THE END OF AN ERA

Bronze Age elites all over Europe strove to acquire wealth in metals and to possess the newest fashions in dress and metalwork in order to emphasize aristocratic appearances and manners. Much material culture in the Bronze Age can be understood broadly as the international language of an elite, who used it in strategies to maintain and extend authority inside society and to sustain alliances with neighboring elites. Ingots of copper and tin are rare, and this suggests that bronze reached Scandinavia as finished objects that were recycled continuously.

Metals moved across Europe as trade in commodities and exchange of gifts. The means of transport were wagons across land and ships on the great rivers of Europe and onward across the Baltic Sea to Scandinavia. Trackways of stones or wood have been excavated, mostly connecting territories across swampy areas, but linear distributions of tumuli across the landscape indicate the existence of major

Fig. 3. Three-aisled Bronze Age longhouse. Modern reconstruction at Hollufgard in Odense, Denmark. KARSTEN KJER MICHAELSEN, ODENSE CITY MUSEUMS. REPRODUCED BY PERMISSION.

lines of communication, in all likelihood earthen roads. Large ships, horses, and chariots are depicted on rock carvings, supplemented by finds of horse bones in settlements and a few boats and wooden wagons from bogs. Horses' bits and bronze fittings for chariots or wagons occur occasionally in burials and sacrificial hoards.

Some people probably made the great journey to faraway places and, as a result, were able to enhance personal power and prestige on their return. The Bronze Age, however, was not characterized simply by peaceful exchanges of ideas and material goods. Hostile encounters also took place—always with serious implications for combatants and noncombatants alike. The huge number of weapons, some cases of skeletal trauma, and pictorial representations of armor and fighting all suggest recurring warfare.

The end of the Bronze Age in Scandinavia can be explained mainly with reference to the social and economic situation in central Europe, where there was a crisis in the supply of metal in the ninth and eighth centuries B.C. Before the end of the eighth century in central Europe iron had taken the place of bronze as a common medium of exchange and measure of value, but in Scandinavia this did not happen until a couple of centuries later, even if iron objects began to appear. The rich Nordic Bronze Age slowly faded and came to an end around 500 B.C. Bronze was increasingly short in supply and the "international" elitist network, which depended on bronze for its existence, simply ceased to exist. From 750 to 700 B.C. new political alliances and social networks were in the making, primarily between the dynastic semi-urban Hallstatt kingdoms and Mediterranean city-states. Scandinavia had become a marginalized region outside the mainstream of events.

See also **Bell Beakers from West to East** (*vol. 1, part 4*); **Bronze Age Coffin Burials** (*vol. 2, part 5*); **Bronze Age Cairns** (*vol. 2, part 5*).

BIBLIOGRAPHY

Hvass, Steen, and Birger Storgaard, eds. *Digging into the Past: 25 Years of Archaeology in Denmark.* Translated by John Hines and Joan F. Davidson. Copenhagen, Denmark: Royal Society of Northern Antiquaries, 1993.

Jensen, Jørgen. *Danmarks Oldtid.* Vol. 2, *Bronzealder: 2000–500 f.Kr.* Copenhagen, Denmark: Gyldendal, 2002.

Kaul, Flemming. *Ships on Bronzes: A Study in Bronze Age Religion and Iconography.* Studies in Archaeology and History 3. Copenhagen, Denmark: National Museum of Denmark, 1998.

Kristiansen, Kristian. *Europe before History.* Cambridge, U.K.: Cambridge University Press, 1998.

Larsson, Thomas B. *The Bronze Age Metalwork in Southern Sweden: Aspects of Social and Spatial Organization, 1800–500 BC.* Archaeology and Environment 6. Umeå, Sweden: University of Umeå, 1986.

Thrane, H. "Bronze Age Settlement in South Scandinavia: Territoriality and Organisation." In *Experiment and Design: Archaeological Studies in Honour of John Coles.* Edited by A. F. Harding. Oxford: Oxbow Books, 1999.

Vandkilde, Helle. *From Stone to Bronze: The Metalwork of the Late Neolithic and Earliest Bronze Age in Denmark.* Århus, Denmark: Jutland Archaeological Society and Århus University Press, 1996.

HELLE VANDKILDE

BRONZE AGE COFFIN BURIALS

A small group of Danish oak-coffin burials in earthen mounds contain excellently preserved bodies of men and women, who lived 3,500 years ago. These finds offer an unexpectedly clear glimpse into the life of a Bronze Age social elite. Information exists concerning 85,000 burial mounds in Denmark, and most of them probably date to the Older Bronze Age (1600–1100 B.C.). Of these burials, a mere eighteen thousand mounds have been preserved in the present landscape, and the number, sadly, is decreasing owing to an inadequate modern heritage law. Several hundred burials have been investigated archaeologically, but processes of decomposition usually mean that organic materials, such as textiles, antler, and wood, do not survive the passing of centuries. On this background the survival of some twenty oak-coffin burials with personalities like the Egtved Girl, the Mulbjerg Man, the Skrydstrup

Woman, the Guldhøj Man, and the Trindhøj and Borum Eshøj bodies constitute a veritable miracle. They are on permanent exhibition at the National Museum of Denmark in Copenhagen.

The phenomenon of oak-coffin burials has been known sporadically in Denmark since the early historical period. When archaeology was scientifically consolidated around the middle of the nineteenth century, the true worth of these occurrences was recognized, and professionals began to supervise excavations. Several finds of oak coffins even then were severely damaged, and sometimes lost to the world, as the result of unprofessional undertakings. Up through the twentieth century, insight and knowledge have increased steadily with respect to technical details, the buried persons, and the society of which they once formed a part. All finds of preserved oak coffins are from the peninsula of Jutland, especially its southern and western parts. The same burial custom, however, with interments in large, hollowed-out oak trunks, occur all over southern Scandinavia, including the adjoining parts of Germany.

In relative chronological terms the oak coffins belong to Nordic Bronze Age period II; a few belong to early period III. Apart from having pinpointed each burial to a specific year, dendrochronology has provided the surprising result that these burials took place within a short time span between 1396 and 1260 B.C. Most of them, notably, date to the span 1389–1330 B.C., which means that these persons must have known each other. Some of the burials were looted in the Bronze Age, suggesting that less fortunate people sought the buried riches or that enemies wished to demolish the social identity and status of the deceased.

The generally well-preserved state of the Jutish coffins and their contents can be explained with reference to chemical processes, which may have been broadly recognized and thus intentionally activated. All mounds in question have the same bipartite construction, with a waterlogged bluish and clayey core containing the coffin and a dry outer mantle of turf. A thin, hard layer of iron pan always separated the two parts, sealing the coffin on all sides and thus hindering decay. It is evident that the sealing took place immediately and could have been instigated by watering the clay core prior to building the turf mantle. This may have been the yearning for an eternal afterlife not unlike what the Egyptians sought to create through the embalming of dead bodies. Holes in the bottom of each coffin point in the same direction, presumably aimed at leading water away from the buried person.

In the year 1370 B.C. a girl about sixteen years old was interred in the hollow of a 3-meter-long oak trunk at Egtved in south-central Jutland. The fully dressed body was placed extended on the back, looking toward the rising sun and wrapped in a large oxhide. When the coffin was opened in 1921, the skeleton had deteriorated because of acidic conditions; however, the skin, nails, and hair were preserved. So was her high-quality woolen dress, consisting of a short blouse with long sleeves and a miniskirt of strings. Her blonde hair was styled in a short-cut fashion, and her body length was estimated to be 1.60 meters. Pieces of cloth were wrapped around the feet. A large bronze belt plate with spiral decoration ornamented her stomach. This plate had been tied to her waist with a belt string, which also held an antler comb. There were bronze arm rings around her wrists, and she also wore an earring. Near her face a small bark box contained personal belongings. At her feet stood a small bucket of birch bark. Upon further investigation, a dried-out substance at the bottom of the bucket turned out to be a kind of honey-sweetened beer. Also at her feet, a small bundle of cloth contained the cremated bone fragments of a five- to six-year-old child, who could not have been her own child. Finally, a blanket of wool covered the body. A flowering milfoil showed that the burial had taken place in the summer. The mound, Storehøj, measured about 4 meters in height and 22 meters in diameter.

At 7 meters in height and 40 meters in diameter, the Eshøj mound stood out from a group of mounds at Borum in eastern Jutland. It had been built over three oak coffins containing a man and a woman, both of middle age, and a young man about twenty to twenty-two years old (probably their son). All of them had been wrapped in oxhides and interred in their finest woolen clothes and with paraphernalia of bronze and wood. Two of these coffins have been dendrochronologically dated to c. 1351 B.C. and 1345 B.C., respectively. The equipment of the woman was similar to that of the Egtved burial, only richer; among the personal belongings were a dagger, a fibula, rings for the neck, fingers,

Fig. 1. Costume of young Danish Bronze Age woman, from Egtved. COURTESY OF THE NATIONAL MUSEUM OF DENMARK. REPRODUCED BY PERMISSION.

and arms, a belt plate, and buttons (so-called *tutuli*), all of bronze. The two men wore loincloths and large kidney-shaped mantles. The older man wore a rounded cap, was clean-shaven, and had manicured hands and nails. The young man carried a wooden sword sheath, which held only a bronze dagger, perhaps because he had not yet earned the right to carry a real sword.

The monumentality and high visibility of the mounds, in addition to the high quality of dress and equipment, leave little doubt that they were reserved for people of high rank. Personal appearance and material culture clearly were very important in building social identities in the domains of gender, age, and rank. The elite built mounds to commemorate their ancestors and to maintain authority in a society with some degree of social mobility. The graded variation in wealth suggests as much. There must have been considerable rivalry within the elite for the control of power sources, such as bronze. The hectic activities in mound construction are one facet of this rivalry; another is the display of warriorhood among males.

See also **Bronze Age Scandinavia** (*vol. 2, part 5*).

BIBLIOGRAPHY

Alexandersen, V., P. Benneke, L. Hvass, and K. H. Stærmose Nielsen. "Egtvedpigen: nye undersøgelser" [The Egtved girl: New investigations]. In *Aarbøger for nordisk oldkyndighed og historie* (1981): 17–47.

Aner, Ekkehard, and Karl Kerten. *Die Funde der älteren Bronzezeit des nordischen Kreises in Dänemark, Schleswig-Holstein, und Niedersachsen.* Copenhagen, Denmark: Verlag Nationalmuseum, 1973–.

Boye, Vilhelm. *Fund af Egekister fra Bronzealderen i Danmark.* Copenhagen, Denmark: 1896; reprint, Århus, Denmark: Wormianum, 1986.

Breuning-Madsen, Henrik, and Mads K. Holst. "Genesis of Iron Pans in Bronze Age Mounds in Denmark." *Journal of Danish Archaeology* 11, nos. 1992–1993 (1995): 80–86.

Glob, P. V. *The Mound People: Danish Bronze-Age Man Preserved.* 2d ed. Translated by Joan Bulman. London: Paladin, 1983.

Hvass, Steen, and Birger Storgaard, eds. *Digging into the Past: 25 Years of Archaeology in Denmark.* Translated by John Hines and Joan F. Davidson. Copenhagen, Denmark: Royal Society of Northern Antiquaries, 1993.

Jensen, Jørgen. *Manden i kisten: Hvad bronzealderens gravhøje gemte* [The man in the coffin: What the Bronze Age mounds concealed]. Copenhagen, Denmark: Gyldendal, 1998.

Sørensen, M. L. S. "Reading Dress: The Construction of Social Categories and Identities in Bronze Age Europe." *Journal of European Archaeology* 5, no. 1 (1995): 93–114.

Thomsen, Thomas. *Egekistefundet fra Egtved fra den ældre bronzealder* [The oak coffin find from Egtved from the Older Bronze Age]. Nordiske Fortidsminder 2. Copenhagen, Denmark, 1929.

Vandkilde H., U. Rahbek, and K. L. Rasmussen. "Radiocarbon Dating and the Chronology of Bronze Age Southern Scandinavia." In *Absolute Chronology: Archaeological Europe 2500–500 BC.* Edited by K. Randsborg. Copenhagen, Denmark: Munksgaard, 1996.

HELLE VANDKILDE

BRONZE AGE CAIRNS

Large tumuli for burials, consisting of stones or turf, are widely characteristic of the Scandinavian Bronze Age, c. 1700–500 B.C. Bronze Age tumuli still form a meaningful part of modern cultural landscapes in many regions of Scandinavia, even if the number has decreased drastically since the Bronze Age. A cairn is a tumulus built of rubble stones collected in the vicinity of the burial. A mound, by comparison, is a tumulus built of earth and turf, which has been cut from adjacent grassland. In general, tumuli hardly ever represent an entire population but were burial places for the privileged few.

Mounds and cairns are parallel phenomena with similar functions and meanings. Owing to natural conditions, stone cairns occur primarily in the rocky north of Scandinavia, whereas turf mounds characterize the agricultural lowlands of southern Scandinavia. Zones of overlap exist, however—for example, in the central Swedish lake district. Moreover, mixtures of cairns and mounds occur: it is not altogether unusual to find a cairn with a thin external layer of turf or a mound with a massive inner core of fieldstones. Likewise, there are cases where a monumental cairn stands solitary in a typical mound region and vice versa.

Such entanglements are rooted not directly in nature but rather in culture and social practice: clearly, the deviating visual effects of turf and rubble were brought to bear in the creation of social identity. More generally, both types of burial relate in different ways to the surrounding landscape, materially and symbolically. According to pollen analyses, the bulk of southern Scandinavian mounds, for example, were built in a period in which there was a predominance of open pastures created by grazing cattle and sheep. Quite possibly, the building of turf mounds mediated and celebrated social power, which was connected to land and livestock. In a similar fashion, cairns may have symbolized domestication of the stony wilderness outside the settlement.

TIME FRAME, CONSTRUCTION, AND ORGANIZATION

The majority of tumuli were erected during the earlier Bronze Age, in the periods IB–III (1700–1100 B.C.). For Denmark it has been calculated that the

Fig. 1. A cluster of prominent Bronze Age burial mounds in the present-day cultural landscape, Skyum Bjerge in northwestern Jutland, Denmark. PHOTOGRAPH BY JENS-HENRIK BECH. REPRODUCED BY PERMISSION.

original number may have been as many as one hundred thousand mounds, most of which were constructed within a fairly short period of about two hundred to three hundred years. In the Late Bronze Age, that is, in periods IV–VI (1100–500 B.C.), existent mounds typically were reused as burial places, but new tumuli to some extent were still constructed. Cairns of the north tend to be slightly later constructions than the mounds of the south.

Tumuli normally were built to cover inhumation burials in oak coffins or stone cists, but they continued in use when the burial custom began to change toward cremation c. 1300 B.C. Apart from the primary, centrally placed burial, a tumulus thus usually includes several graves—inhumations as well as cremations. When new burials were added, the tumulus often was enlarged in height and width, exhibiting several building phases with old and new barrows. The inner structure often is complex, perhaps incorporating a core of stone or clay and frequently one or more circular ring walls of field-

stones at the foot of the tumulus; even dry masonry and wooden posts occur. Tumuli thus embody complicated life histories in addition to the shifting connotations of meaning applied to them by people through the ages.

The shape of most tumuli compares to a cupola or a bowler, but flattened forms also are known. The size of these monuments varies considerably, from about 10 meters to almost 80 meters in width and from about 1 meter to 12 meters in height. A diameter of 15–20 meters and a height of 3–4 meters are most common. The largest ones represent an enormous investment of work, such as: the Bredarör cairn at Kivik in Scania; the Uggårda Röjr on the island of Gotland; the Linkulla cairn on the peninsula of Bjäre in northwest Scania; the Hohøj mound at Mariager Fjord in northeast Jutland; and the Tårup mound and Borum Eshøj in eastern Jutland.

Tumuli typically occur in groups or in rows, occupying the ridge of hills to increase visibility. In this way they dominate the landscape and its inhabitants. Small clusters of tumuli appear to form the cemetery of a single farmstead or a hamlet controlling a larger territory. Such a scattered settlement pattern prevails in the earlier Bronze Age (1700–1100 B.C.), but there also are larger clusters of tumuli. The latter might have been central places of cult and communication and may perhaps have related to a larger, cooperative settlement comparable to what we call a village.

THE BREDARÖR CAIRN AT KIVIK

The Bredarör cairn at Kivik in southeastern Scania in Sweden is a monumental cairn situated in a region otherwise predominated by mounds. This position underscores the exclusiveness of the cairn, its builders, and the person(s) who were buried in the inner grave chamber of rock-carved stone slabs. Otherwise, the location of the cairn in the landscape is strangely inconspicuous, and the Kivik region is marginal in a larger Bronze Age perspective. Our understanding of this extraordinary monument is severely hampered by its unhappy destiny with successive plundering and early excavations. Cult houses, later cemeteries, and other remains of ritual activities surrounding the cairn suggest that the place was attributed central functions.

The cairn has a considerable diameter of 75 meters. It seems to have been flat on top, but the original height can no longer be estimated. Masses of stone covered a cist of about 4 meters in length. The inside of the cist was carved with pictures referring to the life of its first inhabitant(s), funerary games, and a wider Bronze Age cosmology found on rock carvings and on bronze work. The original order of the slabs has been disturbed, and some of them are damaged or have disappeared. Likewise, the burial chamber has been plundered, probably in the Bronze Age as well as in the recent past. A few fragmented remains suggest that in period II of the Bronze Age, c. 1400 B.C., a man was put to rest in the chamber. The size and form of the cist, however, recall a wider tradition of communal gallery graves originating in the Late Neolithic period. This might suggest that the cist at Kivik was intended for a family or leading clan members, rather than one person, and that it was built before period II of the Bronze Age. If not unique, Kivik is at least distinctly removed from the ordinary.

SOCIAL COMMEMORATION

In all likelihood tumuli were constructed for and by a social elite, but this identity should not be understood in an absolutist or static way. The graded content of the burials, among other things, suggests ongoing rivalries internal to the elite and also hints that the border between the elite and non-elite might have been fairly negotiable. Men, women, and children received burials, but the two latter groups are somewhat underrepresented. Males typically were depicted as warriors with swords and other paraphernalia, whereas the personal appearance of females was more peaceful. The social commemoration of certain persons in death—and the overt presentation of certain people in life—evidently were the foremost idea behind the building of tumuli and the material wealth invested in the burials.

The tradition of building tumuli, along with conspicuous consumption in metalwork and other valuables, connects to a larger European trend in material culture and social conduct, which began around 1600 B.C., with the so-called Tumulus culture. Similar material styles and ideologies were emulated effectively across geographical space, indicating the existence of an "international" elite network.

See also **Bronze Age Britain and Ireland** (*vol. 2, part 5*); **Bronze Age Scandinavia** (*vol. 2, part 5*).

BIBLIOGRAPHY

Aner, Ekkehard, and Karl Kerten. *Die Funde der älteren Bronzezeit des nordischen Kreises in Dänemark, Schleswig-Holstein, und Niedersachsen.* Copenhagen, Denmark: Verlag Nationalmuseum, 1973–.

Hyenstrand, Åke. *Arkeologisk regionindelning av Sverige* [Archaeological division of Sweden into regions]. Rev. ed. Stockholm, Sweden: Riksantikvarieämbetet, 1984.

———. "Dolda kallmurar" [Hidden cold walls]. In *Nordsvensk Forntid: Kungliga skytteanska samfundets handlingar, Umeå* 6 (1969), 99–110.

Jensen, Jørgen. *Danmarks Oldtid.* Vol. 2, *Bronzealder 2.000–500 f. Kr.* [The prehistory of Denmark: The Bronze Age]. Copenhagen, Denmark: Gyldendal, 2002.

Kristiansen, Kristian. *Europe before History.* Cambridge, U.K.: Cambridge University Press, 1998.

Larsson, L., ed. *Bronsålderns gravhögar: Rapport från ett symposium i Lund 15.XI-16.XI 1991.* Report series 48. Lund, Sweden: University of Lund, Institute of Archaeology, 1993.

Randsborg, K. "Kivik: Archaeology and Iconography." *Acta Archaeologica* 64, no. 1 (1993).

Vandkilde, Helle. "Social Distinction and Ethnic Reconstruction in the Earliest Danish Bronze Age." In *Eliten in der Bronzezeit: Ergebnisse zweier Kolloquien in Mainz und Athen.* Edited by C. Clausing and M. Egg, Vol. 1, pp. 245–276. Monographien des Römisch-Germanischen Zentralmuseums 43. Mainz, Germany: Verlag des Römisch-Germanischen Zentralmuseums, 1999.

Widholm, Dag. *Rösen, Ristningar och riter.* Acta Archaeologica Lundensia 23. Stockholm, Sweden: Almqvist and Wiksell, 1998.

HELLE VANDKILDE

LATE BRONZE AGE URNFIELDS OF CENTRAL EUROPE

Around 1300 B.C. the prevailing burial rite in much of Europe shifted from skeletal burial under small mounds (called tumuli) and in flat cemeteries to cremation and subsequent burial of the ashes in an urn. In central and parts of southern Europe, such urn burials were grouped together in clusters of dozens, even thousands, of graves. Since they subsequently came to be discovered under agricultural fields, the term "urnfield" came to be applied to such cemeteries, although there is no reason to assume that these places were completely clear of vegetation when they were in use. This burial rite is a defining characteristic of the Late Bronze Age in many parts of continental Europe.

The existence of the urnfields was recognized by nineteenth-century prehistorians, and the East Prussian scholar Otto Tischler (1843–1891) was the first to attribute them to the Bronze Age. Their existence had been signaled centuries earlier, when medieval chroniclers spoke of pots that spontaneously emerged from the soil. We now know that their appearance was the result of the erosion of soil from above the shallow cremation graves. The forms of the metal artifacts found in the burials allowed the German prehistorian Paul Reinecke (1872–1958) to establish the basic chronological position of the urnfields within the Bronze Age and the essential continuity between the Late Bronze Age and the Early Iron Age in central Europe.

NOMENCLATURE

Urnfields represent an unusual phenomenon in European prehistory, since they simply represent a widespread common burial rite shared by peoples with very different artifact types and settlement forms. Despite the fact that German archaeologists often speak of an *"Urnenfelder kultur,"* the urnfields do not constitute an archaeological culture in the traditional sense. Instead, the shared burial rite links a number of regional cultural entities, and thus it is more proper to speak of an "Urnfield complex."

Within the Urnfield complex are a number of distinctive cultural entities. One such group is the Lusatian, or Lausitz, culture, which is widespread over much of Poland and eastern Germany, while another is the Knovíz culture of Bohemia and adjacent parts of Germany. Elsewhere, smaller regional groups have been identified. In general, however, the term "Late Bronze Age" is always a safe characterization that avoids taxonomic nomenclature and its controversies.

CHRONOLOGY

Between 1902 and 1911, Reinecke worked out the basic chronology for the Bronze Age and Early Iron Age of central Europe. He distinguished between a "Bronze Age" and a "Hallstatt Age," the latter named after the immense mountain cemetery south of Salzburg excavated by Johann Georg Ramsauer (1797–1876) in the nineteenth century. Both ages were divided into four stages, labeled A through D, based on grave associations and hoards. These continue to provide a basic yardstick for the relative chronology of central Europe of the second and early first millennia B.C. In general, Reinecke's Bronze D and Hallstatt A and B can be equated with the Late Bronze Age and the associated Urnfield complex.

In calendar years, this corresponds to approximately 1300–750 B.C. It must be noted that the end of the Bronze Age is a very vague and imprecise boundary. Most of the trends in artifact style, settlement form, and burial rite continue straight onward into Hallstatt C of the Early Iron Age. For the purposes of this discussion, these chronological units are primarily of academic interest, although for archaeologists they continue to define an elaborate chronological matrix to which new finds can be connected.

DISTRIBUTION

Urnfields are often considered to be a central European phenomenon, and it is true that they are found throughout Germany, Austria, Slovenia, the Czech Republic, Slovakia, Hungary, and Poland. But they also extend well to the west in France and south into Spain and Italy. In Scandinavia and the British Isles, there was also a transition to cremation burial during the Late Bronze Age, but these areas lack the vast cemeteries with dozens of burials that mark the classic Urnfield expression in central and western continental Europe.

Chronologically, it appears that the switch from inhumation burial under barrows to cremation burial in cemeteries as the dominant mortuary rite occurred first in east-central Europe. From there it spread west and north into Germany and Poland and south into Italy. Finally, in the first decades of the last millennium B.C., it is found in France and northern Spain.

BURIALS

The Urnfield complex, as might be expected, is known primarily through its burials, a trait it shares with many other periods of the Bronze Age in Europe. Unlike the rich skeletal burials of the Early Bronze Age, in which the dead are accompanied by all sorts of trappings of rank and status, most Urnfield cremations are somewhat less impressive by comparison. Each grave contains one or more ceramic vessels containing the ashes of the deceased individual and ash from the funeral pyre. The only artifacts likely to be found in the urn itself are those worn as body ornament, generally bronze pins and jewelry and glass and amber beads. The small pits into which the urns were placed often contain wood ash from the pyre, suggesting that the cremation occurred close to the place of burial. Often, the pits contain supplemental vessels with traces of food offerings, as well as other metal artifacts. At Poing, in Bavaria, parts of a four-wheeled wagon were found in one of the graves, and bronze wagon models have been found in Urnfield burials across Europe.

Although cremation became the dominant burial rite, inhumation continued to be practiced. At Przeczyce in southern Poland, 132 of the 874 burials were cremations, and the rest were inhumations. At Undenheim in Germany, two children were buried uncremated under sturdy wooden mortuary structures in stone-lined pits, accompanied by many vessels and bronze artifacts.

Some Urnfield cemeteries are enormous. The one at Kietrz in the Silesia region of southern Poland has yielded more than 3,000 burials over many years of excavations. A cemetery at Zuchering-Ost in Bavaria is estimated to have contained close to 1,000 originally, while Moravičany in Moravia has yielded 1,260 cremations. Others are smaller, such as the 262 graves at Vollmarshausen in central Germany. Still more have yielded a several dozen or fewer burials. Hundreds of Urnfield cemeteries have been excavated, and probably many more have been destroyed by cultivation and development.

Within some of the Urnfield cemeteries there is evidence that some of the graves were differentiated through the use of mounds or wooden mortuary structures. For example, at Zirc-Alsómajer in Hungary, more than eighty mounds were built over cremation burials, some of which were in small cists made from limestone slabs. At Kietrz, graves were occasionally situated among postholes that suggested the construction of a small roofed timber structure over the pit that contained the urn and grave goods. One of the most monumental Urnfield graves is found at Očkov in Slovakia, where an individual had been cremated on an immense pyre along with many bronze and gold objects whose molten traces were found among the ashes. Vessels that had contained liquids, perhaps associated with feasting, were among the grave goods. A mound about 6 meters high was built over the buried ashes, and a stone wall was built around the mound.

Some of the most unusual Urnfield burials are the so-called "keyhole" enclosures of northwestern

Germany and the Netherlands. At these sites, a central cremation burial is surrounded by a small ditch about 3 to 4 meters in diameter that is extended on one side to enclose an elongated area. At Telgte in northwestern Germany, thirty-five such keyhole ditches (because from above they resemble a large keyhole) were excavated, along with other cremation burials that were surrounded with round and oval ditches.

The adoption of cremation as the dominant burial rite suggests a fundamental change in attitude toward the body's role in the afterlife. When an intact corpse is buried, presumably this is done with the belief that the body plays an important part in the realm the deceased will encounter, whereas cremation suggests that the external form and appearance of the body is not relevant to this spiritual concept. The rapid adoption of cremation as the most common form of burial rite suggests that this change in attitude was quickly and widely accepted across much of Europe.

SETTLEMENTS
Because the Urnfield complex is defined in terms of its burial rite, it is somewhat surprising that a relatively large number of settlements are known. Thus, archaeologists know something about the lives of the people whose ashes are in the urns. Late Bronze Age people in central Europe lived in various types of settlements, some fortified, others not. Many were large open settlements covering many hectares, while some are compact strongholds on naturally defensible locations such as peninsulas and islands in lakes.

At Unterhaching, near Munich, a large, open Late Bronze Age settlement yielded the traces of about eighty houses over an area of about 15 hectares. The houses were rectangular post structures with four main corner posts and several posts along the walls. A settlement of similar extent was found at Zedau in eastern Germany, where seventy-eight small rectangular houses were scattered across the site. Some were small square houses with just four posts, while others had two parallel rows of three posts. At Eching in Bavaria, two small Urnfield settlements of about sixteen houses each were found about a kilometer apart.

A major Urnfield settlement is known from Lovčičky in Moravia. Many of the forty-eight rectangular timber houses had large posts set widely apart, some with a central row of posts for supporting a pitched roof. In a relatively open area at the center of the site is a larger structure with very closely spaced posts that may have served as a communal hall. It measures 21 meters in length, with an interior area of 144 square meters. The village gives the overall impression of having greater structure than sites such as Zedau, which tend to have a scattered layout.

A somewhat different sort of settlement was found at Riesburg-Pflaumloch, in Baden-Württemberg, where the seventeen structures were built during several phases. As at Lovčičky, the posts of the longer houses were spaced widely apart, while smaller structures are interpreted as granaries. Unraveling the stratification of the houses and the sequence of their construction led to the identification of several building clusters, which have been interpreted as loosely connected farmsteads with a main house and several outbuildings.

Among the best-known Urnfield settlements are the fortified villages set on islands and peninsulas in lakes. The Wasserburg at Bad Buchau, on an island in the Federsee in southern Germany, was excavated in the 1920s and 1930s, revealing two successive Urnfield settlements. The first one was founded in the twelfth century B.C., with thirty-eight small, one-roomed houses, most about 4 meters by 5 meters in area. It was enclosed by a palisade with thousands of posts. After a period of abandonment due to rising water levels, a smaller palisaded settlement was rebuilt around 1000 B.C. with nine large, multiroom houses (fig. 1). This second settlement was destroyed by fire early in the first millennium B.C. Many of the houses of the Wasserburg at Bad Buchau were built in a log-cabin style, with timbers laid horizontally on one another. The population of the site during both construction phases is estimated at about two hundred people.

Fortified settlements were also built on higher terrain, on hilltops and plateaus. In many cases, the fortifications were quite elaborate, with their ramparts reinforced using timber structures, stone facing, and sloping banks. Relatively little is known about the settlements in the interior of these fortifications, since archaeologists have typically focused their attention on the ramparts themselves. At the Burgberg, near Burkheim in southwestern Germa-

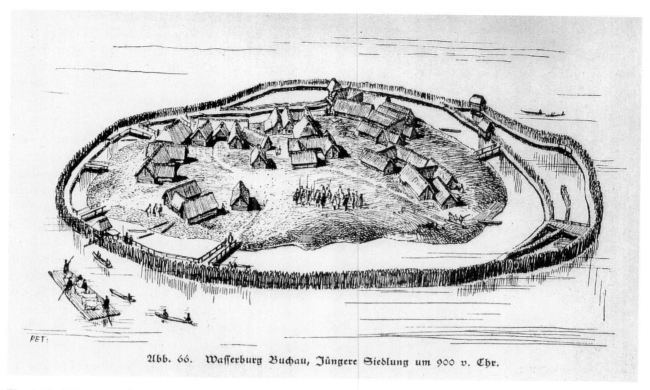

Abb. 66. Wasserburg Buchau, Jüngere Siedlung um 900 v. Chr.

Fig. 1. The "Wasserburg" at Bad Buchau, southern Germany. Reconstruction as envisioned by the excavator of the site, Hans Reinerth. WÜRTTEMBERGISCHES LANDESMUSEUM STUTTGART. REPRODUCED BY PERMISSION.

ny, excavations have revealed hundreds of round pits, interpreted as storage pits or house cellars. Many of the Urnfield fortified settlements of central Europe were destroyed after a very short period of occupation.

SUBSISTENCE

An increase in cemeteries and settlements over the duration of the Urnfield complex suggests that populations grew during this period in many parts of central Europe. It appears, therefore, that settlement was extended into new areas characterized by poorer soils that had not previously been intensively exploited. In order to make use of these soils, new crops were introduced, with millet and rye becoming common alongside the wheats and barleys that had been in use for centuries. Oats were raised for feeding horses. A legume, the horsebean, expanded in use in order to fix nitrogen during crop rotation, besides being easy to grow and nutritious. Generally speaking, Urnfield peoples used many different sorts of field crops depending on what soil conditions occurred in the vicinity of their settlements, and the actual mix of plants varied from site to site.

The Urnfield animal economy was dominated by cattle in temperate Europe and most often by sheep and goats in the Mediterranean basin. These species provided meat and milk, and wool was sheared from the sheep. Oxen and horses were used to pull and carry loads. The so-called Secondary Products Revolution of the fourth millennium B.C. had long been established as integral to the prehistoric economy. Pigs complement cattle at many of the sites in temperate Europe. In general, the animal economy of the Urnfield complex is a continuation of overall trends that began during the Neolithic, with local adjustments to availability of pasture and grazing.

METAL ARTIFACTS

The increasing sophistication in bronze metallurgy that characterizes the second millennium B.C. led to the emergence of many new forms of bronze ornaments, tools, and weapons among the Urnfield communities. Several new techniques appeared. One is the ability to make composite artifacts by casting many small parts that could then be assembled into a whole object. Extensive use was made of

Fig. 2. Antenna-hilt sword from the bog near Bad Schussenried. Swords of this type are primarily found as offerings in bogs, lake, and rivers. WÜRTTEMBERGISCHES LANDESMUSEUM STUTTGART. REPRODUCED BY PERMISSION.

the technique of lost-wax casting, in which a wax model with a clay core was made of the desired object, then covered in clay and fired. The wax melted and ran out, leaving a cavity into which molten bronze was poured. When the outer clay was bro-

ken away, a bronze cast of the original wax form remained. Since the wax could easily be inscribed, it was possible to cast objects with fine surface details. Another new technique was the manufacture of sheet bronze, which could be shaped into complex hollow forms held together with rivets.

Although the range and variety of Urnfield metal artifacts is astonishing, one of its most striking aspects is the expansion in the range and variety of weapons and armor. These have been found primarily in deposits and hoards. Swords were introduced earlier in the Bronze Age, but in Urnfield times they are found with many different lengths and shapes of blades and a wide variety of hilts (fig. 2). Body armor occurs in the form of cuirasses (vests that protect the torso), shin guards, shields, and helmets. The sheet bronze used in this armor was too thin to be of much defense against a sword or spear, so it is assumed that it was largely worn ceremonially as a badge of rank.

Among the most interesting Urnfield metal artifacts are small models of wagons and carts, found largely in southern Germany, Austria, and adjacent areas. Their rolling wheels have four spokes, and on their frame they are often carrying a vessel or cauldron. A particularly distinctive feature is their decoration with stylized birds, apparently waterfowl, which appear to have played a major role in Urnfield symbolism.

SOCIAL ORGANIZATION

Many archaeologists have argued that the Late Bronze Age saw the emergence of a warrior aristocracy, men whose prestige was maintained through success in combat. The principal evidence for this is the elaboration of weaponry and armor and its appearance in elite burials, as well as the widespread occurrence of fortified sites. Some have painted a picture of a society permeated by fear and anxiety, dominated by an armed aristocracy.

Yet most people continued to live in small farmsteads and hamlets much as they had for centuries, and it is difficult to characterize their relationship to the presumed warrior elite and its conflicts. It is possible that they were largely unaffected by them. The variation among graves in the Urnfield cemeteries suggests clear differences in status and wealth, and we can presume a continuation or even elaboration of the differentiation between elites and commoners inferred from the evidence of the Early and Middle Bronze Ages.

CONCLUSION

The Urnfield complex of the Late Bronze Age represents the adoption of a new set of shared values across much of continental Europe, especially a new attitude toward death and the role of the body. It was also a time of technological advances, particularly in the mastery of bronze metallurgy, and of social transformation, quite possibly including the appearance of a class of elite warriors. The Urnfield complex very much set the stage for subsequent developments of the first millennium B.C. The Early Iron Age (also known as Hallstatt C and D) that began around 750 B.C. saw the continuation of the practices of cremation burial and settlement fortification.

See also **Warfare and Conquest** (*vol. 1, part 1*); **Hallstatt** (*vol. 2, part 6*); **Biskupin** (*vol. 2, part 6*).

BIBLIOGRAPHY

Harding, A. F. *European Societies in the Bronze Age.* Cambridge, U.K.: Cambridge University Press, 2000.

Kristiansen, Kristian. *Europe before History.* Cambridge, U.K.: Cambridge University Press, 1998.

Milisauskas, Sarunas. "The Bronze Age." In *European Prehistory: A Survey.* New York: Kluwer Academic/Plenum Publishers, 2002.

Mohen, Jean-Pierre, and Christian Eluère. *The Bronze Age in Europe.* New York: Harry N. Abrams, 1999.

Probst, Ernst. *Deutschland in der Bronzezeit.* Munich: C. Bertelsmann, 1996.

PETER BOGUCKI

BRONZE AGE HERDERS OF THE EURASIAN STEPPES

The Eurasian steppe is a sea of varied grasslands extending from Mongolia to the mouth of the Danube, an east-west distance of about 7,000 kilometers. No surviving inscriptions describe the Bronze Age cultures of the steppe—they are entirely prehistoric. For that reason, they are much less well known than their descendants of the Iron Age, such as the Scythians. Unfortunately, the Bronze Age cultures tend to be seen through the lens of these later horse nomads and their historical cousins—Mongols, Turks, Huns, and others. In fact, horse nomadism of the classic Eurasian steppe type appeared after about 1000 B.C. Before 1000 B.C. the steppe was occupied by quite different kinds of cultures, not at all like the Scythians. It was in the Bronze Age that people first really domesticated the steppe—learned to profit from it. Wagons, wool sheep, and perhaps horseback riding appeared in the steppe at the beginning of the Bronze Age. Chariots and large-scale copper mining arose in the Late Bronze Age. These innovations revolutionized steppe economies, which led to the extension of a single, broadly similar steppe civilization from eastern Europe to the borders of China. Indo-European languages might well have spread through this new community of steppe cultures.

CHRONOLOGY

The steppe Bronze Age was defined by Soviet archaeologists, who did not look to western Europe for guidance. Instead, they matched the chronological phases of the Russian and Ukrainian steppes with those of the Caucasus Mountains—part of both the Czarist Russian empire and the Soviet

Union. The Bronze Age chronology of the Caucasus, in turn, is linked to that of Anatolia, in modern Turkey. As a result, the steppe regions of the former Soviet Union have a Bronze Age chronology that is entirely different from that just to the west in Poland or southeastern Europe, where the western European chronological system defined by Paul Reinecke was used.

The Early Bronze Age of the steppes began about 3300 B.C., perhaps a thousand years earlier than the Early Bronze Age of Poland and southeastern Europe but about the same time as the Early Bronze Age of Anatolia. This might seem a trivial matter, but it has hindered communication between western and Russian-Ukrainian archaeologists who study the Bronze Age. In addition, some influential Soviet and post-Soviet archaeologists were slow to accept the validity of radiocarbon dating, so competing radiocarbon-based and typology-based chronologies have confused outsiders.

Finally, the Bronze Age of the steppe covers such an enormous area that it is impossible to define one chronology that applies to the entire region. In fact, there was a significant cultural frontier in the Volga-Ural region that separated the western steppes, west of the Ural Mountains, from the eastern, or Asian, steppes until the end of the Middle Bronze Age, as defined in the western sequence. In the steppes of northern Kazakhstan, just east of this Ural frontier, the sequence jumps from a local Eneolithic to a brief and poorly defined Early Bronze Age (strongly influenced by the western Middle Bonze Age), followed by the Late Bronze

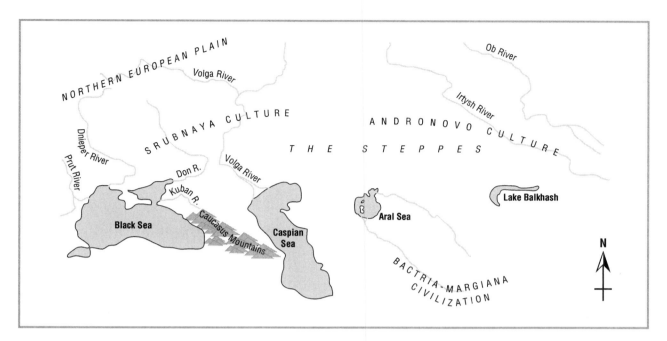

Eurasia about 2000 B.C. showing general location of selected cultures.

Age. It is only in the Late Bronze Age that the eastern and western steppes share the same broad chronological periods.

The sequence of Bronze Age cultures in the western steppes was established in 1901–1907, when Vasily A. Gorodtsov excavated 107 burial mounds, or *kurgans,* containing 299 graves in the Izyum region of the northern Donets River Valley, near Kharkov in the Ukrainian steppes. In 1907 he published an account in which he observed that three basic types of graves were found repeatedly, stratified one above the other: the oldest graves in the *kurgans* were of a type he called pit graves, followed by catacomb graves and then by timber graves. These grave types are now recognized as the backbone of the Bronze Age chronology for the western steppes. The absolute dates given to them here are maximal dates, the earliest and latest expressions. The Pit Grave, or Yamnaya, culture, for example, began in 3300 B.C. and persisted in the steppes northwest of the Black Sea until about 2300 B.C.. (Early Bronze Age). It was replaced by the Catacomb culture in the steppes east of the Dnieper Valley hundreds of years earlier, around 2700 or even 2800 B.C. Catacomb sites lasted until 1900 B.C. (Middle Bronze Age). The Timber Grave, or

Srubnaya, culture came to prominence about 1900 B.C. and ended about 1200 B.C. (Late Bronze Age).

THE ROOTS OF THE STEPPE BRONZE AGE

The period 4000–3500 B.C. witnessed the appearance of new kinds of wealth in the steppes north of the Black Sea (the North Pontic region) and, simultaneously, the fragmentation of societies in the Danube Valley and eastern Carpathians (the Tripolye culture) that had been the region's centers of population and economic productivity. Rich graves (the Karanovo VI culture) appeared in the steppe grasslands from the mouth of the Danube (as at Suvorovo, north of the Danube delta in Romania) to the Azov steppes (as at Novodanilovka, north of Mariupol in Ukraine). These exceptional graves contained flint blades up to 20 centimeters long, polished flint axes, lanceolate flint points, copper and shell beads, copper spiral rings and bracelets, a few small gold ornaments, and (at Suvorovo) a polished stone mace-head shaped like a horse's head. The percentage of horse bones doubled in steppe settlements of this period, about 4000–3000 B.C., at Dereivka and Sredny Stog II.

It is possible that horseback riding began at about this time. Early in this period, perhaps setting in motion economic and military innovations that threatened the economic basis of agricultural villages. Most Tripolye B1–B2 towns, dated about 4000–3800 B.C., were fortified. In the Lower Danube Valley, previously a densely settled and materially rich region, six hundred tell settlements were abandoned, and a simpler material culture (typified by the sites Cernavoda and Renie) became widespread in the smaller, dispersed communities that followed. Copper mining and metallurgy declined sharply in the Balkans. Later, in the Southern Bug Valley, the easternmost Tripolye people concentrated into a few very large towns, such as Maidanets'ke, arguably for defensive reasons. The largest were 300–400 hectares in area, with fifteen hundred buildings arranged in concentric circles around a large central plaza or green.

These enormous towns were occupied from about 3800 to 3500 B.C., during the Tripolye C1 period, and then were abandoned. Most of the eastern Tripolye population dispersed into smaller, more mobile residential units. Only a few clusters of towns in the Dniester Valley retained the old Tripolye customs of large houses, fine painted pottery, and female figurines after 3500 B.C. This sequence of events, still very poorly understood, spelled the end of the rich Copper Age cultures of Ukraine, Romania, and Bulgaria, termed "Old Europe" by Marija Gimbutas. The steppe cultures of the western North Pontic region became richer, but it is difficult to say whether they raided the Danube Valley and Tripolye towns or just observed and profited from an internal crisis brought on by soil degradation and climate change. In either case, by 3500 B.C. the cultures of the North Pontic steppes no longer had access to Balkan copper and other prestige commodities that once had been traded into the steppes from "Old Europe."

After about 3500 B.C. the North Pontic steppe cultures were drawn into a new set of relationships with truly royal figures who appeared in the northern Caucasus. Such villages as Svobodnoe had existed since about 4300 B.C. in the northern Caucasian piedmont uplands, supported by pig and cattle herding and small-scale agriculture. About 3500–3300 B.C. the people of the Kuban forest-steppe region began to erect a series of spectacularly rich *kurgan* graves. Huge *kurgans* were built over stone-lined grave chambers containing fabulous gifts.

Among the items were huge cauldrons (up to 70 liters) made of arsenical bronze, vases of sheet gold and silver decorated with scenes of animal processions and a goat mounting a tree of life, silver rods with cast silver and gold bull figurines, arsenical bronze axes and daggers, and hundreds of ornaments of gold, turquoise, and carnelian.

The *kurgan* built over the chieftain's grave at the type site of the Maikop culture was 11 meters high; it and the stone grave chamber would have taken five hundred men almost six weeks to build. Maikop settlements, such as Meshoko and Galugai, remained small and quite ordinary, without metal finds, public buildings, or storehouses, so we do not know where the new chiefs kept their wealth during life. The ceramic inventory, however, is similar in the rich graves and the settlements—pots from the Maikop chieftain's grave look like those from Meshoko.

Some early stage Maikop metal tools have analogies at Sialk III in northwestern Iran, and others resemble those from Arslantepe VI in southeastern Anatolia, sites of the same period. A minority of Maikop metal artifacts were made with a high-nickel-content arsenical bronze, like the formula used in Anatolia and Mesopotamia and unlike the normal Caucasian metal type of this era. Certain early Maikop ceramic vessels were wheel-thrown, a technology known in Anatolia and Iran but previously unknown in the northern Caucasus. The inspiration for the sheet-silver vessel decorated with a goat mounting a tree of life must have been in late-stage Uruk Mesopotamia, where the first cities in the world were at that time consuming trade commodities and sending out merchants and ambassadors. The appearance of a very rich elite in the northern Caucasus probably was an indirect result of this stimulation of interregional trade emanating from Mesopotamia.

Wool sheep had been bred first in Mesopotamia in about 4000 B.C. The earliest woolen textiles known north of the Caucasus were found in a rich Maikop grave at Novosvobodnaya, dating perhaps to 2800 B.C. Wool could shed rainwater and take dyes much better than any plant-fiber textile. Portable felt tents and felt boots, standard pieces of nomad gear in later centuries, became possible at this time. Wagons also might have been invented in Mesopotamia. Wagons with solid wooden wheels began to appear at scattered sites across southeastern Europe after the Maikop culture emerged in the northern Caucasus. The evidence for the adoption of wagons can be seen at about 3300 B.C. in southern Poland (as evidenced by an incised image of a four-wheeled wagon on a pot of the Funnel Beaker culture), 3300–3000 B.C. in Hungary (seen in small clay wagon models in Baden culture graves with ox teams), and 3000 B.C. in the North Pontic steppes (as indicated by actual burials of disassembled wagons with solid wheels in or above human graves). We do not know with certainty that wool sheep and wagons both came into the steppes through the Maikop culture, but other southern influences certainly are apparent at Maikop, and the timing is right. Numerous Maikop-type graves under *kurgans* have been found in the steppes north of the northern Caucasian piedmont, and isolated Maikop-type artifacts have been discovered in scattered local graves across the North Pontic region.

THE EARLY BRONZE AGE: WOOL, WHEELS, AND COPPER

The Yamnaya culture arose in the North Pontic steppes about when the earliest Maikop mounds were built—3300 B.C., more or less. According to the classic 1979 study of Nikolai Merpert, the Yamnaya began in the steppes of the lower Volga, northwest of the Caspian Sea, and the funeral customs that define the Yamnaya phenomenon then spread westward to the Danube. Merpert also divided Yamnaya into nine regional variants, however, and the relationships between them have become increasingly unclear since 1979. The oldest Yamnaya pottery types defined by Merpert, egg-shaped shell-tempered pots with cord and comb–impressed decoration, clearly evolved from the late-stage Khvalynsk and Repin ceramic types found in the Volga and Don steppes in the earlier fourth millennium B.C. Pots such as these also are found in some Yamnaya graves farther west in Ukraine. Most Yamnaya graves in Ukraine, however, contained a variety of local pottery types, and some of them could be older than those on the Volga. Yamnaya was not really a single culture with a single origin—Merpert used the phrase "economic-historical community" to describe it.

The essential defining trait of the Yamnaya horizon, as we should call it, was a strongly pastoral economy and a mobile residential pattern, combined with the creation of very visible cemeteries of raised *kurgans*. *Kurgan* cemeteries sprang up across the steppes from the Danube to the Ural River. Settlements disappeared in many areas, particularly in the east, the Don-Volga-Ural steppes. This was a broad economic shift, not the spread of a single culture. A change to a drier, colder climate might have accelerated the shift—climatologists date the Atlantic/Subboreal transition to about 3300–3000 B.C.

A more mobile residence pattern would have been encouraged by the appearance of wagons, felt tents, and woolen clothes. Wool made it easier to live in the open steppe, away from the protected river valleys. Wagons were a critically important innovation, because they permitted a herder to carry enough food, shelter, and water to remain with his herd far from the sheltered river valleys. Herds could be dispersed over much larger areas, which meant that larger herds could be owned and real wealth could be accumulated in livestock. It is no accident that metallurgy picked up at about the same time—herders now had something to trade.

Wagons acquired such importance that they were disassembled and buried with certain individuals; about two hundred wagon graves are known in the North Pontic steppes for the Early Bronze Age and Middle Bronze Age combined. The wagons, the oldest preserved anywhere in the world, were narrow-bodied and heavy, with solid wheels that turned on a fixed axle. Pulled laboriously by oxen, they were not racing vehicles. Yamnaya herders probably rode horses; characteristic wear made by a bit has been found on the premolars of horse teeth from this period in a neighboring culture in Kazakhstan (the Botai culture), where there are settlements with large numbers of horse bones. Horseback riding greatly increased the efficiency of herding, particularly cattle herding.

A few western Yamnaya settlements are known in Ukraine. At one of them, Mikhailovka level II, 60 percent of the animal bones were from cattle. A study of animal sacrifices in the eastern Yamnaya region (the Don-Volga-Ural steppes), however, found that among fifty-three graves with such animal bones, sheep occurred in 65 percent, cattle in only 15 percent, and horses in 7.5 percent of the graves. The seeds of wheat and millet have been found in the clay of some Yamnaya pots in the lower

Dnieper steppes (Belyaevka *kurgan* 1 and Glubokoe *kurgan* 2), so some agriculture might have been practiced in the steppe river valleys of Ukraine.

Local sandstone copper ores were exploited in two apparent centers of metallurgic activity: the lower Dnieper and the middle Volga. Some exceptionally rich graves are located near the city of Samara on the Volga, at the northern edge of the steppe zone. One, the Yamnaya grave at Kutuluk, contained a sword-length pure copper club or mace weighing 1.5 kilograms, and another, a Yamnaya-Poltavka grave nearby at Utyevka, contained a copper dagger, a shaft-hole axe, a flat axe, an L-headed pin, and two gold rings with granulated decoration. Dozens of tanged daggers are known from Yamnaya graves. A few objects made of iron are present in later Yamnaya graves (knife blades and the head of a copper pin at Utyevka), perhaps the earliest iron artifacts anywhere.

The basic funeral ritual of burial in a sub-rectangular pit under a *kurgan,* usually on the back with the knees raised (or on the side in Ukraine) and the head pointed east-northeast, was adopted widely, but only a few persons were recognized in this way. We do not know where or how most ordinary people were handled after death. In the Ukraine, carved stone stelae have been found in about three hundred Yamnaya *kurgans*. It is thought that they were carved and used for some other ritual originally, perhaps an earlier phase in the funeral, and then were reused as covering stones over grave pits.

Beginning in about 3000 B.C. rich cultures emerged in the coastal steppes of the Crimea (the Kemi Oba culture) and the Dniester estuary northwest of the Black Sea (the Usatovo culture). They might have participated in seaborne trade along the Black Sea coast—artifact exchanges show that Usatovo, Kemi Oba, and late stages of the Maikop cultures were contemporary. Perhaps their trade goods even reached Troy I. A stone stela much like a Yamnaya marker was built into a wall at Troy I, and the Troy I ceramics were very much like those of the Baden and Ezero cultures in southeastern Europe.

The Early Bronze Age settlement and cemetery at Usatovo, on a shallow coastal bay near the mouth of the Dniester, is the defining site for the Usatovo culture. Two separate groups of large *kurgans* were surrounded by standing stone curbs and stelae, oc-casionally carved with images of horses. In the central graves of *kurgan* cemetery 1 adult men were buried with riveted arsenical copper daggers and beautifully painted pots of the final-stage Tripolye C2 type, probably made for Usatovo chiefs in the last Tripolye towns on the upper Dniester. A few glass beads have been uncovered in Usatovo graves, and some Usatovo riveted daggers look like Aegean or Anatolian daggers of the same period; these objects suggest contacts with the south.

Between about 3000 and 2700 B.C., Yamnaya groups moved through the coastal steppes and migrated into the Lower Danube Valley (especially into northern Bulgaria) and eastern Hungary, where hundreds of Yamnaya *kurgans* are known. This migration carried steppe populations into the Balkans and the eastern Hungarian Plain, where they interacted with the Cotsofeni and late Baden cultures. The graves that testify to the movement were clearly Yamnaya and represented an intrusive new custom in southeastern Europe—some in Bulgaria even contained stelae, and one had a wagon burial, just as in the steppe Yamnaya graves—but the pottery in the graves was always local.

Because the Yamnaya tradition was not identified with a distinct pottery type, it is difficult to say how the Yamnaya immigrants were integrated into Balkan cultures. After the Yamnaya grave type was abandoned, which happened in Hungary before 2500 B.C., the archaeologically visible aspect of Yamnaya material culture disappeared. Nevertheless, some archaeologists see this Yamnaya migration as a social movement that carried Indo-European languages into southeastern Europe.

THE MIDDLE BRONZE AGE: WIDER HORIZONS

The Middle Bronze Age began at different times in different places. The earliest graves assigned to the Catacomb culture date to perhaps 2800–2700 B.C. and are located in the steppes north of the northern Caucasus, among societies of the Novotitorovskaya type that were in close contact with late Maikop culture, and in the Don Valley to the north. Along the Volga, graves containing Poltavka pottery appeared by 2800–2700 B.C. as well; Poltavka was very much like the earlier eastern Yamnaya culture, but with larger, more elaborately decorated, flat-based pots. By about 2600–2500 B.C. Catacomb traditions spread westward over the entire North Pontic region as far as the mouth of the Danube. Poltavka persisted through the Middle Bronze Age in the Volga-Ural region.

The Catacomb culture made sophisticated arsenical bronze weapons, tools, and ornaments, probably using Caucasian alloying recipes. Northward, on the Volga, the Poltavka culture continued to use its local "pure" copper sources, rather than the arsenical bronzes of the south. T-shaped pins of bone and copper, perhaps hairpins, were a common late Yamnaya-Catacomb type. Many metal shaft-hole axes and daggers were deposited in graves. The same kinds of ornate bronze pins and medallions are evident in the Middle Bronze Age royal *kurgans* of the northern Caucasus (Sachkere, Bedeni, and Tsnori) and the settlements of the Caspian Gate (Velikent) on the one hand and the Middle Bronze Age sites of the steppes on the other. These finds imply an active north-south system of Middle Bronze Age trade and intercommunication between the steppes and the Caucasus. Evgeni N. Chernykh, a specialist in metals and metallurgy, has speculated that up to half of the output of the Caucasian copper industry might have been consumed in the steppes to the north. Wagon burials continued in the Catacomb region for exceptional people. In the Ingul valley, west of the Dnieper, as well as in the steppes north of the Caucasus, some Catacomb graves contained skeletons with clay death masks applied to the skull.

Although the Middle Bronze Age remained a period of extreme mobility and few settlements, the number of settlement sites increased. A few small Middle Bronze Age occupation sites are known even on the Volga, a region devoid of Early Bronze Age settlements. A Catacomb culture wagon grave in the Azov steppes contained a charred pile of cultivated wheat grains, so some cultivation probably took place. The emphasis in the economy seems to have remained on pastoralism, however. Near Tsatsa in the Kalmyk steppes north of the North Caucasus, the skulls of forty horses were found sacrificed at the edge of one a man's grave (Tsatsa *kurgan* 1, grave 5, of the Catacomb culture). This find is exceptional—a single horse or a ram's head is more common—but it demonstrates the continuing ritual importance of herded animals.

THE NEW WAVE: SINTASHTA-ARKAIM

At the end of the Middle Bronze Age, about 2200–2000 B.C., the innovations that would define the Late Bronze Age began to evolve in the northern steppes around the southern Urals. Perhaps increasing interaction between northern steppe herders and southern forest societies brought about this surge of creativity and wealth. Domesticated cattle and horses had begun to appear with some regularity at sites in the forest zone by about 2500–2300 B.C., with the appearance and spread of the Fatyanovo culture, a Russian forest-zone eastern extension of the Corded Ware horizon. Fatyanovo-related bronzeworking was adopted in the forest zone west of the Urals at about the same time. In the forest-steppe region, at the ecological boundary, the Abashevo culture emerged on the upper Don and middle Volga. The Abashevo culture displayed great skill in bronzework and was in contact with the late Poltavka peoples in the nearby steppes.

During the Middle Bronze Age some late Poltavka people from the Volga-Ural steppes drifted into the steppes east of the Ural Mountains, crossing the Ural frontier into what had been forager territory. About 2100–2200 B.C., these Poltavka groups began to mix with or emulate late Abashevo peoples, who had appeared in the southern Ural forest steppe. The mixture of Abashevo and Poltavka customs in the grassy hills west of the upper Tobol River created the visible traits of the Sintashta-Arkaim culture. It is more difficult to explain the explosion of extravagant ritual sacrifices and sudden building of large fortified settlements.

Sintashta-Arkaim sites are found in a compact region at the northern edge of the steppe, where the stony, gently rising hills are rich in copper ores. All of the streams in the Sintashta-Arkaim region flow into the upper Tobol on its west side. The known settlements of this culture were strongly fortified, with deep ditches dug outside high earth-and-timber walls; houses stood close together with their narrower ends against the wall. Before it was half destroyed by river erosion, Sintashta, probably contained the remains of sixty houses; Arkaim had about the same. Smelting copper from ore and other kinds of metallurgy occurred in every house in every excavated settlement.

Outside the settlements were *kurgan* cemeteries containing extraordinarily rich graves, accompanied by socketed spears, axes, daggers, flint points, whole horses, entire dogs, and the heads of cattle and sheep. Chariots were found on the floors of sixteen graves of the Sintashta-Arkaim culture, continuing the ritual of vehicle burial that had been practiced in the western steppes, but with a new kind of vehicle. Three chariot burials at Krivoe Ozero and Sintashta are directly dated. They were buried between about 2100 and 1900 B.C., which makes them the oldest chariots known anywhere in the world. There is some technical debate about whether these were *true* chariots: Were they too small, with a car just big enough for one person? Were the wheels too close together—1.1–1.5 meters across the axle—to keep the vehicle upright on a fast turn? Were the hubs too small to maintain the wheels in a vertical position?

These interesting questions should not obscure the importance of the technical advance in high-speed transport represented by the Sintashta-Arkaim chariots. They were light vehicles, framed with small-diameter wood but probably floored in leather or some other perishable material that left a dark stain, with two wheels of ten to twelve wooden spokes set in slots in the grave floor. They were pulled by a pair of horses controlled by a new, more severe kind of bit cheekpiece and driven by a man with weapons (axe, dagger, and spear).

The new chariot-driving cheekpiece design, an ovoid antler plate with interior spikes that pressed into the sides of the horses' lips, was invented in the steppes south of the Urals. It spread from there across Ukraine (through the Mnogovalikovaya culture, which evolved from late Catacomb culture) into southeastern Europe (the Glina III/Monteoru culture) and later into the Near East (graves at Gaza and Hazor). It is possible that chariotry diffused in the same way, from an origin in the steppes. Alternatively, perhaps chariots were invented in the Near East, as many researchers believe. The exact origin is unimportant. What is certain is that chariots spread very quickly, appearing in Anatolia at Karum Kanesh by about 1950–1850 B.C., so close in time to the Sintashta culture chariots that it is impossible to say for certain which region had chariots first.

The Sintashta-Arkaim culture was not alone. Between about 2100 and 1800 B.C., Sintashta-

Arkaim was the easternmost link in a chain of three northern steppe cultures that shared many funeral rituals, bronze weapon types, tool types, pottery styles, and cheekpiece designs. The middle one, with perhaps the oldest radiocarbon dates, was on the middle Volga—the Potapovka group. The western link was on the upper Don—the Filatovka group. The Don and Volga groups had no fortified settlements; they continued the mobile lifestyle of the earlier Poltavka era. This small cluster of metal-rich late Middle Bronze Age cultures in the steppes around the southern Urals, between the Don and the Tobol, had a tremendous influence on the later customs and styles of the Eurasian Late Bronze Age from China to the Carpathians.

The Late Bronze Age Srubnaya horizon grew out of the Potapovka-Filatovka west of the Urals; east of the Urals, the Late Bronze Age Petrovka-Alakul horizon grew out of Sintashta-Arkaim. Many archaeologists have suggested that Sintashta-Arkaim might represent the speakers of Indo-Iranian, the parent language from which Sanskrit and Avestan Iranian evolved. The excavator of Arkaim, Gennady Zdanovich, has speculated that the prophet Zoroaster was born there. Political extremists, Slavic nationalists, and religious cultists have made the site a sort of shrine. These late Middle Bronze Age Don-Tobol cultures need no such exaggeration. As the apparent source of many of the traits that define the Late Bronze Age of the Eurasian steppes, they are interesting enough.

THE LATE BRONZE AGE: THE OPENING OF THE EURASIAN STEPPES

At the beginning of the Late Bronze Age, about 1850–1700 B.C., people across the northern steppes began to lead much more sedentary, localized lives. Permanent timber buildings were erected at settlements where tents or wagons had been used before, and people stayed in those buildings long enough to deposit thick middens of garbage outside and around them. These sites are so much easier to find that settlement sites spring into archaeological visibility at the start of the Late Bronze Age as if a veil had been lifted; they cover a strip of northern steppe extending from Ukraine to northern Kazakhstan. A few Middle Bronze Age potsherds usually are found among the thousands of Late Bronze Age potsherds at Srubnaya sites in the western steppes, suggesting that the same places were being used but in new and quite different ways. We are not sure what that difference was—the nature of the Late Bronze Age economy is fiercely debated.

In the eastern steppes, east of the Urals, the Late Bronze Age witnessed the spread of the Andronovo horizon (1800–1200 B.C.) from Petrovka-Alakul origins. Most Andronovo culture settlements were in new places, which had not been occupied during the preceding Eneolithic, but then the Andronovo horizon represented the first introduction of herding economies in many places east of the Urals. Srubnaya and Andronovo shared a general resemblance in their settlement forms, funeral rituals, ceramics, and metal tools and weapons. We should not exaggerate these resemblances—as in the Early Bronze Age Yamnaya phenomenon, this was a horizon or a related pair of horizons, not a single culture. Still, it was the first time in human history that such a chain of related cultures extended from the Carpathians to the Pamirs, right across the heart of the Eurasian steppes.

Almost immediately, people using Andronovo-style pots and metal weapons made contact with the irrigation-based urban civilizations at the northern edge of the Mesopotamian-Iranian world, in northern Afghanistan and southern Turkmenistan—the Bactria-Margiana civilization—and also with the western fringes of the emerging Chinese world, in Xinjiang and Gansu. These contacts might have started at the end of the Middle Bronze Age, about 2000 B.C., before the Andronovo culture proper began, but they continued through the early Andronovo stages. Once the chain of Late Bronze Age steppe cultures grappled with these civilizations to the east and south, Eurasia began to be, tentatively, a single interacting world.

We have much to learn about exactly how the Srubnaya and Andronovo economies worked. Some western Srubnaya settlements in Ukraine have yielded cultivated cereals, but the role of agriculture farther east is debated. One study of an early Srubnaya settlement in the Samara River valley, east of the Volga, yielded evidence that the site was occupied year-round, or at least cattle were butchered during all seasons of the year. Intensive botanical study recovered not a single cultivated grain, however, and the caries-free teeth of the Srubnaya people buried in a nearby *kurgan* testify to a low-carbohydrate diet. Waterlogged sediments from the bottom of a well at this site, Krasno Samarskoe, yielded thousands of charred seeds of *Chenopodium,* or goosefoot, a wild plant. At least in some areas, then, permanent year-round settlements might have been supported by a herding-and-gathering economy, with little or no agriculture.

During the Late Bronze Age copper was mined on an almost industrial scale across the steppes. Particularly large mining complexes were located in the southern Urals, at Kargaly near Orenburg, and in central Kazakhstan, near Karaganda. The raw copper ore, the rock itself, seems to have been exported from the mines. Smelting and metalworking were widely dispersed activities; traces are found in many Srubnaya and Andronovo settlements. Andronovo tin mines have been excavated in the Zerafshan valley near Samarkand. True tin bronzes predominated in the east, at many Andronovo sites, while arsenical bronzes continued to be more common in the west, at Srubnaya sites.

The combined Srubnaya and Andronovo horizons might well have been the social network through which Indo-Iranian languages—the kind of languages spoken by the Scythians and Saka a thousand years later—first spread across the steppes. This does not imply that Srubnaya or Andronovo was a single ethnolinguistic group; the new language could have been disseminated through various populations with the widespread adoption of a new ritual and political system. The diffusion of Srubnaya and Andronovo funeral rituals, with their public sacrifices of horses, sheep, and cattle, involved the public performance of a ritual drama shaped very much by political and economic contests for power.

Humans gave a portion of their herds and well-crafted verses of praise to the gods, and the gods, in return, provided protection from misfortune and the blessings of power and prosperity. "Let this racehorse bring us good cattle and good horses, male children, and all-nourishing wealth," pleaded a Sanskrit prayer in book 1, hymn 162, of the *Rig Veda.* It goes on, "Let the horse with our offerings achieve sovereign power for us." This relationship was mirrored in the mortal world when wealthy patrons sponsored public funeral feasts in return for the approval and loyalty of their clients. The Indic and Iranian poetry of the *Rig Veda* and *Avesta* offers direct testimony of this kind of system. The people received spectacle with their meat—they witnessed an elaborately scripted sacrifice punctuated by poems full of drama, rich in emotion, occasionally bawdy and earthy, and filled with clever metaphors and triple and double meanings. The best of these verbal displays were memorized, repeated, and shared, and they became part of the collective medium through which a variety of different peoples ended up speaking Indo-Iranian languages across most of the Eurasian steppes.

"Let us speak great words as men of power in the sacrificial gathering," said the standard closing line attached to several different hymns in book 2, one of the oldest parts of the *Rig Veda*, probably composed about 1500 B.C. This line expresses very well the connections among language, public ritual, verbal artistry, and the projection of secular power. A tradition that had begun in the western steppes thousands of years earlier, with simpler animal sacrifices, developed by the Late Bronze Age into a vehicle for the spread of a new kind of culture across the Eurasian steppes.

See also **Domestication of the Horse** (*vol. 1, part 4*).

BIBLIOGRAPHY

Anthony, David W. "Horse, Wagon, and Chariot: Indo-European Languages and Archaeology." *Antiquity* (1995): 554–565.

———. "The 'Kurgan Culture,' Indo-European Origins, and the Domestication of the Horse: A Reconsideration." *Current Anthropology* 27, no. 4 (1986): 291–313.

Chernykh, E. N. *Ancient Metallurgy in the USSR: The Early Metal Age.* Translated by Sarah Wright. Cambridge, U.K.: Cambridge University Press, 1992.

Kuzmina, Elena E. "Stages of Development of Stockbreeding Husbandry and Ecology of the Steppes in the Light of Archaeological and Paleoecological Data." In *The Archaeology of the Steppes: Methods and Strategies.* Edited by Bruno Genito, pp. 31–71. Napoli, Italy: Instituto Universitario Orientale, 1994.

———. "Horses, Chariots and the Indo-Iranians: An Archaeological Spark in the Historical Dark." *South Asian Archaeology* 1 (1993): 403–412.

Lamberg-Karlovsky, C. C. "Archaeology and Language: The Indo-Iranians." *Current Anthropology* 43, no. 1 (2002): 75–76.

Mair, Victor H., ed. *The Bronze Age and Early Iron Age Peoples of Eastern Central Asia.* Washington, D.C.: Institute for the Study of Man, 1998.

Mallory, James P., and Victor H. Mair. *The Tarim Mummies: Ancient China and the Mystery of the Earliest Peoples from the West.* New York: Thames and Hudson, 2000.

Shishlina, Natalia, ed. *Seasonality Studies of the Bronze Age Northwest Caspian Steppe.* Papers of the State Historical Museum, vol. 120. Moscow: Gosudarstvennyi istoricheskii muzei, 2000. (Distributed outside Russia by University Museum Publications, University of Pennsylvania Museum, Philadelphia.)

Rassamakin, Yuri. "The Eneolithic of the Black Sea Steppe: Dynamics of Cultural and Economic Development 4500–2300 B.C." In *Late Prehistoric Exploitation of the Eurasian Steppe.* Edited by Marsha Levine, Yuri Rassamakin, Aleksandr Kislenko, and Nataliya Tatarintseva, pp. 59–182. Cambridge, U.K.: McDonald Institute for Archaeological Research, 1999.

Telegin, Dimitri Y., and James P. Mallory. *The Anthropomorphic Stelae of the Ukraine: The Early Iconography of the Indo-Europeans.* Journal of Indo-European Studies Monograph, no. 11. Washington, D.C.: Institute for the Study of Man, 1994.

DAVID W. ANTHONY

BRONZE AGE TRANSCAUCASIA

Transcaucasia is the territory south of the great Caucasus mountain range that spans the region from the isthmus between the Black Sea and the Sea of Azov in the west to the Caspian Sea in the east. The modern political boundaries of Transcaucasia include the republics of Georgia, Armenia, Azerbaijan, and the area of eastern Turkey and northwestern Iran. Emphasis here is placed on the cultural developments of the area encompassed by Georgia and Armenia, but the archaeological record of the entire region is discussed in the context of overall archaeological trends.

Although Transcaucasia is a region with a unique archaeological history, the material record also reflects some of the shared influences of contact with surrounding territories to the north in the great Caucasus and to the south in the Near East. The span of the Bronze Age (from c. 3500–3300 to 1200 B.C.), in particular, is a period of significant interregional contact, change, and development in nearly all aspects of the way the early Transcaucasian inhabitants lived. Some of these important developments include the invention of transformative technologies, such as metallurgy and wheeled transportation, and changes in the manner in which people built homes, settled, and used the land upon which they lived and established interconnections with surrounding territories. The archaeological history of the entire Bronze Age is of importance for understanding long-term cultural trends and changes, but this article focuses on developments particular to the Early Bronze Age (up to 2200 B.C.). It was during this period that some of the most significant cul-

tural transformations have been recorded and the underpinnings for subsequent cultural, technological, and economic changes were established.

Transcaucasia is a region of vast climatic and ecological diversity, and this diversity had an impact on prehistoric settlement and the emergence of complex society during the Bronze Age. The region is largely mountainous, interspersed with fertile valleys and upland plateaus. Along its western border at the Black Sea there is a lush, subtropical depression in the Colchis region of Georgia. In the east are desertlike, dry steppes bordering the river lowlands in eastern Azerbaijan, and along the shore of the Caspian Sea spreads a broad coastal plain. There are a few seasonally passable routes linking the steppe and the northern, or Greater, Caucasus with the southern Caucasus. To the south in Armenia the terrain is characterized by windswept highland plateaus that connect the area almost without interruption with Anatolia (modern Turkey) and northwest Iran. Transecting the region are two major rivers, the Kura (ancient Cyrus) and the Araks (ancient Araxes) (1,364 and 915 kilometers long, respectively). These rivers, giving name to the Early Bronze Age Kura-Araxes culture, flow from west to east and are joined intermittently by highland-draining tributaries. They link course in Azerbaijan before flowing into the Caspian Sea. The headwaters for both the Kura and Araks Rivers lie in eastern Turkey.

The presence of the rivers and their tributaries is significant for supporting some of the ecological riches of the region, in that they afforded the availability of water necessary for supporting agriculture

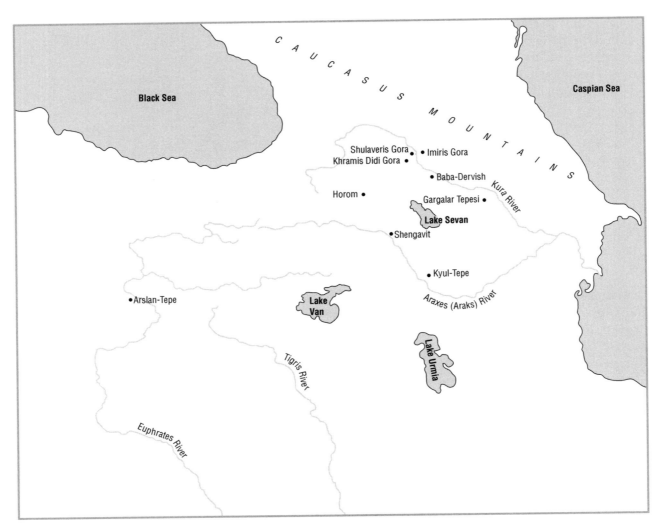

Bronze Age Transcaucasia. ADAPTED FROM KUSHNAREVA 1997.

and for the establishment of permanent settlements along the river courses. As well as being rich in fertile land for practicing agriculture and pasturing animals, Transcaucasia also is rich in other natural resources, such as obsidian (volcanic glass), semiprecious stones, and the very important resource copper.

BACKGROUND ON ARCHAEOLOGICAL RESEARCH
Some explanation of the history of archaeological research in the region is relevant for understanding how archaeologists have come to reconstruct society during the Bronze Age. During the nineteenth century, antiquarians began to investigate the prehistoric riches of the region with the discovery of massive earthen burials called *kurgans*. *Kurgans* are

large circular or square semi-subterranean pits, sometimes constructed in wood and lined with stones, within which were often placed numerous bodies, wagons, animals, jewelry, bronze artifacts, and pottery. The artifacts uncovered in *kurgans* provide the earliest glimpses into the rich archaeological prehistory of the region. During the first half of the twentieth century more systematic excavations in Transcaucasia were implemented, and a fuller picture of the region's archaeological history began to emerge. These investigations were conducted by Russian and Caucasian (Georgian, Armenian, and Azerbaijani) archaeologists.

While the significance of these excavations was recognized and published within the region, these reports often did not circulate among western scholars with interest in European and Near Eastern prehistory. Among the reasons that western scholars did not have access to the archaeological reports from Transcaucasia is that during the Soviet era (1917–1992) members of the scientific community of the Soviet Union remained largely isolated from their European and American colleagues. In addition, the reports of these excavations were published in Russian or in the language of the country where the excavations were conducted. These language barriers further hindered access to what was being recorded of the rich archaeological past. Since the collapse of the Soviet Union, collaborations among western and former Soviet scholars have opened exchanges of archaeological findings, which has afforded a greater understanding of the overall archaeological picture in Transcaucasia. The archaeological history of this region now can be compared more effectively with contemporary prehistoric developments in surrounding regions, such as Europe and the Near East.

CHARACTERIZING THE EARLY BRONZE AGE IN TRANSCAUCASIA

The nature of the development and emergence of the Early Bronze Age Kura-Araxes culture in Transcaucasia is not very well understood, but the archaeological record shows an explosion in the number of settlements across the region. Hundreds of new sites were established in ecologically diverse zones. While excavations at several Early Bronze Age sites, such as Kultepe and Baba Dervish (both in Azerbaijan), Imiris-Gora and Shulaveris-Gora (both in Georgia), Shengavit (Armenia), and Sös Höyük (Turkey) have revealed uninterrupted occupation from the preceding Aneolithic period, the vast majority of these sites represent newfound settlements where none previously existed. In addition to the six sites named, dozens of other sites have been thoroughly excavated, and from these excavations archaeologists are able to interpret much about the culture and economy of the region. Cemeteries have been discovered in association with a few Kura-Araxes settlements, such as Horom in Armenia and Kvatskelebi in Georgia, and the material remains recovered from graves provide an enriched account of the customs of burial as well as a more thorough documentation of Kura-Araxes material culture.

Before the Early Bronze Age, the Aneolithic period (5500–3500 B.C.), which corresponds to the "Copper Age" in southern and southeastern Europe, is characterized by relatively few sites, typically no larger than a hectare in size. The structures built during the Aneolithic Shulaveri-Shomu Tepe and Sioni cultures were constructed from mud brick or wattle and daub, and they typically were rounded, single-room dwellings, sometimes with benches built along the interior walls. The pottery was handmade from coarse clay, and the vessel shapes generally were simple bowls and jars. Stone tools made from obsidian and flint during the Aneolithic are abundant and reflect a sophisticated technology, as do tools made from antler and bone. A limited number of radiocarbon dates of the fossilized remains of plants and animals reveals that as early as the sixth millennium B.C. people inhabiting the region practiced some agriculture and kept livestock, such as cattle, sheep, goats and pigs. They also supplemented their diets by gathering wild cereals and hunting wild game.

Archaeologists typically use the appearance of a more complex copper-based metallurgical technology to mark the chronological and technological distinction between the Aneolithic and Early Bronze Age. There are other significant cultural and economic attributes, such as the increase in the number of sites, intensified agriculture and pastoralism, and changes in ceramic technology, that distinguish these periods. While about a dozen copper artifacts, such as awls and beads, have been excavated from Aneolithic levels at such sites as Khramis Didi Gora and Gargalar Tepesi in the central Transcaucasia, these objects are not typical of the period. It is not until about 3200 B.C. that a more developed copper-alloy metallurgical technology was established in Transcaucasia. The origins of metallurgy in the region are not well known, but the Caucasus Mountains are rich in polymetallic ores necessary for producing metal objects, especially bronze. It is likely that metallurgical technology was adopted from regions outside Transcaucasia, such as northern Mesopotamia or, more likely, the Balkans and areas along the Black Sea, where earlier archaeological evidence of metal production appears. During the early stages of the Bronze Age, metal objects were typically manufactured from a combination of copper and arsenic. The deliberate addition of small amounts of arsenic to copper can make the final object, such as a dagger or a bracelet, stronger than if it were made from copper alone.

While the adoption of metallurgy had a profound effect on the regional economy of Transcaucasia at the beginning of the Bronze Age, there are other significant economic and technological changes evident in the archaeological record as well. The practice of agriculture and pastoralism was intensified during this period. At least six varieties of wild wheat are known to be indigenous to Transcaucasia, although it is likely that the practice of agriculture was introduced from territories to the west and south in Anatolia. Rain-fed agriculture could have been practiced on the central and southern Caucasus plains, where tributary-fed valleys would have been fertile enough to support an agricultural economy. Irrigation would have been required in the eastern region of Azerbaijan, where more desertlike conditions are prevalent; conversely, drainage would have posed a problem in the semitropical Colchis region of Georgia along the Black Sea.

Because of Transcaucasia's ecological diversity, however, it is impossible to define a single economic base that characterizes the entire region during the Early Bronze Age. Pastoralism, whether seasonal or classic nomadism, was certainly a significant component of the economy. Archaeologists have yet to decipher just how prevalent the practice of pastoralism was during the Early Bronze Age and in what manner this way of life coalesced with agriculturally oriented Kura-Araxes people. Still, archaeological evidence in the form of settlement patterns, where sites reveal only single-occupation levels, faunal remains, and portable hearth stands, supports the concept that pastoralism was practiced to some degree.

The earliest Kura-Araxes settlements may indicate a semi-nomadic lifestyle because many of the sites have only single levels of occupation. This suggests that sites were used for a period of time and then abandoned; they do not appear to have been occupied for long periods, which would have necessitated rebuilding of houses and storage facilities. This evidence may reflect seasonal or short-term occupation. Some of the material culture, such as elaborate, yet portable hearth stands, also may be an indication of impermanence (fig. 1).

These conditions are not universal for all Kura-Araxes sites, however. There are many sites, such as Karnut and Shengavit in Armenia, where the houses are constructed from tuff, a local volcanic stone. The investment required to build a home from stone (rather than principally from mud) indicates that the inhabitants may have intended to reside for longer periods of time in a single location. Nonetheless, there is evidence to suggest that the settlements with more deeply stratified layers, reflecting longer periods of occupation, are found mainly in the areas that may have been better suited for agricultural and year-round occupation. Those Kura-Araxes settlements with shallow deposits that appear to reflect seasonal or short-term occupation generally are located instead in areas where the land was better suited for pasturing animals on a seasonal basis. The relationship between the relative degree of permanence among Kura-Araxes settlements in Transcaucasia and zones of ecological diversity in the region remains to be fully investigated.

What clearly appears to be a hallmark of the Early Bronze Age in Transcaucasia, however, is the establishment of many settlements where none previously existed. Rectilinear annexes on the circular dwellings become more common after the first stage of the Early Bronze Age (up to 2800 B.C.). The subsequent addition of rectangular structures has been interpreted, using ethnographic parallels, to suggest a general shift in the economy from one based on nomadism to one that is possibly more sedentary and probably more agriculturally based.

Archaeologists frequently rely on the presence or absence of different types of ceramics at archaeological sites to characterize archaeological cultures, interaction among cultures, and the relative chronological periodization of sites. Kura-Araxes ceramics are unique and very distinctive among contemporary pottery types found in Europe and the Near East. The Early Bronze Age pottery of Transcaucasia is handmade, highly burnished, and red-black or brown-black in color. Vessel forms range in size and shape, but typical forms include carinated bowls and jars with cylindrical necks and flared rims. The Kura-Araxes ceramics from the first two phases of the Early Bronze Age (up to 2500 B.C.) occasionally are decorated with incised lines. Ceramics of the later phase of the Early Bronze Age (2500–2200 B.C.) are more consistently brown-black or red-black in color, extremely highly burnished so as to resemble a metal surface, and occasionally decorated in relief on the exterior surface, with coils of applied clay in the shape of spirals and geometric designs.

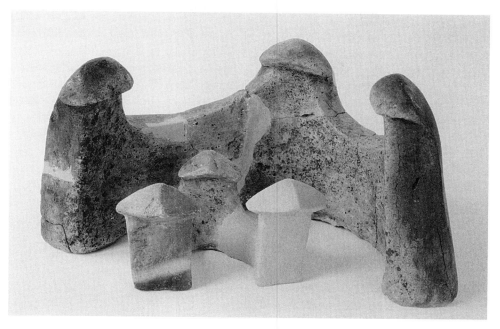

Fig. 1. Two Early Bronze Age portable hearth stands excavated from Sös Höyük in eastern Turkey. Hearth stands such as these examples are characteristic artifacts of early Transcaucasian culture and sometimes also occur in anthropomorphic or zoomorphic forms. COURTESY OF ANTONIO SAGONA. REPRODUCED BY PERMISSION.

Kura-Araxes ceramics have been found across a broad region extending beyond the traditional borders of Transcaucasia well into Iran, northern Mesopotamia, and as far south as Syria and in Palestine, where it is called Khirbet Kerak ware. The expansive presence of this distinctive Kura-Araxes ceramics type across the greater Near East is indicative of the region's contacts with surrounding territories. The economic forces driving the interregional contacts are not well understood, but they may have been connected to numerous complex factors, such as the seasonal migrations of small populations of nomadic pastoralists, the development of metallurgical technology, and an increasing demand for bronze artifacts and expertise in metal technology.

While archaeologists have yet to interpret fully the social and economic relationships between Transcaucasia and its surrounding territories, the discovery of a "royal" tomb at Arslantepe in the Malatya plain of eastern Anatolia reveals a far more complex picture than was recognized previously. Arslantepe was a major urban settlement of the region during the fourth and third millennia B.C., and finds from this site show significant connections with southern and northern Mesopotamia (modern Iraq) as well as Transcaucasia. Discovered in 1996 by a team of Italian archaeologists, the remarkable finds excavated within the "royal" tomb, which dates to 3000–2800 B.C., show a notable influence by bearers of both early Transcaucasia Kura-Araxes and Mesopotamian cultures.

Within the tomb, constructed in a cist form characteristic of some Early Bronze Age Transcaucasian burials, were found numerous Kura-Araxes vessels as well as ceramic types typical of the local tradition. In addition, four juveniles, believed to have been sacrificed, were discovered in the upper portion of the burial, and a single male interred with an extremely rich assortment of metal objects was found within the tomb's central chamber. The metal objects (sixty-four in number) offer the most telling evidence of Transcaucasian influence during this period. These artifacts (jewelry such as a diadem, or headband; spiral rings; and armbands made from silver and silver-copper) are typologically very similar to objects found in Georgia. In addition, many weapons in the tomb, such as bronze spearheads with silver inlay, show clear connections in their metallurgical composition and typology with contemporary Transcaucasian examples.

The finds from the Arslantepe "royal" tomb and the widespread appearance of red-black, burnished Kura-Araxes ceramics suggest that the bearers of the Kura-Araxes culture had far-reaching influence across a wide region during the Early Bronze Age. The command of metallurgical technology as well as the abundance of ores that existed in the Caucasus Mountains, along with the movements of nomadic animal herders from Transcaucasia, may have influenced the economic, political, and social developments in highly significant ways across the Near East.

THE END OF THE EARLY BRONZE AGE

At the end of the Early Bronze Age in Transcaucasia, around 2200 B.C., there was a pronounced change in the archaeological record. Most of the Kura-Araxes sites appear to have been abandoned, and the Middle Bronze Age is known primarily through rich and elaborately constructed *kurgan* burials, of the same type that inspired antiquarians in the early twentieth century to investigate the prehistory of the region. Transportation bears a previously unseen significance at the end of the Early Bronze Age. The domestication of the horse, which probably was introduced from the Russian grassland steppe, had a profound impact on the mobility of Middle Bronze Age peoples, and two-wheeled wagons appeared for the first time in Middle Bronze Age *kurgans*. No simple archaeological interpretation exists to explain the drastic shift of settlement patterns from the end of the Early Bronze into the Middle Bronze Age. A variety of explanations seems possible.

One possibility is that the environment may have become unsuitable to support agriculture, thus forcing or merely encouraging a more nomadic or pastoral-based economy. Another possibility is that dramatic social and political changes in surrounding territories, such as Anatolia and the northern Caucasus, possibly driven by competition for resources and the emergence of incipient state-level political organizations, may have forced changes in how people made a living, settled, stored wealth, and buried their dead. Based on the present evidence, however, such a determination is not made simply, and the result of such a shift is dramatically and swiftly apparent in the material record throughout the Caucasus at the end of the Early Bronze Age.

Ongoing excavations in Transcaucasia continue to provide evidence to further archaeologists' understanding of the prehistory of the region. The finds at Arslantepe as well as the increasing collaboration among Georgian, Armenian, Azerbaijani, and western archaeologists are changing how archaeologists understand the Early Bronze Age of Transcaucasia. The archaeological picture is far more complex than previously was understood. The explosion in the number of settlements, the development of metallurgical technology, the growing reliance on economies of pastoralism and agriculture, and interregional interaction are all component factors in the development of increasingly complex social and political structures during the Early Bronze Age.

See also **Early Metallurgy in Southeastern Europe** (*vol. 1, part 4*); **Iron Age Caucasia** (*vol. 2, part 6*).

BIBLIOGRAPHY

Chernykh, E. N. *Ancient Metallurgy in the USSR*. Translated by Sarah Wright. New Studies in Archaeology. Cambridge, U.K., and New York: Cambridge University Press, 1992.

Frangipane, M. "The Late Chalcolithic/EB I Sequence at Arslantepe: Chronological and Cultural Remarks from a Frontier Site." In *Chronologies des pays du Caucase et de l'Euphrate aux IVe–IIIe millenaires*. Edited by Catherine Marro and Harald Hauptmann, pp. 439–471. Paris: Institute Français d'Étude Anatoliennes d'Istanbul, 2000.

Frangipane, M., et al. "New Symbols of a New Power in a 'Royal' Tomb from 3000 BC Arslantepe, Malatya (Turkey)." *Paléorient* 27, no. 2 (2001): 105–139.

Kavtaradze, Georgi Leon. "The Importance of Metallurgical Data for the Formation of a Central Transcaucasian Chronology." In *The Beginnings of Metallurgy*. Edited by Andreas Hauptmann, Ernst Pernicka, Thilo Rehren, and Ünsal Yalçin, pp. 67–101. Bochum, Germany: Deutsches Bergbau-Museum, 1999.

Kiguradze, Tamaz. "The Chalcolithic–Early Bronze Age Transition in the Eastern Caucasus." In *Chronologies des pays du Caucase et de l'Euphrate aux IVe–IIIe millenaires*. Edited by Catherine Marro and Harald Hauptmann, pp. 321–328. Paris: Institut Français Étude Anatoliennes d'Istanbul, 2000.

———. *Neolithische Siedlungen von Kvemo-Kartli, Georgien*. Munich, Germany: C. H. Beck Verlag, 1986.

Kohl, P. L. "Nationalism, Politics, and the Practice of Archaeology in Transcaucasia." *Journal of European Archaeology* 2 (1993): 179–186.

————. "The Transcaucasian 'Periphery' in the Bronze Age: A Preliminary Formulation." In *Resources, Power, and Interregional Interaction*. Edited by Edward Schortman and Patricia A. Urban, pp. 117–137. New York: Plenum Press, 1992.

Kushnareva, Kariné K. *The Southern Caucasus in Prehistory: Stages of Cultural and Socioeconomic Development from the Eighth to the Second Millennium B.C.* Translated by H. N. Michael. Philadelphia: University of Pennsylvania, University Museum, 1997.

Kushnareva, Kariné K., and T. N. Chubinishvili. *Drevnie kultury yuzhnogo Kavkaza* [Ancient cultures of the southern Caucasus]. Leningrad, Russia: n.p., 1970.

Rothman, Mitchell S. "Ripples in the Stream: Transcaucasia-Anatolian Interaction in the Murat/Euphrates Basin at the Beginning of the Third Millennium B.C." In *Archaeology in the Borderlands: Investigations in Caucasia and Beyond*. Edited by Adam T. Smith and Karen Rubinson. Los Angeles: Cotsen Institute of Archaeology Publications, 2003.

Sagona, Antonio. "Settlement and Society in Late Prehistoric Trans-Caucasus." In *Between the Rivers and Over the Mountains*. Edited by Alba Palmieri and M. Frangipane, pp. 453–474. Rome: Università di Rome "La Sapienza," 1993.

LAURA A. TEDESCO

BRONZE AGE CYPRUS

By the beginning of the Bronze Age, about 3000 B.C., most Mediterranean islands, large or small, had been settled. People were producing their own food and living in the same community year-round. About the same time, Mediterranean societies were becoming increasingly complex, which is evident from such factors as population growth, the production of food surpluses, the use of storage facilities, involvement in long-distance trade relationships, and the establishment of territorial boundaries. These developments occurred because special-interest groups, or possibly even a single local leader, came to control access to various items increasingly in widespread demand on the Mediterranean islands and in the surrounding countries: raw materials (copper, gold, silver, tin), precious goods (ivory, alabaster, faience, lapis lazuli, and other precious or semiprecious stones), and a range of more perishable goods lost to the archaeological record. Intricate and interconnected economic systems also came into operation at this time: from the Levantine coast in the east; through Cyprus and western Anatolia to the Aegean, Italy, and Sardinia; and as far west as Spain. By the end of the third millennium B.C., the trade in metals had become a key factor in promoting social change, and copper from Cyprus was an important component of this Mediterranean interaction sphere.

Cyprus, the third largest island in the Mediterranean (9,251 square kilometers), lies in its northeast corner. The mainland of Syria is approximately 100 kilometers east of Cyprus, that of Turkey about 70 kilometers north, while Egypt lies about 400 ki-

lometers south. The boundary of the Aegean world, at the island of Rhodes, is situated about 500 kilometers west. Archaeological evidence demonstrates that Cyprus increasingly developed trade links and other social contacts with these areas during the course of the Bronze Age. Several important Late Bronze Age (c. 1600–1200 B.C.) Cypriot sites with imported goods—Enkomi, Hala Sultan Tekke, Maroni, and Kition (fig. 1)—had inner harbors situated on large bays or at river mouths, all of which are now silted in or dried up. The material culture of Bronze Age Cyprus—from pottery to seals, from ornate buildings to burial chambers, from copper awls to bronze cauldrons—is among the best known and widely published of any island culture in the Mediterranean.

CYPRUS: THE CULTURAL SEQUENCE C. 2500–1700 B.C.

Toward the end of the fourth millennium B.C., certain innovations such as the cart and the plow, a variety of domesticated animals and their "secondary products" (e.g., wool, leather, and milk), and evidence for the widespread herding of these animals (pastoralism) had appeared in parts of Europe and the Mediterranean. By adopting all or even some of these technological and cultural innovations, people were able to maximize agricultural production and thus ensure a reliable subsistence base. These new technologies represent a phenomenon known as the "Secondary Products Revolution." Along with the emergence of regional trade systems, this revolution brought about changes in the way that people thought about things, and also brought an in-

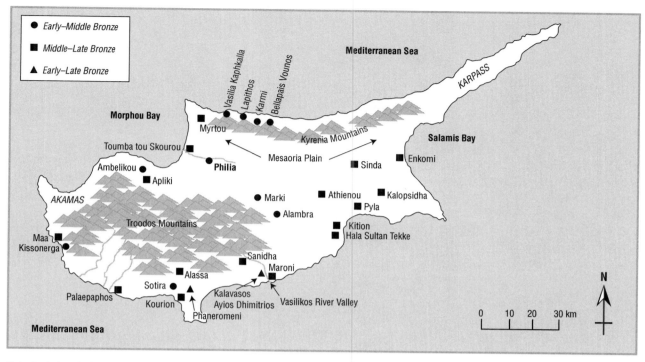

Selected sites in Bronze Age Cyprus. ADAPTED FROM KNAPP 1994.

creased capacity for societies to process and transfer information, ideas, and material goods.

Although such innovations had been adopted in the Levant and the Aegean during the third millennium B.C., initially they seem to have bypassed Cyprus, perhaps as a result of its insularity. Toward the end of the Chalcolithic period (about 2800–2500 B.C. on Cyprus), however, the introduction of the plow and the reappearance of cattle in large numbers demonstrate that the island also had been touched by this Secondary Products Revolution. Excavations at several sites on Cyprus since the 1980s have provided important new evidence for this major economic transformation, evidence that also has helped archaeologists to understand better the transition to the Bronze Age.

The Cypriot archaeological record of this early stage in the Bronze Age also reveals an increased number of ground stone tools used in agricultural production and a growing dependence on domesticated animals at the expense of hunted animals such as deer. This expansion in the agricultural and pastoral sectors of the economy, in turn, served to underpin a key industrial development: the mining and production of copper from Cyprus's abundant ore

deposits. Although the use of copper becomes evident at several sites on Cyprus during the third and especially the early second millennium B.C., expertise in metallurgical technology is best demonstrated by the quality and quantity of metal products found in several tomb deposits along or near the north coast (e.g., Lapithos, Bellapais Vounos, Vasilia Kaphkalla). Almost all foreign imports into Cyprus—pottery, metal implements, stone vessels, and faience goods from the Levant, Egypt, and the Aegean—also were recovered from these north coast sites. Together, the native metalwork and the imports suggest something far beyond local production for local consumption: external demand for Cypriot copper also must have been increasing at this time. Indeed, nineteenth century B.C. cuneiform records from Mari on the Euphrates River in Syria make the earliest reference to copper from "Alashiya," a place-name that virtually all archaeologists and ancient historians now accept as the Bronze Age equivalent of "Cyprus."

Despite the limited evidence for Cypriot overseas contacts during the period between about 3000–2000 B.C., various states and kingdoms in the eastern Mediterranean maintained a high level of demand for imports such as the cedars of Lebanon

Fig. 1. An aerial overview of the excavations at the Late Bronze Age harbor site of Kition, Cyprus. DEPARTMENT OF ANTIQUITIES, CYPRUS. REPRODUCED BY PERMISSION.

or the copper of Cyprus. Because tin was the metal of choice to alloy with copper in order to manufacture bronze, long-distance trade was stimulated even further. Silver produced in the Cycladic islands of the Aegean also became an important commodity, and the products of early Aegean metallurgists helped to expand trade rapidly throughout the eastern Mediterranean. Other goods traded at this time in the Aegean and eastern Mediterranean included wine, olive oil, precious metals, and pottery. Technological innovations of the third millennium B.C., such as the longboat and sail, facilitated the bulk transport of raw materials or manufactured goods on an unprecedented scale. A multitude of harbors and the diversity of trading routes further promoted a budding sense of internationalism.

On Cyprus, the increased size, number, and spread of settlements throughout the centuries between about 2500–1700 B.C. indicate a successful adaptation to environmental constraints imposed by an island ecosystem. The limited evidence for external contacts up to about 1700 B.C. suggests that subsistence needs were met and social networks maintained within the island system. Perhaps because innovations associated with the Secondary Products Revolution reduced the amount of time that had to be devoted to subsistence needs, some people began to specialize in producing goods such as woolens and textiles, stone figurines, shell beads, gaming stones, and a variety of metal tools and implements. Although a large part of the published archaeological data from this period comes from burials, excavations at sites such as Kissonerga-Mosphilia, Sotira-Kaminoudhia, Marki-Alonia, and Alambra-Mouttes are changing that picture dramatically. As a result we are better able to understand issues of chronology, cultural continuity and discontinuity, foreign contacts, and all the developing signs of a more complex social system.

To summarize the earliest phases of the Bronze Age on Cyprus, the Secondary Products Revolution enabled people to utilize their animals more fully and effectively. One result was that more land became available, and some people were able to exploit these economic developments, eventually to establish themselves in positions of social if not political power. The increase in the number and size of sites during the third millennium B.C. indicates population increase; at the same time, some settlements began to show marked differentiation from others. In turn, these developments were linked directly to the increased production of metals and the emergence and expansion of long-distance trade, which was closely associated with the acquisition of imported luxury or prestige goods. Although Cyprus never developed the type of palaces and palatial economies that came to typify Levantine city-states or Aegean citadels, somebody on the island must have managed the increasingly specialized levels of production and overseen the subsistence needs of those specialists who were producing surplus goods and metals for trade. During the third and early second millennia B.C., major social changes took place on Cyprus, when trade and contact with external groups helped to overcome a deep-seated resistance

to social and economic stratification. At the same time, this was a transitional era, when indigenous elites seized the opportunity to formalize, legitimize, and integrate the copper industry that would become so critical in all of the social, politico-economic, and urban developments of the later Middle and Late Bronze Ages.

CYPRUS: THE CULTURAL SEQUENCE C. 1700–1100 B.C.

Throughout the course of the second millennium B.C., states and kingdoms in the Levant and the Aegean, as well as on Cyprus, became entangled in the production, trade, and consumption of utilitarian and luxury goods as well as a range of organic items (e.g., olive oil, wine, honey, spices). Port cities and palatial centers took part in this lucrative international trade and found their political positions enhanced as a result. Some of the best-known trading centers involved were Ugarit (Syria), Enkomi and Hala Sultan Tekke (Cyprus), Tell el-'Ajjul and Tel Nami (Israel), Troy (Anatolia), Kommos (Crete), and Mycenae and Pylos (mainland Greece). Cypriot and Aegean pottery has been recovered everywhere from the southern Levant and Egypt to Sicily and Sardinia; Aegean (Mycenaean) pottery has even been found in Spain. Copper oxhide ingots, which most likely served as a medium for exchange during the Late Bronze Age (c. 1600–1200 B.C.), have been recovered in contexts stretching from the Black Sea and Babylonia to Sardinia.

Since the early 1990s, a number of remarkable finds have helped to extend and refine our understanding of Mediterranean trading systems. Two deserve special mention: The first is the rich and diverse cargo—including Cypriot, Aegean, Egyptian, and Levantine goods—of a Late Bronze Age shipwreck found at Uluburun on the southern coast of Turkey. The second is the fragmentary wall paintings from a Middle Bronze Age palace in Israel (Tel Kabri) and from a Middle to Late Bronze Age palace in the eastern Nile Delta (Tell ed Dab'a), both of which reveal iconographic and design elements common throughout the eastern Mediterranean world. All these goods demonstrate the mobilization of workers and the deployment of craft specialists in a wide-reaching communication system that linked traded goods, ideology, iconography, and sociopolitical status.

To understand how and why Mediterranean peoples became involved in these production and trade systems, it is necessary to realize that trade is a form of social communication, and social resources are as important as natural ones. All goods of lasting value, including prestige or luxury items, are important not only in amassing wealth but also in building social status and creating social or economic alliances. An exceptionally diverse and abundant archaeological record shows clearly that seaborne trade throughout the Late Bronze Age Aegean and eastern Mediterranean had many dimensions: complex in nature and diverse in structure, it encompassed both state-dominated and entrepreneurial aspects. Within the Bronze Age Mediterranean, there were so many different kinds of resources and unique types of goods available, and so many different ways to transport them, that no single overarching system ever prevailed.

On Cyprus itself, several striking changes appear in the archaeological record of the late Middle to Late Bronze Ages (c. 1700–1100 B.C.): (1) urban centers with public and ceremonial architecture ("temples") appear throughout the island; (2) burial practices reveal clear distinctions in social status (e.g., three females found in Tomb 11 at Ayios Dhimitrios were interred with various gold items totaling nearly one pound in weight); (3) writing ("Cypro-Minoan"), on clay tablets, first appears; (4) copper production and export intensified as extensive regional and long-distance trade developed; (5) newly built fortifications and a relative increase in the number of weapons found indicate other kinds of change in Cypriot society. This dramatic trajectory of development and change reveals the island's transformation from a somewhat isolated, village-oriented culture into an international, urban-centered, and highly complex society. The successful exploitation of mineral resources and production of agricultural surpluses meant that political authority, at least initially, had to be centralized. Eventually, the intensified production and trade of copper catapulted Cyprus into the role of the most important purveyor of this metal in the Mediterranean region, a situation that continued at least until the fall of the Roman Empire, some two thousand years later. The name Cyprus, after all, is directly related to the Latin word for copper—*cuprum*.

Newly built port cities (e.g., Hala Sultan Tekke, Maroni, Kition) specialized in trade and prospered as their populations grew. Cuneiform letters sent from "Alashiya" (Cyprus) to the Egyptian pharaoh show that the king of Cyprus wielded considerable authority over copper production and trade. Two cuneiform documents from Ugarit in Syria demonstrate that high-level, diplomatic trade between Cyprus and the Levant continued into the late thirteenth century B.C. Like the dynasts of contemporary western Asia, the Cypriot ruler used state agents to conduct foreign trade. All these documentary records reveal the organizational efficiency, shipping capacity and product diversity that characterized this highly specialized, well-coordinated political and economic system. One of the letters from Ugarit, for example, which states that copper was sent from Cyprus to Ugarit as a "greeting gift," exemplifies a royal correspondence deeply concerned with trade emissaries, the exchange of various goods, and the commercial regulations that kept the entire system functioning.

In tandem with these specialized developments in urbanization, metallurgical production, and international trade, Cyprus's mixed farming economy also underwent some changes. There is evidence, for example, of extensive centralized storage facilities at the site of Ayios Dhimitrios: some fifty massive *pithoi*, or terra cotta storage jars, would have held up to 50,000 kilos of olive oil. The faunal record is less dramatic, but it seems clear that animal exploitation centered on sheep and goats, although cattle remains have been recovered from several sites. This configuration may reflect the dietary preferences of social elites. Overall, this economic system had to be adequately flexible to feed and support the specialists who made up such a key component of the urban economy. One of the more interesting results of the excavation of the Uluburun shipwreck is the appearance of organic goods—coriander, caper, safflower, fig, and pomegranite seeds; olive pits; cereal grains; almond shells; terebinth resin—part of a usually invisible component of trade in resins, oils, fibers, wine, and other foodstuffs. Demand for such goods certainly would have stimulated Cyprus's subsistence economy.

During the three centuries between about 1500–1200 B.C., the archaeological record of Cyprus and the eastern Mediterranean reveals a quantum leap in the production and trade of goods such as Cypriot and Aegean pottery; copper oxhide ingots and metal artifacts; glass products; prestige goods such as ivory, gold, amber, and faience; and various organic goods. Trade goods fluctuated as new opportunities or distinctive products became available. Not only did the burgeoning international system of exchange bring prestige goods to ruling elites, it also brought raw materials to craftspeople and food supplies and basic products to rural peasants and producers. Even if powerful elites controlled local economies, the dynamics of production, distribution, and consumption freed up resources for individual activities within a more structured political economy.

Involvement in trade thus had the capacity to transform social groups, change economic motivations, or inspire individual actions. What had begun as a limited trade in high-value, low-bulk luxury goods (e.g., precious metals in the form of jewelry, semiprecious stones, ivory handicrafts) expanded over time to incorporate the bulk exchange of "nonconvertible" commodities (storage jars, textiles, glass) that were locally produced for export on an interregional scale. The real determinants of economic power and political status, however, were convertible goods, especially metals and the copper oxhide ingots; these were subject to tight control by powerful rulers and may have been traded exclusively through formal gift exchange. Another significant incentive in Middle to Late Bronze Age Mediterranean trade was the desire by elites, especially newly formed elites, to acquire exotic goods from a distance. One of the ways that elites and rulers legitimized their position and consolidated their power was to import luxury goods that could only have been acquired through the production of other goods—whether raw materials (e.g., metal, wood, ivory, ebony) or finished products (e.g., bronzes, textiles, jewelry, decorated chests).

THE END OF THE BRONZE AGE: CYPRUS AND BEYOND

The century between about 1250–1150 B.C. was characterized by a bewildering array of site destructions and demographic movements (involving in part diverse Mediterranean peoples collectively known as the "Sea Peoples") that ended the cooperative and lucrative international relations of the Middle to Late Bronze Ages in the Mediterranean. The "Sea Peoples," and others like them, were more a symptom than a cause of the widespread decline. Behind the widespread movement of peoples—described on Egyptian monumental records and alluded to in the texts of cuneiform clay tablets—was a proliferation of human displacement and ethnic intermixing that spelled the end of an international era. In each country, stable groups like farmers and minor craftspeople remained in place, with their horizons narrowed but subsistence systems still intact.

On Cyprus, if expanding trade relations had once helped to promote social fusion, the natural circumscription of the island and the growing scarcity of land and raw materials (the result of extensive plow agriculture and copper exploitation) eventually may have led to social division and intra-island competition among various factions. The overall political and economic system nonetheless proved to be so stable that the widespread collapse of other states and trading networks in the Mediterranean seem to have had limited effects on Cyprus. Some of the most important developments in early iron technology took place on Cyprus at this very time. While some agricultural and mining or pottery-producing villages were disrupted or abandoned, the major coastal sites of Enkomi, Kition, and Palaepaphos survived the destruction and displacement that occurred elsewhere; they perhaps became new centers of authority, displacing smaller regional centers and managing new Cypriot contacts that were emerging overseas. New maritime trading routes opened to Crete in the Aegean and Sardinia in the central Mediterranean, in the quest for alternative metal supplies or for other resources in demand. As incoming Aegean and Levantine peoples—the latest "colonists" of the island—became acculturated to the Cypriot population, copper production and commercial enterprise seem to have been revitalized, at least in the short term. By 1100 B.C., however, the settlement patterns and political organization that had characterized the Late Bronze Age disappeared, as new social and economic structures dictated the establishment of new population and power centers on Iron Age Cyprus. These new political configurations heralded the rise of Cyprus's early historical kingdoms and the island's tactical and commercial adjustments to the new Age of Iron.

See also **Copper Age Cyprus** (*vol. 1, part 4*).

BIBLIOGRAPHY

Bietak, Manfred. *Avaris: The Capital of the Hyksos. Recent Excavations at Tell el'Dab'a*. London: British Museum Press, 1996.

Broodbank, Cyprian. *An Island Archaeology of the Early Cyclades*. Cambridge, U.K.: Cambridge University Press, 2000.

Gale, Noël H., ed. *Bronze Age Trade in the Mediterranean*. Studies in Mediterranean Archaeology, no. 90. Göteborg, Sweden: P. Åströms Förlag, 1991.

Haldane, Cheryl. "Direct Evidence for Organic Cargoes in the Late Bronze Age." *World Archaeology* 24, no. 3 (1993): 348–360.

Karageorghis, Vassos. *Cyprus: From the Stone Age to the Romans*. London: Thames and Hudson, 1982. (This volume is now quite out of date, yet it still provides the only comprehensive, well-illustrated overview of the archaeology of Cyprus.)

Knapp, A. Bernard. "Archaeology, Science-Based Archaeology, and the Mediterranean Bronze Age Metals Trade." *European Journal of Archaeology* 3, no. 1 (2000): 31–56.

———. "Reading the Sites: Prehistoric Bronze Age Settlements on Cyprus." *Bulletin of the American Schools of Oriental Research* 313 (February 1999): 75–86. (A review article that provides a broad overview of two Early-Middle Bronze Age settlement excavations.)

——— (with Steve O. Held and Sturt W. Manning). "The Prehistory of Cyprus: Problems and Prospects." *Journal of World Prehistory* 8, no. 4 (1994): 377–452.

———. "Spice, Drugs, Grain, and Grog: Organic Goods in Bronze Age Eastern Mediterranean Trade." In *Bronze Age Trade in the Mediterranean*. Edited by Noël H. Gale, pp. 21–68. Studies in Mediterranean Archaeology, no. 90. Göteborg, Sweden: P. Åströms Förlag, 1991.

———. "Entrepreneurship, Ethnicity, Exchange: Mediterranean Inter-Island Relations in the Late Bronze Age." *Annual of the British School at Athens* 85 (1990): 115–153.

———. "Production, Location, and Integration in Bronze Age Cyprus." *Current Anthropology* 31, no. 2 (1990): 147–176.

———, ed. *Near Eastern and Aegean Texts from the Third to the First Millennia B.C.* Sources for the History of Cyprus, no. 2. Altamont, N.Y.: Greece and Cyprus Research Center, 1996.

Knapp, A. Bernard, and John F. Cherry. *Provenance Studies and Bronze Age Cyprus: Production, Exchange, and Politico-Economic Change*. Monographs in World Archaeology, no. 21. Madison, Wis.: Prehistory Press,

1994. (This scientifically based study provides the most comprehensive overview available on "provenance" [origins] on Cypriot pottery, metals, and oxhide ingots, together with a lengthy discussion of Bronze Age trade.)

Manning, Sturt W. "Prestige, Distinction, and Competition: The Anatomy of Socio Economic Complexity in Fourth to Second Millennium B.C.E. Cyprus." *Bulletin of American Schools of Oriental Research* (1993) 292: 35–58.

Muhly, James D. "The Nature of Trade in the Late Bronze Age Eastern Mediterranean: The Organization of the Metals Trade and the Role of Cyprus." In *Early Metallurgy in Cyprus, 4000–500 B.C.* Edited by James D. Muhly, Robert Maddin, and Vassos Karageorghis, pp. 251–266. Nicosia: Pierides Foundation, 1982.

Niemeier Wolf-Dietrich, and Barbara Niemeier. "Minoan Frescoes in the Eastern Mediterranean." In *The Aegean and the Orient in the Second Millennium*. Edited by Eric H. Cline and Diane Harris-Cline, pp. 281–289. Aegaeum 18. Liège, Belgium: Université de Liège, 1998.

Peltenburg, Edgar J. *Lemba Archaeological Project*. Vol. 2.1A, *Excavations at Kissonerga-Mosphilia, 1979–1992*. Studies in Mediterranean Archaeology 70, no. 2. Göteborg, Sweden: P. Åströms Förlag, 1998.

Pulak, Çemal. "The Uluburun Shipwreck: An Overview." *International Journal of Nautical Archaeology* 27, no. 3 (1998): 188–224. (A specialist report on the results of the world's most famous prehistoric shipwreck.)

Sandars, Nancy K. *The Sea Peoples: Warriors of the Ancient Mediterranean 1250– 1150 B.C.* Rev. ed. London: Thames and Hudson, 1985. (This comprehensive study of the multiple reasons behind, and the many different peoples involved in, the "collapse" of states and economies at the end of the Bronze Age, while somewhat out of date, is for both the general reader and the specialist.)

Sherratt, Andrew G. "Plough and Pastoralism: Aspects of the Secondary Products Revolution." In *Pattern of the Past: Studies in Honour of David Clarke*. Edited by Ian Hodder, Glynn Isaac, and Norman Hammond, pp. 261–305. Cambridge, U.K.: Cambridge University Press, 1981. (One of the earliest studies on the Secondary Products Revolution, this specialized article has had a major, far-reaching impact on the study of European and Mediterranean prehistory.)

Sherratt, Andrew G., and E. Susan Sherratt. "From Luxuries to Commodities: The Nature of Mediterranean Bronze Age Trading Systems." In *Bronze Age Trade in the Mediterranean*. Edited by Noël H. Gale, pp. 351–386. Studies in Mediterranean Archaeology, no. 90. Jonsered, Sweden: P. Åströms Förlag, 1991. (A highly specialized study, one of the best and most comprehensive ever written on Bronze Age trade in the Mediterranean.)

Swiny, Stuart. "From Round House to Duplex: A Reassessment of Prehistoric Bronze Age Cypriot Society." In *Early Society in Cyprus.* Edited by Edgar J. Peltenburg, pp. 14–31. Edinburgh: Edinburgh University Press, 1989.

Swiny, Stuart, George Rapp, and Ellen Herscher, eds. *Sotira Kamminoudhia: An Early Bronze Age Site in Cyprus.* Archaeological Reports, no. 8. Boston: American Schools of Oriental Research, 2002.

A. BERNARD KNAPP

THE MINOAN WORLD

FOLLOWED BY FEATURE ESSAY ON:

In the middle of the second millennium B.C. the island of Crete supported the most complex civilization in Europe. With elaborate palaces and well-developed towns, the Minoan civilization was the equal of many in the Near East and North Africa. With the collapse of this culture in the later part of the millennium, the world was left with faint glimpses of their achievements, limited to a few lines in certain Greek histories, such as that of Thucydides, and the references to Knossos and King Minos in such myths as that of Theseus and the Minotaur.

Modern knowledge of the Minoan people did not develop until the later part of the nineteenth century. Spurred on by the discoveries of Mycenae and Troy made by the German-American excavator Heinrich Schliemann, the British excavator Sir Arthur Evans began his remarkable excavation of the palace of Minos at Knossos. Archaeological work has continued on Crete until the present day, with excavations of palaces, villas, and towns and important archaeological surveys of much of the island. The portrait of this civilization that we can piece together is at the same time impressive and frustrating.

We now understand quite a bit about the architecture, diet, ceramic traditions, and so on of these people. It is not known, however, whether the Minoan world was a single culture with variations (similar to the ethnic distinctions that we observe today) or several cultures throughout the island of Crete, sharing in a common elite tradition. Our understanding of the process of cultural development and change is equally uncertain, mainly the product of conflicting arguments over chronology. Dated primarily through ceramic style, Minoan civilization presents problems when we note that some ceramic styles appear to be the result more of locational than of temporal differences. There is controversy concerning the correlation of the Minoan temporal stages to the eruption of the volcano on the ancient island of Thera (now Santorini) in the later seventeenth century B.C. Our dating could well be incorrect by at least a century. Rather than relying on the ceramic identification of Minoan time periods, it is better to refer to a chronology that focuses on large social developments:

Pre-palatial period: c. 3100/3000 to 1925/1900 B.C.

Proto-palatial period: c. 1925/1900 to 1750/1720 B.C.

Neo-palatial period: c. 1750/1720 to 1490/1470 B.C.

Post-palatial period: c. 1490/1470 to 1075/1050 B.C.

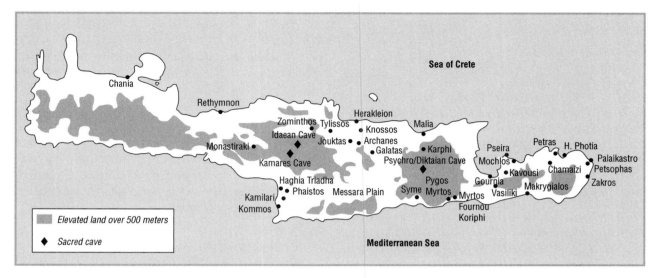

Minoan Crete and selected sites. ADAPTED FROM PREZIOSI AND HITCHCOCK 1999.

FEATURES OF MINOAN SOCIAL DEVELOPMENT

The Neo-palatial period is most commonly considered the zenith of Minoan civilization. At this time there were four large palace centers—Knossos, Malia, Phaistos, and Kato Zakros—as well as large developed towns, such as Gournia, and numerous examples of small isolated farmsteads. Their economic base was a developed agricultural system that utilized wheat, barley, olives, grapes, sheep, goats, and cattle. But just how Minoan complexity fit into this agricultural background is only partially understood.

What we can determine of Minoan social structure derives basically from analysis of the palatial centers. Significant sections of the structure of all the palaces, with the exception of Kato Zakros, were devoted to the storage of large amounts of agricultural supplies. Knossos was by far the largest of the palaces and had the greatest storerooms. Within these rooms were stored massive amounts of olive oil, olives, wheat, and other agricultural items. The presence of these large storerooms gives a glimpse into the probable structure of the Minoan social hierarchy.

The storage and redistribution of agricultural goods are best paralleled in what anthropologists have identified as a social and economic construction in modern societies, the chiefdom. While a direct comparison between these modern social configurations and the ancient Minoans would be misleading, an analysis of just how cultures might use food storage in the development of their social and political structures gives insight into the possible basis for the Minoan political and social order.

Social storage of food often is a measure taken by cultures to moderate the risk of agricultural uncertainty. At times, this storage has been manipulated to afford the armature upon which social and political hierarchy first develops. Such was probably the case with the Minoans. The island is composed of a multitude of microenvironments, rather small isolated areas, that are locked in by topographical features, such as mountains. An important feature of these microenvironments in those times was that each had its own particular reaction to normal interannual fluctuations in rainfall. The result was that Crete often resembled a patchwork of distinct microenvironments with quite different agricultural yields every year throughout the island. Simply put, one microenvironment could have had a bumper crop of wheat while its near neighbors could have been experiencing a serious shortfall in that grain during the same summer.

Social and political hierarchy can develop when a person or a group begins to control agricultural storage within and between these different microenvironments. Often this is seen in the gathering of a certain percentage of the agricultural surplus and ensuring that some of it is redistributed to those people who live in areas with low productivity in a particular year. As one might surmise, therein lies the basis of social indebtedness and the platform for constructing social hierarchy.

The palace of Minos at Knossos best illustrates this economic system. The entire western basement was dedicated to food storage. The rulers of Knossos could either return some food to areas in need or, as can be seen from the plan of the palace, use much of it to support craft specialists, who occupied up to a fourth of the palace, in the production of luxury items for use by the ruling family. This system of centralized redistribution was probably in place throughout the island. Only the palace at Kato Zakros lacks such a distinctive storage capacity.

PRE-PALATIAL DEVELOPMENTS
We know too little about the development of this economic and political system. Our knowledge of Cretan culture before the rise of the palaces is scant, with much of our understanding limited to a few small villages. The most elaborate is Myrtos (c. 2600–2170 B.C.) on the southern coast of Crete. A small village, with up to sixty preserved rooms, Myrtos appears to have been settled by five or six family units, with no identifiable hierarchical relationship. The site was agriculturally based and displayed a range of artifacts, from storage jars to serving dishes. Within each family unit, we have been able identify different types of workrooms, such as kitchens. One unit apparently held a small pottery workshop.

Several common pottery types, most notably, a long-necked, almost bird-shaped teapot, were shared among these Pre-palatial communities, indicating a commonality of design and perhaps function. Regional differences, however, can be seen in distinct variations in tomb types. In the north they were burying the dead in "house tombs," rectangular structures subdivided into different spaces for burial. In the south, specifically the Messara, the common form of burial was the *tholos,* or circular tomb, which presumably was roofed. In general, it appears that both of these tomb types were collective burials, with the family unit or even a larger corporate group using individual tombs. Certain tombs appear to have been used for a millennium, highlighting their importance in the social construction of early Minoan civilization. With the ever increasing complexity of the later early Minoan and middle Minoan periods came an elaboration of tombs, with

an emphasis on ancestry in the struggle to obtain and maintain social hierarchy.

Toward the end of the early Minoan period we see noticeable changes in Minoan culture. In addition to the emphasis on the importance of ancestry, there was a dramatic change in pottery types. The introduction of "Kamares ware," a new light-on-dark style of pottery, as well as the barbotine pottery style took place at this point of transition, marking social change, with a possible emphasis on the new social contexts—both political and religious—where these new pottery types were being used.

PROTO-PALATIAL AND NEO-PALATIAL PERIODS
The Proto-palatial and Neo-palatial periods combine to make the era of the construction of the major palaces of Minoan Crete. Knossos (the largest), Malia, and Phaistos were built shortly after the beginning of the second millennium, in the Proto-palatial period. These sites were to be rebuilt about three hundred years later, in the Neo-palatial period, along with the new construction of the easternmost major palace at Kato Zakros. These locales were the residences of Minoan elites or rulers, but other sites, such as the villa at Hagia Triadha, must equally have been homes to the leading families of Minoan Crete. During this period large towns, such as Gournia, developed around major elite residences. Sanctuaries on mountain peaks also make their appearance at this time.

The period was truly a high point in Minoan architecture. The palaces were often several stories high; that at Knossos, for example, probably was four stories in its domestic quarter. Minoan architects and craftsmen showed an attention to fine architectural detail in wall construction and a keen sense of overall design in layout and technical construction. Light wells were used with confidence to open up the interiors of several palaces. Monumentality was added by the use of grand staircases and imposing walls. Large courts were integrated into the rhythm of palatial construction. Minoans even had plumbing in the palaces and other elite residences.

Among the palaces there is a striking similarity in design and construction, which must have mirrored the similar lifestyles of most of the Minoan aristocracy. The likenesses are remarkable and, except for some differences at Kato Zakros, which was the latest of the palaces, are common features at all the sites. Perhaps the most impressive feature of all the palaces is the central court, a large, rectangular plaza, around which the other sections of the palaces were arranged. The east side of the central court appears to have had a religious character, as evidenced by cult rooms and pillar crypts (sacred rooms with recessed floors and a central post) at Knossos and Malia and the famous throne room—actually a religious installation—at Knossos. As mentioned, agricultural storage was important to the Minoan ruling power, and all the palaces, except Kato Zakros (which might have had storage structures in the form of outlying buildings), had large storage rooms. At Knossos, Malia, and Phaistos these storerooms lie on the ground floor in the wing just to the west of the central court. On the floor above these rooms were the public rooms, or *piano nobile*. These were large reception rooms, perhaps used for public ceremonies.

Each of the four palaces also had a large banquet hall, located on the upper floor, probably to take in a breeze. The hall was not necessarily attached to the public rooms and might have been meant for a more private gathering of elites for entertaining and meals. Residential quarters have been clearly identified at Knossos, Malia, and Phaistos. As we might expect in the layout of private quarters, there is a correspondence in the features of these rooms among similar groups in the same culture. The residential arrangement can be found in a large number of elaborate houses, not just the palaces. That at Knossos is the most elaborate, but it shows the overall regularity of design. Residential space there was composed of a long, triple-divided hall, consisting of a light well, an anteroom, and a back chamber. Running off this hall was access to a religious room, the lustral basin, and to toilet facilities. Within the triple-divided hall, folding doors and upper windows in the wall between the anteroom and the back chamber regulated the light and air coming from the light well.

The palaces themselves were decorated throughout with elaborate frescoes. Favorite themes in the wall paintings were scenes from nature, religious gatherings, palace or community events, and mythological landscapes. The most intricate pottery was used, and possibly manufac-

tured, in the palaces. Several important examples show serving cups, amphorae (large standing containers for oils and water), stirrup jars for perfumed oil, and *pithoi* (storage vessels), decorated with detailed floral designs, geometric patterns, and marine creatures. In addition to this pottery, the palaces also used carved stone bowls, ritual drinking cups (*rhyta*) of carved stone and gold, and cut rock crystal ornaments.

An interesting point in relation to the palaces is the obvious lack of fortifications. We know that the Minoans were not without a military force, as seen in the military themes of their works of art and the chieftain's cup. But we are at a loss to explain why there was no need to fortify the different settlements. It may well have been that Knossos, the largest of the palaces, exercised control of the military, but reference to societies with such political centrality shows that even the subordinate settlements had fortifications. It may well have been that military campaigns on Crete were limited to raiding, which often took place without elaborate fortifications.

Little is known concerning how the common Minoan lived. Perhaps the best-preserved site is that of Gournia. There a relatively large community surrounded what was an elite residence, with its identifiable central court. The town itself was composed of two- or three-room houses, some with upper floors, laid out on compact, paved streets. Unfortunately, the excavation data from Gournia was lost before it could be published.

It was during these palatial periods that the first writing in Europe arose. There is some evidence for a pictographic script, but by far the strongest evidence is for a script dubbed "Linear A," which was discovered in the Proto-palatial period at Phaistos. Large collections of this script, written on clay tablets, have been found at Hagia Triadha and Chania, on the northwest coast. Although it is recognized as a syllabary, attempts to decipher this form of writing have so far proved futile.

We know somewhat more about Minoan religion of this period. A great deal of the religious focus was centered in the palaces, with examples such as the tripartite shrine, the throne room complex, which had a religious function at Knossos. At this time there was a flowering of rituals on hilltops and in caves. The hilltop shrines, known as "peak sanctuaries," number at least fifty and appear along with the development of the first palaces, indicating the strong political function of these sanctuaries as well. Gournia supplies an example of a small town shrine. Figurines, found throughout the palaces, depict women who could have been goddesses or priestesses. One example of the most important figurines, the snake goddesses from the palace at Knossos, depicts women with snakes twirled around their arms and sacred animals, such as owls, on their heads. Male worshippers also seem to be featured, and there are ubiquitous representations of bulls, which have a long history of sacred male identification in the Mediterranean. These figures also appear in stylized form in Minoan culture, as horns of consecration.

Other artifacts indicate that the Minoans regarded trees and the double axe as sacred. We are fortunate to have a sarcophagus from Hagia Triadha, which, on its four sides, depicts events that took place during a funeral. We see worshipers, possible priestesses, and an offering table with a trussed bull waiting to be sacrificed. On a darker note, there is evidence from Knossos and elsewhere that the Minoans also practiced human sacrifice.

During the palatial period, Minoan culture had its greatest contacts with other contemporaneous civilizations in the eastern Mediterranean. The evidence indicates that the most contact Crete had outside its shores was with the Cyclades and Peloponnesian Greece. Finds of Minoan pottery, domestic architecture using the Minoan pier and door hall system, and traces of Linear A script indicate a strong Minoan presence in the Cyclades. Signs of Minoan influence in Greece are directed largely toward the Peloponnese, with a concentration in the Argolid area. The famous grave circles of the elites at Mycenae show numerous works of art, such as sword scabbards and the famous Vapheio cups, that can arguably be attributed to Minoan artists in the employ of foreign elites.

The evidence for Minoan contacts in the rest of the Mediterranean is not as rich. Some Minoan pottery has been found at contemporary sites in western Asia Minor. Small amounts of Minoan goods have turned up in Near Eastern contexts, and tomb paintings from contemporary Egypt depict what appear to be Minoans, the Keftiu, presenting gifts. But we lack a full understanding of the structure of these contacts. While it could have been that Minoans were colonizing parts of the Aegean islands, as well as the Peloponnese, the evidence could just as well indicate that we are witnessing a strong Minoan cultural ascendancy, which foreign elites were copying.

POST-PALATIAL PERIOD

Exact dates may never be known, but sometime near the turn of the second millennium there was an abrupt collapse of a large section of Minoan culture. All the palaces, with the exception of Knossos, ceased to be occupied. Theories to explain this change vary from the devastating effect of the explosion of the volcano on the island of Thera around 1625 B.C. to the possibility of an invasion from overseas. Whatever the cause, most Minoan occupation on Crete was affected by some sort of catastrophe.

Alone of the palaces, Knossos remained occupied. But there is much to suggest that this survival was not Minoan in character. Evidence from burials around Knossos and from the palace itself points strongly to a foreign, Mycenaean presence on Crete. A rise in militarism, represented in artworks, is distinctly non-Minoan but closely parallels that of the Mycenaeans on the Greek mainland. Of great importance is the finding of Linear B writing tablets at Knossos. Linear B is a distinctively Greek script, which also has been found in the archives of Mycenaean palaces, such as Pylos and Mycenae.

While we are almost secure in seeing Mycenaeans in control of parts of Crete at this point, the structure of this control is only vaguely understood. Decipherment of the Linear B tablets at Knossos shows that, economically at least, the palace at Knossos was operating within a structure very similar to that seen at the mainland Mycenaean palace of Pylos. Analysis of the Linear B tablets hints at a condition where Knossos controlled the major part of the island during this period, however.

In the early fourteenth century B.C., Knossos was subject to major destruction, and any Mycenaean presence at the palace disappeared. However, there is some evidence from other sites, such as the port of Kommos and Hagia Triadha, that occupation continued on Crete. Archaeological evidence indicates that at this period Crete was becoming more fragmented in terms of regional art styles as well as social and economic structures.

See also **Knossos** (*vol. 2, part 5*); **Mycenaean Greece** (*vol. 2, part 5*).

BIBLIOGRAPHY

Bennet, John. "'Outside in the Distance': Problems in Understanding the Economic Geography of Mycenaean Palatial Territories." In *Texts, Tablets and Scribes: Epigraphy and Economy*. Edited by J. P. Olivier and T. G. Palaima, pp. 19–41. Minos Supplement, no. 10. Salamanca, Spain: University of Salamanca, 1988.

Betancourt, Philip P. *The History of Minoan Pottery*. Princeton, N.J.: Princeton University Press, 1985.

Cadogan, Gerald. *The Palaces of Minoan Crete*. London: Barrie and Jenkins, 1976.

Cherry, John F. "Polities and Palaces: Some Problems in Minoan State Formation." In *Peer Polity Interaction and Sociopolitical Change*. Edited by Colin Renfrew and John F. Cherry, pp. 19–45. Cambridge, U.K.: Cambridge University Press, 1986.

Dickinson, Oliver T. P. K. *The Aegean Bronze Age*. Cambridge, U.K.: Cambridge University Press, 1994.

Gesell, Geraldine Cornelia. *Town, Palace, and House Cult in Minoan Crete*. Studies in Minoan Archaeology, no. 67. Göteborg, Sweden: Åströms, 1985.

Graham, James Walter. *The Palaces of Crete*. 2d ed. Princeton, N.J.: Princeton University Press, 1987.

Halstead, P. "On Redistribution and the Origin of Minoan-Mycenaean Palatial Economies." In *Problems in Greek Prehistory*. Edited by E. B. French and K. A. Wardle, pp. 519–530. Bristol, U.K.: Bristol Classical Press, 1988.

Manning, Sturt. "The Bronze Age Eruption of Thera: Absolute Dating, Aegean Chronology, and Mediterranean Cultural Interrelations." *Journal of Mediterranean Archaeology* (1988): 17–82.

Peatfield, A. A. D. "Minoan Peak Sanctuaries; History and Society." *Opuscula Atheniensia* 18 (1990): 117–131.

Preziosi, Donald. *Minoan Architectural Design: Formation and Signification*. Berlin: Mouton, 1983.

Preziosi, Donald, and Louise Hitchcock. *Aegean Art and Architecture*. Oxford: Oxford University Press, 1999.

Warren, Peter Michael. *Minoan Stone Vases*. Cambridge, U.K.: Cambridge University Press, 1969.

Whitelaw, T. M. "The Settlement at Fournou Korifi, Myrtos, and Aspects of Early Minoan Social Organization." In *Minoan Society*. Edited by O. Krzyszkowska and L. Nixon, pp. 323–345. Bristol, U.K.: Bristol Classical Press, 1983.

DAVID SMALL

KNOSSOS

The site of Knossos is located some 5 kilometers to the southeast of Herakleion, in the Kairatos Valley on the Greek island of Crete. The earliest Neolithic settlement and the Bronze Age palace are situated on a low hill known locally as the Kephala hill, and the Roman settlement is located to the west, on the lower slopes of the Acropolis hill. The first excavations at Knossos were by Minos Kalokairinos in 1878, on the western side of the mound of Kephala, but the main excavations were undertaken by Sir Arthur Evans between 1900 and 1931.

Knossos is the longest-inhabited settlement on Crete and was preeminent—culturally, politically, and economically—as the largest settlement on the island until the end of the Bronze Age. The Neolithic settlement at Knossos was established on the Kephala hill during the late eighth millennium B.C. or early seventh millennium B.C. by a migrant population probably from Anatolia, and it represents the earliest human occupation attested on the island. Arthur Evans first recognized the existence of a Neolithic settlement beneath the Central Court of the Bronze Age palace in 1923. This he divided into four main phases, based on changing pottery styles. Subsequent excavations by John Evans refined the sequence, with ten strata dating from the Aceramic Neolithic (so-called because of the absence of pottery containers in the material assemblage) through the Early, Middle, Late, and Final Neolithic.

Knossos was an obvious location for settlement, being a naturally protected inland site on a low hill, with a perennial spring and fertile arable land. The settlers brought with them a fully developed Neolithic economy. They reared sheep, goats, pigs, and cattle and grew wheat, barley, and lentils. Stone tools included obsidian from the volcanic island of Melos in the Cyclades as well as flint and chert. During the course of the Early Neolithic, mace-heads became a typical component of the material assemblage. The Neolithic population lived in rectilinear houses built of mud brick or *pisé* (rammed earth) on a stone foundation. Pottery is attested from Stratum IX (Early Neolithic): initially with incised and dot-impressed (*pointillé*) decoration filled with white paste and later with ripple burnished decoration. Equipment associated with textile production (spin-

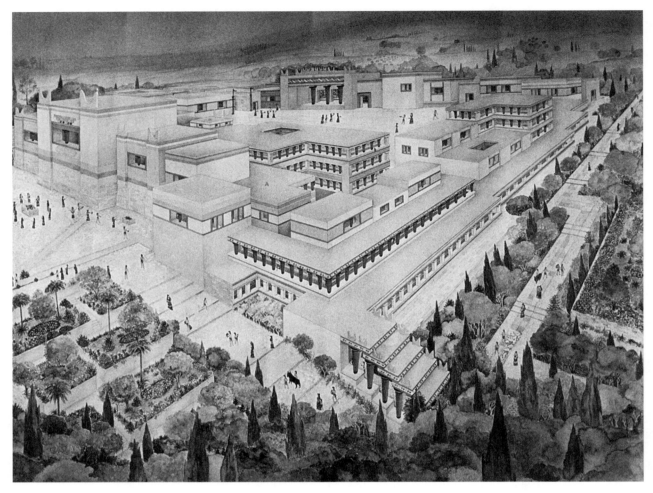

Fig. 1. Artist's reconstruction of the palace of Knossos, built c. 1900 B.C., Kriti, Crete. © GIANNI DAGLI ORTI/CORBIS. REPRODUCED BY PERMISSION.

dle whorls and loom weights) was also introduced in the Early Neolithic period. The symbolic life and religious beliefs of the earliest inhabitants of Knossos remain elusive. Although no adult burials have been found, there are infant and child burials in pits under the house floors in various strata. Figurines are attested from the earliest occupation levels, with a concentration of human and animal terra-cottas in the Early Neolithic II levels.

The Early Bronze Age (Early Minoan or Pre-Palatial) occupation of Knossos is poorly known, being largely obscured by the later construction of the palace, but it has been identified in a number of soundings throughout the site. The remains of the Early Minoan II settlement indicate that it was large

and prosperous. It has been suggested that a partially excavated building beneath the West Court of the palace was the residence of an important inhabitant, possibly the ruler of Knossos. This structure was destroyed by fire and might have been superseded by a large building beneath the northwest corner of the palace in Early Minoan III. The so-called Hypogeum, at the southern limits of the later palace, likewise probably dates to Early Minoan III. It has been suggested that this was an underground, corbel-vaulted granary. Occasional imports from the Cyclades and southern Greece and even stone vases from as far away as Egypt have been found at Knossos, indicating initial trading ventures beyond the island. Internal exchange is illustrated by the presence of significant quantities of luxury pottery imported from the Mesara region of southern Crete and by the Vasilike ware from eastern Crete.

Knossos is perhaps best known for the palace remains on the Kephala hill. Two main phases have been identified: (1) the Old Palace (Proto-Palatial) period, which comprises the Middle Minoan IB, IIA, and IIIA strata, and (2) the New Palace (Neo-Palatial) period, comprising Middle Minoan III through Late Minoan IB. The Old Palace period has traditionally been dated to c. 1900–1700 B.C. and the New Palace period to c. 1700–1425 B.C. New chronometric dates derived from radiocarbon dates from Akrotiri, a site on the nearby island of Thera (modern Santorini) destroyed in a massive eruption in Late Minoan IA, suggest that the duration of the New Palace period should be revised to c. 1690–1500 B.C. The palace at Knossos is one of several palaces identified within the Minoan landscape of Crete: the other principal palaces are at Mallia, Phaistos, and Zakros. Other possible palace structures have been identified at a number of sites in Crete. Although all the Minoan palaces conform to general underlying architectural principles and probably shared similar functions, there are distinct differences most evident in the internal configuration of space.

THE OLD PALACE PERIOD

The origins and function of the Old Palace at Knossos are elusive. Its architectural remains are poorly preserved, whereas those of the immediately preceding phase had been leveled. Certainly the construction of the Old Palace represents the introduction of a new social and architectural concept: a large central building and the use of repeated architectural elements to create ceremonial space. Although the exact plan of the palace is unknown, two phases of construction have been identified. In the earlier phase the palace was laid out around the Central Court (on a north-south alignment). Sir Arthur Evans believed that the palace was laid out in separate blocks of buildings, but it is now accepted that the first palace was envisaged as a single architectural complex. Components of the Old Palace include the initial construction of the Throne Room, several of the shrines along the west side of the Central Court, and the storerooms on the east and west wings of the palace. In the later phase the West Court was laid out with three large circular pits

(*kouloures*), possibly serving as grain silos. Also dating to this phase are the Theatral Area, to the north of the palace, and the Royal Road leading west from the palace.

The Old Palace is generally viewed as an elite residence and a religious or ceremonial center. The use of monumental architecture, in particular cut-stone (ashlar) masonry, was designed to impress the local populace and visiting dignitaries and also illustrates large-scale mobilization of labor. Moreover the palace appears to have played an important economic role, with control over production and redistribution of agricultural staples. In addition to the storage magazines and *kouloures,* the so-called Keep was possibly used to store agricultural produce. By Middle Minoan II there is evidence for the development of a sophisticated bureaucracy, in the form of clay sealings (used to seal shut containers) and "hieroglyphic" clay tablets. It is also suggested that the palace controlled the production of prestige goods. Even so there is only limited evidence for craft production, although some four hundred loom weights were found in the eastern wing of the palace, representing substantial evidence for textile production. Certainly by the New Palace period textile production is central to the Minoan economy, and New Kingdom tomb paintings indicate that woolen cloth was one of the primary Minoan exports to Egypt. Many of these activities are extrapolated from the functions of the New Palaces.

THE NEW PALACE PERIOD

The Old Palace was destroyed at the end of Middle Minoan II, and its reconstruction in Middle Minoan III marks the zenith of Minoan palatial society. The New Palace at Knossos is the largest of the Minoan palaces, covering a surface area of around 13,000 square meters. Much of the extant remains date to Late Minoan IA. The focal point of the palace was the Central Court, a paved open area (54 by 27 meters) on a north-south alignment. The function of the Central Court is unclear, but it probably served as the focus of ceremonial activities, possibly associated with the cult rooms opening onto the west side of the court. These include the so-called Throne Room (possibly the principal shrine), the Tripartite Shrine, and the Temple Repository, the latter where three faience figures of possible snake goddesses were found together with a rich assortment of faience plaques (animals, dragonflies, and richly decorated female costumes).

The ground floor of the palace was devoted to economic activities, namely craft production and storage of agricultural produce. The storerooms (a row of eighteen long, narrow storage magazines containing large ceramic storage jars, or *pithoi*) are restricted to the area of the ground floor immediately behind the west facade of the palace. The walls of the storerooms are blackened by the massive fire that destroyed the palace. The storage area was accessed either via the long corridor from the north or through the Throne Room—the latter approach indicating the extent to which the Minoan economy was embedded within the ceremonial or religious aspect. This symbolic control of the agricultural wealth is reiterated by the presence of pyramidal stands for totemic double axes at the entrance to the storage magazines. To facilitate the redistribution economy, there was a flourishing bureaucracy. Economic transactions were recorded on clay tablets in the Linear A script. Workshops associated with high-status craft production are located at the northeast side of the Central Court.

The suite of rooms located to the southeast of the Central Court, at the foot of the Grand Staircase, has become known as the residential quarters of the Knossian palace elite. These quarters comprise a series of Minoan halls: each hall consists of two adjoining rooms separated by a pier-and-door partition (a *polythyron*) with a light well (a shaft to admit light) at one end. Most notable are the Hall of the Double Axes and the so-called Queen's Hall. The domestic quarters also include a toilet. Indeed Minoan domestic architecture is noteworthy for the development of a sophisticated sanitation system, perhaps best illustrated by the drains at Knossos. A typical feature of the palace is its lavish decoration, namely wall paintings located in both the ceremonial rooms and the private chambers. Themes include processional scenes, bull sports, and richly dressed women.

The main approach to the palace was from the west, and the western facade of the palace was grandly built with ashlar masonry and a line of gypsum orthostats. Large stone "horns of consecration" (a potent Minoan religious symbol, apparently representing stylized bulls' horns) were displayed in places of prominence in the West Court. Raised walkways led across the West Court to the ceremonial southwest entrance. The southwest entrance led into the narrow Corridor of the Procession Fresco (decorated with life-size figures carrying luxurious offerings) toward the Propylaeum and a staircase to the grand reception rooms on the upper stories of the palace and also to the Central Court. A second entrance to the palace was located on the northwest. This entrance was approached via the Royal Road (leading west to the town house known as the Little Palace) and the Theatral Area.

The palace was at the center of a large town, which reached its greatest extent in the New Palace period, possibly covering an area of around 75 hectares. The population has been estimated to have been around 12,000. Several grand town houses have been excavated, such as the South House, the Little Palace, the Unexplored Mansion, and the Royal Villa. Workshops and kilns indicate that the palace did not exclusively control craft production at Knossos. Moreover several of the large houses were decorated with wall paintings, and high-status prestige objects were also found in these buildings. Most notable is the steatite bull's-head vase found in the Little Palace.

The size and grandeur of the town and palace at Knossos indicate the preeminence of the site in Neo-Palatial Crete. The lack of city defenses and the unprotected villas and palace argue for the so-called Pax Minoica, a seemingly peaceful arrangement of political unification and centralization of Minoan Crete ruled from Knossos. In the absence of documents that can be read, this is difficult to substantiate; however, Knossos certainly played a preeminent cultural role on the island. The town was destroyed in a massive conflagration in Late Minoan IB (contemporary with the destruction of the other palace centers around Crete). An unusual discovery in the town to the west of the palace suggests ritual cannibalism of children, possibly to stave off disaster. Yet the palace at Knossos was seemingly unaffected and continued to function into Late Minoan IIIA (the fourteenth century B.C.).

THE END OF THE PALACE PERIOD

The collapse of the Minoan palace centers in Late Minoan IB is usually attributed to an invasion from the Greek mainland and the establishment of a Mycenaean ruling elite. Knossos continued to be an important center in Late Minoan II and III, along-side Khania in western Crete. Parts of the palace were rebuilt and redecorated, and the characteristic griffin decoration of the Throne Room dates to this period. Knossos appears to have been an important religious center, and the Linear B archives (written in an early form of Greek) illustrate the importance of the wool industry at the site. These texts also give the name of Knossos as *ko-no-so*. There is a horizon of wealthy warrior graves in the Knossian hinterland at Zapher Papoura, Ayios Ioannis, and Sellopoulo. Characteristic features include Mycenaean chamber tombs, single inhumation, and distinctive Mycenaeanizing grave goods: a preference for bronze weapons (daggers and swords) and boar's-tusk helmets, hoards of bronze vessels, and large quantities of Mycenaean-style jewelry. The date of the final destruction of the palace at Knossos is unclear due to the vagaries of Sir Arthur Evans's early excavation at the site and in particular the context of the Linear B archives.

The location of the Iron Age settlement at Knossos is unknown, but several important cemeteries have been excavated, such as Fortetsa and Teke. The site continued to be wealthy, receiving imports from Athens and Phoenicia. Most notable is a reused Minoan *tholos* (stone-built circular) tomb, lavishly furnished with gold jewelry. This was used in the ninth century B.C., probably by a migrant Phoenician goldsmith. A sanctuary to Demeter was established in the eighth to seventh centuries B.C. to the south of the palace, and a Hellenistic shrine dedicated to the local hero Glaukos has been found in the western part of Knossos. In 67 B.C. Knossos became a Roman colony (Colonia Julia Nobilis Cnossus), and a large Roman city was established on the lower slopes of the Acropolis hill. Most notable among the Roman remains is the imposing second-century A.D. Villa Dionysos.

See also **The Minoan World** (*vol. 2, part 5*); **Mycenaean Greece** (*vol. 2, part 5*).

BIBLIOGRAPHY

Broodbank, Cyprian. "The Neolithic Labyrinth: Social Change at Knossos before the Bronze Age." *Journal of Mediterranean Archaeology* 5 (1992): 39–75.

Cadogan, Gerald. "Knossos." In *The Aerial Atlas of Ancient Crete*. Edited by J. W. Myers, E. E. Myers, and G. Cadogan, pp. 124–147. Berkeley and Los Angeles: University of California Press, 1992.

Cherry, John. "Polities and Palaces: Some Problems in Minoan State Formation." In *Peer Polity Interaction and Socio-Political Change*. Edited by Colin Renfrew and John F. Cherry, pp. 19–45. Cambridge, U.K.: Cambridge University Press, 1986.

Evans, Arthur L. *The Palace of Minos at Knossos*. 4 vols. London: Macmillan, 1921–1936.

Evans, John. "Neolithic Knossos: The Growth of a Settlement." *Proceedings of the Prehistoric Society* 37, no. 2 (1971): 95–117.

———. "Excavations in the Neolithic Settlement of Knossos, 1957–1960. Part I." *Annual of the British School at Athens* 59 (1964): 132–240.

Evely, Don, Helen Hughes-Brock, and Nicoletta Momigliano, eds. *Knossos: A Labyrinth of History*. Oxford: Oxbow Books and British School at Athens, 1994.

Hägg, Robin, and Nanno Marinatos, eds. *The Function of Minoan Palaces*. Stockholm: Swedish School at Athens, 1987.

Hood, Sinclair, and David Smyth. *Archaeological Survey of the Knossos Area*. Supplement of the British School at Athens, no. 14. 2d ed. London: British School at Athens, 1981.

Hood, Sinclair, and William Taylor. *The Bronze Age Palace at Knossos: Plans and Sections*. Supplement of the British School at Athens, no. 13. London: British School at Athens, 1981.

Manning, Sturt W. *A Test of Time: The Volcano of Thera and the Chronology and History of the Aegean and East Mediterranean in the Mid Second Millennium B.C.* Oxford: Oxbow Books, 1999.

Niemeier, Wolf-Dietrich. "The Character of the Knossian Palace Society in the Second Half of the Fifteenth Century B.C.: Mycenaean or Minoan?" In *Minoan Society: Proceedings of the Cambridge Colloquium*. Edited by O. Krzyszkowska and L. Nixon, pp. 217–236. Bristol, U.K.: Bristol Classical Press, 1983.

———. "Mycenaean Knossos and the Age of Linear B." *Studi Micenei ed Egeo-Anatolici* 23 (1982): 219–287.

Popham, M. R. *The Minoan Unexplored Mansion at Knossos*. Supplement of the British School at Athens, no. 17. London: British School at Athens, 1984.

Ventris, Michael, and John Chadwick. *Documents in Mycenaean Greek: Three Hundred Selected Tablets*. Cambridge, U.K.: Cambridge University Press, 1973.

LOUISE STEEL

MYCENAEAN GREECE

Evidence for the hunter-gatherer population of Greece has been scanty, but intensive research in Epirus (northwestern Greece) and Argolid (Peloponnese, southern Greece) suggests that long-lived successful adaptations probably were widespread on the mainland by the end of the last Ice Age and in the first few millennia of the current warm era (the Holocene, after 8500 B.C.). Nonetheless, the spread of farming and the associated appearance of domestic animals, such as sheep, goats, cattle, and pigs, around 7000 B.C. are understood as marking the colonization of the Balkans, including Greece, by early farming groups migrating out of the zones where these innovations were invented, in southwestern Asia.

These first European farming settlements are best known from their closely packed artificial settlement mounds, or "tells," which mark the great plains of central and northern mainland Greece (notably, Thessaly). In contrast, the equivalent villages or farms on the southern mainland and the Aegean Islands more often are widely scattered and less substantial. Such a distribution encourages the view that this early settled farming era in Greece (the Neolithic) was a time when the centers of population and socioeconomic development lay well north of those regions of Greece that would become the focus of the succeeding Bronze Age and classical civilizations. This view, very much influenced by the comparative ease with which the prominent tells have been identified by archaeologists from early in the twentieth century, may need to be altered slightly as a result of the recent intensive study of the southern Greek landscape, where greater densities of "flat" sites are being recognized.

It may be that tell villages were more stable communities, lasting in one place for hundreds and even thousands of years, while the typical settlement in southern Greece and the islands was smaller and shifted position every few generations. Until late in the Neolithic era (c. 7000–3500 B.C.), however, both types of Greek agropastoral societies sought out well-watered light soils for their hoe- and hand-based farming. In Late Neolithic times, the diffusion—once more from the Near East—of simple plows and animal traction allowed an explosion of settlement across the expanses of fertile hill and plain country of Greece. Here, rainfall was the essential source for plant growth, rather than the lakes, streams, and springs of the preceding era. Since the areas with high water tables are concentrated in the plains of central and northern Greece, it may be that the earlier Neolithic did indeed see a greater population density. Later Neolithic technological changes might have encouraged the south and larger islands to catch up, since their potential for dry farming is much more on a par with that farther north.

Despite claims that the more elaborate village plans on tells in Thessaly suggest the presence of distinct sectors where an elite might have resided, it is not evident that Neolithic society had progressed beyond a social organization of kin groups, clans, and temporary leading families (sometimes called a "Big Man" society), into a more hierarchical stage of chiefdoms dominating one or more villages. Yet finds from a few settlements suggest that populations were well over the two hundred considered by some anthropologists as the maximum feasible for community cohesion, based on a relatively egalitarian type of (face-to-face) organization. In these cases, either some village subdivisions based on real or fictitious kinship (horizontal segmentation) or a power structure grounded in one or more leading families (vertical segmentation) must be suspected. One of the rare settlements that expanded well beyond this threshold population was the great Neolithic village that underlies the later Bronze Age palace at Knossos in Crete. Many researchers have argued that during the three millennia before the inception of the Bronze Age, Knossos grew from a small and simple hamlet of farming colonists into a precociously socially stratified small town.

As for economic development during the course of the Neolithic, there is evidence for a growing range of cultigens and more effective use of domestic animal products. In contrast, the exchange of exotic raw materials or finished artifacts generally tended to become less wide ranging, largely owing to the increasing use of regional rather than imported products.

THE EARLY BRONZE AGE
The main phases and dates for the Aegean region are as follows.

> Neolithic: c. 7000–3500 B.C.
> Early Bronze Age: c. 3500–2100 B.C.
> Middle Bronze Age: c. 2100–1700 B.C.
> Late Bronze Age: c. 1700–1050 B.C.

The Bronze Age periods are given regional names for the Greek Mainland (Early, Middle, and Late Helladic), the Cyclades Islands (Early Cycladic, etc.), and the island of Crete (Early Minoan, etc.). These regional phases are very broadly contemporary.

With the inception of the Early Bronze Age, there are further indications of population growth and more intense colonization of the Greek landscape and clearer, if still localized, signs that in some areas a socially stratified society had begun to take shape. To the continuing impact of plow agriculture in stimulating denser population growth can be added evidence for the cultivation of the olive and

the vine. There is some debate as to how firm the limited data are for such cultivation at this time, however. Much clearer evidence for large-scale reliance on these cultigens for food, drink, and storable trade items derives from the Late Bronze Age two millennia later.

Seafaring boats become more sophisticated, which probably reflects the supplementation of coastal diets with marine food as much as it does the growth of regional and interregional trade. The diffusion of copper and bronze metallurgy into the Aegean, as well as trade in its raw materials and products, added to existing commercial and gift exchange in agricultural surpluses and stone for tools and mills, to create an early "*koine*," or interaction zone, on the southern mainland and the islands. There is, however, no indication of any political aspect to this exchange. Notably, there is much less evidence for complementary zones of economic and cultural exchange to be found in other parts of mainland Greece, such as the northeast and northwest; however, the eastern Aegean islands and the adjacent town of Troy (northwestern Turkey) did develop a significant alternative interaction sphere.

By the third millennium B.C. on the southern mainland, a series of relatively elaborate structures, standing isolated or amid less pretentious houses, have been taken as a group to mark the creation of an elite-focused district power structure. The class was first recognized at Lerna with the House of the Tiles, where associated seal-impressions for stored containers suggest the levying of some kind of tax and its redistribution by a district authority based at the small, walled center. By the latter part of the same millennium, on the Cycladic islands in the south and on some northern islands of the Aegean, there also arose large villages or small towns with well-planned internal layouts and defensive walls, seeming to indicate the central management of local populations by emergent elite groups. Some of these centers, for example, Phylakopi on Melos, seem to be large enough to represent a class of proto-urban community that we can define as the "village-state." Here, largely endogamous marriage created a "corporate community," but one whose size would have required elaborate political management.

On the other hand, throughout this first part of the Bronze Age most of Greece retained a settlement pattern little changed from later Neolithic times. There were two interpenetrating lifestyles: more permanent villages (that is, tells or extensive flat settlements) and short-lived farms and hamlets, without any clear evidence for political stratification. The expansion of trade and population and the limited number of complex communities nonetheless give the impression that in southern Greece and the northeastern Aegean the social and economic bases had been laid for the rise of the first Aegean civilization at the start of the Middle Bronze Age, in about 2000 B.C.

MINOAN CIVILIZATION

That first civilization arose on the island of Crete, and it is typically referred to as the Minoan civilization, after Minos—the mythical king of Knossos, where the most spectacular center of this new culture was located. On the Greek mainland the promising high culture of the Early Bronze Age suffered a severe decline associated with violent destruction at many key sites. Some researchers take the signs of destruction to mark invasion; others link it to a climatic fluctuation, which is seen on a wider front in the eastern Mediterranean. On the islands, however, the small defended townships continued into the new era. It is perhaps less important to explain the delay in reaching civilization on the mainland than to account for why civilization on Crete emerged at all at this time.

First, let us describe the Minoan civilization in its initial phase of florescence—the age of the First Palaces, c. 2000–1800 B.C. The most striking feature is a series of palatial centers of regional administration, the apex of a settlement hierarchy that extended through small towns (which may have had mini-palatial foci) to villages and dispersed hamlets or farms. Few parts of Crete seemed to lie outside the putative control of one of the palaces, but it remains unclear whether the latter formed autonomous princedoms within a unitary culture or were subordinate to the largest and most central example at Knossos in northern Crete. Great similarities in palace design, the use of a common script (Linear A) for recording the economic production of Crete, and vigorous exchange of products clearly indicate that all the palaces were in close and presumably peaceful interaction (fortifications are rare), probably reflecting political alliances sealed by elite intermarriage.

The palaces themselves appear to have been the residences of ruling elites as well as foci for communal celebration and ritual (in the paved courts on their outer faces and the great court at their centers). Major expanses of storage would have served the needs of this elite (consumption, trading capital) and its retinue and servants; and its reserves of oil, wine, grain, and textiles would have been kept full from the tax income of the peasantry. The palaces also acted as manufacturing centers, largely for the upper class (luxury products for rituals, prestigious feasts, and so on). Around most centers, there seem to have developed extensive towns populated by a wealthy middle class (perhaps merchants, administrators, and estate owners) and a farming or servant lower class.

This First Palace period came to a violent end with a catastrophic earthquake c. 1800 B.C. The palaces and lesser centers were rebuilt almost immediately in a very similar or even more elaborate form during the Second Palace period, which lasted until another series of cataclysms c. 1400 B.C., probably caused by invading Mycenaeans (see below). One notable change in this period was the appearance of rural elite residences (perhaps also acting as dispersed administrative centers) in the form of villas across the Cretan landscape.

Although legend tells of a marine empire, or "thalassocracy," associated with Minoan Crete, the available evidence downscales this political structure to a series of zones of decreasing influence radiating out from the island. Islands nearest Crete were transformed into highly "Minoanized" townships, with one or two perhaps receiving actual colonists. Farther away, in the southern Aegean islands and on the adjacent mainlands of Greece and Turkey, Minoan influence is less pervasive, with pottery imports and imitations and the adoption of other cultural features into a predominantly local culture. More distant regions of the Aegean and some parts of the eastern Mediterranean and Italy evidence limited mutual trade with Minoan Crete. Only at the recently excavated Nile Delta palace of Tell el-Dab'a is a stronger form of Minoan influence present, in the shape of frescoes of a highly Minoan character, interpreted as perhaps the result of dynastic intermarriage between Crete and Egypt.

Only for the innermost of the three radii of Minoan influence is political control abroad a possibility. The Minoans required both everyday and precious metals from outside Crete and other materials for elite prestige items. It is difficult, however, to envisage Minoan Crete as a major merchant power rather than as an island flourishing primarily on the income and redistribution of regional production in foodstuffs and textiles. Nonetheless, there are mentions of the Minoans in contemporary state archives in the eastern Mediterranean, suggesting both minor flows of trade and political alliances. Even though the Minoan palaces incorporate elements of traditional Cretan architecture, their design also surely reflects firsthand acquaintance with the very similar, but older, tradition of royal palaces of the city-states of the Levant and parts of Turkey.

Although the clay palace archive tablets are written in Linear A, a hitherto untranslated language, there are close parallels in their form and accounting conventions to the derivative Linear B tablets used by later Mycenaean palaces (which are in readable archaic Greek). Comparison suggests that their content largely focused on monitoring the regional production and distribution of foodstuffs, raw materials, and finished artisan products, as well as equipment for the palace's officials and armed forces. This has reinforced the general view that Minoan (as Mycenaean) palace-focused polities arose and functioned primarily through controlling the people and products of their own territory. Caution is required in this interpretation, because Minoan records remain essentially unread, while the Mycenaean archives almost certainly represent regional management records. We have yet to recover the foreign correspondence that contemporary Near Eastern states of similar scale lead us to expect once existed.

Although the Aegean Islands, especially the Cyclades, were strongly influenced by the Minoans and experienced similarly varying degrees of core-periphery interaction with the following civilization—that of the mainland Mycenaean civilization—they continued to show signs of a vigorous regional culture. This is evident in the typical nuclear island townships that lasted from the later Early Bronze Age into and beyond the Middle Bronze Age. Some would elevate this culture to a distinct Cycladic civilization, even if statehood was confined to small island polities of a thousand or so people at most.

THE RISE OF MYCENAEAN CIVILIZATION

During the peak of the Minoan First Palace civilization in the centuries around 2000 B.C., mainland Greece showed little evidence of complexity above the level of village life in what is termed the Middle Helladic period (regional Middle Bronze Age). As the Minoan Second Palace period developed during the first third of the second millennium B.C., however, there were striking signs of the renewal of regional power structures across the southern mainland. In the western Peloponnese there arose across the landscape, in connection with villages and groups of small settlements, monumental earth burial tumuli with stone "beehive" chambers (tholoi), amalgamating older Cretan communal burial traditions with those of the western Balkans, to mark the emergence of district chiefdoms. In the eastern Peloponnese an alternative elite burial mode, using deep shafts, appeared. This is most notable at the site of Mycenae, where the successive shaft grave circles A and B contain fabulously rich gifts for what can be considered a powerful warrior elite. In the following centuries their descendants developed the associated settlement into a massively fortified palatial center. More subtle changes revealed by settlement archaeology also occurred across this important transformational Middle Helladic era, with the decline across mainland southern Greece of dispersed, short-lived rural sites and a focus on nuclear village and town sites associated with the crystallization of district and regional dynastic elites.

In the following era, the Late Helladic (mainland Late Bronze Age), out of this large network of greater and lesser chiefdoms arose a series of major kingdoms, covering most of southern mainland Greece and centered on palaces with surrounding towns. This relatively uniform civilization (fig. 1) is named Mycenaean after the state center with the highest status in later Greek legends, which are believed to have originated in this period. Still, Mycenae does not have the same archaeological claim to preeminence as Knossos for the Minoan civilization, being neither the largest nor the most magnificent palatial center. On the other hand, Greek myths, such as the siege of Troy, portray the king of Mycenae as merely "first among equals" amid the warrior princes representing the several states of Bronze Age Greece. This view agrees with the archaeologi-

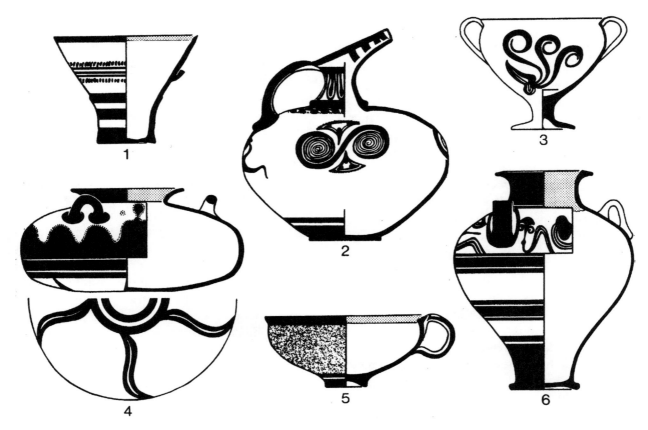

Fig. 1. Characteristic pottery types for Mycenaean Bronze Age civilization on Mainland Greece. FROM DICKINSON 1994. REPRINTED WITH THE PERMISSION OF CAMBRIDGE UNIVERSITY PRESS AND OLIVER DICKINSON. ADAPTED FROM *MYCENAEAN DECORATED POTTERY*, BY P. A. MOUNTJOY.

cal picture for other major centers, such as Thebes, Pylos, and Tiryns.

Several centuries elapsed (c. 1700–1350 B.C.) between the proliferation of chiefly burials in the later Middle Helladic and the construction of the first regional palatial centers, during which we can envisage the emergence of paramount chiefs or kings from competitive networks of district elites. Elite mansions may have appeared first, followed by full-scale palaces with close parallels to obvious older models on Minoan Crete (fig. 2). Distinctive features of the mature Mycenaean major and minor centers were the provision of stone fortifications and a general preference for defensive locations. This militaristic facet was matched by a taste for scenes of warfare in Mycenaean art, which, significantly, was not seen in the more social and ritual art of the Minoans; although it seems too romantic to follow Sir Arthur Evans in imagining a Minoan society lacking internal or external violence. It is reasonable

to see the small number of Mycenaean mainland states as developing in an atmosphere of endemic warfare. To judge by the increasing number and expanding scale of fortifications over time, the threat or practice of major conflicts remained until the end of this civilization, when all the key sites experienced violent destruction (c. 1250–1200 B.C.). During this period of swift decline to disappearance of Mycenaean civilization in the later thirteenth and twelfth centuries B.C., all signs of state-level authority, complex craft skills, and literacy faded away across Greece. This eclipse has led archaeologists to term the following era, up to the beginnings of historic classical Greek civilization in the eighth century B.C., a "dark age."

Despite this emphasis on militarism, which accords with later Greek legends of internal and external conflict, the climax of Mycenaean civilization c. 1450–1250 B.C. vies with the greatest period of the preceding Minoan civilization, which is certainly no

Fig. 2. Reconstruction of the throne room at the Mycenaean palace of Pylos, mainland Greece. © GIANNI DAGLI ORTI/CORBIS. REPRODUCED BY PERMISSION.

coincidence. It has been argued that Mycenaean art, architecture, and settlement organization, as well as political and economic systems, were critically stimulated through increasing contacts with its Cretan predecessor at its height. This contact came mainly through trade but presumably was accompanied by political and perhaps matrimonial alliances. The spectacular prestige objects found in the final Middle Bronze Age and the early Late Bronze Age chieftains' burials of the emergent Mycenaean culture show strong Minoan inspiration, perhaps the employment of Minoan craftsmen, and the likely obtaining of exotic materials via widespread Minoan exchange systems.

Like other core-periphery systems studied globally, the undeveloped margin grew, in turn, into a core in its own right. With many parallels, the process of role inversion may well have been a violent one. The precise historical scenario has been the subject of debate since the early twentieth century. Among the controversies have been the Mycenaean takeover at Knossos, the dating and impact of the volcanic eruption on the island of Thera (Santorini), and the date of the final destruction of the Knossos palace.

At present it seems that the Thera eruption may have occurred in the mid-seventeenth century B.C., destroying a flourishing island township that was a major player in eastern Mediterranean trade with the Aegean world. Probably it did not affect either the emerging mainland Mycenaean chiefdoms or the Second Palace states of Minoan Crete. Not long afterward, however, Mycenaean warriors invaded Crete and destroyed most of its palaces. They assumed control of the island from Knossos and several other former centers, such as Khania, adopting Minoan modes of surplus extraction and adapting Linear A into a script for their own Greek tongue, Linear B. It is probable that these rump Cretan palace centers later were burned down at the same time as the mainland Mycenaean palaces, during the thirteenth century B.C. It is unclear, however, if by then it was Mycenaeans or a resurgent Minoan elite who were in control of Crete.

Thus, through peaceful and forceful means, out of numerous petty chiefdoms arose some half dozen major Mycenaean kingdoms (mainland and Cretan), in the period 2000–1400 B.C., centered on palace towns with a corps of scribes, specialist workers in fine arts, and large, well-equipped armed forces. Mycenaean trade clearly developed beyond that of Minoan and Cycladic trade, both in scale and geographic scope. Existing exchanges with the eastern Mediterranean deepened, and there were stronger links to Italy and sporadic trade with the western Mediterranean islands and Iberia. The needs of the Aegean for working metal (copper and tin) and, equally important, the elite's appetite for raw materials and finished artifacts for prestigious display seem to have been the major stimuli. The Mycenaean palatial economy, like the Minoan, however, appeared to focus primarily on extraction of surplus foodstuffs, perishable and imperishable products (such as textiles), ceramic and metal artifacts, and labor from dependent populations within state boundaries. This allowed elite families and their retinues in major and minor centers to live in luxury and obtain limited imports.

EXPLANATIONS FOR THE ORIGINS OF AEGEAN BRONZE AGE CIVILIZATIONS

The origins of the Minoan and Mycenaean civilizations have been sought in varied factors. Perhaps proximity to older civilizations, such as Egypt, Mesopotamia, and the world of the city-states of the Levant and Anatolia, provided political and economic stimulus and organizational models lacking in more remote areas, such as the central and western Mediterranean and other parts of continental Europe. The undeniable contacts in terms of trade and political interactions offer some support for this "secondary civilization" model for the Aegean. On the other hand, the scale of economic and political exchanges appears to many scholars to be too limited to provide an adequate basis for the complexity of Minoan-Mycenaean society.

An alternative reading emphasizes the head start given to the Aegean through early colonization in the seventh millennium B.C. by incoming village farmers from the Near East. Yet this might lead to the prediction that similar civilizations would arise at appropriately spaced intervals of time farther west and north. In Spain and Portugal this model might

be justified, since widespread village farming was delayed until c. 5000 B.C., and complex cultures of a distinctive local character appeared two to three thousand years later. Moreover, on Malta, the famous Temple societies developed idiosyncratically after some two thousand years of settled farming. With regions of intense farming in the south by the fifth millennium B.C., Italy did not have more than well-planned villages until the final stages of the Bronze Age in the early first millennium B.C. All these examples are complex state societies, whereas this form of complex civilization was achieved early in the course of Minoan civilization.

The concept of "environmental circumscription" might shed additional light. The idea here is that certain cultures are encouraged to adapt into more elaborate social and economic forms through being confined within geographical boundaries or struggling under constraining ecological conditions. Early Iberian complex society and the Malta Temple culture, for example, arose in the context of surprisingly stressful farming ecologies. There is a parallel in the Aegean when we consider that northern and central Greek tell societies failed to achieve state formation (where climatic and soil conditions were generally good), while southern Greece saw the evolution of the Cretan Minoan and the mainland Mycenaean and related Cycladic island civilizations (in environments with a stressful climate and low-resilience soils).

Many scholars tend to combine these elements into a complex interplay of causation: proximity to the Near East gave rise to precocious settled village farming and, later, economic and political stimulation to the development of a stratified and urban society in the Aegean. The concepts of "core-periphery" and "world system" help us model how mobilization of exchange goods, related to political alliances and the flow of prestige goods between elites, could have created, or perhaps enhanced, tendencies in the Aegean toward the elaboration of class societies and administrative central places. A more stressful environment in the southern Aegean and greater access to the Near East would differentiate its path from other regions of the Aegean, with the exception of some northern Aegean islands and the city-state of Troy on the northwest coast of Turkey. Colin Renfrew argued in the early 1970s that olive cultivation, which could have flourished in the south but not over most of the northern Aegean, was a potent element in economic growth in the Bronze Age. Although the scale and timing of large-scale olive cultivation still are disputed, such cultivation seems to have played a major role in sustaining the Mycenaean civilization of the Late Bronze Age. When better paleobotanical evidence becomes available, it may turn out that this factor acted as a significant new force in the rise of small centers of power in the southern Aegean Early Bronze Age and the emergence of the Minoan civilization of the Middle Bronze Age.

What held the Aegean Bronze Age civilizations together as regional state societies? Diverse elements can be suggested. For Cycladic island towns the village-state model may be critical—a centripetal social force (that is, one that turns a community's life intensely in upon itself), which might have been behind numerous cross-cultural small-scale polities of the city-state variety. On Minoan Crete a special emphasis on religious ritual has been offered as a kind of unifying ideology binding different classes together, although one can be somewhat skeptical of a utopian reading for such a highly stratified society. In contrast, the relatively short life and militaristic flavor of Mycenaean society encourage the view that later Homeric descriptions of unstable, aggressive, and competitive warrior elites at the head of these states may reflect actual historical memories. This variety in itself reminds us that history and prehistory are the result of interactions between partially predictable possibilities and unpredictable contingency.

See also **The Minoan World** (*vol. 2, part 5*); **Dark Age Greece** (*vol. 2, part 6*).

BIBLIOGRAPHY

Bintliff, John L. "Settlement and Territory." In *Companion Encyclopedia of Archaeology.* Edited by Graeme Barker, Vol. 1, pp. 505–545. London: Routledge, 1999.

Chadwick, John. *The Mycenaean World.* Cambridge, U.K.: Cambridge University Press, 1976.

Cullen, Tracey, ed. *Aegean Prehistory: A Review.* Boston: Archaeological Institute of America, 2001.

Dickinson, Oliver. *The Aegean Bronze Age.* Cambridge, U.K.: Cambridge University Press, 1994.

Preziosi, Donald, and Louise Hitchcock Preziosi. *Aegean Art and Architecture.* Oxford: Oxford University Press, 1999.

Renfrew, Colin. *The Emergence of Civilisation. The Cyclades and the Aegean in the Third Millennium B.C.* London: Methuen, 1972.

Wardle, K. A., and Diana Wardle. *Cities of Legend: The Mycenaean World.* London: Bristol Classical Press/ Duckworth 1997.

JOHN BINTLIFF

THE EUROPEAN IRON AGE,
C. 800 B.C.–A.D. 400

INTRODUCTION

As citizens living in industrialized societies, it is hard for us to imagine a world without iron. Iron is a part of our everyday lives, from plumbing fixtures to automobiles. The village blacksmith is an almost mythical figure in American folklore, and the iron plow opened the American West to agriculture. Railroad engines were often nicknamed "iron horses." Modern readers may be surprised to learn that iron technology was completely unknown to the builders of the pyramids in ancient Egypt, to the Sumerians of Mesopotamia, and to the Harappans of the Indus Valley. The metals used by these ancient civilizations were entirely based on copper and copper alloys such as bronze.

The beginnings of ironworking represented a fundamental technological revolution for ancient Europe. While sources of copper and tin (which form bronze when alloyed together) were rare in prehistoric Europe, iron ores were ubiquitous. The development of technologies for the smelting and forging of iron led to the greater use of metals for everyday tools such as agricultural implements by Late Iron Age times. In addition, the development of iron technology laid the foundations for the modern industrial world.

CHRONOLOGY

When the Danish scholar Christian Jürgensen (C. J.) Thomsen developed the initial chronological framework for European prehistory, he defined the Iron Age as a period in which iron replaced bronze for tools and weapons. This definition continues to be used by archaeologists and historians. While the Iron Age in central Europe conventionally is dated between 800 and 1 B.C., the beginning and the end of the Iron Age varied from region to region. Archaeological research has shown that iron was in widespread use in the eastern Mediterranean by 1200 B.C. and that iron technology was established in Greece by 1000 B.C. Ironworking became widespread in central Europe around 800 B.C., but the Iron Age does not begin in Scandinavia until about 500 B.C.

Dating the end of the European Iron Age is equally problematic. Since the Iron Age initially was defined as a chronological period in prehistoric Europe, the term Iron Age usually is not applied to the ancient literate civilizations of Greece and Rome. In the European Mediterranean world, the Iron Age ends with the beginning of Greek literature in the Archaic period (eighth century B.C.) and the beginning of Latin literature in the third century B.C. The term "Iron Age" sometimes is applied to the Etruscans, who were literate but whose writings cannot be deciphered by modern scholars. For most of central and western Europe, the Iron Age ends with the Roman conquest during the last two centuries B.C. and the first century A.D. For example, Gaul, including modern France and Belgium, was conquered by Julius Caesar in the middle of the first century B.C., while southern Britain was incorporated into the Roman Empire in the first century A.D. However, many parts of northern and eastern Europe never came under Roman political domination. In Ireland, the Iron Age ends with the introduction of Christianity and literacy by Saint Patrick in the fifth century A.D. In northeastern Europe, the Iron Age continues through the first half of the first millennium A.D. Although these regions were never part of the Roman Empire, they were not immune from Roman influence. In regions such as Germany, Poland, and southern Scandinavia, Roman trade goods appear in archaeological assemblages dating from the first to the fifth centuries A.D. In addition, many non-Roman barbarians served in the Roman army and were exposed to Roman material culture and the Roman way of life. In northeastern Europe, the period from about A.D. 1–400 is termed the Roman Iron Age.

Since the late nineteenth century, the central European Iron Age has been divided into two sequential periods named after important archaeological sites. The earlier period (c. 800–480 B.C.) is known as the Hallstatt period. The later period (c. 480–1 B.C.) is known as the La Tène period and is characterized by a very distinctive style of decoration on metalwork. During the La Tène period, both archaeological and historical information can be used to reconstruct the Late Iron Age ways of life. Archaeological data provide valuable evidence for settlement patterns, subsistence practices, and technological innovations. Late Iron Age peoples also appear in Greek and Roman texts such as historical and geographical works. While the classical authors must be read with caution, these ancient texts do provide some information on social and political organization. The availability of both historical and archaeological information has allowed archaeologists to develop a very rich and detailed picture of Late Iron Age life in Europe.

SOCIETY, POLITICS, AND ECONOMICS

While the traditional definition of the European Iron Age focuses on the adoption of iron technology, the Iron Age was also a period of significant social, economic, and political changes throughout the European continent. During the Iron Age, the Mediterranean region and the temperate European region embarked on different, although interrelated, paths. During the first millennium B.C., urban, literate civilizations developed first in Greece and somewhat later in Italy. With the development of cities, writing, and complex political institutions, the civilizations of ancient Greece and Rome cannot

be considered part of the barbarian world. Thus, they are not explicitly covered in this encyclopedia.

Archaeological and historical sources indicate that the barbarian societies of temperate Europe also experienced significant social, political, and economic changes during the first millennium B.C., and many of these developments are chronicled in this section of the encyclopedia. Moreover, such sources also document a long and complex relationship between the civilizations of the Mediterranean and the barbarian societies of temperate Europe. For example, Greek trading colonies were established in the western Mediterranean by 600 B.C. During the latter part of the Hallstatt period (c. 600–480 B.C.), a wide range of Mediterranean luxury items appear in rich burials in west-central Europe. These include Greek tableware, amphorae (designed to hold and transport wine), and Etruscan bronze vessels. Another example of technology moving between the Mediterranean and temperate Europe can be seen in the fortification walls of the Late Hallstatt town of the Heuneburg, in Germany. They were rebuilt in mud brick with stone foundations. This technique was otherwise unknown in temperate Europe during the middle of the first millenium B.C. but was widespread in the Mediterranean regions. At a later date, Roman pottery and glassware were traded widely outside the empire. However, the nature of Roman and Greek contact with the barbarian world differed in one fundamental way: while the Greek colonies that were established in the western Mediterranean and along the Black Sea were primarily trading colonies, the Romans were more interested in territorial conquest. It is the Roman conquest that marks the end of the Iron Age in much of central and western Europe.

While the historical and archaeological records document extensive contact between the classical and the barbarian worlds, the degree of urbanism is one of the characteristics that distinguishes the Greeks and Romans from the barbarian Iron Age societies of temperate Europe. Urbanism was a central feature of the classical civilizations of the Mediterranean world. Greek political organization was based on the city-state. At ancient Rome's height, it may have been home to a half-million people or more. In contrast, the European Iron Age was overwhelmingly rural. The only exceptions were a small number of commercial towns that developed in west-central Europe in the Late Hallstatt period and the *oppida*—large, fortified settlements of the Late La Tène period. Many archaeologists have argued that the *oppida* represent temperate Europe's first cities. Nonetheless, the vast majority of people in temperate Europe during the Iron Age lived in villages or single farmsteads.

The archaeological record indicates that social and economic inequality was widespread throughout Europe by the Bronze Age. Continuing this trend, the Iron Age societies of temperate Europe and the classical civilizations of the Mediterranean world were non-egalitarian societies characterized by marked differences in social status, political power, and material wealth. In addition, these societies were internally differentiated. While many people may have been engaged in subsistence activities such as farming and raising livestock, craft activities such as metalworking were carried out by full- or part-time specialists. Archaeologists often use the term "complex societies" to describe these stratified and differentiated societies.

Although both the classical and the barbarian worlds can be seen as socially complex, their political organization was quite different. The Romans are a classic example of a state-level society. States have permanent institutions of government that outlast any individual rulers, and they are able to exert military control over a large, well-defined territory. Most anthropologists describe the barbarian societies of temperate Europe as chiefdoms. Chiefdoms are generally smaller than states and have fewer governmental institutions. Their leaders rely more on personal qualities than on an institutionalized bureaucracy. Some archaeologists, however, have suggested that certain Iron Age polities in Gaul may have begun to develop state-level political institutions on the eve of the Roman conquest. Entries in this section and the following one will explore the nature of social and political organization in Europe during the first millennium B.C. and the first millennium A.D.

PAM J. CRABTREE

CELTS

Celts were a people who inhabited western and central Europe during the pre-Roman Iron Age (first millennium B.C.). Nineteenth-century European archaeologists divided Celtic cultural material into two periods: Hallstatt (800–500 B.C.) and La Tène (480–15 B.C.). This division was named for two sites containing objects that display distinctive decorative motifs identified with Celtic artisans. It is also based on the replacement of bronze by iron as the predominant metal for weapons and other tools. Evidence of Celtic culture has been found from the British Isles to western Romania and from the Northern European Plain, south to the Po Valley in northern Italy and into Spain. Investigations of Celtic lifeways and language, as well as their origin and demise, have been undertaken by historians, geographers, archaeologists, and linguists since as early as 500 B.C.

Debate exists as to whether "Celtic" is even a valid referent, as there is no evidence to suggest that populations that have been identified as Celtic considered themselves members of a coherent group. Classical sources referred to the occupants of southern France as Gauls; they, along with the Galatae (Galatians) who invaded Macedonia and Greece, are presumed to be Celts. Julius Caesar recognized similarities between Celts of the British Isles and Gauls, though other sources, including Pytheas of Massalia who sailed the Celtic Atlantic in the second half of the fourth century B.C., failed to make an association between the two groups. Material culture between the insular Celts of Britain and Continental Celts shows a distinct connection, however, with insular Celtic craft producers rapidly adopting Continental styles and then adapting them to their own tastes.

There is a consensus among scholars that the origins of Celtic culture may be found within the Urnfield cultural tradition (also known as the Hallstatt Bronze Age), as early as 1300 B.C. Changes observable both in material culture and settlement distribution took place during the twelfth and thirteenth centuries B.C. at the time of the collapse of the Hittite Empire and the end of the Mycenaean civilization. Movements of large numbers of people along established trade routes are associated with this period, and they may account for the arrival of new skills and ideas, along with archaeologically observable increases in population density, evident from artifacts found in villages that were established at that time.

While proto-Celtic Urnfield populations exhibited a variety of local traditions, subsequent Hallstatt and later La Tène material culture became increasingly homogeneous. Artifacts provide evidence for broadly defined regional traditions such as those seen in Champagne, the West Hallstatt chiefdoms of Baden-Württemberg, the middle Rhineland, the salt mining districts of Hallstatt and Hallein-Dürrnberg, and northern Italy, to name a few. Across western and south-central Europe, burials contained weapon sets adorned with similar patterns, and wealth objects indicate gift exchange relationships with Mediterranean civilizations. At about 500 B.C. a transformation of stylistic elements used to decorate metal and ceramic objects swept across south-central and western Europe. This increasingly uniform cultural material is associated with the beginning of the Late Iron Age and has been identified with "Celtic art."

HISTORICAL DEPICTIONS

The earliest written reference to Celts is from about 500 B.C., when *Keltoi* are introduced in the work of Hecataeus of Miletus, a geographer writing in Greek. In one of his few surviving passages, he indicated that the people living beyond the land of the Ligurians, in whose territory the port colony of Massalia (present-day Marseille) had been established, were Celts. Fifth-century sources such as Hecataeus and Herodotus did not provide ethnographic information about the Celts, though their work makes it apparent that Celts were known to inhabit the periphery of the Greek world. Sources from the fourth century B.C., including Ephorus, Plato, Aristotle, Theopompus, and Ptolemy, characterize Celts in ways that accentuated their fighting and drinking prowess. These descriptions of warrior Celts eager for combat were written during a period of displacement and social upheaval that coincided with Celtic migrations. Rome was sacked by Gauls around 390 B.C., and around 279 B.C. Delphi became the target of Galatian invaders who looted the sanctuary. These attacks immortalized Celts as barbarian aggressors in the psyche of Roman and Greek citizens. At various times throughout the fourth and third centuries B.C. Celts served as mercenaries in Carthaginian, Etruscan, Greek, and Roman armies.

Early historic depictions of Celtic culture indicate that theirs was an oral tradition, carefully managed by priests (druids), bards, and poets. Linguistic studies of Celtic languages began in the eighteenth century A.D. and concentrated on surviving insular Celtic (spoken Celtic languages of the British Isles and Brittany). Celtic languages on the Continent disappeared in antiquity and are only known from inscriptions. Celts were mostly preliterate and adopted Greek and Latin alphabets for writing, beginning in the Late Iron Age. Third- and second-century B.C. inscriptions on pottery and coinage bear Celtic names using Greek and Latin letters. Exceptions to this adapted use of a foreign language for writing exist in several places, however: in Spain, in the form of Celtiberic; in southern France, where the language is Gaulish; and across northwestern

Italy, where Lepontic inscriptions predate Roman influence. Modern linguists speculate that these were languages of Celtic origin that continued to be used as a means of resisting cultural assimilation.

ECONOMY AND SOCIAL ORGANIZATION

Archaeological evidence indicates that the Celtic economy was based primarily on agriculture and maintenance of domesticated stock, though raiding and trading also figured prominently. Wheat and other cereal grains were subsistence staples and were supplemented with legumes, fruits, and berries, both wild and cultivated. Cows, pigs, sheep, and goats constitute the bulk of animal remains at Celtic settlement sites both large and small, but the predominant species vary within different regions. Horses and dogs appear to have had a special place among the Celts and are frequently found in burials with and without human occupants, although occasionally it appears that dogs were butchered for consumption.

Celtic social organization was largely defined by a division of labor between agriculturalists and a warrior elite, although the general population also included specialized craft producers and professionals within the priestly tradition. Some types of specialization are difficult to identify because of the Celtic belief in the ubiquitous nature of magic, which was thought to be present in all kinds of substances, including iron and coral, but could also be invoked by spells, oaths, and incantations. Skills such as the ability to heal were shared by a number of otherwise seemingly unrelated specialists. For example, metalsmiths were presumed to have curative powers, as were druids. Similarly, druids, bards (Latin *vatis*), and poets were all shamans of a sort, though their skills and abilities were assumed to have differed. Often this was expressed as a difference in degree rather than in kind.

A warrior was a type of full-time specialist in the service of a paramount chief. Burials of the warrior aristocracy provide evidence for wealth and the long distance movement of prestige goods. Not least among the remarkable aspects of princely burials (*Fürstengräber*) of the Hallstatt Iron Age is the scale of labor that was mobilized for the construction and furnishing of the graves. In the latter part of the La Tène Iron Age, this practice was replaced by the monumental construction of defensive fortifications surrounding proto-urban settlements called *oppida*.

CELTIC SETTLEMENTS

Iron Age settlement patterns across Celtic Europe vary but reveal several prominent trends. Settlements during the earlier Hallstatt period included enclosed hillforts such as Mont Lassois, the Heuneburg, Ipf, and Hohenasperg in the west, and Závist in Bohemia. Alternatively, ditched and palisaded farmsteads (*Herrenhöfe*) were the dominant Hallstatt form along the Danube in Bavaria and in other locations removed from hillforts. Individual houses on the Continent were square, whereas in Britain they were round. Following the general collapse of the so-called princely seats (*Fürstensitze*) by 450 B.C., centralized settlement disbursed, and most of the elevated hillforts were abandoned. Throughout the beginning of the La Tène period, valley and river terraces provided the location for small villages. Several hundred years elapsed before populations once again aggregated to establish the prominently located and fortified centers that Caesar identified as *oppida*. Like earlier hillfort settlements, *oppida* were ideally situated for defense, trade, and industry.

Production of iron implements—weapons, farm tools, construction tools, and medical instruments—transformed many aspects of society, especially warfare and agricultural practices. Unlike the components of the alloy bronze, iron is plentiful across Europe. Production of iron tools intensified from the Hallstatt to the La Tène, and development of the plowshare and coulter contributed to the movement of farms and villages from the uplands, where light loess sediments had been tilled for millennia, to the heavier but more productive soils of valley bottoms. Enhanced yields provided surpluses that were bartered for items made by the increasingly specialized craft producers. Production and market centers that attracted artisans, traders, and farmers were similar to later emporia. Some even included merchant's stalls, storage facilities, and meeting places, along with residences.

Contact with Mediterranean traders waxed and waned during the centuries of Celtic European domination. The apparent replacement of gift exchange, involving prestige items and luxury goods, by importation of bulk commodities and high-quality goods that were more widely distributed among the population, attests to the strength of a trade infrastructure. Increases in minting and transfer of coinage were promoted by returning mercenaries who had been exposed to civilizations around the Mediterranean, where coins were circulated in true market economies.

ROMANIZATION AND RESISTANCE

Roman conquest of the Celts began in Gaul in the early second century B.C. with the founding of Aquilea in 181 B.C., followed by the annexation of the rest of Gallia Cisalpina (Cisalpine Gaul). The establishment of the province Gallia Narbonensis (Narbonne) in southern France in 118 B.C. was part of the expanding acquisition of territory westward to Spain. Over the next one hundred years Roman provincial governors (proconsuls), including Gaius Marius and Julius Caesar, engaged in a series of battles and skirmishes aimed at gaining and holding territories as far north as present day Holland and east to the Rhine. Further conquest acquired Germany south of the Danube in 15 B.C. and southern Britain in A.D. 43. Continental Celts who had survived the battles for territorial dominion were largely assimilated into the Roman Empire over the next three hundred years as their culture was completely reorganized by Roman occupation. The Roman strategy that utilized preexisting social hierarchies and invested authority in cooperative local leaders served to absorb influential Celts into the new economy and system of government.

Archaeological evidence indicates that resistance to Romanization was present among Celts living on the margins of the empire, or even within it, in areas under weak Roman control. These included remote areas such as the East Anglian fenlands and wetland environments where dwellings on crannogs (artificial islands) made Roman administration nearly impossible. Such enclaves preserved traditional Celtic lifeways into the era of Christianization (in the sixth and seventh centuries A.D.) and beyond. A late form of Celtic writing found mostly on funerary monuments, the so-called Ogham script, was used in the post-Roman fifth to ninth centuries A.D. Stelae bearing this type of inscription have been found in Ireland, Scotland, Wales, the Isle of Man, and in Cornwall. The insular Celts who remained outside the Roman Empire retained their languages, oral histories, and artistic styles into the medieval period. This facilitated a migration of Celtic cultural attributes from Ireland and Britain back to areas under Roman and later Germanic influence, including areas where Celtic cultural practices had nearly been extinguished. The Brythonic linguistic survival on the Breton peninsula resulted from a migration in the fifth century A.D. of Celtic speakers from Cornwall to the Continent. Throughout the spread of Christianity, the monastic tradition preserved Celtic linguistic and artistic expression and disseminated Celtic influenced early Christian ideology across southern Britain and, on the Continent, into northern Italy. Surviving Celtic languages, including Scottish Gaelic and Irish in the Goidelic group, and Welsh and Breton in the Brythonic group, are all descended from insular Celtic culture.

See also **Late Bronze Age Urnfields of Central Europe** (*vol. 2, part 5*); **Hallstatt** (*vol. 2, part 6*); **La Tène** (*vol. 2, part 6*); **Celtic Migrations** (*vol. 2, part 6*); **Oppida** (*vol. 2, part 6*); **Hillforts** (*vol. 2, part 6*); **La Tène Art** (*vol. 2, part 6*).

BIBLIOGRAPHY

Audouze, Françoise, and Olivier Büchsenschütz. *Towns, Villages, and Countryside of Celtic Europe: From the Beginning of the Second Millennium to the End of the First Century B.C.* Translated by Henry Cleere. Bloomington: Indiana University Press, 1992.

Collis, John. *The European Iron Age.* New York: Schocken Books. 1984.

Cunliffe, Barry. *The Ancient Celts.* Oxford: Oxford University Press, 1997.

Dannheimer, Hermann, and Rupert Gebhard, eds. *Das keltische Jahrtausend.* Mainz am Rhein, Germany: Philipp von Zabern, 1993.

Green, Miranda J., ed. *The Celtic World.* London: Routledge, 1995.

Moscati, Sabatino, et al., eds. *The Celts.* New York: Rizzoli, 1991.

SUSAN MALIN-BOYCE

HALLSTATT AND LA TÈNE

Hallstatt is both a cultural tradition, beginning in the Bronze Age around 1200 B.C. and terminating in the Early Iron Age between 500 and 450 B.C., and a type site for which the tradition is named. La Tène (c. 480–15 B.C.) denotes the second period of the central and western European Iron Age, corresponding with marked changes in material culture and mortuary practice that distinguish it from the preceding Hallstatt. It is named for a type site discovered in 1857 along the northwestern shore of Lake Neuchâtel, in the Swiss Alpine lakes region.

HALLSTATT

The site Hallstatt is a large cemetery near the entrance to a salt mine located in the Salzbergtal, a narrow Alpine valley in Upper Austria, in the region of the Salzkammergut. At an elevation of approximately 860 meters above sea level, the Hallstatt cemetery is situated high over a lake and town of the same name. Mining at Hallstatt began at the start of the final millennium B.C., but the majority of the burials in the prehistoric cemetery are dated between 800 and 450 B.C. For this reason, an association between Hallstatt material culture and the beginning of the Iron Age has been made.

The discovery of the cemetery is attributed to Johann Georg Ramsauer, who, in the course of his duties as manager of the Hallstatt mine, was investi-

gating a potential source of gravel in 1846 and uncovered seven burials. Ramsauer reported his find and was referred to Baron von Sacken, the custodian of the Imperial Cabinet of Coins and Antiquities in Vienna. Von Sacken provided financial and tactical support for Ramsauer to excavate at the Hallstatt cemetery annually from 1847 through 1863. Under his direction, some 980 graves were opened, and six thousand objects were recovered for the museum.

Nearly two thousand burials have been excavated at Hallstatt in intermittent investigations that began with Ramsauer in 1846 and ended in 1963. Of those burials for which documentation and provenance information exist, just over half (55 percent) were flat inhumations, mostly oriented east-west, with the body placed on its back. The remaining burials were cremations, ashes and burnt bone heaped into a pile with grave goods, including weapons and objects of personal adornment. In burials containing cremations, personal items and weapons frequently were placed on top of the ashes, surrounded by pottery and other offerings. Weapons at Hallstatt are of bronze and iron and include long and short swords (also identified as daggers) that are associated with both male and female burials.

One-fourth of the buried individuals appear to be males, with a full complement of weapons; these burials have been interpreted as warrior graves. The burial population includes children of all ages, indicating that mining and its attendant activities probably were familially organized. Additionally, there are a few graves that seem to belong to traders or to

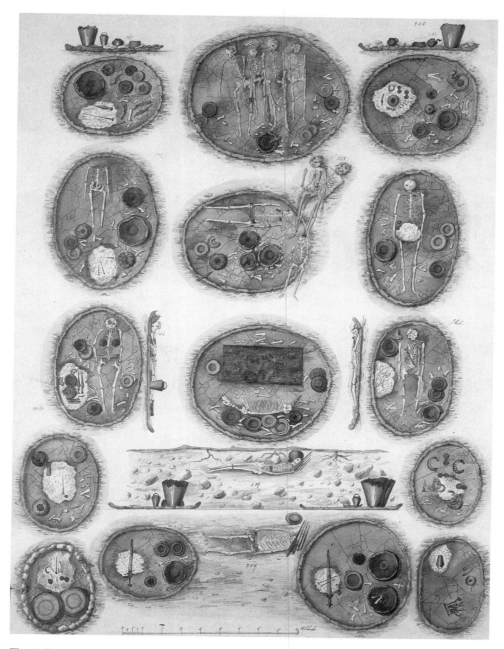

Fig. 1. Ramsauer's excavations included painted illustrations of exposed areas of the Hallstatt cemetery before the artifacts and skeletal material were removed. © NATURHISTORISCHES MUSEUM WIEN, PHOTO: ALICE SCHUMACHER. REPRODUCED BY PERMISSION.

persons from outside the community who died during their stay at Hallstatt and subsequently were buried there.

Stylistic changes in grave goods associated with the Hallstatt burials led to the conclusion that the two burial rites, inhumation and cremation, were contemporaneous and that the cemetery was used over the period in which iron replaced bronze as the dominant metal. This information contributed to the relative chronology developed during the latter half of the nineteenth century; and, at the International Congress of Anthropology and Archaeology held in Stockholm in 1874, a two-division Iron Age, consisting of Hallstatt and La Tène, was accepted.

Imported objects and raw materials emphasize the economic importance of salt mining and reveal a distribution network of cultural material that extended from eastern France across southern Germany, Switzerland, Alpine Italy, Austria, Bohemia, Slovenia, and into western Hungary. Baltic amber, African ivory, Slovenian glass, Hungarian battle-axes, Venetian knives and brooches, and Etruscan drinking paraphernalia are all present at Hallstatt. The site itself is positioned between the broadly defined eastern and western Hallstatt traditions.

Distance from the site influences the density of materials as well as the intensity of stylistic markers associated with the tradition. This factor has contributed to variability between regional chronologies that include Hallstatt as a temporal indicator. The chronological divide within the Bronze Age for French and German archaeologists is due, in part, to distinctions made by Joseph Déchelette, who identified the Urnfield culture period as separate and followed by the Hallstatt, and Paul Reinecke, for whom the Urnfield period in southern Germany was synonymous with Hallstatt A and B (Ha A, 1200–1000 B.C.; Ha B, 1000–800 B.C.). Thereafter, Hallstatt C and D (Ha C, 800–600 B.C.; Ha D, 600–500 B.C.) belong to the Early Iron Age.

Following the terminology developed by Reinecke and modified by Hermann Müller-Karpe, the archaeological evidence for Ha A and Ha B suggests the existence of several cultures subsumed within a generally homogeneous Hallstatt sphere of influence. Regional differences in material culture occur, with widespread individual behavioral expressions regarding funerary rite and settlement. The dominant burial practice during Ha A and Ha B was cremation, in which ashes and calcined bone were placed, with small vessels and personal items, into large biconical urns before burial in occasionally vast Urnfield cemeteries. The cemetery at Kelheim in Bavaria, where Müller-Karpe refined his chronological schema for the period, contained more than 268 burials.

Settlements comprised post-built structures within stockaded and fortified compounds. Earthen fortifications and wooden palisades were utilized to an increasing degree, and in some areas hillforts were established. Both the eastern German Lausitz and the southern Bohemian Knovíz cultures established fortified upland settlements as early as Ha A.

On the whole, however, there are few indicators supporting political organization of the scale that emerges in the Early Iron Age.

The Hallstatt Iron Age (Ha C and Ha D) is a period of extraordinary cultural fluorescence for every part of continental Celtic Europe, with elaborate and richly furnished burials often called chiefly or princely graves and hillfort settlements. Tombs, such as the Hochdorf mound or the burial of Vix, and enclosed fortified hilltops, including the Heuneburg and Hohenasperg (in Baden-Württemberg) and Mont Lassois (in Côte-d'Or), characterize the period and signal the transformation of social organization to a political economy that controlled the movement of luxury goods. A survey of the distribution of imported goods, such as those used for the service of wine as well as the Massiliot amphorae that contained wine shipped into Transalpine Europe, shows that the western and eastern Hallstatt were included in Mediterranean trading and gift exchange.

See also **Hochdorf** (*vol. 1, part 1*); **La Tène** (*vol. 2, part 6*); **Vix** (*vol. 2, part 6*); **Kelheim** (*vol. 2, part 6*); **The Heuneburg** (*vol. 2, part 6*).

BIBLIOGRAPHY

Bibby, Geoffrey. *The Testimony of the Spade.* New York: Knopf, 1956.

Coles, John M., and Anthony F. Harding. *The European Bronze Age.* London: Methuen, 1979.

Kromer, Karl. *Das Gräberfeld von Hallstatt.* Florence, Italy: Sansoni, 1959.

Wells, Peter S. *The Emergence of an Iron Age Economy, The Mecklenburg Grave Groups from Hallstatt and Sticna.* Cambridge, Mass.: Harvard University Press, 1981.

SUSAN MALIN-BOYCE

LA TÈNE

The material recovered at La Tène appears to have had little to do with domestic life, and though there are numerous fibulae (brooches), few objects of adornment are of the type belonging to women. For these and other reasons, the site has been variously interpreted as a military garrison or arsenal, trading center, or votive site. An incomplete inventory of the material from La Tène includes 166 swords and 269 spearheads. The exceptional quantity of artifacts recovered from the lake (especially weaponry) ensured the interest of antiquarians and archaeologists before the end of the nineteenth century, and in 1874 the name La Tène was used to designate the latter Iron Age.

The Swiss Lakes region played an important role in the development of a chronological framework for prehistoric Europe, beginning in 1854 with the first reported discovery of Neolithic Swiss Lake villages. Sites along lakeshores had been dredged for land reclamation during times when water levels were low, and objects well preserved in the fine silts and mud showed that prehistoric communities had constructed entire villages on piles set along the margins of lakeshores. Colonel Friedrich Schwab originally supposed that the material recovered from La Tène on Neuchâtel belonged to this earlier period until he began an inventory of the iron swords and scabbards. In all of the collections of antiquities Schwab assembled before the discovery at La Tène, bronze had been the dominant metal. The piles at La Tène were supports for piers and a double bridge and have been dated using dendrochronology. Dates for piers 3 and 2 of the Cornaux bridge provide evidence for construction or maintenance at 224 B.C. and 120–116 B.C., respectively.

As a term, "La Tène" describes and defines both a time period and a style and has been associated with "Celtic" since its appearance in archaeological parlance. Classical sources describing Celtic territories along the Danube and Celtic migration at approximately 400 B.C. were well known to European antiquarians and archaeologists. Consequently, the Early La Tène also has been called the "early Celtic." This terminology has been particularly popular with art historians, who associated La Tène stylistic elements with Celtic-produced artifacts or "art objects." Materials recovered from La Tène were so well preserved that it was possible to identify and disseminate imagery of the patterns that decorated scabbards and swords. It soon was determined that the "vegetal style" of intertwined plants and elongated animals was a widely distributed motif that occurred from the British Isles across France and southern central Europe, including northern Italy, to the Balkans.

Central Europe has had a usable chronological framework for the La Tène beginning in 1885 with the work of Otto Tischler, who subdivided the period into early, middle, and late periods. When Paul Reinecke constructed his analysis of fibula types at the beginning of the twentieth century, he differentiated the chronological subdivisions for southern Germany from those of western Switzerland and France. His distinctions were based on what appeared to be continuity in the tumulus burial tradition for the earliest part of the La Tène. His solution was to distinguish this phase as La Tène A, followed by B, C, and D, corresponding roughly to the early (B), middle (C), and late (D) horizons used elsewhere in Europe. While this relative temporal sequence has been modified in light of updated research, the La Tène for southern central Europe still is divided into four horizons (A through D).

The European Iron Age typically is divided into early and late periods, corresponding with Hallstatt and La Tène, respectively. The transition from Hallstatt D to La Tène usually is associated with changes in burial rite, from large tumuli to flat inhumation graves. Aspects of the tumulus burial tradition continued, however, in parts of southern Germany, Switzerland, and Austria after its abandonment in other areas. La Tène A originally was intended to cover this anomalous first horizon and was assumed to begin sometime around 450 B.C. Later research placed its beginning at approximately 480/475 B.C., coincident with dating for the Golasecca material culture in northern Italy. A hallmark of the onset of the La Tène is the "early style," with its Etruscan influences. The compass became a design tool, particularly for bronze vessels and ornamental metal disks but also for the occasional ceramic vessel.

The changes evident in material culture and ideology, as expressed in burial treatment, were part of a major transition that is equally evident at the scale of regional settlement. Most of the elevated and fortified settlements, such as the Heuneburg and Mont Lassois, that had controlled the distribution of luxury goods during the preceding Hallstatt period were abandoned, as these apparent centers of power collapsed. Richly furnished burials continued, although the focal area shifted northward to the Hunsrück-Eifel region along the Moselle River. Settlements and burials generally were smaller than

Hallstatt period sites, suggesting more dispersed populations and decentralized social and political power.

La Tène B has a less certain starting date (c. 400 B.C.) associated with the beginning of a major movement among Celtic peoples. This migration, or expansion, depending on the source, corresponded with reduced populations in the Marne, Champagne, Bohemia, and possibly Bavaria. Depopulation is indicated by a decrease in warrior graves and adult male burials in general. Additionally, fewer weapons were deposited in the remaining graves, and the ceramic burial assemblage changed. It was during this period that a considerably less-labor-intensive interment, that of flat inhumation without grave markers, becomes the dominant rite.

La Tène C sometimes is associated with the beginning of the Middle La Tène (280–125 B.C.), because it is when the *oppida* were established. The appearance of these proto-urban settlements signaled a consolidation of power and reorganization of the social and economic structure of Celtic society. Throughout the Middle La Tène, migration and expansion, disruption and resettlement, contributed to an archaeological record that is difficult to unravel. During La Tène C, inhumation burials disappeared altogether as cremation replaced inhumation, even for the social and political elite. This further transition in mortuary practice occurred in conjunction with the formation of nucleated settlements across Europe, and it has been suggested that the total shift to cremation may have been the behavioral expression of the impact of agglomerated settlement on disposal of the dead.

Exposure to Graeco-Italic representation during this period was expressed in the "vegetal style," or continuous plant style. Originally named the "Waldalgesheim style" after the burial from Hunsrück, off the Rhine, the vegetal form can be seen in the decorative repertoire by 320 B.C. This change in motif included stylized palmettes and lotus patterns that garlanded bowls, helmets, and scabbards. These so-called oriental patterns appeared on weapons found at La Tène, which enabled scholars to date the site before dendrochronological confirmation was available.

The Late La Tène (125–15 B.C.) is associated with the rise of Roman colonial interests and their impact on neighboring populations and began with La Tène D1 (125–80 B.C.). La Tène D1 ended with the abandonment of the *oppida* sometime between 80 and 40 B.C. throughout France and Germany, although in Bohemia *oppida* were inhabited until sometime in La Tène D2. Relative chronologies dependent on settlement material, in the absence of burials for this period, are concluded by the disruption of the *oppida* culture. La Tène D3 (50/30–15 B.C.) coincided with the incursion of Germanic populations before the Roman conquest of the region in 15 B.C., which marks the end of the period.

See also **Neolithic Lake Dwellings in the Alpine Region** (*vol. 1, part 4*); **Oppida** (*vol. 2, part 6*); **La Tène Art** (*vol. 2, part 6*); **The Heuneburg** (*vol. 2, part 6*).

BIBLIOGRAPHY

Bibby, Geoffrey. *The Testimony of the Spade.* New York: Knopf, 1956.

De Navarro, J. M. *The Finds from the Site of La Tène.* Vol. 1, *Scabbards and the Swords Found in Them.* London: Oxford University Press, 1972.

Moscati, Sabatino, et al., eds. *The Celts.* New York: Rizzoli, 1991.

SUSAN MALIN-BOYCE

CELTIC MIGRATIONS

Celtic migration refers to the Late Iron Age expansion and resettlement of people affiliated with various Celtic tribes. Historic sources establish the start of this period of upheaval at about 400 B.C. This date is supported by archaeological evidence that indicates an intensive and rapid southward spread of Celtic cultural material and practices. However, archaeological investigations also suggest that 400 B.C. was not the beginning of movement for Celtic peoples and indicate that such migrations were not an isolated phenomenon.

Economic disruption and social transformation were experienced across south-central and eastern Europe throughout the latter half of the final millennium B.C. By the fifth century B.C. population pressure had compelled the Greeks and Phoenicians to establish colonies at coastal Mediterranean sites, such as Massalia (Marseille), Emporion (Ampurias), and Carthage. The fourth and third centuries B.C. were a time of national redefinition and included the consolidation of Greece and Macedonia under Philip II of Macedon, followed by the conquest of Persia and Egypt by his son Alexander III (Alexander the Great). Roman territorial expansion contributed to regional destabilization and population movement throughout Etruria and parts of Iberia, setting the stage for the Punic Wars. Celtic warriors participated in most of these conflicts as mercenaries.

The first wave of historically documented migration is archaeologically evident both at its point of origin (the Champagne region of France) and in the area that was invaded (the Po Valley of northern Italy). Reduced population in Champagne is indicated by the abandonment of settlements and by a decrease in graves, especially those belonging to young adult males. Chariot burials, in particular, practically disappear. Throughout the Cisalpine region (which now forms part of northern Italy), foreign burial practices attest to the arrival of Celts, who established themselves across the plain of the Po River. In Bologna grave markers from the era depict combatants armed with weapons of northern (Transalpine) design. Also burial sites have yielded grave goods that were carried south by the deceased or their acquaintances. Bologna itself was renamed from Etruscan "Felsina" to Celtic "Bononia." Body adornment in the form of bow-shaped brooches (fibulae) of a Transalpine La Tène style are distributed from Champagne and Burgundy across Europe to the Carpathian Basin and south of the Alps throughout Italy.

Not all of the invaders were satisfied to remain in northern Italy. Around 390 B.C. a Celtic invasion force sacked and looted Rome. According to the Roman historian Livy, writing in the first century B.C., the event was witnessed by residents who had taken refuge in the citadel. The city was later ransomed, and the barbarians packed their plunder and left. The effect of the devastation was profound and influenced Roman military commanders in their interactions with Celtic warlords for centuries. Julius Caesar, for example, rushed to meet the Helvetii in 58 B.C. to prevent them from turning south into the Po Valley. Following the battle, he turned the survivors around and provisioned them to make certain that they would continue on their eastward journey back to Switzerland.

The path of migration appears to have first traversed the Alps along the western side of the Italian Peninsula but was soon expanded to include routes south from Bohemia. A delegation of Galatian Celts met Alexander the Great on the banks of the Danube during his campaign in the Balkans in 335 B.C. The source is Ptolemy I, later the ruler of Egypt, who was present on the occasion. Celtic incursion into Thrace, Macedonia, and Greece in about 280 B.C. was the culmination of frequent movements of war parties that had begun nearly a century earlier. Delphi was attacked around 279 B.C. by Brennos, who led his warriors to the temple of the Oracle, which they burned. There is no evidence for Celtic resettlement in Greece, and artifacts associated with the assault on Delphi are few.

Classical sources settled upon various accounts to explain why Celts left their homeland and journeyed south through Alpine passes to establish communities in Italy and Asia Minor. A report by Livy states, "There is a tradition that it was the lure of Italian fruits and especially of wine, a pleasure then new to them, that drew the Gauls to cross the Alps and settle in regions previously cultivated by the Etruscans." The Greek scholar Dionysius of Halicarnassus elaborates on this sequence of events, saying that the Gauls were enticed to Italy with wine, olive oil, and figs and were told that the place was occupied by men who fought like women and would offer no real resistance. According to these two authors, the quality of life available on the Italian Peninsula attracted Celtic immigrants. In another version, the Greek geographer Strabo reports that tribes joined forces in pursuit of plunder. A further account says that population stress prompted consultation with the gods who directed one brother to take his followers to the Hercynian uplands in southern Germany while the other was told to take the more pleasant road into Italy. Scholarly analysis suggests that population growth was a contributing factor, along with a deteriorating climatic phase. These conditions, combined with the disruptions in the traffic of Mediterranean imports that followed the establishment of Roman colonies competing

with the Greek trading post at Massalia, may indeed have been sufficient cause.

It is probable that the migration that began in the Champagne region was motivated by a desire to acquire luxury goods and wine and that it was carried out by young adult males of the warrior aristocracy, as the archaeological evidence indicates. However, movements such as that of the Helvetii included men, women, and children, and they were most likely motivated by other factors that included hardship.

Migration contributed greatly to restructuring Celtic society. Large numbers of Celts were introduced to different lifestyles in the various Mediterranean civilizations. When they returned to their homes north of the Alps (and many of them did) they brought back coinage and an appreciation of its use. They also transported ideas, technologies, and objects that they acquired, along with contacts that enabled them to enter into new trade relationships. Further, the process of migration itself had temporarily reorganized tribal units. During migration, loose coalitions of otherwise distinct groups formed under the leadership of single individuals. Post-migration Celtic Europe during the proto-urban *oppida* phase (150–50 B.C.) reflects these economic and social transformations.

See also **Celts** (*vol. 2, part 6*); **La Tène** (*vol. 2, part 6*); **La Tène Art** (*vol. 2, part 6*).

BIBLIOGRAPHY

Arnold, Bettina, and D. Blair Gibson, eds. *Celtic Chiefdom, Celtic State: The Evolution of Complex Social Systems in Prehistoric Europe.* Cambridge, U.K.: Cambridge University Press, 1995.

Cunliffe, Barry. *Greeks, Romans, and Barbarians: Spheres of Interaction.* New York: Methuen, 1988.

Kristiansen, Kristian. *Europe before History.* Cambridge, U.K.: Cambridge University Press, 1998.

Livy. *The Early History of Rome: Books I–V of the History of Rome from Its Foundation.* Translated by Aubrey de Selincourt. Baltimore, Md.: Penguin, 1965.

Moscati, Sabatino, et al., eds. *The Celts.* New York: Rizzoli, 1991.

Wells, Peter S. *The Barbarians Speak.* Princeton, N.J.: Princeton University Press, 1999.

SUSAN MALIN-BOYCE

GERMANS

The question of the identity of the peoples who were first called Germans is immensely complex. Three main approaches to the subject are historical, archaeological, and linguistic.

HISTORICAL

The earliest description of peoples called Germans is in Julius Caesar's commentary about his military campaigns in Gaul between 58 and 51 B.C. Caesar's remarks formed the basis for later Roman use of the name and thus for subsequent medieval and modern applications. Any discussion of the identity of the early Germans must begin with Caesar. The Greek writer Posidonius (135–51 B.C.) may have mentioned peoples he called Germans, but his works do not survive.

Two assertions by Caesar are of particular importance. One is that the peoples east of the Rhine were Germans, whereas those west of the river were Gauls (whom ancient Greek writers called Celts). The other is that the Germans had a less complex society than did the Gauls. Unlike the Gauls, the Germans had no towns, little agriculture, and less-developed religious rituals, and they spent much of their time hunting and fighting. From Caesar onward, Roman writers called the peoples east of the Rhine and north of the Upper Danube Germans. It is not known what these groups called themselves. It is very unlikely that they thought of themselves as any kind of single people, at least before many of them united to face the threat of Roman conquest.

In his work known as the *Germania*, published in A.D. 98, the Roman historian Tacitus described in greater detail the peoples whom Caesar had called Germans. From the second half of the sixteenth century, when the manuscript of his writing was rediscovered and translated, the account of Tacitus formed the basis for many studies of the early Germans. Much of his description was applied even to groups who lived many centuries after the peoples he called Germans. Well into modern times, scholars interpreted his work as if it were an ethnographic account of peoples in northern Europe beyond the Roman frontier.

Approaches to the writings of Caesar and Tacitus have become more critical. Many historians believe that Caesar's assertions that the peoples east of the Rhine were Germans was politically motivated, to portray the Rhine as a border between Gauls and Germans and thus a cultural frontier at the eastern edge of peoples whom he was fighting to conquer. Much of Caesar's description of the Germans as a simpler people than the Gauls may have been based on long-held Roman ideas about the geography and the peoples of northern Europe. Caesar had little direct contact with groups east of the Rhine, and his remarks about them were made in the context of his primary concern, which was the conquest of Gaul.

A century of critical study of Tacitus has led to the conclusion that his *Germania* should be approached primarily as a literary work, rather than an ethnographic one. Many believe that his descriptions of the Germans tell more about Roman attitudes and values than about the peoples of northern Europe. Whereas Roman writers, following Caesar and Tacitus, regarded Germans and Gauls as distinct peoples, Greek authors, such as Strabo and Cassius Dio, considered them part of the larger group of peoples whom they called Celts. Later Roman and medieval writers built upon the traditions of their predecessors, classifying many peoples identified in later centuries—such as Burgundians, Franks, Goths, and Langobards—as Germans.

ARCHAEOLOGICAL

The archaeological evidence shows a much more complex situation than Caesar and Tacitus describe. When Caesar was writing, between 58 and 51 B.C., the peoples east of the upper and middle Rhine were very much like those west of the Rhine against whom Caesar was fighting. Large fortified towns known as *oppida* dominated the landscape. As at the *oppida* in Gaul, the archaeology shows complex economic and political organization, with mass production of pottery and iron tools, minting of coins, and long-distance trade with much of Europe, including Roman Italy. East of the lower Rhine, however, the archaeology indicates a different kind of society, without the large *oppida* and with smaller-scale manufacturing and commerce. In this region Caesar's assertion about lack of towns corresponds to the archaeological evidence, but his statements about undeveloped agriculture and the major role of hunting are proved wrong by the archaeology. Intensive farming and livestock husbandry had been practiced in the region for some four thousand years before Caesar's time.

The style of material culture, especially metal ornaments and pottery, in much of the region east of the lower Rhine is known as Jastorf, and it contrasts with the La Tène style characteristic to the south and west. Earlier archaeologists have linked La Tène style with Celts (Gauls) and Jastorf style with Germans, but studies show that such direct connections between styles and peoples named by Roman and Greek writers are unwarranted.

Throughout the Roman period (50 B.C. to A.D. 450), the archaeology shows regular interactions—some peaceful, some violent—between the Roman provinces west of the Rhine and the unconquered lands to the east. Many graves east of the Rhine contain fine products of Roman manufacturing, such as pottery, bronze vessels, ornaments, and even weapons. Such settlements as Feddersen Wierde in Lower Saxony show that trade with the Roman world brought both wealth and social change to communities in these regions.

LINGUISTIC

The category "Germanic" as it applies to language is difficult to investigate before the time of the Roman conquests because the Iron Age peoples did not leave writings. Roman and Greek observers did not use language as a criterion in distinguishing the peoples of northern Europe, probably because they did not know enough about the native languages. When runes were developed in northern parts of the continent (by people familiar with Latin), probably in the first or second century A.D., they indicate the presence of a well-developed language that linguists classify as Germanic.

In the Rhineland, where many inscriptions survive from after the Roman conquest, some names can be linked with Germanic and others with Celtic languages. Certain names even combine elements of the two linguistic traditions. Probably in much of temperate Europe at the time of Caesar and Tacitus, many people spoke languages that could not be classified easily as either Germanic or Celtic today but that included elements associated with both of those categories.

See also **Oppida** (*vol. 2, part 6*); **Manching** (*vol. 2, part 6*); **Gergovia** (*vol. 2, part 6*); **Kelheim** (*vol. 2, part 6*); **Langobards** (*vol. 2, part 7*).

BIBLIOGRAPHY

Bazelmans, Jos. "Conceptualising Early Germanic Political Structure." In *Images of the Past: Studies on Ancient Societies in Northwestern Europe.* Edited by N. Roymans and F. Theuws, pp. 91–129. Amsterdam: University of Amsterdam, 1991.

Beck, Heinrich, ed. *Germanenprobleme in heutiger Sicht.* Berlin: Walter de Gruyter, 1999.

Beck, Heinrich, Heiko Steuer, and Dieter Timpe, eds. *Germanen, Germania, Germanische Altertumskunde.* Berlin: Walter de Gruyter, 1998.

Lund, Allan A. *Die ersten Germanen: Ethnizität und Ethnogenese.* Heidelberg: Universitätsverlag C. Winter, 1998.

Pohl, Walter. *Die Germanen.* Munich: R. Oldenbourg, 2000.

Todd, Malcolm. *The Early Germans.* Oxford: Blackwell, 1992.

Wells, Peter S. *Beyond Celts, Germans, and Scythians: Archaeology and Identity in Iron Age Europe*. London: Duckworth, 2001.

PETER S. WELLS

OPPIDA

Oppidum is the Latin word for a defended site, often with urban characteristics, and so, by extension, simply a "town." The modern archaeological usage is based on Julius Caesar's *De bello Gallico,* in which he terms the native urban settlements, such as Genava (Geneva), Vesontio (Besançon), Lutetia (Paris), Bibracte (Mont Beuvray), and Gergovia (Gergovie), *oppida,* although he occasionally calls them *urbs* (city). German and British nomenclature thus uses this word for archaeological sites similar to these historical towns—defended Late Iron Age sites of the second to first centuries B.C. of at least 25–30 hectares, which are found from the Hungarian plain to western France as well as in central Spain. Caesar and other Latin authors also use the term to describe hillforts and small defended urban sites of 5–10 hectares; French nomenclature follows this usage for the towns of southern France, such as Entremont and Ensérune, and the sixth-century Hallstatt hillforts, such as Mont Lassois and the Heuneburg. In Britain the term is used mainly for very large lowland settlements of the first centuries B.C. and A.D., such as Camulodunum (Colchester), which can be as large as 2,000 hectares, defined by linear dikes. In this discussion the British and German nomenclature is used. This essay will discuss *oppida* in Gaul, central Europe, and Britain.

OPPIDA IN GAUL AND CENTRAL EUROPE

Because of their large size and no doubt large populations, the *oppida* must belong to a very different sort of political entity from that of the Mediterranean city-states, or what might be termed tribal states. They bear the name of a tribe rather than of a major town (e.g., the Aedui and the Arverni, compared with the Romans and Athenians). Where the territorial size of the state is known, they tend to be much larger than the city-states. Mont Beuvray near Autun in Burgundy is a good type site. First, Caesar names it as the ancient Bibracte, chief town of the Aedui, who were legal allies of the Romans from at least the second century B.C. Caesar, who spent the winter of 52–51 B.C. in the town writing *De bello Gallico,* tells a little about the state's oligarchic constitution. He mentions the annual election of the chief magistrate (the *vergobret*), the existence of an assembly (*senatus*), and the sources of the state's income (e.g., the annual auctioning of the right to collect tolls from traders).

Mont Beuvray lies in a good defensive position on a hilltop that dominates the Morvan mountain range, and it is visible from a considerable distance in all directions. Although the immediate area is agriculturally poor, there are raw resources, such as iron ore, and the *oppidum* controlled one of the

Some of the principal *oppida* in Europe. ADAPTED FROM WELLS 1999.

major routes from the Mediterranean to the Atlantic, from the valley of the Saône into the Paris Basin via the River Yonne. Dendrochronological evidence shows that the *oppidum* was founded about 120 B.C. and initially was surrounded by a rampart low on the hill, enclosing some 200 hectares. This was a *murus Gallicus,* as described by Caesar, a wall revetted front and back by stone walls and with an internal timber lacing joined with iron spikes where the balks cross. In a *murus Gallicus* the space between the walls is filled with earth and stones, and there is an earthen ramp behind and a ditch (or, in the case of Mont Beuvray, a terrace) in front. Somewhat later the site was reduced in size to 135 hectares with a new *murus Gallicus* rampart, which was repaired regularly, and, finally, in the later first century B.C. by a *Fécamp* rampart—a massive bank of earth with a sloping glacis front (named by Mortimer Wheeler who dug the *oppidum* overlooking the modern-day town of Fécamp). The reason for this series of alterations may have been to make the ramparts more visible from a distance. Certainly, defense is not the only purpose of the "defenses"—the main gate, the *Porte de Rebout,* is much wider than would be needed for defense, and there is no elaborate gatehouse such as those known from many other sites.

The site was a major center for consumption—the annual influx of wine amphorae from western Italy must be numbered in the thousands, but the pre-conquest deposits at Mont Beuvray are poorly known, as they are overlain by masonry buildings of the Augustan period. The site saw a massive investment in public and private buildings in the two generations following the conquest, before the population moved to a less-exposed site 20 kilometers away at Augustodunum (Autun) c. 10 B.C. to A.D. 10.

Several major excavations of *oppida* reveal their internal organization and the range of buildings—Villeneuve–St. Germain near Soissons and Condé-sur-Suippe/Variscourt in France; Staré Hradisko, Hrazany, and Závist in the Czech Republic; and Manching on the Danube in Germany. All of them have produced large palisaded enclosures, which have the appearance of farmsteads, usually with a large timber house and ancillary barns, stables, granaries, workshops, and wells. The largest enclosures are up to 4,000 square meters, but more typically they are about 1,000 to 2,000 square meters. They seem to be elite residences, the equivalent of the courtyard house in the Mediterranean world. They also commonly have evidence of industrial activities, such as bronze casting, ironsmithing, and coin manufacture.

The lower classes lived in smaller timber buildings, typically with a single room, constructed on artificial terraces on hill slopes, or, in the case of Mont Beuvray and Manching, lined along the main thoroughfares. Many people of this class were engaged in manufacturing. Some were bronzesmiths, making such mass-produced items as safety-pin brooches and belt fittings. Others were ironworkers, producing such weapons as swords, iron scabbards, spears, and shield bosses; a wide range of tools for carpentry (drills, hammers, chisels, knives, axes); agricultural equipment (plowshares, sickles, scythes, pruning hooks); house fittings (latch lifters, keys, locks, cauldron hangers), or vehicle fittings for chariots and wagons. Glass was worked to produce multicolored beads, pendants, and bracelets or red glass as an overlay on decorative studs. Wool was spun and woven into textiles, and leather was worked, although little survives of the products themselves. A great range of pottery was made, from basic cooking pots and eating vessels to elaborate painted vessels with geometric and zoomorphic (based on animal forms) decorations. Individual pots, such as specialist cooking pots made of clay containing graphite, could be traded over several hundred kilometers. Thus, *oppida* were important centers of manufacture, linked together by extensive trade networks that saw trade not only in finished goods but also in raw materials, such as metals, salt (Hallstatt, Bad Nauheim), amber, or shale for bracelets and vessels. In some cases, such as Kelheim in Germany and Titelberg in Luxembourg, the *oppidum* encloses or sits on the raw material (in both these cases, iron ores).

Oppida were deliberate foundations, formed at a specific moment in time when the decision was made to found a town and for the population to move in. It implies preexisting knowledge of what a town is like and the necessary economic, social, and political superstructure to support it. Manching is a unique example of a settlement that gradually increased in size until it achieved urban proportions and was given defenses. Lezoux in central France presents the more normal sequence: an open settlement of about 8 hectares in the plain, which was abandoned at the end of the second century B.C. for a defended *oppidum* on a nearby hill. This site, in turn, was abandoned in the late first century B.C. for a Roman town at the foot of the hill.

There are considerable regional variations, however. Sometimes a series of *oppida* replace one another—Villeneuve–St. Germain and Pommiers at Soissons or Corent, Gondole, and Gergovie at Clermont-Ferrand. In many cases, no preceding major settlement is known, and the urban site may represent some sort of synoicism, or joining together into one community, of numerous small settlements. At Roanne and Feurs the early open settlements decreased in size when the nearby *oppida* of Jœvres, Crêt-Châtelard, and Palais d'Essalois were established, but neither site was abandoned and, unlike the local *oppida*, developed into flourishing Roman towns. In some areas, such as Clermont-Ferrand, virtually all the preceding settlements disappeared. In others, such as Champagne, there were many small farms and hamlets in the countryside; indeed, the distribution of rich burials suggests that in northern France this was where many of the elite resided. In still other areas, especially in southeastern France, *oppida* are rare or unknown, and open settlements, such as Saumeray, in the territory of the Carnutes could continue unaffected by the foundation of *oppida* not far away. *Oppida* also could be founded but never attract any permanent occupation.

In Gaul the main period for the foundation of the *oppida* (on the evidence of dendrochronology) is about 120 B.C. This was around the time of the Roman takeover of southern France (125–123 B.C.) and the defeat in 123 B.C. of the Arverni, who, according to the Greek ethnographer Posidonius, had controlled an area from the Atlantic to the Rhine. In central Europe (e.g., the Czech Republic) such sites as Hrazany, Závist, and Staré Hradisko go back a couple of generations earlier, to the early second century B.C., but there is no historical context for their foundation.

The *oppida* played a major role in the events of Caesar's conquest of Gaul, of which the sieges of Avaricum (Bourges), Gergovia, Alesia (Alise–Ste. Reine), and Uxellodunum (Puy-d'Issolud) are the most spectacular. In contrast, when the Romans reached the Danube in 15–14 B.C. many sites, such as Manching, seem to have been abandoned. The gates of Hrazany and Závist, outside the area conquered by the Romans, were hastily blocked just before they were burned down. This event traditionally has been associated with the rise of the Germanic chieftain Maroboduus and the Marcomanni c. 10 B.C., but the archaeological dating now suggests an earlier date for their destruction. In contrast, many of the sites in Gaul, even in areas hostile to Rome, continued in occupation for at least a couple of generations (Gergovie, Mont Beuvray), if not throughout the Roman period (Alise–Ste. Reine). Indeed, many sites can claim continuity of occupation to the present day, among them Besançon (Vesontio), Reims (Durocortorum), Paris, Chartres (Autricum), and Orléans (Aurelianum Cenabum).

The sites in central Spain are less well known and studied; they contrast with the generally smaller Iberian towns of the east and south and the hillforts of the western and northern Iberian Peninsula. Their histories are longer than those of temperate Europe, with sites such as Las Cogotas and La Mesa de Miranda (Ávila) starting as early as the fifth century B.C. A small number of sites figure in the Carthaginian and Roman conflicts: Salamanca (Salamantica) was captured by the Carthaginian general Hannibal in 220 B.C., and Numantia near Soria was the scene of a siege by the Roman general Scipio Africanus in 133 B.C. Typically, these sites consist of two or three defended enclosures with elaborate entrances and large enclosure areas (e.g., La Mesa de Miranda, at 30 hectares; Las Cogotas, at 14.5 hectares; and Ulaca, at 80 hectares). The latter site contains many small stone and double houses, usually with a single room but occasionally with three or four rooms, but there are also ceremonial and religious structures. The associated cemeteries contain some rich burials with weapons and fine bronze jewelry, but the very rich aristocratic burials found in northern Gaul generally are absent, suggesting a less hierarchical society.

OPPIDA IN BRITAIN

The *oppida* of Britain date to the late first century B.C. and early first century A.D. and are confined to the south and east of the country. Generally, they are in low-lying areas enclosing valleys or low ridges between rivers, suggesting that their role was not primarily defensive. In fact, their huge size (300 to 2,000 hectares or more) would have been impossible to man. The linear earthworks, or dikes, even avoid commanding strategic positions, and al-

though they are often massive, with sometimes double or triple lines of ramparts, their function seems rather to impress. They may mark royal properties, and only parts of them were occupied. The richest Late Iron Age burials are associated with them— Lexden at Colchester and Folly Lane at St. Albans. Historical sources and coinage allow researchers to identify up to three generations of dynastic kings, whose names appear on the coins along with the names of the cities, Camulodunum (Colchester), Verulamium (St. Albans), and Calleva Atrebatum (Silchester). Classical sources call Colchester the "capital" of Cunobelin (Cunobelinus, or Cymbeline), "king of the Britons." All the sites produce evidence of extensive trade with the Roman world, with wine and fish paste (*garum*) from Italy and Spain and fine pottery from Gaul and northern Italy. Several developed into major Roman towns.

See also **Germans** (*vol. 2, part 6*); **Manching** (*vol. 2, part 6*); **Hillforts** (*vol. 2, part 6*); **Gergovia** (*vol. 2, part 6*); **Kelheim** (*vol. 2, part 6*); **The Heuneburg** (*vol. 2, part 6*); **Agriculture** (*vol. 2, part 7*).

BIBLIOGRAPHY

Collis, John R. *Oppida: Earliest Towns North of the Alps.* Sheffield, U.K.: University of Sheffield, 1984.

Cunliffe, Barry W. *Iron Age Communities in Britain: An Account of England, Scotland, and Wales from the Seventh Century BC until the Roman Conquest.* 3d ed. London: Routledge and Kegan Paul, 1991.

Cunliffe, Barry W., and Simon Keay. *Social Complexity and the Development of Towns in Iberia, from the Copper Age to the Second Century AD.* Oxford: Oxford University Press, 1995.

Fichtl, S. *La ville celtique: Les oppida de 150 av. J.-C. à 15 ap. J.-C.* Paris: Éditions Errance, 2000.

Hodges, Richard. *Dark Age Economics: The Origins of Towns and Trade A.D. 600–1000.* 2d ed. London: Duckworth, 1989.

Guichard, Vincent, and Franck Perrin, eds. *L'aristocratie celte à la fin de l'Âge du Fer.* Bibracte 4. Glux-en-Glenne, France: Centre archéologique européenne du Mont Beuvray, 2001.

Guichard, Vincent, S. Sievers, and O. H. Urban, eds. *Les processus d'urbanisation à l'âge du Fer: Eisenzeitliche Urbanisationsprozesse.* Bibracte 5. Glux-en-Glenne, France: Centre archéologique européenne du Mont Beuvray, 2000.

Wells, Peter S. *The Barbarians Speak.* Princeton, N.J.: Princeton University Press, 1999.

JOHN COLLIS

MANCHING

Manching is a La Tène period *oppidum* site in Bavaria, Germany, dated from about 250 to 80 B.C., after which time it gradually was abandoned. It is one of a handful of sites of its type that have been investigated systematically, although because of its enormity, only about 3 percent of the settlement has been excavated. It has yielded both cultural material and physical settlement data that inform prehistorians about the organization and function of an *oppidum*. *Oppidum* (plural, *oppida*) is the term that Julius Caesar used to describe large, fortified towns that may have served as administrative centers for the Gallic tribes he had come north to conquer between 58 and 50 B.C.

The role of *oppida* is debated in the archaeological literature mainly because of the structural variability among these settlements, which differ from one another primarily in internal organization. Criteria for identification are based on settlement size, presence of fortification, industrial activities, geographic position, and period of occupation. Generally, the sites are large (hundreds of hectares) and defensively enclosed by earth and timber walls that use ditch and rampart technology. Such sites were located on naturally defended or elevated landscape features that intersected trade routes. They included areas for intensive production of iron implements and pottery. *Oppida* were established and abandoned during the final two centuries B.C., and their distribution across Europe coincides with the occupation of territories by Celtic populations from western France to the Czech Republic.

Manching is exceptional both for the scale of archaeological investigation that has focused on the site and for the wealth and diversity of material evidence collected there. Just south of Ingolstadt in the county of Pfaffenhoffen, this 380-hectare site once was situated on a river terrace along the Danube. The unusual setting (most *oppida* are elevated) was compensated for by its encroachment on a swamp along its northeast side. The supplemental fortification constructed around the exposed portion of the settlement is a 7.2-kilometer-long rampart wall of the *murus Gallicus* type. *Muri Gallici*—timber-laced ramparts fronted by ditches—generally are not seen as far east as Manching. The

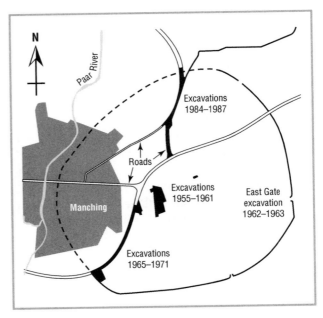

Fig. 1. Site plan showing excavation areas (dark regions) at modern-day Manching, Bavaria. Dark segments of modern roadways show excavation areas necessitated by roadway construction. ADAPTED FROM MOSCATI ET AL. 1991.

Kelheim-type rampart, with its exterior face constructed of vertical timbers and drystone wall (there is no interior walling or timber lacing through the earthen ramp), is more common throughout this area. The site was known from the remains of the wall from the early nineteenth century but was mistaken for a construction of Roman origin and identified only tentatively as Celtic in 1888 by a Romanist familiar with Caesar's *De bello Gallico*. In 1903 Paul Reinecke, working on an inventory of monuments and historic places, recognized artifacts from Manching that were similar to finds from *oppida* in France and Bohemia.

Excavations at Manching have been necessitated by construction projects that started with a military airfield between 1936 and 1938. A central portion of the settlement was destroyed when mechanical equipment was used to strip the area and tear away part of the wall. Efforts to recover artifacts were restricted by the exigencies of impending war, and only those materials that could be rescued from the spoil piles were saved. Subsequently, the airfield was bombed. In 1955 Allied forces decided to rebuild the airfield and, following negotiations with archaeologists, contributed an unprecedented sum of money for investigation of the settlement and of the area that would be affected by renewed construction. Excavation began that year and continued until 1974 under the direction of Werner Krämer. A subsequent excavation was organized in 1984, following a ten-year hiatus, through the Bayerisches Landesamt für Denkmalpflege (the Bavarian department that oversees protection of cultural sites and monuments). This investigation responded to the planned construction of an exit ramp on the secondary roadway that passes through the site (Landstrasse B16) and focused on a previously unexplored tract in the northern part of the settlement. Approximately 1 kilometer long by 35–60 meters wide, a strip running from the center of the roughly circular enclosed area to the wall was examined. A further 6-hectare excavation was begun in 1996. Materials in all these campaigns are consistent with La Tène C1 (280–220 B.C.) through D1 (120–80 B.C.) dates.

Evidence for development of the site shows a multiphase sequence of settlement beginning as early as the third century B.C., making Manching one of the older *oppida*. The earliest settlement is concentrated toward the center of the enclosed area and predates the construction of the wall. A track oriented east-west runs through the old center and provided the foundation for a later main street linking the east and west gates of the *murus Gallicus*.

It is likely that the initial construction of the wall (second half of the second century B.C.) was an expression of prestige that established Manching as a focal point for activities centered on production and exchange. These activities encompassed not only collection of raw materials and manufacture of goods but also feasting and the functions associated with market towns and fairs. The wall itself was rebuilt during the occupation of Manching, as is evidenced by a dendrochronological date for a structure in front of the eastern gate that coincides with its renovation in 105 B.C. It is likely that the function of the wall changed through time from display to defense because a third stage of construction reinforces the entire 7.2-kilometer length of the enclosure. Furthermore, burials of individuals who died of battle injuries attest to an attack on the settlement.

The interior of the settlement seems to have been organized to facilitate trade. Structures include rows of stalls, homes, and even warehouses for the agricultural produce that made up the bulk of exchanged goods. Raw materials used in the production of glass, pottery, iron, and bronze indicate that Manching was a thriving center for craft producers. Coins were recovered from the settlement, as were strikes used to mint coinage. Forty-eight imported amphorae that contained Mediterranean wine during transportation are among the items that were traded. Published volumes covering the analysis of the Manching materials feature bronze finds, tools, fibulae, glass, faunal material, graphite pottery, imported pottery and coarse wares, smooth wheel-thrown pottery and painted pottery, and human burials associated with the settlement.

See also **La Tène** (*vol. 2, part 6*); **Oppida** (*vol. 2, part 6*); **Hillforts** (*vol. 2, part 6*).

BIBLIOGRAPHY

Bott, R. D., G. Grosse, F. E. Wagner, U. Wagner, R. Gebhard, and J. Riederer. "The Oppidum of Manching: A Center of Celtic Culture in Early Europe." *Naturwissenschaften* 81, no. 12 (1994): 560–562.

Collis, John. *Oppida: Earliest Towns North of the Alps.* Charlesworth, U.K.: H. Huddersfield, 1984.

Dannheimer, Hermann, and Rupert Gebhard, eds. *Das keltische Jahrtausend.* Mainz, Germany: Philipp von Zabern, 1993.

Gebhard, Rupert. "The Celtic Oppidum of Manching and Its Exchange System." In *Different Iron Ages: Studies on the Iron Age in Temperate Europe.* Edited by J. D. Hill and C. G. Cumberpatch, pp. 111–120. BAR International Series, no. 602. Oxford: British Archaeological Reports, 1995.

Green, Miranda J., ed. *The Celtic World.* London: Routledge, 1995.

Krämer, Werner. "The Oppidum at Manching." *Antiquity* 34 (1960): 191–200.

Moscati, Sabatino, et al., eds. *The Celts.* New York: Rizzoli, 1991.

Wells, Peter S. *Farms, Villages, and Cities: Commerce and Urban Origins in Late Prehistoric Europe.* Ithaca, N.Y.: Cornell University Press, 1984.

SUSAN MALIN-BOYCE

HILLFORTS

Sites of physical eminence in the landscape have been important throughout prehistory. Hilltops may well have been liminal places where the world of the living met the world of the supernatural, where the dead were laid to rest in a sacred space. They could have been locations for religious gatherings, perhaps at specific times of the year.

Hilltops also could have offered a measure of short-term protection in uncertain times, but a longer-term threat would have called for defensive building. Initially, wooden palisades might have been sufficient, but soon more substantial structures of earth or stone would have to have been built. Many of these sites were never more than places of temporary refuge. There is no doubt that in all areas of Europe such defended enclosures were sites of permanent occupation that often were associated with industrial, commercial, and probably also administrative and ritual activity. Security and defense must be seen as the dominant function of hillforts, but these frequently impressive constructions must have served other, less material purposes. The great sites—Maiden Castle in Dorset, England, as a prime example—possess massive ramparts that appear far larger and more elaborate than was dictated by the needs of military defense. With these sites, considerations of prestige and ostentation may be assumed. Dominating the physical horizon, such great hillforts were tangible statements of tribal power.

It is not completely clear when hillforts in the truest sense first were constructed in continental Europe. As early as the late fifth and early fourth millennia B.C., simple palisaded enclosures were elaborated by the erection of earthworks, often of impressive dimensions, in ostensibly defensive situations. At least a few of them were for protection. In Britain hilltop settlements of the Neolithic, such as Carn Brea in Cornwall and Hambledon Hill in Dorset, suggest a similar function.

Early Bronze Age Europe saw continued, sporadic use of hilltop sites, especially in parts of Germany and farther east, though these were a response to local needs rather than a widespread development. The evolution of hillfort construction on a significant scale across Europe, however, commenced in the later Bronze Age, perhaps at the beginning of the last pre-Christian millennium. There has been considerable discussion concerning the impetus for this trend: population pressure, climatic deterioration, changing polities, security uncertainties, and novel methods of warfare all have been proposed. It is likely that all these factors played a part in this trend to a greater or lesser extent, but significant resources, in both materials and manpower, clearly were involved in their creation.

Within the fortified area at this time, houses frequently were situated along the ramparts or filling much of the internal area in regular, parallel rows. The Wittnauer Horn in Switzerland, a promontory site defended by a massive, timber-framed rampart with an external ditch, is one of the best examples. It originally was proposed that there were two rows of houses, about seventy in all, but research leaves room to doubt this figure and even the contemporaneity of the structures. Differing in internal layout is the contemporary Altes Schloss, near Potsdam in eastern Germany. There, within a roughly pear-shaped enclosure about 100 meters in greatest width, some thirty houses occurred in at least five rows, along with storage pits and a well. Such sites indicate the emergence of agglomerated settlements of considerable size.

Apart from the large-scale excavations of the proto-urban sites of the Late La Tène period, such as Manching in Bavaria and Mont Beuvray in France, emphasis in hillfort excavations over the last half of the twentieth century has concentrated to a large extent on the nature of defensive construction. There was great variety in the details, of course, but, in broad terms, during the Bronze and into the Iron Age there were two essential styles: those with vertical faces and those that originally presented a sloping surface to the exterior. Without excavation, however, it generally is impossible to distinguish between the two.

Among the many forms of timber-laced defenses are those of the so-called *Kastenbau* type, involving boxlike compartments of longitudinal and transverse beams filled with stones and rubble. They were built without the vertical timbers at front or back that are features of the widespread box rampart. These ramparts, of necessity, possessed transverse beams through the body of the rampart to prevent the outward pressure and collapse of the uprights. A variant of this is the *Altkönig-Preist* type (named after two typical examples in Germany), which is characterized by the additional presence of stone walls at the front and the particularly heavy use of internal timbers. Other, less elaborate forms of construction are known, including those where the uprights were secured in position by the transverse lane alone and those with verticals on the front only, the supporting transverses being held in place solely by the weight of the bank. The culmination of timber-laced construction was the massive *murus Gallicus* of the Late La Tène period, which possessed ramparts of nailed box construction with an outer masonry facing and, on occasion, a substantial internal earthen support. Such ramparts enclosed settlements that often were of considerable size, with houses arranged along streets and possessing most of the specialist activities of the true town, including the minting of coins. In Gaul, in the last century before Christ, the Roman general Julius Caesar had no hesitation in using the term *oppidum* to describe them.

Defenses of dump construction consisted of wide, sloping ramparts of piled earth lacking the support of timber elements. More economical to build than were the timber-laced ramparts, a potential weakness was that the outer face, without support, of necessity sloped to the interior. Its height thus was critical, and associated ditches of substantial depth were common, especially in England. In northern France a variant, the so-called *Fécamp* type, possessed shallower but considerably broader ditches. Some British hillforts were constructed with the sloping outer face of the rampart continued by the inner face of the ditch, thus maximizing the defensive potential. Massive ramparts constructed solely of rubble, such as the huge German site of Otzenhausen, also occur. Its prodigious dimensions alone were deemed sufficient for effective defense, but, as elsewhere, the scale of the protective ramparts may well have been intended for more than merely defensive use.

Entrances, potentially the weakest point in the defensive circuit, included angled approaches, overlapping ramparts, mazelike arrangements of strategically placed ramparts, and various timber constructions, including footbridges or towers. Associated especially with the Late La Tène *oppida*, inturned entrances were constructed to create long, narrow passages along which attackers had to progress. Massive timber gateways, sometimes doubled or even trebled, also were present.

The varying types of rampart construction cannot in any way be seen as regular developments over time. It seems more likely that from a number of self-evident structural variables, individual building teams chose specific construction methods that were deemed suitable in the context of the available workforce and for the immediate needs. The Late La Tène *oppida* stand apart, however, as does the spectacular mud-brick wall of the Late Hallstatt Heuneburg hillfort in southwest Germany. The latter, an obvious imitation of a Mediterranean town wall, emphasizes once again that functional considerations alone were not always paramount concerns in defensive construction.

The trend toward hillfort building that gathered momentum across Europe from the later

Bronze Age onward can be mirrored in Britain and in Ireland. In the former area, Rams Hills, Berkshire, and the Breidden, Powys, represent early examples. In Ireland, too, modern investigations show with increasing clarity that the centuries c. 1000 B.C. witnessed a significant explosion in hillfort construction. Rathgall, County Wicklow; Mooghaun, County Clare; and Haughey's Fort, County Armagh, all now yielding radiocarbon dates between 1000 and 900 B.C., are but three examples of this early development. In all cases occupation of some permanence has been recognized.

Britain, with more than three thousand structures of notionally hillfort character, presents acute problems of definition. The classic examples, numbering several hundred, occur in south-central England in a broad band that runs from the southern coast to northern Wales. Construction, as noted, commenced early in the millennium, but the major sites belong to the period from the mid-millennium onward. Timber-laced ramparts of types comparable to those found on the European mainland have been identified (with the notable absence of the *murus Gallicus*) and, of course, massive defenses of earth alone, often in multiple form, are widespread. Entrances of varied complexity occur, including those of inturned form. The latter resemble the inturned entrances in Europe, but it must be stressed that the British forts are not a product of invading groups, as was once believed. They are entirely indigenous developments.

Large-scale excavation at selected sites, including Danebury, Hampshire; Maiden Castle, Dorset; Croft Ambrey, Hertfordshire; and elsewhere, has provided extensive information on the nature of hillforts in late prehistoric Britain. Danebury, a triple-ramparted hillfort of 5 hectares, was subjected to research excavation over twenty seasons, which ultimately exposed 57 percent of the interior. This site has provided us with the most detailed and comprehensive insights into the nature of the late prehistoric hillfort in Britain.

Three main phases of activity, reflected in the three ramparts, were recognized, and dating evidence indicates that the site was in use from about 550 B.C. to the beginning of the Christian era. The innermost, primary rampart is a massive earthen construction with a deep, V-sectioned ditch: from ditch base to the crest of the bank was a distance of 16.1 meters, dimensions surpassed only by the corresponding inner defense at Maiden Castle, which totaled an astonishing 25.2 meters. Initially, there were two entrances and later just one, and they were developed to a level of exceptional defensive complexity, providing complex, mazelike approaches to the interior. Large, strategically placed caches of sling stones underlined the military aspect of the construction.

Within the enclosure, houses, both rectangular and circular, were aligned along streets extending more or less east to west across the interior. Well over one hundred houses were identified, but not all of them were contemporary. Numerous small square or rectangular structures, which may have been grain silos, also were revealed. Most spectacular were the 2,400-odd pits densely concentrated in all excavated zones, superficially resembling the surface of Gruyère cheese. These pits, carefully dug and as deep as 3 meters, generally are seen as having functioned for the storage of grain. In the center were four small rectangular structures, which might have been temples. Extensive evidence for a wide range of secular activities also was brought to light.

The most remarkable feature of Danebury was the evidence for grain storage on what must have been a prodigious scale. The enormous storage capacity implied seems far in excess of the needs of the occupants of Danebury, a number estimated to have been between 200 and 350 at any one time. It has been suggested that the primary function of Danebury was to act as a central place for the storage and protection of grain for the peoples of the surrounding landscape.

Danebury is the classic British hillfort, but it is scarcely typical for the whole island. In Scotland, for example, structures of other types occur, including those with various forms of timber lacing. Most notable, however, are the curious vitrified forts, so called because of the intense burning to which the stones of the ramparts have been subjected. These sites have engendered considerable discussion—accidental burning, hostile action, or even deliberate burning by the inhabitants of the forts have been suggested to explain the vitrification. Hostile action perhaps is most likely, but in any event such ramparts originally must have been laced with timber.

The great southern English hillforts mirror the trend toward centralization, if not urbanization, that had already begun on the European mainland in the latter part of the second century B.C. Belgic influences in southern England advanced this trend a step further, but, as was the case on the mainlaind, it was halted by Roman occupation, soon to be re-born in another guise under the Pax Romana, or age of Roman peace (37 B.C.–A.D. 180).

See also **Maiden Castle** *vol. 1, part 1*); **Hambledon Hill** (*vol. 1, part 3*); **Hallstatt** (*vol. 2, part 6*); **Oppida** (*vol. 2, part 6*); **Manching** (*vol. 2, part 6*); **Danebury** (*vol. 2, part 6*); **The Heuneburg** (*vol. 2, part 6*).

BIBLIOGRAPHY

Avery, Michael. *Hillfort Defences of Southern Britain.* Oxford: Tempus Reparatum, 1993.

Collis, John. R *Oppida: Earliest Towns North of the Alps.* Sheffield, U.K.: University of Sheffield, 1984.

Harding, D. W., ed. *Hillforts: Later Prehistoric Earthworks in Britain and Ireland.* London and New York: Academic, 1976.

BARRY RAFTERY

ORIGINS OF IRON PRODUCTION

FOLLOWED BY FEATURE ESSAY ON:

Iron is potentially superior to bronze and is much more common than copper and tin, bronze's constituents. Iron's workable ores are widespread in Europe and particularly abundant in the Alpine region. The advantage of iron's abundance was offset because ancient technology could not take full advantage of its properties. Furnace temperatures could not reach iron's relatively high melting point. During the Bronze Age, small bits of iron occasionally must have been produced during copper smelting, but metalworkers could not melt it as they could other metals. When iron ore was intentionally smelted in ancient times, the iron was reduced to metal in the solid state, leaving a spongy mass with slag still trapped in pores. Unlike bronze, which could be cast, iron had to be worked in the solid state to turn it into useful shapes. A smith reheated it in a forge to soften the metal to liquefy any trapped slag and then repeatedly hammered it to force out as much slag as possible while shaping the iron into ingots or finished forms. Reheating and hammering were used in working bronze—they improve the metal. Because iron could not be melted, it could not be enhanced by mixing with other metals, and pure iron does not respond favorably to hammering and reheating, as bronze does. Techniques for dealing consistently with molten iron were not developed in Europe until postmedieval times.

Iron in the solid state takes up carbon and forms a product called steel, but this process requires special smelting conditions that did not occur often in ancient furnaces. There is another chance to introduce carbon into iron during forging, but this so-called case hardening is extremely difficult to achieve. Once steel can be produced on a consistent basis, it does have many advantages over bronze. It is almost as hard as bronze and can be further quench-hardened—reheated and dunked into water. The subsequent extremely hard but brittle steel can be reheated again, and a balance can be achieved between hardness and toughness that is vastly superior to bronze. Steel production is, however, a labor-intensive process requiring specialized skill.

Archaeological evidence for iron production takes four forms: production sites (furnaces and forges), by-products (slag and unused ore), tools, and finished objects. Slag has been excavated at numerous Early Iron Age sites, often in fill, but production areas have been identified definitively at fewer than ten sites. Fortunately, these sites span almost the full time and space of Early Iron Age Europe: the earliest is Tillmitsch in the southeastern

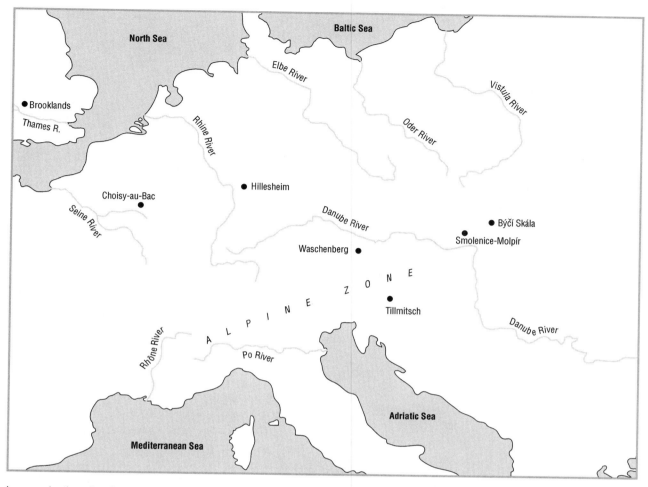

Iron production sites from 800 to 400 B.C.

Alps in Austria, dated to 800 B.C., and the latest is Brooklands in southern England, well outside of the Alpine region and dated to 400 B.C. The map shows these two sites and the five more best-known sites that fall between them chronologically, all within the Alpine zone. In general, these sites were hill-forts involved in long-distance trade with the Mediterranean world. They bear evidence of other craft production, suggesting that they were regional centers with at least part-time artisans trading finished goods to a hinterland. The raw materials they received in return enabled them to support themselves and also to tap into the long-distance trade.

Smelting and smithing took place at the same locations, and smelting was carried out in simple furnaces where the charge was allowed to cool in place. Forges were of uncomplicated open design

not conducive to case hardening. Several dozen slags have been analyzed from some of these sites and from other less well-defined provenances dated to the Early Iron Age. These slags uniformly suggest smelting temperatures of 1,100–1,200°C (2,000–2,200°F), consistent with the type of simple furnace excavated.

Tools—hammers, tongs, and anvils themselves made of iron—are quite rare from Early Iron Age Europe and generally have been found in graves. They, too, reflect a simple technology. On the other hand, by definition, thousands upon thousands of iron objects are known from the Early Iron Age, and by now hundreds of these artifacts have been analyzed. Most of these objects come from graves, a few from settlements, and a handful from the production sites. The earliest iron objects in barbarian Europe are parts of jewelry, sometimes covered with

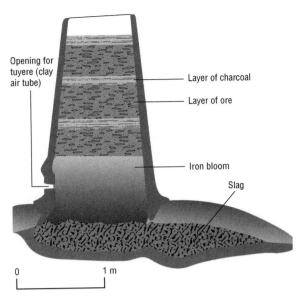

Opening for tuyere (clay air tube)

Layer of charcoal

Layer of ore

Iron bloom

Slag

0   1 m

Fig. 1. Schematic diagram of a typical shaft furnace of the Iron Age. In this case the slag has been tapped off. In some shaft furnaces and in simple bowl furnaces, the slag is allowed to solidify in place, above the iron bloom. ADAPTED FROM HTTP://MEMBERS.AON.AT/DBUNDSCH/LATENE.HTM.

bronze. Weapons are found a bit later, primarily in graves. Agricultural tools date only to the Late Iron Age.

Analysis has shown that the earliest objects, even the weapons, were almost all made of plain iron. They were not intentionally improved during the forging process, although a few were of steel produced accidentally in the smelting process. The few objects exhibiting case hardening or quench hardening were apparently southern imports. Throughout the Early Iron Age, techniques for improving iron developed slowly, and the most sophisticated techniques do not appear until the end of the Iron Age.

During the transition from the Bronze Age to the Iron Age, the barbarians of temperate Europe were in indirect but steady contact with Mediterranean peoples. Iron production was pioneered in the Alpine region c. 800 B.C., at regional centers that already had advanced methods for working in bronze and were in contact with the south. The Greeks had sophisticated steel metallurgy, and objects of trade entered the barbarian world. The northern bronzesmiths would have recognized iron as an occasional by-product of copper smelting that they had not found particularly useful. The presence

of a small amount of Mediterranean iron of superior quality might have spurred barbarian investigations into the new metal, or local conditions brought on by trade and other factors might have led them to experiment with a variety of pyrotechnologies. In any event, there is no evidence that they learned iron production from the south, and sophisticated techniques were developed slowly over a long period of time out of local bronzesmithing traditions. The earliest iron was inferior to bronze and not suitable for many applications, so there was no major technological advantage to adopting it. Iron was at first a decorative material and then came to be used to replace bronze in a few very specific applications, notably in certain types of funerary goods.

Nevertheless, the practice of ironworking spread north and west by a combination of trade and technology transfer. Although in most cases the development continued to be indigenous, in some cases actual migration may have been involved. Ironworking rapidly reached Poland, Germany, and France; it reached northern and western Europe somewhat later. Each local area seems to have developed ironworking according to its own trajectory. Although the use of iron must have had feedback on other aspects of society, it was the other social forces that led to iron production rather than vice versa. The barbarians developed indigenous technology that was to underpin their society from the Late Iron Age until almost modern times.

See also **Early Metallurgy in Southeastern Europe** (*vol. 1, part 4*); **Ironworking** (*vol. 2, part 6*).

BIBLIOGRAPHY

Ehrenreich, Robert M. *Trade, Technology, and the Ironworking Community in the Iron Age of Southern Britain.* BAR British Series, no. 144. Oxford: British Archaeological Reports, 1985.

Geselowitz, Michael N. "The Role of Iron Production in the Formation of an 'Iron Age Economy' in Central Europe." *Research in Economic Anthropology* 10 (1988): 225–255.

Pleiner, Radomír. "Early Iron Metallurgy in Europe." In *The Coming of the Age of Iron.* Edited by Theodore A. Wertime and James D. Muhly, pp. 375–415. New Haven, Conn.: Yale University Press, 1980.

Raymond, Robert. *Out of the Fiery Furnace: The Impact of Metals on the History of Mankind.* Philadelphia: University of Pennsylvania Press, 2000. (Recent general history of metallurgy written for the general public.)

Rostoker, William, and Bennet Bronson. *Pre-Industrial Iron: Its Technology and Ethnology*. Archaeomaterials Monograph, no. 1. Philadelphia: University of Pennsylvania, 1990. (Survey of prehistoric iron production; much material covers Europe but is somewhat technical.)

Scott, Brian G. *Early Irish Ironworking*. Belfast: Ulster Museum, 1990.

Tylecote, Ronald F. *A History of Metallurgy*. 2d ed. London: Institute of Materials, 1992. (General, if somewhat technical, history of metallurgy, including iron and focusing on Europe.)

Wertime, Theodore A., and James D. Muhly. *The Coming of the Age of Iron*. New Haven, Conn.: Yale University Press, 1980. (Collection of regional syntheses about the origins of iron production worldwide plus background essays on method and theory.)

MICHAEL N. GESELOWITZ

IRONWORKING

By about 300 B.C., iron production was common throughout Europe. The abundance of iron ore, however, was offset by the limitations of the bloomery process through which iron was produced. Furnace temperatures could not reach iron's relatively high melting point. When iron ore was smelted, the iron was reduced to metal in the solid state, leaving a spongy mass (called the sponge or bloom) with slag still trapped in pores. A smith reheated the bloom in a forge to soften the metal and liquefy any trapped slag and then hammered it repeatedly to force out as much slag as possible while shaping the iron into ingots or finished forms. The wrought iron so produced was relatively pure and therefore not very hard. The smiths learned that they could harden the iron by placing it in the forge in contact with organic materials. It is now known that this technique, called case hardening, works by introducing carbon into the surface of the iron, converting it to steel. The process was labor-intensive and difficult to control. Furthermore, a great deal of fuel—charcoal, produced from wood—was needed for both smelting and forging. Although wood was readily available in barbarian Europe, procuring the wood represented another labor-intensive step in production.

Ironworking in this early era was carried out in many settlements of various sizes. The level of pro-

duction was small-scale, the political economy had to support a full-time specialist, and the quality of the product could not always be assured. As a result, iron was used primarily for weapons, funerary goods, and other items with a strong political and social component and only to a very limited extent for agricultural tools.

The nature of iron production began to change with the rise of urbanism in Late Iron Age Europe. After about 200 B.C., large, complex settlements began to emerge in specific areas of Europe. These *oppida* were based in part on long-distance trade with the Roman world as well as control of local political, social, and economic networks. Evidence of large-scale iron production occurs on most of these sites, and some even appear to have specialized in iron production. Several well-excavated *oppida* in Bavaria, such as Manching and Kelheim, have provided evidence of every facet of ironworking, from mining through forging, and the analysis of the finds from these sites confirms the view of site specialization and of trade with Rome. The Roman need for iron may have led at least in part to this urban phenomenon. In any event, the formation of large centers with higher population densities and greater social differentiation and specialization certainly allowed and encouraged the support of large-scale iron production, which in turn made iron more important to the economy. Not only do a wider variety of tools and weapons of iron appear, but evidence also includes the appearance of iron bars that seem to have been used as a kind of currency. The use of the iron plowshare almost certainly had a major impact on the rest of the economy. Ironworking also continued to be carried out on the smaller settlements, although their economic relationship to the centers is not clear.

In addition to the changes in the quantity of iron, there were qualitative changes as well. First, the simple shaft furnaces were replaced by slightly more-advanced domed furnaces, which did not create much greater temperatures but were more consistent and had larger capacity. Archaeometallurgical analyses from many parts of Europe have shown that the smiths learned that steel could be reheated and quenched to produce an even harder substance and that the resulting quench-hardened steel could be reheated to achieve a balance between hardness and toughness. This technique was not known in the Early Iron Age and would not have been obvious to early metalworkers because it does not work on other metals such as bronze. The smiths also learned how to weld a steel edge onto a soft iron back without accidentally decarburizing—removing the carbon from—the steel, a difficult process that leads to a superior tool or weapon. Various finds of smiths' tools also attest to the range of techniques available to them. They did not, however, learn to "pile" steel by alternating thin layers of iron and steel, as was done in the Classical world.

There is some debate as to what extent the smiths of the barbarian world developed these techniques independently owing to their long experience with iron and to what extent the technology diffused from the classical world. On the one hand, at the time of the Celtic invasions of Italy in the third century B.C., classical sources make reference to the inferior nature of the barbarians' swords. On the other hand, by the second century B.C., the sources speak of the outstanding quality of the steel from Celtic Iberia. After the Roman conquest of central and western Europe, Noricum—now the province of Carinthia in the Austrian Alps—became the major steel supplier for the empire.

The situation of barbarian iron production outside the Roman *limes* after the Roman conquest until the fall of the empire was a mixed one. Some areas, such as the Holy Cross Mountains in Poland, continued to specialize in and produce large quantities of iron for local consumption and trade with Rome. Other areas underwent a decentralization and technical regression. Still others, such as Ireland and Scandinavia, which had originally been outside the zone of increased and improved iron production, gradually developed their own industries, probably under the influence of their trading and raiding relationships with Roman territories. It is safe to say that, after the fall of the Roman Empire, the barbarian world was everywhere an iron-based economy but one that depended on relatively basic techniques and somewhat decentralized production.

See also **Oppida** (*vol. 2, part 6*); **Origins of Iron Production** (*vol. 2, part 6*).

BIBLIOGRAPHY

Ehrenreich, Robert M. *Trade, Technology, and the Ironworking Community in the Iron Age of Southern Britain.* BAR British Series, no. 144. Oxford: British Archaeological Reports, 1985.

Pleiner, Radomír. "Early Iron Metallurgy in Europe." In *The Coming of the Age of Iron.* Edited by Theodore A. Wertime and James D. Muhly, pp. 375–415. New Haven, Conn.: Yale University Press, 1980.

Raymond, Robert. *Out of the Fiery Furnace: The Impact of Metals on the History of Mankind.* University Park, Pa.: Pennsylvania State University Press, 1986.

Rostoker, William, and Bennet Bronson. *Pre-Industrial Iron: Its Technology and Ethnology.* Archaeomaterials Monograph, no. 1. Philadelphia: University of Pennsylvania, 1990.

Scott, Brian G. *Early Irish Ironworking.* Belfast: Ulster Museum, 1990

Tylecote, Ronald F. *A History of Metallurgy.* 2d ed. London: Institute of Materials, 1992.

Wells, Peter S. *Settlement, Economy, and Cultural Change at the End of the European Iron Age: Excavations at Kelheim in Bavaria, 1987–1991.* Archaeology Series, no. 6. Ann Arbor, Mich.: International Monographs in Prehistory, 1993. (Includes general discussion of the *oppida* and ironworking, including data from other sites, such as Manching, plus specialist reports on the ironworking finds from Kelheim.)

Wertime, Theodore A., and James D. Muhly. *The Coming of the Age of Iron.* New Haven, Conn.: Yale University Press, 1980.

MICHAEL N. GESELOWITZ

COINAGE OF IRON AGE EUROPE

Coinage was an invention of the Greek inhabitants of Asia Minor in the seventh century B.C. Over the next three centuries, the concept spread through the rest of the Mediterranean world, including the Greek colonies of southern France and northeastern Spain, such as Emporion (Ampurias) and Massalia (Marseille), although it was not until c. 300 B.C. that the Romans adopted a regular coinage. At about this time the idea also began to penetrate northward into barbarian Europe. By the second century B.C. some form of coinage was in use over much of the Continent, from the Black Sea and the Danube basin to the Atlantic coast of France and Spain and as far north as Bohemia and central Germany. The inhabitants of southeastern Britain were among the last to adopt coinage and continued to produce it in the first century A.D., after the other coin-using regions had been absorbed into the Roman Empire. Most of the barbarian groups who adopted coinage were Celtic speaking but also included Germans, Iberians, Illyrians, Ligurians, and Thracians.

At the outset Iron Age coinage was either of gold or of silver and derived from Greek models. Precious metal issues in the name of the powerful Macedonian rulers of the late fourth century B.C., Philip II and his son Alexander the Great, were by far the most influential prototypes, but the coins of various Greek colonies also were imitated. Over time distinctive local and regional coinage traditions began to emerge as indigenous moneyers added features and designs of their own. None of the earliest Iron Age coinages is meaningfully inscribed, but from the second century B.C. onward many issuers began to put their names—and sometimes such details as a title or mint name—on their coins. Most legends are in Greek or Latin letters or a mixture of the two, although Iberian, Illyrian, and Italiote scripts were all used in certain areas. As Rome became the dominant Mediterranean power, its coinage also began to be imitated by Iron Age groups. Bronze coinage was a relatively late innovation and essentially was confined to western Europe. Trimetallic coinages are found only in a few parts of southeastern Britain and northern France, whose rulers were effectively already under Roman domination.

Two main and essentially discrete zones of Iron Age coinage can be discerned based on different Greek models. Over a vast area of southern Europe, extending from the Balkans and the Danube basin through the Po Basin in Italy and to the Rhône and Garonne basins of southern France, almost all Iron Age coinages were in silver. Farther to the north, however, in Bohemia, southern Germany, northern France, and eventually Britain they were initially of gold. A third, smaller zone existed in Spain and Mediterranean France west of the Rhône, where from the late third to the early first centuries B.C. numerous groups struck bronze (and occasionally silver) coinages, mostly modeled on the contemporary bronze issues of Roman Spain. None of the peoples inhabiting the north European plain or Scandinavia adopted coinage at this stage, possibly because it did not fit with their dominant ideology or value system.

Region	Bronze	Potin	Silver	Gold
Balkans–Danube Basin	(y)		X	
Alps–North Italy			X	y
Southern France	y		X	
Spain	X		y	
Southern Germany–Czech Republic			y	X
Northern France–Belgium–Luxembourg	X	X	y	X
Southeast Britain	y	y	X	X

X=primary coinage metal(s); y=subsidiary coinage metal(s).
In northwest France, many of the later "gold" coin types were in fact struck from a silver and copper alloy known as billon.

Principal coinages in the different regions of Iron Age Europe.

THE "SILVER" ZONE

The earliest Iron Age coinages began during the late fourth century B.C. in the modern Balkans and were faithful imitations of posthumous silver tetradrachms of Philip II of Macedon, with a bearded head on one side and a horseman on the other. They were not so much a local coinage as substitutes for the real thing. The first unmistakably native coinages emerged in the early third century B.C. They were all based on the same model, except in the regions closest to the Black Sea, where the silver tetradrachms of Alexander the Great or his successor, Philip III Arrhidaeus, provided the preferred model; these portray a seated figure instead of the horseman. A few Greek gold types also were copied in this area, but this production quickly ceased.

Over the next century silver coinage spread through eastern Europe, sometimes employing other Greek models. The overall volume increased markedly, and distinctive regional traditions developed, stylistically much further removed from their prototypes, such as the initially dumpy and later broader *scyphate* (dished) coinages found in the southeastern Carpathians or the facing and double-headed issues found in Moesia. Eventually, in the first century B.C., many groups first abandoned Hellenistic models in exchange for Roman types and added legends; they then stopped striking coinage altogether. Silver fractional units or bimetallic coinages in gold and silver, such as the Biatec series of Bohemia and southern Slovakia, also occur, but bronze coins are seen only in Pannonia.

Elsewhere in the silver zone the initial models were provided mainly by the coinages of various Greek colonies. The Celtic inhabitants of northern Italy adopted silver types imitated from the drachms of Massalia, to which legends in Italiote characters later were added; the Massalia drachms also influenced the weight standard of the first silver coinages of the Rhône Valley. In southwestern France several peoples issued coinages with a distinctive cross-shaped emblem on one side, copied from the Greek colony of Rhode (Rosas) in northeastern Spain. This series probably started in the third century B.C. and lasted to the early first century B.C. The peoples of west-central France opted instead to copy coins issued by the neighboring colony at Emporion; subsequently this coinage provided the model for the first small-scale silver coinages in Britain and northern France.

THE "GOLD" ZONE

In western Europe the earliest Iron Age coinages were gold staters or, more rarely, divisions copied from pieces struck by Philip II of Macedon and his successors from c. 340 B.C. onward, with a head on one side and a two-horse chariot on the other. These imitations even faithfully reproduce the symbols used by particular Greek mints, allowing different groups of primary copies to be identified, dispersed over an area extending from southwestern Germany through northern Switzerland and eastern and central France as far as the Atlantic coast. As in eastern Europe, distinctive regional traditions gradually developed, as, for example, in Picardy, where the designs also were influenced by the Greek coinage of southern Italy, or in Brittany, where debased alloys of silver and bronze replaced gold.

In central Europe developments followed a more diverse pattern. The earliest Iron Age coins in Moravia and Bohemia copy a gold stater of Alexander the Great with Victory standing on one side;

these coins were in their turn copied in other areas, such as the Upper Danube. In the late third century B.C. the Alexander copies were supplanted by Biatec superficially similar types, influenced by both Greek and Roman coinage. These "Alkis" types themselves had various derivatives, including virtually formless coins shaped somewhat like mussels (including ultimately the series mentioned earlier). The influence of late-third-century B.C. Roman coinage also is apparent on a series of tiny gold coins (about $1/24$ of a stater) from southern Germany bearing a double head, soon supplanted by concave coins with affinities to the "mussels" tradition, known as "rainbow cups." The rainbow cup coinage in due course spread into the middle Rhineland and eventually surfaced—in very debased form—in the Netherlands.

The minting of Greek-style gold coinage in western and central Europe apparently began shortly after the initial copying of silver in eastern Europe, suggesting that broadly similar processes were at work. One possibility is that barbarians serving as mercenaries for various Hellenistic rulers in the wars following the death of Alexander the Great in 323 B.C. became accustomed to being paid off in precious metal coins and introduced the concept to their home territories, whence the practice gradually spread. The extensive migrations of Celtic-speaking peoples around the same time may be another relevant factor. Neither idea explains why the peoples over such large regions systematically opted for particular models—although, in more general terms, it is easy to see why motifs such as severed heads, mounted warriors, and chariots on the relevant prototypes must have appealed to them.

LATER DEVELOPMENTS IN WESTERN EUROPE

In the early to middle second century B.C. various peoples in east-central and northern France and the extreme southeast of Britain began to make cast bronze coinage, known as potin after its high tin content. These started as close copies of the bronze coinage of Massalia, but various regional traditions, often with purely native designs, soon emerged. Slightly later several groups in the Rhône Valley and east-central France began striking inscribed silver coinages on a weight standard close to half the Roman denarius (which weighed about 4 grams),

Fig. 1. Silver coin of Biatec, Czech Republic. © COPYRIGHT THE BRITISH MUSEUM. REPRODUCED BY PERMISSION.

many of them clearly directly inspired by Roman types. These so-called quinarius coinages soon spread into other areas, such as the Rhineland, or as in central and western France, stimulated comparable silver coinages on a slightly different weight standard. By the early first century B.C. these new silver coinages had all but ousted gold, apart from in regions north of the Seine (including Britain), where gold remained the preferred metal.

The Roman conquest of France in the middle of the first century B.C. brought further changes.

Fig. 2. Potin coin of the Remi, northern France. © Copyright The British Museum. Reproduced by permission.

Across central France quinarius types proliferated and in places even expanded in volume, while everywhere potin was replaced by struck bronze coinage, which until then had been confined to a few areas, such as western Picardy. Unlike potin, which often circulated over very large areas, many of the new struck bronze issues were quite localized, and some show strong Roman influence. At this stage a few northern rulers, who were probably Roman client

kings (the title commonly given to barbarian rulers who had entered into treaties of friendship with Rome), issued trimetallic sets of gold, silver, and bronze coinage.

With the organization of conquered peoples and Roman allies alike into full Roman provinces, native minting rapidly declined. By the beginning of the first century A.D. most Iron Age peoples inside and beyond the boundaries of the empire had stopped issuing coinage altogether or had turned to producing versions of official Roman bronze types. The sole exception was Britain, where in the regions closest to the Continent, Roman client kings issued coinages with Romanized designs and legends, although the other regional coinages retained their traditional types up until the Roman conquest of the island. Under Roman influence, the kingdoms around the Thames estuary seem to have evolved a more complex system of denominations, with numerous base metal types struck in copper or brass as well as in bronze or at different weights; elsewhere in Britain, however, only gold and silver units and divisions were minted.

THE ROLE OF IRON AGE COINAGE

The function of Iron Age coinage is the subject of controversy. The distribution of different types of coins and the kinds of archaeological sites at which they occur provide the best sources of evidence, but the resultant picture is biased toward the location where the coins finally were abandoned, which is not necessarily where they were used. From studying the contexts of discovery, it is clear that most Iron Age gold and silver finds, and many base metal coins as well, were not casual losses but were deposited intentionally by their users, whether for votive reasons or for security. This applies even to settlement finds. Another problem is that in the earlier period only a tiny proportion of coinage was ever deposited—most of it presumably was recycled—further limiting what can be said about the likely uses.

Because coins were predominantly precious metal and thus presumably of high value, the principal reason for issuing Iron Age coinages cannot have been to facilitate exchange, either local or interregional. Like Greek and Roman coinage, Iron Age coinage is far more likely to have been minted to enable its issuers to make various types of payment as well as providing a convenient store of wealth. While the context in which coinage was adopted suggests that securing or rewarding military services was one of its main functions, the nature of the finds leaves little doubt that gold and silver soon were used in many other forms of social and political transactions between members of the elite, often over long distances, and also as religious offerings to their gods.

Although potin coinages were of base metal, their silvery appearance and widespread distributions imply that they, too, were intended primarily for discharging social and perhaps religious obligations. Most struck bronze coinages, on the other hand, are found close to their places of origin and are associated in particular with the leading centers and settlements. This suggests that they were used in a more limited range of payments than other types of Iron Age coinage and only in places where their face values were guaranteed by the issuers.

See also **Coinage of the Early Middle Ages** (*vol. 2, part 7*); **Agriculture** (*vol. 2, part 7*).

BIBLIOGRAPHY

Allen, Derek F. *The Coins of the Ancient Celts.* Edinburgh: Edinburgh University Press, 1980.

Clogg, P. W., and Colin C. Haselgrove. "The Composition of Iron Age Struck 'Bronze' Coinage in Eastern England." *Oxford Journal of Archaeology* 14, no. 1 (1995): 41–62.

Creighton, John. *Coins and Power in Late Iron Age Britain.* Cambridge, U.K.: Cambridge University Press, 2000.

Fischer, Brigitte. "Les différents monétaires des premières imitations du statère de Philippe II de Macédoine." *Études celtiques* 28 (1991): 137–156.

Haselgrove, Colin C. "The Incidence of Iron Age Coinage on Archaeological Sites in Belgic Gaul." In *Die Kelten und Rom: Neue numismatische Forschungen.* Edited by J. Metzler and D. Wigg. Studien zu Fundmünzen der Antike. Mainz: Academy of Science and Literature (Akademie der Wissenschaften und der Literatur), forthcoming.

———. "The Development of Iron Age Coinage in Belgic Gaul." *Numismatic Chronicle* 159 (1999): 111–168.

———. *Iron Age Coinage in South-East England: The Archaeological Context.* BAR British Series, no. 174. Oxford: British Archaeological Reports, 1987.

Nash, Daphne. *Coinage in the Celtic World.* London: Seaby, 1987.

———. *Settlement and Coinage in Central Gaul c. 200–50 B.C.* BAR Supplementary Series, no. 39. Oxford: British Archaeological Reports, 1978.

Roymans, N. "Man, Cattle, and the Supernatural in the Northwest European Plain." In *Settlement and Landscape: Proceedings of a Conference in Århus, Denmark, May 4–7, 1998.* Edited by Charlotte Fabech and Jytte Ringtved, pp. 291–300. Højbjerg, Denmark: Jutland Archaeological Society, 1999.

COLIN HASELGROVE

RITUAL SITES: VIERECKSCHANZEN

Viereckschanzen is a German word (*Viereckschanze* in its singular form) that may be translated as "rectilinear enclosures." The term refers to enigmatic Late Iron Age "ditch-and-berm" constructions and associated archaeological deposits that are still visible in central and western European landscapes.

CULTURAL AFFILIATION, DATE, AND DISTRIBUTION

The *Viereckschanzen* are associated with pre-Roman Celtic populations living at the end of the Iron Age who produced a material culture known as the Late La Tène culture. Precise dendrochronological (tree-ring dating) measurements of oak timbers preserved in wells at four *Viereckschanzen* in southern Germany (Riedlingen, Fellbach-Schmiden, Plattling-Pankofen, and Pocking-Hartkirchen) range across a 130-year period, from 181 to 51 B.C. These dates correspond to the La Tène C2 and D1 horizons of the central European Iron Age chronology and indicate that the *Viereckschanzen* were contemporaries of the large, defended settlements known as *oppida*.

Southern Germany, including the states of Bavaria and Baden-Württemberg, is the main focus of the distribution of *Viereckschanzen,* where approximately five hundred enclosures have been identified. Significantly smaller numbers of sites are present in the Czech Republic and Moravia (to the east) and in northern Switzerland (to the south). Rectilinear enclosures, known in the French as *enceinte quadrilaterale* or *enceinte carrées,* also exist in eastern and northern France, but these terms are used to describe a variety of sites dating to the final millennium B.C. The classic southern German *Viereckschanze* can be differentiated from Belgic sanctuaries of northeastern Gaul, such as Gournay-sur-Aronde, by the *Viereckschanze*'s larger size and lack of structured deposits of weaponry and animal remains.

DESCRIPTION

The classic *Viereckschanze* is identifiable by its standardized form and construction (fig. 1). A typical enclosure was created by excavation of a steep-sided, V-shaped ditch in a square, rectangular, or slightly trapezoidal form. The excavated soil was placed on the inside edge of the ditch, forming a simple earthen berm or rampart. Ditches were maintained through periodic re-excavation. There is some evidence that a wooden palisade or other superstructure was placed along the top of the rampart to increase the height of the walls. Although the ditch was continuous, a single opening was left in the rampart. This opening was usually in the eastern or southern side of the enclosure, but never to the north. Access to the interior required construction of a wooden causeway over the ditch, which led to a small timbered gatehouse erected within the opening of the rampart. Dimensions of the enclosures range from less than 50 meters to more than 100 meters on a side, but most sites are between 80 and 100 meters across and enclose about 1 hectare. At some sites, a rectilinear palisade predated the ditched enclosure. About 5 percent of all enclosures have one or more internal divisions or external annexes, such as at Plattling-Pankofen in Bavaria and Mšecké Žehrovice in Bohemia (Czech Republic).

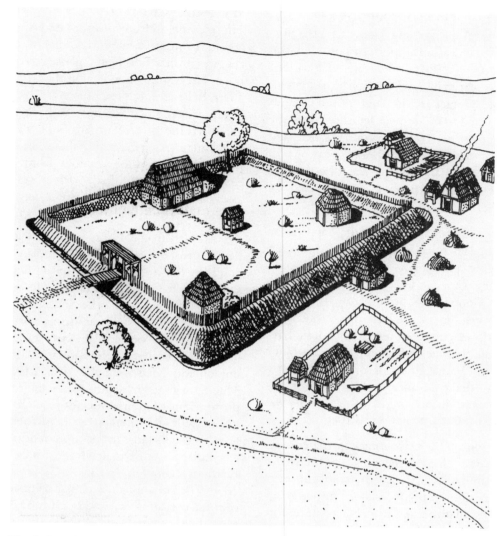

Fig. 1. An artist's interpretation of the *Viereckschanze* at Winden ("Vinida") in southeastern Germany based on aerial photographs and the results of excavations at other enclosures in Germany. The Winden enclosure measures about 80 × 80 meters. The drawing illustrates the characteristic shape and construction of a *Viereckschanze* with an uninterrupted rectilinear ditch, inner walls and gatehouse, and scattered interior buildings aligned with the enclosure's walls. The artist has placed the *Viereckschanze* within a larger settlement following the current interpretation of excavated sites such as Bopfingen-Flochberg. © RUDOLF MÜNCH. REPRODUCED BY PERMISSION.

Viereckschanzen exhibit considerable diversity in the quantity, character, and arrangement of features in their interiors, such as post-built structures, wells, pits, and hearths. Sites such as Holzhausen, Arnstorf-Wiedmais, and Fellbach-Schmiden had few preserved features within their excavated interiors, perhaps an indication of short-term or intermittent occupation. Other sites, such as Bopfingen-Flochberg and Plattling-Pankofen, contained evidence of more intensive, long-term activities and greater accumulation of cultural debris. Well shafts (often wood lined) and distinctive buildings with wraparound porches or ambulatories are known from a number of excavated sites, but they are not found in all enclosures.

PHYSICAL SETTING

Viereckschanzen are found in a variety of landscape settings, including stream terraces, broad loess plains, and upland slopes and ridge crests. A significant number of sites in upland settings were established near natural springs, suggesting that the provisioning of water was an important consideration in site location. Sites in poorly watered locations often had wells placed in their interiors. Most enclosures that remain intact are sited in forested uplands on terrain unsuited to modern agriculture. Since the early 1980s, intensive aerial reconnaissance and large-scale excavations of cultivated portions of southern Germany have led to the discovery of many *Viereckschanzen* that had been leveled by plowing.

The ditch and wall suggest that defense was an important function of a *Viereckschanze;* however, the topographic placement of many enclosures shows that they were not effective fortifications. In southwestern Germany, approximately 40 percent of known enclosures are located on low-lying or sloped terrain, where their interiors would have been vulnerable to attack by ranged weapons (such as javelin, arrow, and slingshot). *Viereckschanzen* generally do not take advantage of the most strategically valuable terrain, so it is likely that defense was not a primary motive for their construction.

The location of *Viereckschanzen* in the cultural landscape provides clues to the nature of the enclosures. Earlier investigators used the distribution of preserved enclosures in the forests of southern Germany to suggest that the sites were placed in remote locations separate from settlement areas. The distribution of known sites extends into the most fertile agricultural regions. Walter Irlinger has pointed out the close geographic relationship between *Viereckschanzen* and undefended rural settlements. These types of site are either found near to one another or are mutually visible and connected through lines of sight. Some enclosures are even located within large settlement complexes, such as at Bopfingen-Flochberg and Plattling-Pankofen.

Viereckschanzen were also placed in apparent reference to older monuments, such as tumulus cemeteries from the Middle Bronze and Early Iron Ages. The situation at the Hohmichele (Heiligkreutztal-Speckhau) in Baden-Württemberg, one of the largest Early Iron Age burial mounds in western Europe, is the most dramatic example of this correspondence between a *Viereckschanze* and earlier burial monuments.

MATERIAL CULTURE

The material culture of excavated *Viereckschanzen* includes common categories, such as pottery, metalwork (bronze and iron), glass, coins, and animal bone. Excavators often lament the lack of finds from *Viereckschanzen,* but excavations of enclosures within larger settlement complexes have yielded more extensive and diverse artifact assemblages. Few detailed analyses of the material culture or even comprehensive excavation catalogs from *Viereckschanzen* have been published, so it is very difficult to assess in what ways the enclosures may be similar to, or different from, other kinds of Late Iron Age sites.

Artifacts from Mšecké Žehrovice apparently reflect a prosperous rural habitation in Bohemia. In contrast, the composition of published ceramic assemblages from some enclosures in southern Germany is different from other settlements of the period. Metalwork, such as tools, weaponry, and jewelry, that is common at larger settlements is rare in *Viereckschanzen*, although small hoards of iron implements have been found in a few enclosures. The faunal assemblages generally reflect normal proportions of animal species (such as pig and cattle) present at contemporary settlements, but there is an unusually large proportion of horse in the small assemblage from the newly excavated enclosure at Plattling-Pankofen. No *Viereckschanzen* have yielded deposits of animal parts that compare to patterns of ritual consumption and sacrifice at Belgic sanctuaries like Gournay-sur-Aronde. Human remains within *Viereckschanzen* are infrequent, although they are relatively common at the larger settlements, such as *oppida*. Celebrated finds of three-dimensional artwork, such as the stone head from outside the Mšecké Žehrovice enclosure and wooden carvings within the well at Fellbach-Schmiden, have generated much interest, but these discoveries are unique and provide little insight into the nature of other *Viereckschanzen*.

HISTORY OF INVESTIGATION AND INTERPRETATION

In the late nineteenth century and early twentieth century, German scholars developed a lively but speculative debate about the date and nature of the *Viereckschanzen*. They were originally interpreted as Roman storehouses or forts and eventually as indigenous Celtic stockyards, farms, cultic places, or fortifications constructed during the Roman conquest.

From 1957 to 1963, Klaus Schwarz conducted the first large-scale excavation of a well-preserved *Viereckschanze* at Holzhausen. Although there were few features and artifacts in the excavated portion of the interior, Schwarz uncovered three shafts (7 to 35 meters deep), a large post-built structure with a wraparound porch or ambulatory, and several hearths and burned areas. Schwarz believed that the *Viereckschanze* represented a Celtic sanctuary, or *temenos,* copied from Mediterranean examples and characterized by a cultic triad consisting of a temple with ambulatory (*Umgangstempel*), a ritual shaft, and devotional offerings or sacrifice. Schwarz's enthusiastic arguments for *Viereckschanzen* as Celtic religious sanctuaries colored their interpretation for the next three decades.

From the late 1950s to the 1980s, substantial portions of several *Viereckschanzen* were excavated in southern Germany. Although interpretations of the sites adhered faithfully to Schwarz's cult model, excavations showed that the interiors were characterized by considerable variability. Investigators discovered shafts similar to those at Holzhausen in a few enclosures (that is, Dornstadt-Tomerdingen, Fellbach-Schmiden, and Arnstorf-Wiedmais) but not in others (such as Ehningen). The discovery of a wooden bucket and well-house timbers in the base of the Fellbach-Schmiden shaft indicated that it was originally a well. Some sites had numerous buildings and associated features, while others were sparsely built or contained no identifiable structures. Buildings with ambulatories were reported at about half of the sites. All *Viereckschanzen* yielded relatively few artifacts compared to other Late Iron Age sites.

In the early 1990s, large-scale excavations in southern Germany (that is, Bopfingen-Flochberg, Plattling-Pankofen, and Nordheim) yielded evidence of *Viereckschanzen* embedded in larger settlement areas, and investigators began to question the assumed cultic nature of the *Viereckschanze*. Also, the cultic triad originally proposed by Schwarz for Holzhausen could not be consistently identified at an increasing number of excavated *Viereckschanzen*. Reflecting on the excavation of Bopfingen-Flochberg, Günther Wieland suggested that *Viereckschanzen* were focal points for groupings of associated farming communities. These "rural centers" embodied a multiplicity of functions: habitation, storage, sanctuary, refuge, communal ceremonies, and the protection of water sources, such as wells and springs. The model of *Viereckschanze* as rural center must be tested against fine-scale chronological studies of feature components at complex sites like Bopfingen-Flochberg. Since the traditional "relative" chronology for the Late La Tène horizon based on artifact typologies ranges across several generations (100 to 150 years), it is possible that individual settlement units and the *Viereckschanze* were actually occupied at different times. Evidence that some enclosures were used as habitations also comes from the eastern limit of the distribution of *Viereckschanzen,* where Natalie Venclová and her colleagues interpret the enclosure at Mšecké Žehrovice in Bohemia as an elite rural-industrial residence.

When pottery assemblages from *Viereckschanzen* are compared to those from other settlements of the time, certain differences between the assemblages may indicate that *Viereckschanzen* were used for communal rituals, such as feasting, which could explain their central role in some Late Iron Age settlement complexes. However, Venclová has criticized the suggestion that pottery from *Viereckschanzen* is distinguishable from domestic assemblages.

The *Viereckschanzen* were prominent elements of the Late Iron Age landscape in southern Germany and adjacent regions, and they probably served multiple functions. They were integrated into contemporary settlement systems and were also placed to take advantage of preexisting funerary monuments. Although there is a range of complexity in interior layout and material culture, all *Viereckschanzen* shared a similar conception, which was the act of enclosing space through construction of a ditch and rampart into which access was restricted. This act of enclosing was based on a tightly controlled construction template that had no uniform defensive purpose but instead created a systematically delineated and enduring place in the landscape.

See also **Dating and Chronology** (*vol. 1, part 1*); **Oppida** (*vol. 2, part 6*).

BIBLIOGRAPHY

Bittel, Kurt, Siegwald Schiek, and Dieter Müller. *Die keltischen Viereckschanzen.* Stuttgart, Germany: Kommissionsverlag K. Theiss, 1990. (A comprehensive catalog of all known *Viereckschanzen* in Baden-Württemberg in southwestern Germany. Includes many informative essays about the construction, layout, setting and topography, artifact assemblages, and chronology.)

Irlinger, Walter. "Viereckschanze und Siedlung—Überlegungen zu einem forschungsgeschichtlichen Problem anhand ausgewählter südbayerischer Fundorte." In *Festschrift für Otto-Herman Frey zum 65. Geburtstag.* Edited by Claus Dobiat and Dirk Vorlauf, pp. 285–304. Marburg, Germany: Hitzeroth, 1994.

Murray, Matthew L. "*Viereckschanzen* and Feasting: Socio-Political Ritual in Iron-Age Central Europe." *Journal of European Archaeology* 3, no. 2 (1995): 125–151. (The only English-language summary of *Viereckschanzen* research; includes an original analysis of ceramic assemblages that suggests *Viereckschanzen* were feasting places.)

Rieckhoff-Pauli, Sabine, and Jörg Biel. *Die Kelten in Deutschland.* Stuttgart, Germany: Theiss, 2001. (A summary of the Iron Age archaeological record in Germany. Provides important background context to the *Viereckschanzen.*)

Schwarz, Klaus. "Die geschichte eines keltischen temenos im nördlichen Alpenvorland." *Ausgrabungen in Deutschland.* Vol. 1. Mainz, Germany: Römisch-Germanisches Zentralmuseums, 1975. (A summary of excavations at the important site of Holzhausen, which was the basis for the persistent interpretation of *Viereckschanzen* as religious sanctuaries until the early 1990s, an idea disputed by Günther Wieland in his 1999 book.)

Venclová, Natalie. *Mšecké Žehrovice in Bohemia: Archaeological Background to a Celtic Hero, 3rd–2nd Cent. B.C.* Sceaux, France: Kronos Editions, 1998. (A comprehensive English-language report of excavations conducted at a multiple enclosure in the Czech Republic; presents the author's belief that the site is an elite rural-industrial household.)

———. "On Enclosures, Pots, and Trees in the Forest." *Journal of European Archaeology* 5, no. 1 (1997): 131–150. (A critique of Matthew L. Murray's idea that feasting can be identified in the ceramic assemblages of *Viereckschanzen* in southern Germany. Argues that the assemblages from *Viereckschanzen* cannot be distinguished from settlement remains.)

Wieland, Günther, ed. *Keltische Viereckschanzen:Einem Rätsel auf der Spur.* Stuttgart, Germany: Theiss, 1999. (Presents the argument that *Viereckschanzen* were central foci within associated rural communities. Provides useful summaries of many of the most important *Viereckschanzen*, including all sites mentioned in this entry.)

MATTHEW L. MURRAY

IRON AGE FEASTING

Communal drinking and feasting, particularly the regulated distribution of alcoholic beverages, were central to establishing and maintaining social relationships in Iron Age Europe and the British Isles. The symbolic concepts and the material culture associated with the distribution of alcohol as a social lubricant characterize intergroup and intragroup competition from the Neolithic until at least the ninth century A.D. on the Continent and into the fifteenth century in Britain and Ireland. There are three primary sources of information on this subject: First there is archaeological evidence in the form of drinking and feasting equipment from burials and, to a lesser extent, from settlements and ritual sites and in the form of iconographic representations of feasts and drinking equipment. Second are Greek and Roman accounts of the drinking habits of the "barbarian" peoples with whom they had increasing contact after the sixth century B.C. And, last, there are the epics, law texts, and other written sources produced by the Celtic- and Germanic-speaking societies in the early Christian period. Scholars have focused their attention on the identification of the alcoholic beverages available, the material culture associated with the production and consumption of those beverages, and their distribution and function in society, including the social conventions and behavioral norms accompanying drinking and feasting. The focus of study includes attitudes toward drinking and alcohol abuse, the ideological significance of the production of alcoholic beverages, the equipment used to dispense and consume it, and the physiological response to alcohol itself.

ALE, MEAD, AND WINE

The alcoholic beverages available to northern and central European peoples before contact with the wine-growing Mediterranean cultures were of two types: honey mead and beer or, more accurately, ale, a fermented barley beverage brewed without hops, an addition to the brewing process that does not appear until historic times. Mead was primarily an elite drink because it was produced from honey taken from the hives of wild bees, the only form of sweetener available to prehistoric European peoples and therefore a valuable commodity. Ale has a very short shelf life in the absence of refrigeration, and without the addition of hops, which acts as a preservative as well as a flavoring agent, this seasonally available beverage was consumed relatively soon after being produced. Wine was a luxury import before the introduction by the Romans of viticulture, the growing of the wine vine, to France and Germany. The different beverages available account in part for the northern European "binge drinking" pattern compared with customs in the Mediterranean, where wine was consumed with meals on a daily basis and moderate consumption patterns tended to be the norm.

CLASSICAL SOURCES

Greek and Roman writers are virtually unanimous in their condemnation of Celtic and Germanic drinking practices. They derogatorily claimed that "barbarians" drank beer by choice; took their wine neat rather than mixed with water, according to the Mediterranean custom; imbibed to excess and engaged in boasting and brawling while under the influence; and were sufficiently addicted to alcohol to be willing to pay exorbitant prices to obtain it. In the fourth century B.C., Plato's *Laws* included the Celts in a list of "six barbarian, warlike peoples who are given to drunkenness, as opposed to Spartan restraint." And according to the Roman historian Ammianus Marcellinus in *Rerum gestarum libri*, calling a fellow Roman a "sabaiarius," or "beer-swiller," was considered an insult. In the first century A.D., Pliny the Elder, another Roman writer, describes the nations of the west as consuming an intoxicant made from grain soaked in water. In *Historia naturalis* he writes that "there are many ways of making it in Gaul and Spain, and under different names, though the principle is the same." The Greek historian Diodorus Siculus, in the first century B.C., describes the Celts in his *Bibliotheca historica* as "exceedingly fond of wine," sating themselves "with the unmixed wine imported by merchants; their desire makes them drink it greedily, and when they become drunk they fall into a stupor or into a maniacal disposition." The historical value of these texts is difficult to determine, partly because so many classical authors borrowed from one another without attribution, particularly in the absence of firsthand knowledge of the peoples they were describing. There is also the obvious propaganda value of denigrating cultures and peoples who were in the process of being conquered or assimilated.

ARCHAEOLOGICAL EVIDENCE

Feasting and the consumption of alcohol are essential components of several European cultural traditions: elite marriage and inauguration rituals, sovereignty and patron-client rituals, death and funerary rituals, and sacrifice and offering rituals. In its sociopolitical manifestation alcohol functioned as a vehicle for maintaining elite prerogatives through feasting and the distribution of liquor to warrior retinues and other clients as an incentive and a reward for service. Sharing food and drink simultaneously communicates messages of membership and exclusion, particularly in Celtic and Germanic societies, where communal feasting served to rank individuals in relation to one another. The structured consumption of alcoholic beverages accompanied most rites of passage, with those of elite groups being most visible in the material culture and the documentary record.

Archaeologically, the elite drinking complex is particularly clearly defined in mortuary contexts. Significantly, when drinking and feasting equipment is not associated with elite mortuary ritual, it appears in the form of votive deposits in rivers, bogs, and springs, an example of the conspicuous destruction of wealth that marks competitive elite signaling behavior in prehistoric Europe. When the energy of a community was invested in elaborate deposition of the dead, however, elite individuals were buried with a standard set of recurring elements that distinguish such graves from the majority of burials.

One of the earliest archaeological examples is a beaker containing mead from a Bronze Age burial at Ashgrove in Fife, Scotland, dated to 1000 B.C. Evidence for fermented ale was found in a vessel of roughly the same date from North Mains in Perthshire, Scotland. Beeswax residue was present in an even earlier ceramic vessel of Neolithic date from Runnymede Bridge in Berkshire, England, suggesting that it originally held mead. One of the latest examples is the Kavanagh Charter Horn, a brass-decorated ivory horn that was the basis of the Kavanagh family's claim to direct descent from the royal house of Leinster as late as the fifteenth century A.D. The geographic range of the sociopolitically significant drinking and feasting complex appears to have Indo-European roots, surviving as a fundamental aspect of cultural identity in northern Europe for much longer than in those areas where it is presumed to have originated.

DRINKING VESSELS

Initially, elite drinking vessels were made of pottery and, more rarely, of exotic materials such as amber or gold, followed by a gradual increase in sheet-metal vessels, with the addition of silver and glass in the Roman and early medieval periods. Occasionally, under ideal preservation conditions, wooden drinking equipment has been documented in archaeological contexts, from finely turned cups and flagons to enormous tuns (casks) or barrels made of wooden staves bound with organic materials or metal. From Neolithic times on, however, there is a pervasive association between drinking and feasting equipment and high rank or status, even though the number and combination of vessel types vary.

The drinking horn is a category of elite symbolism associated with ideologically constituted alcohol consumption that appears consistently from the Bronze Age through the early Christian period; in fact, it is the only item of drinking equipment that is associated with almost every period of later European prehistory. Most drinking horns were made of actual animal horn, the largest coming from the now extinct aurochs, but horns of pottery, bronze, iron, glass, and ivory are known. Genuine horn vessels were in use throughout prehistory and into early medieval times, whereas glass horns made a relatively late appearance, mainly in Roman and early Germanic contexts.

Numerous examples of metal-decorated horns are known, particularly from the Iron Age; most are embellished with sheet gold or bronze. In addition to the nine horns from the Hochdorf burial of the sixth century B.C., near Stuttgart, horns were found in the Early La Tène (fourth century B.C.) Kleinaspergle burial, also near Stuttgart, and a group of five Early La Tène burials from the Rhineland: Reinheim, Bescheid, Schwarzenbach, Hoppstädten-Weiersbach, and Weiskirchen A.D. Saar. Bronze Age examples include the gold-decorated horn from Wismar in Mecklenburg-Vorpommern and a silver-mounted drinking horn, together with other drinking equipment, from the Lübsow burial in northern Germany, of the first century A.D. Adorned pottery drinking horns are documented in the Lausitz culture (Late Bronze Age and Early Iron Age) of northeastern Germany and Poland, with roughly sixty known examples. In Britain silver-gilt-decorated drinking horns are known from two Anglo-Saxon burials of the sixth century A.D., at Sutton Hoo and at Taplow Court.

Drinking horns are found in archaeological contexts throughout eastern Europe, including the Ukraine, Lithuania, Poland, Russia, Hungary, Croatia, and other parts of the former Yugoslavia, as well as in northern Germany and Scandinavia. A drinking horn is depicted in an important seventeenth-century painting from Frisia, in which it acts as a symbol of dynastic succession. Clearly, the symbolic "load" of this particular element of the drinking complex was geographically and temporally resilient. Other indigenous vessel categories were cups, beakers, cauldrons, and various kinds of flagons, including the La Tène *Schnabelkanne,* an Etruscan form that was copied as well as imported by Celtic elites.

DRINKING, FEASTING, AND RITUAL

The alcoholic beverages consumed by European elites were imbued with ritual significance, owing to the pyrotechnic (involving fire) production process, the psychoactive (mood-altering) nature of alcohol, and the relative rarity of some of the raw materials required for production, which could (as in the case of honey or grapes) themselves have symbolic significance. Saint Patrick, for example, is said to have refused to touch honey even when he was suffering from severe privation, because of its pagan ritual significance, and in Ireland both beer and mead are found as elements in personal names. Beer has fairly prosaic associations for today, compared, for example, with wine, which appears as a ritually redolent alcoholic beverage in post-Roman, early Christian Europe at least in part as a result of syncretistic associations between wine, blood, and sacrifice.

In secular as well as religious contexts in Merovingian Gaul, for instance, symbolic exchanges of weaponry, precious objects, and food were a critical component of the creation and maintenance of friendship (*amicitia*) and elite power. The link between drinking equipment and mortuary ritual is present in these early Christian societies until at least the sixth century A.D., both in terms of objects placed in the graves and with respect to the funerary feasts conducted at the grave site. The monasteries took over from Celtic and Germanic leaders as producers and distributors of alcoholic beverages, with feasting continuing as the most important form of gift exchange and patronage. The symbolic link between elites and spectacular drinking vessels of precious metals also was retained, and ritualized presentations of such tableware continued in the Carolingian and Merovingian courts. If given on behalf of the poor, they represented appropriate gifts by laymen or clerics to the church.

In the Celtic as well as the Germanic literary tradition (from the *Mabinogion* to *Beowulf*), drinking vessels sometimes were given names, a phenomenon also associated with weapons, especially swords, underscoring the ritual significance of the equipment used in drinking alcoholic beverages. In early Christian contexts, gifts of feasting and, especially, drinking vessels were thought to retain something of the identity of the person who had bestowed them; it is possible that a similar anthropomorphiza-

Fig. 1. Detail of the silver Gundestrup cauldron, showing a woman's face. THE ART ARCHIVE/ NATIONALMUSEET COPENHAGEN DENMARK/DAGLI ORTI. REPRODUCED BY PERMISSION.

tion of drinking equipment existed in prehistoric Europe.

The iconographic evidence for the ritual significance of drinking vessels, particularly those of metal, consists of a number of so-called cult vessels and other representations of drinking equipment, ranging from the ninth and eighth centuries B.C. to at least the first century B.C. These include vessels that formed part of the feasting and drinking equipment of early monasteries and church leaders. Recurring elements in these "cult" vessels are wheeled vehicles, horses, horned beasts, female figures, and drinking vessels. The silver Gundestrup cauldron found in a Danish bog in 1891 represents a continuation of this tradition; it is dated to the late second century B.C. and may be of Thracian origin, despite its obviously Celtic iconographic elements (fig. 1).

INSULAR WRITTEN SOURCES

In the insular literary tradition, drinking vessels represent the obligation of the ruler to be generous and to provide for his or her people, a constant theme in northern Europe, as it is in most so-called heroic societies. Horns and cauldrons often are "testing" vessels, in the sense that only a true king can drink them dry. The largest of the nine horns in the Hochdorf grave is evocative of such a tradition: at 5.5 liters (ten pints), it had five times the capacity of the remaining eight horns found in the burial. The huge iron horn with its gold decorations hung directly over the "prince's" couch, suggesting that the ability to drink as well as dispense large quantities of alcohol was one of the defining characteristics of a ruler. In one of the best known of the Irish epic tales, *Táin Bó Cúalnge*, also called the "Cattle Raid of Cooley," the king spends a third of the day *oc ól chorma*, that is, "drinking *cuirm*," or beer. This is quite a lot of swigs from the royal drinking horn, calculated on an hourly basis! By drinking from magical horns unharmed, the protagonists in the numerous Irish, Welsh, and Scottish tales that deal with "drinking the feast" of sovereignty confirm their title to the kingship; the horns and other drinking equipment become the symbol of their right to rule.

The symbolic significance of the communal consumption of alcohol as a marker of elite social obligations and prerogatives is a constant element in pre-industrial northern Europe. The composition and meaning of elite drinking equipment appear to have gone through shifts from one structural option to another within the same transformational set, reproducing the basic structure in a novel cultural form. Even though the beverages and vessels may have changed through time—from a stoup of unhopped ale or spiced mead to imported Greek or Roman wine to distilled liquor in a glass cup—the material culture and its ideopolitical significance appear consistently in recognizable form.

See also **Hochdorf** (*vol. 1, part 1*); **Sutton Hoo** (*vol. 2, part 7*).

BIBLIOGRAPHY

Arnold, Bettina. "Power Drinking in Iron Age Europe." *British Archaeology* 57 (February 2001): 12–19.

———. "'Drinking the Feast': Alcohol and the Legitimation of Power in Celtic Europe." *Cambridge Archaeological Journal* 9, no. 1 (1999): 71–93.

Barclay, Gordon J. "Sites of the Third Millennium B.C. to the First Millennium A.D. at North Mains, Strathallon, Perthshire." *Proceedings of the Society of Antiquaries of Scotland* 113 (1983): 122–281.

Biel, Jörg. *Der Keltenfürst von Hochdorf: Methoden und Ergebnisse der Landesarchäologie.* Stuttgart, Germany: Konrad Theiss Verlag, 1985.

Dickson, J. H. "Bronze Age Mead." *Antiquity* 52 (1978): 108–113.

Dietler, Michael. "Driven by Drink: The Role of Drinking in the Political Economy and the Case of Early Iron Age France." *Journal of Anthropological Archaeology* 9 (1990): 352–406.

Dietler, Michael, and Brian Hayden, eds. *Feasts: Archaeological and Ethnographic Perspectives on Food, Politics, and Power.* Washington, D.C.: Smithsonian Institution, 2001.

Effros, Bonnie. *Creating Community with Food and Drink in Merovingian Gaul.* New York: Palgrave/Macmillan, 2002.

Enright, Michael. *Lady with a Mead Cup: Ritual, Prophecy, and Lordship in the European Warband from La Tène to the Viking Age.* Dublin: Four Courts Press, 1996.

Flandrin, Jean Louis, and Massimo Montanari, eds. *Food: A Culinary History from Antiquity to the Present.* New York: Columbia University Press, 1999.

Kaul, Flemming. "The Gundestrup Cauldron Reconsidered." *Acta Archaeologica* 66 (1995): 1–38.

Kaul, Flemming, and J. Martens. "Southeast European Influences in the Early Iron Age of Southern Scandinavia: Gundestrup and the Cimbri." *Acta Archaeologica* 66 (1995): 111–161.

Kendall, Calvin B., and Peter S. Wells, eds. *Voyage to the Other World: The Legacy of Sutton Hoo.* Minneapolis: University of Minnesota Press, 1992.

Nebelsick, Louis Daniel. "Trunk und Transzendenz: Trinkgeschirr im Grab zwischen der frühen Urnenfelder- und späten Hallstattzeit im Karpatenbecken." In *Chronos: Beiträge zur prähistorischen Archäologie zwischen Nord- und Südosteuropa: Festschrift für Bernhard Hänsel.* Edited by C. Becker, M.-L. Dunkelmann, C. Metzner-Nebelsick, H. Peter-Röcher, M. Roeder, and B. Terzan, pp. 373–387. Espelkamp, Germany: Verlag Marie Leidorf, 1997.

Neumann de Vegvar, Carol. "Drinking Horns in Ireland and Wales: Documentary Sources." In *From the Isles of the North: Early Medieval Art in Ireland and Britain.* Edited by Cormac Bourke, pp. 81–87. Proceedings of the Third International Conference on Insular Art, Ulster Museum, Belfast, April 7–11, 1994. Belfast, Northern Ireland: HMSO, 1995.

Sherratt, Andrew. *Economy and Society in Prehistoric Europe: Changing Perspectives.* Princeton, N.J.: Princeton University Press, 1997.

Unwin, Tim. *Wine and the Vine: An Historical Geography of Viticulture and the Wine Trade.* London: Routledge, 1991.

BETTINA ARNOLD

LA TÈNE ART

The European Iron Age, termed the Hallstatt culture after a major Austrian site, began in the latter part of the eighth century B.C. At this early stage the embellishment of items of metal and pottery (and also, though less often preserved, of such organic materials as textiles) was largely geometric, although animals and birds, especially waterbirds, and occasionally humans also were depicted. With respect to humans, there was little attempt at naturalistic representation.

Thus, in the Hallstatt period, abstract decoration, whatever the medium, was just that: decoration and certainly not art. It was not until about the middle of the fifth century B.C., with the blossoming of the second phase of Iron Age culture in Europe (the La Tène culture, named after a site in Switzerland) that a type of decoration developed that, in its beauty, its technical virtuosity, and at times the almost overwhelming power of its personality, may be regarded as art in the truest sense. This rightly has been seen as the first great art of Europe outside the classical world.

ORIGINS

It has been said that La Tène art had no genesis; it came into the world in fully developed form, with a distinctive personality. It is evident, however, that Ionian Greek colonizers in the south of France and Etruscans in northern Italy supplied the models that ignited the creative skills of Celtic craftsmen. The wine trade from these areas acted as the catalyst, introducing, besides the liquid itself—in great quantity—the goblets, flagons, cauldrons, mixing bowls,

and all the appropriate equipment for its proper consumption.

The ruling elite of the Late Hallstatt period was eager to display its wealth and power through its links with the cultured world to the south. Such wealth is evident in the rich graves containing imported Mediterranean produce and is illustrated dramatically by an extraordinary bronze couch, probably of northern Italian manufacture, found in a warrior burial at Hochdorf in southwestern Germany. A mud-brick wall at the Heuneburg hillfort imitates in close detail the defensive construction of the Mediterranean. This was a powerful statement of prestige and wealth.

By 500 B.C. the craftsmen of the Late Hallstatt world had been exposed for more than a century to the best of Mediterranean craftsmanship and art. Nonetheless, for a generation or two this seems scarcely to have impinged on the conservatism of their own artistic repertoire. With the breakup of the old order, however (probably in the second quarter of that century), change and transformation, dramatic in their suddenness, ensued. The old centers of Hallstatt power declined (there is debate as to the reasons for this), and new centers emerged farther north, especially in the Marne region of France and the middle Rhine in Germany. There followed rapid expansion across Europe, sometimes involving entire tribal groupings, into Italy, Greece, and the Balkans and along the Danube as far as Romania. The centuries between 400 B.C. and 200 B.C. have been described as the age of migration, and the Roman commentator, seeing land and plunder as the motivating force, cannot have been far from the truth. Archaeology and the written sources present a consistent picture of expansion and settlement across the European mainland.

The art of these people thus is clearly rooted in the Mediterranean. Elements of earlier Hallstatt geometric ornament survive, of course, but generally as minor background fillers to the larger ornamental compositions. It also has been suggested that elements of eastern inspiration can be detected. Attention has been focused on nomadic horsemen from the eastern steppes, the Scythians, who developed a lively and imaginative animal art. Hints of this art form, such as dragons on a pair of wine flagons of the fourth century B.C. from Basse-Yutz in the Lorraine region of France (fig. 1), have been put forward, but no objects of definitely Scythian manufacture have been found in Celtic areas. Thus, the phrase "orientalizing" is preferred, suggesting that seemingly eastern elements were transmitted not directly but via the southeastern Hallstatt or the northern Italian zones. Chinese silk fragments from several Late Hallstatt tombs are, at any rate, indications of long-distance trading; in this regard the tooth of a mule—a pack animal—from one such burial is interesting. Astonishing, however, are the hen bones that somehow reached the Heuneburg fortress in southern Germany from as far away as India.

LA TÈNE ART

No consideration of La Tène art can commence without reference to Paul Jacobsthal's two-volume 1944 work, *Early Celtic Art*. In the years since it was written it has, not surprisingly, been overtaken in many ways by new discoveries and fresh ideas, but it remains a seminal text. His four divisions of early Celtic art are still the starting point for modern discussion.

In essence, the art form of the La Tène Celts is a curvilinear style growing from the palmettes, lotus blossoms, vine scrolls, and myriad other motifs from the classical world but rendered in uniquely original variations of great imagination and at times bewildering complexity. The compass commonly was used in the early stages, but from the beginning there was a flamboyant exuberance that transcended such mechanical aids. The art of the Celts is unique and essentially different from that of the Mediterra-

Fig. 1. Flagons from Basse-Yutze, France. © ERICH LESSING/ ART RESOURCE, NY. REPRODUCED BY PERMISSION.

nean. The Celtic craftsmen were embarked on their own artistic journey, with the designs of the Mediterranean acting as the catalyst, but no more. It is small wonder that Jacobsthal was moved to remark, "Celtic art has no genesis."

The style is one of light and shade, of twisting shapes, and of meanings that change in the eye of the observer. La Tène art puzzles and tantalizes. Curves combine in birdlike forms, and human faces appear embedded in the seemingly abstract scrolls. There are eyes or pseudo-eyes, at times cartoon-like and at other times glowering in latent menace. Nonetheless, in such apparent ambiguity there is doubt. How intentional are the embedded shapes, to what extent are they no more than forms created by the mere accidental juxtaposition of curving lines? The point is illustrated by the engraved ornament on the bronze covering of an iron sword scabbard from Filottrano in northern Italy, probably of the fourth century B.C., which bears a series of writhing S figures along its length. Where each pair of S figures meets, the line of the *S* ends in the arc of a circle linked by an elongated loop. Here the willing observer can see faces. Is this a deliberate creation, or is it only the eye of the beholder that creates this image? It is quite impossible to decide.

A small sheet-gold fragment from Bad Dürkheim in Germany is unambiguous. A double face, rendered with extraordinary skill, is evident. Viewed from one side there is a mournful, bearded elder. From the other angle, the old man dissolves, to be replaced by an anxious youth. Seamlessly, the beard of the elder has become the elegant coiffeur of the young man.

Our knowledge of contemporary technology rests, to a considerable extent, on the finished objects. These items, of course, are the culmination of complex processes involving the acquisition of the necessary metals and the presence of an organized workshop with furnace, charcoal, and bellows for raising heat to the required level. There must have been apprentices who carried out the basic tasks, learning from the master the many skills necessary for successful work. Artisans needed crucibles of varying sizes and tongs for holding them when they were filled with molten metal. Designs were produced by hammering, casting, or engraving, and many specialist tools were necessary, including hammers, chisels, implements for cutting and chasing, anvils, drills, measuring devices, spatulas for shaping the wax, and much else. In the earlier phases, coral, probably from the Mediterranean, was used; later, red enamel/glass was substituted. Little of this material survives, but an important deposit at Gussage All Saints in southwestern England has yielded the remains of moulds for the manufacture of perhaps fifty matched sets of chariot and horse fittings.

Doubtless, rituals and incantations were needed to ensure success in the work, but most important were the inherited skills of generations, even centuries, of fine metalworking. This was the preserve of an elite, working under the patronage of a powerful ruling class and creating at their behest objects of the highest technical and artistic quality for display and ostentation, for ceremonial occasions, and some, perhaps, for the field of battle. Ultimately, however, the finest material was destined for the Otherworld, through deposition in graves, in water, or in other abodes of goddesses and gods.

Jacobsthal's "early" style, today more commonly termed the "strict" style, is closest to the Mediter-

ranean. Spectacularly rich burials in parts of Germany, France, and Switzerland have yielded the finest objects, one outstanding piece now in the museum of Besançon in France (probably taken from a plundered burial). This Etruscan bronze flagon was transformed by a master artisan through the addition of a web of finely engraved ornament—including palmettes, S scrolls, comma leaves, even the yin-yang symbol—around its sides and on the base. The ornament, delicately traced, washes across the surface in sensuous waves, transmuting the staid container into a Celtic masterpiece. This was an object fit to grace a royal feast.

Abstraction was the essence of this early phase, and the same artistic ethos applied to figural representation. This style was relatively common at this early stage. Safety-pin brooches, the standard Celtic dress fastener (probably deriving its inspiration from northern Italy), combined animals, birds, human faces, and creatures of fantasy, sometimes in combinations of at times bewildering complexity. Belt hooks, often with paired, griffin-like creatures, also belong to this early trend, and these creatures, enclosing smaller human figures, must have had meaning, but a meaning forever denied us. There is much more in metal. In stone, too, there are carved pillars, such as a four-sided example from Pfalzfeld in Germany, combining fleshy S scrolls with a stylized human face on each side. On each there is a so-called leaf crown, resembling a pair of bloated commas. This is a widespread Celtic motif, probably a symbol of divine status. Stones with wholly abstract ornament also are known, especially in northwestern France and, three or four centuries later, Ireland.

The human form, especially the head, is a popular motif, but in true Celtic art the anatomical naturalism of the Mediterranean is never found. There are striking examples. Among the most spectacular is an almost life-size bearded warrior of stone that was found lying beside a rich burial mound of this early phase at the Glauberg in Germany. Although the rendering of form and physique is far from nature, the detailed reproduction of weapons, armor, and a neck ornament is a startlingly faithful copy of known originals. The symbolic leaf crown surmounts this carving, too.

The human representations on a fifth century B.C. sword scabbard from grave 994 at Hallstatt in Austria also are striking. Engraved along its length are variously occupied figures, including both infantry and cavalry, and, in one instance, a prone figure, speared and crushed by one of the mounted warriors. Here, differing cultural traditions are evident, not only Celtic but also some deriving from the elaborately embossed buckets (*situlae*) of a people known as the Veneti of the northern Adriatic.

As Celtic peoples expanded across Europe in the fourth and third centuries B.C., their art developed further along its individual path. The strict style gave way to what Jacobsthal called the Waldalgesheim style, after an exceptionally rich female burial in Germany, which contained native pieces as well as a bucket from southern Italy. Today there is a tendency to use the more neutral term "vegetal style" to describe the new artistic trends, especially in view of the current emphasis on northern Italy as critical in the genesis of the style.

Although Mediterranean elements persisted in this phase of La Tène ornamentation (which may be seen as beginning around the middle of the fourth century B.C.), the art typically was dominated by continuously moving tendrils of varying types, twisting and turning in restless motion across the surface. This is well illustrated on golden torcs from the Waldalgesheim grave, and there are many other examples across Europe that showcase the widespread popularity of the new style. The writhing shapes on a series of bronze mounts said to be from Commachio in northern Italy are similarly fine examples of this stylistic development south of the Alps.

Iron helmets, sometimes with a decorative gold-foil cover, became widespread at this time, from northern Spain as far east as Romania. These items, clearly derived from the Mediterrannean, frequently bear decoration of the highest quality and probably were for parade rather than for the field of battle. One fine example, a gold-plated iron specimen from Amfreville in France, features applied sheet gold decorated with a chased ornament of running, interlinked triskele designs. A spectacular and wholly unique helmet came from a burial of the third century B.C. at Ciumeşti in Romania. A winged bird with hinged, flapping wings—an eagle or raven—mounts the top. This magnificent object, worn by a warrior on horseback wearing chain mail (for such also came from the burial) must have been an object of admiration and awe on ceremonial occasions.

From the third century B.C. onward Celtic art gave way to two stylistic variants, Jacobsthal's plastic and sword styles, terms that remain in current use. The first style is confined largely to personal ornaments, with decoration in high relief. The latter, far more widespread, is found most commonly, though by no means exclusively, on scabbards. The artists of the sword style operated in discrete schools of craftsmanship in different areas of Europe, and individual styles can be recognized. Especially important centers were present in Switzerland and Hungary, but there were others, certainly in parts of France, and there also were insular schools.

There is considerable variety in the art of the scabbards, which is concentrated most frequently at the mouth. Typical of the Hungarian variant are fleshy tendrils that may overlap in their twisting and turning; they occur with lyres of various types and, at times, with tiny spirals. An especially fine example of a scabbard, found at Cernon-sur-Coole in France but certainly Hungarian in inspiration, features a crested bird's head, its beak ending in a tightly coiled spiral. In the Swiss variants of the style, birds' heads are of various types, and there are numerous S figures and tendrils of diverse forms. A distinctive characteristic of the Swiss scabbards is overall stippling, or ring punching (*chagrinage*), which is absent on scabbards of the other groups.

A specific scabbard type, characterized by an opposing pair of so-called dragons or stylized variants of dragons at the mouth, has been a subject of considerable discussion. There are differing versions of this motif—which must have had meaning for the scabbard engravers, as for the owners. Their wide dispersal across the Celtic world, even as far as the River Thames in southeastern England, prompted one commentator to regard this motif as "common Celtic currency."

There is much that could be said about European Celtic art. The diverse iconography, developing from the mid-fourth century B.C., of the extensive coinage of the period merits a chapter of its own. At any rate, by the first century B.C. the momentum of Celtic expansion had run its course, and the burgeoning of Imperial Rome rapidly subsumed the exuberance and individuality of Celtic art. The curvi-

Fig. 2. Detail of a bronze shield from Witham, northern England. © Eric Lessing/Art Resource, NY. Reproduced by permission.

linear art style continued, at times still to a high standard of artistic excellence, but soon decline set in. The rich inhumation burials were a thing of the past, and cremation burials, very often with the simplest of grave goods, increasingly became the norm. On mainland Europe the glory days of La Tène art were numbered.

THE INSULAR WORLD

This spectacular early development of Celtic art on the European mainland is scarcely present on the islands to the west. In Ireland there is certainly nothing dating earlier than about 300 B.C., whereas in Britain there are only occasional items that could be dated earlier. There are, for example, a few scattered trinkets, and it has been claimed that an openwork mount from a hillfort at Danebury in Hampshire, England, dates to the fifth or fourth century B.C. A fragmentary bronze vessel lid (or lids) from Cerrig-y-Drudion in Wales has engraved decora-

tion, predominantly palmettes and lotus blossoms, with a stippled and hatched background resembling early Continental designs. There are, nonetheless, hints of insular manufacture.

The widespread appearance of the new art style in Britain and Ireland once was seen as indicating population intrusion. Apart from accepting the late settlement of southeastern England by Belgic peoples, however, modern scholarship places heavy emphasis on indigenous development. Insular art in the last centuries B.C. thus can be seen as almost entirely a product of local workshops. As on the European mainland, the finest art, notably, is lavished on high-status items, such as weapons, shields, and horse trappings, which clearly reflect considerations of display and ostentation.

There are very few likely imports from this period. One is a gold torc from a bog at Knock, in County Roscommon, Ireland, as is the earlier noted dragon-pair scabbard from the Thames. The latter stands apart from a series of ornate bronze scabbards in Britain and Ireland that have engraved ornament along their lengths, a feature of predominantly insular character. Their decoration, for the most part consisting of wave tendrils, S scrolls, and variants with a bewildering array of minor filling designs (especially in Ireland), is distinct from art on the Continental scabbards. These two insular groups, each characterized by unique and differing forms of chape (the fitting attached at their ends) probably reflect parallel streams of influence from the European mainland. This theory, of course, does not preclude subsequent cross-fertilization between the two islands.

A series of unique bronze shields from Britain (with a single exception, they are shield covers) represents a set of objects of the highest technical craftsmanship and artistic quality. Significantly, almost all are from rivers. Votive deposition thus is a likely scenario—such extraordinary objects probably would not have been used on the field of battle. Exact miniature bronze copies of such shields, including twenty-two from a hoard at Salisbury that was found by illegal metal detecting and then secretly dispersed to collectors worldwide, support the notion that such objects were not primarily for practical use.

The decoration on these shields is as varied as it is magnificent. One of the earliest specimens, a bronze shield boss of spindle form, was found a century ago in the River Trent at Ratcliffe-on-Saor. It features complex designs of Continental sword style derivation, comprising writhing scrolls that undulate across each other in ceaseless motion. On the boss, strange, contorted, stylized quadrupeds lurk in the undergrowth of an otherwise abstract, curvilinear jungle.

There are other fine shields, including three from the Thames and one from the River Witham (fig. 2), each unique and each a product of masterly craftsmanship. There is also a horned fitting of bronze from Torrs in southwestern Scotland, probably a pony cap, with holes for the animal's ears and relief-hammered ornament. The ornamentation includes a variety of interconnecting elements, such as *peltae,* spirals, leaf designs, and pointed-oval motifs, which bend across the bronze in carefully balanced symmetry. A curved pair of horns, possibly the ends of drinking horns, was added to the cap in the nineteenth century. The ornament on these horns is engraved rather than hammered and has much in common with the engraved ornament of the insular scabbards, but the tiny face peering out from the curvilinear undergrowth is unique in an insular context.

Hammered ornament on a bronze disk decorating the mouth of a large, curving, superbly crafted sheet-bronze horn from Loughnashade, County Armagh, Ireland, also is related stylistically to the designs on the Torrs piece, indicating the close relationships between craft centers on the two islands.

Gold is rare in the insular Iron Age, in striking contrast to the extraordinary proliferation of this metal in the preceding Bronze Age. There are, however, several important gold finds, all, apart from the Knock torc discussed earlier, dating to about the last century B.C. In Ireland the most notable finds are the seven gold artifacts discovered together at Broighter in County Derry. Several neck ornaments, a small bowl, a model gold boat, and a beautifully decorated buffer torc were among the items. The torc is adorned with an elegant series of relief trumpet curves and snail-shell spirals, clearly laid out by means of a compass and set against a background web of overlapping arcs, also compass-drawn.

Contemporary with this group, though of entirely local manufacture, is an extraordinary series of

Fig. 3. Engraved bronze reverse side of a mirror from Desborough, Northamptonshire, England. © ERICH LESSING/ART RESOURCE, NY. REPRODUCED BY PERMISSION.

torcs—of gold, silver, electrum, and bronze—found in a series of pits placed randomly together in a field at Snettisham in Norfolk, England. The torcs were both complete and fragmentary, some obviously scrap and others carefully deposited in a tiered arrangement. Ingots and cakes of gold and silver also were found. In all, about 11 kilograms (24 pounds) of gold and 16 kilograms (35 pounds) of silver have been brought to light. The torcs vary in form, some resembling the one from Broighter; the finest are penannular creations of twisted gold strands, some massive and many with ring ends decorated with raised curvilinear ornament of insular type.

As the art of the Continental Celts declined under Roman domination, insular developments continued, especially in Ireland, where Roman legions never trod. Around the time of the birth of Christ, the compass, so important in Early La Tène artistic composition, once more became a dominant element in insular art, which grew increasingly distant from its Continental origins. In Britain at this time a distinctive series of elaborately decorated bronze mirrors occurs, characterized by varied and at times complex combinations of compass-drawn curves, most often filled with incised basketry. Not all are of the highest technical quality, but the best of them, such as that from Desborough in Northamptonshire (fig. 3), are products of exceptional craftsmanship. There are other insular innovations—on both islands—such as bronze horse bits, often with elaborate cast decoration; finely made spun-bronze vessels; and the late, specifically British developments in scabbard decoration. An important artistic creation of this period is a magnificent horned helmet of bronze, also from the Thames, which has enameled ornament and raised curvilinear designs reminiscent of those on some of the Snettisham torcs.

The Roman occupation of much of Britain during the middle of the first century A.D. precipitated a decline in Celtic artistic traditions. In Ireland, however, these traditions continued, eventually receiving new life and vigor through the work of the monastic craftsmen who devoted much of their skill to the glory of God. Metalworking reached new heights of technical and artistic perfection, and the same outstanding skills are displayed in the great illuminated manuscripts and the finely carved high crosses. New motifs were introduced, especially interlacing decoration and animals of many forms, entirely alien to the original Celtic artificer. There were many new mediums, such as millefiori glass and polychrome enamel. By the eighth century Irish craftsmanship had risen to astonishing heights of technical skill and artistic sophistication never again to be achieved.

See also **Hochdorf** (*vol. 1, part 1*); **Irish Bronze Age Goldwork** (*vol. 2, part 5*); **Celts** (*vol. 2, part 6*); **Hallstatt** (*vol. 2, part 6*); **La Tène** (*vol. 2, part 6*); **The Heuneburg** (*vol. 2, part 6*).

BIBLIOGRAPHY

Megaw, M. Ruth, and J. V. S. Megaw. *Celtic Art: From Its Beginnings to the Book of Kells.* Rev. ed. New York: Thames and Hudson, 2001.

Moscati, Sabatino, et al., eds. *The Celts.* New York: Rizzoli, 1991.

Raftery, Barry, ed. (with Paul-Marie Durval et al.) *Celtic Art.* Paris: UNESCO, Flammarion, 1990.

BARRY RAFTERY

IRON AGE SOCIAL ORGANIZATION

The Iron Age in temperate Europe, inland from the Mediterranean basin, lasted for some eight hundred years. Its start is marked by the local adoption of iron to manufacture edge tools, such as axes and swords; there may have been contemporary social changes related to the near collapse of exchange patterns provoked by the declining importance of tin and copper. It ended over much of the Continent with the expansion of the late Roman Republic and, subsequently, the early Roman Empire during the last two centuries B.C. and the first century A.D. In more northerly areas, for instance, Ireland, the influence of Rome was very muted, if never entirely absent. There, many characteristics of the Iron Age either continued into or reasserted themselves during the first millennium A.D. In a real sense, in such areas the Iron Age effectively lasted for several more centuries. Elsewhere, as in southern Germany, the last century B.C. is marked by the arrival of another new population, the Germans, whose appearance broadly coincided with marked changes in the Iron Age archaeological record.

For the period between c. 800 B.C. and the beginning of A.D. 1, the evidence provided by archaeology is complemented by information drawn from other sources. Of very great importance are surviving texts from the classical world. The earliest of them contain scant, almost tantalizing information about conditions in the middle of the first millennium B.C.; written sources thereafter became more numerous, especially from the first century B.C. These texts outline some of the customs and conduct of the peoples with whom the Greek and Latin authors, or their sources, came into contact. Given that they represent more or less contemporary accounts of the Iron Age communities, these accounts have great value, but they cannot be considered dispassionate, unbiased perspectives. On the one hand, they are outsiders' views—descriptions of what anthropologists sometimes term "the Other"—on occasion composed by authors with a vested interest in political affairs within the societies they are describing. The accounts thus display a tendency to focus on characteristics their original readership would have found puzzling, if not unacceptable, thus justifying Roman intervention.

Julius Caesar's description of his conquest of Gaul (corresponding in extent more or less to present-day francophone Europe) is one of the fullest such accounts. Some historians have considered his *De bello Gallico* the unembellished narrative of a straightforward military man, recounting his actual experiences; others argue that it is a consciously literary work that in some respects is simply propaganda. The dominant view sits between these two extremes but would not envisage Caesar's text as "value free." Furthermore, these texts were composed according to the intellectual conventions of their day. Unacknowledged copying of earlier authors was an acceptable practice, allowing for the possibility that descriptions of native societies may have been out of date by the time they were repeated. Far from being attempts at objective ethnography or history, texts were framed within contemporary philosophical perspectives.

A noteworthy example is *Agricola,* the history of Agricola, the governor of Britain, written by his son-in-law, the Roman historian Tacitus. Tacitus recounts the lead-in to his father-in-law's crushing defeat of the Caledonii in Scotland, using simply the auxiliary forces at his command, in the late first century A.D. The speech Tacitus puts into the mouth of the native war leader is not a dispatch from the battlefield but rather an Italian intellectual author's view of what the native leader Calgacus ought to have said: in effect the perspective of an imagined "noble savage." By contrast, the Roman historian Livy's account in *The History of Rome* of the arrival of the Celts in Italy is prefaced by the story of a king in central France, Ambigatus, who instructs his nephew to lead the people southward. Is this an indication of fosterage—the often forcible taking in of the children of people of dependent status—among the elite, a practice later recorded in early historic Ireland? Or is it the pattern of succession? One cannot be sure, for nothing more is known of Ambigatus's family circumstances. As the key individuals in this story are a king and his two nephews (the other being told to lead a portion of the tribe into central Europe) rather than members of a nuclear family, speculations on the relationship between the two generations are possible.

Although literacy made a late appearance in the Iron Age of temperate Europe (which is known, for example, from the evidence of graffiti scratched on ceramics and legends on coins), no contemporary documents from the late pre-Roman barbarian societies of temperate Europe north of the Alps or Pyrenees survive. The archaeological record thus is protohistoric in the sense that it is "text aided" uniquely through external, classical accounts. Because the Roman takeover of temperate Europe was not complete, it has been suggested that more modern literature, eventually written down in early Christian Ireland in the late first millennium A.D., includes elements transmitted orally from much earlier times, in effect providing a window on the Iron Age. Later commentators note, however, that detailed study indicates that this view gives rise to problems, as conscious changes typically are introduced during the transmission process. For this reason, scholars are increasingly cautious about using the Irish evidence to illuminate circumstances—including social conditions—within pre-Roman Iron Age continental Europe and Britain.

Another strand of evidence consists of language, as contained essentially in place, tribal, personal, and similar names as well as in brief inscriptions. This evidence is recorded in Greek or Latin scripts or in local variants of these scripts, as, for example, in the Iberian area of Mediterranean Spain. Many of these western and central European sources indicate languages conventionally ascribed to the Celtic family, beginning with Lepontic in northern Italy and stretching west to Celtiberian in Spain. In the later centuries B.C., such records, once very rare, became more common.

PEOPLES: CELTS AND OTHERS

It has been conventional practice to label the best-fit evidence of material culture with the same name as the language group and, where it is known, the classical term for the people in that area. In this way, the material culture of the Iron Age in west-central Europe attributable to the end of the first Iron Age (or Hallstatt period) and its second Iron Age successor (La Tène culture, from the middle of the fifth century B.C.) have been termed "Celtic." The art of that period, much of it produced for elite patrons and some of it magico-religious in character, is labeled "early Celtic art."

Another, more questionable practice has been to use the classical, or the later Irish, historical sources or the two in combination to provide descriptions of Celtic society as a complement to the evidence furnished by field archaeology. Such social generalizations are idealized: they disregard the real differences through time and from region to region visible in the archaeological record during the several centuries of the Iron Age, and thus they carry inherent dangers. The correlation of a set of material culture with an assumed linguistic affiliation—and beyond that automatically to an ethnic label—often is insecure. To say this is not, however, to deny that there were groups within temperate Europe that their neighbors called Celts or Gauls as well as Iberians, Scythians, and Germans. It is equally unreliable to assume that groups so named also automatically subscribed to a particular ethnically defined form of society, unchanging through the several centuries of the Iron Age.

CHANGES THROUGH TIME AND
THEIR SIGNIFICANCE

By the end of the Iron Age (La Tène D, from the later second century B.C.), the various sources combine to indicate the presence of socially and politically elaborate societies, witnessed, in particular, by the appearance of settlement sites of a scale and complexity not previously encountered. Termed *oppida*, these sites have a strong claim to having been the first indigenous temperate European towns. It would be incorrect, however, to envisage the Iron Age as a straightforward evolutionary sequence from simpler toward increasingly complex societies, numbers of which had crossed or were close to the threshold for definition as a state by the time of the Roman conquest. Most later models of Iron Age evolution suggest that periods and regions marked by increasing complexity were offset by local or regional collapses or reversions. In other areas—parts of northern Britain are a case in point—there is distinctly less evidence for social hierarchies in the available evidence for the later first millennium B.C. than can be gleaned for other areas, such as central France or southwestern Germany. Generally, the rhythm and periodicity of apparent changes and their general scale are matters of debate, as are the mechanisms—internal to temperate European societies or external to them—that lay behind these oscillations.

In most explanations, the nature and scale of contacts between the heartland of the Continent and the civilizations colonizing the Mediterranean (and Black Sea) littorals offer a key driving force underpinning assumed social, political, and economic changes during the Iron Age. Archaeological finds suggest economic contacts, which then can be used to account for social and political developments perceived in that record or in contemporary historical sources. Seaborne colonization by the Greeks, contemporary with the establishment of their leading western colony at Massalia (on the site of present-day Marseilles in southern France) in 600 B.C., is a case in point. Their equivalent establishment of settlements along the northern fringe of the Black Sea and in the Crimea is another example. Also important is Phoenician and subsequent Carthaginian activity, especially in Iberia, which resulted not only in contact with native societies in that area but also in the blocking of Greek access to Iberian metal ores from Galicia and elsewhere. In due course, Roman

conflict with the Carthaginians drew them into military activity in Iberia in late Republican times and set in train their northward expansion from the Mediterranean basin. Another important current was Etruscan colonization of the Po Valley of northern Italy and the head of the Adriatic Sea, which brought them to the ends of the Alpine passes leading from the Continental heartland.

Commodities manufactured in the Mediterranean civilizations appear in autochthonous contexts, including richly accompanied burials that are redolent of high status, for example, in southwestern Germany. It seems excessive, however, to attribute exclusively to these southern contacts the motor for social change in the Continental heartland. Such a perspective implicitly assumes that the constitution of a society necessarily realigns itself on that of an expansive neighbor perceived to be culturally more developed—thus that Hellenization (emulation of Greek traits), like Romanization in subsequent centuries, effectively would be irresistible. The anthropological literature contains many cases that show that in such circumstances the adoption of traits and influences can be highly selective, if they are not entirely rejected.

A refinement of this perspective envisages later prehistoric temperate Europe as a periphery strongly influenced by, if not dependent on, a core area in the Mediterranean civilizations. This application of world systems theory effectively transfers back into the ancient world characteristic patterns that have been recognized in modern times since the great period of European expansion across the world. Given the very different socioeconomic conditions of ancient times, let alone the much more rudimentary nature of transport networks, it is a moot point whether or not such a perspective is realistic for the middle of the first millennium B.C. In any case, a problem of the world systems approach is that it reduces elite decision makers on the assumed periphery to the status of bit actors, puppets on strings pulled from the south, and thus too readily eliminates them as knowing agents in establishing their own destinies.

If this type of approach has any validity, it is most likely to be for the last two centuries B.C., when the archaeological evidence, in particular, indicates that for some regions the scale and frequency of southern contacts were much greater than they were previously. In sum, the change is from exchange dominated by the infrequent arrival of individual high-status items manufactured in the cities of Etruria or in the Greek colonies (a pattern characteristic of the centuries in the middle of the first millennium B.C.) to the arrival of mass-produced goods of distinctly less-elevated status during the century or so before Caesar's campaigns in the 50s B.C.

WINE, FEASTING, AND HORSES AS INDICATORS OF SOCIAL CHANGE

This change is best seen in the accoutrements of alcohol consumption, in particular, the drinking of wine. For much of the temperate European Iron Age (things began to change from about the second century B.C.), wine was essentially an Italian product and the strongest—and probably the most readily storable—drink available. In Late Hallstatt and Early La Tène contexts, in both high-status burials and settlements, fine vessels associated with the consumption of wine occur in small numbers. Direct evidence of the wine itself, in the form of transport amphorae, is rare in areas away from the immediate hinterland of the Mediterranean. By contrast, from the second century B.C. (in La Tène C and D periods), the dominant finds in the archaeological record from some sites and areas of temperate Europe are Italic (made in Italy but not by Italians) wine amphorae. The quantities of discarded examples (each would have held some 25 liters of wine) suggest a level of commercial interaction not previously seen, as well as the much wider role of this exotic commodity in lubricating social and political relationships in inland Europe.

In some cases, the numbers of amphorae, the manner of their discarding, or their association with prolific quantities of animal bones strongly suggest large-scale feasting, a significant activity in cementing social and political obligations in the Iron Age world. There clearly was a major change in the quantities of wine that were accessible and in the social ways this commodity was employed. As ever, the nuances of such differences need to be recognized: both archaeological finds and historical accounts make it plain that southern merchants bringing wine freely traded in certain regions (e.g., marginal to present-day Belgium) while other regions received modest to plentiful quantities.

Other factors profoundly influenced the nature of Iron Age social organization on a wider scale.

Since the Neolithic, the products of agricultural systems had underpinned all communities. In the Iron Age, there is evidence from numerous regions of considerable agricultural diversification as well as the storage of agricultural surpluses, using several different technologies and to an extent not previously encountered in temperate Europe. Such evidence underscores the likelihood of rising populations and of larger aggregations of people resident on some settlement sites than had previously been the case, again with implications concerning the form and operation of society.

In the case of livestock, particular attention needs to be paid to the horse. Westward of the European steppes, evidence for horses is much more widespread in the Iron Age record than in earlier times. One piece of evidence is horse equipment, notably a wide range of horse bits, suggesting subtle control over the ridden horse. There are also bones of the animals themselves and iconographic representations of horses, for example, on high-status decorated metalwork, including appliqué panels and small axes, from certain graves in the cemetery at Hallstatt (in the Salzkammergut, Austria). Both four- and two-wheeled vehicles also are present, as inclusions in elite graves and in more prosaic settings. The ridden horse, horse-drawn chariots and carts, and subsequently, the development of cavalry provided opportunities for a rapidity of overland movement not previously available, and they facilitated the ready exercise of direct political and social control over more extensive territories. Folk migration was an accessible method for social and political change and one to which the classical sources testify, even if some archaeologists believe it was rarely undertaken. Equally, evidence from some areas indicates the emergence of hunting from horseback as an elite sport, unconnected with satisfying subsistence needs.

THE FORM OF SOCIETY—ELITES

There are plentiful indications that European Iron Age societies were hierarchical, although the depth of elaboration of that hierarchy seems to have varied across time and space. For much of the period, the social and political elite groups conformed to what would be anticipated in complex chiefdoms, with succession to important office being determined by real or imagined kinship links. Archaeological evidence suggests that such societies used several methods, including redistribution and gift exchange, to formulate and maintain wider linkages. By the La Tène D period (from the later second century B.C.), in some areas substantial changes had occurred. For certain of the Continental tribal areas (usually known by their Latin descriptor as *civitates*), political command, and by extension, social leadership had shifted from the king and his retinue to an elected magistracy. (The chief of this magistracy was termed a *vergobretus,* a Celtic loanword that appears in Caesar's text.) The magistracy was selected annually from among the oligarchical group that constituted the elite. Place of residence was beginning to oust kinship links, assumed or real, in defining group membership. Caesar's text strongly suggests that both these systems continued during this period, for his account includes plenty of individuals accorded the Latin title *rex,* perhaps a fair reflection of the fluidity of Iron Age political and social relations at this time in the face of powerful external military aggression.

Magistrates appear to have been solely male, whereas women could emerge as the leaders in more conventionally organized societies, as was certainly the case in southern Britain during the first century A.D. That females could hold high rank also is suggested in numerous contexts by the funerary record, where variations in the quality and number of grave goods equally points to subtle gradings within sociopolitical ranks, perhaps akin to what literary texts indicate more particularly for Ireland in the first millennium A.D.

Elite female graves are recognizable from Hallstatt C onward (the eighth century B.C.); they generally are marked by ranges of grave goods in which jewelry (and sometimes mirrors) form a significant component, with weaponry rare or absent. Normally, wealthy female graves are attributed to the sociopolitical elite, as in the rich female grave from Reinheim in Germany. In other instances, it is possible that the wealth in the grave is indicative of a spiritual rather than a political leader. Christopher Knüsel has suggested, for example, that the grave at Vix in Burgundy, dating to the fifth century B.C. (Hallstatt D), held the slightly deformed body of a middle-aged woman whose local importance may have been religious. She is accompanied by a dismantled wagon, a high-quality gold necklet or torc (a rigid

penannular collar or neck ring), and a spectacular imported bronze wine krater, or large vase—the biggest surviving vase from the Greek world. In other instances, grave goods suggest that brides may have been exchanged over considerable distances in continental Europe. Female graves from northeastern France (dating to the third century B.C.) with paired anklets may well contain girls originally from the heartland of central Europe, where this particular fashion was widespread.

The presence of grave goods in some of the relatively rare children's graves suggests that status in the societies to which they belonged was ascribed rather than attained. In some instances, children are accompanied by smaller examples of adult grave goods (e.g., bracelets), and in others their positions within cemeteries or under barrows intimate their significance within their community. As in many ancient societies, infants and young children are underrepresented in the funerary record, but this may be a reflection either of their status or of the use of burial practices less susceptible to archaeological detection. More generally, both inhumation and cremation are encountered, sometimes in the same cemetery (as at Hallstatt), and the change from one to the other need not have any straightforward social significance.

The literary sources provide details of the significance of religious and educational specialists within society, notably the druids. They make it clear, too, that the activities of such elites could extend beyond the polities in which they were based. From numerous areas, archaeological evidence makes plain the fact that many activities had a ritual dimension (including such prosaic acts as the discarding of rubbish in disused underground storage pits within settlements). On some sites—notably, the so-called Picardy sanctuaries of northeastern France—ritualized acts seem to have been key, to judge from the clear patterns in the archaeological finds recovered from them. Deliberately damaged equipment and weaponry, animal bones, and human remains showing a range of postmortem manipulations bear witness to practices involving such religious practitioners that can be gleaned only indirectly. The most famous such locale is a small enclosure within a settlement at Gournay-sur-Aronde, in the valley of a tributary of the River Oise, to the north of Paris.

OTHER GROUPS: WARRIORS, SPECIALISTS, ARTISANS, AND FARMERS

Among other groups prominent within society that can be recognized from the written sources and from the archaeological record are specialists of varying degrees of skill. These people include musicians and poets, craftspeople, and warriors. The accompaniments in male graves indicate that warriors constituted a significant proportion of male adults in some areas. The grave goods that typically identify them are swords (of iron, sometimes encased in elaborate decorated bronze sheaths) and spearheads. Defensive equipment, which is rarer, is dominated by metal shield fittings (usually for shields made of organic materials that have rotted away) and helmets, the latter including ornate examples displaying the status of the wearer rather than simple protective military gear.

It is noteworthy that some of the most elaborate examples of such equipment (for men and sometimes their horses) come from the apparent margins of the Celtic domain, if not beyond. Such places include southern Italy, western France, Romania, and northern Britain, perhaps suggesting that the insignia were of special importance in these peripheral settings. Military protection appears to have been a significant element in the glue that held Celtic societies together, if indications from both earlier Continental written sources and later insular ones are considered. There are hints in the texts of the importance of clientship—the formalization of patron-client relations through the development of mutual obligations. The provision of military protection seems to have been a key component of such arrangements.

There also are signs of profound changes in the nature of the social and political relationships that lay behind the establishment of military forces during the last half-millennium B.C. For the Early Iron Age, it is easy to envisage military service as arising through real or assumed kinship links, clientship obligations, indebtedness, and similar causes and as being both temporary and intermittent in character. By the end of this period, however, there were significant changes. In some instances, armies still had to be called together at moments of crisis by holding a hosting (assembling an irregular army from diverse groups with the express purpose of battle), as

Caesar recounts. In other cases, standing armies were associated with particular *civitates* (or perhaps their constituent parts, the *pagi*), which could be paid in coin, a practice initially learned in mercenary service to the Hellenistic kings around the Aegean. Unsurprisingly, military leadership seems to have been a high-status responsibility and was maintained in Gaul, for example, after its defeat by Rome. Cavalry units, in particular, kept their native commanders and simply transferred their allegiance to their new masters as auxiliary troops.

Specialists also seem to have had considerable, but perhaps variable, status in society. Some are recognizable in death from the equipment placed in their graves, as, for example, the medical doctor of the La Tène C period identified from his instruments at Obermenzing near Munich in Bavaria, Germany. In other cases, tools have been found in workshops or elsewhere on settlement sites. The Late Iron Age toolkit found at Celles in central France is appropriate to marquetry or similar decorative work on furniture, and some of the finest items of early Celtic art, such as the helmet from Agris in western France and a few of the vehicles, imply collaborations among several artisans skilled in different materials or in different trades.

Localized distributions of certain artifacts, such as certain varieties of Late Hallstatt brooches, suggest that they may have been made directly for elite patrons on particular sites. Other types of objects (most particularly in La Tène D) are much more standardized over wide areas of the Continent and may betoken the work of independent craft workers. At some sites, artisans engaged in the same craft are clustered in limited sectors, as in the case of enamel workers found inside the main gate at the La Tène D *oppidum* of Mont Beuvray in Le Morvan, France. Such groupings may be considered socially significant. Overall, however, skilled specialists as well as the general run of artisans must have constituted the dependent classes of later Iron Age societies, as described by Caesar: they probably would have been substantially outnumbered by agricultural laborers, peasants, and small farmers.

SLAVERY

Was slavery a component of Iron Age societies in temperate Europe? For most areas and periods, the evidence is either ambiguous or nonexistent, but there are exceptions. Toward the end of the Iron Age, in western continental Europe and southern Britain, chains and similar accoutrements of slavery become more common in the record and probably are indicative of long-distance movements of slave labor. It often is suggested that captives taken in war were traded down the line across the Continent to the slave-based societies of the Mediterranean even in earlier times. Such captives were exchanged for the luxury products recovered from, for example, rich Hallstatt graves, although the earlier classical sources suggest that servile labor was obtained nearer to hand.

Less certain is the extent to which later Iron Age societies in temperate Europe were themselves slave owning as opposed to exporters of prisoners. Analogy with later Ireland might indicate that slaveholding already was established, and it also is possible that the development of large-scale extractive industries might have relied to some extent on slave labor. Shoe sizes have been pointed to as evidence that children were put to work extracting rock salt at Dürrnberg in Austria, and the open-air gold mines of Limousin in France might have been worked by slave laborers. Overall, we can conclude that in the Iron Age, as in later times, social structures and rates of social change in barbarian Europe probably varied and did not conform closely to a pan-Continental norm.

See also **Celts** (*vol. 2, part 6*); **Hallstatt** (*vol. 2, part 6*); **La Tène** (*vol. 2, part 6*); **Germans** (*vol. 2, part 6*); **Oppida** (*vol. 2, part 6*); **Iron Age Feasting** (*vol. 2, part 6*); **La Tène Art** (*vol. 2, part 6*); **Greek Colonies in the West** (*vol. 2, part 6*); **Etruscan Italy** (*vol. 2, part 6*).

BIBLIOGRAPHY

Arnold, Bettina, and D. Blair Gibson, eds. *Celtic Chiefdom, Celtic State: The Evolution of Complex Social Systems in Prehistoric Europe.* New Directions in Archaeology. Cambridge, U.K.: Cambridge University Press, 1995.

Audouze, Françoise, and Olivier Buchsenschütz. *Towns, Villages, and Countryside of Celtic Europe: From the Beginning of the Second Millennium to the End of the First Century B.C.* Translated by Henry Cleere. Bloomington, Ind.: Batsford, 1991.

Bintliff, John. "Iron Age Europe in the Context of Social Evolution from the Bronze Age through to Historic Times." In *European Social Evolution: Archaeological Perspectives.* Edited by John Bintliff, pp. 157–225. Bradford, U.K.: Bradford University, 1984.

Collis, John R. *The European Iron Age.* London: Routledge, 1995.

Cunliffe, Barry W. *The Ancient Celts.* Oxford: Oxford University Press, 1997.

———. *Greeks, Romans, and Barbarians: Spheres of Interaction.* London: Batsford, 1988.

Dietler, Michael. "Feasts and Commensal Politics in the Political Economy: Food, Power, and Status in Prehistoric Europe." In *Food and the Status Quest: An Interdisciplinary Perspective.* Edited by Pauline Wilson Wiessner and Wulf Schiefenhövel, pp. 87–125. Oxford: Berghahn Books, 1996.

Fitzpatrick, Andrew. "'Celtic' Iron Age Europe: The Theoretical Basis." In *Cultural Identity and Archaeology: The Construction of European Communities.* Edited by Paul Graves-Brown, Siân Jones, and Clive Gamble, pp. 238-255. London: Routledge, 1996.

Gibson, D. Blair, and Michael N. Geselowitz, eds. *Tribe and Polity in Late Prehistoric Europe: Demography, Production, and Exchange in the Evolution of Complex Social Systems.* New York: Plenum, 1988. (Includes Bettina Arnold's essay on slavery.)

Green, Miranda J. *Exploring the World of the Druids.* London: Thames and Hudson, 1997.

Green, Miranda J., ed. *The Celtic World.* London: Routledge, 1995.

James, Simon. *Exploring the World of the Celts.* London: Thames and Hudson, 1993.

Knüsel, Christopher. "More Circe Than Cassandra: The Princess of Vix in Ritualised Social Context." *European Journal of Archaeology* 5, no. 3 (2002): 275–308. (The status of the most important Hallstatt princess reevaluated.)

Kristiansen, Kristian. *Europe before History.* Cambridge, U.K.: Cambridge University Press, 1998.

Kruta, Venceslas. *Les Celtes: Histoire et dictionnaire des origines à la romanisation et au christianisme.* Paris: Robert Laffont, 2000. (Long introductory essay and useful gazetteer.)

Megaw, M. Ruth, and J. Vincent S. Megaw. *Celtic Art: From Its Beginnings to the Book of Kells.* Rev. ed. New York: Thames and Hudson, 2001.

Moscati, Sabatino, ed. *The Celts.* New York: Rizzoli, 1999.

Sims-Williams, Patrick. "Genetics, Linguistics, and Prehistory: Thinking Big and Thinking Straight." *Antiquity* 72 (1998): 505–527.

Wells, Peter S. *Beyond Celts, Germans, and Scythians: Archaeology and Identity in Iron Age Europe.* London: Duckworth Academic, 2001.

IAN RALSTON

GREEK COLONIES IN THE WEST

Between 750 and 550 B.C. a number of Greek cities, both in modern Greece and on the west coast of modern Turkey, established daughter cities along the shores of the Mediterranean, Adriatic, and Black Seas. This process has become known as "Greek colonization." In contrast to colonizing actions of modern nation-states, however, this expansion of individual Greek city-states was not centrally directed, and there was no single purpose. Among the reasons for the establishment of particular towns were overpopulation in the mother cities, need for larger supplies of grain than were available in Greece, and improvement of trade relations with different peoples on and beyond the shores of the Mediterranean Sea. Both Greek historical sources and archaeological investigation provide information about the founding and growth of the new towns and about relations between them and other peoples.

MASSALIA

The most important Greek town established in the western Mediterranean was Massalia, on the site of modern-day Marseille, France's second-largest city. Archaeological evidence from the lands around the mouth of the Rhône River show that, during the second half of the seventh century B.C., merchants from abroad were trading with the indigenous peo-

ples. Pottery, ceramic amphorae that had carried wine, and bronze vessels from Greek and Etruscan workshops appear on settlements and in burials after about 630 B.C., indicating that this region was being opened to seaborne trade by the Mediterranean urban civilizations. It is not known precisely who these early merchants were—probably the peoples called Etruscans and Greeks. They traveled in relatively small ships along the Mediterranean coasts, trading in wine, ceramics, and other luxury goods. Numerous shipwrecks in the shallow waters of the Mediterranean coasts provide underwater archaeologists with rich information about boat technology and about the character of their cargoes.

Around 600 B.C. Greeks from the city of Phocaea, a community in Ionian Greece, now located on the west coast of Turkey, founded Massalia, the first permanent Greek settlement known in the region. The settlers were attracted by the excellent natural harbor, with its entrance protected from Mediterranean storms; the hill to the north that provided ideal settlement land; and the proximity to the mouth of the Rhône River, the principal waterway that linked interior regions of Europe with the western Mediterranean. The site was close enough to the river's mouth to provide easy access and allow control of the river but far enough away to avoid the

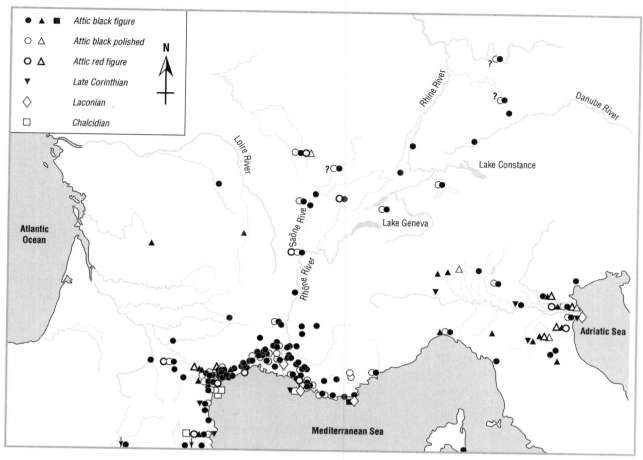

Distribution of Greek pottery of the fourth quarter of the sixth century B.C. (not including east Greek pottery). ADAPTED FROM KIMMIG 2000.

problem of its harbor silting up with riverborne sediments.

Excavations in modern Marseille have yielded abundant evidence of the Greek town, though archaeologists are limited in their investigations by the modern city that overlies the ancient Greek one. For well over a century archaeologists have noted large quantities of ancient architectural remains, pottery from Athens and elsewhere in the Greek world, coins, and other materials from the early settlement. Since the 1960s archaeologists have been able to carry out systematic excavations in parts of the harbor and in places under construction within the ancient town itself. In the harbor they have discovered at least nine ships from the first century of the port's existence as well as warehouses and docks that formed parts of the harbor's infrastructure. Study of archaeological remains within the city of Marseille indicates that this Greek town of the sixth

century B.C. covered some 40 hectares of the hilly land around the harbor and that the town was protected on its northern edge by a massive stone and brick wall.

MASSALIA'S REGION AND DAUGHTER TOWNS

Massalia grew in size and influence and became the principal center along the southern coast of France, from Barcelona to Nice. It dominated an extensive landscape on both sides of the lower Rhône and had an important impact far inland, north and east of the headwaters of the Rhône in the interior of the Continent. French archaeologists have investigated many settlement and cemetery sites in the lower Rhône region northwest of Marseille and found extensive evidence of interaction with the Greek town. Particularly abundant are sherds of ceramic amphorae that had been used to transport wine. Some of the vessels had been manufactured at Massalia; others were imported from elsewhere in the Mediterranean basin. Fine pottery, some made at Massalia and some from as far away as Athens, also circulated from the trade center to communities throughout the lower Rhône Valley. Especially common among the fine ceramics are pitchers, small bowls, and cups—all vessels used in the consumption of wine. The lands around the town of Massalia produced wine, and wine was imported from other regions of the Mediterranean. According to the Greek geographer Strabo, the rocky soils around Massalia would allow the successful cultivation of wine grapes and olives but not grain.

Shortly after they established Massalia around 600 B.C., Phocaean Greeks also founded a new town called Emporion, located on the northeastern coast of Spain, where modern Ampurias is situated. Emporion did not grow as large as Massalia, but around that town, too, is abundant archaeological evidence for interaction with indigenous peoples. Within a century of its establishment, Massalia began founding other daughter towns in the south of France.

MASSALIA AND WEST-CENTRAL EUROPE

In addition to their activities in and around Massalia and along the northern coasts of the western Mediterranean, the merchants based at the Greek port engaged in significant interactions with peoples of interior regions of continental Europe, especially in the region known as west-central Europe, which now is made up of eastern France, southwestern Germany, and northern and western Switzerland. The significance of these interactions between the prehistoric, Early Iron Age peoples of temperate Europe and merchants from the literate civilization of the Greek Mediterranean has been much discussed, and they certainly were of fundamental importance to cultural development within Europe. They also were significant to the Greek world, especially with respect to the trade products that Massalia and its commercial partners acquired through the interactions and in regard to the forming of Greek attitudes toward the non-Greek peoples who lived in the interior of the Continent. The principal concern here is with the effects of these interactions on the peoples of west-central Europe.

Archaeological Evidence for Interactions. The archaeological evidence for interactions between communities in west-central Europe and the Greek establishment at and around Massalia consists largely of objects manufactured in the Greek world that are recovered by archaeologists on settlements and in graves in west-central Europe. The most studied imports are pottery from Athens, pottery from Massalia and from workshops in its region, transport amphorae (some manufactured at Massalia and others brought in from abroad), and bronze vessels (some from Greek workshops and some from Etruscan Italy). Other objects, discussed later, also have significance. All of the imported objects are luxury goods, and all were consumed by the elite groups of Early Iron Age west-central Europe. The great majority of the objects are associated directly with the transportation, serving, and consumption of wine.

The most thoroughly investigated assemblage of Greek imports is from the Heuneburg on the Upper Danube River in the German state of Baden-Württemberg. At Mont Lassois on the upper Seine River in eastern France, even larger quantities of Greek pottery have been identified, and the Vix grave just below the fortified hilltop settlement contained numerous important objects. Between the Heuneburg and Mont Lassois, in the valleys of the Upper Rhine, the Doubs, and the upper Rhône Rivers, Greek imports have been recovered at many other settlements and graves. The Heuneburg and Mont Lassois stand out in being especially well studied and in providing important evidence for both settlement and burial contexts.

A number of different categories of imported Greek pottery have been identified at the Heuneburg, Mont Lassois, and the other sites, including pottery made in and around Massalia, pottery from eastern Greek workshops, and pottery from the center of Attica, Athens. Small numbers of Greek imports are apparent before the middle of the sixth century B.C., but the quantities increased greatly during the second half of that century. The imported Attic pottery has attracted special attention, because it can be dated very precisely and because archaeologists know a great deal about how it was produced and used in its land of origin. To date fifty-eight sherds of Attic pottery have been identified from the materials excavated at the Heuneburg

Fig. 1. Greek *kylix*, or drinking cup, made in Athens and found in the rich burial at Vix. THE ART ARCHIVE/ARCHAEOLOGICAL MUSEUM CHÂTILLON-SUR-SEINE/DAGLI ORTI. REPRODUCED BY PERMISSION.

and more than three hundred at Mont Lassois. The vessel forms represented are part of the Greek wine-serving set—kraters for mixing wine and water (standard Greek practice), jugs for serving wine, and cups for drinking it (fig. 1). Most Attic pottery at these sites dates to the second half of the sixth century B.C., especially to the final quarter (525–500 B.C.). Amphorae used to transport wine from the Mediterranean coast into temperate Europe also are well represented, with fifty-five sherds from thirty-seven amphorae recorded from the Heuneburg, the majority of them dating to the same period as the Attic pottery. Early in the fifth century B.C. the quantities of Greek imports that were arriving into west-central Europe declined, for reasons that are not well understood. The cause of the decline may have lain principally in political and economic circumstances in west-central Europe or in the economic fortunes of Massalia or in a combination of factors.

Bronze vessels are an important category of Greek imports in west-central Europe, but they are much less abundant than fine pottery and am-

phorae. While the imported pottery and amphorae are represented mainly by sherds on settlement sites (though a few complete vessels do appear in graves, such as the two wine cups in the Vix burial), the bronze vessels are found principally in graves. The most spectacular is the Vix krater. Others include the cauldron in the Hochdorf burial; fragmentary sets of tripods and cauldrons from Sainte-Colombe near Vix in France and from Grafenbühl near Hochdorf in Germany; a *hydria* (water jug) from Grächwil in Switzerland; and relatively plain jugs from Ihringen, Kappel, and Vilsingen in the Upper Rhine Valley region.

Other imported luxury items from the Greek world that probably arrived by way of the port of Massalia are small ornaments and lavishly decorated furniture. In the Grafenbühl grave (looted in antiquity) were a small sphinx figure carved from bone and with an amber face. In the same grave and in a grave nearby at Römerhügel were carved amber, bone, and ivory pieces from furniture, perhaps couches. Coral from the Mediterranean Sea was imported in quantity for use as inlay in bronze jewelry.

At the Heuneburg a partly worked coral branch indicates that the material was processed in a workshop on the site. Dyes for coloring textiles, evident at Hochdorf, were imported from the Mediterranean region. Even new foods were introduced to the Early Iron Age centers from the Mediterranean world at this time, including chickens and figs.

Nature of the Interactions. Much debate surrounds the nature of the interactions that brought the imports from the Greek world of the Mediterranean to the communities in west-central Europe. Most often the interactions are referred to simply as "trade," but that term oversimplifies the situation and may not be accurate, if in using that word one thinks of modern trade.

An important factor in attempts to understand why and how Greek luxury imports reached west-central Europe is the concentration of such imports at a few major centers dating to the latter part of the Early Iron Age (550–480 B.C.). The Heuneburg, Mont Lassois, the Hohenasperg (north of Stuttgart in Southwest Germany), Bragny-sur-Saône in eastern France, Châtillon-sur-Glâne in Switzerland, and other sites include hilltop settlements enclosed by fortification walls. Below them are unusually large burial mounds that cover elaborate wooden burial chambers housing rich graves containing Greek imports, gold ornaments, wagons, feasting equipment, and in the case of men's graves, weapons. Thus there is a clear association between high status in Early Iron Age society and the Greek imports. Greek fine pottery, wine amphorae, and bronze vessels are rarely found on typical agricultural settlements or in modestly outfitted graves.

Written Greek sources tell of slightly later times that Greek cities sought to obtain a variety of raw materials through trade. These materials included grain to feed their urban populations, meat and fish, metals (iron for tools and weapons; copper and tin to make bronze for ornaments, statuary, and vessels; and gold and silver for ornaments), timber for building ships and other purposes, salt, pitch and tar, honey, leather, hides and fur, textiles, and perhaps slaves. In some other regions of the greater Mediterranean basin, such as on the north coasts of the Black Sea, appear patterns similar to those at Massalia and west-central Europe, with the establishment of Greek ports and the transmission of Greek pottery and other goods inland to special fortified settlements. One set of interpretations views the Greek imports in west-central Europe as representative of one side of trade relations between elites at the Early Iron Age centers and merchant groups at Massalia. Centers such as the Heuneburg and Mont Lassois can be thought of as collection sites for the accumulation of materials sought by Greek merchants—raw materials, such as honey and furs from the forests, and partly made goods, such as wool textiles from the farming communities. The situation of all of the Early Iron Age centers on major rivers would support this model of economic trade in commodities from west-central Europe in exchange for finished luxury goods from the Greek world. According to this view, the elites at the centers controlled the trade, and thus they acquired and consumed the great majority of the luxury imports. They distributed some imports to the smaller communities that supplied the trade goods; coral inlay on bronze jewelry is well represented not only at the major centers but at many smaller communities as well.

This model is too simplistic, however, and anachronistic. It assumes that trade in the sixth century B.C. operated through exchange principles similar to those of more modern times. Some archaeologists have advocated a prestige-goods model for the exchange. In this view, rather than a barter trade of raw materials for Greek luxury goods, overseen and controlled by local elites, the key factor is the circulation of particular objects that bore high status and prestige in society—the Greek luxuries in Early Iron Age communities. According to this interpretation, the key element was the circulation and display of prestige goods. This model downplays the relationships between the elites at the centers and the smaller communities that produced goods for trade and emphasizes instead the interactions between groups of elites in their competition for status and power at the centers.

Several objects provide important information about the nature of the interrelations between the centers of west-central Europe and the Greek world. The Vix krater has been interpreted as a diplomatic gift from a Greek community to a potentate on the upper Seine, presented in order to seal a treaty or to create a useful relationship. That unique object is much more precious than any other Greek imports in Europe, and it requires a different explanation from the fine pottery, the wine amphorae, and the other bronze vessels. The Greek historian Herodotus, writing around the middle of the fifth century B.C., described a similar vessel that was made to present to a king of a non-Greek people in Asia Minor (modern Turkey). It seems likely that the Vix krater also was made and presented for a particular purpose that went far beyond what would be considered "economic" trade and lay rather in the realm of diplomatic and political relationships.

The clay-brick wall at the Heuneburg similarly provides unique information. The fortification wall surrounding the hilltop settlement at the Heuneburg was built in several phases. In all but one of the phases, the wall consisted of a typical central European earth-and-timber structure. For one phase of construction, however, the wall was built of clay bricks, set on a foundation of cut stone—a technology that was foreign to west-central Europe but at home in the Greek world of the Mediterranean. This wall was about 3 meters thick, and it included 10 rectangular towers on the north side of the site, creating what must have been an impressive view for the inhabitants of the settlement below. The dimensions of the bricks in the Heuneburg wall even match those in contemporaneous walls at Greek cities.

While objects such as Attic pottery and even the Vix krater could have been transmitted to the west-central European centers by indirect trade, without individuals from Massalia and the Early Iron Age centers ever coming directly into contact with one another, the building of the clay-brick wall demonstrates the direct transmission of technical knowledge between individuals of the two societies. Either an architect from the Mediterranean world must have overseen the construction of the wall at the Heuneburg, or someone from west-central Europe must have learned the technique during a visit to a Greek city. Either way, direct interpersonal technology transfer is required to explain the wall.

Transmission of specific technical information from the Mediterranean world to west-central Europe also is indicated by the statue from Hirschlanden, a burial mound near the Hohenasperg hillfort. This life-size statue of a male warrior is sculpted of local sandstone. The modeling of the back and the legs shows familiarity with sculptural traditions cur-

rent during the sixth century B.C. in the Mediterranean world among Greek and Etruscan sculptors but otherwise absent in west-central Europe at this time. Since objects represented on the statue—hat, dagger, and belt—are of local character and the object is made of local sandstone, its local origin is not in question. As in the case of the Heuneburg brick wall, however, the Hirschlanden figure displays technical knowledge brought one way or another from the Mediterranean world.

EFFECT OF THE INTERACTIONS

The role that the interactions between west-central European communities and the Greek world at and around Massalia played in Iron Age Europe also is a greatly debated issue. The principal matter of contention is whether the interactions represented by the Greek luxury goods were an important factor in the emergence of elites in Early Iron Age west-central Europe or whether the emergence of the elites happened as a result of processes internal to European society. Put into simple terms, did the commerce with Massalia "cause" the greater social differentiation that is apparent in the rich graves at the Heuneburg, Mont Lassois, the Hohenasperg, and the other centers? Or did the elites emerge through locally based social changes and participate in trade with the Greeks in order to acquire attractive luxuries?

These questions are difficult to answer. The Greek luxury imports clearly are associated with the elites—the individuals buried in the richest and most elaborate burials. The Early Iron Age centers of west-central Europe rose to importance only during the sixth century B.C., after Massalia had been established and at the time that the first of the imports were arriving. Economic activity flourished at the centers in the final decades of the sixth century B.C., at the same time that the larger numbers of imports were arriving and the rich graves were most lavishly outfitted. Thus it is clear that there was a close connection between the social and political changes in Early Iron Age west-central Europe and the interactions with Greek Massalia. But it is not yet possible to explain exactly how these changes happened.

Some archaeologists argue that these interrelationships can best be understood in terms of core-periphery relations, in which the Greek Mediterranean is viewed as the core and west-central Europe as the periphery. In support of this approach, the archaeological evidence shows similar patterns of importation of Greek pottery, bronze vessels, and other luxury goods at other locations in the greater Mediterranean world, such as Iberia, the east coast of the Adriatic Sea, and the lands north of the Black Sea. These other regions also contain evidence for the same kinds of changes in local societies that are evident in west-central Europe—the appearance of new fortified hilltop settlements, on which Greek imported pottery is found, and increase in differentiation reflected in burial equipment. Thus from the broader perspective of Greek-native interaction all along the north coasts of the Mediterranean and Black Seas, the evidence seems to indicate that similar social changes were stimulated (not to say caused) by the establishment of Greek commercial towns eager to acquire commodities in the interior regions of Europe.

Those that argue in favor of local changes rather than external commerce as the critical factors point out that the total numbers of Greek imports in west-central Europe are small. The fifty-eight sherds of Attic pottery recovered so far at the Heuneburg, for example, represent only about thirteen vessels. Only thirty-seven wine amphorae have been identified from the sherds at the site. Viewed over some fifty or more years of interaction, these numbers of vessels do not indicate a substantial trade. Other investigators counter that in archaeology researchers always work with fragmentary evidence. Perhaps much or most of the importation of Greek luxury goods was in perishable materials, such as the fine textiles in the grave at Hochdorf and the silk from the Hohmichele burial mound at the Heuneburg. If this was the case, then the Attic pottery, wine amphorae, bronze vessels, and other objects are only the most visible signs of interactions, and archaeologists must reckon with much larger quantities of goods that are not as readily recognizable.

These debates are still flourishing. To an extent, new data from excavated settlements and graves will help provide support for one perspective or the other. Much of the debate depends upon how one thinks economic and social systems in the past operated, and thus agreement may never be achieved. In any case, it is clear that the contacts with the Greek world and the emergence of the economic and social centers with their elites were closely interconnected.

Perhaps the most important effects of the interactions were the more subtle ones involving the sharing and exchange of information, ideas, and practices. With any kind of trade or political interaction between groups, information and ideas are passed, resulting in changes in attitudes, beliefs, and values of all parties concerned. One clear example in the case of west-central Europe and the Greek world is the apparent adoption of the Greek practice of the symposium. This was a ritual wine-drinking party in which particular types of vessels were used for specific purposes, and the event served to express social distinctions between members of the elite groups. The sets of feasting vessels that were placed in rich burials such as Hochdorf and Vix provide all of the functions required for the performance of a feast structured like the Greek symposium—large mixing vessels, jugs, and drinking cups. Some of these vessels were Greek and Etruscan imports, and others, such as the horns in the Hochdorf tomb, were local versions. In Greece at the time revelers reclined on couches; perhaps the Hochdorf couch and those represented by ornaments at Grafenbühl and Römerhügel indicate a local use of this item of furniture. It is on this level of practice and performance, with elements from the Greek world and from Early Iron Age west-central Europe integrated into meaningful practices, that much important and exciting research will be done in the near future.

See also **Status and Wealth** (*vol. 1, part 1*); **Hochdorf** (*vol. 1, part 1*); **Iron Age Feasting** (*vol. 2, part 6*); **Vix** (*vol. 2, part 6*); **The Heuneburg** (*vol. 2, part 6*).

BIBLIOGRAPHY

Arnold, Bettina. "'Drinking the Feast': Alcohol and the Legitimation of Power in Celtic Europe." *Cambridge Archaeological Journal* 9, no. 1 (1999): 71–93.

Boardman, John. *The Greeks Overseas: Their Early Colonies and Trade.* 4th ed. New York: Thames and Hudson, 1999.

Brun, Patrice, and Bruno Chaume, eds. *Vix et les éphémères principautés celtiques: Les VIe–Ve siècles avant J.-C. en Europe centre-occidentale.* Paris: Éditions Errance, 1997.

Diepeveen-Jansen, Marian. *People, Ideas, and Goods: New Perspectives on "Celtic Barbarians" in Western and Central Europe (500–250 B.C.).* Translated by Christine Jefferis. Amsterdam: Amsterdam University Press, 2001.

VIX

Dietler, Michael. "The Iron Age in Mediterranean France: Colonial Encounters, Entanglements, and Transformations." *Journal of World Prehistory* 11, no. 3 (1997): 269–358.

———. "Early 'Celtic' Socio-Political Relations: Ideological Representation and Social Competition in Dynamic Comparative Perspective." In *Celtic Chiefdom, Celtic State: The Evolution of Complex Social Systems in Prehistoric Europe.* Edited by Bettina Arnold and D. Blair Gibson, pp. 64–71. Cambridge, U.K.: Cambridge University Press, 1995.

Kimmig, Wolfgang, ed. *Importe und mediterrane Einflüsse auf der Heuneburg.* Mainz, Germany: Philipp von Zabern, 2000.

Kristiansen, Kristian. *Europe before History.* Cambridge, U.K.: Cambridge University Press, 1998.

Moscati, Sabatino, ed. *The Celts.* New York: Rizzoli, 1991.

Pare, Christopher. "La dimension européenne du commerce grec à la fin de la période archaïque et pendant le début de la période classique." In *Vix et les éphémères principautés celtiques: Les VIe–Ve siècles avant J.-C. en Europe centre-occidentale.* Edited by Patrice Brun and Bruno Chaume, pp. 261–286. Paris: Éditions Errance, 1997.

Les Princes celtes et la Méditerrannée. Paris: La Documentation Francaise, 1988.

Shefton, Brian. "On the Material in Its Northern Setting." In *Importe und mediterrane Einflüsse auf der Heuneburg.* Edited by Wolfgang Kimmig, pp. 27–41. Mainz, Germany: Philipp von Zabern, 2000.

Wells, Peter S. *Culture Contact and Culture Change: Early Iron Age Central Europe and the Mediterranean World.* Cambridge, U.K.: Cambridge University Press, 1980.

PETER S. WELLS

VIX

At the small settlement of Vix near Châtillon on the upper Seine River in eastern France, an unusually richly outfitted grave was excavated in 1952 and 1953. Numerous burial mounds are still visible around the fortified hilltop site of Mont Lassois, but the mound above the Vix grave had eroded and was no longer apparent on the surface. Excavations revealed the remains of a mound 42 meters in diameter and probably about 5 meters high, within which was a wooden chamber 3.1 by 2.75 meters in size, covered by a layer of stones. Inside was an undisturbed burial that included the skeletal remains of a woman about thirty-five years of age, buried c. 480 B.C., at the end of the Early Iron Age.

Fig. 1. The Vix krater. THE ART ARCHIVE/ARCHAEOLOGICAL MUSEUM CHÂTILLON-SUR-SEINE/DAGLI ORTI. REPRODUCED BY PERMISSION.

The grave contained goods that characterize rich women's burials of the Early Iron Age, but also unique objects. The woman's body was laid on the box of a wagon in the center of the grave, with her head toward the north. The wagon's detached four wheels had been arranged along the east wall of the chamber. On the western side was an extraordinary assemblage of ceramic, bronze, and silver vessels. Around her neck the woman wore a uniquely ornamented gold ring of exceptionally fine workmanship, weighing 480 grams. At the two terminals were lion paws, tiny winged horses, and intricately incised ornamentation. Gold neck rings are characteristic of richly outfitted Early Iron Age burials in temperate Europe, but the Vix ring is different from all others. The style of ornament suggests connections with Greek and Scythian decorative traditions, but specialists have not agreed on the probable place of manufacture.

Her other personal ornaments are of types common to well-equipped women's graves, but she was buried with more of them, and many are unusually richly decorated. On each wrist she wore three bracelets of schist and one of thin bronze. A necklace was made of amber, diorite, and serpentine beads. On each ankle was a hollow bronze ring. With her were eight fibulae, ornamental brooches, which worked on the principle of the modern safety pin, that were used to fasten garments and for decoration. Two were of iron, the other six of bronze, and some were ornamented with gold, amber, and coral. Amber and coral were both exotic luxuries—amber came from the coast of the Baltic Sea to the northeast and coral from the Mediterranean to the south.

The feasting equipment in the grave consisted of eight vessels, at least six of them imports from the Greek and Etruscan worlds. Two wine cups were products of the luxury ceramic industry in Athens. One was painted in the black-figure style about 525 B.C., and the other was a plain black cup made about 515 B.C. A bronze jug and three basins all may have come from Etruscan workshops in Italy. A silver bowl with a central omphalos, or knob, of sheet gold was 23 centimeters in diameter. The most unusual object in the grave was an enormous bronze krater, a kind of vessel used in the Greek world for mixing wine and water at feasts, made by Greek bronzesmiths.

The Vix krater is 1.64 meters tall and weighs 208 kilograms—the largest metal krater known. It would have held about 1,100 liters, but there is some question as to whether it could, in fact, have been used. It is possible that the weight of so much liquid would have burst the thin bronze. While the body of the krater is hammered sheet bronze, the base, handles, rim, and figures around the neck are all cast. The handles represent figures of gorgons, and the cast bronze figures on the neck are Greek warriors, their horses, and chariots. With the krater was a bronze lid 1.02 meters in diameter, in the center of which stood a figure of a women 19 centimeters tall.

Based on stylistic analysis, art historians believe that the krater was made in a Greek workshop in southern Italy about 530 B.C. This unusually large and finely made object may have been transported in pieces across the Tyrrhenian Sea, up the Rhône Valley, and overland to the headwaters of the Seine and then to Vix. Each of the small bronze figures has a Greek letter on the reverse side and is attached to a spot on the neck with a corresponding letter, as if assembly was required. The most interesting questions are, Why was this very unusual and costly object brought to this place far from the centers of power and wealth of the Mediterranean civilizations? And who was the woman with whom this extraordinary vessel was buried? Most scholarly opinion is that it was a political gift—a present from a powerful Greek group to a potentate in Early Iron Age Europe, perhaps to establish favorable relations for the trade system that is represented so well by Greek and Etruscan luxury goods in this grave and at other sites of the period. At some stage between manufacture and burial, someone removed all of the spears held in the hands of the warriors figured on the neck of the krater. Who might have done this and why?

Archaeological excavations in 1991–1993 uncovered a square enclosure 23 meters on a side, bounded by a ditch, 200 meters southwest of the Vix burial. An opening in the ditch 1.2 meters wide at the center of one side faces the fortified hilltop settlement on Mont Lassois. Animal bones and remains of ceramic bowls in the ditch suggest that rituals associated with funeral rites were conducted in the enclosure. In the ditch just east of the opening were two almost life-size limestone sculptures of seated humans, one of a woman wearing a neck ring resembling that in the rich grave and the other of a man wearing a sword and holding a shield. Apparently these figures were placed at either side of the entrance into the enclosure. The Vix burial and associated enclosure provide unusually rich information about wealth and status, contact with Mediterranean societies, the role of feasting and display in social and political systems, and the character of funerary ritual in Early Iron Age Europe.

See also **Hochdorf** (*vol. 1, part 1*); **Greek Colonies in the West** (*vol. 2, part 6*).

BIBLIOGRAPHY

Chaume, Bruno. "Vix, le Mont Lassois: État de nos connaissances sur le site princier et son environnement." In *Vix et les éphèmères principautés celtiques: Les VIe and Ve siècles avant J.-C. en Europe centre-occidentale*. Edited by P. Brun and B. Chaume, pp. 185–200. Paris: Éditions Errance, 1997.

Joffroy, René. *Le trésor de Vix*. Paris: Fayard, 1962.

———. *La tombe de Vix (Côte-d'Or)*. Vol. 48, fascicle 1. Paris: Monuments et Mémoires (Fondation Eugène Piot), 1954.

Moscati, Sabatino, Otto-Herman Frey, Vencelas Kruta, Barry Raftery, and Miklós Szabó, eds. *The Celts*. New York: Rizzoli, 1991.

Wells, Peter S. *Beyond Celts, Germans and Scythians: Archaeology and Identity in Iron Age Europe*. London: Duckworth, 2001.

PETER S. WELLS

GREEK COLONIES IN THE EAST

The Black Sea littoral, initially called by the Greeks "inhospitable," was colonized intensively by them. Ancient written sources number these colonies between seventy-five and ninety. According to the ancient Greek geographer Strabo, Miletus, the most prosperous city of Ionia (ancient East Greece, the western part of modern-day Turkey), was known to many. Its fame was due mainly to the large number of its colonies, since the whole of Pontus Euxinus (the Black Sea), Propontis (Sea of Marmora), and many other places had been settled by Milesians.

The reasons for Ionian colonization have been argued for many decades as one aspect of the general debate about why the Greeks established so many colonies. Nowadays, most scholars agree that colonization was enforced migration. Ionian cities were situated in favorable geographical locations and possessed large tracts of fertile land. Miletus, called "the pearl of Ionia," was in the Archaic period the center of Greek culture. At the end of the eighth century, Ionians began advancing deeply into the hinterland: Miletus, for example, pushed its frontiers twenty to thirty miles up the river valley. This expansion led to conflict between Lydians and Ionians, with Lydian kings seeking to push the Ionians back toward the coast. The principal outcome was to diminish the amount of cultivable land available to the Ionians. This was the chief reason why from the mid-seventh century, Miletus, which had never undertaken colonization, became the last Greek city to do so.

The struggles between Lydia and Ionia came to an end at the beginning of the sixth century, when Miletus was obliged to accept a treaty reducing its territorial possessions. This, in turn, provoked an internal crisis in Miletus, whose resolution prompted large-scale migration and the establishment of new colonies on the Black Sea. New and hitherto unparalleled difficulties arose in the middle of the sixth century as the expanding Persian empire conquered Ionian cities. Ancient written sources state directly that the Ionians faced a stark choice: death and enslavement or flight. In these circumstances migration was the obvious course, leading to the foundation of more new colonies. This did not mark the end of forced migration: in 499 B.C. an Ionian uprising against Persian rule was crushed, and in 494 Miletus was sacked and burned. In consequence, a final wave of Ionian colonies was established on the Black Sea at the beginning of the fifth century.

Archaeology provides the principal evidence for Greek colonies on the Black Sea. There are a few written sources on the establishment of Pontic Greek cities, but they are contradictory, giving different dates of foundation and mixing myths with other explanations of the colonization process. The first colonies appeared in the last third of the seventh century, and by the end of it Berezan, Histria, Sinope, possibly Amisus and Trapezus, Apollonia Pontica, and the Taganrog settlement on the Sea of Azov had been founded. All were very small, situated on peninsulas. The next wave of colonization dates to the beginning of the sixth century and witnessed the establishment of Olbia, Panticapaeum, Nymphaeum, Theodosia, Myrmekion, Kepoi, Patraeus, Tomis, and others. Hermonassa, on the

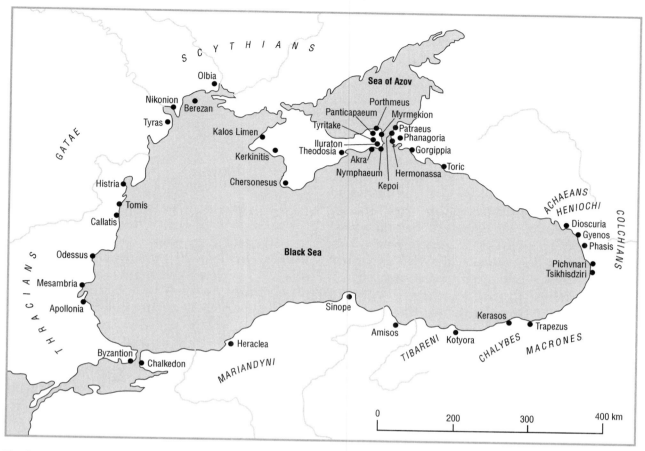

The Black Sea region with major Greek colonies and local peoples. ADAPTED FROM TSETSKHLADZE 1998.

Taman Peninsula (South Russia), was a joint foundation of Miletus and Mytilene in the second quarter of the sixth century.

From the middle of the sixth century, other Ionian Greek cities were in the business of establishing colonies: Teos founded Phanagoria (Taman Peninsula), and the (non-Ionian) Megarians and Boeotians founded Heraclea, on the southern shores of the Pontus c. 556 B.C. The latter colony developed as a major trading center for the whole Pontus and in turn established its own colonies: Chersonesus in the Crimea was founded in the last quarter of the fifth century (where a small Ionian settlement had existed from the end of the sixth century) and, later, Callatis on the western coast. The mid-sixth century also was the period when Miletus established three colonies on the eastern Black Sea (in the ancient country of Colchis)—Phasis, Gyenos, and Dioscurias. The final Ionian colonizers arrived at the end of the sixth/beginning of the fifth century

B.C., establishing new colonies (Mesambria, Kerkinitis, and others) and settling in existing ones. In newly established colonies, Apollo was the major deity, as he was in Miletus.

For their first sixty to eighty years of existence, the colonies looked quite "un-Greek." There was virtually no stone architecture; instead there were pit houses. Nor was there regular town planning. The only colony with fortification walls was Histria. A complete change of appearance took place at the end of the sixth/first half of the fifth century. Pit houses gave way to typical Greek stone dwellings. It is possible to identify clearly standard features of Greek urbanization, such as the agora, *temenos*, acropolis, and craftsmen's quarter, among others. Temples were built in the Ionic and Doric orders. As the result of a change in the local political situation, cities began to construct stone fortification walls. The exception is the region of the eastern Black Sea, where, thanks to natural conditions (wetlands and marshes, for example), temples and fortification walls as well as dwellings were constructed of wood.

Every Greek city became a center of craft production. In Histria and Nymphaeum pottery kilns were found dating from the mid-sixth century B.C.; in Panticapaeum from the end of the century; and in Chersonesus, Gorgippia, Histria, Phanagoria, and Sinope from the fifth to the second centuries. They produced such things as terra-cotta figurines, lamps, loom weights, and tableware; in Heraclea, Sinope, and Chersonesus, amphorae were made as well. Through the migration of Sinopean potters, the Greek cities of Colchis began to produce their own amphorae from the second half of the fourth century B.C. From the fourth century, tiles and architectural terra-cotta were manufactured in Apollonia Pontica, Chersonesus, Olbia, Tyras, and the Bosporan cities (on the Kerch and Taman Peninsulas). The Bosporan cities and Histria produced simple painted pottery, which imitated the shapes of East Greek and Attic pottery.

Nearly every Greek city has left traces of metalworking. In Panticapaeum, for example, workshops were found in two areas. The workshops, which produced iron, bronze, and lead objects (including weapons), contained numerous moulds, iron ore, and slags in the remains of furnaces. In Phanagoria, pottery and metal workshops were situated at the edge of the city. One produced life-size bronze statues. Metalworking in the Pontic Greek cities was based mainly on the use of ingots specially produced for them, for example, in wooden-steppe Scythia for the northern Black Sea cities. The same situation most probably obtained in the other parts of the Black Sea.

Agriculture was the main economic activity. Greek cities established their agricultural territories, called *chorai,* almost immediately. Their size varied over time; initially they were small but grew larger with the appearance of new colonists and the expansion of the cities. In the fourth century B.C. the *chorai* of Olbia and Chersonesus and of the cities of the Bosporan Kingdom each covered an area of about 150,000 hectares and contained several hundred settlements. These rural settlements were sources of agricultural produce for the inhabitants of the cities. There were several settlements specializing entirely in craft production. The wonderfully preserved *chora* of Chersonesus in the Crimea is unique, as is Metapontum in Italy. Chersonesus was situated in the Heraclean Peninsula, approximately 11,000 hectares of which was divided c. 350 B.C. into four hundred lots, each with six subdivisions, to make 2,400 small allotments. They were used mainly for viticulture and growing fruit trees. About 4,000 hectares along the north coast were the basis of the earliest allotments. There was a second *chora* of Chersonesus in the northwestern Crimea, entirely for grain production.

Trade was one of the principal economic activities of Greek cities. The main sources for the study of trade relations are pottery and amphorae. In the seventh and early sixth centuries B.C. pottery from southern Ionia was common throughout the Pontic region; later it was displaced by pottery from northern Ionia. Goods transported in amphorae came from Chios, Lesbos, and Clazomenae. The small quantities of Corinthian and Naucratite goods probably were brought by Ionian merchants, who also were responsible, with Aeginetans, for the appearance of the first Archaic Athenian pottery in the region. In the Classical period Athenian pottery predominates, on evidence from excavation of the Pontic Greek cities. This pottery probably reflects direct links between them and Athens.

Trade between the Pontic Greek cities and the local peoples is an extremely important but complex question. All discussion is based on the finds of Greek pottery made in local settlements, some as far as 500–600 kilometers inland from the Black Sea. Overall, about 10 percent of known and excavated local sites, especially for the Classical period, yield examples, but usually they are few in number (as is the case, for example, in both the Thracian and Colchian hinterlands). At the same time, local elite tombs each provide several examples of Athenian painted pottery. Thus, a simple explanation of the very close trade relationship between Greeks and locals is no longer tenable.

There are other ways in which pottery could have reached local settlements, and the small quantity cannot support the argument that the more examples, the closer and more intense the links. Painted pottery from elite tombs cannot be viewed only from the perspective of trade relationships: it is not known how the locals interpreted the scenes depicted on the painted pottery, which could have been a gift from the Greeks and not traded. Furthermore, the tombs contained jewelry and metal vessels, on which the local elite was much keener, in far greater quantities than pottery.

Over time the composition of imports and exports changed. The best account is found in the *Histories* of the Greek historian Polybius (book 4):

> As regards necessities, it is an undisputed fact that the most plentiful supplies and best qualities of cattle and slaves reach us from the countries lying around the Pontus, while among luxuries, the same countries furnish us with an abundance of honey, wax and preserved fish; from the surplus of our countries they take olive-oil and every kind of wine. As for grain, there is give and take—with them sometimes supplying us when we require it and sometimes importing it from us.

From the start, the history of the colonies is inseparable from that of the local population. Many ethnic groups lived around the Black Sea, among whom the most prominent were the Thracians, Getae, Scythians, Tauri, Maeotians, Colchians, Mariandyni, and Chalybes. From the earliest days of the colonies, locals formed part of their population. For the Archaic period not much is known about the relationship between Greeks and local peoples, although it was most probably peaceful until the end of the sixth century/beginning of the fifth century B.C. Thereafter, local kingdoms grew up, such as the Thracian (Odrysian), Colchian, and Scythian. Relations between these kingdoms and the Greek colonies were at times peaceful and at others hostile. In about 480 B.C. a phenomenon unique for the whole Greek world in the Classical period took place: the Greek cities situated on the Kerch and Taman Peninsulas united, to withstand Scythian pressure, in a single state, known as the Bosporan Kingdom (whose capital was Panticapaeum). The rulers of this state were tyrants. Its final consolidation was completed by the middle of the fourth century B.C. In character it was akin to the kingdoms that mushroomed in the Hellenistic period.

See also **Scythians** (*vol. 2, part 7*).

BIBLIOGRAPHY

Gorman, Vanessa B. *Miletos, the Ornament of Ionia: A History of the City to 400 B.C.E.* Ann Arbor: University of Michigan Press, 2001.

Greaves, Alan M. *Miletos: A History.* London: Routledge, 2002.

Tsetskhladze, Gocha R. "Greek Penetration of the Black Sea." In *The Archaeology of Greek Colonisation: Essays Dedicated to Sir John Boardman.* Edited by G. R. Tsetskhladze and F. De Angelis, pp. 111–136. Oxford: Oxbow Books, 1994.

———, ed. *The Greek Colonisation of the Black Sea Area: Historical Interpretation of Archaeology.* Historia Einzelschriften 121. Stuttgart, Germany: Steiner, 1998.

Tsetskhladze, Gocha R., and J. G. de Boer, eds. *The Black Sea Region in the Greek, Roman, and Byzantine Periods. Talanta* 32/33. Amsterdam: Dutch Archaeological and Historical Society, 2002.

Tsetskhladze, Gocha R., and A. M. Snodgrass, eds. *Greek Settlements in the Eastern Mediterranean and the Black Sea.* BAR International Series, no. 1062. Oxford: Archaeopress, 2002.

GOCHA R. TSETSKHLADZE

IRON AGE FRANCE

Modern France formed part of ancient Gaul, inhabited by Celts, Aquitani, Iberians, Ligurians, Belgae, and Germani. By the time of the Roman conquest most of these peoples spoke Celtic languages, except the non-Indo-European Iberians and probably the Aquitani and Germani. Although Julius Caesar and other historians give firm boundaries between these groups, one should assume neither that they were static nor that ancient authors were knowledgeable. On the south coast historical sources place the boundary between the Ligurians and the Iberians on the Rhône, whereas linguistic evidence from inscriptions suggests that it was the Hérault.

Two "grand narratives" have dominated syntheses of Iron Age Gaul. The first has been the incorporation of Gaul into a Mediterranean world system, with artistic, political, and economic innovations; social hierarchization and urbanization stimulated by trade and Greek colonization; and eventually, the Roman conquest. The second narrative is cultural-historical, the definition of the origin and expansion of the Celts; this viewpoint has come under heavy attack. For instance, the definition of "Celts" as speakers of Celtic languages is a modern one that cannot be imposed on the ancient world; other ethnic groups, such as Ligurians, also may have spoken a Celtic language. Prehistorians also talk of the "Celticization" of western and southern

France during the Iron Age, though what they mean is *latènization*, that is, the adoption of La Tène art styles, ornamentation, and so on. This view often ignores the extremely varied nature of the archaeological record in the different regions, especially the processes of deposition and discovery. The correlation between the Celts and a La Tène culture is no longer sustainable: Iberians in Languedoc and Germans in Jutland were making La Tène artifacts with typical decoration.

Central and western France are largely devoid of burials for the Iron Age. Documentary evidence warns against making simplistic correlations between the occurrence of rich burials and wealth. The king of the Arverni, Luernios, lived in an area where there are no rich burials until after the Roman conquest, and in the fifth century the Bituriges do not have exceptionally rich burials despite the supposed importance of their king Ambigatus. This bias in archaeology has been overcome in part with an increased emphasis on settlement archaeology, stimulated by rescue excavation on major projects for motorways and railways. Where settlement archaeology had taken place, it had concentrated on the defended nucleated hillforts of the south or the urban *oppida* of the Late La Tène, but rescue excavation is revealing many small farming settlements and hamlets. Nonetheless, there are still major voids

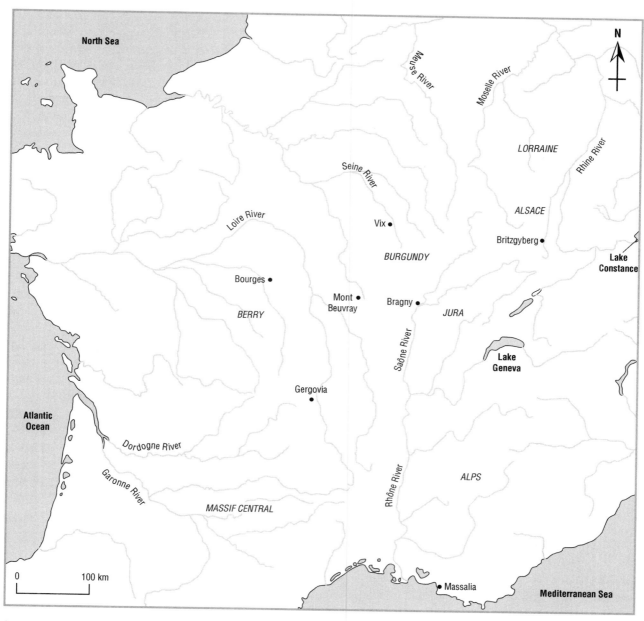

Selected sites in Iron Age France.

in the records, for instance, settlement evidence in the Massif Central.

In France two main patterns can be identified. In the south, on the littoral plains, settlement and political development followed a common Mediterranean pattern with the appearance of numerous small, nucleated settlements, perhaps best described as "city-states," with, initially at least, fairly limited territories. In contrast, the rest of France by the time of the conquest was occupied by "tribal states," much larger territorial entities that only at a late stage in their development acquired urban settlements (*oppida*). The boundary between the two regions lay in the southern foothills of the Massif Central, which, with the Alps and the Pyrenees, formed a major barrier between the Mediterranean and the temperate zones of France but was pierced by two major routes. There was the Rhône Valley in the east and the Carcassonne Gap in the west, though a more central route northward up the Hérault also was used during the Iron Age.

This overview follows the acculturation model while underlining the regional variations and gaps in the evidence and the importance of regional variation. It follows chronological sequence, using the terminology of central Europe. An Early Hallstatt and a later La Tène Iron Age are recognized, though the divisions do not always fit local French developments particularly well.

THE LATE BRONZE AGE
(C. 1000–750 B.C.)

The Late Bronze Age in France, as elsewhere in central and western Europe, presents two disparate images. On the one hand, the settlement evidence often is ephemeral. In the south of France the wooden houses are small, presumably for nuclear family units, and settlements are limited and short-lived, suggesting a shifting pattern based mainly on hunting and pastoralism, with an agricultural component. Over most of France, especially the west and center, burials are virtually unknown, but where they do occur, the so-called Urnfields consist of cremation burials that are poor in grave goods—two or three pots and little else.

In contrast, later research in northern France in the major river valleys has shown evidence that landscapes were highly organized, with linear boundaries formed by alignments of pits. In Britain the Middle and Late Bronze Ages are characterized by enclosed settlements, linear boundaries, and large-scale field systems. This pattern probably holds true for areas of France as well, but unlike Britain, much of the evidence was destroyed in the land hunger of the eighteenth and nineteenth centuries, which saw agriculture spreading to even marginal areas of poor soils and steep slopes. The Late Bronze Age also saw an increase in hillforts such as Fort-Harrouard (Eure-et-Loire), with evidence of dense occupation and industrial activity. Some sites also are known in the Mediterranean littoral, such as the 19-hectare Carsac site or the 5.6-hectare site of Cayla de Mailhac, both lying on the Carcassonne Gap. Although the hillfort of Cayla occasionally was abandoned, its importance is shown in the continuous sequence of burials around the site, reminiscent of the early phases of the cities of central and northern Italy or Greece. As elsewhere, the early burials at Mailhac have no special signs of wealth. Hoards, in contrast, can contain bronze armor and other prestige items.

There are no clearly defined trade routes at this period, except the Atlantic coastal route, where similarities of bronze types, such as carps-tongue swords, show close links between western Iberia, Brittany, and southeastern Britain. All areas are characterized by extensive burial of hoards and the deposition of objects in "watery places," all indicative of deliberate ritual and ceremonial deposition. The affiliations of central and eastern France are more with central Europe, and at this time there is evidence of cross-Alpine trade in prestige goods, such as decorated bronze vessels.

HALLSTATT C (C. 750–600 B.C.)

The Iron Age in France formally starts with the appearance of usable weapons and tools made of iron. Bronze was not vanquished immediately, however. Of the two typical sword types of Hallstatt C, the Gündlingen type is known only in bronze, whereas the Mindelheim type occurs in both bronze and iron. The manufacture of long iron swords implies the mastery of carburization and piling. For France, the Mindelheim swords imply a central European route for the introduction of the new technology. For the south of France, central Italy is a more likely source; one of the early finds, from Grand Bassin I at Mailhac, includes a short "stabbing" dagger, more in the gladius tradition of the central and western Mediterranean, which contrasts with the long "slashing" swords of central Europe.

The Grand Bassin burial also includes an iron horse harness, indicating a major ideological shift away from deliberate destruction of wealth in hoards to a burial context. In these societies it seems that rich objects were deliberately destroyed or buried as a demonstration of social power. In Hallstatt C there is a shift from deposition in rivers or in hoards on dry land to burials of objects to accompany the dead. Thus the Grand Bassin burial also includes an iron horse harness as a symbol of status. During Hallstatt C, burials in France do not compare in wealth with the contemporaneous wagon burials in central Europe or Italy, but the construction of ostentatious burial mounds contrasts with previous Urnfield practice, as does the wider range of grave goods, such as bronze vessels, personal ornaments, and horse harnesses. Most of these burials are extended inhumations, with marked concentrations across the southern parts of the Massif Central and adjacent parts of the Alpine foothills and Jura, in the Berry, Burgundy, Lorraine, and Alsace. In eastern France there are female burials with bronze ornaments (brooches and bracelets), but in central France contemporary female graves are unknown.

Another feature of these tumulus burials is the presence of imported Etruscan bronze vessels. Some, like the bronze cup and incense burner from Appenwihr in Alsace, came over the Alps via northern Italy, but the south of France also was in direct contact with central Italy by sea. Several of the Hallstatt tumuli in the southern Massif Central and the Alpine foothills contain Etruscan bronze bowls or jugs. The main recipients of Etruscan goods, however, were the occupants of the coastal plain, who, from about 630 B.C., were receiving wine amphorae, ceramic tableware (*bucchero*), and, occasionally, Greek vessels. The trade was concentrated around the Rhône delta. There are no obvious port sites, and Etruscan coastal trading is the most likely mechanism for contact. Phoenician trade had mainly bypassed southern France, but some goods, such as Punic wine amphorae, came up the coast of eastern Spain as far north as the Rhône delta, reaching Languedoc in quantity.

The settlement pattern over much of central and western Europe changed during Hallstatt C, with the abandonment of hillforts. Even southern France was affected, with long-lived sites such as Cayla de Mailhac and Carsac showing a hiatus of settlement, though in the case of Mailhac the associated burial sequence is unbroken. The reasons for this shift are unclear, and presumably the majority of the population at that time lived in small farming settlements.

Hallstatt C thus was a period of considerable change with the adoption of ironworking, though initially its impact was more in warfare and prestige items than in the production of tools, such as axes. The occurrence in burials in eastern France of bronze vessels and fine pottery vessels with elaborate painted, stamped, and incised decoration implies a continued interest in feasting. Despite all these changes, there is no need to postulate a change in social structure, though the relationship between the social elites of the Late Bronze Age and Hallstatt C is unclear; they may simply manifest themselves in different ways (deposition in burials rather than hoards). Nonetheless, there are many

blank areas, such as parts of western and northern France, where traditions were different and burials do not occur.

HALLSTATT D (C. 600–475 B.C.)

The major event in sixth-century B.C. France was the founding of Massalia (Marseille) by Greek colonists from Phocaea in Asia Minor. Its impact was not immediate, but until the end of the millennium it played a dominant role, controlling the Rhône route into central Europe. Secondary colonies secured the coast, with Agatha (present-day Agde) at the mouth of the Hérault and Emporion (modern-day Ampurias) commanding the major harbor just south of the Pyrenees. There may have been an early Etruscan enclave at Lattes at the mouth of the Hérault. The sixth century represents continuity, with Etruscan and Punic imports dominating in the south but with Greek ceramics, especially Attic black figure ware, becoming more common. In eastern France rich interments continued to be made but with a shift from the long sword to the dagger. The exception is central France, in the Berry and the Massif Central, where male burials disappear and the early phases of Hallstatt D (D1 and D2) are characterized by female burials with rich sets of bronze ornaments.

The major changes occurred in the last quarter of the century, with the rising importance of Marseille. Along the coast many settlements that were to become major urban centers had been established: Saint-Blaise near Marseille, Béziers, and Montlaurès, the predecessor of Narbonne, all produced black figure ware. Wine production was sufficiently well established for it to be exported in distinctive southern French amphorae. The amphorae are clear indicators of the trade routes into the interior, reaching as far as the Heuneburg on the Upper Danube.

The sixth century was the greatest period of hillfort construction from central Europe to Britain, though the function of the sites varied considerably, from major centers of trade, production, and political power, such as the Heuneburg, to sites briefly occupied in times of danger. Inland this period was the height of development of the *Fürstensitze*, hillforts that acted as magnets for foreign trade and around which rich burials are clustered. The process started in Hallstatt D1 in southern Germany, with the Heuneburg, Asperg, and the Magdalensberg—too early for Marseille to be the cause. Developments in France were later, from about 525 B.C., with three identifiable centers: Bourges in the Berry, Vix at the headwaters of the Seine, and the Britzgyberg controlling the Belfort Gap, where the Rhône/Doubs route meets the Rhine.

Only Vix, with its defended hillfort on Mont Lassois, fits the *Fürstensitz* model closely. The Britzgyberg is a defended site with much imported pottery but no associated rich burials, and Bourges will be discussed in the next section. There were, however, other patterns. The lower Saône has produced rich burials, but they are not clustered at any particular point. They may well have been serviced by the site of Bragny-sur-Saône, an open settlement at the confluence of the Doubs and Saône that not only was in contact with Marseille but also was importing goods across the Alps from northern Italy. It was engaged in iron production and seems to have been a trading emporium rather than a political center.

LA TÈNE A (475–380 B.C.)

For the south, the fifth century represents the culmination of the processes already under way, and by 400 B.C. most of the characteristics of culture up to and beyond the Roman conquest were in place. In the sixth century, settlements such as Tamaris, 40 kilometers west of Marseille, were defended with stone ramparts, with houses built of stone or adobe on stone foundations. No longer were houses individually constructed, but whole settlements were laid out with terraced single-story and usually single-room houses. Most sites are small, between 0.5 and 5 hectares, and may lack features that are associated with urbanism, such as public buildings or industrial areas. Some, such as Nîmes, were to develop into major Roman cities.

Trade was a major activity, and quite commonly 20 to 30 percent of the pottery was imported, especially from Athens, Corinth, and Asia Minor. Rows of subterranean silos for grain are regular features of native sites. Marseille started striking its own coins at the end of the sixth century, and by the fifth century some of the native sites were producing their own. In contrast, the local metalwork was similar to that of inland Gaul—La Tène brooches, belt fittings, swords, and other items—even on Iberian set-

tlements, such as Ensérune. Although the houses give the impression of a relatively egalitarian society, some individuals were distinguished in death by richer grave goods, like the man buried on the ramparts of the Cayla de Mailhac. Many of the cremations at Ensérune are accompanied by La Tène swords and Greek and Etruscan vessels.

The immediate zone of impact of the south seems limited. In the west there are extensive finds up the Aude as far as Carcassonne but not into the upper Garenne; there are no imports in the small hilltop settlements or burials of the Gironde or the foothills of the Pyrenees. Up the Hérault route, pottery reached as far as Sévérac-le-Château, but there is no clear evidence that the gold and silver deposits of the southern Massif Central were yet being exploited. Only along the Rhône was penetration deep, and major settlements developed at Vienne and Lyon, the latter having buildings with painted plaster. Finds are absent from the upper Loire, however, and in the Auvergne only a couple of hilltop sites, Lijay and Bègue, have produced scraps of Attic pottery. Even the routes up the Doubs and the Saône seem to have collapsed in the fifth century, and most of the *Fürstensitze* were abandoned. Only Asperg continued to receive imports, probably over the Alps, as did Bourges, in the Berry.

Bourges lies at the confluence of the Auron and the Yèvre, providing a navigable route from central France to the Atlantic via the Loire. Excavations under the modern town have produced deposits of Hallstatt D3 and La Tène A, including one building with painted plaster. There are areas of intensive occupation, with several workshops engaged in industrial activity, including the production of bronze pins with inlays of amber or coral and exceptionally small, fragile brooches suitable only for the finest cloth. There is also black figure ware as well as Massaliot amphorae, and Bourges has produced more red figure ware than the rest of central and western Europe outside the Mediterranean zone. Associated burials are not rich, though people may have been buried under ostentatious mounds and the cremation placed in Etruscan *stamnoi*, two-handled vases, or flagons. Generally, gold is absent, though one recently excavated grave had a gold pin.

The wealthiest burials of La Tène A are found in western Germany along the Moselle (the Hunsrück-Eifel culture), in Champagne, and in the Ardennes. In Champagne, in Late Hallstatt D, a large percentage of the population adopted inhumation, the women with their bronze jewelry (torcs, bracelets, and brooches) and some men with weapons—in Hallstatt D3 a dagger and in La Tène A spears and a long sword. Some men and women were buried with vehicles, normally four-wheeled in Hallstatt D and two-wheeled in La Tène A, the latter often with elaborate harnesses decorated in the new La Tène art style. There is no focus around individual high-status sites, the majority of the population living on small farming settlements. The Champagne burials lack the rich goldwork of the Hunsrück and have comparatively few imported Mediterranean goods (Etruscan flagons and red figure ware bowls as at Somme-Bionne). These objects probably arrived via the inhabitants of the Hunsrück, who in turn acquired them from northern Italy via routes over the Alps.

Champagne and Southwest Germany are seen as the origin of the La Tène ("Celtic") art style and of the La Tène culture, which from the fifth and fourth centuries spread out in all directions, from Ireland to Romania. It usually is associated with the origin and spread of the Celts, and many maps of the origin of the Gauls who invaded northern Italy show them coming from this area. This, however, is based on a disputed reading of the classical sources. The Roman historian Livy lists the tribes that took part in the invasions, almost all of them located in central France. In his story, Ambigatus, king of the Bituriges, played a key role, and the archaeological record, with the preeminence of Bourges, seems to support this theory. The problem is that Livy places these events around 600 B.C., whereas the Greek historian Polybius and archaeology suggest a date of about 400 B.C.

LA TÈNE B–C (380–150 B.C.)

Within this time span there are thought to have been two important events. First, by the second century B.C., two Celtic tribal entities had appeared in southern France, the Volcae Tectosages and the Volcae Arecomici. Their presence is not detectable in archaeological finds, and there is no evidence of cultural or linguistic change; though La Tène–style metal objects were used and manufactured at sites such as Lattes, this was nothing new. The general trend in both Languedoc and Provence was a general abandonment of lowland sites in favor of small, defended hilltops.

The second event was the territorial expansion of Massalia. Because of increasing conflict with its neighbors, the city entered into an alliance with Rome, which needed a land route across the south of France. Some sites, such as Saint-Blaise, acquired Greek-style defenses, and Greek products almost drove out native products in parts of Provence. The Ligurians had distinctive religious practices, evidenced, for instance, in the stone sculptures of decapitated heads at Entremont. These sculptures probably date to the third century, as does the ritual site at Roquepertuse, with its portico surmounted by a bird of prey and with niches for skulls and seated warriors, possibly "heroes."

In non-Mediterranean Gaul, the areas with rich burials of La Tène A are almost devoid of any burials in La Tène B. Imported Mediterranean goods virtually disappeared; goldwork also largely vanished. In northern France, burials of this period were mainly peripheral to Champagne, in the Paris Basin and northwestern France, and they included a few vehicle burials. The most exotic finds also tended to be peripheral to previous distributions, such as the gold-plated helmets from the river Seine at Amfreville (Eure) and from the cave at Agris in the Charente, both ritual depositions.

In the archaeological record, two new phenomena hint at some sort of state organization. First, from the third century, ritual sites start appearing, especially in Northwest France, such as at Gournay-sur-Aronde and Ribemont-sur-Ancre. Both had square-ditched enclosures containing religious structures, such as wooden buildings. Gournay produced large numbers of mutilated weapons, especially swords. So did Ribemont, though in lesser numbers; here there are buildings in which decapitated bodies were displayed, along with heaps of human femurs. Cult structures also appear on village sites, such as at Acy-Romance in Champagne, which included squatting male burials, probably human sacrifices. Many Roman temples in central and northern France are producing evidence of Middle and Late La Tène activity.

The second phenomenon was the appearance of large, open settlements of proto-urban character. In France the best documented are Levroux in the

Berry and Roanne on the upper Loire, sites of 30 hectares and 10 hectares, respectively, which start during the early second century B.C. (La Tène C1–2). In the fourth century, trade with the Mediterranean virtually faded away, but with the foundation of these sites, contact resumes, as evidenced by the appearance of Massaliot coins and fine Campanian tablewares and wine amphorae from central Italy. Coinage was adopted, initially high-value gold staters imitating those of Philip II of Macedon but later mass-produced cast potin coins, which may have allowed the development of a monetized market economy.

At Aulnat, near Clermont-Ferrand, in the territory of the Arverni, a complex of sites covering 2 to 3 square kilometers appeared in the late third century B.C. The complex includes cult areas, cemeteries (though no rich burials), and a high-status area with goldworking and silver working; coin production; and iron, glass, and other industries. There was also massive deposition of Italian wine amphorae. From the Greek philosopher and historian Posidonius one hears of Luernios, "the richest man of all Gaul," who, in the mid-second century B.C., became king of the Arverni because of his largesse to his followers, "scattering gold and silver" and organizing a feast of food and wine. Posidonius also records that the Arverni controlled an area from the Rhône to the Atlantic, and Aulnat seemed to be the center of their power.

LA TÈNE D (150–30 B.C.)

In 125 B.C. Massalia asked for Rome's aid. By 121 B.C. most of southern France had been conquered, and an expeditionary force under Bituitos, king of the Arverni, had been defeated on the River Isère. Roman power was extended to the headwaters of the Garenne, and a huge treasure at a sanctuary at Toulouse was seized; the Rhône route also was secured as far as Lyon and Geneva. Central and western Gaul was opened up to Italian trade, and the market was flooded with goods. It has been calculated that, in the 140 years it was occupied, the contents of a million amphorae were consumed on the *oppidum* of Mont Beuvray, some 150 a week.

The defeat of the Arverni may have destabilized Gaul—by the time Caesar attacked in 58 B.C., the Aedui and the Sequani were vying for supreme power in central Gaul, though the Arverni, under their leader Vercingetorix, were to play the leading role in the final revolt in 52 B.C. The years around 120 B.C., however, saw a major change in the settlement patterns in Gaul and even east of the Rhine, with the establishment of defended *oppida* often directly replacing the open settlements, though in many areas no urban predecessor can be identified. By this time in central and probably northern France the normal political entity was the tribal state, usually an oligarchic government of a "senate" and annual magistrates, but like their Mediterranean counterparts, these states seem to have been unstable and prone to monarchical takeover.

In Provence and across northern France, burial evidence became more visible, including rich ones with increasing quantities of grave goods from the second century. By the end of the first century B.C., the richest graves included Italian ceramics (black Campanian wares and, later, red Arretine Samian ware); Italian wine amphorae and bronze vessels; local ceramics; weapons, such as swords and spurs; hearth furniture (especially iron firedogs); and highly decorated, bronze-bound wooden buckets, among other items. These burials were associated mainly with smaller settlements, and though it is known that the elite were resident on the *oppida,* the related cemeteries at, for instance, Mont Beuvray and the Titelberg in Luxembourg do not contain the richest burials.

In southern France after the Roman conquest, house structures started becoming more complex. In contrast, from their very foundation, the *oppida* included large, farmlike palisade enclosures, and at Mont Beuvray after 50 B.C. these structures evolved into palatial stone-built Mediterranean style houses, with open courtyards, mosaic pavements, hypocausts, and running water. The smaller houses in the artisan areas also were built independently from one another and were more substantial than their southern counterparts.

The elite were investing in their urban properties but preferred to be buried on their country estates. Both the burial and the settlement evidence document increasing disparities of wealth, similar to what was happening in republican Italy. In Gaul the major change was the way in which wealth was displayed. The huge consumption of wine (and so, presumably, feasting) continued into the Augustan period and then fell off as more money was spent on private luxury, such as houses, or in the public arena on public buildings, such as temples and baths in the towns. In central and northern Gaul, the tribal states became the Roman unit of administration, whereas in southern Gaul, the apparently self-governing towns were too small, and under the reforms of Augustus, towns such as Nîmes became the centers of larger groupings similar to those of the north. Thus, after centuries of contrasting development, under Rome the whole of Gaul began evolving toward a common model.

See also **Hallstatt** (*vol. 2, part 6*); **La Tène** (*vol. 2, part 6*); **Oppida** (*vol. 2, part 6*); **Iron Age Feasting** (*vol. 2, part 6*).

BIBLIOGRAPHY

Brunaux, J.-L. *The Celtic Gauls: Gods, Rites, and Sanctuaries.* London: Seaby, 1988.

———, ed. *Les sanctuares celtiques et leurs rapports avec le monde méditerranéen.* Dossiers de Protohistoire 3. Paris: Éditions Errance, 1991.

Chausserie-Laprée, Jean, ed. *Les temps des Gaulois en Provence.* Toulouse, France: Musée Saint-Raymond, 2002.

Collis, J. R. *The Celts: Origins, Myths, and Inventions.* London: Tempus, 2003.

Cunliffe, Barry W. *The Ancient Celts.* Oxford: Oxford University Press, 1997.

Diepeveen-Jansen, Marian. *People, Ideas, and Goods: New Perspectives on the "Celtic Barbarians" in Western and Central Europe (500–250 BC).* Translated by Christine Jefferis. Amsterdam Archaeological Studies 7. Amsterdam: Amsterdam University Press, 2001.

Gailledrat, Éric. *Les Ibères de l'Èbre à l'Hérault, VIe–IVe s. avant J.-C.* Monographies d'Archéologie Méditerranéenne 1. Lattes, France: Association pour la Recherche Archéologique en Languedoc Oriental, 1997.

Goudineau, Christian. *Regard sur la Gaule.* Paris: Éditions Errance, 1998.

Guichard, Vincent, and Franck Perrin, eds. *L'aristocracie celte à la fin de l'Âge du Fer.* Bibracte 5. Glux-en-Glenne, France: Centre Archéologique Européenne du Mont Beuvray, 2002.

Guichard, Vincent, S. Sievers, and O. H. Urban, eds. *Les processus d'urbanisation à l'Âge du Fer. Eisenzeitliche Urbanisationsprozesse.* Bibracte 4. Glux-en-Glenne, France: Centre Archéologique Européenne du Mont Beuvray, 2000.

Hermary, A., A. Hesnard, and H. Tréziny, eds. *Marseille grecque: La cité phocéenne (600–49 av. J.C.).* Paris: Éditions Errance, 1999.

Py, Michel. *Les Gaulois du Midi: De la fin de l'Âge de Bronze á la conquête romaine.* Paris: Hachette, 1993.

Roymans, N. *Tribal Societies in Northern Gaul: An Anthropological Perspective.* Cingula 12. Amsterdam: University of Amsterdam, 1990.

JOHN COLLIS

GERGOVIA

Between 58 and 53 B.C. Julius Caesar's conquest of Gaul had dealt successively with the east, north, and west of Gaul, but the center had remained virtually unscathed, especially the Massif Central, the homeland of the Arverni, the most powerful tribe in Gaul in the second century B.C. and still a major force in the first century. Among the Arverni, the leader of the anti-Roman group was a young noble, Vercingetorix, who attempted a coup d'état during the winter of 53–52 B.C. but was expelled from the main town, Gergovia. The setback was short-lived; Gergovia was quickly back in Vercingetorix's hands, and he started building a coalition with the neighboring tribal states to oppose Rome.

Caesar was in northern Italy, but he moved swiftly to combat any attack on the Roman province of Transalpine Gaul. He raised an army and, despite the fact that it was winter, crossed the Cevennes into the Auvergne. He moved on to gather his legions, which were in winter quarters around Agedincum (Sens). With these forces he was able to take the offensive, capturing the *oppida* (defended towns) of Vellaunodunum (Château-Landon), Cenabum (Orléans), and Avaricum (Bourges). Sending four legions north under Labienus against the Parisii, Caesar returned with the remaining six to attack Gergovia. Vercingetorix had arrived before him and had installed his troops in and around the *oppidum.*

Caesar describes the town as lying on a high, steep-sided hill, easily accessible only by a col (narrow neck of land joining two pieces of high ground) on the western side. The town was surrounded by a wall, with a second stone wall 2 meters high halfway up the slope; the Gallic forces were camped on the slopes, with garrisons on the neighboring hills. Caesar captured a poorly defended hill at the foot of the town and constructed his "large camp"; he subsequently captured a second hill "facing" the town, on which he built the "small camp," linked with the large one by a double ditch, or "duplex" (Caesar's use of the word "duplex" has been interpreted by some scholars to mean two parallel ditches separated by a pathway, and by other scholars as two ditches on the side facing the enemy protecting the route). Rather than attempt a siege, Caesar launched an attack; though his troops overran the outer wall, attacked the gates, and even mounted the town wall, they were forced to retreat, the only defeat Caesar suffered in the field. It led to a general revolt among the Gauls, and but for a tactical mistake by Vercingetorix, leading to the siege at Alesia, the Romans might well have been forced to retreat from Gaul. The battle of Gergovia had almost changed the course of the history of the Western world.

As early as the sixteenth century the Italian cartographer Gabriele Simeoni located Gergovia on the Plateau de Merdogne just south of Clermont-Ferrand. On the summit there are traces of a rampart enclosing the 75-hectare plateau, with traces of stone buildings, pottery, and Gallic coins. In the 1860s, as part of Napoleon III's research project to identify the sites in Caesar's *De bello Gallico,* Colonel Eugène Stoffel carried out excavations to locate Caesar's siege works. He claimed to have found Caesar's large camp on the Serre d'Orcet and the small camp on a hill overlooking the village of La Roche Blanche, as well as lengths of the double ditch. The plan prepared by Napoleon III for his *Histoire de Jules César* (1865–1866), based on Stoffel's excavations, has illustrated almost every edition of Caesar's *De bello Gallico* since. At a visit by Napoleon III, the village of Merdogne officially changed its name to Gergovie. Unfortunately, the finds from the excavations have been mixed inextricably with those from Alise-Ste-Reine, and no details of Stoffel's excavations were published. The ditches of the large camp were confirmed by excavations in the 1930s conducted by M.-M. Gorce, but his report is fairly schematic and produced no datable finds.

Scientific excavations on the plateau itself between 1932 and 1949 showed that it had been densely occupied in the second half of the first century B.C. and abandoned about 10 B.C. for the new town of Augustonemeton beneath modern Clermont-Ferrand. Only a double stone temple of Gallo-Roman type continued in later use. The excavations located a sequence of small industrial stone buildings on the southern side of the *oppidum,* where the gateway attacked by the Romans probably lay. A second gate of mortared masonry was found in the southwest corner of the site. The ramparts, still visible on the southern and western flanks of the *oppidum,* consist of a dry-stone wall, to whose rear stone buttresses have been added; in front there is a terrace 12.5 meters wide, producing a vertical face some 3 meters high. Nothing, however, dated to the period of the Caesar's attack in 52 B.C.

Several other sites have been suggested, most notably the site of the Côtes-de-Clermont, a volcanic plateau to the north of Clermont-Ferrand with Iron Age occupation as well as a Roman temple and settlement. Several books, including a detailed analysis of Caesar's text, have been published, promoting this alternative site. Excavations by Vincent Guichard from 1992 show that the Iron Age occupation is too early for the period of Caesar, and the claimed "defenses" are part of post-medieval field terracing. The supposed Roman structures on Chanturgue (the "small fort") also are more recent field boundaries, and the layout of the town of Montferrand (the "large camp") relate to the medieval planned town, not a Roman fort.

Changes in the dating of Late Iron Age finds also mean that some from the traditional site can be dated to the middle of the first century. Excavations elsewhere, however, show that there was a succession of sites predating the foundation of Gergovie: an open settlement at Aulnat (second century B.C.), followed by the *oppida* of Corent (c. 120–80 B.C.) and Gondole (c. 80–70 B.C.). Thus, the Greek writer Strabo's statement that Vercingetorix was born at Gergovia is unsupported. Ongoing excavations show that the history of the rampart on Gergovie is more complex than was assumed, with a Late Bronze Age or Early Iron Age rampart preceding the stone wall; the buttresses represent an Augustan reconstruction. Guichard's excavations on the "forts" excavated by Stoffel have confirmed the ditches, with finds typical of the middle of the first century B.C. as well as Roman military equipment (stone ballista balls, iron catapult points). The Lac de Sarliève, which Caesar's large camp overlooks, has been shown by recent excavations to be a post-Roman phenomenon, which accounts for Caesar's not mentioning it. The traditional site thus can be accepted as Gergovia.

See also **Warfare and Conquest** (*vol. 1, part 1*); **Oppida** (*vol. 2, part 6*).

BIBLIOGRAPHY

Brogan, Olwen, and Émile Desforges. "Gergovia." *Archaeological Journal* 97 (1940): 1–36.

Chatelet, P., and H. Chatelet. "Eugène Georges Céleste Stoffel, 1821–1907." *Association site de Gergovie* 14 (1997): 5–20.

Deberge, Yann, and Vincent Guichard. "Nouvelles recherches sur les travaux Césariens devant Gergovie (1995–1999)." *Revue archéologique du centre de la France* 39 (2000): 83–112.

Eychart, Paul. *La bataille de Gergovie (Printemps 52 av. J.C.): Les faits archéologiques, le sites, le faux historique.* Nonette, France: Editions Créer, 1987.

Gorce, M.-M. *César devant Gergovie.* Tunis, Paris: Editions Le Minaret, 1942.

Holmes, Thomas Rice Edward. *Caesar's Conquest of Gaul.* London: Macmillan, 1899.

Napoléon III. *Histoire de Jules César.* 3 vols. Paris: Plon, 1865–1866.

Provost, Michel, and Christine Mennessier-Jouannet. *Le Puy-de-Dôme,* pp. 33–44, 266–291. Carte archéologique de la Gaule Series 63/2. Paris: Fondation Maison des Sciences de l'Homme, 1994.

Texier, Yves. *La question de Gergovie: Essai sur un problème de localisation.* Vol. 251. Brussels: Collection Latomus, 1999.

JOHN COLLIS

IRON AGE BRITAIN

Iron Age Britain is conventionally defined as the period from the first use of iron, c. 750 B.C., to the Roman conquest, which began in southeastern England in A.D. 43. It is known almost entirely through archaeological evidence. Though the existence of Britain was known to the Classical world, it was on the very margin of its knowledge, and most of the classical authors provide little detailed evidence. They regarded the inhabitants of Britain as a separate people from those of Gaul, though they recognized cultural similarities. Julius Caesar was an eyewitness during his invasions of 55 and 54 B.C., and his account is valuable for the parts of southeastern England he visited. The archaeological record is dominated by evidence of domestic settlements, of which several thousand are known, but there is little evidence for burials or ceremonial monuments.

The Iron Age is divided into Early (c. 750 to 300 B.C.), Middle (c. 300 to 100 B.C.), and Late (c. 100 B.C. to the Roman conquest) phases. This scheme is best suited to southeastern England, and elsewhere a simpler division into Earlier (to 300 B.C.) and Later (after 300 B.C.) is more appropriate.

AGRICULTURE AND SUBSISTENCE

Most people in Iron Age Britain were engaged in agriculture, and agriculture was the main source of food. Some coastal sites exploited fish and other marine resources, but wild animals were elsewhere a minimal part of the diet, though some wild plant resources may have been more widely exploited. The landscape of Iron Age Britain, however, had been subjected to more than three thousand years of farming and human over-exploitation had begun to take its toll. Added to this was a long-term climatic deterioration: the warmer and drier conditions of the Bronze Age gave way to a cooler and wetter climate. The combination of human activity and climatic change made some marginal environments, especially upland and moorland areas, increasingly hostile to agriculture. Thus, more emphasis was placed on the lower and more sustainable regions.

Iron Age agriculture involved an increasingly complex strategy for the management of plant and animal resources. The annual cycle of the seasons dominated the rhythms of everyday life, and the critical episodes of sowing and harvesting posed a demand for the maximum labor force. Important changes in the agricultural economy had begun in the Bronze Age and continued throughout the Iron Age. The landscape was increasingly organized and divided, with field systems and other boundaries becoming more common; this organization may have had a functional role in managing crops and animals, but it also may have marked the beginning of more strictly defined rights to the use of land. New crops were introduced; emmer wheat was replaced by spelt, and naked barley by hulled barley. By the end of the Iron Age, bread wheat was also common, probably associated with an expansion of farming into areas of heavier soils. As well as wheat and barley, other crops included peas, beans, and flax.

There were fewer changes in animal-rearing strategies, and most sites have produced evidence for the three main domesticates: cattle, sheep, and pigs. Dogs, horses, and domestic fowl were also kept. Pigs were kept for meat and were killed when they had achieved maximum body weight. Sheep provided meat and milk, but many were kept for longer periods as a source of wool and manure. In the case of cattle, the costs of keeping and feeding them beyond the point where they produced the best meat had to be balanced against their value as a source of milk, leather, and motive power for traction. Actual strategies varied regionally: in southern England, sheep were valued for their manure to support cereal production, while in other regions pigs were more suited to the local environment.

Most agricultural production was for local consumption. Storage of food, as well as seed for the next year, was important, and many sites show evidence of storage in pits or aboveground structures. Salt production became increasingly important, from both seawater and inland mineral sources. It played a major part in the preservation and storage of food, which may have permitted trade in foodstuffs.

Much less is known about how such agricultural produce was transformed into food for consumption. Cereal crops were carefully processed, and the grain ground with querns (grinding stones); a significant technological advance was marked by the introduction of rotary querns in the middle of the Iron Age. Initially, the only method of cooking was over an open hearth, but the development of the closed clay oven in the Middle Iron Age offered a wider range of possibilities. There is little evidence for a change of diet throughout the Iron Age, but by the end of the period some sites showed a dominance of pig similar to the pattern found in continental Europe. At the same time, Mediterranean commodities, including wine and olive oil, were being imported.

SETTLEMENT AND DOMESTIC SPACE

Evidence for settlements is plentiful, but quite varied regionally. One common theme is the presence of roundhouses, up to 15 meters in diameter, though not all such structures may have been used as domestic residences (fig. 1). The houses had a single entrance, orientated toward the east or southeast, for ideological or cosmological reasons rather than for functional purposes. They were mostly built of timber, with wattle-and-daub walls and thatched roofs, though where good building stone was available, this was used for the walls. Regional variations occurred, especially in the later Iron Age: in Cornwall, courtyard houses were grouped around a central open space, and in northern and western Scotland the basic roundhouse plan was elaborated into a stone tower, or broch.

The typical settlement may have contained ancillary structures such as pits and barns in addition to the roundhouses. The sites were sometimes open but often enclosed with a wall or bank and ditch. Isolated settlements of a single household were common, but they could be clustered into larger groups. In eastern England in the Middle and Late Iron Age, larger nucleated clusters of houses were common. In parts of northern Scotland, brochs were surrounded by smaller houses to make villages. The reasons for these complex variations in settlement type remain unexplained. Though settlements were mostly stable and permanently occupied, other sites may have been seasonally occupied for fairs, the extraction and processing of raw materials, or for seasonal grazing.

The most prominent of Iron Age settlements were the hillforts, often very large and elaborately defended enclosures. They were built in different parts of Britain at different periods, and in some regions they are rare or even nonexistent. The earliest were built in the Late Bronze Age, while in southeastern England they all belong to the Late Iron Age. Hillforts certainly had many different functions: some were densely occupied, while others show little evidence of permanent or large-scale occupation and may have been for other purposes such as ceremonial gatherings or temporary refuges.

Much attention has been paid to the hillforts of southern central England, especially Danebury in Hampshire and Maiden Castle in Dorset. Many hillforts were built in this region in the sixth and fifth

Fig. 1. Demonstration area at Butser Ancient Farm in the wintertime. © BUTSER ANCIENT FARM. REPRODUCED BY PERMISSION.

centuries B.C. and show evidence of dense and organized occupation. From the fourth century, however, many were abandoned, while others continued, often enlarged or provided with more elaborate and impressive defenses. These developed hillforts are interpreted as a sign of increasing centralization of political and economic control, but the sequence in this region is not typical of Britain as a whole.

In the Late Iron Age, a new type of site appeared in southeastern England. These are called *oppida* (*oppidum*—the singular form—is the Latin term for town, used by Caesar to refer to similar sites in France). They are large sites, often enclosed with complex earthworks; many were in river-valley locations, and some, such as Verulamium (later St. Albans) and Camulodunum (Colchester), were succeeded by Roman towns. The Iron Age sites contained areas for settlement, craft production, ritual activity, and burial. In some cases, especially at Colchester, the evidence suggests the residence and burial site of a royal elite.

TECHNOLOGY AND PRODUCTION

The production and distribution of manufactured goods became more complex and more specialized during the Iron Age, though with considerable regional variation. There is little evidence of workshops or other places of manufacture, and most of the evidence comes from the finished items themselves or the tools used to make them. New technologies were developed: as well as iron, the manufacture and working of glass for beads, bracelets, and enamel inlays was perfected by the end of the period. New uses were also found for existing technologies: rotary motion was adapted for use in wood lathes, pottery wheels, and rotary querns for grinding grain. Pyrotechnology was also improved: furnaces for smelting iron and ovens for cooking are well documented, and it is possible that pottery kilns were also used by the end of the Iron Age.

Though flint was still used expediently for small tools, and bronze for sheet-metal items and cast ornaments, iron largely replaced them as the basic material for tools and weapons. Iron ores suitable for smelting with the available technology were widespread throughout Britain, which was a major factor in its adoption. Until the Late Middle Ages in Europe, furnaces were unable to produce a temperature high enough to melt iron for casting, so all iron objects were wrought by hammering. There is little evidence for knowledge of techniques such as quenching or tempering, but different ores were recognized as having different properties and selected for different purposes. Tool types suited to iron-working were developed, and by the end of the Iron Age, tools such as axes, hammers, knives, chisels, and reaping hooks were produced in a form that changed little for the next two thousand years. Iron was rare in the early period, though complex objects such as swords and wheel tires were produced, but from the third century B.C. onward it became more common. At the same time, production was increasingly concentrated in the areas with better ores, and their products were distributed over long distances as ingots in standard shapes and sizes. The final manufacture and repair of iron objects was much less specialized, and most sites have produced some evidence of ironworking.

Bronze continued to be used for sheet-metal vessels such as cauldrons and bowls, as well as for a variety of cast objects, including brooches. The copper, tin, and lead used in its production came mainly from western Britain, but in the Late Iron Age brass (an alloy of copper and zinc) was imported from the Roman world. There is no evidence of gold until the introduction of gold coinage in the second century B.C. It is possible, however, that gold may have been more common, but it was recycled rather than deposited. In the Late Iron Age gold and silver coins were produced in much of southern and eastern England, and gold was also used to manufacture torcs (neck rings of twisted metal, see fig. 2).

Stone was quarried to make querns and whetstones. In the Early Iron Age many local sources were exploited, but later production was centered on a restricted number of locations whose products were traded over sometimes very long distances. Salt, whether from marine or terrestrial sources, was also derived from a limited number of locations and exchanged over similar distances.

One of the most common finds on archaeological sites, especially in southern and eastern England and western Scotland, is pottery; elsewhere, however, it is rare or even nonexistent, and its place was presumably taken by containers of organic materials such as wood or leather. Pottery was hand thrown for most of the Iron Age, but in the last century before the Roman conquest wheel-turned vessels were produced. The range of pottery forms varied greatly from region to region and changed through time but included versions of jars and bowls. From about 20 B.C. Roman fine wares were imported and copied, and these included new forms of plates, beakers and cups.

Technologies using organic materials have left little trace apart from their specialist tools. Textile production is indicated by spindle whorls and loom weights, while little survives of leather and basketry. Some of the most complex artifacts would have been made of wood, such as houses, vehicles, and boats, but little evidence survives. Most production would have been for domestic or local use, but there are increasing signs of specialized production and distribution through the Iron Age. The increasingly localized production of iron, stone, and salt has been noted already, and other technologies such as gold, bronze, and glass were probably also dominated by specialists. The growing standardization of pottery forms suggests similar specialist production, while petrological analysis shows that, especially in western Britain, production was largely restricted to a limited number of locations whose wares were widely exchanged.

Some of the finest products of the Iron Age were made for people of high status by highly skilled craft workers. Decorated metalwork such as mirrors, shields, helmets, and sword scabbards, as well as personal ornaments such as torcs and brooches, show an extraordinarily high level of skill; other items such as chariots and coins were also the work of skilled specialists.

RITUAL, RELIGION, AND THE DEAD
For most of the Iron Age throughout Britain there is no evidence of formal burial as a means of disposing of the dead. This does not imply that the dead were not treated with respect, merely that, whatever the rites adopted, they have left no regularly recoverable evidence. Many sites have produced small fragments of human bone, and it is possible that the normal rite in most regions was exposure and excarnation—the body would have been left to de-

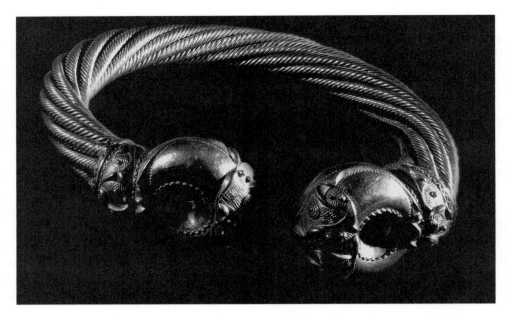

Fig. 2. Gold torc from Snettisham, Norfolk. © ERICH LESSING/ART RESOURCE, NY. REPRODUCED BY PERMISSION.

compose and fragment naturally. There is, however, growing evidence for regional traditions of formal burial.

The best documented is that of East Yorkshire, where from the fourth to the first century B.C. inhumation burials were placed under small square-ditched barrows. Many of the dead were simply accompanied by a pot or personal ornaments, but a few graves were much richer. In these the dead were buried with a chariot and other rich items. This style of burial is similar to that practiced in western Europe, and it was once thought that this indicated an actual migration from the Continent. The burial rite is not identical, however, and other features of the East Yorkshire people, such as houses and pottery, are entirely indigenous. It is now thought that a local group adopted Continental practices. Similar burials are known in smaller numbers elsewhere in eastern Britain, and such imitation of Continental culture may have been more widespread.

Other regional groups of inhumations are known. One in Cornwall is marked by the use of stone cists. Elsewhere, radiocarbon dating is beginning to identify groups of unaccompanied inhumations as belonging to the Iron Age. A small group of burials of males with weapons is also known; such warrior burials are not regional but widely scattered.

From about 100 B.C., cremation burial was adopted in southern and southeastern England. Many of the burials were poorly furnished but a small number contained much richer grave goods, including imported pottery, bronze and silver vessels, and amphorae (wine containers). This burial tradition is very similar to that of western Europe; again, as with the East Yorkshire burials, these were once attributed to immigrants but are now seen as part of a much more complex pattern of social change in the final centuries of the Iron Age.

For most of the Iron Age there are no formal sites of ritual activity separate from the domestic sphere, but domestic life was highly ritualized. Many of the finds from pits, ditches, and houses on settlement sites are not casually discarded rubbish, but carefully selected and deposited items. Human remains are found in storage pits, but so too are placed deposits of animal skeletons, pottery, and querns. Some are the remains of feasting, others may be deliberate deposits as part of ritual practices designed to ensure the continuity of everyday life.

Other deposits away from settlement sites, especially of metalwork, are also best interpreted as deliberate offerings. Many were in rivers or other watery places. At Flag Fen, Peterborough, a long tradition of depositing metal objects, begun in the Bronze Age, continued through most of the Iron

Age. Many of the Iron Age swords and much of the finest metalwork, such as shields and helmets, have come from rivers in eastern England such as the Thames. A Late Iron Age cluster of deposits at Snettisham, Norfolk, was also a votive deposit, though here on dry land. Many gold torcs have been found there.

It is not until the first century B.C. that formal shrines and temples appear, though only in southern England. Some, as at Danebury, are buildings of an unusual rectangular shape within settlements and are thought to have a non-domestic function. Others, such as Hayling Island, Hampshire, are more clearly copied from the Continental style of Roman-Celtic temple. Some of these temples are accompanied by many deposits of coins, metalwork, and other items.

SOCIAL ORGANIZATION

Despite the plentiful evidence regarding everyday domestic, agricultural, and craft activities, it is difficult to define the nature of Iron Age society and social organization. This is partly due to the almost total absence of burials, which elsewhere are an important source of evidence for individual and group identities. As it is, very little is known about how concepts of age, gender, and the family were constructed in the Iron Age. The fact that one of the rich chariot burials in East Yorkshire was that of a female suggests that positions of high status were not exclusively male.

Although not all round structures were necessarily used as domestic residences, the ubiquitous presence of the roundhouse implies a standard residential group, probably a single family. The limited human skeletal evidence shows that survival beyond the age of thirty-five was rare, and so families would seldom have comprised three living generations, though larger groups could have been constructed genealogically.

Two critical questions concern the degree of social differentiation in terms of individuals' status, and the nature and degree of political centralization and regional groups. Where there is burial evidence, as in East Yorkshire or southeastern England in the Late Iron Age, the presence of occasionally much richer graves suggests the existence of some form of social differentiation. Where this evidence is not available, the picture is more difficult to interpret.

The rich metalwork deposited in the rivers of eastern England suggests the presence of an elite, but that is not matched by the settlement record. There is very little differentiation in the size or contents of individual roundhouses, and for most of the Iron Age the archaeological record shows no sign of deposited wealth. Although by the end of the Iron Age it is clear that, at least in the southeast, there were political groupings ruled by kings, it would be wrong to project that type of organization back into the earlier periods. Discerning the extent and nature of any elite remains problematic for much of the period.

Social groupings and social organization above the level of the family are very difficult to determine, and the dominant picture is one of regional variability. Settlements vary from isolated houses to large nucleated villages. Most nucleated sites show little difference between houses, but the broch villages found in parts of northwestern Scotland may have been socially differentiated. A wide variety of community relations may have existed at the local level.

The ability of some Iron Age groups to construct elaborate hillforts, and the presence of the hillforts themselves, have been interpreted as a sign of a hierarchical and politically centralized society. It is not known, however, how the labor for such projects was organized, and the hillforts show little, apart from the defenses, to distinguish them from ordinary sites in terms of architecture or material culture. Even if they are taken as a symbol of political organization, the hillforts were a very regional phenomenon, and societies without hillforts may have been very differently organized.

The archaeological record is characterized by a pattern of regional variation in such themes as settlement type, architecture, burial rites, and pottery styles, but the meaning of such variation is unclear. This variability occurs at different scales: in some cases it may be a response to the availability of environmental resources, or the product of specialist rather than domestic production. Whether any of these patterns of cultural variation should be seen as the material expression of a regional social identity remains to be clarified.

Whatever type of social group existed in the Iron Age, relations between them were not always peaceful. The presence of sling stones, sometimes stockpiled, on many sites indicates warfare, and the available skeletal remains show much evidence of violence.

LATE IRON AGE CHANGES

From c. 150 B.C. many important changes are visible in the archaeological record for Iron Age Britain. The underlying social and cultural changes primarily affected southern and eastern England, but their impact may have been felt much farther afield. The changes affected settlement patterns, material culture, technology, burial, and ritual and political organization. Many of the key elements of these changes have already been noted.

Coinage of gold and cast bronze began to circulate in southeastern England c. 150 B.C. The earliest coins were imported from France, but they were soon imitated locally. By the end of the Iron Age, gold and silver coins were in use over most of southern and eastern England, and in the extreme southeast, bronze coinage was in circulation, too. The gold, silver, and early bronze coins were all of high value and were used for political purposes rather than for commercial transactions; the smaller bronze coins are found mainly on the Late Iron Age nucleated sites and may represent a move toward a money-based exchange system.

Roman amphorae containing wine were imported from c. 100 B.C., first in southern England and then in the southeast. During the first century B.C. other Continental practices were adopted in Britain: cremation burial, wheel-turned pottery, and temples. In other fields, such as the design of swords and brooches, Britain continued to follow prevailing Continental fashions. Roman bronze vessels for serving wine and for washing were imported, and from c. 20 B.C. fine tableware was imported and imitated. Other innovations included the introduction of sets of bronze implements for toilet and cosmetic purposes, suggesting a new concern for the body and cleanliness.

In settlement terms, the most obvious change is the emergence of the nucleated sites, or *oppida*, in the southeast. These represented a strikingly new element in the landscape and a new focus for political and ritual activity.

The explanation of these changes in the archaeology of southern and eastern England has been a major point of debate. Older interpretations tried to account for them as the result of immigration from the Continent, either before or after Julius Caesar's conquest of Gaul in the 50s B.C., but neither the nature nor the chronology of these changes fits well with such an idea. More recent explanations have referred to the political and economic impact of the expanding Roman Empire on regions beyond the military frontier. Critics of these ideas have in turn questioned the quantity of Roman imports and their significance, as well as the rather passive role assigned to Britain in such accounts. They have instead emphasized the developments in indigenous social organization that allowed these emerging contacts with the Roman world to be exploited so successfully.

The problem is undoubtedly complex, involving both indigenous development and interaction with the rapidly changing political structure of western Europe as Rome expanded its empire in the late second and first centuries B.C. It is important to recognize that these changes took place over a long period. Indigenous Iron Age society had been changing through the Middle Iron Age, not least by increased specialization of production, agricultural expansion, and changes in settlement pattern; the sheer quantity of manufactured artifacts increased enormously at that time. The importation and imitation of Roman goods was also a long process, not a single event. It is equally important not to project the post-conquest conditions back to an earlier period: the fact that the site of Iron Age Verulamium (St. Albans) became the site of a Roman town does not imply that it functioned as a town in the pre-conquest period. There is also a question whether the changes in the archaeological record reflect real changes in Iron Age social and economic organization, or in their cultural practices. Politically, the rich burials, the coins, and evidence of the classical authors suggest the emergence of a hierarchical and tribal society ruled by kings. It is possible, however, that changes in practices for the disposal of the dead and the deposition of wealth simply make this pattern of social organization more visible than it had been previously. Perhaps more far-reaching may have been cultural changes such as the adoption of Roman eating habits, including wine, foodstuffs, and tablewares, as well as a concern for bodily hygiene and cosmetics.

When Julius Caesar invaded Britain in 55 and 54 B.C., it had already been undergoing major political and economic changes for a century, at least partly due to contact with the Continent. Caesar's invasions drew Britain, or at least southeastern England, still further into contact with the Roman Empire, with significant effects on indigenous culture. When the final Roman conquest began in A.D. 43, southeastern England fell very rapidly, but resistance was much stronger in the north and west. It took several decades to subdue England and Wales; the northern frontier fluctuated through time, but although much of Scotland was at one time under Roman rule, the whole of Iron Age Britain was never conquered.

See also **Maiden Castle** (*vol. 1, part 1*); **Flag Fen** (*vol. 2, part 5*); **Oppida** (*vol. 2, part 6*); **Hillforts** (*vol. 2, part 6*); **Ironworking** (*vol. 2, part 6*); **Coinage of Iron Age Europe** (*vol. 2, part 6*); **Iron Age Social Organization** (*vol. 2, part 6*); **Danebury** (*vol. 2, part 6*); **Agriculture** (*vol. 2, part 7*).

BIBLIOGRAPHY

Champion, T. C., and J. R. Collis, eds. *The Iron Age in Britain and Ireland: Recent Trends.* Sheffield, U.K.: J. R. Collis, 1996.

Creighton, J. *Coinage and Power in Late Iron Age Britain.* Cambridge, U.K.: Cambridge University Press, 2000.

Cunliffe, Barry W. *Iron Age Communities in Britain: An Account of England, Scotland, and Wales from the Seventh Century B.C. until the Roman Conquest.* 3d ed. London: Routledge, 1991.

———. *Danebury: Anatomy of an Iron Age Hillfort.* London: Batsford, 1983.

Gwilt, Adam, and Colin Haselgrove, eds. *Reconstructing Iron Age Societies: New Approaches to the British Iron Age.* Oxford: Oxbow, 1997.

Hambleton, Ellen. *Animal Husbandry Regimes in Iron Age Britain: A Comparative Study of Faunal Assemblages from British Iron Age Sites.* BAR British Series, no. 282. Oxford: Archaeopress, 1999.

Haselgrove, Colin. "The Iron Age." In *The Archaeology of Britain: An Introduction from the Upper Palaeolithic to the Industrial Revolution.* Edited by John Hunter and Ian Ralston, pp. 113–134. London: Routledge, 1999.

Hill, J. D. *Ritual and Rubbish in the Iron Age of Wessex: A Study on the Formation of a Specific Archaeological Record.* BAR British Series, no. 242. Oxford: Tempus Reparatum, 1995.

James, Simon, and Valery Rigby. *Britain and the Celtic Iron Age.* London: British Museum Press, 1997.

Morris, Elaine L. "Production and Distribution of Pottery and Salt in Iron Age Britain: A Review." *Proceedings of the Prehistoric Society* 60 (1994): 371–393.

Piggott, Stuart. *The Druids.* New York: Thames and Hudson, 1985.

Sharples, Niall M. *English Heritage Book of Maiden Castle.* London: Batsford, 1991.

Stead, I. M. *Celtic Art: In Britain before the Roman Conquest.* 2d ed. Cambridge, Mass.: Harvard University Press, 1996.

———. "The Snettisham Treasure: Excavations in 1990." *Antiquity* 65 (1991): 447–465.

Whimster, Rowan. *Burial Practices in Iron Age Britain: A Discussion and Gazetteer of the Evidence c. 700 B.C.–A.D. 43.* BAR British Series, no. 90. Oxford: British Archaeological Reports, 1981.

TIMOTHY CHAMPION

DANEBURY

The Iron Age hillfort of Danebury dominates the chalk lowland of western Hampshire. Although the hill is not particularly high—only 465 feet above sea level—it can be seen from miles around, and from the hilltop a vast panorama of lowland opens up with distant views of several other contemporary hillforts.

The earthwork fortifications of Danebury occupy the end of an east–west ridge and are very well preserved. Three distinct circuits can be traced. The inner earthwork, which was the main defensive circuit throughout, encloses a roughly circular area of some 12 acres (almost 5 hectares). As originally built the fortification had two entrances on opposite sides of the enclosure, but during the life of the fort one entrance was blocked, whereas the other, on the east side of the fort, was strengthened with forward-projecting hornworks that still dominate the approach. The middle earthwork ran between the two gates and was constructed to create an annex, possibly for corralling animals, sometime during the life of the fort. The outer earthwork is comparatively slight. Unlike the other two earthworks, which comprise a rampart and a ditch, the outer earthwork is really only a ditch with the spoil thrown up in low mounds on both sides. The outer earthwork is the earliest of the enclosures on Danebury Hill and

Fig. 1. Aerial of Danebury showing the 1978 excavations in progess. PHOTOGRAPH BY BARRY CUNLIFFE. COURTESY OF THE DANEBURY TRUST. REPRODUCED BY PERMISSION.

dates to the Late Bronze Age (c. 1000–700 B.C.); it is joined by a linear earthwork boundary that has been traced eastward for several miles toward the valley of the River Itchen.

Excavations at Danebury began in 1969 and continued annually until 1988. During the twenty seasons of work the entrances were examined, the earthwork circuits were sectioned, and 57 percent of the interior of the main fortified area was totally excavated. This work established that within the Late Bronze Age enclosure, defined by the outer earthwork, the first defense, probably a palisaded enclosure, was erected in the sixth century B.C. This first enclosure was replaced a century or so later by the inner earthwork, built originally as a massive timber-faced rampart fronted by a deep ditch. At this stage there were two gates. The earthworks and gates underwent various phases of modification, the most significant coming around 300 B.C., when the rampart was heightened and reconstructed to have a steeply sloping outer face fronted by a deep V-sectioned ditch. From the bottom of the ditch to the top of the rampart measured about 6 meters (20 feet). At this stage the southwest entrance was blocked, and the east entrance began to be massively extended. In this later stage of its life the hillfort was intensively occupied. The end came some time in the first half of the first century B.C., when the gate was destroyed by fire, and there is some evidence to suggest the slaughter of the inhabitants. After this the enclosure continued to be used for another fifty years or so, but activity was at a low level and may have been linked to the continued use of a temple complex in the center of the old settlement.

Throughout its life from c. 500 to c. 50 B.C. the hillfort was occupied. From an early stage a system of roads was established with a main axial street running between the two gates. Even after the southwest gate was blocked the street remained the main axis. Other streets branched out from just inside the main entrance and ran roughly concentrically around the crest of the hill. Amid the streets were arranged circular houses, rectangular post-built storage buildings, and a large number of storage pits. Toward the center of the site, occupying a prominent position directly visible from the entrance, was a cluster of rectangular buildings that were probably the main shrines of the settlement.

There is, throughout the occupation, a sense of order in the layout of the various buildings and activities. In the early stage, when both gates were in use, the main occupation zone lay to the south of the main street, whereas the area to the north was used mainly for storage. After the southwest gate was blocked the order was reversed, suggesting that a major conceptual change had taken place.

In the last two centuries or so of the settlement's life a rigorous order seems to have been imposed. The rows of four- and six-post storage buildings arranged along the streets were rebuilt many times over on the same plots, whereas immediately behind the ramparts—where the stratigraphical evidence is particularly well preserved and the circular houses cluster—it is possible to distinguish six major phases of rebuilding. In this area individual building plots can be distinguished. Although each had a different structural history, their discrete spatial identities were maintained, suggesting continuity of ownership over a long period of time. Arrangements of this kind indicate a high level of centralized control.

The most frequently occurring structures within the fort were storage pits, of which more than one thousand have been examined. For the most part they were probably used for the storage of seed grain in the period between harvest and the next sowing. Experiments have shown that, so long as the pits were properly sealed and airtight, the seed remained fresh and fertile. Evidence from many of the pits indicates that propitiatory offerings were made once the grain was removed, presumably to thank the chthonic (earth) deities for protecting the seed and in anticipation of a fruitful harvest. The offerings vary but include sets of tools, pots, animals complete or in part, and human remains.

Activities carried out within the fort included ironsmithing, bronze casting, carpentry, wattle work and basketry, the weaving and spinning of wool, and the milling of grain. Additional evidence points to the existence of complex exchange systems involving the importation and redistribution of goods, including salt from the seacoast, iron ingots, and shale bracelets. The presence of a large number of carefully made stone weights is clear evidence that a system of careful measurement was in operation. In all probability the hillfort, in its developed state, was a place where the central functions of redistribution were carried out to serve people living in a much wider territory.

The excavation of a number of Iron Age settlements in the landscape around Danebury showed that, although a number of farms existed during the early phase of the fort's existence, after the major reconstruction c. 300 B.C. farmsteads for some distance around were abandoned. This coincides with an increase in the density and intensity of occupation within the fort, the implication being that the rural population coalesced within the defenses. Although this may have been a response to a period of unrest, it could equally be explained as a feature of socioeconomic change resulting in a greater degree of centralization.

See also **Hillforts** (vol. 2, part 6).

BIBLIOGRAPHY

Cunliffe, Barry. *Danebury Hillfort*. Stroud, U.K.: Tempus, 2003.

———. *Danebury: An Iron Age Hillfort in Hampshire*. Vol. 6, *A Hillfort Community in Perspective*. Council for British Archaeology Research Report 102. London: Council for British Archaeology Research, 1995.

BARRY CUNLIFFE

IRON AGE IRELAND

Iron Age Ireland suffers from a paucity of sites and serious dating problems, which makes it difficult to construct a coherent framework within which to attempt interpretation. Thus, the Iron Age lingers in the long shadow of medieval Ireland; the abundant and varied medieval literature and the rich and prolific material culture of the medieval period have strongly affected the interpretation of Iron Age archaeology. Increasingly, however, Iron Age archaeological research is being generated by archaeologists, formulated in archaeological terms, and conducted using an array of archaeological methods, including aerial photography, geophysical survey, and underwater and wetland (i.e., peat bog) exploration. These research agendas do not ignore medieval textual and archaeological evidence; rather, they reflect increasing confidence that a coherent framework for Iron Age archaeology can be constructed.

CHRONOLOGY

To begin with a note about terminology, "medieval" is used here to distinguish the period from the fifth century to c. 1500. In Irish writing, archaeologists normally employ the terms "early Christian" for the fifth century A.D. to A.D. 800, "Hiberno-Norse" or "Viking" for A.D. 800–1169, and "medieval" starting with the Anglo-Norman invasions of

A.D. 1169–1172. For our purposes, we can think of the Iron Age in terms of three periods bounded by the Late Bronze Age, which ended c. 700 B.C., and the early Christian period. There is almost no available data for the Early Iron Age, which spanned c. 700–300 B.C. The Middle Iron Age, or La Tène Iron Age, lasted from 300 B.C. into the first century A.D. It was a time that saw major construction at many sites and the appearance and development of La Tène art, which flourished into the early Christian period. In the Late Iron Age, or Roman Iron Age, contacts with the Roman world, especially with Britain, began, as indicated by imports of various goods. The earliest evidence of writing dates to this time. The period ends with the first recorded Christian missions, about A.D. 431/432.

Archaeologists still depend heavily on conventional dating by stylistic analyses and comparisons, so this discussion will start there. The closing phase of the Late Bronze Age, the Dowris phase, ended c. 700 B.C. The first subsequent datable object is an imported gold torc (neck ring) from Knock, County Roscommon, decorated in La Tène style and with close parallels in the Rhineland from c. 300 B.C. A hoard from Broighter, County Derry, includes a gold torc with spectacular La Tène decoration, which is dated approximately by another item in the same collection, a gold necklace of Mediterranean

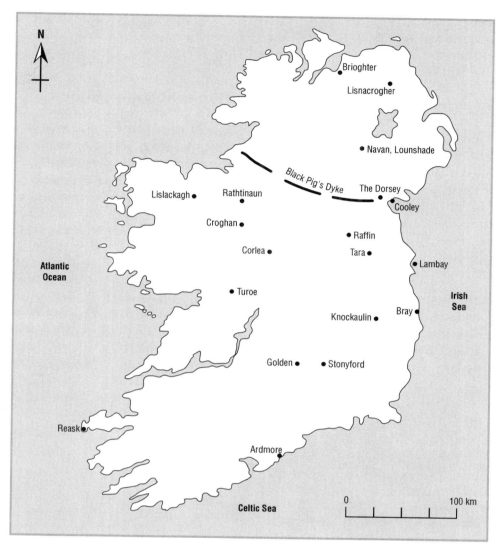

Selected sites in Iron Age Ireland.

origin from the first century B.C. or the first century A.D. As the Roman Empire expanded into Gaul (in the mid-first century B.C.) and Britain (in mid-first century A.D.), increasing contact with the Roman world resulted in the appearance in Ireland of well-dated Roman goods, such as coins and pottery. Coins are not plentiful, though, and most come from isolated hoards, unrelated to sites, while Roman pottery is rare.

Radiocarbon dating has been applied to the Iron Age, of course, but for much of the period the tree-ring samples used for calibration show little difference in amounts of residual radiocarbon over several centuries. In consequence, dates are corre-

spondingly imprecise. Fortunately, however, the dendrochronological sequence for Irish oak makes it possible to date the felling of a tree accurately, often to the exact year. The waterlogged conditions necessary for the survival of wood, which are common in this region, make this technique applicable to many Irish archaeological sites. The contrast in precision between radiocarbon dating and dendrochronology is well illustrated at Navan, County Armagh, where the base of a phase 4 central post has survived. The radiocarbon date for this post is 380–100 B.C., a range of 280 years. Dendrochronology provided a felling date for this post of 95 B.C. (or possibly early 94 B.C.).

SITE IDENTIFICATION

There are two major reasons why so few Iron Age sites are known. The first, paradoxically, is the sheer number of sites. The issue of ringforts, or raths, is particularly important here, for there is hot debate as to whether these enclosed farmsteads are all of early medieval date or whether some may be of the Iron Age. Of those that have been excavated and that can be dated (many cannot), almost all are indeed early medieval. There are, however, some thirty thousand ringforts, of which only about 1 percent have been excavated—hardly a statistically adequate sample. Moreover, there are other types of circular sites of the same general size (e.g., henges, ring barrows, and small monasteries) that are easily confused with ringforts unless closely inspected.

The second reason is that field-walking survey cannot be employed in this context. This method is put to effective use in many parts of the world and simply involves walking over plowed land, looking for scatters of artifacts, typically, potsherds. In Ireland, however, a high percentage of farmland is under pasture, and other large areas are covered by blanket bog. Moreover, the Iron Age is virtually aceramic, which means that there is virtually no chance of finding diagnostic ceramics and little likelihood of finding diagnostic metal artifacts.

EARLY IRON AGE (C. 700–300 B.C.)

Hardly any artifacts can been attributed to this period, and only two sites merit discussion. The first is the crannog of Rathtinaun, County Sligo, where excavation showed a two-phase occupation. Phase 1 contained only Late Bronze Age Dowris-type artifacts, but phase 2 held both Dowris-type artifacts and a few iron objects. Rathtinaun, then, appears to bridge the Bronze Age and Iron Age and should date to the eighth to seventh centuries B.C. Radiocarbon dates, however, indicate that the site was occupied no earlier than the fifth through second centuries B.C.

Second, there is site B at Navan. As at Rathtinaun, phase 3 artifacts were from the Dowris phase, with only a few small iron objects. Phase 3 radiocarbon dates, however, range from the fourth century B.C. into early A.D. times; since the end of phase 3 was followed immediately by phase 4, dated precisely to 95 B.C. (from dendrochronology), it is virtually certain that phase 3 lasted until about 100 B.C. The problems posed by these two sites cannot be resolved at present and so, by the same token, the Early Iron Age remains singularly elusive.

MIDDLE IRON AGE (C. 300 B.C. TO C. A.D. 100)

The date of c. 300 B.C. for the start of this period is based, as noted, on the first appearance of the La Tène art style. Nearly all the Iron Age La Tène decorated objects in Ireland are found on the northern half of the island. The development of La Tène art in this area owes much to close contacts with Wales and northern Britain, just across the Irish Sea. Irish craft workers, however, were not mere imitators, for they produced their own variations of British types as well as some artifact styles unique to Ireland, such as Y-shaped objects, Monasterevin disks, Petrie and Cork crowns, and the so-called latchets. As elsewhere in Europe, La Tène art was displayed mainly on high-status personal metalwork. There are also numerous bronze horse bits, several in pairs, suggesting that the two-horse chariots so well known from Iron Age Britain and the Continent were used in Ireland as well. Some of the enigmatic Y-shaped pieces also occur in pairs and may be components of chariot harnessing. Iron spearheads are known, as are fine bronze spear butts.

To judge by several beautifully decorated bronze scabbards, however, swords were the warriors' pride. Stylistically, they derive from Continental swords of the third through second centuries B.C. The Irish ones are much shorter—the blades ranging from 37 to 46 centimeters; one wonders how they could be used, except as long daggers. Of all the scabbards and swords, only one sword comes from a securely dated context—the excavation at Knockaulin, probably from the first century B.C. or first century A.D.

Although most of La Tène art finds expression on metal items of personal equipment or adornment, there are five La Tène decorated stones; the one at Turoe, County Galway (fig. 1), is embellished most adeptly. There are also numerous querns (grindstones) with La Tène decoration. Many carved stone heads are attributed to the Iron Age, but they bear only the vaguest stylistic resemblance to Iron Age human representations elsewhere.

Almost all decorated metalwork has been discovered accidentally, much of it taken from bogs and lakes. The practice of votive deposits also is known in Britain and on the Continent. In those places, decorated metalwork also appears in burials, however, providing good associations and dating evidence. In Ireland few burials contain such artifacts, and they are virtually absent from the few excavated sites, which makes it doubly difficult to date them or to relate them to other aspects of Iron Age life (and death).

The major sites of the Middle Iron Age are the so-called royal sites. Their commanding locations and large sizes imply that they were the most important sites of the Middle Iron Age, dominating ritual and ceremonial life over considerable areas. Despite their prominence, they have yielded no deposits of high-status valuables. Such items seem to have been reserved for watery places. Significantly, four bronze trumpets with La Tène decoration (and, reportedly, human skulls) were found in the nineteenth century in Loughnashade, a small lake just below Navan. One remarkable exotic import was discovered in a late phase 3 context at Navan (site B), however. This was the skull of a Barbary ape (with a radiocarbon date of 390–20 B.C.), which certainly had traveled a very long way from its homeland in northwestern Africa.

The Dorsey, County Armagh, is a very large, irregular enclosure about 30 kilometers south of Navan. Parts of it run across bog, which preserved timbers from its construction. Dendrochronological dates from these timbers show two phases of building, the first between 159 and 126 B.C. and the second between 104 and 86 B.C. The Dorsey lies close to a section of the Black Pig's Dyke, a series of linear earthworks running east to west across Ireland. This set of earthworks may have marked the southern boundary of Iron Age Ulster, for one section of the dyke is dated by radiocarbon to 390–70 B.C. Other linear earthworks in Ireland may be of the Iron Age also, but none are dated. Trackways constructed across bogland have been dated to the Iron Age by dendrochronology. The best known of these is Corlea, County Longford, where excavation uncovered two stretches of road over 2 kilometers long, with dates of 156 ± 9 B.C. and 148 B.C. Construction required two hundred to three hundred mature oak trees, besides other species.

Fig. 1. Turoe Stone, County Galway, Ireland. A superb example of La Tène art on a granite boulder. COURTESY OF BERNARD WAILES. REPRODUCED BY PERMISSION.

Hillforts are a prominent feature of Iron Age landscapes over much of western Europe, so the sixty to eighty hillforts in Ireland conventionally have been assigned to this period. Of the few excavated so far, however, most appear to be Late Bronze Age rather than Iron Age. Moreover, they are very diverse in size and form. Some are so compact that they could be seen as substantial ringforts or cashels on hilltops, some are large and rambling in plan, and some have ramparts so small (as little as 1 meter high) that probably they were not forts at all. Whether there are really Iron Age hillforts in Ireland is moot. Of the estimated 250 known coastal promontory forts, a few have been excavated, but only Dunbeg, County Kerry, has any dating evidence—a radiocarbon date from the first few centuries A.D., probably Late Iron Age or even early medieval, rather than Middle Iron Age.

Residential sites are very scanty indeed. One site under a ringfort at Feerwore, County Galway, produced a few artifacts for which dating to the second to first century B.C. has been suggested. Two coastal shell-midden sites have radiocarbon dates placing them in the Middle Iron Age, as do two crannogs at Lough Gara, County Sligo. There is one small ringfort known for the period, at Lislackagh, County Mayo, where internal circular structures were radiocarbon dated to 200 B.C. to A.D. 140. A handful of other sites have dates overlapping both the Middle and Late Iron Ages. Despite the limited evidence for daily life in the Middle Iron Age, it is clear that major constructions were undertaken, which implies the mobilization of substantial groups of skilled labor. Particularly noteworthy is the practically simultaneous construction of phase 4 at Navan (95 B.C.) and the later phase of building at the Dorsey (104–86 B.C.). The proximity of these two sites suggests that one authority might have directed construction at both.

LATE IRON AGE (C. A.D. 100 TO C. 550 A.D.)

There is no obvious demarcation between the Middle and Late Iron Ages. Roman material began to appear during the first century A.D., possibly as early as the first century B.C. It is not until the late first century A.D., however, that evidence appears of close (though not necessarily intense) contact with the Roman world, so an arbitrary date of c. A.D. 100 seems suitable. The main issue for consideration is the extent to which interaction with the Roman world promoted changes in Irish society.

J. Donal Bateson has reviewed Roman materials in Ireland in detail, and the total is surprisingly small, considering Ireland's proximity to Roman Britain and Gaul. Clearly, Roman goods were not reaching Ireland in anything like the quantities that reached, say, Germany and the southern Baltic during the same period. Roman imports into Ireland fall into two chronological groups, the first through second centuries and the fourth through fifth centuries. There is very little third-century Roman material, perhaps reflecting the widespread economic contraction of the period, demonstrated, for example, by the contraction of trade from the Continent to Britain. The material in the earlier category consists mainly of coins and fibulae (brooches) and very small amounts of Gaulish Samian (*terra sigillata*) pottery. The objects in this group and their contexts are reasonably consistent with trade and small-scale contacts. The later group, of the fourth through fifth centuries, also includes coins but has significant quantities of silver in the form of ingots and hacksilver (silver artifacts cut into pieces). These items look suspiciously like the result of successful raiding, and we know from Roman sources of this period that the Irish (or Scotti) participated in the frequent barbarian raids on Roman Britain.

There are a very few burials in Roman style. A cremation in a glass container at Stonyford, County Kilkenny, from the first or early second century A.D., and an inhumation cemetery at Bray, County Wicklow, from the second century A.D. both show familiarity with Roman burial practices of the time. Presumably, these are the burials of either Roman immigrants or emigrants returned from the Roman world. Grave goods from the small inhumation cemetery on Lambay Island, County Dublin, show close affinities with items from northern Britain in the late first century A.D., and the people may have been British refugees from the Roman conquest. Inhumation burial with the body extended appears to have become increasingly common through the Late Iron Age, and some such burials are in long cists (graves lined with stone slabs). Because extended inhumation burial began to replace cremation from about the second century A.D. in the Roman Empire, the same shift in Ireland may reflect Roman practice. Dating Irish burials is seriously hampered by the general lack of grave goods, however.

Two other disparate examples of Roman contact come from Golden, County Tipperary, and Lough Lene, County Westmeath. At Golden there was a small Roman oculist's stamp of slate, inscribed along one edge, and at Lough Lene part of a flat-bottomed boat of Mediterranean construction was found. It is assumed to be of Roman date, although its radiocarbon date is 300–100 B.C. (This, of course, dates the growth of the wood and not necessarily the boat's construction.)

There are few remains of residential sites from the Late Iron Age. Traces of occupation from beneath two ringforts have been radiocarbon dated to the third through seventh centuries A.D., whereas dates from several structures on Mount Knocknarea, County Sligo, range from the first century

B.C. to the seventh century A.D. A sherd of Gaulish *terra sigillata* pottery of the first century A.D. was plowed up at the large coastal promontory fort of Drumanagh, County Dublin. This find has fueled suggestions that this site may have been a trading station, and the proximity of Lambay Island, with its cemetery of possible British refugees, lends credence to the theory.

At Tara, County Meath, the Rath of the Synods has yielded intriguing evidence. The finds suggest that the site had four phases of occupation: the first and third were small cemeteries, while the second and fourth were probably residential. Artifacts included some items of Gaulish *terra sigillata* of the first to second centuries A.D., a lead seal, glass beads, and iron padlocks. All the datable objects fall within the first to fifth centuries A.D. It is striking that although several objects certainly or probably are imports from the Roman world, none are definitely of Irish manufacture. This, then, is the most "Roman" site known in Ireland, but it assuredly does not conform to any type of actual Roman site. The location of the Rath of the Synods at a royal site must surely be significant, but how this site should be interpreted is unclear.

Toward the end of the Late Iron Age, perhaps in the fourth century A.D., the first indications of native Irish literacy appear in the form of ogham inscriptions, in which letters of the alphabet are denoted by different combinations of vertical or oblique strokes. The model for an alphabetic script presumably was Roman, and its employment on memorial stones also echoes Roman usage. There is no space here to debate the vexed issue of when the Irish language first entered Ireland, but these ogham inscriptions are the earliest written evidence for the language. The script also demonstrates the presence of Irish settlers in western Britain, where ogham inscriptions (many duplicated in Latin) date to the fifth and sixth centuries, particularly in Wales and southwestern Britain.

DISCUSSION

The picture of Iron Age Ireland sketched here is one dominated by a welter of unassociated objects from chance discoveries, which can be organized into a somewhat murky picture only with difficulty. It is striking that the only really coherent archaeological evidence of Iron Age Ireland comes from larger-scale excavations, such as those of wetland areas and royal sites. Even so, it is still virtually unknown where and how people lived. It is no wonder that the abundant historical and archaeological evidence of early medieval Ireland, highly visible and largely comprehensible, still casts such a long interpretative shadow over the Iron Age.

The traditional or "nativist" view sees Iron Age Ireland essentially as a pagan version of Christianized early medieval Ireland. Thus, the society depicted in the medieval law tracts, for example, provides a template for Iron Age society: the higher ranks, supported by clients and slaves, lived in ringforts, crannogs, and cashels and spent most of their time planning cattle raids. This view is epitomized by Kenneth Jackson's *Oldest Irish Tradition: A Window on the Iron Age,* an analysis of the *Táin Bó Cúailnge* ("Cattle Raid of Cooley," the central tale of the Ulster Cycle of stories). The *Táin* is an account of the raid, organized by Queen Medb (Maeve) of Connacht, to capture the famous brown bull of Cooley in Ulster. In this epic, war chariots, druids, single combat between champions, and cattle raiding are prominent. Jackson argued that these elements of the tale identified a genuine Iron Age oral epic, eventually written down in the eleventh century A.D. Moreover, Medb and her counterpart, the king of Ulster, lived at identifiable sites—respectively, Cruachain (Croghan) and Emain Macha (Navan)—which seems to add authenticity.

The nativist position has come under revisionist fire from both historians and archaeologists. Further textual analysis of the Ulster Cycle shows that it was largely a medieval composition by writers familiar with Latin literature, Greek epics, the Scriptures, and writings of the early church fathers. Similarly, increasingly fine-grained analyses of the aforementioned law tracts show that they were almost certainly composed by monks with a Christian agenda, rather than by secular scholars perpetuating traditional pre-Christian law. The excavation of two of the royal sites since Jackson's work was published shows that there are no satisfactory grounds for regarding them as the royal residences portrayed in the *Táin*. More specifically, Mallory has pointed out that the swords described in the *Táin* were long, resembling medieval swords not the very short swords of Iron Age Ireland.

The revisionists contend that the country underwent a major transformation through the centuries of contact with Rome, culminating in conversion to Christianity and the consequent introduction of literacy. In this scenario the Iron Age is seen as a depressed period when agricultural and pasture lands contracted, as shown by an increase of tree pollen in several pollen diagrams from different parts of Ireland. This contraction began in about the seventh century B.C., perhaps intensified around 200 B.C., and continued until about the third century A.D., when woodland clearance recommenced. This renewed clearance has been attributed to the introduction of the plow with iron share and coulter and of dairying, through contact with Roman Britain. It is thought that productivity of both tillage and livestock thus improved considerably, which increased the wealth of the upper classes and enabled them to invest in clients and to buy slaves. In this way, so the hypothesis has it, the rural economy and society that were so well documented in the early medieval period were triggered by innovations from the Roman world.

We have no satisfactory dating for the appearance of the iron share and coulter, however, and the introduction of dairying is the subject of controversy. Pam Crabtree has argued that the mortality pattern of cattle bones from Knockaulin, probably dating to the first century B.C. or the first century A.D., is consistent with dairying. Finbar McCormick disputed this analysis and went on to propose the hypothesis that dairying was introduced through Roman contacts (i.e., later than the Knockaulin assemblage). In addition, he argued that ringforts—those typical enclosed homesteads of the earlier medieval period—were developed specifically to provide protection for valuable dairy cattle. Milk residues have been identified, however, in British prehistoric pottery. Since this pottery is as old as the Neolithic (fourth through third millennia B.C.), it is plausible to propose that dairying was introduced to nearby Ireland in prehistoric times. Clearly, this debate will continue.

The nativist and revisionist positions are not completely incompatible: the former does not deny that the conversion to Christianity promoted substantial changes in Irish society, nor does the latter deny some continuity from Iron Age to early Christian Ireland (e.g., La Tène art). As archaeological evidence gradually accrues, and textual analysis is pursued, interpretations will improve.

See also **Milk, Wool, and Traction: Secondary Animal Products** (*vol. 1, part 4*); **Trackways and Dugouts** (*vol. 1, part 4*); **Bronze Age Britain and Ireland** (*vol. 2, part 5*); **Irish Bronze Age Goldwork** (*vol. 2, part 5*); **La Tène Art** (*vol. 2, part 6*); **Irish Royal Sites** (*vol. 2, part 6*); **Early Christian Ireland** (*vol. 2, part 7*); **Raths, Crannogs, and Cashels** (*vol. 2, part 7*).

BIBLIOGRAPHY

Bateson, J. Donal. "Further Finds of Roman Material from Ireland." Colloquium on Hiberno-Roman Relations and Material Remains. *Proceedings of the Royal Irish Academy* 76C (1976): 171–180.

———. "Roman Material from Ireland: A Reconsideration." *Proceedings of the Royal Irish Academy* 73C (1973): 21–97.

Copley, M. S., R. Berstan, S. N. Dudd et al. "Direct Chemical Evidence for Widespread Dairying in Prehistoric Britain." *Proceedings of the National Academy of Science* 100, no. 4 (February 18, 2003): 1524–1529.

Crabtree, Pam. "Subsistence and Ritual: The Faunal Remains from Dún Ailinne, Co. Kildare, Ireland." *Emania* 7 (1990): 22–25.

Fredengren, Christina. "Iron Age Crannogs in Lough Gara." *Archaeology Ireland* 14, no. 2 (2000): 26–28.

Jackson, Kenneth H. *The Oldest Irish Tradition: A Window on the Iron Age.* Cambridge, U.K.: Cambridge University Press, 1964.

Kelly, Fergus. *A Guide to Early Irish Law.* Early Irish Law Series, no. 3. Dublin, Ireland: Dublin Institute for Advanced Studies, 1988.

McCone, Kim. *Pagan Past and Christian Present in Early Irish Literature.* Maynooth Monographs, no. 3. Maynooth, Ireland: An Sagart, 1990.

McCormick, Finbar. "Cows, Ringforts, and the Origins of Early Christian Ireland." *Emania* 13 (1995): 33–37.

———. "Evidence of Dairying at Dún Ailinne?" *Emania* 8 (1991): 57–59.

McManus, Damian. *A Guide to Ogam.* Maynooth Monographs, no. 4. Maynooth, Ireland: An Sagart, 1991.

Mallory, James P. "The World of Cú Chulainn: The Archaeology of *Táin Bó Cúailgne*." In *Aspects of the Táin.* Edited by James P. Mallory, pp. 103–159. Belfast, Northern Ireland: December Publications, 1992.

———. "The Sword of the Ulster Cycle." In *Studies on Early Ireland: Essays in Honour of M. V. Duignan.* Edited by Brian G. Scott, pp. 99–114. Dublin, Ireland: Association of Young Irish Archaeologists, 1981.

Megaw, M. Ruth, and J. V. S. Megaw. *Celtic Art: From Its Beginnings to the Book of Kells.* Rev. ed. New York: Thames and Hudson, 2001.

Mitchell, Frank, and Michael Ryan. *Reading the Irish Landscape.* 3d ed. Dublin, Ireland: Town House, 1997.

Raftery, Barry. *Pagan Celtic Ireland: The Enigma of the Irish Iron Age.* London: Thames and Hudson, 1994.

Thomas, Charles. *Celtic Britain.* London: Thames and Hudson, 1986.

Waddell, John. *The Prehistoric Archaeology of Ireland.* Galway, Ireland: Galway University Press, 1998.

BERNARD WAILES

IRISH ROYAL SITES

The Irish "royal sites" are so called because medieval Irish scholars believed them to have been the capitals of pre-Christian high kings of four of the five ancient provinces of Ireland. Croghan (Cruachain) was the royal site of Connacht, Navan (Emain Macha) of Ulster, Tara (Temair) of Meath, and Knockaulin (Ailenn, Dún Ailinne) of Leinster. No early source identifies a royal site for Munster. Various medieval texts refer to the royal sites as former royal residences and burial grounds; venues for major assemblies, including the inauguration of kings; and centers of pagan ritual. Although these sites were invoked as symbols of kingship in medieval Ireland, there is no evidence that they actually were used during the Middle Ages, and the retrospective nature of medieval references to these sites demands caution in assessing their original functions or significance. Archaeology can provide a firmer understanding, and Knockaulin, one of the two extensively excavated sites (with Navan), can serve as an exemplar.

At Knockaulin an oval earthwork encloses c. 13 hectares, with the entrance on the east side of the site. Despite the hilltop location, it was not a defensive site, for the bank is outside the ditch. Geophysical survey showed substantial anomalies only around the center of the site, where subsequent excavation produced the following (simplified) sequence:

Flame (latest): Low mound of burned material, including many animal bones, which suggests periodic feasting

Dun: Central tower and circle of posts dismantled; stone slabs and earth laid over the restricted area of Emerald-phase burning

Emerald: Perimeter wall of Mauve phase dismantled, but central tower and inner circle of posts left standing, despite intense localized burning

Mauve: Double-walled, circular timber structure, c. 42 meters in diameter, enclosing a circle, 25 meters in diameter, of freestanding posts and, at the center, a heavily built timber structure, c. 6 meters in diameter and with buttresses, that may have been a wooden tower

Rose: Figure-eight, triple-walled timber structure with a larger circle, c. 35 meters in diameter, and an elaborate, funnel-shaped entranceway; structure dismantled to make way for Mauve structures

White: Circular, single-walled timber structure, c. 22 meters in diameter; dismantled to make way for Rose structures

Tan (earliest): Neolithic trench and artifacts (fourth millennium through third millennium B.C.)

None of the Iron Age structures (White through Mauve) show evidence of residential or funerary use and must be interpreted as ritual or ceremonial in nature. The White, Rose, and Mauve entrances are oriented toward sunrise around 1 May, the festival of Beltane, the beginning of summer. Radiocarbon dates (Rose through Flame) cluster between the third century B.C. and fourth century A.D., while stylistic parallels for metalwork are mainly of the first century B.C. to the first century A.D. An 8-meter-wide roadway runs through the site entrance toward the timber structures at the center of the site. A radiocarbon sample from sod buried beneath one of the banks at the site entrance suggests that bank construction took place in the fifth century B.C.

The other royal sites share several characteristics with Knockaulin. First, all are on prominent elevated locations with commanding views. Second, all have large enclosures. Those at Navan (c. 5 hectares) and the Ráith na Ríg (Rath of the Kings; c. 6 hectares) at Tara both have internal ditches and external banks. Geophysical survey at Croghan shows a circular anomaly enclosing nearly 11 hectares, probably a silted-up ditch or the foundation for a wooden palisade. Third, the enclosures at Navan, Tara, and Croghan all have mounds. At Navan the mound (site B) has been excavated. Within the Ráith na Ríg at Tara there are two conjoined mounds, while at Croghan the circular anomaly encloses Rathcroghan, a large flat-topped mound. The postulated central timber tower of Mauve phase at Knockauliin might have been equivalent to a mound. Fourth, the roadway through the site entrance at Knockaulin, the roadways at Croghan, and the banqueting hall at Tara may have some equivalence.

Excavation produced further similarities. Navan, like Knockaulin, has a scatter of Neolithic materials, while the Mound of the Hostages at Tara proved to be a Neolithic passage grave. Excavation of site B at Navan has shown that this mound covered a complex sequence of structures. Immediately below the mound was an undoubtedly ceremonial wooden structure of concentric post circles, some 40 meters in diameter (phase 4). At an earlier stage, there had been a series of figure-eight timber structures (phase 3ii) similar to Rose phase structures at Knockaulin, although the Navan structures were smaller and might have been residential rather than ceremonial.

The suggestion that construction of all the enclosure banks and ditches dates to the Iron Age rests on the discovery, in a test trench, of ironworking debris under the bank of the Ráith na Ríg at Tara and the fifth century B.C. date from the site entrance at Knockaulin. The internal structures excavated at Knockaulin and Navan (site B), however, are far more securely dated. At Knockaulin, White through Flame phases are of the Iron Age. At Navan (site B), phase 4 is certainly of the Iron Age, for the central post has been dated by dendrochronology to 95 or 94 B.C. On stratigraphic grounds, the covering mound was not built much later. The preceding phase 3ii probably dates to the Iron Age as well. The Rath of the Synods at Tara has yielded artifacts of the first three to four centuries A.D. No dating evidence is available for Croghan.

The henge monuments of Neolithic Britain and Ireland (fourth millennium through third millennium B.C.) are approximately circular earthworks with external banks and internal ditches. Some enclose circular wooden structures and others stone circles. The similarity of the royal sites to henges can hardly be coincidental, and it seems likely that the royal sites were a revival of henges. This implies that memory of the ritual and ceremonial nature of Neolithic henges survived to the Iron Age. Finally, it is unlikely that the royal sites discussed here were unique in Iron Age Ireland. There are numerous other sites of henge form in Ireland. Many may be Neolithic, but some enclose mounds, and some have roadways, both of which suggest comparison to the Iron Age royal sites. The excavation of Raffin, County Meath, revealed what appears to be a small-scale royal site in use during the third through fifth centuries A.D.

See also **The Megalithic World** (*vol. 1, part 4*); **Iron Age Ireland** (*vol. 2, part 6*).

BIBLIOGRAPHY

Aitchison, Nicholas B. *Armagh and the Royal Centres in Early Medieval Ireland: Monuments, Cosmology, and the Past.* Woodbridge, U.K.: Boydell and Brewer for Cruithine Press, 1994.

Condit, Tom. "Discovering New Perceptions of Tara." *Archaeology Ireland* 12, no. 2 (1998): 33.

Fenwick, Joe, Yvonne Brennan, Kevin Barton, and John Waddell. "The Magnetic Presence of Queen Medb (Magnetic Gradiometry at Rathcroghan, Co. Roscommon)." *Archaeology Ireland* 13, no. 1 (1999): 8–11.

Newman, Conor. "Reflections on the Making of a 'Royal Site' in Early Ireland." *World Archaeology* 30, no. 1 (1998): 127–141.

———. *Tara: An Archaeological Survey.* Dublin, Ireland: Royal Irish Academy for the Discovery Programme, 1997.

Raftery, Barry. *Pagan Celtic Ireland: The Enigma of the Irish Iron Age.* London: Thames and Hudson, 1994.

Waddell, John. *The Prehistoric Archaeology of Ireland.* Galway, Ireland: Galway University Press, 1998.

Wailes, Bernard. "Dún Ailinne: A Summary Excavation Report." *Emania* 7 (1990): 10–21.

———. "The Irish 'Royal Sites' in History and Archaeology." *Cambridge Medieval Celtic Studies* 3 (1982): 1–29.

Waterman, Dudley M. *Excavations at Navan Fort.* Completed and edited by Christopher J. Lynn. Belfast, Northern Ireland: Stationery Office, 1997.

BERNARD WAILES

IRON AGE GERMANY

The nation-state known today as "Germany" is a modern political construction whose boundaries correspond little, if at all, to those of prehistoric populations, including those of the Iron Age. Religious, economic, and linguistic differences subdivide the country, a disunity manifested in a northeast-southwest cultural and religious split that has dominated German history since at least the Early Iron Age c. 800–450 B.C. This essay focuses on developments in the west-central and southwest parts of the modern nation, where contact with the Mediterranean world affected the appearance of proto-urban centers during the Late Hallstatt period (c. 650–450 B.C.) and of large, fortified settlements, termed *oppida* by Julius Caesar, during the Late La Tène period (150 B.C.—the Roman period). The north and northeastern parts of the country are not considered, because their cultural trajectories were quite different, related more closely to developments in Scandinavia and northeastern Europe.

THE EARLY IRON AGE: CHANGE AND CONTINUITY

The transition between the Late Bronze Age (the so-called Urnfield period, which also is designated Hallstatt A and B) and the Early Iron Age (Hallstatt C and D, after the type site Hallstatt in Austria) at first was marked mainly by the appearance of the new metal. The introduction of an ore that was more widely available than copper or tin, and produced more effective weapons and tools than bronze, had led in some areas of Germany to changes in burial ritual and social organization. In place of the large, communal settlements of the Bronze Age, increasing numbers of *Einzelhöfe* or *Herrenhöfe*—large, isolated, fortified farmsteads—suggest that individual families were beginning to profit at the expense of their neighbors in ways not seen during the Late Bronze Age. This emphasis on individual status and social differentiation also is reflected in mortuary ritual. Inhumation gradually replaced the Late Bronze Age cremation rite, with its rows of anonymous urn burials; elaborate wooden burial chambers were constructed to house the dead, who were buried with all their finery and other objects commensurate with their rank and status. In the Early Iron Age, swords appeared in burials as male status markers, rather than being deposited as offerings in bodies of water, in the Bronze Age tradition of communal metal votive deposits. Despite the differences between the Late Bronze and Early Iron Ages, the impression is one of cultural continuity.

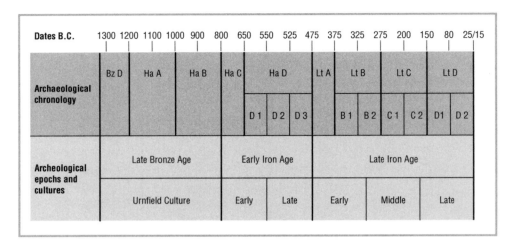

Chronology of Iron Age Germany. ADAPTED FROM SIEVERS IN RIECKHOFF AND BIEL 2001.

THE MEDITERRANEAN CONNECTION

These changes were due to local interactions as well as increased contact with the Mediterranean societies of classical Greece and Etruria. An elite class emerged during the Hallstatt period, driven in part by competition for status symbols, including exotic imports from Greece and Etruria. A suite of high-status markers appeared in burials, including gold neck rings; four-wheeled wagons; imported bronze, gold, or, more rarely, silver drinking vessels; and imported pottery. These graves are found in an area referred to as the West Hallstatt zone: southwest Germany, eastern France, and Switzerland north of the Alps. The East Hallstatt zone, comprising Austria, western Hungary, Slovenia, and Croatia, differed mainly in terms of the weapons buried with male members of the elite: helmets, shields, defensive armor, and axes in the east and swords (Hallstatt C) and daggers (Hallstatt D) in the west. Elite funerary traditions in both zones emphasized the horse and horse trappings as well as four-wheeled wagons and metal drinking and feasting equipment.

There was no hard line between these two regions—the archaeological record of the Early Iron Age in Bavaria and Bohemia, for example, represents a blending of the two cultural traditions, as does the type site of Hallstatt itself. Nonetheless, some geographical barriers seem to have acted as an obstacle to information flow. There was no uniformity between microregions within the West Hallstatt zone, where local variations ranged from different object styles to different depositional patterns. Over time the "zones" become more distinctly different, among other reasons, because of their differing interactions with the Mediterranean world.

IRON AGE ECONOMICS

The Etruscans began explorations beyond the Alps as early as the ninth century B.C., which intensified in the course of the first half of the seventh century. Two primary trade networks linked these regions. The older of the two crossed the eastern Alps or skirted them to the east, to reach the valleys of the Elbe, Oder, and Vistula Rivers that led to the amber sources in the north. The second route crossed the western Alps between Lake Geneva and Lake Constance via several mountain passes, aiming for the Rhine Valley, the English Channel, and ultimately the rich metal (especially tin) sources of the Atlantic coast and the British Isles. The Alpine crossing could be bypassed by the longer but less arduous water route from Etruria via the Greek colony founded at Massalia (modern-day Marseille) in 600 B.C. by Phocaean Greeks and then up the Rhône-Saône corridor to the Danube or the Rhine.

Imports from northern Italy and local imitations of weapons, including swords and helmets, fibulae (safety pin–like clothing fasteners used by the Etruscans as well as the central European Celtic peoples in lieu of buttons during this time), and drinking vessels of metal and pottery testify to this contact. The Celtic-speaking peoples of southern France, with whom first the Etruscans and later the Greeks traded, offered a range of raw materials in exchange for wine, drinking equipment, and other exotica. Burnished black Etruscan *bucchero* ware and Greek black figure and later red figure ceramic drinking vessels were exchanged for the grain, salted meat, copper, gold, silver, lead, tin, graphite, red ochre, and forest products, such as beeswax and timber, to which the central European Iron Age peoples had access.

Initially, this Etruscan trade was intermittent and conducted on a small scale. By Hallstatt C times the peoples inhabiting the southern German part of the West Hallstatt zone undoubtedly were aware of the existence of a new alcoholic beverage and the elaborately decorated and finely made pottery used to consume it. Viticulture, the growing of grapes for making wine, which today is economically important for both France and Germany, was not introduced until the Roman occupation of those countries; during most of the Iron Age, the only alcoholic beverages available were mead and beer.

Information as well as goods traveled in both directions along the tin routes during this period, as evidenced by the distinctive southern German Hallstatt swords in France and copied or imported Etruscan weapons concentrated along the river systems. The oldest known imported Etruscan burial assemblage found in Germany is Frankfurt-Stadtwald grave 12 (dating to the late eighth or early seventh century B.C.), with a bronze *situla* (a bucket-shaped wine-serving vessel), a ribbed metal drinking bowl, and two bronze bowls, probably used to serve food.

Some of the impetus for intensified contact came from the central European Iron Age elites and probably took the form of "down the line" or "stage" trade, in which each link in the chain passes the goods to the next. The Etruscans appear to have dominated the early phase of this interaction, as the archaeological evidence from Massalia indicates. Between 575 and 550 B.C., 27 percent of the pottery in settlement strata were Massaliote wares, 16 percent were Greek, and 57 percent were Etruscan. Only a few dozen Etruscan imports dating to the period between 625 and 540 B.C. are known, however, in the Celtic heartland to the north and east. Some scholars use the term "diplomatic gift exchange" to explain imports found in settlements along the main exchange routes, where local elite satisfaction would have been important in maintain-

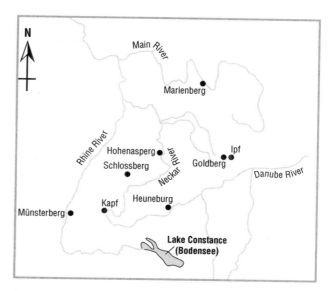

Selected hillforts in the West Hallstatt Zone in southwest Germany. ADAPTED FROM SIEVERS IN RIECKHOFF AND BIEL 2001.

ing a constant flow of valuable goods, such as tin and other ores. This explanation does not fit the case for Etruscan imports in southern Germany, located between the two main trade routes bringing tin and amber to Etruria and initially of little interest to the Etruscan or Greek traders.

SOUTHWEST GERMAN IRON AGE ELITES

This region appears to have developed a nascent elite and an increasingly stratified society mainly on the basis of trade in iron ore, in which this region was especially rich. The wealth concentrated in the hands of a few individuals as a result of this iron industry provided the means to acquire selected and initially rare Mediterranean imports, via the so-called Danube Road linking the two main trade routes already described. An extensive interregional network maintained in part through intermarriage among elites resulted in a cultural and ideological *koine* (a Greek term for a standard language area), reflected in the uniformity of elite material culture across the West Hallstatt area during this time.

Seventeen hillforts, including the Heuneburg in Swabia, have been identified in the West Hallstatt zone, eight of them in Germany. Their identification as *Fürstensitze,* a contested German term for "princely seat," is based on partial excavation or, more commonly, on the basis of stray finds. The

Hohenasperg near Stuttgart, topped by a fortress converted into a minimum-security prison, and the Marienberg in Würzburg, with a massive castle on its summit, are examples of the latter category. The Münsterberg in Breisach, the Kapf near Villingen, the Goldberg and the Ipf near Riesbürg, and the Schlossberg in Nagold also acted as central places during this time and have produced some evidence for imports or elite burials.

Most *Fürstensitze* are located at or near strategic river confluences, natural fords, or areas where rivers become navigable, and all of them appear to have been chosen at least in part for their imposing positions in the landscape. The burial mounds that surround these central places contain wealthy graves as well as graves outfitted quite poorly. This difference apparently reflects a society that was organized into at least three, and possibly four, social strata, variously described as "primary or governing elites," "secondary or nongoverning elites," "nonelites or common folk," and "non-persons." The last category may have included war captives and slaves and is represented most poorly in the archaeological record.

Elite burials containing a mix of imports and items of local manufacture characterize the Late Hallstatt period, exemplified by the interment in 550 B.C. of a local leader at the site of Eberdingen-Hochdorf near Stuttgart and the Vix burial in Burgundy, France, two central burials of the Early Iron Age that escaped the endemic looting in prehistory and in more recent times. These two graves together with a number of partially or mostly looted central burials like those surrounding the Hohenasperg near Stuttgart provide some insight into the Early Iron Age elite subculture. Imported goods, especially drinking and feasting equipment, are a constant feature in these burials, together with the presence of gold personal ornament and a four-wheeled wagon. During the Late Iron Age these ostentatious elite burials disappear, cremation replaces inhumation in many areas, and burial evidence becomes both less abundant and more regionally variable.

GREEKS BEARING GIFTS

Interaction with the Greek world via the trade colony at Massalia began around 540 B.C., a watershed year for Mediterranean sea trade, and lasted until about 450 B.C. The Carthaginian monopoly on the metal-rich Iberian Peninsula following the Battle of Alalia seems to have triggered more extensive exploration by Greek traders of the Celtic hinterland in the last two centuries B.C. Greek amphora fragments and fine pottery wares (first black figure and, later, red figure vessels produced by skilled crafts workers in Athens) are distributed in quantities that diminish with distance from the port at Marseille.

The sudden appearance of Massaliote wine amphorae and Attic black figure pottery in the second half of the sixth century B.C. at distribution centers in Lyon (at the confluence of the Rhône and Saône) and in Burgundy at the hillfort of Mont Lassois (a transport transfer point on the Seine) testifies to the maintenance of this valuable trade route. Supporting evidence is the establishment of an unfortified central place at Bragny in Burgundy (at the confluence of the Saône and Doubs Rivers) around 520–500 B.C., at the peak of the wine export trade. Every liter of wine that was consumed by the southwest German Celtic elites had to pass through Bragny, which has yielded 1,367 amphora fragments to date, twenty-five times the number uncovered at the Heuneburg.

It is doubtful whether anything resembling a regular commercial flow existed. Statistically, based on the number of amphora and drinking vessel sherds found thus far on the Heuneburg, only a third of which has been excavated, no more than two amphorae (roughly 31.5 liters of wine) and two Greek drinking vessels made it as far as the hillfort on the Upper Danube. In other words, Mediterranean contact may have intensified but did not cause the centralization of power and increasing social stratification in the West Hallstatt societies.

SHIFTING CENTERS

By 500 B.C. a group of influential elite lineages had established itself in the central Rhineland, home of the older Hunsrück-Eifel culture. Their presence was manifested in fortified settlements, elaborate mortuary ritual, and impressive weaponry. The Etruscans, who in the meantime had established themselves in the Po Valley and were utilizing centers such as Spina and Felsina (modern-day Bologna) to reach the tin trade routes via the Alpine passes, were quick to recognize a new market for their exotic trade goods. They made use of the so-called Golasecca Celts of the Ticino region as middlemen, who produced many of the bronze *situlae* found in burials in the central Rhineland at the end of the sixth century B.C. Numerous West Hallstatt fibulae dating to this period have been found south of the Alps, testifying to the increased mobility of goods and possibly people from north to south during the La Tène period.

Around 475 B.C. the West Hallstatt zone underwent significant changes as many hillfort centers, including the Heuneburg, were abandoned, probably as the result of internal conflicts and rivalries. New sites were established, and the appearance of a new art style marks changes in ideology during this transitional phase linking the Late Hallstatt and Early La Tène periods. The central Rhineland contact with the Etruscans is evident in the elite graves rich in gold and imported drinking equipment found in this region, while elite burials vanish from the archaeological record in those regions where Late Hallstatt *Fürstengräber* had flourished so recently.

Schnabelkannen, bronze-beaked flagons for serving wine, one of the hallmarks of this time period in the central Rhineland, first appeared at the end of the sixth century B.C. The majority of these vessels are Etruscan imports from the manufacturing center of Vulci, and their distribution indicates that Massalia played no role in the acquisition of these wares. The river system of Moselle, Saar, and Nahe encompasses the elite burials of the younger Hunsrück-Eifel culture (475–350 B.C.).

WOMEN OF SUBSTANCE
Outstanding examples of these mainly female burials, in contrast to the elite graves of the Late Hallstatt period, include Schwarzenbach, Weiskirchen, Hochscheid, Bescheid, Waldalgesheim, and Reinheim. The wealth that appears in elite burials in this region was based partly on river gold and iron ore, possibly even on trade in slaves. The tin trade was its mainstay, however, with elites in the central Rhineland acting as intermediaries between Etruscans and the inhabitants of the region between the Aisne and Marne Rivers (present-day Champagne). The metalworking center of Vulci, as a major consumer of tin, would have been the primary market for the ores that traveled through this region.

The elements of Late Hallstatt paramount elite groups are still present in the Early La Tène female burial of Reinheim (400 B.C.). The body was placed in a large wooden chamber, with an elaborately decorated gold neck ring, a single gold bracelet on the right wrist, three bracelets of gold, slate, and glass, respectively, on the left, and two gold rings on the right hand. Three elaborate fibulae, two of gold with coral inlays, a bronze mirror, and numerous beads of amber and glass also were found. The feasting equipment included two simple bronze plates, probably Etruscan imports, and two gold openwork drinking-horn mounts as well as a gilded-bronze flagon. Reinheim is only one of about half a dozen elaborately outfitted female burials dating to the late fifth and early fourth centuries B.C., also a time of major emigration of men in search of booty and, later, whole tribes in search of new territory.

The Early La Tène elite female burial phenomenon appears to have been partly due to a power vacuum caused by the exodus of large numbers of the elite male population in search of mercenary profits in the south. Some of them would not have returned, either dying abroad or perhaps choosing to marry and remain there. This seems to have provided a brief opportunity for elite women to expand their own spheres of influence, but by Late La Tène B (300–275 B.C.) inhumation graves generally began to disappear, replaced by another mortuary ritual that has left few archaeological traces.

CELTS ON THE MOVE
There are no nuclear places in the Early La Tène central Rhineland comparable to the Heuneburg or the other Late Hallstatt *Fürstensitze*. On the contrary, by 400 B.C. there is evidence for decentralization of the settlement pattern, motivated at least in part by deterioration in the climate that may have led to the Celtic migrations documented in classical sources. Archaeological evidence for depopulation at the beginning of the fourth century B.C. is found in the Champagne region, in Bohemia, and in Bavaria. By the late fourth century and early third century B.C. it also had occurred in eastern France, Baden-Württemberg, and (to a lesser degree) the region between Moselle and Nahe, as cemeteries like the one at Wederath-Belginum attest.

Beginning around this time the Mediterranean world was subjected to what must have seemed a frightening reversal of the traditional interaction with central Europe. The Insubres invaded and occupied Melpum (modern-day Milan) in northern Italy, the Boii took Felsina and renamed it Bononia (present-day Bologna), and the Senoni invaded Picenum as far as Ancona. In the case of the Romans at least, the memory of Celtic marauders on the Palatinate was part of the reason for the military build-up and preemptory territorial expansion that marked their civilization in the centuries after the sack and seven-month-long occupation of their capital by Celtic raiders in 390, 387, or 386 B.C. (Opinions are divided as to the exact year.)

The instability of the Celtic regions during the Early La Tène period resulted in a sociopolitical regression that would last for some two hundred years, when the earlier tendencies toward urbanization finally were realized in the form of the *oppida*. By that time the Romans had conquered the territory taken by the Celts in northern Italy. After crossing the Alps in the first century B.C., they were threatening the Celtic peoples in their home territories, something the Greeks and Etruscans, who were out for economic gain rather than territorial conquest, had never done.

LATE LA TÈNE TRANSFORMATIONS

During the second century B.C. the *oppida* were characterized by large populations as well as craft specialization and a complex economic system made possible by the adoption of coinage (first documented in the first half of the third century B.C.) and writing. There are twenty-three Late Iron Age *oppida* (fortified settlements larger than 15 hectares) in Germany. One of the largest and best documented is the *oppidum* of Manching, near Ingolstadt in Bavaria.

The site flourished mainly because of its strategic location, rich in iron ore, on the Danube at the juncture of several trade routes linking this region to the Black Forest and the river Inn. Along this route, the community transported wine amphorae from Gaul as well as exotic goods from northern Italy. Sometime at the end of the second century B.C. a 7.2-kilometer-long fortification system in the *murus Gallicus* style (Caesar's term for the wood, stone, and earth construction technique he initially encountered in Gaul) was built at the previously unfortified site. It enclosed 380 hectares and held a

peak population of five thousand to ten thousand people between 120 and 50 B.C.

Unlike most of the *oppida* of this period—including the German sites Alkimoenes/Kelheim, the Heidetränk-Oppidum, the Dünsberg, and Creglingen-Finsterlohr—Manching was not located on a promontory or mountain spur, and its walls did not encircle several inhabited peaks. It also seems to have been inhabited by a larger population than other German *oppida*, some of which perhaps operated more as places of refuge for people and their herds during periods of danger. The large population at Manching must have been supported by a sizable hinterland composed of hundreds of small farmsteads and hamlets, judging by the huge quantities of animal bones. Roughly twelve hundred horses, twelve thousand cattle, twelve thousand pigs, and thirteen thousand sheep and goats have been recovered from the 15 hectares excavated since 1955, less than 1 percent of the site.

Another phenomenon associated with the Late La Tène period is the enigmatic and still hotly debated *Viereckschanzen*, rectangular enclosures of varying size that dominated the landscape of southern Germany during this period, clustering especially along the Danube and its tributaries during the second and first centuries B.C. These enclosures consisted of wall and ditch systems 80 meters on a side, on average, and with ditches 4 meters wide and 2 meters deep. Entrances typically were quite narrow, as though to restrict access. No particular direction was favored, but north-facing entrances are not found.

Until the 1950s most *Viereckschanzen* were identified solely on the basis of aerial photographs. In 1957 excavations at the site of Holzhausen uncovered several shafts up to 35 meters deep, and the consensus was that these sites had served a ritual function. Twenty years later excavations at the site of Fellbach-Schmiden, with its wooden carvings of horned animals and a seated human figure, seemed to support this interpretation. At the same time, chemical analysis of one of the deep shafts at the site proved that it had been a well filled in or poisoned with large quantities of manure. Later research has favored the view that these sites, in fact, were fortified small farmsteads, or *Herrenhöfe*, and some may very well have served that function. The possibility of reuse, or multiple uses, of such sites cannot be ruled out. No single theory adequately explains all of the morphologically similar but unexcavated sites that have been placed in the *Viereckschanzen* category.

ROMANS AND BARBARIANS

Most of the *oppida* appeared before the Roman occupation. In the course of the Late La Tène period, however, they undoubtedly were a source of protection against not only Roman military incursions but also the growing Germanic threat from the north. West of the Rhine, Celtic elites in Gaul and Germany responded in a variety of ways to the presence of the Roman occupiers. Political capital could be derived from an external military threat, but at the same time there were benefits to becoming allies of Rome, and Roman citizenship together with Roman customs gradually led to changes in social organization and religious traditions. The heavy yoke of Roman taxation led to intermittent revolts throughout the empire, including in Germany, where one of the most famous uprisings in A.D. 9 eradicated three legions in the Teutoburg Forest under the command of the hapless Publius Quintilius Varus. The abrupt erasure of a major portion of the Roman military forces led the Emperor Augustus to withdraw his troops to the Rhine, ending his expansionist campaign north and east.

Clearly, Augustus had learned what the Celtic groups in the place that the Romans called Free Germany—Germany on the east of the Rhine—already had experienced at first hand: that the Germanic-speaking peoples constituted a seemingly limitless outpouring, pushing south and west in search of land. Beginning with the invasions between 113 and 101 B.C. of the Cimbri, who ultimately terrorized Celtic Gaul at the head of a tribal confederacy intent on territory and plunder, the Celtic-speaking societies in Germany were increasingly caught between several fires. The outcome is indicated by the fact that a Germanic rather than a Celtic language is spoken in Germany today, and the Celtic prehistory of the country is documented only in the archaeological record, presumably to some extent in the gene pool, and by a handful of place names.

See also **Oppida** (*vol. 2, part 6*); **Manching** (*vol. 2, part 6*); **Hillforts** (*vol. 2, part 6*); **Ritual Sites: Viereckschanzen** (*vol. 2, part 6*); **The Heuneburg** (*vol. 2, part 6*).

BIBLIOGRAPHY

Arnold, Bettina, and D. Blair Gibson, eds. *Celtic Chiefdom, Celtic State: The Evolution of Complex Social Systems in Prehistoric Europe.* Cambridge, U.K.: Cambridge University Press, 1995.

Biel, Jörg. *Der Keltenfürst von Hochdorf: Methoden und Ergebnisse der Landesarchäologie.* Stuttgart, Germany: Konrad Theiss Verlag, 1985.

Bittel, Kurt, Wolfgang Kimmig, and Siegwalt Schiek, eds. *Die Kelten in Baden-Württemberg.* Stuttgart, Germany: Konrad Theiss Verlag, 1981.

Collis, John. *The European Iron Age.* London: Batsford, 1984.

Cunliffe, Barry. *The Ancient Celts.* New York: Penguin, 2000.

Green, Miranda J., ed. *The Celtic World.* London: Routledge, 1995.

Krämer, Werner, and Ferdinand Maier, eds. *Die Ausgrabungen in Manching.* 15 vols. Wiesbaden, Germany: Franz Steiner Verlag, 1970–1992.

Rieckhoff, Sabine, and Jörg Biel. *Die Kelten in Deutschland.* Stuttgart, Germany: Konrad Theiss Verlag, 2001.

Schwarz, Klaus. "Die Geschichte eines keltischen Temenos im nördlichen Alpenvorland." In *Ausgrabungen in Deutschland.* Vol. 1, pp. 324–358. Mainz, Germany: Verlag des Römisch-Germanisches Zentralmuseums, 1975.

Sievers, Susanne. "Vorbericht über die Ausgrabungen 1998–1999 im Oppidum von Manching." *Germania* 78, no. 2 (2000): 355–394.

Spindler, Konrad. *Die Frühen Kelten.* Stuttgart, Germany: Reclam, 1983.

Wells, Peter S. *The Barbarians Speak: How the Conquered People Shaped Roman Europe.* Princeton, N.J.: Princeton University Press, 1999.

———. *Culture Contact and Culture Change: Early Iron Age Central Europe and the Mediterranean World.* Cambridge, U.K.: Cambridge University Press, 1980.

Wieland, Günther. *Keltische Viereckschanzen: Einem Rätsel auf der Spur.* Stuttgart, Germany: Konrad Theiss Verlag, 1999.

BETTINA ARNOLD

KELHEIM

Kelheim, a city with a population of about fifteen thousand, is situated at the confluence of the Altmühl River into the Danube in Lower Bavaria, Germany. In and around Kelheim are an unusual number of archaeological sites from the Palaeolithic to the modern day. Particularly important remains date from the Late Bronze Age (a large cemetery of cremation burials) and the Late Iron Age. From about the middle of the second century until the middle of the first century B.C., Kelheim was the site of an *oppidum*, a large, walled settlement of the final period of the prehistoric Iron Age, before the Roman conquest of much of temperate Europe. Just west of the medieval and modern town center is the site of the Late Iron Age complex, set on a triangular piece of land bounded by the Altmühl River on the north, the Danube in the southeast, and a wall 3.28 kilometers long along its western edge, cutting the promontory off from the land to the west. The area enclosed by this wall and the two rivers is about 600 hectares, 90 percent of which is on top of the limestone plateau known as the Michelsberg and 10 percent of which lies in the valley of the Altmühl, between the steep slope of the Michelsberg and the southern bank of the river. Some investigators believe that the settlement that occupied this site was one referred to as "Alkimoennis" by the Greek geographer Ptolemy.

Numerous archaeological excavations have been carried out on sections of the walls, on iron-mining pits on the Michelsberg, and on limited portions of the enclosed land. The western wall, an inner wall 930 meters in length, and a wall along the south bank of the Danube that is 3.3 kilometers in length were constructed in similar ways. Tree trunks about 60 centimeters in diameter were sunk into the ground at intervals of 2 meters or less, and between the trunks the wall front was constructed of limestone slabs to a height of 5 to 6 meters. An earth ramp behind the wall held the stone facing in place and provided access to the top for defenders. Estimates suggest that more than eight thousand trees were felled, some twenty-five thousand cubic meters of limestone were quarried and cut for the wall front, and four hundred thousand cubic meters of earth were piled up for the embankment, representing a substantial amount of labor as well as a significant environmental impact on the surrounding forest.

On the Michelsberg plateau, both within the enclosed area and beyond the western wall, some six thousand pits have been identified from their partially filled remains visible on the surface. Excavations of a few reveal that they are mining pits, cut into the limestone to reach layers of limonite iron ore. Some are of Late Iron Age date and are associated with the *oppidum* occupation; others are medieval. Remains of smelting furnaces near some of the pits have been studied. The principal evidence for the settlement has been found below the Michelsberg plateau, between it and the Altmühl on a part of the site known as the Mitterfeld. Limited excavations on top of the Michelsberg have failed to uncover any extensive settlement remains, but on the Mitterfeld are abundant materials from the Late Iron Age occupation. They are densest in the eastern part of the Mitterfeld and thin out toward the west. Postholes, storage pits, wells, and chunks of wall plaster indicate a typical settlement of the Late La Tène culture, comparable to the site of Manching 36 kilometers up the Danube.

Pieces of ore, slag, and furnace bottoms occur over much of the settlement, attesting to the importance of iron production. Iron tools and ornaments were manufactured on the site, bronze was cast, and glass ornaments made. Tools recovered include axes, anvils, chisels, awls, nails, clamps, hooks, needles, pins, and keys. Vessels, brooches, and spearheads also were made of iron. Bronze ornaments include brooches, rings, pendants, pins, and several figural ornaments, including a small, finely crafted head of a vulture.

The pottery assemblage is typical of the major *oppidum* settlements. Most of the pots were made on a potter's wheel, and they include fine painted wares, well-made tableware, thick-walled cooking pots of a graphite-clay mix, and large, coarse-walled storage vessels. Spindle whorls attest to textile production by the community. Lumps of unshaped glass indicate local manufacture of beads and bracelets. A number of bronze and silver coins have been recovered, along with a mold in which blanks were cast. All of this production of iron and manufacture of goods was based on a solid subsistence economy of agriculture and livestock husbandry. Barley, spelt wheat, millet, and peas were among the principal crops, and pigs and cattle were the main livestock.

Like all of the major *oppida*, the community at Kelheim was actively involved in the commercial systems of Late Iron Age Europe. The quantities of iron produced by the mines and the abundant

Fig. 1. Bronze head of a vulture, from Kelheim. Vultures and other birds of prey became important symbols at the end of the Iron Age. COURTESY OF PETER S. WELLS. REPRODUCED BY PERMISSION.

understood but are subjects of intensive ongoing research.

See also **Oppida** (*vol. 2, part 6*).

BIBLIOGRAPHY

Engelhardt, Bernd. *Ausgrabungen am Main-Donau-Kanal.* Buch am Erlbach, Germany: Verlag Maria Leidorf, 1987.

Pauli, Jutta. *Die latènezeitliche Besiedlung des Kelheimer Beckens.* Kallmünz, Germany: Verlag Michael Lassleben, 1993.

Rieckhoff, Sabine, and Jörg Biel. *Die Kelten in Deutschland.* Stuttgart, Germany: Konrad Theiss, 2001.

Rind, Michael M. *Geschichte ans Licht gebracht: Archäologie im Landkreis Kelheim.* Büchenbach, Germany: Verlag Dr. Faustus, 2000.

Wells, Peter S., ed. *Settlement, Economy, and Cultural Change at the End of the European Iron Age: Excavations at Kelheim in Bavaria, 1987–1991.* Ann Arbor, Mich.: International Monographs in Prehistory, 1993.

PETER S. WELLS

smelting and forging debris indicate specialized production for trade. The site's situation at the confluence of two major rivers was ideal for commerce. The copper and tin that composed bronze had to be brought in, as did the raw glass and the graphite-clay used for cooking pots. Imports from the Roman world include a bronze wine jug, a fragmentary sieve, and an attachment in the form of a dolphin.

As at most of the *oppida* in Late Iron Age Europe, few graves have been found at Kelheim. Without burial evidence, population estimates are difficult to make, but an educated guess might put the size of Late Iron Age Kelheim at between five hundred and two thousand people. Landscape survey shows that when the *oppidum* at Kelheim was established during the second century B.C., people living on farms and in small villages in the vicinity abandoned their settlements and moved into the growing center, perhaps to take advantage of the defense system and for mutual protection. Around the middle of the first century B.C., the *oppidum* was abandoned, like many others east of the Rhine, for reasons and under conditions that are not yet well

THE HEUNEBURG

The Early Iron Age (600–450 B.C.) Heuneburg hillfort in the southwest German state of Baden-Württemberg is one of the most intensively studied Hallstatt period (Early Iron Age) settlement complexes in Europe. It occupies a roughly triangular natural spur about 60 meters above the Upper Danube River some 600 meters above sea level. The 3.3-hectare fortified promontory settlement was associated with a much larger outer settlement, or suburbium, whose precise boundaries are still unknown. The site came to the attention of the international scholarly community when the Württemberg state conservator Eduard Paulus excavated several burial mounds close to the hillfort in 1877, uncovering gold neckrings, metal drinking vessels, and other evidence of elite material culture. Paulus coined the term *Fürstengräber,* "princely burials," to describe these interments, a reference to the wealthy burials excavated by Heinrich Schliemann at Mycenae the year before. All four of the mounds in this group were partially or completely excavated by various researchers between 1954 and 1989. A looted and leveled fifth mound was discovered during excavations to the southwest of the hillfort in 1999.

Unsystematic explorations of mounds within 5 kilometers of the hillfort are recorded as early as the sixteenth century, peaking in the nineteenth century following Paulus's excavations. Looting combined with the gradual destruction by plowing of mounds on arable land has taken its toll on the Early Iron Age burial monuments in this area. Roughly 130 burial mounds, also referred to as tumuli, were known in the Heuneburg area by the end of the 1990s. This probably represents only 10 percent of the original total.

The first exploratory trenching of the hillfort took place in 1921, establishing the contemporaneity of the settlement and the tumuli roughly 400 meters north-northwest of the promontory fort investigated by Paulus. Beginning in 1950, twenty-nine years of systematic fieldwork on the acropolis, led by Wolfgang Kimmig and Egon Gersbach, uncovered a fortification system of air-dried, white-washed mud bricks on a limestone foundation. This arid-climate construction technique is not found on any other temperate European Iron Age site. Far from being especially vulnerable to the wet climate of the region, it actually survived longer than the homegrown wood-and-earth fortification systems that came before and after it. Though relatively fire-resistant, the mud-brick wall was ultimately leveled following a major fire around 540 B.C. that destroyed a significant portion of the hillfort and outer settlement. Additional evidence for contact with the Mediterranean world of the sixth century B.C. was recovered in the form of distinctive Greek imported pottery known as black figure ware, as well as trade amphorae that were probably used to transport wine and olive oil. These imports, combined with the ostentatious wealth of the burial mounds near the hillfort, are the hallmarks of a so-called *Fürstensitz*, or "princely seat." The Heuneburg is one of a small number of such sites in the so-called West Hallstatt Zone (southwest Germany, eastern France, Switzerland north of the Alps).

By 1979, when excavation yielded to analysis and publication of features and finds, just over a third of the plateau had been explored. The site was occupied from the Late Neolithic (fourth and third millennia B.C.) until the medieval period (eleventh and twelfth centuries). Altogether twenty-three separate building phases were identified. The earliest fortification of the plateau dates to the end of the Early Bronze Age to the beginning of the Middle Bronze Age (seventeenth century B.C.). Throughout the thirteenth and twelfth centuries B.C. the site seems to have controlled the economic, social, and religious life of a local microregion. Beginning in 1999, the discovery by Siegfried Kurz of several small settlements in the Heuneburg hinterland dating to this period support this hypothesis of a two-tiered settlement hierarchy for the Bronze Age Heuneburg region.

Population estimates for the Early Iron Age site complex (plateau, outer settlement, associated burial mounds) are complicated by the fact that the outer settlement, which in 2003 was still being explored, and the plateau itself have not been completely excavated. However, the site appears to have housed several thousand people at its peak during the Late Hallstatt–Early La Tène period (seventh to fifth centuries B.C.). Based on the known size of the settlement complex, the evidence for long-distance exchange and the wealth of the surrounding burial mounds, the Heuneburg during its Early Iron Age heyday is interpreted as a central place controlling a large region characterized by a multitiered settlement hierarchy composed of at least three settlement-size categories. The hillfort's strategic position on the Danube, its proximity to iron ore resources, the evidence for various kinds of production activity (especially metalworking and textile production) on a scale consistent with an export trade system, and the size of some of the multi-roomed structures at the site all testify to the sociopolitical and economic importance of the Heuneburg during this period.

The Iron Age burial mounds associated with the Heuneburg echo the social complexity and economic dominance suggested by the settlement record. Following Paulus's excavations in the mounds near the hillfort, no systematic explorations were conducted until Gustav Riek's partial excavation in 1937–1938 of the Hohmichele—at 13.5 meters high and with a diameter of 85 meters, the second-largest known Early Iron Age burial mound in Europe (fig. 1). Although the central chamber had been looted, seven inhumations (body burials) were recovered, including an intact chamber grave (Grave VI) containing the inhumations of a man

Fig. 1. The Heuneburg situated on a hill in the Upper Danube Valley. © Eric Lessing/Art Resource, NY. Reproduced by permission.

and a woman buried with a four-wheeled wagon, bronze drinking vessels, personal ornaments (for both individuals), and weapons (a dagger, a quiver full of iron-tipped arrows, and a bow with the male individual).

Beginning in 1999, excavations by the author and colleagues in two smaller mounds (Tumulus 17 and Tumulus 18) 200 meters from the Hohmichele produced twenty-three new burials. Tumulus 17 Grave 1 contained a bronze cauldron, an iron short sword, two iron spear points, an iron belt hook, and a helmet plume clamp, whereas Tumulus 18, excavated in 2002, produced two burials with bronze neckrings, a costume element that was a marker of elite status in Iron Age Europe until well into the Christian period in Ireland and Scotland. The ongoing search for supporting, smaller settlements in the Heuneburg hinterland (by Siegfried Kurz), the efforts to delineate the boundaries of the outer settlement (by Hartmann Reim), and the systematic ex-

cavation of additional burial mounds (by Bettina Arnold and colleagues) are beginning to fill in the picture scholars have constructed of this dynamic Early Iron Age center.

See also **Hillforts** (*vol. 2, part 6*); **Greek Colonies in the West** (*vol. 2, part 6*); **Iron Age Germany** (*vol. 2, part 6*).

BIBLIOGRAPHY

Arnold, Bettina. "The Material Culture of Social Structure: Rank and Status In Early Iron Age Europe." In *Celtic Chiefdom, Celtic State: The Evolution of Complex Social Systems in Prehistoric Europe.* Edited by Bettina Arnold and D. Blair Gibson, pp. 43–52. Cambridge, U.K.: Cambridge University Press, 1995.

Arnold, Bettina, and Matthew L. Murray. "A Landscape of Ancestors in Southwest Germany." *Antiquity* 76, no. 292 (2002): 321–322. (Additional information is available from the website "A Landscape of Ancestors: The Heuneburg Archaeological Project" at http://www.uwm.edu/~barnold/arch/.)

Bittel, Kurt, Wolfgang Kimmig, and Siegwalt Schiek. *Die Kelten in Baden-Württemberg.* Stuttgart, Germany: Theiss, 1981.

Kimmig, Wolfgang. *Die Heuneburg an der oberen Donau.* Führer zu archäologischen Denkmälern in Baden-Württemberg 1. Stuttgart, Germany: Theiss, 1983.

Kurz, Siegfried. "Siedlungsforschungen bei der Heuneburg, Gde. Herbertingen-Hundersingen, Kreis Sigmaringen—Zum Stand des DFG-Projektes." In *Archäologische Ausgrabungen in Baden-Württemberg 2001,* pp. 61–63. Stuttgart, Germany: Theiss, 2002.

Reim, Hartmann. "Siedlungsgrabungen im Vorfeld der Heuneburg bei Hundersingen, Gde. Herbertingen, Kreis Sigmaringen." In *Archäologische Ausgrabungen in Baden-Württemberg 1999,* pp. 53–57. Stuttgart, Germany: Theiss, 2000.

Rieckhoff, Sabine, and Jörg Biel. *Die Kelten in Deutschland.* Stuttgart, Germany: Theiss, 2001.

BETTINA ARNOLD

IBERIA IN THE IRON AGE

As in other areas of the Mediterranean, the classic European division of the Iron Age into the Hallstatt and La Tène phases is not applicable to the Iberian Peninsula. During the first millennium B.C. this area underwent intense change in which different cultures interacted. The local traditions of the Bronze Age came to an end, and new populations became established. Some of them were of Continental origin, for example, those of the Urnfield culture, the last traces of which are seen in the seventh century B.C. Of greater impact, however, were those of the Mediterranean, beginning with the Phoenicians, who founded their first colonies along the southern coast at the end of the ninth century B.C. The cultural characteristics of the Iberian Peninsula, with its Atlantic, Mediterranean, and Continental influences as well as its local traditions, made the Iron Age a time of complex change that showed little chronological homogeneity. The general features that developed over the long term included the definitive settlement of populations, the marking of political territories, the intensification of agriculture through the introduction of iron tools, the progressive development of social hierarchy, and accompanying ideological changes.

THE ORIGINS OF IRON AGE IBERIA

The arrival of the Phoenicians and the founding of several coastal colonies and trading ports were among the factors that marked the beginning of the Iron Age on the Iberian Peninsula. Important transformations occurred in the economics of the area, accompanied by changes in the political, religious, and social spheres. The Phoenician colonies, among which Gadir (now Cádiz) stands out, assured their subsistence by marking out large catchment areas as well as developing fishing and fish-salting industries. Specialized crafts were developed that introduced new techniques to goldsmithing, the forging of iron, and the making of wheel-turned pottery. In addition to introducing such exotic objects as ivory, alabaster jars, and ostrich eggs, these colonies are attributed with introducing new domestic fauna, such as asses and chickens; expanding wine consumption; and generally incorporating much of the peninsula into the political and commercial dynamics of the Mediterranean.

The economic factors of the Phoenician cities in the Near East were important in the election of the Iberian territories for colonization. The Ríotinto mines in the southwest (Huelva) were considered fundamental to the supply of silver to Tyrus (modern-day Tyre) and Sidon. They would allow commercial strength to be maintained while meeting the increasing tax demands of Assyria. The richness of these mining areas, which were developed in an open-cast fashion, must have been evident to Phoenician metallurgists, because the Huelva mines produced some 2,000 grams per ton of silver and 70 grams per ton of gold.

The mines of the southeast, located around what eventually would become the Carthaginian cities of Baria (present-day Viaricos) and Cartago Nova (present-day Cartagena), also were exploited. The lead ingots obtained in this way were transported by small boats that hugged the coast until they reached the main ports. The seventh-century wreck

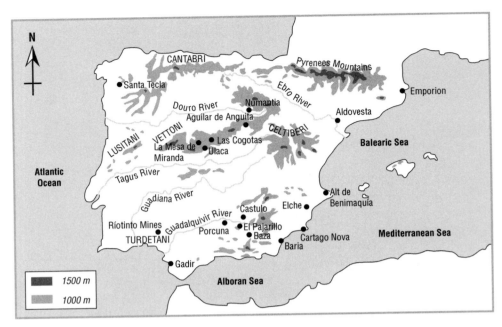

Selected sites and selected populi of Iron Age Iberia.

of one Phoenician vessel at Mazarrón, which has been preserved in excellent condition, was carrying 2,000 kilograms of lead oxide when it sank. The intense mining activity, which reached its peak in the seventh century B.C., caused notable deforestation and the release of important contaminants, as revealed by ice layers in Greenland that correspond to this time.

All this activity implied great change for the indigenous population, which not only saw how part of its territory was progressively occupied but also must have supplied the greater part of the workforce for the mines. The southwest of the peninsula, the hinterland of this colonial world, experienced the upsurge of the "Tartessian culture," which became a mythical reference among the legends of the extreme western Mediterranean. The people of the interior, even those far from the coast, became suppliers of the raw materials required by the Phoenicians as well as a market for the products that the colonists manufactured. Enclaves on the estuaries and along the courses of the main rivers show that Phoenician trade sought out these inland areas. Those on the Sado and Mondego Rivers in western Portugal and on the Aldovesta in the northeast of the peninsula reveal how Phoenician commerce tried to make use of the infrastructure and penetration routes controlled by native populations.

This entire process had a strong ideological impact, which is detectable through the religious changes that took place on the southern and eastern parts of the Iberian Peninsula. Phoenician sanctuaries, such as that of Melkart in Gadir, also were built at the former mouth of the Guadalquivir (Roman Baetis), near Seville. There a sanctuary dedicated to Astarte (Spanish Ashtarte), goddess of fertility and sexual love, was erected, from which a beautiful bronze statuette with a dedication has been recovered. Many other Phoenician divinities were adapted to the religious beliefs of the indigenous populations of the Tartessian area, as evidenced by the palace sanctuary of Cancho Roano in Extremadura. The iconography of the goddess Astarte was absorbed as a representation of the mother goddess venerated over a large part of Iberia. This is palpable proof of the profound political and economic transformations ushered in by the Phoenicians.

The first Greek explorations also made contact with the Tartessian world of the far west. Herodotus (book 1 of the *Inquiries*) indicates that the mythical Tartesian king Arganthonius established good relations with the Phocaeans, to the point that Tartessian silver was used to finance the building of a strong stone wall to protect Phocaea. These contacts have led some authors to establish Tartessus as the site of one of the twelve tasks of Hercules: his fight with the monster Geryon and his dog Orthros, both of whom were killed by the hero, who took from them the herd of red cows he later delivered to Greece.

BIRTH AND DEVELOPMENT OF THE IBERIAN CULTURE

When Phoenician commercial dominance went into crisis at the start of the sixth century B.C., Carthage gained control of the colonial southern peninsula, and some relevant places, such as Gadir, developed as totally independent centers. This same point in time also saw the appearance of certain culturally identifiable groups, such as the Iberians, whose territories extended from southeastern France down to the old Tartessian kingdom (which at this time was given the name Turdetania). The Iberian populations were divided into different political units (the Ilergetes, Lacetani, Edetani, Contestani, Bastetani, and Oretani, among others), in whose territories some very large settlements existed. Stone walls reinforced with towers fortified their towns, and houses of one or two floors lined their stone streets. In eastern Andalusia a system of concentrating the population seems to have existed in the catchment area dominated by the *oppida*. In other locations, such as Valencia, rural settlements abounded next to worked fields. Economic territories revolved around river valleys, religious centers playing an important role in their symbolic definition. This appears to be a case very similar to that described by François de Polignac, the Greek scholar, for the Greek world, as can be appreciated in the iconography of the Iberian sanctuary of El Pajarillo de Huelma and in the large group of sculptures at Porcuna, both in the province of Jaén.

The cultural substratum of the Iberians was influenced strongly by local and Phoenician traditions, but their commercial contacts were with the Greek colonies of the western Mediterranean. Emporion, a Phocaean foundation linked to Massalia as well as to other towns, such as Alonis or Akra Leuke (which have not been located but are cited in texts), was a point at which goods were loaded and Greek pottery, wine, and oil (products highly valued on the Iberian Peninsula) were unloaded. Some trading treaties, such as that of Ampurias, belonging to the second half of the sixth century B.C., were inscribed on lead. This particular treaty accords the shipment of goods from the port of Sagunto. The relationship between Greeks and Iberians was very close, as is seen in the southeast of the peninsula, where a Greco-Iberian language developed, which expressed the local tongue in Ionian characters.

An important economic as well as cultural transformation was the production and consumption of wine. Amphorae of varying Mediterranean provenances have been recovered at the Iberian settlements, but there are signs of developed local production at least from the sixth century B.C. onward. At the fortified settlement of Alt de Benimaquía (Valencia), several pools were dedicated to the treading of grapes, and the wine obtained was stored in amphorae of Phoenician typology. Much of the Greek pottery found on settlements and cemeteries from the fifth century on were linked precisely with the consumption of wine.

After the end of the fifth century B.C., iron tools began to be used in agriculture. This had the effect of intensifying production, which was linked to an increase in the population and in commerce. Calculations of the capacity of the numerous cereal storage pits documented for the area of Emporion in the northeast of Catalonia show it to have greatly exceeded the needs of the local people. Therefore a large part of the stored grain probably was destined for export. In addition the Castulo silver mines in Oretani territory assured the profit of commercial activities. Findings of Attic pottery along the old routes connecting the ports with this city are witness to the intensity of these economic relations.

The social organization of the Iberian peoples has been investigated through the study of their villages and corresponding necropolises. These sites reveal the existence of a warrior aristocracy that always cremated its dead before burying them in tombs. Some of these groups constructed towers or stelae with sculptural decoration playing an important role. Real animals (lions, bulls, and horses) and mythical creatures (sphinxes and griffins) were preferred by Iberian sculptors for the protection of the tombs of important people. Greek and oriental influences can be seen in these decorations.

Among the funerary equipment that accompanied the urns holding the cremated bones, Greek ceramics (kraterae [jars for mixing wine and water], *kylix* [wine cups], and *skiphoi* [cups]) stand out. These items were highly valued for their quality, their shiny varnish, and their iconography and sometimes were imitated by local craftspeople. Iberian ceramics, with their orange hues and red-painted geometric decorations, also were the products of specialized craftspeople. In some areas of the east and southeast figurative themes were developed, with scenes of human activity as well as animal and plant motifs. Iron weapons were important as well, especially the *falcata*, an original curved sword the shape of which has been likened to the Greek *machaira* and which demonstrated mastery of a refined technology.

Iberian religion was of the Mediterranean type. Among the major systems was the veneration of a certain goddess, protector of life and death. She was represented through outstanding sculptures, such as the well-known *Dama de Elche* or the *Dama de Baza*, a large stone statue representing a veiled woman sitting on a winged throne, within which were ashes and cremated bones. These pieces are testimony to the rich clothing worn by Iberian women and the numerous articles of jewelry used on special occasions. Nevertheless those objects typically were not deposited within the grave, suggesting the existence of hereditary transmission systems. The members of these societies are represented in the thousands of stone and bronze votive offerings that have been found in sanctuaries both in rural settings and at the entrance to settlements. Caves in mountainous areas of difficult access were special places of devotion, which suggests a relationship to initiation rites.

THE CENTRAL AND WESTERN AREAS OF THE IBERIAN PENINSULA DURING THE IRON AGE

Other peoples with different roots, normally grouped together as Celts owing to their characteristics and languages of Indo-European origins, occupied the central and western parts of the peninsula. Outstanding among them are the Celtiberi, Vaccei, and Vettoni and farther west the Lusitani. The Iron Age brought about important changes in the economic models characteristic of the western peninsula. At the end of the Bronze Age economic power was based on the control of livestock and trading routes, but during the Iron Age there was a trend toward the intensification and dominance of agricultural production. The transition toward this model was linked to the adoption of definitive sedentary settlements. Warrior groups used their new iron weapons to gain better land.

The introduction of the plow usually is considered a step indicative of the passage from a model of community property to one of privately owned land. The existence of plots dividing up cultivable land as well as separating such land from pasture has been proposed. Crude zoomorphic sculptures from the Vettonian area, representing pigs and bulls (known as *verracos*), are thought to have signaled the claims of particular groups to stock-raising resources, such as winter pastures. Control of the land for agriculture, as a complement to stock raising, led to changes in the relationship between society and its environment, to unequal access to resources, and to progressive social differentiation.

Vettonian settlements were of two basic types, larger ones acting as central hubs and smaller ones basically concerned with agricultural production. Among the former, Ulaca (60 hectares), Las Cogotas (14.5 hectares), and La Mesa de Miranda (30 hectares in maximum extent) stand out, all *oppida*. Vettonian settlements had strong fortifications and dispersed domestic units. The interior of these enormous settlements included not only houses but also centers of worship and sacrificial altars, livestock pens, marketplaces, neighborhoods of artisans with their kilns and metallurgical furnaces, and even quarries. They were so big and their activities so diverse that part of the population might never have needed to leave them in their daily lives. Population-density calculations, based on the number of tombs recovered from the necropolises associated with these settlements, show low values.

At Las Cogotas there are four differentiated areas of graves and nearly 1,500 cremation burials, but because the cemetery was used for a long period of time, not more than 250 people are thought to have lived in this large hillfort at any given time. The existence of separate funerary areas seems to reflect a system of lineal descent in kinship groups whose economy was based on control of different resources, without a remarkable potential of accumulation. Only 15 percent of the burials showed evidence of grave goods, among which 18 percent included such weapons as spears, shields, knives, and swords decorated with silver as well as horse trappings. Most of the dead are accompanied only by pottery vessels, while women might wear spindle whorls, finger rings, and brooches.

Smaller centers show clear differences with the *oppida*. They were open sites placed on the lower parts of the valleys and seem to be small villages or hamlets involved in agriculture, with limited craft production at a familiar level. These farming units complemented stock raising, which was concentrated on the highlands and mountains.

Farther west the Lusitani (to the north of the Tagus River), the Celtici (in the Alentejo), and the Conii (in the Algarve) occupied most of Portugal. A tribal organization dominated the interior areas, the Atlantic coast developing an urban organization more rapidly. Greek products arrived via this route, as witnessed by the necropolis at Alcacer do Sal, although this site also contains clearly western artifacts, such as antenna-hilt swords and printed pottery. Stone walls encircle the settlements, and domestic buildings have circular plans, built with a stone basement and a wooden roof, the floors being thinly paved. No evidence of ironworking is present here until the second half of the first millennium B.C.

The northeast of the Spanish *meseta* was occupied by Celtiberians, who were known, among other things, for their language, which was undoubtedly of Celtic origin. Both their settlements and necropolises suggest that they formed a variety of communities, from small hamlets of five or six houses to villages of twenty-five to thirty domestic units. More exceptional were large settlements with a necropolis like that of Aguilar de Anguita, which had a population of some 400 or perhaps even 600 people. Their characteristic settlement was the hillfort, a permanent village protected by a wall and sometimes by moats and *chevaux-de-frise* (irregular barriers about 50 to 80 centimeters high made up of stones that surround the easiest access to the villages), reflecting Celtic influence. In the interior lived a few families who survived on what the surroundings produced. These self-sufficient units occupied more and more land by a system of segmentation, the "overspill" of the population of one hillfort founding another of the same type in a neighboring area. By the end of the first millennium B.C. the growth of some centers outweighed others

to become "capitals" occupying large extensions of terrain, such as Numantia, which was of extraordinary political importance during the clash with Roman forces.

Celtiberian houses used the defensive wall as their own back wall, and their homogeneity speaks of a society with few social differences. The social model in most of Celtic Hispania was that of warlike tribes, authority resting with the heads of lineages and families. This structure generally prevented any process leading to marked inequality, as witnessed by their housing and the egalitarian nature of most of their burial grounds. The presence of the Romans, however, changed both their political and economic points of reference, with the larger centers starting to become specialized in certain types of work. For the rural hillforts, which became the suppliers of these emerging urban nuclei, this generated a situation of inequality.

Economically the Celtiberians possessed only a limited agriculture, which took advantage of fertile valley bottoms. The main crops were cereals, although the remains found in their villages show that they consumed large quantities of forest products, especially acorns. Their main activity was stock raising, especially goats and sheep, and they must have practiced transhumance to take advantage of better pastures at different times of the year. It has been suggested that these groups performed the same tasks for neighboring populations, such as the Iberians of the east.

Compared with the Mediterranean area, the west of the peninsula appears to have maintained religious beliefs very similar to those of the Indo-European world, worshipping such divinities as Endovellicus, god of health and sometimes of the night, and Ataecina, goddess of agrarian fertility, death, and resurrection. The greater part of these religious forces resided in elements of nature, such as woods, rocks, springs, or rivers. Altars, where animal sacrifices, especially of bulls, pigs, and sheep, were made and where young warriors underwent complex initiation ceremonies, have been preserved both inside and outside settlements.

THE GALICIAN NORTHWEST AND THE CANTABRIAN COAST

The northwest, which includes the north of Portugal and the present Spanish region of Galicia, is separated from the *meseta* and is of difficult and mountainous access. During the Iron Age its development enjoyed a great deal of autonomy. Walled settlements, known as "Galician *castra*," are its most characteristic element. Small in size (0.5–3 hectares), they were situated where they dominated valley areas, their interest being the control of agricultural regions. Unlike anything in the rest of the peninsula, the dwellings they contained were round. Hardly any signs of urban organization can be found beyond the siting of buildings to favor the movement of people and the evacuation of the abundant rain that falls in this area.

These *castra* of the pre-Roman era concentrated families with their own systems of subsistence. No superstructure broke this organization of associated units in which sex and age were the main factors ordering social behavior. The construction and contents of these domestic units show practically no specialization; all incorporate the same basic functional elements. The independence of each family group was limited by the *castra* boundary—the only thing that joined together these poorly united family-autonomous communities.

Roman interests accelerated a substantial change of this simple model. In contrast to the arrangement described earlier, at the end of the Iron Age there was a clear tendency toward intensification and product specialization, which terminated the autarchy of traditional systems. Agriculture and sheep raising, and in many areas the creation of new *castra* linked to mining activities aimed at the Roman market, were factors that provoked notable transformations. Very often the land was redistributed according to Roman interests. Some types of land exploitation, such as gold mines, attained industrial levels of activity. This change opened the way for hitherto unknown social differentiation.

Ideological and functional changes accompanied this new situation. Large nuclei of up to 20 hectares appeared, such as that of Santa Tecla (Pontevedra), leading to a considerable concentration of the population. Their dwellings were more complex, incorporating entrance halls and vestibules as well as sets of rooms arranged around a central patio. Decorative elements appeared in an architecture whose complexity grew—and not simply with respect to housing. The system of defensive walls became a symbol defining both the inside and outside of these *castra*. Finally, the first cemeteries appeared, with graves using stelae of Roman formula. This movement toward complexity and social inequality that had visited other areas of the peninsula in earlier times reached Galicia only now, bringing it into line, if still incipiently, with the general model followed throughout Iberia (although this model did show variations).

Along the rest of the Cantabrian strip the center and west had settlements similar to those of the *meseta* region and Galicia, respectively, with their *castra* and associated farming areas. Archaeological evidence from the Basque country is very limited. Some of the most characteristic structures are enclosures bound by stones, whose value began to be appreciated for the hierarchical control of geographical and productive areas linked to rivers or streams. The difficult mountainous terrain of these lands and their scant economic potential favored a certain isolation, appreciable even in the twenty-first century in the area's pre-Indo-European language.

Although this was still an eminently pastoral society, agriculture continued to gain importance in this period, helped by the manufacture and use of iron tools. It was less noticeable than in other areas, but again it illustrates the changes that led to a reorganization of productive forces, developments undoubtedly accompanied by social adjustment.

THE END OF THE IBERIAN IRON AGE

The Iberian Peninsula was the setting of the Second Punic War between Rome and Carthage (218–202 B.C.). Nearly all the peninsula had come under Punic control after the second treaty between the two powers in 348 B.C. The foundation of New Carthage by the Carthaginian general Hasdrubal was the start of a new policy of territorial domination that looked to local aristocracies for support. Both Hasdrubal and his brother Hannibal married Iberian princesses and were recognized as leaders by the local populations. The growing power of Carthage threatened Roman supremacy. Many of the confrontations between the two powers took place on the peninsula, complicated by fighting, which surely occurred with indigenous groups.

The activity of these two great armies led to the payment of soldiers with coinage, making the domination of mining areas vital. From the point of view of the Iberian peoples, this situation provoked a militarization of human resources and a return of warrior chiefdoms. Men of the Iberian and Celtic areas were used to form part of Mediterranean armies. By the end of the sixth century B.C. they already had served as mercenaries of Carthage, and on other occasions during the fifth and sixth centuries B.C. they served with both Carthaginian and Greek troops at Syracuse. At the end of the Iron Age many of these populations were active as troops in the Carthaginian or the Roman armies, and they also could fight as independent forces when their territory was threatened.

After defeating Carthage in the third century B.C., Rome installed itself first in the Iberian and Turdetanian areas before conquering the rest of the territory. Local resistance was fierce where the existing social structures were incompatible with the Roman state model. A little later, however, the entire peninsula entered a new phase as part of the Roman administration, drawing the Iron Age to a close.

See also **The Mesolithic of Iberia** (*vol. 1, part 2*); **Late Neolithic/Copper Age Iberia** (*vol. 1, part 4*); **El Argar and Related Bronze Age Cultures of the Iberian Peninsula** (*vol. 2, part 5*); **Early Medieval Iberia** (*vol. 2, part 7*).

BIBLIOGRAPHY

Almagro Gorbea, M., and G. Ruiz Zapatero, eds. *Paleoetnología de la Península Ibérica.* Complutum 2–3. Madrid: Universidad Complutense, 1992.

Aubet, María Eugenia. *The Phoenicians and the West: Politics, Colonies, and Trade.* Translated by Mary Turton. Cambridge, U.K.: Cambridge University Press, 1993.

Belén Deamos, M., and T. Chapa Brunet. *La Edad del Hierro.* Madrid: Editorial Síntesis, 1997.

Cabrera Bonet, Paloma, and Carmen Sánchez, eds. *Los Griegos en España: Tras las huellas de Heracles.* Madrid: Ministerio de Educación y Cultura, 2000.

Cunliffe, Barry, and Simon Keay, eds. *Social Complexity and the Development of Towns in Iberia: From the Copper Age to the Second Century AD.* Proceedings of the British Academy, no. 86. Oxford: Oxford University Press, 1995.

Dominguez Monedero, Adolfo J. *Los Griegos en la Península Ibérica.* Madrid: Arco Libros, 1996.

Ruiz, Arturo, and Manuel Molinos. *The Archaeology of the Iberians.* Translated by Mary Turton. Cambridge, U.K.: Cambridge University Press, 1998.

TERESA CHAPA

ETRUSCAN ITALY

The Etruscans originated in central Italy around 900 B.C. and were absorbed into the Roman Empire in the 80s B.C. During the first millennium B.C., they developed the earliest complex society in Italy. In common with other Mediterranean civilizations of their time, the Etruscans lived in city-states, had a specialized agricultural and craft economy, and exchanged goods and ideas with their neighbors. Distinctive to the Etruscans was their religion, social and political structure, and language. There is a wealth of archaeological evidence for Etruscan settlements, economy, society, and culture, including the remains of cities, towns, cemeteries, and everyday objects.

IRON AGE

The traditional Etruscan territory in central Italy is delineated by the Tyrrhenian Sea in the west, the Apennines in the east, and the Arno and Tiber Rivers to the north and south. The Etruscan civilization arose out of the culture and society that developed in this area during the Late Bronze Age (1300–900 B.C.) and Iron Age (900–700 B.C.). During the Iron Age, the roots of Etruscan cities, economy, religion, and language were established.

Settlements. Most of the great Etruscan cities of later times originated as villages in the Iron Age. In southern Etruria, Iron Age villages usually were situated on volcanic tufa plateaus (Veio, Cerveteri, Tarquinia, Vulci, and Orvieto). In central and northern Etruria, villages more often were built on isolated hilltops dominating the sea or inland waterways—Populonium (modern-day Populania), Ve-

tulonia, Volterra, Chiusi, Cortona, and Arezzo. Small farms and hamlets surrounded Iron Age villages. Excavations at Volterra, in northern Etruria, provide archaeological evidence for early settlement patterns in one Etruscan city. During the Iron Age many small villages coexisted on the Volterran hilltop, placed wherever there was relatively flat land and a spring to provide water. Roadways leading into the countryside radiated out from the hilltop in every direction. Along these routes several burial areas developed.

Excavations at Tarquinia, in southern Etruria, have recovered evidence for Iron Age dwellings. Two kinds of huts were found in the Iron Age village: larger oval or rectangular huts, approximately 13 by 7 meters, that could have housed an extended family and smaller huts, approximately 5 by 4 meters, that could have housed a nuclear family. The area between the huts may have been used for growing small cottage gardens and keeping animals and poultry. Drainage channels carried rainwater away from the dwellings and into a central cistern.

Iron Age huts were built on foundation trenches cut into soil or rock. Exterior timber posts were set into holes in the foundation, to support the thatched roof. Walls were made of wattle screens woven from reeds and branches and covered with daub (clay). The door usually was placed at the short end of the structure and sometimes was protected by a small porch. Inside the hut was a central hearth, circular in shape. The interior may have been divided by a screen into a front and a back room.

Cemeteries. Iron Age cemeteries were located outside villages, usually on surrounding hillsides. During the ninth century B.C., most individuals were cremated and their ashes placed into decorated pottery urns. The urns were buried, along with modest grave goods, in tombs cut into soil or rock. Toward the end of the Iron Age new burial customs emerged in central Italy, interpreted as evidence of the development of an aristocracy. By the eighth century B.C., a few rich burials appear among many more common ones, distinguished by their more numerous and expensive grave goods, especially fine metalwork.

Language and Religion. During the Iron Age a common culture developed among the residents of Etruria. The Etruscan language and religion were among the most significant elements in the culture. Etruscan is not an Indo-European language and is not related to the languages of neighboring Italic peoples. The Etruscans learned the alphabet from Greeks who settled in southern Italy and used it to write down their own language. The first texts written in Etruscan date to the end of the Iron Age, around 700 B.C.

The Etruscan religion, as we know it from the historical period, incorporated early cult practices from the Iron Age. The Etruscans believed that divinities determined the course of events in the human world. Etruscan worship took place in sacred groves, caves, and springs, where divinities were thought to reside. The role of Etruscan priests was to learn the will of the gods and then to follow the appropriate rituals and sacrifices. Individual worshippers asked for divine favor by sacrificing animals for the gods, offering them food or drink, or giving them other gifts. A spring at Banditella, near Vulci, was a sanctuary as early as the Middle Bronze Age (seventeenth century B.C.) into Etruscan times, indicating the continuity of religious practices from prehistory into the historic era.

Economy. The Iron Age economy was largely self-sufficient: each Etruscan village produced everything it needed. Agriculture was the foundation of the economy. Farmers grew cereals, legumes, fruits, nuts, and vegetables and raised sheep, goats, and pigs. Villagers also hunted, fished, and gathered in nearby woods and waters. Most tools, utensils, clothing, and other goods were made by each household for its own use. Certain specialized and luxury items were produced in Etruria and distributed throughout central Italy, the Mediterranean, and north of the Alps. By the Iron Age, a specialized metal industry already existed in Etruria. Metals were mined from the Colline Metallifere, or "metal-bearing hills," and fashioned into metal objects in nearby Populonium and Vetulonia. In exchange, luxury objects were imported from Greece, Phoenicia, and Sardinia.

Society. By the end of the Iron Age Etruscan society probably included several classes, linked through patron-client ties. Farmers met their own needs and also produced goods and labor for petty chiefs. In exchange, the petty chiefs provided their clients with protection, communal works, and foodstuffs. The petty chiefs, in turn, were clients of paramount chiefs, who redistributed foodstuffs and prestige goods regionally.

ORIENTALIZING PERIOD
The Etruscan period begins around 700 B.C., when the first surviving historic documents were written in the Etruscan language. Etruscan society evolved directly from the prehistoric Iron Age. Many of the most characteristic features of Etruscan society—settlement in towns, distinctive cultural customs, production of goods for regional and long-distance trade and exchange—were present in incipient form during the Iron Age. Early Etruscans also were influenced by the Greeks, Phoenicians, and other contemporary Mediterranean societies.

The Orientalizing period (700–575 B.C.) is named for the imported goods and foreign styles adopted by the Etruscans during this time. The early Etruscans' economic power was based on mineral and agricultural resources, which they transformed into goods for exchange. They cut a dashing figure across the Mediterranean, renowned for their seafaring skills as traders and pirates. As reflected in their art, monuments, and historical documents, Etruscans of the Orientalizing period were prosperous and cultured.

Settlements. The Orientalizing period saw the transition from village to town life in Etruria. Excavations in Etruscan towns of this period have revealed signs of urban planning and public works, such as streets, drainage channels, reservoirs, retain-

Fig. 1. Etruscan city gate, Volterra, late fourth to early third century B.C. © COPYRIGHT ALINARI/ART RESOURCE, NY. REPRODUCED BY PERMISSION.

ing walls, fortifications, and sanctuaries. Volterra, in northern Etruria, became a small, fortified settlement at this time. In the seventh century B.C., the numerous villages on the Volterran hilltop agglomerated into a single town. In the sixth century a circuit of walls was built to enclose the town, and sanctuaries were demarcated throughout the city (fig. 1). Differences among dwelling and burial types were accentuated, indicating that an aristocracy of prominent families had formed. A similar type of urban development occurred in many other cities in Etruria and Latium (modern-day Lazio), including Roselle, Veio, Vetulonia, and Tarquinia.

Across Etruria there was a significant change in domestic architecture during the Orientalizing period. Stone houses, presumably elite residences, appeared among the thatched huts. Excavations at Poggio Civitate, near Murlo, have uncovered the remains of a princely residence built during the seventh century B.C. The complex at Poggio Civitate was built of rubble foundations, earthen walls coated with lime plaster, and beaten-earth floors. The roof was tiled and decorated with terra-cotta sculpture. The buildings were placed in a U shape around a central courtyard. Two wings of the complex were residential, while the third served as a workshop for crafts made of metal, glass, pottery, wool, and other materials.

A fire destroyed the Orientalizing period residence, and a second complex was built at Poggio Civitate in the early sixth century B.C., or the beginning of the Archaic period of Etruscan history

(575–470 B.C.). The early Archaic building surrounded a central courtyard, with colonnaded porches on three sides. At least twenty-three statues stood on the peak of the roof, including the famous seated "cowboy" figure, with his distinctive hat. Watchtowers were located at two corners of the complex.

Cemeteries. Cemeteries surrounded Etruscan towns. Early cemeteries were placed next to hilltop settlements; as town populations grew during the Orientalizing period, burial areas spread down the hill. The rock-cut Tomb of the Five Chairs at Cerveteri, dating to the second half of the seventh century B.C., provides some insight into burial rites of the time. The main chamber of the tomb held two bodies, while a side chamber provided space for mourners to worship an ancestor cult. Five chairs were carved from rock to hold terra-cotta statues representing ancestors, two women and three men. The ancestor statues sat before rock-carved tables laden with food offerings. A nearby altar held their drinks. Two empty chairs allowed the buried couple to join their ancestors at the feast.

By the seventh century, burials show clear evidence of status differentiation according to gender, socioeconomic status, and region. While existing burial traditions continued, during the Orientalizing period the elite classes began building elaborate chamber tombs covered with tumuli (mounds). Chamber tombs were carved out from soft volcanic rock faces or built from stone slabs or blocks. Their mounds could be as large as 30–40 meters in diameter and 12–15 meters high. A particularly grand example is the Tomb of the Chariots, Populonium, from the middle of the Orientalizing period (mid-seventh to early sixth century B.C.). Under a tumulus 28 meters in diameter, the tomb contained funerary beds for four occupants. At least one woman, with gold jewelry, was buried in the tomb. She was accompanied by men, who were provided with a chariot and two-wheeled carriage.

Religion. Traditional Etruscan worship in open-air sanctuaries continued during the Orientalizing period, but new religious practices also arose. Influenced by Greek ideas, Etruscans began using enclosed structures for worship and representing gods in human form. The earliest known temple in Etruria, built around 600 B.C., was excavated at Veio. It took the form of a large house; a distinctive architectural form would not be developed for Etruscan temples until the Archaic period.

Economy. By the Orientalizing period the Etruscan agricultural system was specialized and intensified, allowing farmers to support the growing town population. Drainage and irrigation techniques improved poor land, and new farming technologies, such as ironclad wooden plowshares, allowed farmers to work more efficiently. Farmers exchanged their surplus subsistence and luxury foodstuffs for craft goods.

Craft production became increasingly specialized and intensified during the Orientalizing period. Etruscans were adept at numerous arts and crafts, including pottery, metalworking, and sculpture. Technological improvements, learned from the Greeks, transformed Etruscan pottery production. Potters purified clay, built vessels on the fast wheel, and fired them at high temperatures in closed kilns. As production became more specialized and intensified during this period, pottery forms were increasingly standardized and distributed in a wide area. *Bucchero,* a kind of tableware with a distinctive gray core, glossy black surface, and stamped or molded decoration, was a famous Etruscan pottery product of the Orientalizing period. Other fine pottery wares included black figure vase painting, produced locally after eastern Greek models.

Metalworking remained an important industry at this time. Bronze was worked into vessels, utensils, armor, furniture, chariots, and carriages. Metalwork ornamentation was inspired by eastern styles, incorporating floral patterns, animals, humans, and divine figures. Etruscan bronze products were exported widely, throughout the Mediterranean and beyond the Alps. Etruria also was famous for jewelry production, particularly ornaments decorated with gold granulation (using fine beads of gold) and filigree (using fine spiral gold and silver wire). Etruscans probably learned these techniques from the Syrians or the Phoenicians.

Trade grew steadily. Beginning in the eighth century, Etruscans had extensive trade contact with eastern Mediterranean cultures, notably Greece and Phoenicia. Recovered shipwrecks were loaded with Etruscan trade goods: pottery and other crafts and amphorae filled with agricultural products, such as pine nuts, wine, and olives. In exchange, the Etruscans imported the eastern luxury goods found in such abundance in aristocratic graves. Etruscan trade was not administered centrally. Instead, many small political units, controlled by the elite, competed on more or less equal terms. The Greeks also established trade towns on the coast of southern Etruria, and Greek craft producers settled permanently to work in Etruria.

ARCHAIC AND CLASSICAL PERIODS

The Etruscan civilization reached its greatest political and economic significance during the Archaic and Classical periods (575–470 B.C. and 470–300 B.C., respectively). During the sixth and fifth centuries B.C., the powerful Etruscan city-states developed and allied themselves in the League of Twelve Cities. The most important Etruscan cities were Cerveteri, Tarquinia, Vulci, Roselle, Vetulonia, Populonium, Veio, Bolsena, Chiusi, Perugia, Cortona, Arezzo, Fiesole, Volterra, and Pisa. (The number of cities in the league varied through time.) Etruscan city-states were autonomous and had their own sociocultural institutions, spheres of influence, and political and economic institutions. Etruscan political organization was generally oligarchic, with important families controlling the territory of individual city-states. A patron-client system linked families within cities and between cities and the countryside.

During the Archaic period the Etruscans expanded beyond their traditional boundaries, in order to establish new commercial bases. They colonized land as far south as Campania, as far north as the Po valley, and east to the Adriatic coast of Italy. Roman annalists report that the Tarquin dynasty of Etruscan kings was established in Rome throughout much of the Archaic period, from 616 to 509 B.C. Many of these colonized lands were lost during the Classical period.

Settlements. During the Archaic and Classical periods, Etruscan towns developed into city-states—urban centers surrounded by regional territories. In Volterra the process of urbanization is visible in increasing settlement density and in the expansion and reorganization of urban space, including the development of public works, places, and cults. A

great wall circuit was begun during the Classical period, with a perimeter of 7 kilometers enclosing an area of 116 hectares. Traces of the wall are still visible at numerous points, including the city gates of Porta all'Arco and Porta Diana. A network of roads connected the foothills and valley bottom to the city.

Excavations at Acquarossa, in southern Etruria, provide evidence for domestic architecture during the Archaic period. Houses were rectangular, built on stone-block foundations. The walls usually were built of sun-dried mud bricks, supported by a wooden framework, covered with plaster, and painted. Roofs were made of terra-cotta tiles and decorated with statues and other terra-cotta ornaments. The floor plan often included a larger central room in front and two or three smaller rooms in the back. Sometimes a porch protected the doorway. The house interior was used for sleeping, protection from bad weather, and storage of tools and foodstuffs. The adjacent outdoor courtyard was where most daily activities took place. Storage spaces and shelters for cattle were carved into rock outcrops next to the houses. Archaic Acquarossa also included one monumental residential building complex constructed after the mid-sixth century: two buildings laid out in an L-shaped plan, with a large courtyard. The complex boasted a portico in front and revetment plaques on the facade, with scenes of banquets, dancing, warfare, and mythical events.

Marzabotto, an Etruscan colony established in northern Italy at the beginning of the fifth century, was laid out on a regular plan—similar to that of Greek colonial towns and quite different from the plans of settlements that developed through time, such as Volterra and Acquarossa. Four main streets, each 15 meters wide, defined the habitation area of Marzabotto. One north-west street ran the length of the town, and three east-west streets crossed it. Minor streets, each 5 meters wide, ran parallel to the main north-south axis, creating rectangular blocks. Marzabotto's city blocks were filled with mud-brick houses and workshops. Craft workshops—including pottery and tile kilns, iron smithies, bronze foundries, and smelting furnaces—faced the street. Living quarters were located in interior courtyards, reached through narrow passageways. Each courtyard had a cistern to collect rainwater running off the tiled roofs.

Cemeteries. Archaic period cemeteries reflect the development of new "middle" classes. Whereas cemeteries of the previous period comprised many humble tombs and a few dominating tumuli, Archaic period cemeteries consisted of many simple, uniform tombs laid on streets. Examples of Archaic cemeteries include the Banditaccia at Cerveteri and Crocefisso del Tufo at Orvieto, both from the sixth century B.C. The streets of Crocefisso del Tufo were laid out in a grid during the later sixth century, and the cemetery was used throughout the fifth century B.C. The small, rectangular tombs were constructed from tufa stone blocks. Their chambers usually have two stone benches for deposition of the dead. The roofs are made of stone slabs and covered with a modest mound and small stone markers (*cippi*). A view down one of the streets gives a sense of how a residential neighborhood in an Etruscan town might have looked.

A Classical period house interior is re-created in the Tomb of the Reliefs, from the Banditaccia necropolis at Cerveteri, built at the end of the fourth century B.C. The underground tomb was carved from tufa stone; then a stucco surface was applied to the walls and painted. The original owners, a married couple, were represented lying side by side in bed. They are surrounded by relief stucco representations of everything they might need to keep house: utensils, tools, vessels, and even a gaming board. The power of the husband, a magistrate, is indicated by his ivory folding chair, trumpet, and weaponry.

Religion and Temples. During the Archaic period Etruscans continued their own distinctive religious practices, although Etruscan divinities were assimilated with the Greek Olympian gods. Again influenced by the Greeks, Etruscans also began building monumental temples. The Temple of Minerva at Portonaccio, Veio, was constructed in the mid-sixth century B.C. and rebuilt at the end of the century. The Tuscan-style temple is oriented to the east, facing a paved piazza. It has a square plan, each side approximately 18.5 meters. The temple was built on a low podium. Steps at the front of the temple led to a deep porch, or *pronaos*. The *pronaos* had two columns with Tuscan capitals; beyond it was placed the sacrificial altar and a sacred pit where libations to the underworld divinity were poured. At the back

of the temples were three *cellae*, or rooms, side by side.

The foundation, walls, and columns of the Temple of Minerva were built of tufa stone blocks. The wooden roof was decorated with terra-cotta sculpture, a famous product of Veio. The revetments were graced with floral ornamentation; the antefixes included heads of nymphs and masks of the Gorgons, the snake-haired sisters of Greek myth. Painted terra-cotta statues, larger than life size, were placed on the roof ridge. The famous statue of Apollo (now in the Etruscan Museum of Villa Giulia, Rome) probably aimed his bow at Heracles, representing the Greek myth of their conflict over the golden-horned hind of Ceryneia.

Sculpture. Etruscan monumental sculpture typically was executed in terra-cotta or bronze. The Etruscan city of Cerveteri was famous for its terra-cotta sculpture during the Archaic period. One well-known example is a sarcophagus depicting a married couple reclining on a bed, placed in a chamber tomb beneath a tumulus in the Banditaccia necropolis around 525 B.C. (now in the Villa Giulia museum, see fig. 2). The husband lies behind his wife, placing his hand on her shoulder. She pours scented oil onto his palm, a rite for the deceased.

The statue of the Chimera (now in the Archaeological Museum, Florence), is a fine example of Etruscan bronze sculpture. The Chimera was a mythological fire-breathing creature with the body of a lion and heads of a lion, goat, and snake. In this representation, the creature is wounded, suggesting that the statue may have been part of a group that included the hero Bellerophon and his winged horse Pegasus. The statue (or group) probably was created as a votive offering in the late fifth century or early fourth century B.C.

Painting. Tarquinia was the main center of tomb painting during the Archaic period. The rock-cut tombs from the Monterozzi necropolis are small, rectangular chambers with shallow ridge roofs. After about 530 B.C. brightly colored paintings covered entire walls of the chambers. The paintings showed mythological scenes, funerary games and ceremonies, banqueting and entertainment, sports, and scenes of the underworld. The Tomb of the Leopards, from the early fifth century B.C., is a vibrant example.

Fig. 2. Sarcophagus of a married couple, Cerveteri, 530–520 B.C. © ARALDO DE LUCA/CORBIS. REPRODUCED BY PERMISSION.

Economy. The Etruscan economy became increasingly specialized and intensified during the Archaic period. New socioeconomic classes emerged, based in the great city-states and trading towns: manufacturers, crafts producers, and merchants. Internal trade throughout Etruria was effected via coastal waters, rivers, and roads. Long-distance trade was completed in emporia, or trade towns, along the Etruscan coastline. Bronze ingots dating to the early Archaic period probably were used as currency in long-distance trade.

Pottery and metalworking remained important Etruscan industries during the Archaic and Classical periods. Early in the Archaic period the Etruscans created their own versions of red figure pottery, modeled after the famous Greek products. Beginning in the fourth century B.C. a distinctive Etruscan product dominated the pottery industry: tableware coated with a glossy black slip, and decorated with stamped and modeled (relief) motifs. Workshops at Vulci and other Etruscan cities worked bronze into chariots, weapons, armor, vessels, and other utensils. Precious metals, such as gold, were made into jewelry.

Society. Etruscan society changed greatly during the Archaic period. Cities and trade towns supported the growth of new socioeconomic classes—merchants, manufacturers, foreigners—that were not bound by traditional patron-client relationships. These new groups shared common political and economic interests that were at odds with the interests of the established Etruscan aristocracy. Their growing influence and power contributed to the dissolution of the traditional Etruscan social system.

CLASSICAL AND HELLENISTIC PERIODS

During the Classical and Hellenistic periods (470–300 B.C. and 300–31 B.C., respectively), the Etruscans' economic power, political autonomy, and distinctive cultural identity gradually eroded, until the Etruscans no longer existed as a separate people. During the Classical period the Etruscan cities engaged in a series of conflicts over sea and land, which ultimately weakened their economic and political significance in Italy.

At the end of the Classical period, the Roman Republic emerged as the preeminent threat to the

266   ANCIENT EUROPE

autonomy of the Etruscan city-states. In 396 B.C. the first Etruscan city, Veio, fell to the Romans after a brutal ten-year siege. With the Battle of Sentinum in 295 B.C., between Rome and the *Quattuor Gentes* (an alliance of Samnites, Gauls, Umbrians, and certain Etruscans), Rome gained supremacy over the entire Italian peninsula. After 270 B.C. relations were largely peaceful between the Etruscans and Romans. Rome began to colonize southern Etruria in the third century B.C. During the second century B.C. the Romans built the via Aurelia, via Clodia, and via Cassia, roads that provided them with communication and control over all of Etruria. By the first century B.C. Etruria was no longer a separate entity, politically or culturally; instead, it was part of the growing Roman state. In 89 B.C. all residents of Etruria were given Roman citizenship and registered in Roman tribes for bureaucratic and voting purposes. By the end of the first century B.C. Etruria for the most part was Latin speaking and assimilated into Roman culture.

Settlements and Cemeteries. The conflicts of the Classical and Hellenistic periods (the fifth to first centuries B.C.) affected the Etruscan city-states differently. Whereas many Etruscan cities in the south were hurt by the maritime and territorial wars, other cities in the north continued to thrive. Volterra was minimally affected by the upheaval during late Etruscan times. The Hellenistic period was, in fact, a time of great urban development and renovation. Public works—including roads, agricultural terraces, city walls, and religious and civic structures—allowed settlement in the Volterra on a far greater scale than before. The city walls, begun during the late Classical period, were completed during the Hellenistic period. The city also was provided with terracing walls, a sewer, and a drainage and canal system. Hellenistic period Volterrans created lavish tombs for their dead in the cemeteries surrounding the city. The Inghirami Tomb from the Ulimeto necropolis, in use from the early second century to the mid-first century B.C., includes several elaborately carved alabaster ash urns, a local artisanal product. The tomb is reproduced in the garden of the Archaeological Museum in Florence.

Etruscan Legacy. Although the Etruscans ceased to exist as a distinct culture in the first century B.C., their people and ideas remained essential to life in central Italy. Etruscans—now Roman citizens—were integrated into the politics, economics, culture, and society of Rome. A few specifically Etruscan contributions to Roman institutions remind us of their presence in later times. The symbols of Roman office—the *fasces* (bundled and tied rods with a projecting axe) and the *curule* (a folding chair)—are derived from Etruscan examples. The Romans adopted rituals of military triumph from the Etruscans. The Roman toga originated as the Etruscan mantle. And many of the most famous architectural and engineering feats of the Romans—houses, temples, tombs, roads, bridges, and sewers—were first achieved in Italy by the Etruscans.

See also **The Italian Bronze Age** (*vol. 2, part 5*); **Iron Age Germany** (*vol. 2, part 6*).

BIBLIOGRAPHY

Banti, Luisa. *Etruscan Cities and Their Culture*. Translated by Erika Bizzarri. Berkeley: University of California Press, 1973.

Barker, Graeme, and Tom Rasmussen. *The Etruscans*. Oxford: Blackwell, 1998.

Boëthius, Axel. *Etruscan and Roman Architecture*. Harmondsworth, U.K.: Penguin, 1970.

Bonfante, Giuliano, and Larissa Bonfante. *The Etruscan Language: An Introduction*. 2d ed. Manchester, U.K.: Manchester University Press, 2002.

Bonfante, Larissa, ed. *Etruscan Life and Afterlife: A Handbook of Etruscan Studies*. Detroit, Mich.: Wayne State University Press, 1986.

Brendel, Otto J. *Etruscan Art*. New Haven, Conn.: Yale University Press, 1995.

Carratelli, Giovanni Pugliese, ed. *Rasenna: Storia e civiltà degli etruschi*. Milan: Libri Scheiwiller, 1986.

Cornell, T. J. *The Beginnings of Rome: Italy and Rome from the Bronze Age to the Punic Wars, c. 1000–263 BC*. London: Routledge, 1995.

Haynes, Sybille. *Etruscan Civilization: A Cultural History*. Los Angeles: J. Paul Getty Museum, 2000.

Lawrence, D. H. *Etruscan Places*. London: Secker, 1932.

Macnamara, Ellen. *The Etruscans*. Cambridge, Mass.: Harvard University Press, 1991.

Pallottino, Massimo. *The Etruscans*. Translated by J. Cremona and edited by David Ridgway. Harmondsworth, U.K.: Penguin, 1975.

Ridgway, David, and Francesca R. Ridgway, eds. *Italy before the Romans: The Iron Age, Orientalizing, and Etruscan Periods*. London: Academic Press, 1979.

Spivey, Nigel J. *Etruscan Art*. New York: Thames and Hudson, 1997.

Spivey, Nigel, and Simon Stoddard. *Etruscan Italy: An Archaeological History.* London: B. T. Batsford, 1990.

Sprenger, Maja, and Gilda Bartoloni. *The Etruscans: Their History, Art, and Architecture.* Translated by Robert Erich Wolf. New York: H. N. Abrams, 1983.

Torelli, Mario, ed. *The Etruscans.* New York: Rizzoli, 2001.

RAE OSTMAN

PRE-ROMAN IRON AGE SCANDINAVIA

The Iron Age in Scandinavia lasted for about fifteen hundred years and archaeologists have divided it into a number of distinct chronological phases. The Early Iron Age, also called the pre-Roman Iron Age or the Celtic Iron Age, spans the first five hundred years of the period, from 500 B.C. to 1 B.C. It was during this time that a technological revolution took place that brought the Bronze Age to an end. Bronze was replaced by iron in most tools and weapons. Like the use of bronze, the use of iron was introduced from central Europe; but iron, unlike bronze, did not need to be imported. Known as bog-ore or lake-ore, it precipitated in small clumps below the peat in marshy pools and was a readily accessible raw material. Plentiful resources existed in southern Norway, Sweden, and Denmark. The ore contained many impurities and was not of very high quality, but the Scandinavians developed efficient techniques for extracting serviceable iron by smelting it in simple furnaces. As the skill developed over the centuries, so did the complexity of the tools and weapons, until they were comparable to many others made elsewhere in Europe.

NECK RINGS

During the pre-Roman Iron Age, society was organized by rank. Neck rings were a marker of elite status. Large bronze neck rings, especially the so-called crown neck rings and individual rings with transverse molded bands, are a characteristic element of the set of finds dating to the pre-Roman Iron Age. Altogether, there are forty-seven such rings from Denmark with clear provenances. There are also three Celtic rings. The majority of the bronze neck rings are bog finds; a few are dry-land finds, but none is a grave find. All are individual finds, that is, they are found without any associated goods. Some arm rings and simple neck rings have also been found. They are also bog finds and occasionally appear in cremation burials. The looped ring, another traditional object of this period, was made either of bronze or iron. The majority of the recovered objects that have been fashioned in this way are made of iron. Large iron looped rings are known only as grave finds; such rings would presumably have rusted away in bogs. Looped rings, with a few exceptions, are known only from Jutland. Small and large looped rings are contemporary to each other, and can be seen in the large ring hoards.

BOG OFFERINGS

When land was drained for modern farming, a number of bog burial grounds were found. Bog offerings are archaeologically recorded as early as Neolithic times and into the pre-Viking period. These votive offerings or sacrifices included weapons and even warships as well as human bodies, animals, and assorted artifacts. It is postulated, based on the variety and type of offerings, that they were of a ceremonial nature, part of a fertility ritual or a ritual to ensure success in battle. The earliest bog offerings in the Neolithic period consisted primarily of stone and flint weapons. In the Bronze Age, there were more elaborate sacrifices. Collections of personal items and household objects, such as cauldrons, were recovered as well. Weapons—swords in particular—have also been found. Very often the blades of these swords have been bent back or otherwise damaged, and some argue that this was done to represent a ritual "killing" of an enemy. Animals, particularly horses, were also slaughtered as part of the ritual.

HUMAN SACRIFICE

Human sacrifice seems to have become widespread in the first century B.C. Most of the evidence comes from Danish bog areas, where the bodies of the men and women who were killed have been preserved in the acid soils of peat bogs under anaerobic conditions. The skin, hair, and, in some cases, stomach contents of these bodies have been preserved by the tannins in the peat soils. This extraordinary state of preservation has allowed archaeologists to learn details about the clothing, hairstyles, and diet of these people. Tollund man, a body discovered at Tollund, Denmark, in 1950, is one of the best-preserved bog bodies. He was unclothed except for a leather girdle and a leather cap that was laced across his chin. His last meal was gruel. Around his neck was a hide rope with which he had been strangled before being submerged in the bog. Tollund man is now on display in the Silkeborg Museum in Denmark.

Another example is Grauballe man, also from Silkeborg, who was found to have eaten a final meal of porridge containing chiefly barley, oats, and emmer wheat, along with some weed seeds, shortly before he had his throat cut. He was killed sometime in the first century B.C.

CAULDRONS, WAGONS, AND WEAPONS

The Roman Iron Age and the Migration period saw a return to sacrificial offerings consisting predominantly of weapons. From the later part of the pre-Roman Iron Age, between nineteen and twenty-one cauldrons have been recovered from bogs or in graves. Few were located on dry land. The cauldrons found in bogs and those found on dry land are all individual finds. Cauldrons from graves frequently contain a rich set of associated finds with a full set of weapons (sword, shield, and javelin/lance) and gold finger rings.

The find material of this period becomes markedly variegated, and various imported luxurious items enter the archaeological record. Particularly striking are the two large Celtic display wagons from the Dejbjerg bog in Denmark. The remains of comparable wagons are also known from two cremation burials, one from Langå on Fyn, and one from Kraghede in north Jutland. Imported swords are also found in both bogs and graves.

Swords tend to be solitary finds. Two major weapon deposits of this period are located at Hjortspring bog and Krogsbølle bog. The great majority of the recoverable archaeological wealth was deposited in hoards during two periods: the early pre-Roman Iron Age and the early Germanic Iron Age. The finds of rings from the early pre-Roman Iron Age are usually interpreted as votive deposits. In the Smederup bog in eastern Jutland, a plank-built well was found not far from the place where great quantities of rings were dug up. It is regarded as a votive well and may therefore emphasize the sacred character of the bog. Artifact studies have shown that artifact types deposited in the bogs of one area are not deposited in graves of the same area.

Two artifacts of great importance have Celtic origins. One is the Gundestrup cauldron, a silver bowl with highly realistic embellishments in relief, including a representation of a human sacrifice; it has been suggested that it was used for catching a victim's blood. Another interesting find is the Hjortspring boat, a war canoe that was unearthed on the island of Als off southeastern Jutland. This canoe carried between twenty-two and twenty-four paddlers and is the oldest surviving example of a boat in Scandinavia. It contained deliberately damaged war equipment, including some single-edged iron swords, which were evidently ceremonial offerings. Studies have concluded that this was a religious deposition of the hoards.

A DECLINE IN POPULATION

One surprising aspect of this period is that it has yielded relatively few archaeological remains. Earlier archaeologists, who worked primarily with grave finds, viewed the pre-Roman Iron Age as a regression period and, in some areas, such as Trøndelag, Norway, it would appear there was virtually no use of iron. This suggests that the population had declined. Although these early centuries remain comparatively obscure, since very few settlements are known from this period, in the 1990s and 2000s, thanks to a change of focus from grave goods to habitation sites, modern archaeological research has been able to contribute tremendously to our understanding of the pre-Roman Iron Age, providing a new picture of society, especially in southern Scandinavia. In fact, settlement development from the Bronze Age to the Early Roman Iron Age now appears to have been continuous. Certainly the climate, which for about two thousand years had been drier than it is now, became both wetter and colder, so that, toward the north, deciduous trees began to disappear and the glaciers began to re-form on the high ground. Investigations of Danish raised bogs have shown that the climate has fluctuated over the past 5,500 years and that these fluctuations lasted for about 260 years. The climatic changes in the final phase of prehistory can be located with great accuracy. A trend toward increased precipitation and lower summer temperatures set in about 600 B.C., just before the transition to the pre-Roman Iron Age. The next fluctuation took place about 300 B.C., and yet another very close to A.D. 0. This climatic deterioration probably affected the efficiency of farming.

LAND-USE PATTERNS

In southern Scandinavia, the late pre-Roman Iron Age was characterized by woodlands that expanded at the expense of open land (pastures, arable land). This may have been caused by a concentration of settlement in permanent farms and villages. This means that the late pre-Roman Iron Age landscape, broadly speaking, was similar to the Late Bronze Age landscape. On a smaller scale, however, it differed in the organization and land-use pattern of its permanent villages: infields with arable fields and meadows around the farms, and outland with pastures and coppiced woods. In general, the transition to the pre-Roman Iron Age in Sweden did not bring about any sudden restructuring of agriculture. The farms were still isolated, with longhouses the same size as they had been during the Late Bronze Age, with room for one extended family.

This was different from Jutland. There, longhouses became much smaller in the pre-Roman Iron Age, with room for only one family household, but with many houses clustered together like villages. In Scania there were no villages prior to about A.D. 500, unlike in other parts of "Denmark." Before that, in the Bronze Age and pre-Roman Iron Age, there were single farms with Celtic fields, probably under shifting cultivation, which slightly

later developed into double or triple farms that seem to have belonged to kin-groups rather than constituting true villages. Nucleated villages were first founded between A.D. 500 and 700. Single farms were not established again with any regularity until the Early Middle Ages.

In Sweden, the excavations of the Skrea project in Halland have unearthed a number of large-scale settlements ranging from the Late Bronze Age to the Early Iron Age. While damage from modern agricultural activities has compromised the preservation of some of the sites, there is still a large quantity of information identifying the settlements as large agrarian units. These settlements are located at dry ridges, often composed of glaciofluvial deposits or other self-draining soil types. Those dry areas were used for living and farming. Vast grounds consisting of heavier soil types suitable for grazing and for hay crops surrounded them. In all archaeological work thus far there has been a clear correlation of site type to soil type. These settlements were inhabited for fifteen hundred to two thousand years, some even longer.

A second type of settlement is smaller and more sporadic. It tends to correlate with different landscape zones, however. Some are on small ridges in otherwise wet areas or in areas with relatively small-scale landscapes. The relationship between the two scales of settlements remains unclear.

Another key site for looking at architecture and settlement is located on the tofts of Lilla Köpinge village. It is in southeastern Scania, near the medieval town of Ystad. It was the subject of intensive investigations, along with Stora Köpinge, which is one of the emporium-like market sites founded in the 800s. Each farm appears to have had its own fixed site, on which several layers of longhouses can be found. The longhouses are relatively large: 17 by 26 by 5.6 meters. Their overall area is not much larger than that of longhouses in the Late Bronze Age, but the greater length of the buildings made it possible to house a greater number of livestock. The farms also had some smaller buildings, including sunken-floor huts, which were used primarily for weaving. In Denmark, the first sunken-floor huts do not appear before the late Roman Iron Age. In the Köpinge area, by contrast, there is concrete evidence dating them to the pre-Roman Iron Age.

MOBILE SETTLEMENTS

One of the observations made for this period is that the settlement was mobile and that villages moved from time to time. Over the long term, they may have come to remain in the same place for longer periods. The greater or lesser mobility of the village communities of this period was first revealed with the extensive excavations at Grøntoft. Grøntoft is a rural settlement in western Jutland dating from about A.D. 200, and it provides invaluable information on these Early Iron Age farmers. The settlers must have lived in buildings very similar to those of their Bronze Age predecessors, grouped in villages surrounded by fences. The excavations reveal a single "wandering village" in the same resource territory for a period of about three hundred years. Grøntoft probably housed about fifty people and about sixty cattle, but it is difficult to know how representative this site is of the period. The houses are of three-aisled construction, which is found at all the Danish Iron Age settlements. This construction dates as far back as the middle of the second millennium B.C. In about 500 B.C., it evolved into a rectangular house shape unvaryingly oriented east-west, with a roof supported by two parallel rows of interior posts. Entrances were found in both long sides of the house. The walls of the houses were sometimes made of massive or light timber and with wattle and daub. There were sometimes also massive earthen and turf walls. The houses were often divided into two sections: the east end sheltered cattle while the west end with the hearth was for human dwelling. The dwelling section often had a clay floor while the barn may have had a stone-paved gutter and stall partitions. At all stages, the village economy strongly emphasized animal husbandry. Houses without stalls did exist, however. When an individual house went out of use, it was torn down and moved to another site within the village territory. The old site was plowed over and the soil was again tilled. The constant moving shifted the original field boundaries marked by balks. The balks (forming the so-called Celtic fields), which were visible at the excavations and thus stem from many phases of cultivation, may have been separated by land left fallow for a period of time. There is evidence of fences dating to roughly 300 B.C.; these were probably used to protect the village and the houses from the cattle.

There are other signs that rural settlements were increasing in number and size toward the end of the Early Iron Age. Many of the Danish settlement sites were excavated in the early 1990s. However, while Grøntoft has the most extensive chronology and has been thoroughly studied, more sites dating closer to the centuries around A.D. 1 provide further information on mobile village communities.

HODDE

Excavations at Hodde, Jutland, began in the 1970s. Hodde is typical of first-century B.C. rural settlement and has many traits that are present in Danish villages up to the beginning of the Viking Age. At its greatest extent, Hodde consisted of twenty-seven farmsteads. Each was composed of a longhouse with dwelling and cattle barn under the same roof, and a few smaller subsidiary buildings, perhaps barns or workshops. A fence surrounded each building complex, and a common fence, pierced by gateways affording direct access from each farmstead to its field, enclosed the entire village. There was an open area in the center of the settlement. One of the farmsteads, larger than the rest, may have been the residence of a chieftain. While some evidence of blacksmithing, pottery making, weaving, and spinning does exist, the primary economic activities were cattle breeding and crop raising, in keeping with the traditions of the Bronze Age but on a much larger scale. Other sites in Jutland show that, alongside such villages, there were also smaller agricultural settlements with only two or three farms, but we do not know why there were such great variations in the scale of settlement in the Danish countryside.

OTHER SETTLEMENTS

The evidence of house construction that is apparent in the Danish material cannot be detected in Köpinge, Scania (Sweden). Instead there are small, gradual changes. Continuity in settlement development in the Köpinge area—as in Denmark—from the pre-Roman Iron Age to the Early Roman Iron Age is apparent, in that many sites date to both periods. No stall partitions have been documented, unlike the case in Denmark. Nor does the relatively regular placement of the pairs of roof-bearing posts give us any guidance about the existence of stalls. Conversely, the length of the houses and the location of the hearths seem to indicate that one end was used as a barn, and that more animals were housed there than was the case in the Late Bronze Age. As with the structure of settlement, the archaeological material clearly demonstrates that these were isolated farmsteads. Only toward the end of the period do we find evidence of agglomerated settlements of two or more farms.

Information about the mobility of the Iron Age village society can also be gleaned elsewhere in Denmark, for example, in the low marsh regions by the North Sea in the south of Jutland, where the large migrating villages are characteristic of the period. At Drengsted, a very small area was found to contain a series of settlements, some with cemeteries dating from the first century B.C. to the fifth century A.D. At Dankirke in southwestern Jutland, a small area was found to contain several settlements, with their cemeteries dating from the same time period. In Grøntoft, Hodde, Drengsted, and Dankirke, the patterns seem to be identical. Over the centuries, mobile village communities centered around large herds of cattle moved around within narrowly defined resource territories.

REGIONAL VARIATIONS

The period of 200 B.C. to A.D. 200 is characterized by a warm, dry climate favorable for cereal cultivation. Descriptions of the cultural landscape and of land use in the Early Iron Age have long borne the stamp of the archaeological material from Jutland and areas preserving a fossilized cultivation landscape, such as Gotland and Östergötland. It is usually thought that most regions in southern Scandinavia underwent the same development at roughly the same time, not just of the cultural landscape but also in social and political terms; it is only as a result of differences in the form of the natural landscape in different regions that this development can be studied today, and then only in certain regions. In recent years large regional and local variations have become more evident, not just between areas with a fossilized cultivation landscape and those without, but also within each category. In Köpinge, it is impossible to know whether the farms in the area cooperated in any form of joint fencing, or what type of cultivation system was used. Analyses of carbonized plant material from the habitation sites show, however, that hulled barley had become the main crop and that weeds like *Chenopodium* had become

more common, which indicates the presence of manured fields. The meadow plants in the material can be interpreted as hay waste and evidence of the stalling of animals. Traces of the production and working of iron have been documented. Iron extraction may also have led to the establishment of special habitation sites, as in the Krageholm area. Manuring and cultivation switch are also seen in the Bjaresjo area of Sweden.

CAIRN FIELDS AND CULTIVATION STYLES

In Norway in the early 1980s, there were systematic investigations of some cairn fields that had previously been interpreted as grave fields. Cairns are formed from clearing a field in preparation for plowing. They are simply rock piles. The typical clearance cairn field is characterized by a dense pattern of small cairns. These may belong to an extensive or to an intensive strategy of cultivation. The two strategies can coexist. Clearance cairn fields are characterized by a lack of internal boundaries, the usual evidence of a permanent arable field. The spatial organization of the cairn fields has no relation to the territorial division of farms from historical times. Phosphate analysis has located several settlements within the same cairn field. There are indications that the settlements had been abandoned and then used as arable fields. In some cases several phases of this cycle can be documented. This phenomenon is similar to what was occurring in the same period in the Danish village of Grøntoft.

Most prehistoric houses are found in Jaeren and Lista in Norway and belonged to the Roman Iron Age and the Migration period. They are three-aisled longhouses with stone walls. It was assumed that these house remains represented the first farms in Norway, which were the result of the climatic change in the pre-Roman Iron Age. That change forced people to house their cattle indoors and to collect winter fodder. Research in the 1990s and early 2000s indicates that the settlement change in southwestern Norway was caused by a shift to a more intensive type of cultivation. No one has found the houses from the first millennium B.C. because the farming system was based on bush fallow and shifting cultivation. In southwestern Norway, it was assumed that the clearance cairn field areas were evidence of extensive cultivation in the Bronze Age and the pre-Roman Iron Age. For a long time, however, settlement history in eastern Norway was written primarily on the basis of place names, graves, and archaeological artifacts. Extensive archaeological investigations in eastern Norway in the 1990s and early 2000s have located an increasing number of Bronze and Iron Age houses. More than twenty different settlement sites have been investigated, partly as research excavations, and partly in conjunction with rescue excavations (e.g., for the new Oslo airport at Gardermoen). These are found primarily in the presently cultivated lands—under the tilth. This means a large material culture is now available, consisting of buildings from the Bronze and Iron Ages.

The study of the principal house types that resulted from these excavations suggests that one principal type dominated from the Bronze Age to the Migration period. The three-aisled buildings were 15 meters long or more. As in contemporary cases from Denmark and Scania, there are indications of separate dwelling and cattle compartments. Each farmstead had two or three houses. This evidence dates the beginning of the "historical farm" to the Bronze Age. The cattle compartments show that cattle were stalled indoors and that winter fodder may have been collected. Within this system it must have been possible to collect manure and spread it on the fields. Therefore there is the possibility that an intensive type of cultivation was associated with the cairns.

The results of these investigations are consistent with the results from the cairns. Many house structures are contemporary with the field clearance cairns. The spatial organization of the cairn fields has no relation to the territorial division of the farms from historical times. At the site of Einang in Valdres, Norway, situated on the outlying lands of three different historical farm territories, the cairn field is located on the hillside, in an area which, in recent times, has been used chiefly as a pasture. The recent farmsteads, by contrast, are located along the valley bottom. They have prehistoric names and, in the graves associated with them, artifacts from the Late Iron Age have been found. In the clearance cairn, conversely, the graves contained artifacts from the Roman period. A pollen analysis shows that this area was cultivated continuously from the Late Bronze Age to the Migration period. The evidence from this locality points to a radical change in the structure of the landscape in the middle of the first millennium.

Sites from northern Norway show mixed economies of farming and fishing and individual farms rather than settlement complexes. Archaeological information coming from sites such as Bleik and Toften in Andøya point to a heavy exploitation of local marine resources and the beginnings of production of cured fish.

See also **Tollund Man** (*vol. 1, part 1*); **Hjortspring** (*vol. 1, part 1*); **Emporia** (*vol. 2, part 7*); **Pre-Viking and Viking Age Norway** (*vol. 2, part 7*); **Pre-Viking and Viking Age Sweden** (*vol. 2, part 7*); **Pre-Viking and Viking Age Denmark** (*vol. 2, part 7*).

BIBLIOGRAPHY

Batey, Colleen E., and James Graham-Cambell, eds. *Cultural Atlas of the Viking World*. London: BCA, 1994.

Becker, C. J. "Früheisenzeitliche Dörfer bei Grøntoft. Westjütland. 3. Vorbericht: Die Ausgrabungen 1967–68." *Acta Archaeologica* 42 (1971): 79–110.

Berglund, Björn E., ed. *The Cultural Landscape during 6000 Years in Southern Sweden: The Ystad Project*. Ecological Bulletins, no. 41. Copenhagen, Denmark: Munksgaard International, 1991.

Callmer, J. "The Process of Village Formation." In *The Cultural Landscape during 6000 Years in Southern Sweden: The Ystad Project*. Edited by Björn E. Berglund, pp. 337–349. Ecological Bulletins, no. 41. Copenhagen, Denmark: Munksgaard International, 1991.

Derry, T. K. *A History of Scandinavia: Norway, Sweden, Denmark, Finland, and Iceland*. Minneapolis: University of Minnesota Press, 1979.

Fabech, Charlotte, and Jytte Ringtved, eds. *Settlement and Landscape: Proceedings of a Conference in Århus, Denmark, May 4–7, 1998*. Moesgård, Højbjerg, Denmark: Jutland Archaeological Society, 1999.

Hedeager, Lotte. *Iron-Age Societies: From Tribe to State in Northern Europe, 500 B.C. to A.D. 700*. Cambridge, Mass.: Blackwell, 1992.

Helliksen, Wenche. *Gård og utmark på Romerike 1100 f.Kr.–1400 e.Kr.: Gardermoprosjektet* [Farm and periphery in Romerike from 1100 B.C.–A.D. 1400: The Gardermoen project]. Varia, no. 45. Oslo, Norway: Universitets Oldsaksamling, 1997.

Hvass, Steen *Hodde. Et vestjysk landsbysamfund fra ældre jernalder* [A western rural society from the Older Iron Age]. Arkæologiske studier, vol. 7. Copenhagen, Denmark: Akademisk forlag, 1985.

Jensen, Jørgen. *The Prehistory of Denmark*. New York: Methuen, 1982.

Myhre, Bjørn. "Agrarian Development, Settlement History, and Social Organization in Southwest Norway in the Iron Age." In *New Directions in Scandinavian Archaeology*. Edited by Kristian Kristiansen and Carsten Paludan-Müller, pp. 224–271. Copenhagen: National Museum of Denmark, 1979.

Näsman, Ulf. "Hus, landsby, bebyggelse [House, rural settlement, and structures]." In *Danmarks længste udgravning: Arkæologi på naturgassens vej 1979–86* [Denmark's longest excavation], pp. 69–86. Copenhagen, Denmark: n.p., 1987.

SOPHIA PERDIKARIS

IRON AGE FINLAND

The topography, natural vegetation, and soil environments of Finland vary substantially. In the southwest region, encompassing the Åland Islands and Varsinais Suomi, a warmer climate marked by the greatest occurrence of deciduous tree growth in Finland led to earlier agricultural development. Safe natural harbors promoted the use of resources from the sea and trade with foreign ships. The west coast of Ostrobothnia had good water access and useful connections with Sweden. The south coast of Uusimaa, on the other hand, was unprotected and forbidding to access by ship. The heavy clay soils found there were unsuitable for cultivation unaided by a plow. Finnish farmers preferred to plant in small forest clearings and to use rotational slash-and-burn methods for preparing the soil. Thus, lighter, fine-grained soils found north of Uusimaa were favored. The interior of Finland, characterized by birch and pine forests and a complex system of lakes and rivers formed amid glacial moraines, was in many places not settled by farmers until the Late Iron Age and medieval times, but its rich hunting and fishing resources were utilized by Finns throughout the Iron Age. The soils of the interior are mostly highly acidic with only a very thin humus layer and are packed in most locations with many surface stones. These soils would rarely be adaptable to intensive plowed-field techniques of cultivation. The waterways were well-used routes of communication, especially during winter months when surfaces were frozen. Finns frequently moved through these water systems while on hunting, fishing, or trading expeditions.

CHRONOLOGY

The five-hundred-year period starting 500 B.C. in Finland is called the pre-Roman Iron Age. For a thousand years prior, the Bronze Age Finns had maintained lively contacts with their Baltic neighbors, including the Scandinavians. Immigrants from Sweden had settled along some of the coastal areas. But in the period after 500 B.C., more Germanic contacts and influences arrived, including a number of loan words and a greater dependence on agriculture. Southern Finns now became more aware of the proto-Saami peoples who lived in the interior. In the Early Iron Age, the Saami lived, herded, and hunted farther south than several centuries later. Their present situation is now far to the north. Other Finnish connections with Finno-Ugric tribes to the east promoted trade of bronze or iron goods.

Some scholars have seen in the archaeological record evidence that the beginning of the Iron Age in Finland is marked by a decline in settlement and a general impoverishment of the population, although the reasons for this having occurred have never been clear. By the late twentieth century, most archaeologists argued for a continuation of population and settlement in Finland. Changing living and burial habits may account for the lessening of some aspects of cultural visibility in the archaeological record. In particular, fewer metal objects have been found from graves of the Early Iron Age, but when archaeologists have focused their search, they have sometimes found dwelling sites easier to

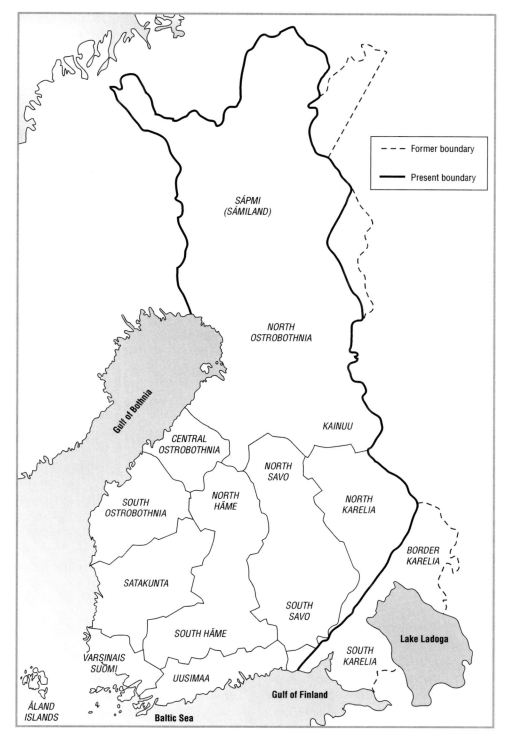

Provinces and traditional cultural regions of Finland. ADAPTED FROM TALVE 1997.

locate than the corresponding burial sites. This experience is the opposite of what Late Iron Age archaeologists have found. Later Iron Age burial sites have been more readily located.

Iron came to Finland c. 500 B.C., and by the Roman period (A.D. 1–400), local iron production is clearly in evidence. Iron tools and weapons were still rare in finds (meaning, for the most part, from

Fig. 1. Provincial Roman glass drinking horn decorated in blue and opaque white, reconstructed from pieces found in fourth-century grave at Varsinais Suomi. NATIONAL BOARD OF ANTIQUITIES FINLAND/HARALD MALMGREN 1966. REPRODUCED BY PERMISSION.

graves), but by the end of the first millennium A.D., all parts of Finland had some iron. It is this lack of metal finds (either of bronze or iron) from the Early Iron Age that has created the impression, perhaps the illusion, that the period was more impoverished than what had come before or what came after. The situation changed within a few centuries, however. Already in the Roman period, material culture, as evidenced by the abundance of artifacts recovered, shows visible prosperity returning to the country.

REGIONS OF FINLAND

During the first millennium A.D., Finnish tribes in the east were moving westward, and new immigrants expanded the existing population of Finland. Other Finns from nearby Baltic lands also moved into Finland. To the west, the population of the Åland Islands and Varsinais Suomi was growing through an influx of Germanic settlers. A 1990s research project conducted around Paimio in Varsinais Suomi included the excavation of a burial ground and dwelling sites near Spurila and a variety of botanical, pollen core, and phosphorus studies that reveal signs of human activity. The burial ground was in use from the first century A.D. into the eighth century. Datable artifacts, mainly brooches, span the period from c. A.D. 100 to 600.

Artifact types indicate connections both with the southern Baltic shore and southern Scandinavia. One dwelling site was dated c. A.D. 400. Pollen cores show intermittent slash-and-burn activity during the early period under consideration here, although the earliest cultivation seems to date from the pre-Roman period. Palaeoethnobotanical studies of plant remains recovered from early soil layers demonstrate that the settlers of Paimio grew mainly emmer wheat and flax. The occurrence of common cultivation weeds also indicates the presence of human agriculture.

Settlement in south Ostrobothnia was limited. At Trofastbacken, Korsnäs, a pre-Roman Iron Age house with hearth, pottery remains, and a wide stone foundation supporting turf walls has been interpreted as a base structure for seasonal activity. Occupied probably only in the spring, this house provided shelter for hunters who came to this locality to hunt seal from the ice surface. Iron Age peoples occupied the coast of northern Ostrobothnia as well. Small settlements dating from the first six centuries A.D. show close Scandinavian ties across the Gulf of Bothnia. A system of barter trade was conducted at numerous points along the shores. One impetus for this trade was the presence of the early proto–market town of Helgö, precursor to Birka in the Lake Mälar region of eastern Sweden. Helgö, which began as early as the fourth century A.D., has been described as a production and trading center supported by chieftains in the area. Ostrobothnians may have been particularly interested in trading with the Swedes for bronze ingots and ornaments. In return they could have offered fur pelts. The Finnish word *raha* has come to mean "money," but originally it meant "fur pelt." Barter trade with pelts could have become so ubiquitous in the region that the pelt itself became a kind of currency.

A similar trade situation developed in the eastern Baltic, across the Gulf of Finland, between Finns and Estonians. Fisherman of individual households or extended families developed and maintained pre-arranged trade relations with household counterparts on the opposite coast by bartering Baltic herring for grain and other cultivated foodstuffs difficult to grow in the coastal soils of southern Finland. This kind of household economy and arrangement for trade relations was typical of the Finns, for whom the extended family or kin group was the most important social and economic unit. Such households might sometimes consist of thirty or more people pooling their labor and production skills.

In what is now known as Russian Karelia, at the eastern side of present-day Finland, pollen and charcoal analysis of lake sediments reveals that there was some human impact in this area during the pre-Roman Iron Age (500 B.C.– A.D. 1), but no significant land clearance occurred until much later, during the Late Iron Age.

THE SAAMI

In A.D. 98, Tacitus, the Roman historian, wrote in his book *Germania* that a tribe he called the Fenni lived at the northern fringes of the Roman Empire. He described the Fenni as wild and very poor, having no weapons, horses, or houses. If his information were to be presumed at all correct, he could not have been talking about the southern Finns, although this description might fit the proto-Saami of northern Finland. Terms such as "Fenni," "Finni," and "Phinnoi" were used by classical writers in the first several centuries A.D. primarily to describe the nomadic people of northern Scandinavia. Since these people were so far away from the writers and their audiences, some of the descriptions are completely fantastical.

The Saami are the indigenous people of Scandinavia. They were a hunting and nomadic herding culture living in symbiosis with the large reindeer herds of the region. Until they were pushed to the northern territories in postmedieval times, the Saami lived as far south as the central interior of Finland. Their skill at hunting the arctic animals whose rich fur pelts were prized as luxury items by Europeans and others farther south forced the Saami into trade relations with both Scandinavians and Finno-Ugric tribes during the Viking and medieval periods.

THE PICTURE FROM ARCHAEOLOGY

Most Iron Age archaeological remains from Finland come from burials. Finnish burials of the period are often found in large stone cairns situated overlooking the sea or a lake. Many of the early cemeteries, from the first century A.D., are found near the mouths of rivers. Some of the largest cemeteries resemble the *tarand* type known from Estonia. This type is characterized by rectangular enclosures outlined on the ground with stones. The cemeteries grew as new rectangles were added. The appearance of *tarand* cemeteries in Finland marks closer contacts with, and also immigration of, Estonian farmers. Various other styles of burial, including inhumations and cremation burials in urns, are known from this time. Over time stone cairns become on average smaller, and various forms of cremation pit cemeteries appear. Archaeologists caution that not all stone cairns of this period contain burials, and some may have nothing to do with human burial.

Not only do certain types of graves characterize the early part of the Iron Age, but grave contents are important as well. During the Early Roman Iron Age, we see for the first time graves including weapons in Finland. These weapon graves occur, for the most part, in coastal areas from the first century A.D. Two distinct groups can be observed among the graves: individuals buried with a spearhead only and others buried with a bigger assemblage consisting often of a sword and shield plus spear. Most of these graves are from southwest Finland and southern Ostrobothnia. Archaeologists sometimes attribute the appearance of weapon graves to the rise of a social class of warriors or special class of persons in authority. However, spears can also be used as hunting weapons and are easier to obtain since they require less skill and labor to be made. The social class of males buried with spears alone is therefore ambiguous. Normally archaeologists assume that individuals buried with weapons are male. Where skeletal remains are adequate, it is usually possible to confirm this by a visual assessment of the bones. With the advent of DNA testing of archaeological remains, however, some surprising gender-role contradictions appeared in Iron Age remains from Europe. Although these exceptions are quite rare, they only serve to emphasize that the bearing of weapons can be a mark of social status and not merely an indicator of occupation.

IRON AGE SOCIETY

The Finnish worldview during the Iron Age was cyclical in type, meaning that all things were seen to progress in cycles. The seasons revolved; life germinated, flourished, and died; and human beings lived to be reincarnated from the kin-based groups of ancestral spirits. Ancestor worship and shamanic communication with the spirit world were major elements of this religion. Carvings on rock, called rock art, may depict the activities of Finnish shamans seeking favors from spirits, such as requests for hunting luck. Shamans would also intervene in order to try to cure illnesses afflicting humans or domestic animals.

The kin group, which was so important socially and economically, also played a religious role. Folklore evidence strongly indicates that pre-Christian Finns did not so much worship generalized ancestors but rather venerated and appealed for help from the ancestors of their own kin group. There was a close and intense relationship between the living community and the family cemetery. This was made closer by the belief that babies born into the family brought back to life in a new identity the spirits of those who had lived before. It was a complex worldview that suited the Finns' annual struggle with the not always kind forces of nature and provided them with a great deal of psychological support. Existence in rural Finland could easily become marginal with one bad harvest, and extended periods of rural famine have been well documented in historic times.

See also **Saami** (*vol. 2, part 7*); **Finland** (*vol. 2, part 7*).

BIBLIOGRAPHY

Hautala, Jouko. "Survivals of the Cult of Sacrifice Stones in Finland." *Temenos* 1 (1965): 65–86.

Hiltunen, Esa, Jukka Luoto. "The Development of the Cultural Landscape in the Paimio River Valley as an Historical and Archaeological Problem." In *Proceedings of the Third Nordic Conference on the Application of Scientific Methods in Archaeology.* Edited by Torsten Edgren and Högne Jungner, pp. 443–450. Helsinki: Suomen Muinaismuistoyhdistys, 1985. (Several other articles in this volume describe various facets of the Paimio Project.)

Huurre, Matti. *9000 Vuotta Suomen Esihistoriaa* (9,000 years of Finnish prehistory). Helsinki: Otava, 1995. (In Finnish.)

Huttunen, Pertti. "Early Land Use, Especially the Slash-and-Burn Cultivation in the Commune of Lammi, Southern Finland, Interpreted Mainly Using Pollen and Charcoal Analyses." *Acta Botanica Fennica* 113 (1980): 1–47.

Kivikoski, Ella. *Die Eisenzeit Finnlands. Bildwerk und Text.* Helsinki: Finnische Altertumsgesellschaft, 1973.

———. *Finland.* Translated by Alan Binns. London: Thames and Hudson, 1967.

Pentikäinen, Juha. *Kalevala Mythology.* Translated and edited by Ritva Poom. Bloomington: Indiana University Press, 1989.

Rausing, Gad. "Hunters and Agriculture." *Fornvännen* 86 (1991): 255–258.

Sarmela, Matti. "Swidden Cultivation in Finland as a Cultural System." *Suomen Antropologi* 4 (1987): 241–262.

Schauman-Lönnqvist, Marianne, Anna-Liisa Hirviluoto, Elvi Linturi, and Pirjo Uino. *Iron Age Studies in Salo 1–2.* Suomen muinaismuistoyhdistyksen aikakauskirja. Helsinki: Finnish Antiquarian Society, 1986.

Taavitsainen, Jussi-Pekka. "Wide-Range Hunting and Swidden Cultivation as Prerequisites of Iron Age Colonization in Finland." *Suomen Antropologi* 4 (1987): 213–233.

Talve, Ilmar. *Finnish Folk Culture.* Helsinki: Finnish Literature Society, 1997.

Tolonen, Kimmo, Ari Siiriäinen, and Anna-Liisa Hirviluoto. "Iron Age Cultivation in South-West Finland." *Finskt Museum* 83 (1976): 5–66.

Vuorela, Irmeli. "Pollen Analysis as a Means of Tracing Settlement History in SW Finland." *Acta Botanica Fennica* 104 (1975): 1–48.

Zvelebil, Marek. "Iron Age Transformations in Northern Russia and the Northeast Baltic" In *Beyond Domestication in Prehistoric Europe: Investigations in Subsistence Archaeology and Social Complexity.* Edited by Graeme Barker and Clive Gamble, pp. 147–180. London: Academic Press, 1985.

DEBORAH J. SHEPHERD

IRON AGE POLAND

As in many other areas of Europe, in Poland there are no archaeological indications for a radical transformation of Late Bronze Age societies entering the new epoch, or Iron Age. Thus, the traditional name "Iron Age," inherited from nineteenth-century archaeology, stresses a symbolical threshold—the introduction of a new raw material that had no immediate impact on cultural development. In fact, in Iron Age Poland, one observes a continuation of the mainstream Late Bronze Age traditions represented by the Lusatian culture, a culture that survived for several more centuries. It blossomed during the Hallstatt period, stimulated by new influences, but did not show evidence of substantial economic or social changes. A more immediate impact on local societies during the Iron Age was exerted by the climatic changes that marked the time, when cooling and higher humidity shortened the growing season, diminished crop yields, and eventually led to the growing role of rye and barley in the diet, at the expense of wheat. One also might stress the part played by the incursions of aggressive Scythians, who started a long sequence of nomadic invasions that penetrated areas north of the Carpathian mountain belt. Still, in the traditional chronological scheme, the introduction of iron defines the major change from the Bronze to the Iron Ages in Poland.

HALLSTATT

The oldest iron objects (decorative pins, axes, swords, and elements of horse harness) arrived in Polish lands during the Hallstatt C period (750–600 B.C.). The presence of these items was the result of lively contacts with the south, which developed through a growing interest in Baltic amber, sought after in the Hallstatt civilization zone. Discoveries of amber "stores" indicate effective organization of trade connections. Apart from scarce iron items that formed the most luxurious group of imports, many bronzes appeared north of the Sudetic and Carpathian Mountains together with new cultural patterns. Contacts with the sub-Alpine region, however, were not equally important for all parts of contemporary Poland during the Early Iron Age. The Lusatian culture that almost completely dominated the area had interesting subdivisions that previewed future regional developments.

In the western part of the country (Silesia, Great Poland, and Kujavia), some dead bodies were placed in richly equipped wooden-chamber graves. In western Silesia skeleton burials reappeared after a 250-year absence. Following new trends, exploitation of salt (in Kujavia) and zinc-lead ores (in Upper Silesia) began. Hallstatt handicraft models were eagerly copied, which is most evident in new forms of jewelry and elegant painted pottery. This was not the case in the areas east of the Vistula River, where imports, however numerous, did not stimulate local producers. Still different was the situation in the north (Pomerania), where contacts with southern Scandinavia and northern Germany prevailed and where the tradition of raised grave mounds survived. There is no evidence that iron-smelting technology was known in Poland during that period.

One interesting aspect of the Early Iron Age was the tendency to build fortified settlements, observed in traces dating to as early as the ninth century B.C. These constructions spread over the western regions of the Lusatian culture and, less densely, in Pomerania. They were of various sizes (0.5–20 hectares) and typically located in positions with natural defenses, such as hills, islands, and peninsulas. Some had a rather irregular inner layout, whereas others were built according to very rigid plans. The famous Lusatian lake stronghold in Biskupin, built during the winter of 738/737 B.C. and discovered in 1933, best represents the latter type. Its defensive function now has been questioned, but the partially reconstructed settlement offers insight into the sophisticated organizational abilities of Early Iron Age societies. More than a hundred large houses (each comprising 72–86 square meters) once stood along eleven broad (wider than 2.5 meters) wood-laid streets. Some 1,000–1,200 inhabitants lived in an area of about 1.3 hectares surrounded by a circular wood-and-earth wall cut by the gate, which opened to a bridge leading to the mainland. Despite attempts to view these settlements as the earliest Polish "proto-urban" structures, the strict egalitarianism evident in the equal quality of all the houses suggests instead that the inhabitants were agriculturalists seeking refuge during uncertain times.

The real threat came with the nomadic Scythians, who, in the late sixth and early fifth centuries B.C., directed their looting raids at southern and central Poland. Burned Lusatian strongholds mark several waves of their deadly raids; characteristic triangular arrowheads are typical finds. The same arrowheads sometimes are found in graves containing the probable victims of Scythian warriors. An outstanding piece of evidence of their presence is the golden treasure from Witaszkowo in southwestern Poland. Such a clear ethnic identification of these finds is supported by parallels from the steppe zone and by Greek written sources.

This favorable situation offered a new avenue of research for archaeologists, who eagerly started seeking indicators of ethnicity in the material culture left by other societies. Thus, many later archeological cultures were given univocal identity corroborated by historical sources. The Celts, Balts, Germans, and Slavs successively became front-stage actors in the processes described by archaeologists studying the following phases of the Iron Age. This tendency can go too far, as when even the traces of small and mysterious tribes are looked for among the archaeological materials. Another effect of this attitude is the frequent application of a very simplified model of culture processes to explain every change effected by migrations.

Pomerania (north Poland), free from the Scythian threat but subject to influences from the Nordic culture of the western Baltic region (southern Scandinavia and northeast Germany), was the first to observe the fall of the Lusatian culture, which was replaced by the Pomeranian culture during the seventh century B.C. This transformation was marked by the appearance of new burial rites. Grave mounds and extensive urnfield cemeteries were replaced by small family grave sites, where rectangular box cairns made of stone slabs housed up to thirty cremation urns. The early phase of this culture showed mysterious affinities with Etruscan traditions, visible in house-shaped and face urns. The latter have ornaments resembling jewelry (e.g., neck rings and pins) affixed to them, or even original personal items—mostly earrings. Expansion of this new culture toward the southeast during the Hallstatt D period (600–450 B.C.) is connected with the disappearance of collective graves and the introduction of another new burial type—the so-called cloche graves, where cinerary urns are covered with larger upside-down pots.

During the same period, northeastern Poland was "invaded" by a West Baltic Barrow culture, associated with the Proto-Balts, who kept this area for almost two thousand years while avoiding adoption of new ideas from their neighbors. These herders lived in small settlements or in little lake dwellings built on artificial islands made of several layers of wooden logs attached by stakes. Their metals were imported, and their dead were cremated and put in urns covered by small mounds.

The fifth century B.C. marked the visible decline of the mighty Lusatian culture. Large defensive agglomerations disappeared, as did specialized pottery making. There is also evidence of regression in metallurgy and impoverishment of grave goods. The aforementioned Scythian attacks and climatic changes are considered the main reasons for the demographic decline and the disintegration of large social structures. This crisis opened the way for the Pomeranian culture to expand over most of the lands between the Baltic Sea and the mountain belt. It promoted broad use of iron in eastern Poland, which had been somewhat underdeveloped earlier. Production of bronze items achieved a very high level of expertise. Pomeranian societies lived in small, nondefensive settlements, where sunken huts were typical dwellings.

PRE-ROMAN IRON AGE

In the south, "Pomeranians" met Celtic newcomers, who had settled in Silesia in the fourth century B.C. About a hundred years later the next wave of the La Tène culture bearers settled in Little Poland. Farther north a small Celtic colony existed in Kujavia. This dispersed northeastern avant-garde of the great European civilization introduced new technological and cultural achievements—very fine wheel-turned pottery, a double-chambered oven for firing pots, production of glass, fine smith techniques, large-scale iron smelting, new decoration motifs, coinage, new arms (long swords and helmets), and the organization of regional cult centers (e.g., the Ślęża Mountain in Silesia, known for numerous stone sculptures). Important progress in agriculture was made possible by improved plowing tools, manuring of fields, and rotational querns. These "Celtic" settlements were rather small, and their inhabitants lived in relative isolation from their autochthonous neighbors, who seemed to ignore the new technological offerings. Typical flat cemeteries with skeleton burials oriented north to south have been found to contain rich goods.

The Pre-Roman Age (earlier called "La Tène period," lasting from 400 B.C. to the turn of the millennium) saw important culture changes elsewhere in Polish lands. During the third century B.C. the last enclaves of the Lusatian culture and the main-

stream Pomeranian culture disappeared, even though its regional survivors lasted until the mid-second century B.C. Those changes were caused by new cultural influences in the west. Along the Oder River, as early as the early third century B.C., Pomeranian societies were replaced by two groups of the Proto-Germanic Jastorf culture, expanding from its cradle in Jutland and northern Germany. It probably was this new influence that prompted further development, resulting in the formation of two new cultures.

Of these two, the Przeworsk culture was the more successful in its territorial expansion and the more durable (lasting more than six centuries). It originated somewhere in central Poland in the second half of the third century B.C. During its early phases it developed under the strong influence of Celtic traditions. In Tyniec, near Kraków, there lived a mixed Celto-Przeworsk society that introduced oats into Polish lands. During this early period cemeteries were flat, with simple pit graves that usually lacked urns. Even stronger was the Jastorfian impact in the north, where the Oksywie culture formed in the lower Vistula region. It is known only from its cemeteries, where women and men were buried according to distinctively different rites. Cremated female bones were put in simple pits, while the males were buried in urns. Stone covers or standing stelae are characteristic of these graves. This culture later gave birth to the Wielbark culture, identified with the Goths. Both Przeworsk and Oksywie cultures sometimes are listed under the common name "Pit Grave culture."

ROMAN AGE

Around the turn of the millennium the great Celtic civilization faded away on continental Europe as a consequence of the strikes made by the aggressively expanding Roman Empire. This resulted in shifts of cultural influence that stimulated development in Polish lands. Thus, the Pre-Roman Age, dominated by the La Tène culture, ended, and Roman Age began, with its promotion of Hellenic-Roman traditions. A Celtic remnant legacy is evident in the technology used by the organizers of intensive iron production centers and in the sustaining of regular trade contacts along the route called the Amber Road. Earlier Etruscan demand for amber was replaced by the still larger demand for this "gold of the north," encouraged by Roman markets always greedy for exotic products. The scope of this import can be inferred from the sizes of amber "stores" discovered along the track, for example, 2,750 kilograms of amber found in Wrocław-Partynice. During the reign of the emperor Nero (A.D. 54–68), a special envoy was sent from Rome all the way to the Baltic coast to study the origin of amber. It was brought back to Rome in such vast amounts that the entire Colosseum was decorated with pieces of this precious material. Thanks to such contacts, in the second century the Greek geographer Ptolemy recorded the name "Calisia," which is believed to represent the predecessor of the contemporary town Kalisz in central Poland.

The decline of the continental Celts allowed for the vigorous expansion of Germanic peoples. Germanic ethnicity is ascribed to two archaeologically distinct cultures that dominated Polish lands during the early Roman Age (A.D. 1–150). The Przeworsk culture expanded east and south, where it replaced societies attached to the Celtic traditions. Its bearers lived in small, semipermanent settlements that consisted of sunken houses. Some of the cemeteries were in use for several centuries. Most burials were simple pit graves, but often richly equipped with pots, tools, weapons, and adornments. Differences in the amount of invested labor and the quality of deposited goods indicate substantial social stratification, with dominant elite members of society buried in "princely" graves equipped with imported status items, among them high-quality Roman glass, silver, and bronze products. These outstanding persons were buried uncremated and separated from the common cemeteries.

Intensive connections with Roman markets that were sending north large amounts of handicrafts and quickly changing local fashions made possible the construction of a very precise chronology for the Roman Age. It is based on detailed classification of metal and glass vessels, *terra sigillata* pottery, fibulae (a type of brooch), belt mountings, and various elements of arms. Similarly to objects discovered at well-dated sites (e.g., Pompeii or briefly occupied army camps), they can be dated precisely within a window of just twenty-five years. This makes the archaeology of the Roman Age an object of envy to those researchers engaged in the study of earlier and

later periods and a research field with great explanation potential that has not yet been fully explored.

This chronological clarity also pertains to studies of the northern neighbor of the Przeworsk culture, the Wielbark culture. This culture represents societies that gave birth to the famous tribes of Goths and Gepids, who migrated southeast in the second half of the second century A.D. Unresolved questions concerning these peoples include their origins (southern Scandinavia or northeastern Poland), the reasons for their departure (economic, climatic, or political), and further development of the region by the lower Vistula (demographic replacement or steady transformation). Expansion and migration of the Wielbark culture enlarged the territory occupied by the West Baltic Barrow culture that moved toward the lower Vistula.

During the younger phase of the early Roman Age (c. A.D. 80–150), the new Luboszyce culture emerged in the region of the middle Oder River. It showed strong affiliations with both the Przeworsk and the Wielbark cultures. Retreat of the latter group toward the southeast opened the way for a stronger influence emanating from the Elbian region in eastern Germany, which led to the formation in western and central Pomerania of the Dębczyno group, known for its late Roman "princely" burials. The late material culture of this area shows Scandinavian connections. Farther east along the Baltic coast the West Baltic Barrow culture established subdivisions that sometimes are identified with the tribes distinguished in written sources as Aestii, Galindai, and Sudinoi.

In A.D. 178 victorious Roman legions of the emperor Marcus Aurelius, fighting the mighty Marcomanni, established bases in Slovakia, thus coming very close to southern Poland. This direct presence lasted only three years and did not interfere with development of the Przeworsk culture. Long and lively contacts with Roman civilization, however, had visible effects in the adoption (since the late second century) of some technical achievements, for example, log-frame construction of houses, advanced goldsmithing techniques, and rotational quern stones. The potter's wheel and effective chamber ovens permitted organization of large centers producing standardized vessels. Ards with iron coulters made possible the plowing of heavier and more fertile soils, and idling of fields resulted in stability and a departure from the slash-and-burn strategy of farming. The really outstanding aspect of the Przeworsk culture was its huge centers of iron smelting. An estimated 400,000–800,000 furnaces concentrated on the northeastern edge of the Holy Cross Mountains, in Mazovia and other smaller centers, must have furnished several million kilos of iron that surely was exported. This "industry" was based mostly on exploitation of surface bog ores, but there also were mines penetrating deeper sources, with shafts dug as far down as 20 meters.

MIGRATION PERIOD

The end of the glorious Roman Age and the beginning of the turbulent Migration period came with the sudden arrival of Asiatic Huns. In 375 they attacked the Ostrogoths, who had settled north of the Black Sea, and triggered massive movements of various peoples that led, in A.D. 406/407, to the fall of the Western Roman Empire and gave way to the establishment of a series of unstable Germanic "kingdoms." The nomads themselves established their center in the steppe zone of Hungarian Pannonia, from where they ruled a multiethnic "empire." Before they were defeated in 454, some of the Huns penetrated Polish lands, which is established by finds of their golden jewelry and characteristic large bronze vessels. Uncertain numbers of inhabitants of Poland took part in those turbulent events of the Migration period, which resulted in demographic declines and visible impoverishment of the area between the Baltic Sea and the Carpathians.

This crisis did not much affect northeastern Poland, settled by the West Baltic Barrow culture peoples, who were stubborn in their attachment to their own traditions. Especially interesting is the Olsztyn group that formed in the Mazurian lake district during the late fifth century A.D. and survived more than two hundred years. Characteristic urns with rectangular "windows"; horses buried under male graves; far-reaching contacts with both western Europe and Scandinavia, as well as with the Danube region and the Black Sea zone; and the interregional character of personal adornments make it one of the outstanding cultures of the Barbaricum around the mid-first millennium A.D.

The end of the Migration period traditionally is set at 568 A.D. with the arrival of the Avars, a new wave of Asiatic nomads who also chose Pannonia as their homeland. The establishment of their new "empire" halted the very promising sociocultural development of earlier times and marked the beginning of the flourishing over vast parts of central and eastern Europe of the Slavs and their culture.

See also **Late Bronze Age Urnfields of Central Europe** (vol. 2, part 5); **Biskupin** (vol. 2, part 6); **Iron Age Ukraine and European Russia** (vol. 2, part 6); **Goths between the Baltic and Black Seas** (vol. 2, part 7); **Slavs and the Early Slav Culture** (vol. 2, part 7); **Poland** (vol. 2, part 7).

BIBLIOGRAPHY

Bielenin, Kazimierz. *Starożytne górnictwo i hutnictwo żelaza w Górach Świętokrzyskich* [Ancient mining and smelting of iron in the Holy Cross Mountains]. Kielce, Poland: Kieleckie Towarzystwo Naukowe, 1992.

Bukowski, Zbigniew. *The Scythian Influence in the Area of Lusatian Culture.* Wrocław, Poland: Ossolineum, 1977.

Gedl, Marek. *Die Hallstatteinflüsse auf den polnischen Gebieten in der Früheisenzeit.* Kraków, Poland: Nakładem Uniwersytetu Jagiellońskiego, 1991.

Godłowski, Kazimierz. *Przemiany kulturowe i osadnicze w południowej i środkowej Polsce w młodszym okresie przedrzymskim i w okresie rzymskim* [Settlement and culture changes in southern and central Poland during the younger Pre-Roman Age and the Roman Age]. Wrocław, Poland: Ossolineum, 1985.

———. *The Chronology of the Late Roman and Early Migration Periods in Central Europe.* Kraków, Poland: Nakładem Uniwersytetu Jagiellońskiego, 1970.

Kolendo, Jerzy. *A la recherche de l'ambre baltique: L'expedition d'un chevalier romain sous Neron.* Warsaw, Poland: Uniwersytet Warszawski, 1981.

Mierzwiński, Andrzej. "Zagadnienie obronności osiedli typu biskupińskiego: O potrzebie alternatywnej interpretacji" [The problem of defensiveness of the Biskupin-type settlements: On the need for an alternative interpretation]. *Przegląd Archeologiczny* 48 (2000): 141–151.

Nowakowski, Wojciech, and Claus von Carnap-Bornheim. *Das Samland in der römischen Kaiserzeit und sein Verbindungen mit dem römischen Reich und der barbarischen Welt.* Warsaw, Poland: Druk; Marburg, Germany: Vertrieb, N.G. Elwert, Verlag, 1996.

Wielowiejski, Jerzy. *Główny szlak bursztynowy w czasach Cesarstwa Rzymskiego* [The main Amber Road during the times of the Roman Empire]. Wrocław, Poland: Ossolineum, 1980.

Woźniak, Zenon. *Osadnictwo celtyckie w Polsce* [Celtic settlement in Poland]. Wrocław, Poland: Ossolineum, 1970.

Przemysław Urbańczyk

Fig. 1. Photo of the reconstructed gateway at Biskupin. COURTESY OF ANTHONY F. HARDING. REPRODUCED BY PERMISSION.

BISKUPIN

Biskupin is the site of a fortified stockade lying in west-central Poland in the lake area (Pałuki) near the town of Żnin. It belongs to a late phase of the Lausitz culture (the main cultural group that covers eastern Germany and western Poland from the Middle Bronze Age onward) and dates to the beginning of the Iron Age.

The site was discovered in 1933 by Walenty Szwajcer (Schweitzer), the local schoolmaster, who saw timbers protruding from the water. Excavation. which began in 1934 and continued until the outbreak of World War II, resumed in 1946 under Józef Kostrzewski and Zdzisław Rajewski of Poznań University; environmental and other small-scale work continued at the site into the 1990s. Because of its waterlogged state, the wood was well-preserved; this led to the recovery of an exceptional quantity and quality of information but also led to many problems of preservation, primarily of the structural timbers. Most of the excavation was subsequently filled in to protect the remains, and a set of reconstructions (houses, gateway, palisaded rampart) was erected at the site. Biskupin has become a major visitor attraction, and it is also a center for experimental reconstructions in ancient technology.

The site lies on a peninsula in Biskupin Lake. The peninsula was probably originally an island about 200 by 160 meters in extent. This area was enclosed by a palisade of rows of stakes driven into the ground at an angle, which served also as a breakwater. Within the palisade was a box-framed rampart of wood filled with earth and sand. A single entrance lay in the southwestern sector and was protected by a gate tower with twin gates. A wooden road ran around the inside of the rampart, enclosing a street system of eleven streets, made of logs laid side by side corduroy style. Along the streets lay houses, more than one hundred altogether; they were typically 9 by 8 meters in extent, built of walls of horizontal logs keyed into uprights, which were then reinforced by pegs. The floor was made of bundles of small branches. Each house had an anteroom and a main room with hearth; a loft ran over part of the main room and was reached by ladder. Smaller animals were probably housed underneath the loft, and a couple of cattle could have been accommodated in the anteroom.

This densely packed village plan has suggested to several scholars that Biskupin represented the beginnings of urbanism on the north European plain. Certainly the settlement must have had a population of many hundreds (possibly even more than one thousand), and the site offers some evidence of craft specialization. Archaeologists have found no indications of buildings for administration, at least in the excavated area, which amounts to about two-thirds of the whole. Nonetheless, the proximity of houses and streets, packed together on a small island in a lake, would have necessitated some form of communal organization, though such proximity would also have brought about many stresses in the village dynamic.

According to the published reports, Biskupin appears to have had two main phases of occupation. In the first phase almost all the structural timber was oak, but in the second phase mainly pine was used, presumably because of a shortage of oak near the site. Since there were more than 35,000 stakes in the palisade alone, and 8,000 cubic meters of timber in each phase of the site, clearly the construction represented a major drain on local woodland and a major effort in terms of labor input and organization.

The material from the site represents a standard domestic assemblage of the late Lausitz culture. In addition to large quantities of pottery, numerous bone and stone tools, clay weights, wooden tools (including a wheel, hoes, plowshares, and paddles), and other organic materials, such as bundles of flax, were found. Metal objects were not so numerous, but both bronze and iron are represented, and bronze was worked on site. Particular houses and areas were designated for particular tasks; thus metalworking debris, weaving equipment, and other craft tools appear in some houses or open spaces but not others.

In terms of artifact affinities, Biskupin has been variously dated to Hallstatt C, Hallstatt D, or a combination of the two. Increasingly, however, opinion favors Ha D. Róza Mikłaszewska-Balcer's (1991) discussion of the pottery from the site, in particular the so-called pseudo-corded ornament, makes the case that the site perhaps began life in Ha C and came to an end at the start of Ha D: this ornament, supposedly typical of Ha D, is relatively rare as a Biskupin artifact, as are examples of encrusted ware that also belong to that phase. Attempts at absolute dating by independent scientific methods have been only partially successful. Radiocarbon dates obtained on samples from a small excavation in 1981 give an apparently clear picture for the early phase (between 850 and 800 B.C. at the 2σ level and 95 percent of the probability distribution), but the dates fall in a wide spread for the later horizon, where the calibration curve is flat (780–470 B.C. at 2σ and 95 percent of probability distribution). Dendrochronological work in the early 1990s on a set of 71 oaks (that is, first phase), comprising 166 rings including bark, spanned the period 747–722 B.C. but with a concentration of timbers felled in 738–737 B.C. The picture presented by published plans and accounts indicates that the separation into an early oak and a later pine phase is not clear-cut, and especially for the second phase it is uncertain how much construction work actually took place. A main construction date in the later eighth century B.C. fits well with the artifactual evidence.

The site's destruction, which seems to have been through abandonment rather than other causes such as fire, may reflect environmental change (rising lake levels), but economic and social pressures arising from the cramped conditions and overexploitation of critical resources may also have played an important part.

See also **Dating and Chronology** (*vol. 1, part 1*); **Hallstatt** (*vol. 2, part 6*).

BIBLIOGRAPHY

Kostrzewski, Józef, ed. *III Sprawozdanie z prac wykopaliskowych w grodzie kultury łużyckiej w Biskupinie w powiecie żnińskim za lata 1938–1939 i 1946–1948* [Third report of excavations at the stronghold of the Lusatian culture at Biskupin in Znin district for the years 1938–1939 and 1946–1948]. Poznań, Poland: Nakład Polskiego Towarzystwa Prehistorycznego, 1950.

Mikłaszewska-Balcer, Róza. "Datowanie osiedla obronnego kultury łużyckiej w Biskupinie" [Dating the fortified settlement of the Lusatian culture in Biskupinie]. In

Prahistoryczny gród w Biskupinie: Problematyka osiedli obronnych na początku epoki żelaza [Prehistoric stronghold at Biskupin: Problems of fortified settlements at the beginning of the Iron Age]. Edited by Jan Jaskanis et al., pp. 107–113. Warsaw: Wydawnictwo Naukowe PWN, 1991.

Piotrowski, Wojciech. "50 lat badań w Biskupinie" [50 years of research at Biskupin]. In *Prahistoryczny gród w Biskupinie: Problematyka osiedli obronnych na początku epoki żelaza* [Prehistoric stronghold at Biskupin: Problems of fortified settlements at the beginning of the Iron Age].

Edited by Jan Jaskanis et al., pp. 81–105. Warsaw: Wydawnictwo Naukowe PWN, 1991.

Rajewski, Zdzisław. *Biskupin: A Fortified Settlement Dating from 500 B.C.: A Guide.* Rev. ed. Poznań, Poland: Wydawnictwo Poznańskie, 1980.

Ważny, Tomasz. "Dendrochronology of Biskupin: Absolute Dating of the Early Iron Age Settlement." *Bulletin of the Polish Academy of Sciences: Biological Science* 42, no. 3 (1994): 283–289.

A. F. HARDING

IRON AGE UKRAINE AND EUROPEAN RUSSIA

The period between about 1000 and 0 B.C. was of crucial importance in the history of the tribes living in the steppe and forest-steppe zones of southeastern Europe (present-day Ukraine and European Russia). It was a difficult period for the people of the region. There were constant movements of population, the appearance of new ethnic groups, Greek colonization, and Roman penetration. Constant movement and migration led new peoples and cultures to appear and others to vanish. Cultures influenced one another, resulting in the creation of new, unique visual art in styles such as Greco-Barbarian, a mixture of Greek and local (non-Hellenic) elements.

This huge region forms the most westerly part of the Great Steppe Zone of Eurasia. In the south, the shores of the Sea of Azov (known in ancient times as Lake Maeotis) and the Black Sea provide a natural boundary. The northern boundary is ill defined, linked to the spread of the chernozem (black earth) that is characteristic of the forest-steppe. The Danube sets the western limit to the region, and, conventionally, the lower Don River is the eastern boundary. Overall the steppes are some 1,000 kilometers east to west, and 500 kilometers north to south: an area that includes the Dnieper basin and the Black Sea lowlands. In times past, this territory was covered in natural, grassy vegetation and forests, encompassing floodplains, terraces, and sandy areas and was watered by the Dnieper, Dniester, southern Bug, Ingul, Ingulets, and many lesser waterways. To the north of the true steppe lies the forest-steppe zone, containing the uplands and middle

reaches of the Dnieper and the southern Bug, and extending to the middle Don. North of the forest-steppe was an area of mixed forest. A characteristic of the forest-steppe is the mixture of large tracts of forest with woodless tracts of meadowland.

The Iron Age in Eastern Europe dates to the early first millennium B.C. Throughout the steppe areas of Eurasia, including those of the northern Black Sea hinterland, it corresponded with the transition from sedentary, pastoral agriculture to the nomadism of animal-rearing tribes. The numerous steppe settlements of the Bronze Age population, surface and dugout, had disappeared by the ninth century B.C.; from then until the late fifth century B.C., tribes moved their herds constantly from one area of pasturage to another. But then the nomads began to settle down. In contrast, the neighboring forest-steppe zone was populated, just as in the Bronze Age, by a sedentary population, albeit one subject to invasion and incursion by marauding nomadic hordes who left their mark on many features of the life and culture of the settled population. The local peoples who inhabited this territory had no writing and have left no written evidence of themselves. We know the names of some groups thanks to authors from the ancient Greco-Roman world and the Near East.

THE CIMMERIANS

The first to be mentioned in such writings are the Cimmerians, to whom the earliest reference is in Homer's *Odyssey*, where they are described as a tribe living in a mythical land of fog and darkness on the fringes of the inhabitable world. Other Greek accounts also mention the Cimmerians, as do some Near Eastern sources. Both tend to concentrate on those aspects of Cimmerian history of direct relevance to other well-known peoples and civilizations, such as Assyria and Phrygia. In general, little is known about the Cimmerians, and for modern scholars they are still enveloped in fog and darkness. A summary of the written accounts is useful, however.

The first Assyrian references to the Cimmerians date from the period between 722 and 713 B.C. During the reign of the Assyrian king Sennacherib (705–681 B.C.), the Cimmerians attacked Asia Minor and destroyed the Phrygian Empire: Phrygia's King Midas committed suicide. This presumably happened in 696–695 B.C., although a date twenty years later is possible. A group of Cimmerians probably settled for some time near Sinope (modern Sinop). The military leader of the Cimmerians in their 679–678 B.C. campaign is called Tuspa in Assyrian records. Another group of Cimmerians probably entered Anatolia from Thrace. This is suggested by the ancient Greek geographer Strabo, writing in the late first century B.C. and early first century A.D. He speaks about an alliance between the Cimmerians and the Thracian Treres and Edoni tribes who later lived in central Bulgaria and in Chalcidice, respectively. The Lydian king Gyges even sought aid against them from the Assyrian king Assurbanapal. An attack on Lydia in 652 B.C. was successful. The Lydian capital Sardis was sacked and Gyges was killed.

Most Cimmerians had left their lands in the Black Sea steppe because of the arrival of the Scythians (see below) from the east, who were in turn under pressure from the Massagetae. This took place before 713 B.C., when both the Cimmerians and, following them, the Scythians reached the region of Urartu. Herodotus, the fifth century B.C. Greek geographer, explicitly mentions the Tyras River (the Dniester) as the place where the Cimmerian kings fought a fratricidal battle and were buried, and from where the common people left their homes. He also describes the Cimmerian's subsequent escape along the Black Sea west of the Caucasus to the area of Sinope. Some Cimmerians, however, remained on the shores of Lake Maeotis (the Sea of Azov). The Cimmerian Bosporus (also

known as the Kerch Strait), Cimmerian Walls, and Cimmerian Peninsula are all in this same area (the Crimea and its surrounds), much farther east than Tyras/Dniester, and equally distant from the River Araxes (now known as the Araks), the original eastern boundary of the Cimmerians. The fratricidal battle of the Cimmerian leaders on the Dniester seems to have marked the last stage of the Cimmerian retreat.

These movements in the Near East are all that we know of the Cimmerians from written sources. It is most probable that the Cimmerians were not a single tribe and that this was a collective name for a large number of tribes living in the steppes of the Ukraine and European Russia. This is a very important point when examining Cimmerian culture and the archaeological evidence for it. The archaeological material does not permit us to single out one culture to which the label "Cimmerian" can firmly be attached. Several generations of archaeologists have sought to provide archaeological evidence of the Cimmerians and their culture but without any positive results. The search for the Cimmerians is based on the proposition that, because the Cimmerians were expelled by the Scythians, any pre-Scythian culture throughout the huge territory mentioned above must be Cimmerian.

Another difficulty is that all these so-called Cimmerian cultures have Scythian features, and their objects executed in Animal Style are extremely close to the Scythian and Near Eastern variants of this type. It is practically impossible with current knowledge to distinguish a Cimmerian culture in archaeological terms. It is so close to Scythian that modern scholars have taken refuge in the labels "pre-Scythian" or "Early Scythian" to describe the cultures of the ninth and eighth centuries B.C.

THE SCYTHIANS

As noted above, the arrival of the Scythians resulted in the expulsion of the so-called Cimmerians. The main sources for knowledge of the Scythians are archaeology and book 4 of *The Histories* by Herodotus. Like the Cimmerians, the Scythians spoke an Iranian-related language, and the term "Scythians" represents a general name for many different tribes, whose individual names Herodotus lists as Royal Scythians, Agricultural Scythians, Callipedae, Alazones, and others. The Scythians came from northern Siberia at the end of the eighth and the first half of the seventh centuries B.C. Initially, they lived in the steppes of the northern Caucasus, not far from the Kuban River. The crucial point in the creation of Scythian culture was the middle seventh century, when a part of their population migrated to the Near East, remaining there, according to Herodotus, for twenty-eight years. Their presence was disastrous for the Near Eastern empires such as the Assyrian. They destroyed Urartu and they raided as far as Egypt. For the Scythians themselves this period was important in the formation of their culture, upon which Near Eastern civilizations had a very strong influence. When the Scythians returned to the Caucasian steppes at the end of the seventh and beginning of the sixth centuries, they possessed a strongly formed culture in which Anatolian/Near Eastern Animal Style had taken root. Scythian tombs dating to the period after their return from the Near East have been discovered in the northern Caucasus. They show how Scythian rulers now imitated those of Assyria, Media, and Urartu, and employed Near Eastern craftsmen to this end.

During the sixth century B.C., thanks to close interaction between the Scythians and the local population of the Kuban region (including the Maeotians), Scythian culture showed increasing signs of Greek influence, but it continued to contain Near Eastern features. The failure of the Persian king Darius I to conquer them in 514–513 B.C. enhanced Scythian self-confidence. At the end of the sixth and beginning of the fifth centuries B.C., they formed their own political entities: one based in the Crimean steppes, not far from the future Bosporan kingdom; the other on the lower Dnieper, not far from Olbia. Classical Scythian culture, which dates from the end of the fifth and beginning of the fourth centuries B.C., when most of the Scythians were becoming a settled agricultural population, is indeed the result of close artistic links between the Scythian and Greek worlds. Nevertheless, it is not particularly difficult to identify Near Eastern traditions within it.

The most characteristic feature of Scythian culture is the tumulus, or *kurgan*. Many of the graves belong to the elite. Altogether, about 3,000 tumuli are known. Over time the incidence of the burial mounds varies. The vast majority, some 2,000, date from the Classical period of Scythian culture, espe-

cially the fourth century B.C., and are concentrated on both banks of the lower Dnieper. This is where Herodotus located Gerrhi, the burial place of the Scythian kings, in the vicinity of the Sea of Azov and the Crimea. In some cases, Bronze Age tumuli were reused, but most were built specially for burying the elite and were constructed in several stages. The main feature of these tombs is the earth mound, the usual height of which varied between 3 and 21 meters and the diameter between 30 and 350 meters. Another characteristic feature is the stone chamber and the *dromos* leading to it; antechambers were rare. Usually, the chamber was rectangular and had a step-vaulted stone roof. The chambers were very large and their height varied between 4 and 14 meters. Some tombs have several chambers. Most tumuli were robbed in antiquity, but the richest to survive untouched contained several dozen gold and silver objects (jewelry, vessels), amphorae, and luxurious Greek pottery. Sometimes horses and slaves were buried with their owners.

GREEK COLONIZATION
The Scythians were the principal local people encountered by the Greek colonists who established settlements on the northern shore of the Black Sea. The relationship between the two groups shaped the history of the Greek cities of the region for several centuries.

The first Eastern Greek settlements in the area, mainly Ionian, appeared in the second half of the seventh century B.C. Not much is known about Archaic colonies, including their layouts; however, the first colonies were quite small. In the sixth century B.C. the area of Panticapaeum (which occupied the site of modern Kerch) was about 7.5 hectares, with a population of about 2,000–3,000. The territory of Olbia in the first half of the same century was 6 hectares; in the second half it was 16.5 hectares. In the middle sixth century, Phanagoria was built on a hill; it covered an area of 20 to 22.5 hectares. It was the only early colony to show evidence of settlement planning and regular streets. The thoroughfares had a width of between 1.5 and 3 meters, and houses were constructed next to each other along both sides of the streets. There is (so far) no evidence of the formation of an agora (marketplace) or *temenos* (sacral place) as a distinct part of any of the towns until the last quarter of the sixth century. Shrines, such as that of Demeter in Nymphaeum, had quite primitive architecture and were not distinguished from dwelling houses. Recent investigation in Berezan has yielded a small temple of the Late Archaic period. Domestic architecture built between the very end of the seventh century and the last quarter of the sixth century B.C. has very distinctive features. So far no aboveground stone dwelling houses are known; instead, so-called dugouts or semi-dugouts predominate. Entire quarters of these pits were found in many Greek cities: in Olbia, for example, there is a street with pit dwellings laid out regularly down one side, and with a few on the opposite side.

The relationship between the first colonists and the local population was quite peaceful. A large amount of handmade pottery has been found in the Greek settlements, representing 12 to 23 percent of the total pottery finds. Because such pottery was mainly a product of the local population, this high concentration seems to indicate that local people lived in the settlements alongside the colonists. Such an arrangement might be evidence of a pacific relationship. Speaking generally, the seventh and sixth centuries B.C. saw no complications in the relations between Greeks and locals. This is indicated by the absence of fortification systems in the northern Black Sea colonies until the Classical period.

In the last twenty-five years of the sixth century B.C., a completely new period in the history of the Greek settlements started. Previously the colonies had not looked very Greek with their pit houses and simple construction, but from the Late Archaic period they exhibited the same characteristic features known in mainland Greece and other areas of Greek colonization. Major cities had designated areas such as an agora and a *temenos*. All houses were built of stone and mud brick. From the end of the sixth century B.C. all houses were aboveground, roofed with tiles, had cellars or semi-cellars, and were rectangular in plan. Some were of two stories; all followed the rules of Greek domestic architecture. Most rich houses were built using the architectural orders and covered up to 550 square meters; some were stucco-clad. The typical small house covered an area of between 80 and 200 square meters; a large one covered from 200 up to 600 square meters. The number of rooms ranged between three and fourteen.

Streets were paved with stones, pebbles and pieces of pottery. By the fourth century B.C. a comprehensive street pattern had formed. Main streets in the various cities were 6 to 11 meters wide; side streets between 4 and 5 meters wide; alleys and passageways between 1 and 1.5 meters across. The terraces on which Olbia and Panticapaeum were constructed were linked by flights of paved steps. Beneath the streets were stone drains and sewers. There were stone-lined wells and water fountains. In Olbia, clay pipes or small stone channels carried water into individual houses from the main channel that brought drinking water into the city. In major cities, stone temples were built in the *temenos,* usually rich in architectural decoration. In Olbia, the agora and *temenos* adjoined. The former extended to 2,000 square meters and was paved with pieces of ceramic, stones, and pebbles. Along the northern coast of the Black Sea the first fortification systems appeared at the beginning of the fifth century B.C., and they were destroyed and rebuilt in various cities between the fourth and second centuries B.C.

THE BOSPORAN KINGDOM

As mentioned above, after the failure of Darius I's Scythian campaign, the Scythians established two political entities—one not far from the Bosporan kingdom and the other near Olbia. It was also during this period that the Odrysian kingdom was created in what is now Bulgaria. War soon broke out between Scythians and the Odrysians but ended quickly in a truce, freeing the Scythians to direct their attentions toward the Greek cities, including Olbia and settlements on the Kerch and Taman peninsulas. The Scythians soon established a protectorate over Olbia.

It was at this time that the Greek cities of the two peninsulas unified into a single state, the Bosporan kingdom, with its capital at Panticapaeum. Although the reason for the unification remains a matter of debate, many scholars link it to the need to combat increasing Scythian pressure on the cities. From this period onward, relations between the Greek cities and the Scythians were characterized by the payment of tribute and the giving of gifts. Strabo, for example, tells us that land for settlement and agriculture was given by local tribal chiefs—that is, the Scythians—either by special agreement or in exchange for a moderate tribute. Furthermore, one inscription of the late fifth century, from Kerkinitis in western Crimea, mentions the payment of tribute to the Scythians.

From the cultural point of view, the political difficulties between the Scythians and Greek cities resulted in the creation of a unique phenomenon: Greco-barbarian art. The Greeks produced many highly artistic objects for the local royal family and elite. From the fifth century B.C., these local upper classes were hellenized—a process that went further in the fourth century. Greek craftsmen were active at the courts of local rulers, who employed them, as in Anatolia, to produce objects in the Greek style but adapted to the tastes of the local elite. Herodotus tells an interesting story about the Scythian king Scyles who had been taught by his Greek mother from Histria to know Greek religion and the Greek way of life. He had a house and a Greek wife in Olbia and regularly stayed there.

The Bosporan kingdom, a unique political entity, was, from its establishment in about 480 B.C., similar in all respects to the Hellenistic kingdoms. It was surrounded by local agrarian population—the Maeotae, Sindians, Dandarii, and others near the Taman Peninsula—and the Nomadic Scythians in the Crimea. From the formation of this state, the relationship between Bosporan Greeks and the local peoples around the Taman Peninsula and the Kuban basin remained peaceful, and by the middle of the fourth century B.C. all of these populations were incorporated into the kingdom. Relations between the Bosporan kingdom and the Nomadic Scythians are not very clear, but they were probably quite hostile, in view of the various earthen fortifications found in the Kerch Peninsula. Another people inhabiting the Crimea were the Taurians. After the establishment of Dorian Chersonesus in eastern Crimea c. 422 B.C., they were pushed back by the colonists into the mountains.

GREEK PENETRATION INTO THE HINTERLAND

In ancient times the northern Black Sea steppes (present-day Ukraine and the south of European Russia) were not just a multiethnic territory but an active contact zone in which interaction between local peoples and between locals and Greek colonists can be studied. The evidence demonstrates not just a trade relationship between Greeks and locals but also how Greeks penetrated deep into the hinterland, even residing in the settlements that formed the political and production centers of local tribes.

The most interesting example of this is the Belsk settlement, situated not far from Poltava in the Ukraine (about 500 kilometers inland from the Black Sea). Some believe it to be the city of Gelonus inhabited by the Budini and the Geloni (one of the Scythian tribes). The site has yielded about ten thousand pieces of Greek pottery dating from the Archaic and Classical periods. To understand what kind of settlement this was, let us turn to book 4 of *The Histories* by Herodotus:

> The Budini, a numerous and powerful nation, all have markedly blue-grey eyes and red hair; there is a town in their territory called Gelonus, all built of wood, both dwelling-houses and temples, with a high wooden wall round it, thirty furlongs each way. There are temples here in honour of Greek gods, adorned after the Greek manner with statues, altars, and shrines—though all constructed of wood; a triennial festival, with the appropriate revelry, is held in honour of Dionysus. This is to be accounted for by the fact that the Geloni were originally Greeks, who, driven out of the seaports along the coast, settled amongst the Budini. Their language is still half Scythian, half Greek. The language of the Budini is quite different, as, indeed, is their culture generally.

The excavator of this site, Boris Andreevich (B. A.) Shramko, indeed believes that he has found a small sanctuary of the sixth through fourth centuries B.C. built with wooden columns. Inside is an altar, and not far away is a pit containing cult offerings. This could indicate a Greek population of merchants and artisans, probably small, from the Archaic period.

From the fourth century and in the Hellenistic period, there is much stronger evidence to demonstrate that Greeks lived permanently in local settlements, establishing their own quarters there. Elizavetovskoe is a settlement on the Don River, at a point where three cultural zones meet—Scythian, Maeotian, and Sarmatian. It dates from the end of the sixth century or the beginning of the fifth century B.C. The important feature at Elizavetovskoe is the presence of a quarter populated by Bosporan Greeks. The quarter dates from the second half of the fourth century B.C., when the acropolis was strengthened with stone towers and walls. Detailed investigation has shown that the Greek quarter was the settlement's trading area and was inhabited by Greeks from the Bosporan kingdom. It ceased to exist at some point at the very beginning of the third century B.C., replaced by a new settlement, a so-called Bosporan trading center (*emporion*), which existed until about 275–270 B.C. The houses of the *emporion* were built of stone in the Greek manner, and the settlement was fortified against the rest of the city, where the local population lived.

Kamenskoe, a Scythian settlement on the Dnieper, far into the hinterland, is another important site. It was the political and economic center of this part of Scythia, covering some 1,200 hectares. There is very strong evidence that Greeks lived in the acropolis from the fourth century B.C.: it had a stone fortification system constructed using Greek techniques, Greek-type stone dwellings, and stone-paved streets. Not far from the acropolis there was a harbor.

Further examples come from the Semibratnoe and Raevskoe settlements, not far from the Taman Peninsula. Unfortunately, neither has been studied very well, and the archaeological investigations that have taken place have not been published in detail. Semibratnoe, situated not far from Gorgippia, yielded very impressive Greek-type stone architecture and a fortification system. An inscription from it demonstrates that it was the residence of the Bosporan governor/prince within the lands of the local population. Raevskoe dates mainly from the Hellenistic period and has Greek-type domestic and public architecture.

Bosporan Greeks in the Hellenistic period were most active in trying to penetrate the hinterland and establish settlements within the territories of the local population. One of the best studied of such settlements is Tanais, not far where the Don flows into the Sea of Azov. Strabo gives a very clear idea of its character:

> On the river and the lake is an inhabited city bearing the same name, Tanais; it was founded by the Greeks who held the Bosporus. . . . It was a common emporium, partly of the Asiatic and the European nomads, and partly of those who navigated the lake from the Bosporus, the former bringing slaves, hides, and such other things as nomads possess, and the latter giving in exchange clothing, wine, and the other things that belong to civilised life.

Archaeological excavation has demonstrated that this settlement was established in the first half of the third century B.C. It had fortification walls and an internal wall dividing the Greek and local sectors.

LATE SCYTHIANS AND THE PONTIC KINGDOM

The period from the late fourth century through the third century B.C. brought massive change. Semi-nomadic Sarmatian tribes moved in from the Volga area, expelling the Scythians and taking over their territory. Some Scythians were assimilated and others were killed; most fled to central Crimea, establishing a new kingdom. The kingdom's capital was Scythian Neapolis (at the site of modern Simferopol), which lasted until the third century A.D. In the literature these Scythians are called "Late Scythians." The rulers and elite of this new kingdom were heavily hellenized. Scythian Neapolis had Greek-type fortifications, public buildings, and sculptural decorations. Soon these Scythians became hostile to the Chersonesus state and its agricultural territories, leading to a war that lasted from the second quarter of the second century to the middle of the first century B.C. The Scythians captured the Chersonesite agricultural territory in northwestern Crimea and surrounded Chersonesus itself. In response, Chersonesus sought the help of Mithridates VI Eupator, ruler of the Pontic kingdom. In about 110 B.C., he sent his general Diophantus to Chersonesus at the head of a Pontic army. Diophantus undertook a number of campaigns against the Scythians, liberating Kerkinitis, Kalos Limen, and other Chersonesite settlements in the northwestern Crimea and capturing various Scythian fortresses in the hinterland. As a result, the Bosporus kingdom, Chersonesus, and, apparently, the Late Scythian kingdom itself, all became part of Mithridates's Pontic domain. Olbia and other cities of the northwestern Black Sea area had probably been incorporated into the Pontic kingdom by the end of the second century B.C.

The Greek cities of the northern shore of the Black Sea played an important role during the wars between Mithridates and Rome. They were Mithridates' principal suppliers of provisions, people, and ships, to which end Mithridates maintained very close contacts with the local barbarian leaders. Mithridates, after being defeated by the Romans and betrayed by his own son, killed himself in Panticapaeum in 63 B.C. The ensuing political chaos witnessed frequent changes of rulers in the major Greek cities of the northern Black Sea, often at the initiative or with the active connivance of Rome. Gradually, Roman appetite and influence grew, but it was not until the beginning of the second century

A.D. that the whole area became fully integrated into the Roman Empire.

See also **Greek Colonies in the East** (*vol. 2, part 6*); **Scythians** (*vol. 2, part 7*).

BIBLIOGRAPHY

Bouzek, Jan. *Greece, Anatolia and Europe: Cultural Interrelations during the Early Iron Age.* Studies in Mediterranean Archaeology, vol. 122. Jonsered, Sweden: Paul Åströms Förlag, 1997.

Davis-Kimball, Jeannine, Vladimir A. Bashilov, and Leonid T. Yablonsky, eds. *Nomads of the Eurasian Steppes in the Early Iron Age.* Berkeley, Calif.: Zinat Press, 1995.

Herodotus. *The Histories.* Translated by Aubrey de Sélincourt. Revised by A. R. Burn. London: Penguin, 1972.

Hind, J. G. F. "Archaeology of the Greeks and Barbarian Peoples around the Black Sea (1982–1992)." *Archaeological Reports* 39 (1992–1993): 82–112.

Reeder, Ellen D., ed. *Scythian Gold: Treasures from Ancient Ukraine.* New York: Harry N. Abrams in association with the Walters Art Gallery and the San Antonio Museum of Art, 1999.

Rolle, Renate. *The World of the Scythians.* Translated by Gayna Walls. London: Batsford, 1989.

Sauter, Hermann. *Studien zum Kimmerierproblem.* Saarbrücker Beiträge zur Altertumskunde 72. Bonn, Germany: R. Habelt, 2000.

Strabo. *The Geography of Strabo.* Translated by Horace Leonard Jones. 8 Vols. London: William Heinemann, 1917.

Treister, Michail J., and Yuri G. Vinogradov. "Archaeology on the Northern Coast of the Black Sea." *American Journal of Archaeology* 97, no. 3 (1993): 521–563.

Tsetskhladze, Gocha R. "Who Built the Scythian and Thracian Royal and Elite Tombs?" *Oxford Journal of Archaeology* 17, no. 1 (1998): 55–92.

———, ed. *North Pontic Archaeology: Recent Discoveries and Studies.* Colloquia Pontica, vol. 6. Leiden, The Netherlands, and Boston: Brill, 2001.

———, ed. *Ancient Greeks West and East.* Mnemosyne Bibliotheca Classica Batava Supplementum 196. Leiden, The Netherlands, and Boston: Brill, 1999.

———, ed. *The Greek Colonisation of the Black Sea Area. Historical Interpretation of Archaeology.* Historia Einzelschriften 121. Stuttgart, Germany: Steiner, 1998.

Tsetskhladze, Gocha R., and A. M. Snodgrass, eds. *Greek Settlements in the Eastern Mediterranean and the Black Sea.* BAR International Series, no. 1062. Oxford: Archaeopress, 2002.

GOCHA R. TSETSKHLADZE

IRON AGE EAST-CENTRAL EUROPE

During the second half of the nineteenth century, when archaeologists developed the outlines of the current system of chronology for prehistoric Europe, they defined the Iron Age as the time when iron came into use as the principal material for making tools. Since iron technology was adopted gradually, defining the beginning of the Iron Age is somewhat arbitrary. There is no break, either in technology or in other aspects of human culture, between the Late Bronze Age and the Early Iron Age. Small iron tools occur on settlements in parts of east-central Europe from 1000 B.C. on, but larger implements do not appear until after 800 B.C. By generally agreed definition, the Iron Age in east-central Europe began about 800 B.C. For the purposes of this discussion, three periods are distinguished: an Early Iron Age, 800–450 B.C.; a Middle Iron Age, 450–200 B.C.; and a Late Iron Age, 200 B.C. to the Roman conquest.

The region of east-central Europe defined here—the Czech Republic, Slovakia, Hungary, and the lands of the former Yugoslavia—includes a variety of different landscapes and was home to distinct cultural traditions during the Iron Age. Except for the Great Hungarian Plain, most of the land is hilly and mountainous. The entire region is dominated by the Danube River valley, and important smaller rivers, such as the Elbe, the Tisza, and the Sava, also played important roles in communities' selection of places to settle and in trade systems. This short review emphasizes patterns that are characteristic of large portions of east-central Europe, while at the same time noting significant variability.

EARLY IRON AGE (800–450 B.C.)
The basic settlement, subsistence, craft-working, and trade systems at the start of the Iron Age were similar to those of the preceding Late Bronze Age. Beginning as early as the ninth century B.C., however, objects associated with horseback riding, such as bits and harness ornaments, indicating links with regions to the east, appeared in graves and in hoard deposits over much of east-central Europe, including the Great Hungarian Plain, western Slovakia, and Croatia. Debate surrounds the question of whether these objects indicate primarily migration of peoples from north of the Black Sea or new contacts made between peoples in these different regions. In the succeeding centuries, horse-riding material of bronze, iron, and bone played an important role in burial ritual and attests to the significance of horseback riding among Early Iron Age elites. In some regions burial practice included the placing of four-wheeled wagons in the richest graves, as in the Bylany culture graves at Hradenín in Bohemia.

In much of Europe, burial practice during the Late Bronze Age was commonly by cremation in flat graves, and in the Early Iron Age inhumation and burying the dead under mounds became widespread. In some places, mounds were erected over individual graves; in others, such as Slovenia, great communal mounds became the rule, with as many as two hundred graves in a mound. These were highly visible structures, meant to be seen by the living. The change to mound burial indicates a new concern with permanent display of status among many of the peoples of east-central Europe.

Hilltop Centers. During the Early Iron Age, the rise to prominence of major centers of political power and of economic activity constituted a change from Bronze Age circumstances. This change is particularly evident in Slovenia, where major fortified hilltop settlements were created at numerous locations during the eighth century B.C. Among the best studied are Magdalenska gora, Most na Soči, Stična, and Vače. Each of these settlements is accompanied by large cemeteries of communal burial mounds. Stična is the most fully investigated. There, the fortified area measures about 800 by 400 meters, and investigators have counted about 150 mounds in the low land around the settlement. One excavated mound at Stična contained nearly two hundred graves, suggesting how large the cemetery, and thus the population, may have been.

Stična and other settlements in Slovenia were centers of iron production, and the graves indicate substantial manufacture of spearheads, axes, horse bits, and other implements from the eighth century B.C. on. Bronze working also was a highly developed craft, with large-scale manufacture of personal ornaments, ornate bronze vessels, and armor, such as helmets and cuirasses. Glass production was a significant industry as well. Hundreds of multicolored beads occur in many graves, and glass beads from this region reached communities all over Europe. Commerce brought amber from the shores of the Baltic Sea, Etruscan pottery and bronze objects, and even ornate feasting equipment from the Near East.

Similar centers emerged in other parts of the region. At Závist in Bohemia, a fortified settlement was established on a hilltop during the sixth century B.C. Workshop evidence shows that a range of goods was manufactured. The community imported amber from the Baltic region and glass beads from centers in Slovenia. The excavators of the site believe that a major ritual complex at the top of the hill, defined by a rectangular enclosure 28 meters on a side surrounded by a ditch dug into the bedrock, was established at Závist. In western Slovakia, a fortified hilltop settlement dating to the seventh and sixth centuries B.C. has been excavated at Smolenice-Molpír. Like other hilltop sites, this one attests to both a central role in production and the presence of high-status individuals buried in nearby cemeteries. Other fortified hilltop centers of this pe-

Fig. 1. *Situla* from Kuffern, lower Austria, fifth century B.C. © NATURHISTORISCHES MUSEUM WIEN, PHOTO: ALICE SCHUMACHER. REPRODUCED BY PERMISSION.

riod include sites at Sopron and Velemszentvid in Hungary.

Figural Art. Among the Early Iron Age peoples of temperate Europe, figural art was a special development in parts of east-central Europe. This artwork includes figurines placed in graves or in deposits, particularly in Slovenia and Hungary. Figures incised on pottery are representative of cemeteries at Sopron in Hungary and at Nové Košariská in Slovakia. The most complex of the figural art, the Situla art of Slovenia and regions to the west, is a specific characteristic of the major centers there, such as Magdalenska gora, Stična, and Vače (fig. 1). Of particular interest for studies of the Early Iron Age are scenes that show people engaged in various activities.

Among the figures incised on pottery, common themes include persons with their arms raised as if in honor of a deity, individuals riding on horseback and driving wagons, and people playing musical instruments, especially lyres. Important scenes figured on pottery from the graves at Sopron include those showing persons spinning and weaving textiles. In the Situla art of Slovenia and regions to the west, a variety of complex activities are represented, among them, scenes that show feasting, hunting, processions, athletic contests, and well-armed troops marching in formation.

Interpretations of these complex representations fall into two main groups. One set views the scenes as pictures of the festive lives of the elites at the centers. The objects shown in the banqueting scenes, in the illustrations of athletic contests, and in the depictions of marching soldiers (such as vessels, helmets, axes, spears, and shields) match objects found in the graves. This provides a clear link between the representations and the local communities at which the scenes were created by craft workers and found by archaeologists. The spindle whorls and looms portrayed in the incised scenes of textile working on the pots at Sopron correspond to implements found in women's burials there and elsewhere.

The other group of interpretations regards these scenes as mythological or religious in nature, not depicting real people but rather telling stories of mythical significance. Specialists have argued that the weaving scenes represent the passage of time or fate and that figures around the weavers can be interpreted in terms of religious ritual. Scenes of feasts, processions, hunting, athletic contests, and marching troops have been understood to exemplify ideas about community solidarity, fertility, death, and rebirth.

Ritual. In the hilly and mountainous regions of east-central Europe, many sites have been discovered at which ritual deposits were made during the Early Iron Age. The practice of placing, dropping, and throwing valued objects into special natural places—springs, ponds, rivers, caves, clefts in cliff faces—as offerings to deities has been done from Upper Palaeolithic times to the modern day. Particular kinds of locations and specific types of objects are favored in different contexts. Many hilltops in east-central Europe apparently were used as places for ritual practice, such as the site of Burkovak, near Písek in Bohemia, where figurines of animals and humans, wheel-shaped clay objects, and pottery have been found in pits. The hilltop at Závist may be another ritual place.

Caves often were used for ritual practice. Bronze jewelry items were particularly common as ritual deposits in caves. Other objects recovered in such contexts comprise tools and weapons, pottery, and human and animal remains. In some caves, evidence of human sacrifice has been identified. Among the best-known sites is the cave at Býčí skála in Moravia, where quantities of materials of varied character were deposited at the end of the Early Iron Age. Personal ornaments of types worn by both men and women were abundant. Weapons were well represented, including daggers, axes, lances, helmets, cuirasses, and arrows. Blacksmiths' tools and fittings from horse harnesses also were present. Fragments of wagons were recovered as well. Bones of cattle, pigs, sheep, and horses were found, as were skeletal remains of men, women, and children, representing at least thirty-seven individuals. Pottery vessels and large bronze containers associated with feasting were part of the assemblage. Among the materials recovered were knives, spindle whorls, harvesting tools, and cereal grains. The assemblage from Býčí skála was removed from the cave in the nineteenth century, and we lack good information about the arrangement of the objects when they were discovered. The different categories of objects found in the cave, however, match those from later, well-documented sites that have ritual associations.

MIDDLE IRON AGE (450–200 B.C.)
The style of ornament known as La Tène, developed in the Rhineland in the early part of the fifth century B.C., appeared in east-central Europe in about the middle of that century. Among the earliest expressions of this new style in the region are fibulae—brooches that work mechanically like modern safety pins—ornamented with human, bird, and mammal heads, a form particularly well represented in Bohemia. From the end of the fifth century B.C. onward, La Tène style, with its curvilinear ornament and stylized animal and human figures, also is seen engraved and incised on weapons, pottery, and other objects. The new style most often is seen on objects associated with elites, in wealthy burials. In some regions, such as Bohemia, there were groups of unusually rich graves, such as those excavated at Chlum, Hradiště, Písek, and Prague-Modrany. At Chlum a dead man was buried within a chamber built of stone, covered by a burial mound. Grave

goods included an imported Etruscan bronze jug, two Greek wine cups, a sword, an axe, a knife, and personal ornaments of gold, silver, and bronze.

New Burial Practices. During the late fifth and fourth centuries B.C., burial practice changed in most parts of east-central Europe, from mound burial to inhumation in flat graves. In many cemeteries, graves generally are well outfitted. Often about half of the men's graves contain sets of iron weapons, including sword, lance, and shield (wood with iron rim). Women's graves characteristically contain bronze and iron jewelry—often complete sets with neck ring, two bracelets, sometimes two leg rings, and several fibulae. Ceramic and, more rarely, bronze vessels occasionally accompany the other grave goods. Burial practices varied somewhat in different regions, but in broad outline the similarities are striking. Among well-documented cemeteries of this period are Bučany in western Slovakia, Jászberény-Cserőhalom in Hungary, Brežice in Slovenia, Karaburma near Belgrade in Serbia, and Jenišův Újezd in Bohemia. One study of several cemeteries in Bohemia found that in those communities, life expectancy for men was forty-two years, and for women it was thirty-eight. Communities were small—individual farmsteads or very small villages, rarely with more than fifty people per settlement. The spread of La Tène style and the adoption of these common burial practices often have been attributed to migrations of Celts from the Rhineland. Modern understanding of the nature of group identity and of the meaning of the name "Celts," however, makes this mechanism of dispersion unlikely. More probably, the new stylistic fashion and burial practice spread because they filled specific social and cultural needs of communities throughout much of Europe.

At the same time that the burial practice changed from tumulus burial to flat grave inhumation, the great majority of the fortified hilltop settlements were abandoned. People who had resided in them moved down into the lower lands. A dispersed settlement pattern characterized the cultural landscape, in contrast to the centralized system based on the hillforts that had dominated many regions during the Early Iron Age. The lavish gold ornaments and ornate bronze vessels from the Mediterranean world were no longer buried with elite individuals, yet differences in burial wealth continued to be sig-

nificant. In the great flat-grave cemeteries, wealth differences between rich and poor graves are subtler than in those from the Early Iron Age, but they are nonetheless evident. Special status is apparent in some men's graves that contain sets of weapons, with swords and scabbards sometimes bearing special ornament. Such ornamentation is especially common in the Carpathian Basin, where opposed pairs of dragons incised on the upper part of scabbards was a special symbol of the warrior elite. Scabbard decoration known as the "Hungarian sword style" appears throughout much of temperate Europe, from England to Romania.

Settlement. Settlements of this period typically were farms and small villages, such as one excavated at Radovesice in Bohemia. Agriculture and crafts were practiced to satisfy the needs of the resident community, with little apparent surplus production for trade. Major centers, such as those of the Early Iron Age, have not been identified for this period, but some specialized production places focused on the extraction of specific resources. At Msec in Bohemia a center of large-scale iron production has been identified, and at Lovosice there is a center for the quarrying of porphyry for making grindstones.

Ritual. During the middle part of the Iron Age, deposits of valuable objects in water best represented ritual practice. At Duchcov in northwest Bohemia, a bronze cauldron was found in a spring with a large number of bronze ornaments in it. They included some 850 fibulae, 650 bracelets, and 100 finger rings. Estimates place the original total number of objects at about 2,500. The site was discovered in 1882 during construction work, and many of the objects were dispersed without record. A complex interpreted as a ritual enclosure has been identified at Libenice, also in Bohemia. A ditch enclosed a long, thin rectangle of land; in the middle of it was a single burial, with a large stone set into the ground nearby.

LATE IRON AGE (200 B.C. TO THE ROMAN CONQUEST)

In the final centuries of the Iron Age, communities larger and more complex than any earlier ones developed throughout much of temperate Europe.

Oppida. The final phase of the prehistoric Iron Age in east-central Europe and as far west as France is characterized by the development of the *oppida*. These were large fortified settlements, usually on hilltops, that had populations substantially larger than any earlier settlements in the region and show evidence of larger-scale manufacturing and trade. Research has shown that the development of these towns was a long and gradual process. Among the principal *oppida* in east-central Europe are Stradonice, Hrazany, Třísov, and Závist in Bohemia; Staré Hradisko in Moravia; Bratislava and Zemplín in Slovakia; Sopron, Velemszentvid, and Budapest-Gellérthegy in Hungary; and Židovar in Serbia.

The reasons that *oppida* developed during the second century B.C. are much debated. Some archaeologists favor a primarily defensive explanation. The second century B.C. was a time of increased violence and migration, and communities banded together, built large fortified settlements, and moved inside to protect themselves against attackers. Others argue for a mainly economic basis. During this time, commerce was expanding rapidly. Roman imports were more common, both at the *oppidum* settlements and elsewhere, and trade with all parts of Europe is evident. Coinage developed late in the third century B.C., and at many of the *oppida*, such as Stradonice, a money-based economy was created. Another explanation is primarily political. Society in temperate Europe was becoming more complicated. The need for both defense against outside aggressors and management of the complex economies gave an advantage to the organization of larger political units. We know that in Gaul during the final century B.C. the *oppida* were the political capitals of the groups that the Romans recognized as tribes. Thus, the *oppida* throughout Europe came into being perhaps in part to serve as centers of political units that were forming at the time.

At excavated *oppida* evidence for extensive ironworking is prevalent. In most cases, iron ores were available on or close to the surface near the settlements. There are abundant remains of smelting slag and furnaces and of tools and debris from the process of forging wrought iron into a wide variety of tools, weapons, building elements, and ornament. In this period, smiths were producing much more iron than in earlier times, and they were fashioning tools that made many tasks more efficient. Iron plowshares made the plowing of fields, including those on rich, heavy loam, much less difficult and

time-consuming. Scythes made harvesting of hay easier than it had been with earlier tools. Nails first appeared in quantities at this time, improving the construction of houses, wagons, boats, and other wooden structures.

While the phenomenon of these large and often commercially and politically central communities suggests similar processes of economic and political change throughout much of temperate Europe, individual *oppida* varied in character. Stradonice was one of the most densely occupied and commercially active centers in Late Iron Age Europe. Unfortunately, the site was extensively excavated under unscientific conditions during the nineteenth century, and good maps or plans do not exist of the settlement or of locations of important finds. The mass of objects recovered on the site, however, indicates the range of manufacturing and commercial activities in which the community was engaged. Ironworking is well represented, and numerous hammers, knives, axes, and other implements were found. Locks and keys suggest an important change in the need for personal security at these large centers.

Potters produced a variety of ceramics, ranging from large, coarse-textured storage vessels to thin-walled, ornately painted vessels thrown on the fast-turning potter's wheel. Fibulae, of which some thirteen hundred specimens are known from Stradonice, were made most often of bronze and iron but sometimes of silver and gold. Certain glass beads and bracelets may have been imported and others made onsite. Communities at some of the *oppida* started minting coins in about the middle of the second century B.C., and at Stradonice bronze, silver, and gold coins are represented. Engagement in commerce with the Roman world is evident in imported ceramic amphorae which probably once contained wine, bronze vessels, and fragments of writing tablets, exemplifying a new technology introduced through trade between the *oppida* and merchants in the Mediterranean Basin.

At the Late Iron Age settlement at Závist, the fortification walls enclose 170 hectares, making this the largest of the *oppida* in Bohemia. Excavations have revealed a site less densely occupied than Stradonice, however, and with fewer archaeological materials. Excavations at Staré Hradisko in Moravia yielded finds similar to those at Stradonice but from a settlement apparently not as densely inhabited. The detailed plans produced by archaeologists show that the settlement was divided into individual units—similar to small agricultural settlements—rather than being designed on a centralized scheme. At Zemplín in Slovakia, the area enclosed by the defensive system is smaller than that at many of the sites to the west, and a substantial settlement lies outside the fortifications. At Židovar in Serbia, excavations have uncovered a fortified hilltop settlement with well-built houses with packed clay floors and, in some cases, stone foundations. Thus, considerable variation in size and character is apparent among these complex Late Iron Age settlements.

In the past, the *oppida* have attracted a great deal of research attention. Later archaeologists have explored the typical small farming communities that are evident throughout east-central Europe, as in other parts of the Continent. Important investigations at the settlements of Strachotín and Boritov in Moravia show that even small communities manufactured pottery and iron tools, and they were connected closely to the large economic and political centers at the *oppida*.

Ritual. At the time that the *oppida* were established in the second and first centuries B.C., rectangular enclosures, usually known by the German term *Viereckschanzen*, became common throughout the same regions. Typically, they are bounded by an external ditch and a wall on the inside; the enclosed area is roughly 90 by 90 meters, though sizes vary. Archaeologists have debated the purpose of these sites. Among the interpretations are enclosed farmsteads, animal pens, small fortresses, and ritual places. Deposits recovered in deep pits on certain sites and in the ditches on others have lent support to the ritual theory. Intensive investigation of many of these enclosures in different part of central Europe, however, has suggested a more complex picture. While many sites yield evidence that strongly supports ritual activity, others include typical domestic settlement debris, such as pottery fragments, animal bones, and scraps from manufacturing processes, very much like the material found on typical habitation sites. Archaeologists are beginning to realize that settlement and ritual places do not need to be viewed as separate. Perhaps in the Late Iron Age, in particular, people often engaged in ritual activity within their settlements.

Fig. 2. Stone head from Mšecké Žehrovice, Bohemia, associated with a pair of rectangular enclosures, first century B.C. COURTESY OF THE NÁRODNÍ MUZEUM, PRAGUE. REPRODUCED BY PERMISSION.

At Mšecké Žehrovice in Bohemia a pair of such enclosures has been excavated. Wooden buildings inside them differ from typical houses of the period and have been interpreted as ritual in purpose. A roughly life-size stylized human head sculpted of stone, with classic La Tène–style scrolled eyebrows and mustache, and wearing a neck ring was found in association with one enclosure (fig. 2). This archetypal example of "Celtic art" supports the interpretation of the Mšecké Žehrovice complex as partly, but not necessarily completely, ritual in purpose.

In this final phase of the prehistoric Iron Age, it became common practice in much of Europe to deposit iron tools in pits in the ground. While the argument can be made for precious metals, such as gold and silver coins, and even for bronze that such hoarding may have been intended to protect valuable materials from theft, in the case of iron this argument is less persuasive. By the final phase of the Iron Age, iron had little value, because it was being produced in such vast quantities. Moreover, unlike gold, silver, and bronze, iron objects rusted quickly in the damp soils of temperate Europe. Iron hoards more likely were ritual in nature.

A cache found at Kolín in Bohemia contained sixty-eight objects, among them implements for use in the hearth, such as vessels; a suspension chain for hanging a cauldron over a fire; and a hearth shovel. Other tools were for ironworking and carpentry. Agricultural tools were present as well—plowshares, hoes, a scythe, and a sickle. Keys, parts of weapons, and attachments from a wagon and from horse harnesses also were present. Comparing the contents of this assemblage with hoards from other sites points up particular themes represented by the objects— hearth and home, nutrition, and transformation (smithing tools to change ore into iron). Not far away, at Stary Kolín, was found a deposit of more than three hundred gold coins, similar to many other coin hoards of this period in temperate Europe.

Writing. At Zenjak in Slovenia was found a deposit of twenty-four bronze helmets, one with writing incised on the brim. The helmet type is common in Slovenia; it is known as a Negau helmet, after the German name for the site. Linguistic analysis of the characters has identified them as part of an alphabet known to have been used in northern Italy at that time, and the inscription is the earliest known in a Germanic language. The meaning of the inscription has been much debated. Some believe it calls upon a god for assistance, whereas others think it designates ownership of the helmet. The fact that the earliest known inscription in a Germanic language should be found far away from the region in which Romans of this period identified Germans adds to the complication of interpreting the significance of this object.

See also **Germans** (*vol. 2, part 6*); **Oppida** (*vol. 2, part 6*); **Ritual Sites: Viereckschanzen** (*vol. 2, part 6*); **La Tène Art** (*vol. 2, part 6*).

BIBLIOGRAPHY

Bouzek, Jan. *Greece, Anatolia, and Europe: Cultural Inter-relations during the Early Iron Age.* Studies in Mediterranean Archaeology 122. Jonsered, Sweden: Paul Åstroms Förlag, 1997.

Collis, John. *Oppida: Earliest Towns North of the Alps.* Sheffield, U.K.: Department of Prehistory and Archaeology, University of Sheffield, 1984.

Guštin, Mitja. "Die Kelten in Jugoslawien: Übersicht über das archäologische Fundgut." *Jahrbuch des Römisch-Germanischen Zentralmuseums Mainz* 31 (1983): 305–363.

Kristiansen, Kristian. *Europe before History.* New York: Cambridge University Press, 1998.

Križ, Borut. *The Celts in Novo Mesto/Kelti v Novem mesto.* Novo mesto, Slovenia: Dolenjski muzej, 2001.

Kruta, Venceslas. *Les Celtes: Histoire et dictionnaire, des origines à la romanisation et au christianisme.* Paris: Éditions Robert Laffont, 2000.

Moscati, Sabatino, ed. *The Celts.* New York: Rizzoli, 1991.

Palavestra, Aleksandar. "Prehistoric Trade and a Cultural Model for Princely Tombs in the Central Balkans." In *Europe in the First Millennium* B.C. Edited by K. Kristiansen and J. Jensen, pp. 45–56. Sheffield, U.K.: J. R. Collis Publications, 1994.

Parzinger, Hermann, Jindra Nekvasil, and Fritz Eckart Barth. *Die Byčí skála-Höhle: Ein hallstattzeitlicher Höhlenopferplatz in Mähren.* Mainz, Germany: Verlag Philipp von Zabern, 1995.

Venclová, Natalie. *Mšecké Žehrovice in Bohemia: Archaeological Background to a Celtic Hero, 3rd–2nd Century* B.C. Sceaux, France: Kronos, 1998.

Wells, Peter S. "The Iron Age." In *European Prehistory: A Survey.* Edited by S. Milisauskas, pp. 335–383. New York: Kluwer Academic/Plenum Publishers, 2002.

PETER S. WELLS

IRON AGE CAUCASIA

The Iron Age (defined broadly as an archaeological period from c. 1200 to 300 B.C.) in Caucasia witnessed a series of remarkable transformations in the social, cultural, and political traditions of the region that have left indelible marks upon the region's cultural landscape and contemporary geopolitics. During this era, small, hierarchical, centralized polities emerged as the dominant features of the region's social order. In some areas, particularly southern Caucasia, these archaic sociopolitical formations subsequently fused into large empires; in other regions, traditions of local control persisted even as contacts with an expanding ecumene—driven by both Greek colonialism and Achaemenid imperialism—brought new social forces and cultural influences into the region. This brief overview provides an orientation to the region's primary sociopolitical transformations. Because the beginning of the Iron Age closely followed traditions established in the Bronze Age, this account begins in the early second millennium B.C. and concludes with a brief historical discussion of post–Iron Age Caucasia from the conquests of Alexander the Great through the Roman defeat of both the Pontic kingdom (66 B.C.) and Tigran II's Armenian empire (65 B.C.).

GEOGRAPHIC ORIENTATION

The Caucasus range traverses more than 1,100 kilometers, from the Black Sea to the Caspian Sea along the northern end of the isthmus that separates the Eurasian steppes from Southwest Asia. Caucasia continues to be shaped by the tectonic action of the Arabian and Eurasian plates, a collision that has thrown up the Caucasus Mountains, folding the un-

derlying bedrock and erecting high volcanic peaks. The volcanic activity that raised peaks, such as Mount Elbrus, Mount Ararat, and Mount Aragats, to name only a few, covered the region with a sea of lava, leaving behind vast deposits of basalt, tuff, and obsidian. Caucasia is an ecologically diverse region with provinces ranging from the subtropical Colchian depression in the west, to the well-watered high mountains in the south, to the arid steppes in the east. Climate is similarly variable, with average annual rainfall varying from about 2,500 millimeters on the Black Sea coast near the modern Georgian city of Batumi to less than 200 millimeters on the Apsheron Peninsula of eastern Azerbaijan. Throughout much of Caucasia, the period of heaviest precipitation is between March and mid-May, but whereas summers are dry, heavy snows can fall in the highlands during the winter.

Distinct geographic provinces within Caucasia are most readily defined in reference to elevation and the Kura and Araxes River drainages. Southern Caucasia is most readily defined as the highland middle Araxes River and its drainages: a region of rugged upland mountains and high plateaus. Average elevation is between 1,200 and 1,800 meters above sea level, dipping below 1,000 meters only in the fertile Ararat Plain. The highlands of northern Caucasia are defined by the upper and middle Kura River and its drainages. North Caucasia should not be confused with the North Caucasus region, which encompasses the northern slopes of the Great Caucasus. Western Caucasia (the Colchian depression, drained by the westward-flowing Rioni and Inguri

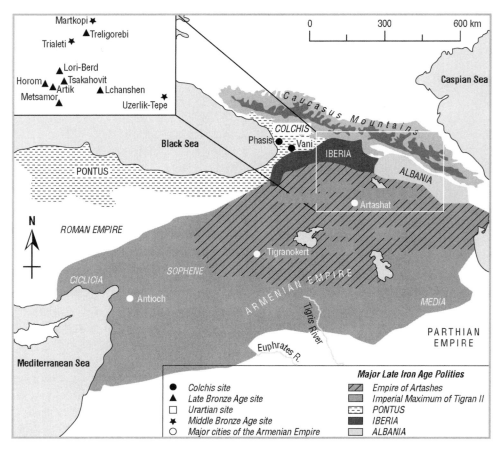

Selected sites and major polities in Bronze Age and Iron Age Caucasia. DRAWN BY ADAM SMITH.

Rivers) and eastern Caucasia (the steppes of Azerbaijan, crossed by the lower Araxes and Kura as they sprint to the Caspian) are both low-lying areas characterized by broad open terrain.

FROM THE MIDDLE BRONZE AGE TO THE EARLY IRON AGE

The end of the Early and beginning of the Middle Bronze Age, across most of Caucasia, was marked by the disappearance of the Kura-Araxes archaeological horizon (defined most readily by distinctive black burnished ceramic complexes) and the large-scale abandonment of settled village communities. Except for the late-third-millennium B.C. layers from the Bedeni sites in southern Georgia, there is little evidence for continuity in Early and Middle Bronze Age occupations, and indeed comparatively few Middle Bronze Age settlements have been documented in Caucasia. As a result, the vast majority of the archaeological record for the Middle Bronze Age comes from mortuary sites. The tombs and

kurgans of Shengavit, Trialeti (old group, a distinctive group of burials within the Trialeti complex), and Martkopi indicate profound social, cultural, and political transformations were under way during the third quarter of the third millennium B.C.

This shift in settlement patterns across Caucasia during the Early to Middle Bronze transition is traditionally interpreted as evidence of the advent of increasingly nomadic social groups predicated upon pastoral subsistence production. The appearance of ox and horse sacrifices in numerous Middle Bronze I and II burials attests to the increased prominence of pastoral production and equestrian mobility within these communities. The shifting subsistence economy was also accompanied by fundamental transformations in the social milieu, changes that centered on emerging radical inequality between a martial elite and the remainder of the social body. The rich inventories of Middle Bronze Age *kurgans* signify a profound departure in social relations from those indicated by the burials of the Kura-Araxes phase. Even more dramatic expressions of this in-equality are visible in the following Middle Bronze II period, when a great part of highland Caucasia was enveloped in the Trialeti-Vanadzor horizon, which was most prominently marked by large burial complexes of unprecedented wealth. The monu-mental construction and rich mortuary goods of tombs from Trialeti, Vanadzor, Karashamb, and Lori Berd as well as the iconography of elite privi-lege portrayed on the metal vessels from Karashamb (fig. 1) and Korukh Tash testify to profound changes in the social orders of Caucasia and provide the initial indications of emergent sociopolitical in-equality in the region.

During the Middle Bronze III period, Caucasia appears to have fragmented into several distinct ma-terial culture horizons. If the earlier Trialeti-Vanadzor sites present a relatively homogeneous horizon style for the Middle Bronze II phase, trans-formations in burial construction and the forms and styles of painted and black ornamented pottery dur-ing the succeeding period indicate the differentia-tion of the region into at least three contemporary, overlapping ceramic horizons: Karmir-Berd, Sevan-Uzerlik, and Karmir-Vank. Karmir-Berd materials largely prevail in the highlands of central-southern and northern Caucasia. The Sevan-Uzerlik horizon tends to predominate in the western steppe of Azer-baijan, the Nagorno-Karabakh highlands, and the Sevan and Syunik regions of Armenia. The Karmir-Vank horizon is best known from the Nakhichevan region of Azerbaijan and the site of Haftavan Tepe in northwestern Iran. These general regional divi-sions cannot be taken as rigid geographic mosaics. Sevan basin sites have also yielded evidence of Kar-mir-Vank and Karmir-Berd painted pottery; Ararat Plain sites have included both Karmir-Berd and Sevan-Uzerlik materials; and Sevan sites contain both Karmir-Berd and Sevan-Uzerlik ceramics. In Georgia, the Trialeti-Vanadzor horizon persists into the Middle Bronze III phase at sites such as Treli, Tsavgli, Natakhtari, and Pevrebi; however, it is also possible to detect the influence of Sevan-Uzerlik complexes as well, represented by black pottery with dotted lines.

During the Middle Bronze III phase, the wealth of the burial inventories seen in the preced-ing phase begins to diminish such that, in the com-plexes represented by Karmir-Berd or Karmir-

Fig. 1. A Middle Bronze Age goblet from Karashamb. COURTESY OF THE INSTITUTE OF ARCHAEOLOGY AND ETHNOGRAPHY, YEREVAN, ARMENIA. REPRODUCED BY PERMISSION.

Berd/Sevan Uzerlik pottery, relatively few bronze artifacts have been recorded. Furthermore, in the complexes that signify the end of Middle Bronze Age, the distinctive painted pottery becomes in-creasingly rare, yielding to the incised gray and blackware ceramics that came to predominate under the Lchashen-Metsamor horizon of the Late Bronze Age.

The first clear evidence for sociopolitical com-plexity in southern Caucasia appears in the Late Bronze Age. The Late Bronze Age is marked most conspicuously by the reappearance of numerous permanent settlements in the form of variably sized stone-masonry fortresses built atop hills and out-crops. These fortified settlements are often associat-ed with large cemeteries, such as Treligorebi located on the outskirts of modern Tbilisi, Georgia. The transition between the Middle and Late Bronze Age is also marked by the gradual introduction of new ceramic forms and decorative styles—most notably the disappearance of painted pottery and punctate designs in favor of suites of black, gray, and buff wares with incised decorations—as well as new approaches to metallurgical production.

Examinations of Late Bronze and Early Iron Age sites in Caucasia began in the late nineteenth century and early twentieth century, when archaeologists and architectural historians embarked on a series of nonsystematic surveys to document the settlement history of the region. To date only a handful of Late Bronze or Early Iron Age settlements, including Metsamor in the Ararat Plain and Tsakahovit on the northern slope of Mount Aragats, have hosted intensive archaeological investigations. Evidence of unfortified settlements remains scarce, even in regions, such as the Tsakahovit Plain, that have hosted intensive systematic archaeological surveys. Archaeological investigations have focused more resolutely on late-second- to early-first-millennia B.C. cemeteries. Large mortuary complexes at Lchashen (on the northwestern coast of Lake Sevan), Lori-Berd (in the Lori-Pambakh region of northern Armenia), and Artik and Horom (both on the lower western slope of Mount Aragats) have provided the most extensive orientation to the material culture of the era as well as the primary bases for periodization.

With the dawn of the Late Bronze Age, the social inequalities visible in the *kurgans* of the early second millennium appear to have been formalized into a tightly integrated sociopolitical apparatus where critical controls over resources—economic, social, sacred—were concentrated within the cyclopean stone masonry walls of powerful new centers. These political centers projected authority well into the hinterlands. Large-scale irrigation facilities first appear in the region in association with Late Bronze Age fortress complexes, suggesting significant centralized control over the agricultural productivity of the region. In addition, vast cemeteries appear coincident with the emergence of Late Bronze Age polities.

In the Tsakahovit region, an archaeological survey conducted in 1998 and 2000 recorded a very high density of Late Bronze Age cemeteries (4.6 per square kilometer) in the mountain highlands immediately surrounding a series of adjacent fortresses. Given the lack of nonfortified settlements in the region, it is quite likely that non-elite populations may have continued the highly mobile ways of life that arose in the Middle Bronze Age, even as elites settled within fortified complexes. It is possible that the explosion in tombs and cemeteries in the Late Bronze Age was part of an effort by emergent sociopolitical authorities to increase the commitments of their subjects to a specific place (through ties between ancestral and descendant families and groups) and thus make them a more stable foundation for the demands of the extractive political economy.

Many of the material culture forms and styles developed in the Late Bronze Age continued into and through the Early Iron Age. Pottery from Early Iron Age levels is typologically distinct from Late Bronze III wares but is quite clearly continuous with Late Bronze Age formal and decorative traditions. The same holds true for fortress architecture, which, while distinct in several morphological features, remains within the building traditions established in the Late Bronze Age. Thus the Early Iron Age is marked archaeologically by the emergence and expansion of iron implements but appears to have been socioculturally continuous with the preceding era. Examinations of materials recovered from mortuary contexts suggest that the Early Iron Age can be divided into two distinct phases: a transitional Early Iron I, dated conventionally to the late twelfth century and eleventh century B.C., and an Early Iron II phase during the tenth and ninth centuries B.C.

THE MIDDLE IRON AGE: URARTU

The florescence of local polities during the Late Bronze and Early Iron Ages was brought to an end in southern Caucasia by Urartian imperial expansion in the early eighth century B.C., providing a rather emphatic terminus for the period visible in the destruction levels at several sites, including Metsamor. The state of Biainili, known to the Assyrians (and hence modern scholarship) as Urartu, appears to have emerged in eastern Anatolia from a group of local polities during the late second millennium and early first millennium B.C. Between the mid-ninth century and the late eighth century B.C., the Urartian kings embarked on a program of imperial expansion, conquering rivals from the headwaters of the Euphrates to the south shore of Lake Urmia. Although a Urartian presence had existed north of the Araxes since the reign of King Ishpuini in the late ninth century B.C., the Urartian occupation of southern Caucasia did not begin until the second decade of the eighth century B.C., when King Argishti I formalized his military conquests through an extensive program of fortress construction in the Ararat Plain.

Although direct Urartian rule in the region was focused in southern Caucasia, the expansion of the empire had profound implications for Caucasia as a whole. The military campaigns of Urartian kings ranged far more broadly than their ambition to govern, and the demands of tribute in the form of goods, livestock, and human captives that they made upon the vanquished must have had considerable implications for local economies of the region. Furthermore, the rise of Urartu profoundly altered trade patterns in the region, as the empire was strategically positioned to regulate north-south exchanges between Caucasia and northern Mesopotamia as well as east-west trade between central Anatolia and northern Persia.

Urartu's imperial era was brought to a close by a series of military defeats in the late eighth century B.C. Urartian military and diplomatic incursions into the southern Urmia basin provoked Sargon II to reassert an Assyrian presence in the region. His campaign climaxed in the defeat of the Urartian army led by King Rusa I. Assyrian intelligence reports indicate that Urartu was also attacked at this time by Cimmerians crossing the Caucasus and destabilized by an insurrection within the Urartian ruling elite that threatened the royal dynasty. Rusa I succeeded in deflecting the Cimmerians and quelling the rebellion, thus preserving the dynasty, but Urartu's era of expansion came to an end, its imperial designs checked by Assyria in the south and Cimmerians moving into Caucasia from the north.

The historical record for Urartu's reconstruction period during the seventh century B.C. is not as rich as that of the preceding imperial phase. But the archaeological record is substantial, indicating a reconsolidation of much of Urartu's territory, a resurgence of Urartian resolve to challenge Assyrian pretensions in the highlands, and a reinvigoration of the power of Urartian central authorities. The reign of Rusa II was the apogee of the reconstruction period. Thanks to foundation inscriptions, five major fortresses, accomplished on a massive scale, are directly attributable to him, including Teishebai URU (modern Karmir-Blur) on the Ararat Plain

near Yerevan (fig. 2). Several additional fortresses in southern Caucasia that lack foundation inscriptions can also be dated to the reconstruction period based upon architectural parallels and ceramic assemblages. Dynastic succession following Rusa II is unclear, leaving some confusion over the last rulers of the empire and the dating of collapse. The fate of Urartu and its possessions in southern Caucasia during the late seventh century B.C. is not well understood. Boris Piotrovskii dated the final collapse of Urartu to 590 or 585 B.C. based largely upon a biblical reference, but this chronology is generally thought to be too long. An inscription of Ashurbanipal, dated to 643 B.C., records the submission of the Urartian king "Ishtar-duri" (Sarduri III or IV) to the Assyrians. Although this event does not provide an adequate date for Urartu's collapse, the empire was never again a significant force in the geopolitics of Southwest Asia.

LATE IRON AGE SOUTHERN CAUCASIA

Investigations of Late Iron Age Caucasia have been accomplished at a number of key sites, including Armavir-Argishtihinili, Erebuni, and Artashat in the Ararat Plain; Horom and Benjamin in the Shirak Plain; Sari-Tepe in western Azerbaijan; and small soundings at Astghi Blur, Jujevan, and Norashen in northeastern Armenia. These sites together provide an orientation to the architecture and archaeological materials of an era during which the rapid decline of Urartu was followed by the emergence of local rulers (including the Yervandid, or Orontid, kings of Armenia) who were subsequently incorporated as satraps of the Achaemenid empire.

During the Late Iron Age, local ceramic traditions from the Middle Iron Age continue, in part, in most sites. In southern Caucasia, preceding Urartian constructions were reoccupied and renovated, often following episodes of destruction that attended the Urartian collapse (e.g., at Armavir-Argishtihinili). The collapse of Urartu appears to have initiated a transformation in settlement patterns, as populations shifted away from the handful of large fortresses that dominated life under the Urartian regime and toward a larger number of small dispersed towns. Throughout the Urartian period, local ceramics in Caucasian regions peripheral to the major centers continued traditions of the

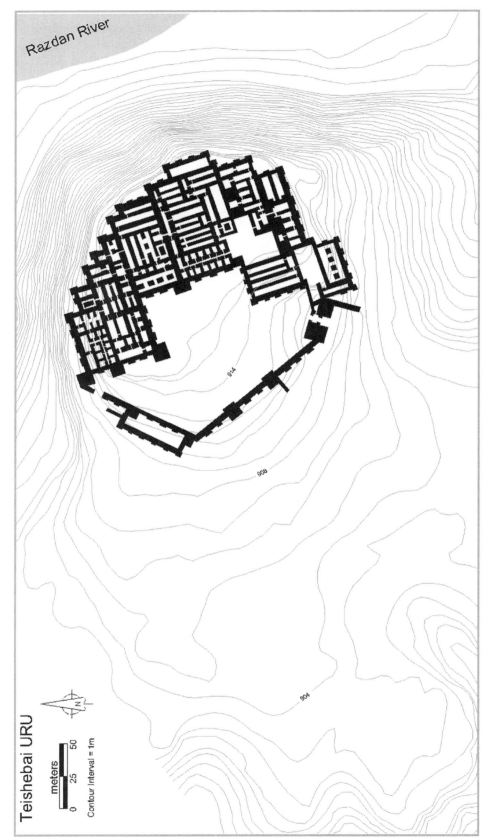

Fig. 2. Site plan of the fortress of Teishebai URU on the Ararat Plain near Yerevan. Courtesy of Adam T. Smith. Reproduced by permission.

preceding Early Iron Age horizons. Following the collapse of Urartu, these pre-Urartian ceramic traditions were partly reenergized, as local wares developed as syntheses of both pre-Urartian and Urartian traditions.

LATE IRON AGE WESTERN CAUCASIA: COLCHIS

Colchis, the easternmost archaic Greek colony, has penetrated the Western imagination largely as a place of myth: home of Medea and destination of the Argonauts. Ancient Colchis was located on the fertile lowlands of the Rioni River drainage of western Caucasia. The region appears to have developed along similar lines as the rest of Caucasia during the Early Iron Age, with the regularization of an entrenched elite, the rise of increasingly large settlements, and the development of a robust metallurgical industry with major centers in Abkhazia to the north and Adzhar to the south. However, the arrival of Greek colonists during the sixth century B.C. brought unique sociocultural and political forces to bear upon the region in the Middle and Late Iron Ages. It has been suggested that it was the prominence of Colchian metallurgy and metalworking that lured not only the Greeks to Caucasia's Black Sea shores—an argument found in the *Geographia* (1.2.39) of the Greek scholar Strabo (c. 63 B.C.–c. A.D. 21)—but also encouraged the northern campaigns of Urartian kings, who referred to the region as "Kulha" or "Qulha." Sarduri II, for example, boasted in his "annals" inscribed on the rock face at Van Kale of having destroyed twenty-two cities in Qulha. Furthermore, the incredible scale of bronze and, later, iron production within the Colchis archaeological horizon has suggested the possibility of close economic and social ties to the prolific metallurgical traditions of the Koban region of the central north Caucasus (North Ossetia).

Despite extensive archaeological and epigraphic research, however, it is not as yet entirely clear as to what kind of sociocultural entity Colchis was. Greek myths suggest a highly centralized kingdom dating back into the late second millennium B.C.; however, Urartian inscriptions indicate a more fragmented political landscape with a number of kings ruling discrete portions of the territory from large fortified settlements (similar to what they encountered in southern Caucasia). Nevertheless, broad similarities

in major material culture classes, including metal and ceramic styles, suggest a degree of sociocultural integration in western Caucasia even if the case for political unification remains unsubstantiated (although substantial disparities in mortuary customs—for example, shaft graves such as those at Dvani in contrast to the dolmens found to the north in Abkhazia—suggests that variation within the Colchis archaeological horizon has been understated).

The dating of the arrival of the Greeks is also a matter of some debate. While the earliest appearance of Greek pottery in the region has been dated to the end of the seventh century B.C., it is not until the mid-sixth century that Colchian sites begin to boast a substantial corpus of Greek wares. Greek settlement in the region was limited to the seacoast and river estuaries. Information about this initial era of colonization comes largely from archaeological sources and a few fragments of mythohistorical sources. However, both do seem to indicate that the vanguard of initial Greek intrusion came to Phasis, at the mouth of the Rioni, from Miletus, on the southwestern coast of Asia Minor. Burials around Vani, the most extensively excavated aboriginal Colchian site, suggest a further intensification of inequality and elite privilege in the era of early Greek colonialism, with extensive and rich burial inventories, including gold jewelry, silver and bronze personal ornaments, and local and imported pottery. The site of Vani itself appears to have been dominated by a local aristocracy that sat at the apex of a stratified social hierarchy. The dramatic expansion in the size and number of large storage jars (*pithoi*) during this period has suggested to some scholars a concomitant increase in the scale of surplus production, increasing demands upon the productive economy from redistributive institutions, or both.

The arrival of Achaemenid imperial forces in Caucasia established Yervandid Armenia as a formal satrap and also reconstituted Colchis geopolitically from a distant periphery to a remarkably cosmopolitan borderland, assimilating and reinventing traditions and practices from Greece, Persia, and the Eurasian steppe as well as the diverse array of social worlds within Iron Age Caucasia. The *Histories* of Herodotus (3.97), from the fifth century B.C., describes the relationship between an autonomous Colchis and the Achaemenid regime as based not on forced tribute but rather regular "presents" of one hundred young men and one hundred young women given to the Persian court. And Colchian soldiers were also listed among the expeditionary force that followed the Persian king Xerxes into Greece. But even at this time, perhaps Colchis's most prosperous era, it appears that the region continued to be ruled by a dispersed aristocracy rather than a single king capable of unifying the region into a single polity.

AFTER THE IRON AGE

The arrival of Alexander the Great's forces in Southwest Asia and the subsequent collapse of Achaemenid power brought about important transformations in Caucasia, including the slow erosion (despite the tenacity of Aramaic in major inscriptions) of Persian cultural influence under the spread of Hellenism; however, it is important not to overstate the significance of the event. Alexander never found his way into Caucasia or the Armenian Highlands of eastern Anatolia, and even if he had, Greek cultural influence was already permeating the region via the long-standing colonies in Colchis. Moreover, Alexander's conquests do not seem to have profoundly reordered the political landscape of Caucasia. By 316 B.C. Armenia was reconstituted as a satrap of Macedonian power, ruled by a king named Orontes, who appears to have been part of the Yervandid dynasty already ensconced in the region during the Achaemenid era. Occasionally the Yervandid kings formally recognized Seleucid suzerainty, but there is little to suggest that the titular overlordship of the Macedonian conquerors made a profound practical difference in Caucasia's sociopolitical order.

In 188 B.C. Artaxias (also known as Artashes) succeeded to the throne of the Armenian kingdom, initiating a new Artaxian dynasty and consolidating much of Caucasia and the Armenian Highlands under his authority. Despite efforts by the weakened Seleucids to reassert their authority over a reinvigorated local dynast, Artaxias was successful in creating an empire that established unified control over a broad swath of Caucasia and eastern Anatolia. Until the first century B.C., the expansion of the Armenian empire under the Artaxian kings was largely unchecked as Seleucid power diminished; however, the emergence of the Parthian dynasty of the Arsa-

cids in Iran and the increasing ambitions of Rome in Southwest Asia signaled trouble not only for the Armenian empire but also for Caucasia's other regimes in Pontic Colchis, Iberia, and Albania. Artaxias's grandson, Tigran II (r. 95–55 B.C.), presided over the largest consolidated polity in Caucasia's history, ruling a territory larger than Urartu that extended from the Caspian in the east, to the Kura Valley in the north, and to the Mediterranean in the west. One result of Tigran II's campaigns in the west was the further Hellenization of the royal court, which had long held to Achaemenid traditions of the early Yervandid era. Tigran was particularly successful in campaigns against Parthia (88–85 B.C.), which brought his armies on the eastern front as far south as Hamadān in Media (northwestern Iran), while to the west his forces reached Syria and the city of Antioch. For thirteen years, a Pax Armenia covered an immense multicultural and multinational empire ruled from the major cities of the empire, such as Artashat, on the northern bank of the Araxes, and Tigranakert, east of modern Diyarbakır. Artashat, occupying twelve hills (approximately 100 hectares), hosted extensive archaeological excavations during the 1970s and 1980s that explored many of the major constructions of the Artaxian period and provided the primary artifactual sources for the period.

Rome, preoccupied in Anatolia by a protracted war with Mithradates of Pontus did not interfere while Tigran's expansionary ambitions were directed against the Parthians and Seleucids. However, by 71 B.C. the imperialists in the Roman Senate sought a more encompassing solution to their problems in the east. A legate of the Roman general Lucullus delivered an ultimatum to Tigran at Antioch to hand over the recently defeated King Mithradates VI of Pontus, who had taken refuge in Armenia. Tigran refused to surrender him. Two years later, in 69 B.C., Lucullus marched on Tigranakert and, after a short siege, succeeded in defeating the main body of the Armenian army and sacking the city. The defeat of Tigranakert prompted the rapid unraveling of Tigran's dynasty, and soon, assailed by both Rome and Parthia, Artaxias's grandson sued for peace (66 B.C.) under terms that left him only the Caucasian and east Anatolian heartland. While Tigran's son Artawazd II (r. 55–34 B.C.) succeeded him on the throne, Armenia was reduced to a buffer

Stonehenge The ritual monument of Stonehenge as it appears today. First built during the Neolithic period, Stonehenge experienced several construction phases before being abandoned in the middle of the second millennium B.C. © BOB KRIST/CORBIS. REPRODUCED BY PERMISSION.

RIGHT: Bronze Age Cyprus A funnel-shaped faience "Rhyton" (ceremonial vessel) of the thirteenth century B.C., from the excavations at Kition, Cyprus. The surface of the vessel is covered with a layer of blue enamel and is divided into three horizontal bands, with the design elements painted in black, yellow, and green, and inlaid with red enamel. © GIANNI DAGLI ORTI/CORBIS. REPRODUCED BY PERMISSION.

LEFT: Bronze Age Britain and Ireland Goldwork and amber necklace from the grave group at Little Cressingham, Norfolk, c. 1800–1500 B.C. These goods were acquired by exchange and indicate the wealth of the deceased. © THE TRUSTEES OF THE NATIONAL MUSEUMS OF SCOTLAND. REPRODUCED BY PERMISSION.

TOP RIGHT: **The Heuneburg** Model of the Heuneburg, Heuneburg Museum. This Early Iron Age hillfort housed thousands of people, c. 600–450 B.C. ROSE HAJDU, FOTOGRAFIE, STUTTGART. REPRODUCED BY PERMISSION.

BELOW: **Etruscan Italy** Fresco of a banquet in the Tomb of the Leopards, Tarquinia, early fifth century B.C. © ARCHIVO ICONOGRAFICO, S.A./CORBIS. REPRODUCED BY PERMISSION.

TOP LEFT: Coinage of the Early Middle Ages Visigothic pseudo-imperial gold tremissis, c. seventh century A.D. THE AMERICAN NUMISMATIC SOCIETY, NEW YORK. REPRODUCED BY PERMISSION.

BELOW LEFT: Migration Period Peoples: Picts Pictish silver hoard from St. Ninian's Isle, Shetland. This hoard of monastic silver is from c. A.D. 800. © THE TRUSTEES OF THE NATIONAL MUSEUMS OF SCOTLAND. REPRODUCED BY PERMISSION.

BELOW RIGHT: Migration Period Peoples: Ostrogoths Ivory of Amalasuntha, queen of the Ostrogoths, c. A.D. 530. Amalasuntha's short reign ended with her murder in A.D. 535. KUNSTHISTORISCHES MUSEUM, WIEN. REPRODUCED BY PERMISSION.

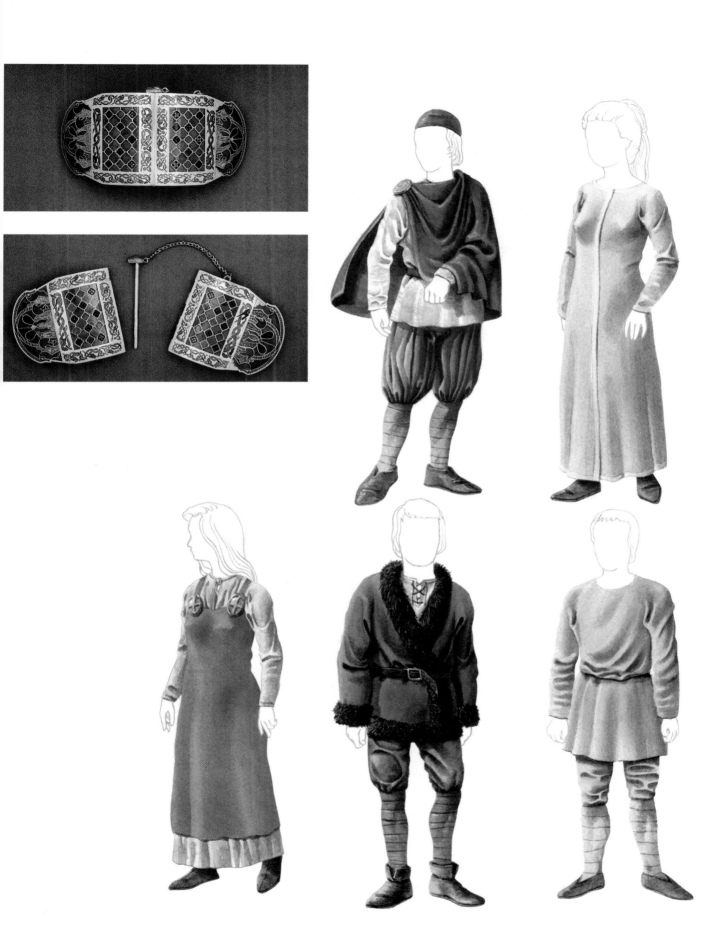

ABOVE: **Tomb of Childeric** Reconstruction of the gold signet ring of Childeric's tomb, fifth century A.D. ASHMOLEAN MUSEUM, UNIVERSITY OF OXFORD. REPRODUCED BY PERMISSION.

RIGHT: **Merovingian France** Reproduction of the mosaic from the sixth-century bishop's palace, part of a complex Merovingian cathedral group. COURTESY SERVICE CANTONAL D'ARCHÀOLOGIE, GENEVA. REPRODUCED BY PERMISSION.

BELOW LEFT: **Hungary** The "victorious sovereign" golden jug from the Nagyszentmiklós hoard, Romania, seventh–eighth century A.D. The iconography of an Avar period goldsmith offers a multitude of historical interpretations. KUNSTHISTORISCHES MUSEUM, WIEN. REPRODUCED BY PERMISSION.

state between Rome and Parthia. Artawazd's participation in raids along the Roman border led to a severe response, as the forces of Marc Antony succeeded in occupying Artashat and carrying Artawazd as a captive into Egypt, where he was eventually executed.

See also **Bronze Age Transcaucasia** (*vol. 2, part 5*); **Greek Colonies in the East** (*vol. 2, part 6*).

BIBLIOGRAPHY

Braund, David. *Georgia in Antiquity: A History of Colchis and Transcaucasian Iberia, 550 B.C.–A.D. 562.* Oxford: Clarendon Press, 1994.

Burney, Charles, and David M. Lang. *The People of the Hills: Ancient Ararat and Caucasus.* New York: Praeger, 1972.

Garsoian, Nina. "The Emergence of Armenia." In *The Armenian People from Ancient to Modern Times.* Vol. 1. Edited by Richard G. Hovannisian. New York: St. Martin's, 1997.

Hewsen, Robert H. *Armenia: A Historical Atlas.* Chicago: University of Chicago Press, 2001.

Khalilov, Dzh A. *Material'naia Kul'tura Kavkazskoi Albanii: Iv V. Do N.E.–Iii V. N.E.* Baku, Azerbaijan: Elm, 1985.

Khalilov, Dzh A., K. O. Koshkarly, and R. B. Arazova. *Arkheologicheskie Pamiatniki Severo-Vostochnogo Azerbaidzhana.* Baku, Azerbaijan: Elm, 1991.

Khanzadian, Emma V., K. A. Mkrtchian, and Elma S. Parsamian. *Metsamor.* Yerevan, Armenia: Akademiya Nauk Armianskoe SSR, 1973.

Koshelenko, Gennadij A., ed. *Drevneishie gosudarstva Kavkaza i Srednei Azii.* Moscow: Nauka, 1985.

Kushnareva, Karine Khristoforovna. *The Southern Caucasus in Prehistory.* Philadelphia: University of Pennsylvania Museum, 1997.

Lordkipanidze, O. *Drevnaya Kolkhida.* Tbilisi, Georgia: Sabchota Sakartvelo, 1979.

Martirosian, A. A. *Armenia v Epokhu Bronzi i Rannego Zheleza.* Yerevan, Armenia: Akademiya Nauk Armyanskoi SSR, 1964.

Piotrovskii, Boris B. *The Ancient Civilization of Urartu.* Translated by James Hogarth. New York: Cowles, 1969.

Pitskhelauri, K. N. *Vostochnaia Gruzia V Kontse Bronzovogo Veka.* Tbilisi, Georgia: Metsniereba, 1979.

Smith, Adam T. "The Making of an Urartian Landscape in Southern Transcaucasia: A Study of Political Architectonics." *American Journal of Archaeology* 103, no. 1 (1999): 45–71.

Smith, Adam T., and Karen S. Rubinson, eds. *Archaeology in the Borderlands: Investigations in Caucasia and Beyond.* Los Angeles: Cotsen Institute of Archaeology at UCLA, 2003.

Tsetskhladze, Gocha R., ed. *The Greek Colonisation of the Black Sea Area: Historical Interpretation of Archaeology.* Stuttgart, Germany: F. Steiner, 1998.

Zimansky, Paul E. *Ancient Ararat: A Handbook of Urartian Studies.* Anatolian and Caucasian Studies. Delmar, N.Y.: Caravan, 1998.

———. *Ecology and Empire: The Structure of the Urartian State.* Studies in Ancient Oriental Civilization 41. Chicago: Oriental Institute, 1985.

ADAM T. SMITH

DARK AGE GREECE

In the late thirteenth and early twelfth centuries B.C. the Bronze Age palace civilization of Aegean Greece went down in flames. Strongly fortified though they were, the urban centers of a series of small Mycenaean states in southern mainland Greece, together with associated regional centers on Crete and lesser Aegean islands, suffered violent destruction, putting an end to their power and unraveling complex political and economic structures. Although the precise origin of the attackers is unknown and other factors may have played a role, at least locally, in some cases (e.g., earthquakes and climatic downturns), it is significant that the fall of Late Bronze Age civilization in the Aegean occurred during a time of equal unrest throughout the eastern Mediterranean. The Hittite civilization in Anatolia suffered a similar fate, and in the Levant and Egypt armies of seaborne raiders and colonists of apparently diverse backgrounds (the "Sea Peoples") sacked towns and threatened the great power of Pharaonic Egypt, leaving a more permanent mark as founders of Philistine city-states in coastal Palestine.

Scholarship nonetheless is inclined, less at present than in the past, to envisage waves of invaders penetrating Greece from outside the Aegean to perpetrate the assassination of the Mycenaean palace kingdoms. However, alternative scenarios of internal civil wars between individual states, or a peasants' uprising, remain mere hypotheses, with only later Greek legend to suggest internal wars. The succeeding archaeological assemblages of the penultimate Bronze Age and Early Iron Age (fig. 1) seem firmly rooted in Mycenaean and, on Crete,

Minoan Bronze Age traditions; so if invaders were a critical element, they must have moved on or been absorbed rapidly into local cultures. In any case, the disruption associated with the violent end to the Mycenaean world was awesome enough to plunge the Aegean into a Dark Age that was to last from c. 1200 to 800 B.C.

Although this Dark Age was perhaps more a half-light than utter blackness, no one would dispute that history leaves us with the extinction of literacy throughout these four centuries. As Anthony Snodgrass pointed out a generation ago, many other striking signs of "de-skilling" characterize this period: the disappearance of elaborate architectural complexes; highly impoverished assemblages of metal; the virtual absence of human representations; a dramatic decline in the number of dated occupation sites; very reduced evidence for foreign exchange compared with the preceding period; and no sign of political centers of regional control. Whatever the reason(s) for the end of the palace states, the reduction in social, economic, and artistic complexity was severe and persisted for many generations.

It seems reasonable to ask why recovery took so long and to link this question to a striking feature of the Dark Age, the evidence for large-scale population movements around the Aegean. Although evidence mainly has been reconstructed from the study of the different ancient Greek dialects, later legends, and a little recorded history, along with certain archaeological support, it appears that during this long, disturbed era few parts of the former

Bronze Age Aegean world did not become involved in folk movements on a significant scale. Some scholars, such as the British historian Robin Osborne, have suggested a link between these migrations and the much better historically attested colonization movements by Aegean Greeks throughout the Mediterranean and Black Sea in the centuries immediately after the Dark Age and in the Archaic and early Classical centuries (the Archaic era is c. 700–500 B.C.; the Classical era is c. 500–323 B.C.; the early Classical era is the fifth century B.C.). The latter generally occurred, however, in times of denser homeland populations and elaborate state organization, so that it seems more appropriate to try to account for the Dark Age migrations in their own unique period context.

Why would whole communities abandon their homelands and risk all to settle far away, especially in an era when organized political authority had collapsed in great violence and insecurity must have been endemic? Violence may indeed have been a central reason. It is true even today that one of the main precipitating factors around the world for the displacement of entire communities, after food starvation and drought, is to escape the arbitrary violence associated with the breakdown of law and order. Generally, this is in the context of civil war or the absence of any centralized control over the use of force. Although there have been attempts to argue that the palace societies were struck by famine or drought, and there is some related evidence from Egypt that could introduce this as one element behind the crisis, no convincing case for prolonged climatic disaster can be found for the Aegean. Other factors must have been critical, even if this is allowed as a potentially secondary contributor. Summarizing a plausible scenario on what remains circumstantial evidence, one might suggest that violent attacks on the Mycenaean state centers by internal forces—with or without assistance from maritime armies of raiders such as the Sea Peoples—caused their definitive removal. This state of affairs ushered in a long period of insecurity that effectively blocked the reconstitution of regional states and the rule of law for centuries to follow.

SHEDDING LIGHT ON THE DARK AGES

One of the seemingly curious aspects of accounts by later, Classical Greek historians of events between

Fig. 1. Protogeometric pot, 975–950 B.C. © COPYRIGHT THE BRITISH MUSEUM. REPRODUCED BY PERMISSION.

the Age of the Heroes (a legendary era essentially rooted in memories of the Minoan-Mycenaean Bronze Age) and their own historic era is that they did not envisage this Dark Age at all. The world of the legendary leaders, associated with major palace centers, such as Thebes or Mycenae, certainly is portrayed in its final phase as riven by warfare, assassination, and internal migrations. It also is conceived as directly giving rise to the elite-dominated world of early historic Greece, from c. 700 B.C. (the Archaic era), with its kings or aristocrats (*basileis*) claiming heroic progenitors for their dynasties. This connection is difficult to accommodate with the archaeological picture just described, with three to five hundred years of an apparent reversion of political and economic organization to a thin scatter of short-lived rural hamlets with narrow horizons and little evidence for any sort of specialization or social stratification. Snodgrass's use of the statistics of Dark

Age cemeteries—their number and size—seemed convincing hard data to argue for tiny, dispersed communities appropriate to such limited achievements.

The first sign that the Dark Ages were merely "dim" came with the spectacular discovery on a small peninsula called Lefkandi jutting out on the mainland-facing shore of the island of Euboea, not far from Athens in southern Greece, of a cemetery that had grown up around a monumental funerary mound. Under the mound an impressive apsidal building was found in 1980 (fig. 2), with a male and female elite burial together with horse graves. The burial has been dated surprisingly early, to about 1000 B.C.—the supposed nadir of Greek culture. Current opinion holds that the great house represents the dwelling of a chieftain's family, namely the elite male and his partner. The gifts and finds from the later community cemetery that grew up beside it indicate exchange with the more advanced Early Iron Age city-states of the eastern Mediterranean, perhaps brought by Phoenician traders to the Aegean. (Their presence is known also at the port of Kommos on the southern coast of Crete at this time.) Nonetheless, Snodgrass had calculated from the size and date range of the Lefkandi cemetery that the population at any one time was only that of a small hamlet—difficult to see as a viable basis for a regional chiefdom.

The key to these accumulating discrepancies would be discovered in the late 1980s by one of Snodgrass's brightest students, Ian Morris. In a book that rewrote at a stroke our understanding of the Dark Age, *Burial and Ancient Society*, Morris showed that the key evidence from cemeteries (settlements being rarely excavated or studied in detail) was, in fact, completely misleading. Through analysis of the structure of the cemeteries and their age, sex, and wealth patterning, he argued that the transitional time between the Mycenaean era and the Dark Age proper—that of the sub-Mycenaean period—saw everyone in a community buried together in cemeteries. With the inception of the full Dark Age or Early Iron Age (proto-Geometric period, c. 1050–900 B.C.), however, formal cemetery burial became reserved exclusively for a social elite. This privileging remained in force in the subsequent Early to Middle Geometric period, but then, in a critical transformational century leading into the

first historic era—the Late Geometric (eighth century B.C.)—there was a dramatic return to social inclusiveness in cemeteries.

The obvious effect of this cycle is to mimic an apparent collapse of populations for the central main era of the Dark Age, bracketed by much higher populations. If one now reconstitutes a significant "invisible" population, this reduces the previous image of extraordinary depopulation. Moreover, and equally important, the evidence of such elite power over burial privileges is predicated on the survival of at least a district elite society throughout the whole Dark Age period. Here the Lefkandi house and subsequent discoveries of similar structures in other parts of Greece fall exactly into place. The Lefkandi chief would have been associated with a much larger support population than the communal cemetery indicates, and one can see the impressive type of residence from which the community was kept under elite sway. One further hint fits well into this new scenario: the term used in our first historic sources from about 700 B.C. for the controlling elite is the *basileis*—princes or lords. The word is used to mean a "minor official" in the preceding Mycenaean state archives. It might be reasonable to suggest that during the catastrophic collapse of palace civilizations around 1200 B.C., regional kingship disappeared, and power fragmented into myriad district chiefdoms. The Lefkandi-type residence would suit this picture very well, as does the survival of the term *basileis* into the earliest historic period.

One other feature of several of the well-studied Dark Age settlements deserves highlighting—their relative impermanence. Important sites, such as Lefkandi or Zagora on the island of Andros, were abandoned by the end of the period. It is important to point out that Morris's corrections to Dark Age population estimates fall well short of bringing them up to Mycenaean or Archaic era levels. Even when one boosts observable cemetery populations by a factor of two, their size and number remain modest and rare across the Greek landscape. The restrictions on architectural complexity and artistic production or trade remain in place, and one must still see a countryside with generally low population numbers and vast empty and uncultivated spaces, later to be filled and exploited to crisis proportions in the historic centuries of Archaic, through Classical, and into Early Hellenistic times (c. 700–300

B.C.; the Hellenistic era is 323 B.C. to 31 B.C. in Greece). In such a landscape, land would not have been of great value, and aspiring chieftains drew their power from controlling a more valuable scarce resource—manpower. In ways still not entirely clear, the Dark Age elite families attached the peasantry to their households. As chiefly power fluctuated from family to family across the landscape or a new elite generation chose to displace the seat of dynastic power from its ancestors, so elite and peasants migrated around the relatively thinly settled countryside. The power clearly was generalized and binding enough to suppress formal burial rights for the lesser folk.

Various theories can be raised to account for the nature of this grip on the working peasantry. A popular model for such a comparatively undeveloped and fragmented society, not far from expanding commercial powers such as the contemporary Phoenicians, would be a core-periphery system. Such a system emphasizes the inflow of eastern Mediterranean prestige goods for the local Greek elite in return for trading out raw materials and surplus foodstuffs that would have been channeled into the local chieftain's trading capital, as a kind of tax from the peasants. As often with this kind of application, the model fails to account for the ways in which elite-peasant dependency arises and is kept from being severed. The brilliant analysis by Hans van Wees of changing fashions in clothing, as portrayed in figured vases from Late Geometric to earliest Classical times (c. 800–480 B.C.), gets much closer to the answer.

A WARRIOR SOCIETY AND ITS LIFESTYLE

Although the main part of the Dark Age shows almost no hint of the representation of people on ceramics, the situation changes dramatically in the critical renaissance of the eighth century B.C. In almost all aspects of life there were major positive changes toward a more populous, politically complex society in most parts of Greece, artistically and architecturally experimental and ambitious. A striking series of large vases of this Late Geometric period give us scenes of everyday life, with a gloss of extra and anachronistic details that come from the popular legendary tales of Troy and the Bronze Age heroic world, clearly underlining claims to heroic

ancestry for the living elite. It is notable that these scenes portray the elite and their male retinue as heavily armed at all times. In the first part of the following period, the Archaic (seventh century B.C.), this remains the typical dress for the elite household. In the final Archaic century (sixth century B.C.), however, the sword and spear and open dress, allowing rapid deployment of these weapons, yield to a tight-fitting male dress copied from the Near East and the disappearance of the sword. By the end of that century, the spear is replaced by a walking stick, still potentially available to fend off vagrants but no longer a serious weapon. At the same time, scenes of the elite dining in Archaic times with series of armor and weapons suspended above them shift by early Classical times to representations of the elite and middle class with a single set of military equipment. This symbolizes the economic and political status of the head of the family as a member of the middle or upper citizen class (the hoplite, who had sufficient income to own the heavy equipment required of the citizen foot soldier in a typical Greek city-state).

What do these transformations in dress reveal about the organization of Dark Age society? Almost certainly, it was one where force was law; mere claim to preeminence was inadequate. Just as the chief and the retinue he sustained always were armed so as to be ready to take on rival families or intruders from neighboring districts, a similar threat of instant violence may have kept the dependent peasantry in their place. They were, after all, the essential foundation for the daily rations, banquets, gifts, and supply of metal that the elite superstructure required for its maintenance. The clashing clans of Romeo and Juliet's Verona come to mind, but closer to this time the return of Odysseus in Homer's epic is a vivid illustration of the period's ethos. In Odysseus's absence during the Trojan War and then on his wanderings around the Mediterranean, a group of other nobles insolently encamp in his palace, hoping to marry the abandoned wife, perhaps already a widow, and squandering Odysseus's resources. Upon their return, Odysseus and his son first remove all the weaponry and armor hanging in the dining-hall—doubtless originally placed there for his own followers—and then massacre the defenseless suitors, rounding that off by hanging the servant girls who had fraternized with the unwelcome guests.

The claims of Dark Age elites to have descended from the royal families of the Mycenaean Late Bronze Age are probably, with some exceptions, as unlikely as they were strongly emphasized by these local chiefly families. With much mobility around the landscape and the limited scope of district warrior-leaders, continuity of actual power and bloodlines is implausible. The aristocrats, who were rather more reliant on a gang of armed followers and their own aggressiveness to claim power over a dependent peasantry, nonetheless were keen to bolster supposed ties to legendary Mycenaean heroes. Hence the later Classical Greek conception that there was no Dark Age was born. This myth allowed Theseus to be both an early Mycenaean Athenian prince who destroyed the Cretan Minotaur (plausibly a memory of the Mycenaean takeover of the Minoan palace at Knossos) and the founder of a unified Attic state focused on Athens in the middle era of the Dark Age, some five hundred years later.

One way to convince people that one's family was in direct descent from Bronze Age heroes would be to identify an elite burial of that era and commence to make offerings to one's supposed ancestors in its precincts. Thus one sees the widespread emergence of hero cults at Mycenaean *tholos* tombs (a massive stone chamber built like a cone-shaped beehive) during the later Dark Age. Another way was to surround oneself with tales and images of the heroic age with which one wanted to be identified. This has two observable facets. First, when in Late Geometric times figural art reappears on a significant scale, with scenes of elite funerals and warfare, the mode of burial and some of the painted accoutrements either deliberately revive customs hitherto kept alive from the Bronze Age only in oral poetry or are pure illustrations to the tales of the *Iliad* and *Odyssey* and related epics and did not actually exist in contemporary society (e.g., giant body shields). Second, when the elite held their regular banquets to entertain and impress their neighbors and reward their retinue, oral poetry would be performed and doubtless continually modified to emphasize the claimed links of the audience to particular heroic figures from their own areas of Greece. By the time Homer wrote down a particular version of the two great cycles linked to the Trojan War (c. 700 B.C., at the emergence of written history), many generations of accretions and deletions are known to have occurred.

The feasting that is so central to Homeric elite gatherings seems to have been equally important to the warrior elite society of the Dark Age. One can suppose that large buildings, such as the Early Dark Age Lefkandi house (or its original, since some scholars suggest that the structure was not necessarily the actual chief's house but a replica built to be destroyed with the chief), were the focus of elite banqueting. These buildings also were repositories of prestigious items obtained by the elite through trade, gift exchange, or dowry as a way to emphasize their relative wealth and status to the impoverished dependent peasants who were their clients. The cult activity of the community almost certainly also was based in the chief's house and under his supervision—a further source of power to reinforce armed might and stores of food and valuables.

The multifunctional community focus represented by the chief's house—symbolic monument, ritual core, storehouse of wealth—and its physical plan are of far more than period interest. In its roles and design elements, this house is directly ancestral to the Archaic and Classical Greek temple. (One common version of the earliest Greek temple plans of the eighth through seventh centuries B.C. is in place at Lefkandi, c. 1000 B.C.—an elongated rectangle to which an apse is added at one end, with internal divisions denoting separate functions.) When the community focus of worship developed apart from the elite dwelling, something seen in several cases in the critical transformational Late Geometric eighth century B.C., it retained the traditional form of a rectangular subdivided building, often with the innermost part ending in an apse. Three key elements can be traced back to the Dark Age elite house—an entry porch, a main room with a focus (originally a hearth and later the cult statue), and an innermost chamber serving as private apartment and treasury.

One other element that is more specific to the Dark Ages and becomes less significant in Archaic to Classical times, as a more democratic society emerges, is the popularity of prestigious feasting vessels, or tripods. For much of the Dark Age, however, the general low level of bronze in society makes large containers too expensive. It is mainly in the final Late Geometric era that growing access to trade and a rising population can be associated with elite investment in great display pieces to show off at the traditional banquets in their households. The tripods, often showpieces at museums today, were large cooking and warming cauldrons for communal eating, highly ornamented and sometimes decorated with appropriate symbols of the warrior elite (e.g., a hero with raised spear, a gesture that is the most common one associated with Homeric warriors). Tripods were suitable gifts between elites and later became a common reward for victors in competitions at the international festivals in pan-Hellenic sanctuaries, such as Olympia.

THE RISE OF THE GREEK CITY-STATE

Classical Greece was divided politically between those regions mostly in the north, where power remained with an elite or even a king, and those largely in the south, where power was vested in the middle or "hoplite" class, only rarely and discontinuously reaching down to the poorest free citizens. Very broadly, the northern regions were dominated by a kind of tribal organization, the *ethnos,* with the south and its more democratic constitutions associated with the city-state, or polis kind of organization. The transformation in Greece, so pregnant for European and later global history, from a common kind of elite politics, found cross-culturally around the world, to a unique experimentation with moderate democracy took place essentially within the Archaic era, but it began in later Dark Age times.

First, the tight control exercised over their peasant clients by the warrior elite seems to have loosened in Late Geometric times with the relaxation of the ban on formal burial. In the following Early Archaic period, military reform occurred widely in Greece: the cavalry and chariots of the rich became subordinated on the battlefield to massed ranks of heavily armed foot soldiers drawn mostly from the wealthier or "yeoman" peasantry. Although Morris, in his pioneering cemetery analysis, suggested that the excluded poor of the Dark Age first won formal burial and soon after became the mainstay of military force in the rising states of Greece, his own statistics tell a different story. He estimated that roughly half the population suffered burial exclusion in the Dark Age, but in the Classical army about half the free population was made up of the aristocrats and middle (hoplite) class, and the other half were lightly armed poorer folk. Effectively, this indicates that the Dark Age elite was a large upper class in a very broad sense, later to form the upper and middle class of Classical times. The Dark Age serf class, even in Classical city-states, normally remained a less privileged class (Athens excepted, and that for a relatively limited part of the general Classical era). This seems to argue that the rise of more democratic institutions in Archaic to Classical times reflects a shift in power from the dominant elite families to lesser, originally dependent elite families, rather than the rise of a hitherto entirely suppressed serf class.

This article has portrayed typical Dark Age landscapes as thinly settled and has concentrated on often rather short-lived chieftain-focused villages. Equally significant is a smaller class of Dark Age settlements of a very different character, usually retaining their uniqueness into the subsequent early historic era. Many key Mycenaean centers shrank to small towns or villages and never recovered greater status or even remained unoccupied (Mycenae and Pylos). A few, however, appear not only to have remained occupied through the Dark Ages and into Classical times but also to have been large clusters of closely spaced hamlets forming a discontinuous town. Athens, Argos, Thebes, and Knossos are four striking examples. This "town in patches" appearance that is seen in the mapped archaeology of Dark Age settlement and cemetery traces at such sites was identified by the Classical historian Thucydides as the "traditional archaic" type of town. It was preserved to his time in the curious amalgamation of close villages that constituted the plan of Classical Sparta. The most likely explanation for this multifocality is that a number of chiefs, with their retinues and serfs, settled in one another's vicinity yet kept a perceptible distance and their own cemetery zones.

In landscapes with mostly smaller communities, the existence of such towns at all times must have exerted a gravitational attraction in their immediate region, with trade opportunities and social possibilities unobtainable elsewhere. Moreover, a warlike elite society sees a virtue in aggression and feuding to enhance status and control over land and people, so that an imbalance of military capability in their favor would have tended to stimulate these larger polities to undertake territorial expansion over lesser polities in their vicinity. Certainly, Athens is remarkable in its feat of taking control of the large region of Attica well before recorded history begins c. 700 B.C., perhaps as early as 900 B.C., and Thebes, Argos, and Knossos all rose to become the most powerful city-states in their regions, though at later dates.

See also **The Minoan World** (*vol. 2, part 5*); **Mycenaean Greece** (*vol. 2, part 5*).

BIBLIOGRAPHY

Bintliff, J. L. "Territorial Behaviour and the Natural History of the Greek Polis." In *Stuttgarter Kolloquium zur Historischen Geographie des Altertums.* Vol. 4. Edited by E. Olshausen and H. Sonnabend, pp. 207–249. Amsterdam: Hakkert Verlag, 1994.

Morris, Ian. "The Early Polis as City and State." In *City and Country in the Ancient World*. Edited by John Rich and Andrew Wallace-Hadrill, pp. 24–57. London: Routledge, 1991.

———. *Burial and Ancient Society.* Cambridge, U.K.: Cambridge University Press, 1987.

Snodgrass, A. M. *Archaic Greece: The Age of Experiment.* Dent: London: Dent, 1980.

———. *Archaeology and the Rise of the Greek State.* Cambridge, U.K.: Cambridge University Press, 1977.

Van Wees, Hans. "Greeks Bearing Arms." In *Archaic Greece: New Approaches and New Evidence.* Edited by N. Fisher and H. van Wees, pp. 333–378. London: Duckworth Press, 1998.

Whitley, J. *The Archaeology of Ancient Greece.* Cambridge, U.K.: Cambridge University Press, 2001.

JOHN BINTLIFF

EARLY MIDDLE AGES/
MIGRATION PERIOD

INTRODUCTION

Most standard prehistories of Europe end with the Roman conquest of central and western Europe in the last two centuries B.C. and the first century A.D. We have decided to extend our coverage of prehistoric and early historic Europe to approximately A.D. 1000 for several reasons. First, the Romans conquered only a part of temperate Europe. While the Romans controlled southern Britain, Gaul, Iberia, the Mediterranean, and parts of east-central Europe, Roman political and military domination never extended to Ireland, Scandinavia, Free Germany (those areas of Germany outside the borders of the Roman Empire), and all of northeastern Europe. Regions such as Ireland and the portions of Germany that bordered the Roman Empire certainly were affected directly by Roman trade, religion, and military activities. However, there were substantial continuities between the Early (or pre-Roman) Iron Age and the Roman Iron Age in many regions of northern and eastern Europe.

Second, the Roman political, military, and economic domination of many parts of western Europe lasted for only about four hundred years. Archaeologically, Britain is the most studied of all the Roman provinces in western Europe. Major programs of excavation in York, Winchester, and London have shown that Roman towns and cities experienced severe depopulation in the fifth century A.D. and that large-scale production of commercial goods such as pottery had ceased by about the year 400. The Roman military withdrew from the province of Britain in the early fifth century, and the residents were forced to see to their own defenses. Similar patterns of political, urban, and industrial decline have been documented throughout the Western Roman Empire in the fifth century. Long before the final Western Roman emperor was deposed in A.D. 476, many of the hallmarks of Roman civilization—military control over a well-defined territory, urbanism, industrial production and exchange, coinage, and literacy—had effectively disappeared in many of the western provinces.

Third, by the sixth century A.D., a series of small successor kingdoms had been established within the boundaries of the former Western Roman Empire. These new rulers modeled themselves on the former Roman emperors. Many, including the Frankish King Clovis, adopted Christianity, and some had served as mercenaries in the Roman army. However, the rulers themselves were drawn from barbarian tribes whose homelands lay outside the boundaries of the former Roman Empire. Moreover, the polities they ruled—Merovingian France, Anglo-Saxon England, Visigothic Spain—were substantially different from the Roman provinces that had existed in these regions a century or two earlier. These Dark Age societies were rural rather than urban. They have much more in common with the barbarian societies of Iron Age Europe than with the Roman societies that immediately preceded them. Since literary evidence and written records are limited, nearly all our information about daily life in these successor kingdoms has been discovered through archaeological research.

CHRONOLOGY

This volume covers only a portion of the European Middle Ages. Traditionally, the medieval period begins with the collapse of the Western Roman Empire in the fifth century A.D. and ends with the European voyages of discovery in the fifteenth and sixteenth centuries. While we begin our coverage of the Early Middle Ages in the early fifth century, we have chosen to end our coverage of medieval archaeology at about A.D. 1000. Archaeological and historical records provide clear evidence for the formation of states in Scandinavia and Poland around this time. With the establishment of institutionalized governments organized on territorial principles, many of the societies of northern Europe no longer can be considered barbarian. In addition, at about this time Christianity was adopted and literacy became widespread in several regions of northeastern Europe, including Poland and Scandinavia. As a result, written records are far more common. The archaeology of the High Middle Ages (c. A.D. 1000–1500) is truly a form of historical archaeology, where documents and material evidence have equally important roles to play.

MIGRATION

Migration or population movement is a well-documented feature of ancient Europe. At the end of the Ice Age (eleven thousand years ago), hunters and gatherers moved into areas of Europe that had been glaciated during the Pleistocene. Both archaeological and skeletal evidence indicates that migration played a role in the establishment of the first farming communities in central Europe. Archaeological, place-name, and literary evidence shows substantial population movements in central Europe during the later Iron Age.

Population movements are also well documented throughout the Early Middle Ages, and the period from A.D. 400–600 often is referred to as the Migration period. In the fifth and sixth centuries A.D., barbarians from outside the Roman Empire—Visigoths, Angles, Saxons, Franks, and others—moved into many regions of western Europe. The nature of these migrations has been debated by both archaeologists and historians for decades. Do they represent large-scale population movements, or are they small migrations of a military and political elite who dominated the local sub-Roman (early

post-Roman, non-Saxon) populations and initiated changes in material culture and ideology? Today, many archaeologists would favor the latter explanation. This chapter profiles many of the Migration period peoples who are known to us through the archaeological record and through historical sources.

Perhaps the best known of the early medieval migrations is the Viking expansion (c. A.D. 750–1050). Eastern Vikings from Sweden established colonies in Russia and the Baltic and conducted trade in distant eastern lands such as Mesopotamia. Western Vikings, from Norway and Denmark, established colonies in Britain, Ireland, Orkney, and Shetland. In addition, Viking colonists settled Iceland in the ninth century and Greenland in about 985. These settlements represent the frontiers of European colonization in the Early Middle Ages. Archaeologists have made extensive studies of the colonial settlements established by both the eastern and western Vikings.

THE REBIRTH OF TOWNS AND TRADE

In A.D. 600 Europe was primarily a rural society. Although many former Roman towns continued to serve as political and ecclesiastical centers, their populations were substantially reduced, and the towns no longer served as major centers of manufacturing and trade. Recent archaeological research in the Mediterranean regions of Europe and North Africa indicates that long-distance trade had declined well before the Islamic conquests of North Africa and Spain in the seventh century A.D.

Beginning in the seventh century A.D. a number of emporia—centers of both long-distance and regional trade—were established along the North Sea and Baltic Coasts from Hamwic (Anglo-Saxon Southampton) in England to Staraya Ladoga in Russia. Major programs of archaeological research have been carried out at these emporia. For example, the Origins of Ipswich project traced the development of this emporium from its establishment in the early seventh century. Ipswich produced pottery, known as Ipswich ware, that was formed on a slow wheel and kiln-fired. This pottery was traded throughout East Anglia, and it also appears at royal and ecclesiastical centers in other parts of England. The trade networks that were established in the Early Middle Ages are entirely different from those that existed during the Roman period. Many Roman trade networks centered on the Mediterranean; early Medieval networks centered on the Baltic and North Sea. Some archaeologists have argued that the establishment of these emporia may be closely related to state formation and the emergence of complex societies in several regions of northern Europe, including England, France, and Scandinavia.

CONCLUSION

Between A.D. 400 and 1000, the European continent was transformed politically, socially, and economically. The breakup of the Western Roman Empire created a power vacuum that was filled by a series of barbarian successor kingdoms. In a period of only six centuries urbanism was established in Europe, both within and outside the former Roman Empire; new patterns of long-distance and regional trade developed centering on the Baltic and the North Sea; and states formed in many regions of Europe. These transformations laid the foundation for the later medieval and modern European worlds.

PAM J. CRABTREE

EMPORIA

The use of the term "emporia" to refer to the specialized trading (and crafting) sites of the late seventh century to the ninth century owes much to Richard Hodges and especially his *Dark Age Economics* (1982). Influenced by anthropologists and economic historians, Hodges saw these emporia as centers created on the frontiers of early medieval kingdoms (but largely divorced from their surrounding hinterland) through which kings funneled and controlled long-distance trade in prestige goods. However, it is important to be aware that contemporaries would not have applied the term "emporium" to all the sites Hodges considers. Eighth- and ninth-century sources do refer to Lundenwic (London, England), Dorestad (Holland), and Quentovic (France) as "emporia," but Hamwic (the best-studied and most-famous of Hodges's emporia) is only ever referred to as a *mercimonium*. Deriving from *merx*, the Latin for goods, merchandise, or wares, this term also relates to trade and exchange but presumably on a different scale or in different goods. As scholars have come to appreciate the comparative rarity of "emporia" in early medieval Europe, so they have gradually come to use the Old English word *wic* to refer to the whole class of such settlements. Contemporaries were more discriminating.

LAYOUT

Hodges used the presence (or absence) of particular classes of archaeological evidence to divide his "emporia" into three types. Type A emporia were characterized by the presence of exotic material culture and an absence of evidence for permanent structures. Sites such as Dalkey Island (Ireland) were thought to resemble the seasonal fairs referred to in, for example, the Icelandic sagas. However, like other archaeologists, he has devoted most of his attention to so-called type B emporia.

These were permanent, strategically located, and in early medieval terms, substantial settlements. Dorestad (Holland) ran for about 3,000 meters along the old course of the Kromme Rijn at the point where it intersected with the Lower Rhine, and the Lek Ribe (Denmark) was situated where a north-south route crossed a ford in the River Ribe, the latter itself connecting the settlement to the North Sea. Similarly Eoforwic (York, England) lay at the confluence of the Rivers Ouse and Foss, close to a natural crossing point of the Ouse and on the line of a Roman road. Hamwic (Southampton, England) covered some 45 hectares of the west bank of the River Itchen, at the point where it flowed into Southampton Water and ultimately the English Channel.

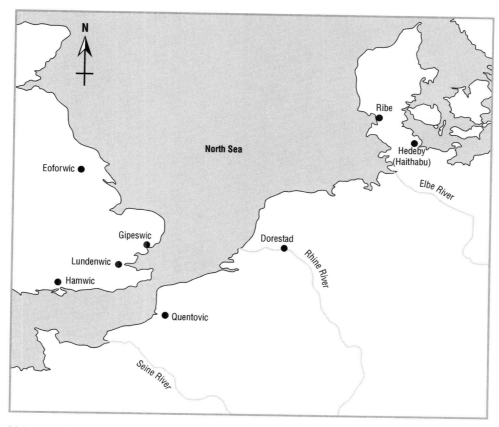

Main emporia (*wics*) of northwest Europe.

Hamwic may have had a population of between 2,000 and 3,000 and, like many other emporia or *wics,* seems to have been planned. Two north-south roads, connected by a series running east-west, formed a gridlike pattern within a defining (not defensive) enclosure. The roads were lined with buildings, and although these did not differ much from those found on contemporary rural sites, a visitor might have been impressed by the number concentrated in one place. Dorestad is characterized by a series of landing piers (about 8 meters wide) stretching into what would have been the River Rhine. They appear to have been lengthened as the river shifted to the east and were major structuring elements in the layout of the settlement—it was divided into 20-meter-wide parcels, each containing two piers, which ran from the riverside, through the harbor area, and into the *vicus* (trading zone) to the west. At Ribe a series of parallel ditches divided the settlement into forty or fifty plots, but here the evidence for permanent buildings is less secure. Most archaeologists argue that planning implies the in-

volvement of a central authority (usually the king) in the establishment and running of the emporia; for example, King Ine of Wessex (688–726) at Hamwic and King Angantyr at Ribe. These (and other emporia) have therefore been seen primarily as royal settlements.

IMPORTS

Type B emporia are also characterized by the presence of significant quantities of exotic material culture. A cowrie shell (from the Red Sea or the Indian Ocean) and the hypoplastron (shell fragment) of a North African green turtle from Hamwic, a bronze statuette of Buddha from eighth-century contexts at Helgö (Sweden), and pieces of carnelian, garnets, and rock crystal at Ribe illumine connections with points far to the south and east (fig. 1). The sharpening stones, soapstone vessels, and whalebone from Ribe, on the other hand, are indicative of connections with the North. They also stand for the furs that flowed from the northern lands, through emporia like Ribe and Birka (Sweden), to satisfy

Fig. 1. Easterly connections—a statuette of Buddha found at Helgö (Sweden). THE MUSEUM OF NATIONAL ANTIQUITIES, STOCKHOLM. REPRODUCED BY PERMISSION.

elite demand in the heartlands of Europe. The bone assemblage from Birka reveals that skins of mountain hare, squirrel, beaver, fox, ermine, pine marten, badger, wolverine, and otter were processed at the emporium. At Eoforwic there is similar evidence for the working of beaver and pine marten skins. The value of these furs should not be underestimated. In the ninth century a Norwegian merchant called Óttar grew wealthy on the tribute he exacted from the Saami, and that tribute included the skins of marten, reindeer, otter, bear, and seal. A large ring-headed pin and part of a fitting for an Irish brooch provide evidence for Hamwic's hitherto neglected westerly connections, while Pictish brooches provide the closest parallels for a gilded, penannular brooch terminal from Eoforwic.

The bulk of the evidence for imports from the major *wics*, however, consists of pottery, mostly from sources in the Rhineland and in northern France and the Low Countries. Kilns discovered near Rouen produced much of the material imported (perhaps via the French site of Quentovic) into Hamwic, although there was also some pottery from Belgium or Holland (or both) as well as Badorf and Mayen wares from the Rhineland. Similarly black and gray burnished wares from northern France or the Low Countries (or both) dominate the imported assemblages from Eoforwic and Lundenwic.

By contrast, the imported pottery from Gipeswic (Ipswich, England) is dominated by the products of the Vorgebirge and Mayen kilns in the Rhineland and thus more closely resembles the assemblages from Ribe and Dorestad. Much of the other "exotic" material culture on these sites can be sourced to the Rhineland—for example, glass vessels, lava quern stones (for grinding grain), and wine barrels (reused to line wells at Dorestad and Ribe). This mention of wine should serve as a reminder that the merchants (and consumers) of early medieval Northwest Europe were probably more interested in the contents than in the vessels (both wooden and ceramic). Analysis of one sherd from Hamwic revealed that the vessel had contained a mixture of meat and olive oil, showing that wine was not the only exotic consumable traded across northwestern Europe.

Although Rhenish quern stones and glass vessels are also found at, for example, Eoforwic and Hamwic, an analysis of the distribution of imported pottery encouraged Hodges to propose the existence of mutually exclusive trading zones—a Rhenish one in the north (including Dorestad, Gipeswic, and Ribe), and a Frankish one in the south (including Hamwic, Quentovic, and now Lundenwic). He believed that the *wics* or emporia were the linchpins of both networks and that they were consciously established by kings in an attempt to exert greater control over an expansion of prestige goods exchange that threatened their position—if they did not control this trade (and the traders), it is argued, then their social inferiors would have had access to the symbols of power. Their position as chief "ring givers," as the sole arbiters of the social hierarchy, would have been undermined. A letter written by Charlemagne, the Carolingian emperor, to Offa, king of Mercia, in 796 reveals some fascinating insights into the nature of this exchange as well as new perspectives on the objects involved.

In this letter Charlemagne refers to Offa's earlier request for some "black stones" of a certain "length" and tells him to send a messenger with details of "what kind you have in mind and we will willingly order them to be given, wherever they are to be found, and will help with their transport." Charlemagne then informs Offa about his requirement for cloaks of a certain size and asked that they "be such as used to come to us in former times." This all reads like a record of one moment in a well-established, routine, and regular system of exchange. The fact that Charlemagne and Offa got involved in discussions about the exchange of items as (apparently) mundane as "cloaks," and the generally accepted argument that the "black stones" were tephrite quern stones from sources in the Eifel mountains (near Mayen in the Rhineland), reinforces the argument that long-distance exchange in the eighth and ninth centuries was directed and controlled by kings (and emperors).

Research since the 1980s, however, while confirming royal interest in long-distance trade, has somewhat modified the impression that this involvement extended beyond prestige goods to utilitarian objects. Thus David Peacock has presented a convincing case that Charlemagne's black stones, rather than being humble lava querns, were in fact antique black porphyry columns from Rome and Ravenna. As such they were laden with the symbolism of empire and antiquity; they were objects of immense political and social value—the "stuff of emperors." In this light it also seems inherently unlikely that the "cloaks" were simple, utilitarian items. They, too, were probably luxury products—perhaps like the late-eighth-century or ninth-century Anglo-Saxon embroideries preserved at Maaseik (Belgium).

Clearly the exchange of prestige gifts did play a significant part in the political strategies of early medieval kings and emperors. However, it now seems that they did not necessarily involve themselves in the trading of quern stones—although the archaeological evidence for them on sites across northwestern Europe is proof that such trading did take place. The question of the "controlling hand" behind that trade, if not always that of the king, is one to which this discussion will return. However, at this point it

should be emphasized that the *wics* were essentially transhipment points. They were places where goods from afar entered the country before, according to the Hodges model, being forwarded to the king for redistribution. One would not expect to find large quantities of prestige goods at these sites—and this is, by and large, the case. The textual references to columns, embroideries (if that is what they are), and slaves (see the Venerable Bede's reference in *Ecclesiastical History of the English People* book 4, chapter 22, to the sale, at Lundenwic, of a Northumbrian slave to a Frisian merchant) thus provide useful illustrations of the kind of trade items that might have passed through the emporia.

PRODUCTION

In his original formulation of the characteristics of type B emporia (in *Dark Age Economics*), Hodges argued that they would have housed a native work force whose role was to produce for "the mercantile community." The "subsidiary" role attributed to these artisans was a product both of the limited amount of evidence (in 1982) for craft production on the *wics* and of the attention devoted to overseas exotica. The idea that these sites were primarily concerned with facilitating the exchange of exotica between elites reinforced the impression that they were largely divorced from the region within which they were situated.

However, as excavation and publication progressed in the years since 1982, and the evidence for craft production on the *wics* accumulated, so it has become clear that scholars have underestimated the significance of production in the Anglo-Saxon economy in general—and on the *wics* in particular. Hamwic (as in so many other respects) provides the best evidence for the range and scale of artisanal activity; this can be used as the framework for a more general consideration of craft production in the main Northwest European emporia. Since 1982 new insights have accumulated into the role of emporia and *wics* in the regional economies of the Early Middle Ages.

At Hamwic, as elsewhere (good evidence comes from Ribe), artisanal activities were carried out in and around the buildings that lined the roads, and all forms of craft working were carried out right across the site, with no clear sign of the zoning of particular "industries." The scale of production within each of the properties differed little from that on contemporary rural settlements, but the possibilities offered by the coexistence in close proximity of many different kinds of craft production probably more than offset this "limitation."

One of the most ubiquitous traces of craft production at Hamwic is the debris from ironworking. This usually takes the form of smithing slag found in association with ore, charcoal, furnaces, and raw iron (the same is true at Gipeswic, Lundenwic, and Eoforwic). As at Dorestad, iron was smelted elsewhere (perhaps at Romsey, 14 kilometers to the northeast) and was transported to Hamwic for the production of a wide variety of objects, including chisels, axes, shears, nails, rivets, needles, keys, bells, and knives (at Eoforwic evidence exists for the plating of some of these objects with tin, tin-lead, and copper). The iron ingots worked at Dorestad probably originated on production sites in the Veluwe region, about 40 kilometers to the northeast. By and large the objects made were similar to those produced at Hamwic, but Frankish swords with inlaid blades (among the most prestigious artifacts of the period) might also have been made here.

The working of copper alloys was the most prevalent of the nonferrous metallurgical crafts on all the Northwest European *wics*. Crucibles, cupels, and molds provide the bulk of the evidence for the production of what seem, for the most part, to have been rather mundane objects—for instance, pins, strap ends, buckle fittings, finger rings, and brooches. There is, however, evidence (usually in the form of molds) for the production of some more decorative (quality) items at Hamwic and Gipeswic; a bone mold for the production of a disk brooch was found at Lundenwic. The bronze workers at Ribe seem to have made jewelry of distinctively Scandinavian type, as if catering for the regional as opposed to the "long-distance" market. Given the rather mundane quality of many of the objects produced on this and other *wics*, one can probably argue that most production of these sites was destined for regional level exchange. This has significant implications for how scholars understand the emporia (see below).

Precious metals were worked on the *wics*. Gold and silver were present in cupels and crucibles from Hamwic, and some evidence exists for gilding. Silver objects are rare (as this would have been transshipment site), but they do seem to have been pro-

duced from the earliest phase of the settlement. Fragments of gold and silver wire and plate from the excavations at Fishergate in York demonstrate that "prestige" objects were being made at Eoforwic, as does an emerald and two fragments of garnet. It seems certain that sceattas (small eighth-century silver coins) were minted at Ribe, Gipeswic, and Hamwic. Glass was worked (rather than made) at Eoforwic, Ribe, and Dorestad, while the latter two have evidence for the production of amber objects.

Despite the fact that, in most cases, little direct evidence exists for the production of pottery at *wics* (see below for the exception), there can be little doubt that it should be added to the range of crafts practiced on them. No kilns have been found at Hamwic, but here, as elsewhere, the vast majority of the pottery was produced from local clays, and small, ephemeral kilns would have sufficed to make it. The facts that some of the Hamwic pottery derived from sources about 20 kilometers away and that the sand- and shell-tempered wares from Eoforwic belonged to widespread ceramic traditions suggest that the *wics* were integrated into regional systems of production and distribution. The production and distribution of Ipswich ware leads to the same conclusion.

Fired in kilns and produced on a slow wheel, Ipswich ware was (mass-)produced in the northeastern part of Gipeswic from the early part of the eighth century. Not only did its manufacture represent a technological advance on any other kind of ceramic production then taking place in England, it was also made in a wider range of forms and achieved a much wider distribution. It is almost ubiquitous on settlements within the kingdom of East Anglia, suggesting that it was made and traded within a regional system focused on the *wic*. Outside the kingdom of the East Angles (it is found as far north as York and as far south as Kent), it is normally found on elite sites and usually in the form of storage vessels. Although, again, the contents may have been more valuable than the vessel, the production and distribution of the latter does suggest that traditional models may have underestimated the significance of trade within and across the kingdoms of England and the role of the *wics* in articulating this "economic" activity. A consideration of the bone objects from the emporia leads to the same conclusion.

At Hamwic cattle bone was the preferred material for the production of combs, spindle whorls, needles, awls, and thread pickers (red deer antler was increasingly used in the ninth century). Although there are some variations (the production of playing counters, amulets, and skates at Dorestad; the latter were also made at Eoforwic), the bone workers on the other *wics* seem to have made a very similar range of products. This implies, again, that production was designed for local or regional consumption—why export a (rather utilitarian) product to a community that also manufactures it? (Combs produced in Hamwic have now been identified in its hinterland—at Abbots Worthy, near Winchester.) The similarity in products created at various *wics* also points to one of the "benefits" of the concentration of different kinds of artisanal activity. There are some signs of the emergence of an integrated system of production in that many of the bone (and other) tools manufactured there were used in other productive processes.

Textile production would seem to have been one of the most important of these. Weaving pits have been identified in the Six Dials area of Hamwic, while more than five hundred loom weights were found on the site of an extension to the Royal Opera House in Lundenwic. Loom weights were also found at Dorestad, while one of the products of this craft (a fragment of a coarse wool textile) was recovered from an early-eighth-century context at Eoforwic. There is evidence for leatherworking at Hamwic and Gipeswic, and shoes were made on the East Anglian *wic*. As already noted, furs were processed at Eoforwic and Birka. In fact these animal "secondary products" provide crucial insight into the function (and rationale) of the emporia; the products were made with tools and materials deriving from animals that were supplied from the surrounding region to the craft workers in the *wic*. These artisans then created objects of varying value. Certain of these, such as the furs and some of the textiles and bone work (an early-eighth-century bone knife handle from Eoforwic was beautifully decorated with scenes of animals in procession) as well as the objects of gold and silver, might have been destined for the elite consumption, prestige goods exchange, or both; the rest (and probably the majority) would have been consumed at the regional level.

RATIONALE AND DEMISE

Classic accounts of the emporia saw them as royally controlled foreign enclaves, situated within, yet separate from, the various kingdoms of northwestern Europe. They were seen as nodes in a pan-European exchange system, operated by elites for the benefit of elites—the driving forces of early European history. Some of the gifts exchanged between the kings of northwestern Europe may have passed through the *wics;* some may even have been made there. However, if the character of the archaeological assemblage in any way reflects the importance of past human activities, it is now clear that artisanal production dominated the lives of most of the residents of early medieval emporia. This production connected them, on a daily basis, with the inhabitants of the surrounding region. It seems likely that the latter "consumed" many of the goods made on the *wics,* although (given the generic nature of these products) this will remain difficult to prove. What is unquestionable, however, is that the artisans (and possibly traders) on the *wic* were provisioned, both in terms of food and raw materials, with resources produced in its hinterland.

The remains of rather elderly cattle, sheep, and pigs dominate the faunal assemblage from Hamwic. These animals had evidently served a useful life elsewhere before being dispatched to the *wic*. The assemblage is noteworthy for the absence of young animals, which would have supplied the better cuts of meat, and for a lack of wild species. It appears that the inhabitants of Hamwic were not able to exercise much choice over the food with which they were supplied, and this is generally taken to support the idea that the *wic* was created, controlled, and provisioned by the king from his other estates in the kingdom of Wessex.

The evidence from other emporia, however, suggests that Hamwic might, to some extent, be exceptional. There is evidence for farms on the edge of Dorestad and Lundenwic, although the faunal evidence from Eoforwic reveals that at least some of its residents had access to fine cuts of meat (although here too they singularly failed to exploit wild resources). All this might imply a greater diversity of supply to these *wics* and less than complete royal control over the activities of its residents. Contemporary texts that refer to ecclesiastical landholding in, and trading from, Lundenwic and the suggestion (based on numismatics) that the bishop of York may have exercised some authority over "economic" activities in Eoforwic open up the possibility that nonroyal elites may have played a greater part than previously expected in the functioning of the emporia.

The discovery that some elite settlements (both secular and ecclesiastical) in England show evidence for intensified production from the end of the seventh century (that is, perhaps just before the emergence of the emporia as a phenomenon) raises the intriguing possibility that their development owed at least as much to the expansion of regional systems of production and exchange as to the king's desire for overseas exotica. Similarly work since the 1980s on the continental European economy has emphasized that, although emporia like Dorestad were important and may have linked regional-level production and distribution to the acquisition of goods from overseas, regional networks were structurally more significant to the development of the Carolingian empire and the Carolingian Renaissance. These networks were frequently focused on old Roman cities and *castella* (forts).

Archaeologists have therefore begun to reassess the significance of the emporia in the economic and political development of the polities that made up early medieval Europe. They were once seen as the "economic" dynamos of early medieval Europe and were thought to be central to the reproduction of kingdoms—they were the places through which kings controlled the importation of the prestige goods that secured and maintained alliances and dependents. As the research accumulates, however, they have come to be viewed as locales articulating overseas trade with the networks of intensified production and exchange being developed around the (usually nonroyal) elites of northwestern Europe. To consider how this new insight affects an understanding of the demise of the emporia, one must return to Hodges's typology.

In fact it can be argued that his type C emporia are not really emporia at all since they are predicated on the demise of long-distance trade. In this event Hodges argues in his *Dark Age Economics* that "the emporium could either be abandoned or it could continue to function within a regional economy." The former (abandonment) was the fate of most of the "classic" emporia, and this generally took place

in the mid– to late ninth century. The Vikings have been blamed for this, as they have been blamed for pretty much anything else that went wrong at this time. They certainly had an effect. Dorestad was regularly sacked from the 830s and was destroyed in 863. Lundenwic was attacked in 842 and 851 and was occupied by a Viking army in 871–872; a deep ditch dug there in the ninth century might be a product of these attacks. Viking disruption of long-distance trade networks may, in fact, have robbed the emporia of their role in linking regional and international "economic" systems. However, one might also argue, as Adriaan Verhulst does in *The Carolingian Economy,* that the emporia's sudden extinction and the continuity of "old *civitates* like Rouen, Amiens, Maastricht . . . Tournai . . . [and] younger towns along the rivers (*portus*) in the interior" demonstrate how ephemeral *wics* had always been. Whatever one's perspective, emporia and *wics* remain among the defining characteristics of their age, and *Dark Age Economics* (despite twenty years of critique) still lies at the heart of archaeologists' attempts to understand them.

See also **Ipswich** (*vol. 2, part 7*); **Viking Harbors and Trading Sites** (*vol. 2, part 7*); **Trade and Exchange** (*vol. 2, part 7*).

BIBLIOGRAPHY

Bourdillon, Jennifer. "The Animal Resources from Southampton." In *Anglo-Saxon Settlements.* Edited by Della Hooke, pp. 177–195. Oxford: Blackwell, 1988. (One of the first and best discussions of the importance of the hinterlands of *wics*, based primarily on the faunal evidence from Hamwic.)

Es, W. A. van. "Dorestad Centred." In *Medieval Archaeology in the Netherlands.* Edited by J. C. Besteman, J. M. Bos, and H. Heidinga, pp. 151–182. Assen, Netherlands: van Gorcum, 1990.

Hill, D., and R. Cowie, eds. *Wics: The Early Medieval Trading Centres of Northern Europe.* Sheffield, U.K.: Sheffield Academic Press, 2001. (Updated proceedings of a conference held in York in 1991.)

Hodges, Richard. *Towns and Trade in the Age of Charlemagne.* London: Duckworth, 2000. (See especially chap. 3.)

———. *The Anglo-Saxon Achievement. Archaeology and the Beginnings of English Society.* London: Duckworth, 1989. (See especially chap. 4. A slightly different perspective on the emporia, with more on artisanal production, but trade and exchange is still central.)

———. *Dark Age Economics: The Origins of Towns and Trade A.D. 600–1000.* London: Duckworth, 1982. (The seminal account of early medieval trade and exchange.)

Jensen, Stig. *The Vikings of Ribe.* Ribe, Denmark: Den antikvariske Samling i Ribe, 1991. (Much of this short, well-illustrated book is about the pre-Viking emporium [or *wic*] site and the kinds of activities that took place on these sites.)

Maddicott, John. "Prosperity and Power in the Age of Bede and Beowulf." *Proceedings of the British Academy* 117 (2002): 49–71. (This overview argues for a relatively prosperous English countryside and emphasizes the significance of the production and exchange of cloth in the eighth century.)

Moreland, John. "The Significance of Production in Eighth-Century England." In *The Long Eighth Century: Production Distribution and Demand.* Edited by Inge Hansen and Chris Wickham, pp. 69–104. Leiden, Netherlands: Brill, 2000. (Moves away from exchange-focused perspectives on emporia, arguing that they were fully integrated into regional economies and may even have been a product of an intensification of agricultural production.)

Morton, Alan. "Hamwic in Its Context." In *Anglo-Saxon Trading Centres: Beyond the Emporia.* Edited by Mike Anderton, pp. 48–62. Glasgow: Cruithne Press, 1999. (One of a number of excellent papers from a Sheffield conference that focused on the hinterlands of emporia.)

Peacock, David. "Charlemagne's Black Stones: The Re-Use of Roman Columns in Early Medieval Europe." *Antiquity* 71 (1997): 709–715. (Makes a convincing case that Charlemagne's "black stones" were in fact porphyry columns rather than lava quern stones.)

Verhulst, Adriaan. *The Carolingian Economy.* Cambridge, U.K.: Cambridge University Press, 2002. (An accessible discussion of the economy of continental Europe in the eighth and ninth centuries that stresses the importance of regional economic networks and sees the emporia as rather "ephemeral.")

JOHN MORELAND

IPSWICH

Ipswich lies at the tidal reach of the Orwell estuary, in southeastern Suffolk, on the shortest crossing of the North Sea to the mouth of the Rhine. Extensive archaeological excavations between 1974 and 1990 have shown that the town is one of the four major craft production and trading settlements of seventh- to ninth-century England (the so-called *wics*, or emporia). The earliest settlement, dating to the seventh century, appears to have covered up to 15 hectares on the north bank of the Orwell, centered on the crossing point of the river that later became Stoke Bridge. Excavations in 1986, west of St. Peter's Street, revealed the first structures and rubbish pits of this date, associated with local handmade pottery and Merovingian (Frankish) black wares, indicating a trading function. Other sites of likely seventh-century occupation have produced few features of this date, but handmade pottery has been retrieved from later contexts, and a hollowed-out tree trunk well discovered at Turret Lane, at the northern limit of the area, gave a dendrochronological date (tree ring date) of A.D. 670 (plus or minus ninety years).

Other elements of this early settlement also have been found. Field boundaries containing cereal remains were excavated at Fore Street, about 200 meters east of the settlement, indicating an agricultural aspect of the local economy. To the north of the settlement is an extensive cemetery. Burials of seventh-century date were excavated at Elm Street in 1975 and at Foundation Street in 1985. The largest group of burials, however, was excavated in 1988 on the Butter Market site immediately north of the early settlement. Here seventy-seven graves were found, despite considerable damage from later occupation. No limits to the cemetery were discovered, and it was clearly larger than the 5,000 square meters excavated. Radiocarbon dates indicate that burial was restricted to the seventh century. Although bone preservation was poor, remains of more than fifty people were recovered, of which it is known that thirty-nine were adults and four were juveniles. Of the adults, research has ascertained that eight were male or probably male and four were female or probably female. All the burials were inhumations, buried with or without coffins in simple graves, in chamber graves, or under small mounds surrounded by ring ditches. Objects accompany nearly half the burials, but the majority of graves were poorly furnished, often with only a knife. Of the more lavishly furnished burials, three dating to the period A.D. 610–670 were accompanied by Continental grave assemblages. The richest was a male buried in a coffin with a sword, shield, two spears, and two glass palm cups.

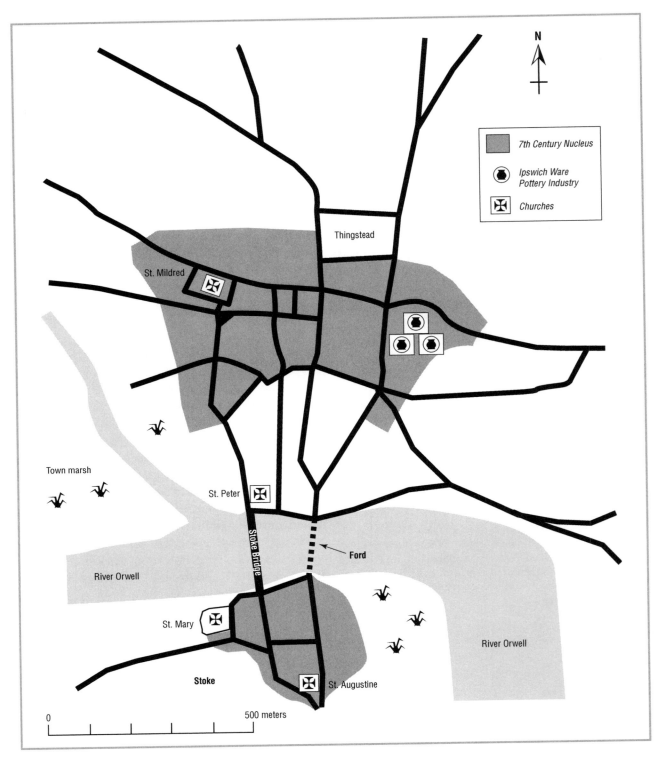

Legend:
- 7th Century Nucleus
- Ipswich Ware Pottery Industry
- Churches

N

Thingstead

St. Mildred

Town marsh

St. Peter

Stoke Bridge

Ford

River Orwell

St. Mary

Stoke

St. Augustine

River Orwell

0   500 meters

Fig. 1. The Middle Saxon emporium of Ipswich. Courtesy Suffolk County Council.

In the early eighth century Ipswich was expanded to a massive 50 hectares by the creation of a virtual new town, to the north of the original settlement, and by expansion south of the river, into Stoke. New streets were laid out on a gridiron pattern, and buildings were constructed on their frontages. Craft activities, including spinning and weaving, antler and bone working, and metalworking, occur on most sites but not in great quantities. Leatherworking, too, must have been common but is represented only on the waterlogged riverfront site at Bridge Street, where a substantial quantity of cobblers' waste was recovered. Other industries, such as shipbuilding and fishing, also may have been important, but direct evidence is lacking. There can be little doubt, however, that the major industry of the town in both the eighth and ninth centuries was pottery production. Evidence of pottery production stretches for about 200 meters on the south side of Carr Street. Ipswich ware was the only wheel-made and kiln-fired pottery produced in England between the seventh and ninth centuries. The industry supplied the entire East Anglian Kingdom with pottery, and it was exported to aristocratic and ecclesiastical sites as far away as Yorkshire and Kent. On the margins of settlement, environmental evidence indicates agricultural activities, including the keeping of livestock and cereal cleaning, but overall the animal bone evidence suggests that meat was imported into the town from the rural hinterland and that Ipswich was a consumer, rather than a producer, of food.

Little is known about any public buildings that may have served the Middle Saxon town. The first Christian churches appear to be associated with the "new town" of the early eighth century. On the basis of their dedications, the churches of St. Peter, St. Augustine, and St. Mildred probably are the earliest. Excavations also have revealed the sequence of waterfront development. The seventh-century harbor looked very different from the present one, being shallow and tidal, as it is farther down the Orwell estuary in the twenty-first century. Since the eighth century there has been continuous land reclamation, as new waterfronts were constructed nearer the center of the river and the land behind them was filled, raised, and developed. The Anglo-Saxon waterfronts were simple timber revetments, no more than 1 meter high, providing protection to the river bank and hard standing for unloading boats.

International trade was important to the Ipswich economy throughout the eighth and ninth centuries. Imported Norwegian hone stones, Rhenish lava millstones, and Frankish pottery are found on all sites throughout the 50 hectares of occupation and in quantities far in excess of finds from rural sites. The dominant trade link is, not surprisingly, with the Rhine and Dorestad, but there are also links with Belgium and northern France. It is assumed that wool or cloth was exported in return. Rhenish imports undoubtedly included wine for consumption by the local aristocracy and early church. The wine itself was transported in wooden barrels, examples of which have been found reused as lining for well shafts. One such barrel from the excavations in Lower Brook Street in 1975 has been dated by dendrochronology to shortly after A.D. 871 and matches the tree ring pattern of the Mainz area of Germany.

By the eighth century a handful of towns had developed around the North Sea and Baltic coast, each with an economy based on commodity production and international trade. In England there is one such place per Anglo-Saxon Kingdom. Gipeswic (Ipswich) served East Anglia and certainly was founded by the East Anglian royal house, the Wuffingas, whose burial ground at Sutton Hoo and palace at Rendlesham lie less than 10 miles northeast of Ipswich, on the east bank of the River Deben. During the ninth century other towns were founded in the region (among them Norwich, Thetford, and Bury St. Edmunds), and Ipswich gradually lost its role as the East Anglian capital. Although it remained a significant international port, its economy otherwise became that of a market town serving southeastern Suffolk.

See also **Emporia** (*vol. 2, part 7*); **Trade and Exchange** (*vol. 2, part 7*); **Anglo-Saxon England** (*vol. 2, part 7*); **Sutton Hoo** (*vol. 2, part 7*).

BIBLIOGRAPHY

Hodges, Richard. *Dark Age Economics: The Origins of Towns and Trade A.D. 600–1000.* London: Duckworth, 1989.

Wade, Keith. "Gipeswic—East Anglia's First Economic Capital 600–1066." In *Ipswich from the First to the Third Millennium*, pp. 1–6. Ipswich, U.K.: Ipswich Society, 2001.

———. "The Urbanisation of East Anglia: The Ipswich Perspective." In *Flatlands and Wetlands: Current Themes in East Anglian Archaeology.* Edited by Julie Gardiner, pp. 144–151. East Anglian Archaeology, no. 50. Dereham, U.K.: Norfolk Archaeological Unit, 1993.

———. "Ipswich." In *The Rebirth of Towns in the West, A.D. 700–1050.* Edited by Richard Hodges and Brian Hobley, pp. 93–100. Council for British Archaeology Research Report, no. 68. London: Council for British Archaeology, 1988.

KEITH WADE

VIKING HARBORS AND TRADING SITES

Our understanding of the harbors and centers of trade dating to the Viking Age is limited, as is information concerning the level and scope of trade and its organization. The difficulty of acquiring and assessing such information stems from the fact that most trading points are known only from scant written records—none of which are from the Viking homelands themselves. A map of the known Viking harbors and towns in the Baltic area shows very few places, sparsely situated. The best examples of early trading centers in the Baltic Sea are Birka (Sweden), Hedeby or Haithabu (Germany), Grobin (Latvia), Wolin (Poland), and Novgorod (Russia). These centers, known from written documents or discovered by chance, give a much too simple picture of the true state of affairs.

Indeed, along the Baltic coast there must have been a vast number and variety of harbors and trading sites of all sizes, from small fishing camps to permanently occupied cities. Surprisingly, there are no confirmed harbors and trading centers, for example, along the eastern coast of Sweden, despite the fact that this region is one of the largest, oldest, and most important cultivated areas in all of Sweden. This situation is more or less mirrored along the eastern Baltic shore as well as along the Norwegian coast. The challenge, then, is to identify the spots not mentioned in written sources, with archaeological fieldwork as our best guide.

The island of Gotland provides good examples of previously unknown harbors. Situated in the middle of the Baltic Sea, it was a true center in the Viking world. Nowhere have so many Viking silver hoards been found as on this tiny island. In all, more

Fig. 1. Discovered in 1999, this hoard is one out of about seven hundred silver and gold hoards from the Viking Age found on Gotland. PHOTOGRAPH BY DAN CARLSSON. COURTESY OF DAN CARLSSON AND THE HISTORICAL MUSEUM OF GOTLAND. REPRODUCED BY PERMISSION.

then seven hundred separate caches of silver and gold give clear evidence of the island's widespread trade connections. Despite the even distribution of this treasure (mostly Arabic coins) over the island, only one known harbor on Gotland dated to the Viking Age—Paviken, on the west coast. It is unlikely that all the hoards could have been distributed over the island from just one harbor. There must have been many more.

Excavation of this site took place at the end of the 1950s and the beginning of the 1960s. Starting in the last decade of the twentieth century an extensive project was carried out on Gotland, with the aim of analyzing and describing the numbers of harbors and trading sites and their structure, development, and spatial organization during the period of approximately A.D. 600–1000. The research was conducted using a combination of methods, both notes and maps in museum archives and field studies. Three main criteria have been used as evidence to locate possible harbors: prehistoric graves

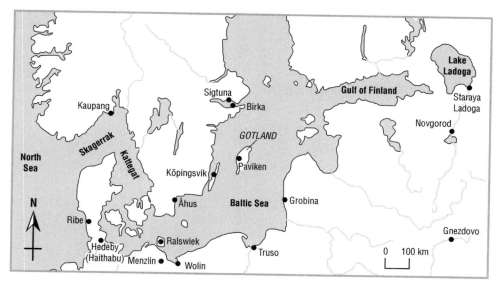

Some Viking harbors and towns in the Baltic Sea region.

or grave fields close to the coast, a shore protected from strong winds, and a situation in the cultural landscape diverging from the normal—for instance, a point where cadastral maps show that several roads converged.

The next step in the project involved phosphate mapping of suspected locations. This mapping identified about sixty places along the Gotlandic coast that showed signs of major or minor activities during the Viking Age. Evaluation of these finds indicated many places that can be interpreted as larger harbors or trading sites, distinguishable from the others in their rich and varied number of artifacts. Boge, Bandlunde, Fröjel, Paviken-Västergarn, and Visby belong to this category. Other, smaller places seem to be fishing harbors for the farmers on the island.

The most extensive investigations of one of these previously unknown Viking trading and manufacturing sites were conducted between 1998 and 2002 at Fröjel, along the west coast of Gotland. At this spot there is an area of 60,000 square meters with many traces of buildings and several grave fields. The archaeological excavations have revealed a harbor and trading center that was active from the late sixth century to approximately A.D. 1180. The harbor's activities peaked during the eleventh century and into the beginning of the twelfth century.

Here is ample documentation of intensive trade and manufacturing—a harbor with connections

both west and east. Coins from Arabia, England, Germany, and Denmark, and jewelry from places as far-flung as the North Atlantic (walrus ivory), the Black Sea (rock crystal), and the area of Kiev in modern-day Ukraine (a resurrection egg) give evidence of distant trade.

The example of Gotland shows clearly that the system of harbors and trading centers in the Viking Age was far more complicated and intricate than one is led to believe from written sources. Jens Ulriksen did the same type of investigation in Denmark in 1997, with more or less the same conclusions. The picture derived solely from written sources is thus far from complete. To understand fully trade and travel patterns in the Viking Age, one must combine the written sources with extensive archaeological fieldwork.

See also **Trade and Exchange** (*vol. 2, part 7*); **Viking Ships** (*vol. 2, part 7*).

BIBLIOGRAPHY

Carlsson, Dan. "Ridanäs"—*Vikingahamnen i Fröjel* ["Ridanäs—the Viking Age harbor in Fröjel]. Visby, Sweden: ArkeoDok, 1999.

Clark, Helen, and Björn Ambrosiani. *Towns in the Viking Age.* Rev. ed. Leicester, U.K.: Leicester University Press, 1995.

"Fröjel Discovery Programme." Gotland University College. http://frojel.hgo.se.

Graham-Campbell, James, Colleen Batey, Helen Clarke, R. I. Page, and Neil S. Price. *Cultural Atlas of the Viking World*. New York: Facts on File, 1994.

Hodges, Richard. *Dark Age Economics: The Origins of Towns and Trade AD 600–1000*. 2d ed. New York: St. Martin's, 1982.

Ulriksen, Jens. *Anløbspladser: Besejling og bebyggelse i Danmark mellem 200 og 1100 e.Kr.* [Seafaring, landing sites, and settlements in Denmark from A.D. 200 to 1100]. Roskilde, Denmark: Vikingeskibshallen i Roskilde, 1997.

DAN CARLSSON

DARK AGES, MIGRATION PERIOD, EARLY MIDDLE AGES

The Middle Ages are sandwiched between the era of classical antiquity and the modern world. The beginning of the Middle Ages is traditionally marked by the fall of the Western Roman Empire in A.D. 476, while Columbus's voyages of discovery mark the start of the modern period. Therefore, most scholars consider the interval between the fifth and the fifteenth centuries A.D. as the Middle Ages or the medieval period.

Most historians, art historians, and archaeologists subdivide the Middle Ages into an earlier and a later period. The Late or High Middle Ages begin in the 11th century A.D. By this time, the Vikings had colonized Iceland and Greenland, and Christianity had been adopted throughout most of central and northern Europe. The High Middle Ages are marked by the growth of urbanism across Europe, the expansion of long distance trade networks, the construction of the great cathedrals, and the establishment of nation-states. Historical records provide valuable information on later medieval life. These European societies of the High Middle Ages have many features in common with the ancient Egyptians, the Maya, and other groups known as civilizations or complex societies. Therefore, the archaeology of the High Middle Ages is not included in this encyclopedia.

The earlier parts of the Middle Ages, on the other hand, have much more in common with the barbarian societies of later prehistoric Europe. These societies were primarily rural and agricultural, and their documentary records are limited or non-existent. As a result, much of what scholars have learned about day-to-day life in the earlier Middle Ages in Europe comes from archaeological surveys and excavations.

Three terms—the Early Middle Ages, the Migration period, and the Dark Ages—have been used to describe the earlier parts of the medieval period. Each term has a slightly different meaning, and the terms can be used differently in different parts of Europe.

EARLY MIDDLE AGES

The Early Middle Ages is a term that commonly is used by art historians and others to describe the period beginning with the collapse of the Western Roman Empire in the fifth century and ending with the rise of the Romanesque style of architecture in the eleventh century. While the term might appear as a straightforward chronological marker, it is most useful in describing regions that were formerly part of the Western Roman Empire. In regions such as Britain, France, and Spain, the replacement of Roman military, political, and economic authority by the barbarian successor kingdoms led to significant social, economic, and political changes. Outside the Roman Empire, however, in regions such as northern Germany and Scandinavia, the first part of this period represents a continuation of the Iron Age way of life. In much of northern Europe, the first four centuries A.D. are referred to as the Roman Iron Age, while the period c. A.D. 400–800 is often termed the Late or Germanic Iron Age. In many parts of northern Europe, the term "medieval" is used only when referring to the period after A.D.

1000, an era that is outside the scope of this encyclopedia.

DARK AGES

The term "dark age" generally is used to indicate a period of time when historical records are limited or nonexistent. For example, the Greek Dark Age begins with the collapse of the Mycenaean kingdoms around 1200 B.C. and ends with reappearance of writing in the eighth century B.C. Historians in the eighteenth and nineteenth centuries A.D. used the term Dark Ages to refer to almost all of the European Middle Ages, from the fifth through the twelfth centuries A.D., and they used the term in a pejorative sense. For these historians, the earlier medieval period was not just a time of limited literacy and few documentary sources; it was a period of intellectual stagnation; the accomplishments of medieval people were deemed far less impressive than those of classical antiquity and the Renaissance. Although there is no question that few contemporary historical sources survive from early post-Roman western Europe, the use of the term Dark Ages is still problematic for two reasons. First, most of northeastern Europe remained nonliterate, essentially prehistoric, throughout almost the entire first millennium A.D. The Baltic regions were well outside the boundaries of the Roman Empire, and these lands were mentioned only peripherally in Greek and Roman sources from the first half of the first millennium A.D. Literacy was introduced to the Baltic regions along with Christianity around the year 1000. Second, the term Dark Age is particularly inappropriate for Ireland between the fifth and the eighth centuries A.D. Christianity and literacy were introduced to Ireland in the 400s. Over the next three centuries the Irish developed the oldest indigenous literary tradition in Europe outside Greece and Rome. Some writers would even suggest that the Irish monks who copied classical manuscripts in their scriptoria actually saved Western Civilization. Irish archaeologists generally refer to the fifth through eighth centuries in Ireland as the Early Christian Period.

Many archaeologists today avoid the use of the term Dark Ages because of its former pejorative connotations. When the term is used, it usually describes post-Roman societies whose social, political, and economic organization differ significantly from the classical world; and it often refers only to the initial part of the Early Middle Ages, usually the fifth to the eighth centuries A.D. Since few historical sources are available to study the economics and politics of the early post-Roman period, archaeology has a crucial role to play in the study of this era.

MIGRATION PERIOD

The Early Middle Ages are sometimes described as the Migration period. In many ways, the first half of the European Middle Ages can be seen as one extended interval of migration. The period begins with the movement of barbarian tribes, such as the Huns, into the territory of the Roman Empire during the fifth century A.D. After the fall of the Western Roman Empire, a series of barbarian successor kingdoms were established in the former imperial territory. These include the kingdoms of the Franks in France, the Visigoths in Spain, the Langobards (Lombards) in Italy, and the Angles and Saxons in southern and eastern Britain. The homelands of these barbarian tribes were located outside the empire, in northern and eastern Europe. Migrations, however, did not cease with the establishment of these successor kingdoms. The Magyars entered the Carpathian Basin in the eighth century, and the Early Slavs expanded into much of east-central Europe in the sixth and seventh centuries A.D.

Perhaps the best known of all the migrating peoples are the Vikings. Beginning in the late eighth century A.D., Vikings from western Scandinavia began to raid, trade, and colonize many regions of the North Atlantic. Norse settlements are well documented in both Britain and Ireland. The Vikings had colonized Iceland by the late ninth century, and about a century later they established two colonies in southwestern Greenland, the westernmost outpost of the medieval European world. Other Vikings migrated eastward, settling in Russia and trading with locations as far away as Constantinople (Istanbul) and Mesopotamia.

Although migration is a fundamental feature of European society between A.D. 400–1000, the Migration period, in the strictest sense of the term, refers to the period between 400–600, when a series of Germanic kingdoms were established in the territory of the former Western Roman Empire. Unlike the term Dark Ages, Migration period does not carry with it a pejorative connotation. For that reason, many scholars prefer it to Dark Ages when discussing the early centuries of the Middle Ages.

BIBLIOGRAPHY

Cahill, Thomas. *How the Irish Saved Civilization: The Untold Story of Ireland's Heroic Role from the Fall of Rome to the Rise of Medieval Europe.* New York: Nan A. Talese, Doubleday, 1995.

Hodges, Richard. *Dark Age Economics: The Origins of Towns and Trade A.D. 600–1000.* 2d ed. London: Duckworth, 1989.

Musset, Lucien. *The Germanic Invasions: The Making of Europe, A.D. 400–600.* Translated by Edward James and Columba James. University Park: Pennsylvania State University Press, 1975.

PAM J. CRABTREE

HISTORY AND ARCHAEOLOGY

The distinction between the fields of history and archaeology is widely recognized to be a result of the scholarly boundaries that place historians and archaeologists in separate academic departments. The hindrance of intellectual exchange between the disciplines has resulted in the development of misunderstandings about philosophical underpinnings, standards of practice, and current inquiry. Moreover, this division between history and archaeology naturalizes modern distinctions between the pasts of literate and nonliterate people. Indeed, a thorough assessment of the relationship between history and archaeology requires an appraisal of the nature of historical and archaeological inquiry, as scholars in each field exhibit fundamental misconceptions about the other discipline.

LITERACY IN EARLY
MEDIEVAL EUROPE

Traditionally, the division between "prehistoric" and "historic" archaeology, with its evolutionary implications, has been based on the presence of writing. In modern studies of the early medieval period, however, this distinction often is obscured, because literate groups, such as the members of the Latinized Christian church, may provide the names and histories by which we know either contemporaneous nonliterate peoples or groups whose symbolic expression remains undeciphered by modern scholars. The archaeology of these peoples has been termed by some scholars "protohistory." The distinction between peoples who produced written records and those who did not underlies the privileged position ascribed to literacy as defining an

evolving "civilization" and nonliteracy as representative of an ahistorical "barbarism."

In a society with limited literacy, such as early medieval Europe, writers generally were drawn from and read by only a small, usually elite, segment of society. Literacy was restricted geographically to religious and urban centers. It is important to acknowledge that documentation is in itself an agent of cultural transformation, as records play a role in the material discourse of power. During the early medieval period, an apparent association with the supernatural afforded an otherworldly authority to the documents created in religious scriptoria.

Documents often were created to maintain and further the economic and administrative interests of certain constituencies. For example, the *Ecclesiastical History of the English People* (*Historia ecclesiastica gentis Anglorum*), written in the first third of the eighth century by the Northumbrian cleric the Venerable Bede, and the sixth-century *History of the Franks* (*Historia Francorum*), by the bishop Gregory of Tours, consciously or unconsciously legitimized the nation-building endeavors of their respective kings, Edwin and Clovis, within the emerging English and Frankish states. These histories presented a spurious political unity that implied, for the benefit of their readers, that these nascent states manifested a cultural homogeneity. Archaeologists seeking a corresponding agreement in material culture patterning must be aware that the documents that direct their interpretations can be misleading. Attempts to relate the tribal groupings recorded in early medieval historical records perpetuate mythic notions of ethnic identity that sometimes find their realization in modern European nationalities. Despite early medieval references to cultural groupings, such as Burgundians, Goths, and Saxons, no evidence exists that these peoples shared a common biological descent. Indeed, ethnicity appears to have been a situational construct that was important within relationships of power and politics. The elite and their interests were most likely to have been the subjects, benefactors, and consumers of the written works in which ethnic labels were recorded.

Because of the centrality of the documentary records in the ongoing activities of church and state, it is impossible to consider any aspect of the early medieval period without acknowledging the power of the written word in our current appreciation of these institutions. Without such awareness, the social, economic, and political organization of the past becomes evidence of evolutionary developments extending from the early medieval period to the modern day. This deterministic presentation of "progress" legitimizes the authority of those powers whose past is recorded and affords modern interests an opportunity to incorporate the legitimacy of a mythic past in the pursuit of their own objectives. The historiography of the early medieval period cannot be separated from Europe's own self-conception, as current political concerns have unconsciously guided interpretations of the past. For example, beginning in the nineteenth century, archaeology presented Europe as the cultural product of conquest and colonization, mirroring the European imperialist experience in Africa, Asia, and the Americas. By the 1960s, this association with militaristic expansionism was superseded by complex processual models. Today, in an environment of individualism and nation building, interpretations emphasizing human agency and cultural identity are evoked.

THE NATURE OF HISTORICAL AND ARCHAEOLOGICAL EVIDENCE

In comparison with texts of later historical periods, those dating to early medieval times (c. A.D. 400–1000) are neither as common nor as specific and typically lack any substantive presentations of individuals. Textual sources during this period include heroic literature, annals, histories and chronicles, saint's lives, charters, wills, pedigrees and genealogies, and laws. Discontinuous in their creation and episodic in their narrative of time and space, documents traditionally have been considered permanent records intended for present and future audiences. In contrast, archaeological information, characterized as cumulative and continuously created, informs on relations and situations in the past. Categories of archaeological data include the excavated remains of settlements, burials, and earthworks, field surveys, and supporting data from specialist analyses (e.g., metallurgical, petrographic, chronometric, and zooarchaeological studies).

Underscoring the importance of the written link between the documentary and archaeological records are inscribed objects. These textual artifacts, such as coins carrying the name and place of the authority under whom they were minted and personal items inscribed with the name of the individual who made, commissioned, or owned the object, occasionally are encountered in contexts associated with nonliterate peoples. It cannot be assumed that the content of the inscription necessarily was understood by those using these objects. The symbolic authority of the written word, however, must have been generally appreciated, as meaningless characters sometimes appear on objects, such as precious metal bracteates, fabricated by nonliterate people. Moreover, the prestige vested in the written word is emphasized by the fact that the members of the elite would have been most likely to have had the resources and relationships necessary to acquire and distribute these valuable goods.

Critical theory has led scholars to understand that the past is a cultural construction and that historians and archaeologists, as well as their source materials, are constrained by biases. The historical records were not created to address the questions that modern scholars pose. Intentional and unintentional biases arise between the situations in which documents were originally created and have been subsequently interpreted. At a fundamental level are errors of translation, as the lack of equivalency in one language can lead to misrepresentation in another. Moreover, the written records often were drafted many years after the events that they describe or, in the case of oral traditions, after the original work was composed. As a consequence, these written works may reflect the political geography and relationships of the time of transcription rather than the period of creation. Not all records from a particular time and place have been preserved, so the picture presented from a reading of the available documents can never be considered complete or even representative. Indeed, early medieval authors were selective in their choice of subjects, often omitting entire categories of people, such as the young, the impoverished, or the disabled, from meaningful mention. The resulting historical narrative often lacks any structure beyond that of chronology, as the events described occur at irregular intervals and are of unknown relative significance.

Without mediation between these two sources of information, our understanding of the archaeological or textual evidence is constrained. For example, the *Beowulf* poem, written down in the eighth century or later, has been used by archaeologists to identify and interpret objects, such as the helmet and standard found in the elite seventh-century ship burial at Sutton Hoo (Suffolk, England). Although the poem and the burial generally are thought to be separated chronologically by at least one century, scholars often treat them as contemporaneous. Moreover, similarities between the literary and archaeological material have been employed to derive the date of the heroic *Beowulf* poem and to guide its translation toward language and concepts framed by the finds at Sutton Hoo. By viewing the Anglo-Saxon epic *Beowulf* and the Sutton Hoo burial as mirrors of each other, we limit our understanding of each in its own right.

RELATIONSHIPS BETWEEN HISTORY AND ARCHAEOLOGY

Archaeology has been famously belittled as the "handmaiden to history" and "an expensive way of telling us what we already know." Indeed, some archaeologists have viewed archaeology during historic periods as most useful as a laboratory in which theories, particularly those developed by prehistorians, can be tested. At the same time, early medieval archaeologists ignore the epistemological implication of this cultural connection across centuries: Is it appropriate—and, if so, under what conditions—to assume a cultural connection from historically documented times into the prehistoric past? Often, little rigor is exercised in assessing the appropriate-

ness of the analogy drawn. This procedure, called by North American archaeologists the "direct historical approach," effectively decontextualizes the past, thereby subjecting it to anachronistic interpretation and obscuring its specific social meaning.

The discipline of history or archaeology is seen by some practitioners in the other field as a fertile source of comparative material to illustrate or interpret research concerns within their own discipline. In the most intellectually arid conception of the relationship between written and artifactual evidence, historians simply have grafted archaeological facts onto a historical framework, and archaeologists have substantiated their findings by drawing facts from the documentary record. Throughout study of the early medieval period, archaeology has been used to illuminate areas of research largely ignored by the written texts, such as technology and economy.

The intellectual conversation between the two disciplines has been characterized as a monologue, as some historians consider archaeology to be irrelevant or overly theoretical. Scholars in both fields complain that in making use of the historian's toolkit, archaeologists demonstrate a limited understanding of the nature of historical inquiry and are unable to keep pace with philosophical and theoretical changes in the historical discipline. Anthropologically related historical approaches that mirror work done by post-processual archaeologists in other parts of the world, such as historical analyses that focus on the cultural construction of language and on the ways in which culture creates, fosters, and challenges inequalities, are largely ignored by those working in the early medieval period.

Using history to frame archaeological questions risks the production of tautologies, or circular arguments. For example, burials found in an area and at a time known from documents to have been inhabited by a certain tribal group generally are deemed to represent the population group. In early medieval England, this unreflective ethnic ascription of cemeteries as Anglo-Saxon has raised critical questions about how Celtic and Germanic ethnic identity was conceived, if at all, by those living in the fourth to seventh centuries and what the cemetery evidence indicates about the fate of the indigenous British population during this time.

PAST APPROACHES, FUTURE DIRECTIONS

During the twentieth century the relationship between archaeology and history reflected wider developments in each field. During the first half of the twentieth century, Anglo-Saxon archaeologists, such as J. N. L. Myres and E. T. Leeds, fashioned an early medieval archaeology that privileged the historical record. Archaeological finds were organized within chronological and typological schema, which were related, in turn, to events, such as battles, and accounts of great men detailed in historical documents.

Into the 1970s and 1980s, archaeological data were viewed as more objective and reliable than historical sources, because it was argued that archaeology produced deposits that were unconsciously created and lacked intentionally communicated messages. Artifacts were seen as the tools by which humans maintain stability within the natural and social environment. Following the positivistic philosophy prevailing in the "New Archaeology" movement at that time, archaeology was positioned as a natural science against which subjective historical facts could be tested.

In the 1980s, however, archaeologists began to complain that historical interests framed the agenda, modes of analysis, and language of archaeological inquiry. As a consequence, it was argued, archaeological research should be guided by its own theoretical premises and executed independently of the historical sources. Rather than chronicling past events of traditional narrative history, with its focus on the elite, the "new medieval archaeology" sought to explicate the social processes affecting the daily lives of the wider population.

The "new medieval archaeology" was itself criticized, however, for conceptualizing change as an adaptive response to external systemic stimuli, thereby denying individual agency and ignoring the discursive relationship between human actions and the structures that they produce. Instead, it was argued that artifacts must be assessed in context, both as the products of actions and as the active agents by which social relations are identified, subverted, and transformed. Particularly in the United Kingdom and Scandinavia, this reassessment of the relationship between history and archaeology revitalized medieval studies. Inspired by anthropologically

oriented historians, such as those engaged in the French *Annales* school, which examined the long-term structures of social and economic history, and by the theoretical agendas of anthropologically trained North American archaeologists, new research cut across traditional disciplinary boundaries and sources to investigate thematic concerns, such as gender, power relations, and cultural identity.

The work of historical archaeologists in the United States was invoked further to demonstrate that the distinction between artifacts and texts is cultural rather than natural. Some archaeologists emphasized that in the same way that historians approach documents, artifacts can be "read," because both sources are components of material culture formed by the imposition of human action on nature. This position considers texts and artifacts equally as the products of thoughtful human action that contain social meaning and are the means by which social relations are articulated and negotiated. Rather than playing a passive role, as labels or markers, artifacts and documents were utilized in the past as expressive media. Written texts, therefore, are fundamentally artifacts and, as such, are not privileged over other forms of material culture in the interpretation of the past. As a consequence, only through examining the specific social contexts of artifacts and documents can we understand their social meaning.

The analytical framework must be derived from a social theory independent of historical or archaeological methodologies. It has been suggested that social reproduction—the renewal and transformation of the social system and its cognitive structure—or the structuring dynamic of power provide organizing principles by which texts and artifacts can be methodologically joined. For example, through reading the changing proportions of different Pictish symbols carved on monumental stones between the sixth and tenth centuries, it is possible to identify a discourse of power. According to this interpretation, changes in the ideological content of these symbols articulate the expansion of dynastic elites in early medieval Scotland and the religious authorities put to their service.

This approach holds more broadly that the processes that produce the archaeological and historical records are often the same, even if their creators or circumstances of origin differ. Thus, the ideological anxieties articulated by the paganism of the seventh-century Sutton Hoo burials also are expressed, at a later time and in a different medium, by the political tension pervading the *Beowulf* poem, thereby uniting these works through a common metaphor or mindset. Indeed, following the writings of postmodern philosophers, the fact that a document shapes reality, thereby transforming it into a monument, is echoed by archaeologists who consider monuments, such as burial mounds, to be documents not only in a metaphorical sense but also as statements of ancestral authority and land tenure.

Rather than ignoring the documentary record or considering it to be all of a piece with the archaeological record, other archaeologists have argued that archaeology and history provide different sets of data that can be related dialectically to expose contradictions. This view holds that because different processes produce them, written and material pieces of evidence are fundamentally independent. In this approach, the interests of the dominant groups, as portrayed in the texts, can be used to investigate the ideological promotion of power and control and the resistance, through the distribution of material culture, among the textually disenfranchised. For example, this type of analysis exposes the contradictions between contrasting religious, political, and social interests vying for supremacy during the sixth and seventh centuries in the emerging East Anglian kingdom. Along with the documented attempts by Frankish and Italian churchmen to bring Christianity to England came a political and ideological alignment with these Continental kingdoms. Despite Continental Christianizing efforts, however, the burials at the East Anglian cemetery at Sutton Hoo exhibit a defiant paganism in their preference for cremation, grave furnishings, and ship burial. The dialectic between the missionary activities of the Christian church, as described in Bede's *Ecclesiastical History of the English People,* and the pagan burial practices has been interpreted as the East Anglian kingdom's resistance to an ideological conquest by Continental powers.

In conclusion, there is no agreement as to whether archaeological and historical inquiries have different source materials, methodologies, or goals. While some archaeologists have sought to validate and integrate the interests of the fields of history and archaeology by identifying commonalties, oth-

ers consider the disciplines to be complementary, and still others argue that archaeology must be released from its historical shackles. Rather than evidence of an inadequate theoretical and epistemological foundation, the lack of a universalizing system within which history and archaeology can be unified has been considered essential for the development of a contextual and pluralistic approach to the early medieval past.

See also **The Nature of Archaeological Data** (*vol. 1, part 3*); **Sutton Hoo** (*vol. 2, part 7*).

BIBLIOGRAPHY

Andersson, Hans, Peter Carelli, and Lars Ersgård, eds. *Visions of the Past: Trends and Traditions in Swedish Medieval Archaeology.* Stockholm, Sweden: Central Board of National Antiquities, 1997.

Andrén, Anders. *Between Artifacts and Texts: Historical Archaeology in Global Perspective.* Translated by Alan Crozier. New York: Plenum Press, 1998.

Austin, David, and Leslie Alcock, eds. *From the Baltic to the Black Sea: Studies in Medieval Archaeology.* London: Unwin Hyman, 1990.

Braudel, Fernand. *On History.* Translated by Sarah Matthews. Chicago: University of Chicago Press, 1980.

Carver, Martin. "Marriages of True Minds: Archaeology with Texts." In *Archaeology: The Widening Debate.* Edited by Barry Cunliffe, Wendy Davies, and Colin Renfrew, pp. 465–496. Oxford: Oxford University Press, 2002.

Driscoll, Stephen T. "Discourse on the Frontiers of History: Material Culture and Social Reproduction in Early Scotland." *Historical Archaeology* 26, no. 3 (1992): 12–25.

———. "The Relationship between History and Archaeology: Artefacts, Documents and Power." In *Power and Politics in Early Medieval Britain and Ireland.* Edited by Stephen T. Driscoll and Margaret R. Nieke, pp. 162–187. Edinburgh: Edinburgh University Press, 1988.

Funari, Pedro Paulo A., Martin Hall, and Siân Jones, eds. *Historical Archaeology: Back from the Edge.* London: Routledge, 1999.

Hodges, R. "New Approaches to Medieval Archaeology, Part 2." In *Twenty-Five Years of Medieval Archaeology.* Edited by David Hinton, pp. 24–32. Sheffield, U.K.: University of Sheffield, 1983.

Knapp, A. Bernard, ed. *Archaeology, Annales, and Ethnohistory.* Cambridge, U.K.: Cambridge University Press, 1992.

Moreland, John F. *Archaeology and Text.* London: Duckworth, 2001.

————. "Method and Theory in Medieval Archaeology in the 1990's." *Archeologia Medievale* 18 (1991): 7–42.

Rahtz, Phillip. "New Approaches to Medieval Archaeology, Part 1." In *Twenty-Five Years of Medieval Archaeology.* Edited by David Hinton, pp. 12–23. Sheffield, U.K.: University of Sheffield, 1983.

Ravn, Mads, and Rupert Britton, eds. "History and Archaeology." Special Issue of *Archaeological Review from Cambridge* 14, no. 1 (1997): 129–135.

Sawyer, Peter. "English Archaeology before the Conquest: A Historian's View." In *Twenty-Five Years of Medieval Archaeology.* Edited by David Hinton, pp. 44–47. Sheffield, U.K.: University of Sheffield, 1983.

Tabaczynski, Stanislaw. "The Relationship between History and Archaeology: Elements of the Present Debate." *Medieval Archaeology* 37 (1993): 1–14.

GENEVIEVE FISHER

STATE FORMATION

To understand the classic archaeological problem of state formation as it was played out in Europe, it is necessary to place it within its wider context. While the terms "state" and "state formation" are still in use, archaeologists today are more likely to discuss states and their immediate predecessors in terms of increasing political complexity, since the line between a so-called chiefdom and a state can become blurred by the context of their development, and it is not always useful to try to pigeonhole such varied political forms.

WHAT IS A STATE?

It turns out to be quite difficult to define a state. In the mid-twentieth century, V. Gordon Childe composed his classic list of state "attributes," which include cities, specialized labor, writing, monuments, and other "markers"; these have proved to be highly problematic, however, since some entities that are clearly states had no writing or cities, while Stone Age farmers built monuments of tremendous size; similarly, many nonstate societies have specialists in various tasks and crafts. However, despite the problems of Childe's original list, it should be noted that many of the characteristics he identified are still recognized as important *variables* in the *study* of states. It is probably safe to say that states are complex political structures in which several administrative or bureaucratic layers are necessary for effective rule, and that they encompass numerous internal groups and stratified social classes over which leaders exercise integrative power in combination with institutionalized coercion.

In addition, while kinship between rulers and other elites is important in many states, the rulers of states rely for the most part on political ties with followers to hold the state together and to perpetuate their power, rather than relying mainly on the support of their own large kin-groups. States are also usually more or less integrated—that is, their "parts" work together relatively smoothly and are more or less controlled by whomever rules. These parts would include, among many other things, the political structure (the chain of command leading from ruler to various bureaucratic specialists), the political economy (taxes, tribute), jurisprudence (lawmaking and lawgiving), communications (roads, bridges, messengers), warfare (commanders, troops, supply lines), and the social and religious institutions partly or completely controlled by the state. When operations are *not* running smoothly, archaeologists can gain useful clues into the process of state formation and development itself, just as a modern economist might interpret a budget deficit as an indication of fiscal problems within a nation. Thus, archaeologists can trace the emergence of a state by monitoring the initial appearance of these institutions and by watching carefully to see who controls them—regional elites or a centralized figure. Often, there are periods during state formation when control of institutions by central authorities is incomplete. This phase may be followed by a consolidation of power or by the collapse of the state.

While today's world is dominated by state political structures, they are in fact a very recent "invention," having emerged from pre-state complex societies in the Near East no earlier than 3600 B.C. They are also a rare occurrence: the archaeological social sequences that have *not* resulted in states far outnumber those that have. Many people believe that state societies are "stable"; in fact, they are one of the least stable forms of government and are highly susceptible to upheaval and collapse. There have been many theories on state formation, and many of the earlier concepts have been characterized as "prime mover" theories because they postulate a single trigger for the rise of all states, such as water control, warfare, trade, the need for record keeping, or demographic pressure. While such theories were popular for a time due to their plausibility and simplicity, archaeological field investigations have shown that one state rarely develops for the same reason as another; even within a single political entity, the causes of state development are complex and multivariate. Today, most archaeologists note the highly contingent nature of states, stressing local conditions and specific "historical" trajectories (even when the states are prehistoric), while at the same time using some generalizations and comparisons across cultures to evaluate how certain factors may influence developing political complexity in similar ways.

HOW ARCHAEOLOGISTS STUDY THE STATE

At the most general level, states can be categorized as either primary or secondary. The first developed where no state had previously existed, as an innovation in sociopolitical evolution; the second, through interaction and association with already-extant states. Those of Europe are secondary states. Why do extant states trigger new state development at their peripheries? One theory is that the presence of a powerful and organized neighbor creates a need in a less complex region to produce "equal" leaders and institutions to cope with and take advantage of nearby states. Another view is that local emerging elites, who already have power in their own societies, achieve greater control by limiting all access to the coveted goods and new ideologies brought by the neighboring state. In addition, if the nearby state presents a threat, leaders grow more efficient and organized to meet the danger. Yet another idea is that a system develops in which the original state stimulates development at its periphery to exploit its

raw materials and resources, yet at the same time tries to limit that development to take advantage of its superior position. Once the process begins, however, it often moves outside the control of the first polity.

Since it is not always easy to identify the process of state formation, or even the existence of a state, on the basis of activities at a single site, the archaeological study of states often takes a regional approach. The reason is clear if one considers the questions important for studying state formation. For example, who controls the economy in a society? Is it individuals, a kin-group, or the political apparatus of a state? To find an answer, one must look at many sites with economic activity and determine whether they are under centralized or individual control. Similar patterns are to be sought for political activity, religious organization, and other institutions likely to be controlled by a ruler or ruling class. In addition, geographers have demonstrated that a bureaucratic hierarchy is often reflected in "size classes" of sites—large centers, small centers, large villages, small villages—even though the officials themselves may not live in these communities, since in some societies elites value spatial separation from commoners as well as economic and political separation. In historically observed chiefly societies, there are centers and satellites, but usually only three classes of sites: primary centers, smaller centers, and small villages or scattered farms. States, however, display at least four types of communities. Thus, if archaeologists observe a change in the organization of settlements over a landscape: for example from many villages, all roughly the same size, to a pattern with various size centers and outlying sites, *and* this is concomitant with apparent increases in stratification, centrally coordinated defense or economic activities, this is often inferred as marking a transition in political organization.

EUROPE'S EARLIEST STATELIKE SOCIETIES

Although Italy and Greece are part of the European sphere today, in ancient times they belonged to a world system centered around Turkey, the Levant, and Asia; hence their earliest phases do not relate strongly to the archaeologic record of the western, northern, and central European world-system. Nevertheless, the earliest state formation sequences in

Europe can be said to be linked to Italy and Greece. The development of Rome itself was secondary in nature, in response to interaction with the Greek and eastern Mediterranean worlds. Rome then developed into an empire—a state that subsumes other civilizations and cultures—and from that position triggered state formation in many other parts of Europe.

Important developments for early European states can be found in the Celtic Iron Age, which began in about 800 B.C. and constituted an ethnolinguistic-political complex encompassing parts of France, Switzerland, southern Germany, the Czech Republic, and other regions. Already, in the Hallstatt period (800–480 B.C.), complex pre-state societies were coalescing as a result of the internal development of a Celtic political elite and interactions with Greek traders in the western Mediterranean who established Massalia (Marseille) at the mouth of the Rhône. During the La Tène period (500–50 B.C.), in the second century B.C., Rome began to expand beyond the Italian peninsula, and, in response, sites called *oppida* emerged north of the Alps throughout much of western and central Europe, spreading to eastern Hungary, Slovakia, Germany, Belgium, and southwestern France. These were fortified central places with nucleated proto-urban populations, often housing a number of industries and the residences of rulers. Clues to their development lie in their defensive locations and walls, their close proximity to mineral-rich areas and good agricultural soils, and their position on trade routes.

The nature of these settlements has been debated: were they city-states, like the small polities of classic period Greece, or were they chiefly societies? *Oppida* such as the well-investigated Kelheim site, with walls that required more than a million person-hours to construct, had populations in the thousands, representing several social classes engaged in many specialized industries, and they appear to have been economic and administrative centers. Evidence at smaller sites indicates that elites may have lived outside the *oppida* as well as in them. This is not at all unusual: in fact, in some states, few elites live in towns. Many archaeologists now classify the *oppida* as archaic or emergent states that were developing independently before Rome's intervention. Their full flowering was cut off in the mid-first century B.C. by the expansion of the Romans through

conquest, and the eventual removal of local rulers and their replacement with Roman officials. Until the collapse of Rome's empire, these regions were provinces within a larger state entity.

Similar developments occurred in Britain, as illustrated by Maiden Castle, a fortified hilltop that was home to as many as four thousand people. The Romans defeated its occupants and their leaders in A.D. 43, an event to which the huge stockpile of weapons found inside and the Roman projectiles found outside bear archaeological witness.

The Celtic culture was not the only one in Europe to have witnessed state formation in the Iron Age. Northern Europe, inhabited primarily by Germanic groups, was never conquered by Rome; and yet, beginning in the first century A.D., interaction with Roman traders and ambassadors seeking wealth and political advantage brought political change to what the Romans called Free Germania, which included much of present-day Germany, all of Denmark, and other Nordic regions. Although the empire planned to conquer this area, it was unable to do so. Thus, unlike the Celtic groups closer to Rome, the peoples of this region retained their independence and built a more politically complex society during the last centuries of the Roman Empire.

POST-ROMAN STATES IN EUROPE

The fall of Rome, like the collapse of any large, integrative political system, had a huge impact not only within its own borders but outside them as well. The post-Roman world consisted of former imperial areas and areas that had never been conquered, and the course of subsequent state formation was different in the two zones because of the preexisting conditions specific to each one. In northern Europe, post-Roman Scandinavians were left in disarray after the imperial collapse, but responded by forming their own, more centralized structures to provide the power and prestige that local leaders had previously acquired from their Roman connections. In the period from A.D. 500 to 1000, they slowly acquired increasingly statelike qualities. Between the eighth and tenth centuries, a settlement system, which included cities, towns, villages, and hamlets, emerged; in addition, a "state" style of runic monuments spread from the epicenter of the state to new regions under its control, and rulers began to mint coins, collect taxes, and mobilize large labor forces for public works projects. Although large labor-intensive projects are possible in many types of societies, the building of the Danevirke, an earthwork many kilometers in length, by the Danes beginning in A.D. 737, and the founding of several market-places and towns that show signs of large defensive works, attest to the emergence of a stronger central authority.

Nearby Slavic peoples, such as the Wends living in the Baltic plain, also began to display more political complexity; administrative centers, markets, and other integrative features arose, often in connection with the coercive power of local rulers, who were linked by marriage to the earliest Danish and Swedish royal lines.

A different series of conditions was found in the Romanized regions after the fall of the empire. Many Germanic and some Slavic peoples flowed onto the Romano-Celtic continent at this time, and, from these old and new societies, new states emerged, often called the "successor states," since they succeeded, or at least followed, the imperial apparatus. The "starting points" of these new polities varied a great deal: in some areas, barbarian Visigoths, Ostrogoths, Vandals, Langobards, Burgunds, and others took up residence and rulership in what is now France, Germany, Spain, Italy, and other nations. Elsewhere, collapsed provinces re-emerged as states. For example, the Merovingian and then Carolingian dynasties of the Franks, though Germanic in origin, came from the Romanized side of the Rhine, while the Visigoth kingdom was created when the Roman government ceded taxes and administration in one area to a Germanic warlord in A.D. 413. As imperial institutions fell apart, a system developed that fused Germanic, Slavic, Romano-Celtic, and Roman elements.

England, a category in itself, was both a former Roman province and a somewhat "de-Romanized" area, since it had been subject to many destabilizing Saxon attacks in the fourth century. It had also lost its Roman connection early. Constantine III, a Roman soldier who became the ruler of the British province, began a campaign in 407 to seize the imperial throne. To back his bid for imperial power, he took the last remaining Romano-British troops with him as he crossed the Channel in his march toward Rome. As a result, the hapless Britons were sudden-

ly forced to organize their own government and military. Archaeological evidence from the terminal Roman sequence shows that the urban centers declined and the many rural villas faded away. Roman artifacts and coins are largely absent from strata more recent than about A.D. 400. By the time the rest of the empire began to collapse in the 450s, Britain had far fewer remnants of Roman structures, such as the imperial church organization, land-ownership systems, and legal practices. Thus, when their new states emerged during the post-Roman period, they had a unique flavor.

The collapse of the Roman Empire in Europe was felt long after the fifth century, as various powers competed for supremacy or at least for a foothold. To take just one example, at least two states, Normandy and Flanders, formed within what would become the kingdom of France in the ninth and tenth centuries. This occurred well before the king of France in the Paris Basin had his own state, which eventually conquered the others. Additional states were formed around very small territories, counties, towns, or even the area immediately around the seats of local nobles. Many archaeologists have found it difficult to classify these areas as they existed in post-Roman times, since they did not display "typical" state features, such as urbanism, yet they were also not "chiefdoms" in the anthropological sense. During the mid- to late twentieth century, archaeologists working with paradigms according to which states were expected to conform to a narrow set of characteristics sometimes called them "post-state societies." However, now that our concept of what a state is and how diversely it can form has been modified, such polities can often be classified as "differently organized" states. For example, structurally, Charlemagne's eighth-century Frankish kingdom was essentially nonurban, and was similar to what is termed a "paramount chiefdom," with the king keeping the allegiance of his vassals with opulent gifts and feasts, yet it was territorially larger than most modern states and had a number of the classic expression of variables usually associated with states. As the Holy Roman Empire expanded and gained new lands confiscated from the conquered, kings began to give land to their vassals instead. This increased the vassals' power in relation to the king's, thus destabilizing the empire and facilitating its further fragmentation.

State formation in Europe may seem at first to be a tangled web of societies that rise, spread, shrink, and fall in a nearly incomprehensible manner. Most people, comparing it to their own experience as citizens of a modern state, would find it highly confusing. In fact, however, this is a short-term perspective. Controlled chaos is the nature of the state, and is more clearly visible to archaeologists, since they have a long-term perspective over many thousands of years with which to make their analysis. Many regions, when viewed from a long-term perspective, have periods of fragmentation into numerous, often warring groups, followed by consolidation into larger entities under unified rule. When Europe and its state formation sequences are viewed in this light, it is clear that, out of many Celtic proto-states, a period of unification emerged, during which they were provinces under Rome. Upon its collapse, these provinces fell back into various polities, which again underwent a fragmented warring era, and then slowly merged back into larger and larger aggregates under the Holy Roman Empire, only to fall back into a series of small states. In northern Europe, the chiefly societies of Scandinavia and northern Germany aggregated into Viking Age states, then were joined together under the Hansa and Kalmar unions, and later divided again. This cycle is seen across the globe, and is just as evident in the Valley of Mexico and the Andes as it is in Europe. Thus, while Europe's various regions have their own unique historical trajectories, whose differences and contingencies are studied by archaeologists, Europe's states can also be compared broadly not only to one another but to cultures as distant as the Aztec and Inca.

See also **Maiden Castle** (*vol. 1, part 1*); **Oppida** (*vol. 2, part 6*); **Kelheim** (*vol. 2, part 6*).

BIBLIOGRAPHY

Arnold, Bettina, and D. Blair Gibson, eds. *Celtic Chiefdom, Celtic State.* Cambridge, U.K.: Cambridge University Press, 1995.

Ehrenreich, Robert M., Carole L. Crumley, and Janet E. Levy, eds. *Heterarchy and the Analysis of Complex Societies.* Arlington, Va.: American Anthropological Association, 1995.

Hedeager, Lotte. *Iron-Age Societies: From Tribe to State in Northern Europe 500 BC to AD 700.* Oxford: Blackwell, 1992.

Hodges, Richard. *Towns and Trade in the Age of Charlemagne.* London: Duckworth, 2000.

Randsborg, Klaus. *The First Millennium A.D. in Europe and the Mediterranean.* Cambridge, U.K.: Cambridge University Press, 1991.

Wells, Peter S. *The Barbarians Speak: How the Conquered Peoples Shaped Roman Europe.* Princeton, N.J.: Princeton University Press, 1999.

TINA L. THURSTON

TRADE AND EXCHANGE

The changing European economy between A.D. 400 and 1000 lies at the nexus of several trajectories of cultural transformation. The major transition from the Roman world to the medieval world is echoed by the geographically ever diminishing economy, from a large-scale interregional trade network to smaller spheres of exchange. In addition, the context of trade within what once had been Roman provinces differed from areas that had been inside the Roman sphere of interaction but outside the Roman purview. Changing connections, changing trade routes, changes in the social, economic, and political context of the marketplace are important considerations. Although historical records give selectively (or arbitrarily) preserved glimpses into these problems, only archaeology can reveal the whole picture, from crafts workshops to marketplace organization, from trade routes to the patterns of interaction between the public, artisans, merchants, and elites of the successor states.

ORIGINS AND CONTEXT OF EARLY MEDIEVAL TRADE

Local trade in early medieval Europe is a continuation of a long tradition of exchange stretching back into prehistoric times, but one of the distinguishing attributes of trade in the Iron Age, Roman era, and Early Middle Ages was the increased mobility of people and goods. Exchange of some type over relatively long distances dates to the Paleolithic, and while recent isotopic analysis of Neolithic skeletons suggests that early farmers were more mobile than previously thought, their travel from upland to lowland and along river valleys was aimed at settling in new places. In the Bronze Age most trade was local, but rare substances, such as bronze and amber, clearly were moved over long distances. Outside the Mediterranean, where trade was organized professionally, goods probably were traded hand to hand by many intervening individuals.

The Iron Age saw a transition to trade as a regular, major part of the subsistence and political economies of European polities. This was due in part to heightened political interactions and improved transport technology, especially in shipping. As in earlier times, Iron Age elites probably controlled importation of luxuries that helped maintain their community status. Later, while still controlling production and trade of the most valuable items, they lost their monopoly over the creation and dissemination of other goods, and the continuing trend from generalist farmers toward economic specialization in various trades and occupations created an artisan class and a market for their output. In the Celtic Iron Age, populous proto-urban *oppida* settlements of continental Europe continued to be the destination for exotic goods. Attached craft specialists created indigenous prestige objects of outstanding beauty for their elite masters, even as others produced less spectacular goods for local exchange and consumption: ceramic vessels, metal tools, and items of clothing and adornment. Eventually, the urban societies of the Iron Age Mediterranean culminated in the market economy of the Roman Empire, where each year professional merchants transported hundreds of thousands of tons of goods in large cargo ships. A vast trading system with com-

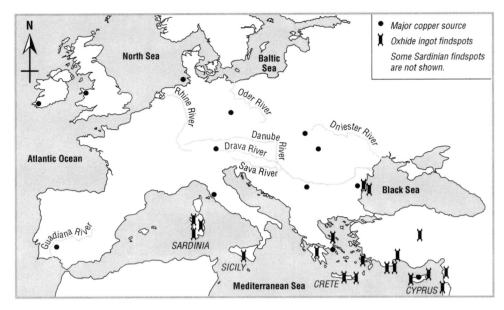

Major copper sources and oxhide ingot findspots.

plex rules and regulations crisscrossed the empire before its decline.

Thus, a combination of earlier trade and exchange traditions combined with the legacy of the Romans influenced the development of early medieval markets. Post-Roman trade varied regionally, depending on whether an area had been part of the former Romanized core, a less Romanized province, such as England or Germania, or a region, such as Scandinavia or the Slavic lands, that was outside the empire but regularly interacted with Rome.

The Roman Empire stretched from Syria to Scotland, but daily governance was conducted at a local level. A Roman *civitas* and its hinterland made up a highly autonomous administrative unit, organized loosely under a provincial governor with a military contingent. When the greater Roman entity became unstable, provinces grew even more autonomous, eventually breaking into regions and then subregions. The post-Roman era is known for its migrations and incursions, as non-Roman outsiders, customarily called barbarians, invaded and seized these fragments of the empire. Many Europeans outside the Roman sphere were content to stay at home, but even so their local economies were affected deeply by the decline of the imperial system. Thus, the question of continuity between the late Roman and early medieval economies during this

period of unimaginable change is an important issue.

THEORIES ON TRADE AND EXCHANGE

The debate has long simmered over urbanism, trade, and markets in post-Roman Europe. Early-twentieth-century historians, most notably Henri Pirenne, combined the documentary record with deductive impressions about the origins of feudalism to formulate several plausible hypotheses about urbanization, markets, and long-distance trade in the post-Roman world. Pirenne's influential thesis proposed that the Roman organization of Europe was never dismantled but persisted far into the medieval period. Only as European trade with the Mediterranean was cut off by Muslim expansion in the seventh century did Germanic rulers of the Dark Ages, such as Charlemagne and his contemporaries, slowly expand their regions' agricultural economies.

The refutation of this theory and a new understanding of markets, money, and manufacturing during the barbarian age have come about largely as the result of the revelations of modern archaeology. The twentieth century saw dramatic changes in urban and marketplace excavation methods. Early civic projects in European towns were conducted by workmen clearing arbitrary layers, keeping sketchy records of the curiosities they unearthed. After

World War II, archaeologists working in bomb-damaged cities primarily used trenches for investigation. As they looked at small bits of deep strata, they could detect a long and complex history at a particular site, and could even date the strata, but they were unable to observe the "big picture." Only in the last decades of the twentieth century, when horizontal excavation became dominant, could large-scale exposure of former surface areas uncover many contemporary structures, features, artifact scatters, and boundaries as well as their patterning and context. By the 1980s archaeologists began to challenge earlier ideas about the complex economics of the early Middle Ages.

ARCHAEOLOGICAL EVIDENCE FOR TRADE AND EXCHANGE IN FORMER IMPERIAL EUROPE

The provinces of Rome had a busy market economy based on import, export, and manufacturing. Trade between provinces was facilitated by shared traditions, rules, and regulations within a single political economy. As the empire's troubles deepened through the course of the fifth century, could producers and consumers maintain the convenience of customary trade, or were they forced or encouraged by changing conditions to find new economic solutions? Archaeological investigations around the Mediterranean and Europe have shown that in contrast to Pirenne's idea of post-Roman continuity, by the late fifth century the Roman world was in decline, leaving a vacuum in which the provinces became disconnected and transformed into regional and subregional systems and in which markets largely lost their character as interregional and long-distance trade centers.

While post-Roman primary documents exist, perhaps the socioeconomic crises are best seen through archaeological evidence. During the imperial era, Rome's Campus Martius was a beautifully planned and maintained monumental landscape. In addition to parade grounds, it held temples, porticoes, baths, the stadium, circus, and several theaters for public enjoyment. By the late fifth century it was despoiled: squatters and craftspeople were camped out in shantytowns within the ruins. One excavation found a glassmaker's stall of the fifth or sixth century supplanted in the seventh or eighth century by a workshop manufacturing religious objects for the clergy and local markets. The extremely local and

limited nature of trade, compared with earlier times, is illustrated by the fact that imported items came from no farther than Sicily. Another indicator of economic decline is coinage. Between the seventh and eighth centuries alone, gold coins dropped from 90 percent to 10 percent content and silver from 70 percent to less than 30 percent, and bronze coins were as thin as paper.

At sites elsewhere in Italy dating to the fifth to seventh centuries, commercial harbors were abandoned, and there is a strong decline in import-trade amphora from Africa and the eastern Mediterranean, indicating that interregional trade had collapsed. On the Adriatic at fifth-century Butrint, fortifications were built against barbarian invaders, palaces were left unfinished, and squatters moved in. Merchants occupied the ruined forums of other towns across Roman Europe, creating makeshift workshops in the rubble of former citadels. While Rome and a few other southern cities maintained a modicum of urban character, western European towns and markets were largely abandoned. Long-distance commercial exchange and the interregional market system had ceased operation.

TRADE, EXCHANGE AND MARKETS OUTSIDE THE FORMER EMPIRE

Archaeological evidence shows regular, active trade between Romans and non-Romans before A.D. 400. In return for elite goods—swords, adornments, wine and serving vessels—non-Roman peoples exported utilitarian wares, such as leather, hide, foodstuffs, and slaves. Modern excavations at elite-controlled ports, such as Gudme-Lundeborg in Denmark, usually show a chieftain's compound with a complement of craftspeople and a harbor during the Roman era.

Rulers in barbarian regions thus became highly dependent on Roman goods for maintaining their social status. After Rome's troubles began and the imperial system began to totter, Roman goods disappeared from these sites, as long-distance trade was curtailed. Despite the cutoff of Roman items, local rulers still needed to impress their peers and over-awe their subjects, so the trade in elite goods could not be allowed to end. Instead, smaller, less ambitious trade networks were formed between the upper classes in Britain, the Low Countries, Scandinavia, and Germanic and Slavic regions. Trade continued at some Roman-era places; more important, however, between A.D. 700 and 1000 a series of new, specialized sites combining crafts production with a trading center appeared. Among them were Ipswich and Hamwic in Britain; Birka, Ribe, Kaupang, and Hedeby in Scandinavia; Quentovic in northern France; Dorestad on the Dutch Rhine; Staraya Ladoga in Russia; and Wolin in Poland. Similar sequences are found in the Czech Republic and northern Germany.

These markets, commonly referred to as emporia, were not the spontaneous efforts of merchants and manufacturers. Local rulers' involvement is apparent in elite-built and maintained fortifications, indicating royal administration and protection, at emporia such as Hedeby, Ipswich, and Hamwic. Ribe and Löddeköpinge in Denmark and Sweden, respectively, had nondefensive boundary markers that probably delimited the area of regulated trade. At Mikulčice in the Czech Republic and at Hamburg, Lübeck, and Brandenburg, Germany, excavations show that local chieftains established fortress-like residences with attached craftspeople in the eighth century, after which non-elite settlements developed around them, leading to urban marketplaces.

Eventually, less luxurious local items were made and traded at these sites, probably because the taxes that kings could collect in a regulated royal market became as important as acquiring their own sumptuary goods. Anglo-Saxon texts confirm that between A.D. 700 and 1000 there was a steady rise in tolls and tariffs on trade. While such documentation is found only in England, scholars believe this was paralleled throughout the emerging successor states, providing a substantial royal income. As these states became important trading powers, new trade routes sprang up, including the Roman-era Rhine-Rhône river route between north and south, which served new trading places, such as Frisian Dorestad on the Rhine, and Roman-Baltic connections via the Oder (Viadna), Dnieper, Dniester, and Prut, the Elbe, Weser (Visurgis), and Eider grew active, serving Hedeby, Hamburg-Bremen, Lübeck, and Wolin. Sea routes continued to connect Atlantic Europe with Britain, and new sea-lanes linked Dorestad, Ribe, and Hedeby with emporia in Sweden and Norway.

NEEDFUL THINGS AND OBJECTS OF DESIRE

Despite the importance of trade to people in the Middle Ages, textual references to early medieval trade remain fairly sparse. Thus, the archaeological examination of ships, wharves, workshops, warehouses, and market organization sometimes is the best option for studying the manufacturers, merchants, and middlemen whose activities were transforming Europe. Through many extensive excavations, archaeologists have discovered what goods were coveted by both rulers and commoners. Precious metals and gems were reserved primarily for the royal and upper classes, as were fine imports of ceramic and glass, wine, textiles, and weapons. Locally produced adornments were skillfully made and available to a larger group of well-off citizens. Production of non-luxury items used by the broader populace is evident, and each trade had its unique artifact assemblage. Weaving tools and loom parts are common, as is the debris from workshops manufacturing combs and pins, in the form of sawed-off bone and horn fragments and partially finished products. Metal casting leaves fragments of crucibles and molds, brooches, and fasteners. Iron yields large amounts of slag, iron bars and rods, tool preforms (blank, pre-formed and unfinished tools), and, in some cases, the tongs and hammers of smiths. Advanced glass industries are evidenced by molten glass wasters and deposits of malformed glass beads; in one case, at the Danish trading site of Dankirke, archaeologists discovered a warehouse of glass drinking horns that had been destroyed by fire. Some sites yield butchered animal and fish bones from purveyors of foodstuffs, and thick dung layers indicate trade in live cattle. Coins, scales, weights, and moneybox keys sometimes are present.

Marketplaces often are ephemeral, with structures resembling fairground stalls and booths. Collections of sunken floored huts often are evident, and at Löddeköpinge, Sweden, the seasonal nature of the marketplace is seen in alternating occupational layers and sterile sand in the floors of these pit houses. On the other hand, many markets were permanent, with continuous occupations by specific workshops and industries. At Ribe and Hedeby, workshop boundaries and property divisions were maintained without change for many generations, reflecting long-term regulation, while the channeling of streams and the gridlike layout of streets and blocks show central planning at Hedeby.

By the end of the first millennium, long-distance and local trade in luxury and non-luxury goods was vital to the economies of medieval states. Taxes and regulations remained, but the specially constructed and maintained royal trading emporia disappeared. They were either supplanted by or transformed into urban markets within the cities of later medieval Europe.

See also **Emporia** (*vol. 2, part 7*); **Ipswich** (*vol. 2, part 7*); **Staraya Ladoga** (*vol. 2, part 7*).

BIBLIOGRAPHY

Callmer, Johan. *Production Site and Market Area: Some Notes on Field Work in Progress, 1981–2.* Lund, Sweden: Meddelanden från Lunds Universitets Historiska Museum (1983): 135–165.

Clarke, H., and B. Ambrosiani. *Towns in the Viking Age.* Leicester: Leicester University Press, 1991.

Fehring, Günter P. *The Archaeology of Medieval Germany: An Introduction.* Translated by Ross Samson. London: Routledge, 1991.

Frandsen, L., and S. Jensen. "Pre-Viking and Early Viking Age Ribe." *Journal of Danish Archaeology* 6 (1988): 175–189.

Hedeager, Lotte. *Iron Age Societies: From Tribe to State in Northern Europe, 500 BC to AD 700.* Translated by John Hines. Oxford: Blackwell, 1992.

Hodges, Richard. *Towns and Trade in the Age of Charlemagne.* London: Duckworth, 2000.

———. "Emporia, Monasteries, and the Economic Foundation of Medieval Europe." In *Medieval Archaeology: Papers of the Seventeenth Annual Conference of the Center for Medieval and Early Renaissance Studies.* Edited by Charles L. Redman. Binghamton, N.Y.: State University of New York, 1989.

———. *Dark Age Economics: The Origins of Towns and Trade AD 600–1000* London: Duckworth, 1982.

Randsborg, Klavs. *The First Millennium AD in Europe and the Mediterranean.* Cambridge, U.K.: Cambridge University Press, 1991.

Sawyer, P. "Early Fairs and Markets in England and Scandinavia." In *The Market in History.* Edited by B. L. Latham and A. J. H. Anderson, pp. 59–77. London and Dover, N.H.: Croom–Helm, 1986.

Schietzel, K. "Haithabu: A Study on the Development of Early Urban Settlement in Northern Europe." In *Comparative History of Urban Development in Non-Roman Europe: Ireland, Wales, Denmark, Germany, Poland, and Russia from the Ninth to the Thirteenth Century.* Edited by H. B. Clark and A. Simms. BAR International Series, no. 255. Oxford: British Archaeological Reports, 1985.

Wells, Peter S. "The Iron Age." In *European Prehistory: A Survey.* Edited by Sarunas Milisauskas, pp. 335–383. New York: Kluwer Academic/Plenum Publishers, 2002.

TINA L. THURSTON

COINAGE OF THE EARLY MIDDLE AGES

In the early centuries of the first millennium A.D. the borders of the Roman Empire divided Europe into two monetary zones: (1) a southern and western zone, in which coins were minted and circulated more or less regularly as an intrinsic part of the economy, and (2) a northern and eastern zone, which made no coins of its own and imported coins sporadically as a result of various interactions, economic and otherwise. This same monetary division of Europe, following approximately the valleys of the Rhine and Danube Rivers, survived the political dissolution of the Roman Empire and was maintained almost until the end of the millennium. It was only in the ninth century and especially the tenth century that lands beyond the Roman imperial frontiers began to produce their own coins to supply a monetized economy.

ROMAN COINAGE IN EUROPE

Coinage was unified throughout the western Roman Empire, with mints scattered across Europe producing coins of various denominations of gold, silver, and copper. Minting, like many other aspects of the Roman state, went through a period of disarray in the third century, to be revived and regularized by the reforms of the Roman emperors Diocletian and Constantine I around A.D. 300. The regular mints of Europe for the next two centuries included Lyons and Arles in Gaul; Trier in Rhineland Germany; Rome, Milan, Ravenna, and Aquileia in Italy; Siscia (modern-day Sisak) in Pannonia; and Thessalonica (now Salonika) in Greece. Spain, which had been an important source of bullion in the earlier empire, lacked a mint in the later period, as did England after the closing of the mint of London in A.D. 325.

The standard coin of the late empire was the gold solidus, which was of pure alloy and an unchanging weight of 24 karats, or $1/72$ of the Roman pound (4.5 modern grams), from its introduction in A.D. 309 well into the tenth century, by which time it was called a *nomisma*. Fractions of the solidus also were minted; in the west the third, or tremissis, was most common (fig. 1). The silver denarius had been the basis of the Roman monetary system during the republic and early empire, but in the fourth and fifth centuries silver coinage was rare. Copper coinage was relatively common, of varying weights and denominations. By the fifth century as many as 7,200 copper *nummi* were needed to buy a gold solidus, with no intermediate denominations available. The obverse of late Roman coins generally bore the image of the reigning emperor, with his name and honorific titles making up the surrounding legend. On the reverse pagan deities gradually gave way to generalized symbolic representations of Roman virtues and scenes of the emperor in military contexts; explicitly Christian imagery was rare.

Beyond the frontiers delimited by the *limes,* or boundaries, along the Rhine and Danube Rivers, Roman coinage was a familiar phenomenon, especially to those in direct contact with the empire. The frontier regions themselves constituted a heavily monetized zone, with coins exchanged to provide for the needs of the soldiers garrisoned there and to pay for commodities imported across the border. Military payments also fueled the export of Roman

356

coinage beyond the frontiers in the form of salaries to individual barbarian soldiers who returned home after service in the Roman army and as payments to federated bands of warriors from outside the empire who were enlisted into its campaigns. Coins also were exported as tribute to barbarian leaders and were carried back home among the booty gained on cross-border raids.

The export of Roman coins to barbarian Europe is attested to by archaeological finds throughout the north and east of the Continent. For the most part copper coins are found nearest to the frontiers, chiefly as stray losses on excavated habitation sites. Gold coins are encountered farther afield, usually buried in hoards varying from a few coins to thousands. Some of these hoards, chiefly in the area north of the Danube, have been identified as salary payments to individual soldiers and as blocks of tribute to such groups as the Huns. Solidi found in Scandinavia constitute a less-clear class of exports; these coins cluster in the period A.D. 454 to 488 and have been interpreted variously as the result of a trade in furs and slaves or sums sent north by federates and invaders.

THE COINAGES OF THE EARLY GERMANIC STATES

The coins produced by the Germanic rulers who succeeded the Roman emperors in Europe followed the form of the earlier Roman examples, if not necessarily retaining their content or function. Again gold coinage dominated, especially the denomination of the tremissis, one-third of the solidus. Silver and copper issues were rare and intermittent. Although the earliest coins were of pure gold, like their Roman predecessors, by A.D. 600 debasements effected by alloying silver with the gold can be noted in many of the issues. The weight of the coinage also underwent reduction; by A.D. 600 the standard of the solidus in Gaul had dropped from 24 karats of weight to 21 karats.

The first issues of the Germanic rulers also followed the imperial example by placing the name and image of the reigning emperor, by that time in Constantinople (modern-day Istanbul), on the obverse of their gold coins. The rarer issues of silver and copper coins sometimes had the name or monogram of the issuing king. Shortly before the middle of the sixth century the Frankish king

Fig. 1. Frisian gold tremissis of Dorestad. THE AMERICAN NUMISMATIC SOCIETY, NEW YORK. REPRODUCED BY PERMISSION.

Theodebert put his own name on his gold issues, thereby provoking an angry response from the Byzantine writer and historian Procopius, who asserted that only emperors had the right to put their images on gold coins. By the end of the century kings of the Suevi and the Visigoths also had replaced the imperial name with their own on their gold coins. Frisian and Anglo-Saxon gold tremisses were modeled on those of Francia; the name of an English king first appears on a coin in the first half of the seventh century. The pseudo-imperial coinage lasted longer in Italy, where the Ostrogothic issues were replaced by those of the Byzantine reconquerors and finally by the Langobards, who put their king's name on the coinage only at the end of the seventh century. Most of these issues followed the Roman and Byzantine imagery of a portrait obverse and a symbolic reverse, with the cross becoming the most common reverse image.

It is evident that a coinage comprising only gold pieces, as was characteristic of most of Europe in the fifth through seventh centuries, was ill suited to a retail economy and would have been outside the daily experience of most people. A great proliferation of mints, especially in the Merovingian and Visigothic kingdoms, implies a change in the circumstances of minting from centralized to local, paralleling changes in the bases of tax collection. This phenom-

Fig. 2. Silver sceatta. THE AMERICAN NUMISMATIC SOCIETY, NEW YORK. REPRODUCED BY PERMISSION.

enon is most apparent in the coinage of seventh-century Francia, where the names of hundreds of mint towns appear on the coins, along with names of thousands of people identified as "moneyers."

Finds of Byzantine gold coins and southern Frankish ones in Frisia (a northern province in modern-day Netherlands) and England suggest a trade route for goods imported from the north to the Mediterranean. Finds of coins of the sixth and seventh centuries are extremely rare beyond the boundaries of the former Roman Empire, however; the few tremisses found in western Jutland seem to tie into the Frisian economic network rather than to a Scandinavian or Baltic sphere.

THE AGE OF SILVER

In the course of the seventh century the gold coinages of Merovingian Francia, of Frisia, and of Anglo-Saxon England gave way to silver issues, and silver remained virtually the only coin metal in Transalpine Europe for the rest of the millennium. In Spain the Visigoths continued to produce debased gold tremisses until Muslim invaders eliminated their kingdom in A.D. 711. The Langobard kings maintained their gold coinages in Italy until Charlemagne's conquest at the end of the eighth century, and the semi-independent Beneventan dukes continued minting gold into the ninth century.

In Francia silver coins moved gradually away from the seventh-century type of portrait and cross with the names of moneyer and mint. By the end of the Merovingian dynasty in the mid–eighth century most denarii were small chunks of silver with simple geometric designs on both faces and few legible inscriptions. The silver coins of Frisia and England in the period, known as sceattas, also were small, thick, and lacking in legends; their imagery in some cases appears to have derived from local artistic traditions (fig. 2). A brief issue of sceattas minted at Ribe on the west coast of Jutland c. A.D. 720 can lay claim to being the earliest European coinage minted beyond the ancient Roman borders.

In the second half of the eighth century silver coinages underwent modifications in appearance and weight standards that resulted in the coin known as the penny (called the denarius in Latin, the denier in French, and the pfenning in German). These innovations appear to have been the initiatives of Carolingian kings, with Pepin the Short, the first of the "mayors of the palace" to take the title of king, standardizing the coinage shortly after becoming king of Francia in A.D. 751 and his son Charlemagne creating a new, heavier penny for his enlarged realm in about A.D. 793 (fig. 3). The coins of the kingdoms that made up Anglo-Saxon England followed a similar pattern of reform and standardization.

By A.D. 800 the silver penny was a broad, well-struck coin weighing between 1.5 and 2.0 modern grams. In England the coins usually featured a royal portrait on the obverse, whereas the Carolingians favored geometric types, especially the monogram of the ruler's name. Anglo-Saxon and Carolingian

Fig. 3. Silver penny of Charlemagne. THE AMERICAN NUMISMATIC SOCIETY, NEW YORK. REPRODUCED BY PERMISSION.

coins bear the names of a substantial number of mints throughout their respective realms, generally coinciding with the main commercial and ecclesiastical centers. No such mints were located north or west of the Roman boundaries of England or beyond the Rhine-Danube frontiers on the Continent.

The standardized silver pennies of the Carolingian empire and of England provided a sound basis for retail and long-distance commerce and facilitated the development of a monetized segment of the economy to supplement the heavily subsistence and manorial agricultural base. The uniformity of the Carolingian coinage broke down with the dissolution of the centralized power of the empire. Counts and dukes and even bishops and abbots took over minting throughout the empire, although they often retained a royal or imperial Carolingian name on their coins. In the course of the tenth century minting began east of the Rhine and north of the Danube, chiefly at mints in Saxony exploiting the newly discovered silver deposits there.

Almost no English or Carolingian coins of the ninth century are found in Scandinavia that would correspond to the well-documented booty seized by Viking raiders and tributes exacted by them; if such wealth reached the Baltic region in the form of coins, these must have been melted rather than buried. A series of coins imitating those of Charlemagne was minted in Jutland, probably at Hedeby (Haithabu in German), in the early ninth century,

but local minting then ceased until about the year 1000.

Large Viking Age hoards are found in the lands bordering the Volga basin, on the eastern shores of the Baltic, and in Scandinavia, especially on the island of Gotland. These comprise Islamic silver dirhams, chiefly of the tenth century; Byzantine silver coins from the same period; and German and English pennies of the late tenth century and the eleventh century. As in the case of the earlier hoards of Roman and Byzantine solidi, these silver finds of the end of the millennium have been interpreted variously as the results of trade, booty, tribute, and the pay of mercenary soldiers. The extent of the use and recirculation of these coins in a local northern economic sphere is difficult to ascertain.

By the end of the first millennium A.D. coinage had spread throughout Europe. The silver penny was struck by royal authority in England and by more localized rulers in France, Germany, and Italy. Minting was initiated in Bohemia in the A.D. 960s, in Kiev in about A.D. 990, and in Hungary and Poland shortly after 1000. In Scandinavia the Hedeby coinage was revived after A.D. 950, and by the year 1000 Danish, Swedish, and Norwegian kings had initiated royal coinages. Not all of these initiatives resulted in continuous minting, and it would not be until the commercial revolution of the twelfth century that Europe could be said to have a fully monetized economy.

See also **Coinage of Iron Age Europe** (*vol. 2, part 6*).

BIBLIOGRAPHY

Bellinger, Alfred R., and Philip Grierson. *Catalogue of the Byzantine Coins in the Dumbarton Oaks Collection and in the Whittemore Collection.* 5 vols. Washington, D.C.: Dumbarton Oaks Research Library and Collection, 1966–1973. (The standard reference work for Byzantine coins. Three volumes pertain to the early Middle Ages: Vol. 1, *Anastasius I to Maurice, A.D. 491–602;* Vol. 2, *Phocas to Theodosius, A.D. 602–717;* Vol. 3, *Leo III to Nicephorus III, A.D. 717–1081.*)

Blackburn, Mark, and D. M. Metcalf, eds. *Viking-Age Coinage in the Northern Lands.* 2 vols. BAR International Series, no. 122. Oxford: British Archaeological Reports, 1981. (A collection of articles surveying the importation of coinage into the Scandinavian and Baltic world at the end of the first millennium.)

Grierson, Philip, and Mark Blackburn. *Medieval European Coinage.* Vol. 1, *The Early Middle Ages (5th–10th Centuries).* Cambridge, U.K.: Cambridge University Press, 1986. (The definitive study of all coinages minted in Europe in the period, with discussion and bibliography summarizing all the important literature to its date of publication.)

Gierson, Philip, and Melinda Mays. *Catalogue of Late Roman Coins in the Dumbarton Oaks Collection and the Whittemore Collection.* Washington, D.C.: Dumbarton Oaks Research Library and Collection, 1992.

Hendy, Michael. "From Public to Private: The Western Barbarian Coinages as a Mirror of the Disintegration of Late Roman State Structures." *Viator* 19 (1988): 29–78.

McCormick, Michael. *Origins of the European Economy: Communications and Commerce, AD 300–900.* Cambridge, U.K.: Cambridge University Press, 2002. (Uses the evidence of the importation of Byzantine and Islamic coins into Europe to argue for the importance of commerce in the Carolingian economy.)

Metcalf, D. M. "Viking-Age Numismatics." *Numismatic Chronicle* 155 (1995): 413–441; 156 (1996): 399–428; 157 (1997): 295–335; 158 (1998): 345–371; 159 (1999): 395–430. (A series of articles examining coinage in the North Sea and the Baltic region from late Roman times to the end of the first millennium.)

Spufford, Peter. *Money and Its Use in Medieval Europe.* Cambridge, U.K.: Cambridge University Press, 1988. (A thorough discussion of the role of coinage in the European economy from the end of the Roman period through the later Middle Ages.)

ALAN M. STAHL

GENDER IN EARLY MEDIEVAL EUROPE

Gender is an underlying structure of everyday life. Anthropological and archaeological studies of gender emerged in the 1960s and 1970s as a result of issues raised by the feminist movement. Sociocultural anthropologists came to realize that women had been either subsumed in the study of "man" or simply ignored altogether. Thus, these new studies emphasized the presence of women in current and past cultures in order to correct for androcentric biases and the previous neglect of women. In the 1980s, with the understanding that women could not be the exclusive focus of research, the field of inquiry turned to gendered studies, dealing not only with women's roles and women's issues but also with the interaction of women and men in society. At the same time, an increasing trend toward alternative issues, such as queer studies, performance studies, and embodiment (particularly its focus on the corporeal aspects of the body), brought about more diverse viewpoints in the fields of archaeology and anthropology.

Archaeological research was somewhat slower than research in anthropology to get on the bandwagon, and early medieval research was slower still, although historical research on women and gender flourished for the later medieval periods, which had plentiful documentary evidence. The seminal publication of Margaret Conkey and Janet Spector's 1984 work on gender and archaeology was followed by a number of studies focused on trying to find women in the archaeological record, often through differentiation of labor. Spurred by the development of new theoretical perspectives within the

framework of post-processual archaeology, the 1990s saw an increased focus on gender rather than women, but a truly unbiased outlook has been difficult to come by. Masculinist as well as feminist perspectives are needed to produce a holistic interpretation of past lives because women cannot be investigated to the exclusion of men. There are also many archaeologists who believe that gender is not something that must be dealt with in a research design. This attitude seems a bit odd, given that in Western society, and indeed any known society, differentiation between sexes and genders are critical components of social, political, and economic activity and of culture and knowledge.

Although it is agreed that gender is culturally constructed and sex is biologically determined, some scholars consider that the concept of a biological distinction between male and female also has a cultural component that guides the outward expression of biological sex. For the purposes of this discussion, however, sex will refer to the biological aspects of the body, whereas gender will refer to the expression of the individual culturally. Biological sex is determined by two chromosomes, X and Y. Normally, a female has two X chromosomes and a male has an X and a Y chromosome. In rare instances, biological sex may not fall within a standard XX or XY chromosomal pattern, or the phenotypic (outward) appearance may not match the genetic designation. There may be a chromosomal designation, such as XXX or XXY, or a situation where an XX fetus is exposed to male hormones in the womb, which can result in the individual having male genitalia. In such a case, the biological sex of an individual does not fit within the norm and may not correspond with the expected gender.

In addition, work in anthropology has demonstrated that most gender systems are not dualistic; that is, there may be a category of individuals in a society who take on a cultural role that differs from the expected role. So while the typical masculine and feminine genders are in the majority, there may be instances where those who do not fit within the expected social identity create other genders, or other identities are created for them. Although it may be difficult to accept that there is, and has been in the past, a multiplicity of genders, it seems likely that gender identities lie on a spectrum of existence rather than existing as discrete categories. Given that biological sex does not always fall into distinct and identifiable categories, it is logical to assume that genders would be just as variable, if not more so.

SOCIAL IDENTITY IN BURIAL CONTEXTS

Gender cannot be analyzed to the exclusion of other aspects of identity or its role in determining societal structures. Gender is inextricably linked with age, status, and power. The complexity of a society may also affect the way in which gender is expressed. The more complex and hierarchical a society is, the more positions within the society are more rigidly defined, and so men's and women's roles may be highly circumscribed.

Status. Understanding the gender structure of past societies seems to be easiest to analyze in a burial context. Burials contain not only bodies, which can give information about health, but often material culture in the form of grave goods. In addition, the landscape of a cemetery (such as where burials are in relation to others and the location of a cemetery within the local topography) may give important clues to a community's view of social identity. It is possible that the spatial relationships of burials to other burials and to the landscape reinforces social hierarchies and social differences within a community. Post-processual and social theory approaches have led to the realization that the social identity of an individual (including gender, status, and power) is not directly reflected through the burial because the individual's representation in death is formed through others in the society who perform the preparation for burial and administer the burial. However, the social structure of a society may be echoed in some form through the representation of its members in death, and so it provides us with many clues that can help to reconstruct it.

Gender in early medieval society has only since the 1990s been approached using archaeological methods and almost exclusively in a burial context. Most information specifically regarding the role and position of women during this period has come through textual information, such as laws, although these often have more to do with women possessing a certain amount of wealth or status. Documentary evidence, such as wills, reveals that medieval women could hold and distribute property, but it is not known if this was common through all social classes. The laws of Aethelbert of Kent, from the seventh century, indicate that women had a number of rights. According to these laws, prospective husbands had to pay a dowry (*morgengifu*), but it went to the bride herself, not her family. This money or property was then hers to do with as she wished. The seventh-century laws of Wihtred of Kent said that a woman was not financially responsible for her husband's crimes if she had no knowledge of them. However, if she participated in any crimes herself, she would have to give up her money and property. Sixth-century Frankish laws only sometimes mention women; they do so in reference to marriage and to criminal activities by women and against women.

Where documentary evidence is scarce or nonexistent, trying to determine such rights through archaeological means can be difficult. The analysis of grave contents shows that the things buried with men and women varied between and among them. Women were often buried with as much wealth as men were, but whether or not the items in a woman's grave were hers during her lifetime or were bestowed upon her in death cannot be known. The same can be held true for men, however.

Other issues with the archaeological analysis of burials stem from assessing the sex and gender of the buried individuals. Traditional thinking, particularly in Continental and British archaeology, has held that weapons found in a grave indicate a male, and jewelry indicates a female. When osteological analysis of a skeleton has disagreed with the material culture found in the grave, the osteological sexing has generally been held to have been wrong. However, there is increasing evidence for occasional aberrations from the normal patterns of mortuary goods. Nevertheless, if a female skeleton has an accompanying weapon, it does not necessarily indicate that the woman actually fought with it. Indeed, Heinrich Härke believes that, even in male graves, the presence of weapons is more likely an indicator of status, power, ethnicity, or all of these. A woman might have been buried with a weapon (most likely a spear) as a mark of her own status in the community, or perhaps the weapon indicates her associated status as the wife or mother of a local chief.

Age. Age, too, might factor heavily in the gender specificity of certain items. Age is closely linked with gender identity. In some cultures, gender has a certain amount of fluidity through the life cycle. There is some evidence for the elderly no longer having such a rigid gender dichotomy in terms of mortuary material culture. Guy Halsall's study of sixth-century Merovingian cemeteries showed that older people tended to have non-gender-specific artifacts, as did children for the most part. A similar practice may be found at early Anglo-Saxon cemeteries, where older male skeletons appear to be buried with very specific female-type artifacts (annular brooches) at certain cemeteries.

Few archaeological assessments of gender include childhood as a focus of interest, mainly because it is difficult to sex juvenile skeletons and hard to find gendered material culture associated with children. DNA analysis has been used to sex children in an Early Anglo-Saxon cemetery, but no gendered patterning in their grave goods was seen. There appear to be no items that are exclusive to children's graves in Anglo-Saxon cemeteries. In addition, it is often difficult to delineate the period of childhood within a culture, particularly if no evidence of a rite of passage to adulthood can be ascertained. In a burial context, children are often identified as male or female if their grave goods fall within the standard typology of weapons or jewelry. Most often, however, children are buried with very little, although there are numerous examples of very lavish children's graves in Anglo-Saxon England. Knives, which are one of the most common items in both adult's and children's graves, do not follow any gendered pattern.

OTHER SOURCES OF EVIDENCE

Osteological analysis, although sometimes unreliable in sexing poorly preserved skeletons, can give other indicators, such as general health, disease, or trauma suffered during an individual's lifetime. In some cultures these may differ among men and women. Wear indicators on bones have been used to identify possible occupations. Dental anomalies (enamel hypoplasia) caused by poor nutrition can demonstrate differences in access to food. Research in pre-Inca and Inca period Peru using stable carbon and nitrogen isotope analysis of male and female skeletons has shown that women and men had similar and then differential access to foods in those periods. Lead and oxygen isotope analysis is being used to try to differentiate the geographical origins of Early Anglo-Saxon settlers in Britain and possibly determine whether or not males and females had different patterns of emigration.

When skeletons are poorly preserved, making osteological sexing difficult, DNA analysis can be used to determine biological sex. This technique has been used to look at issues of gender within the social structure of an Early Anglo-Saxon society at West Heslerton, North Yorkshire, where a fifth- to seventh-century settlement and cemetery were excavated by Dominic Powlesland and Christine Haughton. DNA analysis was done to learn the biological sex of forty-two individuals, and the results were then compared with the gender suggested by the grave goods of each individual. In addition, age, status, and particulars of the burial, such as the position of the body in the grave, were observed in order to produce a representation of the social identity of that person. The majority of skeletons that were determined to be biologically female were buried with jewelry, and the majority of biological males had weapons or no gender-specific goods. Because females tended to be buried with more types of gender-specific items, such as brooches and beads, it was perhaps easier to "see" them, but aside from weapons, which are not common, there were few other male-type goods. However, there were exceptions to the normal pattern. Of the twenty-four individuals buried with at least a spear, three were identified as female through DNA analysis. Another individual, of about eighteen, was found with amulets and jewelry and could not be osteologically sexed. DNA analysis identified him as male, although the grave goods indicate a female; it is possible that he was a spiritual figure within the community. With limited knowledge of the way religious beliefs played out in society before Christianity set in, archaeologists can only surmise the nature of shamanlike roles within communities. Burials found with amulets and other potentially symbolic goods may have signaled that the person buried there played a role as a healer or priest. Tania Dickinson labeled a woman found in one such early Saxon burial as a "cunning woman," a practicer of magic, healing, and divination.

It has been difficult to obtain evidence of gender structures from the archaeological analysis of settlements. Some cultures tend to have distinct segregation of work areas by men and women, and some do not. Some of the easiest gendered artifacts to see from the early medieval period are items having to do with textile production, such as needles and spindle whorls, which are doughnut-shaped objects used as weights when weaving. These are found in graves but are also found in domestic areas. In early medieval Ireland, the presence of these items in household areas indicates that a woman's area of work was directly involved with the home and that this may have been the place where women developed their own social networks. Evidence for gendering food production or food preparation is scarce, both textually and archaeologically. Later Anglo-Saxon texts indicate that lower-status women would have participated in such tasks. In rural farming villages, women would certainly have had to perform these duties, and whetstones are sometimes found in female graves.

Gender is critical to understanding the social structures of past societies. The place of women relative to men in early medieval society has been gleaned mainly from textual sources. These sources have many limitations, but these may now be remedied through archaeological and molecular approaches of study. A critical archaeological analysis of the ways in which gender structured early medieval societies needs to be taken up by researchers. Although there cannot be conclusions that cut across all cultures, at least in some societies women appear to have had a number of rights, many equal to those of men. Yet the ways in which power and status were visibly demonstrated varied between men and women, so one must recognize what these differences mean. One also sees evidence for individuals who did not fit within a conventional gender role. There is still much to be done with regard to understanding how these people negotiated their positions in society, but the first step is acknowledging the complexities of social identity in the past.

See also **Gender** (*vol. 1, part 1*).

BIBLIOGRAPHY

Bitel, Lisa M. "*Tír inna mBan:* Domestic Space and the Frontiers of Gender in Early Medieval Ireland." In *Shifting Frontiers in Late Antiquity.* Edited by Ralph W. Mathisen and Hagith S. Sivan, pp. 242–255. Aldershot, Hampshire, U.K.: Variorum, 1996.

Conkey, Margaret W., and Janet D. Spector. "Archaeology and the Study of Gender." In *Advances in Archaeological Method and Theory.* Vol. 7. Edited by Michael B. Schiffer, pp. 1–38. New York: Academic Press, 1984.

Crawford, Sally. *Childhood in Anglo-Saxon England.* Stroud, U.K.: Sutton, 1999.

Dickinson, Tania M. "An Anglo-Saxon 'Cunning Woman' from Bidford-on-Avon." In *The Archaeology of Anglo-Saxon England.* Edited by Catherine E. Karkov, pp. 359–373. New York: Garland, 1999.

Fell, Christine. *Women in Anglo-Saxon England.* London: British Museum Publications, 1984.

Flaherty, Christine. "Sex, Gender, and Identity in Early Anglo-Saxon England: A DNA and Archaeological Analysis at West Heslerton." Ph.D. diss., Columbia University, forthcoming.

Gilchrist, Roberta. *Gender and Archaeology: Contesting the Past.* London: Routledge, 1999.

Halsall, Guy. *Settlement and Social Organization: The Merovingian Region of Metz.* Cambridge, U.K.: Cambridge University Press, 1995.

Härke, Heinrich. "Early Anglo-Saxon Social Structure." In *The Anglo-Saxons from the Migration Period to the Eighth Century: An Ethnographic Perspective.* Edited by John Hines, pp. 125–170. Woodbridge, Suffolk, U.K.: Boydell Press, 1997.

Hastorf, Christine. "Gender, Space, and Food in Prehistory." In *Engendering Archaeology: Women and Prehistory.* Edited by Joan M. Gero and Margaret W. Conkey, pp. 132–159. Oxford: Basil Blackwell, 1991.

Haughton, Christine, and Dominic Powlesland. *West Heslerton: The Anglian Cemetery.* Yedingham, Malton, U.K.: Landscape Research Centre, 1999.

Knapp, A. Bernard. "Who's Come a Long Way, Baby? Masculinist Approaches to a Gendered Archaeology." *Archaeological Dialogues* 5, no. 2 (1998): 91–125.

Lucy, Sam. *The Anglo-Saxon Way of Death: Burial Rites in Early England.* Stroud, U.K.: Sutton, 2000.

———. "Housewives, Warriors, and Slaves? Sex and Gender in Anglo-Saxon Burials." In *Invisible People and Processes: Writing Gender and Childhood into European Archaeology*. Edited by Jenny Moore and Eleanor Scott, pp. 150–168. London: Leicester University Press, 1997.

Stoodley, Nick. *The Spindle and the Spear: A Critical Enquiry into the Construction and Meaning of Gender in the Early Anglo-Saxon Burial Rite*. BAR British Series, no. 288. Oxford: British Archaeological Reports, 1999.

CHRISTINE E. FLAHERTY

ANIMAL HUSBANDRY

Animal husbandry was well established by the European Iron Age. Two major cultural influences in the barbarian world merged with classical Mediterranean tradition in the Carpathian basin. Areas west of the Danube had close ties with the rest of Europe, most directly with the Hallstatt culture (type site: Austria), extending to Britain between the ninth and fifth centuries B.C. Celtic tribes expanded from their homeland in northern France and southern Germany toward southern Europe and Asia Minor as well as the British Isles between the eighth and third centuries B.C. Meanwhile, the Great Hungarian Plain east of the Danube fell under the influence of pre-Scythian and Scythian cultures from the northern Pontic (Black Sea) region during the Early Iron Age (late seventh century B.C.). From the first century A.D. waves of additional migrations lashed the eastern frontiers of Europe.

Celtic influences met Scythian tradition in the barbarian world of central Europe. Classicism, represented by ancient Greek, Hellenistic, and Roman cultures, flanked these geopolitical developments from the south. Records on animal husbandry originate from the latter, Mediterranean/Pontic, region. Beginning with the description by the Greek historian Herodotus (in the fifth century B.C.) of ferocious "Scythian nomads" of the steppe, classical stereotypes of mobile pastoralists were recycled and homogenized throughout antiquity. Meanwhile, advanced Roman animal breeding is reflected in seminal works by Marcus Terentius Varro, Pliny the Elder, and Columella (first century B.C. to the first century A.D.)

Most differences between the Celtic, Mediterranean, and steppe types of animal husbandry were rooted in their respective geographical environments. Prehistoric agriculture had reached north-central and western Europe millennia earlier across the Balkans. Natural habitats in Mediterranean Europe favored the early establishment of cereal cultivation, viticulture, and the keeping of cattle as well as sheep and goats. People in the Celtic homeland (similarly to northern Germanic tribes inhabiting neighboring areas) had long relied on hunting and pigs, ubiquitous in cool and humid forest regions. Steppe peoples adapted to vast, continental plains by developing mobile pastoralism, with little reliance on cultivation and an emphasis on sheep and goat keeping. Their horses also were used for a great variety of purposes.

Animal keeping, however, should not be viewed with rigid environmental determinism. As empires expanded and reached various areas and people moved around, their traditions blended and interacted, so that by the Iron Age all the important domestic animals were kept in these three cultural regions.

CELTS, GERMANS, AND CLASSICAL TRADITION

Owing to the Celts' sedentary, often urbanized way of life, their animal keeping did not differ markedly from that of the Greeks and Romans. One of the few distinguishing features are the many pig bones at such sites as the Celtic *oppidum* (fortified urban settlement) of Manching in Bavaria and many smal-

Fig. 1. Bronze statuette of a pig, Báta, Celtic. Pigs played an important role in Celtic economy and symbolism alike. PHOTO BY ANDRÁS DABASI. HUNGARIAN NATIONAL MUSEUM. REPRODUCED BY PERMISSION.

ler sites across Europe. Although beef and mutton also were eaten, pork and boar were of special importance. Pig bones commonly occur in Celtic burials. Pork also played a mythical role in divine feasting in the hall of dead warriors (Bruiden in Irish Celtic and Valhalla in Norse mythology). Wild boar, one of the most dangerous game animals in Europe, accompanies Arduinna, continental Celtic goddess of the moon and hunting, often equated with Diana in Roman mythology. Boars are depicted frequently both as decorative motifs and symbols (fig. 1). In such provinces as Pannonia, boars are shown on the tombstones of Romanized Celts.

The small, unimproved Celtic domesticates that have been reconstructed from bone finds (such as those kept by Germans and other peoples in the Barbaricum) often are contrasted with advanced Roman "breeds." This term should be used cautiously when evidence for conscious selection is absent, but the large size and great variation of animal

bones from Roman sites illustrate advanced animal husbandry, as described by classical authors. Representations such as Trajan's Column, from A.D. 113, show livestock whose body conformations appear modern, even by today's standards.

Size differences between the bones from barbarian and classical domesticates are stark. Another sign of developed animal husbandry, a greater diversity in size and shape, is especially striking in dog remains from Roman provincial settlements in present-day Germany and Hungary—lapdogs, greyhounds, and giant forms, exceeding the size of modern-day Alsatians, are represented equally. Such extremes are rare among coeval Celtic dogs in these areas.

"NOMADIC" TRADITION
Peoples from the steppe usually are referred to with the catchall term "nomadic," disregarding the complexity of pastoral societies. While pasturing is cen-

tral to such communities, their seasonal patterns of herding and degrees of sendentariness vary broadly. Theoretically, the entire community of "pure" nomads covered long distances meridionally in a never-ending search for seasonal graze, with no land cultivation. Pastoralism in this extreme form is a highly specialized, precarious way of life. Its stability depends on mobility between different natural habitats, determined by the quality and size of pastures in combination with the speed of movements. Sarmatians, Kalmyks, and some groups of Kazakhs lived this way. The majority of steppe communities, however, included contingents of sedentary agriculturalists as well as major power centers. They could be called, at best, seminomadic. Mobile pastoralism, central to their economy, is a common denominator for past communities. Its technical homogeneity has led to functional similarities between the material and spiritual cultures of many peoples in the vast Eurasian steppe, where perpetual motion greatly intensified contacts and exchange between various groups at all levels.

MOBILE PASTORALISM AND CLASSICAL TRADITION

Scythian tribes included both equestrian nomads and sedentary agriculturalists who inhabited the Eurasian steppe north of the Black Sea. Characteristic of their culture were *kurgans* (burial mounds), many of them in the Dnieper River region, in which Scythian leaders were interred with grave goods of legendary richness, including dozens of horses. Treasures recovered from these graves are decorated with animal motifs showing Greek and Persian influences. Mythical creatures and hunting scenes dominate this artwork, although the evidence for hunting is scarce among the mundane archaeozoological finds.

Scythian settlements between the Dnieper and the Volga region had an overwhelming dominance of domesticates. Sometimes animal husbandry also is represented on precious metal objects. Most famous are the horse-catching scenes on the fourth century B.C. gilded silver amphora from Chertomlyk (near the Dnieper River in the Ukraine) and animals on the gold pectoral from Tolstaya Mogila (some 10 kilometers from Chertomlyk). The latter piece weighs more than a kilogram and has a diameter of more than 30 centimeters. Composed of three ex-

centric circles (joined with the clasp in the back), the outer band of the pectoral is decorated with mythical and wild creatures from griffins to locusts. Separated by a band of floral ornaments, the third, inner band documents the domestic sphere of life. Two Scythians in the center sew a piece of sheepskin, while another milks a ewe (fig. 2). Stylistically, it is likely that a Greek goldsmith in a colonial town in the northern Pontic region made this piece sometime in the fourth century B.C. The figures look Scythian, but it is difficult to tell whether the wild/domestic dichotomy reflects western or eastern traditions.

In a less spectacular form, artifacts decorated in animal style also are known from areas occupied by Scythians in eastern Hungary. Their animal husbandry in the Carpathian Basin can be reconstructed from bone finds at a few rural settlements. In addition to remains of small-bodied cattle, a relatively large number of horse bones (including those of very young foals) occur among the food refuse. The bony cores of large goat horns also point to the eastern pastoral tradition of these communities. A chariot grave with two horses, found at Szentes-Vekerzug on the Great Hungarian Plain, reflects the importance of these animals in all spheres of life.

Having defeated the Scythians in the Pontic region, Iranian-speaking Sarmatian pastoralists reached the Carpathian Basin during the first century A.D., approximately at the time the Romans conquered Celtic areas in its western half, establishing the province of Pannonia. With their westward expansion blocked, Sarmatians and other barbarian tribes spent four centuries in the shadow of the Roman Empire, often in shifting, short-term alliances. This probably strengthened their ethnocultural identity, preserving their eastern pastoral tradition. Small relative frequencies of bones from pig and poultry illustrate this conservative tendency. Although in environmental terms the Great Hungarian Plain represents the westernmost section of the Eurasian steppe, it is far too small for long-distance, nomadic herding. To many steppe peoples who ended up there, it represented a dead end in terms of long-range, annual migrations. Mobility of livestock became less of a priority.

Various written references to the importance of Sarmatian cavalry are in agreement with the high ratio of horse remains in the food refuse at Sarma-

Fig. 2. Highly developed Scythian mobile art often depicted scenes of sophisticated animal husbandry. THE ART ARCHIVE/HERMITAGE MUSEUM SAINT PETERSBURG/DAGLI ORTI. REPRODUCED BY PERMISSION.

tian rural sites. (Among these references are those to the mastering by Germanic Quadi of Sarmatian cavalry tactics, a notation of eight thousand Sarmatian horsemen demanded by the Roman Empire following a defeat in A.D. 175, and the delivery of two thousand mounted warriors to the Romans by the defeated alliance of Sarmatians and Germanic Vandals/Suebians in A.D. 270.) Steppe rituals associated with horses are evidenced by intact horse skulls found at various settlements.

It seems that in peacetime Sarmatians traded livestock and animal products with Roman provinces, in exchange for high-quality Roman craft products (e.g., stamped ware and glass). Sarmatian cattle bones look small and nondistinct. Giant horn cores of rams, however, are indicative of impressive individuals in the sheep flocks. It is difficult to tell whether these animals originated from steppe stocks or represent improved Roman "breeds," adopted by these skillful pastoralists.

POST-ROMAN DEVELOPMENTS

As hordes of Germanic and Asiatic barbarians brought down the Roman Empire in the fifth century A.D., warhorses again best represented barbarian animal husbandry. Mounted warriors literally spearheaded these migrations, in keeping with the tactical necessities of migration through hostile areas. Flavius Vegetius Renatus, in his veterinary handbook on horses, wrote that Hun horses "have large heads . . . with no fat at all on the rump. . . . The leanness of the horses is striking. . . . Their ugly appearance . . . is set off by their fine qualities: sober nature, cleverness and their ability to endure any injury." Note the striking difference between this description, and the coeval, idealized picture of a royal mount from the steppe region.

Between A.D. 567 and 804 Asiatic Avars occupied the Carpathian Basin, creating an ethnically heterogeneous empire, including the ruins of Roman Pannonia. The custom of burying warriors with their horses has preserved hundreds of complete horse skeletons for study. Most were stallions or geldings, more lightly built than modern ponies, on average 135 centimeters tall at the withers. They probably represent animals selected by the practical necessities of light cavalry. Avar warriors introduced stirrups to Europe, which, together with saddles with high pommels, helped mounted archers rise and fire their short reflex bows in almost any direction.

The composition of food refuse from early Avar settlements often resembles that of the Sarmatians, but the growing contribution of pig and poultry over time in grave goods may indicate an increasingly sedentary lifestyle. In comparison with Slavic settlements, Avar period animal bone assemblages look definitely more nomadic. A summary of animal bone percentages from numerous sites of the seventh to ninth centuries, representing various cultures, shows that the significance of horsemeat decreased in an eastward direction across the steppe. Pork was hardly eaten in the east but was important in sedentary Slavic cultures. Beef and mutton show a less consistent pattern.

The next migrants from the steppe, the Magyars, conquered the Carpathian Basin in about A.D. 895. They waged ruthless equestrian raids, rooted in their mobile pastoralist tradition, into much of civilized Europe for more than fifty years. The horse heads and feet buried in some of their graves probably come from skinned animals. Magyar horses therefore are more difficult to reconstruct than their Avar counterparts, to which they are similar in appearance. This does not mean that the two stocks were related, but they probably were shaped by similar military needs.

Early Magyar meat consumption focused on beef and mutton, with an unusually high average proportion of horsemeat. Pope Gregory III banned hippophagy (horse-eating) in Europe in the eighth century, as Germanic tribes were converted to Christianity. As Magyars established a Christian kingdom in Hungary (A.D. 1000), horse eating gradually declined. Pork also started contributing more to the diet, as it had with the Sarmatians and Avars.

Because Magyars (i.e., Hungarians) survived in the Carpathian Basin, there is much speculation about the genetic continuity of their modern domesticates. A mythical animal of the conquering Magyars was, supposedly, a breed of longhorn cattle, which is today called the Hungarian gray. It is reminiscent of the Marreman breed in Italy, which is said to have been introduced by the Huns. This historical confusion is exacerbated by skull finds showing that all peoples of steppe origin (Sarma-

tians, Avars, and Magyars) kept small, short-horned cattle. Archaeological evidence for long-horned animals comes centuries later in the wake of the Middle Ages. Many pastoral communities kept large guard dogs. The striking similarity between a skull from the period of the Magyar conquest (ninth century) and a modern Hungarian *Kuvasz*, however, is rooted more in function than genetic continuity. Owing to their high reproductive rates, dog breeds can change especially rapidly.

See also **Hallstatt** (*vol. 2, part 6*); **Oppida** (*vol. 2, part 6*); **Huns** (*vol. 2, part 7*); **Hungary** (*vol. 2, part 7*).

BIBLIOGRAPHY

Bartosiewicz, László. "A Millennium of Migrations: Proto-historic Mobile Pastoralism in Hungary." In *Zooarchaeology: Papers to Honor Elizabeth S. Wing*. Edited by F. Wayne King and Charlotte M. Porter. *Bulletin of the Florida Museum of Natural History* 44, no. 1 (2003): 101–130.

———. "The Hungarian Grey Cattle: A Traditional European Breed." *Animal Genetic Resources Information* 21 (1997): 49–60.

———. "Early Medieval Archaeozoology in Eastern Europe." In *Bioarchäologie und Frühgeschichtsforschung*. Edited by H. Friesinger, F. Daim, E. Kanelutti, and O. Cichocki, pp. 123–132. Vienna: Institut für Ur- und Frühgeschichte der Universität Wien, 1993.

Bökönyi, Sándor. "Über die Entwicklung der Sekundärnutzung." In *Beiträge zur Archäozoologie und Prähistorischen Anthropologie*. Edited by M. Kokabi and J. Wahl. Stuttgart, Germany: Landesdenkmalamt Baden-Württemberg, Konrad Theiss Verlag, 1994.

———. *Animal Husbandry and Hunting in Tác-Gorsium: The Vertebrate Fauna of a Roman Town in Pannonia*. Budapest, Hungary: Akadémiai Kiadó, 1984.

———. *History of Domestic Mammals in Central and Eastern Europe*. Budapest, Hungary: Akadémiai Kiadó, 1974.

Khazanov, Anatoly M. *Nomads and the Outside World*. 2d ed. Translated by Julia Crookenden. Madison: University of Wisconsin Press, 1994.

Laszlovszky, József, ed. *Tender Meat under the Saddle: Customs of Eating, Drinking, and Hospitality among Conquering Hungarians and Nomadic Peoples*. Krems, Austria: Medium Aevum Quotidianum, 1998.

Matolcsi, János. *Állattartás őseink korában* [Animal keeping in the time of our ancestors]. Budapest, Hungary: Gondolat Kiadó, 1982.

LÁSZLÓ BARTOSIEWICZ

AGRICULTURE

By 1000 B.C. farming, which had originated in Southwest Asia, had been established throughout Europe for millennia. In parts of southeastern Europe agricultural communities existed from 7000 B.C. or earlier, and even in Norway cereal farming was present beginning at least around 2000 B.C. Agricultural changes from around 1000 B.C. to A.D. 1000 therefore represent developments from a long-established tradition. Agricultural systems over this period had two main sets of influences.

BACKGROUND

One set of influences was economic and political. The border between "barbarian" and "civilized" Europe was fluctuating and permeable. In parts of western Europe, for example, agricultural systems that were both more intensive and more extensive developed in the first millennium B.C. to meet indigenous requirements, and subsequently changes were imposed to satisfy the demands of the Roman Empire for larger-scale cereal production. Following the collapse of the imperial economic system in the fifth century, agriculture reverted to subsistence production in some areas. Eventually agricultural systems capable of producing a surplus to support the newly established polities of early medieval Europe were developed. At any given location therefore the economic context of agriculture could vary

markedly through time. Trade in plant products and crops and exchange of knowledge also transpired across the fluctuating cultural contact between civilization and "barbarity" and within the two.

The other major set of influences on early farming systems was environmental. Farmers are pragmatic. They are well aware of the potential productivity of their local environment—its geology, soils, topography, and climate. Although from the beginnings of agriculture cropping systems were almost certainly developed with local adaptations to enhance productivity, it is only in this period that we can unequivocally demonstrate such adaptations in Europe. The effects of climate change over this period are difficult to evaluate. The data currently available are not so regionally precise as to permit discrimination between the effects on agriculture of climatic or cultural change.

DATA SOURCES
Information on early agriculture comes from various sources:

- *Field systems.* These are known both from relict systems in areas which, as a result of climate change, are now too marginal for arable production and from ancient systems now subsumed into modern patterns of field boundaries.

- *Implements.* The artifactual technology of agriculture is known from finds of plows (initially *ards,* which could score only a thin furrow in the soil; later true moldboard plows capable of turning and inverting sod), hand-digging implements (such as spades), and harvesting tools.

- *Crop-processing installations.* These include corn driers.

- *Storage facilities.* In some parts of Europe cereals were stored in belowground silos—during the Iron Age, typically large cylindrical pits—but it is thought that aboveground storage may also have been accomplished in structures marked at many settlement sites by settings of four or nine postholes. Granaries, often with ceramic, basketry, or barrel containers, have been reported from the post-Roman period.

- *Historical sources.*

- *Biological remains.* Most directly these comprise remains of crop plants (macrofossils) preserved by charring (carbonization), as impressions on ceramics, by mineral replacement, and in waterlogged anoxic or oxygen-deficient deposits. Data from palynology (analysis of pollen, spores, and other microscopic entities), entomology (e.g., the presence of scarabaeoid dung beetles or grain pests), and soil science are also very informative. Dating Iron Age deposits by radiocarbon presents difficulties because of a plateau in the calibration curve, therefore palynological analyses of sediment sequences must be linked rigorously to a scientific dating program that permits enhanced precision of calibration by mathematical modeling, as Alex Bayliss has shown. Where this has been done, a detailed picture of land use and agricultural change during the Iron Age can be proposed (as, e.g., at Scole, England, which has been described by Patricia Wiltshire and Peter Murphy).

This article is concerned principally with plant macrofossils, the study of which is known as archaeobotany or palaeoethnobotany, although data from other sources will be mentioned. Cereals and pulses (the edible seeds of legumes) are the domesticated descendents of wild plants native to Southwest Asia. Once they were transplanted to entirely new habitats in Europe, a process of adaptation and intentional human selection began. The full economic potential of the crops available took millennia to realize. Some of the earliest direct evidence for cropping patterns that are closely attuned to local conditions of soil and climate dates from the first millennium B.C.

CROPS, PROCESSING, AND TRADE

Palaeoethnobotanical studies indicate that a wide range of crop species was cultivated during the two millennia under consideration. These included field crops: wheats (einkorn, emmer, durum wheat, rivet wheat, spelt, bread wheat), barley, rye, oats, millets, pulses (peas, horsebeans, vetches, lentils, chickpeas), and fiber and oil crops, such as hemp, flax, and gold of pleasure. The latter is an oilseed no longer grown commercially but well represented, for example, by threshing remains from Iron Age sites in the Assendelver Polders, Netherlands. Some plants that in modern times are generally regarded as weeds may also have been cultivated. In Denmark seeds of *Chenopodium album* L. (a garden weed commonly known as lamb's-quarter or fat hen) have been reported from the gut contents of Iron Age human bodies preserved in peat bogs, and large caches of the seed have been found at settlement sites. Experiments by Paul Stokes and Peter Rowley-Conwy have demonstrated that seed yields comparable to those of cereals may be obtained by cultivating this prolific goosefoot green. Early cultivation of fruits and nuts (including olives, grapes, figs, plums, cherries, walnuts) is evident in regions bordering the Mediterranean, but in the north and west only native wild fruits and nuts have so far been identified from Iron Age sites. Orchard crops and other plants, including culinary herbs (e.g., coriander, dill), spread with the expansion of the Roman Empire. Results from later sites indicate a cessation of fruit and nut cultivation in many areas formerly under Roman control and then reestablishment of production once new trade contacts were established. Orchard crops represented a long-term investment very vulnerable to destruction during conflict, so their apparent absence in these areas in the immediate post-Roman period is unsurprising.

Factors determining the relative economic importance of field and orchard crops were in part environmental, in part economic. The northern and western limits of cultivation for some crops (e.g., ol-

Fig. 1. Late Iron Age British gold coins. These coins of the British king Cunobelin (CVNO) depict cereal ears alongside an attribution to his capital Camulodunum (CAMV). COLCHESTER MUSEUMS. REPRODUCED BY PERMISSION.

ives, lentils) were climatically determined. Rye seems to have reached Europe as a weed in other cereals. By the Iron Age it was being cultivated in some areas, and it spread farther as a result of post-Roman population movements. Its capacity to produce adequate yields on nutrient-deficient upland and sandy soil, by virtue of its extensive root system, made it of great economic importance in parts of North and West Europe. Other marginal soil types occurred in the coastal marshes of Germany and the Netherlands, where there was large-scale occupation from the Iron Age to the Early Middle Ages, eventually associated with mounded settlements known as *terpen* or *wurten*. Archaeobotanical evidence from sites such as the Wurt Elisenhof and the Feddersen Wierde indicates a farming system based on salt marsh grazing and arable production. Barley, a salt-tolerant crop, was the main cereal associated with an early form of broad bean, oats, flax, and where conditions permitted, other crops. Early 1990s excavations at Anglo-Saxon sites dating from around the eighth century A.D. in the fens of eastern England indicate development of comparable farming systems, perhaps independently. Economic change, and in particular a shift to more extensive

forms of production, was associated in parts of Northeast England (and perhaps in the lower Rhineland) with a replacement of emmer wheat by spelt, a hardier crop more tolerant of marginal soils.

Plant macrofossils can also provide information on the economic function and status of sites. It is assumed that the types of plant wastes discarded at a farm (where cereals were being threshed, winnowed, and sieved on a large scale) would differ from those at a higher-status "consumer" site (which might receive only cleaned grain). The relative proportions of grain, chaff, and weed seeds in samples from a site can therefore be informative in terms of the types of activities undertaken there. In fact interpretation is not simple due to the complex range of processes leading to incorporation of macrofossils into archaeological deposits (taphonomic processes). Archaeobotanical results have to be considered alongside other archaeological data and may also draw on ethnographic information from studies of modern peasant agriculture. Martin Jones (1984) has proposed a model for economic interrelationships between Iron Age sites in the hinterland of the hillfort at Danebury, southern En-

Fig. 2. Castle Mall, Norwich. Evidence for Late Saxon malting, using barley and oats. Pictured here are germinated grains of barley (*Hordeum* sp.). Scale: 20 mm. COURTESY OF PETER MURPHY. REPRODUCED BY PERMISSION.

gland, based on sample composition. He proposes that partially processed crops were brought to the hillfort for communal processing and storage. A similar study of plant material from a hilltop settlement dating from the sixth to the ninth centuries in the Biferno Valley, Molise, Italy, produced samples composed mainly of grain with few chaff fragments or weed seeds. This may indicate that the site was not a peasant farming village but a higher-status settlement supplied with largely cleaned cereals by farms in its hinterland.

Evidence also indicates long-distance exchange of crop products. For example, the Roman writer Strabo records grain as one of the exports of Late Iron Age Britain, and the depiction of cereal ears on gold coins issued in the early first century A.D. by the British king Cunobelin could well be seen as a statement of the economic basis of his power (fig. 1). Archaeobotanical evidence for trade in plant foodstuffs is tantalizingly sparse throughout the period under consideration, although exotic cornfield weed seeds in charred grain samples from early me-

dieval Dorestad, Netherlands, suggest importation of cereals from areas farther up the Rhine. It is possible that new techniques, including analysis of DNA and stable isotopes, will enhance understanding of early trade in crops. A few macrofossils of imported Mediterranean foods (e.g., dried figs) have been reported from tenth-century deposits at Cologne, Germany, and York, England, but indications of imported foods are otherwise very rare in North and West Europe before the twelfth century. The highest-status commodity traded appears to have been wine. Remains of Italian amphorae have been reported from Late Iron Age burials in Southeast England (see the report by Rosalind Niblett), and barrels of silver fir originating in the upper Rhine have been found in eighth-to-tenth-century-A.D. deposits at the southern Baltic trading settlement of Hedeby and at Dorestad. As an expression of conspicuous consumption, wine drinking seems to have been the preserve of the warrior and proto-urban elite throughout North and West Europe.

While wine was the drink of civilization (and of those who aspired to it), beer or ale was the common drink of much of Europe. Production of beer from cereal grain involves several stages, the first of which is a controlled germination to allow conversion of starch to sugar that can subsequently be fermented (malting). Finds of charred germinated grains can be evidence for the process (fig. 2). The earliest material reasonably interpretable as malt comprised charred germinated barley grains in pots from a burned first-century-A.D. house at Østerbølle, Denmark. During the Roman period malt was generally produced from wheat, but evidence from cellars of early medieval buildings destroyed by fire at Ipswich, England, indicates that oats and barley were used. Flavorings were commonly added, including hops and bog myrtle. Hops also contain polyphenolic preservative compounds. Large deposits of hop fruits have been reported from ninth- and tenth-century-A.D. contexts at Haithabu, Germany, and in England from a tenth-century boat at Graveney and from contemporary deposits at Ipswich.

Other plant products include medicinal drugs. Seeds of opium poppy have been found in Bronze Age and later deposits throughout much of Europe, whereas *Cannabis* is known from Iron Age contexts in Romania and Hungary and from Roman and later deposits in the north and west. Native wild plants would also have provided a pharmacopoeia, but direct evidence for this is sparse. Patricia Wiltshire found abundant *Artemisia* pollen within corrosion products in the spout of a bronze infusing vessel, which was found in a first-century-A.D. grave of non-Roman native type at Stanway, Essex, in association with a complete set of medical instruments. The *Artemisia* genus of plants includes species that produce antimalarial and vermifuge compounds.

Dyes, too, were produced. Tenth- and eleventh-century Anglo-Scandinavian deposits at York, England, have produced remains of dye plants (madder, dyer's greenweed, woad, and a club moss probably of Scandinavian origin). Colors produced would have varied depending on the mordant, but red, blue, and yellow were certainly available.

Limitations of space preclude discussion of the exploitation and management of natural and semi-natural habitats—particularly woodlands, heathlands and grasslands—but suffice to say that these, too, provided fuel, wild plant foods, drugs, dyes,

tanning agents, and grazing and hay for domestic animals.

See also **Crops of the Early Farmers** (*vol. 1, part 3*); **Danebury** (*vol. 2, part 6*); **Ipswich** (*vol. 2, part 7*).

BIBLIOGRAPHY

Bayley, Justine, ed. *Science in Archaeology: An Agenda for the Future.* London: English Heritage, 1998.

Bayliss, Alex. "Some Thoughts on Using Scientific Dating in English Archaeology and Buildings Analysis for the Next Decade." In *Science in Archaeology: An Agenda for the Future.* Edited by Justine Bayley, pp. 95–109. London: English Heritage, 1998.

Behre, Karl-Ernst. "The History of Rye Cultivation in Europe." *Vegetation History and Archaeobotany* 1, no. 3 (1992): 141–156.

Behre, Karl-Ernst, and S. Jacomet. "The Ecological Interpretation of Archaeobotanical Data." In *Progress in Old World Palaeoethnobotany.* Edited by Willem Van Zeist, Krystyna Wasylikowa, and Karl-Ernst Behre, pp. 81–108. Rotterdam and Brookfield, Vt.: Balkema, 1991.

Crowson, A., T. Lane, and J. Reeve. *Fenland Management Project Excavations 1991–1995.* Lincolnshire Archaeology and Reports Series no. 3. Heckington, U.K.: Fenland Management Project, 2000.

Jones, Martin. "The Plant Remains." In *Danebury: An Iron Age Hillfort in Hampshire.* Vol. 2, *The Excavations, 1969–1978: The Finds.* Edited by Barry Cunliffe, pp. 483–495. Council for British Archaeology Research Report 52. London: Council for British Archaeology, 1984.

Kenward, H. K., and A. R. Hall. "Biological Evidence from Anglo-Scandinavian Deposits at 16–22 Coppergate." *Archaeology of York* 14, no. 7 (1995): 435–797.

Niblett, Rosalind. *The Excavation of a Ceremonial Site at Folly Lane, Verulamium.* Britannia Monograph Series 14. London: Society for the Promotion of Roman Studies, 1999.

Renfrew, Jane M. *New Light on Early Farming: Recent Developments in Palaeoethnobotany.* Edinburgh: Edinburgh University Press, 1991.

Stokes, Paul, and Peter Rowley-Conwy. "Iron Age Cultigen? Experimental Return Rates for Fat Hen (*Chenopodium album* L.)." *Environmental Archaeology* 7 (October 2002): 95–100.

Van der Veen, Marijke. "An Early Medieval Hilltop Settlement in Molise: The Plant Remains from D85." *Papers of the British School at Rome* 53 (1985): 211–224.

Van der Veen, Marijke, and T. O'Connor. "The Expansion of Agricultural Production in Late Iron Age and Roman Britain." In *Science in Archaeology: An Agenda for the Future.* Edited by Justine Bayley, pp. 127–144. London: English Heritage, 1998.

Van Zeist, Willem, Krystyna Wasylikowa, and Karl-Ernst Behre, eds. *Progress in Old World Palaeoethnobotany.* Rotterdam and Brookfield, Vt.: Balkema, 1991. (A comprehensive review of European paleoethnobotany in the 1970s and 1980s.)

Van Zeist, Willem, and W. A. Casparie, eds. *Plants and Ancient Man: Studies in Palaeoethnobotany.* Rotterdam and Boston: Balkema, 1984.

Wiltshire, Patricia E. J., and Peter L. Murphy. "Current Knowledge of the Iron Age Environment and Agrarian Economy of Norfolk and Adjacent Areas." In *The Land of the Iceni: The Iron Age in Northern East Anglia.* Edited by John Davies and Tom Williamson, pp. 132–161. Norwich, U.K.: University of East Anglia, 1999.

PETER MURPHY

MILLS AND MILLING TECHNOLOGY

In the Roman world, water-powered mills that reduced cereal grains to either flour or meal came into use in locations as diverse as Dacia (modern day Romania), North Africa, and the province of Britannia. This relatively widespread distribution has been confirmed by recent archaeological discoveries in the territories that once formed part of the Roman Empire. Both documentary and archaeological evidence attests to their continued use in the various Barbarian kingdoms established after the empire's demise. Several early Latin *vitae,* or saints' lives, for example, composed in the post-Roman period, refer to the use of such mills: the lives of Orientius (c. A.D. 380–426); Romanus (c. A.D. 450); Remigius (A.D. 486–511), and Ursus (A.D. 484–507). Bishop Gregory of Tours also provides an interesting description of the construction of a monastic water mill at Loches (Indre-et-Loire) c. A.D. 500 and mentions the contemporary water mills at Dijon. In documentary sources dating from the sixth to seventh centuries A.D., many of which correspond to the orbit of the Frankish empire, there are, in total, at least sixteen references to water mills in central Europe. The law codes of the Germanic peoples provide further early documentation of the use of water-powered mills in the Barbarian world, and, not surprisingly perhaps, only the tribes that had settled within the frontiers of the Roman Empire made provisions for water mills in their law codes.

These include the *Pactus Alamannorum* (early seventh century), the *Lex Alamannorum* (A.D. 717–719), and the *Lex Baiwariorum* (A.D. 725–728).

The development of monastic estates was perhaps the single most important factor in the spread of water-powered grain mills throughout the barbarian kingdoms prior to the tenth century. Indeed, the growth of the larger religious establishments of the Carolingian period, such as Saint-Germain-des-Prés and Lorsh, where large areas of land were brought under Benedictine control (and from which the order derived substantial profits), effectively increased the demand for mills. The Carolingian countryside, for example, had a particularly high density of mills, and the polyptych of Saint-Germain-des-Prés alone lists a staggering eighty-four mills, most of them situated on smaller streams. The increased use of water-powered mills in this period may also indicate two important developments: a growing need to ensure regular supplies of grain for a rapidly increasing rural population, and its corollary, an expansion in the cultivation of cereal crops.

Two basic types of water-powered mill were used in the barbarian kingdoms, as elsewhere in early medieval Europe, and as they still are used in the contemporary Islamic world. The first of these mills employed a horizontal waterwheel set on a vertical axle, in which one revolution of the waterwheel produced a corresponding revolution of the upper millstone (fig. 1). In the second type of water mill, the motion of a waterwheel set on a horizontal axle was communicated to a pair of millstones via wooden gearwheels set at right angles to each other (fig. 2). A large number of early medieval horizontal-wheeled mill sites have come to light in Ireland, many of which have been dated by dendrochronology to the seventh to eleventh centuries A.D. The huge corpus of Irish mill components includes almost complete mill buildings; the earliest-known examples of horizontal waterwheels; the wooden water-feeder chutes, or penstocks, associated with them; and tentering beams for adjusting the millstones. In England a well-preserved Saxon site, dated by dendrochronology to the ninth century, has been excavated at Tamworth, Staffordshire, while at Earl's Bu in the Orkney Islands the remains of a Viking Age example have come to light. In Denmark wooden structures at Omgard (c. A.D.

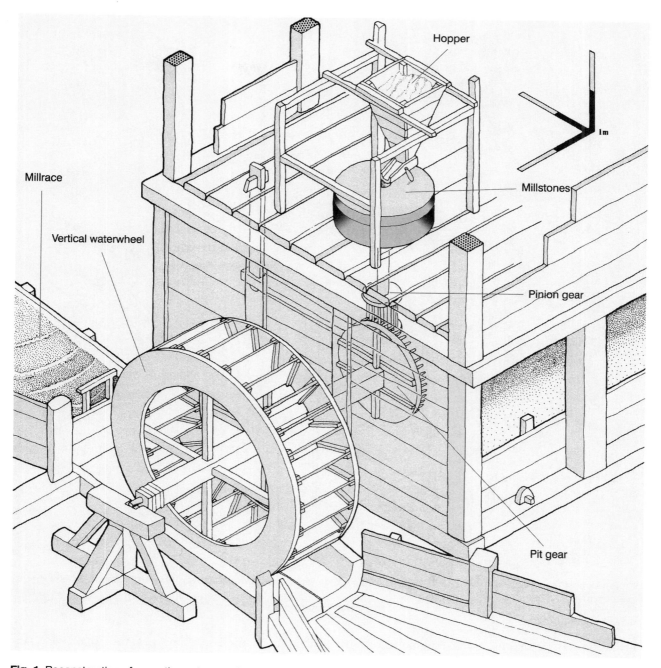

Fig. 1. Reconstruction of seventh-century vertical-wheeled mill at Little Island, County Cork, Ireland. COURTESY OF COLIN RYNNE. REPRODUCED BY PERMISSION.

800) and Ljorring (c. A.D. 960) have been interpreted as the remains of horizontal-wheeled mills.

Vertical-wheeled mills dating to the seventh century have been investigated at Little Island, County Cork, Ireland, and at Old Windsor in Berkshire, England. At Little Island, a double horizontal-wheeled mill and a vertical-wheeled mill (fig. 2) operated side by side, the earliest-known close association of the two types of mill in medieval Europe. As in the case of the majority of the excavated horizontal-wheeled mills, most of the medieval vertical-wheeled mills that have come to light in Europe had

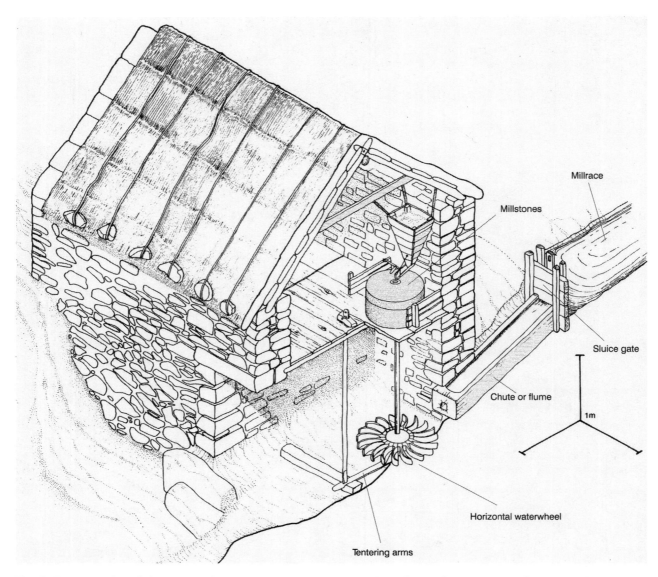

Fig. 2. Reconstruction of ninth-century horizontal-wheeled mill on High Island, County Galway, Ireland. COURTESY OF COLIN RYNNE. REPRODUCED BY PERMISSION.

substantial wooden foundations. Fragments of early medieval vertical waterwheels have also been found at Ardcloyne, County Cork, Ireland (c. A.D. 787) and at Belle-Église (c. A.D. 930–980) in France. Another French site, at Audin-le-Tiche in northeastern France (c. A.D. 840–960), produced physical evidence for a vertical waterwheel with an original diameter of some 1.4 meters.

One should not forget, however, that throughout early medieval Europe simple rotary querns (from O.E. *cweorn, O.H.G. quirn*), which consisted of two small-diameter disk-shaped stones with a central pivot and a wooden crank handle, would still

have been used in many peasant households. Indeed, querns of imported lava from the Mayern-Niedermendig area of Germany are relatively common on Middle to Late Saxon sites in England, while two lava quern blanks were recovered from the Saxon Graveney boat (Kent). During the medieval period, the simple rotary quern underwent an important technical change that made it easier to regulate the distance between the rotating upper and the stationary lower stone. The axle was extended through the base of the lower stone and allowed to pivot on an adjustable beam, which made it possible to exert greater control over the distance between the stones (a process called *tentering*), a factor that directly affected the coarseness of the flour or meal.

BIBLIOGRAPHY

Benoit, P., and Joséphine Rouillard. "Medieval Hydraulics in France." In *Working with Water in Medieval Europe: Technology and Resource Use.* Edited by Paolo Squatriti, pp. 161–215. Leiden-Boston: Brill, 2000.

Holt, Richard. "Medieval England's Water-related Technologies." In *Working with Water in Medieval Europe: Technology and Resource Use.* Edited by Paolo Squatriti, pp. 51–100. Leiden-Boston: Brill, 2000.

———. *The Mills of Medieval England.* Oxford: Basil Blackwell, 1988.

Rahtz, Philip A., and Robert Meeson. *An Anglo-Saxon Watermill at Tamworth.* London: Council for British Archaeology, 1992.

Reynolds, Terry S. *Stronger than a Hundred Men: A History of the Vertical Waterwheel.* Baltimore: Johns Hopkins University Press, 1983.

Rynne, Colin. "Water-power in Medieval Ireland." In *Working with Water in Medieval Europe: Technology and Resource Use.* Edited by Paolo Squatriti, pp. 1–50. Leiden and Boston: Brill, 2000.

———. "The Introduction of the Vertical Watermill into Ireland: Some Recent Archaeological Evidence." *Medieval Archaeology* 33 (1989): 21–31.

Watts, Martin. *The Archaeology of Mills and Milling.* Stroud, U.K.: Tempus Publishing, 2002.

Wikander, O. "Archaeological Evidence for Early Watermills: An Interim Report." *History of Technology* 10 (1985): 151–179.

COLIN RYNNE

MIGRATION PERIOD PEOPLES

Migration or population movement is a well-documented feature of ancient Europe. At the end of the Ice Age (11,000 years ago), hunters and gatherers moved into areas of Europe that had been glaciated during the Pleistocene. Both archaeological and skeletal evidence indicate that migration played a role in the establishment of the first farming communities in central Europe. Archaeological, place-name, and literary evidence document substantial population movements in central Europe during the later Iron Age.

Population movements are also well documented throughout the Early Middle Ages, and the period from A.D. 400 to 600 is often referred to as the Migration period. In the fifth and sixth centuries A.D. barbarians from outside the Roman Empire—Visigoths, Angles, Saxons, Franks, and others—moved into many regions of western Europe. The nature of these migrations has been debated by both archaeologists and historians for decades. Do they represent large-scale population movements, or are they small migrations of a military and political elite who dominated the local sub-Roman populations and initiated changes in material culture and ideology? Today, many archaeologists would favor the latter explanation. This chapter profiles many of the Migration period peoples—including the Saami, of likely ancient, not migratory, origin—who are known through the archaeological record and through historical sources. The Scythians are also included in this section even though they disappear from the historical record at the very beginning of the Migration period, c. A.D. 375.

ANGLES, SAXONS, AND JUTES

In book 1 of his *Ecclesiastical History of the English People* (*Historia ecclesiastica gentis Anglorum*), completed in A.D. 731, the Northumbrian cleric Bede reported that the Germanic settlers of Anglo-Saxon England came from "three very powerful Germanic tribes, the Saxons, the Angles and the Jutes." From the coastal region of northern Germany, now Lower Saxony, came the East Saxons, South Saxons, and West Saxons. The East Angles, Middle Angles, Mercians, Northumbrians, and other Anglian peoples were descended from the people of Angeln, probably in the eastern part of Schleswig-Holstein. The Jutes, who settled Kent, the Isle of Wight, and the area of the West Saxon mainland facing Wight, came from the peninsula of Jutland (in present-day Denmark).

Writing in the middle of the second century A.D., the Roman geographer Ptolemy placed the Saxons at the neck of the Cimbric peninsula, which comprises Jutland in the north and Schleswig-Holstein (present-day Germany) in the south. Fourth- and fifth-century historical sources do not distinguish consistently between the Saxons and Franks, however, by the eighth century these groups had distinct political systems. From the mid-sixth century, the Continental Saxons expanded their territory until its incorporation into the Carolingian empire after the wars of A.D. 772–799.

In Lower Saxony longhouse settlements located on man-made mounds in coastal marshes, such as Feddersen Wierde (figs. 1 and 2) and Flögeln, were in use until the fifth century. A range of building types, including farmhouses, granaries, barns, and outbuildings, were excavated at the Carolingian settlement of Warendorf in Westphalia. In Lower Saxony and extending toward the Rhine, a unique native metalwork style, as demonstrated by supporting-arm and equal-arm brooches decorated with chip-carved surfaces, incorporated Roman influences. The sites at Westerwanna, Issendorf, and Liebenau, dating to the fourth and early fifth centuries, exemplify large Continental cremation cemeteries, which originally appeared in the first century. Inhumation, which emerged in the fourth century, had replaced cremation by the ninth century.

Early Anglo-Saxon cemeteries in England have produced ceramics identical to those found in the Saxon homeland identified by Bede. Fifth-century pottery vessels with "standing arch" designs or bosses from eastern and southern England parallel contemporary ceramics from the traditional homeland of the Saxons. Indeed, the similarity between face masks appearing on vessels from Wehden (Niedersachsen) and Markshall (Norfolk) has led to the suggestion that they were created by the same potter.

Procopius, a sixth-century Byzantine writer, claimed that the Frisians, people living along the coast of Lower Saxony, and Angles settled Britain. In chapter 40 of his account *Germania,* written in the late first century A.D., the Roman historian Tacitus cited the Anglii among the Germanic tribes. From the fourth century, cruciform and small-long brooches characterized a distinctive material culture extending beyond the bounds of modern Angeln. Cremation was the predominant burial practice during the fourth and fifth centuries. According to book 2 of Bede's *Ecclesiastical History,* migration across the channel had depopulated Angeln, a claim that has found some archaeological support. Archaeological evidence indicates that by the sixth century, the large Continental cremation cemeteries were no longer in use, and settlement activity disappeared between the fifth and eighth centuries. A few sixth- and seventh-century hoards, stray finds, and burials, however, argue against Bede's claim of total abandonment. Significant language replacement indicates repopulation in Angeln after the eighth century.

Design motifs on ceramics from the Continental Anglian cremation cemeteries appear on vessels found in southern and eastern England. Pots with horizontal grooves or corrugations around the neck, vertical grooves or bosses ringing the shoulder, and a wider, shallower profile than those from the Elbe-Weser region are found both on the Continent at Hammoor (Germany) and Sørup

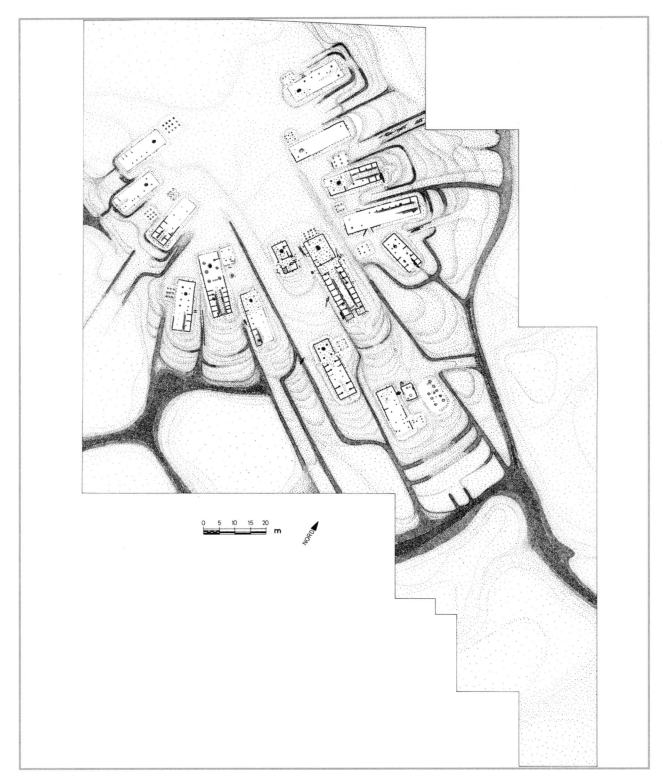

Fig. 1. Site plan of the settlement at Feddersen Wierde. Niedersächsisches Institut für historische Küstenforschung. Reproduced by permission.

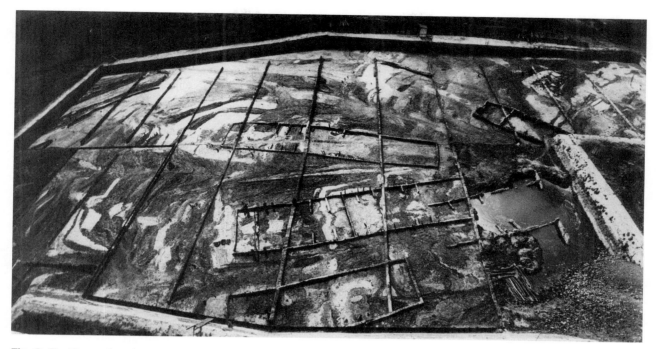

Fig. 2. The Roman Iron Age site of Feddersen Wierde. NIEDERSÄCHSISCHES INSTITUT FÜR HISTORISCHE KÜSTENFORSCHUNG. REPRODUCED BY PERMISSION.

(Denmark) and in England at Caistor-by-Norwich (Norfolk). Cross-headed small-long brooches with spatulate feet and cruciform brooches provide a connection between Angeln and England. Moreover, similarities in the range of artifacts and their proportional occurrence noted between the large cemeteries at Spong Hill (Norfolk) and Bordesholm and Süderbrarup in Schleswig-Holstein have been explained tentatively as the result of migration from the Continent.

Eastern Kent and western Jutland are similarly linked through ceramic and metalwork types. Unlike the areas of England traditionally ascribed to the Angles and Saxons, however, Jutish Kent lacks early burials representative of the earliest settlers. Indeed, burials dating to the fifth and sixth century in Jutland generally are unfurnished. Consequently, little evidence exists for the direct import into Kent of Jutish types of ceramics, bracteates (thin metal plates), and cruciform brooches.

The artifactual diversity of the contact-period Anglo-Saxon cemeteries nonetheless indicates that the Germanic migrants were not culturally homogeneous. Although fifth-century archaeological parallels between England and the Continent are evident

in ceramics and metalwork, it is from the late fifth and sixth centuries in England that ethnic redefinition, manifested by women's dress styles, approximated the Anglian, Saxon, and Jutish groupings described by Bede. Anglian women's primary garment was a tunic dress (*peplos*) secured at both shoulders by small, generally similar brooches. Although the classic *peplos* was sleeveless, the presence of wrist clasps indicates that, in England, Anglian women wore either a long-sleeved version of this dress or a sleeved underdress beneath the sleeveless variant. A third, often larger brooch at the neck, shoulder, or chest either fastened the undergarment to the tunic or closed a heavier outer cloak. In early Anglo-Saxon England, annular, small-long, and cruciform brooches traditionally are associated with women living in the area attributed by Bede to the Angles.

In the Saxon area of England, women's Germanic-type costume incorporated supporting-arm brooches, equal-arm brooches, and saucer brooches similar to those of their Continental homelands, as well as disk brooches. In Kent and the Isle of Wight, the regions traditionally connected with Jutish settlement, women followed a distinctive Continental-influenced dress style that featured a centrally closing garment secured by inlaid brooches. The continuation of these Continental associations into the sixth century is indicated by the importation into Kent of brooches decorated with a southern Scandinavian art style and bracteate pendants. In the late sixth and seventh centuries, access to the wealth of the Frankish kingdom enabled elite women in Kent and the Isle of Wight to adopt other Continental fashions, such as crystal ball amulets and gold-braid headbands (*vittae*).

Today, it is recognized that Bede was describing not the political landscape of the Anglo-Saxon migration, as he claimed, but that of his own time. The Germanic origin myths that legitimized these cultural identities were remembered and exploited into the eighth century.

See also **Anglo-Saxon England** (*vol. 2, part 7*); **Spong Hill** (*vol. 2, part 7*).

BIBLIOGRAPHY

Colgrave, Bertram, and R. A. B. Mynors, trans. and eds. *Bede's Ecclesiastical History of the English People.* Oxford: Clarendon Press, 1969.

Hills, Catherine. "Did the People of Spong Hill Come from Schleswig-Holstein?" *Studien zur Sachsenforschung* 13 (1998): 145–154.

Hines, John. "Culture Groups and Ethnic Groups in Northern Germany in and around the Migration Period." *Studien zur Sachsenforschung* 13 (1999): 219–232.

Pohl, Walter. "Ethnic Names and Identities in the British Isles: A Comparative Perspective." In *The Anglo-Saxons from the Migration Period to the Eighth Century: An Ethnographic Perspective.* Edited by J. Hines, pp. 7–40. Woodbridge, U.K.: Boydell Press, 1997.

Pohl, Walter, and Helmut Reimutz, eds. *Strategies of Distinction: The Construction of Ethnic Communities, 300–800.* Leiden, The Netherlands, and Boston: Brill, 1988.

Welch, Martin. *English Heritage Book of Anglo-Saxon England.* London: B.T. Batsford/English Heritage, 1992.

Wood, Ian. "Before and after the Migration to Britain." In *The Anglo-Saxons from the Migration Period to the Eighth Century: An Ethnographic Perspective.* Edited by J. Hines, pp. 41–54. Woodbridge, U.K.: Boydell Press, 1997.

GENEVIEVE FISHER

BAIUVARII

The Baiuvarii represent the most recent Germanic tribe of the Migration period that played an impor-

tant part in the development of present-day Germany. The first historical record comes from Roman authors of the early sixth century A.D.: Jordanes mentions the tribe in his history of the Goths (551), perhaps reflecting an earlier reference (520) in Cassiodorus. Later the tribe is mentioned by the Gallic Latin poet Venantius Fortunatus (565). The main settlement area of the Baiuvarii included parts of the old Roman provinces of Raetia and Noricum, a territory whose modern appellation, Bavaria, derives from their name. The name "Baiuvarii" probably means "men from the land of Baia," or Bohemia, the old Boiohaemum of the ancient geographers. Identifying the date when these Baiuvarii arrived and the inhabitants they encountered in the Roman territories of Raetia and Noricum was long a subject of constant debate; however, developments in archaeological research in the late twentieth century have yielded new insights, and the understanding of the ethnogenesis of the Baiuvarii has changed radically over the years.

By the 1960s a majority of researchers had observed a distinct gap between late antiquity and the Early Middle Ages. They assumed that the Alpine foothills remained largely unoccupied after the Romans withdrew in 400 until the Baiuvarii, as a fully developed tribe, migrated from Bohemia into the area in the early sixth century. Indeed, for a long time, the archaeological sources remained almost completely silent regarding the fifth century. Since the 1960s, however, archaeological finds have confirmed the account of the Latin scholar Eugippius, who records in his sixth-century *Vita Sancti Severini* that in Raetia, too, Roman rule and border defense ended only around 476 as a direct result of the end of the Western Roman Empire.

Baiuvarian cemeteries have now been discovered that were used as early as the second half of the fifth century and remained in use around 700; examples include the graveyards at Barbing–Irlmauth (Regensburg), Klettham–Altenerding (Erding), Bittenbrunn (in the Neuburg–Schrobenhausen district), Straubing–Bajuwarenstrasse (near Regensburg), and Munich Aubing. Two cases, namely the late Roman forts at Neuburg and Straubing and the early Baiuvarian cemeteries of Bittenbrunn and Straubing–Bajuwarenstrasse, reveal a direct connection between the Germanic allies, who abandoned the forts around 476 and the core of the new settlers who founded the oldest Baiuvarian farming villages. These early cemeteries have one thing in common—the grave goods do not indicate a uniform "early Baiuvarian" culture that would also show close links to Bohemia. The burial offerings rather contain a wide variety of antique objects of Roman, Bohemian, Ostrogothic, Alemannic, and Langobardic origin that strongly suggest that Baiuvarian ethnogenesis is polyethnic in character.

The eponymic core of this process is evident in the archaeologically defined Friedenhain-Prestovice group, which goes back to the Teutons in southern Bohemia. In the fifth century A.D. this group migrated by way of the valley between Cham and Fürth through the Bavarian Forest and into the eastern Bavarian approaches to the Roman *limes* between Neuburg and Passau. They soon provided the majority of the Roman frontier troops, a situation that lasted until the end of Roman rule around the middle of the fifth century. Historically, this group is to be identified as the "Baiuvarii," the "men from Bohemia," who lent their name to this polyethnic tribal structure and represented the nucleus of Bavarian ethnogenesis.

Only in the late sixth century do the grave goods begin to suggest a uniform Baiuvarian cemetery culture, which because of strong Frankish-Lombard influence cannot be distinguished in all respects from neighboring tribes, such as the Alemanni. A difference in the settlement of the land is evident between the north and the south. In the Danube area settlement was continuous from the time of the Romans; in contrast, the Alpine foothills to the south were resettled somewhat later, except for the Roman settlement region around Salzburg.

From the meager historical sources and the insights offered by archaeological research as of the early 2000s, the following model emerges for the Bavarian tribal genesis: when Roman rule came to an end on the Danube around the middle of the fifth century, a polyethnic tribe comprising Roman and immigrant Germanic groups (including Alemanni, Ostrogoths, Langobards, and Thuringians) formed at the turn of the fifth to the sixth century A.D. around Germanic allies who had migrated into the area from Bohemia (the "Baiuvarii"). Particularly important is the fact that the massive and therefore practically indestructible fortress of Regensburg remained in the possession of the allies of

Bohemian origin. Based on written records starting in the Early Middle Ages, this was the royal capital of the early medieval stem duchy of the Agilolfing dynasty.

This Baiuvarian ethnogenesis should not be imagined in a power vacuum or seen as a conscious decision of those involved. It is more likely to have occurred as a result of external influences, namely through the intervention of the Ostrogoths. Under their king Theoderic, the Ostrogoths had conquered Italy from Eastern Rome in 493. The territory they acquired included Raetia up to the Danube, an area that formed part of the diocese of Italy. Ostrogothic rule over the region between the Alps and the Danube ended only in 536. In that year, the Ostrogothic king, Witigis, who was forced to defend Italy against the troops of the Eastern Roman emperor, Justinian, ceded the region north of the Alps to the Franks under their king Theudebert from the Merovingian dynasty. The tribe of the Baiuvarii between the Lech, the Danube, the Enns, and the Alps continued to enjoy substantial independence under the rule of the Agilolfingian dukes, who had many connections with the Langobard dynasty. In the sixth and seventh centuries, settlement expanded rapidly and in northern Bavaria eventually spread across the Danube towards the north. In addition to archaeological finds, historical place-names increasingly testify to these settlement processes in the seventh century. Toward the end of its independence, the stem duchy of Bavaria included the region up to the Enns River and the Bavarian Forest in the east but failed to reach the Main River in the north. The western boundary was formed by a line extending from the Rednitz and Lech Rivers to the upper Inn Valley. In the region of the Alps, the southern area included the upper Etsch Valley and the upper Pustertal Valley.

Regensburg is mentioned as the capital (metropolis) of the stem duchy of Bavaria for the first time in 770. Many ducal palaces and large ducal estates are known to have existed in the eighth century. The earliest known diocesan towns are Eichstätt, Regensburg, Freising, Passau, Salzburg, and Säben. Many monasteries and cloisters, including Mondsee, Mattsee, Chiemsee, and Benediktbeuern, date back to the Agilolfingians. Under Charlemagne a split occurred with the last Agilolfing, Tassilo III, who was deposed in 788. After that, Frankish office-holders ruled in Bavaria.

See also **Ostrogoths** (*vol. 2, part 7*); **Southern Germany** (*vol. 2, part 7*).

BIBLIOGRAPHY

Czysz, Wolfgang, Karlheinz Dietz, Thomas Fischer, and Hans-Jörg Kellner, eds. *Die Römer in Bayern.* Stuttgart, Germany: Theiss, 1995.

Dannheimer, Hermann, and Heinz Dopsch, eds. *Die Bajuwaren: Von Severin bis Tassilo 488–788.* Munich and Salzburg: Amt der Salzburger Landesregierung, 1988.

Dietz, Karlheinz, and Thomas Fischer. *Die Römer in Regensburg.* Regensburg, Germany: Pustet, 1996.

Fischer, Thomas. *Das bajuwarische Reihengräberfeld von Staubing: Studien zur Frühgeschecte im bayerischen Donaraum.* Kallmuenz, Germany: Michael Lassleben, 1993.

———. *Noricum.* Mainz, Germany: Zabern, 1992.

Friesinger, H., and F. Daim, eds. *Typen der Ethnogenese unter besonderer Berücksichtigung der Bayern.* Vienna: Verlag der Österreichischen Akademie der Wissenschaften, 1990.

Geisler, Hans. "Das frühbairische Gräberfeld Straubing-Bajuwarenstraße." *Internationale Archäologie* 30 (1998): 339–342.

Menghin, Wilfried. *Frühgeschichte Bayerns: Römer und Germanen, Baiern und Schwaben, Franken und Slawen.* Stuttgart, Germany: Theiss, 1990.

Reindel, Kurt. "Grundlegung: Das Zeitalter der Agilolfinger (bis 788)." In *Handbuch der bayerischen Geschichte.* Vol. 1. Edited by Max Spindler. Munich: Beck, 1981.

Werner, Joachim. "Die Herkunft der Bajuwaren und der 'östlich-merowingische' Reihengräberkreis." In *Aus Bayerns Frühzeit: Friedrich Wagner zum 75. Geburtstag.* Edited by Joachim Werner, pp. 229–250. Munich: Commission for Bavarian National History, Beck, 1962.

Wolfram, Herwig, and Andreas Schwarcz, eds. "Die Bayern und ihre Nachbarn: Berichte des Symposions der Kommission für Frühmittelalterforschung 25–28 Oktober 1982." *Denkschrift der Österreichischen Adademie der Wissenschaften* 179–180 (1985).

THOMAS FISCHER
(TRANSLATED BY GINA BRODERICK)

DÁL RIATA

One of the peoples of early medieval Scotland, the Dál Riata (or Dalriada) were Gaelic speakers whose territorial base was in Argyll on the West Highland coast. They have provided some of the earliest indigenous historical sources for Scotland, and they participated in the development of the multicultural Insular art style. Their kings are credited with the creation of the greater kingdom of "Scot-land" during the mid-ninth century A.D.

The Dál Riata originated in northern Ireland. Their origin legends claim that Fergus Mór came to Argyll c. A.D. 500. In A.D. 575, at the Convention of Druim Cett, the king of the Scottish Dál Riata surrendered his rights to military service on land from the Irish Dál Riata but retained the rights to their tribute and ship service. Despite this historical evidence, there is debate about exactly how many Dál Riata came to Argyll and under what circumstances. They did speak a Goidelic, or Q-Celtic, language, the ancestor of modern Scots Gaelic, whereas their neighbors the Picts and Britons spoke Brittonic, or P-Celtic, languages related more closely to modern Welsh, which might argue for significant population movement. There is no archaeological evidence, however, to support the theory of a large-scale migration. The archaeological record in Argyll shows considerable continuity with the earlier Iron Age. Nonetheless, it should be kept in mind that there is evidence from early in prehistory for close contact between Argyll and northern Ireland, which are, after all, separated by a mere 19 kilometers (12 miles) of water. In the early twenty-first century most scholars support the idea of a move by the ruling dynasty of the Dál Riata, perhaps under pressure from the powerful Uí Néill, or Ulaid, from their Irish homeland to an area with which they had close connections, perhaps including marriage alliances—very much as some late medieval MacDonalds became the MacDonnels of Antrim.

The Scottish Dál Riata had three, later four, major *cenéla,* or kindreds: Cenél nGabráin, Cenél Loairn, Cenél nOengusa, and Cenél Comgaill, the last of which split from Cenél nGabráin by the eighth century A.D. The names of these groups, some description of their territories, and a census of their military forces are found in the *Senchus fer*

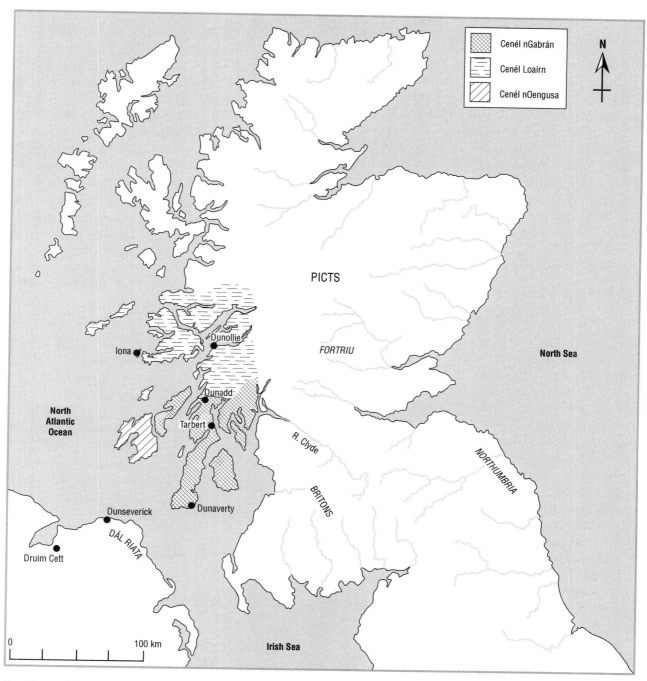

Key sites and kindred territories of early Dál Riata. ADAPTED FROM LANE AND CAMPBELL 2000.

nAlban (History of the men of Scotland), a tenth-century document substantially based on a seventh-century original. The *Senchus* is part king list and royal genealogy, part naval muster: the basic unit of military service was the ship, with two seven-benched ships due from every twenty houses. In the rugged landscape of Argyll, travel by water was easier than by land until well into the twentieth century, and so it is natural that the Dál Riata, with lands in both Ireland and Scotland, should see their navy as more important than their army. The military history of Dál Riata, by land and sea, is found in the entries of various Irish annals, such as the Annals of Tigernach; however, it is widely believed that many of these detailed Scottish entries initially came from an annal compiled at the monastery of Iona in Argyll.

Iona, the birthplace of the Columban tradition of Christianity, no doubt was responsible for first putting so much of Dalriadic history onto parchment. The monastery was founded by Columba (A.D. 521–597) of the northern Uí Néill, who left Ireland (perhaps expediently) in A.D. 563 and associated himself with the politically dominant Cenél nGabráin, consecrating Aedán mac Gabráin (r. A.D. 574–608) king of the Dál Riata at Iona. After Columba, Iona's most famous abbot was Adomnán (abbot A.D. 679–704), who wrote the *Life of St. Columba* about a century after the saint's death.

Iona was a center not only of learning but also of art, with a wide network of international connections that fostered the development of what is known as Insular, or Hiberno-Saxon, art. Although it is commonly called "Celtic," this interlace-rich style is actually a fusion of artistic elements from Celtic, Germanic, and Mediterranean sources. The relative importance of the different elements and the date and location where this hybrid style first appeared are hotly debated, but numerous scholars believe that the Book of Durrow and the Book of Kells, important early Insular manuscripts, may have been produced at Iona during the seventh and eighth centuries A.D. The importance of the Dál Riata in the development of Insular art is supported further by the large number of seventh-century brooch molds and other craft-working materials excavated at the site of Dunadd, the capital of Dalriadic Argyll. In the early medieval period the royalty and nobility of different kingdoms interacted not only in the battles recorded in the annals but also through marriage and other forms of alliance. For instance, Oswald (king of Anglian Northumbria, r. A.D. 634–642) was in exile in Dál Riata earlier in the seventh century and became a Christian while there, and it is from precisely such cross-cultural contacts that the Insular style may have been born.

Politically and militarily the Dál Riata were one of the major powers of North Britain, although there was a period in the mid–seventh century when they may have been under Northumbrian overlordship. Their relations with the Picts, their neighbors to the east, are highly debatable, particularly during the late eighth century and early ninth century:

some scholars believe that the Picts were the overlords of the Dál Riata, whereas others think that a Dalriadic dynasty ruled the Picts. This is the period when the Dál Riata were coming under attack from the sea: the first recorded Viking raid in Scotland hit Iona in A.D. 794. As the Norse gained control of the island fringe of Argyll and the Pictish north, the Dál Riata and Picts amalgamated into a single kingdom, whose first recognized king was Cinead mac Ailpín (more familiarly known as Kenneth mac Alpin, r. A.D. 843–858) of the Dál Riata. Although it is unclear whether this was the result of conquest or assimilation, by the mid-tenth century texts spoke of the destruction of the Picts, and the name of the kingdom itself, Alba, was Gaelic.

See also **Dark Age/Early Medieval Scotland** (*vol. 2, part 7*).

BIBLIOGRAPHY

Bannerman, John. *Studies in the History of Dalriada.* Edinburgh: Scottish Academic Press, 1974.

Campbell, Ewan. *Saints and Sea-kings: The First Kingdom of the Scots.* Edinburgh: Canongate Books–Historic Scotland, 1999.

Foster, Sally M. *Picts, Gaels, and Scots: Early Historic Scotland.* London: B. T. Batsford–Historic Scotland, 1996.

Lane, Alan, and Ewan Campbell. *Dunadd: An Early Dalriadic Capital.* Oxford: Oxbow Books, 2000.

ELIZABETH A. RAGAN

GOTHS BETWEEN THE BALTIC AND BLACK SEAS

In the middle of the sixth century A.D. the monk Jordanes recorded in his *Getica* the detailed history of the Goths. The story describes their crossing the Baltic Sea under the lead of King Berig, a period of time spent on its southern coast, and their later departure (during King Filimer's reign) to the Black Sea, where the Gothic kingdoms subsequently were destroyed by the Huns c. A.D. 375. The Roman historian Tacitus (in *Germania*) confirmed the presence of the Goths in the north, and the astronomer and geographer Ptolemy (in *Geographica*) located them by the lower Vistula River in the late first and the second centuries A.D. Archaeologists supported

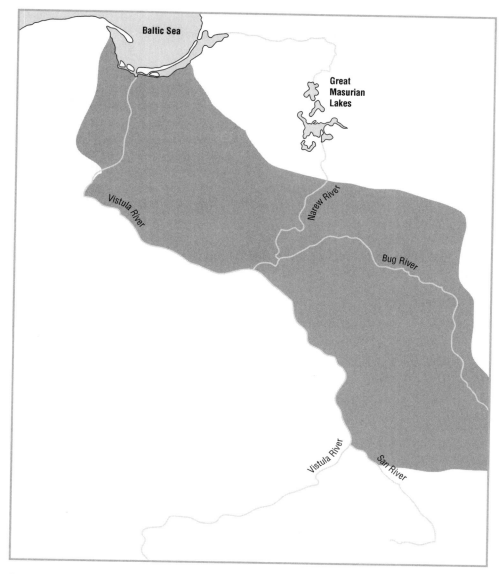

Extent of the Wielbark culture (shaded region) during the third century A.D. and second half of the fourth century A.D.

these written accounts by ascribing to the early Goths the so-called Wielbark culture in Poland (earlier known as the Gotho-Gepidic culture), with its specific cemeteries and characteristic artifacts. The Cherniakhov culture, identified between the Danube and Dnieper Rivers, came to represent later Gothic settlement.

This clear picture has come into question thanks to critical analyses of the historical evidence and precise chronological dating of archaeological finds. Historians have questioned the reliability of Jordanes and concluded that the alleged Scandina-

vian origin of the Goths probably was just a literary motif—a topos introduced in the tribal tradition to give people a feeling of ancient heroic unity. Moreover, an earlier chronology of typical "Gothic" finds in northern Poland, rather than in Sweden, put in doubt the sudden arrival of the Goths in the middle of the first century A.D. Thus, there are no historical or archaeological data to sustain the Scandinavian origin of the Goths as sudden mass invaders of the lower Vistula area.

It should be accepted, then, that Gothic ethnogenesis took place not in Scandinavia but south of the Baltic in the context of the advantageous circumstances of trade contacts with the Roman Empire. Control over the lucrative amber export was both a source of income and a reason for fierce competition among local elite groups, and symbolic expression of group identity played an important role in the formation of the Gothic sense of identity. It was a transformation of local populations of the older Oksywie culture into a new entity that became archaeologically visible as the Wielbark culture around the middle of the first century A.D. Various elements, including Roman traditions, were used to form a specific material culture distinctively different from traditions that prevailed in the Germanic Barbaricum: rich female adornments and handmade pottery and characteristic burial rituals (stelae, pavements and rings of stones—mostly in the early Roman period, the coexistence of cremation and inhumation burials, and poor male graves with no weapons or iron).

Jordanes's description suggests that the early Goths did not differ from other "barbarian" peoples. Like, for example, Langobards, Herulians, or Vandals, they were an opportunistic agglomeration unified by the successes of their military leaders, who legitimized their domination by creating myths of the heroic common past. Some archaeologists also suggest a polyethnic composition of the Wielbark culture. Migration of a political-military center did not mean migration of all inhabitants of a territory controlled by a chief-king. Archaeology does not support Jordanes's report of the well-organized resettlement of the Baltic Goths to the Black Sea in the first half of the third century A.D. It is thought that it was instead a gradual infiltration that began in the late second century A.D., while a substantial part of the population stayed in the north.

After some time there emerged a new elite that also decided to migrate to the south in search of better opportunities. They are identified by Jordanes as the Gepids, which meant "Late Comers." Researchers cannot discern any "Gothic" or "Gepidic" finds in Poland, which means that at the level of the material culture, symbolism, these two ethnic groups did not yet differ there. Thus, the ethnicity of the Gepids must have formed as a result of the decision taken by the second generation of Wielbark leaders to resettle in the late third century and found their new homeland around the Black

Sea. That dramatic decision was taken during a deterioration of the climate in Europe and the economic crisis of the Roman Empire during the period A.D. 235–284. Elites that called themselves "Goths" and "Gepids" decided to leave their Baltic homeland in search of better circumstances to sustain their power status. The warlike mobilization of the migrating population had the effect of uniting people around their leaders, who took responsibility for the prosperity of their followers. Success in subordinating fertile lands lying close to the rich Roman markets reinforced these leaders' power and led to the formation of ruling dynasties.

The region of the lower Vistula still was not emptied, however; indeed, some of the Wielbark cemeteries were used until the fourth century or even into the early fifth century A.D. Continuity has been established by the technological tradition in pottery making that may be traced from the Wielbark culture to the West Baltic culture that expanded toward the lower Vistula at the end of the fifth century. Some studies even suggest that elements of the Wielbark tradition survived until the sixth century.

Thus, the alleged quick resettlement of the Baltic Goths toward the Black Sea as a result of an organized migration led by King Filimer in A.D. 150 must be considered a myth. Instead, archaeologists suggest a slow southern expansion of cultural patterns promoted by Wielbark-Gothic elites. Contacts between the Baltic and Black Sea zones never broke down, however, which resulted in the formation of a huge area inhabited by populations with cultural similarities—biritual cemeteries, male graves with no weapons, and female jewelry.

It seems that the later history of the Goths, who escaped to the west pushed by invading Huns, should be changed or at least supplemented. German archaeologist Eduard Šturms already had suggested in 1950 that some of the Black Sea Goths returned to the north to join those "Goths" who had never left the Baltic zone. There are no written sources to support this claim, but inflow of Byzantine golden coins (dated to A.D. 455–518) to the region of the lower Vistula may indicate such a remigration in the circumstance of the sudden disintegration of the Hun "empire" after A.D. 455.

Thus, modern archaeological knowledge undermines the long-held traditional view of the

Goths as coming from Scandinavia, an already organized "people," to subordinate the region of the lower Vistula, only to migrate later toward the Black Sea and then to the west. Instead, one can envisage a story of a long development and gradual changes with no clear beginning and no end, a story that should not be equated with the heroic history of Gothic kings as described by ancient authors.

See also **Ostrogoths** (*vol. 2, part 7*); **Visigoths** (*vol. 2, part 7*); **Germany and the Low Countries** (*vol. 2, part 7*).

BIBLIOGRAPHY

Bierbrauer, Volker. "Goten. II. Archäologisches." In *Reallexikon der Germanischen Altertumskunde* 12: 407–427. Berlin: Walter de Gruyter, 1998.

———. "Archäologie und Geschichte der Goten vom 1–7 Jahrhundert. Versuch einer Bilanz." *Fruhmittelalterichen Studien* 28 (1994): 51–171.

Godłowski, Kazimierz. *The Chronology of the Late Roman and Early Migration Periods in Central Europe.* Kraków, Poland: Uniwersytet Jagielloński, 1970.

Heather, Peter. *The Goths.* Oxford: Blackwell, 1996.

Kmieciński, Jerzy. "Problem of the So-called Gotho-Gepiden Culture in the Light of Recent Research." *Archaeologia Polona* 4 (1962): 270–285.

Kokowski, Andrzej. *Grupa masłomęcka: Z badań przemiany kultury Gotów w młodszym okresie rzymskim* [The Masłomęcz Group: From studies of changes in the culture of the Goths during the Early Roman Age]. Lublin, Poland: Uniwersytet Marii Curie–Skłodowskiej, 1995.

Okulicz-Kozaryn, Jerzy. "Próba identyfikacji archeologicznej ludów bałtyjskich w połowie pierwszego tysiąclecia naszej ery" [Attempt at archaeological identification of Baltic peoples in the mid-first millennium A.D.]. *Barbaricum* 1 (1989): 64–100.

Wolfram, Herwig. "*Origo et religio:* Ethnic Traditions and Literature in Early Medieval Texts." *Early Medieval Europe* 3, no. 1 (1994): 19–38.

———. *Geschichte der Goten: Von den Anfängen bis zur Mitte des sechsten Jahrhunderts. Entwurf einer historischen Ethnographie.* Munich: C.H. Beck, 1979.

Wołągiewicz, Ryszard. *Ceramika kultury wielbarskiej między Bałtykiem a Morzem Czarnym* [Pottery of the Wielbark culture between the Baltic and Black Seas]. Szczecin, Poland: Muzeum Narodowe w Szczecinie, 1993.

———. "Kultura wielbarska—problemy interpretacji etnicznej" [The Wielbark culture—problems of ethnic identification]. *Problemy kultury wielbarskiej.* Słupsk: Wyższa Szkoła Pedagogiczna (1981): 79–106.

PRZEMYSŁAW URBAŃCZYK

HUNS

The Huns included Asiatic peoples speaking Mongolic or Turkic languages who dominated the Eurasian steppe from before 300 B.C. In the third century A.D. the Great Wall of China, 2,400 kilometers long, was built to fend off "western barbarians." The reverse impact of attacks set off a domino effect of westward migrations. Just after A.D. 370 the Huns crossed the Volga River and conquered the Alans, who had dominated the steppe north of the Caucasus Mountains for millennia. The Huns destroyed the Ostrogothic empire in the Dnieper–Don interfluve in A.D. 375 and defeated the Visigoths at the Dniester River the next year. In his work *Getica* the sixth-century historian Jordanes described a century of Hun subjugation, with Latin translations of passages from eyewitness accounts by the Byzantine Rhetor Priscus. Copies of this compilation biased medieval historiography. Records by a Roman officer, Ammianus Marcellinus, from the late fourth century A.D. form another collection of topics (beginning with the Greek historian Herodotus in the fifth century B.C.) that still may be found in the curricula of many European schools.

Roman infighting in A.D. 395 permitted the Huns to conquer the Roman Balkan provinces and then invade present-day southern Poland. In 406 fleeing German peoples broke into the western Roman Empire at the Rhine. The Huns exploited this situation by offering lucrative mercenary services to the Romans against the intruders. After attacking the Balkans, the Huns moved the seat of their empire into the southern Great Hungarian Plain in about 425. Several late Sarmatian settlements in this area show evidence of violent destruction. The Romans paid Hun mercenaries in money and war booty and provided them access to Roman areas ravaged by Germanic migrations, including Pannonia (A.D. 434). The Huns' expansion is marked by finds in more than 150 archaeological sites across the Carpathian Basin. The finds include large metal cauldrons in Hungary (fig. 1), which are also depicted in rock art in the Altai Mountains in Siberia and southern Russia and western Mongolia.

The empire of the Huns filled a geopolitical vacuum between the two Roman Empires and even acted as a power broker. Huns conducted ambitious

Fig. 1. Several such large "sacrificial" metal cauldrons have been recovered in the Carpathian Basin as well as in Hun territories across Eurasia. PHOTOGRAPH BY ANDRÁS DABASI. HUNGARIAN NATIONAL MUSEUM. REPRODUCED BY PERMISSION.

military campaigns in both directions. They raided Byzantine territories (A.D. 408, 441–443, and 447–449), occupying a series of cities and approaching Constantinople. In 442 the Huns extorted 6,000 pounds of "war compensation" plus 2,100 pounds of gold annually from Byzantium. This was the heyday of their empire. In 445 Attila, the new king of the Huns, attacked the western Roman Empire. He turned back before Ravenna, however, after an earthquake in 447 destroyed the Theodosian Wall in Constantinople (present-day Istanbul), built against the Huns in 408. Damage to the wall left the city vulnerable. The allied Gepid and Ostrogothic infantries slowed Attila's move on Constantinople, allowing months for the reconstruction of the wall. The siege was canceled, but the Huns conducted prolonged peace negotiations with Byzantium. It was then that Rhetor Priscus, who documented the last decades of the Hun empire (434–455), visited Attila's court in 449 with a Byzantine delegation.

Possibly under Byzantine inspiration, Attila moved west in 451, until the Romans and Visigoths and their allies stopped him at Orléans. His army united Gepids, Ostrogoths, Skirs, Alans, and Sarmatians, who faced fellow barbarians in the battle of Catalaunum. Fighting to a draw, the Huns retreated to the Great Hungarian Plain. Early in A.D. 452, Attila raided northern Italy, advancing beyond Mediolanum (modern-day Milan). In the summer, however, he was forced back by heat, epidemics, and the news that Byzantine forces had crossed the Danube River into Hun territory. Early the next year, amid preparations against Byzantine intrusion, Attila died unexpectedly. Subsequent infighting weakened the empire, and even his victorious son could not quell vassals, who defeated the Huns under Gepid leadership (A.D. 455). The Huns fled toward the Pontic steppe. Barbarians emerging after Hun rule finished off both Roman Empires, although written sources attribute much of this destruction to the Huns.

Although western chroniclers of the fifth through seventh centuries detailed Attila's plundering of Gaul and Italy (451–452), the exploits of the Huns in Byzantium remained underrepresented in the historical record. Medieval Catholic propaganda also profited from an unauthenticated encounter between Pope Leo I and Attila. The bishop of Rome became the savior confronting "*flagellum dei*" (scourge of God), Saint Augustine's term for Gothic King Alaric transposed to Attila in medieval Italy. Attila's popular descriptive, "the Dog-Headed," is a reminder of artificial skull deformation, a custom evidenced in fifth-century burials in the Hun confederacy. Attila's life spans nearly a hundred and twenty-four years in documents, of which he spent forty-four as king. In reality, he ruled for eight years before dying at about the age of forty-five.

In German tradition Attila's image varied between bloodthirsty despot and generous monarch. Christian Hungarians started considering Hun ancestry when the *Nibelungenlied*, a High German epic, was written in about 1200. Although the Turkic name Onugarian had been used haphazardly in western sources to denote Magyars (Ungar, Hungar, and Vengr) and other warlike equestrian barbarians, it was not linked specifically with Huns (Hsiung-nu) until the Middle Ages. In about 1283

Simon Kézai, "a loyal priest," crafted an influential legend comparable to the *Niebelungenlied* with a heavy Hungarian emphasis. It was dedicated to King László IV of eastern Cumanian extraction, who was involved in a power struggle with his noblemen and the church. An apocryphal relation to Attila possibly attained paradigmatic significance when steppic tradition had to be reconciled with Christianity.

Despite differences in ethnohistory, language, and physical makeup, the images of Huns and conquering Hungarians hopelessly converged. Coincidentally, both Huns and Magyars launched ruthless raids on their neighbors and beyond from the Carpathian Basin, but with a five-hundred-year time gap between them (Huns in 425–452 and Hungarians in 899–955). Their renowned light cavalry tactics also were similar. By the sixteenth century the Hungarian nobility were considered the glorious descendants of Huns who had *re*-conquered Attila's empire. In the nineteenth century the theory of Hun ancestry spread without social content in the public education system in Hungary, and the myth has become "historical knowledge," periodically resuscitated even today.

In contrast to this passionate historical interest, the Huns have been studied archaeologically in Hungary only since 1932. The three tumultuous decades of their empire left a rich but scattered archaeological heritage in Hungary. (Even in central Asia only a very few Hun finds predate the fourth century A.D.) Stylistically, Alans and Germanic tribes shared many predominantly "Hun" elements in their attire. "Cicada" brooches represent one of the characteristic artifact types. The archaeological traces of the Huns include not only grave goods and hoards but also destruction layers at Antique settlements. Crude architectural structures over such strata often are linked to Hun occupation.

See also **Animal Husbandry** (*vol. 2, part 7*); **Hungary** (*vol. 2, part 7*).

BIBLIOGRAPHY

Bóna, István, *A hunok és nagykirályaik* [The Huns and their great kings]. Budapest, Hungary: Corvina, 1993.

Daim, Falko, ed. *Reitervölker aus dem Osten: Hunnen+Awaren.* Schloss Halbturn, Austria: Burgenländische Landesausstellung, 1996.

Kovács, Tibor, and Éva Garam, eds. *A Magyar Nemzeti Múzeum régészeti kiállításának vezetője (Kr. e.* 400,000–Kr. u. 804) [Guide to the archaeological exhibit of the Hungarian National Museum]. Budapest, Hungary: Magyar Nemzeti Múzeum, 2002.

Lengyel, A., and G. T. B. Radan, eds. *The Archaeology of Roman Pannonia.* Lexington: University Press of Kentucky, and Budapest, Hungary: Akadémiai Kiadó, 1980.

LÁSZLÓ BARTOSIEWICZ

LANGOBARDS

The Langobards, "Long-beards," also known in modern literature as Lombards or Longobards, were not among the many large tribal and confederate groupings who assailed the Roman Empire in its last centuries in the West. Although Langobards are recorded by the Roman historian Tacitus in his first-century ethnographic survey, *Germania* (chap. 40), and noted as "famous because they are so few," later Roman sources pass minimal comment on them, as the Langobards did not force the Rhine or Danube as the Alemanni or Goths achieved in the third and fourth centuries A.D. Although much is written now on ethnogenesis (the creation and formulation of new powers such as the Franks) in these crucial centuries, the Langobards stand out for their antiquity and resilience: Indeed, Tacitus describes how they were a tribe "hemmed in . . . by many mighty peoples, finding safety not in submission but in facing the risks of battle"—this helping them to persist as a name into the Early Middle Ages unlike other tribes listed by Tacitus, as, for example, the Reudingi and Eudoses. Archaeologically, the Langobardic presence in the early Roman imperial period is somewhat uncertain, although urnfields (cremation cemeteries) along the lower Elbe and in Lower Saxony, featuring weaponry as well as Roman imports, are attributed to the tribe. It is disputed how far the archaeological data inform on territory and ethnicity, but indications of change and demographic loss are suggested for the third century. Later textual sources argue for a southeastwardly migration of the Langobards toward Bohemia and thence the Middle Danube. It is doubtful that this movement can be easily tracked through a distinctive cultural residue, such as burial goods, yet any "migration" will have involved much more than the movement and

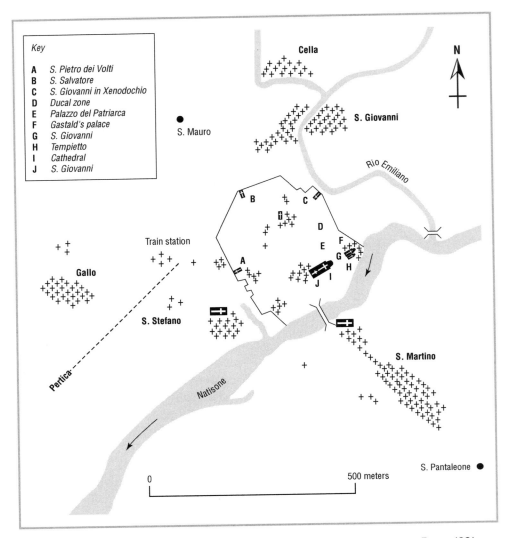

Fig. 1. Site plan showing Cividale and the distribution of cemeteries. ADAPTED FROM BROZZI 1981.

carrying of a name: ancestral bonds and badges of identity and belonging to the Langobardic name should have been preserved through language, titles, artifacts, and ritual, even if these also evolved with time.

Although knowledge of the earliest phases of Langobardic development and history-making remains somewhat insecure, a sixth-century prominence is well attested through both text and archaeology. A contemporary source, the Greek historian Procopius, records alliances forged in the 530s–550s A.D. between the Byzantine emperor Justinian and the Langobards in the context of the Byzantine-Gothic War in Italy (A.D. 534–555). The Langobards in the second quarter of the sixth century occupied the northern portions of former Roman

Pannonia (western Hungary); southern Pannonia was largely ceded, along with much tribute, by Justinian to secure the landward passage of imperial troops to Italy. Langobardic soldiers also fought in the Byzantine armies in Italy, and various chiefs became imperial officers, serving in the Balkans and even in Persia. Procopius records the Langobards as Christian and Catholic allies in the 540s, although Arianism and paganism remain evident into the seventh century.

The late-eighth-century Langobardic historian and poet Paulus Diaconus, writing chiefly for the court of Charlemagne, provides much of the documentation for the subsequent Langobardic occupation of large parts of Italy in opposition to the Byzantines. The Byzantines, who had only defeated the Ostrogoths in the peninsula after a disastrously long and drawn-out conflict, appear little able to counter the Langobardic migration of A.D. 568, despite calling on Frankish support and using gold to buy off Langobardic dukes. Numbers involved in the migration are disputed, but a military component (that is, adult males) is estimated at about forty thousand. By c. A.D. 610 the Langobards held the bulk of northern Italy except for the coastal zones of Venetia and Liguria, and they had limited the imperial forces to a central Italian land corridor linking Rome and Ravenna; the king was based first in Verona, then Milan, and finally settled in Pavia. Territories were divided up chiefly among dukes based in towns and fortresses. Further territorial gains were made in the mid-seventh and mid-eighth centuries when the Byzantine capital Ravenna was occupied. With the ejection of Byzantine rule in central and northern Italy, papal Rome successfully appealed to the Carolingian Frankish court, culminating in Charlemagne's conquest of the *regnum Langobardorum* in A.D. 774. Powerful Langobardic principalities nonetheless endured in central southern Italy, notably focused on Benevento.

Ninth-century Benevento marked a significant Langobardic cultural flourish: in addition to the Langobard's major palace and religious foundations in the city itself, Langobardic princes and elites contributed strongly to monastic seats, notably San Vincenzo al Volturno, which had been founded c. A.D. 703 by three Langobardic brothers and monks. The ninth century witnessed substantial remodeling and aggrandizement of the abbey through Langobardic and Frankish patronage. In particular, excavations have revealed the extensive use of elaborate wall paintings; San Vincenzo also featured a major scriptorium producing high-quality manuscripts, some still extant. In northern and central Italy, eighth-century Langobardic churches and monasteries are attested by text, art, architecture, and archaeology, such as in the royal or ducal cities of Pavia and Verona. Exquisitely ornamented monasteries such as the Tempietto at Cividale and San Salvatore at Brescia survive to reveal not just religious fervor by the Langobardic elites but also a major cultural renaissance, prominent before direct Carolingian influence.

Although walled towns are attested as seats of power (for kings, dukes, lieutenants, and counts), related settlement archaeology remains extremely limited: houses are known in Brescia and Verona, for example, and traces of palaces are claimed for Brescia, Cividale, and Spoleto, but in terms of rural sites, specific Langobardic-period housing is barely known (with the picture even more scarce for Langobardic Pannonia). This deficiency, however, extends also to non-Langobardic sites, including Rome and Ravenna, where sixth-to-eighth-century secular structures remain to be fully identified archaeologically. Excavations at Brescia in particular have shown how towns were severely depleted c. A.D. 600, with open spaces, timber and rubble buildings, robbed classical structures, and burials intruding into the urban confines. Nonetheless, the identification of towns as seats of authority suggests continuity of population, with the bulk of these inhabitants being Italian/Roman and non-Langobardic.

This continuity of population has implications for the chief source of archaeological information for the sixth and seventh centuries, namely burials. Major excavated necropolises include Nocera Umbra and Castel Trosino in central and eastern Italy and Testona (near Turin) and Cividale in the north; a key aristocratic group lies at Trezzo sull'Adda near Milan. Although weapon burials are prominent (and with elite presenting quality "parade" items—gilded or silvered spurs, decorative shields—into the mid-seventh century), attention has increasingly been given to other artifacts, notably dress fittings, can help identify patterns of integration or acculturation between Langobards and natives. The discovery of workshops in Rome that were the source of manufacture for items used in Langobardic territories particularly demonstrates exchange networks in the seventh-century peninsula. These data complement texts such as the Langobardic law codes to provide an ever fuller and more complex image of Langobardic and Langobard-period society and culture.

See also **Coinage of the Early Middle Ages** (*vol. 2, part 7*); **Hungary** (*vol. 2, part 7*).

BIBLIOGRAPHY

Bona, Istvan. *The Dawn of the Dark Ages. The Gepids and the Lombards in the Carpathian Basin.* Budapest: Corvina Press, 1976.

Brogiolo, Gian Pietro. *Brescia altomedievale: Urbanistica ed edilizia dal IV al IX secolo.* Mantua, Italy: Padus, 1993.

(Synthesis of the major excavations and archive data for late antique and early medieval [Langobardic] Brescia.)

Brogiolo, Gian Pietro, Nancy Gauthier, and Neil Christie, eds. *Towns and Their Territories: Between Late Antiquity and the Early Middle Ages.* Transformation of the Roman World, vol. 9. Leiden: Brill, 2000. (Includes articles on the Lombards, their settlement and defense in Pannonia and Italy, and their eighth-century artistic culture.)

Brogiolo, Gian Pietro, and Sauro Gelichi. *Nuove ricerche sui castelli altomedievali in Italia settentrionale.* Florence: All'Insegna del Giglio, 1996. (Detailed discussion of sequences of fortifications, identifying Langobardic contribution.)

Brozzi, Mario. *Il ducato longobardo del Friuli.* Udine: Grafiche Fulvio, 1981. (Useful survey of sources and archaeology for one north Italian region.)

Christie, Neil. *The Lombards: The Ancient Longobards.* Oxford: Blackwell, 1995.

Harrison, Dick. *The Early State and the Towns: Forms of Integration in Lombard Italy, A.D. 568–774.* Lund, Sweden: Lund University Press, 1993.

Hodges, Richard. *Light in the Dark Ages: The Rise and Fall of San Vincenzo al Volturno.* London: Duckworth, 1997.

McKitterick, Rosamond, ed. *The New Cambridge Medieval History.* Vol. 2, *c. 700–c. 900.* Cambridge, U.K.: Cambridge University Press, 1995. (Contains key summary historical papers on eighth- and ninth-century Langobardic and Carolingian Italian society, government, and religion.)

Paroli, Lidia, ed. *La necropoli altomedievale di Castel Trosino: Bizantini e Longobardi nelle Marche.* Cinisello Balsamo, Italy: Silvana, 1995. (A series of papers with full illustrative support linked to reevaluating the finds and population as well as wider context of the well-known Langobardic cemetery of Castel Trosino.)

Roffia, Elisabetta, ed. *La necropoli longobarda di Trezzo sull'Adda.,* Ricerche di archeologia altomedievale e medievale 12/13. Florence, Italy: All'Insegna del Giglio, 1986.

Wickham, Chris. *Early Medieval Italy: Central Power and Local Society, 400–1000.* London: Macmillan, 1981.

NEIL CHRISTIE

MEROVINGIAN FRANKS

The Franks were one of the Germanic peoples who conquered parts of the Roman Empire during the Migration period (fifth century A.D.) and were united into a powerful kingdom covering most of Gaul under King Clovis (A.D. 481/82–511). "Merovingian" is the name of the dynasty he founded (taken from the name of his perhaps legendary ancestor Merovech), which reigned until A.D. 751 and traditionally has been regarded as the first dynasty of the kings of France. (The name France derives from this people.) Who were the Franks, and where did they come from?

The sixth-century bishop Gregory of Tours, the principal narrative source, thought they came from Pannonia (modern-day Hungary and parts of the former Yugoslavia). In the next century a theory emerged that they were descended from the Trojans. The following centuries saw many extravagant developments of these myths of national origin (including notions that the Franks came from Phrygia or from Scandinavia). In 1714 a scholar named Fréret advanced what Patrick Périn has called the "first really scientific theory" of their origin, that they were born of a league of Germanic peoples whose ancestors had fought Julius Caesar. The development of Merovingian archaeology coupled with criticism of the written sources since his day has made this the consensus view.

Julius Caesar, writing in the 50s B.C., and Roman writers of the first century A.D., such as Pliny and Tacitus, describe a number of Germanic peoples and discuss their customs; they make no reference to the Franks. The Franks seem to have emerged as a coalition of smaller peoples mentioned by these authors, such as the Chamavi, the Chattuari, and the Bructeri, living along the Lower Rhine and galvanized to join forces to attack the third-century Roman Empire, weakened by civil war. The new name, which comes from a root meaning "the bold," is cited in connection with a barbarian force defeated near Mainz by the future emperor Aurelian (r. A.D. 270–275), and Franks were exhibited in his triumph. Franks also are mentioned as dangerous pirates, whose depredations, like those of the Saxons named with them, led to the creation of a new system of military defenses along the English Channel. Still others appear at this early date as Roman allies, among them, King Gennobaudes, who concluded a pact (*foedus*) with Rome in A.D. 287–288. By the time the emperors Diocletian (r. A.D. 284–305) and Constantine I (r. A.D.

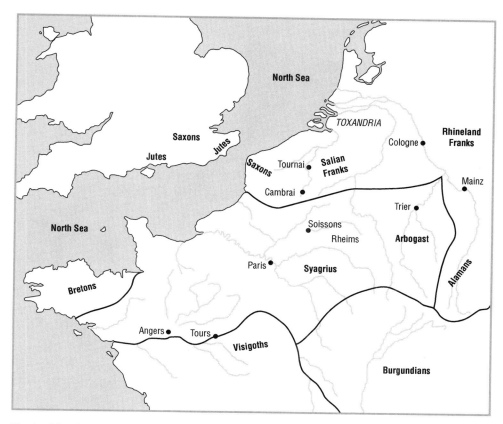

The traditional view of Syagrius's kingdom, stretching across most of northern Gaul. ADAPTED FROM JAMES 1988.

306–337) had restored the frontiers and the empire as a highly centralized and militarized state, the Franks were referred to often in their lower Rhenan homeland, divided into groups of varied and shifting allegiances.

Archaeologists have separated the early pre-Migration Germans into three geographic groupings, primarily on the basis of ceramic types: (1) a northern one, around the northern seacoasts; (2) an eastern one, extending from the Elbe into Bohemia; and (3) a western one, the "Rhine-Weser group." This seems to accord with the traditional division by linguists of northern, eastern, and western dialects of Old Germanic, although the evidence is based on post-Migration sources. The material culture does not itself suggest great differences in lifestyle among these groups. They tended to live in small villages with an economy that combined cereal agriculture with animal husbandry (as Tacitus noted, wealth was measured in cows).

A typical form of Germanic building to the north, well known from such excavations as Bielefeld-Sieker in Westphalia, was a long, rectangular, timber-frame, thatched-roof building shared by people and cattle. Various other timber-post constructions, including rectangular two-room houses and small buildings with dug-out areas underneath (causing them to be misleadingly labeled "sunken huts"), which were used as workshops and for storage, also are well documented. Much of the pottery was handmade; it was often plain but might be decorated with incised linear ornament or crude stamps. Women did the weaving, spinning, and textile production and, along with the slaves, were responsible for the agricultural work, according to Tacitus. Examples of textiles have been found on the "bog bodies," bodies thrown into the swamps or marshes so soft tissue, clothing, and so on have been preserved in this anaerobic environment. The men were responsible for ironworking, a craft of great prestige and technical complexity, largely car-

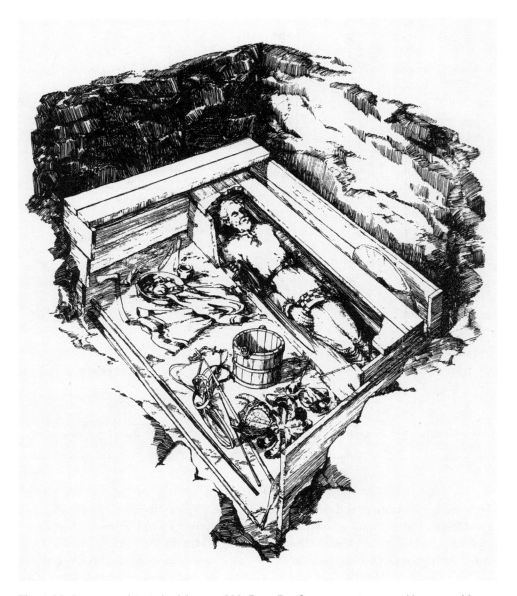

Fig. 1. Morken: a magistrate burial c. A.D. 600. From *Das Grab eines fränkischen Herren aus Morken im Rheinland* (1959). Reproduced by permission of Bohlau Verlag GmbH & Cie.

ried out by local smiths working with small quantities of ore in small ovens. Their supreme product, a sword with a hard cutting edge and a core of softer steel for greater flexibility, proved its worth in battle with the Romans.

Tacitus emphasizes the warrior values of early Germanic society, which was patriarchal in character, based on clan groupings (called *Sippe*), and socially divided into nobles, free warriors, and slaves. His evocation of tribal assemblies, where the free warriors clashed their weapons to voice assent to decisions, misled nineteenth-century scholars eager to

find in them the roots of democratic institutions. Research emphasizes the emergence of war kingship and war bands as a dynamizing force at the time when the Franci and other new, aggressive confederations (Alemani) appear in the written sources. As Patrick Geary points out, the pre-Migration Germanic tribes were unstable groupings whose sense of unity was forged by myths of common ancestry and hence of pure blood. The *thiudans,* a man of noble lineage linked to divine ancestors, was a kind of religious king and a guarantor of law, social order, fertility, and peace. The figure Tacitus called a *dux* (general), chosen to lead the tribe in war and chief of his own band of eager young warriors (a *comitatus*), had become by the third century the forger of a new kind of kingship (suggested by the Celtic loanword *reiks*) and a new kind of cultural identity.

The archaeological signatures of this new identity are the warrior graves and, in particular, what have been called "chieftains' graves." The usual form of burial in the Rhine-Weser culture, and among the Germanic groups in general, had been of cremated remains, often placed in an urn, with few or no grave goods. In the late third century inhumation burials with a rich variety of grave goods begin to appear. In one of the earliest, from Leuna near the Saale River, a man was laid in a carefully constructed wooden chamber with a collection of fine Roman pottery, glassware and metalware, and three silver arrowheads. He also wore spurs; in a nearby pit was found the skull and lower-leg bones of a horse.

In the following century, graves deriving from and often embellishing upon this new funerary model spread through the Germanic regions within and without the Roman frontier along the Rhine, with many of them found in the Frankish territories. Its basic elements are inhumation; burial wearing everyday dress, as indicated by such items as belt buckles; and a funerary deposit consisting of pottery and perhaps glassware and metalware of Roman manufacture, distinctive brooches, and sometimes other personal ornaments in female graves and weapons in many male graves. These weapons might consist of a single spear or axe, but the richest graves might include a panoply (a group of weapons), including a sword and a shield. In about A.D. 350 such graves appear in significant numbers at Roman military sites, such as Krefeld-Gellep and Rhenen on the Rhine frontier, but they also turn up in a variety of funerary contexts across northern Gaul, far from places of Germanic settlement.

Hörst-Wolfgang Böhme, Périn, and other researchers have argued that that these new funerary customs reflect the militarization of the late Roman Empire, a process that drew heavily upon barbarian, and particularly German, manpower. Sometimes this "conscription" was done by force: Constantine settled defeated Frankish groups as a kind of half-free militia (*laeti*) on lands they could farm in return for hereditary military service. Other Franks freely enlisted; Frankish units are known in the Notitia Dignitatum, a muster roll of Roman forces from c. A.D. 400. By that time some Franks, such as Silvanus and Arbogast, held the highest commands: they have been called "imperial Germans." This military service surely encouraged a sense of complex identity: a funerary inscription in Pannonia proudly identifies its author as both a Frank and Roman soldier.

Valor in war always had been the supreme German virtue; the late Roman world provided many more opportunities to make it the route to high status and success. The grave of a military leader buried outside the town of Vermand, in northern Gaul, with his helmet, his display of weapons, and his fine tableware, vividly reflects the material success of one such soldier. It also hints at a double allegiance: to the Roman world he served and to the new military elite, Germanic by the choice of this funerary tradition, to which he belonged. Small cemeteries of barbarian graves from the Namur region (Haillot) to the Somme (Vron) reflect the settling of these Germanic groups within the empire and their defending it.

The complicated events of the fifth century, which led to the breakup of the Roman Empire in the west, served to consolidate this new sense of Frankish identity. Unlike such barbarian peoples as the Huns, sweeping in from the Asian steppes, or the Visigoths, fleeing and fighting and plundering over forty years from the Danube to Italy to end in southwest Gaul in A.D. 418, the Franks had no vast migration to make. Already well established in their homeland, straddling the Lower Rhine frontier and divided into competing groups, their leaders might have expanded their power opportunistically as circumstances permitted or might have had it fall into their hands. The small garrison occupying the fort of Vireux-Moulin, overlooking the Meuse, between about A.D. 370 and 450 is a symbol of this relative stability in a changing world. It is significant that they maintained the furnished burial traditions when these customs already had disappeared in the more Romanized regions south and west.

In 451 some Frankish forces helped Aetius halt the Hunnic invasion of Gaul; it is at about this time that the lineage of Childeric became established in the fortified town of Tournai (Belgium). After his death, his son Clovis defeated the last Roman commander in northern Gaul (A.D. 486), thus launching a career of successful aggression that would leave him, at his death in 511, master of three-fourths of Gaul, from the Pyrenees to the Rhine. Having wiped out the competing Frankish *reiks* lineages, he had become the founder of the Merovingian dynasty. Clovis took two other highly significant steps in the shaping of the Frankish identity. He converted to the Catholic faith, thus opening the way to an enduring alliance between the king and the Gallic church. He also made his capital in Paris, deep in the heart of Romanized Gaul and far from the original Frankish homelands.

Perhaps the most striking archaeological reflection of the reign of Clovis is the revival of the weapons- and ornament-furnished burial traditions and their spread into new regions. Only in the core Frankish regions between the Somme and Rhine did weapons burial continue in the fifth century, an indication that among the Franks it had taken hold as a marker of cultural identity. After the middle of the fifth century, it derived new life from "Danubian influences," such as the colorful gold-and-garnet jewelry style that appears in Pouan and Airan in Gaul. Childeric's grave, whose discovery in 1653 marks the beginning of Merovingian archaeology, was a spectacular restatement of the elite furnished burial.

The many chieftains' graves of the "Flonheim-Gültlingen" type of the late fifth century and early sixth century reflect a greater standardization of the elite burial model. This is particularly notable in the case of the weapons panoply: a long sword, a kind of harpoon called an *angon*, one or more lances, arrows, a shield, a curved throwing axe, and a short one-edged stabbing sword called a *scramasax*. The axe was given the name *francisca* and was described by the mid-sixth century Byzantine writer Agathias as a typical Frankish weapon. Bright polychrome gold cloisonné ornament, which might decorate sword hilts or scabbards, belt buckles or brooches, also are typical of this elite model. Such graves appear as the focal point of new burial groups in established cemeteries, such as Krefeld-Gellep and Rhenen along the Lower Rhine, or as the starting point of new cemeteries, such as Charleville-Mézières or Lavoye, which reflect expanding Merovingian power under Clovis and his sons.

The originality of this "Frankish funerary facies" is underlined by its spread throughout the sixth century. Early archaeologists, among them Édouard Salin, thought that funerary customs were inherited from the distant tribal past and assumed that the other barbarian peoples in Gaul, the Burgundians and the Visigoths, would have their own distinct rites and artifacts. Neither of these groups, however, developed an archaeologically recognizable set of funerary customs, at least before they had been absorbed into the Merovingian kingdom. Cemeteries such as Herpes and Biron in Aquitaine or Brèves and Charnay in Burgundy now are identified either with Frankish groups who had come to hold territory in the conquered areas or with local groups eager to adopt the customs of the victors.

The former case has been argued at Bâle-Bernerring, in Switzerland, where the leading figures were buried in elaborate funerary chambers under mounds, as it is now known that Childeric had been in Tournai. The latter interpretation has been proposed at Frénouville, in lower Normandy, a site that was excavated by the Centre de Recherches d'Archéologie Médiévale of the University of Caen in the 1960s and 1970s. There were distinct late Roman and Merovingian zones in this cemetery, marked by different grave orientations and funerary practices. Still a comprehensive anthropological analysis of the skeletal material, the most thorough and rigorous yet to be completed for any French site, indicates that it is the same population. This suggests that this sixth-century community in the remote Gallic northwest was adopting the vocabulary of new funerary custom to say, in a distorted echo of the Pannonian inscription cited earlier, we are Gallo-Romans and Merovingians, too.

The reign of Clovis also saw the rise of the so-called Salic Law, which, like the codes of the Burgundians and the Visigoths and the parallel codes of the latter groups for their Roman subjects, marks the crystallization of ethnic consciousness. Even after these areas, the Burgundian and Visigothic Kingdoms, roughly modern southeastern and southwestern France, were conquered by the Franks (Aquitaine in A.D. 507 and Burgundian kingdom [Burgondie] in A.D. 536) the principle of the "personality of law" was long maintained; indeed in the seventh century a new law code was promulgated for the Rhenish Franks around Cologne. Gregory of

Tours, writing in the A.D. 570s and 580s, reflects a world where ethnic distinctions, though sometimes mentioned, matter little compared with social striving, political allegiance, and of course, religion.

The conversion of the Frankish elites, at least in a perfunctory sense, advanced rapidly, although this was not understood by archaeologists such as Salin, who tended to interpret furnished burial as a "pagan" rite. The spectacular grave goods that accompanied a woman and a young boy, doubtless of royal rank, who were buried within a funerary chapel in front of Cologne cathedral c. A.D. 530/40 prove the contrary. This is not to deny that some rural magnates might have resisted the new religion for a time; it is plausible that the sixth-century cremation burial under a small tumulus at Hordain, near Douai, represents one such. As Michael Müller-Wille points out, however, the royal example, no doubt enhanced by the prestige of holy men and of ranking churchmen (the two need not coincide), of martyr graves and *ad sanctos* burial (next to or near a martyr or a saint-confessor) encouraged the emerging magnate class to shift to more Christian burial styles. Thus one finds numerous richly furnished elite burials in family chapels: one was built near the older tumulus at Hordain. The ornament might include clearly Christian motifs, such as the cross on the silver locket worn by a girl buried around A.D. 600 in a chapel in Arlon (Luxembourg).

By this time "Frank" referred to those subject to Frankish law, and the connotation of the term had shifted from "the bold" to "the free," that is, free of the tax obligations that the kings tried to impose on their "Roman" subjects. Even as writers, such as Pseudo-Fredegar in the seventh century, were developing myths of Frankish origins, real ethnic distinctions blurred: Roman names appeared in Frankish families and vice versa, and funerary custom was more likely to reflect social distinctions or regional identity or the new association of burial with piety. In practice, Franks had come to signify the elite and free families of the Merovingian kingdoms, particularly of Neustria and Austrasia.

See also **Merovingian France** (*vol. 2, part 7*); **Tomb of Childeric** (*vol. 2, part 7*).

BIBLIOGRAPHY

Böhme, Hörst-Wolfgang. *Germanische Grabfunde des 4. Bis 5. Jahrhunderts zwischen unterer Elbe und Loire.* 2 vols. Munich: Müncher Beiträge zur Vor- und Frühgeschichte, 1974.

Die Franken: Wegbereiter Europas. 2 vols. Mainz, Germany: Verlag Philipp von Zabern, 1996. (Catalog from the Reiss-Museum, Mannheim, of the largest exhibition of Frankish archaeology, with many fundamental articles by leading scholars.)

Geary, Patrick J. *Before France and Germany: The Creation and Transformation of the Merovingian World.* Oxford: Oxford University Press, 1988.

Gregory of Tours. *The History of the Franks.* Translated with an introduction by Lewis Thorpe. Harmondsworth, U.K.: Penguin Books, 1974. (The principal narrative source, written by a Gallo-Roman bishop of Tours during the late sixth century.)

Heinzelmann, Martin. *Gregory of Tours: History and Society in the Sixth Century.* Translated by Christopher Carroll. Cambridge, U.K.: Cambridge University Press, 2001. (Authoritative study of the principal historian of the Franks.)

James, Edward. *The Franks.* Oxford: Blackwell, 1988.

Müller-Wille, Michael. "Königtum und Adel im Spiegel der Grabkunde." In *Die Franken: Wegbereiter Europas.* Vol. 1, pp. 206–221. Mainz, Germany: Verlag Philipp von Zabern, 1996.

Musset, Lucien. *The Germanic Invasions: The Making of Europe, A.D. 400–600.* Translated by Edward James and Columba James. University Park: Pennsylvania State University Press, 1975. (A still-pertinent overview of the period, with an excellent bibliography to 1975.)

Périn, Patrick, and Laure-Charlotte Feffer. *Les Francs.* Vol. 1, *A la conquête de la Gaule.* Vol. 2, *A l'origine de la France.* Paris: Armand Colin, 1997. (Well-illustrated, accessible overview with archaeological emphasis.)

Reichmann, Christoph. "Frühe Franken in Germanien." In *Die Franken: Wegbereiter Europas.* Vol. 1, pp. 55–65. Mainz, Germany: Verlag Philipp von Zabern, 1996.

Riché, Pierre, and Patrick Périn. *Dictionnaire des Francs: Les temps Mérovingiens.* Paris: Bartillat, 1996.

Salin, Édouard. *La civilisation mérovingienne d'après les sépultures, les textes et le laboratoire.* 4 vols. Paris: Picard, 1950–1959. (Although dated and much criticized, this is still a fundamental work by the pioneer of twentieth-century Merovingian archaeology in France.)

Todd, Malcolm. *The Early Germans.* Oxford: Blackwell, 1992. (Archaeological background.)

Zöllner, Erich. *Geschichte der Franken bis zur Mittel des sechsten Jahrhunderts.* Munich: Beck, 1970.

BAILEY K. YOUNG

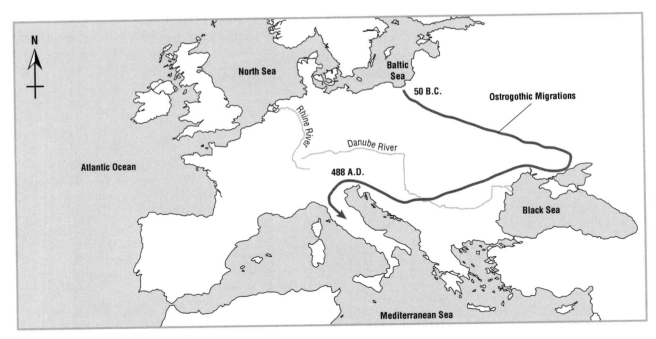

Extent of Ostrogothic migrations. DRAWN BY KAREN CARR.

OSTROGOTHS

The Ostrogoths, like the Visigoths, were an Indo-European group that first appears in the archaeological record in Poland in the first century B.C. From Poland the ancestors of the Ostrogoths seem to have migrated southeast rather than due south, as did the ancestors of the Visigoths, and this is why they are known as the Ostrogoths, or East Goths. They finally settled down to farm in the Ukraine, on the northern shores of the Black Sea. At that time they probably were not unified as a group and did not have a king.

In the course of the fourth century A.D., however, the Huns, leaving eastern Siberia, migrated in a group across northern Asia to the Ukraine, where they pushed the Ostrogoths out of their traditional homeland, forcing them to move to central Europe (modern-day Austria). Even after moving to central Europe, however, the Ostrogoths still suffered from Hunnic harassment, and soon they were taken over entirely by the Huns.

In A.D. 453 Attila, the king of the Huns, died, and his empire collapsed amid squabbling among his weaker sons. The Ostrogoths were able to take advantage of this disunity to break free of Hunnic control and reestablish their independence. According to tradition, they chose as their leaders three brothers, one of whom was Theudemir. By the mid-fifth century A.D., the Ostrogoths increasingly were involved with Roman politics. As a pledge for one of the Ostrogothic arrangements with the Romans, the Ostrogothic king Theudemir sent his own son, Theodoric (Dietrich in German), to live at the Roman court in Constantinople (modern-day Istanbul). Theodoric was eight years old at the time, and he therefore grew up culturally as Roman as he was Ostrogothic. When Theodoric was eighteen, in A.D. 475, his father died, and Theodoric returned home to rule his people.

In A.D. 476 the last of the Roman emperors in the west, Romulus Augustulus, was deposed by Odoacer the Hun, who declared himself king of Italy. The Roman emperor Zeno in Constantinople, to the east, objected to this usurpation and tried to put in his own candidate, Julius Nepos. Zeno, however, lacked the military manpower to send troops to assert his authority in Italy. In 488 he therefore invited the former hostage Theodoric, the young king of the Ostrogoths, to invade Italy at the head of his Ostrogothic army, on Zeno's behalf. Theodoric agreed, and his prompt invasion of Italy was entirely successful. Odoacer was killed, and Theodoric became the leader of Italy as well as the king of the Ostrogoths.

Theodoric was an able and ambitious man, and although he always maintained his allegiance to the Roman emperor in Constantinople, he did very well for himself in the west during his long reign. He married a sister of Clovis, king of the Franks. Theodoric sent one of his own daughters to be married to the Visigothic king Alaric II, and when Alaric was killed in the battle of Vouillé in A.D. 507, he established himself as regent for his young grandson Amalaric. In this way Theodoric was able to rule both Italy and Spain for much of his life, with varying degrees of influence over southern France as well.

Under the rule of Theodoric, Italy seems to have prospered as well. The archaeological evidence suggests that people were still farming and the city of Rome still functioning at this time, although Rome certainly was losing population. Italy also was part of a great Mediterranean world. Despite the takeover of North Africa by the Vandals in A.D. 429, African red slip pottery continued to be imported to Italy throughout the period of Ostrogothic rule.

When Theodoric died in A.D. 526, he left no sons. His grandson Amalaric (a cousin of the child Amalaric above) succeeded him, with Theodoric's daughter Amalasuntha acting as regent for the ten-year-old boy. Under Amalasuntha's guidance, Amalaric was educated in the Roman fashion and learned to read and write. Soon Amalasuntha's influence was shunted aside in favor of less Romanized advisers, and Amalaric was diverted to more military and traditional Ostrogothic pursuits, including heavy drinking. On the death of Amalaric in A.D. 534, Amalasuntha became queen in her own right. She took on her cousin Theodahad as her partner in power, but Theodahad soon had Amalasuntha imprisoned and then, in 535, murdered.

By this time, the Byzantine emperor Justinian I in Constantinople had noticed the weakness and instability of Ostrogothic rule now that Theodoric was dead, and he was preparing to invade. Justinian's army, under the able general Belisarius, conquered North Africa in 533 and then, in quick succession, Sicily and Italy in 536. When Belisarius landed at Naples, the Ostrogoths at first were defeated soundly. Justinian was suspicious of Belisarius' loyalty, however, and recalled him to Italy; the Ostrogoths seized the opportunity to revolt. The war that ensued spanned twenty years and devastated Italy. In the end the Byzantine army prevailed, and the last Ostrogothic king, Totila, was killed in battle in A.D. 552.

See also **Goths between the Baltic and Black Seas** (*vol. 2, part 7*); **Huns** (*vol. 2, part 7*); **Merovingian Franks** (*vol. 2, part 7*); **Visigoths** (*vol. 2, part 7*); **Poland** (*vol. 2, part 7*).

BIBLIOGRAPHY

Heather, Peter. *The Goths*. Oxford: Blackwell, 1996.

Moorhead, John. *Theoderic in Italy*. Oxford: Clarendon Press, 1992.

Wickham, Chris. *Early Medieval Italy: Central Power and Local Society, 400–1000*. London: Macmillan, 1981; rev. ed., Ann Arbor: University of Michigan Press, 1989.

Wolfram, Herwig. *History of the Goths*. Translated by Thomas J. Dunlap. Berkeley: University of California Press, 1988.

KAREN CARR

PICTS

A combination of enigmatic carved stones and a written language (ogham script) that long defied interpretation has ensured the mysterious aura of the Picts. They were first named "Picti" in a Roman panegyric written by Eumenius in A.D. 297, but in terms of their distinctive material culture, the evidence is clearest from the sixth to the ninth centuries. The twelfth-century source *Historia Norvegia* describes the Picts as pygmies who lived underground. The area of Pictish settlement is defined by the distribution of placenames including for example the element "pit" (as in Pitlochry, Pittenweem), as well as by the widespread distribution of the Picts' distinctive symbol stones. The Picts are most strongly associated with the eastern parts of Scotland, such as the regions of Fife and Angus in the south, as well as the northern areas of Scotland including the Sutherland and Caithness regions, and the island groups of Orkney and Shetland. The Roman term may well have been taken from the Picts' name for themselves, the Painted Ones, perhaps due to their distinctive tattoos, but the term is

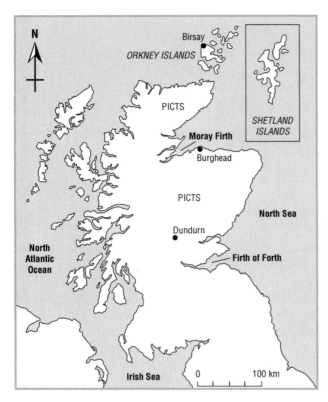

General extent of Pictland.

a general one, encompassing the confederacy of tribes in the north and east of Scotland (e.g., the Caledones and Vacomagii).

THE HOUSES

Writing in 1955, Frederick T. Wainwright described in *The Problem of the Picts,* the lack of evidence concerning settlements and graves that seemed to compound issues of place-names, mysterious symbol stones, and the simple—but seemingly impenetrable—incised line script called "ogham." In Wainwright's era, there were indeed more questions than answers about the Picts. The picture changed beyond recognition, however, with several excavations in the 1970s identifying not only distinctive dwellings but also unique burial sites. In the early 1970s, excavation of a multiphase site at Buckquoy, Birsay, in Orkney revealed the first identified Pictish dwellings, beginning as a simple three-cell stone building and being replaced at a subsequent phase of Pictish activity by more complex multicellular structures of a more anthropomorphic form (suggestive of a human form with a smaller head than body, or of a figure eight in which the upper circle is smaller than the lower). A few years later excavation added to this group a simple figure-eight structure. All these buildings were located on the mainland at Birsay in the northwest corner of mainland Orkney and opposite the major Pictish and Norse center of the Brough of Birsay. The Brough, a small tidal island, had been investigated from the 1930s onward and provided details of extensive metalworking activity in the Pictish period; it produced brooches comparable to those found in the largest and most significant Pictish silver hoard in Scotland—St. Ninian's Isle, Shetland, in 1958. One of the most famous icons of Pictish art was unearthed on the Brough of Birsay during excavations in the 1930s: a shattered grave marker with three warriors and Pictish symbols enigmatically presented on one face.

The identification of trefoil-shaped cellular dwellings (possessing three main cells or rooms off a central larger area with a hearth) as Pictish ensured a reexamination of earlier excavations; many Iron Age broch towers (defensive structures) that had extramural settlement of cellular form (cellular structures built around the tower that post-dated the building and occupation of the tower), such as the broch of Gurness in Orkney, later excavations at the Howe in Orkney, or recent excavations at Scatness in Shetland clearly demonstrate structural sequence and have greatly increased the Pictish corpus. Excavations at Pitcarmick in Perthshire also have been significant because they revealed a rectangular Pictish structure, indicating that not all Pictish buildings are celluar in form. Defended hilltops and promontories were occupied by the Picts as well, and sites such as Craig Phadraig near Inverness, Dundurn in Perthshire, and Burghead on the south side of the Moray Firth, all in mainland Scotland, indicate a need for protection from enemies, both Pictish as well as other neighbors.

THE BURIALS

Mainland Birsay in Orkney also has evidence of the distinctive burial tradition used by the Picts, which had not commonly been identified before work in the late 1970s at Birsay and Sandwick in Shetland in the north and at Garbeg and Lundin Links among others on the Scottish mainland. The body was laid in a simple cist, or stone box, often made of a number of flat stones, without grave goods.

The cist was covered over completely by sand or earth and then a cairn, or mound of stones, was built on top of that, delimited by a squared or rounded curb or sometimes a ditch. In rare instances there is evidence for the presence of a symbol stone on top of the grave (for example at Watenan in Caithness); perhaps more commonly the grave was topped by a cairn made of small white quartz pebbles. Old excavations failed to find the burial beneath the layer of sterile soil or sand beneath the cairn, as in the case of Ackergill in Caithness, excavated in the 1920s.

SYMBOL STONES, OGHAM SCRIPT, AND PORTABLE OBJECTS

The iconic emblem of the Picts is the symbol stone. There are three main types of stone monument: Class 1 is the earliest (dating to about A.D. 400–700) and identifed as minimally shaped with incised symbols of naturalistic form—for instance, animals or crescents and V-rods (two rods set at right angles to each other). Class 2 (dating to about A.D. 700–800s) combines careful shaping of the stone with elaborate and naturalistic elements including human figures and animals, as well as elaborate cross motifs related to the Christian missions to Pictland in c. A.D. 710 of Nechtan (in his attempts to change the Pictish church from Columban to Roman observance). Class 3 (dating to about A.D. 750 onward) is identified by Christian carvings including elaborate crosses and by a complete absence of symbols.

These stones have been studied extensively by many scholars, but there has been no resolution as to their specific function, although tribal boundary stones or naming stones are among the more plausible of suggestions. However, the distinctive symbols associated with the stones, clearly of Pictish origin, can also be found on smaller items of a more portable nature; examples include symbols incised on the terminal of large silver chains such as those found at Gaulcross or Whitecleugh or those engraved on a silver plaque (or earring) from Norrie's Law, all in mainland Scotland.

Other categories of artifact that have been distinguished as specifically Pictish include short composite bone combs, hipped pins (with a slight swelling at mid-point of the shank that prevented slippage during wear) of bone and copper alloy,

penannular brooches as found at St. Ninian's Isle, and simple painted pebbles. A stone spindle whorl, excavated from Buckquoy in 2003, bears an ogham inscription—one of thirty-six such inscriptions identified in Pictland. The ogham script used by the Picts is believed to have originated in Ireland during the first centuries A.D. and is based on single or small groups of strokes that cross a single straight line. Ongoing research seems to suggest that the script originated from a Celtic language.

See also **Dál Riata** (*vol. 2, part 7*); **Viking Settlements in Orkney and Shetland** (*vol. 2, part 7*); **Dark Age/Early Medieval Scotland** (*vol. 2, part 7*); **Tarbat** (*vol. 2, part 7*).

BIBLIOGRAPHY

Ballin-Smith, Beverly, ed. *Howe: Four Millennia of Orkney Prehistory.* Monograph Series, no. 9. Edinburgh: Society of Antiquaries of Scotland, 1994.

Carver, Martin. *Surviving in Symbols: A Visit to the Pictish Nation.* Edinburgh: Canongate, 1999. (An excellent up-to-date summary.)

Dockrill, Steve, Val Turner, and Julie M. Bond. "Old Scatness/Jarlshof Environs Project." In *Discovery and Excavation in Scotland 2002.* Edited by Robin Turner, pp. 105–107. Edinburgh: Council for Scottish Archaeology, 2003.

Forsyth, Katherine. "Language in Pictland, Spoken and Written." In *A Pictish Panorama.* Edited by Eric Nicoll. Forfar, Angus, U.K.: Pinkfoot Press, 1995.

Foster, Sally. *Picts, Gaels, and Scots.* London: B. T. Batsford/Historic Scotland, 1996. (A excellent scholarly summary.)

Friell, Gerry, and Graham Watson, eds. *Pictish Studies: Settlement, Burial, and Art in Dark Age Northern Britain.* British Archaeological Reports, no. 125. Oxford: Tempvs Reparatvm, 1984.

Hedges, John W. *Bu, Gurness, and the Brochs of Orkney.* Part 2, *Gurness.* British Archaeological Reports British Series, no. 164. Oxford: British Archaeological Reports, 1987.

Morris, Christopher D. *The Birsay Bay Project.* Vol. 1, *Brough Road Excavations 1976–1982.* Department of Archaeology Monograph Series, no. 1. Durham, U.K.: University of Durham, 1989.

Ritchie, Anna. "Orkney in the Pictish Kingdom." In *The Prehistory of Orkney B.C. 4000–1000 A.D.* Edited by Colin Renfrew, pp. 183–204. Edinburgh: Edinburgh University Press, 1985. (A full survey of evidence available to 1985.)

———. "Excavation of Pictish and Viking Age Farmsteads at Buckquoy, Orkney." *Proceedings of the Society of Antiquaries of Scotland* 108 (1976–1977): 174–227.

Small, Alan, Charles Thomas, and David M.Wilson. *St Ninian's Isle and Its Treasure*. Oxford: Oxford University Press, 1973.

Wainwright, Frederick T., ed. *The Problem of the Picts*. Edinburgh: Nelson, 1955.

COLLEEN E. BATEY

RUS

The Rus are a people described in historical documents as traders and chiefs who were instrumental in the formation of the ancient Russian state between A.D. 750 and 1000. Historians and archaeologists have studied the Rus and their role in the development of early Russian towns and the Russian state.

HISTORICAL AND LINGUISTIC EVIDENCE

The term "Rus" first appeared around A.D. 830 or 840 in western and eastern historical sources as a designation for traders. Linguistic studies indicate that the word is derived from the Finnish *Ruotsi*, meaning "Swedes." *Ruotsi*, in turn, is loaned from the word that seafaring Swedes used to describe themselves during the pre-Viking period. The sailors used the Old Scandinavian *rodr*, characterizing themselves as a "crew of oarsmen."

From the beginning, then, Rus had both an ethnic and a social (or professional) meaning—indicating both "Scandinavian" and "seafarer." In eighth- and ninth-century historical documents, the ethnic significance of Rus appeared predominant. For example, an entry by Prudentius, bishop of Troyes, for the year 839 in the *Annales Bertiniani* records a diplomatic mission from Theophilus of Byzantium to Louis the Pious of Ingelheim, explaining that men who called themselves "Rhos" were "Swedes by origin." Similarly, Liutprand, Bishop of Cremona, after a visit to Constantinople in 968, mentioned in his *Antapodosis* the "Rus, whom we call by another name: Northmen."

By the mid-tenth century, the term "Rus" had changed in meaning to refer to the ruling class who were instrumental in the establishment of the Russian state in Kiev. Scandinavians were present among the retainers of the early Russian state, but Rus now could be used to refer to all individuals belonging to this elite warrior group, Scandinavian or not. An example of the new social meaning of Rus is found in the Byzantine document *De administrando imperio* from around 950, which describes the Rus in terms of their trade routes and the peoples who owed them tribute. Once Rus lost its ethnic significance, a new term, *Varangian*, was used to specify Scandinavians. The Russian Primary Chronicle, compiled about A.D. 1110, identifies Rurik, the first ruler of Russia, as a Varangian, or Swede.

On the basis of historical sources, eighteenth- and nineteenth-century scholars concluded that elite Scandinavians founded the Russian state, held high rank and status in Russian society, and served as mercenaries in Russia and Byzantium. Later scholars, both historians and archaeologists, have taken a more moderate view, arguing that Scandinavians had a significant role in early Russia but that Slavic, Finno-Ugric, and Baltic peoples who settled in the region also participated in the creation of the early Russian state.

ARCHAEOLOGICAL EVIDENCE

Excavations of early Russian towns provide evidence of the social, political, and economic development of the early Russian state, contributing significantly to our knowledge of the Rus and their activities in eighth- to eleventh-century Russia. The archaeological evidence does not prove the claims of the Russian Primary Chronicle that Swedes founded Staraya Ladoga, Novgorod, and other early Russian towns, but it does suggest that Scandinavians may have had a significant role in their early development. Like the historical data, the archaeological data show a gradual assimilation of the Rus into the multiethnic society of the emerging Russian state.

Archaeological evidence indicates that early Russian towns, such as Rurik Gorodishche and Staraya Ladoga, had multiethnic populations, who participated in an economy focused on long-distance trade and craft production. During the ninth and tenth centuries Rurik Gorodishche, for example, imported goods from the Mediterranean, the Baltic Sea, and Scandinavia. Scales and weights indicate trade, and tools, production debris, and raw materials suggest craft production. Early Rus-

Fig. 1. Traders at a portage point along a Russian river. The boat holds trade goods such as weapons. FROM OLAUS MAGNUS, *HISTORIA DE GENTIBUS SEPTENTRIONALIBUS*, PUBLISHED BY THE HAKLUYT SOCIETY. REPRODUCED BY PERMISSION.

sian towns had a function and nature similar to those of other contemporary Baltic trade towns, including Hedeby and Ribe in Jutland, Birka in central Sweden, and Wolin in modern-day Poland.

Archaeologists have devoted much effort to investigating the ethnic identity of the traders and crafts producers who lived and worked in early Russian towns. Their research shows that Slavic, Scandinavian, Baltic, and Finno-Ugric residents lived side by side and engaged in similar activities, including agriculture, craft production, trade, and military service. Excavated burial sites associated with early Russian towns imply significant cultural contact among the various ethnic groups in ancient Russia. This is seen in the mixture of Baltic, Finno-Ugric, Scandinavian, and Slavic material in cemeteries of the eighth to eleventh centuries—and even within individual graves.

Because of the linguistic and historical evidence suggesting that the Rus were Swedish, careful attention has been paid to the timing and nature of the Scandinavian presence in early Russian towns. Scandinavian artifacts are found in the earliest layers of Staraya Ladoga and Rurik Gorodishche and com-

prise items that probably came to the town as personal possessions, not trade goods. Examples of such finds include humble objects inscribed with runes and characteristically Scandinavian ornaments, combs, footwear, and gaming pieces. One of the most interesting features excavated at Staraya Ladoga is a late eighth- or early ninth-century smithy, containing tools and a bronze figurine of Scandinavian style, hinting that the smith may have been a resident Scandinavian.

Scandinavian graves have been reliably identified in many early towns, among them, Staraya Ladoga and Novgorod on the Volga trade route and Gnezdovo/Smolensk and Kiev on the Dnieper trade route. Based on their burials, the majority of Scandinavians who were active in ancient Russia appear to have been traders and warriors. A limited number of graves include both men and women, intimating that at least some Scandinavians were settled in Russia, living a stable, domestic life. Comparisons of the Scandinavian finds with other graves in Russia and Sweden give the impression that Scandinavians were among the wealthier residents of Russia (but not as wealthy as the elite class of Scandinavia).

THE RUS IN EARLY RUSSIA

Altogether, the historical and archaeological evidence suggests that the Rus were traders and crafts producers, who were important to the economic and political development of early Russian towns. The cultural, social, and political processes of early state development in Russia are reflected both in the changing meaning of "Rus" through time and the increasing homogenization of the material culture. Originally referring to Scandinavian traders, the name "Rus" soon came to mean any member of the urban ruling class, who collected tribute from the peoples settled in early Russia. Both the early Rus traders and the later Rus chieftains were active in and associated with towns. Archaeological finds from burials and towns indicate that these traders and chieftains included Scandinavians, together with other ethnic groups. Both the historical and archaeological evidence show that the legacy of the Rus—the development of towns and a specialized, urban economy—were critical to the formation of the early Russian state, unified under Kiev c. A.D. 1000.

See also **Russia/Ukraine** (*vol. 2, part 7*); **Staraya Ladoga** (*vol. 2, part 7*).

BIBLIOGRAPHY

Melnikova, Elena A., and Vladimir J. Petrukhin. "The Origin and Evolution of the Name *Rus:* The Scandinavians in Eastern-Europe Ethno-political Process before the Eleventh Century." *Tor* 23 (1990–1991): 203–234.

Rahbeck-Schmidt, K., ed. *Varangian Problems.* Scandoslavica supplement 1. Copenhagen, Denmark: Munksgaard, 1970.

Vernadsky, George, ed. *A Sourcebook for Russian History from Early Times to 1917.* New Haven, Conn.: Yale University, 1972.

RAE OSTMAN

SAAMI

The Saami are an ethnic minority living in the arctic and subarctic regions comprising contemporary Norway, Sweden, and Finland as well as Russia's Kola Peninsula. Formerly their settlement area extended farther south to include the western White Sea area of Russia and larger parts of Finland as well as the interior of central and southern parts of Norway and Sweden. Saami language belongs to the Finno-Ugric branch of the Uralic family, most closely (although still distantly) related to Finnish in the Baltic-Finnish language group. According to historical linguists, Saami or Proto-Saami originated due to a linguistic differentiation of a Proto-Finnish language during the Bronze Age or even earlier.

Until the sixteenth century the Saami were predominantly hunters with a subsistence economy based on terrestrial and maritime hunting as well as fishing. The largest sociopolitical unit was the *siida,* the local hunting band composed of five to ten nuclear families. Each *siida* occupied a clearly defined territory where families lived dispersed at various seasonal camps most of the year, aggregating for a longer period only at the common winter site. Exogamy was practiced, forming affinal ties between contiguous groups. Kinship was recognized bilaterally, as by most other circumpolar peoples. During the sixteenth and seventeenth centuries the hunting economy was gradually replaced or supplemented by reindeer pastoralism, commercial fishing, and small-scale cattle husbandry. According to some scholars, however, the transition to reindeer pastoralism had already taken place among the western Saami during the Viking period.

"Saami" (Scandinavian *samer*) is the term properly used to denote the people who have been referred to popularly in the English-speaking West as "Lapps" or "Laplanders." It is a derivative of the self-designating terms *sámit, sáme,* or *saemieh,* reflecting an etymological root that probably means "land." In historical records, however, a number of ethnonyms have been applied to the Saami by outsiders. In Norse sources from the Viking Age and the medieval period, "Finns" (*finner*) is the common term, whereas "Lapps" prevails in Swedish, Finnish (*lappalaiset*), and Russian (*lop'*) sources. It is commonly held that the first written sources mentioning the Saami are descriptions by Tacitus (A.D. 98) and Ptolemy (A.D. c. 100–170) of the "Finns" (Latin *fenni* and Greek Φιννοι/*finnoi*). According to Tacitus the *fenni* live in "astonishing barbarism and disgusting misery" without arms, horses, or houses—their only shelter against wild beasts and rain being a few intertwined branches. For want of iron they tipped their arrows with sharp bone. Even more astonishing to these authors is that the women took part in the hunt on equal footing with men. It is uncertain, however, if these early descriptions of "Finns" actually refer specifically to the Saami or more generally to Finno-Ugric speaking hunters of northeasternmost Europe. A more certain ascription is established by sixth-century Greek and Roman writers adding the term *scrithi* or *scere/cre* to the term *fenni/finnoi*, most notably in the writings of Procopius (*scrithiphinoi*) and Jordanes (*scerefennae, crefennae, rerefennae*). The first term must have been adopted from Norse language, where *skríða* means "to ski"—that is, the combined term means the "skiing Finns." In the Norse culture *skríðfinner* was a common term to designate the mobile Saami hunters due to their skiing skills. This stereotypical ascription is reflected in the Old Norse oath that the enemy shall have peace as long as "falcon flies, pine grows, rivers flow to the sea, and Saami are skiing."

The ethnic origin of the Saami has long puzzled Nordic and European scholars and opinions have changed considerably. Until the mid-nineteenth century it was commonly believed that the Saami were the descendants of the aboriginal Stone Age populations of Scandinavia (and even larger parts of northern Europe). However, as political and scientific currents turned the "noble savage" into the "ignoble," different readings of the archaeological and historical record soon emerged. By the early twentieth century the Saami were almost univocally depicted as an "alien" people who had migrated to Scandinavia from Russia or Siberia during the Iron Age or even as late as the fourteenth or fifteenth century. This doctrine of the Saami as an "eastern other" prevailed in Nordic research well into the post–World War II era.

Most historians and archaeologists have since rejected the migration hypothesis in favor of models claiming local origin. According to the most influential, the formation of Saami ethnicity (and even the introduction of "Germanic" and Norse identity in the north) was related to processes of social and economic differentiation among the hunting societies in northern Fennoscandinavia during the first millennium B.C., processes concurring with increased interaction with the outside world. Regional differences in cultural interfaces and exchange networks promoted different cultural trajectories. The coastal societies along the northwestern coast

of Norway and parts of the Gulf of Bothnia, relating to the South Scandinavian Bronze Age culture, adopted farming and developed chieftain-like systems with a redistributive socioeconomy. Subsequent processes of "Germanization" in the Roman period have been interpreted as a conscious (although imperative) choice among these societies to obtain access to European exchange networks and social alliances. The hunting population in the interior and the far north, however, became involved in exchange networks extending eastward to metal-producing societies in Karelia and central Russia. Relating to these long-distance networks, supplying bronze and iron, as well as to the new socioeconomic and cultural interface caused by the "transformed" coastal groups, ethnic boundaries and symbolic systems of categorization emerged based on a conscious distinction between "hunters" versus "farmers." Thus, according to this model, Saami ethnicity emerged as a social process of identity formation among the "remaining" hunters of the north.

Different suggestions about Saami origin are provided by studies of genetic patterns in modern Saami populations. Based on analysis of mitochondrial DNA it is claimed (although not uncontested) that the Saami hold a unique position in the genetic landscape of Europe. If so, the question remains as to whether this uniqueness is due to their ancient origin (and consequently isolation) or to a foreign origin (and consequently migration)—or if the distinctive Saami genetic makeup even relates to modern social processes of kinship formation.

The Saami's persistence as an ethnic group over time can hardly be ascribed to their isolation. To the contrary, for more than two millennia they have been involved in close interaction with structurally different neighboring societies. During the Iron Age and the medieval period the Saami provided highly valued hunting products such as exotic furs, seal oil, walrus tusks, and probably falcons in return for iron, textiles, and farming products. The character of this early interaction is, however, disputed. According to the "standard view" long held, the Saami were the subject of exploitation and suppression from Norse chieftains and kings: the militarily superior Norse gained access to Saami products through taxation and fierce plundering raids. More recent studies, however, claim that the Saami for the most part interacted in a peaceful and mutually beneficial way with their neighboring societies until the medieval period. Indicative of this is the frequent accounts in the Norse sagas of cooperation and close relations. The sagas emphasize the Saami as good hunters, as helpers, and as skilled boatbuilders, as well as healers, fortune-tellers, and teachers of magic and *seid* (shamanistic practices). Many scholars argue that ample evidence suggests that the Saami and their Germanic or Norse neighbors shared fundamental religious conceptions and values (based in a common shamanistic worldview), which may well have promoted tolerance and smoothed coexistence. As bonds of interethnic dependencies developed during the Iron Age the Saami achieved considerable economic and ideological power. Saami hunting products were crucial to the Norse chieftains' ability to participate in the European prestige-goods economy, and their "magical" knowledge and ritual skills were desired and respected. Studies have argued that during the Viking period these bonds of dependencies were reinforced by ritual gift exchange and interethnic marriages.

Such strategies for strengthening inter-ethnic bonds may partly be seen as a response to the new cultural and socioeconomic conditions that emerged from the tenth century onward. The Saami, who during the Iron Age related more or less exclusively to the redistributive system of neighboring chieftains, now encountered the power politics of surrounding state societies competing for control over their resources. The emergence of the city-state of Novgorod in the east involved the Saami in extensive networks of fur trade. In Norway the northern chieftains were defeated by the emerging all-Norwegian kingdom that simultaneously converted the Norse to Christianity.

The economic, social, and religious changes both in the west and the east had a deep impact on interethnic relations and exposed the Saami to new economical and cultural pressures. The fur trade enforced increased production and pressure on resources while political and religious changes in the Norse society caused severe changes in their long-term social and ideologically embedded relations with the Saami. The archaeological record from the Viking Age and the early medieval period provides some indication of how this "stress" was negotiated within Saami societies. Most notable is the rapid in-

tensification and spread of certain ritual practices, such as burial customs (including bear burials) and metal sacrifices. The formalization and unification of material expressions is also exemplified in dwelling design and spatial arrangements of settlements. This ritual and symbolic mobilization may be read as an attempt to overcome or neutralize the threats from outside. However, archaeological and historical data clearly indicate that Saami societies did change during this phase, and at least in some areas the changes led to more complex social configurations.

See also **Iron Age Finland** (*vol. 2, part 6*); **Pre-Viking and Viking Age Norway** (*vol. 2, part 7*); **Pre-Viking and Viking Age Sweden** (*vol. 2, part 7*); **Finland** (*vol. 2, part 7*).

BIBLIOGRAPHY

Hansen, Lars Ivar. "Interaction between Northern European Sub-arctic Societies during the Middle Ages: Indigenous Peoples, Peasants, and State Builders." In *Two Studies on the Middle Ages*. Edited by Magnus Rindal, pp. 31–95. KULTs skriftserie 66. Oslo, Norway: KULT, 1996.

Hansen, Lars Ivar, and Bjørnar Olsen. *Samenes historie* [History of the Saami]. Oslo, Norway: Cappelen, 2003.

Mundal, Else. "The Perception of the Saamis and Their Religion in Old Norse Sources." In *Shamanism and Northern Ecology*. Edited by Juha Pentikäinen. Religion and Society 36. New York: Mouton de Gruyter, 1996.

Price, Neil. *The Viking Way: Religion and War in Late Iron Age Scandinavia*. Uppsala, Sweden: Uppsala University, 2002.

Olsen, Bjørnar. "Belligerent Chieftains and Oppressed Hunters? Changing Conceptions of Inter-Ethnic Relationships in Northern Norway during the Iron Age and Early Medieval Period." In *Contacts, Continuity, and Collapse: The Norse Colonization of the North Atlantic*. Edited by James Barrett. York Studies in the Early Middle Ages 5. Turnhout, Belgium: Brepols, 2003.

Storli, Inger. "A Review of Archaeological Research on Sami Prehistory." *Acta Borealia* 3, no. 1 (1986): 43–63.

Zachrisson, I. "A Review of Archaeological Research on Saami Prehistory in Sweden." *Current Swedish Archaeology* 1 (1993): 171–182.

LARS IVAR HANSEN, BJØRNAR OLSEN

SCYTHIANS

The Scythians (Assyrian: "Ašguzai" or "Išguzai";
Hebrew: "Askenaz"; Greek: "Scythioi") were a nomadic people belonging to the North Iranian language group. Their earliest mention, by Assyrian
sources, comes from the first half of the seventh century B.C., during the reign of Esarhaddon (681–669
B.C.). The Scythians then appeared in northern
Media, in the Lake Urmia region of Mannea (in
modern-day Iran). They were involved in the Medi-
an-Assyrian conflicts. As Assyrian allies, in 673 B.C.
they helped to suppress a Median uprising under the
leadership of Kaštaritu. They played a still more important role in 653 B.C., saving the Assyrian capital
of Nineveh, besieged by Kaštaritu's army.

At that time the Scythians were a significant military power. Their raiding parties ventured as far as
the borders of Egypt in Syria, even forcing the pharaoh Psamtik I (r. 663–609 B.C.) to pay them ran-
som. In about 637 B.C., during the reign of Ashurbanipal (669–631? B.C.), they played an important
role in defeating the Cimmerians, dreaded invaders
that wreaked havoc across Asia Minor. Earlier still,
the Scythians forced the Cimmerians out from the
lands north of the Caucasus and the Black Sea. It
was Cyaxares (r. 625–585 B.C.), the ruler of Medes,
who finally managed to drive the Scythians out of
the Near East.

ORIGIN OF THE SCYTHIANS

The most important accounts on the origins of the
Scythians can be found in the *Histories* of Herodotus (book 4) relating to "the Scythian-Cimmerian
conflict." According to this Greek historian, the
Scythians, as a migrating people, invaded and conquered the lands north of the Black Sea, forcing out
the indigenous Cimmerians. Herodotus locates
their original dwelling sites somewhere in Asia. He
writes: "The Scythians were a nomadic people living
in Asia. Oppressed by the warlike Massagetae [an-
other nomadic central Asian people], they crossed
the Araxes River [the Volga] and penetrated into
the land of the Cimmerians [who were the original
inhabitants of today's Scythian lands]."

In the absence of historical data, archaeology
has played the main role in determining the Scythians' original "Asian" settlements. During the last
quarter of the twentieth century, exploration
showed that the origins of Scythian culture should
be sought mainly in central Asia, in the upper
Yenissei River basin, the Altai hills, and the steppes
of eastern Kazakhstan. As early as the ninth century
B.C. the Scythians' nomadic ancestors began to migrate westward from those territories, along a
stretch of the Great Steppe, seeking ecological niches to suit their herding economy. This process also
was stimulated by ecological changes, resulting
from the cold, dry climate prevalent since about the
thirteenth century B.C. As a consequence, the steppe
pastures degraded. The westward migration gained
impact in the second half of the eighth century B.C.,
and the mass influx of the Scythian tribes eventually
led to the occupation of the steppes at the foot of
the Caucasus. It was from these regions that the
Išguzai launched their Asian invasions.

Beginning in the first half of the seventh century
B.C. the Scythians gradually conquered the middle
regions of the Dnieper River (which had been penetrated earlier), on the northern edge of the steppe
in the forest-steppe zone. Despite living in strongly
fortified settlements, the native, settled farming
communities had to yield to the military might of
the invading nomads. Around that time, Scythian
expansion also reached into the Transylvania territories, located still farther to the west, in the Carpathian valley. With time, especially after withdrawing
from the Near East, the Scythians increasingly focused their attention on the steppe regions. This
was in part due to climate change and improvement
in the ecological conditions in the steppes north of
the Black Sea. The climate became more humid and
mild, which in Europe manifested itself as the so-
called Subatlantic fluctuation.

Beginning in the mid-seventh century B.C., the
Black Sea region also became more "attractive" as
the result of the founding of Greek colonies on the
north shores of the Black Sea. The oldest among
them, Borysthenes (also the ancient name for the
river Dnieper), on the island of Berezan at the
mouth of the Boh River, dates from about 646 B.C.
Numerous other colonies, for example, Olbia and
Panticapaeum, soon developed into great economic
(production and trade) centers and played an enormous role in the economic and cultural development of the Scythian tribes.

After having been driven out from the Near East in the late seventh century B.C., the Scythians shifted their political center to the Black Sea region. This was not a peaceful process. Its echoes are found in a legend reported by Herodotus (book 4). The legend tells of the "old" Scythians returning from the Near East and fighting with the "young" Scythians, who were the sons of the slaves and wives of the "old" Scythians "left behind in the old country." In the late seventh and early sixth centuries B.C. the military activity of the Scythians was spread over vast territories, reaching west into the Great Hungarian Plain and into what is today southwestern Poland. Gradually, as the result of these processes, Scythian tribes living in the Black Sea region between the Don River and the Lower Danube organized themselves into a proto-state, called "Scythia" by Herodotus. There is no doubt that it consisted of the affluent ethnic Scythians as well as the conquered local peoples, in particular, the settled forest-steppe peoples, who were politically and culturally dominated by the Scythians.

The organization was a sort of a tribal federation. The power was in the hands of the Scythian "kings," local rulers who probably accepted the authority of the leader of the politically strongest tribe. This complex sociopolitical structure of Scythia probably is what Herodotus meant when he talked about the "Royal Scythians" who "consider other Scythians to be their slaves" and about the "Scythian Nomads," the "Scythian Farmers," and the "Scythian Ploughmen" living in the various regions of Scythia. Scythia's political center and, at the same time, a mythical land, Gerrhus, where the Scythian kings were buried, was situated in the lower Dnieper River basin.

SCYTHIAN ECONOMY

Scythian economy was based on nomadic or semi-nomadic animal breeding and herding (horses, cattle, and sheep). Wealth, especially in the case of the Scythian aristocracy, was acquired in wars and pillaging raids and through the slave trade with the Greeks from around the Black Sea. The Scythians also controlled the trade of grain, which the Greeks imported from forest-steppe farming regions. From the Greek colonies the Scythians brought in vast amounts of wine, transported in amphorae. To the great astonishment of the Greeks, the Scythians

drank it without water. Also highly valued were Greek pottery, metal libation vessels sometimes made from precious metals, rich ornaments, and jewelry—often true masterpieces of Greek craftsmanship.

SCYTHIAN CULTURE

Between nomadic "barbarian" civilization and the north Black Sea variant of Greek civilization, certain syncretic cultural phenomena confirm the close coexistence of the two elements. This is evidenced in a specific Greco-Scythian decoration style of metallic objects, vessels, ornaments, and weaponry items produced for the Scythians in Greek workshops. This style combines zoomorphic features characteristic of the Scythian world of cult and magic with mythological scenes and narration describing the life of common mortals, presented in typical situations and settings. Many of the masterpieces, for example, a famous cup from the Kul'-Oba *kurgan,* or a gold pectoral found in Tovsta Mohyla, and a gold comb from the Solokha *kurgan,* are excellent iconographic sources that shed light on Scythian ways, behavior, and appearance.

The unity of the Scythian cultural tradition is symbolized by a characteristic "triad," consisting of a common decoration style dominated by zoomorphic motifs; the manner of restraining horses, reflected in a homogenous bridle set, and, above all, original weaponry—predominantly bows and arrows. The Scythians' use of a hard composite (reflex) bow with a long range and tremendous piercing power, their excellence on horseback, and their ability to shoot from any position—at full gallop without a saddle or stirrups—made the Scythians fearsome warriors. (This also was the case with other Great Steppe nomads.) The Scythians employed distinctive fighting tactics, with warriors arranged in highly mobile groups, skilled in the use of stratagems that exhausted the enemy and that allowed the Scythians to avoid direct confrontation in unfavorable circumstances. The Scythians were formidable enemies, posing a serious threat even to the contemporary world powers. The Assyrians, the Medes, the Urartes, and later the Perses all had firsthand knowledge of the might of the Scythians.

Unquestionably, the Scythians gained their greatest military and political success defeating the powerful Persian army led by Darius I Hystaspis (r.

521–486 B.C.). Faced with this powerful foe, the Scythians applied guerrilla tactics, drawing the enemy far inside the steppe, wiping out smaller regiments, and severing supply lines. Finally, the humiliated Darius was forced to withdraw with the devastated remains of his army across the Danube River into southern Thrace, which was by then a Persian province. As a result of this victory, the Scythians were referred to in the ancient tradition as "invincible." Some time later, in 496 B.C., Scythian warriors followed the same route, reaching the Thracian Chersonesus (or "the Chersonese") in a military expedition.

This direction of Scythian politics continued through the fifth century B.C., when Scythia entered into a closer relationship (both peaceful and bellicose) with the Thracian state of the Odrisses. It was centered in present-day southeastern Bulgaria. This relationship was especially strong (and confirmed by dynastic colligations) around the mid-fifth century, during the reign of Sitalkes, who brought the Odrisses to the peak of their power. Political and economical stabilization in the Black Sea region in the fifth and most of the fourth centuries B.C. favored Scythian economic polarization. The wealthiest "royal" *kurgans* of the Scythian aristocracy date from that period. They are the real "steppe pyramids"—burial sanctuaries of Scythian leaders and rulers. The rulers were buried amid a wealth of funerary offerings and in the company of servants sacrificed especially for the burial. Stone stelae representing armed men, placed on top of the *kurgans*, were the specific apotheosis of a stereotype of a king-warrior and at the same time of a mythical ancestor.

THE FALL OF SCYTHIA

In the second half of the fourth century B.C., however, several factors precipitated a crisis. The development of a dry and warm climate, together with overexploitation of the steppe grazing lands by the great herds, again triggered migration. As a result of these changes, from the second half of the fourth century B.C., the Sauromates and the Sarmates, tribes from central Eurasian steppes, began to venture across the Don River and threaten Scythian territories. Simultaneously, a powerful force arose in southern Europe that eventually changed the world's political order—Macedonia. This period

also witnessed the reign of one of the greatest Scythian rulers, King Ateas (d. 339), an excellent warrior and experienced leader who supposedly ruled over all of Scythia. He fought Philip II (r. 359–336), the king who gave rise to Macedonian power, in a battle in the Lower Danube in which the Scythians suffered a shattering defeat and the aged king (apparently more than ninety years old) was killed in battle.

More defeats followed, such as the one suffered in 313 B.C. at the hands of one of the Diadoches, the Thracian ruler Lizymachos. The Sarmates moving in from the east also were an increasing threat. As a result, during the third century B.C., Scythian territories shrank to the area of the Crimea steppes, where a new political organization appeared with their capital in the so-called Neapolis Scythica. During the second century B.C., it still played a certain political role, fighting for survival with Chersonesus, with the Sarmates, and at the end with the Pontic kingdom of Mithridates VI Eupator (r. 120–63 B.C.). Finally, the influx of Sarmatian nomads into the Crimean region led to the intermixing of both elements. Remnants of the Scythians survived here until the third to fourth centuries A.D., when the Germanic Goths appeared on the scene. In the aftermath of the Hun invasion in 375 A.D. the Scythians disappeared from history.

See also **Iron Age Ukraine and European Russia** (*vol. 2, part 6*); **Huns** (*vol. 2, part 7*).

BIBLIOGRAPHY

Artamonov, Mikhail I. *The Splendor of Scythian Art: Treasures from Scythian Tombs.* Translated from Russian by V. R. Kupilyanova. New York: Praeger, 1969.

Davis-Kimball, Jeannine, V. A. Bashilov, and L. T. Yablonsky, eds. *Nomads of the Eurasian Steppes in the Early Iron Age.* Berkeley: Zinat Press, 1995.

Ghirshman, R. *Tombe princière de Ziwiyé et le début de l'art animalier.* Paris: Scythe, 1979.

Grjaznov, Michail P. *Der Großkurgan von Arzan in Tuva, Südsibirien.* Munich: C. H. Beck, 1984.

Jakobson, Esther. *The Art of the Scythians: The Interpenetration of Cultures at the Edge of the Hellenic World.* New York: E. J. Brill, 1995.

Jettmar, Karl. *Art of the Steppes.* New York: Crown, 1967.

L'or des Scythes: Trésors de l'Ermitage. Leningrad: Bruxelles, 1991.

Reeder, Ellen D., ed. *Scythian Gold: Treasures from Ancient Ukraine.* New York: Harry N. Abrams, 1999.

Rolle, Renate, Michael Müller-Wille, and Kurt Schitzel, eds. *Gold der Steppe: Archäologie der Ukraine*. Neumünster, Germany: K. Wachholtz, 1991.

JAN CHOCHOROWSKI

SLAVS AND THE EARLY SLAV CULTURE

The first certain information about the Slavs dates to the sixth century A.D. The question of the location, time, and course of ethnogenetic processes that shaped the "earliest" branch of Indo-Europeans remains one of the most fiercely discussed issues in central and eastern European historiography. A modest set of primary written sources from that period and a larger but more controversial set of linguistic arguments form the basis of what is known concerning the beginnings of Slavic history. It is mostly thanks to archaeological findings that the understanding of early Slavic culture has broadened in the last fifty years. Authoritative archaeological evidence entered into the discussion on the origins of the Slavs only in the 1960s, when archaeologists began to recognize and analyze assemblages of artifacts from the fifth through the sixth centuries throughout the area between the Elbe and Don Rivers.

According to the "western" thesis, which has not been analyzed properly with respect to the Polish territory, the Slavs' homeland was either in the basin of the Oder and Vistula (perhaps only the Vistula) or between the Oder and the Dnieper. At present, the evidence supporting this hypothesis is weak. Thorough analysis of the findings from the second through the fifth centuries from the area of central Europe, carried out by Kazimierz Godłowski, confirmed the nonindigenous character of Slavic culture on the Oder and Vistula. The fact that the cultural models of two consecutive palaeo-ethnological phenomena were identical—the archaeological findings from the second through fifth centuries in the central and upper Dnieper region and those of the later Slavic structures from fifth to sixth centuries—was also noted by Godłowski. The reliability of the "eastern" concept has been constantly growing, as archaeological source-based research has progressed in eastern and central Europe. The archaeologists' arguments have been confronted with the contents of historical records.

The Byzantines were the first to notice the Slavs—raids from a new wave of barbarians from the north endangered their empire's Danube border. In the first half of the sixth century, Jordanes, in his history of the Goths, pinpointed Slavic settlements in the region surrounded by the upper Vistula, the Lower Danube, and the Dnieper. There, according to Jordanes, along the Carpathian range, "from the sources of the Vistula over immeasurable area, settled a numerous people of Veneti." The Veneti were divided into Sclavenes and Antes—both groups commonly regarded as Slavs. The Sclavenes lived in the area from the Vistula to the Lower Danube, and the Antes inhabited the area to the east of the Dniester, up to the Dnieper. The Byzantine writer Procopius of Caesarea, a contemporary of Jordanes, records in his *Gothic War* (*De bello Gothico*) that "uncountable tribes of the Antes" settled even farther to the east. He recorded that in about A.D. 512 there was "a considerable area of empty land" to the west of Sclavenian settlements (perhaps in Silesia?). It is hard to overestimate the importance of Procopius's words that Sclavenes and Antes spoke "the same language" and that they had long had one common name.

The records of these authors seem to correspond to the area of archaeological phenomena that is identified with the remnants of the Slavs at the beginning of their great expansion. The southern and eastern frontier of Slavdom described in the first half of the sixth century from the Byzantine perspective matches the border of a specific and exceptionally homogeneous cultural province, which can be interpreted only as Slavic. All available excavation materials confirm the division of this province, between the mid-fifth and mid-seventh centuries, into at least three tightly interrelated branches. The historical records allow for the identification of the western group (the Prague culture) with the Sclavenes and of the southeastern group (the Penkovka culture) with the Antes. The name of the third group (the Kolochin culture) is unknown but was perhaps the "Veneti."

These groups represent an identical cultural model. The differentiation of the discussed archaeological units is so slight that it is practically based on a secondary criterion, that is, the differences among the characteristic forms of pottery, which is the only mass finding. The early development stage of all three cultures (the turn of the sixth century) is characterized by a large majority of simple handmade pots without ornamentation.

The boundaries of these cultures were transformed considerably in the late sixth century and into the seventh century. Although the areas occupied by the Kolochin and Penkovka cultures remained the same, the Prague culture spread widely to the west: it encompassed the basin of the Middle Danube and the upper and middle Elbe. At the same time a new phenomenon arose in the basin of the Oder and on the southern coast of the Baltic Sea: the Sukow culture, most likely the younger stage of the Prague culture. Unfortunately, the disappointing state of research on the areas south of the Danube makes it impossible to obtain a clear picture of archaeological structures in the Balkans.

The ethnographic characteristics of early Slavic society captured by historians and archaeologists allow researchers to describe settlement forms; economic structure; the method of artifact manufacture and its stylistic features; some elements of the social system, customs, and beliefs; the funeral rite; warfare; foreign influences; standards of living; and the general level of civilization development. Early Slavic settlements hardly ever were found in the mountains: their traces are rarely seen more than 300 meters above sea level. The areas of fertile soil close to rivers and woods most often were selected. Nondefensive settlements were built along the edges of river valleys. Typical houses were sunken-floored huts on a square plan, with sides from 2.5 to 4.5 meters long. The wooden walls were erected in the form of a log cabin ("blockhouse") or were of pile ("Pfostenbaum") construction. A stone or clay oven typically stood in one corner, although some huts had hearths in the center. According to Procopius, the Slavs "live in pitiable huts, few and far between." The so-called Pseudo-Maurikios, a Byzantine historian writing at the end of the sixth and the beginning of the seventh centuries, says, "They live in the woods, among rivers, swamps and marshes."

Natural forms of environmental exploitation pervaded the economy, which was based mainly on agriculture. The main crops were millet and wheat; breeding cattle was at the forefront of husbandry too. As a result, the inhabitants of rural settlements

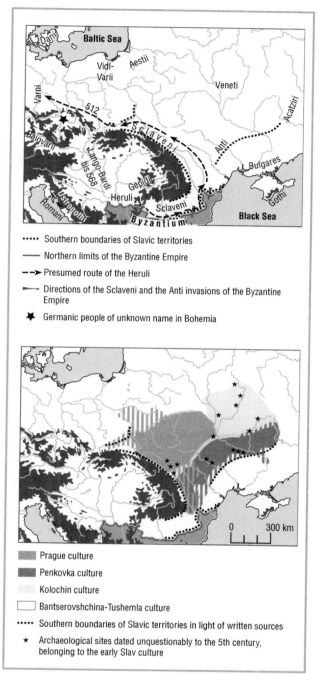

····· Southern boundaries of Slavic territories

—— Northern limits of the Byzantine Empire

--➤ Presumed route of the Heruli

--➤ Directions of the Sclaveni and the Anti invasions of the Byzantine Empire

★ Germanic people of unknown name in Bohemia

◼ Prague culture

◼ Penkovka culture

◼ Kolochin culture

◻ Bantserovshchina-Tushemla culture

····· Southern boundaries of Slavic territories in light of written sources

★ Archaeological sites dated unquestionably to the 5th century, belonging to the early Slav culture

Location of Slavs in the beginning of sixth century A.D. in light of written sources (top) and of archaeological data (bottom). ADAPTED FROM PARCZEWSKI 1993.

were totally self-sufficient, although their lives were of low standard, a fact noted by the Byzantines. According to Pseudo-Maurikios, the Slavs were numerous and persistent; they easily endured heat, chill, and bad weather as well as scarcity of clothes and livelihood.

No form of well-developed handicraft existed, apart from a rudimentary form of ironworking. The models for molten metal ornaments were borrowed from other cultures, as was the handicraft method of pottery production with a potter's wheel (from the sixth and seventh centuries). There are no clear traces of widespread trade. Records exist on the chiefs and tribal elders, who were usually leaders of small tribes. The funeral rite demanded cremation. The remains of human bones, with a few rare poor gifts for the dead, were put in shallow pits, either in a vessel (an urn) or directly in the soil.

The territory of the later—that is, pre–late fifth century—Slavic society is unclear. The ethnogenetic connection between the remains of Slavic settlements from the sixth and seventh centuries and earlier structures can be observed only in the east. The most reliable archaeological guidelines lead to the area of the upper and middle basin of the Dnieper, where a large group of people, whose remains are defined as "the Kiev culture," lived from the second or third century until the beginning of the fifth century. This is, as it were, the matrix of the three early Slavic cultures: the Kolochin culture (taking up almost the same area as the Kiev culture earlier); the Penkovka culture; and, to a large extent, the Prague culture. In the steppe and forest-steppe zones of the Ukraine are concentrated the earliest archaeological assemblages (dated undoubtedly to the fifth century) belonging to these three Slavic groups.

The eastern origin of the Slavs is confirmed directly by one written source. The so-called Cosmograph of Ravenna, writing in the seventh or eighth century, mentions the motherland of the Scythians, the place from where generations of Sclavenes originated. The specific location is unknown but he mentions the vast area of eastern Europe. The land inhabited by the Slavs at the beginning of the sixth century, reconstructed on the basis of archaeological findings, was approximately three times bigger than the area occupied by the Kiev culture in the first decades of the fifth century. New territories were taken over in the south and west—up to the Carpathians, the Lower Danube, and the Upper and Middle Vistula. The second stage of Slavic territorial expansion took place in the course of the sixth and seventh centuries. The population masses concentrated in the Lower Danube moved to the Balkans and occupied land as far as Peloponnese. A steppe people of the Avars, who settled in the Carpathian Basin in about A.D. 568, played a significant role in these events. At the same time other currents of expansion were moving to the west, reaching the eastern Alps and the Baltic Sea and occupying the Elbe basin.

Between the Baltic, the Elbe, and the Danube the newcomers probably encountered largely empty territories. In the Balkans, however, they first devastated the area and suppressed the locals and then, from the end of the sixth century onward, populated the land inhabited by the Greeks, by the remains of the Thracians and Germans, and, in the west of the peninsula, by groups of Romans. One of the mechanisms of the Slavs' demographic success—mass abduction of natives to captivity—is documented clearly in written records. In time, massive territorial growth together with the adoption of diversified ethnic substrates created the conditions for a deepening of the divisions in culture (and undoubtedly language as well) within what had so far been a unified Slavic world.

See also **Scythians** (vol. 2, part 7); **Poland** (vol. 2, part 7); **Hungary** (vol. 2, part 7).

BIBLIOGRAPHY

Baran, V. D., ed. *Etnokul'turnaia karta territorii Ukrainskoi SSR v I tys. n.e.* Kiev, Ukraine: Naukova Dumka, 1985.

Barford, Paul M. *The Early Slavs: Culture and Society in Early Medieval Eastern Europe.* London: British Museum Press, 2001.

Curta, Florin. *The Making of the Slavs: History and Archaeology of the Lower Danube Region, c. 500–700.* Cambridge, U.K.: Cambridge University Press, 2001.

(Note: The opinions of some authors about the localization of Slavs' homeland are in fact widely divergent from the opinions presented in the books of P. M. Barford and F. Curta.)

Godłowski, Kazimierz. *Pierwotne siedziby Słowian.* Edited by M. Parczewski. Kraków, Poland: Instytut Archeologii Uniwersytetu Jagiellońskiego, 2000.

———. "Zur Frage der Slawensitze vor der grossen Slawenwanderung im 6. Jahrhundert." In *Gli Slavi occidentali e meridionali nell'alto medioevo,* pp. 257–284. Settimane di Studio del Centro Italiano di Studi Sull'alto Medioevo 30. Spoleto, Italy: Centro Italiano di Studi Sull'alto Medioevo, 1983.

———. *The Chronology of the Late Roman and Early Migration Periods in Central Europe.* Prace Archeologiczne 11. Kraków, Poland: Uniwersytet Jagielloński, 1970.

Parczewski, Michał. *Die Anfänge der frühslawischen Kultur in Polen.* Edited by F. Daim. Veröffentlichungen der Österreichischen Gesellschaft für Ur- und Frühgeschichte 17. Vienna: Österreichischen Gesellschaft für Ur- und Frühgeschichte, 1993.

———. "Origins of Early Slav Culture in Poland." *Antiquity* 65 (1991): 676–683.

Popowska-Taborska, Hanna. *Wczesne dzieje Słowian w świetle ich języka.* Wrocław, Poland: Ossolineum, 1991.

Sedov, Valentin V. *Vostochnye slaviane v VI-XIII vv.* Moscow: Nauka, 1982.

MICHAŁ PARCZEWSKI

Fig. 1. Rune stone from the Viking period. PHOTOGRAPH BY BENGT A. LUNDBERG. NATIONAL HERITAGE BOARD OF SWEDEN. REPRODUCED BY PERMISSION.

VIKINGS

The precise origin of the word "Viking" remains a mystery. The terms "Viking" and "Viking Age" are associated with a period of almost three hundred years, from the late eighth century to the eleventh century, the last period of the Scandinavian Iron Age. Although we use the term "Viking" to describe the land and people of Scandinavia during that time period, the Northmen or Norse never used that word to describe themselves, and neither did neighboring countries. Some scholars think that the word "Viking" derives from the word *vik,* the Scandinavian word for "inlet" or "creek," but this interpretation is not universally accepted. Whatever its origin, the word "Viking" signifies the Scandinavian fishing-and-farming people who also undertook predatory expeditions to fuel their chiefly economy as well as expand their settlement into new lands. According to Peter Sawyer in his *Kings and Vikings,* "The age of the Vikings began when Scandinavians first attacked western Europe and it ended when those attacks ceased."

RAIDS AND EXPANSION

The Vikings conducted raids to exact tribute. During the Dark Ages, it was commonplace within Scandinavia as well as western Europe and Russia to plunder neighbors, to exact a tribute from them, and to secure their submission—to a large extent interchangeable notions. However, it was a new experience, and to many a shocking one, when the Scandinavians began to extend their sphere of activity so far beyond their own borders. The superior skills in boat making and navigation made this expansion possible. The topography of the Scandinavian countries prohibited travel by land; therefore, the waterways were their highways. This aided in the development of a seafaring culture with extremely accomplished sailors whose nautical expertise was their greatest asset in exploiting new lands. The Vikings settled the previously uninhabited island of Iceland; they developed two settlements in Greenland, which survived for three hundred years before mysteriously disappearing; and they arrived in the New World before Columbus, as seen by archaeological evidence of their presence in the site of L'Anse aux Meadows in Newfoundland, Canada. They helped found many cities in Russia, such as

Novgorod, Kiev, and Staraya Ladoga, and artifactual evidence points to trading with a plethora of places as diverse as Ireland and Byzantium. Their voyages were diverse in nature; the need for productive farmland along with the quest for wealth made the Vikings a mosaic of settlers composed of fighters, traders, and raiders.

DAILY LIFE

The reputation of these Nordic people as fierce warriors and raiders has obscured the more complex aspects of their everyday life for centuries. The Vikings in their homelands adapted uniquely to an arctic culture and exploited an extensive array of available resources. They were fisher-farmers because the warming effects of the Gulf Stream enabled farming much farther north than recorded previously. They fished the rich waters of the North Atlantic for the fish of the cod family, halibut, and wolfish, as well as the local lakes and rivers for freshwater fish such as salmon, trout, and char. They harvested bird colonies for meat (puffins, guillemots, and ptarmigan), eggs (duck, seagull, and cormorant), and eider duck down. They also hunted and scavenged large marine mammals, such as whales (for meat and oil, and for bone to use for structural material and for the creation of gaming pieces, fish net needles, and other implements), and walrus (primarily for their ivory). Their success as traders gave rise to a number of trading towns, such as: Gotland and Birka in Sweden, Hedeby in Schleswig-Holstein, and Kaupang in Norway. These towns became the foci of intense commercial activity and industry, and the goods traded were as diverse as the people who visited. The artifactual evidence (coins, tools, and ornaments) from excavations in these locations point to connections with Russia, Europe and North Africa, and shed light on the transition of Viking life from the farm to the town, and the beginnings of urbanization and city formation.

Archaeology has contributed greatly to the understanding of Viking lifeways. Viking houses were built with timber, stone, and turf. In this class-stratified society, large chiefly estates with good pastureland and large boathouses were the homes for local earls. Inside the houses were central fireplaces for warmth and cooking. Remains of cauldrons and steatite vessels, together with other artifacts such as whetstones for sharpening knives and loom weights from the upstanding looms that women used to weave fine woolen clothing, offer glimpses of domestic life. Implements for farming, hunting, and fishing along with animal bones from middens provide information on activities involving subsistence as well as those involving economy and trade. Charcoal pits, molds, slag, and recovered implements point to highly skilled craftsmanship in metalwork while the Viking ships and their surviving wood ornaments are a stellar example of woodworking. At Oseberg and Gokstad in southeastern Norway, excavations of sunken Viking ships undertaken in the late nineteenth and early twentieth century revealed beautifully crafted sledges and wagons. Fine gold jewelry and inlaid silverwork from finds throughout the Viking world also show a high degree of craftsmanship. Chess games, horse fights, and wrestling were all part of Viking daily life, and finds such as the Lewis chessmen—beautifully carved figurines of walrus ivory—show the Vikings applying their talent as artisans to their entertainment as well as their livelihood.

Military settlements such as Trelleborg in Zealand, Nonnebakken at Odense in Fune, Fyrkat near Hobro, and Agersborg near Limfjorden were all situated to command important waterways that served as lines of communication. The layouts of these camps reflect influences of symmetry and precision of the Roman castra. The Vikings were organized in bands called *lit*, a kind of military household familiar in western Europe. A chieftain might go abroad with just his own men in a couple of ships, but more commonly he would join forces with greater chieftains. These were often members of royal or noble families, styling themselves as kings or earls, and they frequently seem to have been exiles—for example, unsuccessful rivals for the throne—who were forced to seek their fortune abroad. Such men were often willing to stay abroad to serve Frankish or Byzantine rulers as mercenaries, to accept fiefs from them, and to become their vassals. They thereby became a factor in European politics. Vikings were frequently employed by one European prince against another or against other Vikings.

A voting assembly of freemen called *thing* was a governing institution widely used by the ancient Germanic peoples—it served as a forum to settle conflict and to cast decisions on questions relating to fencing, construction of bridges, clearance, pasture rights, worship, and even defense. At the beginning of the Viking Age, there were many *thing* assemblies throughout Scandinavia, and Norse settlers frequently established *things* abroad. The Icelandic *Althing* was unusual, however, in that it united all regions of an entire country under a common legal and judicial system, without depending upon the executive power of a monarch or regional rulers. The *Althing* was established around A.D. 930. Little is known about its specific organization during the earliest decades, because the only description of this exists in writing in Grágás and the sagas. These were not contemporary sources but were compiled by Christian scholars three hundred years after the end of the Viking Age and therefore generally portray the assembly as it was after the constitutional reforms of the mid-960s.

The social stratification of early Viking communities was based on wealth and property. Earls, peasants, and thralls supported the socioeconomic ladder. Women quite often achieved higher status, as evidenced through burial mounds in many parts of Norway. Vikings were intolerant of weakness and it is postulated from later literature that the elderly and infirm were regarded as a burden.

The Vikings, who were probably inspired through their contact with Europe and exposure to the Latin writing system, developed their own alphabet called *futhark* or otherwise known as a runic alphabet. Runes were carved primarily on stone but some have been found in wood and bone. The runes carried a multitude of meanings from the mystical to the mundane. The earliest written sources that provide information about the Vikings (sagas and eddas), were created by Icelandic scribes three centuries after the end of the Viking Age. These sources, along with direct data from environmental and archaeological investigations, help to elucidate the complex and often misrepresented Nordic people.

See also **Viking Harbors and Trading Sites; Viking Ships; Viking Settlements in Iceland and Greenland; Hofstaðir; Viking Settlements in Orkney and Shetland; Viking Dublin; Viking York; Pre-Viking and Viking Age Norway; Pre-Viking and Viking Age Sweden; Pre-Viking and Viking Age Denmark** (*all vol. 2, part 7*).

BIBLIOGRAPHY

Almgren, Bertil, et al., eds. *The Viking.* Gothenburg, Sweden: A. B. Nordbok, 1975.

Batey, Colleen E., Judith Jesch, and Christopher D. Morris, eds. *The Viking Age in Caithness, Orkney, and the North Atlantic.* Edinburgh: Edinburgh University Press, 1995.

Morris, Chris. "Viking Orkney: A Survey." In *The Prehistory of Orkney.* Edited by Colin Renfrew. Edinburgh: Edinburgh University Press, 1985.

Myhre, Bjorn. "The Royal Cemetery at Borre, Vestfold: A Norwegian Centre in a European Periphery." In *The Age of Sutton Hoo: The Seventh Century in North-Western Europe.* Edited by Martin Carver, pp. 301–313. Woodbridge, U.K.: Boydell, 1992.

———. "Chieftains' Graves and Chiefdom Territories in South Norway in the Migration Period." *Studien zur Sachsenforschung* 6 (1987): 169–187.

Nordisk Ministerråd og forfatterne. *Viking og Hvidekrist: Norden og Europa 800–1200.* Copenhagen: Nordisk Ministerråd, 1992.

Sawyer, Peter. *The Oxford Illustrated History of the Vikings.* Oxford: Oxford University Press, 1997.

———. *Kings and Vikings: Scandinavia and Europe,* A.D. *700–1100.* London: Methuen, 1982.

SOPHIA PERDIKARIS

VISIGOTHS

The Visigoths (Good Goths) were located in central Germany when they first came into contact with Roman traders and soldiers in the first century B.C. They were an Indo-European people who seemed to have originated in Poland and not in Scandinavia, as some ancient historians believed. Around 300 B.C. some of these people left Poland for unknown reasons and began migrating south through the Balkans. When they reached the borders of the Roman Empire, the ancestors of the Visigoths found it easier to settle down than to continue south by fighting the Romans, and there they stayed, along the Danube River on the borders of the Roman Empire. They were small farmers, growing mostly wheat and barley.

Throughout the Roman Imperial period, the ancestors of the Visigoths constantly traded with the Romans and intermittently fought with them.

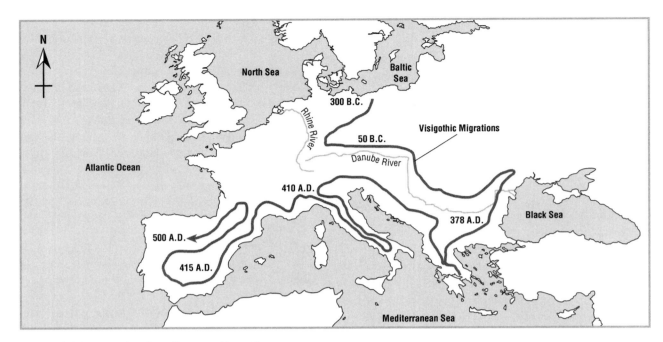

Extent of Visigothic migrations. DRAWN BY KAREN CARR.

Both sides benefited from this exchange of goods and information. It was through this contact that the Visigoths encountered new technologies and products, such as blown drinking glasses and bottles, writing, and poured concrete. In about A.D. 300 the Visigoths converted to Christianity through the missionary work of Roman Arians. The Visigoths also taught the Romans their own military techniques, and in the fourth century A.D. many Roman soldiers on the Rhine and Danube were buried carrying Gothic weapons and wearing Gothic clothing and jewelry.

Starting in about A.D. 200, however, the situation of the Visigoths became untenable. The Huns, leaving their homeland in eastern Siberia, had migrated across Asia and were sweeping down through Europe, pushing refugees ahead of them. The Visigoths, attacked by the Huns, tried desperately to move across the Danube into the safety of the Roman Empire but found themselves trapped between two powerful opponents. Perhaps as a result, they began to develop a more formal identity and leadership. In A.D. 378 the Visigoths took advantage of Roman military mistakes to kill the Roman emperor Valens at the battle of Adrianople, cross the Danube, and take over a piece of the Balkans within the empire. The Romans were unable

to push the Visigoths out but refused to provide the refugees with food, seeds, or tools so that they could reestablish themselves as farmers.

A generation later, the Visigoths were still in the Balkans, struggling as refugees and growing increasingly angry. Their leader, Alaric, demanded food and supplies from the Roman emperor Honorius in Ravenna, but Honorius did nothing. In response, Alaric took his entire people and began moving toward Rome. Meeting no serious opposition, Alaric's army sacked the city of Rome in A.D. 410. The Visigoths stayed only three days, because Honorius immediately cut off food supplies to Rome. When they left, the Visigoths headed south down the Italian coast, apparently hoping to cross the Mediterranean Sea to Africa. Most of Italy's food came from Africa, and the Visigoths thought of it as a promised land. In the toe of Italy, however, a bad storm destroyed the boats they were planning to use, and the Visigoths hesitated, having no experience with seafaring and frightened by the storm. Unexpectedly, Alaric died. Alaric's brother-in-law Ataulf (Ataulphus or Adolf) took over and led the Visigoths back up north and past the Alps into southern France.

In A.D. 409, however, the Vandals, Alans, and Sueves had invaded Spain. Honorius now invited the Visigoths to counterattack and get rid of these people in exchange for the right to settle in southern France. Ataulf accepted the contract, and the Visigoths wiped out the Alans and some of the Vandals. At this point, in A.D. 415, Honorius belatedly realized the danger that the Visigoths would cross from Spain to invade Africa; fearing that the Visigoths would cut off the food supply of Rome, and he hastily recalled them to France, leaving the remaining Vandals and Sueves in place in Spain.

The Visigoths were happy to settle down in southern France, establishing their capital at Toulouse. It seems that they received tax revenues from the whole area, although it is unclear by what mechanism. By the death of King Theoderid in 451, they had established a kingdom essentially independent of Rome and even proposed their own candidate for emperor in the 450s. The Visigoths fought alongside Roman generals against Attila and the Huns in the 460s. Under King Euric (r. 466–484), they established their own laws, with separate codes for the Goths and for their Roman subjects.

After the Vandals abandoned Spain for Africa in A.D. 429, however, the Visigoths gradually expanded into the power vacuum in Spain. At the same time, the Frankish king Clovis was pushing southward from his base in northern France. In A.D. 507 Clovis defeated the Visigoths at the battle of Vouillé and killed the Visigothic king Alaric II. The Visigoths ceded southern France to Clovis and took over Spain instead, establishing their new capital at Toledo in central Spain.

With the death of Alaric, the Visigoths were left with a child king, Amalaric. Amalaric's grandfather was the powerful Theodoric the Ostrogoth, ruler of Italy. Theodoric announced that he would act as regent for his grandson, and in this way the Ostrogoths dominated Spain and the Visigoths for the rest of Theodoric's long life, until A.D. 526. Even after Theodoric died, Amalaric soon was assassinated in favor of another Ostrogothic ruler, Theudis (r. 531–548).

A civil war starting in 549 resulted in an invitation from the Visigoth Athanagild, who had usurped the kingship, to the Byzantine emperor Justinian I to send soldiers to his assistance. Athanagild won his war, but the Romans took over Cartagena and a good deal of southern Spain and could not be dislodged. Starting in the 570s

Fig. 1. Gothic gold eagle fibula with garnet and cloisonné inlays. GERMANISCHES NATIONALMUSEUM. REPRODUCED BY PERMISSION.

Athanagild's brother Leovigild compensated for this loss by conquering the kingdom of the Sueves (roughly modern Portugal) and annexing it, and by repeated campaigns against the Basque separatists. Leovigild's son, Reccared, converted from Arianism to Catholicism, which did much to wear down the old distinctions between Hispano-Roman and Visigoth. This newfound unity found expression in increasingly severe persecution of outsiders, especially the Jews.

After Reccared's death, the seventh century saw many civil wars between factions of the aristocracy. Despite good records left by contemporary bishops, such as Isidore and Leander of Seville, it becomes increasingly difficult to distinguish Goths from Romans, as the two became inextricably intertwined. Despite these civil wars, by A.D. 625 the Visigoths had succeeded in expelling the Romans from Spain and had established a foothold at the port of Ceuta in Africa.

In the late 600s, however, the great Islamic conquest of the Mediterranean coast was in full swing. The Moors, recently converted to Islam, seized the port of Ceuta, attacking unexpectedly on Easter Sunday in 711. Then, in a reprise of the events of the late 500s, one of the Visigothic parties to a civil war invited the Moors to help him, and the Moors invaded Spain. They found no army that could mount any serious opposition, and by 712 Spain was firmly under Moorish control. The Visigoths, by then entirely assimilated with the Romans, retreated to the Pyrenees, from where they began the long, slow process of reconquest.

See also **Huns** (*vol. 2, part 7*); **Ostrogoths** (*vol. 2, part 7*).

BIBLIOGRAPHY

Carr, Karen Eva. *Vandals to Visigoths: Rural Settlement Patterns in Early Medieval Spain.* Ann Arbor: University of Michigan Press, 2002.

Collins, Roger. *Early Medieval Spain: Unity in Diversity, 400–1000.* 2d ed. New Studies in Medieval History. Basingstoke, U.K.: Macmillan, 1995.

Heather, Peter. *The Goths.* Oxford: Blackwell, 1996.

Stocking, Rachel L. *Bishops, Councils and Consensus in the Visigothic Kingdom 589–633.* Ann Arbor: University of Michigan Press, 2000.

Wolf, Kenneth Baxter, trans. and ed. *Conquerors and Chroniclers of Early Medieval Spain.* 2d ed. Liverpool, U.K.: Liverpool University Press, 1999.

Wolfram, Herwig. *History of the Goths.* Translated by Thomas J. Dunlap. Berkeley: University of California Press, 1988.

KAREN CARR

VIKING SHIPS

The region settled by the Vikings during the ninth to eleventh centuries consisted of the Scandinavian Peninsula and Jutland, the Danish archipelago, and islands in the Baltic and the North Atlantic as well as areas along the coasts and larger rivers of Britain, Ireland, northern France, and Russia. There were no overland routes connecting these areas, and consequently all communication relied on the ships and boats that rightfully became a trademark for Viking expansion as recorded in contemporaneous sources and in the archaeological record.

Several ships of the Viking period have been found in graves and as wrecks, and reused ships' parts have been excavated in Viking towns, giving a detailed insight into the boat- and shipbuilding traditions of the period. There are few remains found of Nordic ships from the fifth to eighth centuries, the crucial period during which ship design in this area changed from large rowing vessels of the Migration period to the ships of the early Viking Age, combining propulsion by oars and sail. In contrast, wrecks of the medieval period and later provide evidence for the study of the region's shipbuilding heritage and traditions from the Viking era to the twenty-first century.

All Viking ships were built by the clinker technique—that is, starting from a central keel, with identical stems fore and aft and with the overlapping edges of the planking riveted together. After shaping the lower planks to give the desired shape of the bottom, the floor timbers were inserted and fastened to the planking, with lashings in the early phase and later using treenails. The sides were supported by side timbers and by knees positioned on the deck beams (*biti*) over each of the floor timbers. A light, strong, and resilient hull was evidently the goal of Viking shipbuilders when constructing vessels for various purposes. Oak and pine were the primary materials for the hulls, with ropes of linden bast and sails of sheep's wool. The ships were steered with a side rudder to starboard and propelled primarily by a single square sail stepped amidships in a keelson, a longitudinal timber with the step for the mast. The sail was set from a horizontal yard and adjusted by means of several ropes to bring the ship forward with the wind from astern, abeam, or up to 60 degrees to the wind in tacking. Viking ships had no cabins or weather decks, and all water coming inboard had to be bailed out.

The ships from the large burial mounds in southeastern Norway at Oseberg (c. A.D. 820, excavated in 1904) and Gokstad (c. A.D. 895, excavated in 1880), now exhibited in Oslo, represent the early Viking Age multifunctional ship type. With a length of 21.6 to 24.2 meters, a beam of 5.1 meters, and sides 1.6 to 2.1 meters high amidships, these vessels were propelled equally well by their square-sail of about 90 to 110 square meters or by their 30 to 32 oarsmen. The Oseberg ship is considered the personal vessel for the high-ranking woman buried in it with her elaborately decorated belongings. The Gokstad ship has higher sides and is slightly more robust, making it fit for deep-sea navigation with its crew and a moderate cargo of trade goods or booty.

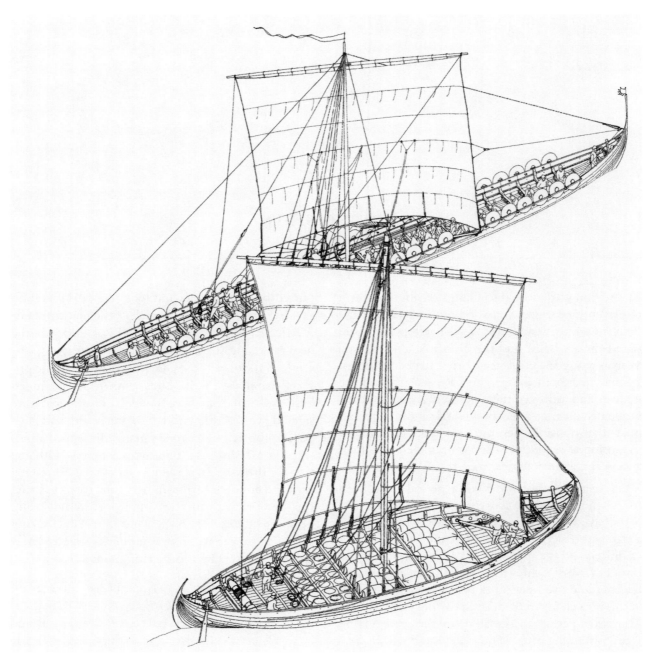

Fig. 1. The Hedeby 1 and Hedeby 3 Viking ships. DRAWN BY SUNE VILLUM-NIELSEN. © THE VIKING SHIP MUSEUM, DENMARK. REPRODUCED BY PERMISSION.

Viking ships of the tenth and eleventh centuries have been found at several sites, the most important ones being Ladby (burial, c. A.D. 925), Hedeby (two wrecks, c. A.D. 985–1025), and Skuldelev (five ships in a barrier, c. A.D. 1030–1050). The Ladby ship imprint in the ground, excavated 1935, is preserved in the Kerteminde region of Denmark, whereas the Hedeby ships, excavated 1979–1980, and the Skuldelev ships, excavated 1962, are exhibited in the Schleswig region of Germany and at Roskilde, Denmark, respectively. Additional evidence comes from excavations in the Viking towns of Hedeby and Dublin.

These ships display the range of types and sizes of vessels that had been developed for different purposes in that period. The primary division was between the relatively long and low "personnel carriers," built primarily to satisfy the requirements for fast propulsion by rowing (demanded by longships used as troop transporters and by boats used for communication and fishing), and the broader and higher "cargo carriers" that required a proper cargo capacity, relying mainly or fully on sail propulsion. This specialization is not found in vessels dating before the tenth century.

The longships that served in the Danish waters, the North Sea, and the Irish Sea are represented by the Irish-built Skuldelev 2 ship and the Hedeby 1 ship (fig. 1) built locally, both about 30 meters in length but only 3.8 meters and 2.7 meters wide respectively and manning about 60 oars each. Skuldelev 5 was a small 26-oared longship for local defense. These three warships represent different levels of craftsmanship, from the royal standard of Hedeby 1 to the "discount version" Skuldelev 5. In the longships, the oars were worked through holes in the ships' sides, and shields could be mounted along the rail. Figureheads were carried on prominent longships, and others had gilt weather vanes, but most longships probably had no decorative flourishes other than their stemposts ending elegantly at a point.

Smaller, boat-sized vessels had their oars mounted along the rails. They could be used as ships' boats, for communication, for general transportation, and for harvesting the sea, such as the Norwegian-built Skuldelev 6.

The cargo-carrying vessels range in sizes from the small Danish-built 14-meter-long general-purpose vessel Skuldelev 3 with a cargo capacity of 4 to 5 tons, to the 16-meter-long Baltic trader Skuldelev 1 (from western Norway) with a capacity of 20 to 25 tons, to the Hedeby 3 ship (fig. 1) with an estimated capacity of about 60 tons. The largest cargo-carrying ships were entirely dependent on sail propulsion, and their hulls were more solidly built than the longships. This type of ship was further developed in size during the eleventh and twelfth centuries to match the needs of trade in this period of urbanization around the Baltic and the North Sea.

The seaworthiness of the Gokstad ship was demonstrated as early as 1893 when a full-scale reconstruction of this ship crossed the Atlantic under sail. Since then several of the ships mentioned here, including all five Skuldelev ships, have been reconstructed at full scale and tested in order to study their potentials for the many needs of the maritime-oriented society of the Vikings.

See also **Viking Harbors and Trading Sites** (*vol. 2, part 7*).

BIBLIOGRAPHY

Bill, Jan. "Ships and Seamanship." In *The Oxford Illustrated History of the Vikings.* Edited by Peter Sawyer, pp. 182–201. Oxford: Oxford University Press, 1997.

Brøgger, Anton Wilhelm, and Haakan Shetelig. *The Viking Ships: Their Ancestry and Evolution.* Oslo, Norway: Dreyers, 1951.

Crumlin-Pedersen, Ole. "Splendour versus Duty: Eleventh-Century Warships in the Light of History and Archaeology." In *Maritime Warfare in Northern Europe.* Edited by A. N. Jørgensen et al., pp. 257–270. Studies in Archaeology and History 6. Copenhagen: National Museum of Denmark, 2002.

———. "Ships as Indicators of Trade in Northern Europe, 600–1200." In *Maritime Topography and the Medieval Town.* Edited by Jan Bill and Birthe Clausen, pp. 11–20. Studies in Archaeology and History 4. Copenhagen: National Museum of Denmark, 1999.

———. *Viking-Age Ships and Shipbuilding in Hedeby/ Haithabu and Schleswig.* Ships and Boats of the North, vol. 2. Schleswig, Germany: Provincial Museum of Archaeology; Roskilde, Denmark: Viking Ship Museum, 1997.

Crumlin-Pedersen, Ole, and Olaf Olsen, eds. *The Skuldelev Ships I.* Ships and Boats of the North, vol. 4.1. Roskilde, Denmark: Viking Ship Museum, 2002.

OLE CRUMLIN-PEDERSEN

JEWELRY

Almost universally, individuals adorn themselves with jewelry that may indicate rank, gender, age, marital status, ethnicity, and religious beliefs—and barbarian Europe was no exception. Jewelry gives an important view into how peoples of the early medieval period from A.D. 400 to 1000 identified themselves and their groups. In the absence of stone architecture and sculpture, jewelry making was a primary art and sometimes is the only medium that has survived from these cultures. Though much of barbarian jewelry comes from loose or undocumented finds, whether accidentally lost or deliberately hidden, examples found in inhumation graves allow archaeologists to re-create details of costumes, since jewelry was used to fasten clothes together as well as to adorn the elite. Some jewelry, such as buckles and brooches, was functional, regardless of the degree of decoration, whereas other types, such as pendants and earrings, were more ornamental and symbolic, distinguishing individuals from each other.

Knowledge of various groups, such as Anglo-Saxons, Burgundians, Franks, Goths, Langobards, Ostrogoths, Vandals, Vikings, and Visigoths, has sometimes been based on spatial distributions of jewelry styles, since these "tribes" had diverse clothing fashions that required distinctive jewelry types to fasten and adorn them. Thus it has sometimes been assumed that peoples can be identified from jewelry found in graves; however, it is difficult to distinguish groups based on artifacts dating to this proto-historic age. As Helmut Roth points out in *From Attila to Charlemagne* (edited by Katharine

Brown, Dafydd Kidd, and Charles T. Little), it is often difficult to establish that an object was produced by, for instance, a Frank, just because it was found in an area later associated with the Franks. Issues of "ethnic" identification are also discussed by Herbert Schutz in the introduction to his *Tools, Weapons, and Ornaments* (2001). Finally, extra caution is necessary when making assertions about ethnicity based on classifications of jewelry without documented provenance.

JEWELRY TYPES

Common jewelry types included hair ornaments and headdresses, straight pins to hold veils and hair ornaments, necklaces of beads and pendants, earrings, brooches, belt buckles, strap ends, bracelets, wrist clasps (cuff fastenings), finger rings, and thin metal plaques sewn to clothing. In particular, brooches (or pins) have been studied and classified according to their myriad forms, including annular (ring), penannular (broken ring), quoit (flattened ring), disk, saucer, bow, cruciform, square-headed, equal-armed, oval, trefoil, bird, and animal types. Several brooch types derive from the Roman fibula, whose name recalls its formal resemblance to the human leg bone. Its function is based on the principle of the modern safety pin; it uses a wire spiral to provide flexibility for opening and shutting and usually has ornamentation on the enlarged head and foot plates that conceal the coiled spring and the catch plate for the pin. Certain types of jewelry were appropriate for particular clothing styles, and as fashions changed, so too did jewelry.

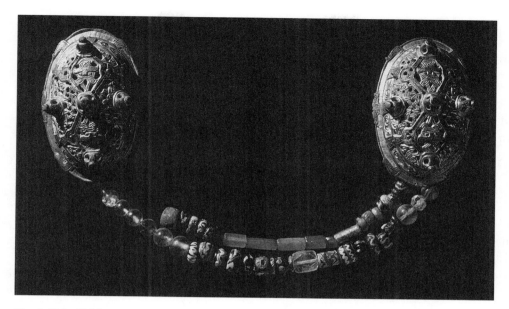

Fig. 1. Pair of Viking cast oval brooches of gilt bronze with silver details and beads of carnelian and glass—some with silver and gold foil, from Birka, Sweden, c. A.D. 900. © TED SPIEGEL/CORBIS. REPRODUCED BY PERMISSION.

RAW MATERIALS

Late Roman styles influenced the types of jewelry that were made, and the gold used in much early jewelry originated from melted down Roman coins. In the Viking Age, silver became more common than gold, as the supply of late Roman coins had long since died out and the source of metal by this time was Arabic silver coins. Copper, bronze, and iron were also used, particularly for functional jewelry. Bone and walrus ivory were carved for pins and rings. Glass, amber, and semiprecious stones (particularly quartz, rock crystal, jet, and garnet) were made into beads and also inserted into metal jewelry. Glass was produced in provincial Roman workshops in the Rhineland, and garnets came to Europe through Roman trade.

CONSTRUCTION TECHNIQUES

The techniques used to produce barbarian jewelry also derive from Roman methods and changed very little throughout the early medieval period, except for the introduction of the draw plate to produce wire (discussed below). The best source of information about production methods often is an examination of the artifacts, though some conclusions can be based on archaeological discoveries of tools and workshop debris. Important early medieval jewelry workshops have been discovered in Scandinavia at Helgö, Birka, Ribe, and Hedeby.

The most common method of jewelry construction was fabrication, which entails mechanical manipulation and joining of sheets of metal by hammering, folding, and soldering. Inscriptions, patterns, and images can be made on sheet metal by chasing or engraving, that is, using a pointed tool to displace or gouge out metal. The sheet can also be impressed with a stamp or die having a relief design, worked in repoussé by having designs hammered from the reverse, or embellished with small hammered punches. The central designs on Scandinavian Migration period (A.D. 450–600) gold pendants called bracteates were stamped with a die, but punches were used around the perimeter of these objects.

Casting was the other major method of jewelry construction. During the early medieval period, a two-piece mold was used rather than the ancient "lost-wax" technique. In casting, metal is melted in a crucible and then poured into the mold; used crucibles with residue as well as broken molds were found at workshop sites such as Birka in Sweden. After casting, rough edges must be filed away and polished; after this cleanup, the piece of jewelry might receive additional embellishment. Often jewelry cast in bronze or silver would be coated with silver or gold respectively to give an impression of a more valuable material.

DECORATIVE TECHNIQUES

Jewelry made by either casting or fabrication may be further adorned by surface decoration, including granulation, filigree, and inlays of stones or glass. Filigree, also known as wire work, consists of patterns of plain or decorative beaded wires soldered to the surface of a piece of jewelry. In the fifth and sixth centuries, wire was made by techniques called strip twisting and block twisting, in which a strip of metal is twisted, rolled, and hammered until it is approximately circular in section like a drinking straw. Drawn wire, manufactured by pulling a thin metal strip through a series of successively smaller round-sectioned holes in a draw plate, gradually replaced strip- or block-twisted wire from the seventh through the ninth centuries in northern Europe.

A decorative technique called granulation consists of soldering small spheres of gold or silver onto the jewelry surface. Granules are simple to produce by heating small pieces of metal until they roll up due to surface tension, but they are difficult to solder into place accurately. They were often used in large quantity and in combination with filigree, so individual mistakes are difficult to see without a microscope while the overall effect is impressive. Both filigree and granulation created glittering effects that are impressive by firelight.

Enameling and inlay of colored stones and cut glass were also used to enhance the surface appearance of jewelry with color, or polychrome, effects. Cloisonné, a technique in which materials are set into small cells (*cloisons*) fabricated by soldering upright strips of metal onto the surface of the jewelry, was often used in the early medieval period. Garnet cloisonné was used extensively on Merovingian jewelry. Well-known Early Anglo-Saxon examples are the shoulder clasps from Sutton Hoo, in which cut garnets as well as millefiori glass, composed of colored glass rods fused together and sliced into thin sections, are placed in cell work. Enameling during the early medieval period was achieved by placing broken or powdered glass within cells, which were then heated, and the glass was allowed to melt and fuse with the metal jewelry surface. Finally, glass was also used to make colorful, patterned beads, as evidenced from workshops at Ribe in Denmark.

See also **La Tène Art** (*vol. 2, part 6*); **Sutton Hoo** (*vol. 2, part 7*).

BIBLIOGRAPHY

Arrhenius, Birgit. *Merovingian Garnet Jewellery: Emergence and Social Implications.* Stockholm, Sweden: Almqvist and Wiksell, 1985.

Axboe, Morten. "The Scandinavian Gold Bracteates: Studies on Their Manufacture and Regional Variations." *Acta Archaeologica* 52 (1981): 1–100.

Bayley, Justine. "Anglo-Saxon Non-Ferrous Metalworking: A Survey." *World Archaeology* 23, no. 1 (1991): 115–130.

Brown, Katharine Reynolds, Dafydd Kidd, and Charles T. Little, eds. *From Attila to Charlemagne: Arts of the Early Medieval Period in the Metropolitan Museum of Art.* New Haven, Conn.: Yale University Press, 2000.

Cherry, John. *Goldsmiths.* Medieval Craftsmen Series. Toronto: University of Toronto Press, 1992.

Coatsworth, Elizabeth, and Michael Pinder. *The Art of the Anglo-Saxon Goldsmith.* Woodbridge, Suffolk, U.K.: Boydell Press, 2002.

Duczko, Wladyslaw. *Birka V: The Filigree and Granulation Work of the Viking Period: An Analysis of the Material from Björkö.* Stockholm, Sweden: Almqvist and Wiksell, 1985.

Hines, John. *A New Corpus of Anglo-Saxon Great Square-Headed Brooches.* Woodbridge, Suffolk, U.K.: Boydell and Brewer, 1997.

———. *Clasps, Hektespenner, Agraffen: Anglo-Scandinavian Clasps of Classes A–C of the Third to Sixth Centuries A.D.: Typology, Diffusion, and Function.* Stockholm, Sweden: Kungliga Vitterhets Historie och Antikvitets Akademien, 1993.

Hougen, Bjørn. *The Migration Style of Ornament in Norway.* 2d ed. Oslo, Norway: Universitetets Oldsaksamling, 1967.

Jensen, Stig. *The Vikings of Ribe.* Ribe, Denmark: Den antikvariske Samling, 1991.

Jessup, Ronald. *Anglo-Saxon Jewellery.* Aylesbury, Buckinghamshire, U.K.: Shire Archaeology, 1974.

László, Gyula. *The Art of the Migration Period.* Coral Gables, Fla.: University of Miami Press, 1974.

Ogden, Jack. "The Technology of Medieval Jewelry." In *Ancient and Historic Metals: Conservation and Scientific Research.* Edited by David A. Scott, Jerry Podany, and Brian B. Considine, pp. 153–182. Marina del Rey, Calif.: Getty Conservation Institute, 1994.

Ryan, Michael. *Studies in Medieval Irish Metalwork.* London: Pindar Press, 2002.

Schutz, Herbert. *Tools, Weapons, and Ornaments: Germanic Material Culture in Pre-Carolingian Central Europe, 400–750.* Leiden, The Netherlands: Brill, 2001.

Suzuki, Seiichi. *The Quoit Brooch Style and Anglo-Saxon Settlement.* Woodbridge, Suffolk, U.K.: Boydell Press, 2000.

Vida, Tivadar. "Veil Pin or Dress Pin: Data to the Question of Avar Period Pin-Wearing." In *Pannonia and Beyond.* Edited by Andrea Vaday, pp. 563–573, 811–815. Budapest, Hungary: Archaeological Institute of the Hungarian Academy of Sciences, 1999.

Whitfield, Niamh. "Round Wire in the Early Middle Ages." *Jewellery Studies* 4 (1990): 13–28.

Wicker, Nancy L. "On the Trail of the Elusive Goldsmith: Tracing Individual Style and Workshop Characteristics in Migration Period Metalwork." *Gesta* 33, no. 1 (1994): 65–70.

Youngs, Susan, ed. *"The Work of Angels": Masterpieces of Celtic Metalwork, Sixth–Ninth Centuries* A.D. Austin: University of Texas Press, 1990.

NANCY L. WICKER

BOATS AND BOATBUILDING

Archaeologists recovered a great deal of information during the last half of the twentieth century concerning the variety of boats used in central and northern Europe c. A.D. 400–1000. Detailed practical studies also have been carried out regarding the methods, tools, and materials used to build boats and ships at this time. The level of study of the material and its geographic spread is very uneven, however; the larger planked craft of southern Scandinavia are fairly well known, but the important shipbuilding traditions to the south, east, and west are far less well known or studied. This essay deals mainly with small boats and boatbuilding but also draws attention to the lesser known larger ships of the Angles, Saxons, Frisians, Slavs, Celts, and others.

Dugout boats, between 2.5 and 7 meters long, were the most common small boats in early medieval central and northern Europe, and many survive in museums across the Continent. Indeed, it is clear that in countries where systematic surveys have been conducted, such as the British Isles, most dated dugout boat finds belong to this early medieval period. The variety of early medieval dugout vessels built in Britain and central Europe was considerable, reflecting local peasant boatbuilding traditions, the function of the craft, and the locally available trees. Most vessels were built from large whole or halved oak trunks between about 0.6 and 1.0 meters in diameter. By the end of the early medieval period in the tenth and eleventh centuries, it is clear that the very highest quality large oak trees were out of reach to small dugout boatbuilders in some in-

tensively settled regions, such as England and Denmark. The best trees were reserved for building the large, high-status planked ships, such as the ninth-century long ship from Hedeby, Jutland. The low status of dugout vessels also is indicated by the lack of historical and pictorial sources for them. On the western fringes of Europe, in parts of Britain and Ireland, it is thought that skin-covered boats ("coracles" and more elongated "curraghs") were used, but the archaeological evidence for them is slight. It also is very likely that rafts were used on some inland waterways where light pines, firs, and spruces grew, in montane central Europe and northern areas.

Detailed experimental work has been done in England in the field of building small early medieval dugout boats (fig. 1), following detailed analysis of evidence, such as surviving tool marks and the trees used. It is clear that such craft were built with axes, adzes, and splitting techniques to remove the waste wood, rather than by fire hollowing. It has been discovered that fire was used in building some dugout vessels, as a means of softening the timber of thin hulls to expand them, as is still done in some parts of the world today. The wider shape, with uplifted ends, produced by this extraordinary process provided a more seaworthy, capacious shape than can be carved from a single log, and it often was extended upward with the use of overlapping planking. It is clear that this method was employed throughout the early medieval period in some areas, such as northwestern Germany, Denmark, England, and the Netherlands and probably elsewhere. An early example of an expanded dugout boat with one added plank on each side is the Vaaler Moor boat from northwestern Germany.

Use of replica craft and desk-based studies have shown that these often humble boats had a key role in developing the early medieval economy in lands with poor roads. They must have been used for expected purposes, such as ferrying, local travel of small numbers of people, fishing, fowling, and hunting, but many also were capable of carrying the equivalent of cart or packhorse loads of local produce or traded goods. For example, the 3.75-meter-long, Clapton boat, dating to the tenth century A.D. and found in London, could carry a crew and as much as 110 kilograms of cargo.

Larger cargo craft based on dugout hulls expanded by fire, extended by planks, and fitted with frames also were used in the Low Countries and around the southern North Sea region. These craft appear to have been known as "hulcs"; tenth-century fragments of such a seagoing trading vessel from the Low Countries were found in London. The most complete inland version of this type of vessel can be seen in Utrecht in the Netherlands. The overlapping planks of the upper hulls were waterproofed in a distinctive manner, with moss held in place by battens secured with small iron staples (*sintels*).

Most large trading, fishing, and war vessels that were built in early medieval northern Europe, however, were made in the clinker-planked "keel" style ("lapstrake"). In this case, a shell of partially overlapping planks was fastened to a central beam (also a "keel") and end posts to form a hull pointed at both ends. The planks were split out of large trees rather than sawn, as in Roman vessels. The use of clinker planks with light frames certainly also was employed late in this period for some quite small boats, such as the 4-meter-long, tenth-century Arby boat from central Sweden.

In the Slav and Baltic lands to the east of Scandinavia and in England to the west, local styles of clinker shipbuilding developed both before and after contact with the Vikings. In both regions the use of wooden pegs ("treenails") to fasten the overlapping boards commonly is found alongside rather heavier frame timbers than were used in the Scandinavian craft. Perhaps the most thoroughly investi-

Fig. 1. Replica of the Clapton tenth-century Anglo-Saxon dugout boat being hollowed out by an axe as dictated by the toolmarks found on the original. COURTESY OF D. M. GOODBURN. REPRODUCED BY PERMISSION.

gated non-Scandinavian-built planked vessel of this period is the Graveney boat, dating to the tenth or eleventh century, which was a small trading vessel. This craft was found in northern Kent in southeastern England in 1970 and had a fairly flat, but rounded bottom with a straight, sloping stern post and an original length of some 14 to 15 meters. Fragments of craft built in the same broad style have been found in London, reused in riverside construction during the tenth century.

Other traditions of planked vessel construction will undoubtedly emerge in the coming years with increasingly systematic archaeological work being carried out on land, sea, and the intertidal zone. One of these new finds being studied in detail is the Port-Berteau II wreck from the Charente River in southwestern France. In this vessel the planking was laid edge to edge, in the manner of carvel-built ships from later medieval times. The boat may even have been built frame first, rather than with framing added to a planked shell, as was typical farther north—even though it initially was dated well before A.D. 1000.

See also **Trackways and Boats** (*vol. 1, part 4*); **Viking Ships** (*vol. 2, part 7*).

BIBLIOGRAPHY

Arnold, Bettina. *Pirogues monoxyles d'Europe centrale: Construction, typologie, évolution*. Vol. 2. Archaeologie neuchateloise, no. 21. Neuchatel, France: Musée Cantonal d'Archeologie, 1996.

———. *Pirogues monoxyles d'Europe centrale: Construction, typologie, évolution*. Vol. 1. Archaeologie neuchateloise, no. 20. Neuchatel, France: Musée Cantonal d'Archeologie, 1995.

Greenhill, Basil. *The Archaeology of the Boat: A New Introductory Study*. London: Adam and Charles Black. 1976.

Litwin, Jerzy, ed. *Down the River to the Sea*. Proceedings of the Eighth International Symposium on Boat and Ship Archaeology, Gdańsk, 1997. Gdańsk, Poland: Polish National Maritime Museum, 2000.

Marsden, P., ed. "A Late-Saxon Logboat from Clapton, London Borough of Hackney." *International Journal of Nautical Archaeology* 18, no. 2 (1989): 89–111.

McGrail, Seán. *Ancient Boats in North-west Europe*. Rev. ed. London: Longman, 1998.

D. M. GOODBURN

CLOTHING AND TEXTILES

Textile and clothing production was an essential domestic industry in preindustrial times. Entire garments are rarely preserved in the archaeological record, but fragments of textiles, textile production tools, written records, and visual representations allow archaeologists to reconstruct how textiles and clothing were produced and worn between A.D. 800 and 1000, that is, the Early Middle Ages in continental Europe and the Viking Age in Scandinavia.

PRODUCTION

Textile production was primarily a domestic industry in early medieval Europe and Viking Age Scandinavia. Archaeological finds, literary and visual representations, and ethnographic analogies to living cultures all suggest that textiles were produced in the household by women. In Europe a few professional centers of production may have existed and may have exported cloth widely. Cloth was also professionally produced in the Middle East, the Near East, and the eastern Mediterranean during this period and was traded with Europe and Scandinavia. In the latter regions, flax fibers were used to create linen cloth and wool to create woolen cloth. Clothing was also made of silk and cotton, but these fabrics were imported from other regions, not produced locally.

In preparation for spinning, wool fibers were combed with wooden combs possessing long iron teeth. Combing aligned the fibers and separated the short fibers from the long. Soft flax fibers were first removed from their tough stem, then combed. Once the fibers were combed, they were ready to be spun into yarn. A distaff held the length of loose combed fibers, and a spindle weighted with a whorl was used to twist the yarn. The spinner held the distaff in one hand, spinning and dropping the spindle to pull and twist the fibers downward into yarn. She or he then gathered the spun yarn into balls or skeins.

Between A.D. 800 and 1000, warp-weighted looms were used to weave fabric throughout most of Europe and Scandinavia. Warp-weighted looms were made of two uprights about 2 meters tall that leaned against a wall or rafter. A crotch at the top of each upright supported a horizontal beam of variable length. The beam had a series of holes to which the warp, or lengthwise, strands of yarn were attached. Loom weights made of stone or baked clay held the warp strands taut. The fabric was woven top to bottom, with the weaver walking back and forth, inserting the weft (crosswise strands) through the warp and beating it upward toward the beam. The weaver wrapped the woven cloth around the beam as she or he worked, so that it would be out of the way.

CLOTHING

Information on early medieval and Viking Age clothing is available through the archaeological remains of textiles, through written sources, and through visual representations. Scandinavian archaeologists have developed a particularly detailed understanding of Viking Age clothing.

A typical female costume in Viking Age Scandinavia consisted of several layers. The first layer was

Fig. 1. Early medieval textile fragments and production implements from York. © YORK ARCHAEOLOGICAL TRUST. REPRODUCED BY PERMISSION.

a linen shift, smooth or pleated, with long sleeves and a long skirt. Over this a Viking woman would have worn a tunic made of imported silk or some other fabric held in place with a pair of tortoiseshell brooches. She might have worn a shirt or caftan over the tunic, fastened with a trefoil brooch, an equal-armed brooch, or a large round fibula. In cold weather she would have added a cape or coat closed in front with a fibula. Finally, her costume would have included leather booties and perhaps a cap or other headgear.

A typical male costume in Viking Age Scandinavia included leggings or wide, knee-length breeches. Along with these, a man would have worn a woolen jacket with overlapping front or a sleeved coat with bronze buttons, similar to a riding caftan. To complete the outfit, he would have had a leather belt, boots, and perhaps a hat or cap.

Both men's and women's clothing was adorned with trimmings and ornamentation made from luxury materials, like silk, precious metals, and furs.

Trimmings included woven bands, braid work, and embroidery.

TEXTILES FROM EARLY MEDIEVAL EUROPE AND VIKING AGE SCANDINAVIA

Several European and Scandinavian archaeological sites are notable for their finds related to early medieval and Viking Age textiles. Oseberg in Norway and York in England have yielded evidence related to textile production, while finds from Birka in Sweden illustrate the richness of clothing between A.D. 800 and 1000.

The Oseberg burial mound in southeastern Norway contained the grave of a wealthy woman buried with a companion in A.D. 834. Among her grave furnishings were textile production tools, including a set of weaving tablets with an unfinished braid still attached.

York was an early medieval urban center, first for the Anglian kingdom of Northumbria (seventh and eighth centuries A.D.) and later for the Scandinavian-controlled Danelaw (ninth to eleventh centuries A.D.). Excavations there have produced evidence of textile production, including raw wool and flax, dye plants, spinning and weaving equipment, and textile fragments (fig. 1.)

Many textile fragments, both local and imported, have been preserved at the Viking Age site of Birka (occupied A.D. 750–970), located on an island 30 kilometers west of Stockholm on the eastern coast of Sweden. Numerous types of linen and woolen fabrics have been recovered, varying in their fiber, fiber preparation, weave technique, and threads per inch and in secondary production techniques, such as dyeing. Silk fabrics also have been recovered at Birka, nearly all of them imported from Byzantium.

PRESERVATION

Textiles are fragile, organic artifacts that often suffer from physical and chemical deterioration. Textiles can be preserved archaeologically if agents of decay are absent or if agents of preservation are present to counteract decay.

Agents of decay include water, which acts as a catalyst for many chemical reactions; oxygen, which also acts a catalyst; pH levels, which affect various textile materials differently; bacteria; salts; temperature; overburden; and organisms. Preserving conditions for archaeological textiles include an absence of oxygen (often due to a waterlogged environ-

ment); an absence of water (in dry environments); and the presence of salts and other residues, which can preserve nearby fabrics by acting as biocides or by impregnating or replacing adjacent textile fibers.

In wet climates, such as in Europe and Scandinavia, textiles are primarily preserved in two environments: in waterlogged sites, where the lack of oxygen prohibits the decay of the fibers by microorganisms; and in close contact with metal objects, where the decay of the metals preserves the textile fibers. At York early medieval textiles survived under waterlogged conditions, while at Birka metallic salts preserved Viking Age textiles.

See also **Emporia** (*vol. 2, part 7*); **Jewelry** (*vol. 2, part 7*); **Anglo-Saxon England** (*vol. 2, part 7*); **Viking York** (*vol. 2, part 7*).

BIBLIOGRAPHY

Cronyn, J. M. *The Elements of Archaeological Conservation.* London: Routledge, 1990.

Geijer, Agnes. *A History of Textile Art.* London: Pasold Research Fund, 1979.

Harte, N. B., and K. G. Ponting, eds. *Cloth and Clothing in Medieval Europe.* London: Heinemann Educational, 1983.

Hoffman, Marta. *The Warp-Weighted Loom: Studies in the History and Technology of an Ancient Implement.* Oslo, Norway: Universitetsforlaget, 1964.

Walton, Penelope, and J. P. Wild, eds. *Textiles in Northern Archaeology. NESAT III: Textile Symposium in York, 6–9 May 1987.* London: Archetype Publications, 1990.

RAE OSTMAN

VIKING SETTLEMENTS IN ICELAND AND GREENLAND

FOLLOWED BY FEATURE ESSAY ON:

Near the close of the eighth century A.D., Nordic pirates, traders, and settlers began the expansion from their Scandinavian homelands that gave the Viking Age its name and permanently changed the development and history of Europe. In the North Atlantic, Viking Age settlers colonized the islands of the eastern North Atlantic (Faeroes, Shetland, Orkney, Hebrides, Man, Ireland) by c. A.D. 800. Iceland was traditionally settled c. 874, Greenland c. 985, and the short-lived Vinland colony survived a few years around A.D. 1000 in the Newfoundland–Gulf of St. Lawrence region. Around A.D. 1000 a common language and culture stretched from Bergen to the St. Lawrence, and colonists drawn from both Scandinavia and the British Isles were attempting the dangerous business of *landnám* (land taking, or first settlement) over a diverse range of island ecosystems.

In some of these island groups (Ireland, Shetland, Orkney, Hebrides, Man) the Nordic voyagers found well-established Iron Age maritime communities similar in many ways to their own, with enough cultural and linguistic overlap to allow widespread intermarriage and political alliance as well as feuding and mutual raiding. In other island groups (Faeroes, Iceland) humanity was either entirely absent or represented by a few (soon departing) hermetical monks, and the Viking Age settlers encountered an essentially virgin landscape. In Greenland and Vinland, contact was with indigenous maritime hunter-gatherers rather than agriculturalists. The Vinland contact rapidly resulted in victory for the local population—hostility of the local *Skraeling* is the only negative factor reported about Vinland in the later saga literature, but it was clearly enough to abort the European *landnám* of continental North America for another half millennium. In Greenland, a still poorly understood contact between Norse settlers and Dorset Paleo-Eskimo hunters resulted in a distribution of Norse farming settlements along the southwest coast and Dorset settlements far to the north in the Thule district. As they had in Iceland and the Faeroes, in Greenland the Norse again took over ecosystems unexploited by large-scale farming and again set up a new cultural and economic landscape.

After the demise of the Vinland settlement shortly after A.D. 1000, Iceland and Greenland were the westernmost outposts of Scandinavian culture in the North Atlantic. As Viking Scandinavia became integrated into European Christendom in the later eleventh century, many new options opened for would-be chieftains and ambitious younger sons in Normandy, England, and even Sicily, and the wind went out of the sails of the Viking Age Atlantic voyages. Greenland survived for another five hundred years before becoming extinct. Iceland, by contrast, remains today a very lively modern descendant of the age of settlement.

DOCUMENTARY SOURCES

Prior to the 1970s most scholars of the Viking period in the North Atlantic were philologists, medieval archaeologists, and documentary historians, and the uneven written record for Viking depredations in Europe and the colorful and diverse saga literature of Iceland tended to dominate discussion of the period (see Adolf Friðriksson, 1994). All of the saga literature of Iceland postdates the events of the *landnám* period in Iceland and Greenland by several hundred years. The rich documentary sources do not begin to become contemporary with the events they describe until the mid-twelfth century, and accounts of earlier times may very well have been heavily shaped by later political and dynastic agendas. Greenland certainly had its own set of sagas, annals, and written historical records, but these were all lost when the settlements became extinct and only a few tantalizing fragments remain. The surviving medieval documentary sources are thus rich and by no means completely analyzed, but it is unlikely that more will be discovered and they are thus essentially a closed body of data.

Since the mid-1970s research focus has shifted, as multiple field projects combining archaeology, paleoecology, and history have been carried out all across the region, producing new troves of data of different kinds not wholly dependent upon later documentary sources. The North Atlantic has become a very active center for field and laboratory research, so that every year new finds are made and new analyses carried out that change and enrich our picture of society of the settlement age and the historical ecology of *landnám*. Rapid expansion of both radiocarbon dating and the use of tephra (ash) from Icelandic volcanoes is providing an increasingly detailed chronology for early settlement in both Greenland and Iceland, and several long-term field projects are concentrating their efforts on early settlement. Thus although archaeology and paleoenvironmental studies increasingly are coming to dominate new research into the essentially prehistoric period of first *landnám,* the written accounts can be reinterpreted in light of fresh evidence to make a renewed contribution.

Both later documentary references and modern genetic studies indicate that many of the participants in each successive westward movement were drawn from previously settled islands—modern Icelanders have a strong British Isles genetic heritage and saga accounts suggest considerable ethnic diversity aboard the *landnám* vessels. Long open-water voyages were always dangerous, and of the twenty-four ships that set out from Iceland to colonize Greenland, only fourteen apparently completed the journey. First settlers had their pick of the best land, but in Iceland and Greenland they also faced a true wilderness without established farms, fields, roads, bridges, or local farming expertise. Domestic animals and human labor would both be desperately scarce in the early years, and saga accounts mention failed *landnám* attempts in Iceland.

EVIDENCE FROM EXCAVATIONS

In Iceland, archaeological evidence for early settlement has appeared in many areas, both along the south coast and in the northern coast and interior. The recent excavations of a nearly complete ninth-century longhouse on Aðalstraeði in the center of modern Reykjavík by Howell Roberts and Mjoll Snaesdóttir and what may be the tenth-century farmstead of Erik the Red himself serve to illustrate the rich evidence for Viking Age settlement in comparatively warm southern Iceland. More surprising has been the discovery of multiple early sites in the more arctic northern interior around Lake Mývatn by a long-term project directed by Orri Vésteinsson and Adolf Friðriksson. These inland high-altitude sites appear to form part of a whole landscape of settlement involving extensive boundary walls, charcoal-burning sites, pagan burials, and what has been identified (somewhat controversially) as a pagan temple at Hofstaðir. It would appear that expansion from the initial settlements along the coast was rapid and that high inland sites were occupied in the first generation of *landnám* in Iceland. Barley growing (for beer as much as bread) was initially practiced in many areas but was later largely discontinued due to both climate change and soil nutrient depletion, and most Icelanders depended on milk, meat, fish, bird's eggs, and a few gathered plants for their basic diet.

By A.D. 930 the Icelanders had set up a self-governing system of local and national *things* (assembly places) intended to regulate competition among chieftains and adjudicate disputes among farmers. The assemblies voted to adopt Christianity as the official religion (although allowing some pagan practice) in 1000, and Icelandic churchmen soon began to contest vigorously with secular chieftains for power, land, and followers. In the thirteenth century competition between great magnate families led to civil war and the loss of independence; in A.D. 1264 Icelanders submitted to rule under the king of Norway. After 1250 fishing played an increasing role in both subsistence economy and overseas trade, and a few fishing towns began in the eighteenth century. The Icelandic population fluctuated around fifty thousand throughout most of the Middle Ages and early modern periods, surviving epidemic disease, volcanic eruption, climate cooling, and repeated famine to regain political independence and prosperity based on commercial fishing in the twentieth century.

In Greenland, settlement took place a century after the Icelandic *landnám,* and settlers following Erik colonized two pockets of rich pasture at the heads of the great fjord systems of the southwest coast. The settlement was divided into a large eastern settlement in the south and the much smaller western settlement farther north in modern Nuuk district. Radiocarbon dates from both settlement areas suggest that, as in Iceland, the landscape filled rapidly, with the eastern settlement probably being settled a generation before the western settlement. Although Greenland is far larger than Iceland, the area holding plant communities rich enough to sustain European domestic stock is far smaller, and the colony seems to have stabilized at a much smaller population level, with estimates ranging from six thousand to around three thousand inhabitants. The Greenlanders were able to set up a chiefly society with assemblies as in Iceland, and they also adopted Christianity around A.D. 1000.

The Greenlandic economy was based partly on domestic stock, but with considerable supplement from hunted caribou and seals. Fishing seems to have played a minor role in Greenland, with walrus hide and ivory, polar bear and fox skins providing the key export products. In 1127 the Greenlandic chieftains traded a live polar bear to the king of Norway to get their own bishop, who appears to have rapidly taken the best land in the eastern settlement

for his manor. By the fourteenth century, Greenland boasted a monastery and nunnery as well as some of the largest stone churches in the North Atlantic. Archaeological evidence also suggests a sharply stratified medieval society, with the bishop's manor providing housing for more than one hundred cattle, whereas most farms had room for only two or three head.

Around A.D. 1200 the Norse and surviving Dorset Paleo-Eskimo were contacted by the Thule Inuit people. Ancestors of the modern Inuit of Canada and Greenland, these newcomers had migrated from Alaska and employed a highly sophisticated arctic hunting technology that allowed them to take baleen whales as well as seals. The dynamics of the Norse-Thule contact is still not understood, but it seems to have been a mixture of friendly and hostile encounters that resulted in a steady migration of the Thule people into the Norse settlement areas in the southwest coast. Around A.D. 1350 the smaller Norse western settlement became extinct, and by around 1450 the larger eastern settlement followed suit. Climate change, Thule contact, and declining connections to Europe all played a role in this sad end, but it also appears that settlement decisions and environmental impacts dating back to the initial *landnám* period created serious vulnerabilities in later Norse Greenland.

FACTORS IN COLONIZATION
Although the perils and opportunities of culture contact, the struggle to set up households and domestic economies, and the politics of land taking probably dominated the minds of the first settlers, environmental factors were also at work in the Norse colonization of the Western North Atlantic. As Norse settlers moved from the long coast of Norway to Iceland and Greenland they cut diagonally across the great arm of the Gulf Stream, the North Atlantic Drift, which brings warm water across the Atlantic to wash the coast of northwest Europe, making grain growing possible above the arctic circle in Norway. As they moved into Iceland and Greenland, the colonists began to leave the main channel of the North Atlantic Drift and enter environments critically different from their homelands. The south coast of Iceland is affected by the North Atlantic drift and is wet and comparatively warm in winter, but the north coast is low arctic, experienc-

ing deep snow and occasional drifting sea ice. West Greenland is affected by a side stream of the North Atlantic drift, but is also fundamentally arctic in climate; for example, it is afflicted by summer drift ice.

Thus it was entirely possible for a Norse colonist to journey hundreds of kilometers southward from an ancestral home in arctic Troms district to reach Iceland or west Greenland and still travel to a colder and more arctic local environment. The environmental differences may have been concealed initially by climate and biogeography. As Paul Buckland has pointed out, the flora of the North Atlantic islands is essentially like that of northwestern Europe, with the biogeographical break occurring between Greenland and Canada. Nordic and northern British settlers in Iceland and Greenland would have encountered fjords, valleys, and mountains covered with the same sort of dwarf willow, birch, grasses, sedges, and flowers so familiar from home. These plant communities formed the basis for northwest European Iron Age agriculture, providing grazing for domestic animals, construction material, fuel for heating and cooking, charcoal for iron smelting, important dietary supplements, and folk remedies for illness and injury. What was less evident to Viking Age settlers was that these familiar plants were all much closer to their biological limits in subarctic Iceland and low-arctic Greenland than they were in north temperate Britain or boreal northern Norway.

Farming practices sustainable for thousands of years in the homelands were to prove unsustainably destructive within a few generations in northern Iceland and Greenland. The deceptive similarity of the western North Atlantic islands was probably enhanced for the Viking Age settlers by the comparatively warm climate of the late ninth and early tenth centuries. Although climatologists no longer believe in a centuries-long, uniformly warm "medieval warm period," high-resolution proxy climate data from both ice and deep-sea cores do suggest that the period of initial *landnám* was warmer and probably more stable than the average for the region, and significantly warmer than the colder periods of the later Middle Ages. In the North Atlantic, a few degrees difference in annual temperature can have a massive impact on the viability of imported crops like barley and on the resilience of local pasture plant communities in the face of grazing pressure.

The western North Atlantic thus may have looked deceptively friendly to Norse settlement in the Viking Age and what was to prove an anomalously warm climate phase contributed to some initial errors in settlement and subsistence choices. In Iceland, rapid deforestation followed first settlement, and pollen studies suggest that 90 percent of the dwarf birch and willow forests present at *landnám* were removed in the first century of settlement. In some areas, rapid soil erosion took place soon after, and many settlement-age sites in Iceland are now located in heavily eroded landscapes. In Greenland, soils are generally less prone to wind erosion, but several studies have indicated a parallel pattern of deforestation and locally significant soil erosion following shortly after *landnám*. Something went wrong when the northwest European Iron Age economy was transplanted to Iceland and Greenland.

ANIMAL EVIDENCE

Zooarchaeology provides good proxy evidence for past economy, and a growing number of large well-excavated animal bone collections from the Viking Age North Atlantic give an impression of the changing economy of the *landnám* period. Domestic animals imported from Europe clearly were both a cultural and an economic necessity. Farm location in both Iceland and Greenland was determined by concentrations of pasture vegetation, and social status seems to have been linked to cattle keeping. There was a relative abundance of domestic animal bones (cattle, horse, dog, pig and "caprine"—that is, both sheep and goats) on sites from Norway, Iceland, and Greenland. The chieftain's farm on the site of Åker in southern Norway probably represents a sort of cultural ideal for aspiring farmers, and it is characterized by a large number of cattle and pig bones and a relatively small number of sheep and goat bones. Late-ninth- to early-tenth-century collections from both northern and southern Iceland show varied success in imitating the Norwegian model, but all show considerable numbers of cattle and pigs.

The later tenth-century collections are all from northern Iceland, and these show a range of different strategies employing different mixes of cattle, pigs, sheep, and goats. By the eleventh and twelfth centuries these northern Icelandic collections began to take on the sheep-dominated character of the later Middle Ages and early modern periods: cattle bones drop in numbers, and pig and goat bones become extremely rare. This shift in farming strategy may in fact be a response to the rapid deforestation and unexpected soil erosion of the first centuries of *landnám*. It is possible that pigs and goats were most responsible for the rapid loss of tree cover in ninth- and tenth-century Iceland and that the loss of woodlands in turn made the keeping of these species uneconomic.

Thus the zooarchaeological record indicates that by the time Erik the Red and his followers were contemplating the *landnám* of Greenland, significant economic change had already taken place on many Icelandic farmsteads. However, the zooarchaeological record from early settlement period phases of Greenlandic sites indicates that the "ideal farm" of the Nordic homelands still exercised a strong hold on the first settlers. Especially at the chieftain's farm at W 51, early layers are rich in cattle and pig bones, and the overall pattern is more similar to that of *landnám* Iceland in the ninth century than to contemporary eleventh-century Iceland. Pigs prospered even more poorly in later Greenland than in Iceland, and the later domestic mammal samples show few or no pig bones and a general reduction in cattle. Imported domestic animals were only a part of the complete subsistence economy, and especially in the early days of *landnám* wild birds, fish, and mammals were critical supplements.

The well-established Norwegian chieftain's farm at Åker may have provided a model for domestic stock raising for the early colonists of southern Iceland at Tjarnargata 4 and Herjolfsdalur, but wild sea birds (including a few of the now-extinct great auk) underwrote the initial survival of these early settlements. The *landnám* settlers in the greater Reykjavík area also apparently made use of now-vanished local walrus colonies, as a few bones of immature walrus have been found at Tjarnargata 4 and an impressive set of tusks were recently recovered from the early longhouse at Aðalstraeði nearby. In northern Iceland, freshwater fish, preserved marine fish, birds, and bird eggs seem to have provided a major supplement on many sites. In Iceland the early reliance upon easily depleted bird and walrus colonies soon shifted toward more extensive use of marine fish, especially cod and haddock, laying the

basis for the large-scale commercial fishing of the later Middle Ages. In Greenland, fish bones are rare finds, but all sites (both early and later) show a massive amount of seal and some caribou bone. Smaller sites in Greenland (like W 48) show an increasing percentage of seal bones through time, a pattern probably mirrored in the 1999 results of isotopic investigation of human bones from Greenland by teams led by Jette Arneborg of the Danish National Museum showing a steady increase in the amount of marine foods consumed in the later Middle Ages.

SETTLEMENT STRATEGIES

Advances in zooarchaeology and understanding of settlement pattern and chronology have prompted some reexamination of the documentary record, and especially of retrospective passages in some of the sagas describing settlement times "long ago." An often-cited passage from *Egil's Saga* (translated in *The Complete Sagas of Icelanders*) describes the establishment of the settlement of the chieftain Skallagrim in Borgarfjörður in southeastern Iceland (emphasis has been added):

> Skallagrim was an industrious man. He always kept *many men with him* and gathered all the resources that were available for subsistence, since at first they had *little in the way of livestock* to support such a *large number of people*. Such livestock as there was *grazed free in the woodland all year round*. . . . There was no lack of driftwood west of Myrar. He had a farmstead built on Alftanes and ran another farm there, and rowed out from it to *catch fish and cull seals* and *gather eggs*, all of which were there in *great abundance*. There was plenty of *driftwood* to take back to his farm. *Whales beached* there, too, in great numbers, and there was wildlife there for the taking at this hunting post: the animals were *not used to man* and would never flee. He owned a third farm by the sea on the western part of Myrar . . . and he planted crops there and named it Akrar (Fields). . . . Skallagrim also sent his men upriver to catch salmon. He put Odd the hermit by Gljufura to take care of the *salmon fishery* there . . . When Skallagrim's livestock grew in number, it was allowed to roam mountain pastures for the whole summer. Noticing how much better and fatter the animals were that ranged on the heath, and also that the sheep which could not be brought down for winter survived in the mountain valleys, he had a *farmstead built up on the mountain,* and ran a farm there where his sheep were kept. . . . In this way, Skallagrim put his livelihood *on many footings*.

The use of marine mammals, freshwater fish, and bird colonies "not used to man," exploitation of upland pastures, and the ecologically sound strategy of diversified resource use ("putting his livelihood on many footings") attributed to Skallagrim are also now clearly reflected in the archaeological record of *landnám*. Equally intriguing are the hints of a centralized settlement strategy involving both initially wide holdings by a single chieftain and careful arrangement of tenant farms to validate and effectively exploit the first comer's claim. The area said in the thirteenth-century saga to have been claimed in the ninth century by the industrious Skallagrim would contain the residences of four major chieftains in the thirteenth century as well as up to three hundred smaller farmsteads. The "Skallagrim strategy" would have the effect of establishing a wide scatter of settlements over a large area (intentionally including many environmental zones). It would also account for some of the unexpectedly early dates for settlements at higher elevations or less-desirable locations documented by archaeology in the late twentieth century and after, suggesting a rapid widespread population dispersal into all potentially habitable sites rather than a more gradual expansion outward from favored coastal locations. The residue of planned settlement expansion may be visible in later patterns of farm settlement in both Greenland and Iceland, which show considerable regularity in farm spacing and may reflect *landnám*-age allotments.

It seems likely that the politics of *landnám* involved the competitive interaction of a range of different strategies by chieftains, middle-ranking farmers, and the lower-ranking servants and slaves whose unsung labor was so vital to the success of the first settlements. Although the process of *landnám* in Iceland and Greenland is only beginning to be understood, research in many interrelated fields is making clear that the first century of settlement saw rapid change and transformation of both nature and human society that was to have profound and lasting impact on the history of the whole region.

See also **Animal Husbandry** (*vol. 2, part 7*); **Viking Settlements in Orkney and Shetland** (*vol. 2, part 7*).

BIBLIOGRAPHY

Amorosi, Thomas, Paul Buckland, Andrew Dugmore, Jon H. Ingimundarson, and Thomas H. McGovern. "Raiding the Landscape: Human Impact in the Scandinavian North Atlantic." *Human Ecology* 25, no. 3 (1997): 491–518.

Arneborg, Jette. "The Norse Settlement in Greenland: The Initial Period in Written Sources and Archaeology." In *Approaches to Vinland*. Edited by Andrew Wawn and Thórunn Sigurðardóttir, pp. 122–133. Reykjavik, Iceland: Nordahl Institute, 2001.

Arneborg, Jette, Jan Heinemeier, Niels Lynnerup, Henrik L. Nielsen, Niels Rud, and Arny E. Sveinbjornsdottir. "Change of Diet of the Greenland Vikings Determined from Stable Carbon Isotope Analysis and C14 Dating of Their Bones." *Radiocarbon* 41, no. 2 (1999): 157–168.

Arneborg, Jette, Jan Heinemeier, Niels Lynnerup, Niels Rud, and Arny E. Sveinbjornsdottir. "C14 dateringer af mennesknogler med de grønlandske nordboer some eksempl." *Hikuin* 27 (2000): 307–314.

Bigelow, Gerald F., ed. *The Norse of the North Atlantic.* Acta Archaeologica, no. 61. Copenhagen, Denmark: Munksgaard, 1991.

Buckland, Paul C. "The North Atlantic Environment." In *Vikings: The North Atlantic Saga*. Edited by William W. Fitzhugh and Elisabeth Ward, pp. 227–268. Washington, D.C.: Smithsonian Institution Press, 2000.

Buckland, Paul C., et al. "Bioarchaeological and Climatological Evidence for the Fate of the Norse Farmers in Medieval Greenland." *Antiquity* 70 (1996): 88–96.

Dugmore, Andrew J., and C. C. Erskine. "Local and Regional Patterns of Soil Erosion in Southern Iceland." In *Environmental Change in Iceland*. Edited by Johann Stötter and Friedrich Wilhelm, pp. 63–78. Münchener Geographische Abhandlungen series B, vol. 12. Munich: Institute for Geography, University of Munich, 1994.

Fredskild, Bent. "Agriculture in a Marginal Area: South Greenland A.D. 985–1985." In *The Cultural Landscape: Past, Present, and Future*. Edited by H. Birks, pp. 28–35. Mons, Belgium: Botanisk Institute, 1986.

Friðriksson, Adolf. *Sagas and Popular Antiquarianism in Icelandic Archaeology*. Aldershot, U.K.: Avebury, 1994.

Hreinsson, Viðar, ed. "Egil's Saga." In *The Complete Sagas of Icelanders: Including Forty-nine Tales*, vol. 1, p. 66. Reykjavik, Iceland: Leifur Eiriksson, 1997.

Jacobsen, B. H. "Soil Resources and Soil Erosion in South Greenland: An Attempt to Estimate Soil Resources in the Norse Period." *Acta Borealia* 1 (1991): 56–68.

Jones, Gwyn. *The Norse Atlantic Saga: Being the Norse Voyages of Discovery and Settlement to Iceland, Greenland, and North America*. New York: Oxford University Press, 1986.

McGovern, Thomas H. "The Demise of Norse Greenland." In *Vikings: The North Atlantic Saga*. Edited by William W. Fitzhugh and Elisabeth Ward, pp. 327–340. Washington, D.C.: Smithsonian Institution Press, 2000.

———. "The Archaeology of the Norse North Atlantic." *Annual Review of Anthropology* 19 (1990): 331–351.

McGovern, Thomas H., G. F. Bigelow, Thomas Amorosi, and D. Russell. "Northern Islands, Human Error, and Environmental Degradation: A Preliminary Model for Social and Ecological Change in the Medieval North Atlantic." *Human Ecology* 16, no. 3 (1988): 45–105. (Reprinted in *Case Studies in Human Ecology.* Edited by Dan Bates and Susan Lees. New York: Plenum Press, 1996.)

McGovern, Thomas H., and Sophia Perdikaris. "The Vikings' Silent Saga: What Went Wrong with the Scandinavian Westward Expansion." *Natural History* (October 2000): 50–56.

McGovern, Thomas H., Sophia Perdikaris, and Clayton Tinsley. "Economy of Landnam: Evidence of Zooarchaeology." In *Approaches to Vinland.* Edited by Andrew Wawn and Thórunn Sigurðardóttir, pp. 154–166. Reykjavik, Iceland: Nordahl Institute, 2001.

Morris, Chris D., and D. James Rackham, eds. *Norse and Later Settlement and Subsistence in the North Atlantic.* Glasgow, Scotland: Glasgow University Press, 1992.

Ogilvie, Astrid E. J., L. K. Barlow, and A. E. Jennings. "North Atlantic Climate c. A.D. 1000: Millennial Reflections on the Viking Discoveries of Iceland, Greenland, and North America." *Weather* 55, no. 2 (2000): 34–45.

Ogilvie, Astrid E. J., and Thomas H. McGovern. "Sagas and Science: Climate and Human Impacts in the North Atlantic." In *Vikings: The North Atlantic Saga.* Edited by William W. Fitzhugh and Elisabeth Ward, pp. 385–393. Washington, D.C.: Smithsonian Institution Press, 2000.

Olafsson, Guðmundur. "Eiriksstaðir: The Farm of Eirik the Red." In *Approaches to Vinland.* Edited by Andrew Wawn and Thórunn Sigurðardóttir. Reykjavik, Iceland: Nordahl Institute, 2001.

Simpson, Ian A., Andrew J. Dugmore, Amanda Thomson, and Orri Vésteinsson. "Crossing the Thresholds: Human Ecology and Historical Patterns of Landscape Degradation in Iceland." *Catena* 42 (2001): 175–192.

Simpson, Ian A., W. Paul Adderley, Garðar Guðmundsson, Margrét Hallsdóttir, Magnús A. Sigurgeirsson, and Mjöll Snæsdóttir. "Soil Limitations to Agrarian Land Production in Premodern Iceland." *Human Ecology* 30, no. 4 (2002): 423–443.

Vésteinsson, Orri. "A Divided Society: Peasants and Aristocracy in Medieval Iceland." In *New Approaches to Medieval Iceland.* Edited by Árni Daniel, Daníel Júlíusson, and Orri Vésteinsson. Glasgow, Scotland: Glasgow University Press, 2002.

———. "The Archaeology of Landnám: The Shaping of a New Society in Iceland." In *Vikings: The North Atlantic Saga.* Edited by William W. Fitzhugh and Elisabeth Ward, pp. 164–174. Washington, D.C.: Smithsonian Institution Press, 2000.

———. "Patterns of Settlement in Iceland: A Study in Pre-History." *Saga-Book of the Viking Society for Northern Research* 25, no. 1 (1998): 1–29.

Vésteinsson, Orri, Thomas H. McGovern, and Christian Keller. "Enduring Impacts: Social and Environmental Aspects of Viking Age Settlement in Iceland and Greenland." *Archaeologia Islandica* 2 (2002).

Wawn, Andrew, and Thórunn Sigurðardóttir, eds. *Approaches to Vinland.* Reykjavik, Iceland: Nordahl Institute, 2001.

THOMAS H. MCGOVERN

HOFSTAðIR

The Viking Age site of Hofstaðir is located in northern Iceland, on the upper Laxá River near Lake Mývatn. The ruins first attracted attention during the late-nineteenth-century Romantic antiquarian revival as a potential pagan temple site. (The name can be translated as "temple farm.") In 1908 the Danish archaeologist Daniel Bruun and the philologist Finnur Jónsson carried out one of the first professional excavations in Iceland on the site, revealing an exceptionally large long hall and a rich midden deposit filling a circular depression just to the south of the hall. Bruun and Jónsson concluded that this great hall was in fact a pagan temple, with a sacred chamber at the north end of a great gathering hall, and for years the site has been used to illustrate discussions of pre-Christian Nordic religion. The original conclusion was disputed by Olaf Olsen, who carried out small-scale re-excavations in the mid-1960s and argued that there were no specialized pagan temple sites but rather chiefly "temple farms" combining many functions.

New international, interdisciplinary investigations began at Hofstaðir in 1992 under the direction of Adolf Friðriksson and Orri Vésteinsson and continued into the twenty-first century. The Hofstaðir excavations have expanded into a regional scale investigation of early settlement and human environmental impact in the Mývatn area. They have also brought the insights of zooarchaeology, archaeobotany, human osteology, tephrochronology, geoarchaeology, and environmental modeling to bear on the complex interactions of human politics, economy, and social organization with soils, vegetation, and a changing climate. Structural work at the Viking Age portion of Hofstaðir was completed in the summer of 2002, and analysis of structures, finds, and chronology continued.

The early-twenty-first-century excavations at Hofstaðir have confirmed Bruun's general conclusion that the main building was an impressively large hall, with four times the floor space of the average Viking Age dwelling. The systematic open-area excavation of Friðriksson and Vésteinsson's teams has added greatly to this picture, documenting a series of outbuildings—some freestanding and others connected to the main hall building. These buildings include an early timber-framed structure (whose sod walls clearly were added later for insulation and probably were not load bearing) with a beam-slot construction not used in later Icelandic structures. This structure changed in use: plant phytolith analysis and soil micromorphological work by Karen Milek (of Cambridge) indicates that what had been a dwelling floor was turned into a hay store. A few meters away a small outbuilding stood beside one of the hall entrances, with a refuse pile nearby. This outbuilding was solidly constructed with a stone-lined trench down the side and a superstructure supported by large posts.

Analysis of the pit fill suggests that this probably was one of the communal privies described in the later saga texts. This substantial and well-built structure certainly was not hidden and, in fact, may have been a mark of status in the Viking Age. Although the interior of the great hall had been damaged by the earlier excavations of Bruun, enough remained untouched to allow documentation and recovery of most of the floor layers and the many postholes penetrating into subsoil beneath. The entire surviving floor deposit has been sampled systematically for soil micromorphology and flotated for botanical and insect remains by Garðar Guðmundsson and should provide new insight into the organization and use of the interior space. The many postholes and stake holes penetrating to subsoil indicate fairly extensive interior partitioning, and bones and small artifacts were deliberately placed at the bottom of several holes before the support was inserted. The great hall was certainly a complex construction that

consumed a great deal of wood as well as turf and stone, representing a major investment of wealth and prestige in this early community.

Just to the south of the end of the great hall was the circular depression (area G) investigated by Bruun and Olsen. Bruun noted the large amount of well-preserved animal bone and described the deposit as a midden similar to those he had encountered in his excavations of Norse sites in Greenland. Expansion of the original trenches into an open-area excavation revealed that the feature was an exceptionally large and deep pit house, an ancient Nordic/Germanic/Slavic building type often found at Early Settlement Age (A.D. 874–930) sites in Iceland. It was filled with stratified layers of well-preserved animal bone as well as bone, stone, and metal artifacts, smithing slag, charcoal, ash, and fire-cracked stones. These deposits are still under analysis, but it is clear from the refuse that Hofstaðir was a full-scale working farm, with bones from all the Norse domestic animals found in all stages of butchery and consumption and extensive evidence of iron smelting from local bog ore. Recovered animal bones will provide a detailed picture of the changing economy at this important site and can be compared with similar deposits (some also filling pit houses) at other nearby Settlement Age sites.

Although Hofstaðir was certainly a chieftain's farm at its height in the late tenth to early eleventh centuries, the artifacts recovered are not particularly rich. A few small fragments of silver jewelry, a classic bronze ring pin, several glass beads, some worn knife blades, and a few single-sided composite bone combs are the exceptional finds; rusted iron nails are by far the most common artifactual finds. Evidence of volcanic tephra found under walls and radiocarbon dates suggest that Hofstaðir was not one of the first farms settled in the area (soon after A.D. 871) and that the peak period of the great hall may date to c. A.D. 950–1000. Its rise to temporary prominence may reflect the dynamic and competitive nature of chiefly politics during the Settlement Age.

The great hall at Hofstaðir certainly marked a briefly substantial chieftain's farm, but it also seems to have had ritual associations. When the hall was abandoned c. A.D. 1000, two sheep were beheaded and the bodies thrown onto the floor, the heads landing nearby. At the same time, skulls of cattle, sheep, goat, and pigs that apparently had been displayed outside along the roof were thrown down into the wall collapse or dumped together in a pit in one of the side rooms of the hall. A sheep skull was placed in each of the doorways, and then the whole farm was moved 150 meters across the home field, where a medium-sized turf farm and a small Christian chapel survived through the medieval period. The Viking Age ruins with the enigmatic great hall were never reoccupied and were left undisturbed for a thousand years.

See also **Viking Settlements in Iceland and Greenland** (*vol. 2, part 7*).

BIBLIOGRAPHY

Friðriksson, A., Orri Vésteinsson, and T. H. McGovern. "Recent Investigations at Hofstaðir, Northern Iceland." In *North Atlantic Environmental Archaeology.* Edited by R. Housely. Oxford: Oxbow Books, 2003.

Vésteinsson, Orri. "Patterns of Settlement in Iceland. A Study in Pre-History." *Saga-Book of the Viking Society* 25 (1998): 1–29.

Vésteinsson, Orri, T. H. McGovern, and Christian Keller. "Enduring Impacts: Social and Environmental Aspects of Viking Age Settlement in Iceland and Greenland." *Archaeologia islandica* 2 (2002): 98–136.

THOMAS H. MCGOVERN

VIKING SETTLEMENTS IN ORKNEY AND SHETLAND

The Orkney and Shetland archipelagos were among the smallest regions settled by Norwegians during the Viking Expansion that took place c. A.D. 800–1100. However, many years of multidisciplinary research have revealed that these northernmost British Isles played significant roles in the politics and economies of the Viking World of the North Atlantic and the North Sea. From their earliest settlements by Neolithic agriculturalists in the fourth millenium B.C., the "Northern Isles of Scotland," as Orkney and Shetland are known collectively, served as the northwestern frontier of the Eurasian landmass, and any westward movements of people, ideas, and domestic plants and animals stopped there. When the islands were settled by the Norse in the early medieval period, their peripheral status was transformed as they became the first stepping stones in an epic transoceanic migration that ended in North America. At that point, Orkney and Shetland became the gateway to the North Atlantic and a crossroads between Britain and Scandinavia.

ENVIRONMENTAL CONTEXT

To better understand the first Viking contacts with Orkney and Shetland and the eventual Norse settlement of the islands, it is necessary to examine the larger geographical contexts of the archipelagos. First, Shetland is the part of Britain which is geographically closest to Norway; as such it was a logical first landfall for Norwegian Vikings who sailed south to British and Irish locations. Thus, Shetland and nearby Orkney were likely staging points for Viking raids in the ninth and tenth centuries A.D., when these attacks were most frequent.

Second, although some archaeological evidence suggests that the islands were settled by people from northern Norway, broader sources point to the west coast of Norway as the home of most of the Viking colonists. The Northern Isles have a gentle landscape compared with much of Norway's mountainous west coast, with relatively richer resources for raising crops and herding domestic animals. However, like the west of Norway, the coastlines of the islands are quite indented, providing residents easy access from the shore to the deep sea. From a Norwegian perspective, Orkney and Shetland would have been desirable lands for practicing the familiar mix of farming and maritime resource exploitation found in most Viking settlement regions.

Third, although Orkney and Shetland are often discussed together, reflecting their sometimes shared political unity as a Norwegian, and eventually Scottish, earldom at various periods, the two archipelagos are geographically quite dissimilar in many ways. Most of the ecological differences are founded, literally, on bedrock. Orkney is underlain largely by the Old Red Sandstone, which breaks down into well-drained, fertile soil capable of supporting productive and stable agriculture. In Shetland, however, the Old Red Sandstone occurs largely in southern Mainland, and much of the rest of the archipelago is blanketed with poorer soils that formed on igneous and metamorphic substrates. These soils have been improved in many places through 5,000 years of cultivation, but in general,

Fig. 1. Aerial view of the Jarlshof site, Dunrossness, Shetland. This long-settled site had an extensive Viking and later Norse settlement, marked by straight walls on the left side of the photograph. © CROWN COPYRIGHT. ROYAL COMMISSION ON THE ANCIENT AND HISTORICAL MONUMENTS OF SCOTLAND (RCAHMS). REPRODUCED BY PERMISSION.

Orkney has always been a better environment for raising crops, while the Shetland landscape has fostered more pastoral adaptations.

The archipelagos' marine environments also differ. Waters of the great North Atlantic current system, which give the British Isles unusually warm temperatures for their northern latitudes, mix with the cooler and less saline North Sea around both Orkney and Shetland. However, Shetland lies quite close to the edge of the European Continental Shelf, where the currents are strongest and where upwelling of nutrient-rich water is greatest, while Orkney is surrounded by relatively shallow waters. The sum of these differences is that Shetland has a more diverse and dynamic marine environment that

has always had the potential to compensate for the region's marginality for cereal agriculture.

HISTORICAL EVIDENCE

There is little straightforward textual evidence regarding the Norse settlement of Orkney and Shetland. Icelandic statesman and historian Snorri Sturluson's *Heimskringla* states that the islands were settled in the reign of the Norwegian king Harald I Haarfager (Finehair) by Vikings wishing to escape his growing political power, but the account was written centuries later by an Icelander with contemporary concerns about Norwegian royal influence. The *Orkneyinga Saga*, the only Icelandic saga that was centered on the Northern Isles, contains little information on the causes and processes of the early

Norse settlement, and largely focuses on the political history of the Orkney Earldom in the eleventh and twelfth centuries. A scattering of other sources touch on the islands' Viking history in discussing the activities of Orkney Earls outside the islands. One such account is found in *Njál's Saga*, which concerns Earl Sigurd the Stout's death in Ireland at the battle of Clontarf in 1014. Written records of life in the islands increased dramatically in number and descriptive content in the later medieval and early post-medieval centuries.

PLACE-NAMES

Place-names are a type of originally verbal evidence that may preserve many cultural continuities from the Viking Period. The place-names of Orkney and Shetland are overwhelmingly Scandinavian in origin, demonstrating that the earlier Pictish language was replaced, not blended, with Old Norse in the decades after the *landnám* (first land-taking). Early place-names may include those incorporating the words or elements "bu" (*bú*), "-bister" (*bolstaðr*), and "skaill" (*skáli*), whereas the names of farms ending with "-ster" (*seter*) and "-gard" or "-garth" (*garðr*) may mark secondary establishments. Although place-names are impossible to date precisely, in some cases they may record changing land use. For example, place-names incorporating the words "pund" and "quoy" refer to livestock pens of various types, pointing to grazing as an early land use. In a more general way, the high density of place-names testifies to a very intensive exploitation of the island landscapes: for example, it is estimated that Shetland has over 50,000 Norse place-names distributed over a total land area of only 1,425 square kilometers.

ARCHAEOLOGICAL EVIDENCE

When the Norse arrived both island groups were inhabited by a Celtic population usually referred to by archaeologists and historians as the Picts. Various forms of archaeological evidence demonstrate strong cultural ties between the Picts of Orkney and Shetland and those of mainland Scotland. (Those on the mainland were first referred to as "Picts" by the Romans in the third century A.D.) Much remains to be learned about the Northern Isles Picts, but archaeological research conducted since the 1970s has shown that there must have been a considerable population in the centuries just before the

Norse colonization. In this regard the Northern Isles of Scotland differed dramatically from the largely uninhabited places that the Vikings later colonized, including the Faroe Islands, Iceland, and Greenland.

However, with the exception of scattered pre-Norse place-names and perhaps some distinctive elements in landholding organization, there are few elements in the cultures of Norse Orkney and Shetland that seem to be holdovers from the Pictish past. The lack of pre-Norse cultural traces in the Viking period has led to speculation that the meeting of the two peoples must have been violent, resulting in the extermination of the Picts. Currently available archaeological evidence regarding this complex issue remains ambiguous, and the nature of Pictish-Norse interaction is still an enigma.

Indeed, the general scarcity of documents relating to local events in the Norse settlement period makes archaeological evidence critically important. Viking-period settlements and burials have been uncovered, either accidentally or through formal excavations since the 1800s, and much has been learned about Norse life in Orkney and Shetland. This brief discussion will outline only the largest and most significant sites and finds that have revealed important information.

The earliest excavated Norse settlements in Orkney include those at Buckquoy, the Brough of Birsay, Pool, Westness, Skaill in Deerness, and Saevar Howe. In Shetland, the only excavated sites with extensive demonstrated Viking period remains are at Jarlshof and Old Scatness. At present, the only relatively well-preserved buildings in Shetland that were not reused Pictish constructions are at Jarlshof. Norse occupation levels at all of these sites were underlain by the remains of Pictish settlements. Yet only at Buckquoy, and possibly Pool, was there plausible evidence of continuities between the Pictish and Norse occupations; others revealed a possible hiatus in settlement before the Norse arrival. Dating evidence for all of the sites varies in quantity and quality. In general, these Viking settlements seem to have begun in the later ninth century, a considerable time after the onset of Viking raids in southern Britain would have brought Norwegians to the Northern Isles. Thus, on the one hand, the long-term assumption that settlement began with Viking raiding in the early ninth century is not supported so far by the archaeological record. On the other hand, further field studies and analyses may change this picture: the settlement evidence for the Northern Isles A.D. 800–1100 is still relatively slight, especially in the Shetland Islands.

Burials also may provide much information about Viking cultures, but this type of evidence is much more common in Orkney than in Shetland. Major cemeteries existed at Pierowall on Westray and at Westness on Rousay. Apparently isolated graves have also been found at other locations in Orkney and in Shetland. Pagan Viking burial forms in the Northern Isles included inhumations in long and short rectangular, stone-lined trenches or cists, flexed burials in stone-lined, ovoid pits, and boat burials that incorporated small, inshore vessels. The variety of included grave goods matches those found in other areas of the Viking World, and typical artifacts include weapons of various sorts and equipment for making textiles. Shetland has far fewer pre-Christian Norse graves than does Orkney, and far fewer than have been found in Norway and Iceland. This is a striking pattern that is difficult to explain: the conditions of preservation and the likelihood of discovering such sites would seem to be the same on Shetland as in the other locations. The acceptance of Christianity by the Norse would have curtailed the equipping of burials with grave goods, but there is no evidence that suggests that the Shetland Norse were Christianized earlier than those of Orkney. Likewise, there is no evidence that Orkney was settled earlier and would thus have had a longer "pagan period," with greater numbers of pagan interments.

REGIONAL ECONOMY

When the regional archaeological evidence is interpreted with the aid of historical records of the Northern Isles and Norway, and with ethnographic information from later centuries, a picture emerges of the ways in which the Norse settlers of Orkney and Shetland provided themselves with food and shelter. However, it is important to recognize that relatively few sites from the 800–1100 era have been thoroughly excavated with modern methods. Even fewer sites contain both well-preserved architecture and bioarchaeological evidence from associated middens, or refuse deposits. Both types of evidence are valuable for reconstructing human economies.

It is likely that current projects, such as the Old Scatness Broch investigations in Shetland and the Quoygrew excavations in Orkney, will produce this type of complementary evidence. (Such sites are more common in Iceland and Greenland, where entire Viking period settlements were quickly abandoned, leaving better-preserved remains.) It is currently impossible to define a typical Viking period settlement type for either Orkney or Shetland. Some excavated settlements apparently supported multiple households in separate but adjacent dwellings, while other sites seem to represent single-household farms. Over time, Orkney and Shetland developed a more concentrated settlement pattern, eventually forming loose clusters of farmsteads similar to what would later be termed townships, but it is difficult to specify the forms these settlement units took in the period between 800 and 1100. Place-name evidence and later settlement distributions suggest that one key requirement for establishing an early Norse farm was proximity to a shoreline where boats could be landed.

Bioarchaeological and artifact evidence from excavated sites indicates that the Viking-period Norse of the Northern Isles relied on diverse sources of food, including domestic livestock, cereals, and wild foods, including fish, seals, seabirds and mollusks. Cattle and sheep were the most important mammals, but some pig bones have been found on all sites. In contrast with Viking Norway and Greenland, there is little evidence that goats were ever important in Northern Isles' economies.

Both the grains and the quern stones used to process them have been recovered from Viking period sites, and they demonstrate that cereals were a key resource in both Orkney and Shetland. *Bere* (two-rowed barley—*Hordeum vulgare*) was the most important crop, as in later centuries. Barley is well suited to cultivation in the archipelagos because it is salt-tolerant, and much sea spray is deposited on the islands, especially in Shetland.

The role of marine fish in Viking and later medieval Orkney and Shetland economies is currently under intensive investigation. Some types of bioarchaeological evidence suggest that fish may have played an important role in Northern Isles economies of the Viking period. But given the limitations of the available evidence it is difficult to sort out the dietary contributions of all of the various categories of marine foods, which also included sea mammals, birds, and mollusks. Also, the environmental contrasts between Orkney and Shetland suggest that the relative importance of marine and terrestrial resources may have differed between the two island groups. Much more archaeological research will be required before this complex issue is resolved, and in the meantime it is probably unwise to generalize about Orkney and Shetland as a single settlement region. Certainly, by the end of the medieval period, fishing for food and for trade was much more important in Shetland than it was in Orkney. In general, it is likely that as more sites are investigated, especially early settlements, Viking Orkney and Shetland will emerge as areas with distinct cultural patterns. These traits were probably fostered by ecological diversity and the lack of later integrating forces such as the medieval church, strong kingdoms, and large, structured market systems.

See also **Picts** (*vol. 2, part 7*); **Viking Settlements in Iceland and Greenland** (*vol. 2, part 7*).

BIBLIOGRAPHY

Ballantyne, John H., and Brian Smith, eds. *Shetland Documents, 1195–1579.* Lerwick, U.K.: Shetland Islands Council and Shetland Times, 1999.

Barrett, James H., Rebecca A. Nicholson, and Ruby Cerrón-Carrasco. "Archaeo-ichthyological Evidence for Long-term Socioeconomic Trends in Northern Scotland: 3500 B.C. to A.D. 1500." *Journal of Archaeological Science* 26 (April 1999): 353–388.

Batey, Colleen E., and John Sheehan. "Viking Expansion and Cultural Blending in Britain and Ireland." In *Vikings: The North Atlantic Saga.* Edited by William W. Fitzhugh and Elizabeth I. Ward, pp. 127–141. Washington, D.C.: Smithsonian Institution Press, 2000.

Bigelow, Gerald F. "Issues and Prospects in Shetland Norse Archaeology." In *Norse and Later Settlement and Subsistence in the North Atlantic.* Edited by Christopher D. Morris and D. James Rackham, pp. 9–32. Glasgow, Scotland: University of Glasgow, 1992.

———. "Sandwick, Unst, and Late Norse Shetland Economy." In *Shetland Archaeology: New Work in Shetland in the 1970s.* Edited by Brian Smith, pp. 95–127. Lerwick, U.K.: Shetland Times, 1985.

Bond, Julie M. "Beyond the Fringe? Recognising Change and Adaptation in Pictish and Norse Orkney." In *Life on the Edge: Human Settlement and Marginality.* Edited by C. M. Mills and G. Coles, pp. 81–90. Oxford: Oxbow Books, 1998.

Buteux, Simon. *Settlements at Skaill, Deerness, Orkney: Excavations by Peter Gelling of the Prehistoric, Pictish, Viking,*

and Later Periods, 1963–1981. Oxford: Archaeopress, 1997.

Crawford, Barbara E. *Scandinavian Scotland.* Leicester, U.K.: Leicester University Press, 1987.

Fenton, Alexander, and Hermann Pálsson, eds. *The Northern and Western Isles in the Viking World: Survival, Continuity, and Change.* Edinburgh: John Donald Publishers, 1984.

Graham-Campbell, James, and Colleen E. Batey. *Vikings in Scotland: An Archaeological Survey.* Edinburgh: Edinburgh University Press, 1998.

Hamilton, John R. C. *Excavations at Jarlshof, Shetland.* Edinburgh: Her Majesty's Stationery Office, 1956.

Hunter, John R. *Rescue Excavations on the Brough of Birsay, 1974–82.* Edinburgh: Society of Antiquaries of Scotland, 1986.

Hunter, John R., Julie M. Bond, and Andrea N. Smith. "Some Aspects of Early Viking Settlement in Orkney." In *The Viking Age in Caithness, Orkney, and the North Atlantic: Select Papers from the Proceedings of the Eleventh Viking Congress, Thurso and Kirkwall, 22 August–1 September 1989.* Edited by Colleen E. Batey, Judith Jesch, and Christopher D. Morris, pp. 272–284. Edinburgh: Edinburgh University Press, 1993.

Kaland, Sigrid H. H. "The Settlement of Westness, Rousay." In *The Viking Age in Caithness, Orkney, and the North Atlantic: Select Papers from the Proceedings of the Eleventh Viking Congress, Thurso and Kirkwall, 22 August–1 September 1989.* Edited by Colleen E. Batey, Judith Jesch, and Christopher D. Morris, pp. 308–317. Edinburgh: Edinburgh University Press, 1993.

Magnusson, Magnus, and Hermann Pálsson, trans. *Njál's Saga.* London: Penguin, 1981.

Nicholson, Rebecca A., and Stephen J. Dockrill, eds. *Old Scatness Broch, Shetland: Retrospect and Prospect.* Bradford, U.K.: Department of Archaeological Sciences, University of Bradford, 1998.

Nicolaisen, W. F. H. *Scottish Place Names: Their Study and Significance.* London: Batsford, 1976.

Owen, Olwyn, and Magnar Dalland. *Scar: A Viking Boat Burial on Sanday, Orkney.* East Lothian, U.K.: Tuckwell Press, 1999.

Pálsson, Hermann, and Paul Edwards, trans. *Orkneyinga Saga: The History of the Earls of Orkney.* London: Penguin, 1981.

Ritchie, Anna. *Viking Scotland.* London: Batsford, 1993.

Sturluson, Snorri. *Heimskringla: The Olaf Sagas.* Vols. 1 and 2. Translated by Samuel Laing. New York: Dutton, 1964.

Waugh, Doreen. "Place-name Evidence for Scandinavian Settlement in Shetland." *ROSC: Review of Scottish Culture* 7 (1991): 15–24.

GERALD F. BIGELOW

EARLY CHRISTIAN IRELAND

Along with all other periods of Irish archaeology, the Early Christian period has been the focus of a great expansion in the level of research since the early 1980s. One of the main trends in contemporary studies has been the increasing secularization of the archaeology related to this period. Increasingly, the academic community is realizing that the monasteries and other religious settlements did not dominate the early medieval Irish landscape, although undoubtedly they were an important component of that landscape. The use of the term "Early Christian" to describe this period is now increasingly being seen as overemphasizing the role of the ecclesiastical sites at the expense of the many other settlement types of the era that had no religious connection. As a result, archaeologists now tend to use the terms "Early Historic" or, increasingly, "Early Medieval" to describe this period.

Generally speaking, the period is thought by most scholars to begin in the fifth century A.D., soon after the coming of Christianity to the island. It ends in the twelfth century with the arrival of the Continental religious orders that broadly overlapped with the coming of the Anglo-Normans in 1169 and 1170. Although Ireland was not part of the Roman Empire, it was intimately involved in the empire's trading connections with Roman Britain and beyond. Thus, it is difficult to be sure when exactly the influence of the Roman Iron Age declines and the Early Medieval period, as such, commences. For instance, archaeologist Nancy Edwards has posed fundamental questions about the origins of this period of Irish history that debate the extent to which the impact of Roman culture and the introduction of literacy and the Christian religion initiated the changes that took place.

CHURCH ARCHAEOLOGY

The church in this period was primarily monastic, and the monastic sites that still survive as ruins in many parts of the island can be seen as a significant reminder of this important phase of Ireland's past. Very little survives archaeologically of the earliest monasteries because their buildings were of wood or wattle-and-mud construction. But it can be argued that some of the small monastic communities established in the western fringes of the country, where stone has always been the principal building material, can give us a good idea of the original appearance of the early monasteries built elsewhere. These include the impressively sited, beehive-shaped dry-stone cells on the island of Skellig Michael, situated in the Atlantic 13 kilometers west of the Iveragh Peninsula in County Kerry. Others are found on the island of Inishmurray in County Sligo. The most famous monastic sites, such as Clonmacnoise in County Offaly and Glendalough in County Wicklow also have the remains of many stone buildings within their monastic enclosures, including churches and round towers. These sites are covered extensively in the later ecclesiastical texts that have survived to the present. Indeed, most of the examples of stone architecture surviving from this period are ecclesiastical in origin, including Cormac's Chapel, built by King Cormac Mac Carthaig on top of the Rock of Cashel in County Tipperary. Dating to the first half of the twelfth century, it is universally considered the most beautiful surviving example of Irish Romanesque architecture. It was in the monasteries that some of the greatest schools of religious manuscript production were located. They produced the masterpieces of illumination, including the Book of Durrow (c. A.D. 650) and the Book of Kells (c. A.D. 800), both on display in Trinity College, Dublin.

It is also important to recognize that there are many other smaller enclosures in the landscape, delineated by either an earthen or stone bank, that originally might have had some kind of monastic function but which have only been identified by aerial photography or field survey. In other words, they do not possess any documentary sources that can positively identify them as such. There are also sites with place names that contain ecclesiastical elements such as "kill" but which, on further archaeological examination, have produced no evidence of ecclesiastical activity. Therefore, it is wise to follow Ann Hamlin's guidance in this by not considering any site ecclesiastical unless it includes clear evidence of a church and burials.

The whole question of urban settlement in this period is also under continuing discussion, especially the extent and nature of indigenous forms of urbanism. Increasingly, it is becoming accepted that some of the larger and more influential monasteries such as Armagh, the ecclesiastical capital of Ireland, were by the tenth and eleventh centuries exhibiting many of the characteristics of urban settlement. Such attributes, including streets and districts with extensive craft production, were largely the norm for the rest of continental Europe. Heather King has located important archaeological evidence of an urban secular settlement alongside the religious core of the monastery of Clonmacnoise, as well as

evidence of an extensive *vallum* that separated the settlement's monastic and secular communities.

RURAL SETTLEMENT

The most ubiquitous settlements during the Early Medieval period were the ringforts. It has been estimated that at least fifty thousand examples survived to be mapped by the Ordnance Survey in the middle of the nineteenth century. These are circular settlements, the design of which varied depending on where they were located. Those in the eastern half of the country had an earthen bank and an external dry fosse (ditch), or rath. Those in the western fringes had a perimeter bank built of dry stone and are therefore known as cashels. These settlements have an average diameter of 30 meters, although there are examples that are much larger and many that possess several lines of defensive banks. While the majority of the ringforts functioned as single-family defended farmsteads of the free element in Irish society, which was largely tribal at the time, with many small kingdoms, the larger ones may also have served as centers for particular tribal groups. Although less than two hundred sites have been excavated, the majority of them appear to have been constructed in the second half of the first millennium. It is thought that few ringforts were built after A.D. 1000, but some were still being utilized after the Norman conquest of Ireland that began in 1169. In addition to the archaeological evidence of this late habitation, there is also contemporary written evidence about the destruction of a particular site in Leinster by the Anglo-Normans as late as the end of the thirteenth century.

Despite the fact that surviving ringforts are so numerous, many aspects of their function and chronology still remain very much an enigma. The remains of circular houses have been discovered in two excavations, and they contained important evidence of some of the occupations and crafts that were carried out in these settlements. At Lisleagh 1 in County Cork, several circular structures were located that measured 5 to 7 meters in diameter. In one example, the buildings were arranged as a conjoined pair in a figure-eight plan. Environmental and artifactual evidence indicates that sheep farming, wool production, and the manufacture of bone combs were among the more important aspects of the economy at the Lisleagh site from the end of the sixth century to the end of the eighth century. The other site with circular houses is located at the northern end of Ireland, at Deer Park Farms in County Antrim. There, a "raised" ringfort with a height of 6 meters was caused by a prolonged occupation of the site from the sixth to the tenth centuries. Altogether, twenty circular wooden structures, all between 5 and 8 meters in diameter, were found throughout the occupation levels of this important site. Among the five that could be identified as houses was an impressive double-walled house some 7 meters in diameter (similar to the Lisleagh houses) with evidence of a bedding area and internal screens surviving within it. In the bedding area, a small brooch stylistically dated to A.D. 800 was located. Souterrains or underground passages were usually made with dry stone walls and a roof, then covered by the earth that had been excavated in order to construct the original trench dug to construct the passage. In many cases the souterrains are found located either close to or actually within ringforts. There is one dendrochronological date from the timbers of a fairly untypical wooden example at the ringfort of Coolcrans, County Fermanagh, which produced a date in the early ninth century. Broadly dated to the first millennium, their original function is not fully clear. They may have provided cold storage for food or acted as refuges when a settlement came under attack.

The other major type of defended enclosure of this period is the crannog, an occupation site on an island situated in a lake, which is either natural or built on artificial foundations. Recent archaeological research has estimated that around two thousand examples were constructed in Ireland, but most are found concentrated in the "Drumlin Belt" in the northern half of the island and especially in the Lakeland area of the northwest. These crannogs are being studied as part of a Lake Settlement research project carried out by the Discovery Programme, an archaeological research company entirely funded by the Heritage Council. The origin of the crannogs is found in the prehistoric period, but they were both constructed and occupied throughout the medieval period and afterward. As with the ringfort, only a small number have been scientifically excavated, but all the evidence to date indicates that in the Early Medieval period they were defended homesteads occupied by the wealthier elements of society. Some

of them, such as Lagore in County Meath, were sites of royal status. At Moynagh Lough, in the same county, compelling evidence indicates that this crannog was an important center for ornamental metalwork production and other skilled crafts, as well as being a traditional farming unit.

There are also other settlement sites of generally a prehistoric provenance that have evidence of sustained occupation during the Early Medieval period. In particular, the promontory forts of Dalkey Island in County Dublin, Dunbeg in County Kerry, and Larrybane in County Antrim were all reinhabited, even if only as temporary refuges in the many uncertain times of this era. Finally, there undoubtedly were settlements either without enclosures or with very flimsy and partial enclosures that have been difficult to identify archaeologically. With the help of aerial photography and increasingly sophisticated remote sensing techniques some of these have been tentatively identified on the landscape. Indeed, some of the Early Medieval law tracts mention the existence of rural nucleated settlements occupied by the unfree members of Irish society (those people who were both economically and legally dependent on a particular lord). These may have consisted of a small cluster of farmhouses with associated outbuildings arranged without any formal organization or layout. Such settlements in upland areas may only have been occupied at particular times of the year, as part of a transhumant system of agriculture.

Archaeologists are also attempting to understand the complexities of past landscapes by viewing them as a whole, thereby getting away from the focus on individual sites that drove much previous research. Utilizing aerial photography and other prospecting techniques, some attempt has been made to examine the layout of fields and other associated enclosures that are thought to date to this period. Two such research projects are in the valley of the River Barrow in the southeast of the country and in the foreshore area of Strangford Lough in County Down.

ARTIFACTUAL EVIDENCE

As regards archaeological evidence, the Early Medieval period in Ireland was largely devoid of ceramic artifacts, as was true for much of contemporary western and northern Britain. One of the few exceptions to this are the surviving sherds of A, B, D, and E ware that were luxury imports from France and the Mediterranean. These date from the fifth to the eighth centuries A.D. The only indigenous pottery type, which was originally called souterrain ware because of its association with these structures, is now better known as early native ware or early historic ware. It is a coarse handmade pottery that has been mainly found on both ecclesiastical and secular sites in the northeast of the country, especially in the two counties of Antrim and Down. There is also some limited evidence of other native, coarse, grass-tempered wares at ecclesiastical sites such as Reask in County Kerry. It would seem, therefore, that wood was used as an alternative to ceramics in this period, as shown from the number of such finds from crannog excavations.

There are also many small, inscribed stone monuments surviving from this period, which are best described as artifacts in their own right. The earliest stone markers generally bear an ogham inscription on them (the oldest form of writing script in Ireland). They mainly date from the fourth to the seventh centuries A.D., are found mainly in the southwest of the country, and are often associated with souterrains. There are also grave slabs, which are found in most monastic sites, usually in the form of flat stones bearing an inscription for a prayer for a particular person along with an inscribed cross. They are generally dated to the end of the Early Medieval period, from the ninth to the twelfth centuries. Undoubtedly the most famous of these decorated stone monuments are the freestanding stone high crosses, the great majority of which are found in monastic sites (fig. 1). They are often elaborately carved, with biblical scenes on their main faces and abstract designs on their sides. There is some evidence that they were originally painted in vivid colors. Most of them are dated from the ninth and tenth centuries. Some of the most impressive examples, possibly still surviving in their original location, are found at Monasterboice in County Louth.

It is in this period that, arguably, many of the finest metalwork artifacts ever produced in Ireland were made. These were fashioned out of bronze, to which precious metals were added. Many of them were manufactured in royal sites such as Tara in County Meath (fig. 2) or in the great monasteries such as Clonmacnoise in County Offaly, on the

Fig. 1. Ninth-century Celtic high cross. © KEVIN SCHAFER/ CORBIS. REPRODUCED BY PERMISSION.

shores of the river Shannon. Some were made in ringforts, such as the beautiful and unique seventh-century gold "wren" brooch found at Garryduff in County Cork. Others were created on crannogs such as Moynagh Lough in County Meath. Until the seventh century many of these metalwork artifacts were still being broadly influenced by the earlier Celtic La Tène style. But from the middle of the seventh century, the increasing influence of continental-European and Anglo-Saxon styles introduced many new motifs and techniques. These can be seen in the Derrynaflan paten of the eighth century and the Tara brooch that was made c. 700. The metalwork of the following four centuries was influenced by the Vikings, with an increased use of silver, as is shown by the large numbers of pennanular (nearly circular) and kite-shaped brooches. In the period leading up to the Anglo-Norman invasion

Fig. 2. The Tara brooch, which is said to come from the royal site of Tara, County Meath, Ireland, ninth century A.D. © ERICH LESSING/ART RESOURCE, NY. REPRODUCED BY PERMISSION.

the construction and repair of many reliquaries took place, including the Cross of Cong.

The evidence for other industries of this period is less apparent, although considerable research has taken place on water-powered mills, both horizontally and vertically driven, and on their ponds and other associated features, which date from the seventh century onward. On the foreshore below Nendrum Monastery, on Mahee Island in Strangford Lough, County Down, there are the remains of three horizontal tidal mills. These were excavated in 1999 and 2000 and date to the seventh and eighth centuries. The mills are of great importance, being the earliest archaeologically dated examples of the use of tidal power in Europe. Other interesting research has targeted the woodworking expertise and woodland management of the time. The expertise of the Early Medieval Irish in wood construction is exemplified by the impressive wooden bridge excavated at Clonmacnoise. Once used to cross the River Shannon, the bridge measures 120 meters

long and 5 meters wide. Its structural oak timbers were dated by dendrochronology to A.D. 804.

THE VIKING AGE

The Early Medieval period underwent a profound change with the coming of the Vikings at the end of the eighth century. In the past their arrival has been used to explain the decay and decline of some aspects of the Irish church at that time. However, modern scholarship has tended to see some of these problems as being present within the church much before the advent of the Vikings. Although Viking raids undoubtedly harmed the more vulnerable monastic communities, attacks on monasteries were not solely confined to outsiders but were also carried out by the indigenous Irish. The other point to stress is that this phase lasted for less than fifty years, until the Vikings started spending winters in Ireland. This led to the construction of *longphorts,* or defended harbors, for their ships. Most of these defensive bases grew into Hiberno-Norse port towns, which were mainly located on the east coast. Two such towns were Annagassan in County Louth, established in A.D. 841, and Dublin.

To the immediate west of Viking-Age Dublin, at present-day Islandbridge-Kilmainham, the largest Viking cemetery outside of Scandinavia was found in the 1840s, when railways were being constructed. The cemetery has been dated by surviving artifacts to the ninth century. Until recently this had caused scholars to debate whether the original *longphort,* built c. 841, was located closer to this cemetery and that the urban settlement of Dublin was established later, around 917, at its present location, farther east and closer to the mouth of the River Liffey. But more recent archaeological excavations have produced both radiocarbon dates and structures and artifacts that indicate a ninth-century settlement at Temple Bar, in the center of the existing city of Dublin. Excavations by Linzi Simpson have shown that Dublin was strongly influenced by Anglo-Saxon culture and society in Britain and was intimately involved in the sociopolitical developments of Danelaw, the northeastern region of England that was centered upon the Viking city of York.

The fusion of Irish and Viking cultures led to the development of an important Hiberno-Norse style that had an important influence on the art of the period, metalwork, in particular. The archaeological record of the Hiberno-Norse towns is very rich, especially as a result of sustained archaeological excavations in Dublin and Waterford. To a lesser extent, Limerick, the only example of a Hiberno-Norse town known on the west coast, has also yielded a rich array of artifacts. Both Dublin and Waterford in this period were laid out with streets lined by single-story mud-and-wattle rectangular houses. Each had a central hearth with fixed wooden benches on either side where the inhabitants slept. Larger dwelling houses were often accompanied by smaller storehouses constructed in the same manner. The many excavations have shown that these urban centers traded extensively with the rest of Viking-Age Europe, as evidenced by the remains of the workshops and their products.

In Dublin, archaeological evidence from the Wood Quay site on the southern quays of the city, excavated by Patrick Wallace in the late 1970s, shows that a stone wall was constructed around the core of the nucleated settlement about 1100. This replaced a large earthen embankment with a wooden palisade on top, which encircled the town from the tenth century. Along the southern edge of the river, docking facilities and buildings were constructed as the river silted up, with nine successive waterfronts being identified archaeologically, dating from 900 to 1300. Subsequent changes in Dublin have been revealed by a large number of excavations both within and outside the medieval walls, many taking place as a result of the redevelopment of the historic core of the city.

Excavations within the stone walls of Waterford by Maurice Hurley have uncovered about 20 percent of the Viking and medieval occupation layers there and have been especially valuable in putting the finds from Hiberno-Norse Dublin into a much broader context. The range and quality of the Viking-Age finds from Dublin may arguably be more impressive than those of Waterford, but Waterford has the richer collection of architectural remains from the High Middle Ages. These include four sunken buildings from the late eleventh century and stone-lined entrance passages to two additional structures. This represents the greatest number of such finds so far located in any Irish urban center. Some limited archaeological evidence from Cork and Limerick has provided insight into the Hiberno-Norse histories of those cities. In Limerick, excavations on the southwestern portion of King's Island, at the lowest fording point across the River Shannon, have revealed occupation layers and signs of construction.

Although each of these Hiberno-Norse towns obviously had a rural hinterland supplying them with many of the commodities that were important to their trading functions, the archaeological evidence for Viking rural settlement is almost nonexistent in Ireland, as is also largely the case in Britain. There is, however, some place-name evidence both in the vicinity of Dublin and Waterford to suggest that the extent of Norse settlement inland from the ports has been largely understated. To reinforce this conclusion, evidence of rural settlement came to light in 2003 as a result of development-driven excavation in the "Dyflinarskí," the area of Hiberno-Norse rural settlement around Dublin.

CONCLUSION

In the twelfth century, ecclesiastical reform was sweeping medieval Europe, so it was hardly surprising that these changes also affected Ireland. The Irish church was finally organized into a hierarchical system of parishes, dioceses, and archdioceses. As a direct result of this reform, many of the monasteries that had been such a mainstay of the Irish church, and which had their origins in Irish society, gradually faded away. They were replaced by the houses of the great Continental orders, as well as by the great cathedrals and parish churches of the Anglo-Norman colony. Of course, this change did not happen immediately. Some Early Medieval monasteries survived the initial Anglo-Norman invasion only to decline as Anglo-Norman diocesan authority grew increasingly stronger in the thirteenth century. In the secular world, it is also important to realize that there were parts of Ireland, especially in the north and the west, that remained under the control of indigenous Gaelic Irish families such as the O'Conors and the O'Briens. In these areas the settlement pattern of the Early Medieval period probably survived and evolved for many years after the fateful year of A.D. 1169, when the Norman conquest of Ireland began.

See also **La Tène** (*vol. 2, part 6*); **Mills and Milling Technology** (*vol. 2, part 7*); **Clonmacnoise** (*vol. 2, part 7*); **Raths, Crannogs, and Cashels** (*vol. 2, part 7*); **Deer Park Farms** (*vol. 2, part 7*); **Viking Dublin** (*vol. 2, part 7*).

BIBLIOGRAPHY

Aalen, F. H. A., Kevin Whelan, and Matthew Stout, eds. *Atlas of the Irish Rural Landscape.* Cork, Ireland: Cork University Press, 1997.

Clinton, Mark. *The Souterrains of Ireland.* Bray, Ireland: Wordwell, 2001.

Edwards, Nancy. *The Archaeology of Early Medieval Ireland.* London: Batsford, 1990.

Fredengren, Christina. *Crannogs: A Study of People's Interaction with Lakes, with Particular Reference to Lough Gara in the North-west of Ireland.* Bray, Ireland: Wordwell, 2002.

Harbison, Peter. *Irish High Crosses: With the Figure Sculptures Explained.* Illustrations by Hilary Gilmore. Drogheda, Ireland: Boyne Valley Honey Company, 1994.

Hughes, Kathleen, and Hamlin, Ann. *The Modern Traveller to the Early Irish Church.* London: S. P. C. K., 1977.

Hurley, Maurice. "Late Viking Age Settlement in Waterford City." In *Waterford History and Society.* Edited by William Nolan and Thomas P. Power, pp. 49–72. Dublin: Geography Publications, 1992.

Kelly, Fergus. *Early Irish Farming: A Study Based Mainly on the Law-texts of the 7th and 8th Centuries A.D.* Early Irish Law Series, Vol. 4. Dublin: School of Celtic Studies, Dublin Institute for Advanced Studies, 1997.

Monk, Michael A., and John Sheehan, eds. *Early Medieval Munster: Archaeology, History, and Society.* Cork, Ireland: Cork University Press, 1998.

ó Cróinín, Dáibhí. *Early Medieval Ireland, 400–1200.* London: Longman, 1995.

Ryan, Michael, ed. *Irish Archaeology Illustrated.* Dublin: Country House, 1994.

Simpson, Linzi. "Forty Years A-digging: A Preliminary Synthesis of Archaeological Investigations in Medieval Dublin." In *Medieval Dublin 1: Proceedings of the Friends of Medieval Dublin Symposium 1999.* Edited by Séan Duffy, pp. 11–68. Dublin: Four Courts Press, 2000.

Stout, Matthew. *The Irish Ringfort.* Irish Settlement Studies No. 5. Dublin: Four Courts Press, 1997.

Wallace, Patrick. "The Archaeological Identity of the Hiberno-Norse Town." *The Journal of the Royal Society of Antiquaries of Ireland* 122 (1992): 35–66.

TERRY BARRY

CLONMACNOISE

Saint Ciarán's monastery of Clonmacnoise (pronounced Klon-mack-noise), founded in the middle of the sixth century A.D., is situated on the east bank of the River Shannon at a point near the center of Ireland, where the Shannon meets the Slí Mhór (the great road) on the Eiscir Riada. The location of the monastery at this crossing point undoubtedly contributed to the fact that the monastery flourished over the following six centuries. It was, as Conleth Manning has described, not only a great monastic center but also a place of learning, trade, and craftsmanship. In the light of the accumulated results of excavations conducted since the late 1970s, one can now legitimately argue that Clonmacnoise was also an urban settlement.

Within the core of the monastic site, excavations took place on the sites of the three High Crosses, which were located to the north, south, and west of the cathedral. Evidence was found for

Fig. 1. Early medieval road at Clonmacnoise, Ireland. COURTESY OF HEATHER KING. REPRODUCED BY PERMISSION.

occupation in this area prior to A.D. 700, followed by a change of use to burial in subsequent centuries. It would appear that on completion of a new cathedral in A.D. 909 King Flann Sinna Mac Maelsechnaill reordered the area to the west of the cathedral by removing older wooden monuments and replacing them with the carved stone crosses.

Two excavations were carried out to the southwest of the monastic site. The first was located about 150 meters from the modern enclosing wall of the old burial ground. It was conducted after the discovery of a hoard of Hiberno-Norse coins beneath the football field of the local national school. The second excavation occurred when the school was enlarged. Although both sites were thought to be within the medieval monastic enclosure, there was no evidence for prolonged activity. The reason for the lack of settlement evidence was explained in 1999, when the enclosing early medieval ditch was located within 100 meters of the monastic site and about 50 meters from the earlier excavations.

Excavations on the site of the new visitor center, immediately west of the monastic core, produced evidence for four phases of early medieval activity. Paths, circular structures, a kiln, and evidence of ironworking were uncovered. Subsequent monitoring of trenches dug for utilities in the adjacent area revealed a continuation of this settlement evidence. Recent excavation on the sloping ground above the Shannon to the north of the visitor center has shown that an extensive area was utilized exclusively for early medieval ironworking. Closer to the Shannon, further settlement features were located. This excavation confirmed the results of geophysical prospecting (the use of noninvasive techniques to identify features below the surface) carried out in the late 1990s.

Dive survey and excavation in the Shannon to the north of the Norman castle revealed substantial remains of a wooden bridge dating to c. A.D. 804, together with eleven dugout canoes and various metalwork finds. Excavations in the northwest corner of the New Graveyard revealed four main phases of activity. The uppermost strata were of the late eleventh century and the twelfth century, characterized by flagged and cobbled areas, pits, well shafts and postholes, below which was the main occupation phase, dating to the ninth and tenth century. The main feature of this period is a metaled road or street more than 18.5 meters in length and about 3 meters in width (fig. 1) running southward from the low-lying callows adjacent to the Shannon toward the core of the monastic site. On either side of the road there was evidence for round houses about 7 meters in diameter, subrectangular structures, corn-drying kilns, hearths for cooking and metalworking, a possible boat slip, a quay, and a number of other features. There is also an earlier phase dating to the seventh and eighth century consisting mainly of stake holes, spreads of burnt soils and charcoal. Monitoring of new graves indicates that settlement extended throughout the area now occupied by the New Graveyard.

Over six thousand objects have been found, and evidence survives for the working of iron, bone, bronze, lignite, glass, silver, and gold. A knife handle with an ogham inscription suggests literacy among the bone workers. Coins dating to the Hiberno-Norse period, together with imported pottery, indicate trade. The quantity of animal bone retrieved from the site has indicated that Clonmacnoise was provisioned in a manner similar to urban centers in Britain and Ireland.

The criteria by which one identifies a town has been the subject of much discussion by archaeologists, but the suggestion put forward here is to use J. Bradley's definitions of a medieval town and a monastic town. In relation to the latter, Bradley noted that "the monastic town is an enclosed settlement, typified by having a major group of ecclesiastical buildings." Because *The Annals of Clonmacnoise* records that Ciaran was buried in the Eaglias Beag (the little church), one can deduce that within seven months of the foundation of the monastery there may have been two churches on the site. An enclosing boundary is recorded in the closing years of the sixth century. Pilgrimage began as early as the seventh century, and pilgrims and guests were lodged in a guesthouse. The Church of Saint Finghin, the Nun's Church, and the Round Tower are mentioned in the eleventh and twelfth centuries. As a center of commerce, Clonmacnoise hosted one

of the great fairs of Ireland. Paved roads were being constructed in the eleventh century, and the extent of the "town" of Clonmacnoise is evident in the twelfth and thirteenth centuries, when 47 houses were burned near the abbot's lodging and 105 houses burned in the "town."

While similar historical facts can be paralleled at some of the other great early Irish monasteries, such as Kells, Armagh, or Durrow, it is only at Clonmacnoise that fairly extensive archaeological excavation has provided the material evidence necessary to fulfill the remaining criteria for a town. This includes proof of settlement complexity, specialized areas for craft working, habitation and burial in defined areas, streets, trade, and enclosure. All of these features date from the A.D. 600s to the late twelfth century.

The documentary evidence for a town at Clonmacnoise is largely concentrated on the eleventh and twelfth centuries, but evidence from the excavations points to a much earlier urban settlement. This affirms an account possibly written in the eighth century that "a shining and saintly city grew up in that place in honour of Saint Ciaran, and the name of the city was Clonmacnois."

See also **Early Christian Ireland** (*vol. 2, part 7*); **Viking Dublin** (*vol. 2, part 7*).

BIBLIOGRAPHY

Bennet, Isabel, ed. *Excavations 1998: Summary Accounts of Archaeological Excavations in Ireland.* Bray, Ireland: Wordwell, 2000.

———. *Excavations 1997: Summary Accounts of Archaeological Excavations in Ireland.* Bray, Ireland: Wordwell, 1998.

———. *Excavations 1996: Summary Accounts of Archaeological Excavations in Ireland.* Bray, Ireland: Wordwell, 1997.

———. *Excavations 1995: Summary Accounts of Archaeological Excavations in Ireland.* Bray, Ireland: Wordwell, 1996.

———. *Excavations 1994: Summary Accounts of Archaeological Excavations in Ireland.* Bray, Ireland: Wordwell, 1995.

———. *Excavations 1993: Summary Accounts of Archaeological Excavations in Ireland.* Bray, Ireland: Wordwell, 1994.

———. *Excavations 1992: Summary Accounts of Archaeological Excavations in Ireland.* Bray, Ireland: Wordwell, 1993.

————. *Excavations 1991: Summary Accounts of Archaeological Excavations in Ireland.* Bray, Ireland: Wordwell, 1992.

————. *Excavations 1990: Summary Accounts of Archaeological Excavations in Ireland.* Bray, Ireland: Wordwell, 1991.

Bradley, J. "The Monastic Town of Clonmacnoise." In *Clonmacnoise Studies.* Vol. 1, *Seminar Papers 1994.* Edited by Heather A. King, pp. 42–56. Dublin: Dúchas, Heritage Service, 1998.

Kehnel, Annette. *Clonmacnois, the Church and Lands of St. Ciarán: Change and Continuity in an Irish Monastic Foundation (6th to 16th Century).* Vita regularis. Ordnungen und Deutungen religiosen Lebens im Mittelalter. Band 8. Münster, Germany: LIT, 1997.

King, Heather A., ed. *Clonmacnoise Studies.* Vol. 3, *Seminar Papers 1998.* Bray, Ireland: Wordwell, in press.

————, ed. *Clonmacnoise Studies.* Vol. 1, *Seminar Papers 1994.* Dublin: Dúchas, Heritage Service, 1998.

Manning, Conleth. *Clonmacnoise.* Dublin: Stationery Office, 1994.

Murphy, Denis, ed. *The Annals of Clonmacnoise: Being Annals of Ireland from the Earliest Period to A.D. 1408.* Translated by Conell Mageoghagan. Dublin: Royal Society of Antiquaries of Ireland, 1896.

Soderburg, John. "Feeding Communities: Monasteries and Urban Development in Early Medieval Ireland." In *Shaping Community: The Art and Archaeology of Monasticism. Papers from a Symposium Held at the Frederick R. Weisman Museum, University of Minnesota, March 10–12, 2000.* Edited by Sheila McNally, pp. 67–77. Oxford: Archaeopress, 2001.

HEATHER A. KING

RATHS, CRANNOGS, AND CASHELS

Raths, crannogs, and cashels are the primary settlement types during the early medieval period in Ireland (c. A.D. 400–800) and also occur in Irish-influenced areas of Scotland and Wales. Until the establishment of Viking cities in the ninth century A.D., Irish society was entirely rural in character with individual farmsteads as the predominant feature of the settlement pattern. The Irish economy was based on mixed farming with cattle as the basis of wealth. This set of circumstances encouraged a dispersed settlement pattern, with each farmstead separated by extensive fields and grazing lands. Although these settlements are considered the classic sites of the early medieval period, the construction of crannogs may have begun in the Late Bronze Age (c. 1200–700 B.C.), and these settlements certainly continued in use through the Viking and Hiberno-Norse periods (c. A.D. 800–1200) and in some areas as late as the sixteenth century.

Raths and cashels together are referred to as ringforts, and they are easily the most common type of early medieval archaeological site. Ringforts were most likely the homes of the majority of the population during the medieval period, and in excess of forty thousand ringforts have been identified in Ireland. Similar in form, both raths and cashels are circular areas surrounded by a bank of earth or stone. Raths are ringforts that have earthen banks and are often surrounded by a shallow ditch. Cashels are stone-built ringforts and usually occur in areas with poorer soil and a natural abundance of stone. Some ringforts have a combination of earthen and stone walls, although these are uncommon.

Ringforts vary widely in size and may also have more than one set of encircling walls. While the largest may have a diameter in excess of 75 meters, the majority are about 25 to 30 meters in diameter. Cashels, however, are on average somewhat smaller. About 20 percent of ringforts are enclosed by multiple banks; these are referred to as multivallate ringforts and were most likely the farmsteads of wealthy or high-status individuals. Regardless of the number of embankments, multivallate ringforts have internal diameters that are not appreciably larger than most single-banked examples and served much the same role.

Ringforts generally functioned as the farmsteads of single families. Excavations have revealed that most contain only a small number of structures, typically a stone or wattle house with a handful of outbuildings. These would have served as the economic center of the farm, and excavations often highlight the self-sufficiency of ringforts as economic units. Raths and cashels would have comprised the home of the inhabitants, enclosures for the farm's animals, a storage place for grain, and workshops for common crafts, such as ironworking. Excavations of higher-status ringforts often reveal a greater range of crafts produced, including the manufacture of objects made of bronze and precious metals. However, the essential function of high- and low-status ringforts varied little.

The actual defensive capabilities of ringforts is debated, with some archaeologists viewing the walls simply as a way to keep animals in the farmyard and having no defensive use, while others have argued for palisaded or hedge-lined embankments with some sort of defensive character. The most defensive element of ringforts, however, was perhaps not in their physical layout but in their distribution across the countryside. Studies have shown that ringforts regularly occur in semiclustered groups. Although quite separated in distance, each ringfort would have been within sight of another, and these clusters often have a larger and presumably more defensive multivallate ringfort within close proximity. This would have created an interlocking community that used the view across the landscape as a type of defense and that would have given the inhabitants time to flee to more defensive positions in the larger ringforts or in the surrounding mountains and bog lands.

Crannogs are artificial islands built in lakes and rivers that are located primarily in the northern and western parts of Ireland. While not as numerous as ringforts (about two thousand Irish crannogs have been identified), these sites are the second most common type of early medieval settlement and have played a central role in understanding the period. They are considered a predominantly early medieval class of settlement, although research in the 2000s has extended the chronology of crannog construction back into the Late Bronze Age and perhaps earlier. The nature of crannog use may have been much different prior to c. A.D. 400, with crannogs perhaps serving a predominantly ritual use in earlier periods or as seasonal dwellings only. Evidence for their use in the Iron Age (c. 700 B.C.–A.D. 400) is very scarce, and it is during the early medieval period that crannogs developed as settlements. Most crannogs are built up on lake and river beds with stones and debris until they emerge from the water, and some have stone causeways built connecting the crannog to the shore. These artificial islands were then sur-

rounded with wooden palisades, and houses and other outbuildings were located inside. Crannogs vary greatly in size and shape but are most commonly oval or round in plan and about 20 meters in diameter.

Unlike ringforts, crannogs were probably not directly related to the farming economy, as their location in the water would make access to fields and animals quite difficult. However, large amounts of animal bones are often found on excavated crannogs, and this is commonly interpreted as evidence of feasting by the occupants. This supports the belief that crannogs were the bases of powerful lords, and some crannogs have been identified by historical documents as royal centers. Excavations of these high-status and royal crannogs have revealed extensive evidence of metalworking, the large-scale manufacture of brooches and other high-status personal objects, and impressive collections of imported goods, such as Continental and Mediterranean pottery. Despite the large amounts of archaeological material commonly found on crannogs, most seem to have no more than one or two small houses and were probably inhabited by a family group. Excavations have traditionally focused on these higher-status sites, but research since the late 1990s has revealed that there are also less-wealthy crannogs. Their role in the early medieval settlement pattern is, however, less well understood.

See also **Celts** (*vol. 2, part 6*); **Early Christian Ireland** (*vol. 2, part 7*); **Dark Age/Early Medieval Scotland** (*vol. 2, part 7*); **Early Medieval Wales** (*vol. 2, part 7*).

BIBLIOGRAPHY

Edwards, Nancy. *The Archaeology of Early Medieval Ireland.* London: Routledge, 1990.

Fredengren, Christina. *Crannogs: A Study of People's Interaction with Lakes, with Particular Reference to Lough Gara in the North-west of Ireland.* Bray, Ireland: Wordwell, 2002.

O'Sullivan, Aidan. *The Archaeology of Lake Settlement in Ireland.* Discovery Programme Monograph, no. 4. Dublin: Royal Irish Academy, 1998.

Stout, Matthew. *The Irish Ringfort.* Dublin: Four Courts Press, 1997.

JAMES W. BOYLE

DEER PARK FARMS

Late in 1984 a rath mound in Deer Park Farms townland in Glenarm, County Antrim, was threatened with destruction in the course of farm improvements. It proved impossible to preserve the monument by negotiation, so four summer seasons of rescue excavations were carried out by the Department of the Environment (Northern Ireland). These revealed a remarkable sequence of well-preserved houses and associated finds. The rath stood at a height of 150 meters above sea level in a north-sloping field overlooking the Glenarm River. The monument was a large flat-topped mound, 26 meters in diameter across the summit and 4.5 meters high. The base of the mound was about 50 meters in diameter and was encircled by a ditch, very wide and deep on the uphill side. Occupation layers were visible at various heights in the mound's sides, showing that it had built up in stages over a period of time.

The surface on which the rath was built revealed several prehistoric features, probably dating from the Bronze Age or earlier. The first feature of the early Christian period was a circular ring ditch, with an overall diameter of 25 meters and an east-facing entrance gap. The ditch was about 2 meters wide and 1 meter deep. It was not accompanied by a bank and may have served to delimit and help drain the site chosen for settlement in the early Christian period, probably in the mid-seventh century. The ditch had silted up or had been deliberately filled in before the rath was built over it.

Before the end of the seventh century the first rath bank was constructed approximately over the site of the primary ring ditch. The external ditch that went with the bank was cut away by subsequent enlargement to obtain material for heightening the rath. Probably at the same time as the first rath bank was built, the first of a long sequence of woven hazel buildings was erected in the enclosure.

After a lengthy period of occupation, perhaps fifty years, the rath was converted into a flat-topped mound and a sloping access ramp of clay and gravel was built over the original east-facing entrance. The outer surface of the mound was encased in a heavy revetment wall of basalt boulders and the ditch was deepened. This main phase of mound heightening was accomplished in several stages. The houses in the final stage of the rath were not abandoned and replaced all at once, as had been presumed on the basis of trial excavations at other rath mounds. Instead, each house was abandoned and its remains covered over only when it reached the end of its useful life. As a result, some new houses stood on isolated platforms overlooking other inhabited houses not yet replaced. Two souterrains were incorporated in a further heightening of the rath, probably by the end of the tenth century.

The hillside site sloped to the north, but the rath entrance faced east, with the result that there was persistent ponding of water against the inner face of the clay bank on the downslope, north side. This resulted in the preservation of an accumulation of organic midden material in this area up to 1.5 meters deep. The heightening of the rath caused a rise in the water table in the mound, which preserved the wickerwork remains of the buried houses in the final phase of the primary, unheightened rath. This well-preserved horizon, dating from the early eighth century, is characteristic of the occupation surfaces of the entire rath.

The most obvious feature of the rath in the early eighth century is, paradoxically, untypical. The entrance, instead of being a simple gap, was inturned. Two parallel banks of earth ran for 6.5 meters into the rath interior. They were stone-revetted on the inner faces and formed a long, stone-paved rectangular antechamber inside the gate some 11 meters by 3.8 meters. A further meter inward from the end of the antechamber was the doorway of the largest house, which stood at the center of the rath. This was of figure-eight plan and the larger component, the main house, was 7.4 meters in diameter. It had a central, stone-curbed, rectangular fireplace, also aligned on the easterly axis of the rath layout. The structure, like all the others found in the rath, was double-walled. The inner wall bore the main weight of the structure, whereas the outer wall, spaced 30 centimeters away, mainly served to retain insulating material—grass, straw, weeds and bracken—in place against the inner wall. The smaller "backhouse," which could be entered only from within the main dwelling, was 5 meters in diameter. Its woven walls interlocked with those of the main house showing that the two elements of this figure-eight-shaped house had been built simultaneously. This figure-

Fig. 1. Wickerwork structures zeta (left) and X (right), early eighth century. The structures were woven together as a conjoined figure-of-eight unit with zeta as the backhouse, which could be entered only from X. The communicating gap was closed by a woven hurdle as zeta was abandoned before X. To the left, in zeta, is a collapsed section of its inner wall, almost reaching the central fireplace. At the bottom right are branches forming the base of a bedding area in the south side of structure X. This composite structure at the center of the rath was clearly the most important in this phase, with smaller dwellings set behind to north and south. © Crown copyright. Courtesy of Chris Lynn, Environment and Heritage Service. Reproduced with the permission of the Controller of Her Majesty's Stationery Office.

eight plan was the normal layout for the main dwelling at the center of the rath in other phases.

The walls were woven using a basketry technique, giving an enormously strong structure. The horizontal component of the wall was woven in spiraling sets of 2-meter-long hazel rods twisted around short uprights, giving the courses of the wall a spiralling rope-like appearance. The surfaces of both inner and outer walls were smooth, because the cut ends of the hazel rods were hidden in the space between the walls. The uprights of the wall were composite: they did not run continuously through the full height of the structure. The first set of pointed uprights was driven into the ground about 25 centimeters apart and rose to a height of about 1 meter. When wall weaving reached this height, the next set of uprights was hammered into

the body of the woven wall alongside the primary uprights. These protruded up for a further meter, wall weaving continued to that height, a further set of uprights was hammered in, and so on. In one area a large panel of pushed-over walling was found, which would have stood to nearly 4 meters in height, showing that the roof was probably constructed in a similar technique to the walls and not as a separate cone of long rafters.

The central house had two bedding areas, one on the north and one on the south, formed of thin branches and twigs alternately laid radially and concentrically against the house walls. These were filled with finer chopped vegetable material. The ends of the bed on the north were protected by wicker screens fixed into drilled holes in oak beams on the floor, forming bed ends. Two stone-curbed paths ran north and south on either side of the entrance to the main house and curved to the west to provide formal access to two other dwellings. The one on the south was a simple single circular house or hut with a central fireplace and a bedding area on the north. The structure on the north was another figure-eight, but smaller than the central one. The western component of this structure at first stood as an isolated single house, but after some time the larger, eastern component was woven onto the front of it. This may reflect a change in the social status of the occupant of the single home, for example maturity and marriage. The complete doorframe of the primary component of the figure-eight was preserved. This was the outside doorframe of the original single house, which then became the connecting door between the conjoined houses. The isolated house on the south may have been occupied by a single or widowed relative of the occupant of the main central house.

One of the most interesting aspects of the excavation is the close correlation between the archaeological evidence from the site and the details of houses, furniture, fittings, and personal equipment and tools given in the contemporary law tracts on status. These specify the equipment and buildings appropriate to hierarchial grades of free farmers who lived in raths. Hitherto, these legal inventories have been considered by archaeologists as somewhat idealized and not a true representation of reality. The occupants of the rath at this phase possessed many artifacts and craft-techniques listed in the law tracts as appropriate to what would now be termed upper-middle-class farmers. They used a coppicing method to grow hazel for their houses and fences, they wore composite leather shoes, they ate a variety of animal products (cow, sheep, pig), and they had access to a water mill for grinding cereals. The wooden hub and two paddles of a mill wheel were found in the waterlogged midden. The rath occupants wore woolen clothes; they plowed the land (as evidenced by two iron plough tips); they made their own stave-built wooden vessels, probably using light from iron candle and rush-light holders also found in the excavation. They had metal cooking pots and hooks for hanging meat, they cultivated woad for dyeing, and they decorated themselves from an extensive range of metal pins and colored glass beads. More personally, evidence suggests that

they and their settlement were occupied by more than sixty species of parasitic and decomposer insect species, in proportions normally regarded as typical of more densely occupied urban sites, such as Viking Age York. From the number of head-louse remains found immediately outside the main central structure, one can picture the family sitting on the end wall of the entranceway combing and grooming one another. Perhaps hair cutting went on at the same time as five locks of cut human hair were found in different levels of the midden nearby.

The deposits in the lower levels of the Deer Park Farms rath were uniquely well preserved, permitting close contact with the life of the people who lived there. In the context of this encyclopedia one is tempted to ask, were these people "barbarians"? What share of their material, cultural inheritance came from a prehistoric insular past and what had been adopted from the Roman world? The round wickerwork houses have not been found in earlier contexts in Ireland, but little is known about houses and settlement in Ireland in the preceding Iron Age. Bronze Age houses, although also of round form, seem to have been made of heavier materials such as stone, clay, and timber. Nevertheless, the round house was essentially a prehistoric form which, uniquely in Europe, survived in Ireland into the historic period. Circular earthworks are known from prehistory but these generally occur in ceremonial or funerary contexts. In turn, this suggests that if there is some continuity with prehistory, the rath enclosures may have had a sacred or legal significance, identifying the special importance of the home place. This could include its significance as the primary domain of women, where household and lighter agricultural crafts were carried out.

Some of the smaller items of equipment found in Deer Park Farms and other raths, such as brooches and iron tools, are of forms that can be paralleled earlier in Roman Britain. Similarly, small enclosed settlements were built in western Britain during the Iron Age and Roman period and some researchers interpret these as being ancestral to Irish raths. The clear view from Deer Park Farms of Slemish, 8 kilometers to the southwest, suggests that the occupants of the rath adhered to the Christian faith of the late Roman Empire, introduced to Ireland by St. Patrick and his contemporaries in the fifth century. Slemish is the prominent hill where St. Patrick is said to have labored as a swineherd some 250 years before the Deer Park Farms rath was built. A small hone, found in the midden layer of the rath, had engraved on it an animal head in the style of the well-known Tara Brooch (from Bettystown, County Meath). Underneath the head is a scratched inscription of seven letters, the earliest archaeological evidence for an awareness of writing in a domestic site in Ireland.

See also **Early Christian Ireland** (*vol. 2, part 7*); **Raths, Crannogs, and Cashels** (*vol. 2, part 7*); **Viking York** (*vol. 2, part 7*).

BIBLIOGRAPHY

Kelly, Fergus. *Early Irish Farming*. Early Irish Law Series, no. 4. Dublin: School of Celtic Studies, Dublin Institute for Advanced Studies, 1997.

Lynn, Chris J., and Jacki A. McDowell. A monograph report by Lynn and McDowell on the Deer Park Farms excavation is at an advanced stage of preparation. Some draft chapters may be consulted on the Internet at http://www.ehsni.gov.uk/built/monuments.

Mytum, Harold. *The Origins of Early Christian Ireland*. London: Routledge, 1992.

Stout, Matthew. *The Irish Ringfort*. Dublin: Four Courts Press, 1997.

C. J. LYNN

VIKING DUBLIN

Forty years of archaeological excavation in Dublin, much of it under the aegis of the National Museum of Ireland, has shed considerable light on the character of this the largest of the Scandinavian-founded urban settlements in the west. Although unconcerted as elements of an overall program and begun in response to building development, in their sum these excavations add up to the most extensive of their time and type undertaken in Europe north of the Alps and west of the Oder. The scale of the total excavated areas together with the waterlogged airless conditions in which as much as 3 meters deep of organic cultural deposits survive means that there is excellent evidence for buildings, town layout, defenses, environment, diet, trade, commerce, and everyday life especially for the three centuries A.D. 850–1150. There are also well-preserved wooden dockside revetments and building and carpentry evidence from the thirteenth to the sixteenth centuries.

Ireland is blessed with rich historical sources including references to the establishment of Dublin in about 840, but it was not until the 1960s at sites like High Street, Winetavern Street, and especially Christchurch Place, all of which were excavated by A. B. ó Ríordáin, that the quality of Dublin's uniquely rich archaeological deposits became apparent. More extensive work by Patrick Wallace on the large Fishamble Street–Wood Quay site from 1962 to 1976 expanded on ó Ríordáin's work, particularly in regard to layout, the succession of town plots and their boundaries, building evidence, and the town's Viking Age port. Work by Clare Walsh at

Ross Road in 1993 gave additional information on the circuit of the earthen defenses that enclosed the early town; the Castle Street and Werburgh Street sites showed that while it was possible to generalize about buildings and town layout, there are variations within the town; and Parliament Street and especially Linzi Simpson's work at Essex Street showed that the earliest settlement in the ninth century must have been at the confluence of the tidal Liffey and its southern tributary, the Poddle. It also showed that the settlement probably expanded southward up the hill from the waterfront and, later, that the early medieval town expanded from east to west. Most significantly, work done from 1996 to 1998 indicates that the main building type, with its tripartite floor space arranged longitudinally between doors in the end walls, was established almost from the beginning and persisted throughout the period up to the twelfth century and possibly beyond (going by the evidence from the parallel Hiberno-Norse town of Wexford) and that the settlement was divided into plots or yards well before 900.

Although Ireland's great monastic "towns" flourished from before the arrival of the Vikings and, with other native settlements of this culturally extraordinary phase of Ireland's history, had some urban traits, it is likely that the *concept* of mainstream urbanism was introduced to Ireland possibly from ninth-century England, with the Scandinavians acting as the catalysts who transferred the idea. Excavations at the other Hiberno-Norse towns—Limerick, Waterford, and Wexford—show that they share many physical traits with Dublin and that it is now possible to speak of the Hiberno-Norse town as a phenomenon in archaeology as well as in history. Revisits to the historical sources as well as excavations at Cork in 2002 and the great monastery at Clonmacnoise in the 1990s show that by the late eleventh–early twelfth century the concept of true urbanism was fully a part of the overall Irish experience.

In its developed form in the later tenth century, Dublin consisted of a number of streets from which radiated several lanes including an intramural variant. The settlement was located around high ground overlooking the tidal and estuarine Liffey near its confluence with the Poddle. In the early tenth century it was defended by a palisaded earthen embankment that encircled the settlement and accommodated ships along its main riverine side. The extent of the defenses on the West is at present unclear. Inside, the settlement was divided into plots of roughly rectangular shape by low lines of post-and-wattle fencing; each plot had its own pathway leading from a street or lane to the entrance of a main building that was located with an end toward the street. At the backs of these main buildings were lesser smaller buildings. It is presumed that plot owners controlled access to the plots, with access to the lesser buildings being difficult: in most cases visitors would have had to walk through the main buildings, which usually straddled the widths of their plots. Cattle were not kept in the plots; it appears that they were not kept in town at all but rather were driven to town in great numbers when it was time for slaughter, judging from the number of bones that have been recovered from the excavations.

Specialized crafts including those of nonferrous metalworking, antler (especially comb) working, woodcarving, and possibly merchandising appear to have been concentrated in different parts of the town. Commerce was regulated, to judge from the hundreds of lead weights (for weighing silver in a bullion economy) that have been recovered; these conform to multiples and fractions of what has been termed a Dublin ounce of 26.6 grams. Ships' timbers, unworked amber, lignite, soapstone, and even walrus ivory testify to the import of bulk commodities; silks (including head scarves), braids, worsteds, English brooches, and coins are among finished products that were imported. Discoveries of runic inscriptions on discarded red-deer antlers and cattle bones show a persistence of close Scandinavian influence two centuries after the initial establishment of the town as a slaving emporium.

In its settled eleventh-century development, Dublin became very rich due to its location on the east of the Irish Sea, then a "Viking lake": it profited from provisioning ships, from the hire of its large mercenary fleet (most notably to the Saxons of the Godwinson dynasty), and from the export of woolens and of manufactured goods like kite brooches, ringed pins, strap ends, combs, and possibly ornaments carved in the local variety of the international Ringerike style, which was so distinctive and prolific that it is now called the "Dublin style."

See also **Viking Ships** (*vol. 2, part 7*); **Early Christian Ireland** (*vol. 2, part 7*); **Early Medieval Wales** (*vol. 2, part 7*); **Viking York** (*vol. 2, part 1*).

BIBLIOGRAPHY

Clarke, Howard B. *Irish Historic Towns Atlas No.11: Dublin, Part 1, to 1610*. Dublin: Royal Irish Academy, 2002.

———. "The Bloodied Eagle: The Vikings and the Development of Dublin, 841–1014." *Irish Sword* 18 (1991): 91–119.

Fanning, Thomas. *Viking Age Ringed Pins from Dublin*. Medieval Dublin Excavations 1962–1981, series B, vol. 4. Dublin: Royal Irish Academy, 1994.

Hurley, M. F., and S. J. McCutcheon. *Late Viking Age and Medieval Waterford Excavations 1986–1992*. Waterford, Ireland: Waterford Corporation, 1997.

Lang, James T. *Viking Age Decorated Wood: A Study of Its Ornament and Style*. Medieval Dublin Excavations 1962–1981, series B, vol. 1. Dublin: Royal Irish Academy, 1988.

McGrail, Seán. *Medieval Boat and Ship Timbers from Dublin*. Medieval Dublin Excavations 1962–1981, series B, vol. 1. Dublin: Royal Irish Academy, 1993.

O'Rahilly, C. "Medieval Limerick: The Growth of Two Towns." In *Irish Cities*. Edited by Howard B. Clarke, pp. 163–176. Cork, Ireland: Mercier Press, 1995.

Simpson, Linzi. *Director's Findings: Temple Bar West*. Dublin: Margaret Gowen, 2000.

Wallace, Patrick F. "*Garrda* and *Airbeada*: The Plot Thickens in Viking Dublin." In *Seanchas: Essays in Early and Medieval Irish Archaeology, History, and Literature in Honour of F. J. Byrne*. Edited by Alfred P. Smyth. Dublin: Four Courts Press, 2000.

———. "The Archaeological Identity of the Hiberno-Norse Town." *Journal of the Royal Society of Antiquaries of Ireland* 122 (1992): 35–66.

———. *The Viking Age Buildings of Dublin.* Medieval Dublin Excavations 1962–1981, series A, vol. 1, 2 parts. Dublin: National Museum of Ireland, 1992.

———. "The Economy and Commerce of Viking Age Dublin." In *Untersuchungen zu Handel und Verkehr der vor- und frühgeschichtlichen Zeit in Mittel- und Nordeuropa.* Vol. 4, *Der Handel der Karolinger- und Wikingerzeit.* Edited by K. Düwel et al., pp. 200–245. Göttingen, Germany: Vandenhoeck and Ruprecht, 1987.

———. "The Archaeology of Anglo-Norman Dublin." In *The Comparative History of Urban Origins in Non-Roman Europe.* Vol. 2. Edited by Howard B. Clarke and Anngret Simms, pp. 379–410. BAR International Series, no. 255. Oxford: British Archaeological Reports, 1985.

———. "The Archaeology of Viking Dublin." In *The Comparative History of Urban Origins in Non-Roman Europe.* Vol. 1. Edited by Howard B. Clarke and Anngret Simms, pp. 103–145. BAR International Series, no. 255. Oxford: British Archaeological Reports, 1985.

———. "Carpentry in Ireland, A.D. 900–1300: The Wood Quay Evidence." In *Woodworking Techniques before A.D. 1500.* Edited by Seán McGrail, pp. 263–299. BAR International Series, no. 129. Oxford: British Archaeological Reports, 1982.

PATRICK F. WALLACE

DARK AGE/EARLY MEDIEVAL SCOTLAND

FOLLOWED BY FEATURE ESSAY ON:

In the later first millennium A.D., Scotland was a complex and dynamic mosaic of political and cultural traditions, where natives and incomers (immigrants) competed for power and influence—a land of "four nations and five languages," in the words of the contemporary Anglian historian the Venerable Bede. The evidence for the various groups contributing to the development of the kingdom of Scotland is uneven, however, both in terms of historical sources and archaeological research. It is therefore necessary to consider the broadest possible range of information to reconstruct the period: archaeology, history, linguistics and place-name studies, and art history provide the most significant evidence.

The early medieval period in Scotland can be divided into three major phases. Limited evidence remains for the post-Roman phase (c. fifth century A.D.), which appears to have been a time of transition, when significant cultural changes took place. The early historic or early Christian phase (c. sixth to eighth centuries A.D.) was a period of interaction and competition, at least among the elites, of four major political or ethnic groups and also saw the establishment of Christianity as the dominant religion. Then came the Viking phase (ninth century through mid–eleventh century A.D.), when a new set of pagans, mainly from western Norway, dis-

rupted earlier patterns, initially through raiding and later by settling in the north and west. Their attacks were surely an important catalyst for the unification of the Dalriadic and Pictish kingdoms into Alba, the kingdom of Scotland.

POST-ROMAN PERIOD

Unlike southern Britain, Scotland never was incorporated fully into the Roman Empire, although the southern lowlands were part of the militarized zone between the Antonine Wall, which ran between the River Forth and the River Clyde, and Hadrian's Wall, now south of Scotland's border. Unlike the situation with the Germanic territories beyond the Rhine frontier, little evidence suggests significant levels of trade across these walls, and so the withdrawal of Rome in the early fifth century was less obviously disruptive in Scotland than elsewhere. It is widely accepted, however, that the people between the walls were influenced significantly by the Roman military presence. In fact, with the recognition that the Picts and the Britons both spoke P-Celtic, or Brittonic languages, some scholars have suggested that cultural differences between the southern Britons and the northern Picts may have been emphasized, if not created, by the adoption of certain elements of late Roman culture, including Christianity, by the Britons.

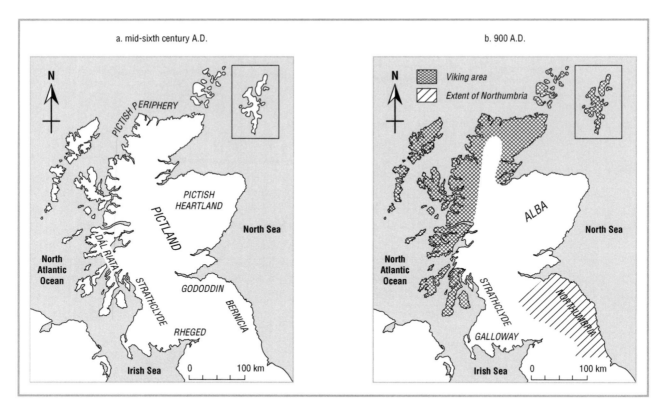

Scotland in the mid-sixth century and c. A.D. 900. ADAPTED FROM FOSTER 1996.

Several small kingdoms are known among the post-Roman Britons. The people the Romans called the Votadini, for instance, appear in the sixth century in the southeast as the Gododdin. In the late Roman period they were based at the Iron Age hillfort of Traprain Law, which has produced a spectacular hoard of Roman silver dated to sometime after A.D. 395; this cache is interpreted either as loot or, more likely, a diplomatic bribe or payment for military services. But Traprain Law was abandoned by the mid–fifth century, and it appears that their new seat of power was at Din Eidyn, modern Edinburgh; excavations in Edinburgh Castle have found evidence for occupation during this period.

Whithorn, in the southwest, was the site of the earliest recorded Christian church in Scotland, the episcopal seat of Saint Ninian, reportedly sent to minister to an already existing Christian community. Dating the activity of any post-Roman figure is extremely difficult, owing to a lack of contemporary documents, but scholarly opinion now places Ninian at Whithorn in the later fifth century. This dating is supported by the site's mid-fifth-century Latinus

stone, an inscribed cross slab with a Latin inscription, including the name "Latinus," and a six-armed Constantinian Chi-Rho Christian cross.

Little evidence exists for the Picts at this period: historically they were the enemies of the Romans, allied with the Scotti (or Irish). Archaeologically there is strong continuity with Late Iron Age culture, particularly in the Northern Isles and Western Isles, although there appear to have been significant changes in settlement types during the later Roman period. Understanding of the Picts, however, is patchy: F. T. Wainwright's pioneering book titled *The Problem of the Picts* was written in 1955, and it is only since the 1970s that excavations have made them less of an enigma.

EARLY HISTORIC OR EARLY CHRISTIAN PERIOD

The Scotti, or at least the Scots of Dál Riata, were one of two groups that first appeared in Scotland during the sixth century, complicating the political picture and contributing new elements to northern British culture. They controlled Argyll, the southern part of the West Highland coast, and retained close ties with their Irish homeland. The other group was the Northumbrian Angles, based at Bamburgh on the northeastern coast of England by the mid–sixth century. The Angles expanded their control over the kingdom of Gododdin by the seventh century and over Rheged, in the southwest of Scotland, by the eighth century, leaving Strathclyde as the only remaining autonomous British kingdom.

The intrusiveness of these groups has long been emphasized by historical tradition, but archaeology warns against exaggerating the differences among the Brittonic Britons and Picts, the Gaelic Scots, and the Germanic Angles. Despite their linguistic differences, the economies and material cultures of these groups were very similar. All of them relied on mixed farming, where cattle were the most important livestock, followed by sheep and pigs; barley and oats were the principal crops; and along Scotland's convoluted coast, fish and sea mammals also were important resources. Most people would have lived on isolated farmsteads or in small, self-sufficient hamlets—there was nothing resembling an urban center in Scotland until the twelfth century. Pottery was uncommon in most of Scotland during this period, and most metal would have been recycled. But excavations at waterlogged sites have produced a wide range of wooden vessels and other organic artifacts.

The scarcity of well-preserved artifacts has left Scottish archaeologists precious little to work with and accounts for the lack of a well-defined chronology for much of later prehistory and the early medieval period until the advent of radiocarbon dating in the mid–twentieth century. The artifacts that are useful for dating, usually because of their wider cultural milieu, were high-status objects: fine metalwork, imported pottery, and sculpture—items associated with the elite rather than with ordinary members of society. Consequently much early medieval archaeology has concentrated on high-status sites, such as fortified settlements and religious centers, although rescue excavations in advance of development or coastal erosion are providing more evidence for the lower classes of early medieval society.

It is important to recognize this bias toward the upper classes not only because it is mirrored in the historical sources (written by and for elites) but also because these were precisely the people most likely to be defining ethnicity in ways advantageous to their own position in the competition for power. Historical, art historical, and archaeological evidence illustrates the ease with which northern British elites mixed and mingled, in political marriage alliances and exile as much as on the battlefield, regardless of linguistic or religious differences. A well-documented example is when Æthelfrith, king of the Angles (r. c. A.D. 592–616), was killed. His sons took refuge in other kingdoms. Oswald (r. A.D. 634–641) went to Dál Riata, and Oswiu (r. A.D. 641–670) married into Irish and British royal houses as well as that of their Northumbrian rival. Eanfrith (r. A.D. 633) had a son who reigned as a king of the Picts. All three were converted to Christianity while in exile, although Eanfrith is reported to have reverted to paganism during his brief reign, and Oswald imported Columban Christianity into his kingdom from Dalriadic Iona with the foundation of Lindisfarne. It was within these dynamic cross-cultural contexts that the Insular art style developed, and it should serve as a warning against the use of simplistic ethnic labels for things as well as people during the early medieval period.

SETTLEMENTS

While the elites were participating in an increasingly shared and internationally connected culture, there are regional differences in the archaeological record, particularly in settlements. In the south, among the British and Angles, slightly different forms of rectangular post-in-ground timber halls have been excavated on such sites as Doon Hill in the east and Whithorn in the west, some defended by palisades; similar forms appear to have been used by the southern Picts. (This thinking is based largely on the evidence of crop marks and soil marks visible in aerial photographs, however, and excavation is needed to confirm the dates of these structures. One such hall, believed to be early medieval, turned out to be three thousand years too old.) In the west, among the Britons and the Scots, are crannogs—natural or modified islands, usually with round timber and wattle houses. These are considered defended settlements because of the water barrier, and examples such as Buiston and Loch Glashan were high-status sites. Along the West Highland coast and in the Northern Isles, duns and brochs, large round drystone structures built in the Late Iron

Age, were reoccupied, often with modifications, or cannibalized for the construction of more modest cellular or figure-of-eight houses. Figure-of-eight houses have been found from the Orkneys to County Antrim, Ireland, illustrating the wide spread of some elements of material culture. It is well to remember that the Picts and Scots were allies against the Romans, and both could assemble substantial fleets of ships, which would have been used to sail between the islands during peace as well as war.

The promontory fort at Burghead, in the northeast, is the largest fortified site of this period in Scotland, and it overlooks an excellent harbor. At least thirty stones carved with Pictish bull symbols were found there, and the wooden framework for its timber-laced ramparts was fastened with nails. The only other known example of nailed timber-laced ramparts is at Dundurn, another Pictish stronghold. Dundurn is a nuclear fort: it has a small citadel at the summit of a hill, with annexes built wherever the hill is relatively level. Britons and Scots as well as Picts used nuclear forts; the type site is Dunadd, the capital of Dál Riata. Fortified sites such as these forts and crannogs would have been the residences of royalty, and these sites have produced evidence for specialized craft working, particularly the production of fine metalwork, suggesting that smiths worked under the patronage or control of kings and other nobles.

ARTIFACTS

Fine metalwork constitutes one of the more distinctive classes of artifacts from early medieval Scotland, like the highly ornamented Hunterston brooch, a pseudo-penannular brooch, one that looks as if it has a gap in the ring, which would be a penannular brooch, but does not. While the Angles have more bow brooches (essentially highly elaborate safety pins), the Celtic groups favored hand pins (large straight pins) and penannular brooches (circular forms with a gap for the pin to pass through). These pins were made of silver or bronze, and some were decorated with gold, enamel, and semiprecious stones or glass. The brooches and pins themselves are rare survivals, and many were chance finds made before the twentieth century. This limits their value as archaeological evidence, but there is lively debate among art historians regarding the origins of different styles, the sources of various decorative ele-

ments, and the social functions of such rich objects. Increasingly these finds are supplemented by the recovery of the molds used to make such objects from sites like the Mote of Mark in the southwest (late sixth century to early seventh century) or Dunadd (seventh century). They can establish conclusively that a particular type was made at a specific place during a given time period.

A larger number of high-status sites have produced small quantities of imported pottery and glass vessel fragments. This material falls into two categories: imports from the Mediterranean dated from the later fifth century to the mid-sixth century and imports from western France dated from the sixth through the seventh centuries. The Mediterranean pottery includes African red slip tableware from Tunisia (A ware), which has been found at Whithorn and Iona, and several types of amphorae (B ware), the earlier forms from the eastern Mediterranean and the later ones from Tunisia. The amphorae would have been shipping containers for commodities like wine or olive oil, and the only other site in Scotland where they have been found is Dumbarton Rock, the capital of Strathclyde. While most of these Mediterranean imports have been found in Southwest Britain and the Scottish examples are best seen as outliers, that is not the case for the later French imports, known as D ware and E ware. D ware is a derivative form of late Roman tableware, dating to the earlier sixth century, and has been found at Dunadd, the Mote of Mark, and Whithorn. E ware is a hard, gritty ware that, like the earlier amphorae, probably was a container. It dates from the late sixth century and possibly into the early eighth century, but most examples in Scotland have been found in contexts dating to the first half of the seventh century. More of this ware has been found in Scotland than anywhere else in the British Isles; Dunadd has the largest collection and Whithorn the second largest, and it has been discovered on at least thirteen other sites, including a couple in the Pictish east.

SCULPTURE

The Picts are associated more commonly with a very distinctive art tradition found mainly on stone—the famous Pictish symbol stones. More than fifty different symbols are known: highly naturalistic figures of animals; recognizable objects, such as combs and mirrors; and abstract figures, the most common symbols being the double disk and crescent, often overlain by linear symbols known as Z-rods and V-rods. The meanings of the symbols and the functions of the stones are a matter of perennial debate; a writing system, totems, marks of rank or occupation, territorial or alliance markers, or memorials for important events or the dead have all been suggested.

Class I stones, where the symbols usually are incised into undressed stone, are believed to date to the sixth and seventh centuries and perhaps earlier and are concentrated in Northeast Scotland. The stones with bulls from Burghead are Class I, and there is evidence that others were associated with burials. The only Pictish carving in Dalriadic territory is a Class I boar carved into the bedrock at Dunadd, which has fueled debate about who was overlord over whom and when. Class II stones, where the symbols typically are carved in relief and accompanied by Christian motifs and scenes of elite activities, such as hunting and war, date to the late seventh century and early eighth century and have been found primarily in southern Pictland. The Aberlemno Kirkyard (Churchyard) stone is a Class II stone: it has an interlace-decorated cross on the front, while the reverse shows an extraordinary battle scene with Pictish symbols in relief above (fig. 1). It has been suggested that this stone commemorates the battle of Nechtansmere (Dunnichen), which was fought nearby in A.D. 685, where the Picts defeated the Angles and killed their king, Oswiu's son Ecgfrith (r. A.D. 670–685), ending Anglian expansion to the north. Secular scenes from these stones have given the clearest images of the people of early medieval Scotland: men armed for war, riding after stags, and drinking from horns; a woman with a large penannular brooch riding side-saddle with a man on horseback barely visible behind her; and hooded clerics with crosiers.

In Dál Riata to the west there was a different sculptural tradition and a distinctive form of inscription used primarily on stone. The Scots were responsible for bringing the ogham script, where short slashes are incised across a baseline, from Ireland, and ogham subsequently was adopted by the Picts. Inscriptions in this style date from the sixth to tenth centuries, but they are difficult to transcribe and translate; few can be read, even by experts. More than 450 early medieval carved stones have

Fig. 1. Battle scene on the cross-slab at Aberlemno churchyard. © CROWN COPYRIGHT. REPRODUCED COURTESY OF HISTORIC SCOTLAND.

been recorded in Argyll, about a hundred from Iona, but many are very simple crosses and difficult to date with certainty. Most attention is given to the elaborately carved crosses that date to the second half of the eighth century, such as Saint Oran's, Saint John's, and Saint Martin's crosses at Iona and the Kildalton cross on Islay. This sculpture almost always is associated with religious sites, and there is little evidence comparable to the hunting scenes on the Pictish stones to suggest that it was an important way for secular elites to display their status. As with the Pictish stones, however, many of the decorative elements on these monuments are shared with the Insular art tradition as it appears on fine metalwork and in Gospel books, such as the Book of Durrow or the Book of Kells. It is now thought that the latter two were created at Iona, which illuminates the interaction between the secular and religious spheres as well as between the different ethnic groups during this time.

RELIGION

The expansion of Christianity across Scotland during this period also has been a topic of continuing scholarly interest. It was Christianity that promoted the literacy that produced the earliest indigenous inscriptions and documents, and even in the post-Roman period some Britons were Christian. The Scots were Christians by the time they were historically active in Argyll, and it was to Dál Riata that Saint Columba came in A.D. 563, founding the monastery of Iona shortly afterward. While Columba's *Life* shows him visiting the pagan king of the northern Picts, there is little evidence for explicitly missionary efforts. Nevertheless both the Angles and the Picts had adopted Columban Christianity before those groups switched to the Roman date for Easter, the Angles in the late seventh century and the Picts in the early eighth century.

Little structural evidence for churches in Scotland has survived, except for Whithorn. In many cases these sites remain in use, and later construction has obliterated the remains of the earliest foundations, although ongoing excavations at Portmahomack, which appears to have been a monastery during the eighth and ninth centuries, will provide better evidence for the Pictish northeast. At Iona part of the *vallum*—the bank and ditch that separated the religious community from the secular world—survives, but texts reveal that the buildings within were built of timber and wattle, which has left no clear trace. Building churches of wood apparently was part of the Irish Columban tradition, although hermits' refuges usually had small, round drystone cells; it was the Roman tradition that encouraged stone construction. In the absence of surviving structural remains, the presence of early churches typically is indicated by place-name evidence—*eccles*- names in British territory and *kil*-names in Dál Riata.

Burials have little to contribute to an understanding of the early historic phase. First of all, the acid soils of Scotland have destroyed most of the skeletal remains. Second, burial practices were quite similar among the different groups, both before and after the adoption of Christianity. Even in the Late Iron Age the most usual rite was extended inhumation in either a simple grave or a long cist, where stone slabs form a rough coffin, without grave goods. The only identifiable characteristic for Christian graves therefore is their east–west orientation. Some Picts did place such graves under low mounds with square stone kerbs (curbs) in the early medieval period. But most such monuments are known only from aerial photographs, and more excavation is needed to confirm the dates.

VIKING PERIOD

At this point a fifth group and sixth language entered Scotland: the Vikings. Unlike the evidence for the Angles and Scots, historical sources provide a definite date for their arrival, for one of the earliest references to these "gentiles" is of their raid on Iona in A.D. 795. By the mid-ninth century the Norse were moving in, rather than making hit-and-run raids, almost entirely in the Northern and Western Isles, which were conveniently placed on the island-hopping sea route from western Norway to Ireland. The intensity of Norse settlement is shown by place names, and in the Northern Isles and northern mainland the local language was replaced by Norn, a dialect of Norwegian. The Scandinavian place-names of Southwest Scotland, however, are not related to this land taking but instead are evidence for settlement during the twelfth century from northern England.

The most alien thing about these Galls, or "foreigners," to the people of early medieval Scotland was their pagan religion—which is why they had no scruples about plundering churches and taking Christians as slaves. The archaeological record provides ample evidence of this in the form of furnished graves for both men and women: the men were buried with their weapons and sometimes with horses or merchants' scales and the women with characteristic oval "tortoiseshell" brooches and tools for making linen. In a few cases men and women have been found buried in small clinker-built boats. These graves provide the best evidence for a distinctly Norse material culture. This is important, because on many sites where rectangular Norse long-house forms replace earlier Pictish cellular structures are found a mix of Pictish and Norse artifact types and even bilingual runic inscriptions. These finds imply that local populations survived, whether as slaves, an underclass below Norse elites, or perhaps as allies and collaborators.

By the late ninth century the Northern Isles were the base of the powerful earls of Orkney, originally from western Norway; by the late tenth century, when they were officially converted to Christianity, their sphere of political control included Shetland, the northern mainland, and the Western Isles. Most of the Viking hoards found in Scotland, which include Arabic coins, ring money (small, irregular silver rings used as a form of currency by the Vikings), and hack silver (pieces of silver cut from larger objects used for the same purpose), date to this later period, from the mid–tenth century into the early eleventh century. Unlike hoards of religious and secular fine metalwork from the earlier period, such as the Saint Ninian's Isle treasure from Shetland, these pieces would have been associated more closely with trading than raiding.

It has been suggested that the hogback monuments found in southern Scotland and dating to the tenth and early eleventh centuries marked the graves of Scandinavian traders from northern England. Once they had become Christians and subscribed to broadly shared cultural values, Scandinavians were simply one more element in Scotland's multicultural mix. The Hunterston brooch mentioned above, a high-status object, has a runic inscription: "Melbrigda owns [this] brooch." The language is Norse, yet Melbrigda is a Celtic name.

CREATING "SCOT-LAND"

While past historians cast the early medieval period as a time of war between monolithic ethnic groups for control over what would become Scotland, with the Dalriadic Scots as the winners, archaeology has shown that the situation was much more complicated and has highlighted the ways in which the different groups contributed to the process of forging a common culture. If there is a large-scale notable trend throughout this period, it is increasing sociopolitical centralization. In the Roman period sources attest to a multiplicity of Pictish tribes; by the early historic phase there are probably three significant Pictish political groups. The hierarchical levels of kingship are evident in Dál Riata, with kings of kindreds, the most powerful of them the Dalriadic overking, and the overkings of the Scots, Angles, and Picts competing for the position of "high king" of northern Britain during the early historic phase. It was only in the Viking phase, as the Norse and their superior sea power annexed the island half of Argyll, that the bonding of these mainland groups into a permanent and internally complex state occurred.

Despite historical uncertainty about the relative power of the Scots and Picts at this time, the Scots moved eastward, and from about A.D. 843 Cinead mac Ailpín (Kenneth mac Alpin) and his descendants ruled both Scots and Picts from Forteviot in southern Pictland. Later historical revision makes it difficult to determine to what extent this was a violent overthrow of Pictish power as opposed to assimilation. Nonetheless by c. A.D. 900 Dál Riata and Pictavia vanish from the sources, replaced by Alba: a nation called by a Gaelic name and using the Gaelic language but with much of its administrative structure apparently derived from the Picts.

See also **Hillforts** (*vol. 2, part 6*); **Dál Riata** (*vol. 2, part 7*); **Picts** (*vol. 2, part 7*); **Viking Settlements in Orkney and Shetland** (*vol. 2, part 7*).

BIBLIOGRAPHY

Alcock, Leslie, and Elizabeth A. Alcock. "Reconnaissance Excavations on Early Historic Fortifications and Other Royal Sites in Scotland, 1974–84: 4, Excavations at Alt Clut, Clyde Rock, Strathclyde, 1974–75." *Proceedings of the Society of Antiquaries of Scotland* 120 (1990): 95–149.

———. "Reconnaissance Excavations on Early Historic Fortifications and Other Royal Sites in Scotland, 1974–84: 2, Excavations at Dunollie Castle, Oban, Argyll, 1978." *Proceedings of the Society of Antiquaries of Scotland* 117 (1987): 73–101.

Alcock, Leslie, Elizabeth A. Alcock, and Stephen T. Driscoll. "Reconnaissance Excavations on Early Historic Fortifications and Other Royal Sites in Scotland, 1974–84: 3, Excavations at Dundurn, Strathearn, Perthshire, 1976–77." *Proceedings of the Society of Antiquaries of Scotland* 119 (1989): 189–226.

Clancy, Thomas Owen, and Barbara E. Crawford. "The Formation of the Scottish Kingdom." In *The New Penguin History of Scotland: From the Earliest Times to the Present Day*. Edited by R. A. Houston and W. W. J. Knox, pp. 28–95. London: Allen Lane–Penguin Press, 2001.

Crawford, Barbara E. *Scandinavian Scotland*. Leicester, U.K.: Leicester University Press, 1987.

Driscoll, Stephen T. "The Archaeology of State Formation in Scotland." In *Scottish Archaeology: New Perceptions*. Edited by W. S. Hanson and E. A. Slater, pp. 81–111. Aberdeen, Scotland: Aberdeen University Press, 1991.

Fisher, Ian. *Early Medieval Sculpture in the West Highlands and Islands*. Edinburgh: Royal Commission on the Ancient and Historical Monuments of Scotland–Society of Antiquaries of Scotland, 2001.

Foster, Sally M. *Picts, Gaels, and Scots: Early Historic Scotland.* London: B. T. Batsford–Historic Scotland, 1996.

Graham-Campbell, James, and Colleen E. Batey. *Vikings in Scotland: An Archaeological Survey.* Edinburgh: Edinburgh University Press, 1998.

Henry, David, ed. *The Worm, the Germ, and the Thorn: Pictish and Related Studies Presented to Isabel Henderson.* Balgavies, U.K.: Pinkfoot Press, 1997.

Hill, Peter. *Whithorn and St. Ninian: The Excavation of a Monastic Town 1984–91.* Stroud, U.K.: Alan Sutton Publishing–Whithorn Trust, 1997.

Laing, Lloyd, and Jenny Laing. *The Picts and the Scots.* Stroud, U.K.: Alan Sutton Publishing, 1993.

Lane, Alan, and Ewan Campbell. *Dunadd: An Early Dalriadic Capital.* Oxford: Oxbow Books, 2000.

Ritchie, Anna. *Viking Scotland.* London: B. T. Batsford–Historic Scotland, 1993.

Spearman, R. Michael, and John Higgitt, eds. *The Age of Migrating Ideas: Early Medieval Art in Northern Britain and Ireland.* Stroud, U.K.: Alan Sutton Publishing; Edinburgh: National Museums of Scotland, 1993.

Wainwright, F. T. *The Problem of the Picts.* Edinburgh: Thomas Nelson and Sons, 1955.

ELIZABETH A. RAGAN

TARBAT

The Gaelic word *tarbat* refers to a dry crossing where boats were hauled across the neck of a peninsula. The Tarbat peninsula in northeastern Scotland juts into the Moray Firth and permitted such crossings between Cromarty and Dornoch Firths. This peninsula contains some of the finest sculpture of the European Early Middle Ages. It is now recognized as the site of the first and so far the only known early monastery in eastern Scotland, land of the lost nation of the Picts.

The sculpture at Tarbat survives in the form of monumental cross slabs, all carved and erected about A.D. 800. At Nigg, at the southern foot of the peninsula, the cross-slab features the biblical king David and the story of St. Paul and St. Anthony in the desert. At Shandwick, the large cross is accompanied by cherubim and seraphim and a mass of intricate Celtic spiral ornament. At Hilton of Cadboll, the cross side of the slab has been erased, but the reverse features a secular scene showing a woman rid-

ing to the hunt accompanied by servants and huntsmen. All of these cross slabs face the sea, and all carry symbols of the Pictish iconic language, symbols that probably represent the names of the persons commemorated.

Archaeological excavation since 1994 at the peninsula's main settlement of Portmahomack has given a context for these remarkable monuments (fig. 1). During the nineteenth century, pieces of carved stone were discovered by gravediggers in the churchyard and surroundings of Portmahomack's church of St. Colman. Among them was a stone carved in relief in insular majuscules recalling the Book of Kells (approximately A.D. 800). In 1984 a buried ditch around the church was discovered by aerial survey. The ditch's D-shaped plan recalled the enclosure that defines the monastery of St. Columba (Columcille) on Iona, an island off western Scotland. It was Columba (according to Adomnán of Iona, his biographer) who had attempted to convert the northern Picts around A.D. 565. Here were clues that Portmahomack might have been a settlement of the first Christians in Pictland.

In 1994 the University of York was invited by a local restoration group (Tarbat Historic Trust) to adopt the site as a research project. After an initial evaluation, the church itself was excavated and its fabric recorded, while outside the churchyard an area of 0.6 hectare was opened, with sensational results. In the church, excavators recorded a sequence of two hundred burials, beginning with sixty-seven graves that were wholly or partly lined with stone slabs (the distinctive "cist" burials of the Picts). These proved to contain the remains of primarily middle-aged or elderly men, the earliest of which has been radiocarbon dated to the sixth century A.D. The later burials, with a more normal distribution of men, women, and children, belong to the twelfth to fifteenth centuries A.D. Six principal phases of church building were distinguished. The earliest stone church is signaled by a single wall and probably dates to the eighth century A.D. It was replaced in the twelfth century by an east-west chapel with a square-ended chancel, which was lengthened and provided with a tower and crypt in the thirteenth century. In the sixteenth century (at the Reformation) the axis of worship was altered to run north-south and a northern "aisle," or quarter, reserved for the laird, was constructed. When the Church of

Fig. 1. Excavations at Portmahomack in 2000. In the background is the church of St. Colman; to the left workshops are under excavation; and in the foreground is the dam for the mill pond. © MARTIN CARVER AND THE UNIVERSITY OF YORK. REPRODUCED BY PERMISSION.

Scotland split in two because of the Disruption of 1843, the axis returned to the east-west. The construction of the present church largely dates from a restoration undertaken in the mid-eighteenth century.

Numerous pieces of carved stone were found to have been reused in the foundations of the eleventh-century church, the majority carrying ornament of the eighth century. As of the early 2000s, more than 150 carved stones had been recovered from excavation in the church or outside it. Many of these are simple grave-markers carrying a cross and recalling examples known from Iona. One massive slab with a lion and a wild boar in relief belongs to a sarcophagus lid, or possibly an altar. Another with a picture of a family of cattle comes from a wall slab, perhaps a *cancellum* (fig. 2). Many other pieces derive from one or more monumental cross slabs that closely resemble those surviving at Nigg and Shandwick.

Excavations in the field next to the church revealed a large segment of an early Christian monastery in plan. Nearest to the church is a workshop area laid out on either side of a paved road. The workshops have produced evidence for the making of objects of silver (cuppelation dishes), bronze (hearths, crucibles, molds, and whetstones), glass (molds), leather (a tanning pit, bone pegs for a stretcher frame, and pumice leather-smoothers), and wood (a chisel clad by ferriferous wood shavings). The objects that were made appear to have been ecclesiastical in nature, since the molds and studs recall reliquaries and liturgical vessels known from the early Celtic world. South of the workshops is a millpond with a dam to provide a head of water for driving a horizontal millwheel. Farther south, still against the enclosure boundary, lie a number of grain-drying pits and the foundations of a timber-framed structure bag-shaped in plan. This was probably a kiln-barn, although its hearth shows evidence

Fig. 2. A family of cattle carved on a slab found at Portmahomack, Easter Ross, eighth century A.D. After the monastery was destroyed by the Vikings, the slab was reused as a drain cover. © MARTIN CARVER AND THE UNIVERSITY OF YORK. REPRODUCED BY PERMISSION.

of use by a blacksmith. The boundary ditch itself was by no means defensive but appears to have been employed in collecting and bringing water to different areas of the monastery.

The male burials, the sculpture, the inscription, the enclosure, and the manufacture of ecclesiastical objects identify the Portmahomack settlement as an early monastery. The earliest burial took place in the sixth century, while the majority of the artifacts, including the sculpture, belong to the eighth century with a terminus around 800. Records indicate that Columba settled in Iona in 563 and took part in an expedition to the northern Picts in 565. He passed up the Great Glen by way of Loch Ness and met the Pictish king Bridei, son of Mailchu, somewhere near Inverness. Although the conversion of the Picts is not claimed in Adomnán's *Life of St. Columba,* he does say that monasteries were founded in Columba's time. Discoveries from the 1990s allow us to identify Portmahomack ("port of Colman"—or Columba) as one of these, established at the opposite end of the Great Glen to Iona, perhaps by Columba himself. By A.D. 800 the whole Tarbat peninsula had emerged as a major ecclesiastical center, its boundaries marked by monumental cross slabs carrying some of the most complex iconography seen

in early Christian art. The end of the monastery and its consignment to oblivion for more than one thousand years remain something of a mystery. Sometime between 800 and 1100, the workshop area was destroyed by fire, and at the same time the monumental cross slabs were broken up and dumped. It seems likely that this targeted attack was the work of the Vikings.

See also **Celts** (*vol. 2, part 6*); **Picts** (*vol. 2, part 7*); **Vikings** (*vol. 2, part 7*).

BIBLIOGRAPHY

Adomnán of Iona. *Life of St Columba.* Translated by Richard Sharpe. Harmondsworth, U.K., and New York: Penguin, 1991.

Bulletins of the Tarbat Discovery Programme. 1995–. Available at www.york.ac.uk/depts/arch/staff/sites/tarbat.

Carver, Martin. *Surviving in Symbols: A Visit to the Pictish Nation.* Edinburgh: Canongate, 1999.

———. "Conversion and Politics on the Eastern Seaboard of Britain: Some Achaeological Indicators." In *Conversion and Christianity in the North Sea World.* Edited by Barbara E. Crawford, pp. 11–40. St. Andrews, U.K.: University of St. Andrews, 1998.

Foster, Sally. *Picts, Gaels, and Scots.* London: B. T. Batsford/
    Historic Scotland, 1996.

MARTIN CARVER

EARLY MEDIEVAL WALES

The archaeology of early medieval Wales has been studied largely within a historical framework primarily derived from sources created late in the period under consideration, about A.D. 400 to 1000, with many of the written sources even later than this and their relevance to earlier periods inferred. Two major themes have emerged from research, that of elite settlements and ecclesiastical archaeology. Elite settlements were first defined at Dinas Powys, Glamorganshire, with the presence of imported vessels and craft production debris. Subsequent excavations have widened the range of such site types, but they have done little to reveal later high-status sites or much of the lower-level settlements of any part of the period. Ecclesiastical archaeology has relied heavily on sculpture and inscriptions but has been augmented by important excavated evidence of burial. Research has also increased the evidence for Viking settlement, and there is lively debate regarding the interpretation of the inscribed stones and sculpture.

POST-ROMAN CONTINUITY

Some late Roman military activity is known at sites such as Cardiff, various locations on Anglesey, and at Caernarfon. These are thought to have been a reaction to Irish raids that led to Irish settlement in several parts of Wales. Even after the Roman military presence ceased around A.D. 410, aspects of Roman life continued into the fifth and sixth centuries, though settlement evidence for this is inconclusive and relies more on later inscriptions discussed below.

Several high-status Romanized sites in southeastern Wales show reuse. At villas such as Llantwit Major there may have been continuity of estates that later came within a monastic context. Other religious foundations were created at Roman sites such as Caer Gybi, Anglesey, in northwestern Wales and Caerwent, Gwent, in southeastern Wales, though in these cases there may have been a considerable hiatus between Roman abandonment and early medieval use. In some cases such as Cold Knap, Glamorganshire, the occupation seems secular, and was set in the ruins of the Roman structures. Here, again, a gap in occupation is suggested. Some continuity of settlement is demonstrated at a few burial locations discussed below, suggesting that estates and communities may have continued, even if the location and nature of settlement sites on those estates altered following the end of the Roman period.

Hillforts in Wales have produced evidence of late Roman occupation, and a few have activity from the early medieval period also, although continuity of settlement or repeated episodes of reuse are both possible. Several native settlements such as Graeanog, Gwynedd, and some of the enclosed farmsteads around Llawhaden, Pembrokeshire, suggest that such sites continued to attract habitation into the fifth and sixth centuries.

The most obvious archaeological evidence for continuity of Roman traditions and elements of culture comes from some of the inscribed stones. Though difficult to date, some from the fifth and

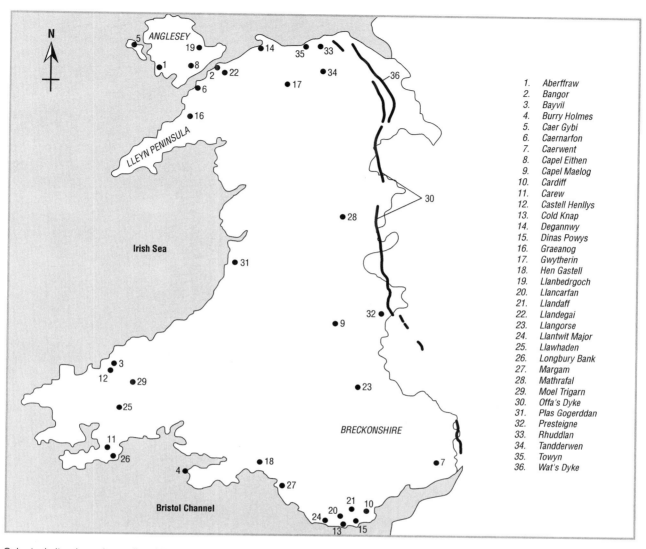

1. Aberffraw
2. Bangor
3. Bayvil
4. Burry Holmes
5. Caer Gybi
6. Caernarfon
7. Caerwent
8. Capel Eithen
9. Capel Maelog
10. Cardiff
11. Carew
12. Castell Henllys
13. Cold Knap
14. Degannwy
15. Dinas Powys
16. Graeanog
17. Gwytherin
18. Hen Gastell
19. Llanbedrgoch
20. Llancarfan
21. Llandaff
22. Llandegai
23. Llangorse
24. Llantwit Major
25. Llawhaden
26. Longbury Bank
27. Margam
28. Mathrafal
29. Moel Trigarn
30. Offa's Dyke
31. Plas Gogerddan
32. Presteigne
33. Rhuddlan
34. Tandderwen
35. Towyn
36. Wat's Dyke

Selected sites in early medieval Wales.

others from the sixth century show clear affiliations with the Roman world. For some, the tradition of inscribed stones in Latin was introduced into Wales from southern Gaul in the fifth century. For others, they demonstrate a more complex pattern with continuity of Christianity and Romanitas within Wales, although with influence from the Continent. The use of Latin titles such as *magistratus* on memorials with crude but clearly Roman-style lettering might be taken to indicate an administrative structure, heavily adapted to more uncertain and less centralized times but which had aspirations to continue the traditions or at least the aura of Roman rule. Charles Thomas has argued that some inscriptions contain complex messages hidden within them, though this has been challenged.

IRISH MIGRATIONS

Inscribed memorial stones form the main archaeological source of evidence for the movement of Irish population, possibly only an elite, from southern Ireland to northwestern and particularly southwestern Wales. Documentary sources also support this interpretation, as do place-name studies. The tribe that moved to southwestern Wales was the Déisi, and Thomas has suggested that the Iron Age hillfort of Moel Trigarn, Pembrokeshire, which was also

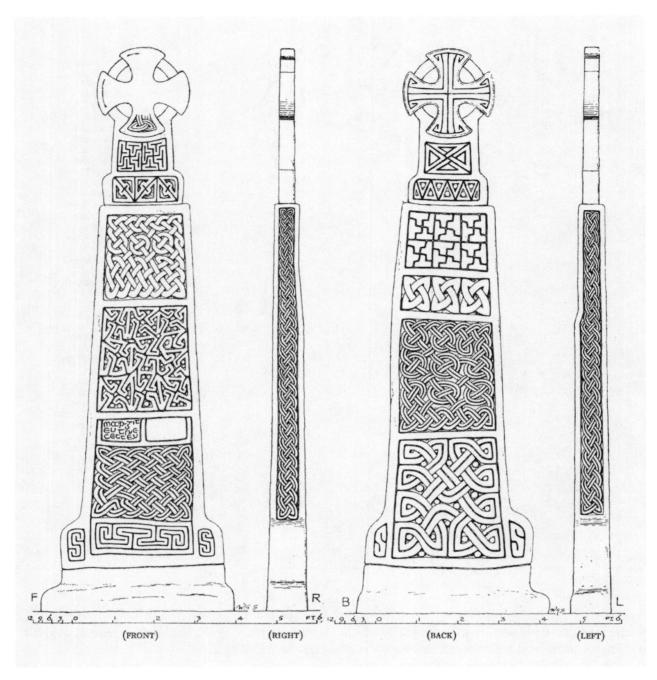

(FRONT) (RIGHT) (BACK) (LEFT)

Fig. 1. Early Christian monuments, Wales. FROM NASH-WILLIAMS 1950. © UNIVERSITY OF WALES. REPRODUCED BY PERMISSION.

used in the Roman period, was perhaps their early base. Excavation at the nearby settlement of Castell Henllys has identified a late Roman or immediately post-Roman refortification of an inland promontory fort. Settlement and control was initially over the northern part of Pembrokeshire, but subsequently

spread east and south. The date of initial settlement is uncertain, but it perhaps first began around A.D. 400.

The earliest inscribed stones are probably those only in ogham, a style of writing that was first developed in Ireland, and with Irish words and names. Later inscriptions, from the later fifth and the sixth centuries, occur bilingually in ogham and Latin, and it is during this phase that obvious Christian features also occur. Irish and British names can now be noted, and relationships between individuals (usually X son of Y) were often recorded.

Less substantial evidence for Irish settlement has also been found in the Lleyn Peninsula of northwestern Wales, and in Brecknockshire (present-day Breconshire) in central southern Wales. In Brecknockshire, a kingdom of Brycheiniog was carved out of territory along the river Usk, and the presence of a number of bilingual inscriptions containing ogham suggests that this was also linked to Irish settlement. This may have been a secondary movement from southwestern Wales. Another piece of evidence that suggests an elite link with Ireland, and one that was continued over generations, is the presence at Brecknockshire of the only known crannog, an early medieval lake settlement of characteristically Irish type, in Llangorse Lake. Excavations there have shown that little survives of the settlement itself, though dendrochronological dates from planking suggest dates of A.D. 890 and 893 for at least one phase of development. Some of the early medieval artifacts recovered from the silts around the crannog are probably earlier in date and suggest a long period of occupation. The finds include items with a clear Irish origin, such as a pseudo-penannular brooch fragment and a fragment of a portable reliquary shrine of the eighth century.

SECULAR SETTLEMENT

A number of sites have been located in Wales that are considered to be elite secular settlements. The first of these to be investigated, and the one that has conditioned interpretations and expectations since, was that of Dinas Powys. Extensive excavation within the interior of the small inland promontory fort located slight traces of two rectangular structures that have been tentatively interpreted as a hall and barn. Little survived within these buildings, but in contrast some middens were excavated that provided rich finds of many kinds.

The early medieval pottery from the site was all imported; it was identified as belonging to four major classes, namely A, B, D, and E, and classified on their form and fabric as defined at the site of Tin-

tagel, Cornwall, where they were first recognized. Class A pottery at Dinas Powys seems to be of early-sixth-century Phocaean Red Slip Ware, originally from the eastern Mediterranean. These fine tablewares comprised bowls and dishes, one of which had stamped designs on the interior base. The B ware sherds were from amphorae vessels, and these have been further subdivided by subsequent scholars into categories such as Bi and Bii as more research on the forms and fabrics in the Mediterranean has allowed distinctive types with particular origins to be identified in Britain and Ireland. Dinas Powys has produced Bi material from the Aegean, Bii sherds date to the middle or later sixth century having come from the eastern Mediterranean, and B Misc, which has not been closely provenanced. In contrast to these Mediterranean products, there were also forty-six sherds of D ware in tableware bowls and in mortaria, mixing bowls of a Roman tradition. These were probably made in France, perhaps the Bordeaux region, and were a rare import to Britain. Dinas Powys also produced Roman-style bowls, storage jars, and pitchers in E ware of the late sixth and seventh centuries. E ware may also have been produced in France.

International contacts are also attested through the presence of glass, which in the 1980s was the subject of reassessment. It can now be seen as material of Continental origin, but not all from the same sources that supplied Anglo-Saxon England, suggesting that some came along the same routes as the imported ceramics.

Leslie Alcock defined Dinas Powys as a *llys* site, the residence of a king or prince, based on evidence from the Welsh Laws, though these only survive in a later form. The *llys* formed the central point within the *maerdref,* land which supported the *llys.* These lands were set within the larger unit, the *commote,* and above that was the *cantref.* This administrative structure was in use by the end of the period under consideration here, though its applicability several centuries earlier is less certain.

The interpretation of Dinas Powys as a high-status site was based on the presence of exotic imported goods and from the way in which the elites in less complex stratified societies controlled production and distribution of craft products such as jewelry. The attribution to a *llys* was additionally based on the faunal assemblage that was thought to match what would be expected if the site had been supplied by food renders as described in the Welsh Laws. Discoveries in the 1990s found B ware ceramics at the nearby monastery of Llandough, which might indicate a high-status ecclesiastical site under the patronage of the Dinas Powys elite. This pairing of major secular and ecclesiastical sites has been suggested as a typical pattern, though this has yet to be firmly demonstrated.

Following the identification of Dinas Powys as a defended elite site, many other forts were proposed as examples of this type. Few, however, have produced conclusive evidence, although some such evidence was recovered below late medieval activity at the hilltop site of Degannwy, Gwynedd. Excavations at Hen Gastell, Glamorganshire, in the early 1990s have located another such site, heavily damaged by quarrying but displaying a range of sixth- and seventh-century finds—Bi, and possibly Bii, amphorae; D and E ware, as well as Continental glass vessels—on a small hilltop location. Craft activity there was demonstrated by the presence of lumps of fused glass. Documentary evidence hints that the major political center in the area may have been at Margam, where a possible secular site and a definite major monastic site with inscribed monuments have been identified.

Another probable high-status settlement has been excavated at Longbury Bank, Pembrokeshire. Again dated to the sixth and seventh centuries by imported ceramics (Ai, Bi, Bii, Biv, D, and E wares) and glass, this was an undefended settlement on a low promontory. This suggests a wider range of types of high-status sites than previously had been considered. Structural evidence was limited: one small building was found, set in a rock-cut platform, but all other settlement evidence had been destroyed by later agriculture. Craft activity was demonstrated by scrap copper alloy and silver, and also crucibles, heating trays, and metal droplets. The early monastic site of Penally lay only 1 kilometer away, and the secular defended site of Castle Hill, Tenby, was only 2 kilometers distant. This suggests that there may have been quite a high density of these higher-status sites in a region, though they may have formed networks of functionally distinct sites used by the same elite group.

Other defended sites such as Carew, Pembrokeshire, indicate that more of the early elite sites may

often lie beneath later castles, and other site types undoubtedly await discovery. For example, sand dunes around the coast contain early medieval artifacts in some numbers, suggesting activity there, and these finds probably represent a category of settlement yet to be revealed through excavation.

Attempts to find later elite residences have not been successful, with documented high-status sites at both Mathrafal, Powys, and Aberffraw, Anglesey, remaining elusive, despite considerable investment in survey and excavation. Within the boundaries of the present Principality of Wales lies the Anglo-Saxon burh at Rhuddlan, with Late Saxon material culture and structures within an urban context of the ninth and tenth centuries, although there is no indication that the native population imitated this settlement form. Anglo-Saxon occupation spread across parts of northeastern Wales, and physical boundaries between the Welsh and the Anglo-Saxon were defined by the construction of linear earthworks. Known as Offa's and Wat's Dykes, they have been subject to much detailed survey and limited excavation beginning in the late 1960s. Although they are extremely difficult to date closely enough to link with specific historical events, they probably belong to the later ninth century.

BURIALS

Evidence for burial in Wales comes from a range of sources. Although the Irish inscribed stones were memorials, not all may have been set up at the burial sites themselves, and the overwhelming majority are now no longer in their original positions. Evidence has therefore mainly come through casual discoveries and archaeological excavations.

Open cemeteries, discovered because of their adjacency to prehistoric remains including barrows and standing stones, have been found at several sites scattered across Wales. The most notable are Capel Eithen on Anglesey, Llandegai in Gwynedd, Tandderwen in Clwyd, and Plas Gogerddan in Cardiganshire. Orientation was roughly east-west, though with a tendency toward a more northeast-southwest alignment. Bone survival was slight, and so sexing of the burials was not possible, but the size of the grave cuts shows that both adults and children were buried at some sites, though others were just for adults. Some of the interments had surviving wooden coffin stains. A few of the graves were surrounded by square structures, but these vary in form within and between sites. Some, such as those at Tandderwen, were clearly ditches that silted up naturally, and the central area may have been covered with a mound. In other cases, there were foundations for a building. At Plas Gogerddan a plank-built structure 4.5 by 3.2 meters could be identified, with a doorway to the east. At Capel Eithen, flooring survived within the wooden structure; this floor sealed the central grave. Graves with rectangular ditches or structures are also known from southern England, and some Anglo-Saxon graves have been noted as parallels. Some burial sites in Scotland also have square barrows, but these seem to be of a different tradition.

The dating of the cemeteries with the square enclosures has primarily been through radiocarbon dating. Coffin stains have been dated approximately to A.D. 430–690 and A.D. 770–1050 at Tandderwen, A.D. 265–640 at Plas Gogerddan, and a more problematic Roman or eighth- or ninth-century date from Capel Eithen. Clearly, most if not all such burials date to the early medieval period in Wales, but more precise chronology for these cemeteries is still uncertain and so their relationship with church burial sites cannot be interpreted.

Some other sites have produced evidence of simple earth-dug inhumation cemeteries, including ones such as that at the Atlantic Trading Estate, Barry. This continued from the second century up to perhaps the tenth century A.D., and may be the cemetery for an estate established in the Roman period with the same family members using it for generations.

A particular form of burial that has been identified for this period in Wales, and which has parallels in southwestern England, Scotland, and Ireland, is the long-cist burial, where stone slabs set on edge have been placed around the edge of the grave and, in some cases, across the top of the inhumation. Long-cist burials occur in cemeteries, with the graves aligned east-west. Many such sites have been recorded, particularly in southwestern Wales, but few have been scientifically examined. One at Bayvil, Pembrokeshire, was set within an Iron Age enclosure, and contained numerous long-cist graves, one dated by radiocarbon to A.D. 640–883. Later examples of long-cist graves have been found at church sites, dated up to the twelfth century, so this

method of burial had a long life and was used in cemeteries with and without churches.

Relatively few early burials have been found at church sites, and only at Capel Maelog, Powys, have extensive excavations allowed a full sequence of site development to be appreciated. Radiocarbon dates suggest that burial began there after the seventh century when a ditch silted up, but unfortunately only one interment was dated. A coffin stain provided a sample from the ninth or tenth century A.D., confirming the early medieval date for the burials. The cemetery was still in use when a church was built on the site in the late twelfth or early thirteenth century. The only other excavated site with a significant number of early medieval burials is that of Berlland Bach, Bangor, Gwynedd. A total of seventy-eight burials have been found; they varied slightly in orientation, and this may relate to their date.

THE CHURCH

Many churches that became part of the parochial system in the Norman period may have been built during the early medieval period. The only early standing fabric from Wales is at Presteigne, Powys, but as the surviving fragments of nave and chancel arch are in the Anglo-Saxon style, they provide no indication of native Welsh ecclesiastical architecture. Wooden churches were probably the normal construction, but only a tiny example at Burry Holmes, Glamorgan, has been excavated. This building was only about 3.4 meters by 3.1 meters and so would be very comparable with timber oratory churches excavated in Ireland and southwestern Scotland.

Inscribed stones from the sixth century onward indicate Christian features not only in the use of the Latin phrase *hic iacet,* "here lies," which occurs elsewhere in Gaul in Christian contexts, but also by definite Christian symbolism. Notable examples include simple crosses with various terminals for the arms, ringed crosses, Chi-Rho symbols (Christograms), and some ringed crosses that resemble a *flabellum* or liturgical fan. Many of these designs can be paralleled in Ireland but that may reflect designs inspired from a common, shared Christian material culture and documentation in Britain, Ireland, and Gaul than on direct copying from one primary source. Historical sources indicate considerable movement of religious personnel within and between these regions, and indeed to other parts of Europe. V. E. Nash-Williams attempted a classification and termed the simple designs associated with ogham and Latin as class 1. Later inscriptions were decorated with various forms of a cross, and some had inscriptions carved with half-uncial style lettering, derived from seventh-century and later manuscript writing; these are termed class 2. The inscriptions are in Latin, with the one exception at Towyn, Merionethshire, which is the earliest surviving example of the written Welsh language.

The latest group of stone sculpture, the class 3 memorials, was carved beginning in the ninth century and continuing until the eleventh century. These are mainly found in southern Wales, where a range of styles is found, with few examples in northern Wales. The class 3 monuments have more elaborate carving than the earlier stones and can be broadly divided into pillar crosses, slab crosses, and cross slabs. Figure representation is rare on the Welsh monuments, and occurs almost completely in the southeast. The main design features were interlace, fret, and key patterns. Though never matching the quality of design and execution of the fine high crosses of Ireland and Scotland, some were substantial monuments.

Many of the early inscribed stones discussed above are now found at ecclesiastical sites, and some may have been erected there. Others, however, have been moved into churches and churchyards in relatively recent times, and so the presence of stones alone does not necessarily indicate an early church site. The likely sites of early churches are suggested by several other features occurring together, such as the use of early saints' names, the presence of a holy spring or well, and a circular or oval churchyard. Some of the major sites can also be linked with documentary references. Aerial photography, particularly in southwestern Wales, has highlighted the presence of outer concentric enclosures around many subcircular churchyards, suggesting possible continuity of late prehistoric and Roman period secular settlements, perhaps given to the church in the early medieval period. These arrangements are also highly reminiscent of some of the concentric enclosures found on Irish monastic sites. As yet there has been insufficient excavation on Welsh sites of this type to determine more regarding their detailed chronology and functions.

Unlike contemporary Ireland, Wales possessed no large monasteries endowed with impressive stone structures. Although there was some sculpture, even this was limited in quantity and quality. Welsh monasteries did contain some small stone buildings, and such institutions owned some relics and libraries, but little survives. A small fragment of a reliquary casket from Gwytherin, Denbighshire, is similar to those surviving in some numbers from Ireland. Fragments of another shrine have been excavated from Llangorse crannog, Brecknockshire, even though that is a secular site.

Welsh monasteries appear relatively impoverished compared with the equivalent contemporary establishments in Ireland and Scotland. This may relate to the relative wealth of such regions, but other factors may have played their part. Welsh cultural expectations were probably that surpluses should be devoted to feasting and almsgiving rather than used for heavy investment in material culture that could be displayed as part of social competition and so survive for archaeological study today. Of particular interest are sculptured crosses of class 3, which, although not numerous and of inferior quality compared with Irish and Scottish high crosses, nevertheless provide evidence for ecclesiastical workshops and patronage.

Written sources late in the early medieval period in Wales survive in some numbers for southeastern Wales, and have been the subject of much scholarship since the 1970s, particularly concerning the charters associated with Llandaff. These demonstrate how Llandaff, and by analogy other successful ecclesiatical sites, became substantial landowners with estates that provided manpower and agricultural produce. Llandaff gained most of its land in the eighth century, and Wendy Davies suggests that this may have been when estates, which had continued intact from the late Roman period, were finally broken up and royalty lost their control of donations to religious houses. At this writing, however, no evidence has come to light that would demonstrate a material shift in ecclesiastical investment in buildings or sculpture at that time.

Scholarship in archaeology and history since the 1990s has highlighted the fact that a Celtic church, distinct from Continental and Anglo-Saxon traditions, never existed. Many administrative powers were held by bishops, though monasteries could be powerful entities. In Wales there could even be some federations of monasteries and dependent churches, as with those linked to Llancarfan, Glamorganshire, but such features also occurred elsewhere in the Christian west. The idea of a Celtic church or a distinctive Celtic Christianity is therefore a modern invention.

VIKING INCURSIONS

Viking raids around the coast of Wales took place in the late tenth and the eleventh centuries and affected monastic establishments in the north, west, and south. A small number of Viking burials have been found, all close to the coast. There were, however, a few Viking settlements, and one was excavated at Llanbedrgoch, Anglesey, in the 1990s. Building 1 of the tenth century was a house 11 meters long and 5 meters wide, with a clear domestic area in the northern part of the structure, with a central hearth and bench or bed areas around the sides. A wide range of artifacts have been recovered from the site, including Hiberno-Norse style artifacts, probably from Viking Dublin, such as ringed pins and an arm-ring trial piece. The Vikings in Wales formed part of a complex network of trading and political links that were built around the two powerful centers of Dublin and York.

CONCLUSIONS

The pattern of adaptation following the collapse of Roman administration, and the movement of warrior elites to take advantage of any instability seen in Wales, can be paralleled elsewhere in post-Roman Britain. The development of a series of small kingdoms ruled from relatively small but sometimes defended settlements, and linked with ecclesiastical sites established out of patronage, can also be paralleled in Ireland and western Britain. There were, however, distinctive features of the Welsh experience in this period, even if these tended toward small-scale solutions that seem unimpressive in archaeological terms. Monasteries never became large centers, and the secular political structure did not become centralized. Expression through material culture never became a cultural strategy, giving the impression that Wales was poorer than it probably was. Only with the coming of the Anglo-Normans

did monumental construction—in castles, churches, monasteries, and planned towns—become an active strategy in Wales, with dramatic remains that now dominate the landscape.

See also **Hillforts** (*vol. 2, part 6*); **Viking York** (*vol. 2, part 7*); **Raths, Crannogs, and Cashels** (*vol. 2, part 7*); **Viking Dublin** (*vol. 2, part 7*).

BIBLIOGRAPHY

Alcock, Leslie. *Economy, Society and Warfare among the Britons and Saxons*. Cardiff: University of Wales Press, 1987. (Updated and expanded version of Alcock 1963.)

———. *Dinas Powys*. Cardiff: University of Wales Press, 1963.

Brassil, K. D., W. G. Owen, and W. J. Britnell. "Prehistoric and Early Medieval Cemeteries at Tandderwen, near Denbigh, Clwyd." *Archaeological Journal* 148 (1991): 46–97.

Britnell, W. "Capel Maelog, Llandrindod Wells, Powys: Excavations 1984–1987." *Medieval Archaeology* 34 (1990): 27–96.

Campbell, Ewan, and Alan Lane. "Excavations at Longbury Bank, Dyfed, and Early Medieval Settlement in South Wales." *Medieval Archaeology* 37 (1993): 15–77.

Davies, Wendy. *Wales in the Early Middle Ages*. Leicester, U.K.: Leicester University Press, 1982. (A comprehensive review by a historian who integrates archaeological evidence effectively.)

Edwards, Nancy, and Alan Lane, eds. *The Early Church in Wales and the West*. Oxbow Monograph 16. Oxford: Oxbow, 1992. (A collection of papers by specialists on various aspects of history and archaeology.)

Murphy, Ken. "Plas Gogerddan, Dyfed: A Multi-Period Burial and Ritual Site." *Archaeological Journal* 149 (1992): 1–38.

Mytum, Harold. *The Origins of Early Christian Ireland*. London: Routledge, 1992. (One section of the book considers the migration of Irish to Wales and the impact of this contact on stimulating change in Ireland.)

Nash-Williams, V. E. *The Early Christian Monuments of Wales*. Cardiff: University of Wales Press, 1950. (The classic work on the stone inscriptions and sculpture, with a detailed catalog and many line drawings; it is due to be replaced by a completely reworked study by Nancy Edwards.)

Quinnell, H., M. Blockley, and P. Berridge. *Excavations at Rhuddlan, Clwyd: 1969–1973: Mesolithic to Medieval*. CBA Research Report, no. 95. London: Council for British Archaeology, 1994.

Redknap, Mark. *Vikings in Wales. An Archaeological Quest*. Cardiff: National Museums and Galleries of Wales,

2000. (A popular account covering many aspects of Viking Age Wales with abundant color illustrations.)

Royal Commission on Ancient and Historical Monuments in Wales. *An Inventory of the Ancient Monuments of Glamorgan.* Vol. 1, part 3, *The Early Christian Period.* London: Her Majesty's Stationery Office, 1976.

Thomas, Charles. *Christian Celts: Messages and Images.* Stroud, U.K.: Tempus, 1998. (A controversial account of the inscriptions and their possible hidden meanings. For a substantial critique, see H. McKee and J. McKee, "Counter Arguments and Numerical Patterns in Early Celtic Inscriptions: A Re-examination of *Christian Celts: Messages and Images,*" *Medieval Archaeology* 46 [2002]: 29–40.)

———. *And Shall These Stones Speak? Post-Roman Inscriptions in Western Britain.* Cardiff: University of Wales Press, 1994. (A detailed analysis of the inscriptions and their archaeological and historical implications.)

———. *Celtic Britain.* London: Thames and Hudson, 1986. (A popular, well-illustrated account covering Cornwall, southwestern England, and Scotland as well as Wales, and so sets Wales in context.)

Wilkinson, P. F. "Excavations at Hen Gastell, Briton Ferry, West Glamorgan, 1991–1992." *Medieval Archaeology* 39 (1995): 1–50.

Williams, George, and Harold Mytum. *Llawhaden, Dyfed: Excavations on a Group of Small Defended Enclosures, 1980–1984.* BAR British Series, no. 275. Oxford: British Archaeological Reports, 1998.

HAROLD MYTUM

ANGLO-SAXON ENGLAND

FOLLOWED BY FEATURE ESSAYS ON:

From an Anglo-Saxon monk, the Venerable Bede (A.D. 673–735), comes the traditional portrayal of the downfall of Roman Britain and the beginnings of early Anglo-Saxon England. Written in the first third of the eighth century, Bede's *Ecclesiastical History of the English People* (*Historia ecclesiastica gentis Anglorum*) was drawn in part from *On the Fall of Britain* (*De excidio Britanniae et conquestu*), a polemical sermon by the sixth-century British cleric, Gildas. Supplementary accounts of the arrival of the Anglo-Saxons come from a ninth-century revision accredited to the Welsh monk Nennius, the late-ninth-century *Anglo-Saxon Chronicle*, and brief references in continental documents.

These sources present a cataclysmic history of battle and bloodshed. According to their account, Roman military forces were withdrawn from the province in the early fifth century, leaving the Britons to defend themselves against barbarian attacks. The Picts and Scots soon after recommenced their raids and were so successful that the Britons called in vain upon the Roman commander in Gaul to aid the native defenses. Although abandoned, the British rallied and overthrew the enemy forces. After a period of peace, ominous rumors led the Britons to hold council over enemy attacks. The head of the Britons' council, Vortigern, then invited the Saxons of northern Germany to protect them. Led by Hengist and Horsa, three ships bearing Saxons arrived on the English coast. The number of Saxons multiplied and, in time, a quarrel about compensation arose between the Saxon warriors and their British overlords. The Saxons rebelled and, during the ensuing destruction, the Britons fled to the safety of the western forests and mountains. The tide of Saxon conquest was halted by the British victory at Mons Badonicus. From the time of that battle to the writing of *De excidio Britanniae et conquestu*, relations between the two groups remained peaceful.

EARLIEST EVIDENCE

The traditional image of the transition from Roman Britain to early Anglo-Saxon England as a period of turmoil and warfare has been supplanted by a more complex and modulated conception of culture change. The eighth- and ninth-century written accounts of the fifth- and sixth-century preliterate Anglo-Saxon past are not always believable, as they incorporate fantastic characters and events and invented chronologies. No longer is the Anglo-Saxon invasion viewed as a single event. Ceramics, belt fittings, and dress ornaments indicate that Germanic people were entering Britain prior to the fifth-century dates calculated from the documentary sources. The lands bordering the North Sea exhibit the earliest archaeological evidence for a Germanic presence in late Roman Britain. Germanic mercenaries in the Roman army were garrisoned at coastal forts and inland towns. The withdrawal of Roman military support from the province in the early fifth century was closely followed by the middle of the fifth century with the appearance of Germanic-style cemeteries. Continental parallels argue for the subsequent immigration into eastern England in the sixth century of people from southern Norway.

The size and character of Germanic populations engaged in this transition remains contested. Some archaeologists argue that a few warrior bands from northern Germany and southern Scandinavia seized control of regional British polities while others consider the discontinuities in material culture and language as evidence of large-scale migration. The lack of any clear continuity of urban life and the evidence for a breakdown in the rural villa system from the Roman to the Anglo-Saxon period indicates a dislocation of the economic structure. Likewise, the replacement of Celtic dialects with Old English speech and the renaming of the landscape with Old English place names indicate extensive Anglo-Saxon settlement. Although the extent and character of British continuity is contested, British kingdoms survived in the highland zone, Wales, and the southwest. Some of these kingdoms, such as Elmet, which lost its autonomy to the Anglo-Saxon king Edwin of Northumbria in 617, were subsumed in the process of political centralization. Recognition that in early medieval Europe ethnic identity was fluid and situational has called for a reassessment of the extent and character of native British survival and assimilation. Indeed, no single model adequately accommodates the regional variability now recognized during the settlement period.

CEMETERIES

Early Anglo-Saxon England remains best known archaeologically through more than one thousand cemeteries, many of which were unsystematically excavated during the eighteenth and nineteenth centuries. Unfortunately, the relationship between cemeteries and the settlements that they served is poorly understood, as few excavations include both types of evidence. However, at Mucking (Essex) and West Heslerton (Yorkshire), the settlements display a structural uniformity that implies a social equality not apparent in the diverse burial assemblages of the adjacent cemeteries.

During the early Anglo-Saxon period (c. 450–c. 650), two main burial practices predominated: cremation and inhumation. Cremation required burning the dressed body of the deceased on a pyre. A selection of the burned bone, generally from the head and chest, was then buried either directly into the earth or enclosed in a ceramic urn, or more rarely, a metal, cloth, or leather container prior to interment. Miniature toilet implements, perhaps serving as symbolic substitutes for the full-scale items, were occasionally included with the cremated bone. Cremation pits, sometimes marked by stones, contained a single deposit or a cluster of vessels. Wooden post-built structures, perhaps housing the cremated remains of a family grouping, have been identified at Apple Down (Sussex) and Berinsfield (Oxfordshire).

Inhumation burials required the dressed but unburned body to be deposited into a rectangular, often wood- or stone-lined pit. Rarely, an elaborate wooden chamber, as at Spong Hill (Norfolk), or a boat, as at Snape (Suffolk) or at Sutton Hoo (Suffolk), was incorporated into the burial structure. At some sites, such as Spong Hill and Morningthorpe (Norfolk), ring ditches enclosed a number of graves. The dead were furnished with weaponry, drinking and eating paraphernalia, foodstuffs, and tools, and in some cases were covered with plant fronds, animal hide, or fabric.

During the course of the sixth century, burial in large cremation cemeteries, such as Elsham (Lincolnshire) and Newark (Nottinghamshire) was generally replaced by the use of numerous smaller predominantly inhumation graveyards, such as Welbeck Hill in Irby-on-Humber (Lincolnshire) and Fonaby (Lincolnshire). The trend toward smaller inhumation cemeteries may reflect a change in the sense of group cohesion from membership within a larger quasi-ethnic group to membership within a localized community or may reflect the waning of ancestral claims to community identity. However, this general pattern should not obscure the fact that in most areas, cremation and inhumation rites were practiced simultaneously, often in the same cemetery, and that cremation continued into the seventh century.

From the end of the sixth century, a marked change occurred in burial practices. This transition is now believed to have connected with structural changes in the political system and in the religious and economic authorities as sources of power shifted from kinship to kingship. Many existing cemeteries were abandoned, and new burial grounds were established. Weapons occurred less frequently in male burials and, when found, were concentrated in well-furnished graves, suggesting that weapon burial shifted to an index of social, rather than "ethnic," concerns. For women, the regional dress styles apparent during the sixth century were replaced during the seventh century with a neoclassical "national" costume influenced by the Frankish kingdom. Throughout the seventh century and into the early eighth century, the appearance of elite, generally isolated graves, interred under newly constructed barrows or inserted into prehistoric monuments and furnished with weapon assemblages, jewelry of gold, silver, and semiprecious stones, and feasting paraphernalia suggest the development of an increasingly ranked society with territorial interests. The symbolism expressed through burial rituals and furnishings at rich barrow cemeteries such as Taplow (Buckinghamshire) and Sutton Hoo may have asserted an independent pagan ideology. At the same time, unfurnished, west-east-oriented supine inhumations became increasingly prevalent. Although associated by past archaeologists with the dictates of Christian burial, these unfurnished graves may represent factors such as the cessation of competitive display as a result of the consolidation of political authority or the transfer of wealth from deposition in graves to the more worldly payments required by political or religious authorities.

The influence of Christian beliefs on cemetery location and burial ritual becomes apparent from the seventh to ninth centuries. While interment in rural cemeteries continued, the new construction of early minster or monastery churches accommodated burials. In the late Anglo-Saxon period (c. 850–c. 1066) the eternal blessings of Christianity were sought by interring the dead in proximity to the church. While a range of burial types—including charcoal burials; interment in wooden chests or coffins, or sarcophaguses, or under grave covers; and graves with stone packing—have been encountered at some churches, other religious foundations, such as the cathedral cemetery at North Elmham (Norfolk), manifest uniformity in burial practice. In the countryside, the fragmentation of large estates from the late ninth century produced a new wave of cemeteries, often associated with churches or chapels, that was complementary to the established pattern of small burial plots within or adjacent to settlements.

Execution cemeteries that served as repositories for those prohibited from burial in consecrated ground appear in the late ninth century. At these sites, perhaps most notably Stockbridge Down (Suffolk), the bodies appear to have suffered violence before or immediately after death. At Banstead Common (Surrey) and Goblin Works, Leatherhead (Surrey), the reuse of early Anglo-Saxon cemeteries may have been an explicit statement in later times of the condemned's exclusion from Christian churchyard burial.

AGRICULTURE

Although the Roman system of food production and distribution is assumed not to have survived the withdrawal of imperial authority, zooarchaeological evidence indicates that the Anglo-Saxon immigrants followed agricultural practices similar to those of Romano-British farmers. In general, the existing coaxial field systems continued in use, and it is postulated that some local Roman estates were transferred intact to their British or Anglo-Saxon successors. At West Stow (Suffolk), a rural settlement in use from the fifth to seventh centuries, Anglo-Saxon plant and animal husbandry evidence indicates a mixed agricultural economy. Plant cultigens included barley (naked and hulled), oats, wheat, rye, hemp, flax, woad, vines, and possibly beans. Although at West Stow sheep or goats numerically predominate, cattle provided the major meat source by weight. Pig and horse were also present.

The Middle Saxon period (c. 650–c. 850) introduced changes in agricultural practices, including new cereal crops, use of water mills and meadows, farming of open fields, production of animal surpluses, and adoption of the moldboard plow, which enabled the increased production of agricultural yields.

SETTLEMENTS

Settlement evidence suggests a range of forms from clusters of small sunken-featured huts (*Grubenhäuser*) to communities of longhouses or halls to royal complexes with public buildings. Building types in early Anglo-Saxon England have been paralleled by those excavated at contemporary continental sites such as Feddersen Wierde, near Bremenhaven (Germany), Wijster (Netherlands), and Vorbasse (Denmark).

Evidence from the early Anglo-Saxon complex at Mucking suggests that rural communities were small, dispersed, and impermanent. At West Stow, roughly contemporary hall buildings, surrounded by sunken-featured huts, are interpreted as single family farmsteads. Finds of loom weights and evidence for animal stalling in the sunken-featured buildings suggest that the general domestic activities conducted in the halls were complemented in these outlying structures by specialized tasks such as textile production or livestock housing. Population estimates for the settlement at West Stow at any time range from twenty to forty individuals.

Bede's account of the villa of *ad Gefrin*, the royal residence of the Northumbrian king Edwin in the late 620s (*Ecclesiastical History of the English People* book 2, chap. 14), provides a context for the archaeological discoveries at Yeavering (Northumberland). The earliest buildings at Yeavering include posthole and plank-in-trench structures similar to those at West Stow and Mucking Subsequent construction of timber halls, a livestock enclosure, and a curved grandstand indicate a change in site function and importance. Yeavering appears to have served as a royal estate center, a type of settlement governed by a peripatetic ruler who received tribute, hosted feasts, and settled disputes during his residence. At Yeavering, the investment of labor and resources in residential and ritual structures implies a belief, if not a reality borne out by the documentary record, that kingship was a permanent office.

Middle Saxon high-status estates also served as industrial and trading centers. Excavations at Flixborough (Humberside) and Brandon (Suffolk) have produced evidence for large-scale textile manufacture, carpentry, bone working, leatherworking, and metalworking. Finds of nonlocal goods indicate that these types of settlements, strategically positioned to exploit local and interregional communications, controlled extractive and exchange networks. The ability of these sites to serve the joint interests of ecclesiastical and political powers may explain the ecclesiastical tenor of some Middle Saxon "productive" sites. In this context, the legitimatization and sanctification of royal authority offered by the Christian church may have facilitated the control of trading networks and the consolidation of land and resources under ambitious rulers.

More important than estate centers were royal centers described as *civitas* or *urbs*. From the seventh century, former Roman towns such as York (Yorkshire) and Canterbury (Kent), functioned as royal centers. Evidence for a diversity of urban settlements appears as early as the late seventh and eighth centuries with the cathedral town of Canterbury, the minster town of Reading (Berkshire), the possibly fortified towns of Cambridge (Cambridgeshire) and Hereford, and trading centers (emporia) at London, Hamwic (Southampton, Hampshire), Ipswich (Suffolk), and York. The population of Hamwic is conservatively estimated to have numbered two thousand to three thousand.

In rural areas, charter evidence indicates the practice of open-field agriculture, with crop rotation and cultivation of narrow common fields, as early as the tenth century. The nucleated villages attributed to this time and earlier are implicit in the communal labor requirements of the open-field system and archaeologically attested by the increase in concentrations of late Saxon pottery. While this settlement shift may have been stimulated by soil exhaustion and population pressures, nucleation may also indicate the attempts of Anglo-Saxon lords to maximize production from their lands. Defended Late Saxon manor houses, such as those at Sulgrave (Northamptonshire) or Faccombe Netherton (Hampshire) anticipate the later fortified Norman manor houses and castles. The development into parish churches of village churches serving the spiritual needs of estate laborers accounts for the frequent corollary between later ecclesiastical parishes and tenth and eleventh century estate boundaries.

Although dispersed rural settlements continued to exist into the Late Saxon period (c. 850–c.

1066), urban settlements assumed increasing importance. While some urban sites developed from ecclesiastical or economic stimuli, a group of fortified towns (*burhs*) were founded in the late ninth century to protect the interests of the West Saxon king Alfred (r. 871–899) against Viking incursions. These planned towns, as listed in the *Burghal Hidage,* include reused Roman walled towns, such as Winchester (Hampshire), newly founded towns located on open sites, such as Oxford (Oxfordshire), and new towns sited on promontories, such as Lydford (Devon) and Lewes (East Sussex). Use of these fortified towns in the early tenth century enabled Edward the Elder (r. 899–924) to conquer the Danelaw lands to the north and to unify the kingdom of England. As well as providing security, these fortified towns structured trade through a network of regional market centers. Towns, such as London, developed a distinctive architecture of timber buildings fronting on graveled streets. The Domesday Book, an assessment roll enumerated under William the Conqueror, indicates that by the late eleventh century as much as one-tenth of the population lived in towns.

TRADE AND EXCHANGE

Anglo-Saxon England was incorporated into larger and overlapping cultural spheres centered in the Frankish kingdom and Scandinavia. The appearance from the late fifth century onward of Anglo-Saxon metalwork in Continental Frankish graves indicates the maintenance through intermarriage, immigration, and trade of close cross-Channel links. Competition for trade goods produced conflicts between local groups and facilitated the concentration of power in the hands of successful leaders. Rulers who could control access to and redistribute luxury imports, exploit relationships with Continental elites, and successfully manipulate the symbolism of new ideas were best placed to promote their own expansionist concerns.

The development of commercial trading centers (emporia) in the seventh and subsequent centuries was one consequence of the increasing sociopolitical elevation and territorial control of the fifth- and sixth-century leaders. Each major Anglo-Saxon kingdom controlled at least one emporium. The rise of the emporia presupposes an integrative process of extracting, processing, and distributing agricultural

products that would have been impossible in the fragmented political circumstances prior to the seventh century. The goods that passed through the emporia were linked to local markets or exchange sites at smaller, probably nonurban settlements. Archaeological finds demonstrate that the Continent supplied Anglo-Saxon England with prestige goods such as precious metals, gemstones, ceramics, jewelry, textiles, glassware, and weaponry, as well as more utilitarian lava quern stones and soapstone vessels. Documentary sources suggest that in exchange the English provided slaves, lead, honey, and textiles.

By the late seventh century, many members of the Anglo-Saxon elite had also adopted a Roman Christian ideology from the continent. A mutually beneficial patron-client relationship existed between the Anglo-Saxon kings and the Christian church. The church promoted the image of the English people in insular literary sources for the purposes of political and religious cohesion. In the late eighth century, the church formalized the sacral role of kingship through ritual anointing and synodic degree. West Saxon and Mercian kings, seeking support for their dynastic ambitions, gave gifts of land and other resources to the church.

Despite the uncertainty surrounding the scale of settlement and disruption effected by the Vikings from the second half of the ninth century, the raids realigned and even enhanced systems of exchange. York, captured by the Vikings in 866, developed into a prosperous market town during the Viking period that produced crafts and traded locally and internationally in raw materials and luxury goods. Documentary accounts identify Danish merchants in York, as well as visits to other late Anglo-Saxon towns by merchants from Ireland, northern France, and Germany.

Early Anglo-Saxon England lacked a coin economy, as Roman coinage did not enter in bulk after the early fifth century and, during the sixth and early seventh centuries, imported Continental coins were valued as ornaments or bullion. The striking of gold *thrymsas* in the southeast, most notably at London, in the seventh century was superseded in the late seventh century by the circulation of debased silver-rich pennies, or sceattas. From the late eighth century, particularly during the reign of Offa of Mercia (757–796), coins often served as potent propaganda by incorporating the name of the issuing king and his people. Edgar's (r. 959–975) major coinage reform, marked by a uniform currency and periodic recoinage, established minting practices that lasted through the Norman Conquest. By c. 973, moneyers at over sixty mints produced a national coinage used for the payment of taxes, fines, and other transactions.

TERRITORIES AND BOUNDARIES

From the late fifth century, the political structure of early Anglo-Saxon England was characterized by groupings that were fluid both in extent and authority. By the late sixth or early seventh centuries, however, archaeological and textual sources indicate that these popular confederations had allied into larger units, presaging the formal kingdoms of the later Anglo-Saxon period. Philological evidence suggests the decline of regional dialects of Old English by 600 in favor of a more uniform English language. The development from popular to territorial concerns may be indicated by the construction of physical boundaries.

The reuse of ancient monuments as early Anglo-Saxon burial sites has been associated with the process of kingdom formation. Initial associations of ancient monuments with large fifth- and sixth-century cemeteries suggest that monument reuse was relevant to the construction of communal concepts of ancestry and identity. During the late sixth and seventh centuries, however, the increasing exclusivity of monument reuse suggests that elites appropriated existing attitudes about the past in order to identify themselves as heirs to a mythically established legacy, thus legitimizing their more worldly political strategies. During later Anglo-Saxon times, ancient monuments continued to be reused as boundary markers.

The modern notion of coherent political units circumscribed by static boundaries is anachronistic in early Anglo-Saxon England. Because, during the seventh and eighth centuries, political authority was vested in individual rulers, the extent of a "kingdom" waxed and waned with the king's career. Central to any consideration of Anglo-Saxon political geography is the putative tax register, the *Tribal Hidage,* believed to have been compiled for the ascendant Mercian overlords in the seventh century. Attempts to reconstruct the political geography of early Anglo-Saxon England generally employ top-

onymic, or place-name, evidence to assign the social units of the *Tribal Hidage* to specific locations. During the Middle Saxon period (c. 650–c. 850), the numerous polities cited in the *Tribal Hidage* had been subsumed by the dominant kingdoms of Mercia and Wessex.

From the eighth and ninth centuries, documentary and archaeological evidence indicates the development of political units whose integrity was not dependent upon personal authority and which outlived the death of their ruler. The obligation to provide men and material for military service and civic constructions appears in eighth-century Mercian charters. The massive linear earthwork known as Offa's Dyke, which runs along the modern English-Welsh border, exemplified the process of consolidation exercised by the Mercian king Offa (r. 757–796). At Offa's Dyke, the labors of individual work crews, identified through archaeological excavation, demonstrate the community discharge of obligations.

THE POLITICAL ORGANIZATION OF ANGLO-SAXON ENGLAND

Bede, writing in the second quarter of the eighth century, used Latin to describe the powerful men of Anglo-Saxon England. Only a few relevant documents, including some Mercian charters and the laws of the Kentish kings, appeared in the vernacular prior to the ninth century. Most Old English texts, such as the laws of Alfred (r. 871–899), the *Anglo-Saxon Chronicle,* and the translation of the *Ecclesiastical History of the English People,* originated in Mercian or West Saxon contexts during the late ninth century.

Three status levels may be inferred from Bede's account: overlord, *rex* (king), and *princips.* At the apex were the overlords, who ruled over many men, including *reges,* or kings. Bede (*Ecclesiastical History of the English People* book 2, chap. 5) enumerated seven overlords who, each in turn, had held sway over the English south of the Humber: Ælle of Sussex (probably late fifth century), Caewlin of Wessex (560–591/592), Æthelbert of Kent (560–616), Rædwald of East Anglia, Edwin of Northumbria (616–633), Oswald of Northumbria (634–642), and Oswy (642–670). This list of overlords reappears in the *Anglo-Saxon Chronicle,* where they are described with the problematic term, "rulers of

Britain" or "wide rulers" (*bretwaldas,* or possibly *brytenwaldas*). In Bede's account, below the overlords were the *reges* of the major kingdoms of Northumbria, Mercia, Wessex, East Anglia, Sussex, and Kent. Bede most frequently described the lesser potentates, who formed the third rung on the ladder of authority, as *princeps.*

Recognizing that political organization was grounded in fluid patron-client relationships can diminish the confusion presented by kingship terminology. The same conditional relationships, in which a ruler's power and prestige grew through his patronage of less-powerful client leaders, characterized relationships between the polities. The successful leaders of the larger extended families expanded their influence—through alliances, exchange, conquest, asylum, and intermarriage—over ever-wider areas. These polities eventually reached such size as to be characterized by contemporaneous writers, such as Bede, as "kingdoms" and "subkingdoms" and their leaders as higher- and lower-order kings.

Among the Anglo-Saxons of the sixth and seventh centuries, a king did not assume his kingdom borne on a well-oiled mechanism of succession. In order to be considered for the throne, contenders had to demonstrate legal title through real or fictitious descent. Gift exchange, motivated by social consumption and extolled in saga literature, structured early medieval society through systems of reward and loyalty. Historical records indicate that by the late eighth and ninth centuries, rulers such as the Mercian king Offa (r. 757–796) exploited genealogical connections and patronage to secure and legitimize their authority. By the tenth century, a monarchy descended from a single lineage and invested with sanctity, whose authority was supported by military force and taxation, heralded the Anglo-Saxon state.

See also **Emporia** (*vol. 1, part 7*); **Ipswich** (*vol. 2, part 7*); **Angles, Saxons, and Jutes** (*vol. 2, part 7*); **Spong Hill** (*vol. 2, part 7*); **Sutton Hoo** (*vol. 2, part 7*); **West Stow** (*vol. 2, part 7*); **Winchester** (*vol. 2, part 7*); **Viking York** (*vol. 2, part 7*).

BIBLIOGRAPHY

Andrews, P., ed. *Excavations at Hamwic.* Vol. 2, *Excavations at Six Dials.* CBA Research Report 109. London: Council for British Archaeology, 1997.

Bassett, Steve, ed. *The Origins of Anglo-Saxon Kingdoms.* London and New York: Leicester University Press, 1989.

Bruce-Mitford, Rupert L. S. *The Sutton Hoo Ship-Burial.* Vols. 1–3. London: British Museum, 1975–1983.

Campbell, James. *The Anglo-Saxon State.* London and New York: Hambledon and London, 2000.

Carver, Martin O. H. *Sutton Hoo: Burial Ground of Kings?* Philadelphia: University of Pennsylvania Press, 1998.

———, ed. *The Age of Sutton Hoo: The Seventh Century in North-Western Europe.* Woodbridge, U.K.: Boydell Press, 1992.

Colgrave, Bertram, and R. A. B. Mynors, trans. and eds. *Bede's Ecclesiastical History of the English People.* Oxford: Clarendon Press, 1969.

Dickinson, Tania, and David Griffiths, eds. *The Making of Kingdoms.* Anglo-Saxon Studies in Archaeology and History, no. 10. Oxford: Oxbow, 1999.

Driscoll, Stephen T., and Margaret R. Nieke, eds. *Power and Politics in Early Medieval Britain and Ireland.* Edinburgh: Edinburgh University Press, 1988.

Graham-Campbell, James, et al. *Vikings and the Danelaw: Select Papers from the Proceedings of the Thirteenth Viking Congress, Nottingham and York, 21–30 August 1997.* Oxford: Oxbow, 2001.

Hamerow, Helena *Excavations at Mucking.* Vol. 2, *The Anglo-Saxon Settlement.* English Heritage Archaeological Report, no. 21. London: English Heritage and the British Museum Press, 1993.

Higham, N. J. *The Convert Kings: Power and Religious Affiliation in Early Anglo-Saxon England.* Manchester, U.K.: Manchester University Press, 1997.

Hines, John, ed. *The Anglo-Saxons from the Migration Period to the Eighth Century: An Ethnographic Perspective.* Woodbridge, U.K.: Boydell Press, 1997.

Lucy, Sam. *The Anglo-Saxon Way of Death: Burial Rites in Early England.* Stroud, Gloucestershire, U.K.: Sutton, 2000.

Lucy, Sam, and Andrew Reynolds, eds. *Burial in Early Medieval England and Wales.* Society for Medieval Archaeology Monograph, no. 17. London: Society for Medieval Archaeology, 2002.

Morton, A. D., ed. *Excavations at Hamwic.* Vol. 1, *Excavations 1946–83, Excluding Six Dials and Melbourne Street.* CBA Research Report, no. 84. London: Council for British Archaeology, 1992.

Reynolds, Andrew. *Later Anglo-Saxon England: Life and Landscape.* Stroud, Gloucestershire, U.K., and Charleston, S.C.: Tempus, 1999.

Sawyer, Peter H., and Ian N. Wood, eds. *Early Medieval Kingship.* Leeds: The Editors, 1977.

Vince, Alan G. *Saxon London: An Archaeological Investigation.* London: Seaby, 1990.

Welch, Martin. *English Heritage Book of Anglo-Saxon England*. London: Batsford, 1992.

West, Stanley. *West Stow: The Anglo-Saxon Village*. 2 vols. East Anglian Archaeology, no. 24. Ipswich, U.K.: Suffolk County Planning Department, 1985.

Yorke, Barbara A. E. *Kings and Kingdoms of Early Anglo-Saxon England*. London: Seaby, 1990.

GENEVIEVE FISHER

SPONG HILL

Spong Hill lies on the southern edge of the parish of North Elmham in central Norfolk, East Anglia, England. It is the site of an early Anglo-Saxon cemetery, known since finds from the site were first recorded in 1711. Following small-scale investigations in the 1950s and in 1969, complete excavation of the cemetery site was carried out between 1972 and 1981 by the Norfolk Archaeological Unit, funded by English Heritage and its predecessors. The project was directed by Peter Wade-Martins, Robert Carr, and (from 1975) by Catherine Hills, with support from many people, including especially Kenneth Penn and Robert Rickett. A team from Warsaw University participated in the early seasons. The site is published in the series East Anglian Archaeology Reports, and the finds are the property of the Norfolk Museums Service.

In addition to the Anglo-Saxon burials, features of prehistoric, Roman, and medieval date were also excavated. Several contemporary buildings lay within the cemetery, and part of a settlement immediately to the west was excavated by Andrew Rogerson in 1984. It is likely that other scattered settlements in the region used this cemetery as their central focus. A prehistoric barrow in the same field may have influenced the choice of site.

The significance of the cemetery lies in its size and near-complete investigation. At the end of the twentieth century it was the largest such site in England to have been fully excavated and published. Although many burials were damaged or incomplete, the overall size, extent, and internal organization of the cemetery can be reconstructed. A minimum of 2,400 cremations, from an estimated original total of more than 3,000, and 57 inhumations were excavated. The original population has been calculated as between 446 and 768 individuals at any one time. The cemetery was in use from the later fifth century and probably throughout the sixth century A.D. There was some chronological zoning, with some early groups of burials in the middle of the site surrounded by later burials in a partly radial development. For a limited period some of the dead, possibly an elite group, were distinguished by being inhumed, buried together on the northeastern edge of the cemetery.

The inhumations survived in the acid sand largely as dark stains with occasional bone fragments but with preserved grave goods, mostly weapons and jewelry. Two large ring ditches, probably originally around barrows, surrounded respectively a pair of inhumations and a single large burial within a timber and turf chamber containing a sword, shield, spear, and bucket. Several apparently female burials were set into the ring ditch.

The cremations were contained in handmade decorated pots, apart from a few deposited in boxes or bags or placed directly in a pit. Analysis of the bones by Jacqueline McKinley showed that many could be aged and sexed. McKinley also reconstructed the cremation and burial ritual. Women's bodies had been laid out for cremation as for inhumation, dressed and wearing jewelry. Men, however, were cremated without the weapons found in a proportion of inhumations. In some cases whole animals, often horses, had also been cremated; in other cases only parts of animals were included, perhaps as food offerings. A selection of the cremated bones had been collected from the pyre, together with the partly melted remains of jewelry and dress fastenings, bags, spindle whorls (large beads, made most often of bone or fired clay, put on the ends of spindles), and glass or metal vessels. Miniature razors, tweezers, and knives, mostly unburned, as well as combs and playing pieces were also included, often but not exclusively with male burials. Through careful sieving many identifiable fragments of objects were retrieved. These finds at Spong Hill, where grave goods were found in about 70 percent of burials, transformed ideas as to the prevalence of grave goods in cremations. Previous distribution maps of early Anglo-Saxon finds were biased against East Anglia, where cremation was common.

Some cremations were buried singly, but many were in pairs or groups. Some pairs contained the shared remains of one individual, whereas in others more than one person, often an adult and a child, had been put into one pot. Some paired burials contained human bones in one pot and mainly animal bones in the second pot.

A majority of the pots were decorated with linear and plastic designs. These included distinctive stamped patterns; some stamps were in the form of animals or runic letters. Many of the stamped pots can be grouped into series related by identical stamp impressions and so identified as contemporary products of individuals or workshops. Some Spong Hill pots can be linked to pots from Lincolnshire and Yorkshire, confirming broad regional connections among East Anglia, the areas around the Wash, and Northumbria.

Analysis of the finds shows clear connections with the regions of northern Germany that the Venerable Bede, the Anglo-Saxon scholar, described as the homelands of the Anglo-Saxons, although the connections are not exclusively with the Angeln region (approximately modern Schleswig-Holstein) that is claimed as the home of the Angles, who are said to have migrated to East Anglia during the fifth century. Many of the brooch types do find their closest parallels in Angeln, but stamped decoration on pots, common at Spong Hill, is very rare north of the Elbe, whereas it does occur in Lower Saxony. Exact parallels for material from Spong Hill can be found around the whole of the North Sea zone, from the Netherlands to Denmark and beyond, from the fifth and sixth centuries A.D. Ivory at the site came ultimately from Africa, via the Mediterranean and probably southern Germany. These connections lasted for generations, suggesting ongoing contact rather than a simple transfer at any one point in time.

Relationships between material culture and ethnicity are complex and not easily unraveled. Peoples and pottery styles cannot be neatly defined and equated. Long-term trading and cultural contacts across the North Sea and the spread of religious beliefs and practices were more important as mechanisms for change than replacement of one population by another. Successful immigrant leaders would have brought their immediate followers from home and would have encouraged others to join them, but they may then have imposed their culture on a population that was still substantially native— and most likely they adopted aspects of native culture themselves. It is probable that some, maybe many, of those buried at Spong Hill had Continental ancestors, whether "Angle," "Saxon," or "Jute," but others—however "Anglo-Saxon" their jewelry seems—may in fact be descendants of Romano-Britons.

See also **Angles, Saxons, and Jutes** (*vol. 2, part 7*).

BIBLIOGRAPHY

Hills, Catherine M. *Origins of the English*. London: Duckworth, 2003.

———. "From Isidore to Isotopes: Ivory Rings in Early Medieval Graves." In *Image and Power in the Archaeology of Early Medieval Britain: Essays in Honour of Rosemary Cramp*. Edited by Helena Hamerow and Arthur MacGregor, pp. 131–146. Oxford: Oxbow Books, 2001.

———. *The Anglo-Saxon Cemetery at Spong Hill, North Elmham, Norfolk, Part I*. East Anglian Archaeology, report no. 6. Norfolk, U.K.: Gressenhall, 1977.

Hills, Catherine M., and Kenneth J. Penn. *The Anglo-Saxon Cemetery at Spong Hill, North Elmham, Norfolk, Part II*. East Anglian Archaeology, report no. 11. Norfolk, U.K.: Gressenhall, 1981.

Hills, Catherine M., Kenneth J. Penn, and Robert J. Rickett. *The Anglo-Saxon Cemetery at Spong Hill, North Elmham, Norfolk, Part V*. East Anglian Archaeology, report no. 67. Norfolk, U.K.: Gressenhall, 1994.

———. *The Anglo-Saxon Cemetery at Spong Hill, North Elmham, Norfolk, Part IV*. East Anglian Archaeology, report no. 34. Norfolk, U.K.: Gressenhall, 1987.

———. *The Anglo-Saxon Cemetery at Spong Hill, North Elmham, Norfolk, Part III*. East Anglian Archaeology, report no. 21. Norfolk, U.K.: Gressenhall, 1984.

Lucy, Sam. *The Anglo-Saxon Way of Death: Burial Rites in Early England*. Stroud, U.K.: Sutton, 2000.

McKinley, Jacqueline. *The Anglo-Saxon Cemetery at Spong Hill, North Elmham, Norfolk, Part VIII*. East Anglian Archaeology, report no. 69. Norfolk, U.K.: Gressenhall, 1994.

Rickett, Robert. *The Anglo-Saxon Cemetery at Spong Hill, North Elmham, Norfolk, Part VII: The Iron Age, Roman, and Early Saxon Settlement*. East Anglian Archaeology, report no. 73. Norfolk, U.K.: Gressenhall, 1995.

CATHERINE HILLS

SUTTON HOO

Sutton Hoo is the name given to a small group of at least eighteen burial mounds located on a terrace 30 meters above the River Deben in Suffolk, south-eastern England. It is interpreted as a burial ground for the pagan leaders of the Anglo-Saxon kingdom of East Anglia, established in the early years of the seventh century A.D. as a reaction to the Christian missions to Kent.

Sutton Hoo was first investigated in 1938 at the behest of the landowner, Edith May Pretty, by a local archaeologist, Basil Brown, who trenched mounds 2, 3, and 4 discovering that each had been dug earlier and inferring their Anglo-Saxon date from scraps of metal. In 1939 Brown returned at Mrs. Pretty's invitation and dug a large trench through mound 1, where he defined a ship some 27 meters long with a collapsed burial chamber at its center. A team of experienced archaeologists led by Charles Phillips of Cambridge University was assembled hastily; this group recovered 267 parts of artifacts made of gold, silver, bronze, iron, wood, textile, and fur—together constituting the richest grave ever excavated in Britain.

The study of the find (between 1945 and 1975) by Rupert Bruce-Mitford of the British Museum included a second field campaign from 1965 to 1971, which completed the excavation of mound 1, confirmed the existence of mound 5, and endorsed the presence of an earlier prehistoric settlement, reported by Brown. In 1983 the Society of Antiquaries of London, in partnership with the British Museum, the British Broadcasting Corporation, and the Suffolk County Council, launched a third campaign. The field team led by Martin Carver of the University of York excavated one fourth of the 4-hectare cemetery, mapped 10 hectares of its surroundings, and surveyed 10 square kilometers of the River Deben. In 1998 the site and its surrounding estates were given into the hands of the National Trust to be cared for in perpetuity, and a visitor center was constructed and opened in 2002.

The third campaign offered a new account of the character, date, and purpose of the Sutton Hoo cemetery. Use of the site had begun in the Late Neolithic to Early Bronze Age (c. 2000 B.C.), when the land was divided into agricultural units. The production of grain then alternated with stock-breeding—a pattern typical of agriculture of the Breckland region (an ancient heath), which continues to the present day. The Anglo-Saxons inherited a landscape of earthworks of Iron Age fields bounded by tracks leading inland from the river. The earliest Anglo-Saxon burials in the area are located near Tranmer House, the site of the visitor center; they date to the sixth century and include cremations, one of which is contained in a bronze bowl placed in the center of small ring ditches.

The Sutton Hoo cemetery itself was a new venture, which began around A.D. 600 about 500 meters farther south. The first burials were cremations in bronze bowls, accompanied by gaming pieces and cremated horses, sheep, cattle, and pigs, placed in pits beneath mounds about 10–15 meters in diameter, laid out in a line (mounds 5, 6, and 7). These burials had been much disturbed by later excavators, but they appear to be the memorials of young men, at least one of whom had blade injuries. The next burial is thought to be mound 17, where a young man was laid in a tree-trunk coffin in about A.D. 610, accompanied by a sword with a horn handle, two spears, a shield, a bucket, a cauldron, and a haversack containing lamb chops. At the head of the coffin was deposited a bridle, saddle, and body harness equipped with silver pendants and gilt bronze roundels, pendants, and strap ends. A stallion was buried in an adjacent pit and is assumed to have lain beneath the same mound.

Two ship burials were added to the cemetery in about A.D. 625. In mound 2 a ship about 20 meters long had been placed over the top of a chamber grave (2 × 6 × 2 meters deep). The person memorialized, probably a man, had lain in the chamber accompanied by a sword, shield, five knives, a cauldron, an ironbound tub, a blue glass jar, and drinking horns. Robbers and excavators had visited the grave at least three times, and the assemblage therefore had to be inferred from scraps and a chemical plot of the chamber floor.

In mound 1 the ship first found by Basil Brown had been positioned in a large trench, and a timber chamber 5.5 by 3 meters had been erected amidships. The dead man probably originally lay in a large tree-trunk coffin (although this theory remains the subject of controversy) with a pile of garments, shoes, and toilet items at his feet. Above him

Fig. 1. The barrow cemetery at Sutton Hoo as viewed from the east. © MARTIN CARVER AND THE UNIVERSITY OF YORK. REPRODUCED BY PERMISSION.

(perhaps on the coffin lid) were items of personal regalia with drinking horns, maple-wood and burr-wood bottles, and a large Byzantine silver dish probably carrying food. The regalia included a sword, a decorated purse, and two shoulder clasps, all made of solid gold inlaid with garnets imported from western Asia, and an iron helmet with bronze zoomorphic decoration. Toward the western end were stacked spears and an iron stand interpreted as a standard or a weapon stand, along with a decorated whetstone, interpreted as imitating an imperial scepter. Three large cauldrons, one with an ornamental iron chain 3.45 meters long, dominated the eastern end.

After these ship burials, burial continued intermittently at the site during the later part of the seventh century. The chamber grave of a woman, subsequently pillaged, originally was furnished richly with silver adornments, including a chatelaine, the symbolic key of a woman of high rank (mound 14),

and two graves of adolescents were accompanied by a knife and a chatelaine, respectively.

In the late seventh or early eighth century the Sutton Hoo cemetery was adopted as a place of execution. Sixteen graves were found around mound 5 and another twenty-three on the eastern edge of the burial mounds, surrounding the site of a tree that was replaced by a post-construction probably representing a gallows. Some of the bodies of the execution victims had had their hands or feet tied, and others had been deposited face down, kneeling, or crouching. Radiocarbon dating suggests that capital punishment was practiced at Sutton Hoo from about A.D. 700 to A.D. 1000, at which point map evidence indicates that the gallows apparently was removed to the site of the new bridge across the Deben, constructed 2 kilometers north. The site then was abandoned, apart from sporadic attention from farmers and warreners, until the sixteenth century, when it was heavily plowed and the majority of mounds robbed by means of a shaft driven from the top. Most mounds were again trenched in 1860; only mounds 1 and 17 were spared.

After the discoveries of 1939 the site was interpreted as the likely burial ground of the kings of East Anglia, the territory in which it lay. The occupant of mound 1 was held to be Redwald, who, according to the Venerable Bede, an English historian of the early eighth century, was a major figure in England up to his death in about A.D. 625. The most recent excavation campaign has broadened this interpretation, showing that Sutton Hoo was part of a general reaction to Christianization, in which pagan Scandinavian practices, such as cremation in bronze bowls and ship burial, were signaled. The making of the mound 1 ship burial itself has been reinterpreted by Carver as a multilayered "composition" in which allusions to contemporary politics are gathered with the aim of declaring ideological alliance with Scandinavia against the Christian Continent. In this sense, the great ship burial is a dramatic statement comparable to the Anglo-Saxon epic poem *Beowulf*, which describes the deeds and deaths of fifth- to seventh-century heroes, including burial in a ship. The pagan alliance failed around the end of the seventh century, at which point the burial ground of pagan kings became a place where the new Christian leaders disposed of dissidents.

See also **History and Archaeology** (*vol. 2, part 7*); **Jewelry** (*vol. 2, part 7*); **Anglo-Saxon England** (*vol. 2, part 7*).

BIBLIOGRAPHY

Bruce-Mitford, Rupert. *The Sutton Hoo Ship-Burial*. 3 vols. London: British Museum Press, 1975–1983.

Carver, Martin O. H. "Burial as Poetry: The Context of Treasure in Anglo-Saxon Graves." In *Treasure in the Medieval West*. Edited by Elizabeth M. Tyler, pp. 25–48. York, U.K.: York Medieval Press, 2000.

———. *Sutton Hoo: Burial Ground of Kings?* Philadelphia: University of Pennsylvania Press, 1998.

MARTIN CARVER

WEST STOW

The excavation of the Early Anglo-Saxon village of West Stow in Suffolk, England, opened a new chapter in the archaeological study of Anglo-Saxon England. Although many pagan Anglo-Saxon cemeteries and burials were excavated throughout the nineteenth and twentieth centuries, very few settlement sites were investigated archaeologically before the 1960s. The site of the West Stow village is on a sandy terrace overlooking the Lark River in Northwest Suffolk. Under the direction of Stanley West, almost the entire Early Anglo-Saxon village at West Stow was excavated during eight field seasons between 1965 and 1972. These excavations shed new light on settlement patterns and subsistence practices of the earliest Anglo-Saxon inhabitants of eastern England.

The West Stow area has long been recognized as an archaeologically important region. In the mid-nineteenth century, workers who were seeking ballast for barges discovered an Early Anglo-Saxon cemetery near the village site. Although the workers collected many Anglo-Saxon artifacts, the cemetery site was never excavated properly. As a result, archaeologists currently are unable to determine which items were buried together. The objects recovered from the cemetery include weapons, jewelry, and a stone coffin. In addition, Roman pottery kilns were found on the site in 1940. The late Roman site of Icklingham, still under excavation, is located about 4 kilometers (about 2 miles) west of the West Stow village. Icklingham is a large open site that may have served as a market center or possibly as the center of a large Roman estate.

A primary goal of the West Stow village excavations was to understand the plan of the Early Anglo-Saxon settlement. Excavations at the site revealed seven small rectangular timber halls surrounded by about seventy smaller buildings. The smaller structures are known as sunken-featured buildings (SFBs), because they were built over roughly rectangular pits that were about 0.5 meters deep. One to three postholes, which would have held upright posts, were sunk into the short ends of the pits. These posts would have supported the roofs of the SFBs. The halls probably were the main farmsteads, and the SFBs seem to have served as workshops and farm outbuildings. For example, large numbers of loom weights were recovered from SFB 15, suggesting that this building may have served as a weaving shed. Based on the number of halls, the West

Stow settlement included about seven individual farms.

Artifactual evidence indicates that the West Stow village was inhabited from the early fifth century to the mid-seventh century. Pottery and metalwork suggest that the village was first occupied in about A.D. 420. The presence of Ipswich ware, distinctive kiln-fired pottery that was produced on a slow wheel, indicates that the village must have been inhabited until about A.D. 650. Detailed chronological analyses indicate that no more than three or four farmsteads were occupied at any one time, so West Stow was probably more of a hamlet than a true village.

One of the main goals of the West Stow excavation was to study Early Anglo-Saxon farming and animal husbandry practices. The technique of flotation was developed in the 1960s to recover small seeds and other plant materials from archaeological soils. West Stow was one of the first sites in Britain where flotation techniques were used. Remains of wheat, rye, barley, and oats were recovered from several of the Anglo-Saxon features at West Stow. Some of the fifth-century features produced the remains of spelt wheat (*Triticum spelta*), a form of wheat that was grown commonly in Roman Britain. The presence of this variety of wheat may indicate some degree of continuity between Roman and Early Anglo-Saxon farming practices. By the seventh century, however, spelt wheat seems to have disappeared from Anglo-Saxon agriculture. It was replaced by other varieties of wheat and rye.

The West Stow site produced more than 180,000 animal bone fragments that could be used to study Anglo-Saxon animal husbandry and hunting practices. These faunal remains have shown that the denizens of West Stow kept herds of cattle, sheep, and pigs. The cattle probably were grazed on the rich pastures along the Lark River edge, while the sheep would have been herded on the drier upland areas behind the site. Pigs were most numerous in the early fifth century; most likely they were herded in the wooded areas along the river terraces. Herding was supplemented by the occasional hunting of red deer, roe deer, and waterfowl; poultry keeping; and fishing for pike and perch in the Lark River. The early Anglo-Saxons also kept a small number of horses. These animals, which were the size of large ponies, may have been used for riding

and traction, but they also were eaten on occasion. The large, straight-limbed Anglo-Saxon dogs were about the size of modern German shepherds. They may have been used as hunting, herding, and guard dogs.

One of the most difficult questions for archaeologists to answer is exactly who lived at the West Stow village. Based on traditional historical evidence, the early Anglo-Saxons were seen as migrants from continental Europe who entered Britain shortly after the withdrawal of Roman military power in about A.D. 410. Later scholarship has suggested that the Anglo-Saxons may have been a small military elite that took control of eastern England in the fifth century. In that case, the denizens of West Stow may have been native Britons who adopted Anglo-Saxon material culture, including pottery, metalwork, and building styles, from their Continental overlords. While it may never be known with certainty who lived in West Stow village, the archaeological evidence for spelt cultivation points to significant economic continuity between the Romans and the early Anglo-Saxons.

A program of experimental reconstruction of the West Stow farm buildings was begun in 1974. Several SFBs and a single hall have been reassembled using early medieval tools and techniques. These buildings currently are part of a county park that is open to the public.

See also **Ipswich** (*vol. 2, part 7*); **Animal Husbandry** (*vol. 2, part 7*); **Agriculture** (*vol. 2, part 7*); **Anglo-Saxon England** (*vol. 2, part 7*).

BIBLIOGRAPHY

Crabtree, Pam J. *West Stow: Early Anglo-Saxon Animal Husbandry.* East Anglian Archaeology 47. Ipswich, U.K.: Suffolk County Department of Planning, 1989.

West, Stanley. *West Stow: The Anglo-Saxon Village.* East Anglian Archaeology 24. Ipswich, U.K.: Suffolk County Department of Planning, 1985.

PAM J. CRABTREE

WINCHESTER

Winchester, Roman Venta Belgarum, the principal royal city of Anglo-Saxon England, is today the administrative center for the county of Hampshire in southern England. To a great extent, the archaeology of Winchester was still terra incognita in 1961 when the first large-scale excavation took place. Nothing certain was known of its origins and almost nothing of the plan or development of the Roman town. As for Winchester after the Romans, it did not exist as an organized field of archaeological enquiry. The contrast between the written evidence for the importance of early medieval Winchester and the virtual absence of an archaeology of that period compelled attention. The aim of the work that the Winchester Excavations Committee began in 1961 was, according to "The Study of Winchester" (1990),

> to undertake excavations, both in advance of building projects, and on sites not so threatened, aimed at studying the development of Winchester as a town from its earliest origins to the establishment of the modern city. The centre of interest is the city itself, not any one period of its past, nor any one part of its remains. But we can hope that this approach will in particular throw light upon the end of the Roman city and on the establishment and development of the Saxon town, problems as vital to our understanding of urban development in this country, as they are difficult to solve. Further it is essential to this approach that the study and interpretation of the documentary evidence should go hand in hand with archaeological research.

It was also realized from the start, as stated in the same publication, that this would have to be "a broadly based exploration of the fabric of the city, across the full range of variation in wealth, class, and occupation. This involved more than gross distinctions between castle, palace, and monastery on the one hand and the 'ordinary' inhabited areas of the city on the other." This was the founding manifesto of urban archaeology, copied in both concept and execution in a multitude of towns and countries.

Eleven years of excavation followed, for ten or more weeks each summer, aided by two-hundred student volunteers from over twenty-five countries working on four major sites and many smaller ones across the city and suburbs. In 1968 the Winchester Research Unit was set up to prepare the results for publication in a series entitled *Winchester Studies*. In 1972, following the end of the major campaign of excavations, the post of City Rescue Archaeologist was set up to make observations of sites threatened

by development and to carry out excavations as needed. That work continues today on a permanent basis as part of the Winchester City Museums Service.

EARLIER PREHISTORIC CONTEXT AND THE IRON AGE

Situated where the River Itchen cuts through the chalk downs on its way to Southampton Water and the sea, the city is a natural focus of long-distance communication from east to west and north to south. The area may have been settled in the Late Neolithic period or perhaps earlier. From the third century B.C., during the Iron Age, people occupied St. Catharine's Hill, on the east bank of the Itchen, south of the later city. The summit of the hill was later encircled by a line of bank and ditch dominating the river valley below, but these defenses were destroyed about the middle of the first century B.C. At that point, the focus of settlement shifted upstream and to the other side of the river, which became the site of the future city. There, a roughly rectangular area of about 20 hectares was enclosed by a ditch and bank with entrances on all four sides through which the major lines of communication had to pass. Now known as the Oram's Arbour enclosure, this was a regionally and strategically important site, as fragments of Mediterranean wine jars (amphorae) show. Occupied for some fifty years, the enclosure was long abandoned when the Romans passed through in A.D. 43.

VENTA BELGARUM

There is no continuity between the Iron Age settlement and the beginning of the Roman city, except that Roman long-distance roads passed through the northern and western entrances of the deserted Oram's Arbour enclosure. Timber buildings in the upper part of the town that date to the 50s of the first century A.D. are the earliest traces of Roman occupation. In the valley floor, a rectangular area of unknown size was defined by a substantial ditch. First identified as part of a small Roman fort, it may have been part of a religious enclosure, as the presence of a later Roman temple and a wooden statue of the goddess Epona suggest.

In the 70s of the first century A.D., a chessboard pattern of graveled streets at intervals of 400 Roman feet was laid out within earth and timber de-

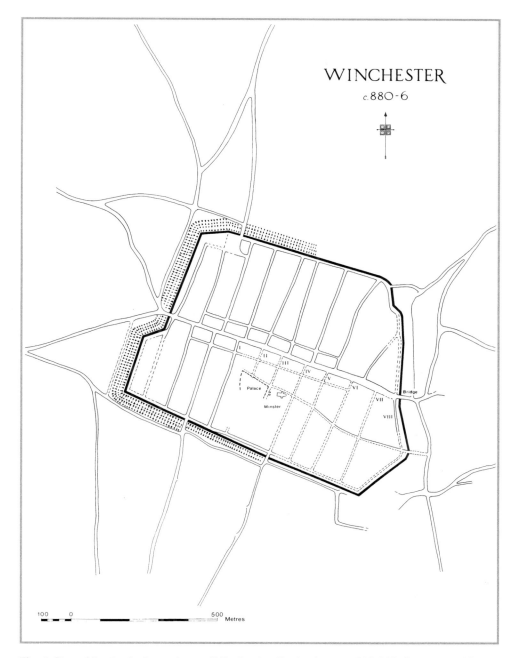

Fig. 1. Plan of the Anglo-Saxon town of Winchester, England, c. A.D. 880–886. COURTESY OF MARTIN BIDDLE. REPRODUCED BY PERMISSION.

fenses. A forum, the settlement's administrative and commercial heart, was later built on a grand scale, filling the central block or *insula,* of the grid. Its construction illustrated that the town was now the capital of the *civitas* of the Belgae, as the name Venta Belgarum (venta, or market, of the Belgae) implies. Timber houses with tiled roofs, painted plaster walls, and mosaic floors were built along the streets. In the 150s and 160s, some of these houses were rebuilt in stone, or on stone foundations, often on a substantial scale. By the end of the second century, water in iron-jointed wooden pipes was fed to parts of the town, implying the existence of an aqueduct, traces of which have been found running along the contours to the north of the city.

By A.D. 200, when the circuit of the defenses was completed, Venta Belgarum, with an area of 58.2 hectares, was the fifth largest city of Roman Britain. In the early third century, the defenses were rebuilt in stone. The streets were kept clean and regularly resurfaced, and houses were still being built and repaired into the first half of the fourth century. Shortly after 350, however, the city underwent a profound change. Major public buildings and the larger townhouses were partly or wholly demolished, and large areas inside the walls were apparently enclosed to form compounds possibly for cattle and sheep awaiting slaughter for hides or shearing for wool. The water supply was reorganized with new iron-jointed wooden pipes, and all parts of the walled area seem to have been more densely populated than before. Varied and intensive industrial activity took place, and the streets continued to be resurfaced. The city walls were strengthened by the addition of external bastions. The cemeteries outside the walls grew greatly in extent: of some 1,300 burials from the Roman era that had been excavated through 1986, more than 1,000 were from the fourth century. In the second half of the fourth century, Venta seems to have become a busier, cruder, more pressured place. A possible explanation is that the city was no longer a civil settlement but a defended administrative base and supply center, dealing with the tax in kind known as the *annona militaris* and engaged in the industrialized production of textiles in a *gynaeceum,* a large-scale textile mill under imperial control.

POST-ROMAN VENTA

The Roman town collapsed in the fifth century. The decline is sharply reflected in the petering out of graves at the limit of the Lankhills cemetery, one of the most poignant images of the end of Roman Britain. Some rough street surfaces were put down during this period and the water supply relaid, but the wooden pipes used for the water supply no longer had iron collars. From this time onward, buildings began to be abandoned and some streets ceased to be used as thoroughfares and were instead taken over for domestic or other use. In the mid-later fifth century the south gate collapsed onto the street, but traffic continued across the uncleared rubble, and two further street surfaces were laid above it. At some date around 600, entry was blocked by cutting a ditch across the street, later re-

inforced by a rough stone wall. The north gate was probably blocked at the same time, so that in the end only one of the five east-west streets and one of the north-south streets of the Roman grid remained in use. The blocking of the gates shows that two centuries after the collapse of the Roman city there was still some authority controlling access to the walled area.

There is evidence from widely spread parts of the city for continuous activity of various sorts through the fifth and sixth centuries. Traces have been found wherever excavation has reached the relevant deposits over areas large enough to allow one to understand what survived and where the sequence was specific enough to provide some idea of the use of the area in spite of the destruction caused by the digging of cellars, wells, and cesspits during the medieval and later periods. The first signs of a barbarian Germanic presence can be dated to the early fifth century, when the Roman city was still at least partly functioning. Small amounts of Early (that is, pagan) Anglo-Saxon pottery have been found on widely distributed sites within the walls, suggesting that there may have been as many as six areas of Germanic occupation at that time. In addition, two later occupations have been indicated by place-name evidence.

Outside the walls, within a seven-kilometer radius of the city, there are seven recorded sixth- to seventh-century Anglo-Saxon cemeteries or isolated burials. Five of these date in whole or in greater part to the pre-Christian period. They form a cluster of a kind unique in Hampshire and rarely paralleled in central-southern England. This demonstrates the relative importance of the former Venta as a focal point in the pre-Christian Anglo-Saxon settlement of Hampshire. Since the early 1970s, discussion has focused on how the town's importance can be explained and what its significance may have been for the foundation of a minster church within the walls in the middle of the seventh century. Some argue that the church was founded only because the West Saxon clergy wished to establish the church within a former Roman town. Others maintain that it was founded to serve an existing center of Anglo-Saxon power and authority within the walled area. The "authority hypothesis" provides an explanation of the archaeological evidence as currently known.

WINTANCEASTER

The arrival of Christianity c. 650 is marked by the building of the church later known as Old Minster in the middle of the town's walled area. Its cross-shaped plan, set out on a modular geometry using the long Roman foot, appears to be derived from northern Italy. This suggests that it was built under the influence of St. Birinus (d. c. 650), the apostle of Wessex, who had been consecrated in Genoa about 630 by Bishop Asterius of Milan. The church was founded by the Anglo-Saxon King Cenwealh of Wessex (r. 643–672), who appears to have endowed it with a large territory around the city. The see of Wessex was moved to Winchester c. 660 and has remained there ever since. Excavation has revealed the long and complicated structural history of the church, but until shortly after 900 it stood almost unchanged. During the greater part of this period, Winchester was not an urban place but a royal and ecclesiastical center. It included a royal enclosure, the cathedral church and its community, a series of high-status private estates, and some service activity, including ironworking, along the east-west axis, now High Street. Only this street and one north-south street survived in use from the Roman period, with a post-Roman street wandering at an angle across the grain of the Roman plan from the southeast corner of the walled area towards the minster and palace in the center.

In 860 Winchester was attacked by the Vikings. There is no record that the church suffered, perhaps because Bishop Swithun (who held his post 852–863) had already put the defenses in order, building a bridge across the Itchen outside the east gate in 859. The bridge may have been part of a larger campaign of defense undertaken by King Æthelbald of Wessex (r. 855–860) that saw the walls and gates repaired.

FELIX URBS WINTHONIA

Modern Winchester has a regular pattern of streets, comprising four elements: High Street running from west to east; backstreets flanking High Street; a series of north-south streets running off to either side of High Street; and a street (now much interrupted) running inside the city walls. When the main outlines of the Roman street plan were worked out in the early 1960s, it became clear that Winchester's present streets were not, as had long been thought, of Roman origin: Roman buildings lie beneath today's streets and Roman streets beneath standing buildings.

Archaeologists then sought to establish when the present street plan was laid out. Coins found in 1963 above and below the second of a series of surfaces of what is now called Trafalgar Street, one of the north-south streets, showed that it was laid in the early tenth century. Excavation below the earthworks of William the Conqueror's castle, built in 1067, showed that another of the north-south streets and part of the street running inside the wall had been resurfaced eight or nine times before being buried below the castle, and that the first surfaces dated to the early tenth century or before. Written evidence showed that some of the present streets were already there by the tenth century. The precinct of New Minster, founded in 901, is defined in terms of the streets on all four sides of its site. The street plan of Winchester is therefore Anglo-Saxon, laid down either by King Alfred (r. 871–899) in the 880s, or (as seems increasingly likely) in the reigns of one or other of his older brothers, possibly Æthelbald.

There can be no doubt that the streets were part of a single deliberate operation. The first surface is everywhere of the same kind, of small, deliberately broken flint cobbles, while a "four-pole" (roughly 1.2 × 5 meters [4 × 16.5 feet]) module of 20.1 meters (66 feet), or one "chain," seems to have controlled the spacing of the north-south streets. Plans of the Winchester type can be seen in a series of other fortified places that were in use by the early tenth century in southern England, some of them on new sites where the street design could not have been influenced by an existing street system of Roman date. Earlier models need not be sought. There is nothing in the regularity of street plans of the Winchester type that was not well known to the hundreds of nameless individuals who in the eighth and ninth centuries had covered England with the vast pattern of rectangular strip fields that were to survive for a thousand years. This is the first great moment of English town planning and one of the earliest schemes of its kind in the post-Roman West.

The streets provided the skeleton upon which a populous and vibrant city emerged during the last century and a half of the Anglo-Saxon state. In about 900, Alfred's wife, Ealhswith (d. 902), established a nunnery, the Nunnaminster, on her property inside the east gate. In 901 her son King Edward the Elder (r. 899–924) founded the New Minster (so-called from the start to distinguish it from the ancient cathedral, henceforth Old Minster) immediately next to Old Minster in the center of the city. In 963 Bishop Æthelwold (who served 963–984) reformed the religious houses of the city, replacing clerks with Benedictine monks. In 971 he relocated his predecessor Swithun from his original grave to a specially made gold-and-jeweled shrine and began the reconstruction of Old Minster on a huge scale. With the dedication of the works of Æthelwold and his successor Ælfheah (served 984–1006) in 980 and 992–994, Old Minster become the greatest church of Anglo-Saxon England. It is also the only Anglo-Saxon cathedral that has been almost completely excavated, its long structural sequence elucidated, and its architectural design restored on paper. It is one of the great and most individual monuments of early medieval Europe.

By the year 1000 the whole southeastern part of the walled area was a royal and ecclesiastical quarter, containing the cathedral and two other minsters, all of royal foundation, the bishop's palace at Wolvesey (where the bishop still resides), and a royal palace to the west of the minsters where the king's treasure was kept for the first time in a permanent location. Winchester was now the principal royal city, the Westminster, of Anglo-Saxon England. It served as a center of learning, music, liturgy, book production and manuscript illumination, metalwork and sculpture, and of writing in Old English and Anglo-Latin. Outside the southeast quarter, the frontages of the streets were becoming fully built up with more than one thousand properties, many parish churches, and a wide range of craft production and industries, not least bullion exchange and minting. This was the golden age of the Old English state, and Winchester was its early capital.

The city was soon to attract the attention of outsiders. In 1006 the people of Winchester, safe behind their walls, watched the Danish Viking army pass on their way to the sea. In 1013 Svein Forkbeard, king of Denmark (r. c. 987–1014) took the city. In the years that followed, his son Cnut, king of England and Denmark (r. 1016–1035), made Winchester the principal center of his Anglo-Danish North Sea empire. He and his family were buried in Old Minster. In November 1066, the principal citizens surrendered the city without a fight to William the Conqueror, heralding a century during which Winchester would remain second only to the burgeoning wealth of London.

See also **Anglo-Saxon England** (*vol. 2, part 7*).

BIBLIOGRAPHY

Biddle, Martin. "The Study of Winchester: Archaeology and History in a British Town, 1961–1983." In *British Academy Papers on Anglo-Saxon England*. Edited by E. G. Stanley, pp. 299–341. Oxford: Oxford University Press, 1990. (Reviews the excavations of 1961 through 1971. Also includes a bibliography of sources published through 1988.)

———. "Excavations at Winchester, 1971: Tenth and Final Interim Report." *The Antiquaries Journal* 55 (1975): 96–126 and 295–337.

———. "Excavations at Winchester, 1970: Ninth Interim Report." *The Antiquaries Journal* 52 (1972): 93–131.

———. "Excavations at Winchester, 1969: Eighth Interim Report." *The Antiquaries Journal* 50 (1970): 277–326.

———. "Excavations at Winchester, 1968: Seventh Interim Report." *The Antiquaries Journal* 49 (1969): 295–329

———. "Excavations at Winchester, 1967: Sixth Interim Report." *The Antiquaries Journal* 48 (1968): 250–284.

———. "Excavations at Winchester, 1966: Fifth Interim Report." *The Antiquaries Journal* 47 (1967): 251–279.

———. "Excavations at Winchester, 1965: Fourth Interim Report." *The Antiquaries Journal* 46 (1966): 308–339.

———. "Excavations at Winchester, 1964: Third Interim Report." *The Antiquaries Journal* 45 (1965): 230–264.

———. "Excavations at Winchester Cathedral, 1962–63: Second Interim Report." *The Antiquaries Journal* 44 (1964): 188–219.

Biddle, Martin, et al. *Object and Economy in Medieval Winchester*. Winchester Studies, vol. 7, pt. 2. Oxford: Clarendon Press, 1990.

Biddle, Martin, ed. *Winchester in the Early Middle Ages: An Edition and Discussion of the Winton Domesday*. Winchester Studies, vol. 1. Oxford: Clarendon Press, 1977.

Biddle, Martin, and R. N. Quirk. "Excavations near Winchester Cathedral, 1961." *The Archaeological Journal* 119 (1962): 150–194.

Clarke, Giles, et al. *Pre-Roman and Roman Winchester: The Roman Cemetery at Lankhills*. Winchester Studies, vol. 3. Oxford: Clarendon Press, 1980.

Collis, John. *Winchester Excavations 1949–60*, Vol. 3. N.p., n.d.

Collis, John, and K. J. Barton. *Winchester Excavations*, Vol. 2, *1949–1960. Excavations in the Suburbs and the West-*

ern Part of the Town. Winchester, U.K.: City of Winchester, 1978.

Cunliffe, Barry. *Winchester Excavations 1949–1960.* Winchester, U.K.: Winchester City Council, Museums and Libraries Committee, 1964.

Keene, Derek, and Alexander R. Rumble. *Survey of Medieval Winchester.* Winchester Studies, vol. 2. Oxford: Clarendon Press, 1985.

Kjølbye-Biddle, Birthe. "Old Minster, St. Swithun's Day 1093." In *Winchester Cathedral: Nine Hundred Years, 1093–1993.* Edited by John Crook, pp. 13–20. Chichester, U.K.: Phillimore, 1993.

———. "Dispersal or Concentration: The Disposal of the Winchester Dead over 2000 Years." In *Death in Towns: Urban Responses to the Dying and the Dead, 100–1600.* Edited by Steven Bassett, pp. 210–247. Leicester, U.K.: Leicester University Press, 1992.

Lapidge, Michael. *The Cult of St Swithun.* Winchester Studies, vol. 4, pt. 2. Oxford: Clarendon Press, 2003.

Rumble, Alexander R. *Property and Piety in Early Medieval Winchester: Documents Relating to the Topography of the Anglo-Saxon and Norman City and Its Minsters.* Winchester Studies, vol. 4, pt. 3. Oxford: Clarendon Press, 2002.

Scobie, G. D., John M. Zant, and R. Whinney. *The Brooks, Winchester: A Preliminary Report on the Excavations, 1987–88.* Archaeology Report, vol. 1. Winchester, U.K.: Winchester Museums Service, 1991.

Zant, John M. *The Brooks, Winchester, 1987–88: The Roman Structural Remains.* Archaeology Report, vol. 2. Winchester, U.K.: Winchester Museums Service, 1993.

MARTIN BIDDLE

VIKING YORK

York was already eight hundred years old when it was captured by the Scandinavian great army in A.D. 866 during the Vikings' attempted conquest of England. Thereafter known as Jorvik, the town remained under Scandinavian control for most of the next eighty-eight years, ruled either by English puppets or Danish or Norwegian kings. In these years it became one of the foremost towns in northern Europe and the central place for a large area of Scandinavian settlements in Northumbria, the northeast of England. After the expulsion of the last Viking king, Erik Bloodaxe, in A.D. 954, Northumbria was incorporated into the kingdom of England but continued to be ruled by earls based in York. The town retained a distinctive Anglo-Scandinavian culture and allegiance for more than a century.

The Roman Ninth legion that founded York had placed the fortress Eboracum where the navigable river Ouse cuts through moraines that give good routes across the broad low-lying Vale of York; the settlement was thus well positioned for good water and land communications. When captured by the Vikings, York was still very much a Roman place. The stone-built defenses, main gateways, and street layout of Eboracum and the nearby civil town Colonia Eboracensis, largely survived into the Viking era. Within the fortress an ecclesiastical enclave had grown up around the church of St. Peter, founded A.D. 627 and since A.D. 735 seat of the archbishop of York, probably with an establishment nearby for the kings of Northumbria. With other churches, domestic occupation, and riverside trading activity, York already had the aspects of a town,

one of very few in England at the time. The Scandinavians, with huge input of effort and materials, transformed this over the next two generations to provide political, military, administrative, religious, industrial, and commercial and trading functions for what was in effect a separate Viking kingdom dependent on Jorvik.

To provide for Jorvik's defense the Roman fortifications were put in order, in some places being heightened with palisaded ramparts over the Roman walls and in others being extended to incorporate and defend a larger area. The town within the defenses was radically replanned to accommodate dwellings for a growing population and for commercial and industrial expansion. The Roman bridge across the river Ouse was replaced by another crossing downstream on the site of the present Ouse Bridge. New streets with Scandinavian names ran down to the crossing: Micklegate ("the great street") from one side and Ousegate ("the Ouse street") and its extension Pavement from the other. Similarly Walmgate led up to a crossing of the tributary river Foss and continued into the town as Fossgate. This concentrated commercial activity along the riversides and on the spur of land between the two rivers. A network of other new streets was laid out in relation to them.

The area is low-lying and has a drainage-impeding clay substrate. Organic debris from the new settlement rapidly caused anoxic (oxygen deficient) ground conditions to develop that preserved archaeological remains very well, especially the normally perishable organic components. The resultant

Fig. 1. Coppergate, York. Excavating post-and-wattle buildings of c. A.D. 930. © YORK ARCHAEOLOGICAL TRUST. REPRODUCED BY PERMISSION.

great depths of stratification therefore contain a uniquely detailed record of life in the commercial heart of a Viking town, although, being under modern York, they are difficult for archaeologists to access.

Excavations along some of the new streets during modern redevelopment have shown that the frontages were divided up into individual properties. Houses were set gable end to the street front on long narrow plots running back into the block. Four such properties were excavated at 16–22 Coppergate between 1976 and 1981. The street and the land divisions here, established by about A.D. 900, have maintained their positions until the present. By A.D. 930 the plots contained post-and-wattle buildings for domestic occupation and industrial scale manufacturing. These were replaced in the 960s and 970s by semisunken two-story plank and post-built oak structures and again in some cases in the eleventh century by further surface-level oak-built structures. Excavations and observations during building developments show that similar Viking Age buildings and layouts exist in many other parts of central York.

People lived in the street-front buildings. Crafts and industries were carried out there and in buildings and open areas behind on the long narrow plots. Such activities at Coppergate included woodworking; production of iron objects; production of copper alloy, silver, and other nonferrous metal objects; craft working of amber and other jewelry, antler combs, and textiles (including spinning, weaving, dying, and the making up of garments); and leatherworking (including shoe manufacture). Die making for coin minting—or minting itself—may also have gone on, Jorvik having produced vast quantities of silver coinage in the tenth and eleventh centuries. The site also contained evidence for regional and international trade. Environmental archaeology has enabled researchers to deduce living conditions, diet, and disease, and cemetery excavations in various parts of Anglo-Scandinavian York have helped determine contemporary demography.

Paganism rapidly gave way to Christianity in Viking York. The former Anglo-Scandinavian cathedral was probably situated north of the present York Minster, whose site was occupied by a high-status Anglo-Scandinavian cemetery. Lesser churches known from documentary and archaeological evidence include one surviving structure, St. Mary Bishophill Junior. Together they imply an Anglo-Scandinavian precursor of the medieval parish system.

Stone sculpture dating to the ninth to eleventh centuries from the Minster and other churches shows that wealthy patrons stimulated a flourishing metropolitan art tradition—also seen on leather, wood and metal objects—reflecting both Anglo-Saxon and Viking traditions and styles. This, along with excavated musical instruments and documented literary works demonstrate cultural aspirations in Jorvik as well as administrative and commercial success.

The Domesday Book drawn up on the orders of the Norman conqueror William I shows that by 1086 Jorvik had become a city of some 1,800 households and perhaps 10,000 people, vast for northern Europe at the time. Repeated attacks or planned attacks by Norwegian armies between 1066 and 1085 suggest continuing Scandinavian links. Jorvik—The Viking City, an underground display on the Coppergate excavation site, provides a full-scale evidence-based simulation of Coppergate in the 970s. Other artifacts from Viking York can be seen in the Yorkshire Museum, York.

See also **Vikings** (*vol. 2, part 7*).

BIBLIOGRAPHY

Addyman, P. V., ed. *The Archaeology of York.* 20 vols. to date. Ongoing series issued in fascicles. York: Council for British Archaeology, 1976–.

Hall, Richard. *Viking Age York.* London: Batsford, 1994.

———. *The Viking Dig: The Excavations at York.* London: Bodley Head, 1984.

Additional information is available at the York Archaeological Trust's website at http://www.yorkarchaeology.co.uk, especially under "Secrets Beneath Your Feet" and "Jorvik: The Viking City."

P. V. ADDYMAN

MEROVINGIAN FRANCE

At the end of the year A.D. 406 a confederation of Germanic peoples, including Vandals, Suevi, and Alans, crossed the frozen Rhine near Mainz and began plundering as far as Spain and North Africa. The Rhine frontier (*limes*) was never to be restored, and the Great Invasions, or Migrations, had reached Gaul. These movements were set off by the arrival from central Asia of the Huns in the 370s, thus provoking the panicked Visigoths to break into the Roman Empire; they were to bring numerous "barbarian" peoples into the western provinces to stay and found new polities. The decisive phase occurred between the 450s, when the collapse of Hunnic power and the accelerating fragmentation of Imperial Rome's authority left the field free for new players, and the years around 600, when major population movements took a hiatus and enduring territorial identities began to emerge in the west.

By that time the most successful barbarian dynasty was clearly that of the Merovingian Franks, reunited under Clotaire II and his son Dagobert in the early seventh century. The lands between the Loire and the Rhine, which had been provinces of Roman Gaul, were becoming known as Francia, the heartland of this "Frankish" power, which extended south into more Romanized regions (Aquitania, Burgundy, and Provence) and eastward into Germanic territories (Thuringia, Alemannia, and Bavar-

ia). What were the roles of the "Franks" and the "Romans" in the development of this new power and of the cultural dynamism that was to carry the Franks to such heights in the oncoming Middle Ages? These questions have been at the heart of historical debates for centuries and have provided the framework for the evolution of Merovingian archaeology. They spring from the paradigm of the decline and fall of the Roman Empire, which first took form under Renaissance historians. When archaeology began to play a role, this paradigm was conceived in terms of identifying the historical actors, already known from the written sources, through studying their graves.

FUNERARY ARCHAEOLOGY

In 1653 during construction near the church of Saint-Brice in Tournai, Belgium, workers came upon a "treasure" of gold and silver coins, along with a profusion of iron and bronze objects—some clearly weapons—and bones, including two human skulls and a horse skull. Thanks to the prompt action of local authorities and the interest taken by Archduke Leopold William in asserting ownership, most of these finds were collected and given for study to the archduke's personal physician, Jean-Jacques Chifflet, who was a noted historian. In 1655 Chifflet published a detailed account of the find, as it could be reconstructed from witnesses and study of the artifacts, each one carefully illustrated.

Chifflet identified the find as the burial of the Frankish king Childeric, on the basis of a gold signet ring that depicted a long-haired warrior holding a spear and that was inscribed "CILDIRICI REGIS." According to the major narrative source for Frankish history, written by Bishop Gregory of Tours (d. 593), Childeric, a ruler of the western Franks, had fought alongside Roman commanders in the later fifth century and had died in A.D. 481/482. His son, Clovis, then attacked and defeated the Roman general Syagrius (486), launching a fighting career during which he eliminated rival Frankish rulers and defeated other barbarian peoples to establish, by his death in 511, the first dynasty to rule France, the Merovingians. The archduke took the Childeric collection with him to Vienna; after his death it was offered to King Louis XIV as a diplomatic present and disappeared from sight until the nineteenth century.

Over the next two centuries, as graves with artifacts turned up in northwest Europe, "antiquaries" argued over their attribution to specific groups of ancient peoples known from written sources. After 1800, early industrialization (the construction of roads and railways) led to the discovery of thousands of graves; this discovery combined with the growth of scientific methodologies and the Romantic enthusiasm for a national past created a climate favorable to the emergence of "national archaeologies." In 1848 Wilhelm and Ludwig Lindenschmidt argued convincingly that the twenty-one well-furnished graves that they had excavated at Selzen (Rheinhessen) must be Frankish because two of them included gold coins of the Byzantine emperor Justinian I (r. 527–565). They published a careful tomb-by-tomb description with sketches depicting all the objects in place.

Between 1855 and 1859 the abbé Cochet published three influential volumes based on his many excavations in Normandy. His approach was more general. He contrasted the indigenous (and pagan) Gallo-Romans, who typically placed offerings of food, tableware, and small coins with their cremated dead, with the invading Germanic warriors, who laid the unburned bodies in graves, along with weapons and, for women, ornaments such as brooches and hairpins. Cochet's methods were crude. He usually did not publish tomb drawings or

site plans or grave assemblages, and he did not pay heed to the chronological dimension of artifacts. For example, his "typical Frankish warrior" was shown carrying weapons of different periods and even female ornaments. Although Cochet rescued Childeric's grave from the obscurity into which it had fallen, he did not appreciate its potential value as a precisely dated closed-finds assemblage. Nonetheless, his enthusiasm for Merovingian archaeology stimulated interest in this new discipline in France and abroad.

In the half-century before World War I thousands of graves were opened, often as the by-product of construction. What may be called the "ethnic paradigm" remained dominant. In 1860 Henri Baudot published an account of graves at Charnay (near Dijon), which he thought must be those of Burgundians before their kingdom was conquered by the Franks in 534. In 1892 and 1901 Camille Barrière-Flavy published material from graves in southwestern France, labeling it "Visigothic" on the principal ground that the Visigoths had ruled this region until their defeat by Clovis in 507. Some researchers developed notions of field methodology and the critical problems posed by the material uncovered. The abbé Haigneré in 1866 published a study of four cemeteries in Boulogne with a list of artifact assemblages for each grave and, for one site, a plan with each grave numbered. In Picardy, Jules Pilloy proposed the first chronological study of Merovingian artifacts. He distinguished an early period that corresponded to the invasions; a second one marking the growth of Merovingian power in the sixth century; a later phase of transition, when weapons such as the throwing axe (francisca) disappeared from grave groups and a new type, a single-edged short sword (scramasax), appeared; and a final phase, characterized by such objects as iron plate buckles with silver and gold inlay (damasquinure), which he took to be Carolingian (fig. 1).

While such men as Pilloy and the abbé Haigneré were laying the foundations for sound research, other diggers were pillaging sites to sell the booty on the expanding antiquities market. The example of Fréderic Moreau illustrates another type of excavator of the day. He worked on a vast scale, opening thousands of graves. Although he was known to present artifacts to visitors, he kept a daily excava-

Fig. 1. Belt buckles and plate, Merovingian era, from Dangolsheim tomb. THE ART ARCHIVE/ ARCHAEOLOGICAL MUSEUM STRASBOURG/DAGLI ORTI. REPRODUCED BY PERMISSION.

tion journal, maintained a restoration laboratory in his house, and privately printed summaries of his work in folio albums with splendid color lithographs. World War I led to a significant decline in Merovingian archaeological activity in France, lasting into the 1960s. Excavations were few and limited in scope; the most important general studies were by foreign scholars, such as the Swede Nils Åberg and the German Hans Zeiss. Édouard Salin kept the French tradition alive. A mining engineer from Lorraine, he began excavating rural cemeteries in that region in 1912 and continued to dig and publish through the 1950s. He gave impetus to technical studies by founding, with Albert France-Lanord, the first laboratory in France specializing in archaeological metallurgy, the Musée de l'Histoire du Fer in Nancy. He proposed an ambitious general interpretation of the Merovingian period founded on graves, written sources, and laboratory analysis. The technical studies of Merovingian metalwork were highly innovative, demonstrating the complex skills that went into making pattern-welded swords, iron belt buckles decorated with patterns of inlaid gold and silver wire, and gold-and-garnet and gold filigree brooches.

Salin's historical vision remained firmly within the boundaries of the "ethnic paradigm": He set out to distinguish Gallo-Roman from Germanic graves on the basis of typical artifacts and funerary customs and to identify the particular groups of "invaders"—Franks, Burgundians, Alemanni, and Visigoths. These groups were presumed to have come into contact with one another at the time of the "Great Invasions" of the fifth century, as distinct groups with fully formed funerary traditions. At a particular site, such as Villey-Saint-Etienne in Lorraine, the archaeologist could discern how, over time, these traditions interacted, giving rise to a new funerary culture in later Merovingian times. Salin stressed that all aspects of this practice—grave construction and orientation, cemetery organization, such traces of ritual activity as fire, and body position—needed to be considered along with the artifact assemblages. Like the abbé Cochet, Salin was deeply interested in what could be learned about ideology and religion from these graves.

Salin's earlier notion of "progressive fusion" overlaps here with the idea of "Christianization." He assumed that the original funerary culture was pagan, the antithesis of the Christian funerary culture practiced by the Gallo-Romans, and that the latter gradually triumphed, leading to the abandonment of the old "row-grave cemeteries" and the disappearance of artifacts from graves during the later Merovingian period. At the end of his career, Salin engaged in the excavation of Merovingian sarcophagi in the crypt of the abbey church of Saint-Denis, associated with King Dagobert (r. 629–639).

During the 1970s and 1980s French archaeology became more professional, and Merovingian archaeology benefited for the first time from leadership based in research organizations. Excavations by the C.R.A.M. (Center for Medieval Archaeological Research) in the Caen region soon corrected the earlier impression that there had been little Merovingian activity in western Normandy; Frénouville was the first Merovingian cemetery in France to be totally excavated and published. In the Rhône-Alps region a group of archaeologists from Geneva, Lyon, and Grenoble excavated numerous early medieval churches and cemeteries in consultation with one another. One of them, Michel Colardelle, published a global study of funerary archaeology in this region from the late Roman to the medieval period.

The intellectual center of the Merovingian revival was the A.F.A.M. (Association Française d'Archéologie Mérovingienne; French Association of Merovingian Archaeology), founded in 1979 by Patrick Périn. Périn's study of a rich early Merovingian cemetery in his hometown of Charleville-Mézières led him to focus on the refinement of chronological systems as the key to progress. He developed an artifact typology based on a series of cemeteries in the Champagne-Ardennes region, studied the frequency of object associations and their changes over time, and proposed a system of phases tied to absolute chronology by well-dated reference graves. Périn also stressed the fundamental importance of using these tools to study the internal dynamics of each cemetery, or its "topochronology."

The decades of the late twentieth century were marked by higher standards of fieldwork, more post-excavation specialist studies, and a much more critical attitude toward the problems of interpreting fragmentary archaeological data in the light of selective written sources. The direct link assumed by Salin between religion and funerary practice has been criticized, for example. Correlations that were drawn between funerary culture and ethnic identity now appear much more complex and ambiguous. The close and careful work of several archaeologists has supported the emergence of a "Germanic" funerary rite within and beyond the Roman frontiers during the late empire (c. A.D. 350–450), which provided the basis for the Frankish funerary rite that emerged and spread under Childeric and Clovis. A generation later, this cultural model was established in newly conquered regions, from Basel in Switzerland to Saintes in Aquitania.

Most researchers now agree that the Visigoths did not have an archaeologically distinct funerary culture while they occupied Aquitania, nor did the early Burgundians in eastern France, except, perhaps, for a few artificially deformed skulls. This is an unusual example of a plausible ethno-cultural conclusion drawn from skeletal data. Other studies have established that, while much can be learned from physical anthropology about ancient population structures, their health, and their relative homogeneity, these data do not lend themselves to ethnic profiling. Funerary practice could, on the other hand, reflect episodic assertions of group or regional identity, such as the belt buckles with Christian iconography that flourished briefly in part of Merovingian Burgundy. Researchers have pointed to the need to allow for the role of ceremony and display, usually archaeologically invisible, in understanding funerary practice. For the region around Metz, for example, the funerary domain might well have been a site of contest among local elite groups struggling for hegemony.

SETTLEMENT ARCHAEOLOGY

Settlement archaeology is a new and rapidly expanding field in France. As late as 1970 fewer than twenty sites were known, and none of them were explored more than partially. Not until 1972 was a Merovingian village—Brébieres, near Douai—excavated and the finds published in France. Between 1980 and 1993, 127 new sites became known, and the number has continued to rise.

This trend reflects the building boom in those years, coupled with legally mandated salvage archaeology, which is carried out with great methodological rigor at a pace and on a scale that dwarfs anything done in the past. For instance, in 1998 a team that included specialists of the prehistoric,

Iron Age, and Roman and Merovingian periods was charged with evaluating and excavating a 237-hectare area at Onnaing (near Valenciennes) before the construction of a Toyota plant. Initial analysis indicated the development of many small settlements in the Late Iron Age and the earlier Gallo-Roman period, with general abandonment of sites before A.D. 200 and reoccupation in one place by a Merovingian settlement with sunken-featured buildings (SFBs). From that time the fertile Onnaing plain was given over to intensive cultivation.

While this example of landscape archaeology that allows us to situate Merovingian settlement in a period of long duration is quite exceptional, it also serves to underline the tentative nature of any general conclusions one might draw today, so soon after the Brebières excavation. The full-scale publication of more recent sites is still awaited. The information now available is unequally distributed geographically. A great density of sites in northern France contrasts with scarcity in western and southern France.

Brebières offers an object lesson in the dangers of drawing hasty conclusions from available data. The excavation disclosed some thirty-one SFBs spread out along either side of a street several hundred meters long. These were small rectangular buildings, 3 to 6 meters long and 2 to 3.5 meters wide, with wattle-and-daub walls and thatch roofs supported by two, four, or six wooden posts set into the dugout floor. There were few fireplaces. Located near a marsh, which was drained by two ditches, this site suggested to some scholars a damp, cramped, and squalid lifestyle, an impression that re-enforced the theory of economic decline and cultural regression following the Great Invasions.

However, it is based on only a partial investigation of the site, for work was limited to a 50-meter-wide band whose surface had been scraped away before the archaeologists arrived. There may have been larger surface-level buildings whose traces had been destroyed, or that lay beyond the excavated area. The SFBs could have been only outbuildings used for storage or workshops, as the discovery of such artifacts as loom weights suggests. Brebières also has to be understood in relation to the nearby royal villa of Vitry-en-Artois (known from written sources), to which it probably belonged. In 1985 more SFBs were found in a rescue operation at

Vitry, as well as posthole alignments, which suggest a ground-level timber-frame house. At Juvincourt-et-Damary (Aisne) three such houses were excavated. The largest (15 by 5 meters) had an entrance porch leading to two rooms, one a living room equipped with a fireplace and the other used for sleeping.

By the mid-1990s many timber-frame buildings had been documented in the northern part of France. More information about the complexities of site evolution also has become available. It has been suggested that Juvincourt, for example, was a hamlet within a polynuclear village. When founded at the beginning of the Merovingian period, it consisted of several surface-level buildings with SFB outbuildings. In the later sixth century, settlement shifted to the north; by the mid-seventh century it had relocated even farther north, with several aligned buildings facing a rectangular enclosure. By the ninth century the settlement had been abandoned.

Excavation of the settlement at Mondeville, near Caen in Normandy, sheds new light on the dynamics of early medieval settlement and its role in the transition from antiquity to the Middle Ages, tying it to the evolution of funerary practice as well. Occupied in the Iron Age, Mondeville became a *vicus* (substantial rural settlement) with houses built on solid stone foundations. By about A.D. 300 these houses were replaced by SFBs: small timber-and-thatch buildings with floors dug into the bedrock. Timber architecture remained characteristic until about A.D. 700, when houses with stone foundations reappeared. This also may have been the time when a church with stone foundations was built within the settlement and burials were made around it, a sign that the traditional separation of the living and the dead was giving way to new Christian attitudes. There is more evidence of this shift at Saleux, in Picardy, a particularly interesting site since the entire settlement, in use from the seventh to the eleventh century, was excavated along with the necropolis of almost twelve hundred graves. At first the dwellings were placed close to the river and the dead buried on higher ground, a good distance to the west. The burial site focused around a special grave housed in a stone sarcophagus and protected by a wooden structure. During the eighth century this structure was transformed into a small timber church, which was later rebuilt in stone; the cemetery was enclosed by a ditch. By then the village itself had advanced to adjoin the churchyard, providing a plausible early example of the typical medieval village, with the living and the dead knit into a seamless community around the parish church.

Was the Merovingian period fundamentally in rupture with antiquity, or should more stress be laid on elements of continuity? Did the basic patterns of medieval life have their roots deep in this period, or did they emerge essentially around the end of the first millennium, after centuries of instability and poverty? Lively debate on such critical questions has replaced the assumption that archaeology's role is merely to provide artifacts that illustrate a historical narrative (whose outline is firmly fixed by written sources) or, at most, to fill in the gaps. In the last decades of the twentieth century there was a fundamental change not only in the scale and precision of excavation but also in the scope of the larger archaeological enterprise, as it has been called upon to collaborate with other disciplines in confronting historical questions. Boundaries once thought secure now seem fluid, as is apparent in the interaction of those "Merovingian archaeologists" primarily concerned with rural settlements and cemeteries, with scholars working on the related problems of cities and Christianity during this period.

URBAN AND CHRISTIAN ARCHAEOLOGY

In 1830 concern for preserving the past, which had been growing since the destructions caused by the French Revolution, led France to create the Commission des Monuments historiques (Historical Monuments Commission), whose trained architects went to work restoring medieval churches. A parallel pursuit, whose origins go back to the Renaissance, was the study of early Christian remains, such as carved sarcophagi and inscriptions. The French presence in North Africa and the Near East also led to pioneering archaeological studies of early Christian buildings, many still standing in part, in the former provinces of the Roman Empire. Because few monuments from that time survived above ground in France itself, interest in the heritage there was slight before the mid-twentieth century. Change began when the fifth International Congress of Christian Archaeology was held at Aix-en-Provence in 1954.

Under the influence of the great historian Henri-Irénée Marrou, the critical centuries from A.D. 300 to 800 were seen less as a time of decadence and collapse (the "Dark Ages") than as a dynamic and creative period (late antiquity) driven by the novel forces released by Christianity. It was clear that any attempt to study this phenomenon archaeologically must involve excavating cities, for they were the heart of the early Christian world. How had the hundred *civitas* capitals of Gaul, the nodal points of the Roman administration that had become in the Christian empire the seats of bishops as well, fared with the barbarian onslaught? Much of the evidence was hidden; the great medieval cathedrals were built atop complex groups of early Christian buildings. A variety of literary sources, inscriptions, sarcophagi, coins, and vestiges of old buildings offered many avenues for research. Given the poverty of resources for excavation in France and the lack of trained excavators and of training programs, what could be done?

By 1986, when the International Congress of Christian Archaeology returned to France (Lyon), impressive progress had been made, thanks to creative and energetic scholarly enterprise and to the growth of publicly mandated salvage archaeology. Since the mid-1970s a group of scholars had been meeting regularly to pursue a critical and systematic study of all the sources, written and material, for each of the Gallo-Roman towns that had become episcopal seats in late antiquity. At the same time research-oriented archaeologists developed focused research programs in partnership with the Archaeological Service of the Ministry of Culture, local and regional authorities, and businesses and private enthusiasts. The most thoroughgoing long-term project has been under way in the city and canton of Geneva since the 1970s, until 1998 under the direction of Charles Bonnet. The archaeology of religious edifices has been a specialty of the Bonnet team. Their most spectacular accomplishment was the thorough excavation of the cathedral and its surroundings, showing how a complex Merovingian cathedral group (including a bishop's palace with a sixth-century mosaic pavement) developed out of late Roman administrative buildings (fig. 2).

While it would be imprudent to draw quick conclusions from the vast amounts of new data generated by this type of work, two general comments

Fig. 2. Mosaic from the sixth-century Bishop's palace. PHOTOGRAPH BY MONIQUE DELLEY. COURTESY SERVICE CANTONAL D'ARCHÉOLOGIE, GENEVA. REPRODUCED BY PERMISSION.

can be made. First, it is clear that the urban component of Merovingian civilization was much more important and dynamic than once was thought and that Christianity was the primary force in the survival and redefinition of these towns. That the overwhelming majority of the Roman *civitas* capitals in Gaul did survive as urban settlements, apparently without any break in continuity, is a clear contrast with the discontinuity found in Britain.

The nature and scale of survival varied dramatically. It was most attenuated in Tours, once a planned Roman town of 80 hectares. By A.D. 500 there remained a 9-hectare walled citadel by the river, where the bishop in his cathedral and the count in his hall kept company. Two kilometers to the west stood a funerary church dedicated to Saint Martin, around which a new community, called by a contemporary the *vicus christianorum* (settlement of the Christians), was emerging. Most of the old

Roman town, between these points, had become fields. The western pole grew rapidly, stimulated by the popularity of Saint Martin's tomb as a goal of pilgrimage; it came to be enclosed within its own wall. In Geneva, around A.D. 500, the bishop's monumental new buildings were filling the walled hilltop citadel; other new churches were revitalizing the *suburbium* (the area around the core) below. Farther out in the countryside churches were going up as well.

This picture leads to the second general observation authorized by recent research: the Christian impact on the rural world. At Sezegnin, about 10 miles from Geneva, a rural cemetery of more than six hundred graves developed around three privileged burials in the center. They were not "elite" graves in the traditional social sense, for they included almost no artifacts, but they were set off by a wooden structure that can be interpreted as a *me-*

moria, a monument to commemorate the honored Christian dead. The fugitive traces of such a structure would have escaped attention in the past, but there is growing evidence in the core Frankish regions to the north that by the later sixth century elite burials were shifting to unmistakable Christian contexts.

A rural cemetery excavated at Hordain (near Douai) shows that an emphatically un-Christian burial style (cremation under tumulus) co-existed c. A.D. 550 with richly furnished (weapons and ornament) inhumation burials in a funerary chapel built in the midst of the cemetery. In Belgium a private funerary chapel at Arlon included an elite warrior grave and that of a young woman buried sometime around A.D. 600 with ornaments that included a Christian silver locket. One of the earliest well-dated examples of richly furnished elite burials in a Christian context (c. A.D. 530/540) comes from the old Roman town of Cologne, capital of the Rhenish Franks. In a chapel within the atrium of the cathedral a young boy was buried with weapons (including a helmet) and furniture (bed and chair); beside him a young woman lay with finery that rivals that of Aregonde in Saint-Denis a generation later. Thus both archaeological finds and written sources associate the Merovingian elites with the towns and stress the vitality of the Christian culture there. Even funerary practices were beginning a gradual shift toward what would emerge in the Carolingian period as a fully Christian organization of death.

See also **Merovingian Franks** (*vol. 2, part 7*); **Tomb of Childeric** (*vol. 2, part 7*).

BIBLIOGRAPHY

Archéologie de la France: 30 ans de découverts. Paris: Réunion des Musées Nationaux, 1989. (Catalogue of the highlights of recent archaeology in France, with useful introductory essays by topic.)

Böhme, Hörst W. *Germanische Grabfunde des 4. bis 5. Jahrhunderts zwischen unterer Elbe und Loire.* 2 vols. Müncher Beiträge. Vor- und Frühgeschichte, no. 19. Munich: C. H. Beck, 1974. (Classic study of late Roman Germanic graves.)

Böhner, Kurt. *Die fränkischen Altertümer des Trier Landes.* 2 vols. Berlin: Germanische Denkmäler der Völkerwanderungzeit, 1958. (First regional relative artifact chronology.)

Bonnet, Charles. *Genève aux premiers temps chrétiens.* Geneva, Swizerland: Fondations des Clefs de Saint Pierre, 1986.

Catteddu, Isabelle. "Le site médiévale de Saleux 'Les Coutures': Habitat, nécropole, et églises du haut Moyen Age." In *Rural Settlements in Medieval Europe.* Edited by Guy De Boe and Frans Verhaeghe, pp. 143–148. Papers of the 1997 Medieval Europe Brugge Conference, vol. 6. Zellik, Belgium: Institute for the Archaeological Heritage, 1997.

Colardelle, Michel. *Sépulture et traditions funéraires du Ve au XIIIe siècle ap. J.C. dans les campagnes des Alpes françaises du Nord (Drôme, Isère, Savoie, Haute-Savoie).* Grenoble, Switzerland: Societé Alpine de Documentation et de Recherche en Archéologie, 1983. (Regional study, integrating artifacts and funerary practices for relative chronology.)

Effros, Bonnie. *Merovingian Mortuary Archaeology and the Making of the Early Middle Ages.* Berkeley: University of California Press, 2003.

Die Franken: Wegbereiter Europas. 2 vols. Mainz, Germany: Verlag Philipp Von Zabern, 1996. (Catalogue from the Reiss-Museum, Mannheim, of largest exhibition ever held of Frankish archaeology, with many fundamental articles by leading scholars.)

Galinié, Henri. "Tours from an Archaeological Standpoint." In *Spaces of the Living and the Dead: An Archaeological Dialogue.* Edited by Catherine Karkov, Kelley Wickham-Crowley, and Bailey Young, pp. 87–106. American Early Medieval Studies, no. 3. Oxford: Oxbow Books, 1999.

Geary, Patrick J. *Before France and Germany: The Creation and Transformation of the Merovingian World.* Oxford: Oxford University Press, 1988.

Halsall, Guy. "Burial, Ritual, and Merovingian Society." In *The Community, the Family and the Saint: Patterns of Power in Early Medieval Europe.* Edited by Joyce Hill and Mary Swan, pp. 325–338. Turnhout, Belgium: Brepols, 1998.

———. *Settlement and Social Organization: The Merovingian Region of Metz.* Cambridge, U.K.: Cambridge University Press, 1995.

James, Edward. *The Franks.* Oxford: Blackwell, 1988.

———. *The Merovingian Archaeology of South-west Gaul.* BAR Supplementary Series, no. 25. Oxford: British Archaeological Reports, 1977.

Lorren, Claude. "Le village de Saint-Martin de Traincourt à Mondeville (Calvados), de l'Antiquité au Haut Moyen Age." In *La Neustrie: Les pays au nord de la Loire de 650 à 850.* Vol. 2. Edited by Hartmut Atsma, pp. 439–466. Sigmaringen, Germany: Thorbecke, 1989.

Martin, Max. *Das fränkische Gräberfeld von Basel-Bernerring.* Basel, Switzerland: Basler Beiträge zur Ur- und Frühgeschichte, 1976.

Mertens, Joseph. *Tombes mérovingiennes et églises chrétiennes (Arlon, Grobbendonk, Landen, Waha)*. Archaeologica Belgica, no. 187. Brussels, Belgium. 1976.

Musset, Lucien. *The Germanic Invasions: The Making of Europe, A.D. 400–600*. Translated by Edward and Columba James. University Park: Pennsylvania State University Press, 1975. (A still pertinent overview of the period; excellent bibliography to 1975.)

Naissance des arts chrétiens: Atlas des monuments paléochrétiens de la France. Paris: Imprimerie Nationale, 1991. (Lavishly illustrated interpretative survey by leading scholars.)

Périn, Patrick. "Settlements and Cemeteries in Merovingian Gaul." In *The World of Gregory of Tours*. Edited by Kathleen Mitchell and Ian Wood, pp. 67–98. Leiden, The Netherlands: Brill, 2002.

———. "Les tombes de 'chefs' du début de l'époque mérovingienne: Datation et interprétation historique." In *La noblesse romaine et les chefs barbares du IIIe au VIe siècle*. Edited by Francoise Vallet and Michel Kazanski, pp. 247–301. Association Française d'Archéologie Mérovingienne Mémoires, no. 9. Saint-Germain-en-Laye, France: Musée des Antiquités Nationales, 1995.

———. *La datation des tombes mérovingiennes: Historique, méthodes, applications*. Geneva, Switzerland: Droz, 1980. (Fundamental for the history and methodology of funerary archaeology.)

Périn, Patrick, and Laure-Charlotte Feffer. *Les Francs, de leur origine jusq'au 6ème siècle, et leur heritage*. 2 vols. Paris: Armand Colin, 1997. (Vol. 1, *A la conquête de la Gaule*; vol. 2, *A l'origine de la France*. Well-illustrated, accessible overview with archaeological emphasis.)

Peytremann, Edith. *Archéologie de l'habitat rural dans le nord de la Gaule du IVe au XIIIe siècle*. 2 vols. Association Française d'Archéologie Mérovingienne Mémoires, no. 13. Saint-Germain-en-Laye, France: Musée des Antiquités Nationales, 2002. (The first general study of the subject, with a complete site catalogue.)

Pilet, Christian. *La nécropole de Frénouville: Étude d'une population de la fin du IIIe à la fin du VIIe siècle*. 2 vols. BAR International Series, no. 83. Oxford: British Archaeological Reports, 1983.

Privati, Béatrice. *La nécropole de Sézegnin (Ive–VIIe siécle)*. Société d'Histoire et d'Archéologie de Genève, no. 10. Geneva, Switzerland: A. Jullien, 1983.

Salin, Édouard. *La civilisation mérovingienne d'après les sépultures, les textes et le laboratoire*. 4 vols. Paris: A. and J. Picard, 1950–1959. (Vol. 1, *Les idées et les faits*; vol. 2, *Les sépultures*; vol. 3, *Les techniques*; vol. 4, *Les croyances*. Although dated and much criticized, still a fundamental work by the pioneer of twentieth-century Merovingian archaeology in France.)

Sapin, Christian. "Architecture and Funerary Space in the Early Middle Ages." In *Spaces of the Living and the Dead: An Archaeological Dialogue*. Edited by Catherine Karkov, Kelley Wickham-Crowley, and Bailey Young, pp. 39–60. American Early Medieval Studies, no. 3. Oxford: Oxbow Books, 1999.

Young, Bailey K. "The Myth of the Pagan Cemetery." In *Spaces of the Living and the Dead: An Archaeological Dialogue*. Edited by Catherine Karkov, Kelley Wickham-Crowley, and Bailey Young, pp. 61–85. American Early Medieval Studies, no. 3. Oxford: Oxbow Books, 1999.

———. "Les nécroples (IIIe–VIIIe siècle)." In *Naissance des arts chrétiens: Atlas du monde paleochrétien*. Paris: Imprimerie Nationale, 1991. (Includes extensive site bibliography.)

———. "Paganisme, christianisation, et rites funéraires mérovingiens." *Archéologie médiévale* 7 (1977): 5–83. (Includes site gazetteer.)

BAILEY K. YOUNG

TOMB OF CHILDERIC

On 27 May 1653 a deaf-mute mason named Adrien Quinquin, working on a construction project near the church of Saint-Brice in Tournai, Belgium, struck gold. As the abbé Cochet reconstructs the story in *Le tombeau de Childéric I*, he was down about 7 or 8 feet in dark earth when a chance blow of the pick suddenly revealed a gold buckle and at least a hundred gold coins. This surprise find caused him to throw down the tool and run about, waving his arms and trying to articulate sounds. The first witnesses who crowded around the trench saw some two hundred silver coins; human bones, including two skulls; a lot of rusted iron; a sword with a gold grip and a hilt ornamented in the gold-and-garnet cloisonné technique and sheathed in a cloisonné-decorated scabbard; and numerous other gold items, among them, brooches, buckles, rings, an ornament in the form of a bull's head, and about three hundred gold cloisonné bees.

The authorities acted quickly to gather together this "treasure," and news of it soon reached the archduke Leopold William, governor of the Austrian Netherlands, who had it sent to him in Brussels. He further ordered that a careful written account of the find be made and confided the collection for study to his personal physician, Jean-Jacques Chif-

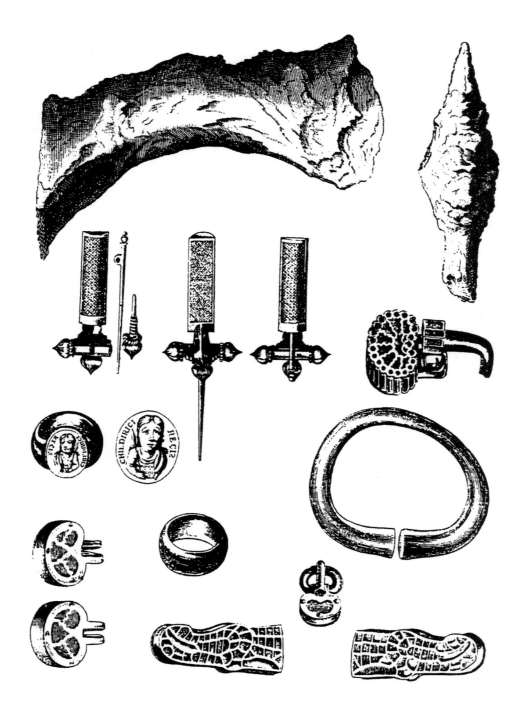

Fig. 1. Childeric's "treasure" from original 1655 plates: weapons. FROM VALLET AND KAZANSKI 1995. REPRODUCED BY PERMISSION.

flet, who also was a historian. The outstanding find was a gold signet ring inscribed with the figure of an armed warrior and the name CHILIRICI REGIS. In 1655 Chifflet published a folio volume of 367 pages with 27 plates of engravings furnishing an excellent visual record of all the artifacts and a careful discussion and interpretative essay identifying the subject as the father of Clovis I, the great ancestor of the French monarchy. This discovery is the starting point of Merovingian archaeology, and

Fig. 2. Childeric's "treasure" from original 1655 plates: fibula, signet ring, cloisonée ornament. FROM VALLET AND KAZANSKI 1995. REPRODUCED BY PERMISSION.

Chifflet's study deserves to be considered the first truly scientific archaeological publication.

This study has proved all the greater a boon because most of the original artifacts have disappeared. The archduke took them home to Vienna when he retired. Upon his death in 1662 they came into the possession of Leopold I, emperor of Austria, who, in 1665, sent them to France as a diplomatic present to young King Louis XIV. The collection survived the French Revolution intact, but one night in 1831 two thieves broke into the Bibliothèque Royal and stole the trove. By the time they were caught, most of the gold objects had been melted down, but a few artifacts, such as the gold cloisonné ornament of the sword, had been thrown into the Seine in leather sacks, and these were recovered.

What do we know of Childeric? The sixth-century ecclesiastic and historian Gregory of Tours tells us something of his life in *Historia Francorum* (The history of the Franks). Childeric may have been the son of Merovech, and he was considered a king so debauched that his own subjects drove him into exile for eight years among the Thuringians, at the court of King Basinus and Queen Basina. During this time the Roman general Aegidius ruled the Franks in his place. Upon his departure from court, Queen Basina followed him. They eventually married, and she gave birth to a son, Clovis. Meanwhile Childeric fought a battle at Orléans against the Visigoths and another at Angers against the Goths and Saxons. When he died in about A.D. 481, his son Clovis replaced him. On the basis of this information and the way in which Gregory recounts Clovis's subsequent (A.D. 486) defeat of Syagrius, Aegidius's son and heir, Childeric often has been presented in history books as a minor Frankish warlord whose power was based on the rather minor and out-of-the-way northern town of Tournai. (This is assumed because of the place of his burial.) He is thought to have played a supporting role to the Roman commanders in northern Gaul, who were attempting to defend what was left of Roman power there from the A.D. 450s to the 480s.

Much can be learned from Childeric's grave. Michel Kazanski and Patrick Périn offer a reconstruction of the burial and comment on how it fits into the complex and changing world of the later fifth century. The polychrome gold-and-garnet ornament so prominent in the grave closely parallels the finds at another contemporary princely warrior grave at Pouan, in Northeast France. The style points particularly to the Danube region, where rich assemblages like those in Pannonia at Apahida (now in Hungary) and Blucina (now in the Czech Republic) define an international barbarian elite style associated with the Hunnic empire. This "barbarian" side of the Childeric assemblage also is reflected in such details as the gold bracelet, which Joachim Werner has shown was the symbol of German royalty, set permanently on the wrist when the king first mounted the throne. In the tradition of late imperial "chieftains' graves," Childeric had a panoply of weapons. No evidence has survived of an *angon*, a kind of harpoon, or a shield, which are typical complements to such an assemblage, but their vestiges could have looked like so much rusty iron to onlookers in 1653.

There was a spear (the figure on the signet ring is shown grasping one, as a symbol of royal authori-

ty) and a throwing axe (francisca)—everyday weapons, balancing the parade-ground pomp of the gold-and-garnet double-edged long sword and the short, single-edged scramasax. The style of the very fine cloisonné ornament on these weapons recalls Byzantine-Sassanid techniques crafted in Byzantine workshops and often distributed as diplomatic gifts. Could Childeric have traveled east and received them, perhaps during his long Thuringian exile? Kazanski sees the Childeric material as reflecting motifs and techniques widespread in the Mediterranean world; he and Périn suggest that at least some of the work may have been done locally for Childeric, perhaps by craftspeople trained in the East. There is thus an international flavor to the barbarian side of the burial.

The Roman side is represented most strongly by a gold cruciform fibula with a finely decorated foot. Such brooches were worn by high-ranking Roman officials, affixing to the right shoulder the official purple cloak, or *paludamentum*. The gold signet ring, too, suggests both the authority of a Roman commander and the technology of writing: it is used to seal orders. The image engraved upon it deftly blends the two sides, Roman and barbarian: the king is depicted as a Roman general with cloak and body armor, but he has long hair. Long hair, a symbol of vitality, was the prerogative of the royal lineage with its claim to divine ancestry.

There were said to have been two human skulls in the grave, one smaller than the other, and this led to suggestions that Childeric had been buried with his wife, Basina. A sphere of rock crystal, always a feminine artifact, was found in the assemblage, but there are no other clearly feminine objects, so this theory seems unlikely. More plausible is the hypothesis that a horse was buried within or near the king's grave (a horse's skull was found). This is a custom with many parallels in the Germanic world, and some of the iron fragments could have derived from harness equipment. Indeed some think the enigmatic decorative objects, the bull's head and the golden bees—finds that remain unique—could have ornamented the royal harness rather than a royal robe, as was long thought.

In the 1980s understanding of Childeric's grave and its significance was revolutionized by a series of excavations led by Raymond Brulet. This research was part of a larger investigation of Tournai, originally a Roman town of secondary importance located at the border of two *civitates,* or states, whose status rose in the late empire until it became the seat of a bishopric. Why was a Frankish war leader like Childeric buried there? Nothing in the meager written sources suggests any specific connection, let alone a reason. What was the context of the grave? Was it isolated, as has often been suggested?

The site of the grave itself is precisely known, thanks to Chifflet, but inaccessible: a house with a deep cellar has replaced it. Brulet was able to excavate underneath the street in front of it, and he obtained permission from the homeowners to dig trenches in their backyards. It soon became clear that Childeric's grave was part of a cemetery where the northern Gallo-Frankish style of furnished burial was practiced: weapons common in men's graves and jewelry in women's graves, with a funerary deposit of late imperial tradition common to both. It is possible, even plausible, that Childeric's was the "founder's grave," the focal point around which the cemetery grew. The two most unexpected discoveries were the monumental conception of the entire tomb and evidence of lavish sacrifice no doubt associated with the funeral. The archaeological features upon which these deductions rest are three pits with several horse burials surrounding the royal grave like satellites and an undisturbed zone encompassing the royal grave itself. This is interpreted as evidence of a monumental tumulus, or grave mound, 20 meters or more in diameter.

Twenty-one horses were packed into the three pits. All of the skeletal material was studied carefully, and carbon-14 tests were run on bones from five animals. The results focus on the later fifth century as the most likely time of burial. The animals themselves were clearly a very selective, not a random, group. Most were geldings—warhorses—and many of the rest were stallions; only one probable mare could be identified. Four were colts, and seventeen were mounts, adults ranging from six to eighteen years old. This seems to have been the royal stable, sacrificed in a lavish gesture at Childeric's funeral.

The king was buried in a stoutly built timber funerary chamber over which the great tumulus was built. It would have been clearly visible from the Roman road, passing a little to the south on its way to the bridge over to the right bank of the Schelde (Escaut) River, where the main part of the town was located. The royal tumulus thus would have become perhaps the most striking monumental feature of the landscape around the town. It fits well with the lavish nature of the grave goods and with the extravagant gesture of sacrificing the royal stable. Was the funerary symbolism meant to recall the mighty figure of Attila, the great war leader in the time of Childeric's youth, who also was buried under a great tumulus and whose funeral featured mounted Huns circling it, singing laments?

Guy Halsall, who has insisted on the need to understand the ceremonial and even theatrical aspects of funerary practice, calls the scale of Childeric's burial display staggering. He also asserts that it was not Childeric but rather his son, Clovis, who created the tomb to demonstrate his right to succession. There is no evidence to support this hypothesis; indeed if Childeric already controlled Gaul as far south as the Loire, as Halsall, following the revisionist thesis of Edward James, argues, the choice of a small town far to the north to make this demonstration seems curious.

Brulet suggests that Tournai may have been where Childeric's ancestors were buried; a contemporary Roman writer, Bishop Apollinaris Sidonius, relates that about A.D. 450 the Salian Franks under Clodio seized the nearby *civitas* of Arras. This is likely to have been Childeric's grandfather, who then occupied the lands as far south as the Somme. As Périn points out, funerary archaeology supports this limit for Frankish power in Childeric's day, and Tournai makes more sense as a central place within it. Childeric's burial always has seemed exceptional for the lavish display of grave goods; Brulet's reconstruction of the funerary environment makes it stand out all the more, accentuating the pagan and barbarian resonance of this cosmopolitan funerary monument.

As imperial authority was fragmenting throughout the western empire and new polities, mostly identified with barbarian leaders and peoples, were emerging to replace it, funerary ritual offered a potent means to claim power symbolically. There is no reason to assume that so successful and decisive a figure as Childeric in the complex and changing political and cultural environment of the day would not have decided so fundamental a matter as his own funeral. Indeed he appears to have fashioned from various traditions (most notably the Germanic "chieftain's burials" that his Frankish ancestors had known for generations) a bold new funerary model fit for a king. Within a few years the astounding success of Clovis, eliminating rival rulers and conquering most of Roman Gaul, changed all the fundamentals of the situation. Clovis centered his new power on Paris, in the Seine basin, far southwest of Tournai. Furthermore, by converting to Catholic Christianity, Clovis turned away from the too pagan funerary model of his father. His own death in Paris in A.D. 511 opens a new funerary chapter, that of royal *ad sanctos* burial (burial next to or near a martyr or a saint-confessor).

See also **Merovingian Franks** (*vol. 2, part 7*); **Sutton Hoo** (*vol. 2, part 7*); **Merovingian France** (*vol. 2, part 7*).

BIBLIOGRAPHY

Brulet, Raymond. "La sépulture du roi Childéric à Tournai et le site funéraire." In *La noblesse romaine et les chefs barbares du IIIe au VIIe siècle*. Edited by Françoise Vallet and Michel Kazanski, pp. 309–326. Association Française d'Archéologie Mérovingienne Mémoire 9. Saint-Germain-en-Laye, France: Musée des Antiquités Nationales, 1995.

———, ed. *Les fouilles du quartier Saint-Brice à Tournai*. Vol. 2, *L'environnement funéraire de la sépulture de Childéric*. Louvain-la-Neuve, France: L'Université Catholique de Louvain, 1990–1991. (Details the excavations of the 1980s, including the original specialist reports.)

Carver, Martin. *Sutton Hoo: Burial Ground of Kings?* London: British Museum Press; Philadelphia: University of Pennsylvania Press, 1998. (See chap. 5.)

Cochet, Abbé. *Le tombeau de Childéric I, roi des Francs, restitué à l'aide de l'archéologie*. Paris: Gerald Montfort, Brionne, 1859. (A nineteenth-century attempt to put the Childeric grave in context.)

Dumas, Françoise. *Le tombeau de Childéric*. Paris: Bibliothèque Nationale, Département des Médailles et Antiques, 1976.

Gregory of Tours. *The History of the Franks*. Translated and with an introduction by Lewis Thorpe. Harmondsworth, U.K.: Penguin Books, 1974. (See book 2, sections 9, 12, and 18 on Childeric and sections 27–43 on Clovis.)

Halsall, Guy. "Childeric's Grave, Clovis' Succession, and the Origins of the Merovingian Kingdom." In *Society and Culture in Late Antique Gaul: Revisiting the Sources*. Edited by Ralph W. Mathiesen and Danuta Shanzer, pp. 116–133. Aldershot, U.K.: Ashgate, 2001.

James, Edward. *The Franks*. Oxford: Blackwell, 1988. (A revisionist view of Childeric.)

Kazanski, Michel, and Patrick Périn. "Le mobilier de la tombe de Childéric I: État de la question et perspectives." *Revue archéologique de Picardie* 3–4 (1988): 13–38.

Müller-Wille, Michael. "Königtum und Adel im Spiegel der Grabkunde." In his *Die Franken: Wegbereiter Europas*, 2 vols. Vol. 1, pp. 206–221. Mainz, Germany: Verlag Philipp von Zabern, 1996.

Périn, Patrick. *La datation des tombes mérovingiennes: Historique, méthodes, applications*. With a contribution by René Legoux. Geneva, Switzerland: Librarie Droz, 1980.

Périn, Patrick, and Laure-Charlotte Feffer. *Les Francs*. Vol. 1, *A la conquête de la Gaule*. Paris: Armand Colin, 1997.

Werner, Joachim. "Neue Analyse des Childerichgrabes von Tournai." *Rheiisches. Vierteljahrsblatter* 35 (1971): 43ff.

BAILEY K. YOUNG

EARLY MEDIEVAL IBERIA

Although early medieval Spain and Portugal may seem to stretch the definition of the "barbarian world" considerably—from the point of view of contemporaries they were perhaps one of the most "civilized" parts of the Western world at the time—they provide an interesting view of the transformation of the classical tradition as it merged with other cultures and gradually developed into new traditions that we recognize in the modern world.

It is only since the last decades of the twentieth century that archaeology has begun to transform our understanding of early medieval Iberia. In the middle decades of the twentieth century, the archaeology of Spain and Portugal was for political reasons somewhat isolated from outside trends and restricted in its discourse. Since the 1980s, medieval archaeology in Spain has benefited tremendously from a great expansion in archaeological research and from active and energetic debate of the theoretical issues. Portuguese archaeology has developed less rapidly, but important new work began to appear in the 1990s. Well-documented salvage excavations in urban centers, more detailed study of the detritus of everyday life (such as utilitarian pottery, animal bones, and traces of irrigation systems), and regional surveys of surface evidence for settlements are among the new forms of evidence available; in part it is the freedom to discuss issues of social theory such as feudalization, structures of state power, and processes of ethnic distinction that has driven this expansion of archaeological research.

HISTORICAL OVERVIEW

A brief overview of the sequence of events known from written historical sources helps to provide a framework for understanding the effects of modern archaeology on our understanding of early medieval Iberia. The Early Middle Ages have rarely been treated as a unified topic by historians; a great divide has traditionally existed between historians who study sources written in Latin and those who study sources in Arabic. The Latin sources tend to be frustratingly sparse and brief, but they are the only evidence for the period before 711 and the principal evidence for northern Spain after that date as well. The Arabic sources are more informative but also more limited in their coverage, and less accessible to most Western scholars. Only the florescence of archaeological research beginning in the late twentieth century has made it possible to transcend this linguistic divide and see the continuities in the Early Middle Ages of Spain and Portugal.

In A.D. 400, Spain and Portugal had been part of the Roman Empire for hundreds of years. A complex provincial administration based in major cities, trade connections with the entire Mediterranean basin, and a cosmopolitan culture combining classical Latin learning with the new imperial religion of Christianity were all part of the legacy of Roman rule. A few years later, however, the defenses of the western Roman frontier collapsed, and the Suevians, Vandals, and Alans, tribes from what is now Germany, entered the Roman provinces. The Suevians, together with fragments of the other tribes,

Selected sites in early medieval Iberia.

took over what is now northern Portugal and northwestern Spain.

As the Western Roman Empire collapsed during the course of the fifth century, the Visigoths (a Germanic tribe from eastern Europe) formed a kingdom in southern France that eventually expanded into Spain. Over the course of the fifth century, the Visigoths extended their control over all of Roman Spain and Portugal except for the Suevian enclave in the northwest. Through a long series of wars with the Suevians, the native tribes of mountainous northern Spain, and eastern Roman armies that attempted to reestablish Roman rule in southern Spain, the Visigothic kings eventually united all of the Iberian Peninsula (together with a small portion of southern France) under their rule by the early seventh century. In doing so they created a tradition of central authority and ideological uniformity, all focused on their capital in Toledo, that gave them the most powerful government in western Europe at the time.

Between 711 and 720, an invasion by a small Arab and Berber army from North Africa overthrew the Visigothic kingdom, and all of Spain and Portugal became part of the Islamic Empire. Arab rule seems to have been established quickly and with little disruption of society, but a series of civil wars among the conquerors over the next several decades may have been more destructive. The developing divisions within the Islamic world soon resulted in the establishment of an independent Arab emirate in al-Andalus, as the Arabs called their Iberian realm, ruled by the Umayyad dynasty. By the tenth century this evolved into an independent caliphate, centered on the city of Córdoba.

Unlike the Visigoths, the Arabs were unable or unwilling to maintain central control in the mountains of northern Spain. Perhaps as early as 718, some Visigothic nobles in the Asturias of northwestern Spain had set up an independent, Christian kingdom. This kingdom gradually extended its control over Galicia, León, and Castille. During the ninth century other small Christian realms were formed by the Franks in Catalonia and the Basques in Navarre. By A.D. 1000, although the Arab Caliphate of Córdoba controlled most of the Iberian Peninsula, the Kingdom of León, the Kingdom of Pamplona, and the County of Barcelona in the north represented the origins of what would, over the course of the later Middle Ages, evolve into the modern countries of Spain and Portugal.

The written sources provide little detail, though, to flesh out this narrative with a deeper understanding of how society worked and how people lived their lives—in other words, the social and cultural processes that guided the course of historical events. Archaeological research is providing new insights into subjects where the texts raise many questions but provide few clear answers, such as the definition and evolution of ethnic and religious identities, the processes of political and social control, and the demographic and economic basis of society.

ETHNIC AND RELIGIOUS IDENTITIES

Ethnic and religious differences such as the distinctions between Catholic Christians and Arian Christians, between Christians and Muslims, between Romans and Goths or Suevians, between Latins and Arabs, or between Arabs and Berbers were of paramount importance from the point of view of the writers of the historical sources, and the persistence of other unassimilated minorities such as Basques and Jews throughout this period added to the diverse mixture. What is not clear is the practical importance that these categories had in reality. They evolved over time, and distinctions that were important in one period became unimportant later on. By showing how these identities affected behavior, archaeology makes it possible to understand their evolution more fully.

Rome's Spanish provinces were among the most romanized parts of the empire, meaning that the native populations had widely adopted Roman culture and ethnicity. The modern Castilian (Spanish), Portuguese, and Catalan languages are all descended from the Latin brought by the Romans, and the Catholic religion of Spain and Portugal was a creation of the Roman Empire. It is not clear to what degree local ethnic identities survived romanization—certainly the Basques in the Pyrenees retained their language and identity, and other peoples in remote parts of the peninsula may have as well. Similarly, scattered pre-Christian religious practices are likely to have carried on for a long time in rural areas, long after the people who maintained them had become nominally Christian. But for the most part, as far as one can see in the available evidence, the Iberian Peninsula in A.D. 400 was inhabited by people who were Roman in ethnicity and Catholic Christians by religion.

The Germanic invasions of the fifth century disrupted this seeming unity by introducing new ruling elites that identified themselves as ethnically Suevian or Visigothic. The Visigoths were also distinct religiously, because they adhered at first to a different theological tradition in Christianity known as Arianism, characterized by an interpretation of the Trinity emphasizing the separateness of its elements rather than their unity as manifestations of a single god. Although the distinction between Arians and Catholics was of great importance to theologians, it seems to have had little practical effect on daily life. There is no way, for example, to distinguish an Arian cathedral from a Catholic one from their archaeological traces, nor do people seem to have made an effort to use clothing, household behavior, or burial rituals to proclaim their identity with one or the other form of Christianity. If there was an effect, it was a negative one—that only after 589, when the Visigothic regime officially adopted Catholicism, was the powerful intellectual tradition of the Hispano-Roman Catholics turned to the active ideological support of the Gothic state.

This conflict, however rarified, may nonetheless have had an effect on the attitudes of the Spanish Church. Jerrilynn Dodds, in *Architecture and Ideology in Early Medieval Spain* (1990), has suggested that the defensive position of the Spanish church, subordinated first to the Arian Visigoths and later to Islam, manifested itself architecturally in a use of constricted, horseshoe-shaped arches and apses as well as screens or barriers separating choir from congregation to create secretive, enclosed spaces for the performance of the liturgy. It is difficult, however, to verify such interpretations of subtle, subconscious meanings.

The Visigoths and Suevians constituted only a small minority of the population. In the fifth century their ethnic identity must have been quite distinct from that of the native Hispano-Roman population, but this identity has left few obvious traces archaeologically. They seem to have adopted the culture of the Roman provinces very rapidly in almost all respects. What were traditionally identified as Visigothic cemeteries in northern Spain, for example, are now thought by many to be related to changes in Roman society, not to Visigothic traditions. A few artifact types may have served specifically to signify this ethnic distinction, such as eagle-shaped brooches, but over time the sense of ethnic differentness between Hispano-Romans and the Germanic conquerors seems to have lost its importance to people. For the most part, the archaeological evidence suggests that the Visigoths and Suevians rapidly assimilated to Hispano-Roman culture. By the seventh century, the ethnic distinction between Hispano-Romans and the Germanic Visigoths or Suevians seems to have merged with and been superseded by concepts of social class and wealth. Like the distinction between Arianism and Catholicism, this ethnic divide does not seem to have had enough practical importance to sustain itself in the long run. In the eighth century and later, Latin Christians in Spain seem to have regarded their Visigothic and Roman pasts as parts of a single cultural heritage.

The social divisions brought about by the Arab conquest proved to be a different matter. Like the Visigoths and Suevians, the Arabs and Berbers were at first a small minority relative to the native population, and initially they brought few significant cultural differences, with the important exception of their religion. Unlike Arianism, Islam manifested its differentness not only in abstract theological concepts but also in many aspects of daily life, from what one could eat or drink, to the daily routine of prayer, to the appropriate placement of the dead in their graves. This religious distinction is not only more visible archaeologically, but it also would have given the boundary between Muslims and Christians more force in processes of cultural change. Cultural assimilation worked both ways in this instance—the Latin Christian population of al-Andalus gradually assimilated to the culture of their rulers, becoming Muslim Arabs, but the Islamic civilization that they adopted was itself heavily influenced by Hispano-Roman culture. The Great Mosque of Córdoba, for example, built in stages from the eighth to tenth centuries, combines elements of Hispano-Roman and Byzantine architectural styles into a building whose function was specifically Islamic (fig. 1).

The immediate effect of the Arab conquest on the archaeological record was probably small, due to the limited numbers of the invaders. It is debated, for example, whether Berber styles of pottery were introduced to Spain in the eighth century. The process of Islamization of the native population, however, had a more prominent impact over time; it is likely that by A.D. 1000 a majority of the population had converted to Islam, and Arabic was probably becoming the most common language.

Food remains provide one way to observe this process. In Roman times, pork was an important source of meat in many parts of Spain, and this continued to some extent through the Visigothic period. After the Arab conquest, the frequency of pig bones in archaeological sites gradually declined, probably indicating conversion of the population to Islam, which prohibits the eating of pork. Pig bones usually continue to be present in small quantities, though, suggesting the presence of a Christian minority even in mainly Muslim communities. An exception that proves the rule is a site in southeastern Spain called the Rábita de Guardamar, a retreat where Muslim warriors could combine asceticism, religious contemplation, and defense of their faith. Not surprisingly, such a specifically Islamic site lacks pig bones.

POLITICAL COMPLEXITY AND THE ORGANIZATION OF SOCIETY

As the rulers changed from Romans to Visigoths to Arabs, the structures of political control and social dominance, unsurprisingly, changed as well. The scanty written documentation gives little insight into the processes of control, however, except to some degree in the caliphate toward the end of the Early Middle Ages.

The Roman government was not the massive bureaucratic system that modern governments are, but by ancient standards it was a powerful and ambitious state. A complex taxation system was administered by professional civil servants, and the proceeds were used to support a standing army, public works such as roads and bridges, and of course the administrative system itself. The government produced massive quantities of coinage as a medium for its taxes and expenditures, and it produced many facilities such as forts and government buildings.

As the Roman Empire disintegrated, its successors such as the Visigoths and the Suevians attempted to retain as much of the Roman administrative system as served their purposes. Invasion and war-

Fig. 1. Rows of columns inside the Mezquita mosque in Córdoba, Spain. © VITTORIANO RASTELLI/CORBIS. REPRODUCED BY PERMISSION.

fare must have disrupted many governmental functions, though, and they had probably already been in decline in later Roman times. In the middle of the fifth century, for example, while the city of Tarragona was still under Roman administration (which lasted there until around 470), what had earlier been public buildings and spaces, such as the provincial forum, had clearly lost their political function and were used as quarries for old building stone and dumping grounds for garbage. In Valencia, the Roman forum was replaced in the fifth century by a church (probably the city's cathedral) and a cemetery, not only indicating the decline of the former civic administration but also symbolizing how the church hierarchy was replacing the old institutions of local authority.

The Suevians and Visigoths, who had no tradition of administrative government, relied on surviving Roman institutions to control and exploit their new territories, but probably at a more limited level of activity. They produced coinage derived from Roman types, but in limited quantities and mostly in gold, suitable for large payments within the rul-ing class but not for everyday use in small transactions. Some public works and state construction projects continued under the Visigoths, but the evidence is much more scarce than for the Roman period; no facilities for a professional standing army are apparent, for example. The state seems also to have been less able to enforce even the policies it was interested in; for example, despite draconian legislation in the seventh century intended to suppress Judaism, Jewish tombstones inscribed in Hebrew were still made.

This decline of state control seems to have affected the entire population in another way. The Roman government had been able to maintain peace and enforce laws well enough for people to live dispersed throughout the country with reasonable security. As Roman rule broke down, however, people tended to live in more clustered settlements, often in defensible locations, in some cases reusing prehistoric hillforts. This change suggests that the people in the countryside were at increased risk from marauders, bandits, feuds, or other forms of small-scale violence.

In sociopolitical organization as in many other things, the Christian north and the Islamic center and south followed different trajectories after the Islamic conquest. This has been made most clear since the late 1970s through studies of the social role of castles.

In much of western Europe, particularly France, medieval castles first appeared as part of a social transformation in which a class of feudal lords emerged during the tenth and eleventh centuries and seized for themselves on a local basis the political powers formerly exercised by the kings as well as by communities of free peasants, who were then reduced to serfdom. Castles served as the focal points of feudal settlement, and thousands were built during the decades around the year 1000. As feudal lords obtained economic power over the peasants, previously dispersed rural settlement was restructured in the form of larger villages located near the castles, so that compulsory labor service was easily accessible to the lords.

This transition to feudalism is generally agreed to have occurred also in Catalonia, which had close ties to France at the time. It is more disputed to what degree these changes happened in other parts of Spain or in Portugal. In the Kingdom of León, castles were built and villages were established as in France, but they seem to have happened separately, not as part of a single, drastic transformation of society. The written sources likewise suggest that neither royal power nor the freedom of the peasantry was so completely usurped there.

In Islamic al-Andalus, as well, castles became abundant, in contrast to their absence in most other Islamic lands at the time. And in some ways these castles may have had functions similar to those of northern Spain, especially in areas where the Muslim elite was formed from converted Hispano-Gothic nobles. Because society was organized differently in al-Andalus, though, the seizure of power by local nobles that was the essence of feudalism did not happen there. Castles in al-Andalus served as defensive refuges and as local outposts of the central administration, so rather than causing a restructuring of rural settlement for the benefit of local lords, they were instead placed where people already were.

POPULATION, TRADE, AND THE ECONOMY

Traditionally, the end of the Roman Empire was imagined in apocalyptic terms of collapse and destruction. Modern research has modified this attitude in many important ways, emphasizing the continuities from Roman times to the Early Middle Ages as well as the creativity and vitality of late ancient and early medieval civilization. Nevertheless, many changes occurred in the material aspects of life. Although there are difficulties with the evidence, the overall pattern appears to be one of economic decline from the later part of the Roman period through the Visigothic period, with gradual recovery beginning in the ninth or tenth century. These trends appear in the evidence relating to rural population, urbanism, and trade.

Under Roman rule, the Iberian Peninsula was densely settled with an assortment of towns and villages, small farms, and large aristocratic villas, most often situated in the best agricultural land. Although many of these sites remained occupied into the fifth and sixth centuries, the number of sites declined, and those that remained were smaller; also, as noted above, new sites were often in defensive locations. By the seventh century, a very different pattern had taken shape: people lived mostly in small sites, which were much less abundant and which were commonly located in mountainous areas or inaccessible hilltops. This pattern, which suggests both a substantial decline in population and a concern with defense instead of maximization of production, continued through the Arab conquest into the ninth century. Only from the late ninth or tenth century does there seem in many regions to have been an expansion of settlement back into lower, more productive, but also more vulnerable areas.

Towns and cities followed a broadly parallel trend. By late Roman times, not only the public buildings but also many residential areas of the towns had fallen out of use, suggesting a diminished number of residents. Although written sources seem to indicate that towns and cities remained important centers of civil and religious administration throughout the Early Middle Ages, the archaeological evidence is sparse. In many urban excavations in Spain, a late Roman level is immediately followed by deposits of the tenth or eleventh century or later, suggesting relatively little occupation during the intervening centuries. Some structures, especially churches, mosques, and fortifications, are known, but the paucity of associated habitation material seems to indicate that the towns remained centers of religious and political activity but were no longer centers of population or economic activity. The few locations where early medieval occupation levels have been found are often restricted in area and associated with defensive locations or religious facilities. In Mérida, one of the few towns where urban excavation has revealed early medieval habitations, they take the form of reuse of semi-ruined Roman buildings, subdivided into small apartments, eventually abandoned, and not replaced with new structures until the ninth century.

The decline in urban occupation is probably related to general changes in the economy during the Early Middle Ages. Under the Roman Empire, the countries around the Mediterranean were linked by active networks of long-distance trade, which can be observed archaeologically in the remains of nonperishable goods such as pottery. Even in the fifth and sixth centuries, pottery types made in what are now Tunisia, Turkey, and other places all around the Mediterranean were regularly available in the coastal cities of Spain and Portugal. After 550, however, these imports rapidly declined, and they ceased entirely by the latter half of the seventh century. Although exchange of goods and ideas did not cease entirely, long-distance trade on a scale large enough to be archaeologically significant did not resume until the tenth century and later.

The economic changes were not limited to overseas trade; the evidence for specialized production and local exchange within the Iberian Peninsula shows a similar pattern. In fact, for a long time this pattern obscured the archaeology of the Early Middle Ages. In previous generations, when medieval archaeology was closely connected with art history, the shortage of finely produced items in early medieval Spain and Portugal, compared to the Roman and late medieval periods, made it difficult to study the period. The Visigothic period was best known from metalwork such as brooches and belt buckles found in cemeteries and from stonecarving associated with churches. So skilled craftspersons continued to exist, but they seem to have been much less abundant than in the Roman period, since few such objects are found in ordinary sites.

Referring once again to the artifacts that are most abundant on archaeological sites, the finely made, decorated table pottery of the late Roman period disappeared after the fifth or sixth century, and then only plain, coarse pottery was made—often without the use of the potter's wheel, which is essential for producing in large quantities—until new styles of decorated tablewares based on eastern Islamic traditions appeared in the late ninth century.

These patterns of economic production are far from the religious and political concerns of the written historical sources, but by elucidating the context in which the recorded events took place, they may provide an essential part of improved explanations of how culture and society changed in Spain and Portugal during the early Middle Ages. Historical events are necessarily shaped by the economic and social context in which they occur, and this context is lacking in the very limited written history of early medieval Spain and Portugal. For example, the inability of the Visigoths to form an effective resistance after their king was defeated at the beginning of the Islamic conquest has been attributed by historians to moral decay or overcentralized rulership. But it may be just as significant that the population of the region was at the bottom of a long process of decline in the eighth century and that economic disintegration would have made coordination difficult. These same factors also raise some interesting questions about the effects of the demographic and economic growth that appeared in the ninth and tenth centuries, such as whether some regions grew earlier or faster and therefore had advantages in political competition. Future archaeological research has the potential to address such questions, which could not even have been asked until the late twentieth century.

See also **Visigoths** (*vol. 2, part 7*).

BIBLIOGRAPHY

Acién Almansa, Manuel. "Poblamiento y fortificación en el sur de al-Andalus." In *Actas del III Congreso de Arqueología Medieval Española*. Vol. 1, pp. 135–150. Oviedo, Spain: Universidad de Oviedo, 1989.

Alba Calzado, Miguel. "Ocupación diacrónica del área arqueológica de Morería (Mérida)." In *Mérida: Excavaciones arqueológicas, 1994–1995*. Edited by Pedro Mateos Cruz, Miguel Alba Calzado, and Juana Márquez Pérez, pp. 285–315. Mérida, Spain: Consorcio Ciudad Monumental Histórico-Artística y Arqueológica de Mérida, 1997.

Barceló, Miquel. "Los *ḥuṣūn*, los *castra* y los fantasmas que aún los habitan." In *Castillos y territorio en al-Andalus.* Edited by Antonio Malpica. Granada: Athos-Pérgamos, 1998, pp. 10–41.

Bazzana, André, Patrice Cressier, and Pierre Guichard. *Les châteaux ruraux d'al-Andalus.* Madrid: Casa de Velázquez, 1988.

Benito Iborra, Miguel. "La evolución estructural de las sociedades históricas del sur de la Comunidad Valenciana." In *Actas del IV Congreso de Arqueología Medieval Española.* Vol. 1, pp. 151–168. Alicante, Spain: Diputación Provincial de Alicante, 1993.

Collins, Roger. *Early Medieval Spain: Unity in Diversity, 400–1000.* 2d ed. New York: St. Martin's, 1995.

Dodds, Jerrilynn D. *Architecture and Ideology in Early Medieval Spain.* University Park: Pennsylvania State University Press, 1990.

Dodds, Jerrilynn D., Bernard F. Reilly, and John W. Williams. *The Art of Medieval Spain, A.D. 500–1200.* New York: Metropolitan Museum of Art, 1993.

Fernandes, Isabel Cristina F., and A. Rafael Carvalho. "Cerâmicas muçulmanas do Castelo de Palmela." In *La céramique médiévale en Méditerranée, actes du VIe congrès de l'AIECM2.* Edited by G. Démians d'Archimbaud, pp. 327–335. Aix-en-Provence, France: Narration Éditions, 1997.

Glick, Thomas F. *From Muslim Fortress to Christian Castle: Social and Cultural Change in Medieval Spain.* Manchester, U.K.: Manchester University Press, 1995.

———. *Islamic and Christian Spain in the Early Middle Ages.* Princeton, N.J.: Princeton University Press, 1979.

Gómez Becerra, Antonio. "El litoral granadino en época altomedieval (siglos VII–XI): Poblamiento, navegación y defensa." *Arqueología y territorio medieval* 7 (2000): 7–21.

Gutiérrez Lloret, Sonia. "De la *civitas* a la *madīna:* destrucción y formación de la ciudad en el sureste de Al-Andalus: el debate arqueológico." In *Actas del IV Congreso de Arqueología Medieval Española.* Vol. 1, pp. 13–35. Alicante, Spain: Diputación Provincial de Alicante, 1993.

———. "Production and Trade of Local and Regional Pottery in Early Medieval Spain (7th–9th Centuries): The Experience of the Southeast of the Iberian Peninsula." *Boletín de arqueología medieval* 6 (1992): 9–22.

Keay, S. J. *Roman Spain.* London: British Museum Press, 1988. (See particularly chap. 9, "The End of Roman Spain.")

Martí, Ramón, and Sergi Selma. "La huerta de la madīna de Šubrub (Segorbe, Castelló)." *Boletín de arqueología medieval* 9 (1995): 39–51.

Olmo Enciso, Lauro. "Consideraciones sobre la ciudad en época visigoda." *Arqueología y territorio medieval* 5 (1998): 109–118.

Ramallo Asensio, Sebastián F. "Arquitectura doméstica en ámbitos urbanos entre los siglos V y VIII." In *Visigodos y Omeyas: Un debate entre la antigüedad tardía y la alta edad media.* Edited by L. Caballero Zoreda and P. Mateos Cruz, pp. 367–384. Madrid: Consejo Superior de Investigaciones Científicas, 2000.

Reynolds, Paul. *Settlement and Pottery in the Vinalopó Valley (Alicante, Spain), A.D. 400–700.* BAR International Series, no. 588. Oxford: Tempvs Reparatvm, 1993.

Ripoll López, Gisela. "The Arrival of the Visigoths in Hispania: Population Problems and the Process of Acculturation." In *Strategies of Distinction: The Construction of Ethnic Communities, 300–800.* Edited by Walter Pohl and Helmut Reimitz, pp. 153–187. Leiden, The Netherlands: Brill, 1998.

Salvatierra Cuenca, Vicente. "The Origins of al-Andalus (Eighth and Ninth Centuries): Continuity and Change." In *The Archaeology of Iberia: The Dynamics of Change.* Edited by Margarita Díaz-Andreu and Simon Keay, pp. 265–278. New York: Routledge, 1996.

Taller Escola d'Arqueologia. *Un abocador del segle V d.C. en el fòrum provincial de Tàrraco.* Memòries d'Excavació 2. Tarragona, Spain: Ajuntament de Tarragona, 1989.

Wolf, Kenneth B. *Conquerors and Chroniclers of Early Medieval Spain.* 2d ed. Translated Texts for Historians 9. Liverpool, U.K.: Liverpool University Press, 1999.

DAVID YOON

PRE-VIKING AND VIKING AGE NORWAY

Norway is a long, narrow, mountainous strip of land on the northwestern edge of the European continent, facing the North Atlantic Ocean. The word means "the way to the north" and originally may have designated the sea-lane along the coast. This is in line with the connections and developments of Norway as a primarily maritime nation through history. Throughout the centuries an exchange of goods, people, and ideas traveled both southward and westward. About the year A.D. 1000 the Christian faith was introduced to Norway from England, but in the later Middle Ages relations with Rome were carried on with Germany as the intermediary. Danish and German influences were long paramount, until new connections with the west were formed in the seventeenth century.

The first evidence of people in Norway dates to 9000–8000 B.C. from the sites of Komsa in Finnmark and Fosna in the Møre area. We do not know who the first Norwegians were, because two different migration routes are possible, one from the north through the Kola Peninsula and one via Sweden and Denmark. The Stone Age in Norway dates from 5000 to 3000 B.C. and is characterized by hunters and gatherers that used coarse tools, especially axes, and had domesticated dogs. During the Late Stone Age (3000–1500 B.C.), domesticated cattle and the beginnings of agriculture made their appearance. This period also marked the first evidence of an artistic tradition. Rock carvings of fish and reindeer have been discovered. The one burial dating from this period, located east of the Oslo-

fjord, is a collective grave. In later time periods single graves came into use.

During the Bronze Age (1500–500 B.C.), there are more extensive settlements and finer tools and weapons. Bronze (a copper and tin alloy) is not indigenous to Norway, and it had to be imported. This metal probably indicates status when found at archaeological sites. From this time period, there are magnificent rock carvings depicting sundials, wheels, oxen and oxen-driven carts, ships, and fish and fishing. All the rock carvings are located on rock faces with water cascading down or in indentations that collect water. A series of large mounds of stone and gravel are preserved from this time period and contain the bodies of powerful chieftains. These mounds also are placed in key locations in the landscape visible by outsiders, possibly as a sign of power and claim on the land. Later in this time period, the tradition moved toward cremation burials, where the remains were buried in urns.

About 500 B.C. iron first came to Norway. The pre-Roman Iron Age, or Celtic Iron Age (500–1 B.C.), primarily is known through archaeological work in southern Norway. Archaeological research in connection with urban development has provided insights on settlement and settlement patterns. It was a challenging time for agriculture, owing to climatic deterioration. The end of this period brought the Scandinavian countries into close association with the Roman civilization. The Roman Iron Age (A.D. 1–400) was marked by trade items from the Roman Empire, and Scandinavians came into contact not just with a different culture but also with Christianity, literacy, and a written alphabet. Both cremation and inhumation burials are found dating to this period. Many of the inhumation burials lie near megalithic monuments, often adorned with runic inscriptions. When the Roman Empire collapsed as the result of pressure from the Germanic migration (A.D. 400–600), a period of unrest also was felt in Norway by new invading tribes, marked by the ruins of local fortresses. This was termed the Migration period. The following period, the Merovingian (A.D. 600–800), saw powerful chieftains in the area, and close contact with the Germanic language–speaking peoples is witnessed in the rise of ornamental art, such as wood carvings, which flourished in the first historic period, the Viking Age.

The Viking Age was the result of linked economic intensification, military and technological advances, climate change, and, particularly, intense competition among chiefly elites and between elites and commoners. The era saw escalating Nordic impact upon northwestern Europe and a dramatic expansion of European settlement into the offshore islands of the North Atlantic. Early in this period, Norwegians settled in the Shetlands and Orkneys and Swedes on the coasts of Finland and Estonia. In these early expansionistic movements, the motive seems to have been more of peaceful integration rather than aggression and war.

The attack on the monastery of Lindisfarne off the coast of Northumberland in 793 marked the beginning of an era that has forever given the Vikings the reputation of raiders. The Viking expeditions were eastward and westward. Swedes who sailed the Baltic and founded the kingdom of Gardarike, with Novgorod and Kiev as the main cities, primarily undertook the eastward expansion. Voyages on the Russian rivers brought them all the way to the Byzantine Empire and Constantinople (modern-day Istanbul), where many of these Vikings entered as soldiers in the Roman emperor's guard and were called Varangians. Some of the Varangians were Norwegians, the most noteworthy of them being the half-brother of Saint Olaf, Harald Sigurdson. He actually became chief of the Varangians and, upon his return to Norway, king. Rich finds of Arabian and Byzantine coins tell of the trade connections between the Orient and the Nordic countries at the time.

Three ship burials dating to the early part of the Viking Age have been unearthed: the Tune, Oseberg, and Gokstad ships. Ships typically were used for the burial of nobles. The fine craftsmanship and flexible frame, in conjunction with a shallow keel, made the Viking boat a formidable tool in surprise attacks. This construction also allowed ease in transport when the waters were too shallow or when a strip of land was blocking the river, as they could be lifted over narrow stretches of land so that the voyage could continue on the other side.

The economic basis of the Viking expansion has attracted a growing body of scholarship, increasingly based upon a rich archaeological record, illustrating that economic power, military power, religious authority, and competitive display were interlocking elements in elite strategies for aggrandizement. They also were key points of friction with the long-established leveling mechanisms of Iron Age Germanic society. Viking Age chiefly economics ultimately was not about money but about honor and power. Wealth generated from successful farming, intensified fishing, loot, trade, or protection selling was not an end in itself but a means to acquire the key elements of chieftainship. Among these prerogatives were well-armed retainers, loyal clients, fine clothing and weapons, exotic objects for display and award, and spectacular architectural settings for glorious feasts and impressive ritual moments. Evidence of ritualistic activity, such as feasting and horse fighting, is evident in materials from the Merovingian site of Åker, near Hamar in Norway.

In arctic Norway, mighty chieftainships grew up on the Lofoten and Vesterålen Islands during the Late Iron Age, creating a power center that was to contest primacy with the expanding petty kingdoms of western and southern Norway for a long time. Research on animal bone material from Iron Age sites (both pre-Viking and Viking) in northern Norway reveals great insight into the structure of political economy of these northern chiefly establishments. Huge boathouses, extensive farms, and at least one large feasting hall at Borg, equipped with imported gold and glass that must have rivaled any similar structure below the Arctic Circle, point to the formation of a political power center in the area. While the warm currents of the North Atlantic drift allowed some barley growing in these offshore arctic islands, most barley production probably was reserved for beer rather than porridge. The majority of the diet was supplied by meat and milk of domestic stock, birds and bird eggs, sea mammals, and, especially, the abundant stocks of marine fish, whose spawning grounds surround Lofoten and Vesterålen.

The development of fishing, in particular, and the building of a monetary economy based on the exchange and trade of a storable product, such as dried fish (stockfish), in the twelfth century A.D. allowed a mercantile connection of these arctic lands with mainland Europe. Royal and church patronage had created a vast investment in the specialized exploitation of the abundant cod stocks accessible from the Lofoten and Vesterålen islands. Settlement pattern, scheduling of subsistence activities, division of labor, gender roles, and relations between Scandinavian and Saami populations all were affected by the profound economic and social transformation. During the Iron Age the Norse were not unfamiliar with the concepts of intensive fishing and the use of stockfish (beheaded air-dried codfish) as an integral part of this multifaceted political economy. Stockfish became the key product that connected this northern land with the mercantile economies of mainland Europe during the eleventh and twelfth centuries.

The difference between the Iron Age and medieval times lies in the focus and scope of the activity as well as the nature of the controlling elements. In both eras, elites were transforming fish into objects of abstract value. In the Iron Age fish was used for prestige by facilitating the purchase of barley for beer making, for getting furs that then were traded for luxury items in distant ports, and, of course, for feeding people both at home and during voyages. All these transactions garnered the ultimate products of "honor," prestige, and lineage power. In medieval times the transformation was of a different nature. Fish no longer was used for acquisition of prestige but rather as money. Fish therefore, did not just change into an object of abstract value but was altered further to become an abstract commodity. Its value went beyond the local and regional level to achieving a truly international scale.

A frequently cited account by a North Norwegian chieftain Ottar (recorded in the court of King Alfred of Wessex in the ninth century) provides a description of chiefly economics, mentioning in-

come from "tribute" collected regularly from the Saami peoples for reindeer farming, and from both the Saami and the Norse for whaling and walrus hunting. According to N. Lund, a wandering Anglo-Saxon scribe noted that this North Norwegian chieftain owned far fewer cattle than any respectable thane of Wessex but was "accounted wealthy in his own country." As King Alfred knew all too well, Nordic seafaring skills allowed for the acquisition of wealth from raiding, protection racketeering (*Danegeld* collection—payment to the Vikings in England and France for not being plundered and for the assurance of defense, if necessary), and large-scale slaving as well as fishing and maritime trade. In the three centuries between A.D. 800 and 1100, Iron Age Scandinavians became major players in the royal politics of northwestern Europe, and for a brief period in the early eleventh century a single Scandinavian dynasty controlled most of England, Denmark, and Norway. Several scholars have argued that the escalating raids and massive wealth generated by Viking activity contributed greatly to social changes that eventually promoted stable monarchies in Scandinavia and thus contributed to the demise of chiefly Viking Age politics in Denmark, Norway, and Sweden by A.D. 1100.

By the tenth and eleventh centuries Norway, as well as the rest of Scandinavia, became Christianized. The early kings used Christianity as an ideological reinforcement for their fledgling states. These kings promoted the development of ecclesiastical centers at foci of secular power, such as Hamar and Nidaros (present-day Trondheim), and the shift from the chieftain's farm to the churchyard marks the beginning of the Middle Ages.

See also **Viking Ships** (*vol. 2, part 7*); **Viking Settlements in Orkney and Shetland** (*vol. 2, part 7*); **Viking York** (*vol. 2, part 7*); **Pre-Viking and Viking Age Denmark** (*vol. 2, part 7*); **Pre-Viking and Viking Age Sweden** (*vol. 2, part 7*).

BIBLIOGRAPHY

Bigelow, Gerald F., ed. *The Norse of the North Atlantic.* Acta Archaeologica, no. 61. Copenhagen, Denmark: Munksgaard, 1991.

Fitzhugh, William W., and Elisabeth I. Ward, eds. *Vikings: The North Atlantic Saga.* Washington, D.C.: Smithsonian Institution Press and National Museum of Natural History, 2000.

Gelsinger, Bruce E. *Icelandic Enterprise: Commerce and Economy in the Middle Ages.* Columbia: University of South Carolina Press, 1981.

Hansen, Jan Ingar, and Knut G. Bjerva, eds. *Fra Hammer til Kors: 1000 år med kristendom Brytningstid I Viken Chr* [From hammers to crosses: 1000 years from the transition to Christianity in Viken]. Oslo, Norway: Schibsteds Forlag A/S, 1994.

Jones, Gwyn. *The Norse Atlantic Saga: Being the Norse Voyages of Discovery and Settlement to Iceland, Greenland, and North America.* Oxford: Oxford University Press, 1986.

————. *A History of the Vikings.* 2d ed. Oxford: Oxford University Press, 1984.

Lund, N. *Two Voyagers, Othere, & Wulfstan at the Court of King Alfred.* York, U.K.: William Sessions, Ltd., 1984.

Midgaard, John. *A Brief History of Norway.* Copenhagen, Denmark: Aschehoug Press, 1989.

Perdikaris, Sophia. "From Chiefly Provisioning to Commercial Fishery: Long-Term Economic Change in Arctic Norway." *World Archaeology* 30, no. 3 (2000): 388–402.

————. "Status and Economy: A Zooarchaeological Perspective from the Iron Age Site of Åker, Norway." In *Debating Complexity.* Edited by D. A. Meyer, P. C. Dawson, and D. T. Hanna. Proceedings of the Twenty-sixth Annual Chacmool Conference. Calgary, Canada: Chacmool Archaeological Association, 1993.

Sturluson, Snorri. *From the Sagas of the Norse Kings.* Translated by Erling Monsen with A. H. Smith. Oslo, Norway: Dreyers Forlag, 1988.

Thurston, Tina. *Landscapes of Power, Landscapes of Conflict: State Formation in the South Scandinavian Iron Age.* Fundamental Issues in Archaeology. New York and London: Kluwer Academic/Plenum Publishing, 2001.

Time-Life Books, eds. *Vikings: Raiders from the North.* Alexandria, Va.: Time-Life Books, 1993.

Urbańczyk, Przemysław. *Medieval Arctic Norway.* Warsaw, Poland: Zaklad Poligraficzny Press, 1992.

SOPHIA PERDIKARIS

PRE-VIKING AND VIKING AGE SWEDEN

Sweden is a long and rather narrow land stretching more than 1,500 kilometers from Denmark in the south to beyond the Arctic Circle in the north. To the west it borders on Norway along a mountainous ridge; to the east it faces the Baltic Sea. The climate and vegetation of the agriculturally rich area of Skåne (Scania) in the south is similar to that of Denmark—to which this province formerly belonged. The open plain of Skåne lies immediately across a narrow waterway from the Danish island of Sjælland (Zealand). The large lakes Vänern, Vättern, Hjälmaren, and Mälaren dominate the middle of Sweden, which is also dotted with thousands of small lakes. The land in the heartland of Sweden is still gradually rising in delayed response to the melt of the weighty ice cap of the Ice Age around 6000 B.C. In areas near the present-day capital Stockholm, the moraine landscape currently rises at a rate of about one-half meter per century, which greatly affects understanding shoreline locations in prehistory. The large islands of Öland and Gotland lie to the east in the Baltic Sea. Their nodal locations have made both islands important trading locations, with Gotland in particular playing an important independent role into the medieval period. Norrland occupies the northern two-thirds of Sweden and is covered by coniferous forests cut by large parallel rivers running from the mountains down to the Gulf of Bothnia. The archaeology of this region has been studied less than the southern parts.

CHRONOLOGY

The final phase of European prehistory is the Iron Age, which follows the Stone and Bronze Ages. The Iron Age in Sweden, which begins around 400 B.C., includes the pre-Roman Iron Age (400 B.C.–A.D. 50), the Roman Iron Age (A.D. 50–400), the Migration period (A.D. 400–550), and the Vendel period (A.D. 550–800) and concludes with the Viking Age (A.D. 800–1050). The later Iron Age and thus the pre-Viking phase begins c. A.D. 400 with the Migration period, when it is possible to recognize evidence of a belief system and artistic traditions that continue through the Viking Age. The entire later Iron Age is in fact a transition from prehistory to the historic medieval Christian period, with the only contemporary writing in an indigenous runic script in which memorial stones and other objects are inscribed.

SUBSISTENCE AND BUILDING CUSTOMS

Fishing and hunting of wild animals, including moose, bear, and reindeer as well as small mammals and birds, remained important throughout the Late Iron Age—especially in Norrland—along with agriculture based on raising cattle, hogs, sheep, and goats and growing barley, rye, oats, and flax on arable land as the climate allowed. Skåne, parts of central Sweden, Öland, and Gotland were the most agriculturally rich areas. In the far north, the nomadic Saami reindeer herders moved into the region, though it is unclear whether their arrival was during the later Iron Age or the medieval period.

Characteristic house types were long rectangular houses like those known at Vallhagar near the west coast of Gotland, dating to the sixth century,

Fig. 1. Viking silver coins and jewelry found at Birka, Sweden. THE ART ARCHIVE/HISTORISKA MUSÉET STOCKHOLM/DAGLI ORTI. REPRODUCED BY PERMISSION.

apparently similar to later Viking Age halls of indigenous longhouse type that are described in saga literature. A northern Swedish farming settlement from the Early Iron Age that has been particularly well studied is that of Gene on the Norrland coast. Iron Age hillforts dot the landscape of central Sweden, the west coast, Gotland, and Öland, and there are a few along the coast of Norrland. In coastal areas, they seem to provide refuge from sea attacks and protect waterways. Stone forts were built on the Baltic Islands, including Torsburgen on Gotland and Ismanstorp and Eketorp on Öland. Hoards of Roman solidi (gold coins) deposited on the Baltic Islands from the late fifth century through the mid-sixth century also reflect unrest in this period.

BURIALS

Burials include both inhumation and cremation during the Late Iron Age, with single mounds gradually replacing mound groups yet with great variation in grave types. At Gamla (Old) Uppsala near present-day Uppsala, two of three prominent, large burial mounds at the end of a chain of mounds excavated in the nineteenth-century were dated to about

A.D. 500 and the mid-sixth century by finds of ornamented gold and bronze fragments damaged by the cremation fire. The three mounds are believed to contain the remains of successive generations of Migration period kings. Several important groups of boat burials have been investigated. At Vendel church north of Uppsala, fourteen such burials contained swords, shields, spears, helmets, domestic animals, and horse harnesses all ornamented in the eponymous Vendel style. At Valsgärde in the same region, burials of both men and women, extending in date from the Vendel period through the Viking Age, were discovered; however, while the men were interred in boats, women were cremated. By contrast, at Tuna in Badelunda in Västmanland, located in the center of Sweden, women were buried in boats and men were cremated. At Anundshög, also in Västmanland, a 15-meter-high unexcavated mound lies alongside large ship-shaped arrangements of stones of a type known from the Bronze Age through the Viking Age. Late Viking Age runic memorial stones were also raised at the site. The construction of large burial mounds represents a concentration of power necessary to command large forces of labor. In the pre-Viking Age, eastern and western Sweden formed separate regions that gradually were consolidated, with the eastern Mälaren region eventually gaining control.

CRAFT WORKING AND ARTISTIC TRADITIONS

Ornamental metalwork is often found in burials but also comes from hoards and bog finds. At the beginning of the Migration period, votive deposits were most often made in watery places—as at Skedemosse on Öland, where gold rings were discovered—whereas deposits of the later centuries were more often made on dry land. Metalwork preserves the characteristically Nordic style of animal ornamentation studied by the Swedish scholar Bernhard Salin, who described Scandinavian Styles I–III, with Style I current in the fifth century, Style II in the sixth and seventh centuries, and Style III from the eighth century into the Early Viking Age.

Migration period ornamentation is usually of gold, made from melted down late Roman solidi, which have been discovered in great numbers on the Baltic Islands. Besides the coins, the gold is found in the form of thin, disk-shaped pendants stamped on one side (known as bracteates), sword pommels, scabbard mounts, and large, extravagantly decorated collars with applied decoration. These spectacular objects, particularly from Norway and western Sweden, display the emergence of Nordic animal ornament called Salin's Style I. Style II is mainly an eastern phenomenon, found in particular on weapons and horse harnesses at sites such as Valsgärde and Vendel in Uppland, with the style often referred to as the Vendel style. Style III is a pan-Scandinavian style, manifested in wood from the Oseberg ship burial in Norway but also in gilt bronze harness mounts from Broa in Halla on Gotland as well as brooches from sites across all of Scandinavia. After the Migration period, the import of Roman gold solidi disappeared and was gradually replaced by silver from melted down Arabic dirhams reaching Scandinavia from an eastern route through Russia. The subsequent Viking styles of ornamentation have been named after the type-sites of Borre in Norway, Jelling and then Mammen in Denmark, and finally Ringerike and Urnes in Norway; however, examples of each of these formal styles are also found in Sweden.

Animal ornamentation dominates artistic production, but there are exceptional examples of figurative art. Large (as high as 2.5 meters), mushroom-shaped raised stones of the Early Viking Age on Gotland (known as picture stones) display narrative scenes of ships, battles, and heroic figures that seem to represent stories known from later saga literature and reflect Continental influence. Gold bracteate pendant amulets of the Migration period also display figures based on Roman emperor portraits that become transformed into images that may represent Nordic deities, and tiny stamped rectangles of gold called *guldgubber* (gold old men), such as from Uppåkra in Skåne, show male and female couples in greatly simplified form. On the whole, however, animal ornamentation decorates surfaces of metal brooches, buckles, and horse harnesses throughout the later Iron Age.

COMMERCE AND THE DEVELOPMENT OF TOWNS

Trading and craft-working sites developed during the later Iron Age, and by the Viking Age, some could actually be called towns. Early market and harbor sites include Åhus and Löddeköpinge in Skåne and Paviken and Fröjel on Gotland. (More sites are found along the coast every year.) Shipping technology was advanced, with the introduction of the sail before the Viking Age. Transportation along waterways of the coast and interior lakes and rivers became more important with increased long-distance trade and exploitation of resources, such as iron and furs, from the mountainous north. Luxury trade from continental Europe and from Asia is evident at some sites, particularly Helgö and Birka, both in Uppland.

Helgö is located on an island in Lake Mälaren west of Stockholm. Excavations of several groups of structures dating from the fifth through eleventh centuries were first directed by Wilhelm Holmqvist and carried out for almost thirty years after the discovery of the site in 1950. Objects of foreign origin include late Roman solidi, a Coptic bronze ladle, a western European Christian crosier, and most remarkably, a sixth-century Buddha statuette from northern India. Bronze-casting workshops in structures on terraces were revealed through the discovery of crucible fragments and ninety thousand mold fragments, particularly for Migration period jewelry types. Debate still centers around the scale and size of the site. Some believe that it was a proto-urban site for trade and manufacture, while others think that it was an exceptional economic site attached to the royal estate of Hundhamra, located on the opposite side of a narrow waterway. The florescence of Helgö occurred before the Viking Age, although it continued as an agricultural site into the eleventh century.

Near Helgö, the site of Birka on the island of Björkö appears to have taken over some of the functions of Helgö in the Viking Age. Birka became a more extensive town and trading site and is associated with the royal manor of Adelsö across a narrow strait. Unlike the other sites discussed, Birka is attested to in a contemporary document, the *Vita Anskarii,* an account of the life of Ansgar, who became bishop of Hamburg and Bremen and whose biography was written by Rimbert, his successor, around A.D. 870. Ansgar was sent in A.D. 820 and again A.D. 851–852 to a place called Birka, which was identified by the seventeenth-century antiquarian Johan Hadorf with the island of Björkö, as known from medieval times. The important complex of finds at Birka has led to its designation as a World Heritage site by the United Nations Educational, Scientific, and Cultural Organization (UNESCO). The occupation layers at Birka are extremely thick and dark—the site has thus been dubbed the "Black Earth"—and the island is dotted with cemeteries including more than two thousand cremations under mounds and one thousand inhumations. Beginning in the 1870s, the island became the focus of numerous excavations, first by Hjalmar Stolpe, who dug in the settlement area and then in the cemeteries, excavating eleven hundred inhumation and cremation graves by standards that were modern for the time. His finds from the cemeteries were not published until a hundred years later and reveal an indigenous population of farmers as well as a number of foreigners, probably merchants and craft workers. Some graves include luxuries and articles of Eastern character. Glass from the Rhineland, Slavic ceramics, Byzantine or Chinese silk, and Arabic dirham coins reflect far-flung contacts. Excavations directed by Björn Ambrosiani in the settlement area during 1990s have led to reassessment of the dating of Birka and the beginning of the Viking Age. Finds of a jetty and workshop dating from about A.D. 750 onward demonstrate that the Viking Age did not begin suddenly in the year A.D. 800. The workshop debris included thousands of mold fragments from bronze jewelry casting, antler scrap from comb making, and glass residue from bead making. These products apparently were made for local markets. Other evidence, namely bones of feet of furbearing animals from the north and iron debris worked from northern bog ore, points to the use of Birka as a center for redistribution of goods for long-range trade. Birka was a bustling trading center into the tenth century but gradually lost its importance as a harbor as the land rose and Lake Mälaren changed from an inlet of the Baltic Sea to an inland lake. The functions of Birka seem to have been taken over largely by the town of Sigtuna, located north of Birka on the Fyris River, during the Late Viking Age.

EXPANSION EASTWARD AND THE COMING OF CHRISTIANITY

Trade goods found in both Sweden and Russia reveal Swedish Viking contacts eastward across the Baltic to Russia and beyond. While western Vikings from Norway and Denmark were reviled for their raids in England and elsewhere, the eastern Vikings seem to have concentrated more on trade and colonization. In reality, most Scandinavians of the Viking Age were farmers who stayed at home. Swedish Vikings known as the Rus were instrumental in the formation of the Russian state and in the foundation of Novgorod and Kiev. They voyaged as far east as Constantinople (modern Istanbul), leaving Norse runic inscriptions as evidence of their travels. Late Viking Age rune stones with Christian crosses and prayers also reveal that many Vikings were becoming Christian during the eleventh century. Although Ansgar's mission to Birka in the ninth century failed to convert the population, contacts with the rest of Christian Europe probably made conversion inevitable. Power shifts from royal manors to ecclesiastical centers of power, such as Uppsala, not far from Sigtuna, and Sweden, become solidly linked with Christian medieval Europe as merchants and clerics move within the European core.

See also **Pre-Roman Iron Age Scandinavia** (*vol. 2, part 6*); **Viking Harbors and Trading Sites** (*vol. 2, part 7*); **Rus** (*vol. 2, part 7*); **Saami** (*vol. 2, part 7*); **Pre-Viking and Viking Age Norway** (*vol. 2, part 7*);

Pre-Viking and Viking Age Denmark (*vol. 2, part 7*).

BIBLIOGRAPHY

Ambrosiani, Björn, and Helen Clarke, eds. *Early Investigations and Future Plans: Investigations in the Black Earth*. Birka Studies 1. Stockholm, Sweden: Riksantikvarieämbetet and Statens Historiska Muséet, 1992.

Baudou, Evert, et al. *Archaeological and Palaeoecological Studies in Medelpad, North Sweden*. Kungliga Vitterhets Historie och Antikvitets Akademien. Stockholm, Sweden: Almqvist and Wiksell, 1978.

Calissendorff, Karin, et al. *Iron and Man in Prehistoric Sweden*. Translated and edited by Helen Clarke. Stockholm, Sweden: Jernkontoret, 1979.

Callmer, Johan. "Recent Work at Åhus: Problems and Observations." *Offa* 41 (1984): 63–75.

———. "Production Site and Market Area." *Meddelanden från Lunds Universitets Historiska Museum 1981–1982* 7 (1983): 135–165.

Clarke, Helen, and Björn Ambrosiani. *Towns in the Viking Age*. New York: St. Martin's, 1991.

Dahlström, Carina. "The Viking Age Harbour and Trading Place at Fröjel, Gotland: A Summary of the Excavation during the Summer of 2001." *Viking Heritage* 4 (2001): 20–22.

Edgren, Bengt, Gustaf Trotzig, and Erik Wegraeus. *Eketorp: The Fortified Village on Öland*. Stockholm, Sweden: Central Board of National Antiquities, 1985.

Hagberg, Ulf Erik. *The Archaeology of Skedemosse*. 4 vols. Stockholm, Sweden: Almqvist and Wiksell International, 1967–1977.

Hodges, Richard. *Dark Age Economics: The Origins of Towns and Trade, A.D. 600–1000*. 2d ed. London: Duckworth, 1989.

Holmqvist, Wilhelm, et al., eds. *Excavations at Helgö*. Vols. 1–14. Stockholm, Sweden: Kungliga Vitterhets Historie och Antikvitets Akademien, 1961–2001.

Jansson, Sven B. F. *Runes in Sweden*. Translated by Peter Foote. Stockholm, Sweden: Gidlunds, 1987.

Jesch, Judith. *Women in the Viking Age*. Woodbridge, Suffolk, U.K.: Boydell Press, 1991.

Larsson, Lars. "Uppåkra: A Centre in South Sweden in the 1st Millennium A.D." *Antiquity* 74 (2000): 645–648.

Nylén, Erik, and Jan Peder Lamm. *Stones, Ships, and Symbols: The Picture Stones of Gotland from the Viking Age and Before*. Stockholm, Sweden: Gidlunds, 1988.

Ohlsson, T. "The Löddeköpinge Investigation II: The Northern Part of the Village Area." *Meddelanden från Lunds Universitets Historiska Museum 1979–1980* 5 (1980): 68–111.

———. "The Löddeköpinge Investigation I: The Settlement at Vikshögsvägen." *Meddelanden från Lunds Universitets Historiska Museum 1975–1976* 1 (1976): 59–161.

Ramqvist, Per H. *Gene: On the Origin, Function, and Development of Sedentary Iron Age Settlement in Northern Sweden*. Umeå, Sweden: University of Umeå Department of Archaeology, 1983.

Roesdahl, Else. *The Vikings*. Translated by Susan M. Margeson and Kirsten Williams. New York: Penguin, 1992.

Roesdahl, Else, and David M. Wilson, eds. *From Viking to Crusader: Scandinavia and Europe, 800–1200*. New York: Rizzoli, 1992.

Sawyer, Birgit. *The Viking-Age Rune-Stones: Custom and Commemoration in Early Medieval Scandinavia*. Oxford: Oxford University Press, 2000.

Sawyer, Peter, ed. *The Oxford Illustrated History of the Vikings*. Oxford: Oxford University Press, 1997.

Stjernquist, Berta. "Uppåkra: A Central Place in Skåne during the Iron Age." *Lund Archaeological Review* 1995 (1996): 89–120.

Widgren, Mats. *Settlement and Farming Systems in the Early Iron Age: A Study of Fossil Agrarian Landscapes in Östergötland, Sweden*. Stockholm, Sweden: Almquist and Wiksell, 1983.

Zachrisson, Inger. "A Review of Archaeological Research on Saami Prehistory in Sweden." *Current Swedish Archaeology* 1 (1993): 171–182.

NANCY L. WICKER

PRE-VIKING AND VIKING AGE DENMARK

Although Danish Vikings are famous in history, much of the Viking Age lacks indigenous documents; thus, "history" largely reflects the views of Denmark's neighbors, leading to the popular connotation of a warrior culture bent on senseless or greedy destruction. In fact, in many ways Denmark was unremarkable during this era: all of the incipient post-Roman European states were equally engaged in mutual raiding, warfare, and conquest. Given the uneven historic record—literate European chroniclers versus largely prehistoric Danes, archaeology, along with careful reading of what documents there are, is the best way to understand circumstances surrounding the formation of Denmark.

Before the Viking era, A.D. 800–1050, economic and sociopolitical development in Germanic Europe, including Denmark, was profoundly influenced by interaction with the Roman Empire, whose borders lay along the Rhine; thus, the period from A.D. 1–400 is called the Roman Iron Age. Many traditions important in the state-building Viking Age are rooted here: the indigenous concept of the Danish provinces as loosely allied chiefly peer polities; the *thing,* a regularly scheduled civic meeting; a social code balancing "ordinary" people with the military hierarchy; and a tradition of long-distance trade. After Rome's fall, a period of post-Roman economic and political reorganization is referred to as the Germanic Iron Age, A.D. 400–800.

Denmark is a small, mostly archipelagic land mass, consisting of the Jutland peninsula, four large islands—Zealand, Fyn, Lolland, and Falster—and 470-odd small islands. Before 1654 Denmark included Scania and Halland, now Sweden. This geography in part determined the location of Roman Iron Age chiefdoms.

DENMARK IN THE ROMAN AND GERMANIC IRON AGES

Roman documents shed some faint light on the region, but like all nonindigenous texts, reflect outside views. Roman-Germanic interaction led to the writing of *Germania* by the Roman politician-historian Tacitus, around A.D. 98, and his description is considered fairly reliable. Tacitus describes a social code wherein leaders did not have unlimited power and required the assent of an assembly in making decisions. Several small chiefdoms operating on these principles coexisted simultaneously in the Roman era, in continual competition, yet interacting via the exchange of Roman goods. In times of warfare with Rome or other "outsiders," a single warlord was selected to lead them collectively for short periods, but the support of his peers was required. If an overly ambitious leader seized too much power, the social code actively encouraged his assassination. Other typical chiefly leveling mechanisms, such as extravagant feasting and the distribution of treasure to followers, kept a balance of power, a tradition that continued in later times.

Tacitus is amply validated through archaeological data. Competing polities and their chiefly centers can be identified by clusters of Roman imports, elite or warrior burials with Roman goods, and sacrificial deposits that were made into water—often the arms and armor of local foes, including Roman-

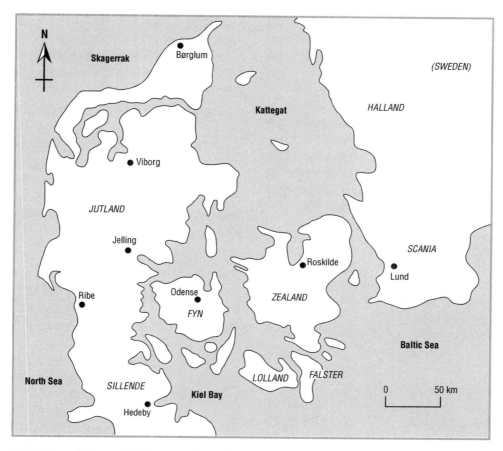

Selected pre-Viking and Viking Age sites in Denmark.

made swords. Some competing centers were located on the large, defensible, fertile islands. Similarly, bountiful Scania and Halland supported local rulers. Jutland was agriculturally poorer but ideal for cattle, and chiefly polities also rose there.

Chiefdoms were based upon what is commonly called a prestige-goods economy. Prestige goods are nonutilitarian objects that are indispensable for social and political relations—in this case, Roman imports of weapons, ornaments, and feasting and drinking equipment. In return, the Romans received leather, fur, meat, cloth, and probably slaves. In Denmark, personal reputation and power were intertwined with the ability and degree to which one could control and own Roman goods, a system that only worked if their flow was controlled by an elite minority. In return for sharing prestige goods with lower-level elites for their own legitimation, chiefs received staple tribute: livestock, grain, and other supplies. Lower-level elite in turn extracted tribute from farmers in return for their services in

defense, upholding law, and overseeing ritual activities. Grave goods reflect this hierarchy: a few have the full complement of prestige items, others less but still rich, while many have small quantities of less valuable Roman items. War chiefs had much power within society but were balanced by the *thing,* a regular meeting of freemen—and possibly some women, if we infer from some later sources—who could vote against the plans of chiefs. In addition, a chief's son was not automatically a chief; all contenders had to prove themselves, leading to a degree of upward mobility in society. One of the greatest changes during the Viking Age was the replacement of this system with a more powerful, centralized leadership and the ascribed inheritance of rulership.

In the Roman era, "Denmark" consisted of many peoples. A long-debated question has thus been "when did the Danes become the Danes?" By combining archaeology and documents, we find that the answer lies in understanding the social and political changes between the Roman, Germanic, and Viking Ages. When Rome fell in the mid-fifth century, so did the prestige economy, but most of Denmark's small realms did not collapse: they reorganized and expanded. A few groups found themselves in disarray and sought new lands, leading to what is called the Migration period, when Langobards, Teutons, and others overran the Continent and staked a claim. Despite this, around A.D. 550, Gothic writings indicate that many small polities in Denmark were being consolidated into bigger political units during the Germanic Iron Age.

DENMARK IN THE VIKING AGE

While historians mark the beginning of the Viking Age in the 790s by the first Danish sea raids on England, archaeologists are less interested in events than in processes, and they track a gradual but significant transition in political and economic organization between the eighth and ninth centuries, and beyond.

In the 700s, Frankish and English records of political, military, and economic interactions with the north describe the Danes as one people ruled by a king, and Denmark as comprising Jutland, all the islands, and Scania. Conversely, other texts state that there were simultaneously two or even three Danish kings, and to further complicate the picture, later *indigenous* chronicles state that there were sometimes one, two, or five kings.

These conflicting representations reflect the fact that protracted conflicts with the Franks elevated the temporary overlord to a more permanent ruler, or king, while the ability to claim this new position still rested on the old traditions of successful warfare, personal reputation, and distribution of wealth to followers. Several early Danish rulers were assassinated by their own people, also after ancient custom. During the 800s, a rapid succession of leaders claimed the Danish crown, fought among each other, and were overthrown, all calling themselves kings in the process. During the ninth and tenth centuries, some failed claimants grabbed parts of Europe as small kingdoms, also perhaps calling themselves Danish kings. Later, when the Danes ruled England and Denmark, a father might make his son a "sub-king" in Denmark. Slowly, Danish kings became more permanent and powerful. Sons began to inherit, some as adolescents or children, a

clear sign of a shift from achieved to ascribed status. To legitimize themselves in a world with new rules, new forms of marking and holding power emerged. One of the most prominent is at Jelling in central Jutland.

Jelling has no habitation: it is a symbolic center consisting of royal monuments and runic inscriptions (fig. 1). Some archaeologists see it as a "nationalist" response to ever-threatening Franco-Germans, others as a king's attempt to firmly legitimize his rule with both monumental architecture and written texts proclaiming his own power. These intertwined purposes are probably both true.

At Jelling, around A.D. 950, King Gorm raised a rune stone to his wife, Thyra, calling her the adornment of Denmark—the first written reference to the kingdom. Olaf Tryggvason's Saga mentions that Gorm (who reigned from about 920 to 950) cleared all remaining "petty kings" from Denmark, conquered the Slavs, and persecuted proselytizing Christians. A second rune stone was raised by Gorm's son King Harald Blåtand, commemorating his parents, his rule of a unified kingdom (from about A.D. 950 to 980), and its Christianization.

Jelling also sports two monumental earthworks: a cenotaph 77 meters across and 11 meters high, and a burial mound 65 meters across and 8.5 meters high, the largest in Denmark. When excavated, no remains, only rich grave furnishings, were found, male and female. When Harald eventually became Christian at about A.D. 970, the mound was carefully opened and his parents' bones were apparently removed to the Jelling church. Traces of this wooden stave church were excavated in the 1980s, yielding the disarticulated bones of an elderly man, clearly in secondary context, perhaps those of Gorm.

Unification of the state can be seen archaeologically. At the transition between the reigns of Harald and his son, Svein Forkbeard, a system of fortified military and administrative centers was established all over the kingdom, dated dendrochronologically to A.D. 980. These so-called Trelleborg fortresses indicate the extent of royal authority at the turn of the first millennium (fig. 2). Likewise, rune stones in a centralized style called "after-Jelling" cover the same geographic range. Also established were so-called magnate sites, estates of high-level elites who oversaw the king's business. Central structures,

Fig. 1. Viking Age stones with runic inscriptions from Jelling, Denmark. COURTESY OF THE NATIONAL MUSEUM OF DENMARK. REPRODUCED BY PERMISSION.

25–40 meters long with slightly curved walls, are called "Trelleborg" houses, since they are nearly identical to the large elite houses found at the Trelleborg administrative sites; so similar, in fact, that some suggest they were designed and built by a royal master-builder. Several have been excavated; in addition to large houses, there is evidence of attached crafts specialists, especially in metallurgy, and extensive barns and stables for many cattle and horses.

ECONOMY AND TRADE IN THE VIKING AGE

Although the Viking Age is traditionally associated with the sack of towns and monasteries in continental Europe and England, archaeologists studying Viking activities in global perspective conclude that they came not from innate hostility toward Christians or outsiders but rather were part of a much larger economic cycle. It is useful to divide Viking contacts with the rest of the world into phases. In early Viking Age expeditions, local chiefs sought wealth during a period of political change: at home,

new, centralized rulers were gaining power, so local leaders sought new means of legitimation, wealth, and fame. Over the course of the eighth to tenth centuries, raiding and trading were predicated mostly upon the economic booms and busts of the Arabian caliphates and the Byzantines, seen in the composition of coin hoards from different eras. During boom periods, chiefs gained wealth by trading to the east. When these sources failed, they gained wealth by both trading and raiding to the west. Kings, charged with ruling at home and defending the borders against the Franks—who were actively trying to conquer Denmark in the first quarter of the ninth century—had little or nothing to do with these opportunistic raids.

In the Middle Viking Age, exiled or defeated royal pretenders sought new territories to overtake and rule, eventually settling in Scandinavian enclaves in Normandy, Ireland, York, the Faeroes, and other northern islands, bringing both conflict and trade with them. Finally, in the Late Viking Age, legitimate Danish kings conquered whole nations,

Fig. 2. The fortress of Fyrkat in Denmark. Courtesy of The National Museum of Denmark. Reproduced by permission.

bringing them under Denmark's imperial sway. While collectively lumped together and called the Viking Age by historians, these phases represent very different strategies and circumstances motivating Viking activity.

The domestic economy consisted of mixed agriculture in the fertile islands, Scania and Halland, whereas husbandry predominated on Jutland. These products were important to the state, but one of the most important props for newly emerging rulers was their ability to control or administer trade. Even after Rome's fall, rulers maintained short-distance trade in luxuries to reinforce their rank in local society, and Jutland lay on sea-trade routes. Beginning around A.D. 700, proto-urban centers called "emporia," with permanent craftspeople and traders, arose to serve as both import and production sites. Precious metals and gems, ta-

bleware and glass, wine, textiles, and weapons came from all over western Europe, while local people worked iron, bone, glass, bronze, clay, and many other materials that are found archaeologically. Extensive workshop quarters have been excavated at sites such as Ribe and Hedeby. Cattle trade is seen in strata consisting primarily of dung from beasts penned for market. In these commercial centers, elites built fortifications, churches for Christian traders, and collected taxes and tolls; in return, merchants could expect protection from thieves, repair and maintenance of harbors and wharves, officials to witness agreements and transactions, and enforcement of the laws of fair trade. The taxes and revenues Danish rulers collected are explicitly referred to in Frankish texts: a series of massive earthworks, collectively called the Danevirke, were constructed by Danish rulers as a defense against the Franks over the course of the eighth and ninth centuries, but these walls also aided taxation on trade by controlling movement across the border.

Between the mid- and late tenth century, many new towns were founded: Viborg, the national *thing* where kings were still "elected" by the people; Ålborg, guarding the inland waterways of the Limfjord; Lund, the Dane's bishopric in Scania with its cathedral; Odense; Roskilde; and others. Just after the millennium, kings extended their power to collect taxes and conscript more military service, and they conferred more power on the growing church. Knut the Great ruled a large empire including England, Denmark, and parts of Norway. All was not quiet at home: several provinces rebelled, hoping to regain autonomy, but the state, forged from the conflicts and resolutions of the Viking Age, had become too powerful to resist. Knut's empire saw the largest extent of Viking Age Denmark; his sons lost their grip on this realm, and by 1042, the last Viking king, whose reign spanned the transition to the Early Middle Ages, was Sven Estridsen, who ruled a Christianized, centralized, and mostly unified Denmark. Sven made a final and unsuccessful attempt to reconquer England in 1069–1070, but with his passing in 1074, the Viking Age was truly at an end.

See also **Emporia** (*vol. 2, part 7*); **Pre-Viking and Viking Age Norway** (*vol. 2, part 7*); **Pre-Viking and Viking Age Sweden** (*vol. 2, part 7*).

BIBLIOGRAPHY

Hedeager, Lotte. *Iron Age Societies: From Tribe to State in Northern Europe, 500 B.C. to A.D. 700.* Oxford: Blackwell, 1992.

Jones, Gwyn. *A History of the Vikings.* 2d ed. London and New York: Oxford University Press, 2001.

Randsborg, Klavs. *The First Millennium A.D. in Europe and the Mediterranean.* Cambridge, U.K.: Cambridge University Press, 1991.

———. *The Viking Age in Denmark: The Formation of a State.* London: Duckworth, 1980.

Roesdahl, Else. *Viking Age Denmark.* Translated by Susan Margeson and Kirsten Williams. London: British Museum Publications, 1982.

Sawyer, Birgit, and Peter Sawyer. *Medieval Scandinavia: From Conversion to Reformation circa 800–1500.* Minneapolis: University of Minnesota Press, 1993.

Thurston, Tina L. *Landscapes of Power, Landscapes of Conflict: State Formation in the South Scandinavian Iron Age.* Fundamental Issues in Archaeology. New York: Kluwer/Plenum, 2001.

TINA L. THURSTON

FINLAND

The Late Iron Age can be said to have begun in Finland around A.D. 400. This last prehistoric period continued as long as eight centuries in parts of eastern Finland. During this time, population expanded, settlements spread, and trade contacts broadened.

WAY OF LIFE

Most Finns continued to live as semisedentary farmers practicing the slash-and-burn technique of field use. This method of agriculture requires that an area of natural growth be burned and the ash used as a supporting nutrient for several seasons of crop growth. When the land no longer produces adequately, it is allowed to lie fallow until it fully regenerates. Traditional Finnish households might move every generation or so in search of fresh arable land.

Slash-and-burn cultivation, which did not require much digging, was an excellent adaptation to most of Finland's southern and central landscape. Large areas of forests were often so stony that permanent clearance and the use of a heavy plow to cut fields of straight furrows was all but impossible. Slash-and-burn cultivation, however, cannot be practiced intensively in just one area, so most of the Finnish population remained dispersed throughout vast wilderness tracts. This dispersal of settlement occurred not only for cultivation reasons but also to gain access to good forest pasturage, hunting lands, and fishing sources. Finnish men might travel great distances during certain times of the year to hunt or fish in wilderness territories. Historical sources suggest that specific areas may have been claimed for use by certain kin- or clan-based groups.

TRADE CONTACTS AND CULTURAL INFLUENCES

The increased raiding and trading activity of the Viking Age began in Scandinavia. Finland, too, was growing restless and making new contacts abroad. Swedish farmers immigrated in earnest beginning around A.D. 400 to the Åland Islands off the coast of Varsinais Suomi, greatly changing the character of the population. More than three hundred Late Iron Age sites are known in the archipelago.

As the first millennium A.D. drew to a close, the focal points of Finnish wealth and influence, based on long-distance trade, migrated eastward to Häme and Karelia. Before the medieval period of Swedish political domination throughout the country, Finland had no centralized towns or government such as were typical elsewhere in Europe. Nevertheless, Finns were still able to organize themselves and recognize leadership on a regional basis in order to maintain systems of defensive hillforts, the distribution of rights to various northern hunting and fishing grounds, and the protection and operation of long-distance trade routes spanning the breadth of the country and beyond. The details of this kind of organization are not known, but it is clear that it existed.

In Finland the commonly recognized archaeological periods are as follows: the Viking period covers the years from A.D. 750 to 1050, followed by the Crusade period from A.D. 1050 to 1150 in western Finland and from 1050 to as late as A.D. 1300 in Karelia. Although Finns were not Vikings in the same sense that the Scandinavians were, they did participate in the eastern trade of furs, silver, and slaves that was a large part of the Viking activity in these regions. The fur trade was already becoming important in Finland in the fifth century and is credited with the growth of settlement and apparent personal wealth in Ostrobothnia and southern Häme. Finnish cultural and trade connections extended from Sweden to northern Norway in the west and to central northern Russia and the eastern Baltic lands to the east. Finnish settlements and cemeteries have been found on the shores of Lake Ladoga in present-day Russian Karelia. Items of jewelry from the Perm region of central Russia have been found in Finnish graves.

Coin hoards from the Viking period, which occur in large numbers in Scandinavia and elsewhere, are much less common in Finland. Not surprisingly, a disproportionate number (nearly a quarter of the total) occur on the Swedish-settled Ålands. These are mostly ninth- and tenth-century hoards of Islamic dirhams, a silver coin minted in vast quantities. The mainland hoards are more recent, from the eleventh century, and contain more western coins. This pattern matches the general pattern for hoards in other northern countries and reflects changing trade relations and silver sources in Russia and the Islamic countries. The Finns did not use the coins as money but rather as either raw silver measured by weight or as ornament. A number of coins have been found in graves as pendants on women's necklaces (fig. 1).

Karelia's first brush with Christianity came from the eastern Orthodox Church of Russia, but the Russians were not intent upon converting the heathens. The Roman Church, on the other hand, reaching Finland via Sweden, was very interested in promoting conversion. Many scholars think that much of Sweden's interest in this endeavor had to do with acquiring control over Finnish territory with the intent to control trade in the eastern Baltic. By converting the Finns to Christianity, the Swedes could make Finland dependent on Swedish ecclesiastical authority. Some western parts of Finland are believed to have become Christian, at least officially, by the year A.D. 1050, at the end of the Viking period. This date is probably rather early, except for a small portion of the population. Over the next century, however, Christian influence—as seen from

the evidence of changing burial rites—clearly increased.

Central and eastern Finland became Christian, under the Roman Church, at progressively later dates. Swedish domination did not touch Karelia until c. A.D. 1300 The interim period in these regions is often referred to as the Crusade period, referring, specifically, to the crusades in Finland led by the Swedes. In Karelia, however, Orthodox influences had some impact when Russian Novgorod, realizing late in the thirteenth century that it was in danger of losing its access to the Baltic Sea because of Swedish encroachments, did finally press for conversion to Orthodoxy in order to gain stronger Karelian support. The Orthodox form of Christianity is still espoused by many Karelians.

HISTORICAL SOURCES

Late Iron Age people in Finland had far-reaching contacts and lived much like their Scandinavian neighbors. The major difference is that continental Europe rarely recorded much information about Finland, and since Finnish society did not develop its own written language until the sixteenth century, no contemporary native sources of value exist. There are a few tantalizing mentions of Finns in Norse sagas, recorded mostly in the thirteenth century, but because Norse terminology often confused the identity of the various cultural groups to the east, the term "Finn" in Norse texts might refer mistakenly to the Saami. At first, medieval Finnish documents were written in Latin or Swedish, for the literate members of the society were often Swedes who were not part of Finnish culture. By the sixteenth century, Finns and others began to write about their ancient culture, but not until the nineteenth century—when folklorists and ethnographers started traveling to the Finnish interior, particularly to Karelia—did many Finnish stories, myths, poems, songs, memories, and other cultural treasures become written texts at last. A central core collection of these poems was first published as the national epic for Finland in the mid-nineteenth century under the title it continues to bear today, the *Kalevala*.

Another group that is occasionally mentioned in saga texts are the Kainulaiset ("Kvenir," in Norse sources). These people are believed to have been certain Finns from the south who (like the northern

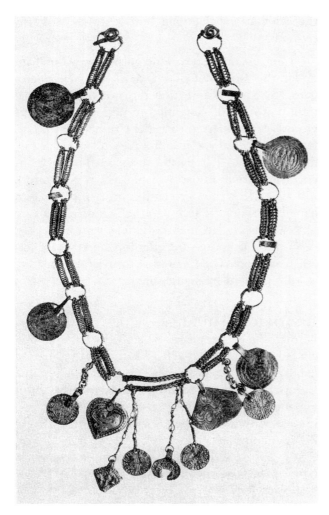

Fig. 1. Pendants made from silver coins, Finland, eleventh century. NATIONAL BOARD OF ANTIQUITIES FINLAND/E. LAAKSO 1950. REPRODUCED BY PERMISSION.

ARCHAEOLOGICAL EVIDENCE

The archaeological remains of Finnish culture from the Late Iron Age primarily consist of burials and a growing list of settlement sites, most notably in the Åland Islands off the southwest coast, which have a more temperate climate than the rest of Finland (marked by a greater percentage of deciduous trees). Island society also prospered from the rich marine environment and an accessible yet protected position between Finland and Sweden. Although ships could carefully navigate the shallow approaches to the Åland harbors, no enemy could stage a swift attack without running aground. Most of the excavated settlement units on the islands are farmsteads resembling contemporary sites in Sweden. A sign of far-flung trade contacts is seen in the "clay paw"–shaped artifacts found in many graves. These have their closest parallel in the Volga area of central Russia. About half of the excavated Iron Age graves belong to the ninth and tenth centuries.

In Varsinais Suomi, similar geological and environmental conditions enabled farmers there to adopt the more intensive methods of plowed field cultivation than seen elsewhere in Finland. It was also possible to keep larger herds of cattle. With greater food production came the possibility of denser settlements and towns. The city of Turku (Åbo in Swedish) in this province was incorporated sometime between 1290 and 1313. Finland's first university arose there. Other early medieval towns were Porvoo, founded in 1347, and Pori, in 1348. Most towns were not founded until the fifteenth century or later. Urbanization came late to Finland.

In southern Häme, near modern Hämeenlinna, a large but historically undocumented occupation site, today called Varikkoniemi, has been excavated. Some believe that the structures found here are the physical remains of a trading station holding a significant level of control over the east-west trade route through Finland's interior. The site may date as early as the Viking period.

The southern Savo region was settled by farmers mostly in the Late Iron Age. A regional survey project conducted in the 1980s noted seven previously registered hillforts and approximately twenty new sites categorized as "ancient guarding posts." There are ninety-four so-called cup-marked stones concentrated in eastern Savo. Many more occur elsewhere in Finland. The cup-marked stones are

Scandinavians) organized into large hunting and trading corporations in order to exploit the more northerly populations' ability to hunt animals producing valuable pelts. The people of Häme, in particular, competed with the Norse in what was referred to in the sagas as the taxation of the "Lapps," now known as the Saami. Finnish traders probably transported many valuable goods from the far north to Lake Ladoga where they met up with Scandinavian and Slavic traders. Another route led from the Ostrobothnian coast to Karelia via the many inland rivers and waterways. Traveling through the interior of Finland in this way was especially useful since difficult seas, lack of harbors, and the presence of pirates in the eastern Baltic made the movement of trade goods there a high-risk proposition.

Fig. 2. Grave 56 from the Luistari cemetery. PHOTOGRAPH BY RAUNO HILANDER 1969. REPRODUCED BY PERMISSION.

recognized as ritual offering places used by the pagan Finnish farmers. In the small depressions, or cup-marks, cut into large boulders, Finns would leave offerings of such things as first fruits from the harvest as a form of thanks to their guardian spirits and ancestors. Pollen studies from soil cores taken at Lake Saimaa show that slash-and-burn cultivation combined with cattle breeding began in southern Savo in the Late Iron Age. Permanent settlement of the area does not seem to have taken hold until the twelfth century. When choosing a dwelling site, Finns sought out fine soils and a close relation to bodies of water. It was more important that a site be suitable for cattle-breeding than for agriculture.

The cemeteries of the Late Iron Age present much interesting information about trade contacts, social organization, and religious beliefs including the process of conversion to Christianity. Finns practiced both inhumation (burial of the intact body) and cremation (burning the body) rites. In a small circumscribed area of western Finland (corresponding to the traditional parishes of Eura, Köyliö, and Yläne), large inhumation cemeteries—the largest cemeteries of any kind in prehistoric Finland—have been found (fig. 2). Many of the dead were accompanied by rich grave goods, and many of these items originated from Scandinavia and western Europe. Males were often buried with impressive sets of weapons including swords and spears. Both sexes were often well ornamented with costly brooches, rings, beads, and other items. Some early-twentieth-century scholars felt that these people were too wealthy and foreign-looking in their dress to be actual Finns, but researchers are now certain that they were truly Finnish. The explanation seems to be that the trade in furs and other valuable goods that had first stimulated settlement in Ostrobothnia was now moving into the interior along the Kokemäki River. These cemeteries represent the settlements of people who operated the gateway to that interior route, which perhaps already reached as far as the Lake Ladoga markets. Such control over valuable long-distance trade would indeed make communities in the area wealthy. Perhaps also, because these Finns dealt so much with foreign traders, they learned about, and chose to adopt, burial practices that are strikingly similar to those used nearby in western Europe. The large inhumation cemeteries found here remained in use until Christian times. Their final phases exhibit the effects of conversion. The latest burials, during the eleventh and twelfth centuries, are significantly lacking in grave goods and demonstrate the Christian teaching that the dead should not take their worldly possessions with them. When the parishes were finally organized, these old cemeteries dating from the pagan centuries were abandoned altogether, and new burials were placed in proper church graveyards.

Although spectacular in the finds they produced, the western inhumation cemeteries do not represent the common burial practice of Late Iron Age Finns. Cremation seems to have been most common, and cremations could be found both in mounds and in low-lying stratified, or layered, areas called field cemeteries. These are unusual in that the cremated remains are scattered about and intermixed with the remains of other cremated bodies. All individuality of burial identity is lost by this mixing. This behavior may reflect a prevailing belief in cyclical reincarnation from a defined ancestral kin group. Individuals who die lose their former earthly identity but are eventually transported into a new earthly form. Thus, the cremation field cemetery symbolizes the merging of kindred spirits in the afterlife.

Other burial types, particularly mound groups, flourish in different parts of the country. Finland is a fascinating place to study Iron Age ritual and religion, for more fragments, both in the ground and in the folklore, can still be uncovered there than in other lands with a longer and more deeply engrained history of Christianity.

See also **Iron Age Finland** (*vol. 2, part 6*); **Saami** (*vol. 2, part 7*); **Pre-Viking and Viking Age Sweden** (*vol. 2, part 7*); **Staraya Ladoga** (*vol. 2, part 7*).

BIBLIOGRAPHY

Edgren, Torsten, ed. *Fenno-Ugri et Slavi 1988: Papers Presented by the Participants in the Finnish-Soviet Archaeological Symposium "Studies in the Material Culture of the Peoples of Eastern and Northern Europe."* Helsinki: National Board of Antiquities, 1990. *Iskos* 9. (Various papers of interest, including many Iron Age papers.)

————, ed. *Fenno-Ugri et Slavi 1983: Papers Presented by the Participants in the Soviet-Finnish Symposium "Trade, Exchange and Culture Relations of the Peoples of Fennoscandia and Eastern Europe,"* 9–13 May 1983. Helsinki: Suomen Muinaismuistoyhdistys, 1984. *Iskos* 4. (Various papers of interest, including many Iron Age papers.)

Grönlund, E., H. Simola, and P. Uimonen-Simola. "Early Agriculture in the Eastern Finnish Lake District." *Norwegian Archaeological Review* 23 (1990): 79–85.

Hirviluoto, Anna-Liisa. "Finland's Cultural Ties with the Kama Region in the Late Iron Age Especially in the Light of Pottery Finds." In *Traces of the Central Asian Culture in the North: Finnish-Soviet Joint Scientific Symposium Held in Hanasaari, Espoo, 14–21 January 1985.* Mémoires de la Société Finno-Ougrienne 194. Edited by Ildikó Lehtinen, pp. 71–80. Helsinki: Suomalais-Ugrilainen Seura, 1986.

Huurre, Matti. *9000 Vuotta Suomen Esihistoriaa.* Helsinki: Otava, 1979. (In Finnish.)

Kivikoski, Ella. *Die Eisenzeit Finnlands: Bildwerk und Text.* Helsinki: Finnische Altertumsgesellschaft, 1973.

————. *Finland.* Translated by Alan Binns. London: Thames and Hudson, 1967.

Lehtosalo-Hilander, Pirkko-Liisa. "Finland." In *From Viking to Crusader: The Scandinavians and Europe 800–1200.* Edited by Else Roesdahl and David M. Wilson, pp. 62–71. New York: Rizzoli, 1992.

————. *Luistari.* 3 vols. Helsinki: Suomen Muinaismuistoyhdistys, 1982. (*Suomen Muinaismuistoyhdistyksen Aikakauskirja* 82, nos. 1–3). (A major inhumation cemetery excavation report in English; burial and artifact catalog in Finnish.)

Meinander, Carl F. "The Finnish Society during the 8th–12th Centuries." In *Fenno-Ugri et Slavi 1978: Papers Presented by the Participants the Soviet-Finnish Symposium "The Cultural Relations between the Peoples and Countries of the Baltic Area during the Iron Age and the Early Middle Ages,"* 20–23 May 1978. Edited by Carl F. Meinander, pp. 7–13. Helsinki: Helsinki University, 1980. (*Moniste* 22).

Odner, Knut. "Saamis (Lapps), Finns and Scandinavians in History and Prehistory: Ethnic Origins and Ethnic Processes in Fenno-Scandinavia." *Norwegian Archaeologi-*

cal Review 18 (1985): 1–35. (Determining ethnicity is a controversial topic.)

Orrman, Eljas. "Geographical Factors in the Spread of Permanent Settlement in Parts of Finland and Sweden from the End of the Iron Age to the Beginning of Modern Times." *Fennoscandia Archaeologica* 8 (1991): 3–21.

Saksa, A. I. "Results and Perspectives of Archaeological Studies on the Karelian Isthmus." *Fennoscandia Archaeologica* 2 (1985): 37–49.

Shepherd, Deborah J. *Funerary Ritual and Symbolism: An Interdisciplinary Interpretation of Burial Practices in* *Late Iron Age Finland*. BAR International Series, no. 808. Oxford: British Archaeological Reports, 1999.

Talvio, Tuukka. "Finland's Place in Viking-Age Relations between Sweden and the Eastern Baltic/Northern Russia: The Numismatic Evidence." *Journal of Baltic Studies* 13, no. 3 (fall 1982): 245–255.

Zachrisson, Inger. "Samisk kultur i Finland under järnåldern." In *Suomen Varhaishistoria*. Edited by Kyösti Julku, pp. 652–670. Oulu, Finland: University of Oulu, 1992.

DEBORAH J. SHEPHERD

POLAND

During the Late Iron Age and Early Middle Ages, the area that makes up contemporary Poland belonged to the outskirts of "civilized" Europe dominated by the Roman Empire. This distant part of the so-called Barbaricum, however, maintained contacts with the lands at the forefront of cultural development. Thus, processes observed in the Romanized parts of the Continent had unavoidable effects in the area north of the Sudetic and Carpathian Mountains. Because written sources are scarce and difficult to interpret, one must rely mainly on archaeological data, with the support of historical anthropology, to piece together a history of Poland from the fifth to the tenth century.

In late antiquity the territories to the north of the Carpathian and Sudetic Mountains faced a serious socioeconomic crisis. In the fifth and sixth centuries this resulted in a retreat from hierarchical authority and a return to an egalitarian form of organization. This process was accompanied by a decrease in widespread exchange, a deterioration of crafts, a reduction in the assortment of metal products, the disappearance of adornments, and a declining quality of pottery production. In general, it was a phase characterized by visible poverty.

This shift might have stemmed from the disruption of long-distance trade connections. Imported Roman products played an important role in the regulation of the social order among the "barbarians" surrounding the Roman Empire. Thus, control over the nodes of the trade network had the weight of a political argument because circulation of prestige objects used for ostentation of status conditioned the sustaining of power relations. Those relatively ranked societies required a steady stream of supplies from the outside; this made them quite sensitive to changes in contacts with the empire, which was the main source of status goods. Those contacts became unpredictable in the wake of the turbulent geopolitical situation in and around the Roman Empire in late antiquity. Historians usually blame this turmoil on the appearance of the Asiatic Huns, who arrived in the eastern European steppe zone in A.D. 375 and subsequently installed the center of their "empire" in the Carpathian Basin. A later breakdown of the transcontinental communication network might have caused barbarian elites to leave distant peripheries in search of closer contacts with still attractive Roman markets.

SUDDEN CAREER OF THE SLAVS

Such new circumstances resulted in radical changes in social organization as well as in the archaeologically observed material culture. The changes discernible from the sixth century onward cannot be reliably explained only by the migration of the Slavs, who settled lands emptied by departed Germanic populations, for example, the Vandals. It is difficult to accept the rather common vision of the whole region between the Vistula and Oder Rivers being suddenly completely depopulated and then resettled by the Slavic newcomers. These changes, however, should be viewed from a much broader perspective.

Archaeological data indicate that from the time of the sixth century, simple societies, based on a

Fig. 1. Example of a Slavic sunken house. COURTESY OF ZBIGNIEW KOBYLIŃSKI. REPRODUCED BY PERMISSION.

nonspecialized, self-sufficient agricultural economy with an egalitarian power structure, became common over vast areas of the northern parts of central Europe. Their uncomplicated socioeconomic organization is indicated by the layout of their settlements, composed of small houses of a uniform type (square, sunken huts with stone ovens in one corner, see figs. 1 and 2) arranged in rows or dispersed irregularly, as well as by analyses of the cemeteries. This stage, commonly identified as early Slavonic culture, was characterized by its small, nondefensive settlements, poor cemeteries with cremation burials, lack of adornments, and technologically primitive pottery of a uniform shape—the so-called Prague type. In a rather short time this simple style of life was adopted by almost all sedentary societies occupying vast areas of central Europe.

The widespread success of the Slavonic culture, measured by its spatial expansion, may seem surprising in light of its poor material equipment and strict egalitarianism. Nonetheless, decentralization of the power structure resulting from a return to the self-sufficient economy of local farming communities had the advantage of durability, stability, and predictability. It was a return to the relationships of solidarity based mainly on kin ties and not on subjugation (even voluntary) to the interests of military elites. Studies of spatial patterns of early Slavic settlements indicate a lack of any territorial organization, which may suggest that expansion of the Slavs and the durability of their decentralized ethnicity were based on the integrative potential of local rural communities and not on some regional power structures. During that silent revolution, in the course of about two centuries, Slavonic culture came to cover huge areas of the Continent—from Schleswig-Holstein in northern Germany to Thessaly in Greece, and from the Ukraine to Bavaria. This rapid expansion of Slavic culture did not result from military aggression or a demographic explo-

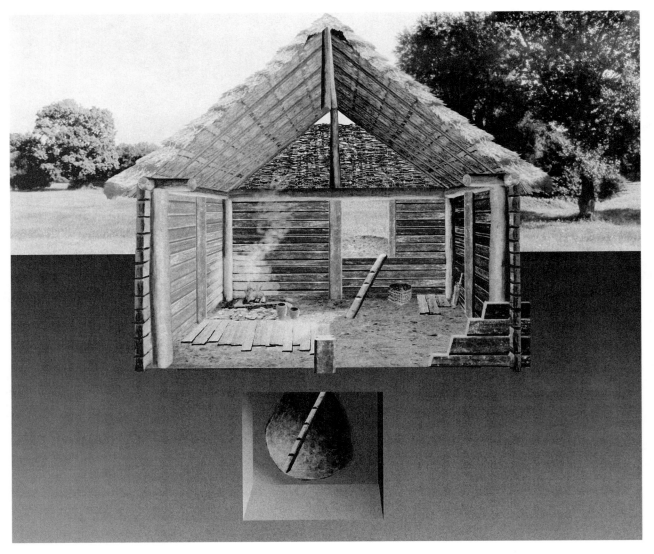

Fig. 2. A reconstruction of an early Slavic sunken-floored hut (Kraków-Wyciąże, Poland). FROM J. POLESKI.

sion but rather from acceptance of a new lifestyle that appeared attractive despite its apparent simplicity. It turned out to be economically effective in the long-term exploitation of various geographic environments.

The age-old controversy between supporters of the "autochthonous," or indigenous, presence of Slavs in the vast lowlands between the Oder and Dnieper Rivers and those who claim that they came from a small "cradle" located between the Carpathians and Dnieper cannot be resolved conclusively. The first group of scholars, stressing continuation of some elements of "Germanic" material culture and

survival of archaic hydronymy is not sensitive enough to the dynamism of the period of great migrations. Their opponents, who concentrate on the breakdown of the ancient social structures of the Barbaricum, overestimate "demographic explosion." Such an uncompromising opposition of "continuity" versus "colonization" is false because both hypotheses are based on radical simplification of the historical process. Sudden expansion of Slavdom cannot be disputed either in cultural terms or by using demographic categories only, and both aspects must be combined. Historical sources, archaeological evidence, and linguistic data suggest that the spreading of Slavic cultural codes was much more extensive than the range of the physical migration of their carriers, who intensively interacted with locally bound populations. Both processes were closely interdependent, and it may be impossible to decide which one was decisive in a given area.

POLITICAL DEVELOPMENT OF THE SLAVS

The early Slavic self-sufficient agricultural economy could not supply much of a surplus, which determined a relatively flat power structure. Apart from economic constraints, there were also geopolitical reasons for political retardation of the Slavs. The most important was the extensive control exerted by the Avars—Asiatic nomadic warriors who settled in the Carpathian Basin in 568 and militarily dominated all of central Europe. It was only after their defeat by Charlemagne in 799 that dynamic changes began to be seen among the Slavs. The collapse of the Avar "empire" and contacts with the mighty Frankish state, which expanded its tributary zone toward the east, initiated a lively process of social hierarchization among the Slavs.

The Polish lowlands had no direct contact with their mighty eastern Frankish neighbor until the mid-tenth century. For this reason, the territory north of the Carpathians did not attract the attention of early medieval chroniclers. The oldest source, written c. 848 by the so-called Bavarian Geographer at the court of the emperor Louis the German, offers very vague information, which reflects little knowledge of the area lying far from the empire's direct tributary zone. Notes on some mighty tribes suggest, however, that centralization of political power took place there as well. It can be assumed that experience of the long-lasting cooperation with the Avars, the establishment of long-distance commercial relations, and development of agrotechnology led, around the mid-ninth century, to the appearance of local chiefdom organizations based on redistribution economy. There are various archaeological indications of such a process.

Great mounds raised in the southeastern Polish highland in the eighth and ninth centuries (in Sandomierz, Kraków, and Przemyśl) are good indications of such a process. These monumental earthworks may be viewed as evidence of attempts to ease the tensions provoked by growing stratification.

None of these mounds contains a grave, which may imply that their main function was to materially manifest the ability to mobilize massive labor input. The aim was to "hide" the proliferating social differentiation behind the traditional symbolism of a burial mound. Such actions can be seen as a form of "propaganda" aimed at social integration despite the progressive stratification. Big mounds also display competition for power by men of status who used them to demonstrate their capacity to mobilize large groups to act collectively. Thus, they indicate periods when new elites symbolically marked their domination.

Arabic written sources address the development of trade relations with the Muslim world, as does the inflow of oriental coins that appeared north of the Carpathian Mountains in three waves during the course of the ninth and tenth centuries. Slaves were probably the main export in that period, although Arabian sources also mention honey, wax, furs, and amber. These commodities left northern central Europe either with Scandinavian merchants via the numerous Baltic trading emporia (e.g., Wolin and Truso), and later along the eastern European river system, or by the transcontinental route (from Spain to Verdun, Mainz, Regensburg, Prague, Kraków, Kiev, the middle Volga, and Khazaria at the Caspian Sea coast) served directly by Arab and Jewish merchants.

Apart from the erection of big mounds and the hiding of silver deposits, archaeological evidence of a new process of power centralization includes the building of earth-and-wood strongholds that began around the mid-ninth century (fig. 3). The strongholds indicate a reorganization of the social space because settlements were concentrated around fortified centers, breaking the older network of agricultural settlement into centralized "cells." As physical and symbolic centers, they fulfilled an important role as nodes of social geography. The strongholds served military functions and were evidence of the wealth of the ruling elite and its capability to execute extensive labor expense. Their construction indicated the economic and demographic potential of the area and might have fulfilled the socially important function of uniting a population around a common goal.

The economic base of a ruling power was supported by attempts to institutionalize ideology,

Fig. 3. Aerial of a small stronghold in Tykocin, Poland. COURTESY OF ZBIGNIEW KOBYLIŃSKI. REPRODUCED BY PERMISSION.

which resulted in the organization of cult centers. Control over these centers was important in sustaining power, because it strengthened political domination by the sacral legitimization of authority. In this respect, large regional cult centers located on "holy" mountains (e.g., Ślęża in Silesia and Łysa Góra in Little Poland) should be viewed, first of all, in terms of political struggle.

"CONSTRUCTION" OF THE STATE
The first written evidence of political organization in Polish lands may be found in the legendary hagiography of St. Methodius, in which "a powerful prince of Vislech" is mentioned. He used to "harass" Christian Moravians and subsequently was defeated and converted to Christianity between 874 and 880. The traditional interpretation of this account as a proof of some "state of Vislane" finds no confirmation in the available data. That "prince" probably was just one of many regional leaders func-

tioning around the border of Great Moravia, which was the main target for looting expeditions.

Despite obvious signs of hierarchization, the Early Middle Ages were still a time when the process of power centralization could have been stopped or even reversed. "Democratic" political institutions avoided the transition to territorial organizations ruled by stable monopolistic centers. That "opposition" had to be broken by ambitious individuals. Seeking exclusive power, they counteracted egalitarian attitudes, while violation of "democratic" mechanisms often was camouflaged by manipulating the common tradition. A distant reminiscence of one such illegitimate takeover of supreme authority is recorded in the dynastic legend of the first ruling Polish dynasty—the Piasts, as cited by the so-called Gallus Anonymus in the twelfth-century *Cronica Polonorum* [Chronicle of the Poles]. The story relates the expulsion of the ninth-century "prince" Popiel because he did not meet the basic requirements of acceptable leadership.

In the words of Gallus Anonymus, when "the Polish principality was not yet so large," Gnezno was ruled by prince Popiel, who had "many noblemen and friends." Once he was not able to "fulfill the needs of his guests," meaning he was unable to give them enough beer and meat; this obligation of a successful leader was met instead by a simple farmer, Piast, whose son Siemowit, "after common approval," was elected the prince of Poland. Popiel was expelled "together with his progeniture." Siemowit "enlarged the borders of his principality" by military means, which was continued by his son Lestek and his grandson Siemomysl. Siemomysl often used to gather together his "earls and dukes" and organize sumptuous feasts, at which the prince asked advice of "the elderly and wise men." He ruled unchallenged for many years, and his successor, Mieszko, also "energetically invaded the neighboring peoples." "Finally, he demanded to marry one good Christian woman from Bohemia," and, with her help, he "renounced the mistakes of paganism."

This is a very good description of the process of stable territorial state formation, in which military expansion helped mobilize the whole population and furnished the economic means to sustain dynastic supremacy. The Piasts were raised to the throne by disillusioned people. The family managed to maintain their position thanks to military successes, which provided material gains and expanded their domain. The leaders continued to seek the counsel of the members of the social elite but were, in fact, beyond their effective control. Mieszko I ultimately reinforced his power in 966 by conversion to Christianity, which offered him ideological legitimacy for unquestioned paramount power.

FOUNDATIONS OF PRINCELY POWER

From such a perspective one must view not only the military but also the political and psychological importance of long wars that mobilized and unified whole societies around victorious chiefs. Wars also had economic importance because booty supported the system of redistribution and gift exchange. War mobilization (against an enemy or for booty) was the best way to maintain the social order. Most im-

portant, however, war gains (horses, cattle, weapons, slaves, precious metals, and so on) made it possible to maintain a retinue. Military leadership, even if temporary, offered very efficient, although short-term, possibilities of strengthening one's status. It also helped limit access to paramount positions to one privileged family.

Apart from the strategy of reinforcing political power by military means, it was also necessary to increase the base of economic power by supplementing war income through trade and systematic coercive exploitation of one's own territory. Thus, the hundreds of strongholds built by the western Slavs from the late ninth century onward did not simply serve military purposes but also were safe places for staple produce. Those staples came from agricultural surpluses collected from the inhabitants of the ruler's own territory. Surpluses were made possible through the agricultural progress achieved in optimal climatic conditions. The growing role of agriculture caused the land to develop into a "commodity" and to become the most important element in determining the power structure. A class of people at first controlling and then possessing the land soon became the main supporters of the state.

Ideological power was strengthened by control over the ceremonial centers and the rituals celebrated there as well as by creating an ethnogenetic tradition. Such a largely legendary tradition was promoted by the privileged elites who, referring to the Indo-European stereotypes, equaled their genealogy with the origins of their peoples in order to legitimize their dominant position. This was aimed at increasing their power over the people and not over territory. In the beginning, those people could have been of many ethnic groups. For this reason, the monarch needed ideological reinforcement that would give his people a feeling of unity. Thus, "ethnic" identity resulted mainly from relationships with a specific leader and his family and not from the fact of living within the same territory or from some commonly experienced past.

THE ORIGINS OF POLAND

It seems that when a territorial authority and the control over the religious sphere are turned into a permanent political center with coercive capability (an "army"), it is only a step away from becoming a state. This breakthrough is difficult to discern from early medieval evidence. For example, the Polish state of Mieszko I (922?–992) seemed to appear ex nihilo, because his home area in Great Poland (Wielkopolska) did not boast any particular concentration of strongholds, no dense settlement, and no rich cemeteries. In the early tenth century various areas (Little Poland, Silesia, Great Poland, Masovia, and Pomerania) showed similar development. Every one of these regions could have emerged as a small state. It seems that the main advantage of Great Poland was its geographical isolation, which limited military dangers. Thus, Silesia offered protection from the direct interventions of the mighty eastern Frankish empire, Little Poland protected from Rus aggression, Pomerania absorbed the activity of the Scandinavian Vikings, and Masovia stood against violent Prussians. Thus the final success of Great Poland was determined greatly by its location, which enabled the Piast dynasty to win the race for stable state formation.

Dendrochronological dates indicate a growing settlement network in Great Poland as late as the mid-tenth century, when Mieszko's state already had entered Continental geopolitics. His strategy was described in 965/66 by the Spanish Jewish merchant Ibrahim ibn Jaqub of Tortosa, who reported on his journey to Prague. He noticed the striking effectiveness of a military model based on the domination of a professional, heavily armed cavalry and the stabilizing effect of the stronghold network. Soon the Polish prince effected an ideological revolution by accepting Christianity as the new state religion in 966. All these measures allowed him to secure unquestionable political domination for himself and his descendants.

There must have been a centralized form of coercion applied, under which old kin-based relationships were replaced with new social hierarchy relationships of political obedience while "democratic" supervision by the common assembly was replaced by norms of the imposed royal law. Military power was applied, which in the core area of the early Piasts' state in the mid-tenth century manifested as the phase of destruction of the old strongholds, which were replaced by new ones. Those new nodes of power often were localized at the same site or nearby the earlier ones.

Mieszko's state was not yet "Poland." It was the state of the Piasts who had executed their dynastic

goals with the support of a military aristocracy. To Ibrahim ibn Jaqub it was obvious in 965 that it was the monarch with his retinue who created and represented the state. Thus he called it "the state of Mieszko." It was not until much later, after stable territorial foundations of dynastic power were laid down, that it was possible to identify the state not personally but geographically. It was recorded in the last quarter of the tenth century, that the name of the central town (Gniezno) was used for identifying the state ruled by the Piasts. In a document written c. 990 and called *Dagome iudex* (the meaning of which remains unknown), Mieszko I described his own domain as *civitas* Schinesghe/Schignesne, that is, "the state of Gniezno." The first coin of his son Boleslav I (r. 992–1025) makes a similar reference, written as "Gnezdun civitas." The general territorial name Polonia appeared as late as about A.D. 1000, when the relatively stable geopolitical structure of central Europe took shape. It was then that the need to attain geopolitical legitimacy forced Boleslav I to introduce a package of commonly accepted attributes of an independent state, that is, an archbishopric, coinage, a territorial name, and a royal crown.

THE REGIONAL POWER

It took three generations of the Piast dynasty to organize a large, stable, strong state, which came to dominate central Europe by the turn of the millennium. Dendrochronology indicates that it must have been Mieszko's father, Siemomysl, who laid the foundations of the dynastic domain in central Great Poland during the fourth and fifth decade of the tenth century. It was in that period when a network of strongholds was created with centers in Gniezno, Giecz, Poznań, Lednica, Moraczewo, and Grzybowo. They were surrounded by dense systems of rural settlements. As the first historical ruler, Mieszko I laid the territorial foundations of the state, which quickly expanded in all directions. Growing in power, he had to enter the geopolitical stage, where he showed skills of an experienced gambler.

Long unnoticed by the German empire, the Piast state emerged in the seventh decade of the tenth century as a military power able to challenge mighty Bohemian and Hungarian princes. Mieszko I started a complex game of alliances aimed at reinforcing his geopolitical position. To balance the expansive strategy of the German church, he asked his closest neighbor, the Bohemian prince Boleslav I, to send a Christianizing mission together with his daughter, Dobrava. The first bishop, Jordan, was responsible directly to the pope, which made the Polish church independent of German supervision. The interdynastic marriage of Mieszko and Dobrava in 965 obliged both courts to maintain political solidarity, which was reflected in their support for the anti-Ottonian opposition.

This alliance lasted as long as Dobrava lived. Mieszko took political advantage of her death in 977 to break the Polish-Bohemian partnership. In 979 he married Oda, daughter of the Saxon margrave Dietrich, and became a close ally of the Ottonian empire. His strategic goal was to challenge Bohemian domination in central Europe. Sometime in the ninth decade he invaded Silesia and Little Poland and included them as southern provinces of his state, despite diplomatic actions taken by the prince of Prague, Boleslav II, the son of the Bohemian prince Boleslav I and Mieszko's own former brother-in-law.

The Piasts' strategy of geopolitical isolation of Bohemia is well reflected in the sequence of quick marriages arranged for Mieszko's oldest son, also named Boleslav. In 984 this Boleslav married the daughter of the Meissen margrave Rikdag. The death of this mighty Saxon aristocrat made possible the annulment of that marriage, which opened the way to finding a new wife for the young prince in 986/87. This time it was a Hungarian princess, who was herself replaced in 988/89 by Emnilda, the daughter of a western Slavonic prince, Dobromir. This clever policy restricted potential partners of Bohemia to pagan Polabians and resulted in Bohemia's loss of its former dominant position.

After Mieszko's death in 992, his son, now Boleslav I, continued the strategy of further expanding and reinforcing his inherited state. Active in all directions, he ran a complex game of military and diplomatic actions. His sister was married first to the Swedish king Eric the Victorious and later to the Danish king Svein Forkbeard. His daughter was sent to Rus as the wife of the prince of Kiev, and his son, Mieszko II, married the German princess Richesa, the niece of the emperor Otto III.

Boleslav's real masterpiece, however, was a summit with emperor Otto III, who came to Gniezno in A.D. 1000. The official reason for this unprecedented visit was a pilgrimage to the grave of St. Adalbert of Prague (originally called Vojtech), who had been killed in 997 during a mission to the pagan Prussians. The emperor substantially reinforced Boleslav I, however, because he brought with him Archbishop Radim (Gaudentius), the half-brother of St. Adalbert, and established an independent church province with a metropolitan seat in Gniezno. Four new bishoprics (in Poznań, Kołobrzeg, Wrocław, and Kraków) formed an administrative network that covered all the lands between the Baltic Sea and the mountain belt. The Polish prince also was freed from the obligation of paying yearly tributes and was elevated to the position of a "brother of the empire," effectively a monarch equal to any other in Europe. Since that time the political name Polonia has been used for the state that has survived to the present.

A review of the origins of the other early states (Bohemia, Hungary, Rus) that constituted eastern central Europe during the tenth century shows a common strategy applied by their leaders, who all achieved stable territorial power. None of them had an overview of the geopolitical situation, and none could foresee the long-range results of their actions. Their ability to organize broad support, their determination in applying coercion, their capacity to muster the necessary means to sustain power, their intelligence in borrowing solutions from more developed neighbors, and simple good luck led to their supreme successes as first monarchs and creators of their states.

One may conclude that Poland emerged in the tenth century as a "private" venture of the Piasts, who managed to defeat local challengers, stop expansion of their neighbors, impose Christian ideology that legitimized monopolistic rules, organize effective exploitation of subjugated territory, and achieve geopolitical acceptance. That state was not an "emanation" of the political striving of a nation. It was just the opposite—the Polish nation was a much later "product" of a state that imposed cultural unification.

See also **Iron Age Poland** (*vol. 2, part 6*); **Slavs and the Early Slav Culture** (*vol. 2, part 7*); **Russia/Ukraine** (*vol. 2, part 7*); **Hungary** (*vol. 2, part 7*); **Czech Lands/Slovakia** (*vol. 2, part 7*).

BIBLIOGRAPHY

Barford, Paul M. *The Early Slavs: Culture and Society in Early Medieval Eastern Europe.* London: British Museum Press; Ithaca, N.Y.: Cornell University Press, 2001.

Fried, Johannes. *Otto III und Boleslaw Chrobry: Das Widmungsbild des Aachener Evangeliars, der Akt von Gnesen und das frühe polnische und ungarishe Königtum. Ein Bildanalyse und ihre historischen Folgen.* Stuttgart, Germany: Franz Steiner Verlag, 1989.

Görich, Knut. *Otto III: Romanus, Saxonicus et Italicus. Keiserliche Rompolitik und sächsische Historiographie.* Sigmaringen, Germany: Thorbecke, 1993.

Kara, Michał. "Anfänge der Bildung des Piastenstaatens im Lichte neuer archäologischen Ermittlungen." *Questiones medii aevi novae* 5 (2000): 57–85.

Kurnatowska, Zofia. *Początki Polski* [Beginnings of Poland]. Poznań, Poland: Poznańskie Towarzystwo Przyjaciół Nauk, 2002.

Labuda, Gerard. *Mieszko I.* Wrocław, Poland: Ossolineum, 2002.

Miśkiewicz, M., ed. *Słowianie w Europie wcześniejszego średniowiecza* [Slavs in early medieval Europe]. Warsaw, Poland: Państwowe Muzeum Archeologiczne, 1998.

Samsonowicz, Henryk, ed. *Ziemie polskie w X wieku i ich znaczenie w kształtowaniu się nowej mapy Europy* [Polish lands in the tenth century and their role in the shaping of the new map of Europe]. Kraków, Poland: Universitas, 2000.

Strzelczyk, Jerzy. *Mieszko I.* Poznań, Poland: Wydawnictwo Wojewódzkiej Biblioteki Publicznej, 1999.

Urbańczyk, Przemysław. *Rok 1000: Milenijna podróż transkontynentalna* [The year 1000: Millennial transcontinental journey]. Warsaw, Poland: DiG, 2001.

———. *Władza i polityka we wczesnym średniowieczu* [Power and politics in the Early Middle Ages]. Warsaw, Poland: Funna, 2000.

———, ed. *Europe around the Year 1000.* Warsaw, Poland: Institute of Archaeology and Ethnology, 2001.

———, ed. *The Neighbours of Poland in the Tenth Century.* Warsaw, Poland: Institute of Archaeology and Ethnology, 2000.

———, ed. *Origins of Central Europe.* Warsaw, Poland: Institute of Archaeology and Ethnology, 1997.

PRZEMYSŁAW URBAŃCZYK

RUSSIA/UKRAINE

The early Russian state emerged between A.D. 750 and 1000, the result of a complex development process. Among the most important factors in this process were the growth of an economy based on craft production and long-distance trade and the rise of urban centers to facilitate the specialized economy and the administration of the nascent state. These factors, in turn, were related closely to connections and interrelationships among peoples living in Russia, the Baltic Sea area, and the east during the eighth through tenth centuries.

Primary historical evidence regarding the origin of the Russian state is scarce, consisting mainly of a single record, the Russian Primary Chronicle. It is thought that the chronicle was compiled in the Monastery of the Caves near Kiev in about A.D. 1110. According to the chronicle account, in the early ninth century northern Russia was divided politically into diverse tribal principalities, all of which owed tribute to the Varangians (Scandinavians). In 859 these principalities rose together against the Varangians and drove them out of Russia. Without a central power, the Russian peoples began to fight among themselves and eventually resolved to invite the Varangians to return and rule over them. Three Varangian brothers accepted the invitation. They moved to northern Russia with their kin and founded cities from which to rule the area. The old-

est brother was Rurik, who located himself in Novgorod or Staraya Ladoga (depending on the particular codex consulted). The two younger brothers also each established a city but died within a few years, leaving Rurik the sole authority over northern Russia. In later years Rurik's successors expanded and consolidated Russian rule. In 882 Oleg, a descendant of Rurik, established himself in Kiev and declared that city the capital of Russia, which it remained until the eleventh century.

Although the Russian Primary Chronicle account has a legendary feel to it, clearly serving to legitimize the rule of the Kievan dynasty over early Russia, it does provides insight into how the early state was formed. The document identifies several key factors in the formation of the early Russian state: early towns, the diversity of peoples who inhabited them, and their economic interrelationships. Archaeological research on the formation of the early Russian state has investigated these key factors, providing a great deal of information about the development of early towns as economic and administrative centers and about the role of the Varangians and other early peoples in the area. Most archaeologists currently believe that the establishment of the early Russian state was a process, not an event, as the Russian Primary Chronicle presents it. The process of state formation, as revealed in the ar-

Early medieval towns in Russia, Scandinavia, and Byzantium.

chaeological record, included the growth of a specialized economy, urbanization, and increasing social stratification.

State development took place between A.D. 750 and 1000 in two primary phases. In the first phase, between about A.D. 750 and 900, appeared such early towns as Staraya Ladoga and Rurik Gorodishche, whose primary function was to facilitate a long-distance economy. The focus of these early towns was on trade and craft production. They had a multiethnic population, which only in later years was controlled by a central administration. In the second phase, from about A.D. 900 to 1000, rose such towns as Novgorod and Kiev, whose primary function was administration. These later towns showed evidence of urban planning, the presence of a ruling elite and a military, and a continuing interest in craft production and trade.

A.D. 750–900

The peoples who settled in northwest Russia before the period of state formation belonged to Baltic and Finno-Ugric ethnic groups. During the eighth century, Slavic peoples were expanding north and settling along the southern coast of the Baltic Sea, while at the same time Scandinavians were moving south into that area. Organized into small tribal principalities, these peoples coexisted in northern Russia. They lived in small villages scattered across the landscape. Their economy was primarily agrarian, with local exchange.

Between A.D. 750 and 900 the characteristic settlement pattern and economy of northern Russia changed rapidly. A number of towns appeared, including Staraya Ladoga, Rurik Gorodishche, and Gnezdovo. These early towns were located at strategic points for facilitating and controlling the growing trade across the Baltic and through Russia to the

Far East. The first towns in northern Russia were different from earlier settlements in two significant ways: their population was more concentrated, and they had a specialized economy focused on craft production rather than agriculture and on long-distance rather than local trade. They also were notable for having a multiethnic population, with individuals from several cultures living side by side and engaging in the same economic activities.

Staraya Ladoga. The earliest known town in northern Russia is Staraya Ladoga, located south of Lake Ladoga at the easternmost point of the Baltic Sea. Staraya Ladoga is important to historians, because it appears in some versions of the Russian Primary Chronicle as Rurik's original seat. To archaeologists it is significant because it is the only northwest Russian medieval town with an unambiguous eighth-century cultural layer and with excellent preservation of organic and metallic materials due to the waterlogged soil. Based on the findings from Staraya Ladoga, archaeologists have reconstructed a great deal of information related to the process of state formation in early Russia, including the development of a specialized economy, the appearance of social stratification, and the role of these factors in the process of urbanization and state formation in Russia.

Staraya Ladoga is situated in an ideal position to monitor access to the main communication routes through Russia, the Dnieper and Volga Rivers. In the mid-eighth century, the earliest settlement at the town developed along the southern bank of the Ladozhka, at the point where the tributary entered the Volkhov River. This location probably was chosen as the best spot for a harbor. The town grew rapidly. During the mid-ninth century, the north bank of the Ladozhka was settled, and by the tenth century the town had expanded to both sides of the Volkhov.

Early development of Staraya Ladoga was haphazard, but after the mid-ninth century there is evidence for town planning and public works, suggesting that a town administration had evolved. The center of Staraya Ladoga was fortified in the second half of the ninth century. In the tenth century, the town's streets were laid out on a grid, and a princely residence was built with provisions for military protection.

More than one hundred and fifty buildings have been excavated at Staraya Ladoga. Almost every excavated building turned up evidence of craft production, suggesting that manufacturing was an important part of the town's economy and that a majority of permanent residents were engaged in craft production. Other activities include agriculture, stock raising, and hunting and gathering, but these appear minor compared with craft production and trade. Staraya Ladoga's economy was organized around two main spheres: a local and regional exchange area and a long-distance exchange area. The local and regional economy centered on manufacturing and trading utilitarian objects and importing prestige goods and raw materials for the elite. The long-distance economy involved exporting furs and other materials, importing foreign prestige goods, and transferring foreign goods to other trading centers in Scandinavia, Russia, and the Near East.

There is no clear evidence to suggest that any particular ethnic group founded or administered the town, or participated significantly more than any other in its core activities of trade and manufacture. In the earliest layers of Staraya Ladoga there are Baltic, Finno-Ugric, Scandinavian, and Slavic materials, integrated throughout the settlement. Over time the material culture began to appear more homogenized, suggesting that the town's diverse ethnic groups were assimilating a new, local identity. Archaeological work carried out throughout the Lake Ladoga region indicates that ethnic integration existed outside the town as well.

There is also evidence of status differentiation among the people of Staraya Ladoga. The town must have had an emerging elite, whose position was communicated clearly and reinforced by their consumption of luxury goods and construction of showy burial mounds. The ordinary folk used utilitarian objects and buried their dead in more humble cremation graves. The elite probably did not organize or control the economy of the town early in its history, but their influence and authority over the town and its activities increased through time. Staraya Ladoga is best understood as a trade and manufacturing town, one link in the network that connected Scandinavia, the eastern Baltic, and the Far East. From its earliest days, the town had far-reaching trade contacts and an economy based largely on commerce and the production of trade goods.

Staraya Ladoga developed around the same time that new peoples were moving into northern Russia, notably Scandinavians and Slavs. These newcomers, together with the existing population of Balts and Finns, played an important role in stimulating trade and the growth of towns and thus ultimately encouraging craft specialization and increasing class stratification. The participation of numerous ethnic groups in the same range of economic activities seems to have contributed to the development of a new local identity and the minimizing of previous ethnic differences.

Rurik Gorodishche. Rurik Gorodishche is located on an island north of Lake Ilmen, which is midway down the Volkhov. In the ninth century Rurik Gorodishche and Staraya Ladoga were the largest settlements in northwest Russia. While Staraya Ladoga served as gateway to Russia from the eastern Baltic, Rurik Gorodishche controlled access to the Russian river routes. Traders heading to the Bulgar state via the Volga or to Kiev and Byzantium via the Dnieper would pass through Lake Ilmen.

Rurik Gorodishche was a trade and craft production center in the ninth and tenth centuries, taking advantage of its location. Craft production seems to have been important to the town's economy, given the quantities of production debris and materials recovered during excavations. Scales and weights indicate that trade also took place in the town. Goods from the Mediterranean, the Baltic Sea, and Scandinavia have been found at the site. The population of Rurik Gorodishche, as at Staraya Ladoga, included many ethnic groups: Finns, Balts, Slavs, and Scandinavians. Evidence from burials, jewelry, and other sources suggests that these groups mutually influenced each other and gradually developed a composite local identity that blended elements from all of the cultures.

Evidence for fortifications and weapons suggest that Rurik Gorodishche ("Rurik's Fortress") was an administrative and military center early in its history. Staraya Ladoga was fortified at about the same time that Rurik Gorodishche was established as a fortified center, perhaps indicating that fortifications were a common precaution or a statement of power in the mid-ninth century.

Archaeological research shows that Staraya Ladoga and Rurik Gorodishche (as well as other early towns, such as Beloozero and Gnezdovo/ Smolensk) share many common features in their development and character: an economy based on trade and craft production, a strategic location along developing trade routes, and a multiethnic population. Other Baltic trade towns manifest these same features, including Hedeby and Ribe in Jutland, Kaupang in Norway, Paviken on Gotland, Birka in central Sweden, and Wolin in Poland.

A.D. 900–1000

By A.D. 900, many towns existed in Russia, including Staraya Ladoga and Rurik Gorodishche. These early towns encouraged the development of a novel specialized economy based on crafts and trade, fostered the interaction of numerous ethnic groups, and depended upon a limited amount of urban administration. Between A.D. 900 and 1000, a new kind of town arose in Russia, which was associated closely with the development of an elite class and a central government. As ethnic differences became less pronounced in urban populations, social stratification became more prominent. Tenth-century towns, such as Novgorod, increasingly served as administrative and economic centers for their territories, encouraging interdependence among the urban and rural settlements. The rise of Kiev in the late tenth century unified Russian towns and their territories under one central administration and further increased the social, political, and settlement hierarchy of early Russia. By A.D. 1000 Kiev effectively served as capital of the early Russian state.

Novgorod. Novgorod was established in the mid-tenth century, two kilometers from Rurik Gorodishche in the Lake Ilmen area of northern Russia. In many ways, early Novgorod resembled its neighboring settlement. Novgorod was home to extensive craft production; about one hundred and fifty workshops have been found so far in the archaeological record. Connections with long-distance trade are indicated by imported objects from the north, south, east, and west. The material culture embraced elements from Slavic, Scandinavian, Baltic, and Finno-Ugric groups, which indicates that there were mutual cultural influences.

Despite the basic similarity between the two towns—a multiethnic population concerned with craft and trade activities—Novgorod had a different character from that of nearby Rurik Gorodishche. Archaeologists have recovered copious evidence of a greater elite presence at Novgorod than at Rurik Gorodishche. In Lyudin End, where the earliest traces of settlement have been found in Novgorod, individual house lots generally fit into one of two types. The first type, a narrow rectangular lot about 15 by 30 meters, is thought to have belonged to regular urban residents. The second type of lot, up to three times as large as the first, has been identified as residences for elite class. The conspicuous consumption of luxury goods in Novgorod also suggests well-developed social differences among the town's population. The evidence for an elite presence is so striking that some scholars have suggested that Novgorod may have been founded as an elite settlement.

In the late tenth or early eleventh century, Novgorod appears to have taken over administrative functions for the Lake Ilmen area and perhaps for all of northern Russia. Novgorod probably also was the religious center of northern Russia, first for the pagan religion and then for Christianity. By about A.D. 1000 Rurik Gorodishche and Novgorod may have had complementary functions, together serving as the urban center of the Lake Ilmen region. Contemporary examples of similar paired settlements have been excavated in other areas of the eastern Baltic, including Hedeby and Schleswig in Jutland and Birka and Sigtuna in central Sweden. In these cases, as in Rurik Gorodishche and Novgorod, the earlier settlement was a craft and trade center particularly reliant on long-distance trade, flourishing from the eighth through the tenth centuries. The later settlement, beginning in the late tenth or early eleventh century, was an administrative and ecclesiastical center. In both Russia and Scandinavia the rise of these urban settlements appears to have been related to the greater sociopolitical and economic changes that played a part in early state development.

Kiev. Kiev is located on a promontory on the west bank of the Dnieper River, about 10 kilometers south of the confluence of the Dnieper and the Desna. From this position Kiev controlled the lower Dnieper. Archaeological evidence indicates that the character and extent of settlement on the Kiev promontory changed dramatically between the be-

ginning of the tenth century A.D. and the first half of the eleventh century. The settlement expanded tenfold, filling the hills of the promontory and stretching along the riverbanks of the Dnieper. Economic specialization increased as craft production, including bronze casting and iron production, flourished. Long-distance trade partners included the Muslim east, the Bulgar state, and the Byzantine Empire.

The town's dense population and specialized economy suggests that Kiev must have been dependent upon tribute or some other means of exacting agricultural and subsistence products from the surrounding countryside. According to the Russian Primary Chronicle, Prince Oleg established Kiev as preeminent over all Russian cities in A.D. 882 and gathered tribute from all the Russian lands. A fortified area was established on Starokievska Hill c. A.D. 900, with large stone structures that may have been princely residences. By about A.D. 1000 this fortress probably served as an administrative center for the area, effectively unifying the scattered settlements in the Kiev area into one urban and tributary unit.

Burial and architectural evidence shows that Kiev was a multiethnic and socially stratified community. Slavic, Baltic, Finno-Ugric, Scandinavian, and Byzantine elements are present in the burial customs and building methods of Kiev during this period. After Kiev was established as the Russian capital, the population of Kiev appears to have become more ethnically homogeneous. This no doubt occurred through natural assimilation of the various groups living in Kiev as well as through the introduction of Christianity. In 988, the Russian Primary Chronicle reports, Prince Vladimir of Kiev introduced the Christian church to Russia. Social stratification, in contrast to ethnic diversity, increased through time.

Archaeological and historical sources indicate that the early Russian state had emerged by A.D. 1000, with centralized rulership at Kiev exercising political and economic control over an extensive area, from the shores of the Gulf of Finland and Lake Ladoga in the north down to the Black Sea in the south. Kievan Russia developed diplomatic and trade relations with its neighbors, including Scandinavia, Europe, the Islamic Caliphate, the Bulgar Khazarate, and the Byzantine Empire. The Russian state also had converted to Christianity, and the lands and peoples under its control were beginning to evince social and cultural institutions considered to be characteristically "Russian."

SUMMARY AND CONCLUSIONS
The development of the early Russian state took place between A.D. 750 and 1000. Several factors contributed to the formation of the state: the growth of early towns as trade and administrative centers, the elaboration of a specialized economy; and the development of social stratification. Between A.D. 750 and 900 the first towns arose in Russia, relying on and encouraging the development of an economy based on craft production and long-distance trade. Early Russian towns, such as Staraya Ladoga and Rurik Gorodishche, share many common features: an economy based on trade and craft production, a strategic location along developing trade routes, and a multiethnic population. As such, they were similar to other trade towns in Scandinavia and northern Europe. The eighth- and ninth-century trade towns created a basis for statehood in these regions, contributing to the expansion of a specialized economy, social stratification, and central administration.

Between A.D. 900 and 1000, a different kind of urban center became established in Russia, administrative and ecclesiastical centers that integrated the urban and rural economy. In Russia and Scandinavia the appearance of these administrative centers settlements resulted from and contributed to the sociopolitical and economic changes associated with the formation of a state. Novgorod served as one such political center, administering taxation and collecting tribute in northern Russia during the tenth century. Kiev in central Russia (now Ukraine) grew alongside Novgorod, eventually surpassing it and all other Russian cities in economic and political importance.

See also **Rus** (*vol. 2, part 7*); **Staraya Ladoga** (*vol. 2, part 7*).

BIBLIOGRAPHY
Brisbane, Mark A., ed. *The Archaeology of Novgorod, Russia: Recent Results from the Town and Its Hinterland.* Translated by Katharine Judelson. Lincoln, U.K.: Society for Medieval Archaeology, 1992.

Callmer, J. "The Archaeology of Kiev to the End of Its Earliest Urban Phase." *Harvard Ukrainian Studies* 11, nos. 3, 4 (1987): 323–364.

Clarke, Helen, and Björn Ambrosiani. "Towns in the Slavonic-Baltic Area." In their *Towns in the Viking Age,* pp. 107–127. Rev. ed. Leicester, U.K.: Leicester University Press, 1995.

Graham-Campbell, James, Colleen Batey, Helen Clarke et al., eds. "Russia and the East." In their *Cultural Atlas of the Viking World,* pp. 184–198. New York: Facts on File, 1994.

Jansson, Ingmar. "Communications between Scandinavia and Eastern Europe in the Viking Age: The Archaeological Evidence." In *Untersuchungen zu Handel und Verkehr der vor- und frühgeschichtlichen Zeit in Mittel- und Nordeuropa.* Vol. 4, *Der Handel der Karolinger- und Wikingerzeit.* Göttingen, Germany: Vandenhoeck & Ruprecht, 1987. (Includes articles in English.)

Ostman, Rae Ellen M. "Our Land Is Great and Rich, But There Is No Order in It: Reevaluating the Process of State Formation in Russia." *Archaeological News* 21–22 (1996–1997): 73–91, 150–155.

Rahbeck-Schmidt, K., ed. *Varangian Problems.* Scandoslavica Supplement 1. Copenhagen, Denmark: Munksgaard, 1970.

Stalsberg, Anne. "Scandinavian Relations with Northern Russia during the Viking Age: The Archaeological Evidence." *Journal of Baltic Studies* 13, no. 3 (1982): 267–295.

Uino, Pirjo. "On the History of Staraja Ladoga." *Acta Archaeologica* 59 (1988): 205–222.

Vernadsky, George, ed. *A Sourcebook for Russian History from Early Times to 1917.* New Haven, Conn.: Yale University, 1972.

Yanin, V.L. "Medieval Novgorod: Fifty Years' Experience Digging Up the Past." In *The Comparative History of Urban Origins in Non-Roman Europe: Ireland, Wales, Denmark, Germany, Poland and Russia from the Ninth to the Thirteenth Century.* Edited by H. B. Clarke and A. Simms. BAR International Series, no. 255. Oxford: British Archaeological Reports, 1985.

RAE OSTMAN

STARAYA LADOGA

Staraya Ladoga, in northwestern Russia, was one of the most important trade and craft production centers of the eastern Baltic during the early Middle Ages. Located at the eastern end of the Baltic, the town was a gateway between the Baltic Sea and Russian river routes to the Black Sea. Staraya Ladoga also is cited by some versions of Russia's earliest historical document, the Russian Primary Chronicle, as the seat of Rurik, Russia's first ruler.

SETTLEMENT

Early settlement at Staraya Ladoga has been thoroughly and systematically excavated, resulting in a detailed picture of life in an eastern Baltic trade town from A.D. 750 to 1200. A total of 3,600 square meters of medieval Staraya Ladoga have been excavated, of an estimated settlement area of 15 square kilometers. The waterlogged soil at the site has resulted in excellent preservation of finds, and dendrochronology has allowed the finds to be dated precisely.

As a result of the extensive excavation program, archaeologists can sketch a clear picture of the development and character of early Staraya Ladoga. The Earthworks Fortress quarter of the town was settled the earliest, beginning in about A.D. 760. This area probably was the most suitable place for a harbor. Settlement expanded into the Varangian Street quarter in about A.D. 842. Once established, these early settlement areas were occupied continuously throughout the Middle Ages. In the ninth and tenth centuries, the trade town began to appear more urban, with more clearly defined areas and functions. Staraya Ladoga was given wooden fortifications in the 860s and stone fortifications in 882. Dwellings and public buildings were concentrated within the town walls. Sacred places and cemeteries were located outside the walls. In the tenth century, a regular street grid was established. At this time the population of the town was slightly more than one thousand persons.

More than one hundred and fifty medieval houses have been excavated at Staraya Ladoga, dating from the eighth century through the eleventh century A.D. The medieval buildings are of two main kinds, a small and a large type. The small buildings are approximately 5 meters square and have a corner hearth. The large buildings measure approximately 13 by 10 meters and have a central hearth. Archaeologists have not found an explanation for the coexistence of the two building types. At one point scholars believed the larger buildings might have predated the smaller buildings, but this hypothesis has been rejected. Likewise, attempts to identify the building types with different ethnic groups living in Staraya Ladoga have been unsuccessful.

One well-preserved building in the Earthworks Fortress quarter is of exceptional size. Built in 894, it measured approximately 17 by 10 meters. A hearth was located in a walled-off interior room measuring approximately 10.5 by 7.5 meters. More than two hundred glass beads and thirty pieces of amber were found associated with the building, suggesting that its occupants were involved in trade. Ibn Fadlan, an Arabic scholar, wrote in 921 or 922 that the Rus traders who sailed down the Volga River built large timber structures that could house ten to twelve people.

Burial mounds were erected along the Volkhov River, in locations where they would be visible from a distance. More than thirty burial mounds are still extant at Staraya Ladoga. It is thought that one of the largest mounds at Staraya Ladoga was built for Oleg (879–912), the ruler who united northern and southern Russia. The cemetery of Plakun is notable for the ten or so Scandinavian boat burials. Other cemeteries at Staraya Ladoga include Baltic, Finno-Ugric, and Slavic burials.

ECONOMY

From its earliest days, Staraya Ladoga's economy was based on trade and the production of trade goods. The town was an important node in the routes between the Baltic Sea and the river routes across Russia to the Far East. Staraya Ladoga controlled a substantial part of the route, from the Baltic to the lower reaches of the Volkhov River. From the lower Volkhov, traders would take either the Volga route to the Caspian Sea and the Islamic Caliphate or the Dnieper route to the Black Sea and the Byzantine Empire.

Silver and trade scales indicate that merchants exchanged goods in Staraya Ladoga. In addition to local trade goods, including crafts, timber, honey, and slaves, goods from other areas also traveled through Staraya Ladoga: furs from Viking Scandinavia, combs from Frisia, beads from the Mediterranean, swords from the Frankish kingdom, and amber from the Baltic. Traders exchanged these goods in the Far East for silver coins, carnelian and rock crystal beads, silk, and warrior-style clothing, ornaments, and accessories.

Local craft production at Staraya Ladoga is indicated by finds of raw materials, tools, various products found at different stages of completion, rejected (flawed) products, and manufacturing debris. Almost every house excavated in the town turned up evidence of such craft production. Glass beads

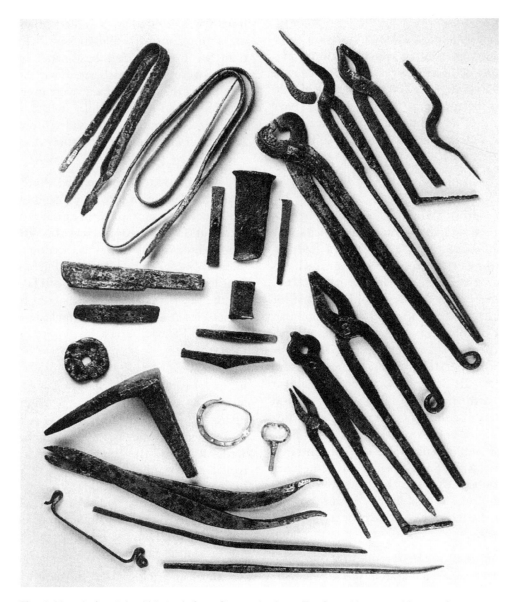

Fig. 1. Hoard of metalsmith's tools from Staraya Ladoga. THE STATE HERMITAGE MUSEUM, ST. PETERSBURG. REPRODUCED BY PERMISSION.

may have been crafted in the glassworks found at Staraya Ladoga. A smithy dating to the 760s was equipped for bronze casting, with a smelting hearth, casting molds, and a collection of twenty-six metalworking tools (fig. 1). Amber was imported from the Baltic and worked at the site. Pottery was manufactured locally, first using hand-built construction and later the fast wheel. Bone and antler were fashioned into numerous objects, including knives and combs. Wooden objects were turned on lathes and carved manually. Textile tools (spindles, whorls, and flax-processing tools) were used to

create the finished cloth found in the town. Leather footwear also was produced in early medieval Staraya Ladoga.

Agriculture, stock raising, gathering, and hunting also occupied the early occupants of the town and its countryside. Agricultural tools, including plowshares, are preserved in the archaeological record. Botanical remains comprise cultivated cereals, such as millet, and locally gathered plants and berries. Animals were raised in cattle pens and sheds. Domesticates included cows, pigs, sheep, goats, hens, horses, dogs, and cats. Hunting equipment and faunal remains of wild game indicate that beaver, fox, hare, moose, deer, wolf, lynx, seal, various birds, and numerous fish were hunted, some for food and some for their pelts.

SOCIETY AND CULTURE

Many ethnic groups lived in early medieval Staraya Ladoga, among them, Balts, Finns, Slavs, and Scandinavians. These groups are distinguished more easily in the early centuries of settlement. Over time, the material culture of Staraya Ladoga became more homogenized. Archaeological research on burials throughout the Lake Ladoga region suggests that ethnic integration existed inside and outside the town. Although it is also known as Russia's first "capital," Staraya Ladoga is best characterized as a multi-ethnic trade town whose residents participated in the international Baltic Sea trade network.

See also **Rus** (*vol. 2, part 7*); **Russia/Ukraine** (*vol. 2, part 7*).

BIBLIOGRAPHY

Clarke, Helen, and Björn Ambrosiani. "Towns in the Slavonic-Baltic Area." In their *Towns in the Viking Age,* pp. 107–127. Rev. ed. Leicester, U.K.: Leicester University Press, 1995.

Uino, Pirjo. "On the History of Staraja Ladoga." *Acta Archaeologica* 59 (1988): 205–222.

RAE OSTMAN

HUGARY

Hungary, the central third of the 300,000-kilometer Carpathian Basin, is divided by the Danube River. The western hilly region (100–600 meters above sea level) is called Transdanubia. The marshy grasslands of the Great Hungarian Plain occupy most of the eastern half. Located at a geopolitical fault line between central Europe and the Eurasian steppe, and marked by a major river as well as a topographic interface, the Carpathian Basin has been divided periodically since prehistory. The historic east-west difference may be detected even today.

From the first century A.D., the paths of Germanic migrations from the north and of Asiatic peoples from the east crossed here in the Barbaricum and, later, over the ruins of the Roman province of Pannonia, leaving overlapping archaeological imprints that made the Migration period one of the least tangible archaeological ages in the region. These peoples are stereotypically described as mobile "nomads," best known for their spectacular pieces of portable art. Germanic peoples for whom there is the best evidence in the Carpathian Basin between the first and mid-sixth centuries included Quadi, Vandals, Gepids, Skirs, Goths, and Langobards. Some arrived from the north, and others followed a detour through the eastern European steppe, from where Asiatic Sarmatians, Alans, and Huns also came. After the late sixth century, Avars, Bulgars, Hungarians, and Cumanians all moved in from Asia. By that time Slavic territory surrounded the Carpathian Basin. Details of this geopolitical picture developed in a subtle chronological sequence. Heterogeneous archaeological sources and emotionally charged historical stereotypes provide only a fuzzy picture of "barbarians," often open to alternative interpretations.

SOURCES FOR THE MIGRATION PERIOD

Migrations left an archaeological record in Hungary that ranges from scarce settlement remains to spectacular hoards. Most field information, however, originates from burials. Most coeval documents chronicled historical events and the life of elites. Our image of barbarians is secondhand, influenced by the ethnocentrism of classical Greek, Roman, Byzantine, or Arabic authors. The word "barbarian" derives from the Greek *barbaros,* meaning "strange" or "foreign."

Interpretations have varied as research has evolved. In conventional terms, the Migration period in Hungary lasted from A.D. 271, when Romans ceded the province of Dacia, to 895, the date of the Hungarian conquest. Archaeologically, however, its beginnings and consequences span well over a millennium. While the historical chronology of barbarian groups is relatively clear, landmark events in the written record do not necessarily mean sudden invasion or complete disappearance of peoples. Mobility depended on the motivations and composition of migrants. Because the length of time that groups stayed also varied, their material cultures are difficult to compare. It is the historical model, therefore, that usually is refined based on stylistic differences between archaeological artifacts.

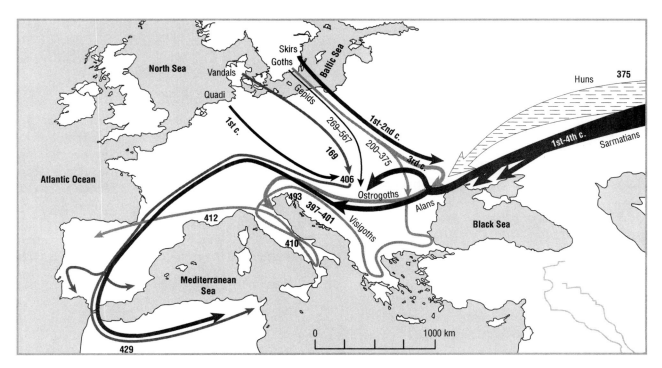

Early Migration period population movements. The migration routes of northern and eastern Germanic tribes as well as Asiatic peoples crossed in the Carpathian Basin. DRAWN BY LÁSZLÓ BARTOSIEWICZ.

Fine-grained absolute chronologies would be fundamental in the archaeology of this hectic period. Poor wood preservation in Hungary limits the use of dendrochronology. Radiocarbon dating, on the other hand, is somewhat inaccurate for later periods. "Typochronology," that is, the interpretation of culture change and ethnic relations using the relative chronology of artifact styles, thus has become the ruling paradigm in Migration period research. Weaknesses in this method are inherent to the finds: various groups are represented by different types of assemblages ill suited to direct comparison. Settlement remains tend to be few and far between, and the comprehensive analysis of cemeteries sometimes is difficult in the absence of proper physical anthropological information. Moreover, high-status grave goods may have remained in use for generations and were circulated over long distances. Antiquarians dug up spectacular hoards during the late eighteenth and nineteenth centuries, before the importance of stratigraphic information was recognized. No researcher can afford to ignore these unique assemblages, but interpretations often are difficult to fit into a systematic picture.

ROMAN PERIOD BARBARICUM

Even before the first-century establishment of the Roman province of Pannonia, inhabited at the time by "native" Celtic tribes, Transdanubia was linked closely to central Europe. The Danube served as a natural boundary for the Roman Empire. During the second and third centuries, the Barbaricum in the Great Hungarian Plain and areas to its north were wedged between Pannonia and the mountainous Roman province of Dacia. Having defeated the Scythians in southern Russia, Sarmatian tribes reached the Barbaricum during the first century as mercenaries for the Quadi, the first northern Germanic group to set foot in the Carpathian Basin. The Sarmatian light cavalry, covered head to toe by fish-scale-like armor, is depicted on Trajan's Column from A.D. 110–113.

Owing to their large population and prolonged presence, Sarmatians are well known from settlement excavations, beyond burials or documented movements. Rural settlements in the Barbaricum show that within a few generations they became sedentary and adopted local technical skills. Thereafter, traditional artifacts from the east indicate another Sarmatian wave. At the turn of the second century, after the Roman occupation of Dacia, Sarmatians spread across the Great Hungarian Plain. Ubiquitous Sarmatian pits dot an entire archaeological time horizon there.

Meanwhile, the Quadi moved south from their first-century territory and remained allied with Sarmatians facing the Romans across the Danube. Hectic relations between Romans and barbarians culminated in two decades of Marcomannic/Sarmatian wars, starting in the A.D. 170s. Finally, the Romans pacified the barbarians and created the province of Sarmatia. Finds show that trade contacts intensified: Roman goods of all sorts, including stamped pottery and a variety of jewelry, commonly occur at Sarmatian sites in the central Great Hungarian Plain. Large, barrel-shaped chalcedony beads may be found in Sarmatian women's graves, and enameled brooches show Celtic influence. Sarmatian pastoralists possibly bartered livestock and foodstuffs for such luxury goods. Weapons as well as settlement features reflect the advanced Sarmatian ironworking.

Vandals were the next northern Germanic group to come after the Marcomannic wars. They occupied northeastern Hungary and raided Roman provinces in the third to fourth centuries. Allied with Iranian-speaking Alans, they moved on to devastate Gaul (406–409), Iberia (409), North Africa (429), and Rome itself (455). Archaeologically, this group is known from burials in the Carpathian Basin. Celtic and Roman decorative art influenced the northern stylistic tradition of their grave goods. Artifacts from "royal" graves of the third to fourth centuries in Ostrovany (Slovakia), found in 1790 and 1865, respectively, have been linked with this group.

The consolidation of China during the third century, along with the hypothesized deterioration of steppe environments, drove Asiatic Huns westward. They crossed the Volga River during the early 370s, forcing eastern Germanic peoples (Goths and Skirs from Scandinavia, who had reached the steppe across the Baltic during the first century A.D.) into the Carpathian Basin. During their westward movement, the Goths, the strongest and most adventurous of the Germans, raided many parts of the Roman Empire throughout the third to fifth centuries. Their eastern confederacy, Ostrogoths, spent

twenty years in Pannonia before forming a kingdom in Italy (493). Western Visigoths were driven into the Balkans in the late fourth century, from where they sacked Rome in 410 and established a kingdom in present-day Spain and southern France.

Skirs surfaced for only a short time in the Carpathian Basin, in alliance with the Huns. The burials of two high-ranking ladies and another woman found in Bakodpuszta were associated with this eastern Germanic tribe. Gold and silver jewelry from these graves postdates Hun rule in the area. (Skirs rose to historical fame when their king Odoaker delivered a coup de grâce to the western Roman Empire by occupying Rome in 476.)

Sarmatians fought bitterly with Germans along their eastern borders during the fourth century and even built a 1260-kilometer-long system of ditches and earthworks, possibly with Roman help, along the northeastern edge of the Great Hungarian Plain. In Pannonia stylistic evidence from potsherds suggests that starting in the 370s, Romans enlisted Hun, Alan, and Germanic *foederati* (mercenaries who retained their tribal organization but acknowledged Roman supremacy) in the defense of the ailing province.

EARLY MIGRATION PERIOD

In 271, the year the Romans ceded Dacia to the Goths, Gepids occupied the upper reaches of the Tisza River. Following the uneasy coexistence of German tribes and Asiatic Sarmatians, as well as Alans neighboring the Roman Empire in the Carpathian Basin, a new Hun invasion reached Hungary in the first third of the fifth century. Renewed incursions by Ostrogoths, Visigoths, Vandals, and Alans (to name but a few) into the Carpathian Basin and the Roman Empire itself were, in part, a consequence of Hunnic expansion. Between 400 and 402 Huns invaded southern Poland, forcing out Germanic tribes and thereby opening up space for subsequent Slavic settlement. During the 410s, their power center moved into the Great Hungarian Plain through the Lower Danube region. Negotiations with the Romans also provided Hun *foederati* access to Pannonia. By this time, haphazardly rebuilt fortifications and intramural burials bear witness to the disintegration of Roman power along the Pannonian *limes*.

Huns organized a tribal confederation in the Carpathian Basin, uniting peoples on the basis of Roman *foederati* rights, filling a geopolitical vacuum between the competing western and eastern Roman Empires. Between 441 and 452 Huns conducted military campaigns in both directions, short of invading Rome itself. After the death of their king, Attila (in 453), however, allies rose and defeated the Huns under the leadership of the Gepids in 454, ending Hun rule in the Carpathian Basin.

The Hun empire that existed for only a single generation yielded numerous artifacts, many of which are commonly associated with oriental, warlike equestrian peoples but came to light as stray finds. Grave goods include metal fittings from high saddles as well as ears of powerful reflex bows (the extreme ends serving for chord attachment, made from antler or bone), double-edged swords, and long combat knives. Gold decoration on these and numerous utilitarian objects, as well as precious metal jewelry acquired as war booty or by punitive taxing, reflect the heyday of the Hun empire. Identifying "Hun" artifacts is difficult because this empire united numerous ethnic groups whose material cultures were similar at the outset. Artifacts were mixed further by diffusion and exchange. After the collapse of the Hun empire, many former vassals formed small "kingdoms." Huns fled toward the Pontic region, from where Ostrogoths came into the Carpathian Basin following a treaty with Byzantium. Archaeologically, this development is shown by jewelry displaying the classic stylistic features of Pontic metal workshops. One technique employed violet-red almandine or garnet in combination with enamel inlay. The Ostrogoths first moved eastward from southern Pannonia in 473 and then left for Italy in 489.

Eastern Germanic Gepids left Scandinavia and regrouped with the Goths in the area of present-day Poland during the Roman period. Pliny, who first mentioned the Goths, placed them in northern Germany. The historian Jordanes in his *Origin and Deeds of the Goths,* however, named their homeland as Scandinavia. Linguistic evidence may suport this, although the Scandinavian origin of the Goths is still impossible to prove. Archaeological evidence points to the Goths having slowly migrated from the Oder-Vistula region to the Ukraine and Scythia.

In the Carpathian Basin they established rural settlements north of Dacia in 269.

Gepids contributed a major contingent to the Hun army during the mid-fifth century, led the usurpation of power that followed Attila's death, and expanded toward the south and east: Sirmium (Mitrovica, Serbia), a Roman imperial town, became the Gepid capital. Important finds of Gepid aristocracy in Transylvania include the royal graves of Apahida and the Szilágysomlyó (Şimleul Silvaniei, Romania) hoards, discovered in 1797 and 1889, respectively, and consisting of Roman memorial gold medallions as well as gold and gilded silver brooches. Gepid cemeteries from the late fifth and sixth centuries contain hundreds of graves. Because many have been robbed, however, they are of limited help in reconstructing socioeconomic differences. High-ranking warriors were buried with long and short swords as well as lances and shields. Commoners were interred with silver and bronze brooches and other clothing accessories. Eagle-headed buckles seem to have been a favorite fashion item. It is possible that Christianity also reached this population through Gothic missionaries during the fourth century. This hypothesis is supported by crucifix motifs in their decorative art. Certain settlement excavations have revealed Gepid houses and adjoining sheds and workshops, containing artifacts related to both household and craft activities. Wheel-thrown, evenly fired, fine Gepid pottery with stamped decoration represents the Celtic-Sarmatian tradition.

After a second-century incursion, the Langobards entered the Carpathian Basin from the north in about 510 and took over urbanized northern Pannonia from other Germanic peoples in 526. At the beginning, they coexisted peacefully with Gepids, who at that time controlled the Great Hungarian Plain and Transylvania. In 535, however, Langobards forged an alliance with Byzantium that allowed them access to southern Pannonia, where they faced Gepids expanding westward. Decades of military skirmishes followed. After 565 Byzantine contacts with the Gepids improved, so that Langobards turned for help to the central Asian Avars, who had just started exploring the possibilities of westward expansion into the Carpathian Basin. From 562 onward, the supreme leader (*khagan*) of the Avars was Bayan Khan, comparable to Attila the

Hun in political stature. The Langobard-Avar alliance defeated the Gepids in 567. Part of the agreement seems to have been that Langobards had to leave Pannonia for Italy the following year.

Langobards were the last Germanic group to rule in the Carpathian Basin. Their material culture in Pannonia is known exclusively from burials. Given the history of Langobard occupation in Transdanubia, the ethnic composition of these cemeteries is complex. Men's burials contained large, double-edged swords, lances, and shields. Women were accompanied by gilded silver jewelry, including brooches decorated with northern as well as eastern stylistic elements.

THE LATE MIGRATION PERIOD

The appearance of Avars in the Carpathian Basin in the last third of the sixth century heralded a new era of centralized rule that united the Carpathian Basin for almost a quarter of a millennium. This is not to say, however, that Avars were an ethnically homogeneous population. The core groups of inner and central Asian extraction were first allied with Byzantium, whose protection they sought against Turkic groups that had forced them westward. As Langobards left for Italy in 568, the consolidation of Avar power began. Large cemeteries from the early Avar period in Transdanubia (Budakalász, Kölked A-B, Környe, and Zamárdi) suggest that the center of the emerging empire was in Pannonia. Aside from Avar finds, such as belt sets, globular earrings, and bead necklaces, grave goods reflect Germanic contacts.

The first sixty years of the Avar empire saw conflicts with Byzantium over Dalmatia and Thrace. Avars occupied the former Gepid capital of Sirmium in 582 and Singidunum (present-day Belgrade) in 584. Avars encouraged the settlement of northern Slavic allies around their empire, to buffer outside attacks. Merovingian contacts are evident from the early seventh century, with other Germanic connections. Amid confrontations and peace treaties, Avars extorted money and gold from Byzantium, whose military priority was securing its eastern border against the Persians. Although some gold solidus coins found in Hungary were trimmed around the edges, an estimated 20 metric tons of Byzantine gold may have reached the Avar empire. In 626 Avar troops laid siege to Constantinople (modern-day Istanbul) in alliance with the Persian navy, al-

though the two forces failed to unite. At that point, the Byzantine emperor Heraclius had had his fill of Avar intimidation and crushed the land offensive. Thereafter, as far as Byzantium was concerned, Avars ceased to exist as a political entity. Trying to compensate for lost revenue, Avars plundered Forum Iulii (Cividale, Lombardy) in 628, straining relations with their western, Germanic allies. Thereafter, they were confined to the Carpathian Basin. Their Slavic and Bulgar vassals also rebelled, weakening the empire from the inside.

Finds from both intact and looted high-status burials in the Great Hungarian Plain (Bócsa, Tépe, Kunágota, and Kunbábony) show that the Avar power center shifted from the right bank of the Danube toward the east during the first half of the seventh century. While the exact social status of the deceased is difficult to establish, there is little doubt that these burials represent the top of the Avar social hierarchy (fig. 1). All graves stood alone, with no permanent markers, such as burial mounds or tombstones. Accompanying burials of complete warhorses was not merely a privilege accorded to leaders; horse skeletons also occur in common warriors' graves. Thanks to the prolonged presence of Avars in the Carpathian Basin, in addition to fifty thousand known burials, there have been discoveries of several of their rural settlements, such as the 150 semi-subterranean houses identified at Kölked.

Early Avar weaponry, horse harness elements, and utilitarian objects tend to reflect oriental traditions, whereas jewelry and other high-status items in treasures (golden bowls and jugs and glassware, for example) represent a variety of artistic elements dominated by late antique and especially Byzantine influences. In comparison with early Avar cemeteries in Transdanubia, however, grave goods in large cemeteries of the Great Hungarian Plain (e.g., Tiszafüred–Majoros) show the declining impact of Mediterranean material culture. This duality in artifact styles confirms written accounts of early Avar history in the Carpathian Basin.

By the late seventh century the initial absence of jewelry and gold objects in graves may be explained by severed Byzantine contacts. In addition to a shift in the orientation of burials, grave goods also changed. These phenomena coincided with the reappearance of Byzantine stylistic features in the grave furniture. Such burials seem to mark the arrival of the Onogur-Bulgarians, a group of Turkic pastoral peoples. They had inhabited the northern Pontic region after 463, until the Khazars destroyed their empire around 670. Some fled to the Lower Danube region, and others reached the Avar empire but maintained intensive contacts with Byzantium.

Large Avar cemeteries from this time, together with evidence for sedentism in settlement materials, suggest that ethnic changes took place peacefully, presumably with the consent of the *khagan*. Historical sources reveal no major military events in the increasingly isolated Avar empire until the end of the eighth century. Burials suggest that equestrian lifestyles were maintained only by the ruling elites, and agriculture seems to have become a dominant occupation among commoners of mixed ethnicity. The integrity of burial rites appears to have declined, and some grave assemblages display signs of impoverishment. A marked change in grave goods is that the pressed metal fittings in men's belt sets were replaced by molded, usually bronze equivalents. Their acanthus motifs gave way to the so-called "griffin and meander" motif. This style was developed to perfection within the Carpathian Basin from evidently Eurasian/Byzantine roots. Floral elements replaced the initial animal fight motifs toward the late eighth century.

Gold objects in the so-called Nagyszentmiklós hoard (Sînnicolaur Mare, Romania), discovered in 1799, display an unusual richness of stylistic elements, dating from the seventh to eighth centuries on a typological basis. Interpretations of this twenty-three-piece "table set" have varied considerably. Researchers largely have accepted that its details reveal the complexity of Avar period mythology, religion, and possibly writing. Its details reflect Byzantine and Sassanian influences, illustrating the rich universe of what is considered late Avar culture today.

After the conquest of Lombardy (774) and the military campaign on Saxony (772–785) by the Frankish king Charlemagne, Frankish expansion from the west first hit the Avar empire in 788. Military campaigns in 791 and 795, together with vicious infighting, weakened the Avars to such an extent that an additional military thrust by Bulgar forces from the south in 804 destroyed their empire. Following these defeats, Charlemagne assigned the territory "Avaria" in 805, between Savaria (Szom-

Fig. 1. Avar Period "fake" golden buckle from a robbed grave in Tèpe, Hungary, mid-seventh century. High-status grave goods have been instrumental in the attempted reconstruction of Avar history. PHOTOGRAPH BY ANDRÁS DABASI. HUNGARIAN NATIONAL MUSEUM. REPRODUCED BY PERMISSION.

bathely) and Carnuntum (Deutsch-Altenburg). Of the Avar *khagans* Theodor was baptised in 803 and Abraham in 805. The Carpathian Basin again became divided: Bulgars took over the eastern section and raided southeastern Pannonia (826–829), dispersing the remaining Avar population. The rest of Pannonia fell into the Carolingian sphere of interest. Avar peoples in western Hungary are last mentioned in 871, as the taxpayers of the Frankish king.

During the 840s the Franks settled the Slavic chieftain Pribina in Mosaburg (Zalavár) in Pannonia. Although his position as head of a "Slavic state" there needs to be confirmed, he undoubtedly ruled an area whose Slavic population had increased in the wake of the Avar period. Pribina and his heir, Kocel, along with Bavarian settlers, may have represented Carolingian rule in the area. Archaeological finds display both Moravian and Carolingian stylistic influences. It appears that Pannonia was largely under Frankish rule between the fall of the Avar empire and the Hungarian conquest.

THE HUNGARIAN CONQUEST

In written sources Hungarians figure as yet another pastoral group from the steppe, often mistaken for Scythians, Turks, or Onugrians. The Magyars did not use the latter name, applied to both Bulgarians and Magyars (i.e., Hungarians), in reference to themselves. During the mid-sixth century eastern Turkic peoples triggered another wave of migrations that brought new peoples to the border between central Asia and Europe. Groups inhabiting the parkland steppe to the north, including the Finno-Ugric–speaking Magyars, also left their homelands for the steppe, which was economically more developed than the Ural region. There are similarities between burials of the sixth to eighth centuries in the Volga and Ural River interfluve and the tenth-century Magyar graves in Hungary. Subsequently, Magyars moved west of the Khazar Khanate north of the Caucasus, where they developed ties with Onogur-Bulgars. Around 850 the Magyars moved farther west, into the Etelköz section of the Dnieper River, seeking independence from the Khazar Khanate. It was there that artifact styles known from burials and settlements of the conquering Magyars in the Carpathian Basin seem to have consolidated.

In 862 Magyars scouted the Carpathian Basin, attacking the eastern Frankish empire. In 881 they returned to join the Moravians against the Franks and then led incursions into Transdanubia (894). Finally, with Turkic Bulgars and Pechenegs on their heels, the entire Magyar tribal alliance, lead by the grand duke Árpád, crossed the Carpathians into the Great Hungarian Plain in 895. The occupation of Pannonia in 900 reunited the Carpathian Basin. The first equestrian burial from the Magyar conquest period was found at Ladánybene–Benepuszta in 1834. The next such burial was discovered at Vereb in 1853, and others soon followed. At the time, however, tenth-century cemeteries of commoners were thought to represent slaves or local Slavs.

Magyar material culture cannot be regarded as a straight continuation of the Avar heritage, although the skull and feet of horses sometimes were included in the graves, possibly as part of the hide. Goldsmithing is well represented by gilded purse covers (e.g., Tiszabezde), some of which may have been made in Etelköz. The style, however, flourished in Hungary. A floral pattern, the so-called palmetta motif, became widespread during the conquest period. Burials also contain objects reflecting ancient beliefs. Bone stick handles carved in the shape of owls' heads were found at Hajdúdorog and Szeghalom.

The mass of precious metal acquired through vicious military campaigns, starting with Italy in 899, gave goldsmithing impetus. The next three fourths of the tenth century became known as the "period of raids." Magyar horsemen destroyed Great Moravia (902) and then turned on the rest of Europe, especially the German provinces, reaching Burgundy in 913 and Bremen in 915. In 924 Magyars simultaneously plundered Italy in the south and Saxony in the north and reached the Atlantic coast as well. It was only the desert that halted their westernmost raid toward the Caliphate of Córdoba (942), and they repeatedly threatened Byzantium (934, 943, 958, 963, and 970) in the east. Military success was related to the mobility of their cavalry compared with the ponderous armies they faced. Aside from brutality, logistical support for such far-reaching campaigns would have been impossible without shrewd diplomacy: not even the most formidable cavalry could have covered such distances crossing purely enemy territory. Raids contributed to the wealth of chieftains and their military entourage. Precious metal artifacts of foreign origin, however, hardly ever occur in Magyar graves. One possibility is that they were melted down.

A devastating defeat by Germans near Augsburg ended westward aggression in 955. Magyars attacked Byzantium until their ultimate conquest in 972. By that time a network of agricultural settlements had developed in Hungary, as the elite warriors of the old order began losing prestige and economic power. These hardships started transforming a mobile Asiatic horde into an established European kingdom.

Hungary was caught between east and west even in peacetime. After 940, a group of Magyar leaders led by Bultsu was baptized in Constantinople. Constantine Porphyrogenitus (Constantine VII, 913–959) stood as godfather. The Byzantine influence among the Magyars was concentrated east of the Tisza River.

In 974, however, the grand duke Géza turned to the Holy Roman Empire and converted to western Christianity, thereby steering the development of his people into the European Middle Ages. After his death, his son István I was crowned in 1000 as the first Christian king of Hungary. The adoption of western Christianity changed material culture. The colorful eastern style disappeared, and ancient beliefs were suppressed. In return for pacification and ideological changes, Magyars survived as a political entity in the Carpathian Basin.

Hungary, however, still faced barbarian threats on the fringes of Europe for centuries. Incursions by Pechenegs and other, smaller groups continued, and "pagan" Magyars also rebelled from within against the new order. Consolidation took several generations. During the 1222–1223 campaign of the Mongol leader Genghis Khan, Turkic-speaking Cumanians moved west from the Pontic steppe, adopted Christianity in 1227, and became Hungarian subjects. Mongols attacked again in 1238, and the rest of the Cumanians fled westward from the Doniec-Dnieper interfluve. In 1239 they crossed the Carpathians. According to the 1243–1244 *Carmen miserabile* by the Italian chronicler Rogerius (later archbishop of Split, Croatia), "because of their great multitude, and because their people were hard and crude and knew no subordination . . . [King Béla IV of Hungary] nominated one of his own leaders to guide them into the center of his country." Cumanians were granted freedom but had to submit to the king and convert to Christianity.

When Mongols reached Hungary in 1241, Magyars thought they spotted Cumanians among the attackers and killed the khan of the new settlers. Cumanians fled southeast, raping and pillaging on their way. Around 1246 the king invited Cumanians back into Hungary. A 1279 decree defined a contiguous Cumanian homeland in the central portion of the Great Hungarian Plain. It prescribed that Cumanians take up a "Christian, sedentary" way of life.

Cumanian cavalry, however, remained instrumental in the royal army until the mid-fourteenth century. Assimilation was accomplished only by the sixteenth century, when permanent settlements became common and Cumanians erected their own churches.

See also **Animal Husbandry; Goths between the Baltic and Black Seas; Huns; Langobards; Ostrogoths; Scythians; Visigoths** (*all vol. 2, part 7*).

BIBLIOGRAPHY

Bóna, István. "Die Awarenfeldzüge und der Untergang der Byzantinischen Provinzen und der unteren Donau." In *Kontakte zwischen Iran, Byzanz und der Steppe in 6.–7. jh.* Edited by Csanád Bálint, pp. 163–183. Budapest, Hungary: Varia Archaeologica Hungariae, 2000.

———. "The Hungarians and Europe in the Tenth Century." In *A Cultural History of Hungary: From the Beginning to the Eighteenth Century.* Edited by L. Kósa, pp. 42–59. Budapest, Hungary: Corvina-Osiris Press, 1999.

———. *The Dawn of the Dark Ages: The Gepids and the Lombards in the Carpathian Basin.* Budapest, Hungary: Corvina Press, Hereditas Series, 1976.

Bóna, István, and Margit Nagy. *Gepidische Gräberfelder am Theissgebiet I.* Budapest, Hungary: Magyar Nemzeti Múzeum, 2002.

Christie, Neil. *The Lombards.* Oxford: Blackwell Press, 1995.

Daim, Falko, ed. *Reitervölker aus dem Osten: Hunnen + Awaren.* Schloss Halbturn, Austria: Burgenländische Landesausstellung, 1996.

Kovács, Tibor, and Éva Garam, eds. *A Magyar Nemzeti Múzeum régészeti kiállításának vezetője (Kr. e. 400,000–Kr. u. 804)* [Guide to the archaeological exhibit of the Hungarian National Museum]. Budapest, Hungary: Magyar Nemzeti Múzeum, 2002.

Laszlovszky, József, ed. *Tender Meat under the Saddle: Customs of Eating, Drinking, and Hospitality among Conquering Hungarians and Nomadic Peoples.* Krems, Austria: Medium Aevum Quotidianum, 1998.

Lengyel, Alfonz, and G. T. B. Radan, eds. *The Archaeology of Roman Pannonia.* Budapest, Hungary, and Lexington: University Press of Kentucky/Akadémiai Kiadó, 1980.

Pálóczi Horváth, András. *Pechenegs, Cumans, Iasians: Steppe Peoples in Medieval Hungary.* Budapest, Hungary: Corvina Press, Hereditas Series, 1989.

LÁSZLÓ BARTOSIEWICZ

CZECH LANDS/SLOVAKIA

The Slavs may have entered the historical scene late, but they did so in an impressive way. Sometime in the fifth century A.D., the expansion of the nomadic Huns in central Asia led to massive ethnic migrations. The Slavs, too, began to move away from their original domiciles in the east of Europe, soon becoming acquainted with the advanced cultural world of the eastern Roman Empire. From A.D. 531 onward, Slavic warriors plundered the territory of the Balkans, leaving terror in their wake. The Slavic expansion to central Europe took a quieter course. There the colonists met only remnants of the original Germanic population in an almost depopulated landscape. At about the beginning of the sixth century, the first wave of immigration arrived in the territories of Bohemia and Moravia. The chronicler Kosmas, who lived and worked during the late eleventh century and early twelfth century, describes the time of the arrival of the Slavs (who were led by their mythical ancestor Čech, or "Czech") and their settlement as idyllic and their life as quiet and peaceful. The results of archaeological excavations suggest that this was the case.

The first Slavic settlements followed the fertile basins of major rivers, and their appearance is remarkably uniform: a group of several countersunk dwellings in plots 3.65 by 3.65 meters in size, all equipped with oven and bed plus storage pits for grain. Traces of internal social differentiation are unclear. Unfortified settlements are laid out in a more or less regular pattern at a distance of about 1.6 kilometers from one another, which gave the individual communities space for fields and pastures. Only occasionally, a grouping of some ten houses appears at a strategic and important site.

THE EMPIRE OF SAMO

The peaceful times did not last long. Apart from the influences of states west and south of Czech territory, social changes in the Slavic world stemmed from a new wave of attacks, this time by the Avars from the steppes of Asia. In A.D. 558 a new series of conflicts with the Roman Empire began. The Germanic Langobards started to leave Pannonia, and the territory was occupied by the Avar ruler. Thus the Czech Slavs gained an unwelcome neighbor in the southeast. The pressure from the incursions of these nomadic horsemen brought about a new wave of Slavic colonists, who arrived in Bohemia and Moravia at the end of the sixth century.

The degree of the Slavs' dependence on the Avars varied. Some Slavic troops even fought in the Avar armies, but at the beginning of the seventh century relations became strained. Led by the merchant Samo, perhaps an emissary of the western Roman Empire, the Slavs rose up and prevailed against the Avars. In A.D. 623 Samo was elected king of a newly established "state," which included modern-day Bohemia and Moravia plus parts of Slovakia and Carinthia (now a part of Austria). Samo's domain probably had its center in the lowlands of southern Moravia.

The independence of this new empire soon became a thorn in the side of its neighbor in the west, the Merovingian western Roman Empire. In A.D. 631 King Dagobert of that empire sent expeditionary troops of Langobards, Alemanni, and Austrasians, with the aim of forcing Samo to submit fully to Merovingian domination. Despite the limited victories by the first two military corps, the expedition was not ultimately successful: the third and main corps of forces was stopped on the border of Samo's empire, at the castle Wogastiburg. The location of the castle is the subject of controversy, but it probably was situated in northwestern Bohemia. Still this is the first time that literary documents mention the existence of fortified seats (that is, castles) in the Slavic world of central Europe.

Samo's empire did not survive its ruler, however, and for the following two centuries accounts of Slavs in Bohemia and Moravia are vague. The reason is clear: after A.D. 680 the newly arrived nomadic Bulgars were wedged between the Byzantine Empire and the Avar territory in the southeast. They cut off the Avars from their rich sources of booty and thus indirectly forced these nomads in the lowlands of Pannonia to adapt to a settled life. Meanwhile the neighboring territories to the west were beset by internal fighting among the Merovingians. Eventually their majordomos emerged as the winners, and Charlemagne began a new era as emperor of the western Roman Empire. Charlemagne did not neglect his eastern neighbors in his policy of expansion. Having defeated the Saxons and the settled Avars, his armies once again set out to the Czech territory in three parts, only to fail again in A.D. 805 at a castle known as Canburg somewhere in the northern half of Bohemia. This time, though, the success of the Slavs did not persist. The Frankish army resorted to the usual strategy of destroying crops, and the following year another expedition forced the Czech Slavs formally to acknowledge their dependence on Charlemagne's empire and to pay taxes.

Still the Dark Ages (the seventh and eighth centuries), from which there are no written accounts, represent a period of lively social changes in the Slavic world. The Canburg castle was just one of numerous castles built—as archaeologists' findings have proved—with growing intensity in these two centuries. The system of forts, which for the most part were situated at the ingresses into and at the peripheries of populated areas, is itself a sign of the social changes taking place that were necessary for the building of such large fortification systems. This building work was probably organized by the emerging local military nobility, as is evident in the finds of both western spurs and eastern jewels and ornaments from the Avar culture. This cultural synthesis gave rise to the first more or less stable state.

GREAT MORAVIA

In A.D. 791 Charlemagne instigated wars with the Pannonian Avars that went on for decades, and it was—among other things—quarrels inside the Avar kingdom that contributed to the definitive victory of the Frankish empire. Charlemagne probably had no idea that in this way he was untying the hands of the Avars' Slavic neighbors in Moravia and western Slovakia. It is no accident that the last appearance of the Avars on the political stage in A.D. 822 is at the same time as the first appearance of the Slavs known as Moravians. That year the Moravians appeared with the Slavs dependent on the empire before the Bavarian king Ludwig the German.

The Moravians, however, had their own idea of dependence on the Frankish empire. Relatively soon they used both the fall of the Avar kingdom and the internal crisis in the Frankish empire to strengthen their hegemony. Mojmír I, the first of the princes (dukes) of the emerging dynasty, appeared in the A.D. 830s; at about the same time, Western Christianity was accepted in Moravia. Apart from the assumption of certain ideological and spiritual values, the acceptance of Christianity in early medieval central Europe meant both juridical protection (though not completely reliable) from the eagerness of the Frankish empire to convert pagans to Christianity and a new sociopolitical system that would strengthen the increasing stratification in Moravian society. But the new state would soon be tested. In A.D. 843 the Frankish empire fell apart, and three years later Ludwig the German, by then ruler of the newly established eastern Frankish empire, attacked Moravia, dethroned Mojmír, and replaced him with Prince Rostislav.

Rostislav's vassalage was fabricated, however. This clever politician formed a coalition with neighboring Slavs and persistently strengthened his position in Moravia. At his behest, a mission of Eastern Christianity came to Moravia from the Byzantine Empire in A.D. 863. This mission did not bring the longed-for independent bishopric to Moravia right away, but it did bring a newly created script based

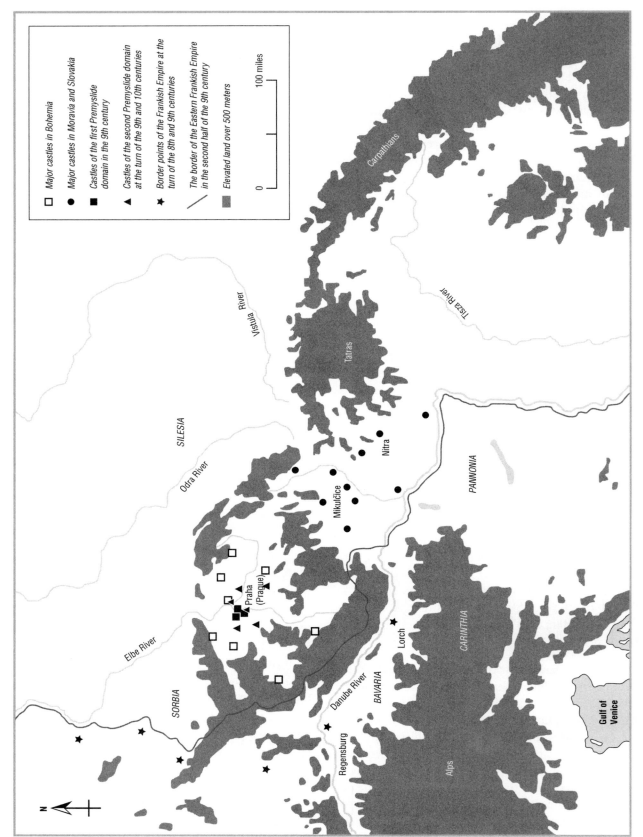

The Czech lands from the arrival of the Slavs to the beginnings of the Czech Premyslide state. DRAWN BY PETR MEDUNA.

on the phonetic transcription of the "universal" Slavic language. In his attempt to gain control over Moravia in the years A.D. 864–874, Ludwig the German made another wrong choice when installing a new ruler. This ruler, Svatopluk, a nephew of Rostislav, managed to occupy and defend Moravian territory with his own forces, and he proved to be a provident politician when he acknowledged his dependence on the eastern Frankish empire, thus showing his loyalty. This ensured him peace, and he could begin to develop further the state concept of his predecessor: formal annexation of neighboring territories, which ensured him revenues to run the state apparatus and allowed him to keep a large professional military retinue.

The social hierarchy in Moravia was a complicated system. At the top of the social pyramid was the ruler, the "chief of chiefs." At the lower levels were magnates and princes from the original tribal nobility and the nongoverning members of the Mojmír dynasty on the one hand and the clergy on the other. Then there was a special group: the military retinue, that is, the state army. The lowest stratum among the free consisted of the rural population. The base of this imaginary pyramid (but not the economic basis) was formed by the unfree domestics, or slaves—that is, those who were not sold to the Mediterranean as a frequent and welcome source of income.

The image of Great Moravia's fame has been made more complete thanks to archaeological excavations in the centers. At the top of an imaginary hierarchy one can put Mikulčice, probably Rostislav's seat of power, referred to by contemporaries as "an unspeakable fort, unlike all ancient forts." Originally an old castle, Mikulčice had almost become a town. Walls several kilometers long of complex tree-and-earth construction and the branches of the Morava River surrounded residences where the highest echelon of the Great Moravian nobility was concentrated. From the windows of his one-story palace, the ruler could enjoy a view of the magnates' estates, filled with light shining off the white walls of churches and reflecting from their varied architecture. The undisturbed peace of this view was enhanced further by the independent housing of the military retinue—uniform barracks-like log cabins, the homes of his well-fed and well-armed mounted warriors situated within sight of the ruler's palace.

Only the smoke from the numerous artisans' workshops might have disturbed the view of the Moravian plains.

The artisans produced a whole range of material goods, instruments, tools, and weapons. The repeated Frankish bans on weapons export to the Slavs and the growing numbers of the warriors soon led to domestic production of high-quality swords for mounted warriors and also of Moravian war axes. These were the main weapons of foot soldiers, that is, free farmers, and they are found among the grave goods at most rural burial places from that time. The craftspeople developed their own style, which borrowed from cultural influences of both the Carolingian world to the west and the Avar and then Byzantine realms in the southeast. In particular, jewelry of exceptional artistic quality and technical achievement defined the development of art handicrafts in central Europe. Products that could not be produced at home came to the central Moravian market mainly with trading caravans. Commodities were imported from places ranging from the Rhineland to central Asia and from Scandinavia to the Mediterranean.

In light of the glory of Great Moravia, one could easily overlook the instability of its whole political system. Territorial expansion brought rulers income in the form of booty from the territories of today's Bohemia, Slovakia, Poland, and Hungary. This made it possible for them to sustain their military retinue. At the same time, it brought about the interior instability of a conglomerate of dependent territories where allies could easily become enemies. The military retinue created its own vicious circle: more expansion led to a larger retinue, which meant further expansion, and so on. In the end, only the most powerful neighbors were left, in the shape of the reconsolidated eastern Frankish empire.

The social structure itself also was a cause of instability. Among the nobility were members of the original tribal aristocracy from the regional dynasties, and the population consisted to a considerable extent of free farmers who worked on their own, not state-owned, land, which provided no tax revenues for the state treasury. A test of Great Moravia's strength came in the A.D. 860s, when nomadic horsemen—this time the Hungarians—once again arrived from the eastern steppes. In the following decades they were both feared raiders and welcome allies of warring European rulers. In A.D. 892 Prince Svatopluk successfully opposed Bavarian-Hungarian aggression, but he died two years later, and the empire, held together only by the power of his personality, slowly began to collapse. His sons, Mojmír II and Svatopluk II, along with the Bavarians and the Hungarians, began to play an intricate political game, with mutual alliances and hostilities. In A.D. 906 this intrigue resulted in a devastating defeat of the allied Moravian-Bavarian army by the Hungarians in the territory of today's Slovakia. Thus under the hooves of Hungarian horses, Great Moravia disappeared from the map of Europe. Soon a close neighbor, Bohemia, found inspiration in its example.

THE BEGINNINGS OF THE CZECH STATE

At the very beginning of the ninth century, Bohemia was in a period of extensive structural changes, among them the planning of castle building. No longer did castles line the perimeters of populated areas; instead, they were built in the centers. The asynchronous development of the individual parts of Bohemia betrayed the slowly emerging regional nobility. A certain emancipation in the material culture was another sign of change: gradually the proportions of men's and women's luxury objects in archaeological finds equalized, which may have been a result of the emergence of regional princely dynasties. There were also transformations in the spiritual sphere, evident in the changeover from cremation to inhumation. In this an effort to sustain and preserve the continuity of family can be anticipated. Gradually impulses from the Christian rite probably became a part of this effort.

In A.D. 845 a group of fourteen Czech princes traveled to Ludwig the German's domain in Bavaria to be converted to Christianity. Like the Moravians, their aim most likely was to avoid giving the Bavarian king an excuse for an attack against pagans. One year later, however, Ludwig the German attacked Christian Moravia, and the Czechs became radical allies of the Moravians. This more or less short-lived period of temporary Christianity in Bohemia gives an important piece of information about the number of magnates ruling in the individual regions of Bohemia. Similar to Moravia, Bohemia was a loosely structured grouping of states, appearing as a unit-ed whole from the outside though territorially divided within.

The present state of archaeological information makes it possible, with varying degrees of detail, to define as many as ten small territorial formations in Bohemia at the time, each dominated by a castle situated in the center of the settlement. It was only a matter of time before one of the regional dynasties tried to seize power in the whole of Bohemia. It did not take long for a suitable candidate to appear. Prince Bořivoj was the first historically documented member of what was to be the Premyslide dynasty of central Bohemia, named after its legendary ancestor Přemysl. Relatively soon this ambitious magnate appeared at Svatopluk's court in Great Moravia, where he was converted to Christianity around the year A.D. 883. This conversion gave him access to the political elite in Moravia, but in Bohemia his baptism brought about a furious reaction and led to civil war. The war made it possible for Svatopluk to launch a military intervention for the benefit of his pretender and temporarily annex Bohemia as a part of the Great Moravian empire. In Bohemia it is possible to trace the close relations with Great Moravia and their varying intensity in this period, mostly in central Bohemia, where Great Moravian jewels and weapons had a strong presence.

Thanks to his firm political position, Bořivoj was able to exercise both his faith and his power. Having built his first church, Saint Clement's, at the Levý Hradec castle in central Bohemia, he immediately built another church consecrated to the Holy Virgin. This church is located in the very heart of the country, at the newly built castle of Prague. From this seat of power Bořivoj's sons, Spytihněv and then Vratislav, began building up the country. The situation abroad was favorable: the eastern Frankish empire to the west was in crisis, and the Great Moravian empire in the southeast was coming to an end.

It was probably the first of the two brothers who used the two peaceful decades of his reign in the years A.D. 895–915 to carry out the fortification of central Bohemia. North of Prague Spytihněv rebuilt the castle of Mělník, originally the center of an independent region. Four more castles were built, each about 12.5 kilometers (about 20 miles) from Prague; thus the Prague basin was surrounded at strategic points by a pentagon of forts. At the same time the building of churches inside the forts also declared the Premyslides' new concept of state. They still were not the sovereign rulers of the whole of Bohemia, however.

Václav, the eldest of Vratislav's sons, was content—just like his predecessors—with formal dependence of the surrounding principalities. His brother, Boleslav, was not so content. In A.D. 935 Boleslav murdered his brother and thus cleared the way to the throne for himself. One year later he launched an attack on one of the neighboring rulers and started both the systematic occupation of Czech territory and a fourteen-year-long conflict with the German emperor Otto I. Throughout Bohemia's territory, the castle network was restructured according to a unified concept. Older castles were abandoned or demolished, and new ones were built close by. They reflected a more or less unified type of fortification, and most of them also had churches. Large settlement groupings began to arise near the newly built castles. In the tenth century the Premyslides deprived the regional nobility of

their power, deployed their own military retinue, built up a new bureaucratic apparatus, imposed taxes on the population, and introduced their own coins, thus laying the foundation of the Czech state.

See also **Slavs and the Early Slav Culture** (*vol. 2, part 7*).

BIBLIOGRAPHY

Bubeník, J., I. Pleinerová, and N. Profantová. "Od počátků hradišť k počátkům přemyslovského státu. Von den Anfängen der Burwälle zu den Anfängen des Přemyslidenstaates." *Památky archeologické* 89, no. 1 (1998): 104–145.

Sláma, J. *Střední Čechy v raném středověku.* Vol. 3, *Archeologie o počátcích přemyslovského státu* [Central Bohemia in the Early Middle Ages. Vol. 3, Archaeology and the beginnings of the Přemysl-Dynasty State]. Praehistorica 14. Prague, Czech Republic: Universita Karlova, 1988.

Třeštík, D. *Vznik Velké Moravy: Moravané, Čechové a střední Evropa v letech.* Prague, Czech Republic: Nakladatelství Lidové noviny, 2002.

———. *Počátky Přemyslovců: Vstup Čechů do dějin.* Prague, Czech Republic: Nakladatelství Lidové noviny, 1997.

PETR MEDUNA

GERMANY AND THE LOW COUNTRIES

According to the standard terminology, the Roman period in the Low Countries and Germany south and west of the Rhine River began with Julius Caesar's conquest of Gaul, completed in 51 B.C. For the next five centuries those regions were under the political control of Rome. Shortly after Caesar's conquest, Rome became embroiled in civil war lasting from 49 B.C., when Caesar led his army across the Rubicon River into Italy, until 30 B.C., with the rise of Octavian, or Augustus, to supreme power in Rome. During this period there is little evidence for major change in the way of life of the peoples of this region.

Roman written sources indicate that, from the time of the Roman conquest, the newly acquired territories were plagued by incursions by groups of Germans from east of the Rhine. The Roman emperor Augustus spent the years 16–13 B.C. in the Rhineland and Gaul, overseeing the creation of military bases on the west bank of the river to protect Gaul. Since the nineteenth century extensive archaeological research has revealed much about the progress of the Roman defensive buildup. Major bases for Roman legions (between five thousand and six thousand men) were established at Vechten and Nijmegen in the Netherlands and at Xanten, Moers-Asberg, Neuss, Cologne, and Mainz in Germany. Beginning in 12 B.C. Roman armies launched a series of campaigns across the Rhine as far east as the Elbe River. Between 12 and 7 B.C. Rome established a series of bases east of the Rhine on the Lippe River to aid in conquests eastward. The base at Haltern, built around 10 B.C. and abandoned in

A.D. 9, is the most extensively excavated early Roman period legionary camp, and its structure provides a detailed view into the character of these complex military institutions that served as towns for the soldiers stationed at them.

Rome's attempts to extend its military conquests beyond the Lower Rhine were brought to an end by an attack on three Roman legions in a place known as the Teutoburg Forest in northern Germany. According to writings by Roman and Greek historians, a Germanic leader called Arminius led the slaughter of three legions of Roman soldiers, together with auxiliary forces—some twenty thousand men. In 1987 the site of this great battle was discovered at Kalkriese near the small city of Bramsche. Excavations begun in 1989 have yielded some of the best information about a Roman battlefield.

As a result of this disaster for the Roman forces in September A.D. 9, Rome gave up its attempts to conquer eastward beyond the Lower Rhine and consolidated its positions along the west bank of that river. The bases that Augustus had established between 16 and 13 B.C. were expanded and strengthened, and new bases were established. The Lower Rhine remained the Roman Empire's frontier for the next four centuries.

DEVELOPMENT OF THE
ROMAN PROVINCES

The Roman bases in the Rhineland had been established in a prosperous region inhabited by peoples commonly referred to as Gauls and Germans. The new communities of soldiers created enormous demand for foodstuffs and raw materials from the countryside. This demand resulted in the beginning of a cash economy in the region and rapid growth in wealth for many local communities. Bases contracted with native communities to supply foodstuffs and critical materials, such as iron and leather. Natives established settlements known as *vici* (singular *vicus*) near the military bases, to provide the soldiers with things they might wish to buy with the money they earned, such as ornaments for their uniforms, trinkets, wine and beer, and other treats. These commercial communities often grew to substantial sizes and produced goods for both military and civilian clienteles.

Substantial towns and cities sprang up near many of the bases, as at Nijmegen around the middle of the first century A.D. The largest Roman city in this region was Colonia Claudia Ara Agrippinensium, modern-day Cologne. A military base was established on the site before the birth of Christ, and a civilian settlement grew close by. The Roman Rhine fleet was stationed at Cologne, just south of the city. In the middle of the first century A.D. Roman Cologne was designated a colonial city, and in about A.D. 85 it became the capital of the province Germania Inferior. In the following centuries it had a population of about fifteen thousand—large for a Roman city north of the Alps. Several thousand more lived just beyond the city walls. The inhabitants of Cologne and other Roman cities were mostly local natives who moved into the new urban centers, attracted by economic opportunities. Except for governmental officials, few persons moved from Italy to take up residence in the new provinces. When scholars refer to the people in Cologne, for example, as Romans, they mean mainly locals who adopted aspects of the Roman way of life, not people who came from Rome.

In the countryside of northern Gaul, Rome introduced the villa system of agricultural production. The villa was an estate, organized around the residence of the owner and his or her family. Residences could be large and ornate if wealthy people owned them, but they also could be very modest. Around the villa were fields, orchards, kitchen gardens, and workshops, usually including a smithy for making iron tools and a pottery for producing the vessels needed. Wealthy owners had tenants who did the agricultural and craft work of the villas. Ideally villas

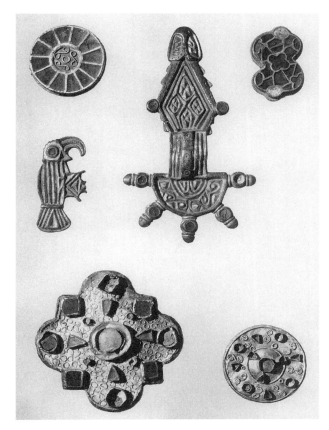

Fig. 1. Frankish jewelry of the sixth and seventh centuries showing the animal-style ornament and gold-and-garnet inlay. RÖMISCH-GERMANISCHES ZENTRALMUSEUM, MAINZ, GERMANY. REPRODUCED BY PERMISSION.

were economically independent units that produced most of what the residents needed, but they also generated surpluses for trade to the cities to exchange for goods manufactured in the urban centers or imported from other regions. In many instances what had been typical houses of the indigenous Late Iron Age populations were transformed over time into versions of the Roman villa, as, for example, at Mayen in the middle Rhineland.

In other aspects of life the archaeological evidence also shows a persistence of indigenous cultural traditions and only a gradual integration of new Roman ideas and practices. Excavations at the large cemetery of Wederath near the Moselle River show that, even in the second and third centuries A.D., elements of traditional funerary ritual were maintained in the arrangement of burials and in the choice of objects to include as grave goods. Places where gods were worshiped also show the complex

Fig. 2. Frankish jewelry of the sixth and seventh centuries. RÖMISCH-GERMANISCHES ZENTRALMUSEUM, MAINZ, GERMANY. REPRODUCED BY PERMISSION.

interplay of new Roman themes and traditional local ones. At Empel in the Netherlands archaeologists found a ritual site at which metal brooches, coins, and other objects were deposited during the prehistoric Iron Age. In the Roman period a typical Gallo-Roman rectangular temple was constructed on the site, and people continued to deposit the same categories of ritual offerings. The deities worshiped also show a melding of local and Roman. At Empel the god to whom the offerings were made was called Hercules Magusenus—a god with both Roman and native names. Well into the Roman period the traditional Rhineland mother goddesses were accorded a special place in the provincial pantheon. At the mouth of the Rhine the Celtic goddess Nehalennia remained the object of devotion for Roman period merchants setting sail into the North Sea.

The first and second centuries A.D. were times of great prosperity in the Roman Rhineland and northeastern Gaul. Natural resources were abundant in the region, and the Rhine offered easy transport of goods. By the middle of the third century

A.D. the period of greatest peace and prosperity had passed. The Roman Rhineland was plagued by incursions by warrior bands from the east, known to the Roman writers as Franks.

ACROSS THE RHINE FRONTIER

From the time of Caesar's campaigns in Gaul (58–51 B.C.), in the lands east of the Rhine, the practice of burying many men with sets of weapons became common. The complete weapon set consisted of a long iron sword, two lances, and a shield. More often a grave contained just one or two lances, sometimes with a shield. Large cemeteries have been excavated at Grossromstedt and Schkopau, both in the former East Germany. Many of the richer weapon graves also contain spurs and Roman bronze vessels. The new role of weapons in burial ritual signals a new importance attributed to military affairs. Perhaps it was a reaction to Caesar's campaigns in Gaul and to his forays across the Rhine in 55 and 53 B.C., but the graves that contain spurs and Roman vessels suggest another reason. In his reports about his conquests in Gaul, Caesar mentioned that he hired German troops to fight with the Roman army, in particular as cavalry, because they were regarded as expert horsemen. Perhaps some of the graves with weapons, spurs, and Roman vessels represent men who served with the Roman army and returned to their homes, ultimately to be buried with signs of their status and of their successful mercenary service to Rome.

This practice of burying sets of weapons, Roman vessels, and sometimes horse-riding paraphernalia with some men continued in fashion throughout the Roman and early medieval periods. In the first century A.D. large cemeteries around the lower Elbe River, such as those at Harsefeld and Putensen near Hamburg, include many examples of this practice. Some graves contain not only weapons and Roman vessels but also elaborate gold and silver ornaments, both local and Roman in origin. These unusually wealthy graves are known as the Lübsow group. Such burials occur across a broad landscape east of the Rhine, from Norway in the north to the Czech Republic in the south to Poland in the east. Their presence shows that significant status differences existed among the peoples east of the Rhine. The similarities in burial structure and in grave goods further indicates that elites in different parts of northern Europe shared common symbols and values that they represented in their burial practices.

Settlements north of the Rhine in the Netherlands and east of the Rhine in Germany remained small throughout the Roman period, most of them farmsteads or very small villages. Many show evidence of interaction with the Roman world across the Rhine. Excavations at Rijswijk in the Netherlands show that between A.D. 30 and 120 the successive generations that inhabited a farm gradually adopted Roman architectural ideas as well as Roman pottery and metal objects. At Wijster in the Netherlands and at Feddersen Wierde on the North Sea coast of Germany, quantities of Roman pottery, coins, brooches, glass beads and vessels, and grindstones from Mayen attest to interactions across the frontier.

The first indigenous form of writing east of the Rhine was created sometime during the first or second century A.D. The earliest runes are short inscriptions incised onto metal objects, especially women's jewelry and men's weapons. Runes were created by people who were familiar with the Latin alphabet of Rome and with the way that the alphabet represented spoken words. The locations of the earliest runes known, such as those on a bronze fibula from Meldorf in Schleswig-Holstein, suggest that this development took place in northern Germany and Denmark.

MEROVINGIAN PERIOD (A.D. 482–751)

The Merovingian period is a historical designation for the Early Middle Ages, named for the founder of the first Frankish dynasty. By the start of this period Roman effective power had disintegrated, though Rome continued to play an important role in the minds of many local leaders. In the Rhineland and the Low Countries the dominant group is known as Franks, whereas east of the Rhineland, in northern Germany, were groups identified as Saxons. Many of the old Roman urban centers, such as Cologne and Mainz, remained significant centers of population, industry, and commerce, though they had declined in population from the early Roman period.

The complex interplay of influences of the Roman world and the new Germanic societies is well illustrated in the grave of the Frankish king Childeric, discovered at Tournai in Belgium. Late Roman written sources reveal that Childeric was a local Frankish king who commanded Germanic troops in the service of the late Roman army, helping to protect the Rhineland from Saxon invasions. He died in A.D. 481 or 482. His grave shows his complex role with respect to Rome and to his Germanic origins. A gold signet ring with his portrait and his name in Latin and a gold fibula of a type traditionally presented by Roman emperors to leaders who provide service to Rome demonstrate his link to the Roman world. His style of burial, however, with a full set of weapons, including a sword in a scabbard ornamented with gold and garnet and a gold bracelet, show that his funeral included the traditional rituals of native practice. Other excavations in Tournai reveal that, as part of his funerary ritual, at least twenty-one horses were sacrificed and buried in three pits around his grave—a practice foreign to the Roman world but common in Germanic societies.

During the latter part of the Roman period a new style of ornament developed that was known as Germanic art. This style became important as a marker of identity among peoples who wanted to distinguish themselves from Roman traditions, and it flourished in the fifth and sixth centuries. Its origins were diverse and reflect the varied influences that formed the societies of the early medieval period. The ornamental technique known as chip carving—removing chips of metal from a surface with a burin—was adopted from Roman techniques used to decorate fittings on soldiers' belts. The characteristic animal ornament derived from earlier artistic traditions in central and northern Europe. In elite contexts, as in Childeric's grave, gold inlaid with garnet was an important new style adapted from traditions associated with the people known as Goths north of the Black Sea. This new style was applied to a variety of objects, especially personal ornaments and weapons.

By the start of the fourth century Christian communities were active in many of the Roman cities in the Rhineland. The archaeological evidence for the adoption of the new set of beliefs and practices is complex. Early churches, objects bearing signs of the cross, and changes in burial practice all provide material evidence for the adoption of the new religion. Just as with Roman religious ritual, however, and its integration with traditional practices (as seen at Empel), the adoption of Christianity resulted in complex patterns of integration of traditions rather than replacement of pre-Christian practices by Christian ones.

For example, excavations at Bonn beneath the modern cathedral have shown that many pre-Christian sculptures, including those of mother goddesses, had been built into the foundation of a fourth-century church. The construction workers may have treated them simply as convenient stone, but more likely they were incorporated, both figuratively and literally, into the new religious structure and its meaning. Early Christian burials often are difficult to distinguish from non-Christian ones. In the course of investigations underneath Cologne Cathedral, archaeologists discovered a woman's grave dating to around A.D. 520 in a chamber within a small church. The woman was outfitted with grave goods characteristic of pre-Christian traditions, including a headband containing gold thread, a box of amulets, a belt with ornate metal fittings, a crystal ball, and vessels made of pottery, glass, and bronze. Although the burial assemblage was not Christian, the location of the grave was. Such ambiguity in burial character is common during this period. While Christianity was being adopted in late Roman cities of the Rhineland, very different traditions were practiced in other parts of northern Europe. For example, at Thorsberg in Schleswig-Holstein large quantities of weapons and ornaments were being offered to native deities in a pond, continuing a practice of great antiquity in the region.

The complexity of the interactions between different groups of peoples and of changing patterns of belief and ritual practice in the Rhineland is illustrated by the cemetery at Krefeld-Gellep, where more than five thousand graves have been excavated. In the third century the cemetery was used by the inhabitants of a small Roman military post and an associated civilian settlement. Burial practice was the standard Roman one of the time, inhumation with no weapons and no unusual wealth in the graves, just a few ceramic or glass vessels and a piece of jewelry or two. During the fourth century the predominant orientation changed from north-south to east-west, and the numbers of grave goods decreased, shifts associated with the acceptance of Christianity. Early in the fifth century, however, a new burial practice appeared in the cemetery, with weapons in many men's graves and sets of Germanic jewelry in women's. This change is interpreted as the result of the arrival of new peoples from east of the Rhine with different practices.

An exceptionally richly outfitted burial dated to about A.D. 525 is representative of a series of sixth-century wealthy men's graves in the Rhineland. Grave 1728 contained objects of a character similar to those in earlier wealthy burials east of the Rhine. Weapons, including many ornamented with gold and garnet; horse-riding equipment decorated with gold and silver; and elaborate bronze and glass vessels from late Roman workshops were present, as were a series of gold and silver personal ornaments. The majority of graves at Krefeld-Gellep during the sixth century were equipped much more modestly, but in contrast to earlier practices, men's graves often contained weapons, and women's often had substantial assemblages of personal ornaments. During the sixth and seventh centuries large cemeteries known as *Reihengräberfelder* (row-grave cemeteries) were common. These often extensive burial grounds, as at Krefeld-Gellep, are made up of thousands of graves, many well outfitted with grave goods, arranged in rows. They are common in the Rhineland and the Low Countries, in regions that had been parts of the Roman Empire, but are rare east of the Rhine.

In the post-Roman period, A.D. 450–800, settlement in the Low Countries and northern Germany was mostly in small villages and trading centers of a regional scale. In a few places, such as Cologne and Trier, urban populations survived, but they declined from their peaks during the first few centuries A.D. In the countryside villas went out of fashion, and architecture returned to traditional building techniques based on wooden posts sunk into the ground, supporting wattle-and-daub walls. At Warendorf near Münster a settlement occupied between A.D. 650 and 800 consisted for four farmsteads at a time. Large, sturdily built post buildings provided for both human habitation and livestock, and smaller structures served as sheds and workshops. Most of the pottery the people used was locally made coarse ceramic, but some finer wares were brought in from the Rhineland. Ironworking is evident, as is weaving. The community produced surplus farm products and traded for glass beads and

Fig. 3. Reconstruction of port of Haithabu in Schleswig-Holstein. WIKINGER MUSEUM HAITHABU. REPRODUCED BY PERMISSION.

vessels and for grindstones made of basalt from the quarries near Mayen.

CAROLINGIAN PERIOD (A.D. 751–911)
During the Carolingian period in the Low Countries and in the German Rhineland, major changes are apparent in political organization, religion, and commerce. The Frankish kings of the Merovingian period gradually created larger kingdoms, and Charlemagne was crowned emperor of the region in the year A.D. 800 by Pope Leo III in Rome. This event symbolized the accumulated power of the Frankish kings, the importance of Christianity to the Frankish world, the recognition in Rome of the significance of Frankish power, and Charlemagne's concern with linking his political and cultural aspirations with those of ancient Rome. He made these connections plain in his capital at Aachen, where his royal chapel was designed on the plan of the church of San Vitale at Ravenna. He even had marble columns transported from Italy to Aachen to emphasize the links between his plans and past Roman greatness. Charlemagne's royal hall, where he exer-

cised his political power, was connected directly to the chapel, providing material expression of the unification of worldly power and religious authority.

Ever larger churches were built as Christianity became an increasingly important feature of life. The tradition of the *Reihengräberfelder* faded into disuse because Christian funerary practices discouraged the placing of objects, especially food and drink, in graves. Cemeteries were established next to churches, and high-status burials for clergy and elite citizens were placed underneath church foundations, with the choicest positions being in front of the altar, a practice known as *ad sanctos*.

During the late Merovingian and Carolingian periods commerce grew. In the Rhineland major pottery industries focusing on export trade grew up on the west bank south of Cologne at Badorf and later at Pingsdorf. Products of these workshops appear throughout the Rhineland and farther afield, in northern Germany, Scandinavia, and Britain. Throughout northern Europe new trade towns developed from the late seventh century.

Dorestad, on a branch of the Rhine in the Netherlands, became the principal port for Charlemagne's kingdom, bringing in goods from all along the North Sea and Baltic coasts and exporting pottery, basalt grindstones, and other products of the Rhineland. Besides being a major transit port, Dorestad also was home to a wide range of industries typical of the trading towns that emerged throughout northern Europe during the ninth and tenth centuries. Craft workers at Dorestad processed metals, carved amber and bone, and wove textiles. Near the southern end of the Jutland Peninsula in Schleswig-Holstein, the port of Haithabu (Hedeby) became a thriving cosmopolitan center, transshipping goods between the North Sea and Rhineland ports and those of Scandinavia and the Baltic lands (fig. 3). Similar developments are apparent at Quentovic in northern France and at Hamburg on the lower Elbe River and Ralswiek on the Baltic coast, both in northern Germany.

Although Aachen was Charlemagne's royal capital, there were still no major urban centers in northern Germany or the Low Countries during this period. The old Roman centers at such places as Cologne and Mainz continued as manufacturing and trading towns but on a much reduced scale from the Roman period. Thriving agricultural villages, such as that excavated at Warendorf, showed a prosperous economy, with active involvement in the commercial systems of the time but no trace of town life, which remained restricted to the coasts and the major river systems. In eastern regions of northern Germany status differences are well represented in settlement systems. At Tornow, for example, a fortress situated above the village included not only substantial defensive works but also sizable storage structures and workshops, all apparently managed by the local elite groups.

By the end of the Carolingian period in the tenth century communities throughout the Low Countries and northern Germany were thoroughly tied into the expanding economy represented at trading towns such as Dorestad, Haithabu, and Ralswiek. In regions west of the Rhine memories of Rome as well as physical remains of the empire had significant influence on thinking about political power as well as on architecture, religion, and art and ornament. In lands to the east, with no direct experience of Roman rule, ideas about the past and its connections to the present were different. The Rhineland was to remain a significant cultural divide between west and east for another millennium.

See also **Germans** (*vol. 2, part 6*); **Merovingian Franks** (*vol. 2, part 7*); **Goths between the Baltic and Black Seas** (*vol. 2, part 7*); **Tomb of Childeric** (*vol. 2, part 7*).

BIBLIOGRAPHY

Erdrich, Michael. *Rom und die Barbaren: Das Verhältnis zwischen dem Imperium Romanum und den germanischen Stämmen vor seiner Nordwestgrenze von der späten römischen Republik bis zum gallischen Sonderreich.* Mainz, Germany: Verlag Philipp von Zabern, 2001.

Fehring, Günter. *The Archaeology of Medieval Germany.* Translated by Ross Samson. New York: Routledge, 1991.

Geary, Patrick J. *Before France and Germany: The Creation and Transformation of the Merovingian World.* New York: Oxford University Press, 1988.

Halsall, Guy. *Settlement and Social Organization: The Merovingian Region of Metz.* New York: Cambridge University Press, 1995.

Hodges, Richard. *Dark Age Economics: The Origins of Towns and Trade A.D. 500–1000.* 2d ed. London: Duckworth; New York: St. Martin's, 1989.

James, Edward. *The Franks.* New York: Blackwell, 1988.

Randsborg, Klavs. *The First Millennium: A.D. in Europe and the Mediterranean: An Archaeological Essay.* New York: Cambridge University Press, 1991.

Roymans, Nico, ed. *From the Sword to the Plough: Three Studies on the Earliest Romanisation of Northern Gaul.* Amsterdam: Amsterdam University Press, 1996.

Theuws, Frans, and Janet L. Nelson, eds. *Rituals of Power: From Late Antiquity to the Early Middle Ages.* Leiden, Netherlands: Brill, 2000.

Wamser, Ludwig, Christof Flügel, and Bernward Ziegaus, eds. *Die Römer zwischen Alpen und Nordmeer.* Mainz, Germany: Verlag Philipp von Zabern, 2000.

Wells, Peter S. *The Barbarians Speak: How the Conquered Peoples Shaped Roman Europe.* Princeton, N.J.: Princeton University Press, 1999.

Wieczorek, Alfried. *Die Franken: Wegbereiter Europas: 5. bis 8. Jahrhundert n. Chr.* Mainz, Germany: Verlag Philipp von Zabern, 1996.

PETER S. WELLS

SOUTHERN GERMANY

Modern southern Germany includes the states of Bavaria, Baden-Württemberg, and the southern part of the state of Hessen. In the south it is bounded by the Alps, Lake Constance, and the east-west section of the upper Rhine River that extends to Basel. In the east it is bounded by the Fichtelgebirge, the Bavarian Forest, and the forest of the Upper Palatinate. The northern margin is formed by the low mountain ranges of the Taunus, the Vogelsberg, the Rhön, and the Franconian Forest. The upper Rhine Plain east of the Vosges Mountains marks the border to the west.

The more important low mountain ranges are the Odenwald, the Spessart, the Steigerwald, the Black Forest, the Swabian Jura, and the Franconian Jura. Fertile agricultural regions are the Wetterau, the Main Valley, the upper Rhine Plain, the central Neckar region, the Nördlinger Ries, and the eastern Danube Valley, called the Gäuboden. Southern Germany shares two of central Europe's largest rivers. The upper course of the Rhine and the western shore of Lake Constance form a vital transport axis in the west. The Danube, the most important natural east-west connection in central Europe, arises in southern Germany. Other significant rivers that also form transport axes are the Main and the Neckar.

HISTORICAL DEVELOPMENT
In late antiquity, the region was clearly divided into two parts. The late Roman Danube-Iller-Rhine *limes* (frontier borderlands) stretched through the provinces of Germania I, Maxima Sequanorum, and Raetia I and II west of the Rhine, south of Lake Constance, and a line extending from Bregenz–Kempten east of the Iller, then along the Iller south of the Danube, and east of the mouth of the Iller. The Germanic tribes of the Alemanni, the Burgundians, and the Juthungi settled to the east and north of this region until the western Roman Empire fell in A.D. 476. From the middle of the fifth century the territory of the Alemanni expanded into the former Roman territory on the left bank of the Rhine and in the south of the Danube. The Lech then formed the boundary of the new tribe of the Baiuvarii, which was under the sovereignty of the Ostrogoths from A.D. 493 to 536 and thereafter was affiliated loosely with the Merovingian kingdom.

As early as A.D. 500, Alemannic sovereignty ceased with the establishment of the Frankish Duchy of Swabia. Toward the end of the sixth century, Frankish expansion also encompassed southern Hessen and northern Bavaria to the Main. Descendants of the Juthungi as well as parts of the Thuringian population then were incorporated into the empire of the Franks or the Frankish duchy. As Frankish colonization continued, Slavic tribes in the eastern part of northern Bavaria also fell under the rule of the Franks by the eighth century. The largely independent Stem Duchy of the Agilolfings in Bavaria was occupied by Charlemagne in A.D. 788 and converted into a duchy dominated by the Franks. What is now southern Germany was occupied at that time by the duchies of Franconia, Swabia, and Bavaria. After the Treaty of Verdun in A.D. 843, southern Germany belonged to the kingdom of East Francia under the Carolingian king Louis the

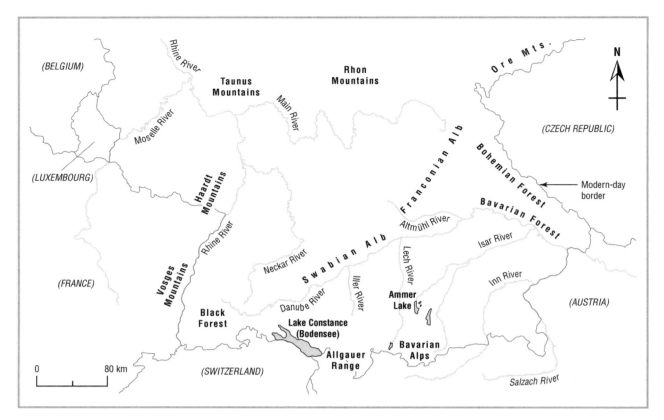

General features of southern Germany.

German. During the tenth century, under Henry I, the Saxon king of the German empire, southern Germany suffered heavily during the plundering raids of the Magyars. These invasions ended in A.D. 955 with the Battle of Lechfeld at Augsburg, under Otto the Great.

ALEMANNI

The tribe of the Alemanni formed in the third century A.D. as a union of several Germanic groups from the Elbe region. After A.D. 233 this new tribe participated decisively in the plundering raids into the *limes* region, the provinces beyond, and Italy. After the fall of the *limes* in A.D. 259–260, the archaeological evidence reveals a lack of continuity of a provincial Roman population. Roman encampments and settlements, including the *villae rusticae* (farms), were abandoned and destroyed. The *limes* region was not resettled until the fourth century, when the Alemanni conquered and occupied it.

Several centers of early Alemannic colonization are ascertainable. These centers include the upper and central Neckar region, the region of Heilbronn,

the area around the mouth of the Neckar, the Brenz Valley and the Ostalb, the Breisgau, and the Tauber Valley, which lies outside the former *limes* region. Especially striking in the Alemannic region are many fortified hilltop settlements. Based on early-twenty-first-century knowledge, the building of the hilltop settlements in the Germanic-Alemannic region of southern Germany on the far side of the late Roman Danube-Iller-Rhine *limes* cannot be linked to older local Germanic traditions. Yet models certainly do exist in the military and civilian hilltop sites that were founded by the late third century in the region of the late Roman Danube-Iller-Rhine *limes*.

The evidence indicates that Alemannic hilltop settlements were not founded until the fourth century and stopped being occupied by the end of the fifth century. Most of these sites were abandoned around A.D. 500, which can be explained by the defeat of the Alemanni by the Franks. There is no evidence of continuity between the Alemannic hilltop settlements and the late Merovingian-Carolingian castles that occasionally followed. The Runder Berg near Urach is the best researched of these sites.

594

In the former *limes* region, Roman villas continued to be occupied. This practice and the use of land cleared by the Romans indicate that there must have been only a short period of time between abandonment and reuse. In southwestern Germany, too, most evidence of Alemannic settlement can be drawn from the form of graves and single, random, or accidental finds. Some larger settlements have been excavated methodically as well. In the settlement of Sontheim, which dates to the first half of the fourth century, excavators identified relatively large post dwellings; smaller economic buildings of post construction, including a round storage building with 7 post holes; and a rectangular area with internal construction (the largest measuring 70 meters) separated from the rest of the settlement by a massive palisade. This is believed to have been the fortified residence of a group having a higher social status. Great quantities of iron slag suggest that ironworking was one of the economic bases for Sontheim.

In the Breisgau, too, large excavations indicate increasing early Alemannic settlement by the fourth century. After the middle of the fifth century, the Alemannic settlement region expanded rapidly. By then it included the Alsace, northern Switzerland, the Swiss Midland, Upper Swabia, the region of Bavarian Swabia up to the Lech, and the Algäu. The Alemanni who carried out this colonization until the seventh century had long been under Frankish rule.

The Alemanni did not enjoy political independence for long. The end of the fifth century was characterized by conflict and defeat of the Alemanni in battle against the Franks. After the defeat of A.D. 496–497 and the suppression of their uprising in A.D. 506, the Alemanni lost their kingdom and their independence. Alemannia became the Duchy of Swabia, a region at times more or less loosely connected to the Frankish empire. Archaeologically this fundamental change is evident in the disappearance of the hilltop settlements of the Alemannic nobility and the end of its cemeteries. At the same time, strategically situated settlements of Frankish warriors and their entourage emerged in the sixth and seventh centuries. Many of their cemeteries are well known. These Frankish officials in Alemannia also included warrior groups of Thuringian origin that became Frankish subjects after the defeat of Thuringia by the Franks in A.D. 531.

JUTHUNGI

The Juthungi generally are believed to have been the eastern subtribe of the Alemanni. Archaeological evidence indicates that they settled in northern Bavaria in the fourth and fifth centuries. This Germanic tribe from the Elbe region is cited for the first and, as far as is known, the last time in the victory monument of Augsburg of A.D. 260, which at the same time reports that the group also was called the Semnones. No written sources on the fate of this tribe exist. The last remaining members of the Juthungi presumably were integrated into the Frankish population in the course of the Frankish development of northern Bavaria in the sixth century.

FRANKS

Starting in the sixth century, colonists from the Frankish heartland along the Rhine settled in northern Bavaria, that is, the Main region around Würzburg and eastward, the Rednitz–Regnitz basin, and the northern foothills of the Franconian Jura in the area of the upper Altmühl. This region was incorporated into the East Frankish kingdom. The same fate befell the present-day Hessen region of southern Germany. These events are not confirmed so much by written sources as by cemetery finds with very distinct Rhenish-Frankish elements.

The Thuringian and Juthungian parts of the population that had previously lived in northern Bavaria apparently were incorporated into Frankish territory without major difficulties. The only evidence of this process is in the archaeological record, primarily in the form of cemeteries and grave goods. These archaeological sources disappeared toward the end of the seventh century as the use of grave goods began to wane. Only in the upper Main area, where the Franks began to colonize the region occupied by Slavic peoples, did the custom of placing burial offerings continue in the Carolingian-Ottonian period. The name "Francia" for this region north and south of the Main—bounded by the Saxons in the north, the Alemanni in the southwest, the Bavarians in the south (the left bank of the Middle Rhine), and the Slavs in the east—does not appear until the eighth or ninth century. It has survived in the names of the Bavarian government districts of Upper, Middle, and Lower Franconia.

BAIUVARII

The Baiuvarii represent the most recent Germanic tribe of the Migration period that was of importance in the development of present-day Germany. The name is preserved in the "Free State of Bavaria." The first historical record dates back to the early sixth century A.D. (alluded to by the historian Jordanes in A.D. 551 or perhaps as early as A.D. 520 by the Roman statesman Cassiodorus and, later, by the Latin poet Venantius Fortunatus in A.D. 565). Their settlement area included parts of the old Roman provinces of Raetia and Noricum. The name Baiuvarii means "men from the land of Baia," or Bohemia—the old Boiohaemum of the ancient geographers.

If one attempts to draw interim conclusions from the meager historical sources and the insights offered by archaeological research, the following model emerges for the Bavarian tribal genesis. When Roman rule came to an end on the Danube around the middle of the fifth century, a polyethnic tribe made up of Romanic and immigrant Germanic groups (including Alemanni, Ostrogoths, Langobards, and Thuringians) formed at the turn of the sixth century A.D. around Germanic allies that had migrated into the area from Bohemia (the "Baiuvarii"). Particularly important is the fact that the massive and therefore practically indestructible fortress of Regensburg remained in the possession of the allies of Bohemian origin. Based on written records starting in the Early Middle Ages this was the royal capital of the early medieval Stem Duchy of the Agilolfings.

Baiuvarian ethnogenesis goes back to the intervention of the Ostrogoths. Under their king Theoderic, the Ostrogoths had conquered Italy from the eastern Roman Empire in A.D. 493. This region included Raetia up to the Danube, which formed part of the diocese of Italy. Ostrogoth rule over the region between the Alps and the Danube ended only in A.D. 536. In that year the Ostrogothic king Witigis, who was forced to defend Italy against the troops of the east Roman emperor Justinian, ceded the region north of the Alps to the Franks under their king Theudebert from the Merovingian dynasty. The tribe of the Baiuvarii between the Lech, the Danube, the Enns, and the Alps continued to enjoy substantial independence under the rule of the Agilolfingian dukes, who had many connections with the Lombard dynasty. In the sixth and seventh centuries settlement expanded rapidly and, in northern Bavaria, eventually spread across the Danube toward the north. Under Charlemagne a split occurred with the last Agilolfingian, Tassilo III, who was deposed in A.D. 788. After that, Frankish officeholders ruled the Duchy of Bavaria.

SLAVS

In northeastern Bavaria, in the present-day government districts of the Upper Palatinate and Upper Franconia north of the Danube, archaeological finds beginning around A.D. 700 indicate a Slavic population that had migrated into the region from Bohemia. By the eighth century, there are also historical sources that confirm the presence of a Slavic population east of the Steigerwald. These Slavic groups were integrated into the Frankish empire and were under the administration of the church. Frankish colonists migrated into their settlement region from the west. In northern Bavaria, Slavs are mentioned as late as the eleventh century. Many place names in northern Bavaria still have Slavic origins.

THE MAGYAR INVASIONS OF THE TENTH CENTURY

Beginning in the late ninth century, the nomadic Magyars (Hungary), horsemen from the Volga-Kama region and originally from central Asia, settled in the central Danube region. They soon began to terrorize southern, central, and western Europe with their highly effective and devastating raids. Especially after the defeat of Bavaria in the Battle of Pressburg in A.D. 907, southern Germany became the focus of the Magyar assaults. In A.D. 926 the German king Henry I paid tribute to purchase a ten-year truce. He used this period to reorganize the German army and build castles. The crushing defeat of Hungary at Lechfeld near Augsburg in A.D. 955 put an end to the Hungarian invasions. The archaeological traces of the Hungarian raids and the German countermeasures have been well summarized in the literature.

CASTLE BUILDING

After A.D. 926, the building of castles in southern Germany was intensified to ward off the Hungarian threat. While castle building in the Early Middle Ages started on the initiative of the king, bishops and monasteries soon added their own fortifications. In the ninth and tenth centuries, the nobility began to erect castles, one of the most important bases of territorial power in the later Middle Ages.

See also **Baiuvarii** (*vol. 2, part 7*); **Merovingian Franks** (*vol. 2, part 7*); **Slavs and the Early Slav Culture** (*vol. 2, part 7*); **Hungary** (*vol. 2, part 7*).

BIBLIOGRAPHY

Archäologisches Landesmuseum Baden-Württemberg, ed. *Die Alamannen*. Stuttgart, Germany: Konrad Theiss Verlag, 1997.

Burns, Thomas S. *Barbarians within the Gates of Rome: A Study of Roman Military Policy and Barbarians, ca. 375–425 A.D.* Bloomington: Indiana University Press, 1995.

Christlein, Rainer. *Die Alamannen: Archäologie eines lebendigen Volkes*. Stuttgart, Germany: Konrad Theiss Verlag, 1991.

Czysz, Wolfgang, Karlheinz Dietz, Thomas Fischer, and Hans-Jörg Kellner. *Die Römer in Bayern*. Stuttgart, Germany: Konrad Theiss Verlag, 1995.

Dannheimer, Hermann, and Heinz Dopsch, eds. *Die Bajuwaren: Von Severin bis Tassilo 488–788*. Munich: Amt der Salzburger Landesregierung, 1988.

Ettel, P. "Der Befestigungsbau im 10. Jahrhundert in Süddeutschland und die Rolle Ottos des Grossen am Beispiel der Burg von Rosstal." In *Europa im 10. Jahrhundert: Archäologie einer Aufbruchszeit*. Edited by Joachim Henning, pp. 365–380. Mainz, Germany: Phillip von Zabern, 2002.

Gradmann, R. *Süddeutschland*. Stuttgart, Germany: Engelhorn, 1931.

Menghin, Wilfried. *Frühgeschichte Bayerns: Römer und Germanen, Baiern und Schwaben, Franken und Slawen*. Stuttgart, Germany: Konrad Theiss Verlag, 1990.

Roth, Helmut, and Egon Wamers, eds. *Hessen im Frühmittelalter: Archäologie und Kunst*. Sigmaringen, Germany: Thorbecke, 1984.

Schlesinger, Walter, ed. *Althessen im Frankenreich*. Nationes, no. 2. Sigmaringen, Germany: Thorbecke, 1975.

Schulze-Dörrlamm, Mechthild. "Die Ungarneinfälle des 10. Jahrhunderts im Spiegel archäologischer Funde." In *Europa im 10. Jahrhundert: Archäologie einer Aufbruchszeit*. Edited by Joachim Henning, pp. 109–122. Mainz, Germany: Phillip von Zabern, 2002.

Teichner, F. *Kahl am Main: Siedlung und Gräberfeld der Völkerwanderungszeit*. Materialhefte zur Bayerishcen Vorgeschichte, series A, no 80. Kallmünz, Germany: Verlag Michael Lassleben, 1999.

Wieczorek, Alfried, Patrick Périn, Karin von Welck, and Wilfried Menghin, eds. *Die Franken: Wegbereiter Europas*. Mainz, Germany: Verlag Philip von Zabern, 1996.

Zeune, Joachim. "Salierzeitliche Burgen im Herzogtum Bayern." In *Burgen der Salierzeit*. Vol. 2, *In den südlichen Landschaften des Reiches*. Edited by Horst Wolfgang Böhme, pp. 177–234. Monographien Römisch Germanisches Zentralmuseum, no. 25. Sigmaringen, Germany: Thorbecke, 1991.

THOMAS FISCHER
(TRANSLATED BY GINA BRODERICK)

GLOSSARY

absolute dating: Dating using a chemical, physical, or biological technique or by reference to dated historical events that produces an age (or range of ages) in years for archaeological remains rather than simply a position relative to other finds. One example of absolute dating is the carbon-14 method. Also known as "chronometric dating."

Aceramic Neolithic: A period in which people relied on domesticated species and lived in permanent settlements but did not extensively use or manufacture pottery. Generally used to specify a portion of the Neolithic in the Near East between approximately 8500 B.C. and 7000 B.C. but also used for similar periods in Greece, Crete, and Cyprus. Also known as the "Pre-Pottery Neolithic."

achieved status: Prestige and social rank acquired through personal deeds. Antonym of "ascribed status."

acropolis: An elevated area of a city containing temples and courtyards. Some have origins as hilltop fortifications.

***ad sanctos* burial:** Positioning of burials around a holy or otherwise revered grave or monument.

adze: A cutting tool with a broad and flat blade that—in contrast to an axe—is hafted with the blade perpendicular to the line of the handle. Commonly used for trimming timbers.

affinal: Of or concerning a relationship formed by marriage.

agora: A forum; an open area for a market and other assemblies.

alignment: Positioning objects, such as standing stones, in a line, often to mark a celestial event or topographical feature.

***allée couverte*:** *See* gallery grave.

alloy: A combination of two or more metals that creates a new metal, as in the mixing of tin and copper to make bronze.

alluvium/alluvial plain: Sediment deposited by flowing water in a riverbed or across a floodplain. The resulting landscape is referred to as an alluvial plain.

amber: Fossilized tree resin. A valued trade item often carved and polished into jewelry, ornaments, and other objects. Most European amber comes from the Baltic region.

amphora (pl. amphorae): A pottery vessel with a narrow neck, two handles, and either a pointed or a rounded base. Used for storage and transportation of goods such as wine, oil, fruit, and salted meat.

AMS radiocarbon dating: A radiometric dating technique that counts individual carbon isotopes. It is faster and requires smaller amounts of carbon than traditional methods of carbon-14 dating (AMS = accelerator mass spectrometry).

androcentric: Male centered.

***Annales* school:** An intellectual perspective emphasizing that different processes operate at different chronological and geographical scales. This school of thought also stresses the need for adopting a multidisciplinary approach to studying the past. Associated with the French historians Marc Bloch, Fernand Braudel, and others known as *Annalistes*.

anoxic: Possessing extremely low levels of oxygen.

anthropogenic: Created by humans. Often used with reference to soils and vegetation.

anthropomorphic: In the shape of or possessing characteristics of a human.

antiquarianism: The study of ancient monuments before the development of modern archaeological techniques. Often associated with a lack of rigorous methods for data collection and hypothesis testing. Antiquarians interpreted prehistoric remains in terms of the historic record, so, for example, they attributed Stonehenge to the Romans or the ancient Druids.

apse: A projecting portion of a building that is semicircular in plan and has a vaulted roof, like the recess extending from the choir of a church.

archaeobotany: The study of plant remains from archaeological sites, including seeds, plant fibers, pollen, and phytoliths.

archaeological culture: A term used to designate a recurring assemblage of material goods associated with a particular time and space. Archaeological cultures are defined by archaeologists and may have little connection to groups or identities recognized by the people using the material goods.

archaeozoology: *See* zooarchaeology.

ard: An early type of plow that cuts into soil without turning it over. Also known as a "scratch-plow."

armature: 1. A stone tool made for hafting. Often used in reference to microliths. 2. A framework, usually one used to support an object during construction.

artifact: An object created or otherwise altered by humans.

ascribed status: Prestige and social rank conferred through heredity. Antonym of "achieved status."

ashlar masonry: A drystone masonry made using squared stones to produce tightly fitting joints and a smooth wall face.

assemblage: A group of artifacts derived from an archaeological feature or set of features.

astragalus: A bone located in the foot that articulates with the tibia (shinbone). One of a group of bones known as "tarsals." Generally called a "talus" in humans.

Atlantic climatic period: A subdivision of the Holocene epoch in northern Europe. Extends from c. 6000 B.C. to 3800 B.C. Relative to modern conditions, a warm and wet (or "oceanic") climate characterized the period. *See also* Preboreal, Boreal, Subboreal, and Subatlantic climatic periods.

auger: A drilling tool used in extracting soil samples. Unlike coring tools, augers disturb the structure and stratigraphy of samples retrieved.

aurochs: The common name for *Bos primigenius,* the wild ancestor of domestic cattle (*Bos taurus*).

Austrasia: The eastern portion of the Frankish empire (the areas under the control of Merovingian and Carolingian rulers).

autochthonous: Term applied to archaeological developments within a particular region as opposed to those introduced from outside that region.

B.P.: A dating convention indicating years before the present, with "present" defined as A.D. 1950.

balk: The unexcavated edge of an archaeological trench or unexcavated areas between trenches. Used to preserve and analyze stratigraphy. Also spelled "baulk."

ballista balls: Objects, generally of stone, propelled from a military engine designed much like a crossbow.

barbotine: A pottery decoration technique in which thick slip is applied to the surface of pottery, often in designs. The result is a roughened surface.

barrow: A round or elongated mound constructed from earth and/or stone, often containing a burial.

basal: Lowest, as in the bottom stratum of an excavation, or earliest, as in the basal phase of construction.

beaker: A decorated pottery vessel, generally in the shape of an inverted bell. Beaker vessels are characteristic of an archaeological culture associated with the spread of copper metallurgy across western Europe.

berdache: A term for groups categorized as neither male nor female, but rather as a third gender or as transgendered. Also known as "two-spirit."

biconical: Double-coned. Possessing a shape that is widest in the middle and tapers toward both ends, as in pottery, or, alternatively, widest at both ends and narrow at the middle, as in some copper objects.

bifacial: Retouching done on both sides (faces) of a stone tool.

biome: A large-scale ecological zone, such as savanna or tundra.

biritual cemetery: A cemetery in which both inhumation and cremation burials are found.

blade: A long, parallel-sided stone tool, conventionally one that is more than twice as long as it is wide and struck from a prepared core, often by indirect percussion.

Boreal climatic period: A subdivision of the Holocene epoch in northern Europe. Extends from c. 8500 B.C. to 6000 B.C. Although the period is part of the trend of increasing temperatures following the end of the last glaciation, relative to conditions in the Atlantic period, a cold and dry ("continental") climate characterized the period. *See also* Preboreal, Atlantic, Subboreal, and Subatlantic climatic periods.

boreal forest: Vegetation that is typical of subarctic areas without permafrost but which have severe winters and a short growing season. Predominant tree species include conifers.

bracteate: A disk-shaped pendant, usually made of gold and decorated with repoussé designs. Also a type of coin.

Breckland: 1. A region in eastern England occupying a portion of Norfolk and Suffolk. 2. (not capitalized) A tract of heathland with thickets of shrubby vegetation, especially heather.

broch: A circular drystone tower with a central courtyard. The wall is generally less than fifty feet tall. Habitation occurred both inside and outside the enclosure. The walls are generally hollow, containing chambers and/or stairways that access a roof walk. Associated with Iron Age Scotland.

bucranium (pl. bucrania): A carved cattle skull used as a decoration on a building.

burin: A chisel-shaped stone tool with a sharp but stout edge. Used for a variety of purposes but conventionally associated with engraving bone, antler, and other materials.

burnished: Polished. Used with reference to the surface of pottery and metal artifacts.

bush fallow cultivation: *See* shifting cultivation.

cairn: A pile of stones. Often used as a term for a barrow made from stone but also used for smaller mounds, such as those produced when clearing a field of stones.

calcine: To heat to drive off impurities or volatile matter. Often used to describe methods for creating lime or refining precious metal.

caprine: A term used to refer to both sheep and goats.

capstone: A stone slab placed horizontally across the tops of orthostats to form the ceiling of a megalithic tomb.

carbon-14 dating: Also known as "radiocarbon age determination." *See* radiocarbon dating.

carburization: A method of heating iron in contact with carbon to produce a steel-like metal.

Cardium: A genus of shellfish commonly known as cockles. Use of their shells for decorating pottery is characteristic of Cardial ware, a Neolithic pottery type in the Mediterranean region.

carinated: A term used in describing the profile of a vessel. A carination is a sharp break in a curve that forms a ridge (an arris), as in the joint between the neck and body of a vessel.

case hardening: A term for various thermochemical methods of hardening the surface of metal. Carburizing is one type.

causewayed enclosure: A monument possessing a series of concentric ditches filled at points to create passages into a central area. Although evidence of permanent structures inside the enclosure is rare, refuse deposited in ditches is abundant. Also known as "causewayed camps."

celt: A polished axe head of either ground stone or metal.

cenotaph: A tomb or similar memorial built for a person whose remains are elsewhere.

chain mail: A protective garment made from loops of metal woven together.

chambered tomb: A tomb with a vault for burials. Often built from megaliths, these tombs can take a variety of forms, including passage graves, dolmens, and gallery graves.

chasing: An ornamental indentation or groove hammered or punched into metal.

chatelaine: An attachment for a purse, set of keys, or other item hung from a belt, particularly a woman's belt.

cheekpiece: 1. An attachment connecting a horse bit to the reins. 2. An attachment to the rim of a helmet that protects the side of the face.

chernozem: A deep, rich, humic soil of dark color, like those associated with prairies and grasslands.

chert: Various types of rock composed of microcrystalline quartz that occur as nodules or masses in a sedimentary environment. Many varieties of chert are prized raw materials for stone tool making. Variation in usage of this term does occur. Technically, flint is one variety of chert, but frequently chert is defined as similar to flint but more coarse grained and less desirable for stone-tool production. Flint and chert are often also used synonymously.

chiefdom: A social organization with a defined leadership organizing the distribution of resources. Generally, surpluses of food and other goods are paid to the chief, who redistributes them to subordinates. Often, chiefdoms have ceremonial centers acting as focal points for group members. Chiefdoms usually are distinguished from states by being smaller in scale and possessing a less complex administrative apparatus.

chronology: An ordering of events into a temporal sequence, as in a timeline.

chronometric: *See* absolute dating.

chronozone: A small stratigraphic unit corresponding to deposits laid down during a chron (the smallest interval of geological time in the hierarchy of the Chronomeric Standard terms).

Cisalpine: Located to the south of the Alps.

cist: A subterranean boxlike structure with sides and a cover built from stone slabs. Used for burial.

city-state: An autonomous political entity composed of an urban center and its hinterland.

***civitas* (pl. *civitates*):** Originally, a self-governing territory in the Roman Empire and the primary urban center in that area. By the early medieval period, the term was used for important ceremonial centers, urban or otherwise.

client king: A ruler subordinate to an overlord. Also known as a "petty king."

clinker technique: A boat-building technique in which the sides of the boat are made of overlapping planks, in the same manner as clapboards on the side of a house. Such boats are also known as "clinker-built."

cloisonné: An inlay technique using gems, glass, or enamel set into a metal framework. *Cloisons* are individual cells in the framework.

coiling: A method of making pottery in which coils of clay are laid on top of each other to create a desired shape. The joints between coils are then smoothed over.

collagen: A protein molecule forming nearly all of the organic content of bone. Collagen gives bones a degree of flexibility and elasticity.

***colonia* (pl. *coloniae*):** A settlement for veterans of the Roman military.

***comitatus*:** Latin for "retinue" or "escort." A group that has sworn allegiance and service to a king, particularly for military duty.

consanguine: Of the same blood; possessing a common ancestor.

context: The find location of an artifact, including its matrix (surrounding soil), its provenance, and its associations with other artifacts.

coppice/coppicing: 1. A forest or grove consisting mainly of slender shoots and small trees. 2. A method of forest management involving cutting trees low to the ground so that they produce small shoots.

corbeled vault/corbel-vaulted: A drystone masonry vault made by setting stones in rings of gradually decreasing diameter until the vault is closed. Also known as a "false arch."

core-reduction technique: A generic term for the various processes of removing flakes and otherwise modifying a core in the process of making stone tools. A core is the nodule of flint or other stone from which flakes are removed as tools are made. *See also* flake and blade.

coring (at a site): The process of retrieving cylindrical samples, generally of wood or soil. In contrast to augers, coring tools tend to remove materials with their structure and stratigraphy undisturbed.

cover sand: A continuous layer of sand, usually deposited by wind. Often causes the rapid burial of archaeological sites and landscapes.

crannog: An artificial island in a lake, usually built as the foundation for a dwelling. Common in the British Isles during the Iron Age and the medieval period. *See also* lake dwelling.

cremation: Incineration of a body.

crucible: A vessel in which compounds, particularly precious metals, are heated or calcined.

cruciform: In the form of a cross.

CT scan: An image produced through computed tomography (CT), which gives a cross-sectional "slice" through an object. CT images are sensitive to materials of various densities so that, for example, when a scanner is used on a body, the image clearly shows both soft tissue and bone. Individual "slices" also can be combined to produce three-dimensional representations. Also known as a "computerized axial tomography (CAT) scan."

cuirasse: A protective garment, usually of leather, covering the torso from waist to neck.

cultigen: A domesticated species for which the wild ancestor is unknown, although the term is sometimes used to refer to cultivated plant species more generally.

cultivar: A horticulturally or agriculturally derived plant species, as distinguished from its wild counterpart.

Danegeld: Payments by Anglo-Saxons in an effort to stop raids by Scandinavians in the late tenth century A.D. Anglo-Saxon coins found in Scandinavia often are associated with these payments.

delayed-return foragers: A group with a hunting-and-gathering system in which return on labor invested in collecting or managing resources is not immediate.

debitage: Waste material created in the process of making and retouching stone tools.

demic diffusion: A wave-of-advance model postulating that a rising population and random migration of small groups drove the spread of Neolithic culture across Europe. Demes are small populations of closely related individuals.

denarius (pl. denarii): A type of coin, usually struck from silver but also from gold. Originally a Roman type of coin, denarii also were minted in the medieval period.

dendrochronology: Tree-ring dating. A dating technique that matches variation in tree-ring width from a wood sample to a master pattern reconstructed from sequences extending from the present backward into antiquity.

denticulate: Serrated or possessing numerous toothlike projections. Used to describe the results of a particular process of retouching the edge of a stone tool.

diffusion: The spread of traits and behaviors through contact between people. Often associated with the belief that traits and behaviors have a single point of origin and appear elsewhere only through imitation.

direct dating: Direct dating applies a technique of absolute dating (such as carbon-14 dating) to an artifact (or organic material) or an ecofact to establish its age rather than relying on the dating of associated material such as charcoal from the same context.

dirham: An Arabic silver coin of the medieval period and later. Also spelled "dirhem."

disarticulated: Disconnected or disjointed. Used particularly in reference to bones moved out of their original relationship with one another.

dolmen: A megalithic monument constructed from upright stone slabs supporting a capstone slab. Also used as a generic term for "megalithic chambered tombs."

downland: An elevated landscape in southern England with rolling hills and a thin layer of soil derived from underlying chalk beds. Owing to extensive grazing, downlands are now associated with low, grassy vegetation; however, before the advent of grazing, downlands were wooded.

droveway: A pathway along which animals are driven or herded, usually defined by earthen banks.

drystone (walling): Stone masonry constructed without the use of mortar.

dugout boat: A boat made from a hollowed-out tree or log.

dump rampart: A defensive earthwork consisting of a wide, flat-bottomed ditch outside a steep bank. Also known as a "*Fécamp* rampart."

dyke: A linear earthwork built as a fortification to protect a large region. Also spelled "dike."

ear spool: An object, usually disk shaped, inserted into a perforation in the earlobe. Perforations can reach several inches in diameter through insertion of increasingly larger spools.

earthwork: A monument constructed from earth and other material piled into a bank or a mound.

ecofact: An item that is neither made nor modified by humans but can provide information on past environments and/or the ways these environments were used by past peoples.

ecotone: An area of transition between ecological habitats or communities.

einkorn: The common name for an early domestic species of wheat (*Triticum monococcum*) and its wild relatives. One of two early types of wheat domesticated in the Near East. *See also* emmer.

electrum: An alloy of silver and gold.

elm decline: A reduction in the prevalence of elms occurring c. 3800 B.C., near the time of the first appearance of agriculture in northern Europe. There has been much debate about whether the change is anthropogenic or due to other factors, such as disease.

emmer: The common name for an early domesticated species of wheat (*Triticum dicoccum*) and its wild relatives. One of two early types of wheat domesticated in the Near East. *See also* einkorn.

emporium (pl. emporia): A trade and manufacturing settlement connected to a long-distance exchange network, often founded and administered through royal control. These settlements were centers of urbanization in medieval Europe, although the status of individual settlements as truly urban is debated.

enamel hypoplasia: A horizontal indentation running across tooth enamel and resulting from a period of malnutrition.

Epipalaeolithic: In Europe this term refers to Palaeolithic cultures existing after the end of the last glaciation. Often used to create a distinction with Mesolithic cultures, but occasionally the terms are used as synonyms. In the eastern Mediterranean the term is used to refer to terminal Pleistocene hunter-gatherers.

epistemology: Study of the basis for and nature of human knowledge, with emphasis on its limitations.

ethnogenesis: A process that results in the creation or redefinition of ethnic identities.

eustasy/eustatic: A rise in sea level.

excarnation: A burial custom involving removal of soft tissue through exposure or other means before deposition of skeletal remains.

extended burial: Deposition of a body in a grave with legs straightened.

faience: A glassy substance made from baked clay and shaped into ornaments, beads, and other jewelry. Also used as a slip on pottery.

faunal analysis: *See* zooarchaeology.

faunal spectrum: The range of animals identified in a zooarchaeological assemblage.

feature: A nonportable component of an archaeological site. Common types include burials, walls, and pits.

Fécamp rampart: *See* dump rampart.

fen: A low-lying marshy area at least partly covered by water, usually with basic or neutral pH (in contrast to a bog, which has acidic pH).

fibula (pl. fibulae): 1. A Latin term for a metal pin with a clasp, used to fasten garments and similar in design to a safety pin. Often highly ornamented with forms specific to a particular time and place. 2. The lateral and smaller of the two bones in the lower leg. Articulates with the tibia (shinbone).

field system: A set of agricultural fields that articulate with one another.

filigree: A decorative design made from fine wire affixed to the surface of an object. Also, other ornamental work intended to resemble such wirework.

firedog: Iron stands for logs burning in a hearth. Also known as "andirons."

flagon: A metal or ceramic vessel with a handle, a spout, and usually a hinged lid.

flake: A thin piece of stone removed from a core in the process of making stone tools. Refers to both pieces used as tools and waste products.

flat grave: A burial executed without a mound or other prominent aboveground structure.

flexed burial: Deposition of a body with the legs pulled up to the torso. The body also is often placed on its side. Also known as a "contracted burial."

flotation: A process for retrieving minute plant remains difficult to recover through hand collection. Sediments are poured into moving water, and the light material is held in suspension so that it can be collected in a fine mesh sieve.

foederatus (pl. *foederati*): Roman irregular troops, drawn from outside the empire and often given land grants in return for service.

foragers: Groups acquiring food and other resources primarily through hunting and gathering.

Free Germany: The area associated with Germanic peoples living beyond the formal boundary of the Roman Empire.

frontlet: A band worn across the forehead.

Fürstengrab (pl. *Fürstengräber*): A German term for a burial possessing unusually rich assemblages of burial goods, commonly associated with the Iron Age. From the German words *Fürst,* meaning "prince," and *Grab,* meaning "grave."

Fürstensitz (pl. *Fürstensitze*): A German term for a defended hilltop settlement possessing a permanent population and associated with unusually rich material culture, commonly of the Iron Age. From the German words *Fürst,* meaning "prince," and *Sitz,* meaning "seat."

gallery grave: A form of chambered tomb with no distinction between the entrance passage and the burial chamber, giving the interior a hall-like shape. Also known as "*allée couverte.*"

geoarchaeology: Archaeological research using the methods and theories of geology and other earth sciences, usually with an emphasis on soil formation processes and postdepositional changes in archaeological deposits.

geochemical: Relating to the chemical properties of geological features or compounds.

Geographic Information Systems (GIS): A database program for mapping and analyzing spatial data. Used, for example, to generate maps illustrating the relationship between the availability of water and the distribution of artifacts in a landscape.

geomorphology: The study of processes creating and reshaping landscapes.

geophysical: Relating to the form and composition of geological features. Often used as a generic term for various noninvasive survey techniques that utilize differences in the physical properties of buried features and surrounding soils, such as resistivity and magnetometry studies.

glacis: A gentle incline, especially the slope below a fortification.

Global Positioning System (GPS): A satellite-based system for determining longitude, latitude, and sometimes elevation.

gold foil: Gold hammered into an extremely thin sheet. Used to gild objects.

grindstone: Stone used for milling grain. *See also* quern.

groove-and-splinter technique: A means of creating elongated plaques of bone, antler, and other materials that can be worked into tools. Parallel grooves are cut into the surface of the material. Beginning at one end of the grooves, the plaque is pried up until it is "splintered" off at the other end of the grooves.

ground-penetrating radar: A noninvasive method of identifying subterranean features in which radar waves are directed into the ground. The reflected energy is measured and analyzed to produce horizontal and vertical maps of subsurface features.

groundstone (tool): A type of stone tool, often an axe, with an edge created by grinding against an abrasive material.

hafting: Placing a point or other tool into another material to create a shaft or handle, as in an axe head affixed to a wooden shaft.

halberd: An axe-like weapon with a pointed blade mounted at a right angle to the shaft. Common in the Bronze Age.

hand axe: A type of stone tool that is bifacially modified, with an edge running around the circumference of the tool. Often teardrop shaped. Also called a biface.

henge: A circular enclosure defined by a bank and ditch, often with the ditch placed inside the bank (the opposite of the arrangement used for defensive purposes). Common internal features include pits, burials, structures, and stone circles. Usually dating to the Neolithic or Bronze Age.

hillfort: An enclosed settlement located on high ground. The enclosure can be defensive and/or ceremonial. Some hillforts appear to have had large numbers of inhabitants. Others have little evidence of habitation.

historiography: The study of how history is written. Particularly, theories about how history should be constructed from the limited knowledge available.

Holocene: A geological epoch extending from the end of the last glaciation, c. 9500 B.C., up to the present. The Holocene in Europe is conventionally divided into the following periods: Preboreal, Boreal, Atlantic, Subboreal, and Subatlantic.

horizontal excavation: An excavation technique that involves removing individual layers by following their horizontal extent before moving on to lower layers.

hunebed: Megalithic tombs of Germany and the Netherlands. Derived from the Old German word *hune*, meaning "big" or "huge."

hypocaust: A gravity-based central heating system developed by the Romans, in which hot air is drawn from a furnace into spaces under a floor.

indirect percussion: A stone-tool production technique. Instead of striking a core directly with a hammer stone, force is directed more precisely by placing an antler point or other material on the core and striking it with a hammer stone. Associated with the production of blades.

inhumation: A burial practice in which bodies are not extensively modified before deposition.

interfluve: The land between two waterways flowing in the same direction.

interglacial: A climatic period with relatively warm temperatures and retreating glaciers that occurs between colder periods when glaciers are advancing.

intramural burial: Deposition of a body within a settlement.

isostasy/isostatic: The rising land levels that occur after glaciers retreat and the Earth's crust returns to its equilibrium position after being pressed down by the weight of ice.

isotopic analysis: Analysis of the combination of isotopes (varieties of an element) within an object. Used to reconstruct diet and provenance.

jet: A type of fossil wood that is dense, hard, and black. Often polished and worked into jewelry.

karst: A landscape with underground streams, caverns, and sinkholes resulting from the erosion of limestone bedrock.

keratinous: Of or relating to the fibrous tissue that characterizes horns, hooves, and fingernails.

kin group: A population of closely related individuals, usually larger than a family group of parents and children. The boundaries of such groups vary from culture to culture.

knap: To remove flakes of stone in the process of making stone tools. An individual who knaps flint is known as a "flintknapper."

krater (pl. kraterae): A vessel with a rounded body and wide mouth, used for mixing and serving wine.

kurgan: A burial mound or barrow, especially in Eastern Europe and Siberia. *Kurgans* gave their name to an archaeological culture in this area that is also characterized by wheeled vehicles and copperworking.

kylix: A drinking vessel usually made of ceramic or metal and with two horizontal handles.

ladder of inferences: A term for the theory that archaeologists confront an ascending scale of difficulty in studying different components of a society. Technological and ecological components are thought to be the least difficult to study. Economic and political organization are thought to be more difficult and ideology or religious beliefs the most difficult. Accordingly, archaeologists must be increasingly circumspect about their interpretations as they ascend these different "rungs." Critics of this theory argue that the perception of increasing difficulty results from archaeologists' approach and is not an inherent property of archaeological data. This theory is also known as Hawkes's ladder, after Christopher Hawkes, who elaborated the theory in a 1954 article.

laetus (pl. *laeti*): A Latin term for a prisoner of war or other non-taxpayer, often from groups outside the Roman empire, recruited into the Roman military. *Laeti* were given grants of land in return for their service.

lake dwelling: A settlement built along the shoreline of a lake, especially in Alpine areas during the Neolithic and Bronze Age. *See also* crannog.

lead isotope analysis: A type of isotope analysis that assesses the prevalence of different lead isotopes in an object made from lead or in other materials containing traces of lead. Used to establish provenance. *See also* isotope analysis.

leister: A fishing spear with several barbed prongs, thrust down over the back of the fish to grip it.

lime: 1. Calcium oxide, at times with other materials added. Used in making mortar. 2. European name for trees of the genus *Tilia*, which flourish in temperate climates. Also known as "linden" in North America.

limes: The fortified Roman imperial frontier, used specifically with reference to the Rhine-Danube frontier in central Europe but often applied to other Roman imperial borders as well.

Linearbandkeramik: An early Neolithic archaeological culture in central Europe characterized by the presence of pottery decorated with incised linear motifs. Also known as the "Linear Pottery culture."

lintel: Wood, stone, or other material placed across the top of an opening in a wall as reinforcement. Also used to describe a megalith resting in a horizontal position across other upright megaliths.

lithic: Made of or relating to stone.

littoral zone: 1. The lands surrounding a body of water. 2. The shoreline between the high and low waterlines.

loess: A dense, pale yellow type of soil consisting largely of glacial debris deposited by wind.

longhouse: A rectangular structure, often constructed using wooden posts, that is relatively long compared to its width. A common dwelling type in both the Neolithic and the Iron Age.

loom weight: An object, usually of stone or clay, tied to the warp strings of a loom to maintain tension during weaving.

lost-wax technique: A method of metal casting in which an object is modeled in wax. Then a mold of clay, sand, or other material is formed around the wax object. When molten metal is poured into the mold, the wax is "lost" and replaced by a metal copy of the original shape.

lur (pl. *lurer*): A long, curved horn made of metal, often cast in sections. Produced in Scandinavia during the Bronze Age.

mace-head: A heavy, blunt weapon similar to a sledgehammer with a rounded head. Often decorated and carried as a symbol of authority.

magnetometry: A noninvasive survey technique that collects data about small-scale changes in the electromagnetic properties of an area to identify subsurface features.

mandible: The lower jawbone.

matriliny: The practice of tracing descent through the maternal line.

matrilocal: A residence pattern in which a married couple lives with or near the wife's family.

megalith: A large, flat stone used architecturally to construct a monument or portion of a monument, such as a tomb, henge, or alignment. Usually not modified by further working.

menhir: A single upright megalith.

meseta: Spanish term for a tableland or mesa. A flat and elevated area that has an abrupt rise from the surrounding landscape. The term is used for areas larger than a butte.

metapodials: Elongated bones located between the wrist and fingers or between the ankle and toes. Known as "metacarpals" in the hand and "metatarsals" in the foot. The number and shape of these bones vary significantly between species.

microburin technique: A technique for producing microliths. A notch is removed from a blade. The blade is then snapped, creating a microlith and a by-product with a burin form (a microburin).

microlith: A small stone tool created by snapping a blade into a series of smaller pieces or removing a blade from a very small core. Usually hafted into wood or other material.

midden: A trash dump. More specifically, an accumulation of debris, usually food and other occupation refuse, deposited in a defined area, such as a hole in the ground or a portion of a settlement.

mitochondrial DNA: A type of DNA existing outside the cell nucleus, where most DNA is located. In sperm, mitochondrial DNA (mtDNA) is located in the region that does not enter the egg. Consequently, mtDNA is inherited matrilineally and is not recombined with each new generation. Since mtDNA has a constant rate of mutation, the difference between the mtDNA of two individuals is a function of the time elapsed since they shared a female ancestor. Best known for its use in identifying a last common ancestor for all modern humans, the so-called mitochondrial Eve.

moraine/morainic: A term used for a variety of landscapes resulting from the accumulation of soil and other material moved and deposited through glacial activity, frequently in the form of linear ridges.

mordant: A substance that combines with dye to create an insoluble compound that fixes to cloth.

moldboard plow: A plow fitted with a blade that turns over the soil as it cuts a furrow. Also known as a "heavy plow" because it is used to farm soils too heavy for an ard.

multivallate/multivallation: Possessing more than one enclosing bank and/or ditch.

murus Gallicus: Julius Caesar's term for ramparts surrounding Gallic towns. They had external faces of timber and stone. They were also reinforced with timbers buried perpendicular to the external face and extending backward into the earthen backing.

necropolis: Greek for "city of the dead." A cemetery, generally one associated with a settlement but located outside its limits.

Neustria: The western portion of the Frankish empire (the area under the control of Merovingian and Carolingian rulers).

New Archaeology: A set of approaches to archaeological interpretation emphasizing the value of hypothesis testing and other scientific methods, the need for incorporating ecology into explanations of social change, and a view of society as composed of interacting subsystems with discrete relationships to one another. Also known as "processual archaeology."

nuraghe (pl. *nuraghi*): Circular stone towers, often with corbeled chambers inside. Associated with the Bronze Age in Sardinia.

obsidian: Volcanic glass, a valued material for stone toolmaking.

ochre: A naturally occurring substance consisting largely of iron oxide. The color of ochre depends on the variety of iron oxide. The most common colors are red and yellow. Used as a pigment and a decoration. Also spelled "ocher."

ogham: A type of script with approximately twenty letters consisting of lines arranged along or across a baseline. Known most commonly from inscriptions along the edge of a stone pillar. Probably originating in the fourth century A.D., ogham is found around the Irish Sea littoral, particularly in Ireland. Also spelled "ogam."

open-cast (mining): A mining technique in which the overburden is removed to uncover the desired material, as opposed to deep mining, which involves tunneling underground.

***oppidum* (pl. *oppida*):** A Latin term for a large fortified settlement of the Iron Age, often located on hilltops and other elevated locations. They acted as centers for habitation, trade, and manufacturing. Julius Caesar used the term to describe settlements in Gaul.

orthostat: An upright stone slab in a megalithic monument.

outworks: A secondary defensive structure, usually an earthwork, constructed beyond or as an extension of primary defenses.

oxhide ingots: An ingot is a mass of metal cast into a convenient and/or standardized shape for storage and transport. Oxhide ingots are cast in a shape reminiscent of the stretched hide of an ox.

oxygen isotope analysis: A technique for reconstructing past climatic conditions. Ocean water and rainwater have different ratios of two oxygen isotopes. In cold periods, when rainwater is locked in glaciers, ocean water has a different ratio than it does during warm periods, when glaciers are smaller and more rainwater returns to the ocean. Changes in the ratio are recorded in the remains of foraminifera, organisms that absorb oxygen isotopes during their life. These organisms fall to the ocean floor at death and are retrieved by coring the ocean floor.

P-Celtic: One of two branches of the Celtic family of languages. Also known as Brittonic, this group includes Welsh, Breton, and Cornish. The other branch is known as Q-Celtic, or Goidelic, and includes Irish, Manx, and Scottish Gaelic. The division is based on phonological differences between the two groups that appear to extend into extinct Celtic languages.

palaeoanthropology: The study of early human and hominid evolution and history, particularly during periods associated with species ancestral to *Homo sapiens*. Palaeoanthropologists often study both human fossils and the archaeological remains associated with them.

palaeoethnobotany: The study of plant utilization and beliefs about plants in ancient societies.

palaeosol: A buried land surface or soil horizon. Indicative of past environmental conditions. Also spelled "paleosol."

palisade: A fence of stakes, usually creating a defensive enclosure.

palmette: A decorative motif in the form of a palm frond.

palstave: A type of axe head with flanges that facilitate hafting.

palynology: *See* pollen analysis.

paramount chiefdom: A disproportionately strong chiefdom, usually with authority over subordinate chiefdoms.

passage grave: A type of chambered tomb with a narrow passageway leading to a central camber.

pastoralism: A social organization based on managing livestock.

patriliny: The practice of tracing descent through the paternal line.

patron-client system: The practice of loaning goods to subordinates. The terms of the loan usually require the return of the original grant plus additional goods and/or services.

penannular brooches: A type of brooch with a circular ring interrupted at one point. The two terminal ends of the ring are often enlarged and highly ornamented.

petroglyph: A drawing carved into rock. Usually reserved for works on large boulders or immobile outcroppings of stone.

phenomenology: The study of the experience and awareness of being human in a material and social world. Also the study of acts of perception and self-awareness and their cognitive implications. In archaeology this perspective has fostered attempts to understand monuments based on the experience of being in a particular landscape and of moving through and around monuments.

phosphate analysis/mapping: Phosphates are abundant in animal waste, fat, and other organic materials. Geochemical analysis identifies concentrations of phosphates in archaeological sites as a method of reconstructing how an area was utilized.

phytolith: A silica structure formed between plant cells. Phytoliths are useful to archaeobotanists because they often have species-specific forms and remain when other portions of plants decay.

piling: A timber driven into the ground to serve as the foundation of a building. Also known as a "pile."

pit house: A structure with its floor dug below ground level, often with timber walls and a gabled roof supported by posts. Also known as a "Grubenhaus" or a "sunken-featured building" (SFB).

pithos (pl. pithoi): A ceramic vessel used for the storage of oil, grain, and other materials. Also used as a container for bodies in certain inhumation practices.

Pleistocene: The geological epoch beginning approximately 1.8 million years ago and ending about ten thousand years ago with the beginning of the Holocene. This period is characterized by alternating periods during which glaciers expanded and contracted. *See also* interglacial.

pollen analysis: The study of pollen with the aim of reconstructing changes in vegetation through time. Also known as "palynology."

polymetallic ores: Ores with more than one predominant metal.

pommel mount: An attachment creating a knob or similar protuberance at the end of the hilt of a sword. Often highly decorated.

postdepositional: Of or relating to occurrences after an object has been buried.

post-processual archaeology: A disparate set of approaches to archaeological interpretation that developed in reaction to perceived limitations in processual archaeology and the scientific method in general. Post-processualists emphasize the influence of assumptions and biases that investigators bring to research and the impossibility of escaping their influence. Instead of attempting to escape those biases, post-processualists advocate use of a defined ideological perspective. This perspective also tends to view artifacts as lacking intrinsic or absolute meaning. They are best understood as evocative of meanings from the contexts in which they were used.

posthole: A pit dug for the insertion of a timber, stone pillar, or other similar upright object. Such pits are then backfilled to pack material around the post. Usage of this term varies. At times its meaning is restricted to only the space occupied by the post itself. That space is often preserved as a darker soil than the fill of the entire pit. Such features are also known as "post pipes" or "post molds." With this usage, the entire hole is generally called a "post pit."

potin: A bronze alloy with a high proportion of tin.

PPNA: An abbreviation of Pre-Pottery Neolithic A, a subdivision of the Aceramic Neolithic in the Near East dated between 8500 B.C. and 7600 B.C.

PPNB: An abbreviation of Pre-Pottery Neolithic B, a subdivision of the Aceramic Neolithic in the Near East dated between 7600 B.C. and 6000 B.C.

Preboreal climatic period: A subdivision of the Holocene epoch in northern Europe. Extends from c. 9500 B.C. to 8500 B.C. During this first period of the Holocene, forests colonized northern Europe. *See also* Boreal, Atlantic, Subboreal, and Subatlantic climatic periods.

preceramic: A term used for an aceramic period of the Neolithic period in Greece, Crete, and Cyprus. *See* Aceramic Neolithic.

pressure flaking: A method for retouching stone flakes by pressing down with a sharpened piece of antler or other similar object, rather than striking the flake with a hammer. The application of pressure detaches a small, flat flake.

processual archaeology: *See* New Archaeology.

provenance: The location where an object was found. In archaeology the find spot of an artifact is usually expressed as a point in the three-dimensional space of an archaeological excavation. Also spelled "provenience."

quern: A grinding stone, usually operated by hand.

rachis: In plant anatomy, the term for the structure that connects a seed casing to the stalk of a plant. This structure is more robust in domestic varieties of wheat than in their wild progenitors.

radiocarbon dating: A radiometric dating technique based on the decay of carbon 14. The amount of carbon 14 in an organism begins to decrease at death because the organism is no longer taking up the isotope from its environment. By measuring the amount of carbon 14, it is possible to estimate the time elapsed since the death of an organism. The primary limitations of the technique are that atmospheric carbon-14 levels vary over time (complicating calculation of how much carbon 14 was in an organism at death) and that it is generally not useful for objects more than fifty thousand years old (owing to the short half-life of carbon 14).

radiolarite: A type of chert formed predominantly from the siliceous remains of a marine zooplankton called radiolaria. Used in making stone tools. *See also* chert.

radiometric dating: An absolute dating technique utilizing the radioactive decay of atoms. Since radioactive isotopes have predictable rates of decay, the amount of an isotope in an object is linked to the age of the object.

ranked society: A society in which access to resources is unevenly distributed. A stratified or hierarchical society.

rath: *See* ringfort.

red ochre: *See* ochre.

redistribution: The collection of goods and subsequent allotment of those goods to group members. Often associated with the development and maintenance of centralized authority in a ranked society. *See* chiefdom.

relative dating: Dating methods that rely on stratigraphy and artifact typology to establish the chronological position of finds in relation to one another but without the assignment of an age in years. Used primarily prior to the development of absolute dating methods such as carbon-14 dating.

repoussé: A decorative technique in which ornamentation is pressed or hammered into the back of sheet metal.

resistivity survey: A noninvasive technique for investigating subsurface features that is based on variation in the resistance to electric current offered by different materials. Resistivity is measured by passing current between two probes.

revetment/to revet: A facing, usually of stone, used to reinforce an embankment.

retouch: Secondary working of a flake or other stone tool to modify its shape or edge quality. Retouching generally involves removing smaller flakes through indirect percussion or pressure flaking.

ringfort: A type of enclosure common in early medieval Ireland, usually 30–40 meters in diameter. Enclosures are defined by banks, ditches, and stone walls. Ringforts were often used as lightly defended farmsteads, although some have yielded little evidence of occupation. Also known as "raths."

roundhouse: A structure with a circular perimeter. A common type of dwelling across northwestern Europe, particularly in the British Isles.

rune/runic: A letter in one of several alphabets used by Germanic groups in the early medieval period. Often found as inscriptions on stones (rune stones).

sarsen: A type of sandstone used in building megalithic monuments.

satrap: Originally a provincial governor in Persia. Used as a generic term for a local potentate.

sceatta: An Anglo-Saxon or Frisian silver coin.

scramasax: A short, single-edged stabbing sword.

scriptorium: An area of a monastery devoted to copying manuscripts.

Secondary Products Revolution: The theory that after an initial period of domestication, when humans used animals for primary products, such as meat and hides, a change occurred in animal exploitation as humans began to use animals as sources of milk, wool, traction, and other "secondary" products. Some argue that no such radical change occurred and that the apparent revolution is only an intensification of previous practices.

semiflexed burial: Deposition of a body with the legs pulled only partially toward the torso. The body also is often placed on its side.

seriation: A chronological ordering of artifacts according to changes in frequency, form, and decoration.

settlement pattern: A characterization of the way in which habitations and other structures are arranged across a landscape, including such variables as form, size, distribution, and density.

shell midden: An accumulation of refuse from the collection and consumption of shellfish. Burials, tools, and other types of refuse are often included.

sherd: A fragment of pottery or worked clay. Also known as "shard" or "potsherd."

shield boss: An attachment to the center of a shield, often dome shaped or pointed.

shifting cultivation: An agricultural system in which areas are cleared of native vegetation, cultivated, and then left unused for a period of time to replenish the soil with nutrients. *See also* bush fallow cultivation and swidden.

ship setting: A Viking period Scandinavian burial monument characterized by an oval arrangement of stones in the outline of a boat, usually with taller stones representing stern and bow posts.

site: Any location where artifacts, ecofacts, or archaeological features are found. Types of sites range from a scatter of a few flints to an entire city.

***situla* (pl. *situlae*):** A bucket-shaped vessel, usually of pottery or bronze.

slag: Refuse from smelting metal. Usually a glassy, porous, and fused material.

sling stone: A rock collected for use as a missile and thrown with a sling. Often found as caches on the perimeter of defended settlements.

slip: Viscous material applied to the surface of pottery before firing. Composed of clay, water, and often colorants or other additives.

smelting/smelted: The process of refining ore in a furnace.

solidus: A Roman gold coin.

sounding: A test pit dug through the layers of a site to allow for preliminary investigation of a site's stratigraphy and underlying features.

souterrains: A subterranean chamber constructed from stone. Common in Ireland, western Britain, and Scotland.

spectrographic analysis: A technique for identifying the combination of elements in an object. Often an object possesses a unique combination of trace elements that allows archaeologists to define its origin. The presence of trace elements is identified by measuring the wavelengths of radiation emitted from samples.

spindle whorls: An implement used in spinning thread and yarn to maintain the momentum of a rotating spindle. Usually made from stone or clay in the form of a disk or sphere with a hole in the middle.

stable carbon isotopes: Forms of carbon that do not naturally undergo radioactive decay. Commonly used in studies of provenance and diet.

stater: A Greek coin of gold or silver.

steatite: A relatively soft type of stone, well suited to carving and working into vessels. Also known as "soapstone."

stela (pl. stelae): A stone pillar, usually with carving and/or inscriptions.

stratigraphy: The layering of sediments into successive strata or the analysis of the results of this process. A cornerstone of archaeological interpretation is that, barring evidence of subsequent disturbance, lower strata were formed in an earlier period than higher strata.

strontium isotopes: Forms of a mineral component of bone that are absorbed from the environment through diet and other means. Used to reconstruct diet.

Subatlantic climatic period: A subdivision of the Holocene epoch in northern Europe that begins c. 800 B.C. and extends to the present. As with the Subboreal, cooler temperatures than are found in the Atlantic characterize the Subatlantic period. *See also* Preboreal, Boreal, Atlantic, and Subboreal climatic periods.

Subboreal climatic period: A subdivision of the Holocene epoch in northern Europe that began

c. 3800 B.C. and ended c. 800 B.C. Cooler temperatures than are found in the Atlantic characterize the period. *See also* Preboreal, Boreal, Atlantic, and Subatlantic climatic periods.

sub-Roman: A term for groups or territories without an Anglo-Saxon material culture in the period following Roman rule in Britain. Used in preference to the term "post-Roman" because many characteristics of Roman culture endured into the medieval period. Also used in preference to "British" or "Celtic" because "sub-Roman" is less ethnically specific and charged by historical debate.

successor states: Political units that emerge after the collapse of an empire or other expansive and centralized organization.

supine: Lying face up with limbs extended.

survey: The process of investigating and recording the archaeological assets of an area, usually without extensive excavation.

swidden: An agricultural field created by cutting, burning, or otherwise removing wild vegetation. Usually part of a shifting cultivation system.

taiga: *See* boreal forest.

taphonomy/taphonomic: The study of the processes affecting the remains of organisms, particularly bones, between death and final embedding in the ground. Relevant processes include gnawing by scavengers and dispersal by flowing water.

tell: A mound in the Near East or southeastern Europe created by building successive settlements, usually from mud bricks, on the same location. Synonymous terms include "tepe" and "hüyük."

temper/tempered: 1. Material, such as coarse sand or ground shell, added to clay in the process of making pottery. The additive makes clay more workable and reduces cracking during firing. 2. The process of hardening metal, particularly iron, by repeated cooling and heating.

tephra/tephrochronology: Particulate material ejected during volcanic eruptions. When it becomes incorporated into sediment in a landscape, tephra can be used to date the formation of that sediment. For relative dating, in areas where the sequence of eruptions is known, it is possible to correlate the stratigraphy of samples from different areas that possess layers of tephra. Tephra is also useful for absolute dating because the unique form of tephra from some individual eruptions is known.

terp (pl. *terpen*): A mound on the coastal plain of the Netherlands and Germany created to raise a settlement above wet ground.

terra sigillata: A type of fine mass-produced Mediterranean tableware pottery. Made with a glossy red slip applied to its surface. Produced and exported across Europe from the first century B.C. through the second century A.D.

terremare: An Italian term for a mound created during the Bronze Age by successive settlements built on the same location.

tholos: A stone chamber capped by a corbeled vault.

Three Age System: The chronology running from the Stone Age to the Bronze Age to the Iron Age. Developed early in the nineteenth century on the basis of the sequence of change in prehistoric tool technology. The defining characteristics of each age have been refined and elaborated considerably since then. For example, the Neolithic is now defined primarily by the use of domestic animals and plants.

toponym: Place name.

torc: A neck ring, often of gold or bronze. Also spelled "torque."

transgression: The flooding of land, usually due to a rise in sea level.

transhumance: The movement of livestock seasonally between upland and lowland pasture.

trapeze: A microlith shaped into the form of a trapezoid (two parallel sides and two convergent sides).

trefoil: A decorative motif in the shape of a trifoliate leaf, such as a clover.

tremissis: A Merovingian gold coin.

trepanation: Medical procedure involving the removal of a piece of a living human's skull. Some skulls bear traces of the survival of multiple trepanations.

trilithon: A megalithic monument composed of two upright stone slabs supporting a capstone slab, most famously at Stonehenge.

tufa: Rock formed of calcium carbonate deposited from ground or surface water, as in the material from which a stalagmite is formed. Used as an architectural material. Archaeologists also analyze samples for data about past climates. Also known as "travertine."

tuff: A geological layer formed of volcanic ash and other material. Also rock composed of compacted or fused volcanic material.

tumulus: A mound constructed from earth or stone, generally circular and containing a burial. Also known as a "barrow" or "*kurgan.*"

tuyere: A nozzle used to direct air from a bellows into a metalworking furnace. Often the only surviving evidence of metalworking.

type site: A find spot that gives its name to, or is used as an exemplar of, a type of settlement, an artifact, or an archaeological culture, usually because it is the location of the first discovery or is the most representative example.

typology: An ordering of objects into categories, usually based on form and decoration.

urbanism: Characteristic of an urban center and the associated ways of life.

urnfield: A cemetery of cremations placed in urns and buried in pits. A burial rite associated with the Late Bronze Age.

***Viereckschanze* (pl. *Viereckschanzen*):** A rectilinear enclosure defined by a bank and ditch. The frequent presence within the enclosure of pits and wells containing votive deposits fosters interpretation of these monuments as ritual enclosures, although some argue that they were habitations as well.

viticulture: The cultivation of grapes.

vitrified fort: A hillfort with an exterior wall face that is smoothed and fused together by heat and wind.

wattle and daub: A technique for constructing walls. Wattles are thin rods or tree shoots woven between stakes planted in the ground. Daub is mud, dung, or another type of plaster spread over the wattling.

wave-of-advance model: A theory that postulates a steady rate of spread, usually of cultural traits, across a landscape over time. Principally associated with the demic diffusion model for agriculture in Europe.

weir: A barrier set in water to channel fish or other quarry into a trap or a fence in tidal areas over which fish can swim in at high tide but cannot swim out at low tide and thus are trapped on the tidal flat.

withe: A slender branch or shoot.

***wurt* (pl. *wurten*):** *See terp.*

zooarchaeology: The study of animal remains from archaeological sites.

zoomorphic: In the shape of or possessing characteristics of an animal.

INDEX

Volume numbers precede the colon. Page numbers in boldface refer to extended discussions of a topic. Page numbers in italics refer to maps, figures, and tables.

pulses, 2:372
rye, 1:**207**; 2:372
vetches, 1:208; 2:372
wheat, 1:**205–206**, *206*; 2:372
Copper Age, 1:358, 361
Bronze Age, 1:208; 2:14, 25, 46, 59
Iron Age, 2:223, 248, 257
Mesolithic period, 1:207, 208
Middle Ages, 2:373, *374*, 375, 448,
491, 500
Neolithic period
Europe, central, 1:337, 380
Europe, eastern, 1:205, 208, 235,
241, 246, 336–337, 356–357,
361
Europe, northern, 1:296, 433
Europe, northwestern, 1:274–275,
276, 277, 279, 283, 289, 290
Europe, southeastern, 1:336, 337
Europe, upland central and
southern, 1:**390**, 397
Europe, western, 1:257
Mediterranean region, 1:204–209,
249, 254, 276, 443, 459; 2:121
Near East, 1:*205*, 1:205–207, 208
Palaeolithic era, 1:208
Crvena Stijena site, 1:172
Cucuteni culture, 1:92, *93, 94,* 354,
355, *355, 358*
Cucuteni-Tripolye culture, 1:**245,
357–359**, 358–359
Cuiry-les-Chaudardes site, 1:274
Cummins, Vicki, 1:96
Curraghmore-16 site, 1:417
Cyprus
Bronze Age, 2:**108–115**, *109*
Copper Age, 1:**347–353**
burials, 1:348
copper artifacts, 1:69, 70
enclosure complexes, 1:348
figurines, 1:348–349, 351–352
settlement structures, 1:349–350,
351, *351*
social systems, 1:**349–350**
trade and exchange, 1:69–70, 352
Neolithic period, 1:**231–232**
Czech Republic. *See also* Moravia
Bronze Age, 2:6, 8, 21
Iron Age, 2:*171*
Middle Ages, 2:155, *155*
Neolithic period, 1:112, *372,* 374,
376–377

D

Dąbki site, 1:135–136

Dál Riata culture, 2:**386–388**, *387,*
469, 471, 475
Dalkey Island site, 2:324
Dalmatia, 1:172
Danebury site, 2:162, 227, **229–231**,
230
Danish National Museum for History,
1:15
Darion site, 1:113, 114
Darius I, 2:291
Dark, Petra, 1:154
Dark Age, 2:**312–318**, 338
Dark Age Economics (Hodges), 2:324,
327, 330
Dartmoor site, 1:129
Darwin, Charles, *On the Origin of
Species by Means of Natural
Selection,* 1:17, 40, 102
Dating methods and chronology,
1:**40–46**
calibration issues, 1:**43–44**, *45*
dendrochronology, 1:**42–43**, *43*
metallurgy industries, 1:66
obsidian used for, 1:45, **68–69**
optical stimulation luminescence
(OSL), 1:45–46
petrographic analysis of artifacts,
1:68
pollen used for, 1:127, 130, 186
pottery used for, 1:66
radiocarbon dating, 1:41–42, 43,
159
stone tools used for, 1:66
thermoluminescence (TL), 1:45–46
Davies, Wendy, 2:486
The Dawn of European Civilization
(Childe), 2:9
Deer Island site. *See* Oleneostrovskii
Mogilnik (Olenii Ostrov) site
Deer Park Farms site, 2:452, **462–
465**, *463*
Déisi culture, 2:481
Dendra site, 1:116
Denmark. *See also specific cultures and
people; specific sites*
about prehistory, origins of, 1:15–
16, 19, 25
Bronze Age
burials, 2:75–76, **80–82**, *81*
clothing, 2:75–76, *81*
coffin burials, 2:5, **80–82**
hoards, 2:27
ritual and ideology, 2:77, 78
settlement patterns, 2:76, 77
settlement structures, 2:77, *78, 79*
social structures, 2:75–76
social systems, 2:5, **75–76**
weapons and armor, 2:10

Iron Age, 2:542–547, *546*
artworks, 1:118
feasting, 2:182, *182*
human remains, 1:26–28, 47;
2:270
political systems, 2:542–547
ritual and ideology, 1:99–100
settlement patterns, 1:77
social systems, 1:77
warfare and conquest, 1:118
Megalithic period, 1:401
Mesolithic period, 1:23, 52, 124,
138, 189, 196
Middle Ages, 2:324, 374
Neolithic period, 1:52, 298, 301–
304, 306, 402, 403, 404
Viking Age, 2:**542–547**
Department of the Environment
(Northern Ireland), 2:462
Deposits of artifacts, 1:76, 315; 2:5,
26. *See also* Bog deposits
Dereivka site, 1:*359,* 360–361
Derevenski, Joanna Sofaer, 1:92
Díaz-Andreu, Margarita, *Excavating
Women: A History of Women in
European Archaeology,* 1:81
Dijon site, 2:376
Dimini site, 1:336, 337
Dinas Powys site, 2:483–484
Diodorus Siculus, 1:113, 118; 2:180
Dionysius of Halicarnassus, 2:150
Discovery Programme, 2:452
Disease and health issues, 1:**377**, 394,
454
Divostin site, 1:337
Dja'de site, 1:*205*
Dnieper-Donets culture, 1:**245–247,
356–357**
Domesday Book, 2:493, 510
Domesticated animals. *See* Animal
husbandry
*The Domestication of Europe: Structure
and Contingency in Neolithic
Societies* (Hodder), 1:84
Doon Hill site, 2:471
Dordogne site, 1:17–18
Dorestad site, 2:324, 325, 328, 329,
330, *357,* 592
Dorsey site, 2:235
Douglass, A. E., 1:42
Dowris site, 2:60
Dowth site, 1:414
La Draga site, 1:163, 249, *249,* 250
Dragsholm site, 1:298, 426
Dreuil-lès-Amiens site, 1:274
Dublin site, 2:454, 455, **466–468**
Duchcov site, 2:299
Dún Ailinne site, 1:25
Dun Troddan site, 1:115

tools, 1:441
trade and exchange, 1:**376**
warfare and conquest, 1:111–112, 367–368
post-Roman period, 2:587–588, 590–591
Roman period, 2:**573–574,** 586–590
Viking Age, 2:349
Europe, eastern. *See also specific countries; specific cultures and people; specific sites*
about prehistory, origins of, 1:18, 20
Bronze Age
burials, 2:17, 93–97, 105
copper industry, 2:9
crops, 1:208
environments, 2:106
farming, 1:434
fortifications, 1:**114–115;** 2:**31–33,** *32*
horses, domestication of, 2:93, 106
metallurgy industries, 2:103–104
political systems, 2:18, 104
pottery industry, 2:96, 104–105
ritual and ideology, 2:26, 32, 99
settlement patterns, 2:15, *93,* 93–94, 95–96, 103, 104
settlement structures, 2:103, 104
social systems, 2:93
steppe herders, 2:**92–100**
subsistence resources, 2:99
tin industry, 2:8
trade and exchange, 2:111–113
Transcaucasia, 2:**101–107,** *102*
warfare and conquest, 1:114
wheeled vehicles, 2:94–95
Copper Age
animal husbandry, 1:358
burials, 1:**341–343,** 358
copper artifacts, evidence of, 1:315
copper industry, 1:317–322, 339
crops, 1:358, 361
environments, 1:**357,** 359
fauna, 1:358
fishing populations, 1:358
flora, 1:358, 361
foraging populations, 1:365
gender roles and relationships, 1:343
gold artifacts, 1:**321,** 341–342, *342*
horses, domestication of, 1:361
kurgan burials, 1:340, 361, 362; 2:94–97
population statistics, 1:359
pottery industry, 1:358, 359, 361, 362

ritual and ideology, 1:360, 361, 363, 365–366
settlement patterns, 1:320, 338–339, 358–359, 362
settlement structures, 1:358
stone tool industries, 1:361
subsistence resources, 1:358, 361, 365
tool industries, 1:315, 318, 339, 341–342
trade and exchange, 1:69, 70, 339, 352, 358
warfare and conquest, 1:112
Iron Age
artisans, 2:293
artworks, 2:*305*
coinage, 2:170
dates for, 2:**289–295,** 303
kurgan burials, 2:291, 304–306
political systems, 2:285, 292–293, 305–307, 309–310
pottery industry, 2:292, 305–306
settlement patterns, 2:291–292, 293–294, 304–306, 307
settlement structures, 2:292
warfare and conquest, 2:290, 294–295, 310–311
weapons and armor, 2:242, 302
Mesolithic period, 1:**183–198**
aquatic resources, 1:184, 186
burials, 1:83, 124, 187, 188, 189, 190, 196
environments, 1:**132–133,** 183–184
farming, 1:186
fishing populations, 1:186
flora, 1:186, 187
foraging populations, 1:184–185, 186–187, 364
horses for subsistence, 1:364
landscape use, 1:**185–187**
pastoralism, 1:362
pottery industry, 1:184–185
ritual and ideology, 1:187, **188–190,** 196
settlement patterns, 1:**184–185,** 187
settlement structures, 1:187
stone tool industries, 1:184–185, 186
subsistence resources, 1:124, 184, 186, 187
trade and exchange, 1:187
Middle Ages, 2:**563–571,** *564*
animal husbandry, 2:570–571
archaeological evidence, 2:**406–407,** 563–564
artworks, 2:412
burials, 2:566, 569

dates for, 2:407
economic systems, 2:**412,** 563–567, **569–571**
environments, 2:413
ethnic identities, 2:563, 564, 565, 566, 571
foraging populations, 2:570–571
fortifications, 2:566, 580
historical evidence, 2:**406–408,** 563
linguistic evidence, 2:**406–408**
metalworking, 2:570, *570*
nomadic tradition, 2:**368–369**
pastoralism, 2:**368–369**
political systems, 2:**556–561,** 564, 566
Russia, 2:*564*
settlement patterns, 2:564–565, **569**
social systems, 2:564, 566
trade and exchange, 2:565–566
urbanization, 2:563, 565
Neolithic period
animal husbandry, 1:326, 328–329, 336–337, 356–357, 361, 362
artworks, 1:361
bog deposits, 1:**298**
burials, 1:297, 305–310, *307,* 360–363, 365–366, 372, 378–382
chronology of, 1:**372–373**
copper industry, 1:315, 318, 379–380
crops, 1:205, 208, 235, 241, 246, 336–337, 356–357, 361
environments, 1:244–245, **356, 357,** 359
farming, 1:185, **223–225,** 243–248, **378–382**
fauna, 1:358, 361, 362
figurines, 1:369
fishing populations, 1:202
flint industry, 1:**376**
flora, 1:357, 361
foraging populations, 1:234–235, 364, 365
horses, role of, 1:364, 366, 367–368
kurgan burials, 1:361, 362
landscape use, 1:129
monumental structures, 1:305–310
pottery industry, 1:185, **235–237,** 238–240, 243, 245, 247, 369–370, 373
ritual and ideology, 1:94, 378–382
salt industry, 1:376
settlement patterns, 1:239, 241, 314, 335–336, 337, 368, **374–375**

──────── ■ ────────

F

Grotta dell'Uzzo site, 1:442
Grotta di Porto Badisco site, 1:446
Grotta Funeraria site, 1:444
Grotta Latronico site, 1:172, 445
Grotta Lattaia site, 1:445
Grotta Marisa site, 1:172
Grotta Pacelli site, 1:446
Grotta Romanelli site, 1:172
Grotta Scaloria, 1:444
La Grotte Gazel site, 1:249, *249*
Guldhøj Man burial, 2:76, 80
Gumelnitsa culture, 1:207
Gundestrup cauldron, 2:182, *182,*
    270
Gündlingen site, 1:74–75
Guðmundsson, Garðar, 2:443
Gussage All Saints site, 1:78
Gyges, 2:290

------------------■------------------

H

Haberey, Waldemar, 1:260
Hacilar site, 1:223
Hadorf, Johan, 2:540
Haervay-Heerweg route, 1:426
Hagar Qim site, 1:452, *453,* 454, *454*
Hagia Triadha site, 2:*117,* 119, 120
Haignerè (abbè), 2:512
Haithabu site. *See* Hedeby site
Hal Saflieni Hypogeum site, 1:452,
    454
Hallgren, Fredrik, 1:433
Hallstatt culture, 2:**144–146, 214–
    216,** 241–245, **281–283.** *See
    also* Urnfield culture
  about, 2:140, 144, 192, 241
  artworks, 1:**117–118;** 2:184–185,
    185, 215
  burials, 1:74; 2:141, 144, *145,* 214–
    215, 216, 242, 244
  dates for, 2:138, 144, 146
  farming, 2:142
  fortifications, 1:114; 2:142
  hillforts, 2:215, 216, 243–244,
    249–252, *251*
  iron industry, 2:216
  ironworking, 2:215
  political systems, 2:142
  salt industry, 1:74
  settlement patterns, 2:142, 215
  settlement structures, 2:146
  social systems, 2:214, 242
  state societies, 2:348
  trade and exchange, 2:146, 215,
    216, 242–243
  warfare and conquest, 1:114, 117–
    118; 2:144

  weapons and armor, 1:117; 2:214,
    242
Halsall, Guy, 2:363
Halstead, Paul, 1:326
Halula site, 1:*205*
Hambledon Hill site, 1:112, **283–
    286,** *285,* 403–404, 160
Hammer site, 1:295
Hamwic site, 2:324–325, 326, 328,
    329, 330
Handsman, Russell, 1:83
Hannibal, 2:258
Hanson, Julienne, 1:56
Hanstedgård site, 1:298
Haraldskjaer Woman, 1:27
Harding, Anthony, 2:12, 15
Hardinxveld-Giessendam site, 1:147
Håga site, 2:75, 78
Harris, Edward, *Principles of
    Archaeological Stratigraphy,* 1:33
Harrison, Richard, 1:459
Hartikka site, 1:190
Hartz, Sönke, 1:296
Hasdrubal, 2:258
Haughey's Fort site, 2:59, 162
Haughton, Christine, 2:363
Le Haut-Mée site, 1:398
Havnelev site, 1:423
Hawkes, Christopher, 1:91
Hayling Island site, 2:227
Hazendonk site, 1:288
Hazleton site, 1:276
Health and disease issues, 1:**377,** 394,
    454
Hecataeus of Miletus, 2:141
Hedeby site, 2:358, 424, *424,* 546,
    591, 594
Heer, Oswald, 1:387
Helgö site, 2:278, 325, *326,* 536–
    537, 539–540
Helmsdorf site, 2:23, 25
Henauhof site, 1:173
Henninge Boställe site, 1:156
Herder, Johann Gottfried, 1:101
Herding, 1:**215–216.** *See also*
    Nomadic traditions; Pastoralism;
    Steppe herders
Heritage Council, 2:452
Hernádkak site, 1:112
Herodotus, 2:203, 254, 290, 293,
    309, 391, 411
Herriko Barra site, 1:160
Herxheim site, 1:111, 264
Herzegovina, 1:337
Hesselø site, 1:423
Heuneburg site, 1:74; 2:161, 200–
    204, 215, **249–252,** *251*
High Island site, 2:*378*

Hillforts, 2:212, 214, 215, 216. *See
    also* Fortifications
Hillier, Bill, 1:56
Hills, Catherine, 2:496
Hipogeo de Longar site, 1:460
Hirschboeck, Katherine, 1:43
Histoire de Jules César (Napoleon III),
    2:220
Historia Francorum (Gregory of
    Tours), 2:521
Historia naturalis (Pliny the Elder),
    2:180
Historia Norvegia, 2:403
The Histories (Herodotus), 2:290,
    293, 309, 411
Histories (Polybius), 2:211
History, field of, 2:**340–345.** *See also*
    Prehistory, origins of
The History of Rome (Livy), 2:192
History of the Franks (Gregory of
    Tours), 2:340
Hjortspring site, 1:**99–100;** 2:270
Hluboké Mašůvky site, 1:376
Hoards
  Bronze Age, 2:26–27, *27,* 33, **60,**
    70, 71, 214
  Iron Age, 2:270, 301–302
  Middle Ages, 2:334, *334,* 404, 535,
    535, 538, *538,* 573
Hochdorf site, 1:76, **79–80,** 96, 118;
    2:181, 201, 204
Hodde site, 1:77; 2:**272**
Hodder, Ian, 1:84, 94, 298
Hodges, Richard, 2:324, 327, 330
Hódmezővásárhely-Gorzsa site, 1:338
Hoëdic site, 1:147, 148, 149, 274,
    275, 309, 400
Hofstaðir site, 2:437, **442–444**
Hohmichele site, 2:250–251
Hohøj site, 2:75
Holland. *See* Netherlands, The
Hollufgard site, 2:*79*
Holmqyst, Wilhelm, 2:539
Holocene era
  aquatic resources, 1:11, 152
  Atlantic period, 1:167, 183, 184
  coastal region, 1:**126–127**
  environments, 1:**8–9,** 11, *48,* 49,
    126–131, 152–153, 168
  farming, 1:8–9, **127–128,** 130, *130*
  fauna, 1:**127,** 152, 181
  foraging populations, 1:9, 10, 127,
    130, 167–182
  landscape use, 1:118–120, 170
  ocean levels during, 1:8, 9, **48,** 171–
    172
  population statistics, 1:9
  Preboreal/Boreal periods, 1:167,
    168, 173, 183, 234

Iron Age *(continued)*
 Mediterranean region, 2:255, 257, 258
 enclosure complexes, 2:**174–178,** *175,* 234, **239–240,** 246, 301
 environments, 1:418; 2:222, **272–273**
 farming
  Europe, central, 2:283
  Europe, eastern, 2:210
  Europe, northern, 2:**273–274,** 276, 372, 548
  Europe, northwestern, 2:**222–223,** 372
  Iberia, 2:255
  Mediterranean region, 2:255, 263, 372
 feasting, 2:**179–183,** *182,* **194,** 218
 field systems, 2:222
 figurines, 2:256, 297
 fishing populations, 2:276, 535
 flint industry, 2:224
 foraging populations, 2:276
 fortifications
  Europe, central, 2:**154–159,** 241, 246–247, **249–252,** *251,* 282, *286,* **286–288,** 301
  Europe, northern, 1:**115;** 2:138–139
  Europe, northwestern, 1:115, 118–120; 2:**157, 160–163,** 451–452
  Europe, upland central and southern, 1:115
  Europe, western, 2:**154–157,** *155,* 212
 Fürstensitze, 2:215–216, 243–244, 250, *251*
 gender roles and relationships, 1:**86–87;** 2:195, **245,** 279, 283
 hillforts
  Europe, central, 2:*243,* 243–244, **249–252,** *251,* **298**
  Europe, northern, 2:550
  Europe, northwestern, 2:**160–163,** 223–224, 235
  Europe, western, 2:212, 215, 216
 historical evidence, 2:**549–550**
 hoards, 2:270, 301–302
 horses, domestication of, 2:**194**
 human remains, 1:26–28, 47; 2:270
 human sacrifices, 2:**270**
 iron industry
  Europe, central, 2:166, 248, 283, 284–285, 297, 300, 416
  Europe, eastern, 2:166
  Europe, northern, 2:269
  Europe, northwestern, 2:166, 224–225
  Europe, western, 2:166, 215

 Iberia, 2:257
 landscape use, 1:24, *61,* 97, 128, *130;* 2:222, **270–272,** 498
 lead industry, 2:253–254
 leather industry, 2:225
 life expectancy, 2:299
 metallurgy industries, 2:210, 216, 217, 263, 266
 migration patterns, 2:**208**
 mining industry, 2:258
 monumental structures, 1:96
 oppida
  Europe, central, 2:**154–159,** *158,* 246, **247–249,** 300
  Europe, northwestern, 2:**157,** 224, 228
  Europe, western, 2:**154–157,** *155,* 218, **219–221**
  Iberia, 2:256–257
 political systems, 2:**138–139,** 194–195
  Europe, central, 2:156, 159, 246, 250, 285, 300
  Europe, eastern, 2:285, 292–293, 305, 306–307, 309–310
  Europe, northern, 2:534, 542–547
  Europe, western, 2:217, 218
  Iberia, 2:255, 257
  Mediterranean region, 2:255, 314, 315–318
 population statistics, 2:249, 250, 256, **270–271**
 pottery industry
  Europe, central, 2:200–203, 283, 300
  Europe, eastern, 2:292, 305–306
  Europe, northwestern, 2:225
  Europe, western, 2:199–200
  Mediterranean region, 2:199–200, 266
 resource use, 1:53–54
 ringforts, 2:235, 236–237
 ritual and ideology
  Europe, central, 2:250, 282, **298, 301–302**
  Europe, northern, 1:93, 94, 96, 99–100; 2:**181–183,** 270, 551
  Europe, northwestern, 2:**225–227,** 235, 237–238
  Iberia, 2:254–258
 royal sites, 2:**239–240**
 salt industry, 2:223
 settlement patterns, 1:58; 2:138–139, **149–150**
  Europe, central, 1:77; 2:**299,** 300–301
  Europe, eastern, 2:208–209, 291–292, 293–294, 304–306, 307

 Europe, northern, 1:77; 2:**270–273, 278–279,** 548
 Europe, northwestern, 1:77; 2:501–502
 Europe, western, 2:212–213, *213,* 215, 217–218
 Iberia, 2:256–257
 Mediterranean region, 2:255, 258, 314–315, 317–318
 settlement structures
  Europe, central, 1:87
  Europe, eastern, 2:209–210, 292
  Europe, northern, 1:95; 2:273, **534–535, 537–538**
  Europe, northwestern, 2:**223–224,** *224*
  Europe, western, 1:75, 76, 87; 2:216, 218–219
  Mediterranean region, 2:257, 258, 316
 slavery, 2:**196–197**
 social systems, 1:62; 2:**138–139, 191–197**
  Europe, central, 1:**79–80;** 2:156, 159, 181, 241–242, 246, 250, 282
  Europe, eastern, 2:304–305, 306
  Europe, northern, 2:269, **279–280,** 535, 548
  Europe, northwestern, 2:181, **227–228**
  Europe, western, 2:214, 216, 217
  Mediterranean region, 1:75, 76, 87; 2:255–258, 266, 314
 state societies, 2:348
 stone industry, 2:225
 stone tool industries, 2:225
 subsistence resources, 2:**222–223, 534–535, 537–538**
 technologies, 2:**224–225,** 248
 textile industry, 2:225, 248
 tool industries, 1:66–67
 trade and exchange
  Europe, central, 2:159, 242–245, 248–249, 250, 283–284
  Europe, eastern, 2:210
  Europe, northern, 2:138, 278–279
  Europe, northwestern, 2:228, 237
  Europe, western, 2:**202–204,** 215, 216
  Iberia, 2:256
 transporation routes, 2:276
 urbanization, 2:138–139, 287, 550
 urnfields, 2:282
 Viereckschanzen, 2:**174–178,** *175,* 246, 247, 301
 warfare and conquest
  Europe, central, 1:**112–113,** 118; 2:246, 247, 282, 300

M

gender roles and relationships, 1:379
landscape use, 1:129
monumental structures, 1:304–310, *307*
ritual and ideology, 1:378–382
salt industry, 1:**376**
settlement patterns, 1:374
settlement structures, 1:374, 379, *380*
trade and exchange, 1:**376**
warfare and conquest, 1:112
Polderweg site, 1:147, 149
Polgár-Csszhalom site, 1:337–338
Polignac, François de, 2:255
Political systems. *See also specific countries; specific sites*
about state societies, 2:**346–350**
about *khagan*, 2:574, 577
Bronze Age
Europe, central, 2:15–16, 18
Europe, eastern, 2:18, 104
Europe, northwestern, 2:**59–61**
Europe, southeastern, 2:15–16, 18
Iberia, 2:**47–49**
Mediterranean region, 2:5, **47–49,** 109, 113
Copper Age
Iberia, 1:460
Mediterranean region, 1:460
Iron Age
Europe, central, 2:156, 159, 246, 250, 300
Europe, eastern, 2:285, 292–293, 305–307, 309–310
Europe, northern, 2:534, 542–547
Europe, western, 2:213, 217, 218
Iberia, 2:255, 257
Mediterranean region, 2:255, 314
Middle Ages, 2:327
Europe, central, 2:385, 398–403, **556–561,** 575–576, 582–585, 592–594, 595–597
Europe, eastern, 2:**556–561,** 564, 566
Europe, northern, 2:418–419, 437–438, 443, 589
Europe, northwestern, 2:388, **494–495**
Mediterranean region, 2:347–348
Neolithic period, 1:389, **432–433, 448–450,** *449,* 451, **460–462**
Polyanitsa site, 1:96, 338
Polybius, 2:211, 217
Pontic-Caspian region, 1:108
Popiel, 2:554, 559
Population statistics. *See also specific countries; specific sites*
Bronze Age, 2:36, 111, 124

Copper Age, 1:359
Iron Age, 2:249, 250, 256, **270–271**
Mesolithic period, 1:148, 158, 160, 161, 165, 166
Middle Ages, 2:492, **530–532**
Porcuna site, 2:255
Pori site, 2:550
Portmahomack site, 2:476–477, *478*
Porto Badisco site, 1:95
Porto Perone site, 2:37, *38*
Portugal. *See also specific sites*
Copper Age, 1:**458,** 460
Mesolithic period
aquatic resources, 1:164
fauna, 1:164
fishing populations, 1:124
midden sites, 1:164–166
population statistics, 1:158, 165
settlement patterns, 1:124, 157–158
social systems, 1:196
stone tool industries, 1:165
subsistence resources, 1:160–161
Neolithic period
artworks, 1:458–459
burials, 1:**458,** 460, 463
dates for, 1:398
farming, 1:202
monumental structures, 1:463
pastoralism, 1:161
political systems, 1:**460–462**
pottery industry, 1:459
settlement patterns, 1:458
social systems, 1:**460**
stone tool industries, 1:160
subsistence resources, 1:160, 249, *249*
warfare and conquest, 1:**460,** *462*
Porvoo site, 2:550
Posidonius, 2:151
Post, Lennart von, 1:19
Post-Roman culture, 2:**348–349, 353,** 369–370
Post-Roman period, 2:**469–470, 480–481, 504–505,** 587–588, 590–591
Postglacial period
ecofacts, 1:**24**
environments, 1:7–8, 118–120, **126–131,** *130, 130,* 183
fishing populations, 1:8, 124, *138,* 184
landscape use, 1:**118–120,** *130, 130*
ocean levels during, 1:124
resource use, 1:142, 154
subsistence resources, 1:142, 143
tool industries, 1:142, 154, *155*
Postoloprty site, 1:374

Potterne site, 2:59
Pottery industry. *See also* Figurines; *specific countries; specific cultures and people; specific sites*
about dating methods and chronology, 1:66
Bronze Age, 2:16–18, **21,** 37–38, 40–41, 46, 96, 104–105
Copper Age, 1:358, 359, 361, 362
Iron Age, 2:199–200, 200–203, 225, 266, 283, 292, 300, 305–306
Mesolithic period, 1:159, 162, 177, 178, 184–185, *278, 279*
Middle Ages, 2:328, *332, 333,* 381, 452–453, 472, 492, 496–497
Neolithic period
Europe, central, 1:185, 202, 238–240, 268, 369–370, 373, *374*
Europe, eastern, 1:185, **235–237,** 238–240, 243, 245, 247, 369–370, 373
Europe, northern, 1:185, 202, 289, 290, 296–298, 432, 434, 436
Europe, northwestern, 1:185, 273–277, 279, 280, 287, 289, 290
Europe, upland central and southern, 1:171, 172, 180, **389,** 395–396, 452
Europe, western, 1:257, 391
Iberia, 1:163, 459
Mediterranean region, 1:249, 255–256, 257, 439, **440–441,** 452; 2:121
Pouech, Abbé, 1:18
Poundbury site, 1:114
Powlesland, Dominic, 2:363
Poznań University, 2:286
Pradestel site, 1:168
Prehistory, origins of, 1:3, **14–21,** 34. *See also* Archaeology; History, field of
Pre-Pottery Neolithic period, 1:207, 208, 231
Predmost site, 1:111
Prehistoric Times (Lubbock), 1:18
Presteigne site, 2:485
Pretty, Edith May, 2:498
Primitive Social Organization (Service), 2:15
Principles of Archaeological Stratigraphy (Harris), 1:33
Principles of Geology (Lyell), 1:17
Prítluky site, 1:114
The Problem of the Picts (Wainwright), 2:404
Procopius, 2:381, 394, 414, 415

Proton-induced x-ray and gamma-ray emission, 1:67–68
Protruding Foot Beaker culture, 1:**470**
Ptolemy, 2:381
Ptolemy, *Geographica,* 2:388
Publius Quintilius Varus, 2:247
Puglisi, Salvatore M., 2:36
Pupicina site, 1:171
Pylos site, 1:114
Pyramids of Egypt, 1:40, 44

Q

Quadi people, 2:573–574
Quanterness site, 1:283
Quentovic site, 2:324

R

Raczky, Pál, *The Late Neolithic of the Tisza Region,* 1:335
Radovanovič, Ivana, *The Iron Gates Mesolithic,* 1:176
Radovesice site, 2:299
Raevskoe site, 2:294
Rainsborough site, 1:115
Rajewski, Zdzisław, 2:286
Ramad site, 1:208
Ramsauer, Johann Georg, 1:17; 2:144
Randsborg, Klavs, 1:100
Rassokhovatka site, 1:370
Rath of the Synods site, 2:237
Rathlin Island site, 1:404
Rathtinaun site, 2:234
Redwald, 2:499
Rega, Elizabeth, 1:86
Regensburg site, 2:385, 593, 596
Reim, Hartmann, 2:251
Reinecke, Paul, 2:86, 147
Remedello site, 1:445
Remigius, 2:376
Rendswühren Man, 1:27
Renfrew, Colin
  "The Autonomy of the South-East European Copper Age," 1:318
  on calibration and dating methods, 1:45
  on copper industry, 1:318, 319
  on Indo-European influences, 1:340
  on megalithic tombs, 1:400
  on populations based on hypogea, 1:454
  on radiocarbon dating, 1:41
  on ritual, evidence of, 1:91

and study of shrines, 1:90
Rerum gestarum libri (Ammianus Marcellinus), 2:180
Resource use. *See also specific countries; specific sites*
  about environments and, 1:**52–53**
  Bronze Age, 1:53–54
  Holocene era, 1:170
  Iron Age, 1:53–54
  Mesolithic period, 1:52, 142, 154
  Neolithic period, 1:52, *53*, 84–85
  postglacial period, 1:142, 154
Rhetor Priscus, 2:391
Rhine and Meuse Valleys, 1:**286–291**
Ribe site, 2:325, 328, 358, 546
Ribeiro, Carlos, 1:164
Rickett, Robert, 2:496
Riek, Gustav, 2:250
Rig Veda, 1:101, 102; 2:99–100
Rijckholt site, 1:404
Rijswijk site, 2:589
Ring of Brodgar site, 1:283
Ringkloster site, 1:135, 295
Rinyo site, 1:283
Ríordáin, A. B. ó, 2:467
Riparo Gabon site, 1:168
Ripiceni-Izvor site, 1:172
Ripoli site, 1:442, 444
Risch, Roberto, 2:47
Ritual and ideology, 1:170. *See also specific countries; specific cultures and people; specific sites*
  about artifacts, and evidence of, 1:**91–92**
  about human sacrifices, 2:**270**
  about Renfrew on evidence of, 1:91
  Bronze Age
    Europe, central, 1:95, 96; 2:**26–27**, 33
    Europe, eastern, 2:26, 32, 99
    Europe, northern, 2:**77–78**
    Europe, northwestern, 2:**57–58**, 62, 68–69
    Europe, upland central and southern, 1:450
    Iberia, 2:**48**, 49
    Mediterranean region, 2:35, 37, 40, 119–120, 123, 124
  Copper Age, 1:92, *93*, 95, 360, 361, 363, 365–366
  Iron Age
    Europe, central, 2:250, 282, **298, 299, 301–302**
    Europe, northern, 1:93, 99–100; 2:**181–183**, 270, 551
    Europe, northwestern, 2:**225–227**, 237–238
    Iberia, 2:254–258, *256*, 257

Megalithic period, 1:95, 97, **411–412**
Mesolithic period
  Europe, central, 1:189
  Europe, eastern, 1:187, **188–190**, 196
  Europe, northwestern, 1:12, **149–151**
  Europe, upland central and southern, 1:170, 177
  Iberia, 1:159, 165
  Mediterranean region, 1:170
Middle Ages
  Europe, central, 2:401, 554, 587–588
  Europe, northern, 2:410, 588
  Europe, northwestern, 2:448, **450–451**, *453*, **456–459, 473–474**, 478, 486–487, 491
Migration period, 2:**270**
Neolithic period
  Europe, central, 1:92, **377–378**
  Europe, eastern, 1:94, 378–382
  Europe, northern, 1:296, 298, 301, **425–426**, 432, 433, 437
  Europe, northwestern, 1:274, 284–285
  Europe, upland central and southern, 1:**391**
  Europe, western, 1:284–285
  Iberia, 1:460, **463**
  Mediterranean region, 1:97, 232, 274, 460, **463**; 2:121
Rive d'Arcano site, 1:171
Roaix site, 1:112
Robb, John, 1:97
Roberts, Howell, 2:437
Robin Hood's Ball site, 2:65
Rocca di Rivoli site, 1:442
Roche, Jean, 1:165
Rock art, 1:18, 85, 188–189, 193, 446, 459; 2:5. *See also* stone carvings; *specific countries; specific sites*
Rogerius, *Carmen miserabile,* 2:579
Rogerson, Andrew, 2:496
Romagnano site, 1:168
Roman culture, 2:**142–143**, 228–229, 236–237, 247, 257, 294–295
Roman period
  about, 1:3, 12, 15, 47, 87
  Europe, central, 2:**573–574**, 586–590
  Europe, northern, 1:62
  Europe, northwestern, 2:501–504, **508–510**
Romanellian culture, 1:172

United Nations Educational, Scientific, and Cultural Organization (UNESCO), 2:540
University of California at Los Angeles, 1:241
University of Frankfurt, 1:261
University of Rennes, 1:410
University of York, 2:476, 498
Uppåkra site, 2:539
Uppsala University, 1:363
Upton Lovell site, 2:66
Ural Mountain cultures, 1:107, 108, 184
Urbanization. *See also Oppida; specific countries; specific sites*
  Anglo-Saxon culture, 2:493
  Iron Age, 2:138–139, 287, 550
  Middle Ages, 2:565
    Europe, central, 2:587, 590
    Europe, eastern, 2:563, 564, 565
    Europe, northwestern, 2:455, **456–459,** *457,* 466–468, 493, **501–507,** *503,* **516–518**
    Europe, western, 2:*514,* **516–518,** *517*
  Viking Age, 2:**539–540**
Urfirnis ware, 1:181
Urnfield culture, 1:24, 114, 116; 2:**86–91,** *90,* 241. *See also* Hallstatt culture
Urnfields, 1:24; 2:4, 38, **87–88,** 214, 282, 393. *See also* Burials
Ursus, 2:376
Ussher, James, 1:14

V

Václav, 2:585
Vadastra site, 1:320
Vače site, 2:297
Vaiale site, 1:168, 170
Vaihingen site, 1:112
Val Camonica site, 1:446
Vale of Pickering Research Trust, 1:155
Valencina de la Concepción site, 1:458
Valsgärde site, 2:535, 538
Vandal people, 2:574
Vænget Nord site, 1:37
Varikkoniemi site, 2:550
Varna site, 1:321, 340, **341–344,** *342*
Varsinais Suomi site, 2:278, *278*
Vasić, Miloje, 1:18
Vasiliev, Igor, 1:365
Västerbjers, 1:432, 433
Västmanland site, 2:535, 538

Västra Hoby site, 1:401–402
Vatte di Zambana site, 1:168
Vázquez, Victoria Villoch, 1:96
Vedas, 1:101, 102
Vedbæk site, 1:138, 309, 420
La Vela site, 1:442, 445
Velatice site, 1:112
Velim site, 1:112
Venantius Fortunatus, 2:384
Veretye site, 1:184
Verhulst, Adriaan, *The Carolingian Economy,* 2:330
Veselovskii, Nikolai, 1:18
Vesely Kut site, 1:358
Vésteinsson, Orri, 2:437, 442, 443
Vészt-Mágor site, 1:339
Viborg site, 2:506
Viereckschanzen, 2:**174–178,** *175, 177,* 246, 247, 301
Vignely site, 1:274
Viking Age
  about regions and
    Europe, northern, 2:**436–444, 533–541,** 544–547, 550
    Europe, northwestern, 2:**445–449,** *446,* **454–456, 466–468,** 469, **474–475**
  artisans, 2:**539,** 550
  burials, 2:534, **538–539**
  Christianity, 2:**540,** 549
  coinage, 2:549, 550
  dates for, 2:548
  economic systems, 2:**539–540, 542–547**
  fortifications, 2:544, *546,* 546–547
  hoards, 2:535, *535,* 538, *538,* 549
  inscribed stones, 2:*542,* 544, *545*
  monumental structures, 2:*542,* 544, *545*
  political systems, 2:541–542, 544–545, *546*
  settlement structures, 2:**534–535, 537–538**
  state societies, 2:349
  stone carvings, 2:*542,* 544, *545*
  subsistence resources, 2:**534–535, 537–538**
  trade and exchange, 2:540, **542–549**
  urbanization, 2:**539–540**
Viking culture
  about Wales and, 2:487
  emporia, 2:**334–336,** *335*
  gender roles and relationships, 1:87
  harbors, 2:**334–336,** *335*
  hoards, 2:334, *334,* 359
  jewelry, 2:427
  settlement patterns, 1:53–54
  settlement structures, 1:53–54

  ships, 2:**423–425,** *425*
  state societies, 2:350
  trade and exchange, 2:**334–336,** *335*
  warfare and conquest, 2:331
Vikletice site, 1:470
Ville-neuve-Tolosane site, 1:443, 445
Villeneuve-la-Guyard site, 1:274, 445
Villey-Saint-Etienne site, 2:513
Vinča culture, 1:*85,* 320, 323
Vinča site, 1:18, 336, 339
Visborg site, 1:422
Visigoth culture, 2:**419–422,** *420, 421,* 514
Vita Sancti Severini (Eugippius), 2:384
Vitelli, Karen D., 1:91
Vix site, 1:75, 76, 87; 2:*201, 205,* **205–207,** 216
Vladar, J., 2:31
Vladimirovka site, 1:368
Vlasac site, 1:124, 175–176, *176, 177*
Volterra site, 2:262, *262, 264,* 267
Von Sacken, Baron, 2:144
Voytek, Barbara, 1:320
Vučedol site, 1:320, 339
Vukovar site, 1:320
Vulci site, 2:266
Vykhvatintsy site, 1:358

W

Waals, Johannes D. van der, 1:470, 476
Wade-Martins, Peter, 2:496
Wagons, 2:55, 98, 106, 270
Wainwright, Frederick T., *The Problem of the Picts,* 2:404
Wales, 2:*480,* **480–484,** *481*
Wallace, Patrick, 2:455, 466
Walsh, Clare, 2:466
Wangels site, 1:295, 296
Waremme-Longchamps site, 1:113
Warendorf site, 2:587, 588, 590, 592
Warfare and conquest, 1:**110–120.** *See also specific countries; specific sites*
  Bronze Age, 1:114; 2:120
  Copper Age, 1:112, **460,** *462,* **464–466**
  Iron Age, 2:196
    Europe, central, 1:**112–113,** 117–118; 2:246, 247, 282, 300
    Europe, eastern, 2:290, 294–295, 310–311
    Europe, northern, 1:118; 2:269–270